S0-DSZ-948

J. B. Francis Herreshoff

NEW ENGLAND FAMILIES

GENEALOGICAL AND MEMORIAL

A Record of the Achievements of Her People in the Making of Commonwealths and the Founding of a Nation

COMPILED UNDER THE EDITORIAL SUPERVISION OF

WILLIAM RICHARD CUTTER, A.M.

CORRESPONDING SECRETARY AND HISTORIAN OF THE NEW ENGLAND HISTORIC-GENEALOGICAL SOCIETY;
LIBRARIAN EMERITUS OF WOBURN PUBLIC LIBRARY; AUTHOR OF "THE
CUTTER FAMILY," "HISTORY OF ARLINGTON," ETC.

VOLUME I

ILLUSTRATED

CLEARFIELD COMPANY

Originally published
New York, 1915

Reprinted for
Clearfield Company, Inc. by
Genealogical Publishing Co., Inc.
Baltimore, Maryland
1996, 1997

International Standard Book Number: 0-8063-4612-4

Made in the United States of America

· FOREWORD

T HE present work, "New England Families," presents in the aggregate a great amount and variety of genealogical and personal information and portraiture. It contains a vast amount of ancestral history never before printed. The object, clearly defined and well digested, is threefold:

First: To present in concise form the history of established families of the region.

Second: To preserve a record of its prominent present-day people.

Third: To present through personal sketches, linked with the genealogical narrative, the relation of the prominent families of all times to the growth, singular prosperity and widespread influence of New England.

There are numerous voluminous narrative histories of this section, making it unnecessary in this work to even outline its annals. What has been published, however, principally relates to the people in the mass. The amplification necessary to complete the picture of the region, old and nowaday, is what is now supplied by these Genealogical and Personal Memoirs. In other words, while others have written of "the times," the province of this work is to be a chronicle of the people who have borne a conspicuous part in founding and developing a nation.

No other region offers so peculiarly interesting a field for such research. Its sons—"native here, and to the manner born," and of splendid ancestry— have attained distinction in every field of human effort. An additional interest attaches to the present undertaking in the fact that, while dealing primarily with the history of native New England, this work approaches the dignity of a national epitome of genealogy and biography. Owing to the wide dispersion throughout the country of the old families, the authentic account here presented of the constituent elements of her social life, past and present, is of far more than merely local value. In its special field it is, in an appreciable degree, a reflection of the development of the country at large, since hence went out representatives of the historical families, in various generations, who in far remote places—beyond the Mississippi and in the Far West—were with the vanguard of civilization, building up communities, creating new commonwealths, planting, wherever they went, the church, the school house and the printing press, leading into channels of thrift and enterprise all who gathered about them, and proving a power for ideal citizenship and good government.

This work everywhere conveys the lesson that distinction has been gained only by honorable public service, or by usefulness in private station, and that the development and prosperity of the section of which it treats has been dependent upon the character of its citizens, and the stimulus which they have given to commerce, to industry, to the arts and sciences, to education and religion —to all that is comprised in the highest civilization of the present day—through a, continual progressive development.

Truly as heroic poems have been written in human lives in the paths of

peace as in the scarred roads of war. Such examples, in whatever line of endeavor, are of much worth as an incentive to those who come afterward, and
such were never so needful to be written of as in the present day, when pes-
simism, forgetful of the splendid lessons of the past, withholds its effort in the
present, and views the future only with alarm.

The custodian of records concerning the useful men of preceding generations, who aids in placing his knowledge in preservable and accessible form, of
the homes and churches, schools and other institutions, which they founded,
and of their descendants who have lived honorable and useful lives, performs
a public service in rendering honor to whom honor is due, and in inculcating the
most valuable lessons of patriotism and good citizenship. The story of the
Plymouth and Massachusetts Bay colonies lies at the foundation of the best
there is in American history, and the names of Brewster, Winslow, Bradford,
Standish, Alden, Warren, Howland—all of whom came in the "Mayflower" and
were prominent in the Old Colony, with Freeman, Gorham and Sears—all these
of Plymouth, and Winthrop, Saltonstall, Dudley, Wilson, Bradstreet, and others,
of the Massachusetts Bay Colony, have an undying fame, and these names are
prominent to-day in the entire world. These early settlers erected an original
form of government, pledging themselves to maintain and preserve all their
liberties and privileges, and in their vote and suffrage, as their conscience might
them move, as to best conduce and tend to the public weal of the body without
respect of person or favor of any man. Their heroism was exhibited in their
conflicts with savages. In statesmanship they builded better than they knew.
Their code of laws known as the "Body of Liberties" has been termed an almost
declaration of independence, opening with the pronouncement that neither life,
liberty, honor nor estate were to be invaded unless under express laws enacted
by the local authorities, and when this bold declaration led to the demand of the
English government that the colonial charter should be surrendered, the colonists resisted to a successful issue. In later days Faneuil Hall became the cradle
of American Liberty, and from its platform were proclaimed the doctrines which
bore fruit in resistance to the Stamp Act, in the Boston Massacre, and the engagement of contesting armed forces at Lexington and Concord and Bunker Hill.

The above applies with equal force to the Providence, Hartford and New
Haven colonies, whose founders partook of the same character as those of Massachusetts. In Providence we find the first colony founded on religious liberty,
and the story of the "Charter Oak" illustrates again the sturdy nature of the
Hartford colonists. From these pioneer settlements spread out a people whose
God-fearing lives and heroic struggles with a savage foe, while conquering the
forest wilderness, bore fruit in establishing a hardy nation and set an example
for succeeding generations.

When came the momentous question whether a free and liberal government
"of the people, by the people, and for the people," was to perish from the earth,
the sons of their illustrious sires were not found wanting in patriotism and devotion, but freely sacrificed comforts, property and life for the vindication of the
principles inherited from the fathers.

Here, too, were developed in highest degree the arts of peace. Religion,
education, science, invention, labor along all the lines of mechanical and industrial progress, here made their beginnings, and, while their ramifications extended
throughout the length and breadth of the land, the parent home and the parent
stock held their pre-eminence, as they do to the present day.

The work has had editorial supervision by an antiquarian and genealogist of high standing, Mr. William Richard Cutter, A.M., corresponding secretary and historian of the New England Historic-Genealogical Society, librarian emeritus of Woburn Public Library, author of "The Cutter Family," "History of Arlington," etc., etc. Efficient aid has also been given by the following named gentlemen: Wilfred Harold Munro, L.H.D., professor of History, Brown University, president of Rhode Island Historical Society, ex-governor Society of Colonial Wars; Samuel Hart, D.D., D.C.L., dean of Berkeley Divinity School, president of Connecticut Historical Society; Ezra Scholay Stearns, ex-Secretary of State, N. H., member American Antiquarian Society, New England Historic-Genealogical Society, New Hampshire State Historical Society, corresponding member Minnesota State Historical Society; John Ellsworth Goodrich, D.D., Latin Professor Emeritus, University of Vermont, vice-president of Vermont Historical Society; Albert Roscoe Stubbs, librarian of Maine Genealogical Society; and John Reynolds Totten, editor of "New York Genealogical and Biographical Record," member of Mayflower Society, etc.

If in any case a narrative is incomplete or faulty, the shortcoming is usually ascribable to the paucity of data obtainable, many families being without exact records in their family line; while, in some instances, representatives of a given family are at disagreement as to the names of some of their forbears, important dates, etc.

It is confidently believed that the present work will prove a real addition to the mass of annals concerning the historic families of New England, and that, without it, much valuable information would be inaccessible to the general reader, or irretrievably lost, owing to the passing away of custodians of family records and the consequent disappearance of material in their possession.

THE PUBLISHERS.

NEW ENGLAND

The following critique was prepared and read by invitation of the president by Mr. William R. Cutter, at the annual meeting of the Rumford Historical Association in Woburn, Massachusetts, on March 26, 1912. This is its first appearance in print.

MATHER

In character not always understood by his contemporaries or by posterity, Cotton Mather probably accomplished more good than he is often accredited with. He was born February 12, 1663; was graduated at Harvard College, 1678; was ordained a colleague with his father, May 13, 1685 (aged twenty-two), and was a precocious scholar.

The diary of Cotton Mather is a minute record of his religious and personal experiences.* The actual interest in original documents is the documents themselves; and this diary, as printed, is furnished with only a few illustrative notes. It is fortunate that in our communities there are societies with means and ability enough to print such valuable sources of contemporary history, from which we learn what the people were thinking of and what they were doing in remote times. In spite of his egregious vanity and excessive egotism, Cotton Mather was the most eminent and learned clergyman of his time in America, pastor of the largest church in Boston, in the habit of preaching to the largest congregations wherever he went, having in his house the largest library or collection of books to be found on this side of the Atlantic, author of more books and tracts than there were days in the year, and vastly learned in ancient and foreign languages. Benjamin Franklin expressed his obligations to Mather's tract, "Ways to do Good," as one of his greatest inspirations to usefulness. Mather had one quality common to the New England clergyman of former days —and that, too, not a bad quality in itself— that of taking an interest in relatives, even to those of a remote degree. He died February 13, 1727-28, one day beyond his sixty-fifth birthday. His life was, therefore, shorter by

*Mass. Hist. Soc. Coll., 7s vii. Diary of Cotton Mather, 1709-1724, Boston; published by the Society, 1912. (Diary, vol. 2).

twenty years than that of his father, and shorter by about eight years than that of his grandfather. His father was president of Harvard College for sixteen years, and his grandfather was the third minister, in succession, of the town of Dorchester. His ancestors were both scholarly and influential. His defects were largely due to the overabundant nature of his qualities. He was three times married, and had fifteen children by his first and second marriages. His last wife, like his second, was a widow at the time he married her. She was uncritical as to his faults, even when entreated to explain them, but owing to an outbreak of insanity, which appears to have gradually come upon her, she became a source of great trouble in his family, and almost drove him distracted himself. He said:

"My glorious Lord has inflicted a new and sharp chastisement upon me. The consort, in whom I flattered myself with the view and hopes of an uncommon enjoyment, has dismally confirmed it unto me, that our idols must prove our sorrows. Now and then, in some of the former years, I observed and suffered grievous outbreakings of her proud passions; but I quickly overcame them with my victorious love, and in the methods of meekness and goodness * * * I do not know that I have to this day spoke one impatient or unbecoming word unto her, though my provocations have been unspeakable, and, it may be, few men in the world would have borne them as I have done. But this last year has been full of her prodigious paroxysms, which have made it a year of such distresses with me as I have never seen in my life before. When the paroxisms have gone off, she has treated me still with a fondness, that, it may be, few wives in the world have arrived unto. But in the returns of them (which of late still grow more and more frequent) she has insulted me with such outrages that I am at a loss which I should ascribe them to—whether a distraction (which may be somewhat hereditary), or to a possession whereof the symptoms have been too direful to be mentioned.

In the first place she took such an objection against his writings (evidently of the diary variety) that he was obliged to lay them where he thought she could not find them. For fear of what might happen, he wrote not one disrespectful word of this "proud woman" in all the papers. But, nevertheless, by rummaging she found them, and hid them, and informed him that he would never see them any more. He offered to blot out with the pen whatever she would not have there, but unavailingly. She gave him to understand that she might return the papers of the four or five preceding years which she had got into her possession. Mather claimed that they were of more value to him than any temporal estate he could pretend unto. He began to believe that before another birthday (he was in his fifty-sixth year) his life would be finished. His theme was upon the article of "Good Devised," which stood for it three hundred and sixty-five times in a year. He concludes by saying that "while those who destroyed Jeremiah's roll got nothing by it, so this unhappy woman will get nothing by what she does unto mine."

He was also in a continual anguish of expectation that his wife, by exposing her madness, would bring ruin on his ministry, and he was also troubled about what might occur when her own reputation was made public. His family, too, were made unhappy by her furious and froward conduct. He even resorts to the use of the Latin and Greek languages to express her unaccountable passions. They seemed little short of Satanical, and on one occasion, after unrepeatable invectives, he was compelled by her to rise at midnight and retire to his study; while she, calling up two other persons, went over to a neighbor's house for a lodging. She told numberless lies, "which a tongue set on fire of hell would make no conscience of." He claimed that there was no other husband who treated his wife with greater efforts to please her and make her comfortable at home and reputable abroad. She invented occasions for outrages, and then at lucid intervals would be filled with expressions of the most enamored fondness. The poor husband, at last, when rebuking her lying tongue, used terms which he had not been used to. She was the most heavy scourge that he had ever met withal. But, at last, came the occasion of her recovery. "In the evening of the day," says her husband, "my poor wife, returning to a right mind, came to me in my study, entreating that there might be an eternal oblivion of everything that has been out of joint, and an eternal harmony ever afterwards."

Out of Cotton Mather's fifteen children a number of whom died young, there was one son who was a very bad young man, who gave his father much anxiety—an example of the saying, "ministers' sons and deacons' daughters." After a scandalous career he was reported lost at sea in the West India Islands. His vessel had been out five months on a compara-

tively short voyage, and had not arrived. An untrue rumor was brought to his father that the son was yet living, but in a day or two it was found that the news applied to another vessel. Surely the life of Cotton Mather was very human!

In Cotton Mather's writings we discover coincidences between his times and ours. He mentions cold weather in winter and hot weather in summer. He caught cold from going out damp winter evenings. On one occasion he was attacked by a painful malady, which I should diagnose as the tic-douloureux. He wrote:

"I have been for some time afflicted with grievous pains in my head * * * A neighboring minister last night asked me, whether the Dragon (that is the Devil) might not be, by the wise permission of Heaven, taking some revenge upon me, for some notable mischief, which my head may have lately done unto his kingdom. * * * All methods and medicines for my cure fail me. I have used unguents, and plasters, and cataplasms, and epispastics, and sinapisms, and cathartics, and what not, but all to no purpose.* My physicians are of no value. My pains this morning are more violent than they use to be. I lie down like a stag in a net, with a very despairing discouragement. However, I thought I would make one more experiment. (In his characteristic way, he commended his case to his Maker). Behold, I had no occasion for any further application. My pains immediately went off. And as yet (I write the day following) I have no return of them." "After two or three days of unaccountable repose, I suffered some return of my pain * * * and I put on an epispastic, which suddenly and mightily relieved me."

He was an admirer of the rainbow in the sky, and preached a sermon and wrote a book upon the subject. The fuel of the people was wood, and the wooden city of Boston was subject to conflagrations, in which many buildings were destroyed. His aged father was worried because his people wanted to swarm into a new church (people at that day, as well as this, were desirous of a change), and he did what he could to comfort him. For the restraining of profaneness in a considerable number of unruly children on the Lord's Day in his congregation, he found a person to look after them whom he accordingly employed and rewarded for that service. In 1713 he wrote:

"There are knots of riotous young men in the town. On purpose to insult piety, they will come under my window in the middle of the night, and sing profane and filthy songs. The last night they did so, and fell upon people with clubs, taken off my wood-pile."

At about this time an epidemic of the measles in Boston caused the deaths of five mem-

*In present day terms, unguents are ointments, cataplasms are poultices, epispastics are blisters, and sinapisms are cataplasms with a mustard ingredient, i. e., a mustard poultice.

bers of his family, including his second wife. This occasioned him to give a list of the names of his children, and this mathematical calculation upon their number: "Of 15, dead 9, living 6."

"Some foolish and froward people in the flock fall out about their seats. I must use the methods of prudence and piety to manage such roots of bitterness." [We shall hear some more about this subject of seating the meeting-house, later on.]

"This day [August 14, 1716,] a singular thing befell me. * * * I was prevailed withal to do a thing, which I very rarely do; not once in years. I rode abroad with some gentlemen and gentlewomen, to take the country air, and to divert ourselves at a famous fish-pond. [Spy Pond, now in Arlington.] In the canoe on the pond my foot slipped, and I fell overboard into the pond. Had the vessel been a little further from the shore, I must have been drowned. But I soon recovered the shore, and going speedily into a warm bed, I received no sensible harm."

His wife, too, had premonitions "all the former part of the day and all the day before" that this "little journey" would have mischief attending it.

I have discovered in writing the "History of Arlington," that there was, at a very early period, a house very near the shore of this pond devoted to the public entertainment of such visitors as might come to it. The deep waters of this very dangerous lake have probably engulfed, from Mather's day to this, more drowned persons than any similar body of water in this vicinity.

I am very glad that I have had the opportunity to examine closely the pages of these memorial records of the experiences of Cotton Mather. The process of examination has been a mental stimulus as well as recalling to my mind certain religious beliefs which found rigid followers in the days of my childhood. Cotton Mather said on one occasion:

"I feel a very sensible rebuke from Heaven upon me, in shutting me out from the service of the flock. On the last Lord's day I was compelled into sitting still [his father and he were joint pastors of the same church] out of a compliment to a person, who had been asked by my father to preach for him, and yet arrived not so soon, but that my father fearing his failing had got another to supply his room. The young man, to whom I thus, in civility, gave way, was also one, whom for the vanity of his character I did least of all desire to see in our pulpit. This Lord's day I am arrested with a cold, and a cough, and am withal so hoarse, that I am laid by from all public ministrations."

Who is there who has not had differences, certainly in opinion, if not otherwise, with the body of his numerous family relations? Mather had certainly in his schemes of doing good included them in the number of his beneficiaries. On one occasion he writes:

"I am sorry that among my personal enemies, I must now reckon some of my relatives. Unaccountable creatures! But I have a little penetrated into their inexplicable character and conduct. I must watch over my spirit, and study to carry it as well unto them, as if they were better affected towards me."

On another occasion he said:

"I observe a great number of people in the flock, whose employments are so circumstanced, that while their hands are employed, their minds are very much at leisure; and others, in whose business both hands and minds are so. I would in a sermon propose methods for these neighbors to redeem this time."

People of this kind are not scarce now.

Cotton Mather also had a practice of writing out his sermons fully in order that the copy might be used for publication, and he sometimes wrote English sentences in the Greek character, in which manner their meaning was obscured to the ordinary reader.

There is no more interesting part in the book than that describing Cotton Mather's experience during the terrible visitation of Boston by the smallpox in the year 1721, a time when vast numbers of the people were lying sick of that loathsome disease, and an equally large number died. The disease was apparently brought by a vessel of war which lay in the harbor, on board of which were two or three men sick with the pestilence. Mather's life was in extreme danger from the horrid venom of the sick chambers, which he made it his duty to enter on his pastoral visits. Mather called the attention of the physicians of Boston to the "new method" of inoculation for this dire disease, used by the African people and Asiatics, in their own countries, which he had read about in letters from Constantinople and Smyrna, as published by the Royal Society in London. As soon as his project was made public a storm of opposition arose on the part of the New Englanders. The chief moral reason brought against inoculation was that it was a heathen practice, and it was unlawful to learn of the heathen, and, absurd as the argument seemed, its defenders could only point out in reply, that all of the physicians of antiquity were heathen, and that the colonists of New England had learned from the Indians a corrective to snake bites and the practice of smoking.

Mather also prepared a little treatise on the smallpox, first awakening the sentiments of piety which it calls for, and then exhibiting the best medicines and methods which the world had yet had for the managing of it; and, finally, adding the new discovery to prevent it in the way of inoculation. He instructed the physicians in this new method used by the Africans and Asiatics to abate the dangers, and infallibly to save the lives of those that have the smallpox in the natural way. But a horrid clamor was raised against him, and a strange possession from the evil one took possession of the people on this occasion; they raved, they railed, they blasphemed; they talked not only like idiots, but also like frantics; and not only himself, but the physician who began the experiment, were objects of their fury; their furious obloquies and invectives. "This cursed clamor of a people strangely and fiercely possessed of the Devil," he said, "will probably prevent" the saving of the lives of Mather's two children from the smallpox in the "way of transplantation;" another way of describing the operation or process of inoculation. After ten remarkable experiments in his own neighborhood it was decided that his son should undergo the operation of receiving the smallpox in the new way; privately, if possibly the child should die under it. So it was done, not so skillfully as he had wished, but successfully. Thereupon, in the words of Mather:

"The town became a hell on earth, a city full of lies, and murders, and blasphemies, as far as wishes and speeches can render it so; Satan seemed to take a strange possession of it, in the epidemic rage against that notable and powerful and successful way of saving the lives of people from the dangers of the small-pox."

The situation grew still darker. "This miserable town," said Mather, "is a dismal picture and emblem of Hell." He arraigns the church members as having a fearful share in the false reports, and murderous wishes, and the "rage of wickedness among us" was "beyond what was ever known from the beginning to this day." Mather acknowledged in his own hand that in his remarks on the folly and baseness of an absurd and wicked people that he used "too bitter terms." Such terms as miserable, and detestable, and abominable, as applied to the town, seemed to fall easily and naturally from his lips.

He received a kinsman into his house who was under the inoculation of the smallpox, to whom he gave the use of his chamber. This poor man in the night, as it grew towards the morning, while lying in this room, narrowly escaped being killed by a murderous bomb which some malicious person threw through the window intending it for the unpopular Mather. The circumstances were these:

"Toward three o'clock, in the night, some unknown hands threw a fired (or lighted) granado (hand grenade) into the chamber where my kins-man lay, and which uses to be my lodging-room. The weight of the iron ball alone, had it fallen upon his head, would have been enough to have done part of the business designed. But the Granado was charged, the upper part with dried powder, the lower part with a mixture of oil of turpentine and powder, and what else I know not, in such a manner, that upon its going off, it must have split, and have probably killed the persons in the room, and certainly fired the chamber, and speedily laid the house in ashes * * * The grenade, in passing through the window, had by the iron in the middle of the casement, such a turn given to it, that in falling on the floor, the fired wild-fire in the fuse was violently shaken out upon the floor, without firing the grenado."

When the missile was taken up there was found a paper so tied with string about the fuse that it might outlive the breaking of the shell, on which paper was written an opprobrious and insulting message.

I have been requested by your president to examine the second volume of Cotton Mather's Diary, lately issued from the press, to discover further facts, if any, concerning the connection of this celebrated man with Woburn. As there was no index to the first volume, a comprehensive index in the second volume covers all the contents of the first. In the Woburn Journal for August 4, 1911, I attempted some review of the first volume, under the heading of "Cotton Mather and Woburn," and described certain events in the history of the Woburn First Parish Church, whose early records of those days are now missing, and may be regarded as altogether lost. The substance of what I found in Mather's record was a reference to an evil spirit at Woburn (some reference, perhaps, to the performance of a personal devil, for our forefathers heartily believed in such things); to an account of a sermon preached by Mather at Woburn in 1703, forestalling the settlement of a new minister there—a species of fast for that purpose, that a desirable minister might be had, and an account of an assault upon the action of Mather in reference to the conduct of a wicked man in the Woburn church; a man whom the church had censured for his impious conduct, and who had applied to Mather to help him out of trouble, and Mather had rendered a decision against him. Next Mather was a member of a council held at Woburn to settle the disturbances and differences among the brethren. In the second volume of the Diary we find an account of two visits which Mather had made to this place to settle differences among the rather violently disposed Woburn people.

Those who read Mather's reflections on various subjects will be more appreciative of their real value if the person has had some experience, however small, of the puritanical training once accorded to persons residing in this section. Puritanism is a fact whose conditions can be traced to the early history of Greece and Rome. Its conditions are the converse of luxury and vicious living. It is found where a people live the simple, dutiful life of their ancestors, and mainly in the rural portions of the land, away from the enervating influences of the cities. The influences of New England puritanism existed in modified form in Woburn until after 1840.

In justice to Cotton Mather it was his intention to do good to all his fellow mortals in whatever state and condition, and, in illustration, note what he says at the beginning of his fifty-first year, or at the opening of 1713:

"Not one day has passed without some contrivance to do good, invented and registered: besides multitudes of such not entered in these poor memorials. Not one day has passed without being able to say at night, something of my small revenues dealt out unto pious uses. Never any time spent with any company without some endeavor of a fruitful conversation in it."

No wonder such a man is said to have placed the sign over his study door: "Be short;" he was so busy about many things.

And now what did he say in his second volume of Diary about Woburn, vol. 2, p. 125. Visit, Nov. 4, 1711:

"God has blessed my applications unto Woburn, for the bruising of Satan, who had begun to raise grievous contentions. It was thought that it would be a confirming and finishing stroke on that good work, if I would give a lecture unto that people. I assign a time for it; purposing to preach as charming things as I can unto them, on Romans, 15-14, *I am persuaded you are full of goodness.*"

Wise Cotton Mather! Three days afterward, on Wednesday, November 7, 1711, he writes: "This day I accomplished my purpose for Woburn, and had many smiles of Heaven on my journey. Some that were surprising ones."

A reference to Sewall's "History of Woburn," p. 186, shows that the trouble had some reference to the "disorderly seating of many persons in the house of God."

On a second visit, vol. 2, p. 167, February 7, 1711-12, Wednesday. "I preached the lecture at Woburn on Rom. 15, 14. *Being Full of Goodness.*" An extension of the same subject and on the same text. When the character of the controversy is understood the implied sarcasm of the text is refreshing, showing that Mather was not slow in turning a ridiculous situation into a lesson of enlightenment.

Examining the work of Sewall, we find that at bottom the case was one arising from notions of family rank and station brought over from England, where distinctions of that kind had long been created and cherished, and to which our earliest ancestors here had attached an inordinate importance, and were jealous of any neglect of them by others. Thus the sentiments with regard to rank and condition in society held strongly, while other praiseworthy qualities had been neglected. The superiority of family was strong in many minds, and that when seating the meetinghouse was done, after repairs and enlargement had been made, a change was made in the method, which became very unpopular, which was explained by the following petition from the town records: Many inhabitants were much "aggrieved at the disorderly seating of many persons in the house of God, the ancient behind the backs of the youth, which they apprehended not to be according to the law of God, which requireth the youth to rise up before the hoary head, and to honor the person of the old man." In this case the seating had been done on this foolish principle. Namely, to prefer those first who had done the most by their contributions to the building of the original house, and, second, those who had contributed the most towards its recent repairs and enlargement, and, finally, those who paid the largest taxes. Thus the front seats were awarded to the wealthy and liberal, though young, before the aged members of the church and community, who were poor. Hence there resulted, and justly, much murmuring and discontent, and a row also resulted, which Cotton Mather's eloquence seems to have quelled.

Henry Seggerman was SEGGERMAN born in Bremen, Germany, and lived and died there. He was not in active business. He married Johanna Hildebrand. They had two children, Louise, and Henry, mentioned below.

(II) Henry (2), son of Henry (1) Seggerman, was born in Bremen, Germany, and came to this country in 1850 when a young man. He located in New York City and became a prosperous and prominent merchant. He was a Democrat in politics and a German Lutheran in religion. He died in 1888.

He married, in New York City, Martha Strong Gleason, who was born on Staten Island, New York, daughter of Daniel and Helen (Vanderburgh) Gleason, granddaughter of James and Martha (Strong) Vanderburgh, descendant of Peter Brown, who came in the "Mayflower" (see Strong and Brown). Children: Anna, born 1856; Frederick Krueger, mentioned below; Louise Norton, 1863; Victor, August, 1865.

(III) Frederick Krueger, son of Henry (2) Seggerman, was born in Yonkers, New York, February 7, 1857. His early education was received at St. John's College, which he attended until he was twelve years old, when he went abroad and became a student at Keilhan high school, near Rudolsbadt, Germany, an institute founded by Froebel, of kindergarten fame, graduating after a five-year course in 1874. After his return to this country he started in his business career as clerk for the Decastro & Donner Sugar Refining Company. Afterward he was in the employ of the firm of Havemeyer & Elder, sugar refiners, and clerk for the firm of L. W. Minford & Company, of New York. He founded the firm of Seggerman Brothers in partnership with his brother. Afterward the business was incorporated under the name of Seggerman Brothers, Incorporated, and he is president of the company, which imports and deals in coffee and also handles California products. He is one of the leading merchants in his line of business in New York. He is also vice-president of the Wisconsin Condensed Milk Company, which has factories at Burlington, Wisconsin, Pecatonica and Grey's Lake, Illinois, and vice-president of the McCann-Frazier Company, of Philadelphia, Pennsylvania. He is a member of the Chamber of Commerce of New York, the Knollwood Country Club, the New York Athletic Club, the Baltusrol Golf Club, the New York Wool Club, the Mayflower Society of New York, the Society of Mayflower Descendants and Squadron A Club of New York. In politics he has been an independent Democrat, but he voted for Theodore Roosevelt and William H. Taft for president. He served four years in the Seventh Regiment, New York National Guard, and for three years in Squadron A, New York National Guard. He is a communicant of the Protestant Episcopal church. His home is at 309 West Eighty-first street, and his offices at 91 Hudson street, New York.

He married, October 18, 1887, Annie Hawthorne Timpson, who was born in a house on Eighteenth street, New York, in 1866, daughter of Alfred H. and Ellen (Mather) Timpson, granddaughter of General Mather, of Windsor, Connecticut. Her father was cashier of the Continental National Bank of New York, and was for ten years a member of the famous Seventh Regiment, New York National Guard. Children of Mr. and Mrs. Seggerman: 1. Frederick Timpson, born in New York City, 1890; graduated from Princeton University; member of Ivy Club and of Squadron A; associated in business with his father. 2. Kenneth Mather, born in New

York City, 1892; member of class of 1913, Princeton University; member of the Cottage Club.

(The Brown Line).

(I) Peter Brown, the immigrant ancestor, was born in England, and came in the "Mayflower" with the Plymouth Company in 1620. He was unmarried when he came, but within the next thirteen years had married twice. He was admitted a freeman in 1633. Mary and Martha Brown, probably his wife and daughter, had shares in the division of cattle with him in 1627, and it is believed that the name of his first wife was Martha, that Mary and Priscilla were her daughters, and the two mentioned in the history of Governor Bradford as married in 1650. In 1644 the daughters were placed in the care of their uncle, John Brown, a leading citizen of Duxbury. Peter Brown died in 1633, before October 10, and his estate was settled by the court November 11, 1633. He had several children.

(II) Peter (2), son of Peter (1) Brown, was born in 1632. He settled in Windsor, Connecticut, and lived to be nearly sixty years old. He died at Windsor, March 9, 1692, leaving an estate of £409 to be divided by thirteen children. The famous Abolitionist, John Brown, was a descendant, through his son John, grandson John and great-grandson John, whose son Owen was father of Captain John. Abigail, his daughter, born 1662, married Samuel Fowler, born 1683, and their daughter Isabel married Ezra Strong (see Strong).

(The Strong Line).

(II) Samuel Strong, son of Elder John Strong (q. v.), was born August 5, 1652, and died at Northampton, Massachusetts, October 29, 1732. He married (first), June 19, 1684, Esther, daughter of Deacon Edward Clapp. She died January 26, 1698, and he married (second), October 28, 1698, Mrs. Ruth Wright, widow of Joseph Wright. Samuel Strong was a farmer. Children, born at Northampton, by first wife: Esther, April 30, 1685; Samuel, January 21, 1687; Susannah, February 26, 1688; Abigail, January 1, 1689, died young; Abigail, November 23, 1690; Christian, March 1, 1692; Nehemiah, 1694-5; Ezra, mentioned below. Children by second wife: Mary, May 19, 1701; Joseph, May 9, 1703; Josiah, August 17, 1705; Deacon Samuel, February 11, 1712-13.

(III) Ezra, son of Samuel Strong, was born in Northampton, October 14, 1697. He married December 14, 1720, Isabel Fowler, born February 1, 1700, died December 27, 1723, daughter of Samuel and Abigail (Brown) Fowler. He married (second), May 27, 1736, Miriam, daughter of Robert Jr. and

J. K. Seggerman

Carleton Coat of Arms.
Original in possession of W. Dudley Carleton.

Rebecca (Rust) Dank. Ezra was a farmer at Northampton and Southampton. Children: Ezra, mentioned below; Benoni, born December 23, 1723. Children by second wife: Miriam, February 14, 1737; Isabel, May 12, 1744; child, died August 29, 1746.

* (IV) Ezra (2), son of Ezra (1) Strong, was born at Pittsfield, Massachusetts, January 17, 1721. He married, November 5, 1741, Mary King, born February 24, 1719, died at Benson, Vermont, daughter of John and granddaughter of Fearnot and Mary (Fowler) King. Children, born at Westfield: Captain John, mentioned below; King, December 4, 1744; Asa, December 16, 1746; Eleanor, October 9, 1748; Silence, November 26, 1750; Warham, January 31, 1753; Huldah, October 2, 1757; Ozem, December 1, 1760; Russell.

(V) Captain John Strong, son of Ezra Strong, was born in Pittsfield, October 13, 1742. He was graduated at Yale College in 1766 and became a lawyer in Pittsfield. He was an officer in the American army during the revolution, and contributed funds to the support of the government so generously that at the end of the war he was bankrupt. He removed to Shodack, New York, and Albany. Children: 1. Hannah. 2. Martha, married, in 1805, at Kinderhook, New York, James Vanderburgh, a merchant of Troy, New York, where he died in 1828; children: Margaret, Maria, Cornelia, married Charles M. Parker; Julia, married ——— Arnold; William, Helen, married Daniel Gleason (see Seggerman); Catherine, married ——— Evarts. 3. Margaret. 4. Charles. 5. Joseph. 6. John, died unmarried. 7. James.

This ancient family is now
CARLETON represented in New York
by William Dudley Carleton, of the law firm of Jones & Carleton. Mr. Carleton has been for several years in active general practice in the city of New York, where he ranks as one of the highly esteemed members of the bar. The history of the Carleton family is traced through the following generations, the name being derived, according to some authorities in England, from the place name. Carleton is from the Saxon word "ceorl," husbandman, and "ton," or town. The coat of arms is as follows: Escutcheon: Argent, a bond sable, three mascles of the field. Crest: Out of a ducal coronet, or, an horse's head couped. Motto: *Aut mors aut Gloria.*
(I) Baldwin de Carleton, of Carleton, near Penrith, Cumberland, England, 1066. (II) Jeffrey de Carleton. (III) Edward de Carleton. (IV) Henry de Carleton. (V) Gilbert de Carleton, married ——— Fitzwilliam.
(VI) William de Carleton was justice's

counsellor of Edward, the king's son and lieutenant, while the sovereign, Edward II. was absent in foreign wars. William de Carleton also served on a commission to reconcile the king and the barons. He was chancellor of the exchequer, and interceded with the king in behalf of the Earl of Norfolk and Hartford. William de Carleton married Helena, daughter of Geoffrey de Stanton.
(VII) Adam de Carleton married Sarah, daughter of Adam de Newton. (VIII) Adam de Carleton married Sinella ———, supposed to have been a Plantagenet. (IX) John de Carleton was conspicuous as commissioner with the chief men of England in making treaty with Flanders. (X) Henry de Carleton was of county Lincoln, thirteenth of Richard II.; married Alicia ———. (XI) Sir Thomas de Carleton. (XII) Sir Walter de Carleton, married ——— Fieldman. (XIII) Thomas Carleton, of Sutton, Lincolnshire, married ——— Shorne. (XIV) John Carleton, of Sutton and Walton-upon-Thames, died 1450; married Anne Skepwith. (XV) John Carleton married Alice Danield.
(XVI) John Carleton lived in 1500; married Joyce, daughter of John and Margaret (Culpepper) Welbeck, cousin of Queen Catherine, wife of Henry VIII.
(XVII) Edward, fifth son of John Carleton, settled in East Clandon, Surrey, in 1571, and is ancestor of the Carletons of London, Surrey, Arundel and America.
(XVIII) Erasmus, son of Edward Carleton, was a citizen and mercer of St. Bartholomew, London; married Elizabeth ———.
(XIX) Edward, son of Erasmus Carleton, was born in 1605, in England, and is the immigrant ancestor of the American family. In 1638-39 he settled on the plantation of Rev. Ezekiel Rogers, and became one of the founders of the town of Rowley, Massachusetts, where next to the minister he was the largest landowner. He was given the title of "Mr.," usually reserved for ministers and people of high social or official standing. He was admitted a freeman May 18, 1642; deputy to the general court in 1644-45-46-47; commissioner to hear small causes in 1648. He returned to England, and died there about 1661. He married Eleanor Denton (Carth originally, of old Roman ancestry). He left an estate in New England, a part of which his son John obtained. Christopher and Hannah Babbage and Jeremiah and Nehemiah Jewett received letters of administration on behalf of the children of Hannah Carleton, his widow, November 29, 1678. Children: John, mentioned below; Edward, born October 28, 1639; Mary, June 2, 1642; Elizabeth, March 26, 1644.
(XX) John, son of Edward Carleton, was

born in 1630, in England, and was one of the leading men of the town of Haverhill. He married Hannah, born June 15, 1640, in England, daughter of Joseph and Mary (Mallinson) Jewett. Joseph Jewett was the son of Edward Jewett, of Bradford, West Riding of Yorkshire, baptized December 31, 1609; married, October 1, 1634, Mary Mallinson. Children of John Carleton and his wife: John, born 1658; Joseph, March 21, 1662; Edward, mentioned below; Thomas, born September 9, 1667. All these children were born in Haverhill, and in that town John Carleton, the father, died January 22, 1668.

(XXI) Edward, son of John Carleton, was born March 22, 1664, in Haverhill, and settled in Bradford, Massachusetts, where his descendants have been numerous to the present time. He married Elizabeth ———. Children, all born at Bradford: Edward, February 20, 1690-91; Benjamin, mentioned below; Nehemiah, April 15, 1695; Nathaniel, 1697, baptized June 20, that year; Ebenezer, December 22, 1704; Mehitable, March 8, 1707.

(XXII) Benjamin, son of Edward Carleton, was born April 23, 1693, and married (first) Abigail Dudley (?), who died June 29, 1726, in her twenty-seventh year. He married (second) Elizabeth ———. Children, born at Bradford, the eldest by first wife, the others by second wife: Dudley, mentioned below; Reuben, June 2, 1732; Abigail, May 13, 1734; Mary, December 4, 1736; Hannah, April 24, 1740; Phoebe, July 9, 1742; Benjamin, December 16, 1745; Joseph, October 22, 1748. Benjamin Carleton, the father, died at Bradford, May 3, 1772, in his eightieth year.

(XXIII) Dudley, son of Benjamin and Abigail (Dudley?) Carleton, was born January 5, 1721-22, and his name appears in the revolutionary rolls of Massachusetts as one of a list of men serving as a committee for Essex county to raise recruits for the campaigns in New York and Canada. He married, February 25, 1745, Abigail Willson, of Bradford, who died October 2, 1799, aged seventy-four years. Children, born in Bradford: Rebecca, May 26, 1746; Dudley, May 16, 1748; Abigail, March 30, 1750; David, December 7, 1751, soldier in the revolution; Hannah, January 7, 1753; Michael, mentioned below; Moses, January 17, 1759; Mercy, September 17, 1760; Edward, July 2, 1762; William, June 1, 1764; Ebenezer, April 4, 1766; Phoebe, March 4, 1769.

(XXIV) Michael, son of Dudley and Abigail (Willson) Carleton, was born May 23, 1757. Bradford, his native place, is now part of Haverhill. He married, November 20, 1795, at Haverhill, Ruth, born August 12, 1778, at that place, daughter of Nathaniel and Lydia (White) Ayer. Nathaniel was a son of David and Hannah (Shepard) Ayer, and was born February 24, 1734-35. David was a son of Nathaniel and Esther Ayer, and was born May 2, 1714. Nathaniel was born November 5, 1676, son of Nathaniel and Tamsen (Thurlow) Ayer. Nathaniel was born March 13, 1654-55, son of John Ayer Jr., and grandson of John Ayer, the American immigrant. Children of Michael and Ruth (Ayer) Carleton, born at Haverhill: Michael, April 8, 1796, died April 13, 1796; William, mentioned below; David, April 17, 1799; Nathaniel, November 29, 1800; died December 8 following; Nathaniel, 1807, died at Fayetteville, North Carolina, April, 1833.

Michael Carleton was a soldier in the revolution, a private in Captain John Davis' company, Colonel Jonathan Cogswell's regiment, stationed near Boston in 1778; also in Captain Stephen Webster's company, Colonel Jacob Gerrish's regiment, October 14 to November 22, 1779, a regiment raised in Essex and Suffolk counties to re-enforce Washington's army. There was another Michael Carleton, of Andover, in the revolution. (See Mass. Soldiers and Sailors in the Revolution under Carleton and Calton, pp. 36 and 103, vol. iii). Ebenezer Caltran (misspelling for Carleton) was in Captain John Bodwell's company, Colonel Jacob Gerrish's regiment, from April to July, 1778, and was stationed at Cambridge. Michael Carleton died, according to his gravestone, at Bradford, June 20, 1836, and his widow passed away September 13, 1847.

(XXV) William, son of Michael and Ruth (Ayer) Carleton, was born May 20, 1797, at Haverhill, where he served seven years as apprentice to a tinman. At twenty-one he went to Charlestown to follow his trade, and after a few years opened a small shop and store on Washington street, Boston, where he began the manufacture of handlamps. He prospered and gradually enlarged his business until his manufactory gave employment to about three hundred workmen. The following incident illustrates his native force of character. Two years after the erection of his first factory he determined to introduce power, and had an engine built by M. W. Baldwin, founder of the Baldwin Locomotive Works, in Philadelphia. When it had been put into operation it was visited by many mechanics, and greatly excited their admiration. Among these visitors was Otis Tufts, a machinist, of Boston, who immediately began the construction of an engine on the same model, thus inaugurating the building of stationary steam engines in Boston. When experiments were undertaken for the introduction of illuminating gas into Boston, Mr. Carleton entered into the manufacture of gas fixtures, and having difficulty in obtaining suitable castings for this and other purposes of his business, started a brass foundry of his own. During the remainder of his life he was engaged in the manufacture of a great variety of small brass works, and at the time of the introduction of kerosene oil he was the first to enter this field. He was a large exporter, sending his goods to nearly all foreign countries, and continued in the supervision of his large enterprise until his eightieth year, retaining both mental and physical faculties. No incident of his life better illustrates his character than the following. In his latter days he carried on his business for several years at an annual loss of not less than $10,000 rather than economize for his own advantage by the discharge of his employes. Mr. Carleton's benevolence began early in life and increased with his income, embracing not only the poor at home, but the needy far away. He affiliated with the Masonic fraternity and was a member of the Congregational church, to the work of which he was a liberal contributor. His gifts to foreign missions, to home missions and to the cause of education in the west and south were very large, but the one generous deed for which his name will be inscribed in history was the donation to Carleton College, Northfield, Minnesota, in 1871, of $50,000. The amount was bestowed without the least ostentation, without any conditions, and in the most available form; other gifts were added, and from him and other members of his family the college received in all nearly $70,000. The trustees unanimously requested permission to bestow his name upon the institution which, previous to the period of his aid, looked only to the heroic efforts of a few earnest and devoted men. It is now one of the noblest of our western institutions of learning.

Mr. Carleton was president of the Charlestown Gas Light Company and the Sandwich Glass Company. He married (first) Lydia Hunting, of an old colonial family, and they were the parents of a son, William Edward, mentioned below. Mr. Carleton married (second), March 11, 1875, Susan Willis, a niece of his first wife. Miss Willis was born in April, 1818, in Shutesbury, Massachusetts, her father being a cousin of the poet, N. P. Willis. The first of her ancestors in this country, John Hunting, came to Dedham, Massachusetts, in 1638, and was one of the founders and the first ruling elder of the church in that place. Mrs. Susan (Willis) Carleton was a most lovely character. She and her husband were united in their benefactions to Carleton College, and

it is difficult, if not impossible, to say to which of these two the institution owes most. Mrs. Carleton died March 23, 1876, and Mr. Carleton passed away December 5, of the same year. Quiet and simple in manner, retiring in disposition, yet decided in character, he was a man of unswerving integrity and earnest Christian faith.

(XXVI) William Edward, son of William and Lydia (Hunting) Carleton, was born September 6, 1835, in Boston, Massachusetts. He received his education in the private schools of Boston, and later attended the Lawrence Scientific School of Harvard University. He was a member of the Bunker Hill Monument Association. Mr. Carleton married, November 21, 1877, Bertha Jane, born January 15, 1848, in Bangor, Maine, daughter of Dudley Franklin and Dollie (MacQuesten) Leavitt, of that city. Mr. and Mrs. Carleton became the parents of the following children: William Dudley, mentioned below; Guy Edward, born November 15, 1879, in the home at Monument Square, in Charlestown, now part of Boston, graduate of Harvard University, class of 1902, and Ruth Ingersoll, born at Charlestown, May 5, 1889. Mr. Carleton died May 20, 1910, leaving a name in all respects worthy of his noble ancestry.

(XXVII) William Dudley, son of William Edward and Bertha Jane (Leavitt) Carleton, was born September 11, 1878, at Charlestown, and attended private schools in Boston, and also the Boston Latin School, from which he graduated in 1898. The same year he entered Harvard University, completing the four years' course in three years, and graduating in the class of 1901, *cum laude*, with the degree of Bachelor of Arts. After taking a graduate course in New College, Oxford University, England, he returned to this country and entered Harvard Law School, from which in 1905 he received the degree of Bachelor of Laws. During the next three years he was in the law office of Lord, Day & Lord, New York City, and in June, 1908, formed a partnership under the firm name of Jones & Carleton, with E. Powis Jones, since which time he has been in general practice in New York. In February, 1906, he was admitted to the New York bar.

Mr. Carleton is a member of the Bar Association of New York, the Harvard Club of New York, the Bunker Hill Monument Association and other organizations. He is well known for his ability as a lawyer and as a public speaker. While at college he received the first prize in the Boylston prize-speaking contest. In politics he is an Independent. He is a communicant of the Protestant Episcopal church.

NEEDHAM The surname Needham is English in origin. Needham was a market town in county Suffolk, England, and a parish in the county of Norfolk, England, and it is probable that the families of that name took it, after the Norman fashion, from these towns. The family of the Earl of Kilmorey, to take one instance, took their name from Needham in the county of Derby, England, where they are supposed to have resided during the reign of Edward III., and possibly even earlier. Other derivations of the name are from the Saxon, neat; Danish, nad, a herd, and ham, a village. In another sense it may denote a clean, fair town. The Needham families of the United States are the descendants of several early immigrants. Chief among them were John Needham, of Boston; Edmund Needham, of Lynn, and Anthony Needham, of Salem, Massachusetts. John Needham, of Boston, was born in 1674, died February 24, 1742, having married Mary Jefts, February 26, 1702, the next generation finding them at Billerica, Massachusetts, and Tewksbury, Massachusetts. Edmund Needham came from London about 1639 and died at Lynn, Massachusetts, May 16, 1677, having married a lady of the baptismal name of Joan. There were several other settlers of a somewhat later date whose descendants are scattered throughout America. The Needhams, descendants of Anthony, were among the first settlers of Salem and the towns in its vicinity and in Hampden county, Massachusetts.

(I) Anthony Needham, first immigrant ancestor of the American branch of the Needham family here dealt with, was born in England in 1628, died after September 6, 1705, at Salem, Massachusetts. He was among the number of municipal officers organized under an act of incorporation by the people of the town, and he was also lieutenant in the troop of horse raised by the Salem authorities. He was in religion a Quaker Puritan, and when in England, which he is supposed to have left about 1650, he took with his family, according to tradition, an active part in the reformation work under Cromwell. He married, January 10, 1655, at Salem, Massachusetts, Ann Potter, who died after July 16, 1695, and by whom he had twelve children, namely: 1. Rebecca, born December 21, 1656; married Michael Chapleman, in January, 1675. 2. Hannah, born June 30, 1658. 3. Elizabeth, born October 1, 1659. 4. Provided, born February 12, 1661, died unmarried. 5. Anthony, mentioned below. 6. Mary, born February 3, 1665, died unmarried in 1742. 7. George, born March 26, 1667, died unmarried. 8. Isaac, born April 15, 1669,

died in May, 1750. 9. Abigail, born May 31, 1671; married Thomas Gould in 1691. 10. Thomas, born July 25, 1673, died in 1752. 11. Dorothy, born August 25, 1675; married William Brown, of Ipswich, Massachusetts. 12. Rachel, born March 17, 1677; married William Small, February 21, 1712.

(II) Anthony (2), eldest son of Anthony (1) and Ann (Potter) Needham, was born April 11, 1663, died in 1758. He married, January 3, 1695, at Salem, Massachusetts, Mary Swinerton, born May 17, 1670, by whom he had five children, namely: 1. Anthony, mentioned below. 2. Humphrey, born in 1698. 3. Ruth, born about 1700, died June 8, 1748, at Brimfield, Massachusetts; married Benjamin Warner, of Brimfield, Massachusetts, April 11, 1733, at Salem, Massachusetts. 4. Rebeckah, born about 1704; married Jonathan Felton, January 18, 1719. 5. Jasper, born June 15, 1707, died October 3, 1794.

(III) Anthony (3), eldest son of Anthony (2) and Mary (Swinerton) Needham, was born November 23, 1696, died July 2, 1763, at South Brimfield, Massachusetts. He removed from Salem to Brimfield, Massachusetts, and was the first white settler in the town. He was the first town clerk, selectman and representative to the general court from Brimfield from 1730 to 1740. He had numerous land grants in Brimfield, and was a leader in the pioneer work of clearing the wilderness and building up a prosperous community. When a body of municipal officers was organized in 1762 by the authorities of the district of South Brimfield he was elected to one of the leading positions. He took much interest in military affairs and became captain of a troop of horse. Wales, Massachusetts, was a part of Brimfield, Massachusetts, from 1731 till 1828, and a small moss-covered stone erected in his memory in the old burying ground in Wales, bearing the most ancient date of any stone there, tells that he died July 2, 1763, aged sixty-seven years. He married, June 10, 1722, at Salem, Massachusetts, Mary Moulton, born September 30, 1702, died in 1790, and by whom he had eleven children, namely: 1. Anthony, born May 18, 1723, died in 1783 at Hopkinton, Massachusetts. 2. Mary (Molly), born June 21, 1725; married Benjamin Cooley, at Brimfield, Massachusetts, February 14, 1744. 3. Hannah, born in March, 1727, died August 16, 1781; married William Carpenter, at Brimfield, Massachusetts, April 28, 1743. 4. Ruth, born January 16, 1729; married Israel Kibbey, at Brimfield, Massachusetts, June 7, 1756. 5. Naomi, born June 5, 1731, died December 10, 1772, at Brimfield, Massachusetts; married Joseph

Munger, at Brimfield, Massachusetts, June 7, 1756. 6. Nehemiah, mentioned below. 7. Abigail, born November 10, 1736, died December 11, 1736. 8. Jasper, born July 31, 1738, died December 14, 1821. 9. Jeremiah, born June 17, 1741, died in August, 1815, at Wilmington, New York. 10. Daniel, born September 10, 1743. 11. Abner, born December 17, 1746, died June 20, 1800.

(IV) Nehemiah, second son of Anthony (3) and Mary (Moulton) Needham, was born April 4, 1734, died in 1783. He served with his brother Anthony, who was a lieutenant of the South Hampshire Regiment in the French and Indian war, and who responded as captain to the Lexington Alarm, April 19, 1775, in both the French and Indian and the revolutionary wars. With them in the revolutionary war were also their younger brothers, Jasper, Jeremiah, Daniel and Abner. He married (first), June 21, 1758, at Brimfield, Massachusetts, Eunice Fuller, who died in 1778, at South Brimfield, Massachusetts, and by whom he had seven children, namely: 1. Eunice, born June 24, 1759, died November 16, 1837, at Brimfield, Massachusetts; married Robert Andrews, April 18, 1781. 2. Mehetable, born January 17, 1762; married (first) Ebenezer Moulton, December, 1786; married (second) Amos Green, September 11, 1828. 3. Jonathan, mentioned below. 4. Robert, born November 27, 1766, died in 1820, at Stafford, Connecticut. 5. Susanna, born December 14, 1769; married David Brown. 6. Nehemiah, born October 16, 1772. 7. Abigail, born June 20, 1775. He married (second), March 10, 1779, at South Brimfield, Massachusetts, Lydia Blodgett, by whom he had two children, namely: 8. Sarah, born December 29, 1779; married William Gilbert Jr., November 10, 1800, at Marlboro, Vermont. 9. Samuel, born May 22, 1782, died February 17, 1813.

(V) Jonathan, oldest son of Nehemiah and Eunice (Fuller) Needham, was born May 21, 1764, died December 8, 1811, in Calvert county, Maryland. He was a large trader in cattle and also did a large business in real estate. When the revolutionary war was in progress he served along with his brother Robert in spite of their youth. He married, May 30, 1786, at South Brimfield, Massachusetts, Eunice, daughter of Captain Asa Fisk, of South Brimfield, Massachusetts, land owner and farmer, after whom was named Fisk Hill. There were five children of the marriage, the mother dying after ten years of married life. She was born October 24, 1768, died January 20, 1797. Children: 1. Roswell, born August 8, 1787, died April 8, 1870. 2. Sally, born March 29, 1789. 3. Asa, born May 18, 1791,

died February 11, 1874, at Baltimore, Maryland. 4. Jonathan, mentioned below. 5. Chester, born October 10, 1795, died November 7, 1850.

(VI) Jonathan (2), third son of Jonathan (1) and Eunice (Fisk) Needham, was born June 21, 1793, died January 24, 1862, at Wales, Massachusetts. He was a deacon of the Baptist church for twenty years, and served in the war of 1812. He married, December 21, 1816, at South Brimfield, Massachusetts, Lodisa Pratt, born May 3, 1799, died November 19, 1873, at Wales, Massachusetts, by whom he had three children, namely: 1. Asa H., born April 6, 1821, died April 27, 1849, at Baltimore, Maryland. 2. Eunice M., born April 8, 1827, died September 29, 1843, at Wales, Massachusetts. 3. Henry M., mentioned below.

(VII) Henry M., son of Jonathan (2) and Lodisa (Pratt) Needham, was born November 23, 1829, died August 12, 1890, at Wales, Massachusetts. He was educated at Union College and subsequently at Harvard Law School. From his graduation to his death he practiced law in New York City and resided at Brooklyn, New York. He married, July 6, 1864, at St. Albans, Vermont, Helen E., born October 3, 1840, died August 23, 1903, at Brooklyn, New York, daughter of Henry T. Chapman, of Brooklyn, New York. They had three children, all born at Brooklyn, namely: 1. Helen P., born April 10, 1865; married George C. Flynt, of Monson, Massachusetts, June 21, 1892, at Brooklyn, New York. 2. Henry Chapman, born November 8, 1866; received his degree of LL. B. from Columbia Law School in 1888; is a practicing attorney in New York City, devoting his attention almost entirely to real estate and probate work. 3. George A., born September 12, 1868; after completing his course at the Adelphi Academy, Brooklyn, entered the employ of Herring & Company, manufacturers of safes and bank vaults; later, and upon the sale of that company to the so-called trust, he with others organized the Remington & Sherman Company, manufacturers of safes and vaults; he is vice-president of the company and an engineer of ability.

PATTERSON This ancient Scotch name, long honorably known in "Thistle Kingdom," was transported to Northern Ireland at a very early day in common with many other Scotch names, forming a population now popularly known as the Scotch-Irish. These settlers on the lands of Antrim, Derry and other Northern Irish counties preserved the traditions, customs and habits of thought of their ancestry in such marked degree that it has often been said of them, "They were more Scotch than the Scotch." The United States owes many of its best citizens to this sturdy blood which was lured to our shores by the prospects of religious liberty and practical opportunity.

(I) In Argleshire, Scotland, dwelt John Patterson, who settled in Northern Ireland during the first half of the seventeenth century. Little can now be shown regarding his descendants, but it was known that he had a son Robert, mentioned below.

(II) Robert, son of John Patterson, resided in Northern Ireland, married, and among his children was a son Alexander, mentioned below.

(III) Alexander, son of Robert Patterson, was born in Northern Ireland. He came to America with the immigrants who settled Londonderry, New Hampshire, locating there in 1721. No record of his wife appears, and only one of his children is known, Alexander, mentioned below.

(IV) Alexander (2), son of Alexander (1) Patterson, was born at Bush Mills, Northern Ireland, in 1714, died in Strafford, Vermont, in 1802. In early life he accompanied his father to Londonderry, New Hampshire. He appears but little in the records of that town, in which he served as surveyor of highways in 1753-55. About the year 1764 he visited the town of Henniker, New Hampshire, where he appeared leading a cow and carrying a bag of meal. He built a shanty of boughs for protection while locating his lands and beginning a clearing. In the spring of 1765, with his sons, Joseph and Isaac, he visited the location, which is on the north side of the Contoocook river, and there they began a clearing in earnest. At that time his family was in Pembroke, New Hampshire, whither he returned in time to gather his hay crop. After this was accomplished he returned to Henniker with his sons, and they then burned off the clearing already made and prepared the ground for a crop the following year. They built a log cabin, in which they settled with the entire family in the fall. The snows of the ensuing winter were very deep, and for a period of six weeks they saw no person outside of the family. Mr. Patterson became a leading citizen of Henniker, where he served as selectman in 1772-73, and from which town he went out as a revolutionary soldier. In 1799 he removed to Thetford, Vermont, and shortly afterward to Strafford, same state, where his death occurred. He and one of his sons responded to the alarm following the battle of Lexington, and his name appears among the signers of the Association Test in 1776.

He married Elizabeth Arbuckle, who was born in 1720 on board ship while her parents were removing from Scotland to America. She is described as a "pert little woman, straight as an arrow, of great activity, running over with humor, and of an excellent education for her day." Her name is the only one of a female which appears on the call to Rev. David McGregor to become first pastor of the West Parish of Londonderry, New Hampshire. She taught one of the first schools in Henniker. Children: Lydia, Mary, Joseph, mentioned below; Margaret, Sarah, Isaac, Josiah, died young; Josiah, Robert, Alexander, James.

(V) Joseph, eldest son of Alexander (2) Patterson, was born in Londonderry, New Hampshire, in 1750, died in Henniker, New Hampshire, January 16, 1831. He resided on the homestead in Henniker, and was an industrious, successful and useful citizen, acquiring the title of honorable, which was an unusual honor in his time. He enlisted for three months' service, September 20, 1776, in Captain Emery's company, Colonel Baldwin's regiment, and participated in the battle of White Plains, October 28, 1776, having been shot through the neck. He lost most of his accoutrement on account of this injury, and the state subsequently granted him five pounds and fourteen shillings. He married Susannah, daughter of Captain William and Naomi (Bell) Duncan, of Londonderry, and granddaughter of George and Margaret (Cross) Duncan and of John and Elizabeth (Todd) Bell, who were among the leading citizens of Londonderry. Children: Abraham, Elizabeth, Polly, Joseph, William, mentioned below; Samuel, Rachel, Susannah, George, Anna, Margaret.

(VI) William, third son of Joseph Patterson, was born in Henniker, New Hampshire, November 4, 1784, died in Lowell, Massachusetts, April 26, 1862. He resided on the paternal homestead until 1843, when he removed to Manchester, New Hampshire, and later to Lowell, Massachusetts. He was connected with the operation of various mills, and is described as an energetic and industrious citizen. He was captain of the Henniker Militia Company. He married (first) Lydia Joslyn, born September 19, 1787, in Henniker, New Hampshire, where she died March 12, 1816, daughter of James and Sarah (Wetherbee) Joslyn. He married (second) August 29, 1820, Frances Mary Shepard, of Holderness, New Hampshire, born April 20, 1795, died June 19, 1858. Children of first wife: 1. Mary, born 1811, died March 24, 1812. 2. Alonzo, born March 21, 1813, died July 18, 1885; resided in Henniker, where he served as selectman and was otherwise prominent. 3. George W., born March 12, 1815, died July 19, 1895. Children of second wife: 4. Lydia A., died young. 5. James Willis, born July 2, 1823, died May 4, 1893; professor in Dartmouth College, member of congress and United States senator from New Hampshire. 6. Sophia Anne, born October 23, 1825, died February 21, 1877; married Charles Wilkins; resided in California. 7. Joseph D., died young. 8. Harriet W., born March 25, 1830, died January 13, 1910; married Charles Smith, of Lawrence, Massachusetts. 9. Joseph, died young. 10. Frances Jane, died young. 11. John Bartlett, born August 9, 1836. 12. Charles Henry, mentioned below.

(VII) Charles Henry, youngest son of William Patterson, was born in Henniker, New Hampshire, January 20, 1840. He was educated in the public schools of Manchester. Later he entered Dartmouth College, from which he was graduated in 1864 with the degree of Bachelor of Arts. Very shortly afterwards he entered the public service, being employed in the war and treasury departments at Washington, D. C., from 1864 to 1866. During this period he pursued the study of law and attended lectures at the Law School of Columbian University, Washington, from which he graduated with the degree of Bachelor of Laws in 1866. He was immediately admitted to the bar in Washington, but never engaged in the active practice of his profession. He was employed in a clerical position in the office of the assistant treasurer until 1868, when he received promotion to an official position, which he resigned in 1882 to become assistant cashier of the Fourth National Bank of New York. In 1887 he was appointed cashier of the same institution, and in 1910 became vice-president, in which capacity he is serving at the present time (1912). Mr. Patterson is a member of the Presbyterian church, and in politics is a Republican.

Mr. Patterson married, November 17, 1868, Frances Anne Holden, of Lowell, Massachusetts, born September 25, 1843, daughter of Frederick Artemas Holden, and granddaughter of Artemas Holden. Children: 1. Frederick Holden, born June 27, 1870; graduate of Columbia University; lawyer by profession; married, October 17, 1900, May C., daughter of James W. Corsa; child, Shepard Holden, born December 6, 1901. 2. Edith, born August 26, 1874; married, June 1, 1901, William N. Shaw; child, Mary Elizabeth, born June 24, 1908. 3. Roswell Miller, born Sep-

tember 15, 1876; graduate of Yale College; lawyer by profession; married, October 22, 1910, Antoinette Sexton.

WITHERBEE Frank Spencer Witherbee, born at Port Henry, New York, May 12, 1852, comes from an old New England family, and is a direct descendant of John Witherbye, who was born in the county of Suffolk, England, about 1650, and came to America in 1672. His name first appears at Marlboro, Massachusetts, as having married May A., daughter of John Howe, a prominent citizen of that place. He fought in "King Philip's War," and on March 26, 1676, when at church, was attacked by the Indians, who also set fire to his house. He was later one of the founders of the town of Stow, Massachusetts, and in 1688 was elected a selectman of that town, where he died about the year 1711.

(II) Thomas Witherbye, son of John Witherbye, was born in Sudbury, Massachusetts, January 5, 1678, died January 23, 1713. He resided in Marlboro, Massachusetts. He married, February 20, 1699, Hannah, born August 4, 1677, daughter of John and Lydia Wood, of Marlboro. She married (second), August 8, 1716, Moses Leonard. Children of Thomas and Hannah (Wood) Witherbye: Mary, born June 10, 1700; Hannah, June, 1702; Thomas, March 4, 1705; Silas, of whom further; Submit, March 9, 1710.

(III) Captain Silas Witherbye, son of Thomas Witherbye, was born in Marlboro, Massachusetts, July 20, 1707, died at Shrewsbury, March 10, 1783. He married, August 20, 1738, Thankful Keyes, born at Marlboro in 1709, died in Shrewsbury, June 12, 1782, daughter of Major John Keyes, known at that time as "the famous Major."

(IV) Lieutenant Thomas Witherby, son of Captain Silas Witherbye, was born in Grafton, Massachusetts, June 1, 1747, died May 9, 1827, in Shrewsbury, whither he had removed in 1777. He married, January 2, 1770, Relief Huston, of Dunstable, New Hampshire, born in May, 1749, died December 23, 1813. Children: Lewis, born December 2, 1770; Jonathan, of whom further; Thomas, born February 13, 1774; Sally, born September 10, 1775.

(V) Jonathan Witherbee, son of Lieutenant Thomas Witherby, was born in Fitzwilliam, Massachusetts, March 3, 1772, died in Bridport, Vermont, August 18, 1820. He married, October 30, 1795, at Shrewsbury, Massachusetts, Virtue Hemenway, born in Shrewsbury, January 23, 1775, died there, May 10,

1849, daughter of Silas and Mary Smith Hemenway.

(VI) Thomas Weatherby, son of Jonathan Witherbee, was born in Shrewsbury, Massachusetts, April 2, 1797, died at Port Henry, New York, August 12, 1850. He married, November 4, 1819, Millie Adams of Bridport, Vermont, born in Dublin, New Hampshire, July 2, 1799, died at Port Henry, New York, May 27, 1879, daughter of Timothy Adams, who was a descendant of Henry Adams, of Quincy, Massachusetts, the ancestor of the two Presidents Adams.

(VII) Jonathan Gilman Adams Witherbee, son of Thomas Weatherby, was born in Crown Point, New York, June 7, 1821, died at Port Henry, New York, August 25, 1875. He was one of the principal pioneers of the iron ore industry of Lake Champlain, and one of the founders of the firm of Lee, Sherman & Witherbee, established in 1849, and merged into the firm of Witherbee, Sherman & Company in 1862, which was incorporated under the same name in 1900, and is now one of the largest producers of iron ore in this country. He was a man of wide influence in both business and political circles. He married, May 13, 1846, Charlotte Spencer, born in Vergennes, Vermont, February 15, 1827, and at this time (1912) is still living. Her father was Jonathan B. Spencer, born in Vergennes, Vermont, in 1796, died at Westport, New York, in November, 1875. He was one of the pioneers in developing the lumber districts of Canada and the Western States. He served with distinction in the war of 1812, and for his services received a tract of land in the state of Iowa. His wife was May (Walker) Spencer, born in Vergennes, Vermont, April 6, 1802, died in Westport, New York, in July, 1895, at the age of ninety-three years, and with scarcely a gray hair in her head.

(VIII) Frank Spencer Witherbee, son of Jonathan Gilman Adams and Charlotte (Spencer) Witherbee, was born, as stated at the beginning of this article, at Port Henry, New York, May 12, 1852. He was educated in various private schools and at Yale University, from which he was graduated in the class of 1874 with the degree of Bachelor of Arts. Since 1875 he has devoted himself chiefly to iron mining at Port Henry, New York, having succeeded his father in the copartnership of Witherbee, Sherman & Company in that year. Upon the incorporation of that company in 1900 he was elected its first president, which office he still holds. He is also president of the Lake Camplain & Moriah Railroad Company, and of the Cubitas Iron Ore Company, and vice-president of the Cheever Iron Ore Com-

pany. He was formerly president of the Troy Steel Company and vice-president of the Tennessee Coal, Iron and Railroad Company, both of which companies are now a part of the United States Steel Corporation. He is a director of the Equitable Life Assurance Society, the Chatham and Phenix National Bank, and the Fulton Trust Company, of New York City; and of the Citizens' National Bank, Port Henry, New York, and the Central Hudson Steamboat Company.

He has traveled extensively in the United States, Canada and Europe. He is a Republican in politics, and has taken an active part in public affairs. He represented New York state on the Republican National committee during the second Harrison campaign, was for many years a member of the Republican state committee of New York, and was frequently a delegate to National, state and other nominating conventions of the Republican party. In the first Harrison election he was chosen as a presidential elector from New York state. He was a prime mover in securing the legislation to create an Adirondack State Park and to complete the State Barge Canal. He served five years in the New York state militia. He is a member of the Presbyterian church. He is a director of the American Iron and Steel Institute and a member of the American Institute of Mining Engineers, Lake Superior Mining Institute, New York Chamber of Commerce, Metropolitan Museum of Art, American Museum of Natural History, New York State Historical Association, American Scenic and Historic Preservation Society, Sons of the Revolution and American Geographic Society. He is a member of the following clubs: Union, University, Metropolitan, Republican, Down Town and Railroad (New York City); Tuxedo, Sleepy Hollow Country, Travellers' (Paris), and Benedict (Port Henry, New York). His residences are at No. 4 Fifth avenue, New York City, and at "Ledgeside," Port Henry, New York.

He married, April 25, 1883, Mary Rhinelander, daughter of Lispenard and Mary (Rhinelander) Stewart (see Stewart V). Children: Lispenard Stewart, born in New York City, June 1, 1886, died February 8, 1907; Evelyn Spencer, born at Port Henry, New York, July 8, 1889.

(The Stewart Line).

(II) Charles Stewart, the pioneer ancestor, son of Robert Stewart, came from the north of Ireland with the Scotch-Irish in 1750 and settled in Hunterdon county, New Jersey. He was commissioned by congress, June 18, 1777, as commissary of issues in the army of the

United States and served as such during the remainder of the revolutionary war. He was the male representative of his grandfather, a Scottish officer of dragoons, wounded in the battle of the Boyne in Ireland, fighting with the army of William III. At a later date he made his home in county Donegal, Ireland.

(III) Robert Stewart, brother of Charles Stewart, lived at Londonderry, Ireland, and at Hunterdon county, New Jersey; died in 1785.

(IV) Alexander L., seventh child of Robert Stewart, was born May 31, 1775. He married, January 27, 1803, Sarah, daughter of Anthony Lispenard (see Lispenard IV). Children: 1. Helen, born February 28, 1805; married James Watson Webb, of New York, and among their children was General Alexander S. Webb, of civil war fame, president of the College of the City of New York. 2. Mary Jordan, married, February 14, 1826, Stephen Hogeboom Webb. 3. Sarah A., married (first) John Skillman, and (second) Rev. Charles Samuel Stewart. 4. Lispenard, of whom further. 5. Eliza (or Elvia), born March, 1812, died unmarried, February 22, 1866. 6. Amelia Barclay, born November 6, 1814, died April 14, 1826. 7. Matilda Wilson, born February 6, 1816; married Herman C. LeRoy.

(V) Lispenard, son of Alexander L. Stewart, was born in New York City, August 9, 1809. He married, June 4, 1834, Louisa Stephania Salles, who died September 7, 1837. He married (second), December 22, 1847, Mary Rogers Rhinelander (see Rhinelander IV). Children by first wife: 1. Louisa Stephania, born at Paris, May 21, 1836; married, May 21, 1861. John B. Trevor and had Helen and Henry G. 2. Sarah Lispenard, born April 9, 1837; married, April 20, 1864, Frederick Graham Lee. Children by second wife: 3. William Rhinelander, born December 3, 1852; married, November 5, 1879, Annie Armstrong and had Muriel, Anita and William R. 4. Lispenard, born July 19, 1855; state senator, prominent in business and public life. 5. Mary Rhinelander, born March 3, 1859; married, April 25, 1883, Frank Spencer Witherbee (see Witherbee VIII).

(The Lispenard Line).

(I) Antoine L'Espenard, who came from a family of French extraction claiming descent from the ancient nobility of France, left Rochelle in his native country in 1669 for America with his wife Abeltie, and in 1670 he was a settler at Albany, New York. A treaty of neutrality between the English and French, dated November 16, 1686, stipulated that the

Indian trade should be free to the colonies of both nations and that neither French nor English should interfere in the warfare among the Indians. Antoine L'Espenard was the representative of the English government dispatched by Governor Dongan from New York to Governor Denonville in Canada. He was selected, it is believed, because he was an intimate acquaintance of the governor and doubtless spoke his language perfectly. L'Espenard ascertained during his mission that the French were preparing to make a winter expedition on snow shoes against Albany to burn the city, because the inhabitants had aided the Seneca Indians. L'Espenard warned Colonel Peter Schuyler at Albany, then mayor of the city, and Schuyler moved promptly against the French settlements at the north end of Lake Champlain and won a victory. For a few years L'Espenard lived at Saratoga and he was one of the French settlers taken to Albany when the war between the French and English colonies came in 1690. He was released immediately with other French known to be friends of the English. Soon afterward he joined the Huguenot colony at New Rochelle, New York, and, according to tradition, he was joined by Baroness L'Espenard, probably a relative. He resided on what is now Davenport's Neck on Long Island sound. When he was eighty-one years old he was granted by the freeholders of New Rochelle land upon which to build a grist mill, which he erected on the east side of the Neck, then called Leisler's and LeCount's Neck, and the family mansion stood at the easterly end of the millpond. L'Espenard died at New Rochelle in his eighty-sixth year. His will was recorded in Albany and a second will was dated April 3, 1685, in New York. These wills bequeath to wife Abeltie and children—David, Anthony, of whom further; Johannes, Cornelia, Margarita and Abigail.

(II) Anthony Lispenard, as the name has been spelled since the days of the pioneer, son of Antoine L'Espenard, was born October 31, 1683. He married, November 7, 1705, Elizabeth Huygens de Klyne, daughter of Leonard and granddaughter of Barrentsen Huygens de Klyne, of New York. Elizabeth was baptized March 29, 1688 (Reformed Dutch Church, New York). Anthony died in the seventy-fifth year of his age and his will was dated August 16, 1755. Children: Anthony, Magdalen, Leonard, of whom further; John, Elizabeth, David, Abigail, Maria and Susannah.

(III) Leonard, son of Anthony Lispenard, was born December 14, 1714. He married, in 1741, Alice, daughter of Anthony and Cornelia Rutgers. His wife inherited from her father, who died in 1746, a third of one large landed estate known as the Rutgers Farm, a portion of the extensive grant of land which Anthony Rutgers received from George II. In an orchard on this farm on East Broadway, New York, Nathan Hale, the American spy, was hanged. Leonard Lispenard purchased, September 28, 1748, from the sisters of his wife, the other two-thirds and became sole owner of this farm. Leonard Lispenard was an important merchant in New York, and for some fifty years he held important offices of trust. From 1750 to 1762 he was an alderman and was one of the committee of the common council to draft an address in honor of Lord Amherst for his success in the war against Canada in 1760. He was a member of the Twenty-eighth session assembly, province of New York, 1759; twenty-ninth session, 1761-63, delegate to the "Stamp Act Congress" which met in New York in 1765, and in the same year he was one of the twenty-eight delegates from New York City who united with delegates from eight other colonies in a futile effort to secure the repeal of certain obnoxious laws. In 1773 he was president of the New York Marine Society. He was an original member of the Society of the New York Hospital and one of its governors from 1770 to 1777, and from 1780 to 1787. He was a member of the "Committee of Fifty-one," elected May 14, 1774, to act on the impending crisis, and one of the "Provisional Committee" which met in New York, April 20, 1775; member of the "Committee of One Hundred," chosen May 5, 1775, to control all general affairs relating to public interests; deputy to the revolutionary congress in New York in 1775. He was regent of the University, and governor, trustee and treasurer of King's College, now Columbia University. As a member of the "Committee of Observation" he was active in political movements and influential in molding public sentiment. When the news of Lexington came a small body of men, including Anthony and Leonard Lispenard, seized a sloop laden with provisions for the English at Boston and threw the cargo overboard, and on April 23, 1775, captured a thousand stands of arms and sent them to the American army. Leonard Lispenard, who was then holding a commission as colonel of militia under the king, resigned. On his way to Boston to take command of the army General Washington and his party, June 25, 1775, were entertained at the house of Colonel Lispenard at what is now the corner of Hudson and Desbrosses streets. Lispenard died February 20, 1790, was buried in the family vault in Trinity churchyard. His es-

tate was bounded on the north by Canal street, south by Reade street and extended from the Hudson river to West Broadway. Lispenard, Leonard and Anthony streets were named for the family.

Children: Leonard, born 1743, graduate of King's College, 1762, merchant, member of chamber of commerce, owned the property at Davenport's Neck, where he had a summer residence; Cornelia, married, February 5, 1759, Thomas Marston; Anthony, of whom further.

(IV) Anthony (2), son of Leonard Lispenard, was baptized in the Reformed Dutch church, New York, December 8, 1742. He married, December 10, 1764, his cousin, Sarah, daughter of Andrew Barclay, a New York merchant, after whose family Barclay street was named. The wife of Andrew Barclay was Helen Roosevelt, niece of Rev. Henry Barclay, rector of Trinity Church, New York. Her sisters were Mrs. Augustus Van Courtland, of the Manor of Van Courtland; Mrs. Frederick Jay, Mrs. Beverly Robinson and Mrs. Bayley, whose descendant, James Roosevelt Bayley, was Roman Catholic Archbishop of Baltimore and Primate of America. Anthony Lispenard was the proprietor of extensive breweries and mills on Greenwich road near the foot of the present Canal street. It is said that he was captain of militia at the beginning of the revolution and sided with the colonies against the king.

Children: Thomas and Anthony, died unmarried; Alice, died unmarried in 1886; Leonard, married Ann Dorothy Bache; Helen Roosevelt, married, in 1792, her cousin, Paul Richard Bache; Sarah, married, January 27, 1803, Alexander L. Stewart (see Stewart IV).

(The Rhinelander Line).

(I) Philip Jacob Rhinelander, immigrant ancestor, was born about 1650 on the Rhine in France, died in New Rochelle, New York. His native place was four miles above Oberwessel. He came with the Huguenots in 1686 and settled in New Rochelle on Long Island sound. He became an extensive land owner.

(II) William, son of Philip Jacob Rhinelander, was born in New York City. He invested largely in real estate and was trustee of the family. He married Magdalen, daughter of Stephen Renaud, of New Rochelle.

(III) William (2), son of William (1) Rhinelander, was born in New York City in 1753, died there in 1825. He possessed much real estate and was trustee of the Rhinelander estate. He married Mary, daughter of Christopher and Mary (Dyer) Roberts, granddaughter of John Dyer and descendant of Colonel Roberts, a line officer in the revolution, also of Huguenot ancestry.

(IV) William Christopher, son of William (2) Rhinelander, was born in New York City in 1791, died there in 1878. He was trustee of the family estates under his father's will. He was quartermaster and lieutenant in Colonel Stone's regiment in the war of 1812. He married, in 1816, Mary Rogers, descendant of John and Mary (Pierrepont) Rogers. Mary Pierrepont was a niece of Benjamin Franklin. Children: Mary Rogers, married Lispenard Stewart (see Stewart IV); Julia, died young; William, trustee of the Rhinelander estates, married, June 1, 1863, Matilda Cruger, daughter of Thomas J. Oakley, chief justice of the supreme court, 1846-57; member of congress 1813-15; Serena.

WILLIS George Willis, the immigrant, was born in England in 1602. He came to New England in 1636 or earlier and settled in Cambridge, Massachusetts. He was a mason by trade and in Cambridge engaged in the manufacture of brick. In 1636 he was a proprietor of the town of Cambridge, and he was admitted a freeman of the colony, May 2, 1638. He petitioned to be excused from training in 1662. He was probably a brother of Michael Willis, cutler, of Dorchester. There were at least seventeen emigrants bearing the name of Willis in Massachusetts and Plymouth colonies before 1650, and it is, of course, impossible to trace the connection between them, if any existed. George Willis acquired considerable land in Cambridge, Brookline, Billerica and vicinity. He resided on the west side of the common in Cambridge. In 1638 he was a deputy to the general court. He married (first) Jane Palfrey, widow, who had children John and Elizabeth Palfrey. The son, John Palfrey, who came to America and joined the church at Cambridge, December 10, 1658, is the progenitor of the Palfrey families in this country. On joining the church in 1640 Jane Willis spoke of formerly being in Newcastle and Heddon, England. George Willis married (second) Sarah ———, who survived him. He died September, 1690. Children of George and Jane Willis: John, born in 1630; Nathaniel, mentioned below; George; Thomas, born December 28, 1638, at Cambridge; Roger, in 1640, settled in Sudbury; Stephen, October 14, 1644.

(II) Nathaniel, son of George Willis, appears to have left practically no record behind him. He owned land in Dorchester. The family history names as his children: Nathan-

iel, mentioned below; John, married Rebecca Tufts; Andrew, married Susanna ———.

(III) Nathaniel (2), son of Nathaniel (1) Willis, is believed to have had these children: Charles, mentioned below; James, Richard, had a son William at Boston.

(IV) Charles, son of Nathaniel (2) Willis, married, in 1727, Anna Ingalls, probably daughter of John and Sarah (Russell) Ingalls. Her will proved in 1765 mentions only two children: Charles, mentioned below; Anna, born December 29, 1731.

(V) Charles (2), son of Charles (1) Willis, was born in Boston, August 21, 1728. His father appears to have died when he was a child and he was brought up in Boston in the bookstore of John Phillips and Nathaniel Belknap on Cornhill. He was a sailmaker. He married Abigail Belknap, born May 2, 1730, daughter of Nathaniel and Rebecca (Bailey) Belknap, granddaughter of Joseph and Abigail (Buttolph) Belknap and great-granddaughter of Abraham Belknap, of Boston, ancestor of Rev. Dr. Jeremiah Belknap, of Boston, author of "The History of New Hampshire." His mother was daughter of John Bailey and granddaughter of the gifted Rev. Thomas Bailey, of Watertown. Children: Charles, born 1753; Nathaniel, mentioned below; Abigail, married, 1785, Lieutenant Isaac Collins.

(VI) Nathaniel (3), son of Charles (2) Willis, was born February 7, 1755, died in Ohio, April 1, 1831.

He was a printer by trade. From June, 1774, to January, 1784, he published the *Independent Chronicle,* a Whig newspaper, in Boston, printed in the same building in which Benjamin Franklin had worked at his trade. He was an active man, a fine horseman and a leader of the patriots. He took part in the Boston tea party and was adjutant of the Boston regiment sent on an expedition to Rhode Island under General Sullivan in the revolutionary war. In 1784 he sold his interest in the *Independent Chronicle* and became one of the pioneer journalists of the frontier. He removed first, however, to Winchester, Virginia, where he published a paper for a short time; then to Shepardstown, where for a time he published a paper, and thence in 1790 to Martinsburg, Virginia, where he founded the *Potomac Guardian* and published it until 1796. In that year he removed to Chillicothe, Ohio, and established the *Scioto Gazette,* the first newspaper in what was then known as the Northwest Territory. He was printer to the government of the territory and afterward held an agency in the post office department. He bought and cultivated a farm at Chillicothe, where his death occurred.

He married (first) at New London, Connecticut, Lucy Douglas, born September 22, 1755, at New London, daughter of Nathan and Anne (Dennis) Douglas, granddaughter of Thomas and Hannah (Sperry) Douglas and great-granddaughter of Robert and Mary Douglas, first of Ipswich, Massachusetts, then of New London. She died in Boston, May 1, 17—. He married (second), January 18, 1789, Mary Cartwell, at Winchester, Virginia, born September 7, 1770, died September 9, 1844. Children by first wife: Andrew and Mary, died young; Nathaniel, mentioned below; Rebecca, born July 28, 1782. By second wife: Elijah C., born January 9, 1790; Sarah A., May 10, 1791; Mary A., February 12, 1793; Eliza A., October 7, 1795; Catherine C., May 12, 1797; Martin C., February 19, 1799; Julia A., March 29, 1801; Matilda, November 22, 1802; Henry C., February 5, 1805; James M., January 20, 1808; Madeline C., October 19, 1811.

(VII) Nathaniel (4), son of Nathaniel (3) Willis, was born in Boston, June 6, 1780, died May 26, 1870. He remained there until 1787, when he joined his father in Winchester, Virginia, and was set to work folding newspapers and setting type. At Martinsburg, a few years later, he became postrider and with his time-honored tin horn used to deliver the papers from saddle-bags through the country round about. A sketch of the old office of the *Potomac Guardian* made by Porte Crayon is in the possession of Richard Storrs Willis, of Detroit. At the age of fifteen Nathaniel returned to Boston and entered the printing office of his father's old newspaper, the *Independent Chronicle*, working in the same pressroom in which his father and the great Franklin had worked in their day as apprentices. He also found time while in Boston to drill a militia company, the Fusiliers. In 1803, at the request of a Maine congressman and others of the Republican party, he established at Portland, Maine, the *Eastern Argus*. Party feeling was vehement and the controversies in his newspaper soon involved Willis in costly libel suits. After six years he sold the newspaper to Francis Douglas. At this time, through the influence of Rev. Dr. Edward Payson, the editor turned his attention to religion. From 1810 to 1812 he made efforts to establish a religious newspaper in Portland, but secured no substantial support. In the meantime he supported himself by publishing tracts and religious books. In January, 1816, he started the *Boston Recorder*, which he asserted to be the first religious newspaper in the world. He conducted this paper until 1844, when he sold it to Rev. Martin Moore, and it still lives in the

Congregationalist and Boston Recorder. Willis also originated the idea of a religious paper for children. *The Youth's Companion*, which he commenced in 1827 and edited for about thirty years, was the first and remains today perhaps the best and most successful publication of its kind.

Charles Dudley Warner wrote of him:

The elder Willis, though a thoroughly good man and good father, was a rather wooden person. His youth and early manhood had been full of hardship; his education was scanty, and he had the formal and narrow piety of the new evangelicals of that day, revolting against the latitudinarianism of the Boston Churches. He was for twenty years deacon of the Park Street Church, profanely nicknamed by the Unitarians Brimstone Corner. * * * His rigidity was, perhaps, more in his principles than in his character, and his austerity was tempered by two qualities which have not seldom been found to consist with the diaconate, namely, a sense of humor—dry of course to the correct degree—and an admiration for pretty women, or, in the dialect of that day, for female loveliness.

Mr. Willis married (first) Hannah Parker, who was a native of Holliston, Massachusetts, "a woman whose strong character and fervent piety were mingled with a playful affectionateness which made her to her children the object of that perfect love which casteth out fear." The testimony to her worth and her sweetness is universal. The Rev. Dr. Storrs, of Braintree, in an obituary notice written on her death in 1844, at the age of sixty-two, spoke of her as "the light and joy of every circle in which she moved; the idol of her family; the faithful companion, the tender mother, the affectionate sister, the fast and assiduous friend." She was born January 28, 1782, died in Boston, March 21, 1844, daughter of Solomon and Elizabeth Parker, descendant of John Parker, a pioneer of Hingham. Mr. Willis married (second), July 8, 1845, Susan (Capen) Douglas, widow of Francis Douglas. She was born October 11, 1790. Children: 1. Lucy Douglas, born May 11, 1804; married Josiah F. Bumstead. 2. Nathaniel Parker, mentioned below. 3. Louisa Harris, born May 11, 1807; married Rev. L. Dwight. 4. Julia Dean, a talented writer in her brother's paper; never married. 5. Sarah Payson, born July 9, 1811; a prolific and successful writer for children under the name of "Fanny Fern;" married Charles Eldridge. 6. Mary Perry, born November 28, 1813, died unmarried, March 22, 1853. 7. Richard Storrs, born February 10, 1819; editor of the *Musical World*, author of "Our Church Music," a poet and musical composer of note; married Jessie Cairns. 8. Ellen Holmes, born September 23, 1821, died February 5, 1844; married, June 12, 1843, Charles F. Dennett.

.

(VIII) Nathaniel Parker, son of Nathaniel (4) Willis, was born in Portland, Maine, January 20, 1806. He began his school life under the instruction of Rev. Dr. McFarland, of Concord, New Hampshire. Afterward he attended the Boston Latin School, Phillips Academy of Andover, Massachusetts, and Yale College, from which he was graduated with high honors in the class of 1827. While in college he began to write under the signature of "Roy," and he published various religious articles and won the first prize offered by Lockwood, the publisher, for the best poem contributed to his gift book, "The Album." After leaving college he became the editor of the "Legendary" and the "Token," a series of sketches and tales, published by S. G. Goodrich, known as "Peter Parley." In the following year, 1828, he established the *American Monthly Magazine,* and conducted it for two years and a half, when it was merged with the *New York Mirror,* and the interesting literary partnership of the editors, Nathaniel P. Willis and George P. Morris, began. Willis went abroad as soon as the partnership was launched and contributed to the *Mirror* the piquant sketches called "Pencillings by the Way," while traveling. He made a long and interesting journey through all the countries of the Continent. During his foreign residence he wrote for the *New Monthly Magazine* the tales and sketches of "Philip Slingsby."

In 1837 Mr. Willis returned home and made his home near the village of Oswego, New York, at "Glenmary." The sudden loss of his income by the death of his father-in-law and the failure of his booksellers, five years later, compelled him to return to the city. For a time he was associated with Dr. Porter in the publication of the *Corsair,* a weekly critical journal. While in London soon afterward he published a collection of stories, poems and letters under the title of "Loiterings of Travel," and another volume, "Two Ways of Dying for a Husband," which contained his plays, "Bianca Visconti" and "Tortesa the Usurer," and when he returned he found the *Corsair* had failed and he engaged with General Morris in the publication of the *New Mirror,* first as a weekly, afterward as a daily. The *New Mirror* passed into other hands while Willis was sick abroad, and upon his return he was again associated with General Morris in the publication of a weekly, the *Home Journal.* As editor and contributor in New York, and at his second country place, "Idlewild," on the Hudson, Willis toiled faithfully through the twenty-one years of life that remained to him. During the civil war he

went to the front as correspondent of his paper. He died at "Idlewild," January 20, 1867.

A recent writer says of his early life:

He figured to some extent in the more fashionable society of Boston, gave great care to his dress and personal appearance, and drove a high-stepping bay horse which he named Thalaba. For frequenting the theatre and neglecting his duties in Park Street Church, he was excommunicated from the church. In England Lady Blessington and other persons of less notoriety and perhaps a secure position took him up and made much of him. To women particularly, and often to older women, he was here, as elsewhere, very attractive. He was given the entrée of the best clubs, and found it as easy as it had been at New Haven to make himself agreeable to everybody. No, not everybody, for when his Pencillings were reprinted in England there were those who took him roundly to task for some of the things he had said. He fought a duel with Captain Marryat, the author.

He was unquestionably among the foremost poets and writers in this country in his day. No complete edition of his works has been published. Thirteen volumes published by Scribner contained a large part of his writings. A bibliography is given in the biography written by Professor Henry A. Beers, edited by Charles Dudley Warner, and published in the "American Men of Letters" series of the *Riverside Press* in 1885. This list describes twenty-nine books, besides nine others that he edited and wrote in part.

He married (first) in England, Mary Leighton Stace, daughter of a British army officer who won distinction in the battle of Waterloo, commissary-general in command of the arsenal at Woolwich. She was a woman of great beauty, grace and sweetness of character. He married (second), October 1, 1846, Cornelia, an adopted daughter of Hon. Joseph Grinnell, of New Bedford, Massachusetts, a congressman from Massachusetts. She was born March 19, 1825, died in 1904. Child by first wife: Imogene, born June 20, 1842. Children of second wife: Grinnell, mentioned below; Lillian, born April 27, 1850; Edith, born September 28, 1853; John Bailey, born May 30, 1857.

(IX) Grinnell, son of Nathaniel Parker Willis, was born at 19 Ludlow place, New York City, April 28, 1848. He attended the public schools of New Bedford, Massachusetts, and the Friends Academy of that city. He is a partner of the firm of Grinnell Willis & Company, merchants and agents of the Wamsutta Mills, 44 and 46 Leonard street, New York City. Mr. Willis has inherited the literary tastes of his father and has written some poetry, but his life has been devoted mainly to business. He married, October 24, 1874, Mary Baker Haydock, born March 13,

1849, daughter of Robert and Hannah (Wharton) Haydock. Children: Hannah Haydock, born in New York City, December 31, 1875; Cornelia Grinnell, born in New York City, August 31, 1877; Joseph Grinnell, born in Germantown, Pennsylvania, July 24, 1879.

This name is usually written HELMS Helme, but that branch of the family which located in Orange county, New York, early in the eighteenth century, seems to have changed the final letter and their descendants have adhered to the new form. The name is found very early in Rhode Island, and was identified with the settlement of eastern Long Island soon after the pioneers located there. Down to a very recent date it has been conspicuous in connection with the history of Orange county, New York.

(I) Thomas Helme was in the town of Brookhaven, Long Island, before 1680. He was among the original proprietors of the town and was one of the second patentees. With Richard Woodhull he was appointed to lay out Little Neck in 1687, was commissioner in 1690 and justice of the peace in 1691. On December 27, 1686, he was appointed one of the seven trustees of the freeholders and commonalty by Governor Dongan, of New York. He was president of the board of trustees in 1694-95 and 1698; justice of the peace in 1701-06, trustee in 1702 and a member of the commission to lay out highways in 1704. In 1687 and 1691 he was town clerk of Brookhaven.

(II) Thomas (2), son of Thomas (1) Helme, was born about 1680, and resided in Brookhaven.

(III) Phillips Helms, son of Thomas (2) Helme, born June 14, 1703, in Brookhaven, was probably named in honor of Rev. Mr. Phillips, long pastor of the church at Seatucket. He married Johanna, daughter of Andrew Miller, a prominent citizen of Brookhaven, and they had sons: Anson, William and Thomas.

(IV) William, second son of Phillips and Johanna (Miller) Helms, was born September 10, 1758, in Brookhaven, and settled in the present township of Monroe, Orange county, New York. Many others of the name are found in that vicinity about the same time. In 1775 Vincent Helms was constable of the town of Monroe and Thomas Helms was his bondsman. The neighborhood where the family was located, south of Mombasha Lake, was known as Helmsburg. William Helms was a private in the revolutionary army, and helped forge the Hudson river chain. He married Eleanor, daughter of Hugh Dobbins, from Ireland.

(V) William (2), son of William (1) and Eleanor (Dobbins) Helms, was born about 1780, in Monroe, where he resided engaged in farming. He was an active member of the Methodist church, a man of standing and influence in the community. He married Elizabeth Helms.

(VI) Uriah, son of William (2) and Elizabeth (Helms) Helms, was born January 1, 1800, in New York City, and died in St. Louis, Missouri, in the fall of 1881. He was a merchant in New York City, dealing in fancy goods. He was a member of the Presbyterian church, and a Democrat in politics. He married Amy, eldest daughter of Amos and Rosetta (Lewis) Whitney, born January 5, 1805, in Yorktown (see Whitney V).

(VII) Rosetta Lewis, only child of Uriah and Amy (Whitney) Helms, was born in New York City, and was educated at Rutgers Female College, from which she graduated in 1853. She is a graduate of the New York University Woman's Law class of 1902, and member of the Alumni Association. She is a member of St. Mark's (Protestant Episcopal) Church, Brooklyn, New York, where she resides; of the Rutgers Alumnæ Association; charter member of the Chiropeon Club, of Brooklyn; member of Colony, No. 8, Society of New England Women, of Brooklyn; of the Sunshine Society, of Fort Green Chapter, Daughters of the American Revolution, and of the National Society of Patriotic Women. She married, March 22, 1866, Charles Winter, who was born in New York City, May 9, 1832, son of Isaac Winter, who came from Prussia. Charles Winter was a marine engineer during the civil war, and was employed in the quartermaster's department of the ship "Fulton." He was ten years a member of the Seventh Regiment, N. G. S. N. Y., and was a member of the Marine order. He died December 26, 1889.

(The Whitney Line).

The surname Whitney, originally written de Whitney, is said to have been derived from the name of the parish where the castle stood. Aluard, a Saxon, held the land before the conquest, but at the time of "Domesday Survey," A. D. 1086, it was waste, without an owner, save the king, as lord paramount. A grandson, or great-grandson of Sir Turstin, one of the conqueror's knights, known as Turstin of Fleming, sometime between 1100 and 1200, engaging in the border wars, built a stronghold and took up his abode at Whitney, on the banks of the Wye, and thus far after the custom of the period acquired the surname of de Whitney. The first mention of a de Whitney

Rosetta Lewis Winter

in any extant record is that of Robert de Wytteneye, in the "Testa de Nevil," A. D. 1242. (I) Henry Whitney was born in England about 1620. No record has been found of the time of his arrival in this country, but the town records of the town of Southold, Long Island, show that on October 8, 1649, he with Edward Tredwell and Thomas Benedict bought three-fourths of William Salmon's land at Hashamommock, now Southold, Long Island. The town records of Huntington, Long Island, show that he was an inhabitant of that place August 17, 1658, when he bought of Wyandance, sachem of Pemmanake, "three whole necks of land for the use of the whole town of Huntington." He built a gristmill there for Rev. William Leverich, and the dispute that followed over payment finally led to the dismissal of the minister from his parish. Once he was in court for grinding corn in the absence of the owner of the mill which he formerly owned, but he proved that the grinding was necessary and that no harm had been done the property, and he was acquitted. He removed to Jamaica, Long Island, where he bought a tract of land of Richard Harker. His name appears several times on the town records there as a member of important committees. He made a contract July 24, 1665, with the town of Norwalk, Connecticut, to build a "corne" mill there and received a grant of land from the town for that purpose, and also grants of a home lot and of several other pieces of land. He probably died at Norwalk in 1673. His will was dated June 5, 1672. He was admitted a freeman October 11, 1669. His will shows an only son John, mentioned below.

(II) John, son of Henry Whitney, was born before his father went to Southold, died in 1720. He had a grant of land January 20, 1665, at Norwalk, where he settled with his father. He was also a miller and millwright, and succeeded his father as owner of the Norwalk mill and homestead. He built a fulling mill and in the deed of his mills and land to his son, July 8, 1712, attempted to entail the estate. John Jr. reconveyed the land to his father and his father deeded it to his second son Joseph, May 20, 1713, on condition that he support his parents the remainder of their days. His administrator was appointed October 11, 1720. He married, March 17, 1674-75, Elizabeth Smith. Children: Not in order of birth: 1. John, born March 12, 1676-77; married March 4, 1709-10, Elizabeth Finch; lived in Norwalk, where he died February 3, 1712-13. 2. Joseph, March 1, 1678-79; millwright; married July 6, 1704, Hannah Hoyt. 3. Henry, February 21, 1680-

81; a weaver by trade; married June 14, 1710, Elizabeth Olmstead; died at Ridgefield, Connecticut, April 26, 1728. 4. Elizabeth, 1684; married Joseph Keeler, a prominent citizen of Ridgefield, Connecticut, where both died. 5. Richard, April 18, 1687; a miller; married, April 7, 1709, at Fairfield, Hannah Darling, who died October 20, 1774; lived at Fairfield. 6. Samuel, 1688; married, January 18, 1721-22, Anna Laboree; resided at Stratford, Connecticut; he died there, December 6, 1753. 7. Anne, 1691; married, October 13, 1709, Matthew St. John, one of the original settlers of Ridgefield, Connecticut; settled in Sharon, Connecticut, in 1745; she died May 9, 1773. 8. Eleanor, January 27, 1693; married, June 13, 1717, Jonathan Fairchild; she died January 25, 1777. 9. Nathan, mentioned below. 10. Sarah, married, June 13, 1717, Samuel Smith, one of the proprietors and first settlers of Ridgefield, Connecticut. 11. Josiah, married, October 30, 1729, Eunice Hanford; no record of their births or deaths has been found.

(III) Nathan, son of John Whitney, was born at Norwalk, Connecticut, about 1690. He was admitted a freeman December 9, 1728. Real estate was deeded to him February 5, 1718-19, by Joseph Keeler, Henry Whitney and Matthew St. John, brothers and brothers-in-law. He was a farmer at Ridgefield, Connecticut. His wife bore the name of Sarah. The dates of their deaths are not known. Children: 1. Mary, born December 29, 1715; married Isaac Keeler. 2. Eliasaph, February 3, 1716-17; bought house at Stamford, May 13, 1742; was a tanner and shoemaker; deacon of the church at what is now Darien; wife and he lived together seventy years; he died May 17, 1817, age one hundred years three months three days. 3. Eliakim, November 13, 1718; tanner, currier and shoemaker; married (first), May 10, 1744, at Stamford, Mary Beachgood; (second) Mary Gorham, January 15, 1775; he died in Malta, New York, about 1811. 4. Sarah, October 25, 1720. 5. Nathan, August 13, 1722, died young. 6. Nathan, June 11, 1724; removed to Cortlandt, New York. 7. Seth, mentioned below. 8. Josiah, June 12, 1729. 9. Jeremiah, September 18, 1731; died 1810; settled at Cortlandt Manor, now Yorktown, New York, in 1747; married Eva Youngs. 10. Uriah, November 12, 1737. 11. Ann, August 31, 1739; died young.

(IV) Seth, fifth son of Nathan and Sarah Whitney, was born February 8, 1726, in Ridgefield, and died before May 30, 1807, in what is now Yorktown, New York. He was a tanner, currier and shoemaker, and in 1758 was residing on Cortlandt's patent in the neighborhood now known as Crompond, in the town of Yorktown, where he purchased a fine farm which is still in possession of his descendants, and built a house which stood for more than a century. His house was attacked by Tories during the revolution and his arms taken away. Subsequent to this another party approached his house and one of its members, Joseph Hueson, attempted to enter by a rear window, believing that Mr. Whitney was entirely without means of defense. The latter had, however, mounted an old bayonet upon a strong staff, and with this he stabbed Hueson, who fell within the window. The other members of the party then seized Whitney and took him into his yard, where he was struck on the head with a pistol and left for dead; the scar caused by this blow remained with him until death. The diary of Rev. Silas Constant shows that he sometimes held religious services in Seth Whitney's house. The last-named married (first) Sarah Moe, probably from Greenwich, and (second), March 21, 1787, Elizabeth Wright; his third wife, Anna (Smith) was the widow of ——— Jump and Captain Trowbridge, of Bedford. She died, June 29, 1819. Children of Seth Whitney: Sarah, born April 3, 1750, married Joseph Fowler; Mary, married, 1790, Samuel Beadle; Ezra, a bachelor, resided with his brother Seth in Yorktown; Abijah, lived in Yorktown, as did also Seth, born May 13, 1765; Amos, mentioned below.

(V) Amos, youngest son of Seth and Sarah (Moe) Whitney, was born December 15, 1767, in Yorktown, where he was a farmer, residing on the western part of his father's homestead, and died February 2, 1844. He was buried in Crompond East graveyard, near the site of the old Congregational church, where he was admitted a member July 26, 1788. He married, January 21, 1800, Rosetta Lewis, born April 3, 1779, daughter of David Lewis, of Waterbury, Connecticut (see Lewis V). She was admitted to the Crompond church March 27, 1802, and died September 3, 1868. Children: Lewis, born October 18, 1801, died in Harlem, New York; Amy, mentioned below; Seth, December 25, 1808, was a farmer in Yorktown; Silas Constant, August 13, 1810, was a farmer in Yorktown; David, October 26, 1813, was a farmer at New Castle Corner; Sarah Jane, December 24, 1819, became the wife of William Edward Blakeney, and resided in Caldwell, New Jersey.

(VI) Amy, eldest daughter of Amos and Rosetta (Lewis) Whitney, was born January 5, 1805, in Yorktown, and became the wife of Uriah Helms, of New York City. He was a grandson of William Helms, a native of New York state, who served as a private soldier in the revolutionary army and assisted in forging the chain which the colonists stretched across the Hudson river in the hope of preventing the ascent of British forces. He married Eleanor, daughter of Hugh Dobbins, a native of Ireland. Their son, William Helms, was born near Monroe, in Orange county, New York, and was a farmer and member of the Methodist church. He married Elizabeth Helms, and they were the parents of Uriah Helms, born January 1, 1806, in New York City, where he was a fancy goods merchant, and died in 1881. He was a member of the Presbyterian church, and in politics a Democrat. He removed in 1859 to St. Louis, Missouri, where he remained until after 1874. He married, in January, 1831, at Crompond, Amy Whitney, as above noted. She died October 9, 1849, and was buried in Crompond East Graveyard. Their only child, Rosetta Lewis Helms, married Charles Winter (q. v).

(The Lewis Line).

This is one of the oldest names in English history and one of the most numerous and distinguished in American history. It is claimed by many genealogists that the name was originally spelled Louis, and was known in France as early as the eighth century, when that country was a part of the Roman Empire. Genealogists also attempt to establish the fact that all of the Lewis name in America descended from one common stock of Huguenot refugees who fled from France on the revocation of the Edict of Nantes in 1685; but the records show that in many countries of England there were many of the name to be found centuries before that event, and indeed there were many of them in Virginia previous to 1685. The name of Louis in continental Europe and Lewis in England is too old and too numerous to be traced to a common origin. The name, doubtless, had a common origin, but it would be worse than useless to attempt to trace it. Indeed, the name Lewis is too numerous in America, too widely dispersed, and traceable to too many different sources, to admit of any "common origin" theory even here. It is asserted that General Robert Lewis was the first of the name in America known to history or genealogy. He was a native of Brecon, Wales, and came here in 1635, with his wife Elizabeth, sailing from Gravesend, England, in April of that year, and settling in Gloucester county, Virginia. These facts are all denied, and even his existence is doubted. But the proofs are substantial, and he may be accepted as a fact.

Amos Whitney

The records of Massachusetts Bay colony name Humphrey Lewis in May, 1629. There were several others among the earliest in New England, including John Lewis, who was in Charlestown, Massachusetts, as early as 1634, Edmond Lewis among the early settlers of Watertown and Lynn, Benjamin Lewis, who was at New Haven, Connecticut, before 1669, and John Lewis at Westerly before 1690. William Lewis and his wife and only son William came to Boston in 1632 in the ship "Lion." The family is exceedingly numerous in New York, there being several Lewis Associations, and had a periodical published called "The Lewis Letter." In the Mohawk Valley, David Lewis kept an inn near Schenectady in 1713. Lewis county, New York, is named in honor of Major-General Morgan Lewis, of French ancestry, son of Francis Lewis, a signer of the Declaration of Independence. He was a famous general in the revolutionary and 1812 wars with Great Britain, and governor of New York, 1804-07, defeating Aaron Burr.

(I) John Lewis crossed the Atlantic in the ship "Hercules" in 1635 with his wife Sarah. He came from Tenterden, county Kent, England, bearing a certificate of character from the mayor and vicar of Tenterden. He is supposed to have been a brother of George Lewis, who was in Plymouth as early as 1634, and later resided in Scituate, Massachusetts. John Lewis resided for a time in Scituate, whence he removed to Boston, and there his wife died July 12, 1757. Their sons John and Joseph settled in Windsor, Connecticut, where the former purchased in 1678 an island at Poquonnock Falls.

(II) Joseph, son of John and Sarah Lewis, resided in that part of Windsor which is now Simsbury, and married, in Windsor, April 30, 1674, Elizabeth Case. Children recorded at Simsbury: Elizabeth, born March 20, 1675; Joseph, mentioned below; John, January 8, 1781. There were undoubtedly others whose names were not placed on the records.

(III) Joseph (2), eldest son of Joseph (1) and Elizabeth (Case) Lewis, was born March 15, 1676, in Simsbury, and settled in Waterbury, Connecticut, where he was a cloth-weaver, and acquired what was considered wealth in his time, dying November 29, 1749, at Waterbury. He married, April 7, 1703, Sarah, daughter of Abraham and Rebecca (Carrington) Andros, born March 16, 1684. After his death she married, in 1750, Isaac Brunson, and died March 6, 1773. Joseph Lewis' first child, a daughter, died aged twenty-six days. Others recorded in Waterbury: Joseph, born March 12, 1705; Sarah, April 29, 1708; John, mentioned below; Mary, June 10,

1714; Rev. Timothy, August 6, 1716, died at Mendham, New Jersey; Samuel, July 6, 1718; Abram, February 1, 1720.

(IV) John (2), second son of Joseph (2) and Sarah (Andros) Lewis, was born April 12, 1711, in Waterbury, and died there February 24, 1799. He married (first), December 4, 1734, in Waterbury, Mary, daughter of Samuel Munn, of Woodbury, Connecticut, baptized in December, 1711, died September 30, 1749; (second), May 29, 1750, Amy, daughter of Captain Samuel Smith, of New Haven (see Smith III). Children of first wife: David, died aged eighteen, in 1754; John, born December 10, 1740; Sarah, April 9, 1743. Children of second wife: Ann, born May 24, 1751; Samuel Smith, September 17, 1753; David, mentioned below.

(V) David, youngest child of John (2) and Anna (Smith) Lewis, was born April 11, 1756, in Waterbury, where he resided. No record of his wife appears in that town, but the following children are shown: Sylvester, Martha, Rosetta, David, Chester, Isaac, Betsy, Sylvia, Joseph, John, Hannah, Warren.

(VI) Rosetta, second daughter of David Lewis, was born April 3, 1779, in Waterbury, and was married January 1, 1800, to Amos Whitney, of Yorktown, Westchester county, New York (see Whitney V).

(The Smith Line).

(I) Thomas Smith, immigrant ancestor, came from England in the ship "Hector," which came to New Haven, Connecticut, leaving London, England, in 1637, and wintered at Boston, Massachusetts. He was one of the youngest persons on the ship. He was born in 1634, died at East Haven, Connecticut, November 16, 1724. It is thought by some that his father, who accompanied him, was Charles Smith. He married, in 1662, Elizabeth, born 1642, died 1727, only daughter of Edward Patterson. Thomas Smith proceeded to the rights of his father-in-law among the proprietors of New Haven. Children: John, born March, 1664; Anna, April 1, 1665; infant, 1667; John, June 14, 1669; Thomas, died young; Thomas, January 31, 1673; Elizabeth, June 11, 1676; Joanna, December 17, 1678; Samuel, mentioned below; Abigail, August 17, 1683; Lydia, March 24, 1686; Joseph, 1688; Benjamin, November 16, 1690.

(II) Samuel, son of Thomas Smith, was born at New Haven, June 24, 1681. He married, 1708, Anna Morris, born 1686, died October 19, 1743, daughter of Eleazer Morris, granddaughter of Thomas Morris, who signed the Plantation Covenant in New Haven in 1639. Children: Patterson, born October 17,

1709; Abel, mentioned below; James, June 14, 1713; Benjamin, September 20, 1716; Anna, May 17, 1719; Sarah, April 6, 1725; Daniel, August 6, 1727; Thankful, August 27, 1729; Samuel, June 11, 1732.

(III) Anna, eldest daughter of Captain Samuel and Anna (Morris) Smith, became the wife of Captain John Lewis (see Lewis IV).

PUTNAM The lineage of a very large part of the Putnams of New England is traced to John Putnam, the immigrant, the ancestor of several prominent citizens of the early days of Massachusetts. The name comes from Puttenham, a place in England, and this, perhaps, from the Flemish word putte, "a well," plural putten, and ham, signifying a "home", and the whole indicating a settlement by a well. The name has also been connected with the family name of Put, which is still in existence in certain villages in Friesland, and which may very possibly have been borne by some of the Friesland followers of Hengist and Horsa. Some four or five years after the settlement of Salem, Massachusetts, it became necessary to extend the area of the town in order to accommodate a large number of immigrants who were desirous of locating within its jurisdiction, and as a consequence farming communities were established at various points, some of them being considerable distance from the center of population. Several families newly arrived from England founded a settlement which they called Salem Village, and the place was known as such for more than a hundred years. It is now called Danvers. Among the original settlers of Salem Village was John Putnam. He was the American progenitor of the Putnams in New England, and among his descendants were the distinguished revolutionary generals, Israel and Rufus Putnam. Much valuable information relative to the early history of the family is to be found in the "Essex Institute Collection." In common with most of the inhabitants, they suffered from the witchcraft delusion, but were not seriously affected.

(I) The first ancestor of whom definite knowledge is obtainable is Roger, a tenant of Puttenham in 1086.

(II) The second generation is represented by Galo, of the same locality.

(III) Richard, born 1154, died 1189, presented the living of the church of Puttenham to the prior and canons of Ashby.

(IV) Simon de Puttenham was a knight of Herts in 1199.

(V) Ralph de Puttenham, a journeyman in 1199, held a knight's fee in Puttenham of the honor of Leicester in 1210-12.

(VI) William de Puttenham is the next in line.

(VII) John de Puttenham was lord of the manor of Puttenham in 1291 and was a son of William. His wife, "Lady of Puttenham," held half a knight's fee in Puttenham of the honor of Wallingford in 1303."

(VIII) Sir Roger de Puttenham, son of John de Puttenham and Lady of Puttenham, was born prior to 1272, and with his wife Alina had a grant of lands in Penne in 1315. He was sheriff of Herts in 1322, in which year he supported Edward II. against the Mortimers. His wife, perhaps identical with Helen, is called a daughter of John Spigornel, and was married (second) to Thomas de la Hay, king's commissioner, knight of the sheer, in 1337, who held Puttenham with reversion to the heirs of Roger Puttenham, and land in Penne in right of his wife.

(IX) Sir Roger de Puttenham was pardoned by the king in 1338, probably on account of some political offense. The next year he was a follower of Sir John de Molyns, and was knight of the shire from 1355 to 1374. He had a grant of remainder after the death of Christian Bordolfe of the manor of Long Marston, in 1370-71. He had a second wife, Marjorie, in 1370.

(X) Robert, son of Sir Roger de Puttenham, in 1346, held part of a knight's fee in Marston, which the Lady of Puttenham held. He was living in 1356.

(XI) William, son of Robert de Puttenham, of Puttenham and Penne, was commissioner of the peace for Herts in 1377, and was called "of Berk Hampstead." He was sergeant-at-arms in 1376. He married Margaret, daughter of John de Warbleton, who died in 1375, when his estates of Warbleton, Sherfield, etc., passed to the Putnams. They had children: Henry, Robert and William.

(XII) Henry Puttenham, son of William and Margaret (Warbleton) de Puttenham, was near sixty years of age in 1468, and died July 6, 1473. He married Elizabeth, widow of Jeffrey Goodluck, who died in 1486, and was probably his second wife.

(XIII) William, eldest son of Henry Puttenham, was in possession of Puttenham, Penne, Sherfield and other estates. He was buried in London and his will was proved July 23, 1492. He married Anne, daughter of John Hampden, of Hampden, who was living in 1486. They had sons: Sir George, Thomas and Nicholas.

(XIV) Nicholas Putnam, third son of William and Anne (Hampden) Puttenham, of

Penne in 1534, bore the same arms as his elder brother, Sir George. He had sons: John and Henry.

(XV) Henry, youngest son of Nicholas Putnam, was named in the will of his brother John, in 1526.

(XVI) Richard, son of Henry Putnam, was of Eddelsboro in 1524, and owned land in Slapton. His will was proved February 26, 1557, and he left a widow Joan. He had sons: Harry and John.

(XVII) John, second son of Richard and Joan Putnam, was of Wingrave and Slapton; was buried October 2, 1573, and his will was proved November 14 following. His wife Margaret was buried January 27, 1568. They had sons: Nicholas, Richard, Thomas and John.

(XVIII) Nicholas, eldest son of John and Margaret Putnam, was of Wingrave and Stukeley; died before September 27, 1598, on which date his will was proved. His wife Margaret was a daughter of John Goodspeed. She married (second) in 1614, William Huxley, and died January 8, 1619. Children of Nicholas and Margaret Putnam: John, Anne, Elizabeth, Thomas and Richard.

(I) John, eldest son of Nicholas and Margaret (Goodspeed) Putnam, was of the nineteenth generation in the English line, and first of the American line. He was born about 1580, and died suddenly in Salem Village, now Danvers, Massachusetts, December 30, 1662, aged about eighty-two years. It is known that he was a resident of Aston Abbotts, England, as late as 1627, as the date of the baptism of the youngest son shows, but just when he came to New England is not known. Family tradition is responsible for the date 1634, and the tradition is known to have been in the family over one hundred and fifty years. In 1641, new style, John Putnam was granted land in Salem. He was a farmer and exceedingly well off for those times. He wrote a fair hand as deeds on file show. In these deeds he styled himself "Yeoman"; once in 1655, "husbandman." His land amounted to two hundred and fifty acres, and was situated between Davenport's hill and Potter's hill. John Putnam was admitted to the church in 1647, six years later than his wife, and was also a freeman the same year. The town of Salem in 1644 voted that a patrol of two men be appointed each Lord's day to walk forth during worship and take notice of such who did not attend service and who were idle, etc., and to present such cases to the magistrate; all of those appointed were men of standing in the community. For the ninth day John Putnam and John Hathorne were appointed. The following account of

the death of John Putnam was written in 1733 by his grandson Edward: "He ate his supper, went to prayer with his family and died before he went to sleep." He married in England, Priscilla (perhaps Gould), who was admitted to the church in Salem in 1641. Their children baptized at Aston Abbotts, were: Elizabeth; Thomas, grandfather of General Israel Putnam, of the revolutionary war; John; Nathaniel, mentioned below; Sara; Phœbe; John.

(II) Nathaniel, third son of John and Priscilla Putnam, was baptized at Aston Abbotts, October 11, 1619, and died at Salem Village, July 23, 1700. He was a man of considerable landed property; his wife brought him seventy-five acres additional, and on this tract he built his house and established himself. Part of his property has remained uninterruptedly in the family. It is now better known as the "old Judge Putnam place." He was constable in 1656, and afterwards deputy to the general court, 1690-91, selectman, and always at the front on all local questions, whether pertaining to politics, religious affairs, or other town matters. "He had great business activity and ability and was a person of extraordinary powers of mind, of great energy and skill in the management of affairs, and of singular sagacity, acumen and quickness of perception. He left a large estate." Nathaniel Putnam was one of the principals in the great law suit concerning the ownership of the Bishop farm. His action in this matter was merely to prevent the attempt of Zerubabel Endicott to push the bounds of the Bishop grant over his land. The case was a long and complicated affair, and was at last settled to the satisfaction of Allen and Putnam in 1683. December 10, 1688, Lieutenant Nathaniel Putnam was one of the four messengers sent to Rev. Samuel Parris to obtain his reply to the call of the parish. Parris was afterwards installed as the minister of the parish, and four years later completely deceived Mr. Putnam in regard to the witchcraft delusion. That he honestly believed in witchcraft and in the statements of the afflicted girls there seems to be no doubt; that he was not inclined to be severe is evident, and his goodness of character shows forth in marked contrast with the almost bitter feeling shown by many of those concerned. That he should have believed in the delusion is not strange, for belief in witchcraft was then all but universal. The physicians and ministers called upon to examine the girls, who pretended to be bewitched, agreed that such was the case. There can be no doubt that the expressed opinion of a man like Nathaniel Putnam must have influenced scores of his neighbors. His eldest brother had been dead seven years, and he had succeeded to the position as head of the great Putnam family with its connections. He was known as "Landlord Putnam," a term given for many years to the oldest living member of the family. He saw the family of his brother, Thomas Putnam, afflicted, and being an upright and honest man himself, believed in the disordered imaginings of his grandniece, Ann. These are powerful reasons to account for his belief and actions. The following extract from Upham brings out the better side of his character: "Entire confidence was felt by all in his judgment and deservedly. But he was a strong religionist, a lifelong member of the church, and extremely strenuous and zealous in his ecclesiastical relations. He was getting to be an old man, and Mr. Parris had succeeded in obtaining, for the time, possession of his feelings, sympathy and zeal in the management of the church and secured his full coöperation in the witchcraft prosecutions. He had been led by Parris to take the very front in the proceedings. But even Nathaniel Putnam could not stand by in silence and see Rebecca Nurse sacrificed." A curious paper written by him is among those which have been preserved: "Nathaniel Putnam, senior, being desired by Francis Nurse, Sr., to give information of what I could say concerning his wife's life and conversation. I, the above said, have known this said aforesaid woman forty years and what I have observed of her, human frailties excepted, her life and conversation have been to her profession, and she hath brought up a great family of children and educated them well so that there is in some of them apparent savor of godliness. I have known her differ with her neighbors, but I never knew or heard of any that did accuse her of what she is now charged with." In 1694 Nathaniel and John Putnam testified to having lived in the village since 1641. He married, in Salem, Elizabeth, daughter of Richard and Alice (Bosworth) Hutchinson, of Salem Village. She was born August 20, and baptized at Arnold, England, August 30, 1629, and died June 24, 1688. In 1648 both Nathaniel and his wife Elizabeth were admitted to the church in Salem. Their children, all born in Salem, were: Samuel, Nathaniel, John, Joseph, Elizabeth, Benjamin and Mary.

(III) Captain Benjamin Putnam, youngest son of Nathaniel and Elizabeth (Hutchinson) Putnam, was born December 24, 1664, at Salem Village, and died at the same place about 1715. He was a prominent man in Salem and held many town offices, being tithingman of the village in 1695-96; constable and collector in 1700; selectman in 1707-13, and was often on the grand and petit juries

He was chosen to perambulate the bounds between the towns of Salem and Topsfield, which was his last appearance on the records, in 1712. He held the position of lieutenant and captain; served in the Indian war and received the titles in 1706-1711. It appears that he was imprisoned at one time, but for what cause does not appear. Among the signatures to the certificate of character of Rebecca Nurse, appear the names of Benjamin and his wife Sarah. Rev. Joseph Green, in his diary, mentions calling on "Landlord Putnam," and that he was very sick and out of his head. December 30, 1709, he was chosen deacon of the church of the village. His will dated October 28, 1706, was proved April 25, 1715. He gives to his son (Minister at Reading) "one hundred and fifty pounds for his learning." "Overseers, Uncle John Putnam and Captain Jonathan Putnam." All his children but Josiah are mentioned. He was married August 25, 1686, to Elizabeth, daughter of Thomas Putnam (according to Colonel Perley Putnam), but on the Salem records the births are recorded as by wife Hannah. His first wife died December 21, 1705, and he married (second) July 1, 1706, Sarah Holton. His children were: Josiah; Nathaniel; Tarrant; Elizabeth; Benjamin; Stephen; Daniel, mentioned below; Israel; Cornelius.

(IV) Rev. Daniel Putnam, sixth son of Benjamin and Hannah (or Elizabeth) (Putnam) Putnam, was born November 12, 1696, in Salem, Village, and died June 20, 1759, at Reading, Massachusetts. His father left him in his will "one hundred and fifty pounds, for his learning." In 1718 the North Precinct of Reading voted to give him twenty acres of land if he would be their minister, also "to build Mr. Putnam an house 28 feet long, 19 feet wide and 15 feet stud, a lenter on the back side 10 feet stud, three chimneys from the ground, and chamber chimney, and convenient parlor and convenient well, in lieu of the 100 pounds, if Mr. Putnam finds nails and glass for the house." He was not ordained until 1720, at which time the church had thirty-nine members. He was their minister thirty-nine years, and added one hundred and ninety-four persons to the church, baptized four hundred and ninety-one, and married one hundred and eleven couples. He married, February 25, 1718, Rebecca Putnam, born August 16, 1691. Their children were: Rebecca; Daniel, mention below; Aaron, died young; Sarah; Hannah; Elizabeth; Mary; Joshua; Aaron; Bethia; Susanna.

(V) Deacon Daniel (2) Putnam, eldest son of Rev. Daniel (1) and Rebecca (Putnam) Putnam, was born November 8, 1721, in Reading, died November 5, 1774, in the same town. He was elected deacon of the church in North Reading in 1754; was selectman of Reading in 1763-68-71, and in 1773 represented his town in the general court. June 4, 1774, Hannah Putnam, spinster, was appointed administratrix on his estate. He married Hannah, daughter of Henry and Hannah (Martin) Ingalls, of North Andover, Massachusetts, who was born September 12, 1723, and died May 11, 1761, in Reading. Their children were: Henry, mentioned below; Daniel; Joshua; Rebecca; Aaron; Sarah.

(VI) Henry, eldest son of Deacon Daniel (2) and Hannah (Ingalls) Putnam, was born May 7, 1755, at North Reading, and died November 27, 1806, at the same place. He was a man of influence in the community, and was chosen deacon of the church in 1778. He responded to the Alarm of April 19, 1775, and served nine days in Captain John Flint's company. He married (first) November 9, 1775, Mary Hawkes, of Lynnfield, Massachusetts, who died January 21, 1794; (second) Lucy, daughter of Peter and Ann (Adams) Tufts, of Charlestown, who married (second) in June, 1811, Jacob Osgood. She cared for James Otis, the patriot, for many years, and he was killed by lightning in her house.

(VII) Henry (2), son of Henry (1) and Mary (Hawkes) Putnam, was born June 28, 1778, died in January, 1827, in Brunswick, Maine. He was graduated from Harvard College in 1802; served in many town offices in Brunswick, and in 1808 was named as chairman of a committee to petition the president to withdraw the Embargo Act. He was representative from Brunswick, in 1813. He married, September 13, 1807, Catherine Hunt, daughter of Joseph Pease Palmer, of Roxbury, Massachusetts, who was born in 1783 and died December 12, 1889. She taught school in Brunswick from 1807 to 1825, when she removed to New York. Children: Henry, born 1808, died 1815; Catherine, 1810, died 1827; George Palmer, mentioned below; Elizabeth, 1816, died 1875; Anne, 1819, died 1869.

(VIII) George Palmer, son of Henry (2) and Catherine Hunt (Palmer) Putnam, was born February 7, 1814, in Brunswick, Maine, and died December 20, 1872, in New York. He received his early training with his sisters in his mother's school, a well-known and popular institution of Brunswick. He enjoyed the sports of the times and region, skating on the Androscoggin river in winter and boating up and down the same in summer. When he was eleven years of age he was offered an apprenticeship in Boston to the mercantile business by the husband of his mother's sister, John

Gulliver. The latter's son, John Putnam Gulliver, was of the same age as young Putnam, and they became companions in the business training and work of the store. This establishment was devoted chiefly to carpets and its owner was a man of strict puritanical views. The boys slept together in the rear of the store and were chiefly occupied in keeping the place in order. There were few holidays and the business day was a long one. The Sabbath was observed with full New England strictness, including morning and evening prayers at home, Sunday school and two long church services. No reading was permitted on the Sabbath except works of a devotional character, and there were very few books then available to the young men. Young Putnam had a strong taste for reading and in later years he often referred to the "literary starvation" which he suffered in Boston, and also referred to the compunctions of conscience he experienced when surreptitiously reading a volume of Miss Edgeworth's tales. This belonged to the forbidden class of fiction and its reading was looked upon as a frivolity.

He remained with his uncle in Boston about four years, and decided in 1829 to try his chances of securing a livelihood in New York. Here he very soon became engaged in literary work, and during the first years after his arrival, when he was fifteen years old, he began a historical manual which was completed in three years' time. In 1833 he completed and published through West & Trow a weekly chronicle entitled the *Publishers' Advertiser*. He undertook to review the current publications which in that year included the first volume of Bancroft's "United States," Abbott's "Young Christian," Mrs. Sigourney's "Sketches," and Cooper's "Letters to My Countrymen." His first introduction to the book trade was made very shortly after his arrival. He speaks of his first studies as conning paragraphs in the papers beginning "Boy Wanted." His second application was made at a little book and stationery store on Broadway, near Maiden Lane, where he engaged himself to do errands, sweep, etc., for which he was to receive a wage of twenty-five dollars per year and board in the family of his employer, George W. Bleecker, who lived over his store. For a short time he was engaged as a canvasser in the interest of a quartomonthly published by Mr. Bleecker, which took him on a cruise up the Hudson river. He was subsequently employed as first clerk in the Park Place House, an emporium of literature and art, and still later was general clerk and messenger for Jonathan Leavitt, in a two-story building at the corner of John street and

Broadway, Mr. Leavitt being the leading publisher of theological and religious books.

About this time Daniel Appleton, founder of the great house of D. Appleton & Company, became connected with Mr. Leavitt. In that era an edition of one thousand copies of a new book was the average, and those of five hundred copies were as usual as any exceeding two thousand. After Mr. Appleton had established his own business, he and Mr. Leavitt published jointly an edition of one thousand copies, including some four hundred pages, prepared by young Putnam, entitled "Chronology, an Introduction and Index to Universal History." It had been prepared originally for his own benefit as a reference. It was his custom in these times to repair to the Mercantile Library, then recently opened, after the closing of the store where he was employed, which was usually after nine o'clock. He read almost exclusively works of history. In the shop of Mr. Leavitt he was advanced to two dollars per week, and after a few months to four dollars. With this large income he felt able to rent a seat in the church. In 1833 he entered the employ of Wiley & Long, publishers and booksellers. In 1840 he became a partner, and the firm was styled Wiley & Putnam, Mr. Wiley being about one year the senior of Mr. Putnam. At that time the Appletons and I. & J. Harper were the leading publishers in New York, and the principal retail booksellers were Stanford & Swords. A very large portion of the books then sold in New York were imported from England. In the firm of Wiley & Putnam the publishing division was in charge of the junior partner, while the senior gave his attention chiefly to the selling. Mr. Putnam held to the view that irrespective of nationality or political boundaries contemporary authors should receive the returns secured from the publication of their works, and he became intimately associated with Bryant, Matthews, Halleck, Cooper & Fay. In 1840 he made his first business journey to England in the effort to establish a closer relation between the book trades of the two countries. In 1841 he made a second journey to London and established a branch house in that city in Paternoster Row, the old-time center of the London book trade. The business of this agency was the sale of American books and the purchase of English publications for sale in the United States. Thus began the great publishing house now having a world-wide reputation and known as G. P. Putnam's Sons, and which still maintain a London publication office. The firm of G. P. Putnam was established in 1848 and in 1853 began the publication of *Putnam's Monthly.*

In 1862 Mr. Putnam was appointed by President Lincoln collector of internal revenue of New York and this position he acceptably filled for three years. His activities in connection with the spread of literature and art were numerous, and he was one of the founders, and at the time of his death honorary superintendent, of the Metropolitan Museum of Art. In 1872 he was chairman of the American committee on art at the Vienna Exposition. His literary work was early recognized by Bowdoin College, which conferred upon him in 1853 the honorary degree of Master of Arts. The career of Mr. Putnam furnishes an excellent example of the fact that a liberal education is not indispensable in the development of one's best powers, if he be an earnest and painstaking student. He was accustomed to refer humorously to the granting of this degree as a reward for his service in spreading the alarm on one occasion, when a fire broke out in the college buildings at Brunswick, while he was a small boy.

Mr. Putnam organized in 1837 the earliest of the American copyright Leagues or Associations, and he was from that date until the year of his death, 1872, the secretary and the working man in the series of Leagues and Associations which had for their purpose bringing the United States into copyright relations with Europe, and securing for authors on both sides of the Atlantic, irrespective of political boundaries, the returns due to them for their labor.

He married in May, 1841, in New York, Victorine, born 1824, daughter of Joseph Haven, and his second wife, Mary Parsons Tuttle. Joseph Haven was a son of Samuel Haven, a merchant of Boston, and was engaged in the china trade of that city. He became broken in health and died there while his daughter Victorine was an infant. The children of George Palmer and Victorine (Haven) Putnam were: Mary Corinna, born 1842, married, 1873, Abram Jacobi, M. D.; George Haven, mentioned below; Edith G., born 1846; John B., born 1848; Amy V., born 1850; Irving, born 1852; Bayard, born 1854; Kingman, born 1856; Ruth, born 1860; Herbert, mentioned below; Sidney, born 1869. Several of the children were possessed of literary taste and have contributed more or less to American literature.

Among the principal works issued by the father were: "American Facts," London and New York, 1846; "The World's Progress," a manual of historical reference, New York and London, 1832-1871; "Tabular Views of Universal History." This constitutes the second division of "The World's Progress," and has been issued in successive editions from 1832 to 1908. The last edition is rewritten and brought down to date. The elder son is the author of: "The Question of Copyright," New York and London, 1892; "Authors and Their Public in Ancient Times," New York and London, 1898; "The Artificial Mother," New York and London, 1884; "Books and their Makers in the Middle Ages," New York and London, 1900; "The Censorship of the Church, a Study of the Prohibitory and Expurgatory Indexes," with reference to their influence on the production and distribution of books, two volumes, New York and London, 1906-07; "Authors and Publishers," a manual of suggestions for beginners in literature (written in coöperation with J. B. P), 1899, New York and London; "Abraham Lincoln; the Peoples' Leader in the Struggle for National Existence," 1910. John Bishop Putnam, the second son, co-author of "Authors and Publishers," is also the author of "A Norwegian Ramble." He is the founder and president of the Knickerbocker Press. Ruth Putnam is the author of "William the Silent," two volumes, 1900, New York, Amsterdam and London; "Medieval Princess," 1905, New York and London; "Charles the Bold of Burgundy," 1908, New York and London. Mary Putnam Jacobi, M. D., who died in 1905, had had a distinguished career as a physician. She was the first woman to secure admission to, and a degree from, the School of Medicine in Paris. She was the author of a number of medical treatises, and was a constant contributor to the scientific journals.

(IX) George Haven Putnam, Litt. D., eldest son of George P. and Victorine (Haven) Putnam, was born April 2, 1844, in London, and was educated at Columbia University, New York, at Gottingen and Paris. He enlisted in 1862 in the One Hundred and Seventy-Sixth Regiment New York Volunteers and was promoted successively to sergeant, lieutenant, quartermaster, adjutant, and was on retiring commissioned major. He served in the Army of the Gulf, and later under Sheridan, in Virginia, and participated in the engagements of the Red River campaign, and of Sheridan's campaign in the Shenandoah Valley. In 1865 he was appointed deputy collector of internal revenue and served until 1866. In 1866 he was admitted a partner in his father's publishing house, which is now incorporated under the style of G. P. Putnam's Sons and of which he is head. The establishment occupies quarters, extending from Twenty-third to Twenty-fourth street, near Fifth avenue, and in the Putnam Building in Forty-fifth street, near Fifth avenue. Mr. Putnam has taken active part in copyright legislation. He reorganized in 1886 the Publishers' Copyright League, of which he has since been secretary and working member. He was interested in taking up the copyright work that his father had originated, and the League of which he was secretary was finally able to bring about in 1891 the international copyright legislation for which the earlier Putnam had worked for forty years. He is himself the author of numerous volumes bearing upon the relations of author and publisher, as well as of a memoir of his father, which was printed in two volumes for private circulation. He has received honorary degrees from Bowdoin College, the University of Pennsylvania and Columbia University. He is a member of the Century Association, and of the City, the Authors' and the Economic clubs of New York, and of the Legion of Honor (France).

He married (first) in July, 1869, Rebecca Kettell Shepard, who died in July, 1895. He married (second) April 27, 1899, Emily James, daughter of Judge James C. and Emily (Adams) Smith, a graduate of Bryn Mawr, and from 1894 to 1900 dean of Bernard College. His children by his first wife were: Bertha Haven, Ethel Frothingham, Corinna Haven and Dorothy Leslie. By his second wife: Palmer Crosslett, born July, 1900.

(IX) Herbert Putnam, Litt. D., son of George Palmer Putnam, was born September 20, 1861, in New York City, and graduated from Harvard College in 1883. He was librarian of Minneapolis Athenæum and Public Library from 1884 to 1891; was librarian of the Boston Public Library from 1895 to 1899, and in 1899 was appointed Librarian of Congress, and was delegate to the International Library Conference in 1897, and president of the American Library Association in 1898. He was admitted to the bar in 1886.

Mr. Putnam married, in October, 1886, Charlotte Elizabeth, daughter of Charles W. Munroe, of Cambridge, Massachusetts. Their children are: Shirley and Brenda.

HOLBROOK The family of Holbrook is ancient and distinguished in England. The ancient coat-of-arms is: A chevron between three martletts. Several other coats-of-arms were borne by different branches of the family in England.

(I) Thomas Holbrooek, or Holbrooke, the immigrant ancestor, aged thirty-four, of Broadway, England, with wife Jane, aged thirty-four, and children, John, aged eleven; Thomas, aged ten; Anne, aged five, and Elizabeth, aged one, came from Weymouth, England, about 1628. He settled at Weymouth, Massachusetts, in 1640, and was on the committee to lay out the way from Braintree to Dorchester. He was admitted a freeman, May, 1645. He was selectman several years. His will was dated December 31, 1669, with codicil, December 31, 1673. He died 1674-76. His widow Jane died before April 24, 1677, when administration of the estate was granted to his son John. Children: John, born 1617; Thomas, mentioned below; Captain William, died 1699, lived at Scituate; Ann, married ——— Reynolds; Elizabeth, married Walter Hatch; Jane, married ——— Drake.

(II) Thomas (2) Holbrook, son of Thomas (1) Holbrooek, or Holbrooke, lived at Scituate, Weymouth and Braintree, Massachusetts. In 1653 he bought a farm of fifty-three acres in Braintree, and later became the owner of much real estate. He married Joanna ———, who survived him. He made his will, July 25, 1695, and administration on his estate was granted his widow, August 19, 1697, and his eldest son, Thomas. In the will he mentions Thomas as his eldest son, and Peter, to whom he gives "all that estate of lands and meadows in Mendon which he had formerly purchased of his brother William." Children: Thomas, buried at Braintree, December 20, 1728; John, born October 15, 1653, at Braintree; Peter, mentioned below; Joanna, born October 30, 1656; Susanna, married Andrew Willet, of Boston; Joseph, born February 12, 1660, died young.

(III) Deacon Peter Holbrook, son of Thomas (2) Holbrook, was born September 6, 1656, died 1712-13. He settled in Mendon, where he inherited lands from his father, most of which was afterwards included in Bellingham. He was an important man in his time. His will was made January 16, 1711-12, and proved May 29, 1713. He married (first) Alice ———, who died April 29, 1705. He married (second) Elizabeth Pool, who survived him, and married (second) Robert Ware, of Wenham, and died 1724. Children: John, born September 24, 1679, at Braintree; Peter. October 16, 1681, Mendon; Silvanus, August 15, 1685; Joannah, March 7, 1686-87; Richard, May 30, 1690; Eliphalet, mentioned below; William, March 28, 1693-94; Samuel, February 27, 1695-96; Mary, October 14, 1702.

(IV) Eliphalet, son of Deacon Peter Holbrook, was born January 27, 1691-92, died October 19, 1775, at Bellingham. He is called "yeoman." He married, November 17, 1716, Hannah Rockwood, born August 15, 1692. Children: Ebenezer, born June 3, 1717, at Mendon; Seth, February 26, 1721, at Bellingham; Eliphalet, mentioned below; Noah, December 6, 1727; Caleb, January 14, 1731; Elijah, May

6, 1736, died May 2, 1740; Joanna, July 21, 1738.

(V) Eliphalet (2), son of Eliphalet (1) Holbrook, was born October 25, 1725. He died intestate, and administration was granted his son Henry, on whom the homestead was settled, April 10, 1778. He married, November 26, 1753, Abigail Wight, who died September 3, 1808. Children: Olive, born April 4, 1755; Henry, mentioned below; Martha, October 11, 1758; Caleb, November 1, 1760; Peter, November 23, 1762; Seth, July 17, 1765; Nathan, July 24, 1768; Peruda, March 24, 1770; Eliab, February 20, 1772, died October 16, 1775; Eliphalet, February 9, 1774, died October 15, 1775; Abigail, June 9, 1776, died aged six weeks; Abigail.

(VI) Ensign Henry Holbrook, son of Eliphalet (2) Holbrook, was born August 27, 1756, died at Bellingham, his native town, October 1, 1833, aged seventy-seven. He was a soldier in the revolution in the company of Captain Jesse Holbrook on the Lexington Alarm, April 19, 1775, and served from May 9 until August of that year in Captain Samuel Cobb's company, Colonel Joseph Read's regiment. He was also in Captain Jesse Holbrook's company, Colonel Wheelock's regiment in 1776 on the Rhode Island Alarm; in Captain Samuel Fiske's company, Colonel Ephraim Wheelock's regiment, in Rhode Island in 1777; also in Captain Amos Ellis's company, Colonel Benjamin Hawes's regiment, in Rhode Island in 1777-78, and in Captain Nathan Thayer's company, Colonel Ebenezer Thayer's regiment in the Continental army in New York in 1780. He married (first) December 20, 1780, at Bellingham, Elizabeth Cook, born July 16, 1753, died at Bellingham, August 4, 1803 (gravestone). He married (second) Eunice Badger, born June 17, 1769, died March 10, 1818. Children, born at Bellingham: Eliphalet, April 13, 1782; Eliab, mentioned below; Anna, March 29, 1786; Henry, July 31, 1790.

(VII) Eliab, son of Ensign Henry Holbrook, was born at Bellingham, May 6, 1784. He married there (intentions dated October 15, 1809) Betsey Ide. Children, born at Bellingham: Elizabeth, June 25, 1811; Lurania, October 31, 1815; Eliab, mentioned below.

(VIII) Eliab (2), son of Eliab (1) Holbrook, was born at Bellingham, October 8, 1817. He married (first) April 25, 1839, Hannah Pickering, who died January 9, 1841, daughter of Ellery Thayer. He married (second) June 23, 1842 (intention at Bellingham, May 15, 1842), Julia Ferry Morse. She was born July 9, 1817, daughter of Eliakim Morse (see Morse VI). Child of first wife: Helen

Angelia, born at Bellingham, April 26, 1840.
Children of second wife, born at Bellingham:
Hannah Elizabeth, August 23, 1843; Gilbert
M., March 31, 1845; Hiram Pond, February
15, 1848; Edward, mentioned below.

(IX) Edward, son of Eliab (2) Holbrook,
was born at Bellingham, July 7, 1849. He
attended the public schools of Bellingham and
Hopkinton, Massachusetts, and after his
schooling became a clerk in the store of Bigelow, Kennard & Company, dealers in watches,
jewelry and silverware in Boston. From the
age of sixteen to twenty-one he was with this
house, and then he became a salesman for the
Gorham Manufacturing Company, manufacturers of silverware, in 1870. He subsequently
became the agent of the company in New
York, in 1887 was elected treasurer of the
company and in 1894 president. Since then he
has filled both offices and he is one of the best
known and most prominent silver manufacturers in this country. The period covered by
this connection with the Gorham Manufacturing Company has marked an epoch in the development of the silverware industry, more
important than any that has occurred during
the past century, as the growth of that industry has been of larger extent during the time
of Mr. Holbrook's official connection with the
Gorham Manufacturing Company, than for
all of the one hundred years previous and
during this remarkable development of the
manufacture of silver as an industry.

He was one of the charter members and
organizers of the Silversmiths Company of
the United States in 1905 and became its first
president, an office he is still filling. He is a
director of the Rhode Island Hospital Company of Providence, Rhode Island; of the
Merchants National Bank of New York City;
of the Harriman National Bank of New York
City; of the Garfield Safe Deposit Company
of New York City; of the American Brass
Company, the leading brass manufacturing
concern of the United States; of the American Coal Company, and the General Fire Ex-
tinguisher Company. He is a member of the
Union League of New York, the Union Club,
the Metropolitan Museum, New York, the
New England Society of New York, the Hope
Club of Providence, Rhode Island, the Pilgrims, an American Club of London, England.
In politics he is a Republican. Mr. Holbrook
is one of the few Americans who have had
conferred upon them the medal of the Legion
of Honor of France by the French government.

He married, February 18, 1874, in Boston,
Frances, born in 1854, daughter of John J.
Swift, of Boston. Her father was president
of the Boston & Fitchburg Railroad Company.
Her mother, Mary (Hichborn) Swift, was of
the old Hichborn family of Boston, to which
Admiral Hichborn belongs. Children: 1. John
Swift, born in Boston, March 4, 1875; mar-
ried, in April, 1907, Grace, daughter of John
J. Sinclair, vice-president of the Gorham
Manufacturing Company. 2. Lilian, born
March 7, 1878; married, January 3, 1906, the
Count Guillaume de Balincourt, and now resi-
dent of Neuilly sur Seine, France.

(The Morse Line).

(I) Samuel Morse, the immigrant ancestor,
was born in England in 1586. He sailed for
New England in the ship "Increase," April 15,
1635, and settled first at Watertown, and in
the following year, 1636, at Dedham, Massachusetts. He was admitted a freeman there,
October 8, 1640. Afterward he removed to
the adjoining town of Medfield, where many
of his descendants have lived. He was a town
officer of Dedham and one of the proprietors.
He died April 5, 1654, and his will was proved
January 30, 1655. He married, in England,
Elizabeth ———, who died at Medfield, June
20, 1655. She was forty-eight years old when
she emigrated. Children, born in England:
John, 1611; Daniel, 1613; Joseph, mentioned
below; Abigail, married Daniel Fisher, of Dedham; Mary, married Samuel Bullem; Jeremiah, went "east."

(II) Joseph, son of Samuel Morse, was
born in England in 1615, and came to this
country with his parents in 1635. He lived
first in Watertown, but soon removed to Dedham, where he received, August 18, 1636,
twelve acres of land for a home lot. He married, in Watertown, September 1, 1636, Hannah Phillips. He died in Dedham and his
widow married (second) November 3, 1658,
Thomas Boyden. She died in Medfield, October 3, 1676. Children, born at Dedham: Samuel, March 10, 1639; Hannah, August 8, 1641;
Sarah, September 16, 1643; Dorcas, August
23, 1645; Elizabeth, September 1, 1647; Joseph, September 26, 1649; Jeremiah, mentioned below.

(III) Jeremiah, son of Joseph Morse, was
born at Dedham, March 10, 1651, died February 19, 1715-16. He resided at Dorchester and
Medfield. He married Elizabeth, born in 1659,
died April 25, 1733, daughter of Francis and
Sarah Hamant. Children, born at Medfield: Elizabeth, June 22, 1678; Jeremiah, October 31, 1679; Elizabeth, February 24, 1681;
Mary, March 5, 1685; Timothy, December 27,
1687; Benjamin, mentioned below; Captain
Samuel, September 24, 1694; Abigail, October
16, 1696, died young; Jedediah, 1700; John,
1704, resided at Wrentham.

(IV) Benjamin, son of Jeremiah Morse, was born at Medfield, August 31, 1692. He settled in early life at Wrentham, an adjacent town. He married (first) March 15, 1714, Sarah, born at Dedham, December 18, 1694, died at Wrentham, February 20, 1725-26, daughter of Peter and Abigail Fales. He married (second) February 14, 1727, Sarah Blake, of Wrentham. Children, born at Wrentham: Benjamin, March 6, 1716; Hannah, December 17, 1720; Peter, October, 1723; Joseph, August 22, 1728; Sarah, December 30, 1730; Nathan, December 23, 1733; Moses, mentioned below.

(V) Moses, son of Benjamin Morse, was born at Wrentham, June 17, 1739. He was a farmer at Wrentham. He married there, June 4, 1766, Lydia Daniel. Children, born at Wrentham: Rhoda, March 5, 1767; Darius, May 29, 1769; Aaron, August 24, 1771; Lydia, October 26, 1775; Jacob, January 25, 1778; Eliakim, mentioned below; Polly, July 1, 1784.

(VI) Eliakim, son of Moses Morse, was born at Wrentham, Massachusetts, October 8, 1780. He married Lucinda Pond, born at Franklin, Massachusetts, July 5, 1787, daughter of Eliezer and Huldah (Hill) Pond. They lived for a time at West Springfield, Massachusetts. They settled in Oakham, Worcester county, Massachusetts. Children except four eldest, born at Oakham: Lucinda, June 13, 1809, at Franklin; Elvira Metcalf, November 4, 1812, at West Springfield; John Morman, February 1, 1814, at West Springfield; James, February 14, 1816, at West Springfield; Julia Ferry, born July 9, 1817; married Eliab Holbrook (see Holbrook VIII); Hiram Conant, February 3, 1821; Electa Bothwell, May 30, 1822; Jasper Pond, February 8, 1824; Sabra Aldens, August 18, 1827.

The name Mead is the English MEAD form of the Norman de Prato, Hervey de Prato in 1200, in Normandy, was King John's knight and the custody of Rouen Castle was given to his brother. In 1180-95, there is found in the Norman records the names of William, Robert, Matilda, Roger and Reginald de Prato, and in 1198 those of Richard and Robert de Prato. The following year, in Essex, England, occurs the name of Roger de Prato, and the same year also that of Walter de Prato in Hereford, England.

De Prato as translated into English became Mead, Meade, Mede and Meads. The first of the Mead or Meade family who came originally from Somersetshire into county Essex was Thomas Meade, Esq., who in the reign of King Henry VI. settled at Elmdon. The coat-

of-arms is thus described: Sable, a chevron between three pelicans or vulnant gules.

(I) William Mead, the immigrant ancestor, was a brother of Gabriel or Goodman Mead, and came with the latter in the ship "Elizabeth," 1635, from England. Goodman Mead remained in Massachusetts, but William went into the Connecticut Valley, and settled first in Wethersfield, and in 1641 removed to Stamford. He received from the town of Stamford, December 7, 1641, a home lot and five acres of land. His wife died in Stamford, September 16, 1657, no record of his death has been found. Children: Joseph, born in 1630; Martha, about 1632; John, mentioned below; Son, died in 1658.

(II) John, son of William Mead, was born about 1634, died February 5, 1699. He lived in Stamford until 1657, when he, with Joseph his brother, removed to Hempstead, Long Island. In 1660 he again removed to Old Greenwich, Connecticut, and October 26th of that year bought land from Richard Crab. In 1670 he was propounded for a freeman of Greenwich, and in 1679-80-86 was a member of the assembly. About 1672 a number of citizens of Greenwich, together with some from other colonies than Connecticut, bought from a few Indians a tract of land within the bounds of Greenwich, then called Horseneck, and now known as Greenwich Borough. These purchasers were twenty-seven in number, and were called the "27 proprietors of 1672." On the list are the names of John and Joseph Mead. In 1691 John Mead with his son John, and others, was appointed on a committee to procure materials and build a new meeting house. He married, in 1657, Hannah, daughter of William Potter, of Stamford, and through her received a considerable amount of property. Children: John; Joseph; Hannah; Ebenezer, mentioned below; Jonathan; David; Benjamin, mentioned below; Nathaniel; Samuel; Abigail; Mary.

(III) Ebenezer, son of John Mead, was born in 1663, died in 1728. He is on the list of voters in Horseneck in 1688, and on the tax list of Greenwich in the years 1694-95. The following year he was appointed by the town to keep the tavern, which stood on the same site for nearly two hundred years, and had a thrilling history during the colonial and revolutionary wars. He married, 1691, Sarah Knapp, of Stamford. Children: Ebenezer, mentioned below; Caleb, born 1694; Sarah, 1696; Hannah, 1698; Jabez, 1700; David, 1702; Abigail, 1704; Susanna, 1706; Jemima, 1708.

(IV) Ebenezer (2), son of Ebenezer (1) Mead, was born October 25, 1692, died May

3, 1775. He married, December 12, 1717, Hannah Brown. Children: Ebenezer, born October 8, 1718; Silas, May 22, 1720; Rev. Abraham, December 5, 1721, died 1743; Jonas, December 25, 1723; Rev. Solomon, December 25, 1725; Deliverance, mentioned below; Dr. Amos, February 22, 1730; Edmund, 1732; Hannah, December 5, 1734; Jabez, November 4, 1737; Jared, December 15, 1738; Captain Abraham, December 14, 1742.

(V) Deliverance, son of Ebenezer (2) Mead, was born May 4, 1728, died May 3, 1785. He married, June 11, 1759, Abigail, born February 22, 1738, died April 28, 1807, daughter of Captain Isaac Howe. Children: Elizabeth, born April 19, 1760; Sarah, November 7, 1761; Rachel, August 25, 1763; Hannah, August 10, 1765; Jabez, February 13, 1767, died October 29, 1769; Robert, November 22, 1768; Mary, March 25, 1771, died November 11, 1776; Huldah, February 26, 1773; Ephraim, mentioned below; Jabez, August 22, 1777; Zenas, December 10, 1779.

(VI) Ephraim, son of Deliverance Mead, was born March 15, 1775, died July 16, 1850. He married Azuba, born January 9, 1787, died January 21, 1861, daughter of Jonah Mead. Children: Mary H., born February 2, 1810; Huldah, February 5, 1812; Thirza, July 26, 1814, died April 14, 1830; Jane, July 23, 1817; Elthea, July 26, 1820, died April 5, 1830; Isaac Howe, mentioned below.

(VII) Isaac Howe, son of Ephraim Mead, was born July 4, 1823, died December 13, 1889. He married Mary E., daughter of Zophar Mead, of New York City, mentioned below. Children: Ephraim, September 7, 1856; Elbert L., September 11, 1857, died young; Dr. Clarkson S., February 19, 1859; Willard H., April 26, 1860; Spencer P., mentioned below; Thomas M., May 25, 1865; Amos H., February 1, 1869.

(VIII) Spencer Percival, son of Isaac Howe Mead, was born at Greenwich, Connecticut, March 23, 1863. He was educated there in the public schools, at the Greenwich Academy and at the New York Law School, from which he was graduated in the class of 1893, with the degree of LL. B. In the same year he was admitted to the bar in New York and he practiced in that city for six years. For several years he was in the employ of the Lawyers' Insurance and Trust Company of New York. He has been keenly interested in local and family history and is the author of "Ye Historie of ye Town of Greenwich, Conn." and "History and Genealogical Record of the Mead and Reynolds Families in America." He has contributed much to current literature. He is a member of the New England Society

of New York, the Sons of the Revolution, the Society of Colonial Wars. He was made a Mason in Acacia Lodge of Free Masons, of Greenwich, Connecticut, and has taken all the degrees in Scottish Rite Masonry, including the thirty-second. He is unmarried.

(III) Benjamin, son of John Mead, was born in May, 1666, died February 27, 1746. He married (first) May 10, 1700, Sarah Waterbury, of Stamford, Connecticut, born August 15, 1677; (second) Rachel Brown, of Rye. Children of first wife: Benjamin, mentioned below; Sarah, born June 3, 1702; Eliphalet, March 14, 1704, Elizabeth, November 2, 1705; Keziah, February 10, 1707. Children of second wife: Rachel, May 30, 1717; Obadiah, February 20, 1719; Zebediah, August 16, 1720; Nehemiah, 1721; Mary, 1724; Hannah, 1726.

(IV) Benjamin (2), son of Benjamin (1) Mead, was born March 18, 1701, died October 22, 1782. He married, November 18, 1728. Martha Ferris, born November 8, 1708, died November 6, 1797. Children: Benjamin, born August 15, 1729; Thaddeus, November 16, 1730; Martha, July 18, 1732; Sarah, August 10, 1735; Elizabeth, October, 1737; Sylvanus, mentioned below; Gideon, April 18, 1741; Mary, September 29, 1743; Rachel, August 31, 1745.

(V) Captain Sylvanus Mead, son of Benjamin (2) Mead, was born January 19, 1739, died in 1780, in the revolution. He married Sybil, daughter of Jonas Wood, of Huntington, Nassau Island, now Long Island. Children: Whitman, mentioned below; Platt, born June 16, 1768; Gideon, November 1, 1771; Asel, May 1, 1774.

(VI) Whitman, son of Captain Sylvanus Mead, was born May 3, 1764, died January, 1795. He married, 1787, Rachel, daughter of Deliverance Mead, mentioned above. Children: Mary, born February 14, 1788; Zophar, mentioned below; Whitman, August 5, 1792.

(VII) Zophar, son of Whitman Mead, was born December 20, 1790, died October 3, 1838. He married, April 26, 1820, Martha, born February 14, 1799, died May 29, 1869, daughter of David Seaman. Children: Araminta, born March 6, 1821; Marie A., June 7, 1822, died young; Mary E., October 18, 1823, married Isaac Howe Mead, mentioned above.

BRITTON

William Britton, the pioneer ancestor in this country, came from Bristol, England, and settled in Newport, Rhode Island. The family name in England was Summerill, but this son William, before leaving England, took his mother's family name which was Britton. This change of name is proven by letter written from father to son. He was a sea captain. He married, on Sunday, May 22, 1785, at Newport, Elizabeth Clarke, daughter of Audley and Margaret (Howland or Hulin) Clarke (see Clarke IV). Children, born at Newport: William, mentioned below; Margaret, April 15, 1787; Eliza, April 15, 1790, died August 23, 1791; Eliza, September 17, 1793, died September 16, 1794; Nathaniel Mumford, May 22, 1795; Eliza, August 21, 1798; John Henry, January 15, 1803, died July, 1816; John Henry, September 5, 1805, died September, 1819. William Britton died at Esopus, Ulster county, New York, November 1, 1836. His wife was born in Newport, Rhode Island, July 28, 1765, died October 21, 1819.

(II) Captain William (2) Britton, son of William (1) Britton, was born at Newport, Rhode Island, March 6, 1786, died in New York, May 27, 1857. He was a sea captain. He married (first) April 5, 1804, Ann Price; (second) Sarah Packer, who was born in England. Children: Mary Ann, born September 26, 1805; William Audley, mentioned below; John Price, May 16, 1813.

(III) William Audley, son of Captain William (2) Britton, was born at Newport, Rhode Island, April 11, 1811. He was educated in the public schools. He engaged in business as a banker in Mississippi, and died in New York City in 1874. He married, July 16, 1844, Mary Ann Adams, born April 23, 1822, in Durham, New York, daughter of Reuben and Almira L. (Mills) Adams, and a descendant of George Adams, of Watertown, Massachusetts. Almira L. Mills was a descendant of Peter Wautrous Van Der Meulen (Dermenen), who came from Holland and whose name was anglicized to Mills. Children: Charles Price, mentioned below; Reuben Adams, born in Kent, Connecticut, in 1849, married Matilda Dunbar, of Natchez, Mississippi, and had a daughter Gladys.

(IV) Charles Price, son of William Audley Britton, was born at Kent, Connecticut, June 27, 1845. He attended the district schools in Connecticut, and private schools in New York City. Afterward for a time he was a clerk, and at the time of his marriage he was admitted to partnership in the dry goods jobbing firm of William I. Peake & Company. After five years in this firm he became in 1871 a stock broker and has continued in that business to the present time. His office is at 111 Broadway, New York City. His firm is Charles P. Britton & Company. He is a member of the Sons of the Revolution, the Society of Colonial Wars, the New England Society of New York, the Union League Club of New

York. In politics he is an Independent. He was formerly in the state militia and is now a veteran member of the Seventh Regiment, New York National Guard. He is a communicant of the Fifth Avenue Presbyterian Church.

He married, September 5, 1866, Caroline Berry, born in Kent, Connecticut, in October, 1846, daughter of John Clark and Ann (Marsh) Berry. Children: 1. William Adams, born in Kent, August 17, 1868, died in Asheville, North Carolina, September 29, 1888. 2. Mary Marsh, born in New York City, March 13, 1873, died November 20, 1875. 3. Henry Berry, born September 5, 1878, a graduate of Columbia University, class of 1901, a mechanical engineer by profession, now a partner in his father's firm of Charles P. Britton & Company, stock brokers; married Marian W. G., daughter of Horace S. and Fanny (Griswold) Ely; children: Charles Price, born October 11, 1909; Horace Ely, born October 9, 1910.

(The Clarke Line).

The name Clarke is derived from the Latin word, "clericus," meaning a priest, or one connected with the service of the church. At first the name was used to designate those in clerical orders, but was later given to all who were able to read and write.

(I) Jeremiah Clarke, the immigrant ancestor of the Newport branch, came to America before 1638, and in that year was admitted an inhabitant of the island of Aquidneck, later Newport, Rhode Island. He and eight others signed a compact at Portsmouth, April 28, 1639, preparatory to the settlement of Newport. The same year he was present at a meeting of the inhabitants, and was made treasurer. He held various important positions in the town; 1639-40 constable; 1642, lieutenant; 1644, captain; 1644-45-46-47 treasurer for Newport; 1647-48-49 treasurer for the four towns of the colony. In 1648 he was an assistant and became president regent, with the power of governor under this title. In March, 1640, he had land recorded to the amount of one hundred and sixteen acres, and that same year was chosen with two others to lay out the remainder of the lands at Newport. He married, before leaving England, Frances, born 1611, died September, 1677, daughter of Lewis Latham, sergeant, falconer to King Charles I., and widow of William Dungan, performer of St. Martin's in Field Parish, London. She came to New England with her second husband, Jeremiah Clarke, and her four children, one son and three daughters. She married (third) Rev. William Vaughan. Jeremiah Clarke died in Newport, January, 1651-52. Children: Walter, born 1637; Mary, 1641;

Jeremiah, mentioned below; Latham; Weston, April 5, 1648; James, 1649; Sarah, 1651.

(II) Jeremiah (2), son of Jeremiah (1) Clarke, was born 1643, died January 16, 1729. In 1666 he was a freeman. In 1696-98-99-1700-01-02-03-04-05, he was deputy. He was ordained deacon of the Second Baptist Church in 1701. He deeded one-half of his lands in Providence and in Connecticut to his son James, September 17, 1691, and on the same date, the other half of the above lands to his son-in-law, Jeremiah Weeden, for three pounds, and the sum of three pounds annually during the life of Jeremiah and his wife Ann. He married Ann Audley, who died December 15, 1732. Children: Jeremiah; Henry, mentioned below; James; Samuel; Weston; Frances, born December 15, 1669; Mary, died 1756, married Jeremiah Weeden; Anne, born 1675; Sarah, died 1729.

(III) Henry, son of Jeremiah (2) Clarke, married Judith Peckham. Children: James, married Catherine Magee; William, married Diana Davis; Anne, married William Pike; Hannah, married Richard Moore, January 9, 1734; Judith, married Job Hubbard; Audley, mentioned below.

(IV) Audley, son of Henry Clarke, of Newport, Rhode Island, was born about 1738. He married, at Newport, December 7, 1760, Margaret Hulin, or Howland, and she died November 4, 1784. He is in the census of Newport as having one male over sixteen, one female over sixteen, and two females under sixteen, in 1774. Children: Henry, born at Newport, October 19, 1761; Olive, March 26, 1763; Elizabeth, July 28, 1765, married, Sunday, May 22, 1785, William Britton, of Bristol, England (see Britton I); Sarah, July 29, 176—.

LOCKWOOD The name of Lockwood is of ancient origin, and dates back over eight hundred years, when it is mentioned in Domesday Book. During the reign of Edward III., 1327-77, a John Lockwood was attached to the royal party, fought at Naseby, and was wounded there. There were families of the name in county Essex and county Northampton as early as 1530. At that date Rev. Richard Lockwood, rector of Dingley, in Northamptonshire, had a coat-of-arms granted to him, as follows: Argent, a fesse between three martletts sable.

(I) Robert Lockwood, the immigrant ancestor, came from England about 1630, and settled first in Watertown, Massachusetts, where he was made a freeman, March 9, 1636-37. About 1646 he removed to Fairfield, and was made a freeman of Connecticut, May 20, 1652. His name is recorded as a settler in Fairfield as early as 1641, and in May, 1657, he was appointed sergeant there. He died in 1658, and an inventory of his estate was made September 11th of that year. He is supposed to have lived for a time in Norwalk, Connecticut. While living in Watertown he was executor of the estate of one Edmund Lockwood, supposed to be his brother. His wife was Susannah, who survived him, and married (second) Jeffrey Ferris. She died at Greenwich, December 23, 1660. Children, the first six born in Watertown: Jonathan, September 10, 1634; Deborah, October 12, 1636; Joseph, August 6, 1638; Daniel, March 21, 1640; Ephraim, mentioned below; Gershom, September 6, 1643; John; Abigail, married John Barlow, of Fairfield; Sarah; Mary, married Jonathan Huested.

(II) Ephraim, son of Robert Lockwood, was born in Watertown, Massachusetts, December 1, 1641. He removed with his parents when a child to Fairfield, and afterward lived in Norwalk, Connecticut. His name appears in the list of home lots there, and he was made a freeman, October, 1667. He bought the home lot of Jonathan Marsh, December 30, 1664. He married, June 8, 1665, Mercy, daughter of Matthias Sention Sr., of Norwalk. The name is now written St. John. Children: John, born March 19, 1666; Daniel, August 13, 1668; Sarah, November 3, 1670; Ephraim, May 1, 1673; Eliphalet, mentioned below; Joseph, April 1, 1680; James, April 21, 1683; Edmund, died unmarried; Mary, married Joseph Garnsey; Abigail, married ——— Cook.

(III) Deacon Eliphalet Lockwood, son of Ephraim Lockwood, was born February 27, 1675-6, died October 14, 1753; born and buried in Norwalk. He was representative from Norwalk to the general assembly in May, 1724. He married, October 11, 1699, Mary, born about 1673, died March 6, 1761, daughter of John Gold, of Stamford, Connecticut. Children, born in Norwalk: Hannah, July 28, 1700, died July 16, 1712; Damaris, November 7, 1701; Son, born November 28, died December 20, 1703; Mary, November 4, 1704; Eliphalet, June 2, 1706; John, January 8, 1707-08; Mercy, April 11, 1709, died October 1, 1712; Peter, mentioned below; Hannah, July 12, 1712, died October 27, 1713; Abigail, October 17, 1716.

(IV) Deacon Peter Lockwood, son of Deacon Eliphalet Lockwood, was born in Norwalk, March 16, 1710-11, died in Danbury, Connecticut, in 1775. He was representative from Norwalk six times between the years 1755 and 1764. Before he removed to Danbury he had been appointed deacon. His will was made August 26, 1775, and proved November 1, 1775. He married (first), September 8, 1737, Abigail Hawley, died June 6, 1749, daughter of Rev. Thomas Hawley, of Ridgefield, Connecticut. He married (second), January 1, 1750-51, Elizabeth, born February 17, 1727-28, daughter of David and Laurana (Bill) Lambert, and granddaughter of John Bill, of Lebanon, Connecticut. He married (third) Hannah Fitch. Children of first wife: Abigail, born October 17, 1738; Eliphalet, October 17, 1741; Hannah, September 23, 1743; Mary, August 31, 1745; Dorothy, December 7, 1747, died June 23, 1750. Children of second wife: Lambert, December 14, 1753, died January 1, 1754; Dorothy, August 10, 1755; Lambert, mentioned below; Gould.

(V) Lambert, son of Deacon Peter Lockwood, was born in Norwalk, July 17, 1757, died February 11, 1825. He was assistant quartermaster-general in the revolution, and his widow received a pension at the rate of $600 a year. During the British attack on Danbury, April 26, 1777, he was sent by Colonel Cook, then in command there, to General Silliman for arms and ammunition, but coming suddenly upon the British troops near Reading Church, was made a prisoner. He was recognized by General Tryon, the British commander, as a young man who had formerly given him aid when his carriage broke down while passing through Norwalk, and was consequently taken under the general's protection. In the latter's hasty retreat from Danbury, however, he was interrupted while writing a protection for him, and left him to take care of himself. He was a merchant by occupation, and about 1792, with J. S. Cannon, built a store and wharf at Bridgeport, and ran a packet sloop, the "Juba," to New York. In 1794 he removed from Wilton to Bridgeport, and lived on the north side of State street. When the Bridgeport Bank was incorporated in 1806 he was a subscriber, and February 3, 1807, was elected a director. In 1811 he was first clerk of the Bridgeport and Stratford Burying Ground Association. He was a pewholder in the old Congregational church in 1835. Two of his sons were clergymen. He was a public-spirited man, of fine presence and agreeable manners. He married, December 5, 1793, Elizabeth, born March 1, 1771, died February 3, 1846, daughter of Rev. Azel Roe, of Woodbridge, New Jersey. Children: Rebecca Roe, born 1794; Frederick, April 7, 1796; Peter, February 9, 1798; Roe, mentioned below; Elizabeth, 1802.

(VI) Roe, son of Lambert Lockwood, was born in Bridgeport, 1800, died in 1871. He removed to New York. He married, June 19, 1821, Julia G. Gouge, of Bridgeport. Children: George Roe, mentioned below; Frederick, died young; Catharine G., born August 31, 1825; Julia, January 19, 1828; Elizabeth Roe, December 25, 1839; Louisa Matilda, February 17, 1841.

(VII) George Roe, son of Roe Lockwood, was born June 7, 1848, Mary Elizabeth, born 1826, in Hartford, daughter of Richard and Martha (Smith) Bigelow. She was the granddaughter of John and Clarissa (Hillyer) Bigelow, great-granddaughter of John and Hannah (Wadsworth) Bigelow, great-great-granddaughter of Timothy and Abigail (Olcott) Bigelow, great-great-great-granddaughter of Jonathan and Mabel (Edwards) Bigelow, great-great-great-great-granddaughter of Jonathan and Rebecca (Shephard) Bigelow, and great-great-great-great-great-granddaughter of John Bigelow. Children, born in New York City: Ella, October 2, 1849; Richard Bigelow, December 7, 1850; Mary Elizabeth, May 17, 1854; George Roe, mentioned below.

(VIII) Dr. George Roe (2) Lockwood, son of George Roe (1) Lockwood, was born March 7, 1861, in New York City. He attended the public schools and was graduated from the College of the City of New York in the class of 1881 with the degree of Bachelor of Arts. He studied medicine in the College of Physicians and Surgeons of Columbia University and received his degree of M. D. in 1884. He spent a year abroad, traveling and studying in the medical schools and hospitals of the old world and since his return has been in practice in New York City, making a specialty of diseases of the stomach. He is on the staff of the Bellevue Hospital of New York City. He is a member of the American Medical Association, and the city, county and state medical societies.

He married, November 4, 1893, Elizabeth, born in New York City, 1872, died August 19, 1911, daughter of Horace and Melvina (Brown) Dennett, of New York.

SIMMONS　　Albertus Simon appears to be the immigrant ancestor of this family. He was of Dutch ancestry and settled in Rensselaerwyck, in or near what is now Troy, New York, then in Albany county. He was born in 1728. At an early date families of English ancestry named Simmons appeared in New York and the name Simonds was common in Massachusetts. Simonds is also an English surname. While all have a similar derivation from the personal or baptismal name Simon, which dates back of Biblical times, and while Simon became a surname in this family, it may have been a patronymic for several generations earlier. It is impossible to trace many of the early Dutch families of New York, because for several generations they continued to use patronymics instead of surnames.

But before the revolution Simon was well established as a surname and in New York state we find Antras, Battis, Henrich, Jacob and John Simon, evidently of Dutch stock, in the American army. Henry, or Heinrich, and Jacob, were living in Rensselaerwyck, Albany county, when the first federal census was taken in 1790, doubtless the same Simons who served in the revolution. Peter and Helmers also were heads of families in the same locality, and Albertus Simon, of Rensselaerwyck, had four males over sixteen, three under that age and six females in his family. Judging from the fact that he had so numerous a family living in 1790 at home, we are led to the conclusion that, if he were the immigrant, he must have had brothers or relations of the name who settled in the same section.

(II) Christian John Simon, one of the younger sons of Albertus Simon, was born at Rensselaerwyck, New York, probably about 1775. He married Patience Safford, of Greenwich, New York, now Washington county.

(III) Joseph Ferris Simmons, as the name is now spelled, son of Christian John Simon, was born in 1818, in the town of Brunswick, Rensselaer county, New York, died July 8, 1879. He married Mary Sophia Gleason, born 1819, died July 5, 1872, daughter of Samuel Gleason, of Shaftsbury, New York. Children: 1. Joseph Edwards, who was president of the Fourth National Bank of New York City; president of the New York Chamber of Commerce in 1909-10; president of the New York Stock Exchange; grand master of the Free Masons of New York State; president of the Board of Education of New York City; his son, Joseph F. Simmons, is a member of the New York Sons of the Revolution. 2. Dr. Charles Ezra, mentioned below. 3. Emma Kate, born in Troy, New York, March 2, 1850; married Charles R. Flint, born in Thomaston, Maine, late of Brooklyn and New York.

(IV) Dr. Charles Ezra Simmons, son of Joseph Ferris Simmons, was born in Troy, New York, August 16, 1840. He attended a private academy at Troy, the Sand Lake Boarding School, and in 1857 entered Williams College. After three years at Williams he entered Beloit College at Beloit, Wisconsin, and was graduated in the class of 1861 with the degree of Bachelor of Arts. He studied

for a year at the University of Guttenburg, Germany, and in 1862-63 was a student at Jefferson Medical College of Philadelphia, Pennsylvania, and in 1863-64 at the College of Physicians and Surgeons of Columbia University, from which he was graduated in the class of 1864 with the degree of M. D. From the time of his graduation until 1868 he practiced in Troy and since then in New York City. He is a member of the Medical Society of Greater New York, of the New York Medical Society, the New York Academy of Medicine, the American Medical Association and the Alumni Association of Williams College of New York. He was commissioner of charities and corrections from 1885 to 1895 in New York City, appointed originally by Mayor Grace and reappointed by Mayor Grant. He has written from time to time various medical monographs and was the first to report a case of quinine blindness. He is a member of the Old South Dutch Reformed Church of New York City. In politics he is an independent Democrat, but was formerly an active member of Tammany Hall and held the office of Sachem in that organization.

He married, June 29, 1865, Sarah Ruby Gould, born July 6, 1842, daughter of Jacob Gould, of Rochester, New York. Children: 1. Edward DeForest, born at Rochester, May 18, 1866; unmarried; a real estate dealer in New York City. 2. Mary Sophia, born June 20, 1868; married Henry King Browning, a merchant of New York City; children: Adelaide Scott Browning, born March 31, 1892; Marjory Hull Browning, born June 8, 1893; Catherine Simmons Browning, born April, 1895; Natalie Hull Browning, born September, 1896. 3. Ruby Gould, born October 21, 1874, in New York City.

NORTON The name of Norton is of ancient origin and the many distinct families in America bearing it are undoubtedly descended from the same source. Their lineage can be traced back to Le Signr de Noruile (Norvile), who crossed the channel with the Norman Conqueror and subsequently served as the latter's constable. This de Norvile married a lady of the famous house of Valois. Dr. Norton, of London, England, has made much research to discover the earliest origin of the family and finds it first in Norway, whence came a large portion of the inhabitants of Normandy, France, the original home of William the Conqueror. In Norway it had its present form, but the influences of the French language changed it somewhat, being made Nordville and Norvile. A few generations after its arrival in England it was changed to the original form of Norton. The senior William D. Norvile was chamberlain of William the Conqueror at the time of the conquest. A descendant of Cantable de Norville in the sixth generation, anglicized the name into its present form of Norton. Professor Charles Eliot Norton, of Harvard University, is a lineal descendant of the constable in the twenty-first generation. In addition to Norton street, a prominent London thoroughfare, there are in England several important rural communities of this name—Chipping Norton, Sedbey Norton, King's Norton and Phillip's Norton, all of ancient origin and doubtless deriving their name from some prominent family or individual. Several immigrants of this name are mentioned in the early colonial records of New England. Captain Walter Norton arrived in America in 1630. George Norton, of Salem, Ipswich, and other places, who came from London, was made a freeman in 1634, and died in 1659. William Norton, of Hingham and Ipswich, born in England, 1610, came in the "Hopewell" in 1635, and took the freeman's oath the same year. Rev. John Norton, brother of William, born in 1605, probably in London, emigrated to Massachusetts Bay in 1635, shortly after graduating from Cambridge, and located in Ipswich. In 1656 he became pastor of the First Church in Boston, and was noted for his piety and learning. Nicholas Norton, who is thought to have come from the county of Herts, was of Weymouth, Massachusetts, as early as 1638, removed to Martha's Vineyard, and his descendants are still found there. A Francis Norton was admitted a freeman at Weymouth in 1642. Major Peter Norton, an efficient officer in the revolutionary war, was a son of Ebenezer, grandson of Joseph, and great-grandson of Joseph, the Martha's Vineyard settler.

(I) Nicholas Norton was born in 1610, in England, and settled in Weymouth, Massachusetts, among the pioneers. February 20, 1639, he bought of Richard Standerwick of Broadway, Somersetshire, a clothier, all the cattle in the hands of Mr. Hull, in New England. He was a prominent citizen and held various town offices. He removed to Martha's Vineyard, and died there in 1690, aged eighty years. Children: Joseph, mentioned below; Nicholas; Isaac, born at Weymouth, May 3, 1641; Jacob, March 1, 1644.

(II) Joseph Norton, born about 1640, was a son of Nicholas Norton, and may have been a nephew of some of the other immigrants mentioned in a preceding paragraph, though no actual proof of relationship has been found. He settled in Salisbury, Massachusetts, in the vicinity of which the Nortons named above

settled. He took the oath of allegiance and fidelity in 1677, and was a soldier against the Indians in 1697. He died November 16, 1721, at Salisbury. He married, March 10, 1662, Susanna, daughter of Samuel and Dorcas Getchell, who died his widow August 19, 1724. Children, all born at Salisbury: 1. Son, 1662, died young. 2. Samuel, October 11, 1663; a soldier in service at Wells, Maine, in 1696. 3. Joseph, August 14, 1665. 4. Priscilla, December 16, 1667; married John, son of Robert Ring. 5. Solomon, mentioned below. 6. Benjamin, March 24, 1671-72, died October, 1693. 7. Caleb, June 25, 1675; married, March 6, 1699-1700, Susanna Frame; was a soldier in 1697-98, and subsequently removed to Brunswick, Maine. 8. Flower, November 21, 1677. 9. Joshua, October 13, 1680, died January 22, 1692-93.

(III) Solomon, fourth son of Joseph and Susanna (Getchell) Norton, was born January 31, 1670, in Salisbury, and resided in that town, where he died May 2, 1721. His wife bore the baptismal name of Sarah, and they had children in Salisbury: Miriam, born December 4, 1695; Benjamin, mentioned below; John, January 14. 1701; Maria, November 9, 1704; Gideon, August 1, 1711.

(IV) Benjamin, eldest son of Solomon and Sarah Norton, was born February 24, 1699, in Salisbury, and settled in Newbury, where he died February 27, 1756. He married (first) in Newbury, June 14, 1722, Margaret Richardson, born September 27, 1699, in Newbury, daughter of Joseph and Margaret (Godfrey) Richardson, and died there November 11, 1742. There were six children of this marriage: Judith, 1723; Joshua, November 4, 1728; Hannah, died young; Benjamin, August 11, 1734, died young; Hannah, March 5, 1737; Miriam, August 6, 1739. Benjamin Norton married (second) December 5, 1744, Mercy Shute, born April 18, 1710, in Malden, Massachusetts, daughter of Richard and Lydia Shute. Children recorded in Newbury: Mary, born September 12, 1745; Benjamin, mentioned below; Sarah, May 24, 1751.

(V) Benjamin (2), third son of Benjamin (1) Norton and second child of his second wife, Mary Shute, was born January 16, 1747, in Newbury, and died April 28, 1816, in Newburyport. He was a private in the brigantine "Freedom," commanded by Captain John Clouston, in June, 1776. He married, November 26, 1775, in Newburyport, Sarah Wyatt, born February 7, baptized February 8, 1776, in the Third Church of Newbury, daughter of John Wyatt, and died March 7, 1834, in Newburyport. Children: Benjamin, born July 21, 1777; Joshua, died young; Sarah, November

3, 1780; Hannah, August 11, 1782; Catherine, February 27, 1784; Joshua, January 5, 1786; Stephen, January 8, 1788; Mary Brown, October 31, 1790; William, January 8, 1792; Elizabeth, February 18, 1794; Daniel, mentioned below; Charles, May 4, 1798, the last not on Newburyport records.

(VI) Daniel, sixth son of Benjamin (2) and Sarah (Wyatt) Norton, was born February 18, 1796, in Newburyport, and was engaged in the sailmaking business during the greater part of his active career. He removed to Boston about 1830, and died at Melrose, Massachusetts, August 3, 1884. He married (first) in Newburyport, August 19, 1819, Jane Cheever, born there July 17, 1801, daughter of John and Sarah (Hidden) Cheever, and died October 2, 1820, in Newburyport. Their only child, Jane, born September 9, 1820, died 1897, married Samuel Francis Hunt, of Cambridge, who died the same year; they had four children: Charlotte Jane, born June 30, 1846; Francis Edgar, June 20, 1848, married Rebecca Franklin Nickerson, January 15, 1885; Abigail Elizabeth, died in second year; Alfred Herbert, September 15, 1861, married, April 4, 1900, Kathryn Cecilia Kyle, of Brooklyn, New York, and has children: Alfred Herbert, born June 1, 1901; William Edgar, July 11, 1906; both in Colorado Springs, Colorado. Daniel Norton married (second) in Newburyport, March 20, 1822, Mary Carr, born September 3, 1800, on Carr's Island, Newburyport, Massachusetts, daughter of Levi and Mary (Putnam) Carr, and died in Charlestown, Massachusetts, August 2, 1877. Mary (Carr) Norton was a lineal descendant of George Carr, one of the Mayflower colony, who was born about 1598-99 in England, and was ship carpenter on the Mayflower. He married (first) in England, Lucinda Davenport, who came to America with him and was one of the forty-one who died at Plymouth in the succeeding winter. A few years later he settled at Ipswich, Massachusetts, where he was found of record as early as 1633 and had a house lot in 1635. He removed to Salisbury, Massachusetts, where he received land in the first division in that town in 1640-41-44, and his name appears in most of the early lists of citizens. In 1640 the town granted him Carr's Island, and he established a ferry there in 1641. In 1662 it was agreed that he should have a common right in Amesbury when any of his sons came to live there, and he received land in 1668. The records give him the title of "Mr.," which was given in those days only to the most prominent citizens. He agreed to keep the ferry in Amesbury at Goodwin's Landing in April, 1670. He died April 4,

1682, in Salisbury. He had married (second) Elizabeth, supposed to have been a daughter of Elder Thomas Oliver, of Boston, as James Oliver, the latter's son, is spoken of in the records as a brother-in-law of George Carr. She survived him, was a member of the Salisbury church in 1687, and died May 6, 1691. Her will was made March 18, 1684, and proved June 30, following her death. Children: Elizabeth, George, Richard (died young), William, James, Mary, Sarah, John, Richard and Anne. Daniel and Mary (Carr) Norton had children: 2. Daniel, born June 4, 1823, died March, 1900; married Hannah Higgins, of Charlestown, who died in 1897; children: i. Ellen Wade, died at the age of twenty-three years; ii. Alice May, born May 22, 1857, married John Randall Heath, of Jamaica Plain, Massachusetts, and had a son Donald, born June 24, 1883; iii. Ada L., June 16, 1859, married Winthrop Messenger, of Melrose, Massachusetts, and has children: a. Winthrop Norton, born October 1, 1883; b. Stuart, February 14, 1891; c. Hazel, September 17, 1893. 3. Mary Elizabeth, June 29, 1826; married (first) January 31, 1847, Allen F. Eastman, who died March 6, 1890; their daughter, Mae Aphia, died in her second year. She married (second) December 18, 1902, John Mitchel Osgood, who died October 14, 1908. 3. Clarissa Ann, February 12, 1829, died June 24, 1909; married July 31, 1857, Edward John Norris, died 1906; children: i. Walter Eliott, died in fourth month; ii. Webster, born October 20, 1859; married Margaret Stetson; iii. Clara Augusta, November 21, 1861, married Arthur E. Roberts, and had daughters: Marjorie, born December 27, 1890, and Emma Norris, died in second year; iv. George Lincoln, January 11, 1866, married Rachel Parker; v. Walter Henry, March 6, 1870, married July 6, 1897, Effie Louise Shapleigh, and has children: a. Elizabeth, born August 8, 1898; b. Katherine, June 7, 1901; c. Edward John, March 21, 1908; d. Emerson Shapleigh, October 31, 1911; vi. Emma Josephine, February 5, 1874, died 1910. 4. Hannah Bartlet, August 24, 1832; married January 15, 1852, Thomas L. Summers; died January 16, 1854. 5. James Carr, February 9, 1835, died at age of twelve days. 6. Sarah, August 15, 1836; married October 5, 1856, Thomas L. Summers, who died January 11, 1886; children: i. Hannah Frances, born July 5, 1857; married March 26, 1890, William Merritt; ii. Arthur Warren, May 21, 1859; married Mabel Bond, and has children: Grace B., born March 31, 1897; Arline W., December 7, 1898; Arthur Warren, April 18, 1902; iii. Mary Eunette, February 24, 1864. 7. Caroline Duntlin, August 2, 1839; married Thomas

W. Griffith; children: i. Mary Eliza, born January 8, 1866, married, August 12, 1890, James Arthur Crawford, and had children: Allen F. E., died in sixteenth year; Phebe Hooper, born March 12, 1896; ii. William Henry, December 13, 1868; married October 2, 1890, Abbie Boston, and has children: Emory, born March 28, 1891; Florence May, January 23, 1893; Harold, February 21, 1895; Ralph, December 21, 1898. 8. William Edward, mentioned below.

(VII) William Edward, youngest child of Daniel and Mary (Carr) Norton, was born June 28, 1843, in Boston, and was educated in the public schools of Charlestown. For a number of years he attended the Lowell Institute science lectures and art classes, and was one of the founders of the life classes at that institute. Mr. George Hollingsworth and Mr. Carleton, art instructors there, were Mr. Norton's first teachers in art. He studied anatomy under Dr. Rimmer, of Boston, and also pursued that subject in the Harvard Medical School, the Royal Academy in London and the Beaux Arts in Paris. When quite young he learned the trade of house sign and decorative painting, but his wonderful artistic talent fitted him for more interesting and higher work. When a mere boy he manifested a talent for art and had a wonderful knack of drawing, especially of horses and ships. In order to satisfy his craving for knowledge of ships and the ocean, he went to sea as a sailor. Returning to Boston he studied painting under the renowned George Inness, of that city, and took a studio, soon becoming known as a marine painter. He made two more voyages as a sailor prior to going to London, England, in 1877, and in 1878 exhibited three pictures at the Royal Academy, following which he went to Paris for further study under Jacquesson de la Chevreuse and A. Vollen, and at the Beaux Arts. Some three or four years later he visited Italy and other parts of Europe and afterwards opened a studio in London, where he lived until 1902. At the Salon in Paris in 1895, Mr. Norton received honorable mention, and while in Europe he was a constant and regular exhibitor in the Royal Academy in London, in the Paris Salon, and in many of the public art galleries of other countries. In the United States he has been awarded three gold medals for his work, besides two Osborne prizes, $500 each, and the Jordan prize, $1,000. Since 1902 he has been a resident of New York City, his studio being located at No. 1931 Broadway. Mr. Norton's paintings have been chiefly marine views and scenes pertaining to and having to do with the sea and sailors. One of his well-known paintings is "The Eng-

lish Channel," which adorns the Chamber of Commerce at Boston, and he also painted the celebrated picture entitled, "Fight of the Alabama and Kearsarge," which is owned by the Historical Society of Portland, Maine. "Fish Market, Dieppe France," which hangs in the public library at Malden, Massachusetts, was executed by him, as was also "Crossing the Grand Banks," which is in the Abbot Hall, Marblehead, Massachusetts. Essex Hall, Salem, Boston Art Club, Boston Athletic Club, and Black Heath Art Club of London own examples of his work. Three more of his famous pictures are: "The Thames from London Bridge"; "Tranquillity"; "Midst Fog and Ice." In political conviction Mr. Norton is a stalwart Republican, and in religious matters he is independent. He is affiliated with the Masonic fraternity, having been made a Mason in Winslow Lewis Lodge at Boston, in 1877. He is a member of the Salamagundi Club of New York, and the Boston Art Club, and was formerly a member of the Natural History Society, Papyrus Club, and the Boston Yacht Club of Boston. He is a member of the National Geographic Society of Washington, D. C.

He married, September 23, 1868, Sarah Dorcas Ryan, of Grand Manan, New Brunswick, Canada, where he passed several summers sketching the rugged and picturesque scenery of that locality. Mrs. Norton was born October 3, 1846, and died in New York May 15, 1904. Children: Gertrude Maud, born October 27, 1871, in Charlestown, Massachusetts; Florence Edith, July 1, 1879, in Paris France.

KINNEY   The surname Kinney is identical with Kenney, Kenny, Keney, Kinnee, Kene and Keny, and the spelling is found varied still more in the early records.

(I) Henry Kinney, immigrant ancestor, was born in 1624, of English ancestry in Holland. According to some accounts he was born in Norfolk, England, but came from Holland to America. He was first at Roxbury, Massachusetts, where he was placed in apprenticeship to William Park, of Roxbury, by Vincent Potter, probably a relative. Kinney removed thence to Salem, Massachusetts, about 1653. His wife Ann was admitted to the Salem church, August 24, 1654. Children and dates of baptism: John, September 10, 1654; Mary, July 3, 1659; Sarah, June 29, 1662; Elizabeth, May 1, 1664; child, May 12, 1666; Thomas, mentioned below.

(II) Thomas, son of Henry Kinney, was born at Salem, January 1, 1655-56, in what is now Danvers, Massachusetts. He resided at Salem village, now Danvers. He married,

W. E. Norton

May 23, 1677, Elizabeth Knight, who died in 1694. Among their children was Thomas, who removed to Preston, Connecticut, in 1715; Joseph, mentioned below.

(III) Joseph, son of Thomas Kinney, was born at Salem, September 7, 1680, died in 1745. He came to Preston, Connecticut, in 1706, was a farmer at Preston, and his farm adjoined that of his brother Thomas. He was captain in the colonial troops in the Indian wars. He married, in 1704, at Salem, Keziah Peabody, born 1686, at Topsfield, died at Preston, daughter of Jacob and Abigail (Towne) Peabody, of Topsfield, granddaughter of Francis Peabody, the immigrant. Children, baptized at Preston (church records) : Abigail, September 15, 1706; Jacob, July 2, 1707; Zipporah, May 8, 1709; Daniel, July 8, 1711; Child, October 18, 1713; Eunice, April 1, 1716; Joseph, mentioned below; Ezra, September 20, 1727.

(IV) Joseph (2), son of Joseph (1) Kinney, was born at Preston, Connecticut, baptized there May 4, 1718, died in Vermont. He married (first) at Preston, now Griswold, Sarah Blunt, who died in 1754. He married (second) 1755, at Norwich, Jemima (Newcomb) Lamb, born in 1730, at Lebanon, Connecticut, died in Vermont, daughter of Hezekiah and Jerusha (Bradford) Newcomb, and widow of Jonathan Lamb, of Norwich. She was a descendant of Governor William Bradford, who came in the "Mayflower." She was admitted to the church at Preston with her husband, May 30, 1756. They came thither from the East Norwich Church. Children, baptized at Preston (church records) : Joseph, May 30, 1756; Jonathan, September 25, 1757; Daniel, October 28, 1759; Jonathan, mentioned below; David, June 13, 1762; Bradford, mentioned below.

(V) Rev. Jonathan Kinney, son of Joseph (2) Kinney, was baptized at Preston, Connecticut, June 13, 1762. He removed to Vermont with his parents. He lived for ten years at Bethel, Vermont. In 1793 he came to Plainfield, Vermont, and began to clear a farm on Lot No. 4, working through the week and spending his Sundays at the home of Seth Freeman. He built a frame house in 1794 nearly opposite the H. Q. Perry house, and his was the first frame house in the town of Plainfield. In February, 1795, his family moved into the new house. He was the first minister of the Congregational church. He died at Berlin in 1838. Deacon Justus Kinney afterward lived on his farm. Justus, a child of Rev. Jonathan Kinney was the first person buried in the town. He died March 6, 1796. David, another child, is mentioned below.

(V) Judge Bradford Kinney, brother of

Rev. Jonathan Kinney, was baptized at Preston, Connecticut, September 15, 1765. He came to Vermont with the family during or just after the revolution. He lived at Royalton until about 1795 when he came to Plainfield, Vermont, and settled. He was the first representative to the legislature; magistrate and a citizen of prominence. The Vermont revolutionary rolls show that Peabody, Jesse, Jacob, Daniel, Benoni and Seth Kinney (or Kenney) were soldiers and all were of this family. Seth was also in a Connecticut regiment.

(VI) David, son of Rev. Jonathan Kinney, was born at Plainfield, Vermont, October 29, 1787. He was educated in the public schools, and followed farming in his native town. He married and among his children was William Henry, mentioned below.

(VII) William Henry, son of David Kinney, was born at Plainfield, Vermont, May 11, 1836, and is now living in that town. He was educated there in the public schools, and followed farming all his active life. In religion he is a Congregationalist, and in politics a Republican. He married Sarah Jane, daughter of Rev. Joel Fisk (see Fisk XIII).

(VIII) William Chapman, son of William Henry Kinney, was born at Plainfield, Vermont, October 29, 1864. He was educated in the public schools of his native town and at St. Johnsbury Academy, Vermont, entering Dartmouth College in 1883 and graduating with the degree of Bachelor of Arts in the class of 1887. He then became clerk in the Hanover National Bank, and subsequently in a similar position in the National Bank of Commerce of New York City. Thence he entered the employ of the well-known banking firm of Harvey Fisk & Sons, New York, January 1, 1888, and he is now cashier of the house. He is a member of the Dartmouth College Club of New York City, the Vermont Society of New York, the Union League Club of New York and the New England Society of New York. His home is at Plainfield, New Jersey, and he is a member of the board of health of that city, and president of the Muhlenburg Hospital of Plainfield. He is secretary and treasurer of the Greeley Square Realty Company of New York, and secretary and assistant treasurer of the Hudson Companies of New York. He is a member of the Crescent Avenue Presbyterian Church of Plainfield. In politics he is a Republican.

He married, December 10, 1890, Belle Harriet, born January 7, 1866, daughter of John H. and Ann E. George, of East Hardwick, Vermont. Children: George Montgomery, born at Plainfield, February 29, 1892, died

May, 1897; William Chapman, born at Plainfield, New Jersey, June 7, 1900.

(The Fisk Line).

The surname Fisk or Fiske has been in use from the earliest times in England. The records show that in May, 1208, the Duke of Lorraine granted land in Digneveton Park, to the men of Laxfield, the list including one Daniel Fisc, who is supposed to have been the grandfather of Lord Symond Fisk, from whom the American family is descended, as given below.

(I) Lord Symond Fisk was proprietor of the Manor of Stadhaugh, parish of Laxfield, Suffolk, England, 1390-1422. He married (first) Susannah Smith, (second) Katharine ———. His will was proved at Norwich, February 26, 1463-64. Children: William, married Joan Lynne; Jeffrey, married Margaret ———; John; Edmund, married Margery ———; Margaret, married ——— Dowsing or Dowling.

(II) William, son of Lord Symond Fisk, was born at Stadhaugh. He married Joan Lynne, of Norfolk. He died before his wife, who made her will, July 15, 1504, which was proved February 28, 1505. Children: Thomas, William, Augustine, Simon, mentioned below; Robert, John, Margery, Margaret.

(III) Simon, son of William Fisk, was born at Laxfield. His will was dated July 10, 1536, and proved July 13, 1538. He died in June, 1538. He married Elizabeth ———, who died in Halesworth, June, 1558. Children: Simon, mentioned below; William, Robert, Joan, Jeffrey, Gelyne, Agnes, Thomas, Elizabeth, John.

(IV) Simon (2), son of Simon (1) Fisk, was born in Laxfield. His will was dated January 26, 1605, and he died that year. Children: Robert, John, George, Nicholas, Jeffrey, Jeremy, William, Richard, Joan, Gelyne, Agnes.

(V) Robert, son of Simon (2) Fisk, was born at Stadhaugh about 1525, died in 1600, and his will was proved July 28, 1600. He married Mrs. Sybil (Gould) Barber. For some time he lived in the parish of St. James, South Elmham, England. Sybil, his wife, was in great danger at the time of the religious persecution, 1553-58, as well as her sister, Isabella (born Gould), who was confined in the castle of Norwich, and escaped death only through the intervention of her brothers. Robert Fisk fled to Geneva during the reign of Bloody Mary, on account of the religious faith that he held. The progeny of three sons settled in New England. Children: William, Jeffrey, Thomas, Eleazer, died in England in 1615; Elizabeth, married Robert Bernard.

(VI) William, son of Robert Fisk, was born in Laxfield, in 1566. He married (first) Anna, daughter of Walter Anstye, of Tibbenham, county Norfolk, England. He married (second) Alice ———. He also had to leave his home on account of his religion. His will was proved May 17, 1623. Children: John, mentioned below; Nathaniel, Eleazer, Eunice, Hannah, Hester, Mary.

(VII) John, son of William Fisk, was born at St. James, England, died in 1633. He married Anne, daughter of Robert Lantersee. Children: John, born 1601; William, mentioned below; Anne, married Francis Chickering; Martha, married Captain Edmund Thompson; Nathan, died in infancy; Eleazer, born in England.

(VIII) William (2), son of John Fisk, and the immigrant ancestor, was born in England about 1613, and came to this country in 1637. He had a grant of land in Salem, Massachusetts, that year, and was freeman, May 18, 1642. Soon after he removed to Wenham, where he was first town clerk, 1643-60. In 1647 he was elected representative to the general court and was reëlected until 1652. In 1643 he received permission to keep an ordinary, and in 1646 was licensed to "sell wine and strong water." He married at Salem, 1643, Bridgett Muskett, of Pelham, England. After his death, 1654, she married (second) November 4, 1661, Thomas Rix, of Salem, surgeon. He died suddenly September, 1654, and letters of administration were granted his widow, July 16, 1654. Children: William, mentioned below; Samuel, born in Wenham, married Phebe Bragge and Hannah Allen; Joseph, married Elizabeth Haman; Benjamin, married Bethusha Morse; Martha, born in Wenham.

(IX) Deacon William (3) Fisk, son of Hon. William (2) Fisk, was baptized in Wenham, June 4, 1642-43, died February 5, 1728. He married there, January 15, 1662, Sarah Kilham, born 1649, died January 26, 1737, daughter of Austin Kilham, the immigrant, who settled in Wenham before 1645; married Alice ———. William Fisk was a weaver by trade and held a number of town offices; representative, 1701-04-11-13-14; moderator, 1702-03-12-13-14. He was called lieutenant, and was elected deacon of the church in 1679. Children: Sarah, born February 5, 1664; Ruth, March 2, 1666; Samuel, May 8, 1667, died young; Martha, May 5, 1668; Joseph, February 10, 1669, died young; Samuel, February 16, 1670; Joseph, April 14, 1672; Benjamin, March 22, 1674; Theophilus, July 28, 1676; Ebenezer, February 10, 1677, died June 7, 1678; Ebenezer, mentioned below; Jonathan,

July 22, 1681, died February 14, 1705; Elizabeth, December 12, 1684.

(X) Ebenezer, son of Deacon William (3) Fisk, was born in Wenham, March 22, 1679, died September 30, 1771. He was a farmer by occupation, and held various town offices. He was elected deacon, May 16, 1739, and resigned "by reason of age" in 1758. He married (first) in Wenham, May 24, 1710, Elizabeth, daughter of Jacob Fuller, of Salem, from whom was descended the celebrated Margaret Fuller. She was born 1686, died August 25, 1732. He married (second) December 1, 1733, Mrs. Martha Kimball, who died March 28, 1764. Children: Sarah, born July 15, 1711; Jonathan, December 11, 1713; Ebenezer, mentioned below; Elizabeth, October 12, 1718; Jacob, December 26, 1721; Mary, January 27, 1723; William, November 30, 1726; Mercy, March 9, 1728; Lucy, April 22, 1732.

(XI) Ebenezer (2), son of Ebenezer (1) Fisk, was born in Wenham, Massachusetts, July 2, 1716, died in 1804. He was one of the first settlers of Shelburne, Massachusetts, about 1760, and its first constable. Before settling in the latter town, he had lived in Upton, Grafton and Hardwick, Massachusetts. He married, in Upton, Massachusetts, January 28, 1739, Dorcas Tyler, an aunt of President John Tyler. Children: Dorcas, born October 17, 1640; Elizabeth, January 28, 1743; Jonathan, September 17, 1746; Ebenezer, September 9, 1749; Levi, December 16, 1751; Abigail, October 7. 1755; John, September 27, 1757, Grafton; Simeon, July 15, 1762, Hardwick; Moses, mentioned below.

(XII) Deacon Moses Fisk, son of Ebenezer (2) Fisk, was born September 13, 1764, in Shelburne, died February 5, 1847. He married, June 2, 1789, Hannah Batchelor, born in Upton, May 14, 1770, died in Waitsfield, Vermont, in 1854. He settled in Waitsfield, where he and his wife were among the original members of the Congregational church. Of this church he was a deacon for fifty-five years. Children: Joel, born July 16, 1790, died July 18, 1795; Perrin, July 6, 1792; Moses, July 25, 1794; Joel, mentioned below; Harvey, April 12, 1799; Lyman, October 15, 1801; Betsey, May 8, 1804; Anson, October 31, 1806; Jonathan, May 6, 1809; Elvira Eliza, August 20, 1811 (twin); Horace Alonzo (twin), August 20, 1811; Emily, January 12, 1817.

(XIII) Rev. Joel Fisk, son of Deacon Moses Fisk, was born in Waitsfield, Vermont, October 26, 1796, died December 16, 1856. He fitted for college at Montpelier Academy, read theology with Rev. Charles Walker, of Rutland, Vermont, 1825-26, and graduated from

Middlebury College, Vermont, in 1825. He was settled successively at Monkton, Vermont, 1826-30; New Haven, Vermont, 1830-32; Essex, New York, 1832-44; as missionary at Phillipsburg, Canada East, 1844-45, and Plainfield, Vermont, where he died. He married, October 15, 1826, Clarinda Chapman, born June 21, 1803, died January 15, 1878. Children: Pliny, born May 10, 1828; Clarinda Chapman, November 27, 1829; Harvey, April 26, 1831; Sarah Jane, December 12, 1835, married William Henry Kinney (see Kinney VII); Mary I., April 9, 1838; Daniel C., November, 1840; Richard Henry, November 17, 1842.

RICHARDS Joseph Richards married Agnes ———, who was buried March 31, 1608. They lived in North Leigh, Oxfordshire, England.

(II) William, son of Joseph Richards, was baptized May 20, 1586. He lived in North Leigh, Oxfordshire, England. His wife died about July 18, 1632.

(III) Dr. Joseph (2) Richards, of Newgate, in the parish of Whitney and county of Oxford, England, son of William Richards, was baptized April 27, 1628, died in 1710-11. He was the immigrant ancestor, and he settled on five hundred acres of land near Chester, Delaware county, Pennsylvania. His will is recorded in Philadelphia, dated July 6, 1710-11, proved February 10, 1711-12. In his will he mentioned his children and grandchildren. He was buried at Old Chichester, Delaware county, Pennsylvania. He married Jane ———. Children: Joseph, married Mary ———; Nathaniel, mentioned below; Ann, married (first) Anthony Weaver, and (second) Humphrey Scarlott; Susanna, married James Lowne, and had four or more children.

(IV) Nathaniel, son of Dr. Joseph (2) Richards, died in 1700. His will was dated December 26, 1699. He married Mary, daughter of Richard Mason. Children: William, probably died young; Nathaniel, mentioned below; Elizabeth, married, about 1716, Roger Kirk; Mary, probably died young.

(V) Nathaniel (2), son of Nathaniel (1) Richards, was probably the only son in this generation to continue the family name. He died in 1730. He married Margaret, who died December 5, 1796, aged ninety, widow of William Carpenter. She left one hundred and thirteen descendants. She was daughter of Allen and Sarah (?) Wiley, and was born about 1706. Children: William Richards, married (first) April 13, 1751, Joanna Jenkins, and (second) May 10, 1759, Jane Miller; Nathaniel; Isaac, mentioned below.

(VI) Isaac, son of Nathaniel (2) Richards,

was born in 1727, died in 1821, aged ninety-four. He was only three years old when his father died. He married (first) January 17, 1753, Mary Gregg, of Hockessing. She was daughter of Thomas Gregg, who married, February 10, 1729, Dinah Harlan, and who died September 1, 1748; Dinah was daughter of Michael, died 1729, and Dinah (Dixon) Harlan, married January, 1690; Dinah Dixon was daughter of Henry Dixon; Michael Harlan was son of James Harlan. Thomas Gregg was son of John, born about 1668, died 1738; married, 1694, Elizabeth, daughter of ———— and Elizabeth (Fox) Cocke; John Gregg was son of William, who died July 1, 1687. Isaac Richards married (second) November 10, 1763, Rebecca Miller. Children by first wife: 1. Thomas, mentioned below. 2. Nathaniel, born September 21, 1756. 3. Isaac, born April 18, 1759, died June 22, 1854; remained on homestead at Toughkenamon, Pennsylvania; married (first) Ann Pusey, and (second) Tamsen Hoopes. 4. William, born January 17, 1761. 5. Mary, March 1, 1762. 6. Lydia, twin of Mary.

(VII) Thomas, son of Isaac Richards, was born June 10, 1755, died February 8, 1837, aged eighty-two years. He moved to Cecil county, Maryland, taking his family, about 1795. He married, September 23, 1779, at Uwchlan Meeting, Hannah Cox, born about 1753, died August 7, 1823, aged seventy years, daughter of Lawrence and Sarah (Edge) Cox; Lawrence Cox is said to have come from England to Willistown, where he died about 1760; he married at Middletown Meeting, February 5, 1739, his second wife Sarah, who died December 6, 1805, daughter of John and Mary (Smedley) Edge; John Edge was born May, 1685, died about 1734, married, August, 1709, Mary, born February 3, 1690, daughter of George Smedley, died 1723, and Sarah Kitchin, married 1687; John Edge was son of John and Jane Edge; and this John who was born about 1646, died May 10, 1711, was son of George Edge. Children: 1. Sarah, born 1781, died 1828; married, May 18, 1797, William Moore, born February 24, 1771. 2. Isaac, born 1783, died December 15, 1832; married Lydia Wood, born 1774, died June 19, 1839. 3. Hannah, born September 19, 1785, died November 25, 1859; married, 1819, Samuel Taylor, born April 2, 1768, died April 22, 1852, son of Elisha and Elizabeth Taylor; children: Isaac R., Samuel H., Sarah. 4. Thomas, mentioned below. 5. Mary, born May 7, 1790, died February 14, 1828; married, September 15, 1819, Abraham Metcalf, son of Abraham and Mary Metcalf. 6. Jacob, born September 4, 1793, died August 6, 1881; married, November 4,

1819, Sarah B. Taylor, of Kennett; died March 7, 1868. 7. Rachel, born November 16, 1798; married, 1823, Mahlon McMillan, son of Thomas and Ruth (Moore) McMillan.

(VIII) Thomas (2), son of Thomas (1) Richards, was born November 11, 1787, died October 9, 1868, aged eighty-one. He married, April 14, 1814, Orpah Stubbs (see Stubbs). Children: 1. Ruth Hannah, born May 20, 1816, died February 3, 1909; married Amos Preston, died August 27, 1875, and had two sons, Thomas and Albert W., and a daughter Elizabeth. 2. Isaac Stubbs, mentioned below. 3. Joanna A., born July 10, 1822, died 1855; married Isaac Jackson.

(IX) Isaac Stubbs, son of Thomas (2) Richards, was born September 7, 1819, died April 19, 1864. He married, March 11, 1841, at Oxford, Chester county, Pennsylvania, Mercy Ann Reynolds (see Reynolds VI). Children: 1. Ruthanna, born 1843, died March 6, 1896; married Joseph R. Coates, born May 12, 1834. 2. Joseph Thomas, mentioned below. 3. Louis Henry, born 1847, died 1895; married, October 29, 1885, Rebecca Williamson; child, Arthur Louis. 4. Isaac Stubbs, born 1848, died August 19, 1880; married, February 25, 1874, Margaret Deal, and had no children. 5. Jacob Granville, born 1851; married (first) December 26, 1872, Jennie Elizabeth Langdon, and (second) Mae V. Pennington; had four sons by first wife, William, Harry F., Joseph T. and Hampton, and three daughters and one son by second wife, Mae Ruth, Josephine Mercy, Granville P. and Margaret S. 6. William Franklin, born January 12, 1855, died July 19, 1859. 7. Mercy Ann, born and died September 24, 1859.

(X) Joseph Thomas, son of Isaac Stubbs Richards, was born near Rising Sun, Maryland, February 12, 1845. He was educated largely at the West Nottingham Academy, Maryland, Rev. S. A. Gayley, president, and George K. Bechtel, a graduate of Princeton College, principal, and finishing at Polytechnic College of Pennsylvania, of which Dr. A. L. Kennedy was then president. After mastering the profession of civil engineering, he entered the employ of the Pennsylvania Railroad Company in 1869 as a rodman and transitman during the construction of the railroad shops at Altoona, Pennsylvania. He was made supervisor of a division of the main line from Harrisburg to Newport in 1870, leaving this position in 1871 to become chief engineer of the Kent County railroad, on the Eastern Shore of Maryland. After the construction was completed the board of directors elected him to fill the position of superintendent, secretary and auditor. He managed the railroad for about one year, and returned to the Pennsylvania railroad in 1873 as chief of locating engineers for the surveys of three routes over the Allegheny Mountains, intended to form a connecting link between the Bedford division and the main line at Altoona and Johnstown, Pennsylvania. After finishing the surveys, with estimates of cost, the work was abandoned because of a financial panic in 1874, and he resigned and accepted the position of mining engineer for the Cambria Iron Company at Johnstown, Pennsylvania. He returned to the Pennsylvania railroad in 1875. He was for one year supervisor of the main line from Newport to Granville, and early in 1876 was promoted to be assistant engineer in charge of constructing the system of tracks, bridges and stations for the Philadelphia Centennial Exposition. After the Centennial year he was appointed principal assistant engineer of the United New Jersey Railroad and Canal Company, with office at Jersey City, New Jersey, continuing in that position until 1883, when he was made assistant to the chief engineer with office at Philadelphia. In 1885 his title was changed to assistant chief engineer. In 1893 the maintenance of way department of the railroad was created and he was made the engineer to organize and manage this department, including all lines east of Pittsburgh and Erie to New York and Washington, becoming chief engineer of the department for the entire system in 1903. This position made him the operating engineer for the company and a staff officer of the general manager, and besides caring for the buildings and tracks, he had charge of such construction work as came under the department of the general manager. Mr. Richards has been deemed an authority on railroad engineering, both in construction and maintenance, for many years, and has written quite extensively on the economy and efficiency of this department of railroading. His address to the American Civic Association at the annual meeting in 1907 at Brown University, Providence, Rhode Island, on "The Railroad as a Factor in Civic Improvement," has been republished extensively throughout the country. The efficiency of his organization was exemplified in the repairs after the Johnstown Flood in 1889, when he had about nine thousand organized for the emergency work of rebuilding the lost bridges, buildings and roadbed. In the beginning of this disaster he rebuilt 1,100 feet of the railroad bridge over the swollen waters of the Susquehanna river at Montgomery, Pennsylvania, in three days and a half, and the entire line from Philadelphia to Johnstown was opened for traffic in fourteen days. Another item of efficiency work done under Mr. Richards' direction was in 1897, when the old metal span of 286.3 feet of double-track bridge over the Schuylkill river at Philadelphia was moved twenty-seven feet, replaced by the new structure moved the same distance, without interrupting the regular schedule of trains. The longest interval between trains was thirteen minutes, but the actual time taken to move the old and new spans was but two minutes and twenty-eight seconds. Mr. Richards, at the request of President Frank Thomson, wrote an account of this feat to answer the criticism of an English technical journal, in which it was called an incredible feat and described as "credible, if credible" because "nothing of the kind has ever been done." The journal published Mr. Richards' account, stating that it was a case like Columbus' egg—easy enough when you understand it. Mr. Richards was for a number of years the designing and constructing engineer for the new piers at New York and Philadelphia for the International Navigation Company. The steel pier No. 14 in New York, north of Cortlandt street, North river, was, when finished, considered by a committee of experts, as the most complete in its appointments for steamships of any building in the harbor. He coöperated with the late president, Alexander J. Cassatt, of the Pennsylvania Railroad Company, in planning much of the construction work on the system during his administration, and all the operating details of stations and yards were entrusted to Mr. Richards. The new station constructed by the Terminal Company at Washington, D. C., and owned jointly by the Pennsylvania Railroad Company and the Baltimore & Ohio Railroad Company, built to accommodate all the main lines entering Washington from the south, was planned by a committee of which Mr. Richards was chairman. He was also chairman of various committees of operating officers in charge of thè plans and construction of the new Pennsylvania Railroad Station in New York City. This station presented many new problems, the tracks being forty-two feet below the street level, with numerous supports located at the track level for the station building, and the tracks were arranged for operation either by tunnel engines or multiple-unit trains. The United States Mail Building was constructed over the tracks also. In such a vast expenditure of money it was necessary to secure the greatest possible efficiency and capacity. The architects of the station reported direct to the railroad committees, which had to harmonize many differences of opinion between architects and engineers. The perfect order and train service at the opening of the station demonstrated that every feature of the great undertaking had been worked out successfully.

Mr. Richards is first vice-president of the West End Trust Company; former president of the Engineers Club of Philadelphia; member of the Union League of Philadelphia, the Historical Society of Pennsylvania, the American Society of Civil Engineers, the American Society for Testing Materials, the American Railway Engineering Association, the American Forestry Association, the American Railway Association, and a member of the Board of Trustees of the Jacob Tome Institute of Port Deposit, Maryland. In National politics he is a Republican; in religion he is a member of the Society of Friends, as his family has been since early in the seventeenth century.

He married, November 26, 1873, Martha Elizabeth Ernest, born December 5, 1848, daughter of Henry Wooster and Mary Ann (Walters) Ernest. Children: 1. Mercy, born February 11, 1875; married, June 3, 1896, Norman Sturgis Essig, D. D. S., born November 6, 1869; children: Charles James Essig, born March 12, 1898; Joseph Richards Essig, January 14, 1902. 2. Mamie, October 18, 1876, died August 30, 1877. 3. Joseph Ernest, born March 8, 1881; married, March 18, 1905, Catharine Louise Fletcher, born March 28, 1886; children: Philip and Herold, born January 26, 1909, died next day; Christine Louise, January 11, 1910. 4. Amy, born September 12, 1883; married, February 2, 1909, Edwin Oberlin Fitch Jr., United States navy, born January 6, 1882; child, Susanna Fitch, born November 3, 1910. 5. Martha, born February 20, 1888, died October 21, 1888.

(The Stubbs Line).

(I) Thomas Stubbs, who died in 1763, married, in 1720, Mary Minor.

(II) Daniel, son of Thomas Stubbs, died April 6, 1808. He married, January 20, 1751, Ruth Gilpin, born October 23, 1736, died July 27, 1781, daughter of Joseph Gilpin, born January 21, 1703, died December 31, 1792, married, October 17, 1729, Mary, daughter of Vincent Caldwell, born 1673, died January 10, 1720, married, 1703, Betty Pierce; Betty Pierce was born September 18, 1680, died October 27, 1757, daughter of George Pierce, died about 1734, married, December 1, 1679, Ann Gainer. Joseph Gilpin, father of Ruth, was son of Joseph Gilpin, born April 8, 1663, died 1739, married, December 23, 1691, Hannah Glover, born 1675, died 1757; Hannah was daughter of George and Alice (Lamboll) Glover. Joseph Gilpin, father of Joseph Gilpin, was son of Thomas and Joan (Bartholomew) Gilpin.

(III) Joseph, son of Daniel Stubbs, was born May 27, 1761, died August 4, 1856. He married, May 4, 1786, at Little Britain Meeting, Ruth, daughter of Moses Pyle, of Little Britain, who died January, 1784; Moses Pyle married, October 9, 1741, at Londongrove Meeting, Mary Cooke, his second wife, born August 4, 1719; she was daughter of John Cooke, born July 2, 1696, died 1759, married, October, 1718, Elinor Lansdale, born in Lancashire, daughter of Thomas and Margaret Lansdale. John Cooke was son of Peter Cooke, who married, October 7, 1695, Elinor Norman. Moses Pyle was son of John Pyle, born June 8, 1687, died 1752, married, 1710, Lydia Thomas, died before 1716, daughter of Peter Thomas, who married, February 15, 1686, Sarah Stedman, daughter of ———— and Elizabeth Stedman. John Pyle was son of Robert Pyle, who was baptized December 29, 1660, died in 1730, married, September 16, 1681, Ann, daughter of William Stovy, who died November 7, 1705. Robert Pyle was son of Nicholas Pyle, baptized March 12, 1625, died August, 1691, married, September 22, 1656, Edith Musprat, who died June, 1676.

(IV) Orpah, daughter of Joseph and Ruth (Pyle) Stubbs, was born August 8, 1791, died September 16, 1853. She married, April 14, 1814, Thomas Richards (see Richards VIII.).

(The Reynolds Line).

(I) William Reynolds, the first ancestor known in the direct line, married Margaret Exton.

(II) Henry, son of William Reynolds, was born in 1655, died August 7, 1724. He married, November 10, 1678, Prudence Clayton, who died about 1728, daughter of William and Prudence Clayton.

(III) Henry (2), son of Henry (1) Reynolds, was born August 16, 1693, died December 17, 1779. He married, 1717, Hannah Brown, born October 31, 1701, died December 12, 1731-32, daughter of William Brown, born January 29, 1658, died June 23, 1746; he married (third) 1699, Catharine Williams, mother of Hannah; William Brown was son of Richard Brown, who died September 28, 1662, and his wife, Mary Brown.

(IV) Jacob, son of Henry (2) Reynolds, was born September 14, 1728, died February 6, 1799. He married, August 10, 1751, at East Nottingham, Rebecca Day, born about 1735, died September 14, 1785, daughter of John Day, who died 1775, and who married at Nottingham Meeting, April 21, 1733, Lydia Ross; she was born July 7, 1708, died March 1, 1799, daughter of Alexander Ross, who died 1748, and who married, 1706, Katharine Chambers.

(V) Jacob (2), son of Jacob (1) Reynolds, was born November 10, 1755, died February 2, 1811. He married, at West Nottingham Meeting, October 19, 1785, Esther, born May 12, 1763, daughter of John Taylor, who died 1772, married at Birmingham Meeting, May 13, 1762, as his second wife, Mary Jackson. Mary Jackson was daughter of Samuel Jackson, of Marlborough, who died June 9, 1745, and who married at New Garden Meeting, September 16, 1727, Mary Chambers, born January 7, 1707, died October 4, 1787; Mary was daughter of John Chambers, born December 28, 1662, son of William Chambers; John Chambers married, April 13, 1699, Deborah Dobson, daughter of Richard Dobson. Samuel Jackson was son of Thomas Jackson, who died in 1727. John Taylor, father of Esther Taylor, was son of Richard Taylor, born November 26, 1702, died September 2, 1744, married, 1735, Eleanor ———, who died 1793. Richard Taylor was son of Joseph Taylor, who died March 30, 1744, and who married, January 16, 1700, Elizabeth Haines, who died June 21, 1743; Joseph Taylor was son of Abiah Taylor, who married, January 17, 1663, Alice ———.

(VI) Jacob (3), son of Jacob (2) Reynolds, was born May 8, 1791, died May 12, 1869. He married Anna Moore (see Moore IV). Their daughter, Mercy Ann Reynolds, born May 29, 1816, died February 5, 1885, married Isaac Stubbs Richards (see Richards IX).

(The Moore Line).

(I) Andrew Moore, of Sadsbury, was born in 1688, died in 1753. He married (second) April 24, 1725, Rachel Halliday, born October 25, 1704, died in 1785, daughter of William Halliday, who died in 1741, and who married at Moate Meeting, Ireland, September 2, 1698, Deborah Woodsworth.

(II) Joseph, son of Andrew Moore, was born July 13, 1736, died July 13, 1805. He was of Londongrove. He married at Sadsbury Meeting, January 22, 1756, Jane Marsh, born February 18, 1735, died November 15, 1779, daughter of Henry Marsh, of Sadsbury, Chester county, Pennsylvania, who died about 1803, fought in the revolution, married at Christ Church, Philadelphia, August 1, 1734, Anne Stuart, born June 4, 1712. Henry Marsh was son of William Marsh, died 1744, and Sarah ———. Anne Stuart was daughter of Alexander Stuart, who died November 5, 1714-15, and who married, 1708, Mary Baily, born September 10, 1688, died 1741; Mary Baily was daughter of Joel Baily, who was baptized January 29, 1658, and died 1732; Joel Baily married, 1687, Ann Short.

(III) Joseph (2), son of Joseph (1) Moore, was born April 11, 1767, died December 13, 1850. He was of West Nottingham, Maryland, and he married at West Grove Meeting, October 27, 1791, Mercy Cutler, born October 12, 1773, died November 7, 1822, daughter of Benjamin and Susanna (Dunn) Cutler; Benjamin Cutler was of Buckingham and Londongrove, born in 1740, died September 6, 1794, married, July 25, 1770, Susanna Dunn, born September 3, 1751, died October 18, 1823. Susanna Dunn was daughter of Ralph Dunn Jr., born October 2, 1716, died August 23, 1797, married Anna Heaton, born July 5, 1726, died August 16, 1813, daughter of Robert and Susanna (Carter) Heaton; Susanna Carter was daughter of James and Susanna (Griffith) Carter; Robert Heaton Jr. was son of Robert and Grace (Pierson) Heaton. Ralph Dunn was son of Ralph Dunn Sr., who died March or April, 1727, and who married Sarah, widow of Thomas Searl, and daughter of John and Jane (Cutler) Naylor. Benjamin Cutler was son of Benjamin Cutler, born July 7, 1709, died 1769, married, December, 1731-32, Mercy Bills, who died November 21, 1749; Mercy Bills was daughter of Nathaniel and Mary (Gardner) Bills; Nathaniel Bills was born June 25, 1677, died 1729, and was of Shrewsbury, New Jersey; he was son of Thomas Bills, who died February 2, 1721, and who married (second) May 2, 1676, Johanna Twining (see Twining II). Benjamin Cutler was son of John Cutler, who married, April 17, 1703, Margery, daughter of Cuthbert and Mary Hayhurst.

(IV) Anna, daughter of Joseph (2) and Mercy (Cutler) Moore, was born August 31, 1793, died September 19, 1874. She married Jacob Reynolds (see Reynolds VI).

(The Twining Line).

(I) William Twining, immigrant ancestor, was born in England. He settled in this country, as early as 1643, when he was a freeholder at Yarmouth, on Cape Cod, Massachusetts. Family tradition makes of him a Welshman and another tradition asserts that he came from Yorkshire. He appears in the list of those able to bear arms in 1643, and in 1645 he was one of five sent out against the Narragansett Indians. He removed to Eastham, an adjacent town, in 1644, and he was constable there in 1651. He died April 15, 1659, at Eastham, aged about sixty-five. He married, in 1652, at Orleans, Anne Doane, who died February 27, 1680. She must have been a second wife. Children: William, mentioned below; Isabel.

(II) William (2), son of William (1)

Twining, was born soon after 1620, probably in England, and died at Newtown, Bucks county, Pennsylvania, November 4, 1703. He was admitted a freeman, June 3, 1652; was on the grand jury in 1652 and in 1667-68-71. He was deacon of the Eastham church as early as 1677. About 1695 he became a Friend and decided to leave New England, where Quakers were sorely persecuted, and he settled on the banks of the Delaware in Pennsylvania with part of his family. His will was dated June 26, 1697, proved April 8, 1705, bequeathing to grandson William, son of Stephen; daughters Joanna, Mehitable, daughters of his daughter, Anne Bills; to William Twining, his lands in Eastham and county of Barnstable, Massachusetts; to Elizabeth Rogers, his daughter, land at Truro. He married Elizabeth Deane, daughter of Stephen Deane, of Plymouth, whose widow married Josiah Cooke. She died at Newtown, Pennsylvania, December 28, 1708. Children: Elizabeth, married, August 19, 1669, John Rogers; Anne, married, October 3, 1672, Thomas Bills; Susanna, born February 25, 1654; Joanna, born May 30, 1657, married Thomas Bills (see Moore III); Mehitable, married Daniel Deane; Stephen, born February 6, 1659; William, born at Orleans, February 28, 1664.

HOWE   The surname Howe was originally identical with Howe, Hoo, Hough, Howes and other variations, including the Norman-French forms of de la How, de How, de Hoo, etc. The oldest English forms are doubtless Hoo and How. The name was spelled How in New England until comparatively recent date. John How, immigrant ancestor of a large part of the American families of this surname, is believed to be the son of John How, of Warwickshire, England, and grandson of John How, of Hodinhall, said to be connected with Sir Charles How, of Lancaster, who lived during the reign of Charles I. John How, the American immigrant, was born in England, and was among the earliest settlers of Watertown, Massachusetts; was admitted a freeman, May 13, 1640, and was at Sudbury as early as 1639, and a selectman of Sudbury in 1642. He was also among the first settlers of Marlborough, Massachusetts. Abraham How, of Marlborough, another early settler of Marlborough, was probably related. There were several other Hows in Massachusetts before 1650. A branch of the English family settled in the north of Ireland and thence scattered through that country as well. In 1890 we find the record of sixteen births in Howe families in Ireland, six in Ulster province.

(I) Francis Howe, of this Irish branch of the family, a descendant of John How, was born in Tullee, county of Roscommon, Ireland, died at New London in 1899. When but seven years old he came to this country with his widowed mother. He made his home in Stonington, Connecticut. At fourteen he was apprenticed to the captain of a whaling ship. At twenty he returned from a three years' voyage as master of his ship. In religion he was a Roman Catholic, in politics a Democrat. He married Ann Larkin, born in county Clare, Ireland, a daughter of Patrick and Anne (Winter) Larkin. Children: Thomas, born in Groton, Connecticut, and resides at New London; Mary Ellen, born at Stonington, Connecticut and now resides at New London; Frank, mentioned below.

There is a family tradition that Francis Howe was of the same stock as Sir William Howe and Lord Howe who led the British forces in the revolution, and if this tradition is well founded there is reason to believe that he was also related very distantly to the old New England families of this surname. It is likely that all the Hows came originally from the same stock. The coats-of-arms tend to support this belief, the various families bearing the same armorials in many cases.

(III) Frank, son of Francis Howe, was born at Stonington, Connecticut, April 11, 1856. He attended the public schools of Groton and New London, Connecticut. Early in life he developed a talent for music. Finally deciding upon the cornet, he studiously applied himself, and at the age of sixteen had become so proficient as a musician that he appeared professionally as a cornetist. At the age of twenty he appeared first in Philadelphia with the Third Regiment Bank, C. N. G., and appeared as a solo cornetist at the Centennial Exposition. In 1879 he began his business career as a clerk in the Boston carpet house of John & James Dobson, Philadelphia. He won promotion from time to time. He left to become the Boston sales agent of another Philadelphia firm, Coffin, Altemus & Company, dry goods commission merchant. Thence he went to Chicago to conduct a branch store for this firm. While living in Boston he developed somewhat a talent for playing and he was Dick Deadeye, at the old Globe Theatre in Boston, in Gilbert and Sullivan's "H. M. S. Pinafore," in the same amateur cast in which Richard Mansfield played Sir Joseph Porter at the time Mansfield had not yet entered into prominence as an actor. In 1883 Mr. Howe made his first venture as a theatrical manager at McVicker's Theatre, Chicago, producing "Iolanthe," the first performance in Chicago of this operetta.

From that time he has continued in the theatre business with eminent success. In 1895 he became the sole lessee of the oldest theatre in America, the Walnut Street Theatre of Philadelphia, erected in 1808, and at the same time he became also lessee of the Park Theatre, Board street and Fairmont avenue, Philadelphia, which was opened in 1889, and which was the most pretentious and most modern that the city knew at that period.

Some of the most famous productions in America were made at the Park Theatre during his management. Notable among them being "The Fencing Master" by Reginald De Koven, A. M. Palmer's famous stock company, together with many well remembered musical productions and dramas. Not long afterward he disposed of the lease of the Park Theatre, but he has retained the Walnut Street Theatre and conducted it with gratifying success to the present time. It was during Mr. Howe's lesseeship of the historic Walnut Street Theatre that some of the now most famous actors and actresses made their first successes. Notable among these were David Warfield, Willie Collier, Dan Daly, Ethel Barrymore, George Cohan, Helen Ware, Robert Mantell. In 1900 he induced Mr. William Weightman, the capitalist, to build the beautiful Garrick Theatre in Philadelphia, of which Mr. Howe became lessee and manager. This theatre was opened October 11, 1901; Richard Mansfield in Booth Tarkington's "Monsieur Beaucaire" was the stage offering. From that date until the fall of 1911, he directed the policy and management of this house, which in that time became one of the most popular and successful playhouses of that city and now has an international reputation. Mr. Howe was gifted with that ambitious characteristic that caused him to first study the wants of his patrons and then see that they got the nature of entertainments that appealed to them. He avoided the licentious and his patrons were insured of the highest class in the art of music and the drama. This is borne out in the fact that on the stages he directed such artists as Mansfield, Mme. Modjeska, Mme. Janauscheck, Wilson Barrett, Julia Marlowe, Agnes Huntington, Marie Tempest, E. H. Sothern, Joseph Jefferson, Fanny Davenport, Chauncey Olcott, Ethel Barrymore, and other stars fondly remembered by theatre visiting people of Philadelphia, made their appearance. Mr. Howe is a member of the Lambs Club of New York City, and he is president of the Theatrical Managers' Association of Philadelphia. In politics he is Republican, in religion a Roman Catholic.

He married, April 16, 1890, Florence Leigh, born in 1870, in Jersey City, New Jersey, daughter of Frederick and Wilhelmina (Melber) Leigh. Mr. and Mrs. Howe have no children.

FROTHINGHAM William Frothingham, immigrant ancestor of all the colonial families of this surname, was born in England about 1600, and came from the vicinity of Holderness in Yorkshire, the ancient seat of the family, which probably came thither from Scotland. The name spelled Fotheringham was common in Forfarshire, Scotland, before 1300, at the very beginning of the use of surnames. In the ancient History of Scotland by John Lesley, vol. i., p. vi., the family of Fodringhame together with Crychton, Giffert, Manlis, Borthik "and others" are said to have come from Wugre (Hungary) under Malcolm, King of Scotland, with his wife Queen Margaret. But Hailes raised a doubt of the accuracy of the statement. Indeed, it seems that the final syllable indicates a local origin of Fotheringham, though the surname may have been a place name taken by a Hungarian noble after the custom of the time, eventually becoming the family name.

William Frothingham came from England in Winthrop's fleet, and was one of the proprietors of Charlestown, Massachusetts, in 1630. He was admitted a freeman, March 6, 1631-32. With his wife Anne he was admitted to the church in Boston in 1630 and joined the new church at Charlestown in 1632. He was an adherent of Rev. John Wheelwright who founded Exeter, brother of the celebrated Mrs. Hutchinson, but Frothingham finally renounced his beliefs and remained in the established church of the Puritans at Charlestown. His wife Anne died July 28, 1674, aged sixty-seven years (see gravestone). He had a grant of land from the town on the Mystic side (Woburn) of ten acres. His house and four acres of land were bounded on the north by the Mystic river, east by homesteads of George Bunker and Thomas Ruck; west by E. Mellows and Abraham Pratt. He had eight other parcels of land on record. His will is dated September 31, 1651, and was proved February 6, 1652. The document itself has been in the possession of the family many years, though the records show that it was proved properly. He bequeathed his property to his wife, and the inventory places a value of fifty pounds on his house and orchard. His widow bought a house and land in Charlestown in 1656 of Grace Palmer. Her will, dated October 4, 1672, was proved October 6, 1674, be-

1—4

queathing to her sons Samuel, J. Kettell, Peter and Nathaniel Frothingham, and Thomas White, who received her house orchard and barn. Children, born in Charlestown: Bethia, born February 7, 1631; John, August 10, 1633; Elizabeth, March 15, 1635; Peter, April 15, 1636; Mary, April 1, 1638; Nathaniel, mentioned below; Stephen, November 11, 1641; Hannah, March 29, 1642; Joseph, December 1, 1645; Samuel.

(II) Nathaniel, son of William Frothingham, was born in Charlestown, Massachusetts, April 16, 1640, died there December 12, 1688. His gravestone is preserved. He died the same day as his brother, Peter Frothingham. He joined the church with his wife, January 22, 1670-71. He lived in Charlestown and was granted two common rights there in 1681. He owned land on what is now called Bunker Hill. He was a legatee of the estate of William Croft, of Lynn, in 1689, or rather his eldest son was, together with the eldest children of his brother Peter. His estate was divided in 1708. He married, February 6, 1667, Mary Hett, and she married (second) in 1694, Samuel Kettell. Children: Mary, born September 25, 1668, died January 9, 1679; Nathaniel, April 16, 1670, died July 28 following; Nathaniel, mentioned below; Hannah, November 26, 1673, died young; Thomas, December 2, 1675; Joseph, October 31, 1677; Benjamin, December 26, 1679; Eliphalet, September 5, 1681; Mary, November 14, 1682; Hannah, May 30, 1685; Abigail, May 10, 1687; Abiel (daughter), May 26, 1689, died June 5, 1689.

(III) Nathaniel (2), son of Nathaniel (1) Frothingham, was born July 2, 1671. He was admitted to the church with his wife, February 17, 1705-06. He was a carpenter. His name was on the tax lists of 1727 and 1729. In 1696, with his father's heirs, he deeded land to Kidder which had been inherited from his father. He bought of his brothers Benjamin and Thomas, in 1702, one-half house joining the north end of his father's house and land below, fifty-two feet broad, and in 1708 he bought of heirs of his father, one-third of an orchard. There are recorded also many other purchases made by him at different dates. His will was dated June 16, 1725-26, and proved August 24, 1730. He bequeathed to his wife and three daughters all the estate during his wife's life, and afterwards it was to be divided among all the children. On June 9, 1760, Benjamin Frothingham was appointed executor of his estate. He married, April 12, 1694, Hannah Rand, who died April 23, 1760, aged eighty-seven, according to her gravestone. He died July 31, 1730, aged fifty-nine (grave-

stone). Children: Hannah, born June 8, 1695, died August 15, 1714; Elizabeth, January 20, 1696-97; Nathaniel, mentioned below; Mary, January 19, 1700; Joseph, July 15, 1703; Sarah, December 8, 1705; Benjamin, April 6, 1708; Thomas, January 3, 1709-10; Ruth, August 10, 1712.

(IV) Nathaniel (3), son of Nathaniel (2) Frothingham, was born December 7, 1698, died May 7, 1749, aged fifty, according to his gravestone. He was taxed in 1727-48. In 1723 his father deeded to him a lot of land, and some purchases of other lands are recorded, as well as land which he sold. He was a painter. His widow was made administratrix, May 22, 1749, and the inventory amounted to one thousand four hundred and sixty-six pounds. He married, July 27, 1721, Susanna Whittemore. She married (second) Stephen Badger, in 1756. Children: Nathaniel, mentioned below; Joseph, born January 15, 1723-24; Susanna, October 23, 1725; Hannah, October 17, 1727; William, October 16, 1729; Jabez, July 23, 1731, died November 30, 1748; Jonathan, August 15, 1733; James, August 22, 1735.

(V) Nathaniel (4), son of Nathaniel (3) Frothingham, was born June 2, 1722. He lived in Charlestown and Boston and was a coachmaker. In the shops at one period were four of the family bearing the name Nathaniel, each designated by some peculiar, significant term. He was taxed from 1756 to 1773. In 1746 his father deeded to him one-half house. In 1784 he deeded to his son Nathaniel a lot, and in 1786 he bought a house of Nathaniel and Hepzibah Rand. In 1788 he bought of Nathaniel Prentiss a house and one acre of land partly in Cambridge and partly in Charlestown. In 1796 his son Ebenezer with his heirs sold land to Page; Nathaniel Frothingham's executors in 1798 sold land to Nathaniel Prentiss, and also to John Page, and to Richard Frothingham in 1799. Nathaniel Frothingham married (first) March 1, 1743-44, Mary Whittemore, who died December 18, 1763, aged forty (gravestone). He married (second) in 1765, Ruth Taylor, who died October 12, 1800, aged sixty-one, and on the gravestone is written: "Husband and two wives were all buried here." He died in West street, Boston, March 14, 1791, aged sixty-nine. Children: Nathaniel, baptized February 24, 1744-45; Nathaniel, mentioned below; Richard, March 15, 1748; Mary, baptized July 14, 1754; Ebenezer, December 13, 1756; child, December 11, died December 12, 1758; Susanna, September 19, 1763; Katharine, May 14, died October 1, 1765; Thomas, November 30, 1767; Peter, November 24, 1775.

(VI) Nathaniel (5), son of Nathaniel (4) Frothingham, was born April 6, 1746. He was a coachmaker in Boston. This Nathaniel Frothingham was one of those patriots who took part in the Boston Tea Party, and disguised as Indians threw the tea overboard in Boston Harbor. In 1784 his father deeded him land on Main street. In 1785 he bought land with cellar of B. Bradish. He bought of Ebenezer Frothingham his levy on Soley & Stearns, and in 1801 he sold land to John Larkin. He married (first) May 16, 1771, Rebecca Austin. He married (second) December 22, 1785, Mary Townsend, who died October 12, 1800, aged forty-two (suicide). He married (third) May 2, 1804, Lydia Kettell. Children: Nathaniel, born 1779; Rebecca, 1781; Samuel, mentioned below; Mary, 1789; Susanna, 1792; Ruth, married John Redman, builder; others who died young.

(VII) Samuel, son of Nathaniel (5) Frothingham, was born at Charlestown, March 4, 1787, died in 1869. He located in Boston, became cashier of the State Bank, and latterly for many years the president of the institution. He was one of the prominent citizens of Boston taking part in many civic activities. He married, in 1810, Eliza Atkins, born in 1792, died in 1850. Children: Samuel, Harriet, Eliza, Theodore, of whom further; Henry; Cornelia, married Joshua H. Wolcott (see Wolcott VII).

(VIII) Theodore, son of Samuel Frothingham, was born July 5, 1818, in Boston. He received his education in Boston, and after leaving school went into the dry goods business in that city. In 1859 he removed to Philadelphia, continuing in the same kind of business of which he had already made a success, and there he resided until his death. Mr. Frothingham was one of the original members of the Union League Club, and was a very well-known and conspicuous citizen. He married, February 4, 1845, Mary Frances Wolcott, who was from Litchfield, Connecticut. She was born July 9, 1823, at Litchfield, died April 10, 1898, in Philadelphia. Children: 1. Mary Goodrich, born March 1, 1846; married Charles A. Brimlay, died July 15, 1911. 2. Theodore, mentioned below. 3. E. Cornelia, born December 22, 1853. 4. Bessye Wolcott, born January 15, 1857; married Percival Roberts Jr. 5. Harriet Wolcott, born December 28, 1860; married Dr. Herbert Norris.

(IX) Theodore (2), son of Theodore (1) Frothingham, was born in Boston, Massachusetts, March 22, 1848. He was prepared for college under Reginald Chase, in Philadelphia, and matriculated at Harvard College, joining as sophomore the class of 1870. He graduated with his cousin, Roger Wolcott. After he left college he engaged in business in Philadelphia as a ship broker and commission merchant until the year 1886. He then became connected with the Solicitors' Loan and Trust Company as secretary, and later as vice-president and treasurer; secretary and assistant treasurer of the Schuylkill River East Side Railroad Company since 1886; president of the Commercial Trust Company from 1894 until 1900; vice-president and treasurer of the Philadelphia Securities Company since 1898, and secretary and treasurer of the Assets Realization Company since 1900. He was director of the Young Men's Christian Association for a number of years, and was also director of the Philadelphia Orthopedic Hospital for many years, being for three years its treasurer. He has been director of the Pennsylvania Institute for the Deaf and Dumb for the past ten years, and as director has been connected with a number of other corporations. He was vice-president of the Harvard Club of Philadelphia from 1892 to 1895, and president from 1895 to 1898. He was second vice-president of the New England Society of Pennsylvania from 1901 to 1903, and president from 1903 to 1906. He is a member of the Rittenhouse, Philadelphia, Country and other clubs.

He married, May 22, 1888, Lucy Jaudon Harris, of Philadelphia. They have five children: Theodore, born April 19, 1889; Thomas Harris, April 5, 1891; Huntington Wolcott, September 19, 1893; William Bainbridge, October 30, 1898; Dorothea, May 6, 1909.

Mrs. Theodore Frothingham was the daughter of Captain Thomas Cadwalader Harris, United States navy, and Mary Louise Bainbridge Jaudon. She was born in Philadelphia, December 23, 1866. The father of Captain Thomas Cadwalader Harris was Dr. Thomas Harris, born January 3, 1784, who was the first surgeon-general of the United States navy. He practiced for many years in Philadelphia, and was a prominent man of his time. The father of Dr. Thomas Harris was William Harris, born in Chester county, Pennsylvania, in 1757, and was a revolutionary officer, later serving as brigadier-general. He was a member of the legislature during the years 1779-80, and 1810-11-12. He died September 4, 1812. This patriot was the son of Thomas Harris, born in 1722, who came in 1747 from Ireland, and settled in Chester county, Pennsylvania.

(The Wolcott Line).

(I) John Wolcott lived and died in Tolland, Somersetshire, England. His will, dated February 9, 1571, was proved April 11, 1572. Children: John, mentioned below; Alice, Mary.

(II) John (2), son of John (1) Wolcott, lived at Tolland, where he died March 2, 1618. He owned mills and other property at Tolland. William and Thomas Wolcott were in Tolland as early as 1526, but the relationship is not known. John Wolcott married Joan ———, who died April 5, 1637. Children, baptized at Lidiard, a parish adjoining Tolland: Christopher, died March 25, 1639; Henry, mentioned below; John, died February 17, 1652.

(III) Henry, son of John (2) Wolcott, was baptized at Lidiard, England, December 6, 1578. He came with the first company to Dorchester, Massachusetts, though it is said he came first in 1628. He came with part of his family in the ship "Mary and John," landing at Nantasket, May 30, 1630. He was an original settler and proprietor of Dorchester, and was on the first list of freemen, October 19, 1630. He was a leading citizen and selectman and in other important positions. In 1636-37 he moved with many neighbors to Windsor, Connecticut, and was a member of the first general assembly in 1637; in 1643 he was elected to the house of magistrates, serving the remainder of his life. He was a wealthy and influential man, owning a good estate in Somersetshire, England, at his death. He was called a "man of fine estate and superior abilities." He died May 30, 1655. He married, January 19, 1606, in England, Elizabeth Saunders, born 1582, died at Windsor, July 5, 1655, daughter of Thomas Saunders. Children: John, baptized at Lidiard, England, where he died; Anna, Henry, baptized January 21, 1610-11; George, Christopher, Mary, Simon, mentioned below.

(IV) Simon, son of Henry Wolcott, was born in 1624-25 in England. He was prominent in public life. In 1668 he was on a committee of the general court to further planting. In 1671 he moved to Simsbury, and was captain of the train band there, August 11, 1673; selectman, 1674. He and his neighbors were driven from home during King Philip's war. In 1680 he was one of the 'six in the colony called "Mr." He married (first), March 19, 1657, Joanna Cook, born August 5, 1638, died April 27, 1657; (second), October 17, 1661, Martha Pitkin, who came from England with her brother William, attorney-general and treasurer of the colony. Simon Wolcott died September 11, 1687, and his widow married (second) Daniel Clark, and died October 13, 1719. Children: Elizabeth, born August 19, 1662; Martha, May 17, 1664; Simon, June 24, 1666; Joanna, June 30, 1668; Henry, May 20, 1670; Christopher, July 4, 1672; Mary, 1674; William, November 8, 1676; Roger, mentioned below.

(V) Governor Roger Wolcott, son of Simon Wolcott, was born January 4, 1679, at Simsbury, Connecticut, and he was the foremost man of the day in the colony. He received school instruction from his parents. After his mother married (second) Daniel Clark, he went to live with her in her new home. In 1690 he learned to write and read; in 1694 he was apprenticed to a clothier or fuller to learn the trade, and January 2, 1699, he engaged in business as a clothier on his own account, and became very successful. He was elected selectman of Windsor in 1707; deputy to the general assembly in 1710. He took part in the expedition against Canada in 1711 as commissary of Connecticut stores. He was elected councillor in 1714; judge of county court in 1731; of superior court in 1732; deputy governor and chief judge of superior court in 1741. He was commissioned major-general of the colonial army by Governor Shirley, of Massachusetts, and Governor Law, of Connecticut, and led the Connecticut troops in the expedition against Cape Breton in 1745, then being sixty-seven years old. In 1750 he was elected governor of Connecticut. He published three books, "Political Meditations," 1720; "A Tract on a Controversial Letter on the New England Churches," 1761, and "Letter to the Freemen of Connecticut," 1761. He died May 17, 1767. He married, December 3, 1702, Sarah Drake, born May 10, 1686, daughter of Job Drake. Children: Roger, Elizabeth, born April 10. 1706; Alexander, January 20, 1708; Samuel, January 9, 1710; Alexander, January 7, 1712; Sarah, born and died December 10. 1713; Sarah. January 31, 1715; Hepzibah, June 23. 1717; Josiah, February 6, 1719; Erastus, twin, February 8, 1721; Ephraim, twin of Erastus; Oliver, mentioned below; Ursula, October 30, 1734.

(VI) Governor Oliver Wolcott, son of Governor Roger Wolcott, was graduated at Yale College in 1747. Soon afterward he was commissioned captain and marched to the defense of the northern frontier in the French and Indian war. He studied medicine for a time. In 1751 he was appointed the first sheriff of Litchfield county. He was active in support of the movement in the colonies against British misrule and was a member of the continental congress in July, 1775, and was one of the signers of the immortal Declaration of Independence. When he returned to Litchfield he carried with him the leaden statue of King George from New York and had it converted into bullets to shoot at the king's soldiers. He was commissioned by Governor Trumbull and the committee of safety, August 15, 1776, to command fourteen regiments. In November, 1776, he again attended Congress, and in 1777 he attended the session at Baltimore. He was commissioned brigadier-general, January 17, 1777, and commanded a brigade under General Gates. He attended congress at Yorktown in 1778. In the summer of 1779 he commanded a division of militia defending the seacoast. Early in life he was a member of the Connecticut general assembly, and from 1774 to 1786 an assistant or councillor and while councillor was also chief judge of the court of common pleas. For many years he was judge of probate also. He served in the provincial militia in all grades to the rank of major-general. During the war he contributed liberally to the patriots' cause from his own fortune. In 1782-83 he occasionally attended congress. In 1785 he was commissioner of Indian affairs for the northern department and was engaged in making peace with the Six Nations. In 1786 he was elected lieutenant-governor of Connecticut and re-elected annually until he became governor. He was a delegate to the state convention to ratify the federal constitution in 1787; was presidential elector in 1796 and voted for Adams and Pinckney. From 1796 until he died he was governor of the state. He married, January 21, 1755, Lorraine, daughter of Captain Daniel Collins, of Guilford. Children: Oliver, born August 31, died September 13, 1757; Oliver, born January 11, 1760, also governor of Connecticut; Laura, December 15, 1761, married William Moseley; Mariann, February 16, 1765, married Chauncey Goodrich; Frederick, mentioned below.

(VII) Frederick, son of Governor Oliver Wolcott, was born November 2, 1767, died at Litchfield, May 28, 1837. He graduated from Yale College in 1786 with first honors. He began to study law, but gave it up on account of ill health. In 1793 he was made clerk of the court of common pleas, and in 1798 clerk of the superior court of Litchfield county, an office he filled until 1836. In 1796 he was made judge of probate, an office he also filled as long as he lived. He represented the town often in the general assembly. In 1808 he was presidential elector. From 1810 to 1823 he was a state senator, and during the last six years was a fellow of Yale College. He and his brother Oliver were engaged for many years in the manufacture of woolen cloth at Wolcottville, Connecticut, and in farming. They imported Devon and Durham cattle and Merino sheep. Twice he declined the nomination

for governor when his party nominee was elected. All his life he was a student and a scholar, continuing to study and read the ancient classics.

He married (first), October 12, 1800, Betsey Huntington, born November 8, 1774, died April 2, 1812, daughter of Colonel Joshua Huntington. He married (second) Sally Worthington (Goodrich) Cooke, a daughter of Rev. Samuel Goodrich, of Berlin. She was born August 7, 1778, and died September 14, 1842. Children by first wife: 1. Mary Ann Goodrich, born August 9, 1801. 2. Hannah Huntington, January 14, 1803. 3. Joshua Huntington, born August 29, 1804; married (first), November 12, 1844, Cornelia, daughter of Samuel Frothingham, of Boston (see Frothingham VII). She died June 1, 1850, and he married (second), November 12, 1751, a sister of his first wife; his only surviving son was Governor Roger Wolcott, of Massachusetts, born July 13, 1847. 4. Elizabeth, born March 6, 1806. 5. Frederick Henry, born August 19, 1808. 6. Laura Maria, August 14, 1811. Children by second wife: 7. Charles Moseley, born November 20, 1816. 8. Chauncy Goodrich, born March 15, 1819, died young. 9. Henry Griswold, born November 4, 1820. 10. Mary Frances, born July 9, 1823; married, February 4, 1845, Theodore Frothingham, of Boston (see Frothingham VIII).

HOYT Hoyt is the surname of an ancient English family. As the old English word *hoit rom hoyt* means to leap or to caper, it is probable that some early progenitor of the family was noted for his agility or good spirits. In America the name has been spelled in more than thirty different ways. The Hoyt family in this country seems to have sprung from two men, Simon Hoyt and John Hoyt, between whom no relationship has been traced, although they were perhaps brothers. Simon Hoyt was in Salem, Massachusetts, as early as 1629. He was the emigrant ancestor of most of the Hoyts of Western Massachusetts, Connecticut and Eastern New York. The descendants of John Hoyt embrace most of those bearing the name in Eastern Massachusetts, Maine and New Hampshire. In other parts of the country there are numerous members of both branches.

(I) John Hoyt was probably born in England about 1610. He was one of the earliest settlers of Salisbury, Massachusetts, and obtained lands at the "first division," in 1639 or 1640. A few years later he removed across the Powow river to the west parish of Salisbury, his family being one of thirty that removed to settle it, and he sold his house on the east side in 1647. This west parish was named Amesbury in 1668 by the general court. In both Salisbury and Amesbury John Hoyt seems to have been prominent. He was at an early date appointed sergeant of the Salisbury military company. In the Amesbury records his name is frequently mentioned as prudential-man, selectman, constable, juror, moderator of a town meeting, etc. In old deeds he was styled "planter." He died February 28, 1687-88.

John Hoyt was twice married, both of his wives being named Frances. He had five children by his first wife, who died February 23, 1642-43, viz.: Frances, John, mentioned below; Thomas (twin), born January 1, 1640-41; Gregorie (twin), January 1, 1640-41; Elizabeth, February 23, 1642-43; and eight children by his second wife, viz.: Sarah, January 16, 1644-45; Mary, February 20, 1645-46; Joseph, born and died in 1648; Joseph, born November 27, 1649; Marah, November 24, 1653; Naomi, January 23, 1654-55; Dorothie, April 13, 1656; Mehetabel, October 25, 1664.

(II) John (2), eldest son of John (1) Hoyt, was born in Salisbury about 1638. In old deeds, of which he gave and received a large number, he is sometimes called a planter and sometimes a carpenter. He lived in Amesbury and there held the offices of "standing lot-layer," constable and "Clarke of ye market." He was "upon ye request and choyce" of the town licensed for several years to keep the town ordinary or inn. He was killed by the Indians in Andover, on the road to Haverhill, August 13, 1696. He married, June 23, 1659, Mary, daughter of William and Rachel Barnes. She survived him many years, and it is probable that she is the Granny Hoyt who tried the experiment of using the powder-horn in kindling the fire and thus gave rise to the expression current among her descendants: "Quick as Granny Hoyt's powder-horn." John Hoyt had ten children: William, born September 5, 1660; Elizabeth, February 8, 1661-62; John, March 28, 1663; Mary, October 11, 1664; Joseph, mentioned below; Sarah; Rachel, June 28, 1670; Dorothie, January 29, 1673-74; Grace, March 29, 1676; Robert.

(III) Joseph, son of John (2) Hoyt, was born July 14, 1666. He appears to have lived at the homestead of his grandfather, John Hoyt, in Amesbury. He held the offices of tythingman and selectman. He married, October 5, 1702, Dorothy Worthen, and died in 1719 or 1720. He had eight children: John, born July 2, 1703; Mehetabel, November 25, 1705; Joseph, January 10, 1707-08; Ezekiel, mentioned below; Judith or Juda, February

22, 1711-12; Nathan, February 16, 1714; Moses, March 23, 1716; Dorothy, August 23, 1718.

(IV) Ezekiel, son of Joseph Hoyt, was born in Amesbury, January 7, 1709-10. He was a tanner, and seems to have been a man of considerable means. He removed about 1739 to that part of Salisbury which became South Hampton, and thence, about 1748, to Brentwood, New Hampshire, where he died in 1754. He married, December 25, 1735, Rebecca Brown, of Newbury. He had seven children: Judith, born November 25, 1736; Mary, October 11, 1739; Sarah, March 22, 1741-42; Dorothy, June 10, 1744; Ezekiel, January 27, 1746-47; Ezekiel, September 3, 1749; Joseph, mentioned below.

(V) Joseph (2), son of Ezekiel Hoyt, was born November 3, 1751, in Brentwood, New Hampshire. He settled in Sandwich, New Hampshire, and died there May 12, 1788. He was one of the signers of the Association Test issued by the New Hampshire committee of safety in April, 1776, which was as follows: "We the *Subscribers*, do hereby solemnly engage, and promise, that we will, to the utmost of our Power, at the Risque of our Lives and Fortunes, with ARMS, oppose the Hostile Proceedings of the British Fleets, and Armies, *against the United American COLONIES.*" He married, August 25, 1774, at Epping, New Hampshire, Betsy, daughter of Daniel and Huldah (Eastman) Folsom. His widow died July 16, 1834. He had five children: Huldah, born April 25, 1775; Ezekiel, January 27, 1777; Daniel, mentioned below; Joseph, July 31, 1780; Josiah, May 14, 1786.

(VI) General Daniel Hoit (as he spelled the name), son of Joseph (2) Hoyt, was born in Sandwich, October 26, 1778. He was a merchant in Sandwich, for many years president of the Carroll County Bank, and a prominent public man in New Hampshire. He was elected fifteen times to represent his native town in the lower house of the state legislature, first in 1807, and was senator four years and a member of the governor's council two years. He was general of the state militia, and always went by the name "General." He early identified himself with the Liberty or Free Soil party, and was for several years their candidate for governor. Two years of his life was spent in Ohio. He married (first) Sarah (Sally), daughter of Moses and Elizabeth (Batchelder) Flanders, January 21, 1805, and (second) Betsy Emerson, of Chester, December 10, 1838. His first wife died May 31, 1837. He had five children, all by his first wife: Eliza Flanders, born April 9, 1806; Julia

Maria, November 15, 1807; Albert Gallatin, December 13, 1809, a distinguished artist; Otis Gray, August 12, 1811; William Henry (Harrison), mentioned below.

(VII) Rev. William Henry (Harrison) Hoyt, son of General Daniel Hoit, was born in Sandwich, January 8, 1813. He dropped the name Harrison early in life. Later he changed the spelling of his surname from Hoit to Hoyt. He was graduated at Dartmouth College in 1831, and after pursuing a course of study at Andover Theological Seminary and at the General Theological Seminary in New York, he was ordained a minister of the Protestant Episcopal church in 1836. During the next two years he was a professor at Bishop Hopkins's seminary in Burlington, Vermont, and rector of the Episcopal church in Middlebury, and from 1838 until 1846, when he left the ministry, he was rector of St. Luke's Episcopal Church in St. Albans. Soon afterward he became a convert to the Roman Catholic faith, studied law and was admitted to the bar. In 1860 he removed from St. Albans to Burlington, where he was editor and proprietor of the Burlington *Sentinel,* which was at one time carried on by John G. Saxe, the poet. He removed to New York City about 1868. After the death of his wife, in January, 1875, he became a Catholic priest, being ordained in May, 1877. On December 8, 1883, while celebrating mass in St. Ann's church, on Twelfth street, New York, he fell insensible before the altar, and died four days later. He was a man of scholarly attainments, a fine linguist, and possessed of qualities of heart that endeared him to all who knew him. He married, August 21, 1838, Anne, daughter of Eleazer Hubbell and Fanny Fay (Follett) Deming, of Burlington. He had eleven children: Charles Albert, born July 27, 1839; William Henry, March 26, 1841; Francis Deming, November 29, 1843; Anna Deming, May 22, 1846; Mary Elizabeth, February 4, 1848; Julia Catherine, January 20, 1850; Jane Frances, April 10, 1851; George Aloysius, December 14, 1852; Frederick Alphonsus (twin), mentioned below; Edward Vincent (twin), October 12, 1854; Henrianna Maria, October 1, 1858.

(VIII) Frederick Alphonsus, son of Rev. William Henry Hoyt, was born October 12, 1854, in Burlington. He received his education at the College Ste. Marie, in Montreal, Canada, and at the College of St. Francis Xavier, in New York. He was for many years in the insurance business in New York, where he resides. He married, April 4, 1883, Florence Sarah, daughter of Captain Peter Umstead Murphey, of the United States and Confederate navies, and Emily Rennie (Patrick) Murphey. He has four children: William Henry, mentioned below; George Aloysius, born July 21, 1885; Charles Albert, July 28, 1888; Florence Fredericka, January 24, 1891.

(IX) William Henry, son of Frederick Alphonsus Hoyt, was born in New York City, January 10, 1884. He studied at private schools in New York and Montreal, Canada, and received the degree of A. B. from Fordham College in 1902, A. M. from the University of Vermont in 1906 and LL. B. from Harvard University in 1910. Since his admission to the bar in 1910 he has been in general practice in New York City, with the firm of Hawkins, Delafield & Longfellow, but making a specialty of the legality of municipal bonds. He is a diligent student of North Carolina history, and has written several books and articles on that subject, including "The Mecklenburg Declaration of Independence; A Study of Evidence Showing that the Alleged Early Declaration of Independence by Mecklenburg County, North Carolina, on May 20th, 1775, is Spurious" (G. P. Putnam's Sons, 1907); "The Murphey Papers: Being the Correspondence, Public Papers and other Writings and Collections of Archibald Debow Murphey, of North Carolina, 1777-1832" (North Carolina Historical Commission, 1912), and the article on Judge Murphey in "The Biographical History of North Carolina" (vol. IV., Greensboro, North Carolina, 1905). He married, December 9, 1911, Josephine Dorothea, daughter of William Allen and Annie Josephine (Cassidy) Butler.

JOHNSON Thomas Johnson, the immigrant ancestor, was one of three brothers, Robert, John and Thomas, who came to America in 1638. Although no definite proof has been found, the records seem to show that they were undoubtedly brothers. They came from Kingston-on-Hull and landed at Boston, being Puritans under Ezekiel Rogers, a Cambridge graduate and clergyman, of Rowley, in Yorkshire. Thomas and Robert settled in New Haven, and John, after remaining there a short time, moved to Rowley, Massachusetts, where Ezekiel Rogers and his followers had settled. Thomas was drowned with Thomas Ashley in New Haven harbor in 1640. He married Helena ————. Children, according to Ralph Dunning Smyth, the Guilford historian: Thomas, of New Haven, Connecticut, and Newark, New Jersey; Daniel, of New Haven;

Jeremiah, of New Haven and Derby, Connecticut; William, mentioned below. Savage also adds a John, of Guilford.

(II) William, son of Thomas Johnson, was born in England, October 10, 1635. He was sometimes called Wingle or Windle on the records, and has also been confused with his cousin William, of Guilford, son of Robert, the immigrant. According to tradition, the family came from Cherry-Burton, a village about three miles from the town of Beverly, Yorkshire, about six miles north of Rowley, England. William married (first) in America, in December, 1664, Sarah, daughter of John and Jane, or Jeanne, (Wollen or Woolin) Hall. She was born in 1643, and baptized by Rev. Mr. Davenport, in New Haven, August 9, 1646. According to Ralph D. Smyth, he married (second) Abigail ———, but she was not mentioned in his will, and all of his children were by his first wife. He owned land in Wallingford, Connecticut, although he lived in New Haven, where many deeds of land to and from him are recorded. He was a husbandman and planter. In 1670 he was one of about forty who signed the original compact for the settlement of Wallingford and became original proprietors. He had a lot of land about twenty rods square assigned to him there, which he sold in 1694 to Isaac Curtis. He died in 1716 and his will, dated March, 1716, was proved in August, 1716, his son Isaac being named executor. Children by first wife: Lieutenant William, born September 5, 1665, died 1742; John, born July 20, 1667; Abraham, 1669; Abigail, December 6, 1670; Isaac, of Woodbridge, Connecticut, deacon and captain, born October 27, 1672, died October 23, 1750, married, April 25, 1693, Abigail, daughter of John Cooper, from whom descended Andrew Johnson, LL. D., president of the United States; Sergeant Jacob, mentioned below; Sarah, November 6, 1676; Samuel, September 3, 1678; Mary, April 1, 1680; Lydia, July 7, 1681; Hope, May 10, 1685, died same month; Elizabeth, May 10, 1685, twin of Hope; Ebenezer, April 5, 1688.

(III) Sergeant Jacob Johnson, son of William Johnson, was born in New Haven, September 25, 1674, died July 17, 1749. He was sergeant of the Wallingford trainband, and was referred to by that title in a deed in 1752 and also in probate records. In 1721, 1732, 1733 and 1736 he was deputy to the general court from Wallingford. He owned much land, leaving an estate valued at over fourteen thousand pounds, including four hundred acres and several slaves. His will was dated June 3, 1749, and his sons Abner and Caleb were executors. He married (first),

December 14, 1693, Abigail, daughter of John and Abigail (Merriman) Hitchcock. She died January 9, 1726. He married (second) Dorcas Linsley, of Branford, Connecticut. Matthias Hitchcock, father of John, was one of the original signers of the "fundamental agreement" of the New Haven colony. John Hitchcock was an original proprietor at Wallingford, 1670. His wife Abigail was daughter of Captain Nathaniel Merriman. Abigail Hitchcock was born in New Haven, April 10, 1674. Children by first wife: Reuben, born August 27, 1694; Deacon Isaac, February 21, 1696; Enos, 1698, died 1786; Abigail, 1699; Captain Abner, August 2, 1702; Lieutenant Caleb, 1703; Israel, 1705; Daniel, mentioned below; Sarah, 1710; Rev. Jacob, at Wallingford, April 15, 1713.

(IV) Daniel, son of Sergeant Jacob Johnson, was born in 1709, died October 14, 1780. He was a trial justice under the king. He married, December 24, 1732, Joanna Preston, who was born March 18, 1714, died January 18, 1781. Children: Charles, born November 13, 1735, died at sea; Captain Solomon, mentioned below; Joanna, April 4, 1743; Lieutenant Daniel, March 24, 1746; Israel, July 8, 1748; Justin, March 4, 1752; Abigail, December 23, 1753; Joshua, July 26, 1757; Mindwell, May 19, 1758; Rebecca, March 29, 1759.

(V) Captain Solomon Johnson, son of Daniel Johnson, was born May 4, 1740, died April 4, 1799. He lived in Wallingford. He served in the revolution and was a sea captain. He married, December 6, 1765, Mary Barker, who was born March 10, 1742. died September 7, 1825. Children: John Barker, and Charles, mentioned below.

(VI) Charles, son of Captain Solomon Johnson, was born in Wallingford, May 3, 1767. died September 22, 1848, in Durham, New York. He was captain of a troop of horse in Durham. He left Wallingford about 1792. and became a farmer in Durham. The following certificate in the handwriting of Charles Johnson is in the possession of his great-grandson, Edward Hine Johnson, of Philadelphia: "I do hereby certify that Ezekiel Smith has been enrolled and served in a uniform company of cavalry for fifteen years previous to the date hereof. Durham, September 5, 1811. Charles Johnson, Captain." Ezekiel Smith was the maternal great-grandfather of Edward Hine Johnson, mentioned below. (See Colonial Records of Connecticut, vol. 6, p. 233; vol. 7, p. 420; vol. 8, p. 27.) He married Elizabeth Rice, of New Haven. She was born October 22, 1769, and died December 25, 1840. Child: Solomon Rice, mentioned below.

(VII) Solomon Rice, son of Charles Johnson, was born in Durham, New York, in August, 1797, died November 5, 1833, in Durham. He was a farmer in Durham. He married, October 12, 1828, Mary Whittlesey, of Saybrook, Connecticut. She was born December 12, 1797, and died December 3, 1829. Child: Solomon Whittlesey, mentioned below.

(VIII) Solomon Whittlesey, son of Solomon Rice Johnson, was born at Durham, November 5, 1829. He resided in New York City and Brooklyn, and was one of the founders and third president of the American News Company. He married, September 15, 1853, Adelaide Hine, who was born in Cairo, New York, February 12, 1830, died December 15, 1898. Children: Edward Hine, mentioned below; Agnes, born January 28, 1860; Mary, June 9, 1861; Adelaide, December 7, 1869, died March 28, 1888.

(IX) Edward Hine, son of Solomon Whittlesey Johnson, was born in New York City, June 29, 1854. He received his early education in private schools, where he prepared for college. In 1873 he entered Yale College and was graduated with the degree of Ph. B. in the class of 1876. He then entered the service of the American News Company of New York. He remained with this company, of which his father was president, until 1884, when he came to Philadelphia, Pennsylvania, to take charge of the Central News Company. Since then he has been manager of this company and has resided in Philadelphia. He is a member of the University Club, the Philadelphia Country Club, the Corinthian Yacht Club of Philadelphia, the Society of Colonial Wars, the Sons of the Revolution, the New England Society of Philadelphia. In politics he is a Republican, but he is independent in municipal politics. He is a communicant of St. James' Protestant Episcopal Church.

He was married, December 12, 1883, in St. Mark's Church, Philadelphia, by Rev. Dr. Nicholson, to Frances Van Leer, who was born in Philadelphia, October 27, 1858, daughter of George H. Earle. Children: Edward Earle, born in Philadelphia, October 31, 1884, and associated with his father in the management of the Central News Company of Philadelphia; Florence Earle, December 8, 1892.

Thomas Miller, yeoman, of MILLER Bishops Stortford (called usually Stortford), England, had by his wife Bridget, daughter of Thomas Jernegan (see Jernegan XVI), the following children (Hert. Ant., 3, p. 265): 1. John, see No. 2. 2. Thomas, mentioned in his brother's will and in that of John Gace, where he is called

"Maister Thomas Miller," evidently a clergyman; his wife's name was Matilda (Hert, Ant., vol. 2, p. 342). 3. Agnes, married, May 1, 1584, John Gace, whose will is dated 29 August, 44 Elizabeth (1601), proved 20 September, 1602, mentions wife Agnes and "John Miller the Elder" and "Maister Thomas Miller." Agnes had previously married a man named John Dennison, buried December 4, 1582, by whom she had: i. George, mentioned in stepfather's will. ii. Edward, also mentioned in same will. iii. William, also mentioned in same will, married at Stortford, November 7, 1603, Margaret Monck, and came to New England, 1631, settling at Roxbury; wife died 1645, he died 1653 (N. E. Reg., vol. 46, pp. 352-53, and vol. 47, pp. 110-11). iv. Elizabeth, married ——— Crouch. 4. Bridget, married George Abbott (Hertford Antiquary, 3, p. 225). 5. Margaret, married Edward Hake (ibid. 3, pp. 225). 6. Elizabeth, married Thomas Sprenger (ibid. 3, p. 85). 7. Jane, married Richard Meade (ibid. 3, p. 85).

(II) John Miller, of Stortford, son of Thomas and Bridget (Jernegan) Miller, was a butcher, as shown by his will. He married Elizabeth, daughter of Richard Jardfielde, of Stortford, and sister of John and George Jardfielde (Hert. Ant., vol. 3, p. 271). Mr. Miller's will is dated 26 March, 1601, proved November 9, 1602. Hertford Antiquary, vol. 3, page 85, mentions "my poor Aunt Holly (probably his father's sister); wife Elizabeth; eldest son John to have orchard and dovehouse in it, situated near Hockerell bridge now on tenure of Nicholas Wilsemer; and six closes of land which my father bought of the Willie daughters beyond Waightfield; daughter Agnes Miller a message in Stortford where John Moulton now dwelleth and the meadow purchased of Thomas Meade; daughter Sarah Miller, land in the Great Halfe, purchased of Thomas Jernegan; daughter Katherine Miller; brother-in-law Richard Mead; daughter Ursula to have land in Great Halfe bought of William Brett; son William house in Stortford wherein Richard Burges now dwelleth and land in Sheeplo, late bought of Thomas Wilesmer, also house in Little Hadham; three eldest daughters, Joane, Margaret and Jane; servant Luce Wilesmer. Debts owing to me by the Rt. Hon. Edward Lord Morley and his sons. Brother Thomas Miller and brother-in-law Thomas Sprenger, to be executors."

(III) John Miller Jr., son of John and Elizabeth (Jardfielde) Miller, of Stortford, married, and had children (according to parish records which run back to 1561, Rev. Henry Tydd Lane, Vicar of St. Michaels,

Bishops Stortford, Hertfordshire, England) :
1. John, born 1605-06; matriculated in Caius
College, Cambridge, 1623; graduated A. B.
1627; probably came to New England in 1635;
was at Dorchester, 1636; lands in South Boston, 1637; was in Roxbury, 1638; Rowley,
1639; freeman 22 May, and became minister
there, and was also first town clerk; in 1642
he was called to Yarmouth, Cape Cod, but was
back in Roxbury in 1647; wife's name Lydia,
she died 7 August, 1658, and he died at Groton,
12 June, 1663 (Savage, vol. III., p. 209) ; had
children: i. John, born in England, March,
1632; married, 24 December, 1659, Margaret,
daughter of Josiah Winslow. ii. Mehitable,
born 12 July, 1638; married John Crow. iii.
Lydia, born 12 April, 1640; married ———
Fish. iv. Faith, born 1642; married, 3 August, 1664, Nathaniel Winslow. v. Hannah,
born 1644; married, 22 May, 1666, Joseph
Frost. vi. Susannah, born 29 August, 1647;
died 14 October, 1669. vii. Elizabeth, born 13
October, 1649; married Samuel Frost. viii.
Mary, born 1651; married, 8 November, 1677,
John Whittemore. 2. Thomas, see No. 4. 3.
Alexander (?).

(IV) Thomas Miller, son of John Miller
Jr., was born at Bishops Stortford, about 1609-
10; came to Massachusetts with brother John
in 1635, but did not settle in Dorchester, as
the list of inhabitants of that town in January,
1636, contains only John and Alexander. The
first notice we have of Thomas Miller is that
he was enrolled as a freeman at Boston, 22
May, 1639; residence Rowley (Gage's Rowley,
p. 131). The following items are from the
Rowley Town Records: "Thomas Miller
granted one house lott, containing one acre
and a half, bounded on North side by Mr.
Tenney's lott, and east by the street, 10 May,
1643." "Thomas Miller granted two acres of
salt marsh lying on south side of Humphrey
Rayners' salt marsh; in the marsh field the
southwest end abutting on an Island, the northeast end on John Scales' salt marsh." "Thomas
Miller granted four and one half acres of upland joining to the rod of ground on east side
of Francis Parratt's planting lott in north east
Field, the south end abutting upon a cart path
near Satchell's Meadow, the north end on
some ground not laid out." "Thomas Miller,
an acre of rough marsh in the field called the
Marsh, the west end abutting on upland of
Humphrey Reyners, the south side lying along
by a cowpath." "Thomas Miller, two acres
lying on North side of James Bailey." All
these of the same date, 10 May, 1643. 1648:
"Thomas Miller has no. XX 6 rail length and
no. XXXI ten rail length of the public fence."

"Thomas Miller allowed 2s. 6d. for going to
Ipswich for Deacon Mighill and £15 for fencing horse pasture and £10 lent him." 1650.
1651: "Thomas Miller, 10s. for work about
mill." 1661, January 28, "Thomas Miller sold
his lotts to Ezekiel Northend." The New England Register, vol. 14, p. 139, gives us Thomas
Miller, Middletown, Connecticut, 1670, assessed value of real estate £50. The Town
Records of Middletown, Connecticut, vol. 1,
p. 8, show deal on the 9th day of June, 1654.
"Thomas Miller, late of Rowley, Massachusetts, rec'd lands in Middletown," and that he
brought letters of recommendation from the 1st
Church of Rowley to the 1st Church of Middletown. The New England Register, vol. 14, p. 67,
containing the town records of Middletown,
shows that Capt. Thomas Miller, as he is
styled, first married Isabel ———, who died
in 1660, having had one child: 1. Anne, who
married, in 1653, Nathaniel Bacon. Captain
Miller married (second), at Middletown. June
6, 1666, Sarah, daughter of Samuel Nettleton,
of Milford, settled there 1639. Captain Thomas
Miller died in Middletown, August 14, 1680,
above 70. By second wife had: 1. Thomas
Jr., born May 6, 1666; married, 1688, Elizabeth Turner, and died September 24, 1729. 2.
Samuel, born April 1, 1668; married, 1702,
Mary Eggleston, and died April 11, 1738. 3.
Joseph, born August 21, 1670; married, 1701,
Rebecca Johnson, and died in December, 1717.
4. Benjamin, born July 20, 1672; see No. 5. 5.
John, born March 10, 1674; married, 1700,
Marcy Bevin, and died May 3, 1745. 6. Mar-
garet, born September 1, 1676. 7. Sarah, born
January 7, 1678; married Smith Johnson. 8.
Mehitable, born March 28, 1680. Captain Mil-
ler's widow married (second) Thomas Harris.

(V) Benjamin Miller, son of Thomas and
Sarah (Nettleton) Miller (Senior so-called in
Middletown records), born July 30, 1672; married, 1700-01, Mary Basset, born 1674, died
December 5, 1709, aged 35; had at his death,
September 12, 1737: 1. Benjamin Jr., see No.
6. 2. Daniel, born 1704; died unmarried, September 26, 1736, aged thirty-two. 3. Thomas,
born 1706; married Love ———, and had; i.
Abigail; ii. Thomas; iii. Hannah; iv. Elizabeth; v. Lydia; all baptized with mother, December 9, 1737.

(VI) Benjamin Miller Jr., born 1702;
wife's name, Hannah; married about 1730, and
had: 1. Benjamin (3d), see No. 7. 2. Thankful, born May 12; died December 8, 1733. Mr.
Miller removed to New Hampshire in 1737-
'38, as in the latter year we find him at Newington (New Hampshire Town Papers, vol.
XIII, p. 260), and was there in 1753 (ibid.

Historical Pub Co   W.T. Barnes NY

vol. XII, p. 717), and as late as 5 June, 1783 (vol. XIII, p. 50). We have been unable to find the date of his death or that of his wife.

(VII) Benjamin Miller (3d), was born between 1731 and 1735. He was in Newington, New Hampshire, prior to 1775, when he removed to Brookfield, Massachusetts, but returned to New Hampshire about 1778-80, settling at Lyme, where he probably died. He married, in 1773, Esther, daughter of Elijah Clapp. Children: 1. Elijah, see No. 8. 2-3. Benjamin and Esther, twins, baptized at Brookfield, Massachusetts, June 23, 1776; Esther married at Brookfield, January 21, 1794, Sewell Gleason, her residence given as Lyme, New Hampshire. 4. A daughter, baptized August 31, 1777, name probably erased.

(VIII) Elijah Miller, son of Benjamin and Esther (Clapp) Miller, was born at Newington, New Hampshire, in 1774, as his recorded age at death in the New Hampshire State Official Register was sixty-three. He was baptized June 23, 1776; died January 10, 1837. He was then in the town of Lyme, New Hampshire, from 1780 to 1798, when he removed to Hanover, and married there Eunice, daughter of David and Susanna (Durkee) Tenney; she was born in Hanover, December 21, 1783 (see Tenney), died February 21, 1870. Mr. Miller also held several local offices in Hanover town and Grafton county, and was state senator June 23, 1829, to June 2, 1830, and from that date to June 1, 1831; and was a member of the governor's council 1834-35-36, and died, according to New Hampshire Official Register of 1851, January 10, 1837, aged sixty-three. He was a man of ability and distinction. In politics he was a Democrat, in religion a Unitarian. By occupation he was a farmer. Children: Patia, Benjamin D., Elijah Tenney, of whom further; Esther, John A., Eunice.

(IX) Elijah Tenney Miller, son of Elijah and Eunice (Tenney) Miller, was born at Hanover, New Hampshire, August 15, 1815, died May 30, 1892. He married Chastina C. Hoyt, born about 1826, daughter of Benjamin and Abigail (Strong) Hoyt (see Hoyt). Children: Fayette M., born July 25, 1844; Susan A., born March 22, 1847, married David C. Tenney, of Hanover, and died 1873; Charles Ransom, see forward.

(X) Charles Ransom Miller, son of Elijah Tenney and Chastina C. (Hoyt) Miller, was born at Hanover, New Hampshire, January 17, 1849. He attended the public schools of Hanover, the Kimball Union Academy at Meriden, New Hampshire, and the Green Mountain Institute at South Woodstock, Vermont, where he completed his preparation for college. He entered Dartmouth College and was graduated in the class of 1872 with the degree of Bachelor of Arts. In 1905 he was honored by his *alma mater* with the degree of Doctor of Laws. From the time of his graduation from college until 1875 he was on the editorial staff of the *Republican*, at Springfield, Massachusetts, and rose to the position of city editor of that newspaper. In July, 1875, he became exchange editor of the *New York Times*, and since then has been connected with that newspaper. He was foreign editor for a time, then editorial writer, and since April, 1883, has been editor-in-chief. From 1881 to 1883 he was editorial writer. He is also vice-president of the New York Times Company. During the period of Mr. Miller's editorship *The Times* has become one of the foremost newspapers of the country. In the opinion of many of the best judges it is the best newspaper in New York City, and the success of the newspaper under the policy of "All the news that's fit to print" has been a wholesome example and inspiration to editors and publishers of newspapers throughout the whole country. In politics Mr. Miller is an Independent, and in religion non-sectarian. He is a member of the Century Club, the Metropolitan Club, the Ardsley Club, the Garden City Golf Club, the Blooming Grove Hunting and Fishing Club of Pike county, Pennsylvania.

He married, October 10, 1876, Frances Ann Daniels, born April 8, 1851, died December 8, 1906, daughter of Francis Cotton Daniels, a descendant of Rev. John Cotton, the Puritan divine. Children: Madge Daniels, born October 28, 1877; Hoyt Miller, born March 18, 1883, in New York City. Mr. Miller resides at 21 East Ninth street, and his office is in the Times Building, New York City.

(The Jernegan Line).

(I) Sir William Jernegan, of Horeham, county Suffolk, Knight, married Isabella, daughter of Thomas Aspall, of Aspall, and had issue a son and heir.

(II) Sir Hubbard Jernegan, of Horeham, Knight, married Maude, daughter of ———— Harlinge, and had a son and heir.

(III) Sir Hugh Jernegan, of Horeham, Knight, married Ellen, daughter and heir to Sir Thomas Inglethorpe, Knight, and had: Sir Walter (see No. 4); Jane, married John Leyston.

(IV) Sir Walter Jernegan, of Somerleton, Knight, married Isabel, daughter and heir of Sir Peter Fitz Osborne, of Somerleton, and became possessed of that estate in her right, and had a son and heir.

(V) Sir Peter Jernegan, of Somerleton, Knight, married Ellen, daughter of Sir Roger Huntingfelde, Knight, by Joyce d'Eugaine. (This Sir Roger, who died in 1301, was great-grandson of William de Huntingfelde, who was one of the twenty-five barons who compelled King John to sign Magna Charta at Runnymede, June 15, 1215; Burke's Extinct Peerage, 1866, p. 293). Had a son and heir.

(VI) Sir John Jernegan, of Somerleton, Knight, married Agatha, daughter of Sir ——— Shelton, Knight, and had a son and heir.

(VII) Sir John Jernegan, of Somerleton, Knight, married Jane, daughter and co-heir of Sir William Kelvedon, Knight, and widow of Loudham, and had two children: Sir John (see No. 8); Jane, married Sir Gilbert Debenham.

(VIII) Sir John Jernegan, of Somerleton, Knight, married, Margaret, daughter of Sir Thomas Vise de Lou, Knight, and had three children: Thomas (see No. 9); Elizabeth, married John Gonvyle; Alice, married John Cleresbys.

(IX) Sir Thomas Jernegan, of Somerleton, Knight, married Love, daughter of ——— Apleyard, Esq., and had two children: John (see No. 10), and Margaret.

(X) Sir John Jernegan, of Somerleton, Knight, married Jane, daughter of Sir John Davell, Knight, and had a son and heir.

(XI) Sir John Jernegan, of Somerleton, Knight, married Isabel, daughter and heir of Sir Jervis (Gervaise) Clifton, Knight, and had five children: Edward (see No. 12); Sir Richard; ——— ———, married ——— Palmer; ——— ———, married ——— Scott; ——— ———, married ——— Haslake, of Norfolk.

(XII) Edward Jernegan, of Somerleton, Esq., married Margaret, daughter of Sir Edmond Bedingfelde, of the county of Norfolk, Knight, and had, by this marriage, seven children: John (see No. 13); Thomas, Oliffe, Sir Robert, Nicholas, Edward, Margaret, married (first) Edward Lord Grey, (second) ——— Barkley, (third) Edmond Bellingham. He married (second) Mary, daughter of Richard Scroope, of Bolton, and had four children more: Sir Henry, Ferdinando, Edmond, Mary.

(XIII) Sir John Jernegan, of Somerleton, Knight, married Bridget, daughter of Sir Robert Drury, of Hawsted, county Suffolk, Knight, and had five children: George (see No. 14); Robert: John (see No. 14), Hertfordshire line; Anne, married Sir Thomas Cornwallis, of Broome, county Suffolk, Knight; Eliza, married Sir John Sulyard, of Wetherton, county Suffolk, Knight.

(XIV) George Jernegan, of Somerleton,

Esq., married Eley, daughter of Sir John Spelman, of Nasborough, county Norfolk, Knight, by Elizabeth, his wife, daughter and heir of Sir Henry Frowyke, of Gunnersbury, county Middlesex, Knight, and had ten children: 1. John, son and heir, married Catherine, daughter of John Lord Cobham, and had, in 1561, Middlesex, Knight, and had ten children: 1. Elizabeth. 2. Robert, living 1561. 3. Walter, living 1561. 4. Thomas, living 1561. 5. George, living 1561. 6. Henry, living 1561. 7. Eley, married Arthur Jeunye, of Knotishall, county Suffolk. 8. Anne, married Lyman Broke. 9. Elizabeth, living 1561. 10. Margaret, living 1561.

(XIV.) John Jernegan, founder of the Hertfordshire line, third son of Sir John Jernegan and Bridget Drury (see No. 13), removed to Hertfordshire, settling at Little Wylmondeley, where his maternal grandfather, Sir Robert Drury, Knight, owned lands in 1516. In the Hertford Genealogist and Antiquary, vol. 1, p. 78, we find the following Feet of Fines, Trinity Term, 8 Henry VIII (1516): "Robert Drury, Kt. William Drury Esqr., son of Robert Drury, Kt. John Jernegan, Esqr. (grandson), John Vere. Philip Calthorp, Kt. George Waldegrave, Esqr. Philip Butler, Esqr. Edward Greene, Esqr. Robert Norwicke, Esqr. and Francis Mountford, Esqr." Giles Alyngton and Mary (Drury) his wife were joint tenants and owners of the Manor of Little Wylmondeley, and six messuages, lands and rents in Great and Little Wylmondeley, and the advowson of the Priory of Wylmondeley.

John Jernegan married ———, daughter of Thomas Parsons, of Stortford, and acquired lands there. He had four children: 1. Thomas (see No. 15). 2. Henry, whose wife was Anne, daughter of George Ellyott, of Farnham; owned lands there, 1579 (Hert. Gen. Ant., vol. 2, p. 255), lived at Stortford, 1596 (ibid. vol. 3, p. 226). 3. Mary, married Thomas Bartlett. 4. Anne, married Robert Baspole.

(XV) Thomas Jernegan settled at Stortford, married Elizabeth, daughter of William Snowe, of that place, and had evidently but one daughter and heiress.

(XVI) Bridget, daughter of Thomas Jernegan, married Thomas Miller, of Stortford, and her son, John Miller, was co-tenant with his grandfather, Thomas Jernegan, in lands at Stortford, in 1598. (Hert. Gen. & Ant., vol. 3, p. 265.)

(The Hoyt Line).

(II) Thomas Hoyt, son of John Hoyt (q. v.), was born January 1, 1640-41. He was apprenticed to Walter Taylor, who seems to have been a disorderly character, for Thomas Hoyt and Thomas Jonson, two of his apprentices, ran away from him because of his treatment of them, and April 12, 1664, the Salisbury court decreed that he be fined for using "cursing speaches to his servants"; John Hoyt, father of Thomas, was "admonisht for enterjeining his son", who evidently ran home, and the two servants were each fined for leaving Walter Taylor. On December 5, 1677, he took the oath of allegiance before Captain Thomas Bradbury, at Salisbury. Shortly after 1680 he moved to Amesbury, where in 1685-86 John Hoyt deeded him land at "Bugsmore," there. On November 29, 1689, there was a Thomas Hoyt, of Amesbury, who married Mary Nash, and it must have been this Thomas. He died January 3, 1690-91. His son Thomas was administrator of his estate, March 31, 1691. An inventory of the estate of Thomas Hoyt was taken March 31, 1691.

He married Mary, daughter of William and Elisabeth Brown, of Salisbury. Children, born at Salisbury: Lieutenant Thomas; William, born October 19, 1670, died October 29, 1670; Ephraim, mentioned below; John, born April 5, 1674; William, April 8, 1676; Israel, July 16, 1678; Benjamin, September 20, 1680. Born at Amesbury: Joseph, about 1684; daughter, Deliverance, May 2, 1688, died May 9, 1688, called second daughter, on records; Mary, born October 1, 1690, died January 20, 1690-91, possibly child of a second wife.

(III) Ephraim Hoyt, son of Thomas and Mary (Brown) Hoyt, was born at Salisbury, October 16, 1671, and died in 1741 or 1742. In January, 1702-03, he petitioned the town of Hampton for a piece of land to cultivate for two or three years, at the end of which time he would return it to the town, and he doubtless lived in that part incorporated as Hampton Falls in 1712, for he was taxed there in 1727 and 1732. In June, 1741, he deeded to his son Ephraim his homestead in Hampton Falls, and in August, 1742, his widow Elisabeth relinquished her right of dower. He married (first) Hannah Godfrey, of Hampton, April 25, 1695, and (second), August 12, 1736, another Hannah Godfrey, and (third) Elisabeth Macrest, or Macree, September 4, 1738. Children by first wife (baptismal dates): Ephraim, mentioned below; Benjamin, December 16, 1716; Hannah, December 16, 1716; Mary, November 3, 1717; Huldah, November 3, 1717; David, September 2, 1722; Jonathan, September 2, 1722; Nathan, September 23, 1722; John, September 23, 1722.

(IV) Ephraim Hoyt, son of Ephraim and Hannah (Godfrey) Hoyt, was born at Hampton Falls, and baptized there December 16, 1716. He lived in Hampton Falls until about 1757, when he moved to Chester, New Hampshire, where he lived until his death, between February and April, 1767. In 1727 he was taxed at Hampton Falls, and also in 1732. His will was dated February 16, 1767, and proved April 29, 1767. He married (first) Sarah Clough, of Salisbury, January 3, 1726-27, (second) Abigail Welch, October 31, 1754, (third) Susanna ———. Children, by first wife: William, mentioned below; Lydia, baptized January 15, 1744; Hannah, born February 5, 1730-31; Reuben, March 21, 1732-33; Sarah, August 2, 1735; Ephraim, February 28, 1737-38; Mary, January 28, 1739-40; Benjamin. By second wife: Philip, born February 13, 1756, at Hampton Falls; Samuel, July 4, 1758, at Chester, New Hampshire; Thomas, who may have been a child of third wife.

(V) William Hoyt, son of Ephraim and Sarah (Clough) Hoyt, lived in Exeter, New Hampshire. He served in the French and Indian war, and also in the revolution. He was killed in battle, July 5, 1777. He was certainly a brother of Reuben, of Salisbury and Enfield. He is very likely the one who married Sarah Smith, daughter of Benjamin Smith. Children: Benjamin, mentioned below; Nicholas (Smith?); Abraham, born January 25, 1764; Sarah, January 25, 1764; Elisha, died when about fourteen; William.

(VI) Benjamin Hoyt, son of William and probably of Sarah (Smith) Hoyt, was born about 1755. He was in the battle when his father was killed, during the revolution, but was unable to find the body. He moved to Hartford, Vermont, with his mother. He died February 25, 1830. He married (first) Isabella Elliot, of Exeter, (second) Widow Mack, (third) Widow Smith. Children, by first wife: Benjamin, mentioned below; Lucy E.

(VII) Benjamin Hoyt, son of Benjamin and Isabella (Elliot) Hoyt, was born October 10, 1779. He died August 9, 1844, his wife surviving him. She moved to Enfield, New Hampshire. He married Abigail Strong, of Plainfield, New Hampshire, about 1807. Children: Abigail, born 1809; Isabella, 1811; Mary, 1814; Benjamin; Lucius C.; George E., 1820; Eliza, 1823, married George Clark, of Enfield, New Hampshire; Chastina C., 1826, married Elijah Miller, died July 9, 1849 (see Miller).

(The Tenney Line).

(IV) Joseph Tenney, son of Elder Samuel Tenney (q. v.), was born in Bradford, March 16, 1698-99, and married there, February 14, 1722-23, Abigail, daughter of John and Isabella (———) Wood, born there, December

14, 1700. She united with the First Congregational Church, September 7, 1718, and he July 6, 1718. In 1723 he removed to Norwich, Connecticut, and that same year was admitted to the colony. Later he removed to Woodbury, Connecticut, where he died April 20, 1775. Children, born in Norwich: Joseph, April 22, 1724; Anne, February 5, 1726-27; John, mentioned below; Sarah, September 17, 1731; Asa, September 4, 1733; Elijah, June 25, 1735; Jesse, June 14, 1739, died in infancy; Jesse, April 20, 1741; Hannah, April 24, 1743.

(V) John Tenney, son of Joseph Tenney, was born in Norwich, Connecticut, September 2, 1729, and died February 19, 1810. He married, March 11, 1755, Olive Armstrong, born in Woodbury, July 5, 1736, died April 18, 1806. May 5, 1760, he bought land in Woodbury. In 1770 he removed to Hanover, New Hampshire, where he went by ox-team. He bought there, November 16, 1770, three hundred acres of land located on Moose Mountain, afterwards known as Tenney Hill. Children, first four born in Norwich: Silas, April 15, 1757; Lydia, May 12, 1758, died March 7, 1759; David, mentioned below; Reuben, July 29, 1760; Lydia, October 23, 1761; Eunice, January 27, 1763; Andrew, October 13, 1764; John, July 9, 1767; Truman, April 14, 1769, died January 17, 1776; Asa, November 30, 1772, died January 23, 1776; Truman, April 10, 1778.

(VI) David Tenney, son of John Tenney, was born in Norwich, May 15, 1759, died March 14, 1851. He lived at Hanover, on a portion of the land formerly belonging to his father, and came there with his parents when eleven years of age. He was a soldier in the revolution, and a pensioner of that war. His record as given in the "History of Hanover" is as follows: David Tenney, private in Captain Edmund Freeman's Hanover company, Colonel Jonathan Chase's regiment, June 27 to July 3, 1777; David Tenney, of Captain Freeman's Hanover company, at a military court testified that he was present at the surrender of General Burgoyne, October 17, 1777, their company having left home on September 22 and being discharged October 19; on January 21, 1780, the town of Hanover raised nine men to form Captain Timothy's Bush's company, of whom David Tenney was one, and they served six weeks and three days, receiving forty-eight shillings per month and twelve shillings bounty; on July 3, 1780, David Tenney again enlisted, for three months.

David Tenney married (first), in Hanover, December 5, 1782, Susanna Durkee, born November 7, 1765, died February 11, 1788. He married (second) April 9, 1789, Anna Jacobs,

born August 23, 1765, died May 8, 1813. He married (third) May, 1824, widow Priscilla (Smith) Dole, who died at Newbury, Vermont. Children, born probably at Hanover: Eunice, December 21, 1783, married Elijah Miller (see Miller); Elisha, May 26, 1785; Sheldon, May 18, 1786; Susanna, January 3, 1788. Children of the second wife: Lucy, February 7, 1790; Vina, May 28, 1791; Seth, October 8, 1792; Elijah, August 22, 1794; David, April 9, 1796; Anna, August 26, 1798; Olive, March 22, 1800; Percy, March 24, 1802; Joseph, April 15, 1804.

DUGAN James Dugan was born in county Tipperary, Ireland, in 1836, died in Webster, Massachusetts, in 1908. He came to this country in 1852, and made his home in Webster, Worcester county, Massachusetts, where he was employed throughout his active life. In religion he was a Catholic, in politics a Democrat.

Mr. Dugan married (first) Margaret Spencer, born in Worcester, June 26, 1843, died 1871, daughter of William and Mary Spencer. Her sister Jane was born in that city, February 26, 1846. Michael Spencer, of this family, married Mary Dugan. John Spencer married Jean Brien. Mr. Dugan married (second) Jane Breen, born in Ireland in 1831, and is now living in Webster, Massachusetts. Children by first wife: 1. Mary Alice, born 1867, died in 1899; married Henry Andre, and had children: Frederick, James, John, William and Mary Andre. 2. Dr. William J., mentioned below. 3. John William, died unmarried. Child by second wife: Lawrence J., born November 17, 1874; a prominent citizen of Webster, a leading Democrat, formerly representative to the general court for the district comprising the towns of Webster, Oxford and Dudley, Worcester county, Massachusetts; married ———; children: James and Margaret.

(II) Dr. William J. Dugan, son of James Dugan, was born September 18, 1869, at Webster, Massachusetts. He attended the public schools and the Webster high school, completing his preparation for college at Phillips Academy, Exeter, New Hampshire. In 1893 he entered Jefferson Medical College of Philadelphia, and was graduated with the degree of Doctor of Medicine in 1896. For sixteen years he has been connected with the out-patient department of that institution, and he is now in the neurological out-patient department of the same college, assistant neurologist and lecturer on electro-therapeutics. He is a member of the American Medical Association, the Pennsylvania State Medical Society, the

Philadelphia County Medical Society, the Medico-Legal Society of Medical Jurisprudence, the Pathological Society, the Neurological Society, the Philadelphia Psycho-Therapeutic Society, the American Electro-Therapeutic Society, the Medical Club of Philadelphia, the New England Society of Philadelphia, the Phillips-Exeter Alumni Association, and the Jefferson Medical Alumni Society. He is the author of a medical work entitled "Manual of Electro-Therapeutics," published by the F. A. Davis Company, Philadelphia, in 1910. Within a year it has been adopted as a textbook by twenty medical colleges in the United States. He is a specialist with extensive experience in diseases of the nerves, having his offices in the Flanders building, Fifteenth and Walnut streets, Philadelphia. His residence is at Overbrook, No. 1908 North Sixty-third street. He is one of the best known specialists in electro-therapeutics and electro-physics. In religion he is a Roman Catholic, in politics a Republican.

He married, April 12, 1899, Nan Marie, born in Philadelphia, March 25, 1883, daughter of Bernard and Ella Marie (Howell) Gillespie. Dr. and Mrs. Dugan have no children.

THAYER The surname Thayer was originally Tayer, Tawier and Tawyer, and is a trade name for one who dresses skins. The letter "h" was not added until after the family came to New England, and in the Mendon line that letter was silent as in Thomas, until quite recently. The home of the family in England was Thornbury, in the western part of Gloucestershire, a short distance from the river Severn, eleven miles north of Bristol. The name is now extinct in Thornbury. The spelling Theyer and Thayern, with the same root form "Taw" has long been used by the family at Brockworth, Gloucestershire, a parish twenty-five miles northeast of Thornbury, and there was a family of Tawyer at Raounds in Northamptonshire, about eighty miles northeast of Brockworth and one hundred and five miles from Thornbury; also a family of Thayer at Great Baddow and later at Thayden Garnen in county Essex, afterwards of London; but no connection between these families has been established, so far as is known. In an account of "Able and Sufficient Men in Body fit for His Majesty's Service in the Wars, within the County of Gloucester in the Month of August 1608," given in three classes, namely, those about twenty years, those about forty years, and those between fifty and sixty years of age, there appear in Thornbury, Edward, John, Nicholas and Richard Tayer, all of the second

class; in ———comb, eight miles northeast of Thornbury, John Thayer, of the second class, and in Brockworth and its vicinity, John Theyer of the first class, Richard, Roger, Thomas, Walter and William Theyer of the second class, Gabriel, Giles, John Thomas of the first class, and William Thayer of the second class. The Thornbury parish register begins in A. D. 1538, with breaks from 1645 to 1660 and from 1679 to 1684 (see "New England Register," 1906, page 283, for copy of baptisms, etc.).

John Thayer or Tayer was baptized January 4, 1557-58, and another John, son of Thomas, October 15, 1558. The godfathers and godmothers are given, but as a rule the parents' names are omitted. A Richard Tayer or Tawier was baptized August 2, 1562, and a Thomas, February 12, 1569-70. It is probable that either Thomas or Richard was father of the American ancestors, Richard and Thomas. The will of Thomas was dated February 13, 1622, and proved May 20, 1623.

(I) Richard Thayer, immigrant ancestor, settled in Boston, Massachusetts, and his son Richard settled in Braintree. He was born and baptized in Thornbury, Gloucestershire, England, April, 1601, and came to America in 1641, bringing with him, according to a deposition of his son Richard, eight children. He was a shoemaker by trade. He married (first) in Thornbury, April 5, 1624, Dorothy Mortimore. He married (second) Jane Parker, widow of John Parker, and in 1658 joined her in a deed to her Parker children. He died before 1668 (see Suffolk Deeds V., 446). Children: Richard, mentioned below; Cornelius; Deborah, baptized February, 1629-30; Jael, married, March 17, 1654, John Harbour Jr.; Sarah, married, July 20, 1651, Samuel Davis; Hannah, married, May 28, 1664, Samuel Hayden; Zachariah, died July 29, 1693; Abigail, died August 6, 1717; Nathaniel, born about 1650.

(II) Richard (2), son of Richard (1) Thayer, was baptized February 10, 1624-25, died at Braintree, Massachusetts, August 27, 1695. He married, December 24, 1651, Dorothy Pray and lived in Braintree. She died December 11, 1705. Children: Dorothy, born August 30, 1653; Richard, mentioned below; Nathaniel, January 1, 1658; Abigail, February 10, 1661; Joannah, December 13, 1665; Sarah, December 13, 1667; Cornelius, September 18, 1670.

(III) Richard (3), son of Richard (2) Thayer, was born August 31, 1655, died December 4, 1705, or September 11, 1729. He married, July 16, 1679, Rebecca Micall, and lived in Braintree. She was born January 22,

1658. Children: Rebecca, born August 16, 1680; Benjamin, October 6, 1683; Richard, January 26, 1685; John, mentioned below; Mary, February 10, 1689; James, November 12, 1691; Deborah, April 11, 1695; Anna, November 14, 1697; Gideon, July 26, 1700; Obediah, May 1, 1703, died April 5, 1721.

(IV) John, son of Richard (3) Thayer, was born January 12, 1688, died September 10, 1745. He married, May 26, 1715, Dependence French, and lived in Braintree. Children: John, born February 18, 1716; John, July 27, 1717; Benjamin, January 11, 1720; Obediah, December 31, 1721; Micah, October 31, 1723; Richard, December 15, 1725, died January 30, 1727; Richard, mentioned below; Abiah, June 25, 1729; Simeon, March 22, 1732; Elijah, July 16, 1736.

(V) Richard (4), son of John Thayer, was born January 26, 1727. He married, 1752, Susan Randall, and settled in Randolph, Massachusetts. Children: Randall, born June 8, 1753; Susannah, June 14, 1754; Rhoda, September 9, 1755; Richard, September 13, 1757; Barnabas, October 12, 1759; Rebecca, April 12, 1761; Sarah, October 19, 1763; Bezer, mentioned below; Phineas, March 7, 1767; Jonathan, January 9, 1769; Luther, July 17, 1771; Anna, January 24, 1773.

(VI) Bezer, son of Richard (4) Thayer, was born at Randolph, March 5, 1765. He married, 1788, Eunice Howard, and lived in Randolph. Children, born in Randolph: Eliphalet, mentioned below; Loring, July 18, 1791; Charlotte, March 8, 1793; Bezer, March 30, 1795; Eunice, July 20, 1797; Harriet, August 10, 1799; Minot, April 5, 1801; Azel, December 26, 1802; Jason, November 28, 1804.

(VII) Eliphalet, son of Bezer Thayer, was born at Randolph, July 4, 1789, died June 29, 1867. He was a farmer. He married (first) March 28, 1813, Mary Davenport Vose, and lived at Dorchester, Massachusetts. His wife died October 20, 1829 (see Vose VI). He married (second) Jane Hunt, September 26, 1832. Children by first wife: Henry Vose, born January 26, 1814; Edward Loring, December 3, 1815; Warren, August 28, 1817; Richard C., mentioned below; Lydia Caroline, September 8, 1822; Child, August 11, 1824; Hannah Vose, September 9, 1825. Children of second wife: Martha Jane, March 1, 1834; George, August 1, 1835; Alice, September 12, 1837; Seth, December 9, 1839.

(VIII) Richard C., son of Eliphalet Thayer, was born at Dorchester, October 5, 1819. He married, October 31, 1841, Julia A. C. Wadsworth, and lived at 3 Lyon Place, Boston, Massachusetts. Children: Richard Loring, born March 6, 1843; Frank James, mentioned below; Henry B., March 3, 1854; Charles Vose, September 24, 1856.

(IX) Frank James, son of Richard C. Thayer, was born in Somerville, Massachusetts, September 15, 1852. He was educated there in the public schools. His occupation is foreman of Boston postoffice. In religion he is non-sectarian, and in politics independent. He resides in Somerville. He married Susan Waddington Holden. Among their children was Albert Roland, mentioned below.

(X) Albert Roland, son of Frank James Thayer, was born in Roxbury, Boston, Massachusetts, January 14, 1878. He attended the public schools of his native place. He started in the banking business as messenger for the Blackstone National Bank, corner of Hanover and Union streets, Boston. Afterward he was a clerk in the Second National Bank of Boston, and held various positions of trust there during the six years following. For three years he was with the banking house of E. H. Rollins & Sons, of Boston and New York, and two years with the banking house of Thomas Newhall, banker and broker, of Philadelphia, Pennsylvania. When Mr. Newhall became a member of the firm of Edward B. Smith & Company, Chestnut street, corner of Broad, Philadelphia, on December 1, 1909, Mr. Thayer became connected with the company, and has been salesmanager of the bond department since January, 1910. In politics he is independent, and in religion non-sectarian. He is a member of the New England Society of Philadelphia. His home is at 1843 North Thirteenth street, Philadelphia.

(The Vose Line).

(I) Robert Vose, immigrant ancestor, was born in Garston, near Liverpool, county Lancaster, England, about 1599, died in Milton, Massachusetts, October 16, 1683, son of Thomas and Anna Vose. In July, 1654, he purchased of the heirs of "Worshipful John Glover" one hundred and seventy-four acres of land in Dorchester, afterwards Milton, on the easterly and southerly sides of "Cobert Baddocks River." A part of this land has remained in the family for two and a half centuries. Robert Vose was a prominent man in the town. He was one of the three petitioners for the incorporation of Milton. He gave to the town in 1664 eight acres of land for church purposes near Vose's lane and Center street, now occupied in part by the Blanchard house. He was active in church affairs. He lived in the old Glover house, near the junction of Canton avenue and Brook road. He married Jane ———, who died in October, 1675. Children: Edward, born 1636; Thomas, mentioned below; Elizabeth, married, December 9, 1657, Thomas Swift; Martha, married Lieutenant John Sharp, of Muddy Brook (Brookline), who was killed in the Sudbury fight by the Indians.

(II) Thomas, son of Robert Vose, was born about 1641, died April 3, 1708. He was a man of more than ordinary standing in the town. For many years he was town clerk and under his management the records were kept systematically and carefully. He was an officer in the French and Indian war and went on the expedition to Canada. He was representative to the general court. He married Waitstill Wyatt, who died January 8, 1727, aged eighty-four years. Her mother, Mary Wyatt, was ninety-two years of age when she died, and the Dorchester town records say that "she was instrumental for the bringing into the world of one thousand one hundred and odd children." Children: Elizabeth; Henry, mentioned below; Jane; Thomas, married Hannah ———.

(III) Lieutenant Henry Vose, son of Thomas Vose, was born April 9, 1663, died March 26, 1752, aged eighty-nine. He married Elizabeth Babcock, born October 24, 1666, died November 18, 1732. Children: Waitstill, Robert, mentioned below; Mary, Elizabeth, Martha, Abigail, Hepzibah, Beulah, Thomas.

(IV) Lieutenant Robert (2) Vose, son of Lieutenant Henry Vose, was born October 25, 1693, died April 20, 1760. He married, September 14, 1721, Abigail Sumner, born January 31, 1699-1700, died December 20, 1769. Her brother, Seth Sumner, was great-grandfather of Hon. Charles Sumner and of General Edwin Vose Sumner, of the United States army. Robert Vose occupied the farm on the corner of Brush Hill road and Atherton street, Milton, which remained in the possession of the family until about 1880. His sons were remarkable for their height. Children: Othniel, Waitstill, Robert, Henry, Samuel, mentioned below; William, James, Elizabeth, Abigail, Thomas, Joshua, Benjamin.

(V) Samuel, son of Lieutenant Robert (2) Vose, was born May 13, 1730, at Milton, died there November 9, 1804, aged seventy-four. He married Sarah ———. Children, born at Milton: Susanna, April 3, 1756; Samuel, mentioned below; Ann, October 27, 1762.

(VI) Samuel (2), son of Samuel (1) Vose, was born at Milton, March 6, 1760. He married Miriam Billings (see Billings IV). Children, born at Milton: Peter, October 8, 1777; Charles, June 14, 1783; Lydia Billings, March 11, 1792; Mary Davenport, at East Windsor, Connecticut, January 22, 1794, married at Milton, Eliphalet Thayer (see Thayer VII).

1—5

(The Billings Line).

(I) Roger Billings, immigrant ancestor, was a carpenter by trade, and a proprietor of Dorchester, Massachusetts, in 1640. He was admitted a freeman, May 18, 1648. He bought of the Indians a tract of land two and a half by two miles, part of which was taken off in establishing the Rhode Island line. In 1662 he was one of the petitioners for six miles square for a township at Warranoco. He died November 15, 1683, aged sixty-five years (gravestone). His will was dated February 2, 1680, and November 13, 1683, and proved December 13, 1683. He married (first) Mary ———, who died in 1644; (second) Hannah ———, who died May 25, 1662; (third) Elizabeth, daughter of John Pratt. Children: Mary, born July 10, 1643, died December 10, 1643; Mary, baptized November 23, 1645, married, December 16, 1663, Samuel Belcher; Hannah, married, February 24, 1665, John Penniman; Joseph; Ebenezer, baptized October 26, 1651, married Hannah Wales; Samuel, baptized October 26, 1651; Roger, mentioned below; Elizabeth, born October 27, 1659; Zeppora, born May 21, 1662, died October 8, 1676; Jonathan, died January 14, 1677.

(II) Roger (2), son of Roger (1) Billings, was born November 16, 1657, died January 17, 1717-18. He settled in Canton, Massachusetts. He was married, January 22, 1678, by Governor Bradstreet, to Sarah Paine, who died September 19, 1742, aged eighty-four, daughter of Stephen Paine, of Braintree, Massachusetts. Children: Hannah, born January 21, 1679; Joseph, mentioned below; John, March 10, 1683; Roger, January 9, 1685; William, July 27, 1686; Sarah, February 27, 1687-88; Stephen, August 27, 1691; Mehitable, January 21, 1693-94; Moses, November 20, 1696; Ann, August 4, 1698; Abigail, February 15, 1700; Elizabeth, June 21, 1701; Isaac, July 9, 1703; Daughter, alive 1742.

(III) Joseph, son of Roger (2) Billings, was born at Milton or Canton, May 27, 1681. He settled at Milton, and died there January 18, 1765. He married Ruhamah Babcock, who died there February 2, 1740, aged fifty-four. Children, born at Milton: Hannah, February 25, 1707; Joseph, June 17, 1708; Benjamin, September 6, 1711, died October 28, 1711; Sarah, born November 6, 1712, died September 21, 1714; Patience, March 21, 1717; Ebenezer, mentioned below; John, born May 29, 1722; Ruhamah, February 19, 1725.

(IV) Ebenezer, son of Joseph Billings, was born at Milton, September 19, 1719, died September 16, 1766. He married (first) Jerusha ———. He married (second) at Milton, February 23, 1749, Miriam Davenport, who died

December 19, 1785 (see Davenport III). Children of first wife: Jerusha, born February 8, 1745, died young; Jerusha, October 29, 1746, died November 5, 1746. Children by second wife: Mary, November 5, 1750; Hannah, November 5, 1752; Joseph, March 26, 1757; Lydia, March 21, 1760; Miriam, April 10, 1763, married Samuel Vose (see Vose VI); Benjamin, October 26, 1765.

(The Davenport Line).

The English ancestry of the famous Rev. John Davenport, founder of New Haven, Connecticut, has been traced for many centuries in England. The Davenport surname is traced to the earliest period of the use of hereditary family names. Besides Rev. John Davenport, Captain Richard Davenport, of Salem, and Thomas Davenport, mentioned below, were in Massachusetts before 1640. The families used the same coat-of-arms, indicating common ancestry, but the relationship has not been traced.

(I) Thomas Davenport, immigrant ancestor, came from England to Dorchester, Massachusetts, where he was admitted to the church, November 20, 1640. His wife Mary joined the church, March 8, 1644, and died October 4, 1691. He was admitted a freeman, May 18, 1642, and was elected constable in 1670. He probably lived on the east slope of Mount Bowdoin, near Bowdoin street and Union avenue. He bought a house and land of William Pegrom, November 26, 1663, and of William Blake, February 5, 1666. His will was dated July 24, 1663, bequeathing his homestead to his son John after his wife's death. He died November 9, 1685. His estate was appraised at three hundred and thirty-seven pounds, sixteen shillings, eight pence. Children, born at Dorchester: Sarah, December 28, 1645; Thomas, baptized March 2, 1645, killed in the Narragansett fight in King Philip's war, December, 1676; Mary, baptized January 21, 1649; Charles, baptized December 7, 1652; Abigail, baptized July 8, 1655; Mehitable, February 14, 1657, died October 18, 1663; Jonathan, March 6, 1659; Ebenezer, April 28, 1661; John, mentioned below.

(II) John, son of Thomas Davenport, was born in Dorchester, October 20, 1664, died at Milton, Massachusetts, March 21, 1725. He inherited the homestead after his mother's death, and after she died he moved to Milton, where his name is first found on the tax list of 1707. In Milton he lived on the old farm still standing on the Isaac Davenport estate, owned by the family. His will is in the probate office of Suffolk county. He married Naomi, who died January 7, 1739, supposed to have been the Naomi, daughter of Timothy

Foster, of Dorchester, who was born there February 11, 1668. Children, born in Dorchester, except the last: John, mentioned below; Samuel, October 20, 1697; Ephraim, baptized August 6, 1699; Joseph, born August 30, 1701; Stephen, October 8, 1703; Mehitable, August 30, 1705; Benjamin, August 12, 1707.

(III) John (2), son of John (1) Davenport, was born in Dorchester, June 10, 1695, died at Stoughton, Massachusetts, July 20, 1778. He married, in Milton, June 10, 1725, Mary, daughter of Joseph Bent. She was baptized January 28, 1699, died July 20, 1768. Children, all born in the part of Stoughton now Canton: Mary, November 19, 1729; Miriam, April 15, 1732, married, February 23, 1749, Ebenezer Billings, of Milton (see Billings IV); Mariah, November 13, 1735; John, November 1, 1737; Mehitable, April 30, 1740.

(Genealogy by Mrs. M. H. O. France-Rice, of South Montrose, Pa.)

BUNNELL The Bunnell family dates back to Normandy, France, where they were called La Bunnells. When they came to England is not known, but a Bunnell historian visited England from Connecticut many years ago, and traced the family back to the eleventh century, when William La Bunnell came to England from Normandy as aide-de-camp on the staff of William the Conqueror in 1066. Their coat-of-arms is still preserved, but the French La was dropped. The ancestry is traced from three brothers, William (mentioned below), Solomon and Benjamin, who came from Cheshire, England, in 1638, and settled at New Haven, Connecticut. When the first census was taken in 1790 in the Thirteen Colonies, there were Bunnells recorded in every state, and their descendants are widespread. Beginning with the first at New Haven, historians wrote of them as "being without exception men of character and piety, who used every opportunity to promote education and religion, and were the first in all history to adopt a written constitution and to refuse compensation for public service."

(I) William Bunnell, the immigrant ancestor, came with his brothers Solomon and Benjamin from Cheshire, England, in 1638, and settled in New Haven, Connecticut, where he married, in 1640, Anna, daughter of Benjamin Wilmot.

(II) Benjamin, eldest son of William Bunnell, was born in 1642, and married Rebecca, daughter of Peter Mallory. They had ten children.

(III) Benjamin (2), son of Benjamin (1) Bunnell, was born about 1676. Children: Rebecca, born 1701; Hannah, 1702; Benjamin,

1704; Solomon, mentioned below; Gershom, 1707; Nathaniel; Isaac, 1713.

(IV) Solomon, son of Benjamin (2) Bunnell, was born in 1705. He married Mary Holdren, about 1737, and moved from New Haven about 1740 to Kingwood, New Jersey. His brother came with him as far as Elizabeth, New Jersey, where he located, and spelled his name Bonnell. About 1760 Solomon moved to Middle Smithfield, Bucks (now Monroe) county, Pennsylvania, where he died in 1779. Children: 1. Isaac, born July 13, 1738; married Lanah Barkalve, 1766, and had eight children. 2. Solomon, married Eleanor Fox, two children. 3. Benjamin, mentioned below. 4. Rachel, married Benjamin Brink, one child. 5. Patty (Martha), married (first) Robert Hanners, and (second) John Lock, three children. 6. Polly (Mary), married Elias Daily, three children; returned to Connecticut. 7. Lizzie (Elizabeth), married Benjamin Drake. 8. Rebecca.

(V) Benjamin (3), son of Solomon Bunnell, was born November 10, 1742, in Kingwood, New Jersey. He married Catharine Barry (Barre) in 1778. When about eleven years old he came with his parents to "The Hollow," in Monroe county, Pennsylvania, where he later inherited a part of his father's farm. Catharine Barry was daughter of James and Hester (Bryant) Barry, of Bucks county, Pennsylvania. She was born November 26, 1759, and died September 5, 1843, and was buried in the Bunnell Cemetery at "The Neck," Wyoming county, Pennsylvania. At the beginning of the revolutionary war, Benjamin was induced by his father to remain at home, care for the family and attend the farm, while he entered the service. After his father's health failed the records show that he enlisted in 1778, remaining to the close of the war. He took his newly wedded wife to a fort in New Jersey, where their eldest child Polly was born. By his military service Benjamin's health was a great deal impaired for future usefulness. Children: 1. Mary (Polly), born August 5, 1778, died January 24, 1838; married John Jayne, father of David, Benjamin, and Aaron. 2. Elizabeth, February 13, 1780; married William Jayne, in 1797, had twelve children, among whom was son Allan, born June 20, 1812, married Margaret Hankinson, of New Jersey, and left a property valued at about $250,000, at Meshoppen, Pennsylvania, when he died. 3. Esther, 1781; married Moses Kennedy; went to Ohio early in 1800. 4. Rebecca, October 17, 1782, died July 7, 1850; married Moses Bartron, of Russell Hill, Wyoming county, Pennsylvania, nine children. 5. Martha, October 12, 1787, died January 19, 1856; married, July

10, 1810, John Place; lived on homestead at Middle Smithfield, where Frederick Place, a grandson, now resides. 6. Benjamin, October 29, 1788, died February 27, 1880; married Mary Eve Ozies, in 1806; died at Bunnell Hill, Wyoming county. 7. John, August 13, 1790, died August 11, 1872; married Mary Place, July 10, 1810, fourteen children; was first class leader in Methodist church founded at Vosburg in 1816, was converted at a camp meeting in 1815. 8. Solomon, mentioned below. 9. Isaac, February 18, 1795, died June 26, 1832; married, 1815, Anna Overfield, granddaughter of Nicholas DePue, of Minisink, eight children. 10. Catharine, March 13, 1797, died February 20, 1892; married (first) Dr. Elijah Carney, of Mehooany, and had Benjamin; married (second) Benjamin Crawford, and had four children. 11. James, May 29, 1799, died March, 1879; married Lovisa Russell, nine children. 12. Gershom, December 15, 1803, died June 8, 1855; married Sarah Kellogg, January 1, 1823, two children.

(VI) Solomon, son of Benjamin (3) Bunnell, was born July 21, 1792, and died May 22, 1874. He married Eleanor Place, August 19, 1812, at Middle Smithfield, and with his five other brothers, became pioneer farmers in Wyoming county. He located on a farm overlooking Black Walnut Bottom, which is noted as having been a camping ground, August 4, 1779, for General Sullivan's army on its way to destroy the Indians at the Great Lakes. Children: 1. Elizabeth, married Ansel Gay, when fourteen years old, and had seventeen children. 2. Anna, born August 17, 1814, died January 2, 1817. 3. John, mentioned below. 4. James, died May 28, 1884, aged nearly sixty-seven years; married Mary Ann Luce, nine children, of whom two, Carrie and Ella, are now living. 5. Mary Ann, July 10, 1819, died August 10, 1820. 6. Eleanor, married William Cooley, of South Auburn, Susquehanna county, Pennsylvania, four children. 7. Aurelia, married Isaac Carter, November 25, 1851, died October 27, 1867; four children. 8. Phœbe, March 11, 1825, died February 11, 1826. 9. Infant daughter, born and died January 15, 1830. 10. Infant daughter, born May 7, died May 8, 1832.

(VII) John, son of Solomon Bunnell, was born May 20, 1816, and died January 23, 1887. He married, May 19, 1836, Laura M. Whitcomb. Children: 1. Alrisa Leaman, born January 5, 1840; married (first) Etna Storm, and had Frank Wesley, and died in 1864; married (second) Alice Williams, and had daughter Jessie. 2. Wesley, October 12, 1841; married Hannah A. Hadlock, and had Clarence Udell; died October 12, 1903. 3. Henry Clay, mentioned below. 4. Albert, May 11, 1845; married Harriet A. Overfield, six children; died October 7, 1906. 5. George Marble, January 13, 1849, died April 28, 1849. 6. Amma Delphine, December 12, 1855; married Henry Bacon, October 8, 1877; seven children.

(VIII) Henry Clay, son of John Bunnell, was born May 20, 1843. He married, February 6, 1866, Lydia Martha Overfield (see Overfield IV). He is now living in Scranton, Pennsylvania. He was a farmer and county commissioner. Children: 1. William Overfield, mentioned below. 2. Dana Whitcomb, born September 29, 1870, died January 7, 1877. 3. Annie Laura, November 12, 1872, died May 14, 1875. 4. Mary Otta, February 27, 1876; a trained nurse of Scranton, Pennsylvania. 5. Hartley John, August 14, 1878, died September 8, 1882. 6. Harry Wesley, May 9, 1883, died February 17, 1888. 7. Infant son, June 9, 1887, died same day.

(IX) William Overfield Bunnell, son of Henry Clay Bunnell, was born at Meshoppen, Wyoming county, Pennsylvania, July 22, 1867. He received his early education in the public and private schools of his native place. At the age of sixteen he became a clerk in the drug store of N. & E. H. Wells, in his home town, and continued for two years there. Having a natural inclination toward surgery and medicine, he was often called upon to assist in operations, and at an early age acquired much practical knowledge of the profession he afterward followed. On account of ill health at the age of eighteen years, he returned to his father's home and for three years assisted him in the stone quarrying and lumbering business. When he came of age he began at the bottom of the ladder in the railroad business as brakeman on the Lehigh Valley railroad, and soon won promotion to the position of conductor. When the railroad extension was built from Sayre to Buffalo he was placed in charge of some of the construction work. Leaving the railroad business soon afterward, he resumed the study of medicine under the instruction of Dr. Jacob Biles, at Meshoppen, and a year later entered the Eclectic Medical School at Cincinnati, Ohio, taking four full lecture courses and graduating with the degree of doctor of medicine June 5, 1894. He passed the examinations of the State Medical Board with an exceptionally high average, receiving marks of 100 per cent. in five branches. After serving in the Eclectic Medical School two terms as prosector of anatomy and assistant demonstrator of histology, he was appointed to the chair of diagnosis and hygiene in the Medical School of Lincoln University at Lincoln, Nebraska. He resigned on account of ill-

ness and returned home. After he took two full courses of lectures at the Golden Cross Medical College, at Chicago, and received the degrees of D. O. and D. A. O. He then opened an office at Wilkes-Barre, Pennsylvania, making a specialty of diseases of the eye, ear, nose and throat. After three years he found the confinement to office practice was again undermining his health, and he turned to general practice in the country, locating at Conyngham, where he had to be outdoors much of the time. His health improved and he decided to make a specialty of medical jurisprudence, and he began to study law in the office of Vosburg & Dawson at Scranton, Pennsylvania. After two years he entered the Indiana Law School of Indianapolis University, Indianapolis, and took three full courses of lectures, not missing a lecture or failing in a recitation during his course. He was graduated in due course with the degree of LL. B. in 1908, and was admitted to the bar and to practice in the supreme court of Indiana and in the United States circuit court. While a law student he read law in the office of Colonel James A. Rohback, the dean of the Law School. After practicing law a short time in Indianapolis, he returned to Conyngham as clerk in the office of John Kelly, making a special study of Pennsylvania statutes and practice, and was admitted to the bar in Luzerne county, March 14, 1910, by the late Judge John Lynch. He opened an office at 12 Swartz Block, Hazelton, Pennsylvania, and another at 105 Coal Exchange Building, Wilkes-Barre. Dr. Bunnell is one of the few successful men following two difficult professions, law and medicine, and has made an enviable reputation in medical jurisprudence. His residence is at No. 256 North Washington street, Wilkes-Barre, Pennsylvania.

He is a member of the Pennsylvania Medical Association and vice-president of the Physicians and Surgeons Mutual Insurance Association of the United States. He has contributed frequently to medical journals. He is prominent in a number of fraternal organizations. He joined the Ki-Men-Chee Tribe, Improved Order of Red Men, at Meshoppen, Pennsylvania, and was the founder of Sha-Man Tribe of this order at Conyngham. The name "Sha-Man" is the Indian term for "medicine man," the lodge being named in honor of its founder, Dr. Bunnell. He was district deputy for one term. He is also a member of Conyngham Lodge, No. 208, I. O. O. F.; Wyoming Valley Encampment, No. 25, I. O. O. F.; Canton, No. 31, Patriarchs Militant, I. O. O. F.; Goldie Lodge, No. 108, Daughters of Rebekah; Patriotic Order Sons of America,

Camp No. 206, being chief surgeon of the Second Regiment, Military Reserves of the same, with the rank of major. He is also a member of Diamond City Court, No. 46, Tribe of Ben-Hur, being medical examiner of the same. He was the organizer of Power City Lodge, No. 202, Loyal Order of Moose; a member of Haymakers Association, No. 165½, I. O. R. M., and various other orders, being a member in all of fourteen different organizations. In religion he is a member of the Christian Church. In politics Dr. Bunnell is a Republican.

He married (first) March 20, 1895, Eloise Hines, who was born at Lacyville, Wyoming county, Pennsylvania, in 1873. He married (second) August 15, 1902, Rose Pease, who was born at Dayton, Ohio, in 1873. Child by first wife: Marjorie Elizabeth, born January 2, 1896. Children of second wife: William Henry, born July 28, 1904; Harry Albert, September 2, 1906, at Conyngham.

Mrs. Bunnell was the founder of Shahoctee Council, Daughters of Pocahontas, at Conyngham, Pennsylvania, the name "Shahoctee" meaning medicine woman, and this lodge was named in honor of Mrs. Bunnell, who was a professional nurse before her marriage.

(The Overfield Line).

(By Mrs. M. H. O. France-Rice).

The Overfields or Eberfields are a numerous and well-known family in Germany, where there are large historic towns of the same name. The first written mention of the family in America is in the book, "The Great Indian Walk and Life of Edward Marshall," by his descendant, William J. Buck, in regard to Marshall's walking a vast tract of land from the Indians in Eastern Pennsylvania in 1737. He married Elizabeth Overfield, or "Ueberfeldt," about 1734; her parents were located on the east bank of the Delaware river, in New Jersey, above Easton, Pennsylvania, in the famous Minisink regions. The name of Elizabeth's father is not known, but he was born near Stuttgart, Germany, and emigrated to America in 1722.

(I) Paul, brother of Elizabeth Overfield, was born in 1715, in Germany, and when seven years of age came with his parents to America. He married Rebecca Marshall, sister of Edward, the noted Indian walker. He died in Middle Smithfield, Monroe county, Pennsylvania, in 1800, aged eighty-five. Children: Abner; Benjamin, mentioned below; Sarah; Mary; Rachel; Paul Jr.; William; Martin.

(II) Benjamin, son of Paul Overfield, was born in 1751, in Middle Smithfield, and died

October 27, 1813, in Braintrim, Luzerne (now Wyoming) county, Pennsylvania. He enlisted in the Continental army in 1776, and was in the battles of Trenton and Princeton, New Jersey. He also fought at Chadd's Ford and Germantown, Pennsylvania. He and his brothers Abner and Martin were in the forces when General Sullivan was dispatched by General Washington in the summer of 1779 to raid the Indians in Genesee Valley, New York. His brother-in-law, Moses Van Campen was quartermaster. During this excursion from Easton, Pennsylvania, Benjamin located his homestead in the fastnesses of the wilderness along the Susquehanna river at Brick Chapel, as it is now known, Wyoming county, Pennsylvania. He and his brothers Abner and Martin were in the Fifth Battalion of Northampton county, and were honorably discharged in 1781. He removed his family to the new home in the spring of 1794. He married (first) ——— Gonzales, a descendant of Spanish nobility. He married (second) Margaret Henshaw. Children by first wife: William; Emanuel, married Sarah Shields, and moved to Canada; Martin, married Susan Shinks; Rebecca. married Thomas Marshall; Elizabeth, married David Daily, moved early "to the Ohio"; Eleanor, married ——— Bowman, had son Erastus, married (second) Daniel Cooley, of South Auburn, Susquehanna county, and had five or six children. Children by second wife: Paul, mentioned below; Sarah, born June 15, 1794, in new home, married John Sterling, of Black Walnut.

(III) Paul, son of Benjamin Overfield, was born May 22, 1792, and married, June 18, 1812, Lydia Lacey, whose father, Isaac, came from Connecticut. They lived on the original homestead of their pioneer ancestors, and twelve children were born. Children: 1. William, mentioned below. 2. Susannah, born October 22, 1816, died 1819. 3. Harriet, January 12, 1818, died February 6, 1881; married Rev. Almon G. Stilwell, in 1840, nine children. 4. Sarah E., February 28, 1820, died June 21, 1902; married Rev. Henry Brownscombe, August 21, 1843; four children, all deceased. 5. Benjamin, March 28, 1822, died March 5, 1904; married Lois Ann Camp, March 2, 1847; nine children, all married. 6. Margaret, April 16, 1824, died December 13, 1875; married John C. Sturdevant, September 27, 1848; two sons. 7. Anna, May 20, 1826; married John C. Bertholf, November 30, 1863; one child. 8. John Lacey, July 16, 1828, died November 19, 1889; educated at Wyoming Seminary and Trinity College, Hartford, Connecticut, class of 1856; entered the law firm of Scudder & Carter, of Greater New York, and after four years practiced law as a profession in New York and Brooklyn; married (first) Augusta Dean, one son Alam, 1861, and both died; married (second) Olivia Binns, and had Leonidas, Louise, Mortimer, and Chauncey Percy, in business at Salt Lake City, Utah. 9. Eliza Rebecca, September 3, 1830; married Edmund C. Bunnell, February 6, 1851; seven children, all married. 10. Nancy Maria, September 24, 1832, died May 13, 1876; married George W. Smith, November 23, 1852; he was in civil war. 11. Lydia Martha, born November 28, 1836, died August 6, 1846. 12. Infant son, born and died same day.

(IV) William, son of Paul Overfield, was born October 10, 1813, and died March 6, 1898, aged eighty-four. He was a farmer and expert fruit grower; also a pioneer in Susquehanna county. He married Anna Bunnell, February 22, 1836; she was daughter of John and Mary (Place) Bunnell; she died March 11, 1854; her father was one of the six brothers who came from near Stroudsburg, Monroe county, to Wyoming county, Pennsylvania, in 1813. He married (second) November 17, 1854, Minerva H. Reeney, who died January 20, 1884. Children: 1. Mary Harriet, the family historian, born March 26, 1837; was graduated from Wyoming Seminary, June 23, 1859; married (first) John M. France, March 26, 1861, and had one child (Lydia M., born September 27, 1862, who married Henry R. Decker, of South Montrose, Pennsylvania, October 5, 1883); she married (second) W. Henry Rice, of Solebury, Bucks county, Pennsylvania, November 23, 1887, and he died February 22, 1909. 2. Lydia Elizabeth, born February 26, 1839, died August 8, 1839. 3. Sarah Helen, June 6, 1840, died August 1, 1847. 4. Paul James, February 6, 1842, died November 2, 1882; served three years in civil war, from 1862 to 1865; married Sarah Roe, December 30, 1872; seven children (the eldest, Peter D., being noted for football at Pennsylvania University, now judge by appointment of President William H. Taft at Valdez, Alaska, and married Virginia Beale Leckie, of Virginia, April 28, 1906). 5. John Bunnell, January 14, 1844; served in civil war, was treasurer of Wyoming county one term; married Julia Johnson, January 24, 1866, had four children, died in Pasadena, California, where he now lives with his second wife, Josephine Nye, whom he married January 1, 1908. 6. Lydia Martha, December 29, 1845; married Henry Clay Bunnell, February 6, 1866 (see Bunnell VIII). 7. Ettaline A., March 28, 1848; married Henry Low Lott, January 11, 1865; four children. 8. Charles Nezbert, May 5, 1850; married Amanda Ace, January 1,

1879; six children; he was helpless with paralysis for a number of years and is now deceased. Children by second wife: 9. Seth Lee, October 12, 1855; married Mary Boyhen, April 7, 1875; seven children. 10. William Grant, February 18, 1857; located early in Puyallup, Washington; married Addie Stone; six children. 11. Annie Minerva, May 11, 1858, died October 1, 1863. 12. Infant son, born August 28, died September 18, 1859. 13. Gilbert, January 18, 1861; married Deborah Nye, September 26, 1886; have son George at Pasadena. 14. Henry Dean, June 25, 1862, died January 7, 1864. Four unrecorded and unnamed infants were born.

RUSSELL John Russell, immigrant ancestor, came to New England and settled first at Cambridge, where he was a proprietor in 1635. He was admitted a freeman, March 3, 1635-36, and was a town officer and clerk of the writs. He was a subscriber to the orders drawn up for the town of Woburn, at Charlestown, in 1640, and was one of the first settlers of Woburn. He was a proprietor there in 1640. He was selectman of Woburn for several years, and in 1644 was appointed on a committee for distribution of land. He was deacon of the church, but afterwards became a Baptist, and about 1669-70 was admitted to the Baptist church of Boston, which at that time met for worship at Noddle's Island. He was later chosen elder of this church. For his change of faith he was summoned before the court at Charlestown in 1671 and sent to prison, but soon released. He died June 1, 1676. His will was dated May 27, 1676. He married (first) Elizabeth ———, who died December 16, 1644. He married (second) May 13, 1645, Elizabeth Baker, who died January 17, 1689-90. Children: Samuel, born 1636; John, mentioned below: Mary, married, December 21, 1659, Timothy Brooks.

(II) John (2), son of John (1) Russell, was born about 1640, died December 21, 1680, aged forty years, and was buried in King's Chapel burying ground, Boston. He settled first in Woburn, and later removed to Boston where he was ordained to succeed Elder Gould as minister of the Baptist church, July 28, 1679. During the short period he was in office, he wrote a treatise in answer to some harsh reflections in a publication by Rev. Dr. Increase Mather, asserting "The Divine Right of Infant Baptism." The answer was entitled "A Brief Narrative of some considerable passages concerning the First Gathering and Further Progress of a Church of Christ in Gospel Order, in Boston, in New England, etc." It was dated in Boston, May 20, 1680, and sent to London for publication. He married, October 31, 1661, Sarah, daughter of John Champney, of Cambridge. She died at Woburn, April 25, 1696. Children: John, mentioned below; Joseph, born January 15, 1663-64, at Woburn; Samuel, February 3, 1667-68, died December 1, 1668; Sarah, February 10, 1670-71; Elizabeth, February 19, 1672-73; Jonathan, August 6, 1675; Thomas, January 5, 1677-78; Ruth.

(III) John (3), son of John (2) Russell, was born August 1, 1662, died July 26, 1717. He married, December 21, 1682, Elizabeth Palmer, who died about 1723. He died before she did, as the Woburn records say that "Widow Elizabeth Russell" is named in the province tax in 1723, but not in that of 1724. Children, born in Woburn: John, September 20, 1683; Joseph, October 3, 1685; Stephen, August 25, 1687; Elizabeth, June 21, 1690; Samuel, July 16, 1692; Sarah, October 15, 1694; Son, August 19, 1697, died September 12, 1697; Ruth, January 16, 1699; Jonathan, November 7, 1700; Mary, March 2, 1703, died November 27, 1709; Thomas, mentioned below.

(IV) Thomas, son of John (3) Russell, was born in Woburn, Massachusetts, June 26, 1705, died before 1790. He moved from there to Sherborn, Massachusetts, where he settled on the southeast side of Course brook, and lived there the remainder of his life. He married Hannah, daughter of Isaac Cooledge, Esq., of Sherborn, and Hannah (Morse) Cooledge; Hannah Morse was daughter of Captain Joseph and Hannah (Badcock) Morse. Thomas Russell's wife, Hannah, died December 21, 1800, aged ninety years. She was niece of Mary Cooledge, wife of Deacon Jonathan Russell. Children, born in Sherborn: Joel, March 7, 1733-34; Rebecca, April 20, 1735; Isaac, September 27, 1736; Hannah, January 27, 1738-39; Hannah, February 21, 1740-41; Isaac, November 21, 1742; Thomas, mentioned below; Hannah, May 11, 1746; Sarah, September 28, 1748; Isaac, March 8, 1750; Hannah, April 2, 1752; Samuel, November 18, 1754.

(V) Thomas (2), son of Thomas (1) Russell, was born December 13, 1744. He was a soldier in the revolution in Captain Benjamin Bullard's company, Colonel Pierce's regiment, April 19, 1775; also in 1776-77. He married Abigail ———. Children: Daniel, born April 7, 1775; Joseph, November 1, 1776; Arnold, mentioned below; Thomas, baptized March 4, 1781; Nabby, born May 30, 1783; Shubael, baptized November 20, 1785.

(VI) Arnold, son of Thomas (2) Russell, was born in Sherborn or vicinity, and was baptized August 23, 1778. He removed to

Albany county, New York. He married ———, and among his children was Zenas Henry, mentioned below.

(VII) Zenas Henry, son of Arnold Russell, was born in Albany county, New York, in 1806, died May 11, 1878. He was a successful business man of Honesdale, Pennsylvania, the first vice-president and second president of the Honesdale National Bank, of which he was one of the original incorporators, of which his son is now president. The bank was organized in 1836 under a state charter, and now has a capital of $150,000, with a surplus of nearly $200,000. Mr. Russell was one of the early pioneers of Northeastern Pennsylvania, and for a number of years was successfully engaged in the mercantile business in Honesdale. He was one of the organizers of the Grace Episcopal Church, and continued a liberal supporter of the same up to the time of his death, being senior warden of the church at the time of his death. He married Lucy Waite Forbes, who passed away April 22, 1891, a descendant of Daniel Forbes, the pioneer of the family, who was born at Kinellar, Scotland, about 1620, and settled during the civil war in England at Cambridge, Massachusetts, where he died in October, 1687. Through the Waite family she was descended from the same stock as Chief Justice Waite, of the United States supreme court. Her parents lived at New Bedford, Massachusetts. Children: Sophie C., married Robert J. Menner, and she is now deceased; Annie E., married William H. Dimmick, and she is now deceased; Julia A., died in infancy; Henry Zenas, mentioned below.

(VIII) Henry Zenas, son of the late Zenas Henry Russell, was born at Honesdale, Pennsylvania, April 3, 1851. He was educated in the public schools of his native town. He is president of the Honesdale National Bank, treasurer of the Honesdale Consolidated Light, Heat and Power Company, and is one of the most prominent business men and financiers of this section. In politics he is a Republican. He is a member of Grace Episcopal Church, of which he has been senior warden and treasurer for a number of years. He is a member of the Exchange Club, of Honesdale.

He married (first) May 15, 1884, Jessie A. Wood, born in Honesdale, died February 24, 1908. He married (second) September 22, 1909, Mrs. Jessie (Ball) Dolmetsch, born at Goshen, New York, daughter of Henry and Margaret Ball. Children by first wife: 1. Zenas Henry, born February 25, 1885; married Isabelle Crooker, of Mt. Vernon, and they reside at Manchester, New Hampshire, where he is connected with the Amoskeag Company; they are the parents of two sons, Henry Z., 2d, and Malcolm Story Russell. 2. Sophie Menner, born December 3, 1886; married Clinton I. Dow, and they reside at Manchester, New Hampshire, where he is connected with the Amoskeag Company. 3. Marietta, born June 19, 1889. 4. Lucy Forbes, born October 7, 1891. 5. Milton Dimmick, born April 1, 1895.

POND   Samuel Pond, immigrant ancestor, was born in England, and was one of the early settlers of Windsor, Connecticut. He died March 14, 1654, and his inventory was filed March 19, 1654. He left sixty-two acres of land. He married, November 14, 1642, Sarah ———. Children: Isaac, born at Windsor, March 16, 1646; Samuel, mentioned below; Nathaniel, December 21, 1650, killed by the Indians, December 19, 1675, in King Philip's war; Sarah, February 11, 1652.

(II) Samuel (2), son of Samuel (1) Pond, was born at Windsor, March 4, 1648. He was one of the signers of the "New Plantation and Church Covenant" of Branford, Connecticut, January 20, 1667. He was propounded for freeman in 1672. He was a deputy to the general court from Branford in 1678-82-83-87, and was lieutenant of the military company in 1695. He married, February 3, 1669, Miriam Blakeley. Children, born at Branford: Nathaniel, 1676, died 1679; Abigail, 1677; Samuel, July 1, 1679; Josiah, September 25, 1688; Lois, 1690; Moses, mentioned below; Miriam, 1696; Mindwell, 1698.

(III) Moses, son of Samuel (2) Pond, was born and baptized in 1693. In 1747 he made his will at Branford, Connecticut, then aged fifty-four years, and bequeathed to wife Mary and ten children: Aaron, Gad, Asher, Paul, Samuel, Mary, Bathsheba, Lois, Rachel, Mindwell. He was a cordwainer. He resided for a few years at Haddam, then at Branford, where he had a farm. He was administrator of the estate of Isaac Tyler, of Haddam, who died January 22, 1718, and he was guardian of a minor son, Israel Tyler. He married, January 7, 1718-19, Mary, daughter of Elijah Brainerd, and granddaughter of Daniel Brainerd (p. 42 "Brainerd Genealogy"). She lived at Haddam, Middlesex county, Connecticut. Children: Aaron, mentioned below; Moses, born 1721; Mary, 1723; Bathsheba, January 2, 1724-25; Gad, August 12, 1727, at Branford; Asher, August 12, 1727; Lois, June 20, 1730; Rachel, May 26, 1733; Paul, May 12, 1736; Samuel, June 24, 1739; Mindwell, July 12, 1742.

Elijah Brainerd, son of Daniel Brainerd, married (first) September 28, 1699, Mary Bushnell, born March 10, 1675, daughter of Joseph and Mary (Leffingwell) Bushnell. She died September 11, 1735. Elijah Brainerd married (second) Margaret ———, September 6, 1738. The will of Elijah Brainerd, who died April 20, 1740, according to the Hartford probate records, bequeaths to his daughter, Mary Pond, and mentions the "right of Moses Pond" in describing land.

Daniel Brainerd, father of Elijah Brainerd, and the immigrant ancestor, was born probably at Braintree, county Essex, England, about 1641, and was brought to this country when about eight years old and lived with the Wadsworth family in Hartford, Connecticut. He remained there until 1662, when with others he took up land and made Haddam his permanent home, although at that time it was an unbroken wilderness. His children were baptized in the Middletown church, eight miles from home. He married (first) Hannah Spencer, born about 1641, at Lynn, Massachusetts, daughter of Gerrard and Hannah Spencer, of Cambridge and Lynn, Massachusetts, and Haddam, Connecticut. She died about 1691. Daniel Brainerd married (second) March 30, 1693, Elizabeth (Wakeman) Arnold, daughter of Samuel and Elizabeth Wakeman, both natives of England. Samuel Wakeman died at the Bahama Islands in 1641. Daniel Brainerd married (third) November 29, 1698, Hannah (Spencer) Sexton, born April 25, 1653, daughter of Thomas and Sarah Spencer, and widow of George Sexton. Deacon Daniel Brainerd died April 1, 1715, and is buried in the old burial ground at Haddam. His home was on Lot No. 5½ and was bounded west by the main street, north by land of John Bailey, east by the river and south by Joseph Stannard's place. Deacon Brainerd was constable, surveyor, fence viewer, assessor, justice of the peace and on town committees to lay out land, etc., deputy to the general assembly in Hartford and he was elected by that body in 1669 a commissioner. He was deacon of the old church at Haddam. Children by first wife: Daniel, born March 2, 1665-66; Hannah, November 20, 1667; James, June 2, 1669; Joshua, July 20, 1671-72; William, March 30, 1673-74; Caleb, November 20, 1675-76; Elijah, about 1677-78; Hezekiah, May 24, 1680-81.

(IV) Aaron, son of Moses Pond, was born at Haddam, October 1, 1719. He married, January 23, 1744-45, Martha ———. They had Moses, mentioned below, and perhaps other children.

(V) Moses (2), son of Aaron Pond, was born at Haddam, January 7, 1745-46. He was living at Southington, Hartford county, Connecticut, in 1790, when according to the first federal census he had in his family two males over sixteen, three males under sixteen and three females. His name appears in November, 1793, on a list of subscriptions for music in the church at Wolcott, Connecticut. According to the town history of Wolcott (p. 196) Colonel Moses Pond kept a hotel, afterward owned by Lucius Tuttle. Of his family Moses joined the church at Wolcott in 1828; Moses J. Pond was baptized at Southington, an adult, April 6, 1834; Naomi Pond was baptized at Southington in 1827; Lois Pond in 1826. Moses Pond was a soldier in the revolution (pages 562 and 622, Connecticut revolutionary records), a private in the Sixth Brigade, Connecticut seacoast guard. He was credited to Farmington, and was of the Fifteenth Regiment, Colonel Noadiah Hooker, in 1780. He was in the same regiment in 1779, Captain Beecher's company, and was detached with others to serve in the battalion of Lieutenant Colonel Mead from July 29, 1779, to the following March and was credited to Farmington parish. Southington was formerly part of Farmington. He married and among his children was Alpheus, mentioned below.

(VI) Alpheus, son of Moses (2) Pond, was of Southington, Wolcott and Bristol, Connecticut. He died in Wolcott, Connecticut, at the age of sixty-seven years. He married Betsey Peck, and she died aged forty-four years. Their children were Julia, born in 1814; Lois, 1815; Henry, 1817; Roswell, 1819; Alvin P., mentioned below; Almeron, 1822; Hiram, 1825; Lucinda, 1827; Phœbe, 1829; Oliver, 1831; Emeret, 1835; Leontine, 1838.

(VII) Alvin Porter, son of Alpheus Pond, was born at Wolcott, Connecticut, December 19, 1820, died at Southington, Connecticut, March 16, 1883. He was educated in the public schools, and followed the trade of a mechanic. He married (first) Emeline Thirza Clark, born May 19, 1826, daughter of Jesse Clark, of Clark Farms, Southington, Connecticut. She died November 8, 1867. Their only child was Charles Harvey Pond, mentioned below. Mr. Pond married (second) Mary Ann Frost, by whom he had one son, Elbert A., born December, 1874, now living in New Britain, Connecticut.

(VIII) Charles Harvey, son of Alvin Porter Pond, was born at Southington, Connecticut, December 15, 1847. He attended the public schools of his native town and Lewis Academy, also of Southington. He began his business career as a clerk in the hardware house of George B. Curtiss Company, in New York, in 1865. In 1868 he was employed at Bristol, Connecticut, in connection with the Curtiss Company, and in the following February he returned to Southington in the employ

of the Aetna Nut Company, as bookkeeper and secretary, remaining in this position until 1873, when he went to Ohio in the employ of the Gerard Rolling Mill Company at Gerard, Ohio, and in 1874 became the junior member of the firm of Taylor, Mitchell & Pond, at Massillon, Ohio, manufacturers of merchant iron and "T" rails. He was traveling salesman during part of the time and engaged in office work part of the time. In 1879 he again returned to Southington, Connecticut, and engaged in business with J. B. Savage in the manufacture of forgings. In 1887 the business was removed to Scranton, Pennsylvania, and was incorporated as the Scranton Forging Company, using drop and trip hammers for the work formerly done by hand. Mr. Savage became president and Mr. Pond secretary and manager of the company. Mr. Pond became president in 1890, and since then has been at the head of the concern. The business has flourished and is one of the prominent industries of the city of Scranton. In addition to this business Mr. Pond is financially interested in various other industrial corporations, and is a director in several companies. He is a director of the North Scranton Bank. In religion he is a Presbyterian, and for twelve years he was treasurer of the Green Ridge Presbyterian Church, of which he was also a trustee for many years. He is also a member and ex-president of the New England Society of Northeastern Pennsylvania. He is a member of the Scranton Board of Trade, and of the Green Ridge Club. In politics he is a Republican.

He married, December 15, 1874, Harriet I., born at Southington, Connecticut, December 16, 1850, daughter of Samuel H. and Helen (Lee) Finch. Children: 1. Harry Orlo, born at Massillon, Ohio, October 15, 1875; associated in business with his father; member of the Green Ridge Club. He married, October 5, 1911, Helen M. Heimbach, of Scranton. 2. Charles Wilcox, born at Southington, February 4, 1879, died January 24, 1900, in Scranton.

MATHEWSON   James Mathewson, the immigrant ancestor, may have been the James Mathews or Mathewson who was in Charlestown, Massachusetts, in 1634, and in Yarmouth prior to 1639; was constable of Yarmouth 1639-40, and on the list of those able to bear arms at Yarmouth in 1643.

James Mathewson settled in Providence, Rhode Island, as early as 1658. He bought land there of Thomas Angell, January 27, 1658, and of John Brown, February 24, 1668.

He was a deputy to the assembly in 1680. His will was dated August 24, 1682, and proved October 17, 1682. He married Hannah, daughter of John Field; she married (second) Henry Brown, and died in 1703. Children: Ruth, married Benjamin Whipple; James, born August 11, 1666, died January 7, 1737; John, died September 18, 1716; Isabel, married John Brown; Thomas, mentioned below; Lydia; Zachariah, died January 5, 1749; Daniel, born January 28, 1683 (posthumous).

(II) Thomas, son of James Mathewson, was born at Providence, Rhode Island, April 1, 1673, and died October 23, 1735. He lived at Providence and Scituate, Rhode Island. He had a deed dated December 2, 1707, of four acres from William Field, who calls him brother-in-law, and Thomas Field, father of William, confirmed the deed, the consideration of which was "good will and respect." His widow Martha was appointed administratrix November 10, 1735. He married Martha Field, who died in 1735, daughter of Thomas and Martha (Harris) Field. Children: Thomas, mentioned below; Amos.

(III) Thomas (2), son of Thomas (1) Mathewson, was born about 1700, at Providence or Scituate. He married Sarah ———. Children, recorded as born at Scituate: Philip, September 4, 1737; Thomas, January 8, 1739 (either he or his father died July 8, 1743; if the son, there must have been another Thomas born about 1743-44); Thomas, mentioned below.

(IV) Thomas (3), son of Thomas (2) Mathewson, was called Jr. in the records, indicating that his father was alive after he grew to maturity. He married (first) Hannah ———, and (second) Sarah, daughter of Captain Stephen Smith (by Jeremiah Angell), at Scituate, July 30, 1769). He removed to Vermont. Children by first wife, born at Scituate, Rhode Island: Elizabeth, November 12, 1764; Elisha, April 17, 1767. Children of second wife: Abigail, May 14, 1770; Charles, mentioned below.

(V) Charles, son of Thomas (3) Mathewson, was born October 26, 1784, and died August 24, 1870. He was a farmer at Wheelock, Vermont. He married Sarah Williams, born October 7, 1797, died October 1, 1872. Children, married at Wheelock, Vermont: Charles M., born January 7, 1819, died June 21, 1849; Sarah Ann, born February 5, 1820, died August 5, 1840; Azro Buck, mentioned below; Melina, born October 13, 1825, died October 12, 1840; Asher A., born March 15, 1827; Harley P., born December 14, 1829; Athelia E., December 4, 1830, died April 25, 1873; Arthur W., November 14, 1832; Rosilla M.,

October 2, 1834, died September, 1836; Epaphras C., September 25, 1836; Ozias D., February 15, 1839, died May 14, 1862.

(VI) Azro Buck, son of Charles Mathewson, was born at Wheelock, Vermont, February 7, 1822, and died July 18, 1884. He married, April 13, 1853, Amelia Sias, who was born in Boston, July 19, 1827, daughter of Rev. Solomon Sias, one of the founders and first publishers of *Zion's Herald*, a religious newspaper of Boston. His father, Captain Benjamin Sias, born June 14, 1747, married December 25, 1771, died December 21, 1799, lived at Canterbury and London, England, and Loudon, New Hampshire; he was captain of the Tenth Company, Colonel Thomas Hickney's regiment of New Hampshire militia, as shown by a return of the commanding officers, March 5, 1776; also captain of a company in Colonel David Gilman's regiment, "destined for New York," mustered and paid by Colonel Thomas Stickney, December 5, 1776; also captain of a company of men which marched from Loudon to reinforce the garrison at Ticonderoga, July 2, 1777; also captain of a company in Colonel T. Stickney's regiment under General John Stark, which joined the Northern Continental army, July 20, 1777, and was also at Bennington, September 3, 1777, in Stark's brigade. He was of a party of volunteers who went to Fort Edward when General Burgoyne was taken in October, 1779. He was also captain of a company in Colonel Moses Nichols' regiment in the Rhode Island expedition in August, 1778, and captain at the forts in Piscataqua harbor, September 2-27, 1779. The record given herewith is an abstract from the Revolutionary War Rolls preserved in the archives of New Hampshire, as certified by the secretary of state, Edward N. Pearson.

Captain Benjamin Sias married Abigail Moore, who was born March 2, 1754, and died February 16, 1822. Children: Jeremiah, born June 5, 1773, married Abigail ———, March, 1799, and died November 25, 1833; Samuel, born December 23, 1775, married, 1802, Sally Chamberlain, and died December 18, 1857; Archelaus, born August 29, 1778, married Polly Glines, and died December 5, 1860; Rev. Solomon, born February 25, 1781, married Amelia Rogers (see Rogers), July 31, 1825, and died February 12, 1853; John, born January 16, 1785, married Betsey Cheney, and died July 15, 1864; Hannah, born June 1, 1787, died unmarried, January 31, 1811; Abigail, born July 31, 1789, died in childbirth, June 30, 17—; Enoch Wood, born September 1, 1792, died in infancy, September 20, 1793. Children of Azro Buck and Amelia (Sias)

Charles F. Mathewson

Mathewson: Amelius Sias, born May 26. 1856, died November 11, 1870; Charles Frederick, mentioned below; Lillie Blanche, born September 19, 1862; Nellie Kate, born March 1, 1867, died April 6, 1895.

(VII) Charles Frederick, son of Azro Buck Mathewson, was born in Barton, Vermont, May 3, 1860. He attended the public schools of his native town and entered Dartmouth College, from which he was graduated with the degree of Bachelor of Arts in the class of 1882, of which he was valedictorian. He was first in scholarship in his class, and won prize awards in Greek, Latin, mathematics and oratory. He was elected to the Phi Beta Kappa. He began to study his profession at the Columbia Law School, from which he received his degree of LL. B. in 1885. In the same year he was admitted to the bar in New York City and began to practice. He has devoted his attention particularly to corporation business, and has built up a handsome practice. He is a partner in the law firm of Krauthoff, Harmon & Mathewson. He is a director of the Caledonian-American Insurance Company, the New York & Queens Electric Light & Power Company and the Columbia Trust Company of New York; a member of the New York Law Institute, and the Bar Association of New York City, in which he has served on the executive and grievance committees. In politics he is a Republican. He was active in various lines of athletics while in college, and since graduating has continued to take a lively interest in outdoor sports, especially golf and tennis. He was president of the Dartmouth Alumni Association from 1894 to 1896. Since 1904 he has been an alumni trustee of Dartmouth College, from which he received the honorary degree of Master of Arts in 1908, and in 1912 he received from Middlebury College the honorary degree of LL. D. He was formerly president of the Metropolitan Association of the Amateur Athletic Union. He is a member of the New England Society of New York, of which he is one of the trustees; of the Vermont Society, of which he is president; the Dartmouth Club of New York, of which he was the first president; the University Club of New York; the University Club of Boston; the Down Town Association; the Delta Kappa Epsilon fraternity of the council of which he is president; St. Andrew's Golf Club; the Apawamis Club, and the Automobile Club of America. In religion he is a liberal.

He married, December 8, 1886, Jeanie Campbell Anderson, who was born in Portland, Maine, January 8, 1852, daughter of General Samuel J. and Jane Wade (Dow) Anderson. (For a partial account of her ancestry see appended sketches).

(The Rogers Lines).

Two lines of Rogers ancestry met in Amelia Rogers, who married Rev. Solomon Sias, as stated above. The first of these, her paternal line, was a family connected with the history of Newbury and Newburyport, formerly part of Newbury, Massachusetts, from the early colonial days.

(I) Robert Rogers, founder of this family, was born in England, in 1625, and died December 23, 1663. He came first to Boston, and removed in 1651 to Newbury. He married Susanna ———, of Newbury. Children: Robert, born April 28, 1650; Thomas, of whom further; John, born March 13, 1653-54; Susan, born February 6, 1656, died September 4, 1657.

(II) Thomas, son of Robert and Susanna Rogers, was born at Newbury, July 9, 1652, and died October 15, 1735. He married Ruth Brown, probably the daughter, born May 26, 1662, of Isaac and Rebecca (Baily) Brown; she died February 1, 1730. Children: Thomas, born August 14 or 15, 1678; Susanna, born March 17, 1681-82; Robert, born April 5, 1684; John, born July 11, 1686; Isaac, born June 21, 1691; Stephen, baptized August 20, 1693; Daniel, born November 14, 1695; Daniel (second), born November 14, 1698; Jonathan, of whom further; Ruth, born October 30, 1715.

(III) Jonathan, son of Thomas and Ruth (Brown) Rogers, was born at Newbury, June 18, 1702. He was a captain in the English provincial army. He married, intention July 12, 1735, Margery Stevens, of Boston. Children: Jonathan, born June 16, 1736; Robert, born April 21, 1738; Benjamin, of whom further; Margery, born May 2, 1742; Hannah, born March 18, 1744-45.

(IV) Benjamin (1), son of Jonathan and Margery (Stevens) Rogers, was born at Newbury, January 27, 1739-40, and died April 10, 1812. He married, April 22, 1762, Mary, daughter of Joseph and Tamzen, also called Thomasin (Gerrish) Stevens, who was born June 23, 1741, and died about 1813. Children: Benjamin (2), of whom further; Mary, born February 10, 1780.

(V) Benjamin (2), son of Benjamin (1) and Mary (Stevens) Rogers, was born in Newbury (in what is now Newburyport, as it is very probable that some, at least, of the former entries may be), January 22, 1763, and died in Boston, April 27, 1806. He married, August 26, 1788, Amelia, daughter of Elihu and Elizabeth (Cogswell) Hewes, one line of whose ancestry is given hereinafter; she was born at Ipswich, Massachusetts, September 11, 1761, and died at Newbury, Vermont, October 30, 1850. Children: Amelia, born in 1789, died in 1856, married Rev. Solomon Sias, of whom above; William Cogswell, born January 11, 1800, died July 13, 1862, married Caroline Dudley.

One line of Amelia Hewes, by which she was descended from another Rogers family is as follows:

(I) John Rogers, the first member of this family about whom we have definite information, was born about 1500. He lived in the north of England. He was put to death at Chelmsford, England, in 1575, being the first to suffer for religious nonconformity in the reign of Queen Mary. He married, May 8, 1541, Agnes Carter.

(II) John (2), son of John (1) and Agnes (Carter) Rogers, was born September 10, 1548, and died in 1601; his will was recorded in October, of that year. He married Mary ———, who was born about 1550, and died in 1579.

(III) Rev. John (3) Rogers, son of John (2) and Mary Rogers, was born at Moulsham, Chelmsford, England, in 1571, and died October 18, 1636. He was a distinguished Puritan, and preached at Dedham, England. He married Elizabeth (Gold) Hawes.

(IV) Rev. Nathaniel Rogers, son of Rev. John (3) and Elizabeth (Gold-Hawes) Rogers, the first member of this family in America, was born at Haverhill, England, in 1598, and died at Ipswich, Massachusetts, July 3, 1655. He came to America November 17, 1636. Like his father, he was a Puritan; from 1638 he was minister at Ipswich. He married, January 23, 1625, Margaret, daughter of Robert Crane, who was born at Coggeshall, England, about 1610, and died at Ipswich, Massachusetts, January 23, 1675-76. Children: John (4), of whom further; Nathaniel, born September 30, 1632, died June 14, 1680; Samuel, born January 16, 1634, died December 21, 1693, married (first), December 12, 1657, Judith Appleton; (second), November 13, 1661, Sarah Wade; Timothy; Ezekiel, married Margaret (Hubbard) Scott; Margaret, married Rev. William Hubbard.

(V) Rev. Dr. John (4) Rogers, son of Rev. Nathaniel and Margaret (Crane) Rogers, was born at Assington, England, January 23, 1630-31, and died July 2, 1684. In June, 1676, he was elected president of Harvard College, but declined; in April, 1682, he was elected again and was installed August 12, 1683. Of this institution he was himself a graduate, and he had assisted his father and other ministers; he was also a physician. He married, in 1660, Elizabeth, daughter of Daniel and Patience (Dudley) Denison, who was born April 10, 1642. Her mother was daughter of Thomas Dudley, of whom hereafter. Children: Elizabeth, born February 3, 1661, died March 13, 1754, married, November 23, 1681, John Appleton; Margaret, born February 18, 1664, died June 7, 1720, married (first), December 21, 1682, Thomas Berry; (second), November 25, 1697, Rev. John Leverett, a president of Harvard College; Rev. John (5), of whom further; Daniel, born September 25, 1667, died December 1, 1722, married Sarah Appleton; Rev. Nathaniel, born February 22, 1669, died October 3, 1723, married Sarah Purkess; Patience, born in 1676, died May 2, 1731, married, April 15, 1696, Benjamin Marston.

(VI) Rev. John (5) Rogers, son of Rev. Dr. John (4) and Elizabeth (Denison) Rogers, was born at Ipswich, July 7, 1666, and died December 28, 1745. He was a minister at Ipswich. He married, March 4, 1691, Martha, daughter of William and Mary (Laurence) Whittingham, who died March 9, 1759. Children: Rev. John (6), born about 1692, died in 1773, married, October 16, 1718, Susannah Whipple; Martha, born November 2, 1694, died August 25, 1727, married, June 24, 1714, Thomas Berry; Mary, died October 18, 1725, married John Wise; William, born June 19, 1697, died July 29, 1749; Rev. Nathaniel, born September 22, 1701, died May 10, 1775, married (first), December 25, 1728, Mary (Leverett) Denison; (second) Mary (Burnham) Staniford; Richard, born December 2, 1703, died November 26, 1742, married Mary Crampton; Elizabeth, born July 20, 1705; Rev. Daniel, born July 28, 1707, died in 1785, married Anna Foxcroft; Elizabeth, of whom further; Samuel, born August 31, 1709, died December 21, 1772, married, June 1, 1735, Hannah Ruhami.

(VII) Elizabeth, daughter of Rev. John (5) and Martha (Whittingham) Rogers, was born at Ipswich, Massachusetts, July 28, 1707. She married, March 14, 1727-28, Francis Cogswell.

(VIII) Elizabeth, daughter of Francis and Elizabeth (Rogers) Cogswell, was born in Ipswich, December 17, 1729. She married, in October, 1756, Elihu Hewes, who was born in England, about 1727, and died at Hampden, Maine, about 1808. Child: Amelia, of whom above.

Mrs. Mathewson's ancestry is an interesting one in many lines. Eligibility to the Colonial Dames is well established. Some of the most prominent families in colonial history are included, and some of the most notable men of early New England. The following ancestry can show, from necessary limitations of space, but a partial list of these; various other lines can be easily traced.

(1) Captain Roger Dudley, the first member of this family about whom we have definite information, was born in England about 1550; it is probable that he was killed at the battle of Ivry, in 1590. Children: Thomas, of whom further; at least one daughter.

(II) Thomas, only son of Captain Roger Dudley, the immigrant, was born in Northamptonshire, England, in 1576, and died at Roxbury, Massachusetts, July 31, 1653. In England he was a page in the family of William Lord Compton, afterward Earl of Northampton, and later steward to the Earl of Lincoln. With Winthrop and a party of four vessels he came in 1630 to America on the *Arabella,* sailing April 8, arriving June 12. He settled first at Cambridge, removed to Ipswich, and finally resided at Roxbury. In May, 1634, he was elected governor to succeed Winthrop, and was re-elected in 1640, 1646 and 1650. For thirteen years he was deputy-governor, and for five years assistant. He was one of twelve men appointed by the general court in 1636 to establish Harvard College, and he signed its charter in 1650. In March, 1644, he was appointed sergeant major-general of the colony, being the first to hold this position; he held it for four years. He married (first) Dorothy, daughter of Edmund Yorke, who was born in Northamptonshire, England, in 1582, and died at Roxbury, December 27, 1643; (second) Catherine (Dighton) Hackburn, who died August 29, 1671. She married (first) Samuel Hackburn, (third) Rev. John Allen. Children, six first named by first, others by second, wife: Rev. Samuel, born 1610, died February 10, 1683, married (first) Mary Winthrop, (second) Mary Byley, (third) Elizabeth ———; Anne, of whom further; Patience, born 1615, died February 8, 1689-90, married, October 18, 1632, Daniel Denison; Sarah, baptized July 23, 1620, died 1659, married (first) Benjamin Keane, (second) Thomas Pacy; Mercy, born September 27, 1621, died July 1, 1691, married Rev. John Woodbridge; Dorothy, died February 27, 1643; Deborah, born February 27, 1645, died November 1, 1683; Joseph, born September 23, 1647, died April 2, 1720, married Rebecca

Tyng; Paul, born September 8, 1650, died December 1, 1681, married Mary Leverett.

(III) Anne, daughter of Governor Thomas and Dorothy (Yorke) Dudley, was born in England, about 1612, and died September 16, 1672. She married, in England, in 1628, Simon, son of Rev. Simon and Margaret Bradstreet, who was baptized at Horbling, Lincolnshire, England, March 18, 1603-04, and died March 27, 1697. He matriculated at an English college, but did not finish his course, perhaps on account of his father's death. He came to America with Governor Winthrop in the *Arabella.* He was one of the founders of Newtown, now Cambridge. For a while he resided probably at Salem, certainly, at Ipswich, removing in 1648 to Andover, where he was one of the first settlers and the leading citizen. Among his important offices and functions were these: secretary of colony, from 1630-34; one of the commissioners of the united colonies, in 1643. In 1653 he successfully opposed a projected war on the Dutch and Indians. He was a commissioner with regard to the boundary between New Amsterdam and New Haven in 1650, and the next year a commissioner concerning the jurisdiction of Massachusetts over York and Kittery, Maine. About 1662 he went to England to answer charges against the colony. He was deputy governor 1673-79; he was assistant fifty years together. From 1679 he was governor of the colony until the dissolution of the charter in May, 1686. Although then almost ninety years old, he was active in resisting Andros; and when Andros was imprisoned he took charge of the government. The old charter was restored and he was governor of Massachusetts and New Hampshire until May, 1692. The general court, in consideration of his long and extraordinary service, voted £100 toward defraying the expenses of his interment. He was buried in the Charter burying ground at Salem. His wife, Anne (Dudley), was the first American poetess. Her poems were first published in London in 1650; a second edition was brought out in Boston in 1678. Among her descendants have been William Ellery Channing, Oliver Wendell Holmes, Richard H. Dana and Wendell Phillips. Governor Bradstreet married (second) Ann (Downing) Gardner, who married (first) Joseph Gardner. Children, all by first wife: Samuel, of whom further; Dorothy, died February 26, 1672, married, June 25, 1654, Rev. Seaborn Cotton; Sarah, married (first) Richard Hubbard, (second) Samuel Ward; Rev. Simon, born 1638 or 1640, married, October 2, 1667, Lucy Woodbridge; Hannah, died 1707, married, June 14, 1659, Andrew Wiggin;

Mercy, born about 1647, died October 5, 1715, married, October 31, 1672, Nathaniel Wade; Dudley, born 1648, died November 13, 1702, married Ann (Wood) Price; John, born July 22, 1652, died January 11, 1718, married, June 11, 1677, Sarah Perkins.

(IV) Samuel, son of Governor Simon and Anne (Dudley) Bradstreet, died in August, 1682. He graduated in 1653 from Harvard. He was a physician in Boston. From 1657 to 1661 he was in England. He removed to the island of Jamaica, and there died. He married (first) Mercy, daughter of William Tyng, (second) Martha ———. By his first wife he had five children, the three children of his second wife were living with their grandfather, Governor Bradstreet, at the time of the latter's death. Among these children were: Elizabeth, born January 29, 1663; Annice, November 17, 1665; Mercy, of whom further.

(V) Mercy, daughter of Dr. Samuel and Mercy (Tyng) Bradstreet, was born November 20, 1667. She married Dr. James, son of Peter and Sarah (Newdigate) Oliver, who was born March 19, 1659. He lived in Cambridge.

(VI) Sarah, daughter of Dr. James and Mercy (Bradstreet) Oliver, married, in Boston, August 12, 1714, Jacob, son of Johannes and Elizabeth (Staats) Wendell, who was baptized at Albany, New York, August 11, 1691. Coming to Boston in his youth, he had entered the counting-house of John Mico, a well-known merchant. He afterward entered business on his own account, and became one of the most prominent citizens of that day. From 1737 to 1760 he was of His Majesty's council; in 1735 and 1745 he was commander of the Ancient and Honorable Artillery. He was in 1733 director of the first banking institution in the province. Children: Jacob (2), of whom further; Mercy, born June 22, 1717; Elizabeth, January 20, 1718; Sarah, March 3, 1720, married Rev. Dr. Abiel Holmes, was mother of Oliver Wendell Holmes; Mercy, born April 10, 1722; Mary, January 14, 1723; Katharine, June 17, 1726; John Mico, May 31, 1728, married Katharine ———; Ann, December 7, 1730; Oliver, March 5, 1733, married, 1762, Mary Jackson; Abraham, born November 2, 1735, whose youngest child, Margaret, married William Phillips, and was grandmother of Wendell Phillips; one other daughter.

(VII) Jacob (2), son of Jacob (1) and Sarah (Oliver) Wendell, was born September 4, 1715. He married, in Boston, December 9, 1736, Elizabeth Hunt. She married (second), at Windham, Maine, August 12, 1766, Rev.

Thomas Smith, father of her daughter's husband, her son-in-law officiating.

(VIII) Elizabeth, daughter of Jacob (2) and Elizabeth (Hunt) Wendell, was born about 1742, and died October 16, 1799. She married, in Boston, October 8, 1765, Rev. Peter Thacher, son of Rev. Thomas and Sarah (Tyng) Smith, who was born June 14, 1731, and died October 26, 1826. He graduated from Harvard in 1753. After teaching school several years he became pastor of the church at New Marblehead, now Windham, Maine, September 22, 1762. He was dismissed from the charge in 1790, but continued to reside at Windham and to be prominent both in the church and in the town. He married a second time, but had no children by this marriage. Children: Elizabeth Hunt, born August 17, 1766; Sarah, April 9, 1768; Lucy, of whom further; Thomas, born October 2, 1770, died February 27, 1802; John Tyng, born March 6, 1772; Mary, July 6, 1774; Peter, November 6, 1775, died November 9, 1775; Ann Wendell, born March 28, 1777; Rebecca, June 15, 1778, died April 19, 1782; Susanna Wendell, born March 31, 1780; Rebecca, September 25, 1783, died October 31, 1808.

(IX) Lucy, daughter of Rev. Peter Thacher and Elizabeth (Wendell) Smith, was born August 24, 1769, and died April 17, 1844. She married, April 13, 1788, Abraham, son of Abraham and Ann (Collins-Cloutman) Anderson, who was born June 18, 1758, and died September 3, 1844. His father was one of the leading men of New Marblehead. Children: Peter Smith, baptized May 17, 1789, married Susan ———; John, born October 8, 1791; John, of whom further; Betsy, born November 19, 1795; Edward, born September 3, 1802; Abraham, born September 18, 1805.

(X) Hon. John Anderson, son of Abraham and Lucy (Smith) Anderson, married Ann Williams Jameson.

(XI) General Samuel Jameson, son of Hon. John and Lucy (Smith) Anderson, lived in Portland, Maine. He married Jane Wade, daughter of John and Sarah (Brooks-Wade) Dow. Child: Jeanie Campbell, born in Portland, Maine, January 8, 1852, married December 8, 1886, Charles Frederick Mathewson, of whom above.

(The Dow Line).

The surname Dow first occurs in the Hundred Roll of the thirteenth century at the time surnames were coming into use in England. It is undoubtedly derived from the Scotch word Dhu, signifying black. The ancestors who adopted the surname were probably of a swarthy complexion, or living in a place popularly known as a "black" region. Such members of the family as came early to England, in the southern counties, were called "Dove" by the people who spoke Norman-French, and this pronunciation and its written form gave rise to the design of doves upon the coats-of-arms of various branches of the family, a custom known as canting in heraldry. The Dutch "Douw" is the same name, probably having the same origin. From John Dow, of Tylner, county Norfolk, England, born July 7-25, 1561, the immigrant to America, Thomas Dow, is believed to have descended.

(I) Thomas Dow, the immigrant ancestor, was born in England, and was among the early settlers of Newbury, Massachusetts. He was admitted a freeman June 22, 1635. He bought a house and land at Newbury in 1648. Afterward he removed to Haverhill. He married Phebe ———. He died May 31, 1654. His will was dated May 29, 1654, and proved April 8, 1656, bequeathing to wife Phebe, sons John, Thomas, Stephen (mentioned below), Mary and Martha, all under age Children, born at Newbury: Stephen, mentioned below; Mary, April 26, 1644; Martha, June 1, 1648.

(II) Stephen, son of Thomas Dow, was born at Newbury, March 29, 1642, and died at Haverhill, July 3, 1717. He was admitted a freeman of Haverhill in 1668. He married Ann Story. He was selectman in 1685; grand juror in 1692. He and his son were in the Sixth garrison in 1697, and his daughter Martha was killed by Indians. Children, born at Haverhill: Ruhamah, February 24, 1663; Samuel, January 22, 1665; Hannah, July 1, 1668; Stephen, mentioned below; Martha, April 1, 1673; John, July 13, 1675.

(III) Stephen (2), son of Stephen (1) Dow, was born at Haverhill, September 18, 1670. He was with his father in the Haverhill garrison in 1697, when his sister and twenty-six others were slain by Indians. He married Mary Hutchins. Children, born at Haverhill: Timothy, September 4, 1698; Nathaniel, mentioned below; Mary, April 18, 1701; Elizabeth, February 29, 1703-04; Richard, February 15, 1705-06; David, December 25, 1714; Jonathan, September 11, 1718; Stephen, October 13, 1722.

(IV) Nathaniel, son of Stephen (2) Dow, was born at Haverhill, August 11, 1699. He married Mary Hendrick. Children, born at Haverhill: Daniel, June 28, 1728; James, September 2, 1731; Amos, March 12, 1734-35; Jeremiah, mentioned below.

(V) Jeremiah, son of Nathaniel Dow, was born at Haverhill, Massachusetts, March 14, 1737-38. He lived at what is now Salem, New Hampshire. He was first in the Provincial

service at Crown Point in 1762 in the French and Indian war; afterward he was in Captain Dearborn's company, Colonel Stark's regiment, and in Captain Henry Elkin's company, enlisted for the defense of Piscataqua harbor in the revolution, November, 1775. He was captain of a company in 1776, and in Lieutenant-Colonel Welsh's regiment at the battle of Bennington and at the surrender of General Burgoyne. The family possesses papers relating to Captain Dow, dated 1758, a lieutenant's commission under George III, and a captain's commission granted for some act of bravery by the Continental Congress during the revolution were preserved, together with a stirring letter from his commanding officer in the revolution urging him to enlist more men, but were lost or stolen from the Polytechnic Institute of Louisville, Kentucky, where they were deposited by one of the Dow family for safe-keeping while he was living at Louisville. Jeremiah Dow married, at Bradford, Massachusetts, May 1, 1766, Lydia Kimball, a descendant of Richard Kimball, the pioneer. She was born at Bradford, March 8, 1749, and died March 12, 1826. They had seven children.

(VI) Aquila, fifth child of Jeremiah Dow, was born at Salem, New Hampshire, April 23, 1771; married, June 25, 1794, Delia Dow. They had seven children.

(VII) John Dow, son of Aquila Dow, was born April 17, 1799; married Sarah (Brooks) Wade, of Medford, Massachusetts, a grandniece of Governor John Brooks, of Massachusetts. They had six children. Their eldest, Jane Wade, married Samuel Jameson Anderson, of Portland, Maine, and their youngest child, Susan Jameson Anderson, married Frank Eliot Sweetser, and their eldest, Jeanie Campbell Anderson, married Charles F. Mathewson, of New York. (See Mathewson VII.)

KINGSLEY Stephen Kingsley, the immigrant ancestor, settled first in Braintree, Massachusetts, as early as 1637, coming from England. Many of his descendants because of the prejudices of the revolutionary period against the word "King," have followed the spelling Kinsley. John Kingsley, of Dorchester; Richard and Roger Kingsley also, are believed to be descended of Stephen Kingsley, who was a proprietor of the town of Braintree, and was admitted a freeman May 13, 1640. He removed to the adjacent town of Dorchester, and bought half of the Hutchinson farm, February 23, 1656. Returning to Braintree, he sold his land in Milton, formerly Dorchester, May 11.

1670. He was an elder of the church, and a deputy to the general court. His will, dated at Milton, May 27, 1673, and proved July 3, 1675, bequeathed to his son John, sons-in-law Henry Crane (ancestor of United States Senator Crane), Anthony Gollifer and Robert Mason; to the three children of his son Samuel, to the son at the age of twenty-one and the daughters at the age of eighteen. He married Elizabeth ———. Children: Samuel, mentioned below; John, daughter, married Henry Crane, born at Braintree, August 30, 1640; daughter, married Anthony Gollifer; daughter, married Robert Mason; Mary.

(II) Samuel, son of Stephen Kingsley, was born in England, probably about 1636, died May 22, 1662, before his father. He lived at Milton, Massachusetts. He married Hannah, daughter of Captain Richard and Alice Brackett. Children, named in the will of their grandfather, Stephen Kingsley; Samuel, mentioned below; two daughters.

(III) Samuel (2), son of Samuel (1) Kingsley, was born at Braintree or Dorchester, August 16, 1662, died December 17, 1713, at Easton, Massachusetts. His estate was divided in 1722, when the youngest son, Benjamin, came of age. He lived in South Bridgewater, Massachusetts, where he bought the Jeduthan Robbins place, adjoining that of Thomas Washburn. After he settled in Easton. He married Mary, daughter of John Washburn, who died at Easton, February 28, 1740. Children, probably born at Easton: Samuel, mentioned below; Hannah, married, February 2, 1714, Edward Hayward; Sarah, married, 1715, Josiah Hayward; Mary, married, 1716, Thomas Willis; Susannah, married, 1729, Samuel Packard; Abigail, married, 1728, William Hayward; Bethia, married, 1732, William Brett; Benjamin, born in Easton, died in 1759, married (first) Priscilla Manley, (second) a Widow Perkins.

(IV) Samuel (3), son of Samuel (2) Kingsley, was born in Bridgewater, Massachusetts, about 1690. He settled early at Easton, where his homestead is described as west of the Littlefield place, near the railroad, southeast of Cranberry Meadow. Afterward he removed to Norwich, Connecticut. In 1741 he and his wife, then of Norwich, deeded land in Bridgewater to their "brother," Joseph Packard, of Bridgewater, son of John Packard. This deed identifies this Samuel Kingsley completely. John Packard was a son of Samuel and Elizabeth Packard, the former of whom died at Bridgewater in 1684. John Packard, father of Mary, wife of Samuel Kingsley, married Judith, daughter of John and Judith Winslow, and granddaughter of John and Mary (Chilton) Winslow. Mary Chilton came with her parents, James and Mary Chilton, in the "Mayflower." John Winslow came in the ship "Fortune," in 1621, to Plymouth. All the descendants of Samuel and Mary (Packard) Kingsley are eligible to the Mayflower Society. Children of Samuel and Mary (Packard) Kingsley, born at Easton: Nathan, March 6, 1715, married Betty Dunbar; Samuel, December 12, 1716, died in Worcester, on his way from Deerfield to his family in Bridgewater, September 25, 1773, married Sophia White; Mary, February 28, 1719; John, May 20, 1721, married Thankful Washburn, settled in Charlemont, Massachusetts; Hannah, January 3, 1724, Amos, March 26, 1726; Silence, August 30, 1727; Daniel, mentioned below.

(V) Daniel, son of Samuel (3) Kingsley, was born at Easton, Massachusetts, August 25, 1731. He went with his parents to Norwich, Connecticut, about 1746. In 1756 he deeded land in Norwich. He sold land there, December 29, 1761, and with wife and four children located in Charlemont, Hampden county, Massachusetts, where he became a prominent citizen. In 1770 he was one of the largest property owners in Charlemont, as the tax list shows. The others were Othniel Taylor and Aaron Rice. He married, at Norwich, February 15, 1753; Eunice, daughter of Joseph and Ruth (Post) Bingham. Children, born in Norwich: Stephen, December 6, 1753; Hannah, May 13, 1756; Lois, December 9, 1758; Samuel, February 19, 1761. Born at Charlemont: Daniel, April 22, 1764; Nathan, mentioned below; John. Daniel Kingsley and his sons Stephen, Daniel and Nathan, served in the revolutionary war.

(VI) Nathan, son of Daniel Kingsley, was born in Charlemont, about 1765. He removed with his father and brothers to Bennington, Vermont, about 1780. Daniel Sr. and Daniel Jr. drew land in Cambridge, Vermont, now Chittenden county, August 28, 1783. Daniel Sr. had lot No. 1; Daniel Jr. lot No. 44, and Stephen lot No. 47. In 1790 there were three heads of family of this surname in Cambridge, Nathan and his brothers, Stephen and Daniel. Nathan had in his family three males over sixteen, of whom two were doubtless brothers, one son under sixteen, and three females. Stephen had three males over sixteen, three under that age and four females. Daniel had one female. Nathan Kingsley was one of the prisoners' guard under Lieutenant Joseph Wickwire at the schoolhouse in Bennington, 1781. He was also in Captain Peleg Matteson's company, marching to the northward in 1781 (pp. 423-519). Vermont Revolutionary

Rolls). He married Lydia Pearl. Children: Hiram, Pearl, Nathan, mentioned below; Lydia, born 1797, married —— Aycox.

(VII) Nathan (2), son of Nathan (1) Kingsley, was born in North Hero, Vermont, in 1791. He married, in 1816, Lois Hazen, who was born at North Hero, Vermont. Children: Lavinia, born in 1817, married Jed Martin; Fessenden G., 1819, married Mary A. Parks; Madeleine, 1821; Lydia, 1823; Hiram Pearl, mentioned below; Diadama, 1827, married Dan Hazen; Diana, 1829, married Alson Wheeler; Darwin, 1832, married Martha Bell; Laura, 1835, married Dan Hazen; Rosina, 1838, married William McGregor; Cecelia, 1840, married William H. Babcock.

(VIII) Hiram Pearl, son of Nathan (2) Kingsley, was born in Alburgh, Vermont, April 26, 1825, died November 30, 1882. He married Celia Permilla La Due, born at Alburgh, in 1831, now (1912) living at Burlington, Vermont, daughter of Abraham and Permilla (Ames) La Due, of French Huguenot ancestry. Her brother, Phineas, is now (1912) living at Alburgh. Children of Mr. and Mrs. Kingsley: Flora Ann, born 1853, married (first) S. C. Dodds, (second) W. W. Sawyer; Darwin Pearl, mentioned below; Lena, 1859, married J. A. Dodds; Naomi, 1864, married W. W. Sawyer; Emmett E., 1868, died 1874.

(IX) Darwin Pearl, son of Hiram Pearl Kingsley was born at Alburgh, Vermont, May 5, 1857. His boyhood was spent on his father's modest farm, bordering on Lake Champlain, and like the other boys of the neighborhood he received his early education in the district schools of his native town during the winter terms. He was the prize scholar of his school district, however, and when he was examined by the county superintendent for a certificate as a teacher he met with no difficulty. But instead of teaching school he determined to have a college education, and in order to prepare he went to the academy at Barre, Vermont, of which Dr. J. S. Spaulding was then principal. He could expect but little assistance from his father, and he depended upon his own exertions to pay his way. He worked at various occupations out of school hours, taught school in winter and worked at farming in summer, and to save expenses boarded himself. He managed thus to get through the preparatory school and won distinction for scholarship. Where the money was to be found for his college expenses he did not know, but again he succeeded in providing for himself. A good friend offered to lend him small sums of money, from time to time, providing Mr. Kingsley would take out a policy of insurance on his

life for one thousand dollars, stating that while he was perfectly willing to trust him to repay the loans, he wanted to be protected against the contingency of death. This was probably the first time that life insurance had been brought to the attention of Mr. Kingsley, and this policy, which meant a liberal education to him, when he wanted it more than anything else, doubtless had an influence upon his subsequent career in the life insurance business. By economies similar to those that he exercised in the academy, Mr. Kingsley completed his freshman year with a total outlay of $165 for college bills, books, clothing, board, and during the second year he spent but ten dollars more. During his junior and senior years his financial circumstances were better, and he was enabled to live more as other college boys lived and to enter more into the life of the institution. He was elected to the Phi Beta Kappa of the University of Vermont, and competed in the first contest in oratory in 1878, winning the first prize. That competition is now known as the "Kingsley Prize Speaking," and is a regular feature of commencement week at his alma mater. He was graduated in the class of 1881 with the degree of Bachelor of Arts.

Immediately after graduation he went to Denver, Colorado, but not liking the city for a home, he went further and located in what is now the city of Grand Junction, Colorado. At that time it was a settlement of tents and log huts, and the Ute Indians had but recently taken themselves out of the Valley of the Grand to their reservation in Utah. In 1882, after a few weeks in Grand Junction, he purchased an interest in The News, which is now the leading newspaper in that section of the state. The newspaper brought him into public life, and two years later he was elected a delegate from Colorado to the Republican national convention which nominated James G. Blaine for president. In 1886 he was nominated on the Republican ticket for state auditor and was elected, being also ex-officio state superintendent of insurance in 1887-88. As an editor Mr. Kingsley had all the experience peculiar to the management of a frontier newspaper. In standing for what he thought was right in politics and in local government, he had to defend himself not only with pen and voice, but with his fists.

At the end of his term as state auditor he had another important decision to make. He had intended to study law and expected to have time for reading law while holding this office, but he found that the conscientious performance of his official duties occupied all his time. As superintendent of insurance he

i—6

came into contact with insurance men and thus acquired an inside knowledge of the business. Various life insurance companies offered opportunities to him, and in the end he gave up the ambition to become a lawyer to engage in business in the service of the company of which he is now president. In January, 1889, he took his family to Boston, and in the language of life insurance men began with the rate book, then managed an office, then had charge of the business in several states. Upon the election of John A. McCall as president of the New York Life Insurance Company, Mr. Kingsley came to New York City to take charge of the agency department under George W. Perkins. In this department he made a remarkable record in securing new business and increasing the efficiency of the agents, especially from 1892 to 1905. The agents were brought together in clubs and conventions for conference and instruction.

At banquets and conventions the ability of Mr. Kingsley as a speaker was of inestimable value. He preached life insurance with a zeal and enthusiasm that inspired his men. A volume of his addresses was issued by the company some years ago under the title, "The First Business of the World." An additional volume entitled, "Militant Life Insurance," was issued in 1911. Incidentally he became widely known among the agents in the field, and he won a reputation for uprightness and fair dealing, as well as for energy, thoroughness and executive ability. He was made superintendent of agencies, then third vice-president, then vice-president of the company. Since 1901 he has devoted most of his time to the financial department. He began to attend the meetings of the finance committee, and early in 1905 was made a member of the committee. From the beginning of 1906 until he was elected president, June 17, 1907, he had sole charge of mortgages on real estate and of the real estate of the company. Under his administration the New York Life Insurance Company has maintained its leadership, enjoying rapid growth and the public confidence, notwithstanding the assaults made upon it and other great life insurance companies. He was called before the Armstrong committee in the investigation by the state and came through the ordeal without criticism.

Mr. Kingsley is a director of the Citizens' National Bank of New York, National Surety Company, New York Trust Company, Louisville & Nashville Railroad Company and member of the New York Chamber of Commerce, New York Society Sons of the Revolution, Vermont Society of New York, Tuna Club (California), American Museum of Natural History, Burns Society, St. Andrews Golf Club, University Club, Union League Club of New York, Sleepy Hollow Country Club, National Golf Links, Lake Champlain Association, Hobby Club, New England Society. In religion he is a Unitarian, but not a church member. His wife was brought up in the Roman Catholic faith, and his children attend the Presbyterian church. His home is at Riverdale-on-the-Hudson.

Mr. Kingsley has always found time for out-door recreation and athletics. In college he was a football and baseball player. He is a member of the famous Tuna Club, and in his rooms at No. 346 Broadway has a fine specimen of tuna caught with rod and reel at Catalina Islands, California. Since about 1895 he has played golf at every opportunity. His library indicates his fondness for good books, and he is something of a collector. He has all four of the Shakespeare folios, including three of the 1632 folio and other Shakespereana of interest. He has also a small collection of first editions of Tennyson and Dickens. He has been a trustee of the University of Vermont since 1897.

Mr. Kingsley married (first), June 19, 1884, Mary M., born November, 1863, died August 21, 1890, daughter of Ossian and Susan T. (Walton) Mitchell, of Burlington, Vermont. He married (second), December 3, 1895, Josephine I. McCall, born in Albany, New York, March 14, 1873, daughter of John A. McCall. Child by first wife: Walton Pearl, born in Colorado, August 10, 1886; graduate of the University of Vermont (1910). Children of second wife: Hope, born November 3, 1897; Darwin Pearl Jr., June 15, 1899; John McCall, February 28, 1903; Lois, August 3, 1905.

When surnames were generally WAITT introduced into England in the eleventh century those who held an office, in most cases, added its designation to their Christian names; thus Richard, the minstrel-watchman, became Richard le Wayte, afterward contracted to Richard Wayte. The name has since been spelled Wayt, Wayght, Waight, Wait, Waitt, Weight, Waiet, etc. The word is derived from the old high German, wahten, to keep watch; and is common in this sense of guard, or watchman, to all the Teutonic languages; the German wacht, Dutch vaght, Swedish wakt and English watch. When used as a verb its meaning is "to stay in expectation of;" as a noun it denotes "a minstrel watchman." The original Waytes were found in England immediately after the Norman Conquest, only among the retainers of the kings, princes and great barons; but their rank gradually degenerated with that of the other orders of minstrels until the name was applied only to those itinerant musicians who, in most of the large towns of England, go around the principal streets at night, for some time before Christmas, playing popular tunes, calling the hour and expecting a gratuity. These are the "Christmas waits," or wandering melodists.

In A. D. 1075, William the Conqueror gave the earldom, city and castle of Norwich, in England, to Ralf de Waiet, son of Ralf, an Englishman, by a Welsh woman; Ralf de Waiet married Emma, sister of Roger, Earl of Hereford, cousin of the Conqueror. This is the earliest record found in regard to the family and the source from which all by the same name seem to trace their origin, down through Ricardus le Wayte of the county of Warwick, a lineal descendant. Thereafter the name was written Wayte almost exclusively until different persons of the name came to New England, when the forms Waite or Wait were generally used. The kindred were pretty freely distributed throughout the central portion of southern England, extending to northern Wales, the land from which the progenitors of the present family came to the New World. The arms of the family are as follows: Argent, chevron gules between three bugle horns, stringed, sable, borne by the name Wayte; crest, a bugle horn, stringed, sable, garnished. Motto: Pro aris et focis (For our homes and altars). The bugle portrays the musical element of the family and tends to support the tradition that the original Waytes were musician attendants upon the king and his knights.

The earliest settlers of this name in America were three brothers, cousins of the regicide judge, Thomas Wayte: Richard, born in 1596; Gamaliel, born in 1598, and Thomas, born in 1601, who came over from Wales or south England in the year 1634, and landed at Plymouth, Massachusetts. The two eldest settled first in Plymouth and then Boston, while the youngest, Thomas, went on to Rhode Island, settling at Portsmouth, all of them leaving descendants. Another early settler of the name was John, son of Samuel Wayte, of Wethersfield, England, who came over about 1638, and was one of the first settlers of Malden, Massachusetts. He attained great influence in the community, and with Joseph Hills, his father-in-law, bore the highest honors and responsibilities in the town from the time of its incorporation; his name is perpetuated in "Wayte's Mount." He left a son, Samuel, who inherited house and lands, and who in turn left descendants. Other early settlers of

this name were: Richard, born 1608, of Watertown, Massachusetts, 1637; Thomas, of Ipswich, 1658; Alexander, of Boston, 1637; George, of Providence, 1646; John, of Windsor, Connecticut, 1649, and Benjamin, of Hatfield, 1663; the latter having been a famous Indian fighter and finally killed by them.

These all became prominent in the history of the colonies, and many were soldiers and officers in the war of the revolution; in later days descendants of these early progenitors have become conspicuous in the history of the country and in public affairs, the name being found in all professions and in all walks in life, especially in legal ranks, where they are among the first citizens of the state.

(I) Among these descendants was Samuel Waitt, of Barnstable, Massachusetts, grandfather of Arthur M. Waitt; he was a chocolate manufacturer in Boston. He married Persis Hallett, whose father flew the first Seamen's "Bethel Flag" in the world.

(II) Robert Mitchell, son of Samuel Waitt, was born in Rhode Island, in August, 1824, died May 7, 1900. He was a sea captain in early life and later became inspector of United States customs at Boston, Massachusetts. He married Ellen, born December 7, 1831, died August 11, 1911, daughter of Captain Mathias and Mary (Cobb) Hinckley, of Barnstable, Massachusetts, and a descendant of Governor Thomas Hinckley, of Massachusetts Colony.

(III) Arthur Manning, son of Robert Mitchell and Ellen (Hinckley) Waitt, was born in East Boston, Massachusetts, October 24, 1858. He was educated in the public schools of East Boston and the English High School of Boston, and in 1875 he entered the Massachusetts Institute of Technology, one of the best technical schools in the country, graduating in 1879 at this institution, obtaining the degree of S. B. in mechanical engineering. He at once entered the railway service and until 1881 was draughtsman in the car and locomotive department of the Chicago, Burlington & Quincy Railroad; from that date to 1882 he was draughtsman in the car and locomotive department of the Eastern Railroad, and from then until 1884 chief draughtsman of the locomotive department of the same road. From 1884 to 1887 he was general foreman of the car department of this railroad; and from 1887 to February 1, 1889, was assistant master car builder of the Boston & Maine Railroad. From February 1, 1889, to October, 1889, he was assistant manager of the Pullman Car Works, and from that date to October, 1892, he was assistant general master car builder of the Lake Shore & Michigan Southern Railway. He then became general master car builder of the same road, continuing until April, 1899; from then until March, 1903, he was superintendent of the motive power and rolling stock of the New York Central & Hudson River Railroad. From September, 1903, to January, 1905, he traveled in Europe and the United States studying electric traction; from January, 1905, to date he has been consulting engineer and specialist in New York City, and is now (1912) president of the Standard Third Rail Company, at No. 165 Broadway, New York City.

He is a member and former vice-president of the American Society of Mechanical Engineers; former member and president of the American Railway Master Mechanics' Association; former president and member of the Western and Central Railroad Club; member of the American Institute of Electrical Engineers, and of the Master Car Builders' Association. He is also a member of the following clubs: Machinery, Transportation, Engineers, Technology and the New York Railroad. He has taken all the degrees in Free Masonry up to and including the thirty-second degree, and is a member of the Lake Erie Consistory; Iris Lodge, Free and Accepted Masons, Cleveland, Ohio; Webb Chapter, Royal Arch Masons, Cleveland, Ohio, and of the Oriental Commandery, Knights Templar.

Mr. Waitt married (first), in Boston, October 20, 1886, Maude, born in Canada, January 20, 1865, daughter of Roscoe and Sarah Gleason. He had one child by this marriage, Weymer Hinckley Waitt, born in Boston, September 7, 1887. The son was educated in the public schools of Cleveland, Ohio, and at MacKenzie private school at Dobbs Ferry, New York, and subsequently spent a year in study at the Massachusetts Institute of Technology, in Boston; also one year at Columbia University. He married Frances C. W. Haines, of New York City, and has no children. Mr. Waitt married (second) in New York City, April 6, 1906, Mrs. Anna S. Milbury, widow of Dr. Frank S. Milbury, of Brooklyn. She was born in Breslau, Germany, April 1, 1867, and is the daughter of Adolph Schoeps. Mr. Waitt has no children by his second marriage. He has a handsome residence in Sharon, Connecticut.

POST

The Post family is of ancient German origin. As early as A. D. 980 we find among the conquerors of Nettelburg, later known as Shaumburg, Herren Von Post, and in 1030 Adolph Post was a member of the Reichstag of Minden. From the local name Von Post doubtless came the surname Post, for in the same town, Ludwig and Heinrich Post, in 1273, appear as witnesses to a deed, and this Heinrich was progenitor of a prominent German family.

(I) Goossen Post, a descendant of Heinrich Post, and from whom the American family is traced by the family historian in an unbroken line, is mentioned in 1376 as one of the anzienlijkste Arnhemsche burgers. Arnheim is in that part of Netherlands called Gelderland. He had wife, Jantje, daughter of Peter and Jane (Rapalje) Van Zul. They had sons: Peter, mentioned below; George.

(II) Peter Post, son of Goossen Post, owned land in 1399 in or near Elspet, and is thought to have married Annatie, daughter of George and Else (Meyers) Suydam, of Zwolle. Children: Peter Arnold, mentioned below; George, said to have emigrated to England and to have settled in county Kent about 1473, and his will was filed at Canterbury, 1502; Jan.

(III) Peter Arnold Van Der Poest, son of Peter Post, is given in the Post Genealogy as son of Peter, and his birth year as 1500, but it is probable that some generations were missed in the search. Goossen Post must have been born about 1325 to be a city officer in 1376, and his son Peter, who owned land in 1399, was born, say as early as 1365. Peter Arnold would be, according to this reckoning, over a hundred years younger than his father. Peter Arnold married Marragrietje, daughter of Jan Bogert, and had sons: Jan, whose daughter Sarah married in Maidstone, Kent, September 15, 1607, Isaac Clark, or Clerk; Panwell, mentioned below.

(IV) Panwell Van Der Poest, son of Peter Arnold Van Der Poest, married, February 7, 1571, Susannah, daughter of Abraham Van Gelder. Children, baptized at the Dutch Church, Austin Friars, London: Abraham, October 6, 1573; Sarah, same date; Susanna, January 18, 1578; Jan, November 5, 1579; Arthur, mentioned below.

(V) Arthur Post, son of Panwell Van Der Poest, was baptized August 26, 1580. He married, February 2, 1614, in Maidstone, Kent, Bennet, daughter of Richard Lambe. That he was the father of the American pioneer, Richard, is deduced from a "deed" dated June 14, 1644, "being of grete age Arthur Post gives to my cousin Richard Van Mulken; my second son Stephen and his wife Margaret; lands, tenements and hereditaments in Estling, formerly in the possession of my eldest son Richard, being now of New England, or some parts beyond the seas. Panwell, my younger son, to have my wearing ap-

parel." (Phillips Coll. Mss. in Mulken Gen.
Mss. XXII, 4). This must mean will, not a
deed in the proper sense of the word.

(VI) Richard Post, immigrant ancestor,
son of Arthur Post, of England, is said by the
genealogy and other authorities to have settled
first at Lynn, Massachusetts. Richard Post
or Poast, lived at Lynn and Woburn, Massachusetts, it is true, and was a taxpayer in 1643.
But we have record that he married in Lynn
or Woburn, February 27, 1649-50, Susanna
Sutton, and that in the same locality a Richard
Post married, November 18, 1662, Mary Tyler. The records seem to show, however, that
Richard Post went with the pioneers from
Lynn to Southampton, Long Island. He shared
in every division of the common land, and
from 1643 to 1687 he was prominent in the
records of the town. It is true that he may
have returned to Lynn for two wives, but it is
not known that the Southampton man had
any other wife than Dorothy (given in some
works as Johnson). He was constable, marshal, magistrate, lieutenant, commissioner to
treat with the Indians, on a committee to settle a dispute between the town and Captain
Topping, patentee under Governor Andros'
patent. The original homestead of Post was
on the east side of Main street and has lately
been owned by Captain Charles Howells and
Henry Post. Before he died he deeded land
to his sons, John and Joseph Post, daughter
Martha, wife of Benjamin Foster, and grandson, Benjamin Foster Jr., April 17, 1688. He
died in 1689. Children: Martha, married Benjamin Foster; Joseph, was in business in Talbot county, Maryland, in 1675, returned to
Southampton and died there November 10,
1721, aged about seventy-one years, leaving
a will; John, mentioned below.

(VII) Captain John Post, son of Lieutenant Richard Post, was born about 1650, doubtless at Southampton. He was progenitor of
all the Post families of eastern Long Island;
Montrose and Honesdale, Pennsylvania; Palmyra and Newburg, New York, and California. The homestead of Captain John Post, bequeathed to his son, Captain John Post, was
on the east side of Main street, Southampton,
and the railroad station occupies part of it at
present. He was one of the purchasers of the
house and lot bought for and dedicated to the
use of a Presbyterian parsonage "forever,"
and the property is still owned by the church.
His will was dated December 9, 1687, and
proved at Southampton, March 21, 1687-88,
bequeathing to five sons and three daughters,
homestall, close at the head of the creek, a
fifty-pound commonage, the house and home
lot formerly his father's, the close that was

his father's between the Mill path and Cobb's
Pound path, close at Long Springs and his
fifty-pound allotment at Mecox; land at Hog
Neck, west of Canoe place and in Great place.
He died in 1687. He married, in 1671, Mary
————. Children: Mary, Captain John, men-
tioned below; Jeremiah, settled in Hempstead;
Sarah; Dorothy, Martha, Deborah, Richard,
lived at Hempstead, became a Friend.

(VIII) Captain John (2) Post, son of Captain John (1) Post, was born in 1673, at Southampton, died there in 1741. In 1690, when he
was about seventeen years old, he was trading
land, and in 1692 he was buying and selling
land and his name was on the tax list. In 1712
he was a trustee and proprietor and purchased
for the town the North End Burying Ground
in which his Uncle Joseph was the first man
buried. From 1714 to 1739 he was many times
elected to public office, serving as trustee, collector of taxes, assessor, commissioner on disputed boundaries and captain of the military
company (as shown by the records at Albany).
He died in 1741. He married Mary Halsey.
Children: John, born 1700, died 1792, married Abigail Halsey; Joseph, born 1704, died
1780; Isaac, mentioned below.

(IX) Isaac, son of Captain John (2) Post,
was born in 1712, died May 8, 1785. He married Mary Jessup, and among his children was
Isaac, mentioned below.

(X) Isaac (2), son of Isaac (1) Post, was
born in 1741, died in 1788, killed by a fall
from a tree. He married Agnes, born June 1,
1764, died May 2, 1834, daughter of Joseph
and Deborah (Hudson) Rugg (see Rugg II).
His widow married (second) Bartlett Hinds,
born April 4, 1755, and had two children: Richard Hinds, born December 17, 1795, and Bartlett Hinds, born June 7, 1797 (see Hinds V).
Children of Isaac and Agnes Post; Isaac, mentioned below; David, born July 26, 1786, died
February 24, 1860.

(XI) Isaac (3), son of Isaac (2) Post, was
born August 12, 1784, in Southampton, Long
Island, New York, died in Montrose, Pennsylvania, March 23, 1855. He was one of the
early settlers of Northeastern Pennsylvania,
coming to Montrose in the early part of 1800,
where he became one of the prominent men of
the community. He conducted a general store,
and also kept an inn. He took a foremost
part in every good project in the community,
and was instrumental in establishing the first
bank in that section. He held various offices
of honor and trust, was major of the Second
Battalion of the State Militia in 1811, and was
also inspector of the Second Brigade; he was
treasurer of Susquehanna county in 1812; a
member of the state legislature from Susque-

hanna county in 1828; and associate judge of Susquehanna county in 1837. He was a member of the Masonic organization, holding membership in Hiram Lodge, No. 131, of Newburg, New York. He married, in 1805, Susannah Hinds, the ceremony being performed by Thomas Tiffany, Esq. She was born November 10, 1782, died November 15, 1846, daughter of Bartlett Hinds (see Hinds V). Their children were: Mary Ann, born March 6, 1806, died April 17, 1806; William Leander, April 26, 1807, died February 26, 1871; Albert Lotan, March 25, 1809, died December 6, 1886; Mary Susannah, May 25, 1811, died March 23, 1812; Susannah Jane, April 4, 1813, died February 9, 1819; Agnes Ann, September 25, 1815, died June 22, 1816; Isaac Lucius, mentioned below; Jane Amanda, November 14, 1820, died October 25, 1903, unmarried; Elizabeth Vallonia, July 4, 1825, died October 4, 1853, she married Gordon Dimock, M. D., of Montrose, Pennsylvania, who was a surgeon in the civil war; George Leonidas, September 24, 1828, died December 5, 1841.

(XII) Isaac Lucius, son of Isaac (3) Post, was born July 11, 1818, in Montrose, Pennsylvania, died December 8, 1899. His education was acquired in the district schools. During the civil war he served in the paymaster's department of the Army of the Cumberland, under Colonel Asa Holt Jr., and after the war, in 1865, he removed to Scranton, Pennsylvania, where he was for a number of years engaged in the insurance business, and where he also served as justice of the peace and alderman. He was active in the Pennsylvania Avenue Baptist Church, of Scranton. He was a very stalwart Republican, and was instrumental in bringing Congressman Galusha A. Grow before the public, assisting materially in raising the funds for his campaign. Mr. Post was married, July 28, 1846, by the Rev. H. A. Riley, at Montrose, Pennsylvania, to Harriet Amanda, born February 26, 1828, died at Scranton, November 22, 1895, daughter of William and Amanda (Harris) Jessup (see Jessup-Rugg IV). To this union was born one son, Isaac, mentioned below.

(XIII) Isaac (4), son of Isaac Lucius Post, was born November 21, 1856, at Montrose, Pennsylvania. He attended the public and high schools of Scranton and Professor H. H. Merrill's Academic and Primary Training School. He began his business career, October 1, 1873, as messenger boy of the Third National Bank of Scranton, and a year later, December 2, 1874, became messenger of the First National Bank of Scranton. His ability and fidelity to duty were rewarded by promotion and he was advanced by various steps to

positions of larger responsibility. He became assistant cashier, January 4, 1886, and in October, 1891, cashier, a position he has filled since then with conspicuous ability. He enlisted in the Scranton City Guards during the labor disturbances of 1877, in Company A, and with the other members of the company was mustered into the Thirteenth Regiment, National Guard of Pennsylvania, October 10, 1878. He was discharged May 25, 1885, with the rank of first sergeant. In politics he is a Republican; in religion a Presbyterian, being a member of the First Presbyterian Church, of which he served as trustee for several years.

He married, February 16, 1887, Emily Pierson, born at Roselle, New Jersey, April 14, 1861, daughter of Hiram Pierson and Caroline Elizabeth (Shnyder) Baldwin, the former late general passenger agent of the Central Railroad of New Jersey. Children: Margaret Baldwin, born April 12, 1889; Evelyn Jessup, February 22, 1892; Norman Baldwin, January 3, 1896, died March 26, 1900, at Scranton; Carolyn Elizabeth, August 27, 1897.

(The Rugg-Jessup Line).

Charles Rugg married Agnes, daughter of Lord Norman, according to family tradition, of Exeter, England. It was a runaway match and the young couple came to America, where Rugg became a manufacturer of cloth with mills at North Side, about three miles from North Sea, Long Island, New York. Afterward they returned to England.

(II) Joseph, son of Charles Rugg, married (first) in England, ———— ————; (second) Deborah Hudson. After coming to America Joseph Rugg lived at North Sea, Long Island, and both he and his wife died at North Sea and are buried there. Deborah died in 1808, at the home of her daughter, Phila Harris. Children of first wife: Silas, died on board a British prison ship at Brooklyn in the revolution; Sally, married ———— Wooley, at Southampton, New York. Children of second wife: Polly, born 1761, married Samuel Scott; Agnes, born June 1, 1764, married Isaac Post (see Post X); Phila, mentioned below; Phebe, born July 12, 1774, married Luke Foster, of Cincinnati, Ohio; Jerusha, born 1776, died January 8, 1822, married ———— Voorhees; Jerusha; Joseph.

(III) Phila, daughter of Joseph Rugg, was born May 8, 1766, died December 26, 1831. She married, January 15, 1792, Henry Harris, born August 16, 1764, died November 21, 1851. Children: Harvey, born October, 1792, married Sarah Scott; Mary, born August 17, 1794, married Huntting Cooper, March 29, 1821, and died at North Sea, April 5, 1860;

Ann, born June 1, 1796, married, in 1826, Samuel Hodgden; Amanda, mentioned below; Joseph, born December 30, 1802, married, in 1831, Harriet White, and died January 15, 1879; Phebe, born December 28, 1804, married, April 19, 1861, Huntting Cooper, and died September 19, 1890; Harriet, born May 28, 1807, married, May 15, 1847, Moses Cass Tyler, of Montrose, Pennsylvania.

(IV) Amanda Harris, daughter of Henry and Phila (Rugg) Harris, was born August 8, 1798, at North Sea, Long Island, died June 13, 1883. She married, July 4, 1820, William Jessup, born June 21, 1797, in Southampton. Children: 1. Jane Rose, born June 29, 1821, died in Jersey City, October 1, 1864; married Javan Butterfield Salisbury. 2. Mary Sophia, born March 20, 1823, died in Montrose, December 19, 1893; married, at Montrose, May 26, 1841, Francis Blake Chandler. 3. Fanny, born March, 1825. 4. Harriet Amanda, born February 26, 1828; married Isaac Lucius Post (see Post XII). 5. William Huntting, born January 29, 1830; married, October 5, 1853, at Scranton, Sarah Wilson Jay. 6. Henry Harris, born April 19, 1832; married (first) October 7, 1857, Caroline Bush; (second) October 1, 1868, Harriet Elizabeth Dodge; (third) July 23, 1884, Theodosia Davenport Lockwood. 7. Samuel, born December 21, 1833; married, September 2, 1862, Ann Eliza Jay. 8. Fanny Mulford, born October 29, 1835, died unmarried. 9. George Augustus, born February 5, 1838; married, September 28, 1864, Ellen Beardsley. 10. Phebe Ann, born September 5, 1840, died April 25, 1872; married, September 11, 1861, Alfred Hand 11. Huntting Cooper, born February 18, 1843; married, at Clarksville, Tennessee, December 27, 1865, Marina Modena Cobb.

(The Hinds Line).

The surname Hyne, Hine, Hinds is variously spelled. It is derived from the trade or occupation, like many other English surnames. A hyne, hine, or hind was a tiller of the soil, peasant, farmer. The surnames Haynes, Haines, Hine and Hinds may have had different origins, but for a long time the spellings were used interchangeably in England and America, and it is not possible to separate the families by the surnames. In fact nine different ways of spelling their name are still found among the descendants of William Hinds, the immigrant.

(I) William Hinds, immigrant· ancestor, was born in England. He settled in Salem, Massachusetts, in 1644, or earlier. He came over with his sister Margaret, aged thirty, in the ship "Paull" of London. He was thirty-five years of age at the time. He served as a soldier in Salem. He was admitted to the church there, November 14, 1647. On November 25, 1647, he gave a letter of attorney to Thomas Hines or Haynes, merchant of London, for collection at Danes Halle, Bedfordshire, England, his former home. He mortgaged land at Salem in 1647, and the mortgage was discharged in 1660. He owned land in common with Richard Hinds at Salem. Both were related, no doubt, to Robert Hines, who was in Salem in 1648. William Hinds removed to Marblehead and married Sarah, daughter of Richard Ingersoll. Children: William, mentioned below; Francis, born about 1670.

(II) William (2), son of William (1) Hinds, was born about 1655 in Salem. He was a soldier in King Philip's war in 1675 and was present at the taking of the Narragansett fort. Over fifty years later, in 1728, he had a grant of land in payment for his services in the Narragansett grant, at what is now Amherst, New Hampshire. He married (first) Abigail, daughter of Samuel and Sarah (Hubbard) Ward, and granddaughter of Samuel and Frances Ward, of Hingham. Abigail joined the church, May 19, 1684, at Salem, and was one of the original members of the Marblehead church. She died in 1688, and he married (second) Elizabeth ———. Children of first wife: John, born February 14, 1682; Abigail, January, 1684; Rebecca, April 7, 1686; William, baptized July 22, 1688. Children of second wife, born at Marblehead: Richard, baptized January 6, 1694-95; Joseph, baptized March 21, 1701; Benjamin, born September 3, 1705.

(III) John, nephew of William (2) Hinds, probably son of Francis Hinds, was born about 1685. He went to Bridgewater when a young man, and married there, August 11, 1709, Hannah, born April 26, 1787, daughter of John and Hannah Shaw, great-granddaughter of Abraham Shaw, the immigrant, of Dedham. Children, born at Bridgewater: Hannah, 1710; Elizabeth, 1712; Abigail, 1714; John, 1716; Ebenezer, mentioned below; Susanna, 1722.

(IV) Rev. Ebenezer Hinds, son of John Hinds, was born in Bridgewater, July 29, 1719, died at Fairhaven, Massachusetts, April 19, 1812. He was a farmer in Bridgewater until he was over thirty years of age. He was baptized by immersion in 1749 by Rev. Ebenezer Moulton, pastor of the Baptist church at Brimfield, and the same year began to exercise his gifts in prayer and exhortation. In 1749 he was called to distant points to preach and baptize, above eighty miles, it is said, so his reputation must have extended rapidly. He baptized ten in Bridgewater and three in Raynham the first year. He joined the Second Baptist Church of Boston, March 3, 1751, then under the pastorate of Rev. Ephraim Bond. He preached at the house of Thomas Nelson, of Assawomsett Neck, in 1753, and afterward regularly. He was ordained the first pastor of the Second Baptist Church of Middleboro, January 26, 1758. This church was organized November 16, 1757. A house and barn were bought for a parsonage at Lakeville, called Beech Woods. He continued as pastor upwards of forty years and spent the best part of his life in Middleboro, and his church enjoyed a season of healthful growth and prosperity, the denomination gaining strength rapidly. Mr. Hinds contributed greatly to the growth of his sect and his pulpit was a stronghold. His pastorate closed when he was seventy, but he continued to preach from time to time and retained his physical and mental vigor. Even after he was eighty years old he would mount his horse unaided, ride long distances to hold religious services or assist at ordinations. He went as chaplain with Captain Benjamin Pratt's company to Lake George in 1758 in the French and Indian war. Elder Hinds deeded his house to the church and society, November 2, 1805.

He married (first) Susannah Keith, of Bridgewater, born 1727, daughter of John and Hannah (Washburn) Keith, and granddaughter of Rev. James Keith. She was buried near the present Congregational church in Bridgewater. He married (second) in 1751, Lydia Bartlett, who died May 12, 1801. Her brother Richard was a soldier at Annapolis Royal in 1775 under Colonel Winslow in seizing and disposing of the neutral French.

The epitaph of Elder Hinds on his tombstone in the old Middleboro graveyard reads: "In memory of Rev. Ebenezer Hinds, who died April 19, 1812, in the 94th year. 'I have fought a good fight. I have finished my course, I have kept my faith, henceforth there is laid up for me a crown of righteousness'." That of his wife: "Sacred to the memory of Mrs. Lydia, wife of Rev. Ebenezer Hinds. She died May 12, 1801, in her sixty-seventh year. 'Give her of the fruits of her hands, and let her own works praise her'." Children of first wife: Keziah, born 1745; Salome, 1747; Child, died in infancy; Child, died in infancy. Children of second wife: Ebenezer, born January 25, 1753; Bartlett, mentioned below; Susannah, May 16, 1757; John, September 19, 1759; Leonard, August 19, 1761; Lydia, August 1, 1763; Preserved, February 27, 1765; Abanoam, June 19, 1768; Keziah, March 19, 1772, died August

12, 1774; Hannah, born May 12, 1773; Richard, September 11, 1775.

(V) Bartlett, son of Rev. Ebenezer Hinds, was born in Bridgewater, April 4, 1755, died December 11, 1822. He was a soldier in the revolution in Captain Wood's company. He went to Pennsylvania and became the first settler in Montrose, Susquehanna county. He was involved in the controversy between settlers who were divided over the question whether Connecticut or Pennsylvania had jurisdiction over their land and he was once the victim of a persecution and assault by a mob (see p. 40, Hinds Genealogy). Bartlett Hinds was one of the three county commissioners elected when Susquehanna county was organized in 1812. He married (first) December 1, 1780, Ruth Pickens, of Middleboro, daughter of John Pickens (see Pickens II). He married (second) Agnes (Rugg) Post, widow of Isaac Post, she was born June 1, 1764, died in May, 1834 (see Post X). Children of first wife: Susannah, born November 10, 1782, died November 15, 1846, married Isaac Post (see Post XI); Conrad, January 5, 1785. Children of second wife: Richard, born December 17, 1795; Bartlett, June 7, 1797.

(The Pickens Line).

(I) Thomas Pickens, immigrant ancestor, came from the north of Ireland with the Strowbridges, McCulloys and a few other Scotch families about 1718 with the earliest Scotch-Irish pioneers. They came from Ballygully, near Coleraine, Ireland. With Pickens came also his wife, Margaret (Steele) Pickens, and their children: Jane, Andrew and James Pickens, and after a rough and tedious voyage of eleven weeks they landed at Boston. They lived at Milton, near Boston, at Freetown on Cape Cod and finally at Middleboro, in Plymouth county. Thomas Pickens bought land in Middleboro, December 26, 1732, of Barnabas Eaton (see Middleboro History and Strowbridge Genealogy, p. 17, which contains a letter written by one of the third generation). In 1736 Thomas Pickens, of Middleboro, deeded land to John Dunham. In 1739 Thomas Pickens, of Middleboro, deeded to son James. Thomas Pickens died before November, 1739. The son James died March 22, 1800, in his eighty-fourth year. In this country Thomas and Margaret Pickens had: Martha, John, mentioned below; Margaret, Thomas.

(II) John, son of Thomas Pickens, was born about 1725. He married Ruth Cushen. They lived in Middleboro and their daughter Ruth, born April, 1759, married Bartlett Hinds (see Hinds V).

Sergeant Richard Hildreth, immigrant ancestor, was born in the north part of England, in 1615, died in 1688. He settled first in Cambridge, Massachusetts, and was admitted a freeman there, May 10, 1643. He removed to Woburn, Massachusetts, and was one of the grantees of Chelmsford, Massachusetts. By 1663 he had no less than eight grants of land from the general court, amounting altogether to one hundred and five acres. The "History of Westford" says:

The Hildreth homestead was about midway between the centre and south villages of Chelmsford. This family also spread into Westford. A tract of land containing about five hundred acres on the east side of the town came into their possession. It is not easy to give the exact boundaries. It included the houses with land attached of Augustus Bunce, George Porter Wright, the Drew Brothers, (Thomas and George), Isaac G. Minot and Julian Hildreth. Providence Meadow was its northwest limit and the house of Edward Symmes stands not far from the east border. The Hildreths also took up two or three farms south and east of Tadmuck hill or that spur of it known as Prospect Hill. Four or five houses there were at one time known as "Hildreth Row." Richard Hildreth had a special grant of one hundred and fifty acres of land from the general court in 1663 on account of having lost the use of his right hand, presumably in the service. He was accused in 1670 by Rev. John Fiske, of Chelmsford, of having used "reproachful speech concerning the church" and was disciplined by the church. Previously he had been charged by Deacon Esdras Reade in 1656 and 1661 with the use of similar "seditious language" and was ordered to appear before the church authorities, but he refused to obey the order. His will was dated February 9, 1686, and proved some time after his death in 1688. He left land in Chelmsford to his son Ephraim, who was then living in Stow, including the homestead and the seven acres north of the Great Pond, eighteen acres south and seventeen acres east of it.

He married (first) Sarah ———, who died 1644; married (second) Elizabeth ———, who died at Malden, August 3, 1693, aged sixty-eight years. Children of first wife: James, born in Woburn, 1631; Ephraim, born in Cambridge or Woburn, married Anna Moore, of Lancaster. Children of second wife, born at Woburn: Elizabeth, September 21, 1646; Sarah, August 8, 1648. Born at Chelmsford: Joseph, April 16, 1658, married, December 12, 1683, Abigail Wilson; Persis, February 8, 1660; Thomas, February 1, 1662; Isaac, mentioned below; Abigail, married Moses Parker.

(II) Isaac, son of Richard Hildreth, was born in July, 1663, and lived at Woburn in 1695. It is believed that he removed to Stow, Massachusetts, or vicinity. He married Elizabeth ———. Two children were born at Woburn: Persis, November 25, 1691; Joanna, November 16, 1695.

(III) Isaac (2) Hildreth was a grandson of Richard Hildreth and doubtless son of Isaac (1) Hildreth, of whom little is known. He was born about 1700 in Stow or vicinity, and was among the early settlers and proprietors of the town of Petersham, Worcester county, Massachusetts. His son Isaac appears to have succeeded to his homestead and there is no record of his death in the vital records of Petersham or the probate records of the county of Worcester. It is surmised that he returned to Stow and probably died in Middlesex county. The Hildreth family before 1700 lived at Chelmsford, Dracut, Concord, Stow and vicinity. All of the name are descended from Richard Hildreth. From this section came a large part of the original settlers of Petersham. The earliest authentic list of the proprietors of the town of Petersham was prepared December 14, 1750, by Thomas Adams, clerk of the proprietors, giving the names of forty-seven settlers with the proprietor's rights on which they located. Isaac Hildreth's name is misspelled "Hilldrake," a not uncommon spelling, however. He or his son Isaac deeded to Isaac Jr. land in Petersham, November 28, 1753. Children: 1. Isaac, born about 1725; lived and died at Petersham; his will was dated May 8, 1764, bequeathing to wife Esther and minor children whose names were found to be Isaac, Jesse, Joshua, Esther and Rachel (see Worcester County Probate Records, No. 29, 302 A). 2. Samuel, mentioned below. 3. John, born about 1735-45; lived in Petersham; married (intention dated February 6, 1768) Elizabeth Farr, of Chesterfield. 4. Elizabeth, married, November 4, 1762, Jonas Davis, of Chesterfield, New Hampshire. 5. Jonathan, settled in Westmoreland, New Hampshire, as early as 1751, coming from Petersham and settling in Chesterfield, New Hampshire, about 1763; married three times, wives named Mary, Phebe and Dinah; was selectman and left many descendants. 6. Edward, settled in Chesterfield as early as 1767, when he married Sarah Whitney; he died January 21, 1821, aged eighty years, and had many descendants at Chesterfield and vicinity. 7. William, came from Petersham to Chesterfield; married, 1768, Joanna Bingham. There may have been other daughters.

(IV) Samuel, son of Isaac Hildreth, was born in 1735 at Stow or vicinity, in Massachusetts. He married (first) in 1759, Hannah Farr, who died at Chesterfield in December, 1786, aged forty-five years. He settled there before 1767 on the farm now or lately owned by Hermon C. Harvey and formerly by Marshall H. Day. Samuel Hildreth was selectman of Chesterfield in 1776-78. He died in

1812, in his seventy-seventh year. The Farr or Farrar family came from Stow to Petersham among the early settlers. Hannah (Farr) Hildreth probably died before 1787, as her name does not appear on the following described deed, signed by her husband. Samuel Hildreth, Daniel Farr, Edward Hildreth 2d. and Sarah his wife, Mary Farr, all of Chesterfield, New Hampshire, and Patience Farr, of Boylston, Massachusetts, quitclaimed to Samuel Farr, of Boylston, all their rights as heirs-at-law of "their father Daniel Farr" whose home is described as in the "north part of Shrewsbury, now Boylston," the deed being dated April 26, 1787, and witnessed by Jonathan Hildreth and Samuel Hildreth Jr., at Chesterfield (recorded at Worcester). Samuel Hildreth signed the Association Test in 1776 and his descendants are eligible to the Sons and Daughters of the Revolution. Children of Samuel and Hannah Hildreth: Leah, born October 4, 1760; Samuel, mentioned below; Daniel, May 18, 1765, died 1781; Isaac, September 19, 1767, married Hannah Farr; Hannah, October 29, 1769; Susanna, October 2, 1771, died 1774; Joel, December 28, 1773, married Anna Bowker and died in Lynn, Massachusetts; Susanna, July 8, 1776; Elijah, July 7, 1779; Daniel, September 30, 1781, married Susanna Fairbanks; Persis, July 8, 1782, married John Rugg, of Salem, Massachusetts. Samuel Hildreth married (second), at Petersham, January 10, 1788, Sally Bosworth.

(V) Samuel (2), son of Samuel (1) Hildreth, was born at Chesterfield, October 25, 1762, died there April 12, 1802. His first wife died in 1790, and he married (second) Jerusha ———. Children, born in Chesterfield: Daniel, February 27, 1790, a prominent citizen of Beverly, Massachusetts, where he died in August, 1860; Alvin (?), born May 28, 1792; Samuel, mentioned below; Paul, April 19, 1798, died in Danvers, Massachusetts; Thirza, May 20, 1801, died August 19, 1816.

(VI) Samuel (3), son of Samuel (2) Hildreth, was born in Chesterfield, New Hampshire, October 3, 1794, died in Lynn, Massachusetts. For a time he was a farmer at Springfield, formerly Protectworth, New Hampshire. The census of 1790 shows that at Cornish, adjacent to the present town of Springfield, lived Samuel, who then had four males over sixteen, one under sixteen and two females in his family, and Joel, who had two males under sixteen and one female. At Chesterfield Edward, Isaac, Jesse, Ichabod, Lotan, Martin, Reuben, Samuel and William were at that time heads of families. He married (first) Polly, daughter of David Morgan. Chil-

dren: David Morgan, mentioned below; Thirza J., born 1824, married, May 30, 1844, James L. Alger, at Lynn. He married (second) Elizabeth ———; child, Caroline Louisa, born September 14, 1836.

(VII) David Morgan, son of Samuel (3) Hildreth, was born at Springfield, New Hampshire, December 28, 1821. He was educated in the public schools of Lynn, Massachusetts, whither his father came in 1827 when he was six years old. Throughout his active and useful life he was engaged in the hotel business. He was proprietor of the famous St. Charles Hotel in New Orleans, before the civil war, and also conducted for a time the Royal Hotel of New Orleans. He remained in New Orleans after the war began, and was living there when it was surrendered to the federal army. Subsequently he gave up business there and spent two years in Spain with his family. He returned to this country, October 21, 1864, and conducted the New York Hotel, which became headquarters for visiting southerners, especially those from New Orleans.

He married (first), September 28, 1841, at Lynn, Elizabeth C. Washburn, who died August 19, 1849, aged twenty-seven years. He married (second) Annie Lloyd Mudge, born in Portland, Maine, October 14, 1830, daughter of Solomon Hinkley and Susan (Hodgkins) Mudge, of Providence, Rhode Island. Child of first wife: Sally Elizabeth, born at New Orleans (recorded at Lynn), August 7, 1849. Child of second wife: Walter Edwards, mentioned below.

(VIII) Walter Edwards, son of David Morgan Hildreth, was born in Oakdale, Madison county, Illinois, where his parents were then living, October 21, 1857. He was educated in various private schools and in Columbia College, from which he was graduated in the class of 1877 with the degree of Bachelor of Arts. For a time he followed his profession as civil engineer and then became financially interested in various mining industries. When his father died he succeeded to his hotel business, and is at present president of the Breslin Hotel Company and manager of Hotel Breslin, Broadway, New York City. He is president of the Urbana Wine Company. He is a member of the Columbia University Club and the University Club. In politics he is a Democrat.

He married, March 4, 1886, Hanie Hammond Lawson, born at Woodbury, Connecticut, May 4, 1857, daughter of Robert C. Lawson. Children: Ruth Lawson, born May 10, 1893; Hanie Dorothy, November 13, 1894.

There are several different ways of spelling this surname, among them Twichell, Tuchill, Twitchwell and Twitchell.

TWITCHELL

(I) Joseph Twitchell, immigrant ancestor, settled in Dorchester, Massachusetts, in November, 1633, died September 13, 1657. He was made freeman, May 14, 1634. He had land assigned to him in Dorchester, February 18, 1635-36. He was admitted to the church, January 8, 1644. He signed a deed of land, May 24, 1656. The inventory of his estate was presented December 26, 1657, by Timothy Wales and Benjamin Twitchell, probably a brother.

(II) Joseph (2), son of Joseph (1) Twitchell, was an early settler in Sherborn, Massachusetts. He married Lydia ———, who died between 1715 and 1730. He had one hundred acres of the first grants in Sherborn, and June 12, 1682, united with the others in paying off the Indian claims. In 1686 he was rated to extinguish the Indian claim to the remainder of the lands. He built his house near Royal Stone's house in Sherborn. Children: Patience, born December 2, 1678; Content, January 25, 1680; Charity, December 7, 1682; Sarah, November 15, 1684; Lydia, October 11, 1686; Joseph, mentioned below; Ephraim, October 24, 1695.

(III) Joseph (3), son of Joseph (2) Twitchell, was born September 3, 1688, died January 31, 1728. He lived in Sherborn, where he was born. He married, March 27, 1717, Elizabeth, born in Sherborn, July 22, 1696, died there March 31, 1782, daughter of John Holbrook, who was born in Sherborn in 1674, died there February 28, 1740; he married Silence Wood, born in "Bullard's Fort," February 22, 1675, the day after her father's death, and her mother died a few days later; she died in Sherborn, May 11, 1756; she was daughter of Jonathan Wood, born in Dorchester, Massachusetts, January 3, 1651, and killed by the Indians on the bank of the Charles river, February 21, 1675-76. Jonathan Wood was son of Nicholas Wood, freeman of Dorchester, June 2, 1641, who died in Natick Bounds, February 7, 1670; the inventory of his property was dated 1649; he married Mary Williams, of Roxbury, died February 19, 1663, daughter of Robert Williams, who came to Roxbury in 1637, was made freeman, May 2, 1638, and is said to have come from Norwich, county Norfolk, England, with wife Elizabeth (Stratton, by family tradition), who died July 28, 1674; he died September 1, 1693. John Holbrook was son of Thomas Holbrook, born about 1727. Thomas Holbrook married,

in Weymouth, January 26, 1669, Margaret Bouker, who died April 9, 1690. Thomas Holbrook was son of John Holbrook, of Dorchester, who was made freeman, May 13, 1640, and later removed to Weymouth, Massachusetts. Children of Mr. and Mrs. Twitchell: Joseph, mentioned below; Deacon Jona, July 22, 1721.

(IV) Joseph (4), son of Joseph (3) Twitchell, was born February 13, 1718, at Sherborn, died there March 12, 1792, from apoplexy. He was captain of the militia, and commissary for the army in the revolution. He served as town clerk, representative and magistrate. He married (first) Deborah Fairbanks, June 28, 1739. They were admitted to the church, July 27, 1740. He married (second) Deborah (Sanger) Fasset, January 1, 1786. His first wife was daughter of Eleazer Fairbanks, born in Sherborn, December 29, 1690, died there September 19, 1741; he was a captain; he married, in Sherborn, December 25, 1712, Martha Bullard, born in Sherborn, February 11, 1695, daughter of Hon. Samuel Bullard, born in Sherborn, December 26, 1667, died December 11, 1727, married, June, 1690, Deborah Atherton, born in Lancaster, Massachusetts, June 1, 1669. Hon. Samuel Bullard served as captain, and was assessor five years, selectman nineteen years, representative in 1708-09 and 1723-24-25; he was son of Benjamin Bullard. Deborah Atherton, wife of Samuel Bullard, was daughter of James Atherton, born in England, came to Dorchester, then Lancaster, 1654, and finally Sherborn, Massachusetts, where he died in 1707; he married Hannah ———. Eleazer Fairbanks was son of George Fairbanks, born in England, came with his father to Dedham before 1641 and settled in 1657 in Sherborn, where he died January 10, 1682, married Mary ———. He was son of Jonathan Fairbanks, born in Yorkshire, England, married, in Halifax Parish, Yorkshire, May 20, 1617, Grace Smith, of Warley, England, came to New England before 1641 and settled in Durham, Massachusetts, died December 5, 1668. Children of Joseph Twitchell by first wife: Captain Samuel, born August 24, 1740; Joseph, November 27, 1741; Elizabeth, July 27, 1743; Eleazer, January 22, 1744-45; Ezram, June 23, 1746; Martha, December 16, 1747; Deborah, March 26, 1749, died May 13, 1752; Abel, May 28, 1751; Deborah, December 23, 1752; Molly, May 17, 1755; Amos, December 28, 1756; Eli, February 17, 1759; Peter, mentioned below; Jule, March 18, 1766.

(V) Peter, son of Joseph (4) Twitchell, was baptized August 30, 1760, died in Bethel, Maine, November 18, 1855. For over forty years he was a vegetarian in diet. In 1851 he was able to walk for miles to church and back and stand during the delivery of the sermon. He was a soldier in the revolution. He married (first), May 8, 1783, Sarah Bullard, who died September 20, 1791. He married (second) Amy Perry, January 10, 1793, born in Sherborn, January 10, 1774, died in Bethel, October, 1835 (see Perry VI). Children by first wife: Almond, born July 10, 1784, died November 18, 1792; Jona, 1789; Eli, died of small-pox, September 26, 1792; by second wife: Eli, born July 22, 1794; Julia, April 10, 1797; John Adams, mentioned below.

(VI) John Adams, son of Peter Twitchell, was born in Sherborn, September 7, 1798, died in Bethel, Maine, April 13, 1877. He married, in Bethel, June 17, 1823, Roxanna Howe, born in Bridgton, Maine, June 13, 1800, died in Bethel, February 22, 1888 (see Howe VII). He had a son, John Quincy Adams, mentioned below.

(VII) John Quincy Adams, son of John Adams Twitchell, was born in Bethel, Maine, May 18, 1838, died in Portland, Maine, February 29, 1896. He married ——— ———. Children: Frederick, died in infancy. Gertrude Marble, born in Portland, Maine, 1872, died in 1906. Arthur C., mentioned below.

(VIII) Arthur C., son of John Quincy Adams Twitchell, was born at Portland, Maine, October 12, 1874. He attended the public schools of his native city and prepared for college at St. Paul's School, Concord, New Hampshire. He entered Williams College and was graduated in 1898 with the degree of Bachelor of Arts. For a time afterward he was in the employ of the International Paper Company of New York City, but soon resigned to become the manager of the M. B. Fuller Company, of Scranton, Pennsylvania. After two years with that concern, he became purchasing agent of the Temple Iron Company. He is also general manager of the Winton Coal Company, of Scranton, with offices in the Mears Building. He is a director of the Dime Deposit and Discount Bank of Scranton. He is a member of Peter Williamson Lodge, No. 323, Free and Accepted Masons, of Scranton; of the Sons of the Revolution, the Colonial Society, the Scranton Club, the Country Club and of Kappa Alpha, a college fraternity. In politics he is a Republican. He attends the Presbyterian church.

He married, April 5, 1899, Frances A., born July 27, 1875, daughter of Byron Manning and Frances (Silkman) Winton, and granddaughter of W. W. Winton. Mr. and Mrs. Twitchell have no children.

(The Perry Line).

(I) John Perry, immigrant ancestor, came to Roxbury, probably coming over in the "Lion" in 1632. He was made freeman, March 4, 1633. He died September 21, 1642.

(II) John (2), son of John (1) Perry, was born in Roxbury, Massachusetts, September 2, 1639, died in Sherborn, before 1715. He married, in Sherborn, Massachusetts, May 23, 1665, Bethiah Morse, born in Sherborn, March 24, 1646, died in 1717, daughter of Daniel Morse, who was born in England in 1613, died at Sherborn in 1688; he settled first in Watertown, Massachusetts, where he was made freeman, May 6, 1635; he married Lydia Fisher in Dedham, where he lived for a time; she was sister of Anthony Fisher Sr., and she died at Sherborn, January 29, 1691. Daniel Morse was son of Samuel Morse, the immigrant, who came in the "Increase" from London in 1635, aged fifty, with his wife Elizabeth, aged forty-eight; he died December 5, 1654, and she died June 20, 1655.

(III) Nathaniel, son of John (2) Perry, was born in Sherborn in 1683, died there September 7, 1756. He married Abigail Mason, who died March 15, 1729.

(IV) Nathaniel (2), son of Nathaniel (1) Perry, was born in Sherborn, January 2, 1717, died there January 24, 1754. He married Elizabeth Soughton, from Watertown, Massachusetts.

(V) Edward West, son of Nathaniel (2) Perry, was born in Sherborn, March 8, 1743, died there June 5, 1810. He was a soldier in the revolution. He married, in Sherborn, September 4, 1771, Esther, born in Sherborn, May 26, 1751, died there March 12, 1813, daughter of Captain Edward Learned, born in Sherborn, December 2, 1705, died there September 9, 1775; he married (third), August 25, 1748, Mrs. Sarah (Fuller) Pratt, born in Newton, Massachusetts, October 20, 1720, died at Sherborn, January 11, 1783. Captain Learned was son of Benoni Learned, born in Charlestown, Massachusetts, December 4, 1656, died April 10, 1738; he married (second) Sarah More, born in Sudbury, Massachusetts, March 3, 1684, died at Sherborn, January 25, 1737. Benoni Learned was son of Isaac Learned, of Woburn and Charlestown, born in England, freeman, 1647, died November 27 or December 4, 1657, married, July 9, 1646, Mary Stearns. Isaac Learned was son of William Learned, of Charlestown, 1632, when he and his wife, Judith (Goodith) Learned joined the church; he was made freeman, May 14, 1634, and was selectman in 1636; he settled in Woburn in 1641, died April 5, 1646.

Mrs. Sarah (Fuller-Pratt) Learned, wife of Captain Learned, was daughter of Captain Jonathan Fuller, who was born in Newton, Massachusetts, January 7, 1687, died there December 1, 1764; he married, October, 1718, Sarah Mirick, born in Newton, March 6, 1695, died September 21, 1772, daughter of John Mirick, of Newton, who married, in 1682, Elizabeth Trowbridge, born in Dorchester, October 12, 1660; John Mirick died July 11, 1706, son of John Mirick, who was in Charlestown before 1643. Elizabeth Trowbridge was daughter of Lieutenant James Trowbridge, who was baptized in Dorchester in 1638, freeman, 1665, selectman, clerk of the writs, deacon, representative 1700 and 1703; he lived in the part of Cambridge that became Newton, and died May 22, 1717; he married, in Dorchester, December 30, 1659, Margaret Atherton, born there and died in Cambridge, June 17, 1672, daughter of Major Humphrey Atherton, of Dorchester, 1636; freeman, May 2, 1638, and of the artillery the same year, its captain in 1650, often selectman, and representative nine years, from 1638, but not in succession; major-general in 1656, died September 17, 1661. Lieutenant James Trowbridge was son of Thomas Trowbridge, of New Haven, Connecticut, 1640, who, according to tradition, first settled at Dorchester, coming from Taunton, county Somerset, England, about 1637, and returned home about 1644, leaving his three sons, and died in Taunton, England, February 7, 1672.

Captain Jonathan Fuller was son of Joseph Fuller, born in Cambridge, February 10, 1652, died February 7, 1699; married, February 13, 1680, Lydia Jackson, born in Newton, 1656, died April 13, 1700; Lydia was daughter of Edward Jackson, of Cambridge, baptized in Stepney, Whitechapel parish, London, England, February 3, 1604-05, came to New England about 1643, freeman, 1645; representative, 1647, and fifteen years more, died in the village, now Newton, July 17, 1681; married (second), March 14, 1649, Mrs. Elizabeth (Newgate) Oliver, born in England, 1618, died in Newton, September 30, 1709. Edward Jackson was son of Christopher Jackson, of Stepney, Whitechapel parish, London. Elizabeth (Newgate) Oliver was daughter of John Newgate, born in Southwark, near London Bridge, 1580, come to Boston with wife and children; merchant there in 1632, freeman, March 4, 1635; representative, 1638, died 1665; widow Ann died in 1679.

Sarah More, wife of Benoni Learned, was daughter of Jacob More, born in Sudbury, April 28, 1645, married there, May 29, 1667, Elizabeth Looker. Jacob More was son of John More, of Sudbury, 1643, wife Elizabeth ———; married (second), November 16, 1654, Ann Smith, settled in Lancaster, died November, 1703.

Mary Stearns, wife of Isaac Learned, was baptized in Neyland, county Suffolk, England, January 6, 1627; she married (second) John Burge, of Chelmsford, Massachusetts; she died in 1663; daughter of Isaac Stearns, of Watertown, freeman, 1630; May 18, 1631, Isaac was on the first jury that tried a civil cause in New England, and he died June 19, 1671, leaving wife Mary.

Joseph Fuller was son of John Fuller, of Cambridge, died February 7, 1699; widow Elizabeth died April 13, 1700.

(VI) Amy, daughter of Edward West Perry, married Peter Twitchell (see Twitchell V).

(The Howe Line).

(I) Abraham Howe, immigrant ancestor, was of Roxbury. He was made freeman, May 2, 1638, and died in Boston, November 20, 1683. His wife died December, 1645.

(II) Abraham (2), son of Abraham (1) Howe, was born in England.

(III) Isaac, son of Abraham (2) Howe, was born in Charlestown, Massachusetts, March 30, 1656. He married, in Ipswich, Massachusetts, May 11, 1685, Deborah, daughter of James Howe Jr., who was born about 1634, married Elizabeth Jackson, was made freeman, 1669; and granddaughter of James Howe, of Roxbury, freeman, May 17, 1637, of Ipswich, 1648, died May 17, 1702, married Elizabeth Dane, daughter of John Dane, who was of Roxbury; came from county Essex, England, 1636, with his first wife Frances; two or more children born in England, at least Elizabeth and John; married (second) Widow Chandler, who died September 14, 1658.

(IV) Jacob, son of Isaac Howe, was born in Charlestown. His intention of marriage was made January 20, 1721, with Eleanor Sherwin, born in Ipswich, June 28, 1696. She was daughter of John Sherwin, of Ipswich, who was born in 1644, died October 15, 1726, married (second), September 30, 1691, Mary Chandler, born in Andover, Massachusetts, in 1659, daughter of William Chandler, who was born in Roxbury, December, 1636, and married, August 24, 1658, Mary Dane, born in Ipswich in 1639, died May 10, 1679, daughter of John Dane Jr., of Ipswich; John Dane Jr. was born in Colchester, England, 1613, made freeman, June 2, 1641, was a surgeon, and died September 29, 1684. William Chandler was son of William Chandler, of Roxbury, 1637, who died January 19, 1642.

leaving a widow Annis or Hannah, who married (second), July 2, 1643, John Dane.

(V) Jacob (2), son of Jacob (1) Howe, was born in Charlestown, February 9, 1724, died in Ipswich, August 1 or 9, 1806. He married, November 21, 1751, Lydia Davis, born in Ipswich, October 9 or 19, 1731, died there February 2, 1808.

(VI) Jacob (3), son of Jacob (2) Howe, was born in Ipswich in 1759, died in Paris, Maine, January 30, 1830. He was a soldier in the revolution. He married, 1782, Bettee Foster, born in Boxford, Massachusetts, August 10, 1763, died in Farmington, Maine, daughter of Moses Foster, who was born in Boxford, March 2, 1739, was a soldier in the revolution, married, September 29, 1761, Hannah Putnam, born in Danvers, Massachusetts, in August, 1743, and who married (second), October 23, 1777, Reuben Burnham, of Bridgton, Maine. Moses Foster was son of Jeremiah Foster, who was born in Boxford, May 4. 1701, and whose intention of marriage with Abigail Wood was published in Boxford, October 31, 1731 ; she died July 27, 1750, and he died August 15, 1785. Jeremiah Foster was son of Timothy Foster, who was born in Rowley Boxford, now Boxford, in 1672, died there in 1751 ; he married Mary Dorman, who died before 1718, daughter of Ephraim and Martha Dorman, of Topsfield, Massachusetts, and granddaughter of Thomas Dorman, of Ipswich, who was made freeman, March 4, 1635, and died in Topsfield, April 25, 1670. Timothy Foster was son of William Foster, who was born in England in 1633, died May 17, 1713; he married, May 15, 1661, Mary Jackson, born February 8, 1639. William Foster was son of Reginold Foster, of Ipswich, 1638, born in England, and died between March 5 and May 30, 1681; he married Judith ———, who died in October, 1664.

Hannah Putnam, wife of Moses Foster, was daughter of William Putnam, who was born in Salem Village, now Danvers, March 3, 1712; he married Ruth Leach ; he was son of Bartholomew Putnam. Bartholomew Putnam was born in Danvers in October, 1688 ; he married Mary Putnam, who was born in Danvers, February 2, 1691, and was sister of General Israel Putnam, and daughter of Lieutenant Joseph Putnam, who was born in Salem, Massachusetts, September 4, 1669; Lieutenant Joseph Putnam married, April 21, 1690, Elizabeth Porter, born October 2, 1673, daughter of Israel Porter, of Salem ; Israel Porter married, November 20, 1672, in Salem, Elizabeth Hathorne, born in Salem, July 22, 1649, daughter of Major William Hathorne or Hawthorne, of Salem, 1636. Major Haw-

thorne came in the "Arabella" with Winthrop in 1630 and was made freeman, May 14, 1634; he was representative for Salem for many years, and speaker in 1644 and six years later ; he was assistant or councillor in 1662-79, and military commander as captain or major in King Philip's war; he died in 1681. Israel Porter was son of John Porter, of Hingham, 1635, who was representative in 1644 and removed to Salem that year ; he died September 6, 1676, and his widow Mary died February 6, 1685.

Lieutenant Joseph Putnam, father of Mary Putnam, was son of Lieutenant Thomas Putnam, of Lynn and Salem, who was made freeman, May 18, 1642, and died May 5, 1686; he married (second), November 14, 1666, Mrs. Mary Veren, widow of Nathaniel Veren, and she died March 16, 1694.

Bartholomew Putnam was son of Lieutenant James Putnam, who was born in Salem Village, September 4, 1661 ; he married Sarah ———. Lieutenant James was son of Captain John Putnam, who was born at Aston Abbots, county Bucks, England, and baptized May 27, 1627 ; he came to Salem about 1640, where he married, September 3, 1652, Rebecca Prince ; he was representative in 1680-86-91-92. Captain Putnam was son of John Putnam, who was born in England in 158—, died in Salem Village, now Danvers, December 30, 1662 ; he married in England, before 1612, Priscilla Deacon ; he was a well-to-do farmer.

(VII) Roxanna, daughter of Jacob (3) Howe, married John Adams Twitchell (see Twitchell VI).

——————

Thomas Pope, immigrant ancestor, POPE was born in 1608, died in Dartmouth, Massachusetts, in October, 1683. He settled in Plymouth, Massachusetts, where he was taxed on January 2, 1632-33. and again on January 2, 1633-34. On October 6, 1636, he received a grant of five acres of land "at the fishing point next Slowly field, and said Thomas be allowed to build." On June 7, 1637, he volunteered to go under "Mr. Prence," on an expedition against the Pequots. On August 29, 1640, he sold his property at the fishing point to John Bonham, and on November 20 of that year he was granted five acres "of meadowing in South Meadows toward Gavans Colebrook meadows." In August, 1634, he was among those men able to bear arms. He was chosen constable, June 4, 1645, and was on a jury in August, 1645. In 1646 he was at Yarmouth. On June 1, 1647, an action for slander was brought against him, confessed, authors and defendants were brought in equally guilty, and damages paid. In July, 1648, he was chosen surveyor of highways, and again on June 6, 1651. On July 26, 1652, and in 1656, he was "on an Enquest". In December, 1663, he and Gyles Rickard were arrested "for breaking the King's peace by striking each other, and were fined three shillings and four pence". On February 7, 1664, and May 2, 1665, he was disputing with John Barnes in regard to a boundary line. He was made freeman in 1668. In 1673 he petitioned for a grant of land at Saconnett, now Little Compton, Rhode Island, but was unable to secure the grant. He was granted permission by the court to look for land, undisposed of, and he secured a large tract on the east side of the Acushnet river at Dartmouth, where he moved doubtless about 1674. In July, 1675, his son John, aged twenty-two, his daughter Susannah and her husband Ensign Jacob Mitchell, were killed by King Philip's Indians, "early in the morning as they were fleeing on horseback to the garrison, whither the Mitchell children had been sent the afternoon before". The Dartmouth settlement was abandoned soon after this, because of the danger from the Indians, and no attempt seems to have been made for about three years to settle there again. On June 12, 1676, several Indians who had been captured and sent in by Bradford and Church, were brought before the court; one of them, John-num, was accused of being concerned in the murder of Jacob Mitchell and his wife and John Pope, and was put to death. On July 13, 1677, other Indians were put into slavery as a punishment for the outrages committed at Dartmouth. Thomas Pope's will was dated July 9, 1683. Isaac and Seth Pope were appointed administrators on his estate, November 2, 1683. Isaac inherited the homestead of one hundred and seventy-two acres, comprising a large part of the thickly settled portion of Fairhaven, Massachusetts.

Thomas Pope married (first) in Plymouth, January 28, 1637, Ann, daughter of Gabriel and Catherine Fallowell, of Plymouth. He married (second) in Plymouth, May 19, 1646, Sarah, daughter of John and Sarah (Carey) Jenney, of Plymouth. Child by first wife, born in Plymouth: Hannah, 1639. Children, born in Plymouth, by second wife: Seth, mentioned below; Susannah, 1649; Thomas, March 25, 1651, probably died young; Sarah, February 14, 1652; John, March 15, 1653; Joanna, died about 1695; Isaac, born after 1663.

(II) Seth, son of Thomas Pope, was born in Plymouth, January 13, 1648, died in Dartmouth, March 17, 1727. According to tradi-

tion, about 1670 he came to Sandwich, Massachusetts, as a peddler, and the constable, following a regulation then in force, ordered him to leave, lest in future he might become a charge on the town, and the records confirm the story in part. He left, saying he would come back and buy up the town. He took a boat at Monument and went along the coast to Acushnet, settling within the present limits of Fairhaven. He was very successful in business, and became one of the wealthy and influential men in the colony. On March 8, 1678-79, he was given an allowance by the court to pay him for expenses and time taken in returning guns to the Indians after King Philip's war. On June 2, 1685, he was chosen selectman at Dartmouth, and on March 4, 1686, he took the oath of fidelity. He was again selectman on June 2, 1686, and on June 4 was commissioned lieutenant. In 1689 and 1690 he was chosen representative from Dartmouth to the general court at Plymouth; he was magistrate for Bristol county, July 7, 1691, and justice of the peace in Dartmouth, May 27, 1692. He was named as one of the fifty-six proprietors of Dartmouth in the confirmatory deed of Governor Bradford in 1694. On June 12, 1695, he appeared in Boston to urge an abatement of taxes in behalf of his townsmen. He had a wharf and warehouse at Acushnet, and in 1698 was part owner of the sloop "Hopewell," and in 1709 of the sloop "Joanna and Thankful." In 1700 he purchased a large amount of realty in Sandwich, including the gristmill, fulling-mill and weaving-shop, carrying out his promise made to them thirty years before; the property at the time of his death was valued at three thousand four hundred and sixty pounds. He owned a large amount of real estate in Dartmouth, including several farms and dwelling houses, a saw and gristmill, a store and warehouse, and other property amounting to more than fifteen thousand pounds.

He married (first) Deborah Perry, born in 1655, died February 19, 1711. He married (second) Rebecca ———, born 1662, died January 23, 1741. Children by first wife, all born in Dartmouth except the first, and perhaps the second: John, mentioned below; Thomas, September 1, 1677; Susannah, July 31, 1681; Sarah, February 16, 1683; Mary, September 11, 1686; Seth, April 5, 1689; Hannah, December 14, 1693; Elnathan, August 15, 1694; Lemuel, February 21, 1696.

(III) John, son of Seth Pope, was born October 23, 1675, after his parents were driven from Dartmouth by the Indians; it has not been found where they remained the two or three years they were away from Dartmouth, but perhaps they were at Plymouth or Sandwich, or possibly in Rhode Island. He died in Sandwich, November 18, 1725, and his gravestone there still exists, probably the oldest one in America. He married (first), about 1699, Elizabeth, daughter of Mrs. Patience (Skiff) Bourne, of Sandwich, and she died April 15, 1715. He married (second), October 3, 1717, Experience (Hamblen) Jenkins, of Barnstable; she was born March 28, 1693. Children by first wife, all, except perhaps the first, born in Sandwich: Seth, mentioned below; Deborah, January 6, 1702-03; Sarah, March 25, 1705-06; Elizabeth, January 3, 1706-07; Thomas, 1709; Mary, December, 1713. Children by second wife: Ezra, April 3, 1719; Joanna, March 3, 1721-22; Charles, February 28, 1724-25.

(IV) Seth (2), son of John Pope, was born in Sandwich, January 3, 1701, died in 1769. He often held public offices in the town. In 1749 he moved to Lebanon, Connecticut, where he had a farm at the north end of Town street, which he sold in the spring of 1759. He then bought a large tract on the borders of Plainfield and Voluntown, Connecticut, now in the village of Sterling Hill. In 1760 he was on the list of taxpayers in Plainfield, and April 28, 1762, he was admitted an inhabitant of Voluntown. On March 1, 1762, he conveyed his homestead to his sons Seth Jr. and Gershom. He married, June 22, 1719, Jerusha, daughter of Gershom and Mehetable (Fish) Tobey, of Sandwich. She was born March 23, 1697-98. On October 3, 1769, his son Seth was appointed administrator of his estate. Children, born in Sandwich: Ichabod, September 5, 1720, died young; Elizabeth, October 3, 1721; Deborah, February 23, 1725; John, April 24, 1727; Mehetable, May 27, 1729; Seth, mentioned below; Gershom, December 18, 1733, died young; Elnathan, August 16, 1735; Ichabod, January 27, 1740; Gershom, August 22, 1743.

(V) Seth (3), son of Seth (2) Pope, was born April 19, 1731. He went with his father to Lebanon, Connecticut, in 1749, where he married, about 1750, Martha, born November 6, 1734, daughter of Ebenezer and Lydia (Lothrop) Bacon. On March 1, 1762, he received from his father the homestead in Voluntown. He was killed by being run over by a cart, in September, 1774. Children: Ansel, born 1751; Lothrop, 1753; Hannah, 1757; Seth, died August, 1802; William, 1763; Esther, married Philo Hamlin, of Bloomfield, New York; Lydia, February 28, 1767; Martha, married (first) John Fairchild and (second) Tyrranus Collins; Ebenezer, mentioned below.

(VI) Captain Ebenezer Pope, son of Seth

(3) Pope, was born April 3, 1772, died March 8, 1841. He lived until 1784 in the family of his maternal grandfather, Ebenezer Bacon, of Lebanon. From 1795 to 1809 he lived in Alford, where he carried on a small ironworks, and in 1809 he moved to Great Barrington, Massachusetts, where for many years he was a prominent citizen and Mason. He served several times as selectman in Alford and Great Barrington, and three times was elected to the state legislature. In 1827, because of financial trouble, he moved to Verona, New York, returning in 1831 and settling in West Stockbridge, Massachusetts, where he died. He married (first), December 17, 1800, Keziah, born in 1776, died February 6, 1804, daughter of Simon and Anne Willard; Simon Willard was son of Simon, son of John, son of Simon Willard, of Kent, England, born 1605. He married (second) Rhoda Willard, sister of Keziah, born 1782, died January 13, 1813. He married (third) Mrs. Zady (Prindle) Tobey, born April 5, 1777, died February 5, 1864. Children born in Alford by first wife: Ebenezer, mentioned below; Keziah, born February 6, 1803. Children of second wife, born in Alford and Great Barrington: Abby, August 20, 1805; Amanda, November 4, 1806; William, July 21, 1808, died January 15, 1884; Martha, June 30, 1810; John Willard, October 1, 1812, died February 16, 1813. Children of third wife, born in Great Barrington: John, August 2, 1814; Harriet, July 24, 1817; Seth Griswold, December 14, 1819, died October 26, 1911.

(VII) Ebenezer (2), son of Captain Ebenezer (1) Pope, was born in Alford, Massachusetts, October 22, 1801, died in Union township, New Jersey, December 12, 1878. He was a farmer and a blacksmith. In 1809 he went with his father to Great Barrington, and in 1827 to Verona, New York. In 1831 he returned to West Stockbridge, and afterward lived in Great Barrington until 1867, when he moved to Union township with his sons, and lived there the remainder of his life. He married, at Great Barrington, January 27, 1840, Electa Leonard, born December 19, 1803, died in Elizabeth, New Jersey, February 27, 1878, daughter of William and Mary (Leonard) Wainwright. Children, born in Great Barrington: Franklin Leonard, born December 2, 1840, died October 13, 1895; William, born and died November 27, 1842; Ralph Wainwright, mentioned below; Henry William, November 2, 1848, at Elizabeth, New Jersey, married in Pittsfield, May 10, 1870, Lucy Delia Porter, born April 23, 1851; children: Grace Electa, born June 11, 1871.

William Henry, August 20, 1873, Irving Wainwright, September 29, 1875, Florence L., June 8, 1892.

(VIII) Ralph Wainwright, son of Ebenezer (2) Pope, was born in Union township, New Jersey, August 16, 1844. He received his early education in the public schools at Great Barrington Academy and Amherst Academy in Massachusetts. He learned the art of telegraphy and became an operator in the employ of the American Telegraph Company at Great Barrington, Massachusetts, and Providence, Rhode Island, from 1861 to 1864. He studied the principles of electricity and electrical engineering, as then practiced in connection with telegraph business largely, and he must be numbered among the pioneers in electrical engineering. In 1858 he mastered the working of the Hughes printing telegraph. In 1861 he had charge of the Morse telegraph office at Great Barrington, and in 1862-63 he was in the employ of the American Telegraph Company in its New York, New Haven and Providence offices. In 1865 he was one of that band of telegraph pioneers who went into the forests of British Columbia to construct an overland telegraph system with Europe by way of Alaska and Siberia. In 1867 he was with the Bankers' & Brokers Telegraph Company, remaining until 1872, when he became an inspector of the Gold & Stock Telegraph Company. He was promoted to the office of deputy superintendent of this company in 1880, when the apparatus then used by that company was at that date probably the highest development of electro-mechanical art. While with the Bankers & Brokers Company in 1867 he was also assistant editor of *The Telegrapher*. In 1882 he became manager of the Union Electric Manufacturing Company of New York. In 1884 he was associate editor of *The Electrician and Electrical Engineer*. In 1885 he was elected secretary of the American Institute of Electrical Engineers, organized the preceding year, and he continued in this office until he resigned and retired August 1, 1911.

In 1890 Mr. Pope founded the monthly journal, *Electric Power,* and in 1891 he became editor for electrical terms in the Standard Dictionary. In 1893, under direction of the council, his quarters as secretary were established in the rooms of the American Institute of Electrical Engineers in the Electrical Building of the Columbian Exposition, and he was appointed on the committee of judges for the Department of Electricity. While at the Exposition at Chicago he personally met more than two-thirds of all the members of the In-

stitute, and ever since then he has kept up a large personal acquaintance among the members of the American Institute of Electrical Engineers. Mr. Pope had visited a majority of the sections of the Institute and many of the branches, and made a study of their requirements and growth. Upon his retirement from the office of secretary, the Institute, being unwilling to lose his services entirely, made him honorary secretary with the duty of organizing and visiting the various sections and branches, a task for which his knowledge of the members, of electrical science and of the Institute itself, pre-eminently qualified him. At the time of his retirement, a committee on resolutions, consisting of John J. Carty, George A. Hamilton and David B. Rushmore, made a report, from which we quote the following:

For more than twenty-six years, Mr. Ralph Wainwright Pope has faithfully and loyally served the American Institute of Electrical Engineers as Secretary and for the twenty-seventh consecutive year he has again been elected to the office of secretary. The Board of Directors and the membership at large are of the opinion that his continuous and honorable service he has attained such a position in the regard and affections of the members of the Institute that he is entitled to some relief from the active executive duties of his arduous position. Therefore, to carry out his own expressed wishes, his resignation as secretary has been accepted. In accepting his resignation, the board of directors, in order to give expression to their own feeling of gratitude as well as the feeling of the membership at large, and in order to reward such long and distinguished service, has appointed him to the position of Honorary Secretary, in which capacity the Institute may still have the benefit of his long experience in its affairs.

In thus complying with the natural and just desire of Mr. Pope, the board of directors has thought it well to mark this change by this minute, expressing its good will and appreciation, and by pointing out that the term of Mr. Pope's service in the Institute covers many of the most important developments in electrical engineering, and that this period has witnessed the growth of the Institute from the humblest beginning to its present flourishing condition.

Mr. Pope is a member of the Engineers' Club, the New York Electrical Society, associate of the American Institute of Electrical Engineers, honorary member of the Franklin Institute, and of the Association of Railway Telegraph Superintendents. In politics he is an Independent Democrat, and in religion a Protestant Episcopalian.

He married (first) Alice E. Judson, born September 4, 1849, died October 27, 1880, daughter of Azariah and Ellen Judson. He married (second), February 6, 1884, Ruth E. Whiting, born 1846, died 1901, daughter of Gideon M. and Louisa Whiting, of Great Barrington, Massachusetts. He married (third), October 1, 1902, Katherine A. (Cain) Durant, formerly of Clyde, New York. Children, all by first wife: 1. Ellen Lowrey, born at Elizabeth, New Jersey, May 26, 1870; married Horace Russ Wemple. 2. Frank Judson, born at Elizabeth, July 27, 1873; married Mary E. Russell, of Great Barrington. 3. Gertrude Castle, born in Elizabeth, September 24, 1876, died February 1, 1890.

JOHNSON William Johnson, the immigrant ancestor, was born in Kent, England, according to tradition, and was an early settler of Charlestown, Massachusetts. He was admitted a freeman March 4, 1634-35, and was with his wife Elizabeth received into the Charlestown church February 13, 1634-35. He was a planter. He made a deposition, now on file, December 29, 1657, stating his age as fifty-four years, from which we learn that he was born in 1603. In early family records it is stated that "he was a Puritan of good parts and education, and brought with him from England a wife and child and means." As early as 1638 he was assessed for ten separate parcels of real estate in Charlestown. His homestead is described: "One dwelling house with garden plot and yard—half a rood of ground by estimation more or less—situate in the middle row, butting southwest upon the street path—northwest upon Bark Street bounded on the southeast by Rice Cole and on the northwest by Thomas Carter." He afterward appears to have possessed, for the time and place, a large estate, a part of which by deeds of gift or otherwise he distributed among his family and the remainder he bequeathed to them by will dated December 7, 1677. He died December 9, 1677, his widow in 1685, leaving six sons and a daughter. John Johnson, of Haverhill, and Zechariah Johnson, of Charlestown, were appointed administrators of the estate of their father and mother, April 12, 1686, and the estate was divided April 13, 1686, between the administrators and their brothers Isaac, Jonathan and Nathaniel. Children: John, blacksmith, of Haverhill; Ruhannah, baptized at Charlestown, February 21, 1634-35; Joseph, mentioned below; Elizabeth, baptized March 17, 1639, married Edward Wyer; Jonathan, baptized August 14, 1641; James, baptized August 21, 1643; Nathaniel; Zechariah, aged thirty-three in 1679; Isaac, aged twenty-two in 1671.

(II) Joseph, son of William Johnson, was born in Charlestown, and baptized there by Rev. Thomas James, February 12, 1636-37. He was one of the founders and proprietors of Haverhill, Massachusetts, whither he and his brother John removed from Charlestown. He held various town offices. He married (first), April 19, 1664, Mary Soatlie, who died March 22, 1664-65, (second), in 1666, Hannah, daughter of Ensign Thomas Tenney, of Rowley, England. He and his sons owned three hundred acres of excellent land, on which part of the city of Haverhill now stands. "These Johnsons," says a tradition, "were noted for having highly cultivated farms which were enclosed by stone walls, while those of their neighbors were fenced with logs." He and wife Hannah quitclaimed rights in his father's estate to brother Isaac in 1681. He died November 16, 1714, leaving a widow and a large family of children. Children, born at Haverhill: Joseph, October 15, 1667; William, January 15, 1668; Thomas, mentioned below; Zechariah, April 16, 1672; John, November 9, 1673; Hannah, June 10, 1675; Mary, June 4, 1677; Jonathan, April 24, 1679; Elizabeth, February 28, 1680; Nathaniel, August 15, 1683; Zechariah, August 26, 1687.

(III) Thomas, son of Joseph Johnson, was born in Haverhill, December 11, 1670. He was a town officer; one of the founders of the Haverhill North Parish church, of which he was elected deacon March 23, 1732, and of which his own family at its foundation constituted a fifth of the membership. He married, May 1, 1700, Elizabeth, eldest daughter of Cornelius and Martha (Clough) Page, granddaughter of John Clough, of Salisbury, Massachusetts, who came from London in 1635 in the ship "Elizabeth." Johnson died February 18, 1742, and his widow June 12, 1752. Children, born at Haverhill: Mehitable, February 26, 1700-01; Cornelius, January 17, 1702-03; Thomas, January 6, 1704-05; Abigail, May 15, 1707; Ruth, August 24, 1709; John, mentioned below; Jabez, April 24, 1716; Jeremiah, June 30, 1717; Elizabeth, January 2, 1719-20. Two others.

(IV) Hon. John Johnson, son of Deacon Thomas Johnson, was born at Haverhill, North Parish, November 15, 1711, and was one of the founders and earliest settlers of Hampstead, New Hampshire, formerly part of Haverhill. He procured the charter for the town and was paid his expense by vote of the town May 30, 1750. He was chosen on the first board of selectmen. Soon afterward he was appointed by the royal governor, Benning Wentworth, a magistrate, and he was one of the justices of the court of general sessions at Portsmouth for the Province of New Hampshire.

He married (first), November 25, 1731, Sarah Haynes, who died September 20, 1750, daughter of Thomas and Hannah Haynes, of Haverhill, west parish. She was a sister of Joseph Haynes, of Haverhill, a deputy from that town to the First Provincial Congress at Salem, 1774, a delegate to the convention in Essex county at Ipswich, September 6-7, 1774, "to consider and determine on such measures as shall appear to be expedient for the country to adopt in the then alarming crisis." He married (second) Sarah Morse. He died April 1, 1762, leaving five surviving sons, all of whom adhered to the cause of the patriots during the revolution. Children of first wife, born at Haverhill: 1. Jesse, October 20, 1732; a member of revolutionary committees, and the state legislature. 2. Sarah, July 9, 1734. 3. Miriam, March 22, 1736. 4. Colonel Caleb, February 3, 1737-38; commanded a company in the revolution. 5. Moses, April 13, 1740; died young. 6. Colonel Thomas, March 21, 1741-42; settled at Newbury, Vermont; captain of a company in the revolution, distinguished himself at the taking of Ticonderoga and at the siege of Mount Independence in the autumn of 1777, when he was for a time an aide on the staff of General Lincoln; captured in the spring of 1781 by the British and taken to Canada, released on parole October 5, 1781; afterward colonel of militia. 7. Ruth, February 3, 1743-44. 8. Elizabeth, March 6, 1744-45. Born at Hampstead: 9. Moses, October 11, 1748. 10. Haynes, mentioned below. Children of second wife, born at Hampstead: 11. Sarah, December 29, 1751. 12. Ruth, April 23, 1754. 13. Elizabeth, twin of Ruth. 14. Peter, June 7, 1756; soldier in the revolution, wounded in the arm at battle of Bunker Hill; soldier in the company of his brother, Captain Thomas at Ticonderoga, and pronounced by his brother "brave as a lion." 15. John, August 18, 1757, died young. 16. Judith, April 4, 1758. 17. John, February 9, 1760. 18. Tammie, July 6, 1761.

(V) Haynes, son of Hon. John Johnson, was born at Hampstead, New Hampshire, August 28, 1749. At an early age he went from Hampstead with his elder brother Thomas as one of the first settlers in that part of the Connecticut Valley known then as the "Coos" or "Cohass" country, which included the Ox-bow and other rich meadows in the present town of Haverhill, New Hampshire, and Newbury and Bradford, Vermont. These meadows were first discovered in the spring of 1752 by John Stark, afterwards the famous general in the revolution, who, captured by the Indians while hunting on Baker's river, in Rumney, New Hampshire, was taken through these meadows to the home of the St. Francis tribe of Indians in Canada. It was not until 1762, however,

that a settlement was made there, and the town of Newbury was chartered in 1763. At the first town meeting of Newbury held at Plaistow, New Hampshire, June 13, 1763, Jesse Johnson, brother of Haynes, was elected town clerk, and another brother, Caleb, was elected constable. The town of Mooretown, subsequently Bradford, received its charter in 1770, and at an annual town meeting, May 1, 1775, it was voted to raise a stock of ammunition and Haynes Johnson and Benjamin Jenkins were made "a committee to look out and procure a stock of powder, lead and flints." While actively engaged in his duties on this committee he was taken ill and died at Concord, New Hampshire, September 2, 1775. He married Elizabeth Elliot. His young wife, who was with him when he died, was obliged to take her three young children, the youngest less than a month old, all on the same horse, and return to her father's home in Hampstead, a distance of more than thirty miles through a wilderness, mostly by a blazed trail. She afterwards returned to Newbury, Vermont, and married Remembrance Chamberlain, by whom she had a large family of children. It is a remarkable fact that for many years after her death nearly all of the large farms in the Connecticut Valley between Newbury and Bradford were owned and occupied by her descendants. Children of Haynes and Elizabeth Johnson: Jonathan, died January 19, 1812; Jesse, born March 27, 1772, died July 18, 1830; Haynes, mentioned below.

(VI) Captain Haynes (2) Johnson, son of Haynes (1) Johnson, was born in Newbury, Vermont, August 13, 1775, and died November 1, 1863. He settled on a large farm on the Connecticut river, in the town of Bradford, Vermont. He was for a long time captain of the Bradford militia company, and was all his life prominent in town and military affairs. He married, April 8, 1802, Jane, daughter of Captain Ezekiel Sawyer, then of Bradford, formerly of Rowley, Massachusetts, where he had served his country in the revolution as an officer in the army. His wife died May 31, 1869, aged eighty-seven years. He built a large mansion on the homestead. He and his wife were members of the Congregational church of Bradford. Children, born at Bradford: Ezekiel, September 26, 1803, married, February 27, 1827, Nancy Rogers, of Newbury; Mary, twin of Ezekiel; Eliza, February 18, 1808, married Earle Paine; Haynes C., April 4, 1811, married Harriet Willard, and had part of his father's homestead; Hannah, October 10, 1813, married William Peters; Thomas, mentioned below; Jane Ann, February 22, 1819, married Dan W. Shaw; Clarissa

P., July 18, 1825, married John Richardson; Edmund Elliot, November 27, 1827, had part of his father's homestead.

(VII) Thomas, son of Captain Haynes (2) Johnson, was born at Bradford, Vermont, December 13, 1816. He attended the public schools of his native town, and when a young man left home to work in Boston and Charlestown, Massachusetts. In 1856 he purchased and settled on the large river farm in Bradford, Vermont, adjoining the place on which he was born, and there spent the rest of his life. He died March 6, 1894. The farm is beautifully located near Rowell's Ledge, and was formerly known as the Rowell place. The local newspaper, at the time of his death said: "Mr. Johnson was an upright man in all his dealings, and was one of the most respected and substantial citizens of Bradford. He was one of the best representatives of the old class of citizens who made Vermont what it is." He married, February 12, 1862, Harriet E., daughter of Christopher and Emily (Walker) Avery, of Corinth, Vermont, a descendant of Captain James and Joanna (Greenslade) Avery, who were among the first settlers of New London, Connecticut. Her maternal grandfather was a lieutenant in the revolution. Children of Thomas and Harriet E. Johnson: Frank Verner, mentioned below; Charles Forster, born August 6, 1865; Herbert Thomas, January 27, 1872.

(VIII) Frank Verner Johnson, son of Thomas Johnson, was born at Bradford, Vermont, March 12, 1863. He attended the public schools of his native town and the Bradford Academy, Vermont, graduating in the class of 1882. He then entered Dartmouth College and was graduated in the class of 1886 with the degree of Bachelor of Arts. In 1889 he entered the Law School of Columbia College in New York City, and was admitted to the New York bar in May, 1891. For many years during the earlier period of his professional career he was the New York attorney of the Travelers' Insurance Company of Hartford, Connecticut, and devoted a large part of his time to the defense of negligence actions on behalf of policyholders in that company. He entered upon the general practice of law in New York, and has been especially successful in the field of trial attorney. He is a member of the New York Bar Association; the Association of the Bar of the City of New York; the New York County Lawyers' Association; the Manhattan Club of New York; the Dartmouth College Club of New York; the Founders' and Patriots' Society, and of several college fraternities. He is a communicant of the Protestant Episcopal church.

He married, April 19, 1893, Evelyn Webber, born August 29, 1866, daughter of Christopher and Julia (Cooper) Webber, of Rochester, Vermont, granddaughter of Christopher Webber Sr., a lawyer of Vermont. Children, born in New York City: Evelyn, April 29, 1894; Frances Virginia, July 3, 1895, died in August, 1896.

CLARK   Lieutenant William Clark, the immigrant ancestor, came to New England in the ship "Mary and John," which sailed from Plymouth, England, March 20, 1633, and arrived at Nantasket, May 30, 1636. He settled at Dorchester, where he and his wife Sarah were members of the church in 1636, and where he was a proprietor. He was selectman in Dorchester, 1660, and April 28, 1661, was dismissed from the church to join in forming a church at Northampton, whither he moved about 1669. He was lieutenant of the Train Band of Northampton in August, 1661. He was allotted twelve acres of land which included part of the site of Smith College, and which remained in the family many generations. He put up a log house, which was burned in 1681 by a negro slave. He then built another which stood until 1826. "He was a leading citizen," frequently selectman, and fourteen years deputy to the general court. He was of Deerfield in 1673, and owned lot No. 38 in 1683. He returned to Northampton, where his wife Sarah died September 6, 1675, and he married (second) Sarah Cooper, widow of Thomas Cooper, who was killed by the Indians at Springfield in 1675. He died July 19, 1690, aged eighty-one, and his wife died May 8, 1688. About 1880 a fine monument was erected by his descendants near his grave in Northampton. Children: Sarah, born June 21, 1638, died young; Jonathan, born October 1, 1639; Nathaniel, born January 27, 1642; Experience, born March 30, 1646; Rebecca, born about 1649; John, mentioned below; Samuel, baptized October 25, 1653; William, born July 3, 1656; Sarah, born March 9, 1659; perhaps, Increase, born March 1, 1645.

(II) John, son of Lieutenant William Clark, was born in 1651, died at Windsor, Connecticut, on his way home from Boston, from "fatigue and cold taken in a snow storm, September 3, 1704." He inherited the southerly six acres of the homestead. His house stood just beyond that of the president of Smith College in Northampton. He was prominent in church and town affairs, and was four years deputy to the general court. His sons, six in number, each married and outlived their wives. Each of his five married daughters also out-

lived their husbands, and all the children lived to be over eighty years of age, all living when the youngest was seventy years old. He married (first) July 12, 1677, Rebecca Cooper, of Springfield, who died May 8, 1678. He married (second) March 20, 1679, Mary Strong, who died December 3, 1738, aged eighty-four, daughter of John and Abigail (Ford) Strong. Children: Sarah, born April 20, 1678; John, born December 28, 1679; Nathaniel, born May 13, 1681; Ebenezer, born October 18, 1682; Increase, mentioned below; Mary, born October 27, 1685; Rebecca, born November 24, 1687; Experience, born October 30, 1689; Abigail, born March, 1692; Noah, born March 28, 1694; Thankful, born February 13, 1696; Josiah, born June 11, 1697.

(III) Increase, son of John Clark, was born April 8, 1684, at Northampton, Massachusetts, in the homestead on Elm street, where at last accounts descendants were still living. The initials "I. C." in a prominent place in one of the rooms, before the house was repaired in later years, were probably those of Increase Clark. In 1735 and 1739 he was selectman of Northampton and held other offices. He lived on the homestead sixty-five years and died there in 1775. He married at the age of twenty-six, in 1710, Mary, daughter of Isaac Sheldon, whose home lot was the sixth on Elm street proceeding north from King street. Among his children were: Deacon Simeon, who settled in Amherst and had a numerous posterity; Elijah, mentioned below.

(IV) Deacon Elijah Clark, son of Increase Clark, was born, lived and died on the Elm street homestead. He was born in 1730, died in 1791. He was honored by various town offices. He was chosen deacon of the church in 1785, at the age of fifty-four, and served the remainder of his life. During the revolution he served on the town committee of fifteen and his services entitled his descendants to membership in the Sons and Daughters of the American Revolution. Three of his sons were also deacons, two in the same church. Of his children, Eli, the second son, moved to Marcellus, now Skaneateles, New York, in 1801, and was one of the pioneers of that section, journeying thither by ox-cart through the wilderness. Experience, the only daughter, married Justin S. Smith, had eleven children, and lived on her father's homestead for many years. Luther, mentioned below. Calvin, born 1770.

(V) Deacon Luther Clark, son of Deacon Elijah Clark, was born in 1767, in the old Judson Smith house in Northampton, died October 17, 1855, aged eighty-eight years. In 1812 he bought the homestead on Mill river. He took part in Shay's rebellion. He held town

offices fifty years, and was deacon of the church. He married Polly White. He left four living sons.

(VI) Bohan, son of Deacon Luther Clark, married and among his children was Luther Clapp, mentioned below.

(VII) Luther Clapp, son of Bohan Clark, was born in Northampton, July 4, 1815. He was educated in the public schools of Northampton, Massachusetts. For many years he was a banker at St. Louis, Missouri. He married Julia Crawford, born October 2, 1823, daughter of David Crawford, of Putney, Vermont. Her father was brigade major on the staff of General Winfield Scott, United States army, during the war of 1812. David Crawford married Nancy Campbell, who was born in Vermont. Children of Luther C. Clark: George Crawford, mentioned below; Ellen White, deceased; Arthur Campbell; Louis Crawford; Julia Goodman, married Samuel P. Blagden; David Crawford.

(VIII) George Crawford, son of Luther Clapp Clark, was born in St. Louis, Missouri, August 3, 1845. He attended private and public schools in New York City and was graduated with the degree of Bachelor of Arts from the College of the City of New York in the class of 1863. Since that time he has been in the banking business in New York City. He is the senior partner of the firm of Clark, Dodge & Company, bankers and brokers, 51 Wall street. His father was also a banker in New York, and his son, George C. Clark Jr., is a member of the firm of Clark, Dodge & Company, the third generation to follow this business in New York City. He is a director of the Northern Securities Company; the Chicago, Burlington & Quincy Railroad Company; the City Investing Company; the Norfolk & Southern Railway Company; the Atlantic Mutual Insurance Company, and of the Seamens Bank for Savings of New York. He is treasurer and director of the Brearley School (Limited) and of the General Memorial Hospital; member of the Metropolitan Museum of Art, New England Society of New York, American Museum of Natural History, Union Club, Century Club, Racquet and Tennis Club, University Club, Down-town Club, Riding Club, New York Yacht Club. His home is at 1027 Fifth avenue, New York City.

He married, November 4, 1875, Harriet Seymour, born August 18, 1853, daughter of James G. and Charlotte (Seymour) Averell, of Ogdensburg, New York. Children: 1. George Crawford, born February 8, 1878; married Gertrude Sard, of Albany, New York, and they have two children: George Crawford, 3d, and Caroline. 2. Edith Gilbert, married

Reginald Fincke; children: Reginald Jr. and Nancy Gilbert. 3. Marian Averell. 4. James Averell, born 1894.

The name Highet seems to have HIGHET originated in the neighborhood Ayr, Scotland, where members of the family have been prominent and influential, acting well their part in all the walks of life, proving themselves of the highest type of manhood by their useful lives in the communities in which they resided.

(I) John Highet, the progenitor of the line here under consideration, is a native of Ayr, Scotland, born May 17, 1737. His entire life was spent in his native land, and he was noted for integrity and uprightness of character. He married Jane McGregor and among their children was John, mentioned below.

(II) John (2), son of John (1) and Jane (McGregor) Highet, was born at Ayr, Scotland, May 20, 1782, died in June, 1833, in New York City. He was reared, educated and married in his native land, from whence he emigrated to the United States in 1819, locating in Baltimore, Maryland, his purpose in coming to this country being to erect a carpet mill, which was the first of its kind, he being a skillful mechanic or machinist. After a residence of eighteen months in Baltimore, he removed to New York City and there spent the remainder of his days. He was interested in the welfare of the cities in which he made his home, and was honored and respected by his neighbors. He married, at Ayr, Scotland, December 7, 1819, Janet Thomson Wilson. Children, all born in the United States: Mary, died young; John, drowned in early life; Mary Jane, married James B. Burgess; William Wilson, mentioned below; Margaret Primrose, married Charles Stevens; Robert Bennett, married Mary Hill. Of these children only two are living at the present time (1912) William Wilson and Robert Bennett.

(III) William Wilson, son of John (2) and Janet Thomson (Wilson) Highet, was born in New York City, March 29, 1829. He obtained a practical education in the public schools, and his active career has been devoted to carriage manufacturing. He has resided in New York City and Poughkeepsie. Throughout his life he has been public-spirited and enterprising, ever forward in advancing the interests of the localities in which he has resided. He married, March 29, 1853, Ellen Adams, born in June, 1830, daughter of Galen Thompson and Mary Ellen (Fletcher) Porter, the latter of whom was a daughter of Elisha Fletcher (see Porter VII). Children: Carita, married Joseph LeRoy Porter; Ella, married

Raymond L. Donnell; Frank Brewster, mentioned below.

(IV) Frank Brewster, son of William Wilson and Ellen Adams (Porter) Highet, was born in Poughkeepsie, New York, February 10, 1858. He attended the public schools of New York City, thereby preparing himself for an active and useful life. He is now serving in the capacity of secretary and treasurer of Gardner, Highet & Company, of New York, manufacturers of feather stitch, cotton braid and fancy narrow fabrics. He is a communicant of the Protestant Episcopal church, and in politics is an adherent of the Republican party. He is a member of the New York Society of the Sons of the Revolution, New York Historical Society, Metropolitan Museum of Art, New England Society of New York, Ardsley Club and the Greenwich Country Club. His home is in Greenwich, Connecticut.

Mr. Highet married, April 16, 1885, Isabella Boudinot Servoss, born in New York City, daughter of Elias Boudinot Servoss, and a descendant of Elias Boudinot, president of the continental congress when peace was declared.

(The Porter Line).

(I) Richard Porter, immigrant ancestor, was born in England and sailed for this country from Weymouth, England, March 30, 1635. With others in the same company he settled in Weymouth, Massachusetts. His home was not far from the site of the meeting house in the north parish. In 1661 he was on a committee to repair the meeting house. He married Ruth ———. Children: John, mentioned below; Ruth, born October 3, 1639; Thomas, married Sarah Viniv; Mary, married John Bicknell. Richard Porter died in 1689. His will was dated December 25, 1688, and proved March 6, 1689.

(II) Sergeant John Porter, son of Richard Porter, lived in Weymouth and was one of its leading citizens, having many grants and buying much land. In 1693 he built the first saw mill in what is now South Abington at "Little Comfort." In 1696 he sold half of his mill to Joseph Josselyn. He held various town offices and served on committees to fix town boundaries. He married, February 9, 1660, Deliverance, daughter of Nicholas and Martha (Shaw) Byram. Children: Mary, born October 12, 1663; Susanna, June 2, 1665; John, July 2, 1667; Samuel, mentioned below; Nicholas; Ruth, September 18, 1676; Thomas; Ebenezer; Sarah. Sergeant Porter died at Weymouth, August 7, 1717; his widow September 30, 1720. His will was dated February 8, 1715-16.

(III) Samuel, son of Sergeant John Porter,

was born about 1670. He was a town officer of Weymouth in 1705. About this time he removed to Abington, where he was schoolmaster in 1712, and by trade a shoemaker. He was selectman in Abington, 1714, and for three years afterward; assessor in 1716. We know he taught school there in 1724 and 1727. He was one of the original members of the Abington church. He married Mary, daughter of Jacob and Abigail (Dyer) Nash, of Weymouth, about 1698. Children, born at Weymouth, except the three younger who were born at Abington: Samuel, mentioned below; Mary, October 5, 1701; David, 1702; Jacob, August 10, 1704; Hannah, December 16, 1716; Abigail, June 23, 1719. Samuel Porter died at Abington, August 31, 1725, and his will is dated August 24, 1725.

(IV) Samuel (2), son of Samuel (1) Porter, was born at Weymouth, May 14, 1699. He lived in Abington and Bridgewater. He married (first) July 2, 1722, Sarah, daughter of Joseph and Sarah (Ford) Josselyn, of Abington. He married (second) May 31, 1764, Ruth Reed, widow, of Bridgewater. He and wife Sarah deeded land in Bridgewater, December 1, 1742, to his brother Jacob. Children: Sarah, born May 26, 1723; Mary, February 9, 1725; Samuel, October 12, 1727; Joseph, mentioned below; Ebenezer, September 12, 1731; Mary, August 3, 1733; Adam, February 24, 1735; Hannah, February 18, 1736; Betterus, September 23, 1737; Noah, May 13, 1740; Jonathan, August 27, 1741: Deliverance, July 19, 1742; Abigail, July 7, 1743; Tabitha, 1744; Sarah.

(V) Lieutenant Joseph Porter, son of Samuel (2) Porter, was born February 27, 1730. He lived at Bridgewater and Stoughton, Massachusetts. He bought a house in what is now West Bridgewater, April 9, 1765, and sold it April 2, 1777, removing then to Stoughton. He was a soldier in the revolution in Captain William Briggs' company, Colonel Joseph Read's regiment, from May to August, 1775, credited to Stoughton. He was also in Captain Simeon Leach's company, Colonel Benjamin Gill's regiment, marching from Stoughton to Braintree in 1777, and was corporal in Captain James Endicott's company in 1778. The genealogy states that he was a lieutenant in the time of the war. He married, January 25, 1763, Elizabeth, born July 4, 1733, daughter of Samuel and Content (Whitcomb) Burrill. She was a teacher at Abington before marriage, a woman of remarkable beauty. Children, of whom the first seven are recorded at Bridgewater: Elizabeth, born November 8, 1753; Joseph, June 10, 1754; Hannah, July 21, 1758; Robert, March 30, 1762; Isaac, mentioned be-

low; Content, February 5, 1767; Mehitable, April 15, 1769; Lebbeus, April 22, 1771; Cyrus, 1774. Lieutenant Porter died January 15, 1803; his widow died March 26, 1822, aged eighty. His will was dated February 16, 1802.

(VI) Isaac, son of Lieutenant Joseph Porter, was born February 23, 1765, at Bridgewater. He was admitted to the North Bridgewater Church in 1780. He resided in Bridgewater and Middleborough; was surveyor of highways in Bridgewater in 1797. He married Susannah, born December, 1763, died October 29, 1841, daughter of Reuben and Anna (Perkins) Packard, of Bridgewater. Children, of whom the first five were born in Middleborough and the others in Bridgewater: Susanna, born April 17, 1788, married Galen Thompson; Isaac, April 20, 1790; Sybil, April 13, 1792; Rhodolphus, January 25, 1794; Samuel, May 12, 1796; Reuben, March 23, 1798; Martin, July 21, 1800; Ira, April 5, 1803; Anna, April 20, 1805; Galen Thompson, mentioned below.

(VII) Galen Thompson, son of Isaac Porter, was born in Bridgewater, November 5, 1807. He was a real estate dealer in Harlem, New York City. He married, September 13, 1829, Mary Ellen, daughter of Elisha and Abigail R. (Day) Fletcher (see Fletcher VII), of Lancaster, Massachusetts. Children: Ellen Adams, born June, 1830, married, March 29, 1853, William W. Highet, of New York (see Highet III); John Holmes, February, 1832, married Louisa J. Ayers, and died June 5, 1875; Emma, October, 1834, died December 17, 1834; Mary Emma, March, 1837, married Marcellus E. Randall, September 8, 1854; Anna Perkins, November, 1839, married, March 30, 1862, Lewis W. Stetson, and died March 7, 1869; Galen Thompson, June, 1842, died at St. Thomas, West Indies, September 15, 1866, purser in United States navy; David Fletcher, December, 1844, married, August 13, 1869, Fannie E. Leggett, of New York; Harriet Augusta, September, 1847, married Elihu L. Tompkins, of White Plains, September 27, 1865; Frank, died February 25, 1852.

(The Fletcher Line).

(I) Robert Fletcher, the immigrant, was born in England in 1592, died at Concord, April 3, 1677, aged eighty-five. His will was dated February 4, 1672, then "aged about fourscore". The family tradition fixes his birthplace in Yorkshire. He settled in Concord, Massachusetts, in 1630, and became well-to-do and prominent. He was appointed by the general court a constable for Concord, November 2, 1637; was one of the founders of the town of Chelmsford, Massachusetts. He married ——— ———. Children: Luke, born in England; William, mentioned below; Caroline; Francis, 1630; Samuel, 1632.

(II) William, son of Robert Fletcher, was born in England in 1622, died November 6, 1677. He came to Concord with his father. He was admitted to the church there, was made a freeman, May 10, 1643; selectman, 1655, of Chelmsford, the first town meeting being at his house. In 1673 he was appointed a commissioner or magistrate for Chelmsford. He owned the land on which the city of Lowell is located, and a part of the original lot near the meeting house in Chelmsford is still owned by his descendants and has been in the possession of the family two hundred years and more. He married, October 7, 1645, Lydia Bates, of Concord, who died October 12, 1704. Children: Lydia, born January 30, 1647; Joshua, mentioned below; Paul; Sarah; William, born at Chelmsford, February 21, 1657; Mary, October 4, 1658; Esther, April 12, 1662; Samuel, July 23, 1664.

(III) Joshua, son of William Fletcher, was born at Concord, March 20, 1648, died November 28, 1713. He was admitted a freeman, March 11, 1689. He married (first) May 4, 1668, Grissel Jewell, who died in January, 1681. He married (second) July 18, 1681, Sarah Willey. Child of first wife: Joshua, born about 1669. Children by second wife: Paul, 1682; Rachel, June 27, 1683; Timothy, October, 1685; John, May 7, 1687; Joseph, June 10, 1689; Sarah, January 21, 1690; Jonathan; Jonas, 1694; Elizabeth, June 10, 1698.

(IV) John, son of Joshua Fletcher, was born in Chelmsford, May 7, 1687. He married, in 1712, Hannah Phelps, of Lancaster, Massachusetts, where he settled and built a house on George's Hill, directly west of the present meeting house. The homestead remained in the family until 1868. His wife died April 10, 1737, aged fifty-one. Children, born in Lancaster: John, Timothy, Robert, Joshua, mentioned below; Lydia, Hannah, Ruth.

(V) Joshua (2), son of John Fletcher, was born in Lancaster, December 26, 1724, died November 13, 1814. He was born and always lived on the homestead on George's Hill. At the time of the revolution he was on the committee of safety and his service makes eligible his descendants to the Sons and Daughters of the American Revolution. Though more than fifty years old, he responded to the Lexington Alarm and joined the Lancaster company. He married, May 15, 1748, Mary, daughter of Ebenezer and Sarah Allen. She died July 25, 1813, aged eighty-six. Children, born at Lancaster: Joshua, February 25, 1749; Timothy,

September 20, 1750, a soldier in the revolution; Phineas, May 29, 1753; Elisha, June 18, 1755; John, October 1, 1757; Mary, June, 1760; Peter, September 5, 1762; Rufus, mentioned below; Anne, born September 29, 1767; Sophia, November 22, 1769; William, August 9, 1772.

(VI) Rufus, son of Joshua (2) Fletcher, was born at Lancaster, October 14, 1764. He lived on part of the homestead on George's Hill and died there September 28, 1851, a humble and devoted Christian. He married, June 29, 1786, Mary Sawyer. Children: Elisha, mentioned below; Sophia, October 18, 1788; Artemas, October 10, 1790; Cynthia, January 31, 1792; Christopher, April 6, 1794; Rufus, June 9, 1795, died young; Rufus, March 30, 1797; Mary, December 25, 1799; Elijah, August 23, 1802, died young; Lewis, December 19, 1805.

(VII) Elisha, son of Rufus Fletcher, was born September 4, 1787, at Lancaster. He was a mason by trade. He found employment in New York City and when about to move his family thither he was killed by the fall of a building, October 11, 1816. His widow died in 1865. He married Abigail R. Day in 1809. Children: Mary Ellen, born September 6, 1810, married, September 13, 1829, Galen Thompson Porter (see Porter VII); John Day, April 29, 1813; Elisha Rufus, born in Gloucester, November 16, 1816; David Boynton, twin of Elisha Rufus, married Sarah A. Smith.

———

DAVIES   This family is of Welsh origin and was first known under the name of Davies in 1581, when Robert ap David of Gwysany assumed it, and received confirmation of the family arms and grant of crest and motto. From the best information that can be obtained, it appears that John Davies, the immigrant, was the only son of Thomas Davies, fourth son of Robert Davies of Gwysany Castle in the parish of Mold, Flintshire, England. The family for years has ranked among the first of North Wales. They derived an unbroken descent from the famed Cymric Efell, Lord of Eylwys Eyle, who lived A. D. 1200, son of Madoc ap Meredith, Prince of Powys Fadoc, sixth in descent from Merwyn, King of Powys, third son of Rodic Maur.

(I) John Davies, the immigrant ancestor, was born in England, in Kingston parish in 1680, and came to America in 1735 with his wife, Catherine Spenser. He settled in the western part of Litchfield county, Connecticut, and purchased one hundred and sixty acres of land from Thomas Lee for one hundred and fifty pounds, within the present town of Washington. Within fifteen years after his arrival he was owner of a large and valuable tract containing nearly a thousand acres of the best land in Litchfield county. In religion he was Episcopalian, being one of the founders of the Episcopal church at Litchfield. On April 4, 1747, he conveyed to Mr. Samuel Cole, as trustee for the church, a tract of fifty-two acres of land in Litchfield, to be held for the use and benefit of the minister of the church. At his request the church was named St. Michael's, and the first service held April 23, 1749. In 1747 Mr. Davies gave to his son a tract of four hundred and thirty acres, and in 1750 he gave to his grandsons, John, Thomas and William, one hundred and twenty acres of land. His wife died several years before he did, but the exact dates are unknown. He had only one child, John.

(II) John (2), son of John (1) Davies, was born in England, in 1711, died May 19, 1797, aged eighty-six years. He was educated at the University of Oxford, and in 1734, married Elizabeth Brown, who died about 1739. He married (second) in England, 1744, Mary Powell, who died December 15, 1801, aged seventy-five years. He made two or more voyages to America before he finally settled here in 1747 on the land given him by his father. As a member of the Episcopal society in Litchfield he was influential. Like his father, he did not appear to have much interest in taking part in public affairs. During the French and Indian war, 1757, he purchased a large tract of land in Saratoga county, New York, and went there to take possession, but was kept from his purpose by hostile Indians, and returned to Connecticut in 1758. He and his family were Tories, and the property of his sons John and William was confiscated, and John was fined and imprisoned for a year in Litchfield jail for giving aid to the royal cause. His young son David narrowly escaped death for the same reason, but was pardoned on enlisting in the continental army during the war, it is written, although his name does not appear on the war rolls. After the separation of Birch Plains of "Davies Hollow" from the township, the family withdrew from the church and built one principally at their own expense near their homes. Children, by first wife, born in England: John, mentioned below; Thomas, born January 2, 1737; William, born 1739, died in infancy. Children, by second wife, born in England: William, born January 29, 1744; Mary, March 17, 1745, died young; James, 1746, died in infancy; Walter, June 22, 1747. Born in America: Catherine, born July 20, 1751; Elizabeth, July 3, 1753; Ann, November 18, 1755; James John, Decem-

ber 31, 1757; David, March 14, 1759; Rachel, August 20, 1761; George, February 12, 1764; Thomas, May 30, 1766.

(III) John (3), son of John (2) Davies, was born at Kingston, county of Hereford, England, June, 1735, and was brought to America by his father when young. In 1750 his grandfather conveyed to him a tract of land, and in 1758 his father gave him sixty acres. During the revolution he was imprisoned for aiding England's cause, as well as being deprived of his property. He was active in the organization of the Church of St. John, founded by his father. In 1793 or 1794 he opened a store in the town of Washington, in partnership with his son Thomas John. They also purchased cattle in the country which they sold in New York. This enterprise was successful until the summer of 1798, when there was an epidemic of yellow fever in New York, and the cattle drove sent there was an entire loss to him. This last blow seems to have discouraged him, and he died April 18, 1799, aged sixty-four. He married, in 1763, Eunice Hotchkiss, of New Haven, who died March 29, 1824, aged seventy-nine. Children: Elizabeth, Thomas John, Eunice, Esther, all born before 1774.

(IV) Thomas John, son of John (3) Davies, was born at Davies Hollow, November, 1767. He lived near his father. As the rest of the family had been, he was an Episcopalian, and in August, 1796, he was elected chorister. In 1798 he met with reverses in business and determined to start again on the shore of Black Lake, St. Lawrence county, New York. In 1800 he removed his family there and made a home in the wilderness. Soon many families were settled near, and Mr. Davies always had a leading part in the community. In politics he was a Democrat and for ten years held the office of sheriff of St. Lawrence county, and served for several years as county judge. Two sons, Charles and Thomas, he sent to the United States Military Academy at West Point. He died April 18, 1845, aged seventy-eight, and was buried on his own grounds at Black Lake. He married, December 29, 1792, Ruth Foote, daughter of Captain John Foote, of Watertown, Connecticut, who died September 21, 1852. Children: Belvidere, wife of George Ranney; John Foote, Charles, Henry E., mentioned below; Thomas Alfred, and Eunice Ruth.

(V) Henry Ebenezer, son of Thomas John Davies, was born at Black Lake, February 8, 1805. At the age of fourteen he entered the family of the late Judge Alfred Conkling, at Canandaigua, to prepare for the profession of the law. On becoming of age he was admitted to the bar in Albany county, April, 1826. He began his professional career in Buffalo, then a small village on the western frontier. His first important case was between the owners of uplands who wished to extend warehouses into the river and shut off ancient rights of way and by the aid of old residents, including the Seneca Chief, Red Jacket, establishing the fact that the right of way had existed from time immemorial, Mr. Davies won his case and his victory resulted in his election in the following year as city attorney. In the winter of 1829-30 he removed to New York City and soon after formed a partnership with his uncle, Samuel A. Foote, and the firm continued until 1848, when Mr. Foote retired. Among the clients of the firm were various large corporations, including the Erie Railroad Company. Mr. Davies next entered into partnership with Hon. William Kent, and the firm lasted until 1853. His next partner was Henry J. Scudder, son-in-law of Prof. Charles Davies. When Mr. Davies was elected a justice of the supreme court in 1855, James C. Carter, who had been a clerk of the firm, was admitted to partnership and the firm became Scudder & Carter.

Mr. Davies was always a Whig in politics and was an able public speaker and campaigner. In 1840 he was elected assistant alderman of the City of New York from the Fifteenth Ward and in 1842 was chosen an alderman. At this time, he was chairman of the committee in charge of celebrating the introduction of Croton water in the city. In 1850 he was appointed corporation counsel and he held the office three years. One of the most important services he rendered in this office was in successfully defending Mayor Cornelius W. Lawrence in suits for damages caused by the blowing up of buildings to check a conflagration, upon order of the mayor. After he retired from this office he made, at the request of the common council, a compilation of the statutes relating to the city with its ancient and modern charters. In the summer of 1855, he accompanied abroad Millard Fillmore, former President of the United States, whose friendship he had formed in early life, continuing until his death. In the same year he was elected to the bench of the supreme court. During his term of office he presided at two celebrated murder trials, those of Cancemi and Burdell, and in the general term concurred in the decision that slaves brought into the state became free. In the fall of 1859 he was elected justice of the court of appeals for eight years, during the last two of which he was chief justice. He wrote the opinions of the court in many most important cases, such as that of Kortright vs. Cady (21 N. Y. 343),

establishing the point that tender of the amount due on a mortgage destroys the lien thereof; People vs. The Canal Appraisers (33 N. Y. 461), establishing the law relating to navigable streams; Dealfield vs. Parish (25 N. Y. 9), discussing the matter of testamentary capacity. Probably no opinion ever caused him more thought and study than that written in Metropolitan Bank vs. Van Dyck (27 N. Y. 400), sustaining the legal tender acts of the nation. He gave to the government unfaltering support during the civil war, and his conviction that the constitution conferred extraordinary powers on the government in time of war found expression in his opinions, especially in the legal tender case. At the end of his term, he declined reëlection and resumed his practice in partnership with Judge Noah Davis until the latter was reëlected to the bench in 1872, and afterward with his son, Julien Tappan Davies. He was counsel for the Mutual Life Insurance Company and other large corporations, but devoted himself mainly to chamber practice and to service as referee in important cases. The day before he was stricken with his last illness he sat for many hours as one of the commissioners to determine the feasibility of constructing the Broadway Arcade Railroad. He was a director of the Institution for the Instruction of the Deaf and Dumb, and during the last year of his life its president. In 1870 he became dean of the Law School of the University of the City of New York and continued in this office as long as he lived. He received the honorary degree of LL. D. from the university and also from Amherst College.

"Judge Davies was conspicuous," wrote his son, Henry Eugene Davies, in the Davies genealogy, "during his long and busy life for sterling integrity and devotion to the interests committed to his charge. His capacity for labor was prodigious and sustained by a constitution of iron that gave him enormous powers of endurance. During the Cancemi trial, after five days spent until a late hour in presiding, at half-past seven on a Friday evening he commenced to write his charge. He finished it as he was summoned to breakfast at eight o'clock the next morning, having labored all the night without intermission for sleep or refreshment. From this, and from other similar herculean labors, he never suffered any inconvenience or felt that he had sustained a strain, until some two years before his death, when age slowly claimed him as its own. Yet he retained great vigor until the day when he was fatally attacked, some two weeks only before his death. * * * In person he was strongly and heavily built, though of medium stature.

He possessed the powerful body with large organs and short limbs, characteristics of his Welsh ancestry. His head was large, with a brain fully developed, and a countenance full of benignity, though stern in such times as called for an exhibition of strength. He was genial in manner and friendly with all men. His sole pleasure was the professional one of whist. Temperate indeed, almost abstemious in his habits, simple in his tastes, earnest in his professional duties, the two leading motives of his life were devotion to duty and love of his family. True to the church of his ancestry, and following their lead, he gave to St. Luke's Church at Mattewan, in Dutchess county, the land upon which its edifice is erected. Under the shadow of its eaves he rests—wife, children and grandchildren reposing around him. The memory of his pure, strong, loving spirit is the most precious heritage of his living descendants." He died in the city of New York, December 17, 1881.

He married Rebecca Waldo Tappan, born in Boston, 1815, died February 24, 1884, daughter of John and Sarah (Salisbury) Tappan. John Tappan was born July 26, 1781, son of Benjamin (5), (Benjamin (4), Samuel (3), Peter (2), Abraham (1) Tappan), married, September 30, 1805, Sarah, daughter of Samuel Salisbury, granddaughter of John, and great-granddaughter of Nicholas Salisbury. Elizabeth (Sewall), wife of Samuel Salisbury, was a daughter of Samuel (6), (Rev. Joseph (5), Samuel (4), Henry (3), Henry (2), Henry (1),) Sewall. Elizabeth (Quincy) Sewall, wife of Samuel, was a daughter of Edmund and Elizabeth (Wendall) Quincy. Sarah (Salisbury) Tappan died August 28, 1839, after having eleven children, and he married (second), September 22, 1841, Mrs. Hannah (Pomroy) Edwards. John Tappan was sent by the United States government to London as a delegate to the International Convention of Peace in 1843. Children of Mr. and Mrs. Davies: 1. General Henry Eugene, born in New York City, July 2, 1836; entered the service as captain in 1861 and rose to the rank of major-general in 1865, resigning January 1, 1866; lawyer in New York City; author of Davies' Genealogy; public administrator 1866-69 in New York City; assistant district attorney 1870-73; died September 6, 1894; married, August 10, 1858, Julia Rich. 2. William Gilbert, born March 21, 1842; a lawyer; married, December 15, 1870, Lucy C., daughter of Hon. Alexander H. Rice. 3. Julien Tappan, mentioned below. 4. Theodore, October 22, 1847; was in the diplomatic service; journalist; died March 15, 1875. 5. Francis Herbert, September 15, 1849; married, April 27, 1876, Cornelia

Scott, daughter of Henry S. Rokenbaugh; died February 27, 1906. 6. Helen, June 9, 1851. 7. Lucy, March 7, 1853; married, April 21, 1875, Dr. Samuel Swift, died February 4, 1897.

(VI) Julien Tappan Davies, son of Hon. Henry E. Davies, was born in New York City, September 25, 1845. He attended the schools of his native city and the private school of Dr. Reed at Walnut Hill, Geneva, New York. He entered Columbia College in 1862 and was graduated in the class of 1866. In the summer of 1863, while a student in college, he joined the Twenty-second Regiment of New York State Militia, and took an active part in the Pennsylvania campaign of the Civil War, ending at the Battle of Gettysburg. On leaving college he devoted himself to the study of law in the office of Hon. Alexander W. Bradford. Under the will of Judge Bradford, Mr. Davies succeeded to part of his law practice, and soon afterward became associated with his father, Judge Davies, who retired from the bench of the Court of Appeals, January 1, 1868. With these fortunate connections he established an active and prosperous professional career and gained a deservedly high reputation as one of the leading lawyers of New York City. In politics he is a Republican. In religion a member of the Episcopal church. He has been for many years counsel for the elevated railways of New York; has been since 1881 a trustee of the Mutual Life Insurance Company of New York. His office is at 34 Nassau street, New York. He is now a partner in the firm of Davies, Auerbach, Cornell & Barry.

He married, April 22, 1869, Alice, born January 12, 1847, daughter of Hon. Henry H. Martin, a descendant of Captain John Martin, of Woodbury, Connecticut. Children: Julien Townsend, born February 20, 1870; Alice, died in 1885, aged fourteen; Helen, died in 1877, aged five; Thomas Alfred, died in 1877, aged four; Ethel, born March 19, 1876; Frederick Martin, born September 12, 1877; Cornelia Sherman, born October 21, 1882.

HUBBARD The surname Hubbard dates from the first use of family names in England, and was doubtless in earlier times a personal name. Some writers think it a modification of the Danish name Hubba, made famous by one of the sea kings who conquered part of England. Several forms of spelling survive, Hubbard and Hobart being the most prominent as surnames, Hubert and Herbert as personal names. In old records some fifty different spellings have been found, and as late as the

colonial period in America the variations are
very numerous. The English family has always been prominent, and many of the
branches have ancient coats-of-arms. We find
the records mentioning a John Hubbard, born
about 1235, living in Rye, Norfolkshire, England, and from him a numerous posterity residing in that section of the country.

(I) George Hubbard, immigrant ancestor,
was born in England in 1601, probably in the
eastern or southeastern part. He settled in
Hartford, Connecticut, before 1639. Another
George Hubbard, who settled in Wethersfield,
Connecticut, was doubtless a relative, but not
his father. William and Thomas Hubbard,
also of Hartford, were among the early settlers,
and they seem also to be closely related. George
Hubbard came with the first settlers overland
from the Massachusetts Bay Colony. He was
given six acres of land "by courtesy of the town,
with privilege of wood & keeping cows on the
common", and lived on a lot adjacent to land
of James Ensign and George Graves on a
road that ran parallel with the Connecticut
river, from the south meadow to George
Steele's place. In 1640, after his marriage, he
was assigned a home lot and land on the east
side of the Connecticut river. In 1649 he was
fined ten pounds for exchanging a gun with
an Indian, it being against the law to furnish
arms or ammunition to the savages. He removed in March, 1650-51, with about fifteen
other settlers and their families, to Mattabesit,
later called Middletown, Connecticut. He was
licensed as an Indian agent and trader as early
as 1650. He was admitted a freeman in 1654.
He owned much land on both sides of the
river, living on what is now Main street. He,
together with Thomas Wetmore and two
others, gave land for the second meeting-
house. He was the first sexton of the first
meeting-house, and his son Joseph beat the
drum to call the people to meeting or to warn
them against hostile Indians. His will, dated
May 22, 1681, states his age as eighty years.
His inventory is dated May 13, 1685, and
states that he died March 18, 1684. In 1640
he married Elizabeth, daughter of Richard and
Elizabeth Watts; she died in 1702. Children:
Mary, born at Hartford, January 16, 1641-42;
Joseph, December 10, 1643; Daniel, mentioned
below; Samuel, May, 1648; George, December
15, 1650; Nathaniel, December 10, 1652;
Richard, July, 1655; Elizabeth, January 15,
1659. One record says that George Hubbard
"was highly respected and of marked integrity and fairness."

(II) Daniel, son of George Hubbard, was
baptized at Hartford, December 7, 1645, and
died at Haddam, November 9, 1704. He set-

tled in Haddam about 1700. He took part in
the war of 1690. He married (first), Feb-
ruary 24, 1669-70, Mary Clark, who died De-
cember 24, 1673. He married (second)
Sarah Cornwell, born at Middletown, Octo-
ber, 1647, daughter of Sergeant William and
Mary Cornwell. Child of first wife: Daniel,
mentioned below. Children of second wife:
Margaret, born July 20, 1675, married John
Ward; Mary, January 16, 1678; Jacob; Sarah,
March 10, 1680; Mehitable, August 18, 1683;
Mary, March 23, 1686.

(III) Daniel (2), son of Daniel (1) Hubbard, was born at Hartford, Connecticut, December 16, 1673. He removed with his family to Haddam, where he owned considerable
land, and was regarded as a well-to-do and
prominent citizen. He married (first), December 8, 1697, Susannah Bailey, of Haddam.
In his will, which was proved January 14,
1756, he bequeathes to his second wife, Bathsheba Hubbard. Children: Mary; Daniel, born
1701, died March 11, 1765; Susannah, 1703,
married ―――― Crampton; Elizabeth, 1706,
married Ebenezer Munger; Hannah, 1708,
married, June 13, 1734, Elisha Cone; Martha,
1710, married Abraham Stone; Thomas, mentioned below.

(IV) Thomas, son of Daniel (2) Hubbard,
was born in 1714 at Haddam, Connecticut. He
was an extensive land owner and conducted a
grist mill. He married (first) Elizabeth Snow.
He married (second), at Haddam, Sarah
Walkley. Children, born at Haddam: Agnes,
1736, married Lewis Smith; Thomas, mentioned below; Hannah, 1741, married John
Brainerd; Daniel, 1742, married Anna Woodruff.

(V) Thomas (2), son of Thomas (1) Hubbard, was born at Haddam, Connecticut, in
1738, died there June 6, 1803. He was a soldier in the revolution, according to the genealogy. He was wealthy for his day, owning
considerable land and a grist mill. He married,
November 6, 1771, Sarah Boardman, born in
1752, died at Haddam, 1829. Children, born
at Haddam: Zerviah, baptized October, 1772;
Amasa, mentioned below; Hannah, baptized
1777; Jemima, 1778; Jerusha, baptized June,
1780; Daniel, baptized February, 1782; Samuel Boardman, baptized June, 1784; Damaris,
baptized January, 1787, married Jonathan
Burr; Juliana, 1788, married Elisha Clark;
Sarah and Elizabeth, twins, 1790; Maria, 1793,
married Herman Brainerd.

(VI) Amasa, son of Thomas (2) Hubbard,
was baptized at Haddam, Connecticut, September, 1775. He married (first) Elizabeth
Burr; married (second) Deborah Coates;
married (third) Hannah, daughter of David

Hubbard. Children, born at Haddam: Samuel, about 1802, died young; Clarissa, 1805, married Joseph Arnold; Thomas, 1806; Dr. Samuel Thomas, mentioned below; Rev. Jonathan, 1810, graduate of Princeton University, resided at Granville, New York, married Mary Fish and had children, Jane, Frederick and Martha; Daniel, 1812, died in 1835; Alburn, 1816, resided at Haddam, married (first) Cynthia Bonfoey and (second) Mary Smith and had children: Eleanor, Frank, Florence and Frederick.

(VII) Dr. Samuel Thomas Hubbard, son of Amasa Hubbard, was born at Haddam, Connecticut, February 19, 1808. He was educated at the Garfield grammar school, Middletown, and Suffield Academy, Suffield, Connecticut. He studied medicine with Amos S. Miller, of New York, graduating at the College of Physicians and Surgeons of the University of the State of New York in 1835. He was a prominent physician of New York City, and in addition to his private practice held the position of physician to the Presbyterian Hospital, consulting physician to the New York Dispensary. He was a member of the Medical Society of New York County, the New York Academy of Medicine, the Medical Journal Association, the Medico-Legal Society, the Society for the Relief of Widows and Orphans of Medical Men, and of the Physicians' Mutual Aid Association. He was president of the first-named society in 1866-67: vice-president of the second-named from 1873 to 1876, corresponding secretary from 1853 to 1858, trustee from 1862 to 1873, and re-elected in 1876. He also served as trustee of the College of Physicians and Surgeons of Columbia University, New York. Dr. Hubbard married, in 1850, Mary Hearn Hustace, of New York City, born 1826, daughter of Benjamin and Ann (Hearn) Hustace, of New York. Children: Walter Comstock, mentioned below; Emily, born 1853; Samuel Thomas Jr., mentioned below; William, born 1857, died in 1884.

(VIII) Walter Comstock, son of Dr. Samuel Thomas Hubbard, was born in New York City, June 26, 1851. He attended private schools and the Mount Washington Collegiate Institute, from which he was graduated in the class of 1865. After completing his studies he engaged in the shipping and commission business in New York City and subsequently became a cotton merchant. In partnership with his brother, Samuel Thomas Hubbard, they established the firm of Hubbard Brothers & Company, cotton merchants and brokers, New York City. He acted as president of the Cotton Exchange of New York City in 1905-06-07. He is a member of the Chamber of Commerce, the Union Club, the Union League Club, of New York, St. Nicholas Club of New York, New York Yacht Club, Seawanhaka Yacht Club, Larchmont Yacht Club, New England Society of New York and St. Nicholas Society, Sons of the American Revolution, and the Society of Colonial Wars. Mr. Hubbard married, in May, 1872, Helen Ingalls, daughter of Alfred A. Valentine, of New York, who came thither from Rhode Island. Children: 1. Dr. Ernest Valentine, graduate of Columbia College and the College of Physicians and Surgeons; a physician in New York City; married Mary Cheatham, of Nashville, Tennessee. 2. Edith Ingalls, married Duncan Sterling, of New York. 3. Ralph Hustace, graduate of Columbia College; married Etta Fleming, of New York City.

(VIII) Samuel Thomas Jr., son of Dr. Samuel Thomas Hubbard, was born in New York City, 1855. He completed his studies in private schools. He is a member of the firm of Hubbard Brothers & Company, cotton merchants and brokers, New York City. He is a member of the Cotton Exchange of New York City, serving as president of the same for two terms, and is also a member of the Chamber of Commerce, the New York Club and the New York Yacht Club. He married Elizabeth A. Van Winkle, of New York City. Children: William Hustace, Samuel Thomas, Elizabeth and Margaret.

FAIRBAIRN Fairbairn is an ancient Scotch surname meaning "fair child." The old coat-of-arms of the Scotch Fairbairns is described: Gules an eagle; wings endorsed or, a bordure ermine. Crest: a griffin passant sable. Motto: *Semper eidem* (Always the same). The family is also found in England. Among the famous men of the family may be mentioned Andrew Martin Fairbairn, who was born in Scotland, November 4, 1838; D. D. University of Edinburgh, 1878; M. A. Oxford May 17, 1887. He was a minister of the independent church at Bathgate, West Lothian in 1860; at Aberdeen in 1872; became principal of Airdale College, in 1884, and of Mansfield College, Oxford, in 1886; received the honorary degree of D. D. from Yale University in 1889; was Muir lecturer on philosophy and history of religion at Edinburgh University from 1878 to 1883, and was chairman of the Congregational Union of England and Wales in 1883. Children: John Shields, born at Bathgate, December 21, 1868, graduate of Magdalen College, B. A. 1891, with honors in physiology;

Andrew, born at Bathgate, October 1870, graduate of the Oxford High School and Wadham College, B. A. 1892.

John Fairbairn was born in Nenthorn, Roxburghshire, Scotland, in 1714; married Helen Anderson, of Cralny, and died at Galashiels in 1796; children: Walter, died young; William, of Galashiels, died in 1809; Andrew, mentioned below; Peter, secretary to Lord Seaforth, died in 1823.

Andrew Fairbairn, son of John Fairbairn, was born at Smailholme, Roxburghshire, February 10, 1758; married, December 12, 1783, Margaret Henderson, of Jedburgh, and died January 14, 1844. Children: Sir William, made baronet November 2, 1869, for eminent service as engineer and scientist; Thomas, drowned in 1812; Sir Peter, mayor of Leeds.

(I) George Fairbairn, who was closely related doubtless to the Roxburghshire family from which Sir William Fairbairn descended, was born at St. Boswell's parish, Roxburghshire, Scotland, in 1670, and died in his native place. He married Jenett Caile, born 1673, in the same parish.

(II) William, son of George Fairbairn, was born in 1709 in St. Boswell's parish and died there in 1789; married Ann Cranston, born 1700 and died in 1778 in Crasting parish, Roxburghshire, daughter of Robert and Isabella Cranston.

(III) William (2), son of William (1) Fairbairn, was born at Cron (?) Flats, Bothwell parish, Roxburghshire, Scotland, July 13, 1762, and died February 18, 1843. In 1796 he came to Philadelphia, Pennsylvania, and engaged in business as a printer and book publisher. He published an edition of Burns' poems in this country at the same time that they were published in England for the benefit of the poet's family.

He married Mary Mott, who was born at Poughkeepsie, New York, December 23, 1776, and died in New York City, February 1, 1840, a daughter of Henry Mott, born about 1746, and Elizabeth (Newcomb) Mott (see Newcomb V).

(IV) Robert Brinckerhoff, son of William (2) Fairbairn, was born at Greenwich Village, New York, May 27, 1818, and died January 27, 1899, at Brooklyn, New York. He received a public school education and then took special training in the Mechanics' School, after which he entered a bookstore in Franklin Square, where for three years he received a useful and educational training, which he always declared was of great value to him the rest of his life. In 1834 he entered Bristol College, Pennsylvania, ith the view of studying for the Episcopal ministry. When that

institution ceased to exist he was transferred to Washington (now Trinity) College, at Hartford, Connecticut, from which he was graduated in 1840 with the degree of Bachelor of Arts. He then studied at the General Theological Seminary in Chelsea Square, New York, from which he was graduated, and in 1843 was ordained deacon, immediately entering on the rectorship of Christ Church, Troy, New York. After being very successful there and rescuing the church from debt, restoring a property worth $20,000 to the vestry, he went to Stillwater, on the upper Hudson, as rector of St. John's Church there, but not long after this he decided that he was more fitted naturally for a teacher, and he combined the duties of the ministry with that of teaching.

In 1853 he became the principal of the Catskill Academy, and for nearly ten years held that office, resigning to accept a position as professor of mathematics in St. Stephen's College at Annandale-on-the-Hudson. This institution had been established as a training college for the ministry for only three years; the Rt. Rev. Horatio Potter was its founder, but it very likely was not started with definite views as to its purpose, and the result was that it had not made as much progress as it should, though under the direction of able men. After one year there, Dr. Fairbairn was appointed the warden, as the presiding officer was called, after Oxford fashion. He seemed to have a definite idea of what the institution was to do. His view was that it was an undergraduate college, in which the education and training of young men who intended to study theology was to be conducted, and though he did not have adequate means to carry out his purpose, he was never discouraged. With the help of several faithful professors he made the college a power in the church, and at the end of twenty-eight years could name nearly two hundred men prominent in the church who had received their preparation at his college.

He is the author of several works, among which are "The Child of Faith," "College Sermons," "The Doctrine of Morality in Its Relation to the Grace of the Gospel," and twenty-five pamphlets on educational and religious subjects. In 1864 the degree of Doctor of Divinity was given him by Trinity College, and also by St. Stephen's College in 1874. He was one of the sixty persons on whom a doctor's degree was conferred by Columbia College at its centennial anniversary in 1887. He also received the degree of Doctor of Laws from Delaware College in 1876.

He married Juliet Arnold, daughter of Anson and Sally (Gardner) Arnold (see Arnold XXIII). She was born at Troy, June 3, 1822, and died in August, 1893, at Annandale, New York.

(V) Dr. Henry Arnold Fairbairn, son of Robert Brinckerhoff Fairbairn, was born at Catskill, New York, May 5, 1855. He attended the Annandale parish schools and St. Stephen's College of Annandale, graduating with the degree of Bachelor of Arts in 1875. In 1878 he received the degree of Master of Arts from his alma mater, and in 1910 the honorary degree of Doctor of Letters. He received his medical education at the University of Virginia, receiving the degree of Doctor of Medicine in 1878. In the same year he located in Brooklyn, New York, where he has been practicing to the present time (1912). For many years he has been among the foremost physicians of Brooklyn. Formerly he was a surgeon of much skill and reputation, but in later years he has devoted his practice chiefly to internal medicine. He has a very large practice and is popular not only among his patients, but among a large circle of friends and acquaintances. He is a member of the Board of Regents of the Long Island College Hospital; attending physician of St. John's Hospital of Brooklyn; attending physician of the Brooklyn Hospital; consulting physician of the Long Island State Hospital; consulting physician of the Long Island College Hospital; consulting physician of the Swedish Hospital; consulting physician of the Hebrew Orphan Hospital. He is a trustee of St. Stephen's College of Annandale. He is a director of the Home Trust Company of Brooklyn. In politics he is a staunch Republican. He is a communicant of the Church of the Good Shepherd (Protestant Episcopal), and was formerly a vestryman and for many years delegate to the Diocesan Councils. He is a member of the Union League Club of New York and the Authors' Club of London; the New York Academy of Medicine, the Kings County Medical Society, the New York State Medical Society, of which he is a member of the publication committee; the American Medical Association, the Victoria Institute of London, England, and the New England Society of New York. He published a biography of his father under the title of "The College Warden" (1899), and has written extensively for the medical journals on the subject of Internal Medicine, and published many pamphlets on medical subjects.

He married, February 7, 1888, Alice Le-Fevre (see LeFevre). Children: 1. Robert LeFevre, born January 2, 1889, educated at Brooklyn Polytechnic Institute; Adelphi Academy, from which he was graduated in 1905; Columbia College (A. B. 1910); the School of Mines of Columbia University, graduating in 1913; member of the Sigma Alpha Epsilon fraternity; secretary of the Civil Engineering Society of Columbia. 2. Ruth, born December 16, 1889. 3. Russel Arnold, born January 3, 1891, graduate of Adelphi Academy in 1909 and from Columbia University School of Mines, 1912; member of Sigma Alpha Epsilon fraternity. 4. Agnes Lathers, born July 30, 1892, student at Packer's School, class of 1912.

(The Newcomb Line).

Captain Andrew Newcomb, the immigrant ancestor, came from the "west of England," according to tradition, perhaps from Devonshire or Wales. He was very likely among the earliest settlers of New England. The first mention of him was in 1663, in Boston, Massachusetts, when he married his second wife, Grace, widow of William Rix or Ricks. He was called a mariner or sea captain, and doubtless had always had this occupation. In the Charlestown records for February 28, 1666-67, mention is made of his taking horses on his ship for John Ely and Elikim Hutchinson; on August 28, 1679, in the New York Colonial Manuscripts at Albany, Andrew Newcomb is named as Master of the sloop "Edmund and Martha," then in New York and bound for Boston, probably from Virginia, a part of the lading being tobacco. Philip Foxwell deposed that Andrew Newcomb was in Saco river from Boston, October, 1684, and this is the last record of him until his will was proved two years later. His second wife, Grace, was born about 1620-25, and had by her first husband, William Ricks: Elisha, John, Thomas and Ezekiel, born in Boston between 1645 and 1656. On February 14, 1672, agreement was made that Andrew Newcomb and Grace should occupy William Ricks' house during their lifetime; that John and Thomas Ricks should have the new house near the former, near the water-mill in Boston, each to have a half of the land, paying to Newcomb twenty pounds each. On April 13, 1681, he bought of Simon Lynde and Sarah, wife of Joseph Goodale, the administratrix of Thomas Ricks, the right to redeem an estate in Boston mortgaged to Lynde by Thomas Ricks in 1677. On April 14, 1681, he and his wife sold to John Ricks all right in the house near Mill Bridge, that had been owned by Thomas Ricks, deceased. His will was dated January 31, 1682-83, and proved December 9, 1686. He doubtless died in November, 1686, though he may have died a year earlier at sea. Although his son Andrew was not mentioned in his will, many facts show that he was doubtless his son. Children of first wife: Andrew, mentioned below; Susannah, born between 1635 and 1650. Child of second wife: Grace, born in Boston, October 20, 1664.

(II) Lieutenant Andrew (2) Newcomb, son of Captain Andrew (1) Newcomb, was born about 1640, and was living in America as early as July, 1666, when he attended a meeting at the Isle of Shoals, near Portsmouth, New Hampshire, of several merchants and men engaged in the fisheries, for the purpose of fixing the price of fish. The first record of land purchased by him was April 20, 1669, at Alfred, York county, Maine, when he, of Kittery, York county, a fisherman, bought of Daniel Moore, of Portsmouth, blacksmith, a dwelling-house in Kittery and six acres adjoining the house at Emberrys (Emery) Point. The place is situated on the southeast side of the mouth of the Spinney Creek, bounded on the west by the Piscataqua river. Andrew Newcomb served as constable, and in 1671 was living at the Shoals. In June, 1673, he was called before the county court at Dover, New Hampshire, to answer a complaint of Francis Small for withholding the "Hull of a fishing shallop of sd Smalls receiued of Thomas Trickie by virtue of sd Small's order", but finally the case was withdrawn as there was no cause of action. On July 19, 1673, a deed is recorded at Exeter, New Hampshire, in which he sold a house on Hog Island to Henry Platts. About 1675 he seems to have moved from the Shoals to Edgartown, Martha's Vineyard, Dukes county, Massachusetts, where he remained the rest of his life, dying between March 7, 1703-04, and October 22, 1708. He was one of the proprietors of Edgartown and had several shares in the divisions of land there, also making many purchases of land. He sold the land in 1700 which is the famous camp-meeting ground on Martha's Vineyard. He served as juror at quarter court, September 26, 1677, at Edgartown, also December 28, 1680; was foreman of the jury September, 1681, and foreman of the grand jury, March 7, 1703-04; in 1681 was constable, and was chosen townsman May 10, 1693, overseer, March 16, 1693-94; on April 13, 1691, was chosen lieutenant and was in command of the fortification that year. He very likely was a merchant for several years. He was well-to-do and a prominent man in Edgartown. The land on which the court-house now stands belonged to him.

He married (first) Sarah ———, about 1661, and she died about 1674. He married (second) in Edgartown, in 1676, Anna, daughter of Captain Thomas and Anna (Baker) Bayes; she was born about 1658, and died in

the summer of 1731 or in September of that year, aged about seventy-three, having survived her husband for many years. Her name is on the oldest list of church members which has been kept there, July 13, 1717, and also in the list of January 24, 1731. Children of first wife: Simeon, born about 1662; Andrew, about 1664; Simon, mentioned below; Thomas, about 1668; Sarah, about 1670; Mary or Mercy, about 1672; Peter, about 1674. Children of second wife: Anna, 1677; Elizabeth, 1681; Joseph, 1683; Emblem, about 1685; Tabitha, about 1688; Hannah, about 1694; Zerviah, 1698-99; Mary, about 1700.

(III) Simon, son of Lieutenant Andrew (2) Newcomb, was born about 1666, probably at Kittery, York county, Maine, or perhaps on one of the islands of the Shoals, near Kittery. His father moved to Edgartown when he was about eight years old, and here he lived until 1713, when he moved to Lebanon, New London county, Connecticut, where he remained the rest of his life. The first time his name was on record was May 10, 1690, when he was named in the will of William Vinson, of Edgartown, to see that it was carried out. He owned several shares of land on the Island of Chappaquiddick, where he kept large numbers of cattle and sheep. He also received several shares from 1695 on, in Edgartown, as a proprietor, and he bought much land at Pohoggannut, near Job's Neck. He bought of his father the land called Job's Neck, or Sopataming. Other purchases and grants to him are also recorded, and there are records of the land sold by him, also. His first purchase in Lebanon was September 26, 1711, when he bought of Israel and Mary Phelps, a farm of about 160 acres, on which he lived in Lebanon for nearly a third of a century, leaving it by will to his son Simon. He gave farms to his sons, and made several purchases in Lebanon. In 1710 he was chosen field driver in Edgartown, and was made freeman there; in 1714 was surveyor of highways; grand juryman, 1718; served on various committees and helped in settling town boundaries. · His will was dater July 23, 1741. He died January 20, 1744-45, aged seventy-nine.

He married about 1687, Deborah ———, who died in Lebanon, June 17, 1756, aged ninety-one. Children: John, born about 1688-89; Thomas, mentioned below; Hezekiah, 1693-94; Obadiah, 1695; Deborah, 1696-97; Sarah, about 1698; Benjamin, about 1700; Elizabeth, 1701-02; Simon, about 1705.

(IV) Thomas, son of Simon Newcomb, was born in Edgartown, in 1691-92, died in 1761. About 1714 he settled in Lebanon, Connecticut, where he lived until 1739, moving then to Salisbury, Connecticut. He was a cordwainer, being also engaged to a large extent in mercantile business until 1739, for over twenty years. His account book of 1735-1739 is still preserved. In 1737 he gave Hannah Harsel pay for schooling his children. About twenty purchases of real estate are recorded in Lebanon, the first being September 29, 1718, on Chestnut Hill, now in the town of Columbia. The largest purchase was for 200 acres. On December 8, 1729, he was elected surveyor of highways, and between March 19, 1738-39, and October 11, of that year, moved to Salisbury, where he was one of the original proprietors. He was moderator of the first town meeting, November 9, 1741, and first chosen selectman. In 1745 he united with the Salisbury church by letter from the First Church of Lebanon; in 1746 moved to Crum Elbow Precinct, or "Little Nine Partners," Dutchess county, New York, about ten miles east of Poughkeepsie, where he was one of the "Little Nine Partners" to a large tract granted by the government. He gave a farm to each of his sons. He lived in Charlotte Precinct, in the town of Pleasant Valley, and was buried in the Washington Hollow churchyard.

He married (first) at Nantucket, Massachusetts, December 28, 1712, Eunice, daughter of Dennis and Catharine (Innes) Manning, of Nantucket, born about 1685, died December 7, 1715. He married (second), January 17, 1720, Judith, daughter of Benjamin Woodworth, of Lebanon. Children of second wife: Cyrenius, born April 16, 1721; Azariah, May 18, 1722; Keziah, November 14, 1723; Zaccheus, February 19, 1724-25; Adonijah, February 3, 1726; Thomas, mentioned below; Judith, May 21, 1733; Simon, January 9, 1736; Deborah, June 21, 1738, died in Salisbury, June 24, 1739.

(V) Thomas (2), son of Thomas (1) Newcomb, was born November 11, 1730. In 1739 he went with his father to Salisbury, and in 1746 to Dutchess county, New York. He lived at "Little Nine Partners," or North East Precinct, after his marriage. He married Bridget Gardner, of Rhode Island, and she married (second) Dr. Corkins; they lived in Susquehanna, and when the fort was taken by the Indians they just escaped with their lives. Children: Elizabeth, married Henry Mott, of Poughkeepsie, their daughter Mary married William (2) Fairbairn (see Fairbairn III); Judith, born September 23, 1759, married James Newcomb; Nancy, married —— Wilcox, of Ferrisburg, Vermont; Gardner, "moved west," had a son who was a Baptist deacon.

1—8

(The Arnold Line).

The family of Arnold is very ancient, having its origin among the princes of Wales. According to a line recorded in the College of Arms, they trace from Ynir, King of Gwentland, who flourished about the middle of the twelfth century, and who was descended from Ynir, the second son of Cadwaladr, king of the Britons. This Cadwaladr built Abergavenny, county Monmouth, and its castle was afterward rebuilt by Hamley ap Hamlet, ap Sir Druce of Balladon, in France, and portions of the walls still remain. The coat-of-arms is: Gules, a chevron ermine between three pheons or. Crest: A lion rampant gules, holding in his paws a lozenge or. Motto: *Mihi Gloria Cessum.*

(I) Ynir, King of Gwentland, married Nesta, daughter of Jestin ap Curgan, king of Glamorgan.

(II) Meiria succeeded his father and married Eleanor, daughter of Ednivid ap Jorworth, of the house of Trevor.

(III) Ynir Vichan, king of Gwent, married Gladice, daughter of Rhys Coch ap Maenerch, Lord of Ystradyw, in Brecknockshire.

(IV) Carador ap Ynir Vichan, Lord of Gwent, married Nesta, daughter and heiress of Sir Rydereck le Gros, Knight.

(V) Dyfnwall ap Carador, Lord of Gwent, married Joyes, daughter of Hamlet ap Sir Druce, Duke of Balladon, in France.

(VI) Systyl ap Dyfnwall, Lord of Upper Gwent, married Annest, daughter and heiress of Sir Peter Russell, Knight, Lord of Kentchurch, county Hereford.

(VII) Arthur ap Systyl married Jane, daughter of Lein ap Moreidhec, Lord of Cantreblyn.

(VIII) Meiric ap Arthur married Annest, daughter of Cradock ap Einen ap Golhroyn.

(IX) Qwillim ap Meiric, Esq., married Jane, daughter and co-heir of Ivor ap Syssylht, Lord of Lyhs Taly-hont.

(X) Arnholt ap Qwillim ap Meiric, Esq., married Janet, daughter of Philip Flering, Esq.

(XI) Arnholt ap Arnholt Vychan, Esq., married Sybil, daughter of Madoc ap Einen ap Thomas.

(XII) Roger Arnold of Llanthony in Monmouthshire, was the first of the family to adopt a surname. He married Joan, daughter of Sir Thomas Gamage, Knight, Lord of Coytoy.

(XIII) Thomas Arnold, Esq., succeeded to Llanthony and other estates in Monmouthshire. He married Agnes, daughter of Sir

Richard Warnstead, Knight. Children: John of Hingham and Over; Richard, mentioned below.

(XIV) Richard Arnold moved to Somersetshire in the parish of Street. He married Emmote, daughter and heiress of Pearce Young, of Damerham, Wiltshire.

(XV) Richard (2) was eldest son and heir of Richard (1) Arnold, and removed to Dorsetshire and was seated at Bagbere, in the parish of Middleton, otherwise Milton Abbas. He was Lord of the Manor of Bagbere and had estates at Alton Pancras, Buckland Newton, Cheselbourne, Melcombe Horsey, and other places in that county. He was also the patron of the churches of Blandford and of Bingham Melcombe. His manor house at Bagbere was standing until 1870, when it was demolished and a farm house erected on the site. A small part of the ancient building is incorporated in the new house. His will was dated May 15, 1593, and proved July 9, 1595. He desires to be buried "in the Parishe Churche of Milton in the Ile called Jesus Ile as we goe to the Tower". He married twice.

(XVI) Thomas (2), second son of Richard (2) Arnold, is mentioned in his father's will. He lived some time at Melcombe Horsey, and removed to Cheselbourne on one of his father's estates. The family register of the baptisms of his children was prepared and brought to America. He married (first) Alice, daughter of John Gulley, of North Over, parish of Tolpuddle, near Cheselbourne. Children of first wife: Thomasinel Joanna, baptized November 30, 1577; Margery, baptized August 30, 1581; Robert, baptized 1583; John, born 1585; William, June 24, 1587. Children of second wife: Elizabeth, 1596; Thomas, mentioned below; Eleanor, baptized July 31, 1606.

(XVII) Thomas (3), son of Thomas (2) Arnold, was the immigrant ancestor. He was born in 1599 at Cheselbourne, county Dorset, England, and baptized April 18, 1599. He came to America in the ship "Plain Joan" in May, 1635, settling at Watertown, Massachusetts, and on May 13, 1640, was made freeman. He was deputy to the general court in 1666-67-70-71-72, and in 1672 was a member of the town council. There are records of his buying and selling land in Watertown at various times. He died in September, 1674, at Providence, Rhode Island, and his wife and children settled his estate as he had directed by oral will. He married (first) ———, and (second) Phebe Parkhurst, who died in 1688, daughter of George and Susanna Parkhurst. Children: Thomas, born May 3, 1625, died young; Nicholas, 1627, died young; Susanna.

By second wife: Richard, mentioned below; Thomas; John, February 19, 1648; Eleazer, June 17, 1651.

(XVIII) Richard (3), son of Thomas (3) Arnold, was born March 22, 1642, at Providence, and died April 22, 1710. He served as deputy to the general assembly in 1671-76-79-80-81-96-98-1700-01-02-05-07-08, and was assistant in 1681-82-83-84-85-86-90-98-99; on May 6, 1685, was on a committee to draw up an address of congratulation to King James II. on his peaceable succession to the throne; on December 22, 1686, was appointed a member of the council of Governor Andros; was on the town council in 1700-01, and in 1707-08 was a speaker of the house of deputies. His will was dated June 8, 1708, proved May 10, 1710. He married (first) Mary Angell, who died in 1695, daughter of Thomas and Alice Angell; (second) Sarah ———, who died in 1712. Children by first wife: Richard, John, mentioned below; Thomas, born March 24, 1675; Mary. By second wife: Jonathan.

(XIX) John, son of Richard (3) Arnold, was born November 1, 1670, at Providence, died October 27, 1756. He was a miller. In religion he was a member of the Society of Friends, and on December 9, 1719, was appointed to build their meeting-house. In 1731-32 he was a member of the town council at Smithfield, Rhode Island. About 1712 he built his corn and fulling mill on the island near Woonsocket Falls. His will was dated May 5, 1753, and proved November 1, 1756. He married (first) Mary Mowry, born 1675, died January 27, 1742, daughter of Nathaniel and Joanna (Inman) Mowry; (second), October 31, 1742, Hannah Hayward. Children of first wife: William, born December 9, 1695; John, July 27, 1697; Daniel, May 1, 1699; Mercy, December 22, 1701; Anthony, March 12, 1704; Seth, mentioned below; Israel, Anna, Susanna, Abigail.

(XX) Seth, son of John Arnold, was born at Providence, Rhode Island, September 6, 1706.

(XXI) Seth (2), son of Seth (1) Arnold, as born at Providence or Smithfield, about 1728. He settled at Smithfield and married, October 25, 1750, Mary Cargill. Children, born at Smithfield: George, mentioned below; Phebe, June 2, 1755; James, November 27, 1763; Anthony, May 28, 1769; John, died February 22, 1752 (an older son).

(XXII) George, son of Seth (2) Arnold, was born October 11, 1751, at Smithfield. He married Elizabeth ———. Children, born at Smithfield: Phebe, born September 27, 1777; Hadwen, June 20, 1779; Oliver, February 27, 1781; Elizabeth, March 24, 1783; Margaret,

February 21, 1785; George, January 1, 1787; Anson, mentioned below; Maria, September 17, 1791; James, September 12, 1793; Sarah H., August 7, 1795.

(XXIII) Anson, son of George Arnold, was born at Smithfield, Rhode Island, March 8, 1789, died at Catskill, New York, April 19, 1855. He married Sally Gardner, born July 15, 1795, died at Troy, New York, May 9, 1859, daughter of Nathaniel Gardner. Their daughter Juliet married Robert Brinckerhoff Fairbairn (see Fairbairn IV).

(The LeLevre Line).

Peter LeFevre, the first of this family in America, was born at Havre de Grace, France, whence he fled with other Huguenots to San Domingo, West Indies. Among his children was John, mentioned below.

(II) John Jacques, son of Peter LeFevre, was born in 1753, died in 1837. He removed from San Domingo to New Rochelle, New York, where the Huguenots had made a settlement before 1700. He married Susanna Coutant, of an old New Rochelle family (see Coutant III). She died in 1802. Children: Peter E.; Prosper; John W., mentioned below; Benjamin Drake.

(III) John W. LeFevre, son of John J. LeFevre, was born about 1780-90.

(IV) Peter Edward, son of John W. Le-Fevre, was born at New Rochelle, New York, September 6, 1810, died there December 24, 1886. He was a master mariner and at one time superintendent of the Ocean Steamship Company, of New York. During the Civil War he commanded the "Vanderbilt" when that vessel was sent to prevent the Confederate iron-clad "Merrimac" from coming out of Hampton Roads. His home was in New Rochelle and he was captain of a militia company there. He was a Democrat of the old school. In religion he was a Methodist.

He married at Rye, New York, April 6, 1848, Mary Ann Mount, a daughter of Forman Marshall Mount, who was born May 4, 1793, at Allentown, New Jersey, and died at Rye, May 14, 1827, also a shipmaster. Forman Marshall Mount married, December 25, 1819, at St. Mary's Church, Rotherhith, E., London, England, Mary Ann Russell, who was born at Nantucket, Massachusetts, May 10, 1803, and died on Easter Sunday, April, 1882, at New Rochelle. Forman Mount, father of Forman Marshall Mount, married April 6, 1760, Margaret Edwards. Michael Mount, father of Forman, was born in 1730, and died February 4, 1815; married Mary Forman, who died September 12, 1809, aged seventy-five years, daughter of Ezekiel Forman, born October 31,

1706, died October 3, 1745, granddaughter of Samuel and Mary (Wilson) Forman, great-granddaughter of Aaron and Dorothy Forman. Aaron's father was Robert, of Flushing, 1645. Richard Mount, father of Michael, died 1777. Mary Forman's mother was Elizabeth Seabrooke, born 1713, died May 16, 1791, daughter of James and Hannah (Grover) Seabrooke, granddaughter of Thomas and Mary Seabrooke and of Joseph and Hannah (Lawrence) Grover, great-granddaughter of James Grover on one side and of William and Hannah Lawrence on the other.

A daughter of Peter Edward LeFevre, Alice, married Dr. Henry Arnold Fairbairn (see Fairbairn V).

(The Coutant Line).

John Coutant, the immigrant ancestor, was born in France in 1658, and came, about 1689 from Saint Arville, France, with the first settlers from Rochelle, France, to the settlement at New Rochelle, New York. His name is spelled Contin, Coutin, Couton and in various other ways in early records. He married Susanna Bonnefoy, who was born in 1660. His name appears prominently in New Rochelle records. Children: John, mentioned below; Isaac, John Jr., Peter, Judy, Hester.

(II) John (2), eldest son of John (1) Coutant, was born about 1690. He is mentioned in the will of Ambrose Sicard, of New Rochelle, August 27, 1733. The will of his brother Isaac, dated December 8, 1747, and proved November 29, 1766, bequeaths to wife Catherine and children—Jacob, Isaac, John (if he ever returns), Catherine, Esther, Susanna and Miriam. Isaac was witness of Pierre Perott's will at New Rochelle, May 26, 1730, and of Lewis Guion's will, November 23, 1732. Catherine Coutant, widow of Isaac, was legatee under the will of Mar LeFevre, of New Rochelle, dated April 17, 1753, proved May 11, 1753, "the best of my diamond rings," and Jacob and Jane Coutant were witnesses of this will.

(III) Isaac, son of John (2) Coutant, was born in New Rochelle, in 1723, and died in 1802. He married Fannie Badeau, of another French Huguenot family, who was born in 1732, died December 17, 1825. Their daughter Susanna, born about 1760, married John LeFevre (see LeFevre II).

The name of Burke, Bourke or BURKE Bourck, was originally written de Burgh, and under that form is an ancient name, and signifies "pertaining to a city." It is of much note in the old world, and may be traced back to the eighth century.

Its head was Charles, Duc d'Ingheim, fifth son of the Emperor Charlemagne. In the fourth generation from him is Baldwin de Bourg, his great-grandson, a renowned Crusader, whose son Baldwin founded the house of Blois in France, and was a progenitor of the noble families of Burgh and Vesey, in Ireland. Early in the fourteenth century lived John, Earl of Comyn and Baron of Tonsburgh in Normandy, and a descendant of the above, "who, being general of the king's forces, and governor of his chief towns, obtained the surname of de Burgh." The name is mentioned in very early English history, and its owners verify their descent from the old crusader by deeds of bravery, piety and loyalty to their king. The most celebrated was Hubert de Burgh, who became king's justiciar of England under Henry III., was made Earl of Kent, and received in marriage the eldest sister of the King of Scotland. In the reign of Henry II. a branch of the de Burghs went over into Ireland, and from that time down figures in Irish history. It is frequently involved in the wars and struggles which harassed that riotous kingdom, and in most cases is found on the side of law and order.

(I) Richard Burke, the immigrant ancestor, is supposed to have been born about 1640, in England, and died at Sudbury, Massachusetts, 1693-94. October 24, 1670, he bought one hundred and thirty acres of land in Sudbury, and March 1, 1685-86, he was granted by the town of Stow thirty acres of upland and swampland for a house lot. July 26, 1687, he had another small grant of land in Stow. He married, in Sudbury, June 24, 1670, Mary Parmenter, born in Sudbury, June 10, 1644, daughter of John and Amy Parmenter, and granddaughter of Deacon John Parmenter, born 1588, who was one of the first settlers of Sudbury, 1639. She survived her husband, and afterward married ——— Allen. Children, born in Sudbury: Richard, mentioned below; John, married Rebecca ———; Joseph, born April 1, 1676; Mary, September 25, 1680; Jonas, January 4, 1683-84; Thomas, November 1, 1686.

(II) Richard (2), son of Richard (1) Burke, was born in Sudbury, April 16, 1671. He lived at Stow, Sudbury and Brookfield, Massachusetts. His name appears upon the records of Stow as late as 1705; in 1708 he is called of Sudbury, and in 1720 had a grant of land in Brookfield. He married Abigail, daughter of Jonathan and Mary Sawtell, and granddaughter of Richard Sawtell, a proprietor of Watertown, 1636-37, and one of the first settlers of Groton, where he was town clerk for the first three years after its organization.

Her father was also an original proprietor of Groton. She was born there March 5, 1671-72, and died in Sudbury, April 1, 1716 (?). Children, first three born probably in Stow, last three in Sudbury: Abigail, married John Parmenter; Richard, lived in Brookfield, married Mary ———; Jonathan, mentioned below; Sarah, born 1708; Keziah, February 24, 1710-11; Uzziah, twin of Keziah.

(III) Jonathan, son of Richard (2) Burke, was born in January, 1701, and died in Windsor, Vermont, May 18, 1775. He lived in Brookfield, where his name appears on the records as late as 1748, at which time he purchased real estate in Brimfield, Massachusetts. July 10, 1759, he conveyed to his son Jonathan eighty acres of land in Brimfield, and was later of South Brimfield, which was incorporated September 18, 1762. He was often appointed on committees on town and church affairs in the two latter towns. December 15, 1769, he was living in what is now Westminster, Vermont. He served in the colonial wars, 1722-24; in Major John Chandler's company, August 18 to November 26, 1722; January 8, 1724, on the frontier; in garrison at Brookfield, Massachusetts, April 13 to November 20, 1724. (Authorities: Temple's "History North Brookfield, Massachusetts," quoting from muster rolls among Massachusetts archives in State House, Boston; Burke Alvord Memorial; Hemmenway's Gazeteer). Jonathan married May 10, 1731, in Northampton, Massachusetts, Thankful, daughter of William and Ann (Webb) Wait; she was born in Northampton, January 27, 1706 (?), and died in Windsor, January 29, 1783. Children, all but the youngest, born in Brookfield, the latter in Brimfield: Keziah, March 3, 1732; Jonathan, February 26, 1733-34; Simeon, May 3, 1736; Jesse, mentioned below; Isaiah, June 13, 1740; Richard, "deceast April 13, 1741"; Solomon, born December 2, 1742; Silas, November 22, 1744; Elijah; Anna, September 2, 1728.

(IV) Captain Jesse Burke, son of Jonathan Burke, was born in Brookfield, April 8, 1738, and died in Westminster, Vermont, January 20, 1811. He was one of the first settlers of Westminster, and a large landowner. He was proprietor of a large part of the land comprised in the lower settlement of the East Parish of that town. In the political agitation which preceded the outbreak of the revolution he was early allied to the side of the patriots, and was captain of the first military company raised in the vicinity. He was a friend and confidant of Ethan Allen, of revolutionary fame, and during the collision between the people of Vermont and the authorities of New York, prior to the independence and admittance of Vermont into the Union as a state, had the latter as a guest at his house. He was a man of marked decision of character, of integrity and intelligence. He married May, 1761, in Brookfield, Leah (Jennings) Rice, widow of Charles Rice. She died August 5, 1811, aged seventy-four years, gravestone record. Children, born in Westminster: Anna, married (first) Calvin Chaffee, (second) —— Cobb; Joseph, born June 22, 1762; Jonathan, married May 26, 1811, widow Laurana Butterfield; Eliab, born 1766; Jesse, born December 20, 1770; Eli, born October 21, 1771; Elijah, mentioned below.

(V) Elijah, son of Captain Jesse Burke, was born in Westminster, March 3, 1774, and died March 21, 1843. He was a farmer by occupation, and in early life was very active in that line. He was among the first to engage in the introduction and growth of merino sheep in Vermont, and for many years was owner of large flocks of that valuable animal. He was much respected by his fellow-townsmen, and was often tendered public offices, all of which, except the most humble and practically useful, he invariably declined. He married, September, 1795, Grace, daughter of Moses and Lucy Jeffers, of New London, Connecticut; she was born September 14, 1777. Children, born in Westminster: Russell, mentioned below; Rhoda, June 25, 1799, died March 18, 1818; Elijah, March 31, 1802, died August, 1804; George Emery, born October 27, 1803; Udney, September 1, 1806; Edmund, January 23, 1809; Thales, January 31, 1811; Gratia, March 22, 1815; Catharine, May 5, 1817.

(VI) Russell, son of Elijah Burke, born in Westminster, March 26, 1797, and died in Springfield, Vermont, October 4, 1852-55. He married, August 18, 1822, Eliza Williams, born March 15, 1803. Children: Russell Williams, born July 5, 1825, died June 19, 1826; Russell Williams, born April 3, 1827; John Westfield, September 4, 1829, died July 26, 1830; John Westfield, June 2, 1831, died April 20, 1832; Harriet Eliza, March 2, 1833, died March 16, 1833; Harriet Eliza, May 14, 1834, died April 14, 1838; George Henry, February 23, 1837, died August 6, 1839; George Henry, born June 5, 1839; Charles Clinton, of whom further.

(VII) Charles Clinton, son of Russell Burke, was born at Springfield, Vermont. He was educated at the Kimball Union Academy, Meriden, New Hampshire. From Meriden he went to Boston and began his business career there with a wholesale provision house. After living in Boston about two years he went to

the oil regions, arriving at Titusville, Pennsylvania, in the early sixties. Crude petroleum was then being produced in great abundance. There were, however, few refineries in the country, and few men with practical knowledge of that branch of the business. In order to become proficient in it he placed himself under the tuition of a well-known chemist of the oil fields. After obtaining from him the general methods of refining, he supplemented this course of instruction by sending to Pittsburgh for a German chemist whose services he utilized in the manufacture of various products from petroleum. Although he had not then attained his majority, Mr. Burke associated himself with others and secured a factory, which he reconstructed, and long afterward this plant was totally ruined by fire. Mr. Burke removed later to Pittsburgh and remained there several years as a refiner. In 1871 he established himself in New York and became an owner in an oil refinery on Newtown creek. This plant was successfully operated under his management until about 1883. In that year he was elected president of the Eagle Oil Company, with works at Communipaw, New Jersey. He has originated several grades of lubricating oil which are celebrated for their excellent qualities, and has received letters patent for various valuable improvements in machinery. Mr. Burke is a director of the Fulton Trust Company, of New York, having been one of its founders. He has served as vice-president and president of the New York Produce Exchange, and is also treasurer of the New England Society of New York, and a member of the Union League Club.

Mr. Burke has been married twice—in 1872, to Miss Elsie P. Ely, a daughter of the late Abner L. Ely, of New York; and in 1886, to Miss Elizabeth S. Cass, a daughter of General George W. Cass, of Pittsburgh. Mr. Burke has several sons and daughters, and resides at Plainfield, New Jersey.

(The Williams Line).

The Williams family of Wales and England is of great antiquity. The surname is derived from the ancient personal name William. Sir Robert Williams, ninth baronet, of the house of Williams of Penrhyn, was a lineal descendant from Marchudes of Cyan, Lord of Abergelen in Denbighshire, of one of the fifteen tribes of North Wales that lived in the time of Roderick the Great, King of the Britons, about A. D. 849. The ancient Williams coat-of-arms of the Welsh family is: Sable a lion rampant argent armed and langues gules. The crest is a moor cock. The seat of the family was at Flint, Wales, and in Lincoln-

118   NEW ENGLAND.

shire. Oliver Cromwell, the Protector, was a Williams by right of descent, and was related to Richard Williams, who settled in Taunton, Massachusetts, as shown by the following pedigree. Alden de Cromwell lived in the time of William the Conqueror, and from him descended ten Ralph de Cromwells in succession, the last of the name dying without issue. The seventh Ralph de Cromwell married, 1351, Amicia, daughter of Robert Berer, M. P. Robert Cromwell (1) was a Lancastrian, killed in the wars in 1461. From him the line to Oliver Cromwell and Richard Williams is definitely known. William Cromwell (2), son of Robert (1), left a daughter Margaret, who was ancestor of both Cromwell and Williams. John Cromwell (3) married Joan Smith. Walter Cromwell (4) married ——— Glossop. Katherine Cromwell (5), daughter of Walter (4), married Morgan Williams, fifth from Howell Williams, mentioned below. Sir Richard Williams (6), son of Morgan and Katherine (5), born about 1495, married Frances Murfyn. After reaching mature years Sir Richard took the name of Cromwell, under the patronage of his mother's brother, Thomas Cromwell He lived in Glamorganshire, Wales. Sir Henry Cromwell (7), alias Williams, son of Sir Richard (6), was called the "Golden Knight" of Hinchenbrook, Huntingdon; married Joan Warren. Robert Cromwell (8), alias William, was of Huntingdon, a brewer, married Elizabeth Stewart. Their first child was Oliver, the Great Protector. Oliver Cromwell used the alias in his youth, and in some deeds his name is found Oliver Williams, alias Cromwell. Howell Williams (1), Lord of Ribour, was progenitor of the Williams family of Wales. Morgan Williams (2) married Joan Batten. Thomas of Lancashire (3), son of Morgan (2), died in London. John Williams (4), son of Thomas (3), married Margaret Smith; died at Mortlake, 1502. Their son John, born 1485, married Joan Wykys, daughter of Henry Wykys, of Bolleys Park, Chertney, and sister of Elizabeth Wykys, who married Thomas Cromwell (brother of Katherine, mentioned above), secretary to Henry VIII., Lord Cromwell, of Oakham, Earl of Essex. Richard Williams (6), born at Rochampton 1487, settled at Monmouth and Dexter; died 1559. John Williams (6), son of Richard (5), was of Huntingdonshire, near Wotton-under-Edge, Gloucester; died 1577. William (7), son of John Williams (6), was also of Huntingdon; married, November 15, 1585, Jane Shepherd; second, December 4, 1603, Jane Woodward His first child by the second marriage was Richard Williams, who settled in Taunton, Massachusetts. The Williams families of America descend from more than a score of different immigrant ancestors. That several of them were related to Richard of Taunton, mentioned above, seems certain, but the degree has not been traced in the various instances.

(I) Roger Williams, son of James and Alice (Pemberton) Williams, born 1599, in Wales, was a very bright youth and engaged the favorable notice of prominent men in London through whom he secured excellent educational facilities. He was ordained a clergyman of the Church of England, but soon became an extreme Puritan and migrated to New England. For his opposition to the New England theocracy he was driven from Salem, taking refuge at Plymouth, where he studied the Indian dialects. Banished from the colony in 1635, accompanied by a few adherents, he escaped in midwinter to the shores of Narragansett Bay, where he purchased lands of the Indian chiefs, founded the city of Providence, and established a government of pure democracy. In 1654 he was elected president of the colony, and his death occurred in 1683. He married Mary Barnard, who died in 1676, and had children: Mary, born 1633, died 1681; Freeborn, 1635-1710; Providence, 1638-1686; Mercy, 1640-1705; Daniel, 1642-1702; Joseph, mentioned below.

(II) Joseph, youngest child of Roger and Mary (Barnard) Williams, was born December 12, 1643, in Providence, died there August 17, 1724. He married, December 17, 1669, Lydia Olney, born 1645, died September 9, 1724. Children: Joseph, born 1670, died young; Thomas, mentioned below; Joseph, November 10, 1673; Mary, June 16, 1676; James, September 20, 1680; Lydia, September 26, 1683.

(III) Thomas, second son of Joseph and Lydia (Olney) Williams, was born February 16, 1672, in Providence, and died there August 27, 1724. He married Mary Blackmar, who died July 1, 1717. Children: Joseph, died July 17, 1750, Thomas, Stephen, John, Abigail, Jonathan, Mary.

(IV) Stephen, third son of Thomas and Mary (Blackmar) Williams, was born in Providence, was a house carpenter in that town, and died there May 26, 1745. He married, June 28, 1736, Jemima, whose surname is not shown in the records. Children: Isaiah, born January 15, 1738; Katherine, April 28, 1739; Jonathan, mentioned below.

(V) Jonathan, second son of Stephen and Jemima Williams, was born May 20, 1741, in Providence, and settled in Douglas, Massachusetts, before 1659, dying there February 16, 1803. He resided in East Douglas, and the records show that his wife's name was Esther. Children recorded in Douglas: Samuel, born September 29, 1769; Jonathan, mentioned below; Thaddeus, February 4, 1774; Amos, October 21, 1776; John Nason, May 23, 1780; Jesse, July 20, 1789.

(VI) Colonel Jonathan (2), second son of Jonathan (1) and Esther Williams, was born March 11, 1772, in Douglas, and resided for a short time in Grafton, Massachusetts, whence he removed to Grafton, Vermont, remaining there but a brief period. About 1796 he settled at Springfield, Vermont, where he bought land of Joseph Selden and built what was later called the Dr. Eleazer Crain house, situated where the Brown residence now stands. In 1800 he built the part of the tavern house to the east and west, known so long as Black River Hotel and Springfield House, and for a time he kept the hotel. In 1803 he built on the site of Leland's block, a building which he occupied as a hat shop; later he built below the lower bridge the house now owned by the Olneys, and the George O. Henry house, known for a long time as the Williams Tavern, where he and afterwards his son Luke kept a public house. He was engaged with Ethan Allen in running the fulling mill on the west side of the river in 1797. In 1812 he built the woolen mill at the lower bridge, where he manufactured cloth, and which was afterwards run by his son. For several years he was constable of the town, and he was a man of great executive ability and enterprise, of much influence in public affairs. He was colonel of the Second Regiment of state militia and enlisted in the war of 1812 with General John Perkins, Jonathan Chase and others. At the close of the war he had charge of paying off the soldiers. He married Betsey Kidder, and she died January 23, 1841. Children: Elias, born in Grafton, Massachusetts, September 4,.1794; Luke, born in Grafton, Vermont, March 29, 1796; Henry, December 11, 1797; Frederick, died in infancy; Frederick, June 11, 1801; Eliza, March 15, 1803, married Russell Burke (see Burke); Lucretia, December 8, 1806; Nancy, December 20, 1808; Harriet, December 24, 1810; Jonathan, January 2, 1813; George N., October 9, 1814; Sarah, August 13, 1816; Louisa, October 18, 1818.

CHAMBERLIN Henry Chamberlin, the immigrant ancestor, came from Hingham, county Norfolk, England, arriving in New England, August 10, 1638, in the ship "Diligent," accompanied by his mother Christian, his wife Jane, and two or more children. His mother was probably the "Mrs. Chamberlin, widowe, sister of Mr. Israell Stoughton," who received an allowance from Mr. Andrews' gift by the governor and deputies of Massachusetts Bay Colony, May 14, 1645. She died at Hingham, Massachusetts, April 19, 1659, aged eighty-one. Henry Chamberlin, in common with many others, came to New England to escape religious persecution. He settled in Hingham, Massachusetts, where he had a grant of a house-lot in 1638. He was made freeman March 13, 1638-9, and lived in Hingham until 1660. On February 4, 1660, he deeded land in Hingham to Daniel Cushing, and in this deed and others he was called blacksmith and shoemaker. About 1661 he moved to Hull, where he lived until his death, July 15, 1674. He called himself blacksmith from 1660 until his death. His will was made December 8, 1673, and his widow with her sons deeded his property in Hingham to Thomas Sawyer, March 3, 1674-5. Children, perhaps not in order of birth: Susannah, born about 1616; Henry, eldest son; William, mentioned below; Daniel, baptized at Hingham, England, May 15, 1632, buried there May 19, 1632; Mary, perhaps twin, baptized at Hingham, England, May 15, 1632, buried there May 25, 1632; John, baptized at Hingham, England, November 15, 1633; Ursula, born about 1634; Faith; Daniel (2), baptized at Hingham, Massachusetts, September 26, 1641; Nathaniel, baptized at Hingham, Massachusetts, November 26, 1643, not mentioned in his father's will; Ebenezer; probably a son died at Hingham, October 28, 1646.

(II) William, son of Henry Chamberlin, was born doubtless about 1620. On November 9, 1647, he bought a house and lot from Francis Smith, in Boston, situated on Washington street, and bounded on the west by the "Common," and on January 4, 1648, he deeded this back to him and before August 27, 1654, moved to Hull, settling on the east side of Quaker Lane. In 1657 he was granted by the proprietors eleven lots of land in Hull, and also had his deed from Thomas Jones, of Langley's Island, confirmed by them. About 1658 he was a selectman, and June 5, 1662, was one of the appraisers of Thomas Loring's estate. In 1669 he was townsman. He died at Hull, October 22, 1678, and his estate was valued at £529, provision being made by him for the care of his father and mother. He married (first), about 1651 (name unknown), who died at Hull about 1660, and he married (second), about 1661 (name unknown). Children by first wife, probably born at Hull: William, April 9, 1652; John, baptized at Hingham, August 27, 1654; Job, born about 1656; Nathaniel, September 4, 1659; Freedom, about 1660. Children by second wife, born at Hull: Benjamin, baptized at Hingham, May 18, 1662; Joseph, mentioned below; Mary, born about 1672, and Sarah, born about 1676.

(III) Joseph, son of William Chamberlin, was born at Hull about 1665, and died at Colchester, August 7, 1752, aged eighty-seven years. He was buried in the old parish cemetery in Colchester village. In 1685 William James, of Scituate, was his guardian. On March 30, 1687, he deeded to his brother William, of Hull, weaver, land on Pettox Island which had been his father's, his brother Freedom's and finally his own. In the deed he called himself cordwainer. About 1688 he moved to Hadley, Massachusetts, and before 1701 migrated to Hatfield, Massachusetts. As early as 1704 he moved from Hadley or Hatfield to Colchester, Connecticut. On May 29, 1693, he executed a power of attorney to his brother William. On May 31, 1695, his wife Mercy quitclaimed her interest in his estate to Nathaniel Chamberlin, weaver, and John Collier, husbandman, both of Hull. He was a petit juror at Hadley in 1701, and in 1705 his taxes at Hadley and Hatfield were referred to. The first mention of him in Colchester was April 1, 1703, when the proprietors granted land they had formerly given him to Thomas Day, and October 30, 1704, they granted him twenty acres on Wigwam Hill. Stiles says that he lived for a time in Wethersfield, Connecticut, but of this no proof has been found. Until his death he was very prominent in Colchester, where he served as selectman in 1705, 1706, 1716-18, and perhaps other years, was licensed to keep the ordinary in 1710, and continued to keep a tavern until 1748. At the expense of the province he entertained the French ambassadors when they passed through Colchester to and from New London in 1711. He was admitted a freeman December 31, 1712. His home was on the main road leading from New London to Hartford, and about a mile north of the present village of Colchester. He married, at Hadley, June 8, 1688, Mercy, daughter of John and Frances (Foote) Dickinson; she was born at Wethersfield, Connecticut, about 1668, and died at Colchester, June 30, 1735. Joseph Chamberlin died at Colchester, August 7, 1752, and was buried there. Children: William, of Colchester; Sarah, born at Hadley, November 2, 1690, died young; Sarah (2), born at Hadley, March 10, 1693; Elizabeth, born about 1695; Joseph, mentioned below; John, born at Hatfield, March 4, 1700; Benjamin, born about 1701; Freedom, born at Colchester, April 15, 1705, and John (2), born at Colchester, January 31, 1707-08.

(IV) Joseph (2), son of Joseph (1) Chamberlin, was born about 1697, at Hadley or Hatfield, and settled in Colchester. His wife Lydia died there March 3, 1730, and he probably married (second), July 12, 1738, Hannah, widow of Aaron Gillett. October 18, 1749, Hannah Stores quitclaimed to Joseph Chamberlin and wife. Children of first wife: Lydia, born October 20, 1721; Joseph, mentioned below; Job, born February 8, 1725-26; Jonathan, July 1, 1728; Jonathan (2), February 22, 1729-30, died young.

(V) Joseph (3), son of Joseph (2) Chamberlin, was born at Colchester, April 11, 1724, and appears to have settled near his grandmother's home, in the neighborhood of Hadley or Hatfield, where his father and some of his uncles and aunts were born. He married, February 7, 1762, at Sunderland (which was incorporated from Hadley in 1714), Eunice, born July 31, 1739, daughter of John and Mary (Cowles) Amsden, of Deerfield. The marriage is also given in Deerfield, as are the births of the children. On his wedding day Joseph Chamberlin bought lot 18, on the west side of Sunderland; he purchased it of Gideon Henderson, and in August of the same year sold it to Nathaniel Barstow. He owned other land, perhaps inherited from his father or grandmother, and his farm remained until recently in the possession of his descendants. Children: Luther, mentioned below; Mary, born at Sunderland, August 24, 1764, died June 11, 1766; Joseph, born April 3, 1766, died at Cannonville, or Trout Creek, Delaware county, New York.

(VI) Luther, son of Joseph (3) and Eunice (Amsden) Chamberlin, was born about 1763, and was probably still a child when his parents removed to Vermont, appearing to have resided both at Guilford and Brattleboro. Joseph Chamberlin was a lieutenant in Colonel Timothy Church's regiment, of Brattleboro. The farm of Joseph Chamberlin at Guilford was in the territory over which New York and New Hampshire claimed jurisdiction and granted land titles for many years, and Vermont and New Hampshire also had a controversy over this territory. Luther Chamberlin married Temperance Pollard, and about 1790 went with his wife to New York state from Brattleboro, Vermont, settling on part of lot 66, in the northern part of "Jericho" (now Bainbridge), on Stockwell's creek. This was part of the land originally granted to his father, but Luther did not remain there long, preferring to migrate to a fine farm on the west side of the Susquehanna river, some six miles further south. A little settlement which had already begun to grow just at the northern line of this farm was known a little later as South Bainbridge, and is now Afton. Here were born and reared several children, among them a son, Joseph Pollard, mentioned below, and a daughter, Eunice, named in honor of her grandmother. Luther Chamberlin died about 1838, his wife having passed away in 1828.

(VII) Joseph (4) Pollard, son of Luther and Temperance (Pollard) Chamberlin, was born in 1795, at South Bainbridge, and spent his entire life on the farm. He became a very prominent man in the community. As justice of the peace he tried Joseph Smith, the founder of Mormonism, for false pretense. He was sheriff of the county, 1843-46, and served as assemblyman in 1834, in the fifty-seventh session of the legislature, and 1852 in the seventy-fifth session, he was again a member of the assembly. He was urged to become a United States senator, and the gubernatorial nomination was tendered him by both political parties, but he declined to assume the burdens which his acceptance of these honors would have involved. A man of generous impulses, he gave liberally to all projects for the betterment of the neighborhood, but when it was decided to rename the village and many desired to call it Chamberlin or Chamberlinville, he gave his influence in favor of Afton. He married, February 19, 1824, Margaret, daughter of Benjamin Carpenter; children: Jeanette, born November, 1825, died December 5, 1851; John Clark, born May 14, 1828, died January 27, 1903; Joseph (5) Pollard (2), born June 1, 1830, died May 13, 1897; Emma, born August 27, 1832, died July 27, 1908; Henrietta, born September 18, 1837, now living in Colorado; Ralph, born March 18, 1840, died December 26, 1891; Horace Stowell, mentioned below. Mrs. Chamberlin died August 22, 1848, and the death of Mr. Chamberlin occurred November 21, 1857.

(VIII) Horace Stowell, son of Joseph (4) Pollard (1) and Margaret (Carpenter) Chamberlin, was born August 6, 1842, at Afton, New York, and received his education in the public schools and at the Delaware Literary Institute, Franklin, New York. After completing his course of study he returned to his native place, and in January, 1866, opened a general store. In 1871-72 he was supervisor of the town, and was urged to accept a nomination for the assembly, an honor which he declined, having little inclination for political life. In 1875 he engaged in the commission business in Scranton, Pennsylvania, an enterprise which was most successful. Eventually he sold out and became general manager of the B. G. Carpenter wholesale and retail house-furnishing, gas-fitting, plumbing and metal-

work establishment in Wilkes-Barre, Pennsylvania, to which city he removed his family in 1876, making it his home for the remainder of his life. Mr. Chamberlin married, February 13, 1866, in St. Paul's Protestant Episcopal Church, Oxford, New York, Mary M., born August 22, 1845, only child of Amos A. and Lucy L. (Palmer) Hitchcock, and they became the parents of one son: Rollin Smith, mentioned below. The death of Mr. Chamberlin, which occurred January 20, 1900, was an irreparable loss to his family and friends. He was a man of strong domestic affections, finding his highest happiness at his own fireside. The loss to the community in general was recognized as one of exceptional magnitude, as appears by the following extract from an obituary notice published in one of the Wilkes-Barre papers:

Mr. Chamberlin is dead after a brave but short struggle with pleuro-pneumonia. This announcement comes with unusual sorrow,—he was one of Wilkes-Barre's best known and most highly esteemed citizens. In him seemed embodied the qualities of an ideal manhood, and those who knew him best were most sincere in their admiration for him. For many years he had been with B. G. Carpenter & Company. His figure was familiar to all, his greeting sincerely pleasant, and to be in his presence, whether in a business or social way, was to be in the company of a thorough gentleman. Men such as he stand out prominently in the community,—not, perhaps, for great, illustrious deeds, but for the nobleness of mind and soul that rise above the vanities and fame of earth.

(IX) Rollin Smith, only child of Horace Stowell and Mary M. (Hitchcock) Chamberlin, was born June 2, 1867, in Afton, Chenango county, New York, and received his education in the public schools of Wilkes-Barre, Pennsylvania. When a very young man he became a night operator for the Bell Telephone Company, and in 1889 was made manager of the Wilkes-Barre exchange. A few years later he was promoted to the position of district superintendent, and in 1902 became general superintendent, with headquarters at Harrisburg, Pennsylvania. He held this office for eight years, retiring when the state system was absorbed by the Philadelphia Bell Telephone Company. In 1911 he was made superintendent of the Scranton district of the Consolidated Telephone Company, with headquarters in the handsome Republican Building on Washington avenue. His administration was marked by a wonderful increase in the number of subscribers and a great improvement in the efficiency of the service of the system. Mr. Chamberlin is an energetic, magnetic and thoroughly capable executive head, and a most genial and approachable gentleman, with bubbling good humor and a kind word for every one. So satisfactory was his management of affairs in this district that he was promoted in 1911 to the general superintendency, with offices in Philadelphia. He is a Republican in politics, belongs to the Engineers' Club, of Pennsylvania, and is a member of St. Stephen's Protestant Episcopal Church, of Wilkes-Barre.

Mr. Chamberlin married, June 6, 1894, Helen Louise, born September 12, 1872, at Wilkes-Barre, daughter of David L. and Polly A. (Griffin) Patrick, of that city. Children: Esther Margaret, born May 12, 1900, at Wilkes-Barre, and Helen Louise, born September 7, 1908, at Harrisburg.

PACKARD Samuel Packard, immigrant ancestor, came to New England with his wife and one child in the ship "Diligent," of Ipswich, John Martin, master, in 1638. He came from Windham, a small hamlet near Hingham, county Norfolk, England, and settled in Hingham, Massachusetts. He moved about 1660 to Bridgewater, Massachusetts, and held office there in 1664. In 1670 he was licensed to keep the ordinary. His sons, and probably he himself, were soldiers under Captain Benjamin Church in King Philip's war in 1675-76. His will was dated 1684. Children: Elizabeth, born probably in England, married, 1665, Thomas Alger, of West Bridgewater; Samuel Jr., born in Hingham, Massachusetts, married Elizabeth Lathrop; Zaccheus, mentioned below; Thomas, born in Hingham, living in Bridgewater in 1673; John, born in Hingham; Nathaniel, married a daughter of John Kingman; Mary, married Richard Phillips; Hannah, married Thomas Randall; Israel; Jael, married John Smith; Deborah, married Samuel Washburn; Deliverance, married Thomas Washburn, brother of Samuel Washburn.

(II) Zaccheus, son of Samuel Packard, was born in Hingham, Massachusetts, died in Bridgewater, August 3, 1723. He married Sarah, daughter of John Howard, of West Bridgewater. Children, born in Bridgewater: Israel, April 27, 1680; Sarah, August 19, 1682; Jonathan, December 7, 1684; David, February 11, 1687; Solomon, mentioned below; Deacon James, June 2, 1691; Zaccheus Jr., September 4, 1693; John, October 8, 1695; Captain Abiel, April 29, 1699.

(III) Solomon, son of Zaccheus Packard, was born at Bridgewater, Massachusetts, March 20, 1689, died in 1723. He married (first), in 1715, Sarah, daughter of John Howard. He married (second) Susanna, daughter of Samuel Kingman. Children, born at Bridgewater: Sarah, 1719, married Isaac Ful-

ler; Jacob, mentioned below; Nathan, 1722; Susanna, 1724, married Joseph Alden; Joanna, 1725, married Israel Allen; Martha, 1727, married Isaac Alden Jr. and Israel Bailey; Solomon, 1729; Nathan, 1733; Benjamin, 1734, married Ruth Leach; Zebulon, 1736; Micah, 1738, went to Maine.

(IV) Jacob, son of Solomon Packard, was born in Bridgewater, Massachusetts, in 1720, died in 1777. He married, in 1742, Dorothy, daughter of Mark Perkins. Children, born at Bridgewater; Jacob, Asa, mentioned below; Oliver, Mark, Hezekiah, graduate of Harvard, 1787, minister of Chelmsford, D. D., died in 1849; Rhoda, married Abijah Stowell; Dorothy, married James Richards; Phebe, married Henry Thayer.

(V) Rev. Asa Packard, son of Jacob Packard, was born at Bridgewater, Massachusetts, in 1758. At the age of fifteen he was a fifer in the revolutionary army and at the battle of Harlem received a severe wound that was nearly fatal from a musket ball in his back above the hip. But he recovered and served again later in the war. The records show that Asa Packard, of Chesterfield and Bridgewater, was a fifer in Captain Robert Webster's company of militiamen, General Pomeroy's regiment, in the Lexington Alarm, April 21, 1775, and that he continued in this company through the summer under Colonel John Fellows to October 8, 1775. He is known to have served, as stated, in 1776. He was in Captain Nathan Packard's company, Colonel Eliphalet Cary's regiment, in the summer of 1780 in Rhode Island; also in the Tenth Company, of Plymouth county, and his service is reported as eight months at Roxbury, twelve months at York, fifteen days at Bedford and five days in Rhode Island (Mass. Soldiers and Sailors in Rev.). He graduated from Harvard College in 1783 and became a minister at Marlborough, Massachusetts, March 23, 1785. He continued there until the church and society were dissolved and was dismissed at his own request. In 1808, two years later, he was settled over the west or seceding parish and stayed there until May 12, 1819. He then removed to Lancaster, Massachusetts, where he lived until his death, March 20, 1843, aged eighty-five years. He fell dead while listening to a letter from his brother, having been in his usual good health to the very end of life.

He married Nancy, daughter of Josiah Quincy, of the famous old Braintree family of that surname. She died February 3, 1844, aged eighty years. Children: Ann Marsh, born August 7, 1791, died June 6, 1796; Elizabeth Quincy, November 2, 1792, died in 1816;

Frederick Adolphus, mentioned below; Asa, January 24, 1796, married Lydia Blake, of Shrewsbury, and died in 1851; Ann Marsh, March 17, 1798, married James G. Carter, and died December 15, 1853; Ruth Freeman, March 22, 1800, married, April 12, 1831, Rev. George Trask.

(VI) Frederick Adolphus, son of Rev. Asa Packard, was born at Marlborough, Massachusetts, September 26, 1794, died November 11, 1867. He graduated from Harvard College in the class of 1814 and studied law. After he was admitted to the bar he settled in general practice at Springfield, Massachusetts. He represented that town in the general court in 1828. In 1829 he removed to Philadelphia, Pennsylvania, and became editor of the American Sunday School Union publications. He received the degree of LL. D. from Princeton University. He married, May 5, 1822, Elizabeth Dwight, born February 16, 1798, died at Philadelphia, July 5, 1862, daughter of Hon. John and Sarah (Dwight) Hooker, descendant of several of the leading families of that section (see Hooker VIII). Children: 1. John Hooker, died in infancy. 2. Frederick, born at Springfield, July 24, 1828; a lawyer at Appleton, Wisconsin; died at Philadelphia, July 18, 1862; married, November 2, 1852, Ellen Louisa, daughter of Isaac and Susan (Mitchell) Hall. 3. Mary Hooker, born at Philadelphia, August 30, 1830; married, April 12, 1854, Samuel Clarke Perkins, son of Samuel Huntington and Mary (Donnell) Perkins. 4. John Hooker, mentioned below. 5. Lewis Richard, born at Philadelphia, August 22, 1836; graduated from Yale in 1856, Ph. D., studied for the ministry, but gave it up, was tutor, then assistant professor, and finally Hillhouse Professor of Greek in Yale; director of the American Archæological School at Athens, 1883-84; died October 26, 1884, at New Haven; married, December 29, 1870, Harriet Moore Storrs.

(VII) Dr. John Hooker Packard, son of Frederick Adolphus Packard, was born at Philadelphia, August 15, 1832. He was graduated from the University of Pennsylvania in 1850 and from his alma mater received the degree of Doctor of Medicine in 1853. He was resident physician of the Pennsylvania Hospital in 1856, and in general practice in Philadelphia until the time of his death, May 21, 1907. He was a member of the County, State and National Medical Societies. He was demonstrator of anatomy in the University of Pennsylvania in 1862-63; acting assistant surgeon in the United States army in the service during the civil war, 1861-65; surgeon to the Episcopal Hospital, 1863-84; surgeon to the

Women's Hospital in 1876-77, and to the Pennsylvania Hospital from 1884 to 1896. He wrote on many medical and surgical subjects for medical journals from time to time. He was the author of books on "Minor Surgery," "Lectures on Inflammation," "Operative Surgery." He translated into English "Malgaigne on Fractures." From 1868 to 1871 he was editor of the Medical Directory of Philadelphia. He retired from active practice several years before he died.

He married, June 3, 1858, Elizabeth Wood, born at Philadelphia, May 2, 1835, died March 11, 1897, in that city, daughter of Charles Stuart and Juliana (Fitz Randolph) Wood. Children, born in Philadelphia: 1. Elizabeth Dwight, April 6, 1859. 2. Charles Stuart Wood, mentioned below. 3. Frederic Adolphus, mentioned below. 4. John Hooker, born May 9, 1865; married, June 15, 1889, Agnes, born July 7, 1868, daughter of Richard A. and Susan Price (Toland) Tilghman; children: Joan Hooker, born December 24, 1890, and John Francis Randolph, June, 1893. 5. Francis Randolph, mentioned below. 6. George Randolph, mentioned below.

(VIII) Charles Stuart Wood, son of Dr. John Hooker Packard, was born in Philadelphia, June 2, 1860. He attended the public schools and prepared for college at Rugby Academy. He was a student in the University of Pennsylvania, from which he was graduated in 1880 with the degree of Bachelor of Arts. After leaving college he became secretary and treasurer of the Philadelphia Warehouse Company. After four years in this position he became treasurer of the Washington Manufacturing Company in 1886 and continued there until 1892. Since then he has been with the Pennsylvania Company for Insurances on Lives and Granting Annuities, as auditor in 1892-93, treasurer, 1893-99, and president and director since 1899. He is an officer of various other insurance and financial corporations, director of the Farmers' & Mechanics' National Bank, of the Insurance Company of North America, of the Philadelphia Savings Fund Society, the Philadelphia Contributionship, the Penn Mutual Life Insurance Company, the Philadelphia Warehouse Company, the Fourth Street National Bank, the Franklin National Bank, the Chesapeake & Delaware Canal Company, Lehigh Coal & Navigation Company, Westmoreland Coal Company, Philadelphia Rapid Transit Company. He has been a trustee of the University or Pennsylvania and director and treasurer of the University Athletic Association. He is a member of the Philadelphia Club, the Racquet Club, the Rittenhouse Club, St. Anthony's Club and the Country Club. In religion he is an Episcopalian. His residence is at 326 South Twenty-first street and De Lancey Place, and his office at 517 Chestnut street, Philadelphia.

He married, April 14, 1882, Eliza Gilpin, born February 18, 1860, at Alexandria, Virginia, daughter of Samuel and Maria (Williams) McLean, of Warrenton, Virginia. Children: 1. Elizabeth Routh, born March 31, 1883, died July 11, 1883. 2. John Hooker (3), April 4, 1884; married, October 8, 1907, Mildred, daughter of Edwin N. Benson, of Philadelphia.

(VIII) Frederick Adolphus Packard, M. D., son of Dr. John Hooker Packard, was born November 17, 1862, died of typhoid fever, November 1, 1902. He was graduated from the College Department of the University of Pennsylvania in 1882, and from the Medical School of the University of Pennsylvania in 1885. He graduated at the head of his class in medicine. After serving as resident physician in the Hospital of the University of Pennsylvania and in the Pennsylvania Hospital, he practiced in Philadelphia. He was visiting physician to the Children's Hospital, the Episcopal Hospital, the Philadelphia Hospital and the Pennsylvania Hospital. He was a trustee of the University of Pennsylvania. He was also at one time or another president of the Philadelphia Pediatric Society and the Pathological Society, a member of the Association of American Physicians and the American Pediatric Society. He married, June 1, 1893, Katherine, daughter of Dr. Edward Shippen.

(VIII) Francis Randolph, son of Dr. John Hooker Packard, was born in Philadelphia, March 23, 1870. He graduated from the Biological School of the University of Pennsylvania in 1889, and from the Department of Medicine at the University of Pennsylvania in 1892. Served as resident physician at the Pennsylvania Hospital from 1893 to 1895. During the Spanish-American war he was commissioned as lieutenant and assistant surgeon of Second Pennsylvania Volunteer Infantry. Since 1899 Dr. Packard has devoted himself exclusively to the practice of diseases of the nose, throat and ear. He is a member of the American Laryngological, Rhinological and Otological Society, the American Medical Association and the College of Physicians; chief to the Out-Patient Department for Diseases of the Nose, Throat and Ear at the Pennsylvania Hospital; laryngologist to the Children's Hospital of Philadelphia, the Bryn Mawr and Chestnut Hill Hospitals; consulting aurist to the Pennsylvania Institution for the Deaf and Dumb; also lecturer on the History of Medicine in the University of Pennsylvania. From 1901 to 1906 Dr. Packard edited the American Journal of the Medical Sciences. He is the author of a History of Medicine in the United States, published by the J. B. Lippincott Company, 1901; a text book on Diseases of the Nose, Throat and Ear, of which several editions have been published. He is a member of the Philadelphia, University and Franklin Inn clubs, and lives at 304 South Nineteenth street, Philadelphia. He married (first) Christine Curwen, June 1, 1899, who died May 16, 1901, without issue. Married (second) Margaret Horstmann, February 10, 1906. They have three children: Margaret, born February 26, 1907; Ann, May 18, 1908; Elizabeth, April 25, 1912.

(VIII) George Randolph, son of Dr. John Hooker Packard, was born September 25, 1872. He has been engaged in the fire insurance business. He married, October 31, 1895, Elizabeth Waln Wistar, daughter of T. Wistar Brown. Children: Mary Farnum, born November 9, 1896; Elizabeth Wood, December 25, 1897; Ruth, November 14, 1900; George Randolph Jr., November 17, 1905.

(The Hooker Line).

(VI) John (3) Hooker, son of Hon. John (2) Hooker (q. v.) was born March 6, 1695-96, at Farmington, died at Kensington, August 3, 1766. He was a justice of the peace and a prominent and active man in the business of the town. He married, July 4, 1728, Mercy, (Mary), born at Kensington, September 29, 1703, died there in 1782, daughter of Deacon Thomas and Mary (Thompson) Hart, of Kensington, Connecticut. Children, born at Kensington: John, mentioned below; Seth, born December 8, 1731; Ashbel, April 18, 1737; Elijah, April 12, 1746.

(VII) John (4), son of John (3) Hooker, was born at Kensington, March 19, 1729-30. He was graduated from Yale College in 1751. He was ordained at Northampton, Massachusetts, December 5, 1753, and remained there for twenty-four years, until his death of smallpox, February 6, 1777. He married, December 10, 1755, Sarah, born January 27, 1732, at Springfield, died at Northampton, April 5, 1817, daughter of John and Mary (Pratt) Worthington, of Springfield. Children, born at Northampton: Mary, September 10, 1756; Sarah, January 30, 1757; Seth, October 26, 1759; John, mentioned below; Lucy, baptized August 19, 1764, died June 30, 1766; William, November 26, 1766; Thomas, May 20, 1770; John Worthington, baptized April 12, 1772; Lucy, July 16, 1775.

(VIII) John (5), son of John (4) Hooker, was born at Northampton, August or October 8, 1761, died at Springfield, March 7, 1829. He was graduated from Yale College in 1782. He settled at Springfield and became a lawyer and judge of the court of common pleas. He was a deacon of the First Congregational Church, and a member of A. B. C. F. M. He married, February 9, 1791, Sarah, daughter of Colonel Josiah and Elizabeth (Buckminster) Dwight, and died at Springfield, September 5, 1842. Children, born at Springfield: John, December 15, 1791; George, March 17, 1793; Sarah, October 16, 1795; Josiah, April 17, 1797; Elizabeth Dwight, February 16, 1798, married Frederick Adolphus Packard (see Packard VI); Mary, September 14, 1799; Richard, July 15, 1801, died April 24, 1802; Clarissa, February 11, 1804, died October 8, 1804; Worthington, March 13, 1806; Richard, April 10, 1808.

SARGENT William Sargent, progenitor of the American family, was born in Exeter, England, in 1610, and is said to have gone to the Barbadoes with his father when he was quite young and to have been brought up there. He returned to England where, according to tradition, he married Mary Epes against family opposition and we are told that she stole away from home in the habit of a milkmaid to become his wife, and that they left England and settled at Bridgetown, Barbadoes. The fact that Mary Epes was an ancestor of this family through the marriage of William Sargent Jr. tends to disprove the tradition, however. The name Epes doubtless comes into the Sargent family through the Duncan marriage.

(II) William (2), son of William (1) Sargent, was the American immigrant. He was born at Bristol or Exeter, England, and went to Bridgetown, Barbadoes, with his parents. He appears first in New England at Gloucester and was called William Sargent (2) to distinguish him from another William Sargent of that town. It is not known that they were related. William Sargent (2) was a mariner and owned a sloop. He had a grant of land of two acres in 1678 on Eastern Point and built his house there. He died prior to January, 1707, and the probate records support the belief that he was lost at sea. He married, June 21, 1676, Mary, daughter of Peter and Mary (Epes) Duncan (see Duncan II). She died February 28, 1724. Children: Fitz William, born January 6, 1678, died January 28, 1699; Peter, May 27, 1680; Mary, December 29, 1681; Daniel, October 31, 1685; Jordan, January 22, 1687, died 1689; Epes, mentioned below; Ann, born August 6, 1692; Andrew, August 21, 1693; Samuel, 1694, died October 11, 1699; Fitz John, 1696, died January 20, 1697; Machani, April 9, 1699, died same day; Jabez, January 30, 1700, died next day; Fitz William, October 21, 1701; Winthrop, March 11, 1703.

(III) Colonel Epes Sargent, son of William (2) and Mary (Duncan) Sargent, was born July 12, 1690, died of small-pox, December 6, 1762, aged seventy-two years, was buried in Gloucester. He was a prominent citizen, a wealthy merchant, for several years one of the magistrates, deputy to the general court in 1744. After his second marriage he removed to Salem and was active in town and military affairs; colonel of his regiment, justice of the general sessions and held other offices of trust and honor.

Colonel Sargent married (first), April 1, 1720, Esther, born July 1, 1701, died July 1, 1743, daughter of Florence and Elizabeth Maccarty. Her father was a butcher by trade, was one of the founders of the first Protestant Episcopal church in New England. Colonel Sargent married (second), August 10, 1744, Catherine Brown, of Salem, Massachusetts, widow of Samuel Brown, who was born April 7, 1709, and graduated from Harvard College in 1727. She was a daughter of John Winthrop, granddaughter of Waitstill Winthrop, great-granddaughter of Fitz John Winthrop, who was governor of Connecticut. Governor Fitz John Winthrop was a son of Governor John Winthrop, of Connecticut, and grandson of Governor John Winthrop, the first governor of Massachusetts Bay Colony. Children by first wife: 1. Epes, born February 27, 1721; was a loyalist in the revolution; removed to Boston and thence to Nova Scotia; married Catherine Osborn. 2. Esther, September 20, 1722. 3. Ignatius, July 27, 1724. 4. Thomas, April, 1726, died April 24, 1727. 5. Winthrop, mentioned below. 6. Sarah, August 6, 1729. 7. Daniel, March 18, 1731, died in Boston, February 18, 1806; a successful merchant; father of Henry Sargent, a famous painter, and of five other prominent men. 8. William, June, 1733, died 1736. 9. Benjamin, October 18, 1736. 10. Mary Ann, December 1, 1740, probably died young. Children by second wife: 11. Paul Dudley, born in 1745 in Gloucester; colonel in the American army in the revolution; afterward a farmer at Sullivan, Maine, and represented that town in the general court, was judge of probate, of common pleas, and held other offices under the state and federal government; died September 5, 1827. 12. John, December 24, 1749; was also a loyalist and removed to Nova Scotia. 13. Catherine, died in infancy. 14. Ann, died young. 15. Mary.

(IV) Winthrop, son of Colonel Epes and
Esther (Maccarty) Sargent, was born in
Gloucester, March 6, 1727, died there December 3, 1793. He followed the sea and early in
life became a master mariner and commanded
a vessel. In later years he was a merchant.
He was an officer in a sloop-of-war at the taking of Breton in 1745 by Admiral Warren and
General Pepperell. He was a patriot during
the revolution, one of the committee of safety
of Gloucester in 1775 and government agent
on Cape Ann throughout the war. In 1778
he was a delegate to the state convention to
ratify the federal constitution. He was a parishioner of Rev. John Murray, of Gloucester,
and one of his warm friends and supporters.
We are told that he was "much respected for
general benevolence." He married Judith, born
September 25, 1731, in Gloucester, died July 1,
1793, daughter of Thomas and Judith (Robinson) Saunders, granddaughter of Captain Andrew Robinson, of Gloucester. Her father,
Thomas Saunders, was lieutenant of the ship,
"Merry Making," in 1725, and for many years
was in the service of the province in command
of a government vessel. On one voyage he
was taken prisoner by the French and Indians,
but made his escape, taking with him a bag of
the enemy's gold containing about $200.
Thomas Saunders, father of Thomas Saunders, appears in the records of Cape Ann as
early as 1702, and in 1704 was granted an acre
of land between the head of the harbor and
Cripple Cove; in 1706 he was granted some
flat land on the shore for his business as shipbuilder, and in 1725 he commanded the ship
"Merry Making," of which his son was lieutenant. Children, born in Gloucester: 1. Judith,
May 5, 1751, died in 1821; married (first), October 3, 1769, John Stevens, who died March
8, 1786, and (second) John Murray, by whom
she had Julia Maria Murray. 2. Winthrop,
May 1, 1753, died at New Orleans, June 3,
1820; commanded a company in Colonel
Crane's regiment in the revolution and took
part in the battles of Trenton, Brandywine and
others; was major, adjutant-general after the
war and fought against the Indians under
Pontiac; was governor of the Northwest Territory; in 1796 was appointed governor of .
Mississippi and made his home near Natchez
until his death; also charter member of the
Order of Cincinnati, certificate of membership
dated October 31, 1786, ten years after the independence of the United States. 3. Esther,
May 1, 1755, died November 30, 1811; married John Stevens Ellery; children: John Stevens Ellery, Sarah Ellery, who married Ignatius Sargent. 4. Catherine, July 5, 1758, died
June 15, 1759. 6. Sarah, July 12, 1765, died

September 6, 1766. 7. Fitz William, mentioned below. 8. Sarah, December 3, 1771,
died October 5, 1775.

(V) Fitz William, son of Winthrop and
Judith (Saunders) Sargent, was born at
Gloucester, August 14, 1768, died at Newton,
Massachusetts, October 6, 1822. He was a
prudent and enterprising merchant in Glouces-
ter, but was for many years a sufferer from
rheumatism. He married, September 3, 1789,
Anna, who died August 5, 1860, aged ninety-
one years, daughter of Thomas and Sarah
(Sawyer) Parsons (see Parsons IV). Chil-
dren: 1. Anna Maria, born July 11, 1790, died
August 27, 1794. 2. Winthrop, mentioned be-
low. 3. Sarah, September 24, 1793; married,
January 2, 1817, Samuel Worcester (see
Worcester VII). 4. Judith, April 12, 1795;
married (first) David Williams, who died
May, 1821, and (second), May 6, 1824, David
Worcester, who died July 25, 1845. 5. Juliana,
March 27, 1797, died April 5, 1842; married,
December 19, 1820, Edward B. Babbitt. 6.
Fitz William, December 18, 1799, died Octo-
ber 23, 1818. 7. Thomas Parsons, September
24, 1801, died September 26, 1801. 8. Mary,
July 4, 1806, died aged ninety-two years.

(VI) Winthrop (2), son of Fitz William
and Anna (Parsons) Sargent, was born at
Gloucester, January 20, 1792. He succeeded
his father in business and was known as the
"Gloucester merchant." In 1829 he removed
to Philadelphia, Pennsylvania. He was representative from Gloucester to the general
court in 1823. In Philadelphia he became active in the Presbyterian Board of Foreign
Missions and in church work. He continued
to live in Philadelphia until his death, except
for a few years spent in Byfield parish, Newbury, Massachusetts, at the home of his son,
Gorham Parsons Sargent. He married, May
17, 1814, Emily Haskell, of Gloucester. Children: 1. Anna Maria, born June 6, 1815; married, November 22, 1848, Moses Allen Lowe;
children: Eliza, married Waldo B. Smith;
Lucy, Winthrop, David L. and Anna. 2.
Emily, April 6, 1817; married, September 19,
1841, Henry Pleasants, M. D.; children: Mary
Haskell, born August 2, 1842, died September
10, 1843; Israel, October 2, 1843, died November 27, 1847; Emily Sargent, September 15,
1845; Sally, December 30, 1848; Elizabeth
Byrd, July 10, 1851; Henry, September 12,
1853. 3. Fitz William, January 19, 1820; a
physician; married, November 27, 1850, Mary
Newbold Singer; children: Mary Newbold,
born May 3, 1852, died July, 1853; John Singer, January 12, 1856; the artist now residing
in London; Emily, January 29, 1857; Mary
Winthrop, 1865. 4. Winthrop, mentioned be-

low. 5. Henry, June 2, 1825; married, Octo-
ber, 1864, Sophie H. Malin. 6. John Haskell,
February 8, 1828; married, June 2, 1853,
Frances Eugenia Hall. 7. Thomas Parsons,
July 19, 1830; married, December 13, 1854,
Jane Elizabeth Goodall. 8. Gorham Parsons,
December 10, 1834; married, January, 1865,
Caroline B. Montmellin.

(VII) Dr. Winthrop (3) Sargent, son of
Winthrop (2) Sargent, was born in Gloucester, July 8, 1822, died in Roxbury (Boston),
Massachusetts, March 16, 1896. He was graduated from Dartmouth College with the degree
of Bachelor of Arts in 1844, and studied his
profession in the Medical School of the University of Pennsylvania, graduating in 1847.
He practiced medicine for several years in
Montgomery county, Pennsylvania, and in
1855 located in Philadelphia, where he continued to practice medicine and minor surgery,
and there he took rank among the most successful physicians of his day. In 1862 Dr.
Sargent was surgeon-in-chief of the United
States Military Hospital at Kingsessing, and
later in the civil war was a contract army surgeon. He was a member of the American
Medical Association, the Medical Society of
the State of Pennsylvania and served as its recording secretary and corresponding secretary,
one of the founders, secretary and president
of the Montgomery County Medical Society,
member and for several years censor of the
Philadelphia County Medical Society, fellow
of the College of Physicians and Surgeons of
Philadelphia. He married (first), in Philadelphia, November 16, 1847, Elizabeth Browne,
born August 6, 1822, died April 25, 1864. He
married (second), November 7, 1876, Anna C.
Caldwell, born in New Orleans in 1836, daughter of William W. and Jane (Wheelright)
Caldwell, of Newburyport, Massachusetts.
Children, all by first wife: 1. Samuel Browne,
born December 13, 1848. 2. Winthrop, mentioned below. 3. Jane Tunis, January 28, 1856;
married Edward Worcester. 4. Fitz William,
January 4, 1859; married (first) Kate E.
Cowdrey, October 6, 1886, died October 27,
1891, and (second) Hattie Barnes, October 1,
1894. 5. Katie, May 15, 1862, died May 25,
1862. 6. Elizabeth Browne, October 26, 1863,
died April 10, 1890; married Theodore Worcester, January 15, 1890.

(VIII) Winthrop (4), son of Dr. Winthrop (3) Sargent, was born in Gwynedd,
Montgomery county, Pennsylvania, August 18,
1853. He was educated in public and private
academies. He was engaged in various enterprises, and in his younger days was on the
office force of the Pennsylvania Railroad Company, stationed at Altoona, Pennsylvania. His

time in later years has been given largely to
real estate and the management of property.
In 1911 was appointed by Governor Tener a
member of The Chestnut Tree Blight Commission. His office is in the Real Estate Trust
Building in Philadelphia. His home is at Haverford, a suburb of Philadelphia, and he has
also a summer residence at Bass Rocks,
Gloucester, the ancient home of the Sargent
family. He is a member of Merion Cricket
Club of Haverford, Philadelphia Country
Club, Radnor Hunt Club, Historical Society
of Pennsylvania, Union League of Philadelphia, Racquet Club of Philadelphia, the Engineers' Club of New York and Essex County
Club of Manchester, Massachusetts.

He married, October 20, 1886, Emma, born
January 25, 1861, in Maine, daughter of Rev.
Samuel Howard and Elizabeth Ann (Scott)
Worcester (see Worcester VIII). Children:
1. Winthrop, born August 21, 1887, Bridgewater, Massachusetts; a graduate of Haverford College, 1908, with honors; obtained the
degree of M. A. at Harvard University, 1909;
married, July 6, 1910, Frances Rotan; child,
Winthrop, born July 12, 1911. 2. Samuel
Worcester, April 13, 1889, at Philadelphia;
graduate of Harvard University, June, 1911;
married, June 5, 1911, Marion Bigelow. 3.
Gorham Parsons, August 18, 1891, at Bridgewater, Massachusetts; class of 1914, Dartmouth College. 4. Fitzwilliam, October 10,
1892, at Bridgewater, Massachusetts; class of
1914, Harvard University. 5. Richard Milne,
January 6, 1899, died January 9 of that year.

(The Duncan Line).

(I) Captain Nathaniel Duncan, immigrant
ancestor, was born in England, and was one
of the original church colony which came in
1630. He was a merchant and a person of
some distinction as shown by the title "Mr."
which was at that time reserved for clergymen,
scholars and men of high standing. He came
to America in the sloop, "Mary and John."
He was admitted a freeman of Massachusetts
Bay Colony, May 6, 1635. He was one of the
seven signers of the second church covenant in
1636. He held the offices of selectman,
auditor and deputy to the general court. He
removed to Boston and was received with his
wife in the Boston church, March 7, 1646.
We are told that he was "learned in Latin and
French; a very good accountant." "My son
Nathaniel Duncan and his children are legatees in the will of Ignatius Jordan (Jurdaine),
of Exeter, England, March 1, 1635;" and from
this fact it is presumed that Duncan's wife
Elizabeth was a daughter of Ignatius Jordan.
He was lieutenant of the first company in Dor-

chester, 1636, afterward captain. He became auditor general for the county. Nathaniel Duncan died in 1668 and the inventory of his estate was filed January 26, 1668, by James Trowbridge, administrator. Children: Nathaniel, member of the Boston Artillery Company in 1642; Peter, mentioned below.

(II) Peter, son of Captain Nathaniel Duncan, was born about 1630 in England or soon after coming to New England. He was a member of the Boston Artillery Company in 1654. He removed to Gloucester, Massachusetts. He married Mary Epes, daughter of the widow, Martha Epes (who was second or third wife of Samuel Symonds, Esq., of Ipswich). Children: Mary, married William Sargent (see Sargent II); Martha, born November 10, 1655; Elizabeth, February 28, 1657, died young; Elizabeth, August 30, 1661; Ruth, July 27, 1663; Peter, November 2, 1665; Priscilla, January 9, 1667; Margery, January 8, 1670; Daniel, May 19, 1672.

(The Parsons Line).

The name of Parsons, which is very ancient, is recorded in various counties of England and Ireland. In 1290 Walter Parsons lived at Mulso, Ireland, where some of the family owned and still own the castle of Ross and were viscounts and earls of Ross. Sir John Parsons was mayor of Hereford in 1481. In 1546 Robert Parsons, a famous Jesuit, lived at Bridgewater, was educated at Oxford, had to flee from the country because of religion, founded an English college at Rome and was well known as a writer. Charles I., in 1634, knighted Thomas Parsons, a royalist. Sir John and Sir Humphrey Parsons were lord mayors of London in 1704-31-40. The coat-of-arms which is entitled to be used by the American branch of the family, and which was granted Sir Thomas Parsons, is as follows: Gules two chevrons ermine, between three eagles displayed or. Crest: An eagle's leg erased at the thigh, standing on a leopard's head—gules.

(I) Benjamin Parsons, immigrant ancestor, came to America with his older brother, "Cornet" Joseph Parsons, sailing from Gravesend, England, for Boston in the "Transport," July 4, 1635. He was one of the first settlers at Springfield, Massachusetts, in 1639, and was a prominent citizen there. He was a deacon of the church, and held many important town offices. He married (first) Sarah, daughter of Richard Vore, of Windsor, Connecticut; Richard Vore was a member of Rev. John Warham's church, and came with him to Windsor in 1635. She died in Springfield, January 1, 1676. He married

(second), February 21, 1677, Sarah, widow of John Leonard, and she died in 1690. He died in Springfield, August 24, 1689. Children by first wife: Sarah, born August 18, 1656; Benjamin, September 15, 1658; Mary, December 10, 1660, died January 27, 1662; Abigail, January 6, 1662; Samuel, October 10, 1666; Ebenezer, mentioned below; Mary, December 17, 1670; Hezekiah, November 24, 1673; Joseph, December, 1675.

(II) Ebenezer, son of Benjamin Parsons, was born in Springfield, November 17, 1668. He was a deacon of the church in West Springfield for fifty-two years and highly respected. He married Margaret, daughter of Samuel and Katherine Marshfield, who came from Exeter, England, with Rev. John Warham and settled in Windsor, Connecticut. Children: Ebenezer, born January 12, 1691; Margaret, September 19, 1693; Jonathan, July 16, 1695, drowned July 1, 1703; Benjamin, December 15, 1696; Caleb, December 27, 1699; Sarah, February 4, 1703; Jonathan, mentioned below; Abigail, October 21, 1708; Katherine, October 16, 1715.

(III) Rev. Jonathan Parsons, son of Ebenezer Parsons, was born in West Springfield, November 30, 1705, died there July 19, 1776. He was graduated from Yale College in 1729, and then studied theology with Rev. Elisha Williams, president of Yale College, and with Rev. Jonathan Edwards, of Northampton, Massachusetts. He was ordained minister at Lyme, Connecticut, March 17, 1730. In 1746 he moved to Newburyport, Massachusetts, and officiated as minister of the church there until his death; he was buried in the tomb by the side of Rev. George Whitfield, who had died at his house not long before. He was one of the famous preachers of his day, and published two volumes of his sermons, besides several occasional and other sermons in pamphlet. He married (first), December 14, 1731, Phebe, daughter of John Griswold, of Lyme, Connecticut, and sister of Governor Matthew Griswold. She died December 26, 1770. He married (second) Lydia Clarkson, widow of Andrew Clarkson, of Portsmouth, New Hampshire. She died April 30, 1778. Children by first wife: Marshfield, born 1733; Jonathan, 1735; Samuel, 1737; Thomas, mentioned below; Phebe, 1748; Lucia, 1752; Lydia, 1755. Rev. Jonathan Parsons had thirteen children, but six of them died in infancy.

(IV) Thomas, son of Rev. Jonathan Parsons, was born in Lyme, Connecticut, April 28, 1739. He was a mariner, living at Newburyport, Massachusetts, and although he was reported as missing it is believed that he was murdered while on board his ship, in February, 1772. He married (first) Mary Gibson. He married (second) Sarah Sawyer, of Newbury, Massachusetts; she was born March 25, 1740, daughter of Enoch Sawyer, who was born June 22, 1694, died at Newbury, November 15, 1771; he was a physician of great ability; he married Sarah Pierpont, born in Reading, Massachusetts, October 3, 1697, died 1773, daughter of Rev. John Pierpont. Child by first wife: Jonathan Gibson. Children by second wife: Sarah, married Gorham Parsons; Anna, married Fitz William Sargent (see Sargent V); Mary, married Ignatius Sargent.

(The Worcester Line).

(I) William Worcester, immigrant ancestor, came from England and was pastor of the first church in Salisbury, Massachusetts, some time in 1638 and 1640. He died there October 28, 1662. He married (first) Sarah ——, who died at Salisbury, April 23, 1650. He married (second), July 23, 1650, Mrs. Rebecca Hall, who died at Ipswich, Massachusetts, February 21, 1695, widow of Henry Bylie, John Hall and William Worcester; her fourth husband was Samuel Symonds, deputy governor of the colony.

(II) Samuel, son of William Worcester, was born in England, lived in Salisbury and Bradford, Massachusetts, died February 20, 1680-81. He was in business in Towley as "partner in a sawmill." He married, November 29, 1659, Elizabeth, daughter of Francis Parrott, of Rowley, born May 1, 1640.

(III) Francis, son of Samuel Worcester, was born in Rowley, later Bradford, died December 17, 1717. He was an innholder and yeoman there. He married, January 29, 1690-91, Mary, daughter of Peter Cheney, of Newbury, born September 2, 1671; she married (second), December 8, 1726, Joseph Eaton, of Salisbury.

(IV) Francis (2), son of Francis (1) Worcester, was born in Bradford, June 7, 1698, where he lived until 1722, and then lived in Concord and Littleton; he was a blacksmith. He then preached in Boxford and was ordained at Sandwich in 1735. He then moved to Exeter, New Hampshire, and from there to Plaistow, New Hampshire, and in 1750 to Hollis, New Hampshire. He married (first), April 18, 1720, Abigail Carlton, of Rowley, who died July 25, 1774, aged seventy-eight. He married (second) Mrs. Martin. He died October 14, 1783.

(V) Noah, son of Francis (2) Worcester, was born in Sandwich, October 4, 1735. He lived in his father's home until his death at Hollis, August 13, 1817. He was an officer in the revolution. He married (first), Febru-

I—9

ary 22, 1757, Lydia, daughter of Abraham Tyler, of Hollis, born October 11, 1733, died July 6, 1772. He married (second), September 29, 1772, Hepzibah Sherwin, born in Boxford, April 30, 1746, died July 2, 1831.

(VI) Noah (2) Worcester, D. D., son of Noah (1) Worcester, was born in Hollis, November 25, 1758, died in Brighton, October 31, 1837. He served in the revolution as fifer and fife major. He lived in Plymouth and Thornton, New Hampshire. He was a shoemaker, teacher and preacher, being licensed in 1786, and preached at Thornton and Salisbury, New Hampshire; in May, 1813, he moved to Brighton, Massachusetts, becoming editor of a new periodical, the Christian Disciple. In 1791 he received an A. M. from Dartmouth College, and in 1818 the degree D. D. from Harvard College. He married (first), November 25, 1779, Hannah, daughter of Moses Brown, of Newburyport, born May 6, 1760, died November 16, 1797. He married (second), May 23, 1798, Hannah, daughter of Jeremiah Huntington, of Norwich, Connecticut, born March 24, 1764, died January 16, 1832.

(VII) Samuel (2), son of Noah (2) Worcester, D. D., was born in Thornton, New Hampshire, August 31, 1793, died in Bridgewater, Massachusetts, December 25, 1844. He was pastor of the New Jerusalem Church, Bridgewater, Massachusetts. He published several valuable school books. He married, January 2, 1817, Sarah, daughter of Fitz William Sargent, of Gloucester, Massachusetts, born September 24, 1793 (see Sargent V).

(VIII) Samuel Howard, son of Samuel (2) Worcester, was born in Gloucester, Massachusetts, February 16, 1824. He lived in Cambridgeport and Bridgewater. He was a student at Brown University, from which he received degrees of B. A. and M. A. He was a teacher at the academy at Framingham, Massachusetts, and was pastor of the New Jerusalem Church in Baltimore, Maryland. He married (first), September 22, 1844, Jane Ames, daughter of Calvin Washburn, of Bridgewater, born March 9, 1821, died December 11, 1854. He married (second), October 11, 1855, Elizabeth Ann, daughter of Townsend B. Scott, of Baltimore. Emma, child of second wife, married Winthrop Sargent (see Sargent VIII).

CLARK   The Clark family located at Portsmouth, New Hampshire, at an early date. Judging from the names they were closely related to the Clarks of Haverhill and vicinity, but no proof of the relationship has been found. There were also

Clarks at Kittery, Maine, an adjacent town. Edward Clark had land assigned to him at Portsmouth, October 19, 1659. He was drowned June 17, 1675. He left a widow, Mary, and two children, John and Sarah, by his first wife. By his second wife he had three young children whose names are not given. John Clark, probably a relative of Edward Clark, believed to be a brother, was in Portsmouth, according to the town records, as early as February 4, 1660. His will was dated April 25, 1700, proved February 4, 1701, bequeathing to sons, Jacob and Joseph.

(I) Josiah Clark, born 1650 or earlier, doubtless in England, was of age in 1671, when with Samuel Clark, both in John Hunking's division, he subscribed to the fund for the support of Mr. Moody, the minister. Samuel, Josiah, John and Edward were very likely brothers. Nothing further is found on the records of Samuel and Josiah (p. 12, vol. I, "New Hampshire Gen. Recorder").

(II) Josiah (2), son of Josiah (1) Clark, was born about 1685, probably at Portsmouth, but the vital records are incomplete. He married, April 21, 1715, at Portsmouth, Mary Wingate (p. 43, vol. V, "New Hampshire Gen. Recorder"). Josiah Clark joined the North Church, Portsmouth, July, 1715, with wife Mary. Children: Josiah, mentioned below; John, married, November 26, 1747, at Newington, Abigail Peverly, and had at Portsmouth, Elizabeth, baptized November 27, 1748; probably other children, including Andrew, who married Mary ———, and had William and Mary, baptized December 7, 1735, at Portsmouth.

(III) Josiah (3), son of Josiah (2) Clark, was born about 1720-25. He married, January 14, 1748, at Newington, New Hampshire, Mary, daughter of Josiah and Abigail (Nelson) Moses, of Portsmouth, born April 9, 1724 (p. 175, vol. II, "New Hampshire Gen. Records"). Both were of Portsmouth. Children of Josiah and Abigail Clark, born at Portsmouth: John, baptized December 25, 1748; Josiah, baptized July 29, 1750; Andrew, mentioned below (pp. 87, 89, 91, "New Hampshire Gen. Records").

(IV) Andrew, son of Josiah (3) Clark, was baptized at Portsmouth, New Hampshire, April 15, 1753, at the North Church. He was a member of the South Church, Portsmouth. He had a son Andrew, mentioned below.

(V) Captain Andrew (2) Clark, son of Andrew (1) Clark, was baptized at the South Church, Portsmouth, March 26, 1780. He followed the sea, became a master mariner and was lost at sea about 1815. His will was proved July 17, 1816. He bought his house

at Portsmouth by deed dated March 17, 1810. He married, about 1805, Phebe Ann Pearce Roach, born February 16, 1784, daughter of Captain Thomas and Phebe (Pearce) Roach, granddaughter of Captain William and Mary (Buss) Pearce. Captain William Pearce married at Portsmouth, March 28, 1763, Mary Buss, and they had Phebe, born in 1766; Anne, 1767, and Elizabeth, 1768. Captain Pearce married (first), January 4, 1755, Phebe Haines. Mary (Buss) Pearce died in July, 1788, aged fifty-four. Captain Thomas Roach died November 4, 1824; he ran away from school, according to family history, and was found on board Captain Pearce's vessel after it left Calais, France. It is related that Captain Pearce wrote to the boy's people, and that they answered that as he had run away he could stay where he was, and he became a seaman, and finally mate under Captain Pearce and married his daughter. He was afterward master mariner himself and a shipowner. Captain Roach was an open-hearted, hospitable man of gentlemanly tastes, of considerable wealth. He owned a slave Dinah who married a slave of Captain Pearce; they lived in a little house at the rear of Captain Roach's house, which was at the corner of Daniel street and South, now Chapel, street. In 1810 Captain Roach sold his house or part of it to his son-in-law, Andrew Clark, for $1,300, having in 1808 bought a farm at Newington, about three miles from Portsmouth. A brother of Captain Roach came from France and visited him at Newington, where Captain Roach lived the life of a gentleman, entertaining much, especially the sea captains in port at Portsmouth. His gravestone is in the family cemetery on his farm. Among the French Spoliation Claims was one of $700 for the loss of Captain Roach's vessel, "The Two Sisters." Children of Captain Andrew (2) and Phebe Ann (Pearce) Clark; Andrew Jr., born at Portsmouth, March 9, 1806; Joseph Stevens, mentioned below; Mary Ann, born August 9, 1810.

(VI) Joseph Stevens, son of Captain Andrew (2) Clark, was born at Portsmouth, New Hampshire, August 13, 1808, died February 8, 1877. He was educated in the state of Maine. He was an accountant by profession and afterward engaged in the lumber business. He resided at Mendon, Worcester county, and at Worcester. He married (first), name unknown; (second), August 12, 1851, at Mendon, Mercy Maria Aldrich, born at Mendon, January 26, 1824 (see Aldrich VI). Children, recorded in Worcester: Charles Edwin, mentioned below; William Augustus, born June 14, 1856; Lucinda Aldrich; Fred

Chas. E. Clark

W.; Ella M.; the last three named were born near Woonsocket.

(VII) Charles Edwin, son of Joseph Stevens Clark, was born at Mendon, but recorded in Worcester, Massachusetts, April 23, 1854. His early childhood was spent in Worcester, whence the family removed to Woonsocket, Rhode Island, where he attended the public and high schools. His business career began in Philadelphia, Pennsylvania, where he spent ten years in the woolen trade. In 1893 he became engaged in the dental manufacturing business, forming the Pennsylvania Dental Manufacturing Company, a corporation of which he is president and treasurer. In politics Mr. Clark is a Republican and a member of the Union League Club. He attends the Presbyterian church and is a trustee of the Tabernacle Presbyterian Church. He is a member of the New England Society of Philadelphia and Sons of the Revolution. His offices are at 1317 Sanson street, his home at 4115 Walnut street, Philadelphia, and his summer home is at Strafford, Pennsylvania.

He married, February 13, 1880, Nancy Warner Skinner, born in Northampton, Massachusetts, December 29, 1853, daughter of William and Nancy (Warner) Skinner, of Northampton. Her father was born in London, England; her mother was of an old Hampshire county, Massachusetts, family. Children, born in Philadelphia: 1. Raymond Skinner, born December 22, 1880; married, October 3, 1911, Helen Ashton Burt, of Wheeling, West Virginia; he was a student at Harvard University from 1899 to 1901; since then has been with his uncle's firm, William Skinner & Sons, of New York. 2. Herbert Skinner, born September 16, 1886; graduated from Harvard College in 1909 (A. B.), and since then has been associated in business with his father, living in Philadelphia. 3. Charles Edwin Jr., born August 12, 1887; graduated from Princeton class of 1911, as civil engineer; now employed by the Pennsylvania Railroad Company.

(The Aldrich Line).

(I) George Aldrich, immigrant ancestor, was born in Derbyshire, England, about 1605, died at Mendon, Massachusetts, March 1, 1682. He was a tailor by trade. He sailed for America, November 6, 1631, and settled first in Dorchester, Massachusetts, becoming a member of the church there, with his wife Catherine, in 1636. He was admitted a freeman, December 7, 1636. From about 1640 to 1663 he lived in Braintree, Massachusetts, and finally settled in Mendon, where he was one

of the first seven settlers, and here he lived the remainder of his life. He sold his place in Braintree, June 9, 1663, to Richard Thayer. His will, dated at Mendon, November 2, 1682, was proved April 26, 1683, and he bequeathed to his wife and children: Joseph, John, Jacob, Mary Bartlett, Mercy Randall and Martha Dunbar. He married, in England, September 3, 1629, Catherine Seald, born in 1610, according to her deposition, June 18, 1670, when she gave her age as sixty years. She died at Mendon, January 11, 1691. Children: Abel; Joseph, born June 4, 1635; Mary, June 16, 1637, died young; Meriam, June 29, 1639, died young; Experience, September 4, 1641, died December 2, 1641. Born in Braintree; John, April 2, 1644; Sarah, January 16, 1645; Peter, April 4, 1648; Mercy, June 17, 1650; Jacob, mentioned below; Martha, July 7, 1656.

(II) Jacob, son of George Aldrich, was born in Braintree, Massachusetts, February 28, 1652, died at Mendon, October 22, 1695. He settled at Mendon and was a farmer, living on the old homestead. He married, November 3, 1674, Huldah, born June 16, 1657, daughter of Ferdinand and Huldah (Hayward) Thayer, of Braintree. Children: Jacob, born May 8, 1676; Abel, January 27, 1678; Seth, July 6, 1679; Huldah, November 17, 1680; Rachel, February 22, 1682, died November 25, 1690; Sarah, October 24, 1683; David, May 23, 1685; Peter, October 17, 1686; John, November 27, 1688; Moses, mentioned below; Mercy, February 17, 1692, died March 18, 1693; Rachel, December 27, 1695.

(III) Moses, son of Jacob Aldrich, was born April 1, 1691. He married, April 23, 1711, Hannah White, born December 9, 1691, daughter of Joseph and Lydia White, of Mendon. Children: Abigail, born September 18, 1712; Mary, February 15, 1714; George, January 13, 1715; Mercy, November 28, 1717; Robert, December 11, 1719; Lydia, October 28, 1721; Thomas, February 24, 1723; Caleb, mentioned below; Luke, February 29, 1727; Alice, May 2, 1730; Moses, April 19, 1732; Aaron, January 23, 1733.

(IV) Caleb, son of Moses Aldrich, was born January 13, 1725, died November 8, 1809. He was a prominent man and held both town and state offices. He was a justice of common pleas from 1781 to 1787. He married, January 1, 1747, Mary Arnold, born in 1732, died in 1816. Children: Susannah, born November 25, 1748; Thomas, April 7, 1750; William, April 3, 1752; Hannah, February 2, 1754; Naaman, mentioned below; Joel, June 2, 1758; Augustus, May 9, 1760; Mary, September 8, 1763; Caleb, September 27, 1764;

Moses, March 15, 1767; Lydia, May 29, 1769; Arnold, August 1, 1773.

(V) Naaman, son of Caleb Aldrich, was born May 6, 1756, died October 19, 1824. He married, June 6, 1776, Mercy Arnold, born August 4, 1757, died February 25, 1826, daughter of Stephen and Rachel (Arnold) Arnold. Children: Mark, born October 13, 1777; Luke, mentioned below; Lucy, July 25, 1782; John, January 20, 1785; Peleg, November 25, 1787; Alpha, August 30, 1790; son, May 11, 1793, died December 28, 1793; daughter, December 13, 1794, died January 13, 1795; son, August 21, 1796, died October 18, 1796; Louis, February 18, 1799; Maria A., June 9, 1802.

(VI) Luke, son of Naaman Aldrich, was born March 22, 1780, died August 16, 1867. He married (first), April 23, 1800, Nancy Nichols, born about 1773, died March 24, 1819, aged forty-six. He married (second), November 23, 1820, Lucinda Thayer, born about 1791, died February 6, 1859, daughter of Seth and Sarah (Holbrook) Thayer, of Milford, Massachusetts (see Thayer VII). Children by first wife: Mercy, born May 19, 1801; Lucy, January 20, 1803; Stephen A., February 17, 1805; Harriet, February 4, 1807; Eliza, May 12, 1809; Alpha, May 15, 1812. Children by second wife: Seth T., November 1, 1821; Mercy Maria, January 26, 1824, married Joseph Stevens Clark, died November 18, 1902 (see Clark VI); Edwin R., July 25, 1826; Benjamin F., May 2, 1828; Sarah Ann, April 3, 1831; Moses, February 8, 1834.

(The Thayer Line).

(I) Thomas Thayer, immigrant ancestor, came from Thornbury, England, and settled in Braintree, Massachusetts, in 1630. He married Margery Wheeler, who died December 11, 1672, and he died April, 1672. He was a shoemaker. His will was dated September 13, 1665. Children: Thomas Jr., Ferdinando, mentioned below; Shadrach.

(II) Ferdinando, son of Thomas Thayer, was born in England. He settled in Mendon, Massachusetts, about 1668, where he had a large family, and where he died March 28, 1713. He was in Mendon before King Philip's war, and his name was on the minutes of the first town meeting there, June, 1667, as selectman. He had a tract of land set off for him in January, 1674, as well as other lands also, and after the Indians burned the town, he returned again and took lands which included a forty-acre house lot, May 26, 1686. He married Huldah Hayward, of Braintree, and she died in Mendon, September 1, 1690. Children, about half of them born in Braintree and the remainder in Mendon: Sarah, Huldah, Jonathan, mentioned below; David, died 1674; Naomi, Thomas, Samuel, Isaac, Josiah, Ebenezer, Benjamin, David.

(III) Jonathan, son of Ferdinando Thayer, was born March 18, 1658, and lived in Mendon. He married, June 22, 1679, Elizabeth French; she died October 3, 1703.

(IV) Jonathan (2), son of Jonathan (1) Thayer, was born December 8, 1690, died April 27, 1747. He married (first), Sarah Bailey, and she died in 1712. He married (second), October 1, 1714, Bethiah Chapin, born in Medfield, Massachusetts, February 16, 1693, died in 1734, daughter of Captain Seth Chapin, of Braintree, who was born August 4, 1668, and married Bethiah Thurston, March 25, 1691; Captain Seth Chapin was son of Josiah Chapin, Esq., who was born in England in 1634, and married Mary King, of Weymouth, November, 1658. Josiah Chapin was a lawyer and surveyor and held the highest municipal and civil positions, dying at the age of ninety-two years; he was son of Samuel Chapin, who came with his wife Cicely from England to Roxbury, Massachusetts, in 1636, and settled at Springfield, Massachusetts, where he was prominent in church and state. Jonathan Thayer married (third), September 4, 1735, Rachel Holbrook. He had fourteen children.

(V) Seth, son of Jonathan (2) and Bethiah (Chapin) Thayer, was born July 27, 1725, died April 17, 1819. He served in the revolution as private on the Lexington Alarm, April 19, 1775, under Captain William Jennison, marching from Mendon to Roxbury and Cambridge, and he served eleven and a half days. His name is on the list of officers chosen by the company, July 9, 1776, as first lieutenant on Muster and Pay Roll of "Capt. Lieut. Seth Thayer's Co.", Lieutenant-Colonel Nathan Tyler' regiment, for service in Rhode Island on the alarm of December, 1776. He enlisted December 8, and was discharged January 23, 1777. His name is on a resignation dated at Mendon, November 1, 1779, as first lieutenant of Fifth Company, Third Regiment in Worcester county, Colonel Nathan Tyler, and the resignation was accepted by the council, November 16, 1779. He married his third cousin, Judith Thayer, of Braintree, in 1751. She was born December 25, 1734, died January 1, 1823, daughter of John and Lydia (Wales) Thayer.

(VI) Seth (2), son of Seth (1) Thayer, was born July 27, 1765, died in 1819. He settled at Bear Hill, Milford, Massachusetts. He married (first) Elizabeth Daniels, of Holliston, Massachusetts, April 27, 1786, and she died in 1787. He married (second), April 19, 1790, Sarah Holbrook, of Bellingham, Massachusetts, and she died in Milville in 1844. She was daughter of Seth Holbrook, who served in the revolution and drew a pension. Seth Holbrook was born November 24, 1751, and lived in Bellingham; he married his second cousin, Dinah Holbrook, and he was son of Seth, who was son of Joseph, son of Joseph, son of Peter, son of Thomas, son of Thomas Holbrook. Seth Holbrook served as a private on the Lexington Alarm, in Captain Jesse Holbrook's company, from Mendon, and he was a corporal in Captain Cobb's company, Colonel Read's regiment, 1775; he was sergeant in Captain Samuel Cowell's company, Colonel L. Robinson's regiment, 1776; corporal in Captain Job Knap's company, Colonel Job Cushing's regiment; sergeant in Captain Amos Ellis' company, Major Seth Bullard's regiment, 1780; sergeant in Captain Amos Ellis' company, Colonel Dean's regiment for service in Rhode Island, Fourth Suffolk County Regiment.

(VII) Lucinda, daughter of Seth (2) and Sarah (Holbrook) Thayer, married, November 23, 1820, Luke Aldrich (see Aldrich). She was born in 1791, died February 6, 1859.

Joseph Bemis, immigrant ancestor of this family, was born in BEMIS England in 1619. He came to Watertown, Massachusetts, as early as 1640, and died there August 7, 1684. He was accompanied by his sister, Mary Bemis, who married at Watertown, March 20, 1644-45, William Hagar. Joseph Bemis was selectman of Watertown in 1648-72-75. He was a blacksmith, as well as a farmer. His will was dated August 7, 1684, and proved October 7, 1684. His widow administered the estate, which was divided November 18, 1712, soon after her death. Children, born in Watertown: Sarah, January 15, 1642-43; Mary, September 10, 1644; Joseph Jr., twin, October 28, 1647, buried November 4, 1647; Ephraim, twin of Joseph, buried November 4, 1647; Martha, born March 24, 1649; Joseph Jr., December 12, 1651; Rebecca, April 17, 1654; Ephraim, August 25, 1656; John, mentioned below.

(II) John, son of Joseph Bemis, was born in Watertown, in August, 1659, died October 24, 1732. He married (first), at Watertown, about 1680, Mary, daughter of George and Susanna Harrington. He married (second), January 1, 1716-17, Mrs. Sarah (Holland) Phillips, widow of Jonathan Phillips, who was born November 16, 1663, died February 1703-04. She was born in Watertown, November 30, 1662, died before 1726, daugh-

ter of Nathaniel Holland and his second wife, Sarah (Hosier) Holland. He married (third), at Watertown, May 30, 1726, Judith (Jennison) Barnard, who was born at Watertown, August 13, 1667, died there, daughter of Ensign Samuel Jennison, who was born in 1645, died October, 1701, and his wife, Judith (Nacomber) Jennison, who died March 1, 1722-23. She was the widow of James Barnard. John Bemis owned land in Marlborough before April 26, 1701, when he sold it. Children of first wife: Beriah, born June 23, 1681; Susanna, December 24, 1682; Joseph, November 17, 1684; Samuel, 1690; Lydia, 1692; Hannah, October 9, 1694, died October, 1700; Isaac, 1696; Jonathan, April 30, 1699, probably died young; Jonathan, November 17, 1701; Abraham, November 26, 1703; Susanna, December 3, 1705; Hannah, December 3, 1707.

(III) John (2), son of John (1) Bemis, was born in Watertown, October 6, 1686. He married (first), May 8, 1710, Hannah Warren, born January 25, 1690-91, daughter of Daniel Warren, who was born October 6, 1653, and his wife Elizabeth (Whitney) Warren, born June 9, 1656. He married (second), April 2, 1713, Anna Livermore, born 1690, daughter of Samuel Livermore, born 1640, died 1690, and his wife, Anna (Bridge) Livermore, born in 1646, died August 28, 1727. After John Bemis died, his widow married, December 5, 1769, Josiah Smith. Child of first wife: John, mentioned below. Children of second wife: Anna, born April 29, 1714; Josiah, February 29, 1715-16; Abraham, December 27, 1717; Grace, November 5, 1719; Lydia, April 5, 1721; Abijah, March 16, 1722-23; Elisha, March 20, 1725-26; Elizabeth, March 23, 1727-28; Nathaniel, May 6, 1730; Susanna, April 3, 1732; Phineas, March 24, 1734.

(IV) John (3), son of John (2) Bemis, was born at Watertown, February 11, 1711-12. He was a surveyor of highways and soldier in the French War, 1656. He married, February 16, 1731, Hannah Warren, born April 28, 1715, daughter of Captain Daniel Warren, born April 30, 1686, and his wife, Hannah (Bigelow) Warren. Children, born in Watertown: John, August 28, 1732; Timothy, March 6, 1734-35; Anna, September 30, 1736; Elizabeth, January 17, 1738-39; Lydia, June 10, 1741; Abigail, September 1, 1743, died July 25, 1750; Nathaniel, mentioned below; Sarah, September 27, 1748; Henry, January 28, 1750-51; Jeduthan, June 10, 1753; Mary, May 16, 1755; Daniel, March 5, 1758.

(V) Sergeant Nathaniel Bemis, son of John (3) Bemis, was born at Watertown, Massachusetts, March 12, 1745. He married, 1765, Esther Cox, born October 4, 1743, daughter of Elisha and Anna Cox, of Weston, Massachusetts. He served in the revolution as a sergeant in Captain John Walton's company at Cambridge, 1778. In another list, year not given, he was of Weston, as a private in Captain Charles Miles' company, Colonel Jonathan Reed's regiment. Children: Lucy, born August 5, 1766; Nathaniel, May 8, 1770; Lot, August 5, 1772; Polly, November 22, 1777; Elisha, January 22, 1780; Charles, mentioned below.

(VI) Charles, son of Sergeant Nathaniel Bemis, was born January 9, 1785, died in 1877 at the age of ninety-two years. He married, December 20, 1807, Betsey Jones, born December 24, 1781, daughter of Lieutenant Eli Jones, of Lincoln, who was born in 1756, died May 9, 1811, a Bunker Hill soldier, and his wife, Anna (Brown) Jones, who was born June 26, 1763 (see Jones V). Children: Emily Jones, born November 29, 1808; Charles Winslow, May 15, 1811; Dexter, May 3, 1813; Eli Emery, July 17, 1815; Betsy Jane, December 24, 1817; Royal, mentioned below; Luke, November 10, 1822; John, June 26, 1825, died in infancy.

(VII) Royal, son of Charles Bemis, was born at Lincoln, October 1, 1820, died April 13, 1910. He was brought up on his father's farm, and educated in the public schools of his native town. He was for a time a manufacturer of boots and shoes, afterward a manufacturer of watch tools, and finally engaged in the business of florist at Waltham, Massachusetts. He married (first) Mary Ann Bond, who died in April, 1849. He married (second) Susan Warren Durgin, daughter of David and Sarah (Oddway) Durgin. She had several sisters and brothers, Nathaniel, Joseph, Sarah, Sutton, Aurexene, Robinson and a sister who is now living, Mrs. Oliver Treadwell, of Naples, Maine. Children of second wife: Arthur Herbert Lincoln, now living in Williamstown, Massachusetts; Susie Bell, born in Waltham in 1862, married Frank Lamb, of Naples, Maine, where she is now living; Dr. Royal Warren, mentioned below.

(VIII) Dr. Royal Warren Bemis, son of Royal Bemis, was born at Waltham, January 16, 1868. He attended the public schools of his native town, and fitted for college in the Waltham high school. He entered the Jefferson Medical College at Philadelphia in 1889, and was graduated with the degree Doctor of Medicine in 1892. During the next three years and a half he was an interne at the Municipal Hospital of Philadelphia. Since then he has been in general practice in Phila-

delphia. His offices are at 2512 North Fifth street. He has been on the staff of physicians at St. Christopher Hospital for Children, Philadelphia, since 1898, and on the staff of the Stetson Hospital, Nose and Ear Department, since 1901, and for several years on the staff of the Roosevelt Hospital. He is a member of the Philadelphia County Medical Society and was chairman of the Kensington branch in 1899; member of the Philadelphia Medical Club, County Medical Society of Philadelphia, the Pennsylvania Medical Society and the American Medical Association; member of Medico-Legal Society; of the Clinical Society of Philadelphia; of the Philadelphia Laryngological Society; of the Pediatrical Society. He was a member of the Board of Health of the city of Philadelphia for two years. He is a medical examiner for the Royal Arcanum. In addition to his extensive general practice he makes a specialty of diseases of the nose and ear. In politics he is a Republican. He is a communicant of the Methodist Episcopal church.

He married, August 5, 1896, Gertrude L. Foster, born at Lynn, Massachusetts, March 8, 1872, daughter of Handley and Elizabeth (Kilpatrick) Foster. They have a daughter, Marion Elizabeth, born July 29, 1898, in Philadelphia.

(The Jones Line).

(I) William Jones, immigrant ancestor, lived in Charlestown, Massachusetts, as early as 1658, when he owned fifteen acres of land and two and a half of commons. His will, dated March 4, proved March 28, 1678, left all his property to his son Thomas, mentioned below. "Old Father Jones near 90 died March 8, 1677-8," at Charlestown. He may have been the same William Jones who lived in the adjoining town of Cambridge and was a proprietor there in 1635, coming from Sandwich, England, a painter by trade, whose wife Margaret came in the ship "Hercules" in March, 1634. She was accused of being a witch, tried, convicted and hanged by the superstitious authorities in 1648. Her husband desired soon afterward to ship for the Barbadoes, but was imprisoned, and unless he is the William Jones, of Charlestown, described above, nothing more is known of him. There was no other William Jones in Massachusetts before 1650.

(II) Thomas, son of William Jones, was born in 1645 (aged twenty-four in 1669). He was a bricklayer by trade. It is a significant fact that Thomas Jones, as the record shows, went to the Barbadoes and returned, was married in Charlestown and again went to sea, although he was a bricklayer or mason by trade. He died in Charlestown, November 28,

1679, leaving five children aged one to ten years. He married Sarah Crouch after 1669, and she married (second) Thomas Stanford. He owned and sold land in Charlestown. His widow, administratrix of his estate, was granted two commons in 1681. The probate records proved that his son Thomas was living in Sherborn when heirs sold land in Charlestown in 1695. Children, born in Charlestown: Sarah, April 24, 1670; Mary, May 13, 1672; Thomas, mentioned below; William, October 4, 1676.

(III) Thomas (2), son of Thomas (1) Jones, was born in Charlestown, July 3, 1674, baptized October 11, 1674, died at Sherborn, May 25, 1729, aged fifty-six years. He owned land in Charlestown. He settled in Sherborn, Middlesex county, Massachusetts, and in 1721 was the largest taxpayer there. He shared in the New Sherborn or Douglas grant in 1730. He married Elizabeth ———. Children, born in Sherborn: Jonathan, December 13, 1701; Eli, mentioned below; Thomas, May 27, 1706; Elizabeth, May 27, 1711; Aaron, April 11, 1713, died 1742; Jonathan, lived at Holliston, formerly Sherborn.

(IV) Eli, son of Thomas (2) Jones, was born in Sherborn, December 5, 1704. He married, May 15, 1729, Mercy Underwood, born April 3, 1709, daughter of Joseph and granddaughter of Joseph Underwood. She died at Holliston, January 31, 1754. Children, born at Holliston: David, February 17, 1731; Hannah, August 6, 1734; Thankful, April 6, 1738; Miriam, June 1, 1743; Mercy, September 18, 1745; Mary, baptized June 3, 1750; Eli, mentioned below; Abel, baptized September 24, 1758.

(V) Lieutenant Eli (2) Jones, son of Eli (1) Jones, was born at Holliston, April 24, 1756, died at Lincoln, Massachusetts, May 9, 1811, aged fifty-five years (gravestone). He was a soldier in the revolution in Captain Abraham Pierce's company on the Lexington Alarm, was at Bunker Hill and in the same company, Colonel Samuel Thatcher's regiment, in 1776; also in Captain Joseph Fuller's company, Colonel Samuel Bullard's regiment, August 20 to November 29, 1777, at Stillwater; also in Captain Edward Fuller's company, Colonel William McIntosh's regiment, March-April, 1778; also in the Continental army, enlisting July 19, 1779, at the age of twenty-three years. He was five feet, seven inches and a half in height. He served in Colonel Bradford's company and regiment (Fourteenth) to April, 1780. He was commissioned lieutenant, July 15, 1780. In 1780 he was in Captain James Cooper's company, Colonel Gamaliel

Bradford's regiment (Fourteenth), and again for six months in 1781 under Colonel John Brooks. He lived in Weston and afterward in Lincoln. He was warden in Weston in 1786, fence viewer in 1790, and owned a pew in the church in 1800.

He married, at Waltham, Massachusetts, August 23, 1780, Anna Brown, born June 24, 1763, died in Lincoln, Massachusetts, April 14, 1857, aged ninety-four years, daughter of Colonel Abijah Brown, who fought at Bunker Hill, a prominent figure in revolutionary days. Children, born in Weston and Lincoln: 1. Betsey, born December 24, 1781, died July 15, 1874; married Charles Bemis (see Bemis VI). 2. Nancy, born March 25, 1783, died September 26, 1851. 3. William, born September 16, 1785. 4. Polly, born September 29, 1788, died August 26, 1848. 5. Sally, born October 12, 1790. 6. Susan, born October 30, 1793, died March, 1886. 7. Rebecca, born March 23, 1795. 8. Sophia, born June 27, 1797. 9. Hannah, born September 27, 1799. 10. Levina, born January 24, 1802. 11. Eli, born May 13, 1804. 12. Almira, born July 12, 1808, baptized July 17, 1808; married Jonas Hastings.

GIFFORD William Gifford, the immigrant ancestor, was born in England, and appears to have been for a short time at Stamford, Connecticut, and about 1647 his name appears in the court records there. He certainly settled in the Plymouth colony soon afterward, and in 1650 was a member of the grand inquest at Plymouth. He continued to reside in Sandwich, Massachusetts, until his death, with the exception of five years between 1665 and 1670 when he with George Allen and the sons of Peter Gaunt, all of Sandwich, together with others, were first proprietors and settlers of Monmouth, New Jersey, having purchased the land of the Indians, and to whom the Monmouth Patent was granted April 8, 1665. They were adherents of the Quaker faith, and suffered severely from persecution and vexatious arrests and suits in Massachusetts and New Jersey. Gifford owned land in Massachusetts, Rhode Island and Connecticut. His Massachusetts possessions consisted of land in Sandwich, Falmouth and Dartmouth. He gave by will to his sons Jonathan and James land at Falmouth, and deeded to sons Robert and Christopher lands at Dartmouth, Massachusetts, both of whom built houses on their property. Robert continued at Dartmouth, but Christopher moved to Little Compton, Rhode Island. Both have descendants in Southern Massachusetts and Rhode Island. William probably deeded his Connecticut lands to his son John, who gave by will 100 acres in Connecticut to his son Samuel, and 200 acres to his grandsons. He died April 9, 1687. He married twice. His second wife was Mary Mills, whom he married July 16, 1688; she died February 10, 1734. Children of first wife: John, died 1708; Hananiah, married Elizabeth ——; William, died 1738; Christopher, born July, 1658, died November 22, 1748; Robert, born 1660, died 1730; Patience, died 1673, married Richard Kirby. Children of second wife: Mary; Jonathan, born May 14, 1684; James, born March 10, 1685-86.

(II) Robert, son of William Gifford, was born in 1660, died in 1730. He resided at Dartmouth, Massachusetts. He married Sarah Wing, born February 2, 1658, daughter of Stephen and Sarah (Briggs) Wing. He married (second) Elizabeth ——. Children, born at Dartmouth: Benjamin, Jeremiah, Stephen, Timothy and Simeon.

(III) Jeremiah, son of Robert Gifford, was born at Dartmouth; he married Mary ——. Children, born at Dartmouth: Jonathan, March 25, 1704; Gideon, March 19, 1705-06; John O., March 7, 1707-08; Sarah, October 3, 1710; Elizabeth, October 13, 1712; Joseph, twin of Elizabeth; William, January 19, 1714; Benjamin, May 14, 1717; Isaac, May 16, 1717 (sic), died March 3, 1812; Peleg, mentioned below; Margaret, April 15, 1722; Adam, January 3, 1725; David, April 5, 1728.

(IV) Peleg, son of Jeremiah Gifford, was born at Dartmouth, December 1, 1719.

(V) Elihu Gifford, as far as is known only son of Peleg Gifford, was born at Dartmouth, October 9, 1747, and died December 3, 1846(?). He was a captain in the revolution. He married Abigail Chase. Children: Isaac, born July 16, 1769, died February 14, 1850; Parnel, March 12, 1772, married John Wood, of Dartmouth; Abraham, January 6, 1774, died August 13, 1861; Elihu Jr., October 1, 1776, died in the West Indies, 1798; George Washington, mentioned below; Polly, born January 20, 1780, died June, 1830, married Elihu, son of David Gifford, of Dartmouth; Paul, born October 31, 1782, died June 25, 1854; Pardon, twin with Paul, died June 7, 1854; Abigail, January 4, 1785, died in November, 1854, married Francis Tripp, and (second) Benjamin Howland; Benjamin, July 1, 1787, died March 1830.

(VI) George Washington, son of Elihu Gifford, was born at Dartmouth, February 8, 1778, and died in February, 1816. He married Judith Palmer, and lived at Mattapoisett, Massachusetts. Children: Frederic; Holder; Gideon; Elihu; Captain Peleg W., born 1805, died 1889, married Amelia Hammond; George Washington, mentioned below; Mary H., born in 1814, at Newport, married Arnold M. Barker, November 10, 1839, and died February 4, 1874, had four children.

(VII) George Washington (2), son of George Washington (1) Gifford, was born at Mattapoisett, Massachusetts, February 4, 1812. He followed the sea and became a master mariner. He died in 1885. He married Ann Grant, born June 15, 1842, daughter of Thomas and Elizabeth (Diman) Grant. Children: 1. George Barker, mentioned below. 2. Mary E., born December 4, 1862, at Assonet; married James H. Breck, of Springfield, Massachusetts, and had Robert G. Breck, born 1891. 3. Ann E., born September 29, 1864; married Frank L. Blackwell, of Fairhaven, Massachusetts, and had Malcolm Gifford, born January 9, 1897, at Bristol, Rhode Island. 4. Charles H., born in Rehoboth, Massachusetts; married Elizabeth Ellis, of Fair Haven; children: Ruth Gifford, born 1891, and Frances Gifford, born 1895. 5. Grace B., born at Rehoboth, March 8, 1870; married Albert A. Chamberlain, of Springfield, Massachusetts; children: William, born 1895, and Gifford Chamberlain, 1900.

(VIII) George Barker, son of George Washington (2) Gifford, was born at Assonet (Freetown), Massachusetts, January 15, 1861. He was educated in the public schools of Fair Haven and Rehoboth, Massachusetts. After leaving school he was employed in a furniture repairing store, and afterward was clerk in a general store at New Bedford, Massachusetts. In 1878 he entered the employ of the Standard Oil Company as a helper in the machine shop, and was promoted in time to the position of foreman and afterward superintendent. During the thirty-three years in which he has been connected with this great corporation his rise has been steady. At the present time he is manager of the works of the Standard Oil Company at Bayonne, New Jersey, with offices at 26 Broadway, New York City. He is a member of the Jersey City Club, the Newark Bay Club, the New England Society of New York. He attends the Baptist church, and in politics is an independent Republican. He married, November 1, 1883, Minnie Van Cott, born in Brooklyn, New York, September 9, 1862, daughter of George W. and Hester (Strickland) Van Cott. They have one son: George Barker Jr., born in Brooklyn, December 7, 1886, educated in the public schools and at Pratt Institute, Brooklyn, a mechanical engineer by profession.

Geo. B. Gifford

The surname Tracy is taken TRACY from the castle and barony of Tracie, near Vire Arrondissement of Caen. The first of the name of whom there is record is Turgis de Tracie, who, with William de la Ferte, was defeated and driven out of Main by the Count of Anjou in 1078, and was in all probability the Sire de Tracie mentioned below, in the army of Hastings. The coat-of-arms of the family was borne in the middle of the twelfth century, and was as follows: Or, an escallop in the chief dexter, between two bendlets gules. Crest: On a chapeau gules turned up ermine an escallop sable, between two wings expanded or.

(I) Sire de Tracie is mentioned as being in the army of Hastings in 1066, an officer in the army of William the Conqueror.

(II) Henri de Tracie was his son, and was Lord of Barnstable. He settled in County Devon, and was the only man of noble birth in that county who stood firm for the king during the invasion of the Empress Maud, and received as a reward the Barony of Barnstable. He died about 1146.

(III) Grace de Tracie, daughter of Henri, married John de Sudely, and her second son inherited her estates and assumed her name.

(IV) William de Tracie, son of Grace, lived in the reign of Henry II., and held the Manor of Toddington. He was one of the knights who, in 1170, at the instigation of Henry II., assassinated Thomas á Becket, Archbishop of Canterbury. He is described as "a man of high birth, state and stomach, a favorite of the king and his daily attendant." In 1171 he was created justiciary of Normandy, serving about five years. He then returned to England and during the reign of King John, took up arms against him, and his lands were confiscated. They were later restored, however. Late in life he founded and endowed a chapel to Thomas á Becket in the conventual church at Tewkesbury, indicating his repentance. He died at Morthoe, County Devon, in 1224.

(V) Sir Henry de Tracy of Toddington was his heir, and died about 1246.

(VI) Sir Henry de Tracy was his eldest son and died 1296.

(VII) Sir William de Tracy, Esq., of Toddington, was high sheriff of Gloucestershire, and was called to the privy council of Henry IV.

(VIII) William de Tracy inherited the Toddington estates and was sheriff of Gloucestershire. He died 1460.

(IX) Henry Tracy, Esq., was his eldest son, and married Alice, daughter and co-heiress of Thomas Baldington, Esq.

(X) Sir William Tracy of Toddington was his eldest son, sheriff of Gloucestershire during the reign of Henry VIII. (1513). He was one of the first to embrace the reform religion in England, as shown by his will, dated 1530. He married Margaret Throckmorton.

(XI) Richard Tracy was his third son and inherited the Manor of Sathway. He was highly educated and wrote several treatises on religion. He was sheriff of Gloucestershire. He married Barbara, a pupil of Fox, the Martyrologist. He died 1569.

(XII) Samuel, son of Richard Tracy, had a son, Stephen, mentioned below.

(XIII) Stephen, son of Samuel Tracy, and himself the immigrant ancestor, came to Plymouth, Massachusetts, on the ship "Ann," Captain William Prince, in 1623, with his wife and infant daughter. His name is on the list of freemen, in 1623. He settled first on the south side of Plymouth and shared in the division of cattle in 1627. Soon after, he removed to Duxbury, and in 1634, was appointed one of five to lay out highways. He served as a constable in 1639, and was one of five to select a site for a meeting house. He was a grand juror in 1639-40-42, and was arbitrator by order of the governor. Before 1654, he had returned to England, for a power of attorney is in print which authorizes John Winslow to dispose of Tracy's property in New England. This instrument bears the date, March 20, 1654-55, at New London. In it he calls himself an inhabitant of Great Yarmouth, in County Norfolk, and states that he has five children in New England. There is no further record of him, and it is probable that he never returned.

He married, 1621, in Holland, Triphosa La———. Children: Sarah, born in Holland, married George Partridge; John, mentioned below; Rebecca, born at Plymouth; Ruth, Mary, Thomas.

(XIV) John, son of Stephen Tracy, was born at Plymouth, 1623, and died at Windham, Connecticut, June 30, 1718. He married Mary Jane, daughter of Governor Prince and Mary Collins, his second wife. He was representative in 1683 and 1686, deputy in 1677 and 1692. Children: John; Alphea; Stephen, mentioned below.

(XV) Stephen, son of John Tracy, was born 1673, died December 14, 1769. He married, January 26, 1707, Deborah Bingham. Children: Mary, August 26, 1708; Prince, January 27, 1710-11; Deborah, January 8, 1714; John, April 25, 1718; James, January 15, 1720; Nathaniel, January 2, 1722; Thomas, mentioned below.

(XVI) Thomas, son of Stephen Tracy, was

born August 19, 1725, and died at Hartford, Vermont, February, 1822. He married, October 28, 1751, Elizabeth, daughter of Joseph and Elizabeth (Allen) Warner. Children: Mary, November 12, 1752; Andrew, August 1, 1754; Deborah, March 10, 1756; Susannah, July 7, 1758; James, January 28, 1760; Thomas, September 4, 1761; Joseph, mentioned below; Elizabeth, April 15, 1765.

(XVII) Joseph, son of Thomas Tracy, was born July 18, 1763, and died April 10, 1829. He married, December 26, 1792, Ruth Carter. Children: Joseph Chester, November 3, 1793; Ebenezer Carter, mentioned below; Myron, April 20, 1798; William Warner, December 12, 1801; Ira, January 15, 1806; Samuel, April 14, 1808; Stephen, February 25, 1810; Ezra Carter, January 5, 1812.

(XVIII) Ebenezer Carter, son of Joseph Tracy, was born January 10, 1796, died at Windsor, Vermont, May 15, 1862. He married, September 13, 1832, Martha Sherman Evarts (see Evarts VI). Children: Martha Day, October 1, 1833, died November 2, 1852; Jeremiah Evarts, mentioned below; Anna, October 23, 1836; William Carter, July 14, 1838, killed in the Civil War, January 23, 1864; Roger Sherman, August 10, 1840, died October 22, 1841; John Jay, December 23, 1843; Charles Walker, June 28, 1847.

(XIX) Jeremiah Evarts, son of Ebenezer Carter Tracy, was born January 31, 1835, at Windsor, Vermont. He attended the public schools of his native town and began to study law in the office of his uncle, Hon. William M. Evarts, of New York City. He attended Yale Law School and was graduated with the degree of Bachelor of Laws in 1857. He was admitted to the bar in New York and became a clerk in the office of Mr. Evarts. Since June 1, 1859, he has been partner in the firm and its successors. The present firm is Evarts, Choate & Sherman, one of the best-known law firms in the United States and second to none in the importance of its clientele and in the personnel of the partners comprising it. Mr. Tracy was one of the founders of the Bar Association of New York City and is a member of the New York State Bar Association and the New York Lawyers' Institute. In politics he is a Republican, and in religion a Presbyterian.

He married, September 30, 1863, Martha Sherman, daughter of Rev. David and Mary (Evarts) Greene. Their home is in New York City. Children: Emily Baldwin, born November 30, 1864; Howard Crosby, August 1, 1866, now of Plainfield, New Jersey; Evarts, mentioned below; Mary Evarts, December 22, 1869, now in Yokohama, Japan; Robert

Storer, October 6, 1871, deceased; Margaret Louisa, May 11, 1873, now of Muncie, Indiana; Edith Hastings, December 13, 1874, now of New York; Martha, April 10, 1876, of Philadelphia; William Evarts, September 24, 1878, of Telluride, Colorado.

(XX) Evarts, son of Jeremiah Evarts Tracy, was born in New York City, May 23, 1868. He attended the public schools and entered Yale University, from which he was graduated with the degree of Bachelor of Arts in the class of 1890. He went abroad and studied until 1894 at L'Ecole Nationale et Speciale des Beaux Arts in Paris. He traveled extensively in Europe and America, including the British possessions and South America and visited the important buildings and architectural masterpieces of the world. He is a partner of the firm of Tracy, Swartout & Litchfield, architects, of New York City. The firm has made a specialty of public buildings, clubs, banks, hotels and courthouses. Some of the notable buildings designed by this firm are the Yale Club, the Home Club and Hotel Webster, in New York City; the National Metropolitan Bank of Washington, D. C.; the Connecticut Savings Bank of New Haven, the Somerset county courthouse, New Jersey; the Minneapolis Club, Minneapolis, Minnesota; United States Post Office and courthouse, Denver, Colorado; armory, Washington, District of Columbia. In politics he is a Republican. He is a member of the Beaux Arts Society, the Architectural League of New York, the American Institute of Architects and the Metropolitan Club of Washington, the University Club of New York, the Yale Club of New York and the Plainfield Country Club.

He married at Plainfield, New Jersey, June 23, 1904, Caroline Frederica Streuli, daughter of A. F. Streuli, of Zurich, Switzerland. Her father came to America in 1866 and settled in Philadelphia, where he married Caroline Hooper, of an old American family. Mr. Streuli came from an old Swiss family, the ancient home of which was build in the year 800 and is still in the possession of the Streuli family. In olden times, the Catholic church paid an annuity to the family for sheltering pilgrims to the Convent of Einsedeln, and the annuity is still paid to the family by the papal government. One of the provisions of the contract stipulated that the family should entertain any religious pilgrims passing through the country. Mr. and Mrs. Tracy have no children.

(The Evarts Line).

John Evarts, the immigrant ancestor, was admitted a freeman at Concord, Massachusetts, in March, 1637-38. He lived there some years and then removed to Guilford, Connecticut. He took the freeman's oath there, February 5, 1651-52, and in 1655, appears as the defendant in two civil suits. He purchased John Mepham's allotment at Guilford, July 29, 1651, and in 1667, was appointed tythingman. He is said to have lived some time in New Haven. He died May 9, 1669. He married (first) Elizabeth ———, (second), May 27, 1663, Elizabeth Parmelee, who died in November, 1688, widow of John Parmelee. Children of first wife: 1. James, mentioned below. 2. John, born at Concord, February 29, 1639-40; died December 28, 1692. 3. Judah, born at Concord, October 27, 1642; died November, 1696. 4. Daniel, born 1645; died December 5, 1692. 5. Elizabeth, married, 1665, Peter Abbott; she was killed by her husband at Fairfield, and he was executed for the offense, October 16, 1667.

(II) James, son of John Evarts, was born in 1638, died in April, 1682. He married, in 1660, Lydia, daughter of Richard Cuttridge. Children: Mary, March 26, 1661, died young; John, 1664; Lydia, 166—; James, 1667, mentioned below; Joseph, 1669, died December 21, 1679; Jonathan, died unmarried, October, 1696; Judah, 1673; Mary, May 1, 1674; Hannah, September 23, 1677; Joseph, February 24, 1679-80; Dorothy.

(III) James (2), son of James (1) Evarts, was born in 1667, died January 3, 1739. He was a farmer and lived in East Guilford, Connecticut. He married, March 7, 1694, Mary Carter, who died March 30, 1751. Children: Mary, December 7, 1696; Jonathan, April 12, 1699; Mindwell, August 16, 1705, died December 31, 1736; James, April 21, 1713, died April 6, 1721; Elinor, December 9, 1714; Reuben (twin), March 25, 1719, mentioned below; Elizabeth (twin), March 25, 1719.

(IV) Reuben, son of James (2) Evarts, was born March 25, 1719, died July 31, 1776. He married, June 5, 1751, Honor, daughter of Jeremiah Evarts, son of John (III), son of James (II). Jeremiah was born May 21, 1702, died September 14, 1751, married, June 8, 1726, Jerusha Blinn. She married (second) Deacon Thomas Stone, of East Guilford. Children of Reuben and Honor Evarts: James, mentioned below; Elizabeth, December 15, 1755; Jeremiah, February 25, 1761; Reuben, January 7, 1763; John, December 16, 1765.

(V) James (3), son of Reuben Evarts, was born at East Guilford, May 15, 1752. He was a farmer and lived in Georgia, removing there in 1787 and also in Sunderland, Vermont. He married Sarah, daughter of Timothy Todd. Children: Jeremiah, mentioned below; another son and three daughters.

(VI) Jeremiah, son of James (3) Evarts, was born February 3, 1781. He became a lawyer in New York City and for many years was secretary of the American Board of Commissioners for Foreign Missions. He married Mehitable Barnes, daughter of Roger Sherman. Children: Hon. William Maxwell, the eminent lawyer; Martha Sherman, married, September 13, 1832, Ebenezer Carter Tracy (see Tracy XVIII).

INGRAHAM The English ancestry of the American Ingrahams has been traced with what appears to be good authority to very ancient times. Randolph, son of Ingel'ram or Ing'-ram, was sheriff of Nottingham and Derby in the reign of Henry II., A. D. 1133-89. He had two sons, Robert and William. Robert Ingram, knight, son of Randolph, was of so much importance in the reign of Henry III. that the Prior and Convent of Lenton granted to him a yearly rent out of their lands in Shaynton and Nottingham, in recognition of his military service in their defense. His arms are painted in Temple Newsham or Newsam, England, which is an immense estate, six miles long and four wide, about four and a half miles east of Leeds. It is now called the Ingram estate, and at first it was a settlement of Knights Templar in the twelfth and thirteenth centuries. After their dispersion it was granted by Edward II. to Sir John Darcy and descended to Sir Thomas Darcy, who was beheaded by Henry VIII., and the estate was forfeited to the Crown. In 1554 it was again granted by Edward II. to Mathew, Earl of Lennox, and here was born his son, Henry Darnley, who later married Mary, Queen of Scots. The estate descended to their son, James I. of England, and from him to his kinsman, Esme Stuart, Duke of Lennox, from whom it passed to Sir Arthur Ingram, the first of the Lords Viscount Irwin, one of the conditions being that the room in which Lord Darnley was born should remain unaltered, and this room is still called the "King's Chamber."

(I) Sir Arthur Ingram, who is supposed to have been born about 1570, was celebrated for his valor as a cavalier. He was a near relative of Wentworth, the celebrated Earl of Stafford. He married (first) Eleanor, daughter of Sir Henry Slingsby, and (second) Lady Katherine, daughter of Thomas, Lord Viscount Fairfax, of Gilling. Sir Arthur died in 1655. His portrait, in cavalier costume, that of the first Viscount Irwin in full armor, and that of Henry, the second Viscount Irwin in half armor, all nearly full length, were in the collection of the Bishop of California, William

Ingraham Kipp, D. D., LL. D., who died in 1894. His sons were Henry and Arthur Ingraham.

(II) Henry Ingraham or Ingram, son of Sir Arthur Ingram, was born between 1595 and 1600. At the time of the restoration, six years after the death of his father, Ingram was created a Peer of Scotland by Charles II. with the title of Viscount Irwin, by letters patent dated May 23, 1661, as a recompense to the family for their loyalty. He married Anne, daughter of Montacute, Earl of Manchester, a leader in Parliament. The male branch in England descended from Sir Henry, the second Viscount Irwin, and became extinct with Charles Ingram, ninth Viscount Irwin, who died in 1778. His daughter, the marchioness of Hartford, and Lady William Gordon, successively inherited Temple Newsam, and from them it passed to their sister, Mrs. Hugo Maynell, whose son took the name of Ingram, and his descendants are the present owners of the family estate.

(II) Arthur Ingraham, of Barrowby, son of Sir Arthur Ingram, and brother of Henry Ingraham or Ingram, was born between 1595 and 1600. He married a daughter of Sir John Mallory, about 1615, and the genealogists agree that from him the Ingraham family of America is descended.

(III) Richard Ingraham, son of Arthur Ingraham, came to America between 1638 and 1642. He settled in Rehoboth, Massachusetts, where he was a proprietor in 1645. Some years later he moved to Northampton, Massachusetts, where in 1668, late in life, he married (second) Joan (Rockwell) Baker, daughter of William Rockwell and widow of Jeffrey Baker, of Windsor, Connecticut. By this marriage he had no children. The name of his first wife is not known. He contributed a sum at the time of the general subscription for the support of Harvard College in 1672-73. He died in August, 1683, and his widow died September 16, 1683, both at Northampton. He may have been a brother of Edward, who came to America in 1635. Among his children were: William, of Boston; John, of Hadley; Jarrett, mentioned below.

(IV) Jarrett, son of Richard Ingraham, was born in 1640-42, probably in Boston. His name first appears in the records of the town of Boston for 1662, May 28, when he married (first) Rebecca, daughter of Edward Searles, Governor John Endicott performing the ceremony. Soon afterward he removed to Rehoboth. He was there certainly in 1665 when his second child was born and his name appears on the list of those who drew lots for meadow land in the North Purchase of Reho-

both, now the town of Attleboro, May 16, 1668. He removed with his family to Swansea, Massachusetts, about 1672, and was one of the early settlers of that town. He returned to Rehoboth, however, about 1690, and his wife Rebecca died there August 19, 1691. He married (second), April 22, 1692, Waitstill, widow of Joseph Sabin. He died at Rehoboth, January 11, 1717-18, and his widow November 15, 1718. Children of Jarrett and Rebecca Ingraham: Margaret, born in Boston, January 17, 1662-63. Born in Rehoboth: Rebecca, May 1, 1665; Mary, September 10, 1667; Ephraim, June 22, 1669; Mercy, July 13, 1671. Born in Swansea: Hannah, December 29, 1673; John, May 5, 1676; Joseph, January 14, 1677; Benjamin, mentioned below; Jeremiah, July 12, 1683; Nathaniel and Elizabeth, August 12, 1686. Child by second wife, at Rehoboth: Obadiah, September 21, 1696.

(V) Benjamin, son of Jarrett Ingraham, was born about 1679. His father's will dated April 16, 1714, proved February 3, 1717-18, mentions him after Joseph. Benjamin Ingraham married (first), at Rehoboth, March 20, 1712, Patience Ide, who died in November, 1716, leaving one child, Benjamin. He married (second), May 15, 1718, Elizabeth Sweet. He lived for some years in Rehoboth, presumably on property deeded to him by his father and mentioned in the will. He removed to Woodbury, Connecticut, where he died in 1741. Child by first wife: Benjamin, mentioned below. Children by second wife, born at Rehoboth: Henry, March 15, 1719-20; Juniah, January 21, 1721-22; Jeremiah, February, 1723-24; Job, March, 1726; Patience, May 21, 1728; Elizabeth, October 10, 1730; Betty, March 25, 1733.

(VI) Benjamin (2), son of Benjamin (1) Ingraham, was born at Rehoboth, August 25, 1714. He went to Woodbury, Connecticut, with others of the family. He married, in Woodbury, February 18, 1732, Hannah Tomlinson, and resided in Woodbury until 1745, when he removed to Chatham, Columbia county, New York. Children: Hannah, born February 6, 1743, married Joshua Barrett; Samuel, January 6, 1745; Abijah and Benjamin were Tories and removed to Nova Scotia during the revolution; John, mentioned below.

(VII) John, son of Benjamin (2) Ingraham, was born about 1735. He removed to Columbia county, New York, and according to the first federal census in 1790, was living at Canaan in that county and had in his family two females. In the same town the Gibbs family settled. He married Julia ——— (probably a Gibbs).

(VIII) Nathaniel Gibbs, son of John Ingraham, was born in 1761, died August 24, 1827, aged sixty-six. He married (first) Juliana, born August 18, 1766, died December 28, 1797, eldest daughter of Dr. Daniel Redfield, son of Daniel Redfield, of Guilford, Connecticut. He married (second) Elizabeth Phoenix, (see Phoenix IV). Children by first wife: Ezra L'Hommedieu; Nathaniel Gibbs, United States consul at Tampico; Martha (Patty), married Alexander Phoenix; Samuel Dana; John Redfield; David Gelston; Benjamin Gale; Fred Redfield. Children by second wife: Daniel Phoenix, mentioned below; Sidney; William; DeWitt, died young.

(IX) Daniel Phoenix, son of Nathaniel Gibbs Ingraham, was born in New York City, April 22, 1800. He married, in Guilford, Connecticut, January 25, 1838, Mary Hart Landon, of Guilford, Connecticut, born February 25, 1815. Children: Daniel Phoenix Jr., born February 17, 1839, died September, 1902, was an attorney in New York City, married Annie E. Lent, and had seven children: Nathaniel Gibbs, James Lent, Landon, Virginia, Daniel Phoenix, Anne Von Lent, Arthur; George Landon, mentioned below; Arthur, mentioned below.

(X) Judge George Landon Ingraham, son of Daniel Phoenix Ingraham, was born August 1, 1842. He attended the public schools and was graduated from Columbia College Law School with the degree of LL. B. in 1869. He was elected judge of the superior court of the city of New York in January, 1883. In May, 1891, he was appointed justice of the supreme court of the first New York district and elected the following November for the remainder of the term of his predecessor. In November, 1905, he was reëlected for a full term of fourteen years. In politics he is a Democrat. He is a member of the Century Club, the Manhattan Club, the Metropolitan Club, the New York Yacht Club, and the Tuxedo Club. He married, December 4, 1872, Georgina Lent. Children: Nathalie and Phoenix.

(X) Arthur, son of Daniel Phoenix Ingraham, was born in New York City, September 26, 1849. He attended the public schools of his native city and Dr. D. W. Dwight's private school and entered Columbia College in 1866, graduating in the class of 1870 with the degree of Bachelor of Arts. He entered the employ of Jay Cook, the famous banker, Wall street, New York City, and continued there for two years. Since then he has not been in active business, devoting his time to the management of his investments. He is a member of the St. Nicholas Society, New England Society of

New York City, University Club, Racquet Club, New York Yacht Club, Manhattan Club, Larchmont Yacht Club, Cuttyhunk Fishing Club, Whist Club, Wamsutta Club of New Bedford, Massachusetts, and Maryland Club of Baltimore, Maryland. In politics he is a Democrat. He is unmarried.

(The Phoenix Line).

(I) Alexander Phoenix, the immigrant ancestor, probably of Scotch ancestry, settled in New Amsterdam, now New York, in 1643. In 1652 he removed to Rhode Island, where he purchased large tracts of land in Narragansett. He was living near Wickford, Rhode Island, as late as July 29, 1679. The surname is believed to be originally Fenwick. The name of his first wife is unknown. He married (second) Abigail Sewall, probably daughter of Thomas Sewall, and born August 14, 1650. She was living May 23, 1717, when mention was made of her grandson, Charles Brown, son of her daughter Abigail. She had other daughters, whose names are not known. Children: Jacob, mentioned below; Alexander, married in New York, October 29, 1704, Hester Van Vorst.

(II) Jacob, son of Alexander Phoenix, was born in New Orange, now Albany, New York, and baptized in the Dutch church at New Amsterdam, October 8, 1651. He purchased, November 2, 1685, the bouwerie known as Klinkenbergh, behind the present city of Albany, and January 11, 1686, a house on the north side of Beaver street, between Broadway and New street, where he lived until his death. He was a member of the Dutch church of New York, June 2, 1686; freeman of New York, 1698; was living as late as June 24, 1727. He married, June 4, 1686, Anna (Van Vleeck) Beeck, in the Dutch church of New York. She was the widow of William Beeck and daughter of Tielman Van Vleeck, the first sheriff and president of the court at Bergen, New Jersey, by his wife Magdalena. Children: John, baptized at the Dutch church, New York, January 12, 1687; Alexander, baptized May 5, 1689, died young; Alexander, mentioned below; Jacob, baptized November 4, 1694, married Elizabeth Beek.

(III) Alexander (2), son of Jacob Phoenix, was baptized in New York, December 5, 1690. He was a freeman of New York City in 1732; member of the Blue Artillery Company in 1738. His will was proved September 20, 1770. He married (first) at New York, May 30, 1712, Margaret Comfort. He married (second) at New York, July 19, 1723, Elizabeth (Burger) Bockee or Bocquet, widow of Jacob Bockee or Bocquet, and daughter of

George and Elizabeth (Thomas) Burger. She was born July 31, 1692, married (first) June 8, 1717, and died February 28, 1757. Children by first wife: Jacob, baptized in the Dutch church, New York, April 29, 1713; Gerard, baptized August 3, 1715; Mary and Anna, twins, baptized April 14, 1717; Gerard, baptized January 3, 1720; Telamon, baptized January 7, 1722. Children by second wife: John, baptized April 12, 1724; Alexander, baptized December 11, 1726; Anna, baptized April 8, 1730; Catharine, baptized October 17, 1733; Daniel, baptized March 31, 1736, died young; Daniel, mentioned below.

(IV) Daniel, son of Alexander (2) Phoenix, was baptized at the Dutch church, New York, July 13, 1737. He was a trustee of the Wall Street Presbyterian Church from 1772 to 1812; member of the general committee of one hundred, May 5, 1775, and on the committee to receive General Washington at the end of the revolutionary war, 1783; New York city treasurer from 1784 to 1809; governor of New York hospital in 1787; secretary of the New York Insurance Company, 1795-99; trustee of the New York Society Library, 1795 to 1810; director of the Manhattan Company, 1803 to 1810. He died in New York City, May 16, 1812. He married (first) Hannah (license dated February 8, 1770), daughter of Timothy and Mary (Platt) Tredwell, of Smithtown, Long Island. He married (second) Elizabeth, daughter of Dr. Zophar and Rebecca (Wood) Platt, of Huntington, Long Island (license dated November 2, 1772). She died in 1784. Children, all by second wife: 1. Gerard, born July 10, 1774, at New York. 2. Elizabeth, born April 23, 1776, died December 1, 1844; married, December 1, 1798, Nathaniel Gibbs Ingraham (see Ingraham VIII). 3. Alexander, born February 28, 1778, near Madison, New Jersey; pastor of Congregational church at Chicopee, Massachusetts; married (first) Martha (Patty), daughter of Nathaniel Gibbs and Juliana (Redfield) Ingraham, born July 9, 1786, died January 31, 1810 (see Ingraham VIII). 4. Sidney, born October 7, 1779. 5. Rebecca, born January 17, 1781. 6. Jennet, born July 15, 1782. 7. Amelia, born March 30, 1784.

The Goodhue family is one
GOODHUE of English extraction and the earliest date to which it has been traced in England is 1280 A. D. In the eighth year of the reign of King Edward I., in various public records, are found the names of Wills Godhewen and Robs Godhewen (William and Robert Goodhue), both of the county of Kent. The name has been spelled

Godhewen, Goodhugh, Goodhug, Godhewyn, Godhew and Godhill. It is of Saxon origin, the first syllable "God" being Saxon for "good." It seems quite probable from all that can be learned regarding the ancestry of this family that William Goodhue, who came from England to America in 1635-36, and settled in Ipswich, Massachusetts, was a descendant of Wills Godhewen, of Kent, mentioned above. His name William, his origin from Kent, and the fact that in his day the name was frequently written Goodhew, are evidences of some weight. Robert and William Goodhew, of 1280, were agriculturists.

Concerning the coat-of-arms of the Goodhue family there is extant a record of arms granted to one branch of the family in 1738 and to another in 1790. Those granted in 1738, on petition of Mary Goodhugh, widow of Richard Goodhugh, of Under River, in the parish of Seale, in the county of Kent, are described as follows: "Gules, a chevron vaire between three talbots passant, argent; crest of adoption, a talbot as in the arms. Motto: *Nec invedis, nec despicio*. Of the arms granted in 1790 the following description is given: "Or on a chevron between three griffins' heads, erased gules, a swan's neck also erased, ducally gorged gold; on each side of the field a bee volant. Crest, a young shepherd leaning on the stump of a tree, playing a flute, his dog by his side. Motto: *Dieu avec nous* (God with us)."

(I) William Goodhue was born in England about 1612-13. He immigrated to America in 1635-36. Before leaving England he married Margery Watson, of Kent, who died at Ipswich, Massachusetts, August 28, 1668. She was the mother of all his children—two sons and one daughter. His second wife was the widow, Mary Webb, whom he married at Ipswich, February 7, 1669-70; she died September 7, 1680. July 26, 1682, William Goodhue married the widow, Bethiah Grafton, whose death occurred December 6, 1688. His fourth wife was Remember Fisk, of Wenham, Massachusetts, who survived her husband and died at Ipswich, February 16, 1701-02. They were married in 1689. Children by first wife: Joseph, mentioned below; William, born in 1645; Mary.

(II) Joseph, son of William and Margery (Watson) Goodhue, was born in 1639, at Ipswich, Massachusetts. He married (first) July 13, 1661, Sarah, daughter of John Whipple, one of the elders of the church. After his marriage Joseph inherited his father's farm and dwelling. He married (second) October 15, 1684, Rachel Todd, a widow, who died at Ipswich in 1691. He married (third) Mercy

Clarke, likewise a widow, July 4, 1692. He died at Ipswich, September 2, 1697, at the age of fifty-eight years. When death called him he was moderator, selectman, assessor, representative to the general court and a deacon of the First Church. His children by first marriage were: Joseph, born May 13, 1662, died young; Mary; Sarah; Margery; Susannah; Elizabeth; John, mentioned below; Hannah, born July 20, 1681; William. Children by second marriage: Ebenezer, born July 25, 1685; Joseph, 1687; Benjamin, January 25, 1690, died December 3, 1697. Child of third marriage: Samuel, born April 6, 1696.

(III) John, seventh child of Joseph and Sarah (Whipple) Goodhue, was born in 1679. He married, in 1711, Sarah Sherwin, of Ipswich. Children: Sarah, born in 1713; Hannah, September 4, 1715; John, July 13, 1718; Elizabeth, December 28, 1719; John, mentioned below.

(IV) John (2), youngest son of John (1) and Sarah (Sherwin) Goodhue, was born in January, 1721, and was well known as Lieutenant John Goodhue. He resided at Ipswich and died there January 15, 1815. He married, in 1743, Elizabeth Lampson, and had ten children: John, mentioned below; Elizabeth, born July 13, 1746; Sarah, March 6, 1747; Lucy, May 6, 1750; Ebenezer, 1754; Ephraim, January 16, 1757; Priscilla; Abner, January 18, 1762; Eunice, March 4, 1764; Daniel, August 27, 1769.

(V) John (3), son of John (2) and Elizabeth (Lampson) Goodhue, was born in Ipswich, Massachusetts, April 23, 1745, died May 4, 1817. He married (first) August 27, 1772, Mercy Lampson, who died October 16, 1777; (second) Mary Potter, who died October 5, 1821. Children by first marriage: John, born at Ipswich Hamlet, February 21, 1774; Eunice, February 12, 1776. Children by second marriage: Thomas, December 28, 1779; Isaac, mentioned below; Ephraim and Manasseh (twins), July 30, 1783; Polly, June 3, 1785.

(VI) Isaac, second son of John (3) and Mary (Porter) Goodhue, was born June 13, 1781. He married, September 16, 1802, Sarah Henfield, of Salem, Massachusetts. He married (second) in September, 1819, Mary Learock, of Salem, who died June 7, 1856. He was noted for his great philanthropy and public spirit. Children of first wife: Margaret; Benjamin S., born June 16, 1812; Sarah Tarrant, January 16, 1814; Mary Eliza, March 15, 1818. Children of second wife: Jane Catherine, August 9, 1822, died 1840; Lydia B., October 6, 1824; Jane Gage, January 14, 1826; Henry A. and Ellen A. (twins), February 1, 1828, Henry A. is mentioned below; Isaac W.,

November 3, 1831, died at sea; Samuel D., December 1, 1833, died January 10, 1880; Ardelia, born in Portland, Maine, October 31, 1835, died April 22, 1841.

(VII) Henry A., son of Isaac and Mary (Learock) Goodhue, was born February 1, 1828, died August 8, 1880. He was a furniture merchant at Meriden, Connecticut, during his active life, and he was a soldier in the Mexican war. He married Emma Burdette, born at Elmira, New York, July 27, 1837, daughter of Samuel Burdette. Children: Henry A. Jr., born December 25, 1860, died in 1865; Isaac Walter, mentioned below; Delia A., March 11, 1873.

(VIII) Isaac Walter, second son of Henry A. and Emma (Burdette) Goodhue, was born in Boston, Massachusetts, November 22, 1862. He received his preliminary educational training in the public schools of Meriden, Connecticut, and subsequently he was prepared at private schools for entrance to the Crozer Theological Seminary, at Chester, Pennsylvania. He was graduated from that institution in 1890, with the degree of Bachelor of Divinity. He was ordained to the Baptist ministry in 1890 and became pastor of the Baptist church at Bristol, Pennsylvania. While living in Meriden, Connecticut, he was secretary of the Young Men's Christian Association of that city. He was pastor of a large church in Philadelphia, Pennsylvania, in 1898, and for several years was pastor of Ascension Church in New York City, being vice-president of the Young People's Society of the latter church. He is a life member of the Foreign Missionary Society.

Notwithstanding the marked success of Mr. Goodhue in the ministry and as a pulpit orator, because of circumstances, he determined to leave the ministry and take up the study of law. Consequently he entered the law department of Columbia University, New York City, in 1898, and was graduated therefrom in 1900 with the degree of Bachelor of Laws. He was admitted to the bar in 1901 and at once began the practice of civil law in New York City, with offices at 43 Wall street. Then followed what is quite unusual, a man educated and trained in one profession and eminently successful in the same, changing to another and quite different calling and also meeting with unqualified success in it. This has been the case with Mr. Goodhue. He is president and a director of the Continental Talc Company and in connection with his law work is a member of the New York County Bar Association, the New York State Bar Association and the National Bar Association. He is also a member of the Alumni Association of Columbia University and belongs to the Republican Club of New York. He has completed the circle of York Rite Masonry, being affiliated with Kane Lodge, No. 454, Free and Accepted Masons; Royal Arch Masons, and Couer de Lion Commandery, Knights Templar. He is likewise a member of Ancient Arabic Order Nobles of the Mystic Shrine, and of the Independent Order of Odd Fellows.

Mr. Goodhue married and has one child, Walter Kendall, born at Waterbury, Connecticut, May 14, 1885.

DEARDEN   Simon Dearden, the ancestor of this family, lived and died in England. He married Harriett Sinneston, and they had a son, William, of whom further.

(II) William, son of Simon Dearden, was born in Manchester, England, August 25, 1817, died in July, 1894. He came to the United States and entered mercantile life at Springfield, Massachusetts, after a similar career at Lowell, Northampton, England. He was a man of great business ability, and was also possessed of a brilliant mind and considerable literary talent. He married Sarah Faraday, born in Shropshire, England, in 1818, died in 1856. They had a son, Robert Rowland, of whom further.

(III) Robert Rowland, son of William Dearden, was born in Lowell, Massachusetts, March 23, 1845. He attended the public schools of his native city, followed by a course in the English and Classical Institute at Springfield, Massachusetts. After the completion of his education, he immediately became associated with his father in business at Springfield, continuing thus for a few years, but being of a literary turn of mind mercantile pursuits were extremely distasteful to him, and in 1867 or 1868 he went west and entered the publishing business in Chicago. He associated himself with the Blanchard Publishing Company, who issued maps and lithographs, and subsequently bought out the concern. He also associated himself with William F. Brewster, of the same firm, in the publication of the *Northwestern Review;* in 1869 he bought out the interests of Mr. Brewster, changing the name to the *United States Review,* and removing the enterprise to Philadelphia, Pennsylvania, in 1875. Mr. Dearden has maintained his active connection with this paper which has become the well known insurance organ of the United States, with a circulation in every state in the Union, and has been largely responsible for the immense growth of the insurance business in America, carrying information into countless homes in regard to methods employed and benefits to be derived. As an insurance journalist, Mr. Dearden has shown himself to be in the leading ranks of the profession. He is president of the corporation which manages the *Review,* of which he is the editor, and his son, Robert Rowland Dearden Jr. is secretary and manager of the business.

Soon after his removal to Philadelphia, Mr. Dearden entered political life, and was first elected to represent Philadelphia in the Pennsylvania legislature in 1882, and was reëlected in 1884-86-88-90, serving continuously for eight years as a representative of the city; for four years he was chairman of the important committee of appropriations. He was also chairman of the house insurance committee in 1885, and in 1890 was unanimously chosen as a candidate for receiver of taxes of Philadelphia, on the Municipal League ticket, but he declined the nomination. He was again elected to the house of representatives in 1906, representing the twenty-second and forty-second wards of Philadelphia, the Germantown district, and has been reëlected in the same capacity in 1907-09-11, serving until the present time, being a strong member of the Republican party.

He has been a well known speaker on the stump for many years, and has made for himself a name as a writer on semi-literary subjects. During his early life, while out in the west at Omaha, then considered one of the frontier posts of civilization, he was a contributor to the *Springfield Republican,* depicting western life as he saw it. Mr. Dearden is a member of the Presbyterian church, and was for a time one of its trustees; he is a member of the American Academy of Political and Social Science, and of the Columbia Club, of which he was president for four years. He resides with his family at Oak Lane, corner of Sixty-ninth avenue and North Eleventh street, Philadelphia.

Mr. Dearden married, November 5, 1867, Ella Sherwin, daughter of Horace and Lydia (Sherwin) Chapin, the latter having been born in Vermont, July 19, 1845. Mr. and Mrs. Dearden have three children: 1. Grace Ella, born in Chicago, April 10, 1869; married William Elton; children: William Dearden, Rowland Faraday and Roberta Chapin Elton. Mrs. Elton died March 15, 1907. 2. Robert Rowland Jr., born in Chicago, January 3, 1871; he is secretary and manager of the corporation which publishes the *United States Review,* of which his father is president, as previously stated. He married Lotta Sutliffe; children: Robert Rowland 3rd, John Edward and Catherine. 3. Edward Chapin, born in Evanston,

Illinois; married Elizabeth Blaborn, daughter of the well known oil cloth manufacturer. They have one child, Edward Chapin Jr.

BULL On both the paternal and the maternal sides, the Bull family of New York traces its origin to several of the oldest and most distinguished New England families of the colonial and revolutionary periods, the Bulls, the Lanmans, the Trumbulls, the Boylstons, the Coits and others.

(I) Henry Bull, a native of South Wales, was born in 1610, died in 1693. He came to America in 1635 and was the progenitor of all the Bull families of New England. After a short residence in the Massachusetts Bay Colony he went to Rhode Island, being one of the followers of Roger Williams. With seventeen associates he purchased land in 1638 and joined in the settlement of Newport, being at once one of the leading men of the new colony. He was chosen sergeant of the town, with the care of the prison included in the duties of his office; while in 1689, when he was nearly eighty years of age, he accepted election as governor, when the duty of restoring the charter privileges of the colony after the fall of Andros made the office one of arduous labor and heavy responsibilities, so much so, in fact, that two others declined to serve in that capacity. He was admitted a freeman in Massachusetts, May 17, 1637. He was one of the fifty-eight followers of Wheelwright and Mrs. Hutchinson, disarmed by order of the general court. Henry Bull was one of the founders of Portsmouth, Rhode Island, having been associated in that enterprise with men from Boston and vicinity; this was in 1638. In the following year he became one of the founders of Newport. He was elected corporal of the train band, June 27, 1638; chosen sergeant, November 24, 1638, and in 1641-42 he was designated as sergeant assistant. In 1655-57 he was one of the six commissioners from Newport to the general court of election at Providence, and from 1666 to 1681 represented Newport in the general assembly. In 1674-76 he was assistant, and in 1685-86 and 1689-90 governor of Rhode Island.

Henry Bull, according to the Friends' Records "aged about eighty-four years, departed this life at his own home in Newport, he being the last man of the first settlers of this Rhode Island, 22nd. 11mo. 1693-4." He was buried in the Coddington ground, the old "Quaker Cemetery on Farewell Street" in Newport. The records of deeds indicate that he owned considerable property. The house

1—10

that he built on the easterly side of Spring street is still standing and is in the possession of his descendants, it being the only one remaining of those built by the original settlers. On July 18, 1906, the Rhode Island Historical Society unveiled a tablet, attached to the house and inscribed: "The Gov. Bull house, the oldest house in Rhode Island. Built in part in 1639 by Henry Bull, Governor under the Royal Charter of the Colony of Rhode Island and Providence Plantations, in the years 1685-6 and 1690."

He married (first) Elizabeth ———, who died October 1, 1665, and was buried at Newport. He married (second) at Sandwich, Massachusetts, Esther Allen, born December 18, 1648, died February 26, 1676, daughter of Ralph and Esther (Swift) Allen. He married (third) March 28, 1677, Ann Clayton, widow of Governor Nicholas Easton. She died January 30, 1707, and was buried in the Coddington cemetery at Newport. Children: Jireh, mentioned below; Elizabeth, married ——— Allen; Amey, married Edward Richmond.

(II) Jireh, son of Henry Bull, was born at Portsmouth, September, 1638, died in 1684 in Kingstown, probably. He was one of a company who purchased land in the Narragansett Country, June 29, 1660, and he signed articles relating to the Westerly lands, March 22, 1661. He bought five hundred acres at Pettequamscott and thereafter seems to have resided on the west side of the bay except during King Philip's war. He and two others were appointed on a commission to the Indians, August 19, 1669. By appointment of the governor he was a conservator of the peace in 1669-70, 1678 and 1683. He was assessor or rate-maker for Pettequamscott in 1670; was appointed lieutenant and took the oath of fidelity, May 19, 1671; was appointed one of the commissioners to adjust the Connecticut boundary line, May 14, 1672. Roger Williams in a letter dated June 27, 1675, to John Winthrop, written from Richard Smith's at Narragansett, says: "Just now comes in Sam Dier in a catch (ketch) from Newport, to fetch over Jireh Bull's wife and children and others of Pettequamscott." This was on account of King Philip's war and in December following Bull's garrison house was burned, ten Englishmen and five women and children were killed, but two escaping. After the war Jireh Bull returned to his home and five hundred acres of land were laid out to him December 5, 1679. During the war he was probably at Newport, for he was on a commission appointed April 4, 1676, to make a census of the island, and August 24, 1676, he served on a court-martial to try Indians. In 1683 services of the Church of England were read at his house. He died in 1684.

The name of his wife is unknown. It is thought that she was Katherine ———, on whose estate administration was granted August 16, 1713. Children: Henry, of Kingstown, born 1658, died 1691; Jireh, mentioned below; Mary, 1663, died June 13, 1754, married John Coggeshall; Ephraim, of Kingstown, born 1669, died 1721; Ezekiel, of Kingstown, born 1671, died September 7, 1727.

(III) Jireh (2), son of Jireh (1) Bull, was born in 1659, died July 16, 1709. He married (first) Godsgift, born August 27, 1658, died April 23, 1691, eighth child of Governor and Damaris (Westcott) Arnold. He married (second) Sarah ———. Children, born at Westerly, by his first wife: Jireh, 1682, died 1709; Benjamin, married, December, 1710, Content James; Benedict, mentioned below.

(IV) Benedict, son of Jireh (2) Bull, was born in 1687 in Rhode Island. He settled in Milford, Connecticut, about 1711. He married Sibella Bryan. Children, born at Milford: Benedict, 1717, killed in childhood by a fall; Sibella, February 14, 1719-20; Jireh, mentioned below; Benjamin, October 10, 1721, twin of Jireh, married (first) December 22, 1748, Esther, daughter of Solomon Baldwin, (second) April 11, 1754, Anna Platt; they lived at Milford; Godsgift, February 24, 1724; Content, about 1725, married a Mr. Bryan, of Milford.

(V) Jireh (3), son of Benedict Bull, was born at Milford, Connecticut, October 10, 1721. He married Sibella, daughter of Jeremiah Peck. Children, born at Milford: Sibella, married Daniel Buckingham; Jabez, mentioned below; Jerusha, married David Noble; Content, married David Baldwin; Henry, born 1754; Jeremiah, born March 10, 1757.

(VI) Jabez, son of Jireh (3) Bull, was born at Milford, Connecticut, January 19, 1747. In 1790 Jeremiah Bull was head of a family at Milford, according to the first Federal census. Anna Bull (doubtless widow of Benjamin) was living with one male over sixteen and two females in her family, in 1790. Benjamin and Temperance Bull were also heads of families in Milford. Hinman calls Jabez "Benedict Jabez," as if he had assumed the name. Jabez Bull married Naomi Bridge. Children, born at Milford: James, married a Miss Bryan; Lucy, married William Atwater; Jireh, mentioned below.

(VII) Jireh (4), son of Jabez Bull, was born in Milford about 1770-80. He married Elizabeth Atwater, probably a sister or near relative of William Atwater, who married Lucy Bull. One child, Frederic, mentioned below.

(VIII) Frederic, son of Jireh (4) Bull, was born in Milford, Connecticut, July 17, 1800, died in 1871. He was a prominent business man in New York City for more than a third of a century preceding his death at his country seat in Montclair, New Jersey, in 1871. He was head of the New York family bearing the name. He married Mary Huntington Lanman, born May 28, 1804, at Norwich, Connecticut, and died in 1880 (see Lanman). The ceremony was performed in 1829. Children: Sara, Elizabeth, Mary H., Caroline W., Abigail T., Frederic, William Lanman, mentioned below; Anna C.

(IX) William Lanman, seventh child and youngest son of Frederic and Mary Huntington (Lanman) Bull, was born in New York City, August 23, 1844. After a good preparatory education he completed his studies in the College of the City of New York, from which he was graduated in 1864. He then began his business career by entering the banking house of Edward Sweet & Company, the senior partner of this firm being a brother-in-law of Mr. Bull. In 1867 he became a partner in the firm, a relation that he has maintained uninterruptedly down to the present time, a period of forty-five years. Outside of his banking business Mr. Bull has been otherwise prominent in business and in social life. Twice he has been president of the New York Stock Exchange and his important railroad connections have included membership in the directorates of the Northern Pacific, the East Tennessee, Virginia & Georgia, the New York, Susquehanna & Western, and the Atchison, Topeka & Santa Fe railroads. He is a valued and appreciative member of the following prominent organizations: The Chamber of Commerce, Society of Mayflower Descendants, Museum of Natural History, Metropolitan Museum of Art, Historical Society, Sons of the American Revolution, New York Zoological Society and others, and is affiliated with the following clubs: Century Association, Grolier, Union, Metropolitan, Republican, Ardsley, Church, City Midday, Alpha Delta Phi, Manhattan Society, and the Phi Beta Kappa honorary fraternity. The Bull home is at 805 Fifth avenue, New York.

William Lanman Bull married, February 15, 1871, Sarah Newton, born March 28, 1851, daughter of Henry Rossiter and Sarah (Newton) Worthington, and granddaughter of Admiral Newton, of the United States navy. The father of Mrs. Bull was one of the most successful inventors and manufacturers of his generation. He invented the steam pump and was the pioneer in the manufacture of pumping machinery. He was born in New York in 1817, and died in New York, in 1880. His father was Asa Worthington, a prominent merchant of New York, who was for many years in the South American trade and was United States consul at Lima, Peru. The American founder of the Worthington family came over in 1649. He was descended from Sir Nicholas Worthington, of Worthington, England, who fell at Naseby, defending the cause of King Charles. The mother of Mrs. Bull was a daughter of Commodore John T. Newton, United States navy; Commodore Newton had a long and notable career. Born in Alexandria, Virginia, in May, 1793, he died in Washington, D. C., in July, 1857. He was appointed midshipman in 1809, lieutenant in 1813, commander in 1827, captain in 1837, and commodore in 1857. He saw service on the "Hornet" in the war of 1812, commanded the steamships "Fulton" and "Missouri," had charge of the Pensacola, Florida, and the Portsmouth, New Hampshire, navy-yards, and was flag officer of the home squadron in 1848-52. Children born to Mr. and Mrs. Bull: 1. Frederic, mentioned below. 2. Henry Worthington, born March 27, 1874, at Montclair, New Jersey; married Maude Livingston, in March, 1906. 3. William Lanman Jr., born July 16, 1880; married Matilda E. Heppenheimer, in 1904; they have one child, Elizabeth W., born November 25, 1904.

(X) Frederic (2), son of William Lanman Bull, was born at Montclair, New Jersey, December 11, 1871. He attended the Cutler School in New York City and the Stevens' Technological School, in which he took the mechanical engineering course. For five years he practiced his profession in New York City, in the employ of the Henry R. Worthington Company. He became a clerk in the banking house of Edward Sweet & Company, 34 Pine street, New York City, in 1898, and in the following year was admitted to partnership in the firm, continuing in that capacity to the present time (1912). Mr. Bull is a member of the Union, Racquet, City Midday, Westminister Kennel and Knickerbocker clubs; the Brook Club of New York; New England Society of New York; Metropolitan Club of Washington, D. C. In politics he is a stalwart Republican, and in his religious faith is a communicant of Grace Protestant Episcopal Church of New York.

He married, October 2, 1895, Helen, born in Brooklyn, New York, October 15, 1871, daughter of Jeremiah Potter and Margaret Downing (Lanman) Robinson. Children: Frederica, born June 30, 1896; Helen, November 6, 1900.

(The Lanman Line).

The Lanman family, to which Mrs. Frederic Bull belonged, was of English origin. Its founder in this country was James Lanman, of London, 1692-1775, who came to America about 1700 and settled in Boston. In 1714 he married Joanna, daughter of Dr. Thomas and Lucy (Gardner) Boylston, of Roxbury, Massachusetts. He removed to Plymouth, Massachusetts, in 1724, and there his son, Peter Lanman, 1725-1804, was born. Peter Lanman married, in 1764, Sarah Spalding Coit, daughter of Colonel Samuel Coit, of Preston, Connecticut. During most of his life Peter Lanman was a prominent shipping merchant at Norwich, Connecticut, where he died. The Coit family was derived from the oldest settlers in Connecticut. Colonel Samuel Coit, the great-grandfather of Mrs. Frederic Bull, was a resident of Plainfield and Preston (now Griswold), Connecticut. He was born in Plainfield, in 1708, and his wife, whom he married, in 1730, was Sarah Spalding, daughter of Benjamin Spalding, of Plainfield. He was several times a member of the general assembly of the state and a judge of the county court. His daughter Sarah was born in 1743. The parents of Colonel Coit were the Rev. Joseph and Experience (Wheeler) Coit, of New London, Connecticut. The Rev. Joseph Coit, born in 1673, was the son of Joseph Coit, of New London, who died in 1704, and his wife, Martha Harris, daughter of William and Edith Harris, of Wethersfield, Connecticut; he was a grandson of the founder of the family in America, namely, John Coit, who came hither from Wales, in 1630, and settled in Salem, Massachusetts, afterward removing to New London. The wife of John Coit was Mary Gennes. He died in 1659 and his wife died in 1676.

Peter Lanman, of Norwich, Connecticut, 1771-1854, was a son of Peter and Sarah Spalding (Coit) Lanman. His wife was Abigail Trumbull, 1781-1861, daughter of David Trumbull, whose father was Jonathan Trumbull, governor of Connecticut from 1769 until 1783, and through the whole period of the American revolution a trusted supporter and confidential adviser of General Washington. The wife of Governor Trumbull was Faith Robinson, a direct descendant of John Alden and Priscilla Mullins. Mary Huntington Lanman, who married Frederic Bull (see Bull VIII), was the daughter of Peter and Abigail (Trumbull) Lanman.

EATON Francis Eaton, the immigrant ancestor of this family, came from England to Plymouth, Massachusetts, in 1620, in the "Mayflower," and signed the famous compact on board that historic vessel. He was a carpenter by trade. He was admitted a freeman in 1633, and March 25, 1633, was rated at nine shillings. His wife Sarah, son Samuel, and infant, came with him. His wife died before 1627; Bradford says she died "in the generall sicknes which was in the winter of 1620-21." He married a second wife, who died soon, and he married (third) Christian Penn, who came over in the "Ann," in 1623. He removed from Plymouth to Duxbury, where he died in the latter part of 1633. Administration on his estate was granted to Thomas Prence and John Doane, November 25, same year. In July, 1634, his widow married Francis Billington, by whom she had eight children. Children of Francis Eaton, by first wife: Samuel, born in England or Holland, 1620. By second wife: Rachel, born in Plymouth, 1624-25, married, March 2, 1645, Joseph Ramsden. By third wife: Benjamin, of whom further. There were two other children, one an "ideote," and another who probably died without issue.

(II) Benjamin, son of Francis Eaton, was born in Duxbury, Massachusetts, about 1627. He was apprenticed or bound out February 11, 1635, for fourteen years, including two years at school, to Bridget Fuller, widow. In 1648 he was of Duxbury, and in 1650 of Plymouth, and was admitted to the first church there, March 19, 1693. He married, December 4, 1660, Sarah, daughter of William Hoskins; he was a grantee of Middleboro, but never lived there. Children: William, born about 1662, will proved March 18, 1690-91; Benjamin, of whom further; Ebenezer, born about 1667; Rebecca, married Josiah Richard.

(III) Benjamin (2), son of Benjamin (1) Eaton, was born at Plymouth, in 1664. His trade was that of "housewright" at Kingston, then a part of Plymouth. His will was dated April 3, 1745, and proved December 20 same year. He married (first) December 18, 1689, Mary Coombs, who had twelve children by him. He married (second) Susanna ——, who died April 13, 1739, aged seventy years. Children, born at Kingston: William, June 1, 1691; Hannah, February 16, 1692; Jabez, February 8, 1693, died young; Daniel, 1694; Sarah, October 20, 1695; John, October 6, 1697; Benjamin, 1698; Francis, of whom further; Elisha, about 1702; Mary, married Zachariah Souls; Elizabeth, married Cornelius Sturtevant; David, born about 1709.

(IV) Francis (2), son of Benjamin (2) Eaton, was born about 1700, at Kingston, and lived at Middleboro, where he died before 1748. He joined the church there, September 30, 1733. He married (first) Thankful Alden, and (second) in 1727, Lydia, daughter of John Fuller. Among their children was John, of whom further.

(V) John, son of Francis (2) Eaton, was born about 1730. He lived for a time at Pelham, Massachusetts. He married Patience Shelley. Among their children were Dr. Eliphaz and Jairus, both further mentioned below.

(VI) Dr. Eliphaz Eaton, son of John Eaton, was born at Pelham, March 3, 1773. He married, in 1797, Polly Barnes, a native of Greenwich, Massachusetts. They resided a few years at Hartford, Vermont, and then moved to Barnard, where he studied medicine. Dr. Eaton practiced at Eden for a time, and in 1805 located at Enosburg, where he practiced about sixty-five years, the first physician of the town, and for many years the only one. Children: Amanda, died at Enosburg, April 19, 1823, aged twenty-four years; Sophia, died June 3, 1821, aged twelve years; Oren, died August 23, 1803, aged sixteen months; Horace, of whom further; Maro, lived in Magnolia, Iowa; Aley, died September 4, 1855, aged forty-seven years; Rollin, died in Philadelphia, October 13, 1858; Sophia, wife of D. C. Harwood; Anne, wife of Henry Dixon, of Bennington. Dr. Eaton died November 22, 1846, and his wife January 29, 1865, aged eighty-seven years.

(VII) Dr. Horace Eaton, son of Dr. Eliphaz Eaton, was born at Barnard, Vermont, June 22, 1804. He was educated in the public schools and at St. Albans Academy; taught school for a time, and entered Middlebury College. He studied medicine in his father's office, and graduated from the Medical College at Castleton, Vermont. He practiced with his father at Enosburg, and afterward with his brother, Dr. Rollin Eaton. He was town clerk several years, representative in the state legisláture six years, state senator six years, lieutenant-governor five years, governor two years, state superintendent of schools five years, and a member of the constitutional council. He was six years a professor in Middlebury College. He married (first) August 14, 1831, Cordelia H. L. Fuller; (second) Edna Palmer. From his epitaph we quote: "Enlightened, learned and conscientious, he discharged the duties of every station with eminent ability and uprightness. This monument is erected by his friends in token of his great merit as a public man and a citizen."

(VI) Jairus, son of John Eaton, settled early in the nineteenth century in Enosburg, Vermont. He married Lucy Bennett, and they joined the Methodist class there in 1813. Among their children were two sons who entered the ministry of the Methodist Episcopal church: Jairus and Bennett, both further mentioned below.

(VII) Rev. Bennett Eaton, son of Jairus (1) Eaton, was born at Enosburg, Vermont, December 31, 1806, died at Crescent, New York, March, 1872. He was educated in the public schools, and received the degree of Master of Arts from Middlebury College. He was repeatedly a member of the Vermont legislature, representing his native town. He united with the Methodist Episcopal church of Enosburg in November, 1827, and was soon after chosen class leader. He gave up that office to go out as a traveling preacher in his denomination. He was for a time pastor of the Enosburg church, and wrote a historical sketch of the church in that town for "The Vermont Historical Magazine," and in 1866 published "An Essay on Death, its Author and Cause." He married, about 1829, Betsey Maria, born January 21, 1809, daughter of Joel and Hannah (Billings) Webster. Children: Rev. Joel Webster Eaton, D. D., born September 21, 1831; Rev. Homer Eaton, D. D., LL. D., of whom further; Lucy Maria Eaton, born December 5, 1836.

(VIII) Rev. Homer Eaton, D. D., LL. D., son of Rev. Bennett Eaton, was born at Enosburg, Vermont, November 16, 1834. He attended the public schools of his native town, the Bakersfield (Vermont) Academy, and the Methodist Theological Seminary at Concord, New Hampshire, from which he was graduated in 1857. In the same year he was admitted to the Troy annual conference of the Methodist Episcopal church, and his first pastorate was in the city of Troy, New York. In 1861 he was chosen first assistant secretary of the conference, and was secretary from 1870 to 1877. In 1872 he was a delegate to the general conference of the Methodist Episcopal church, held at Brooklyn, New York, and by that body was appointed one of the fraternal delegates to the general conference of the Methodist church in Canada. He was reserve delegate to the general conference in 1876, and delegate to each of the general conferences in 1880-84-88-92-96-1900-04-08-12. In 1881 he was a delegate to the Methodist ecumenical conference held in London, England, and again in 1901. He was elected agent of the Methodist Book Concern in 1889, and since then has had charge of that immense publishing business, with headquarters in New York City, the annual sales of

which amount to more than a million dollars annually. Since 1896 he has been treasurer of the board of foreign missions of the M. E. church and has traveled in Europe and Asia in the interests of that board. During his ministerial life he was successively pastor of many of the principal churches in his conference, and has for a long time ranked among the foremost clergymen of his denomination in the country. In 1878 he received the degree of Doctor of Divinity from Syracuse University, and later was honored with the degree of Doctor of Laws by the same institution. Dr. Eaton's office is at 150 Fifth avenue, New York City.

Dr. Eaton married, April 28, 1858, Hannah, born March 19, 1834, daughter of Jacob and Rowena (Keith) Saxe, of Sheldon, Vermont, granddaughter of John Saxe, of German ancestry (see Saxe III).

(VII) Rev. Jairus (2) Eaton, son of Jairus (1) Eaton, was born at Enosburg, Vermont, December 8, 1808, and died at Warren, Vermont, December 25, 1861. He was a preacher of the Methodist Episcopal church at Enosburg, and in various other parishes in Vermont, and for several years represented Warren in the legislature. He married, July 4, 1832, Hannah Giddings, of Bakersfield.

(The Saxe Line).

(Compiled by John W. Saxe, Esq., Boston).

(I) John Saxe, immigrant ancestor, was born in Langensalza, near Saxe-Gotha, Germany, in 1732. He came to Philadelphia about 1750. He married, November 18, 1771, Catherine Wever, born in 1744, at Rhinebeck, New York. After the revolution he joined a company of many German loyalists from Dutchess county, New York, who were on their way to Messisquot Bay, now Phillipsburg, Canada, finally settling at Saxes Mills in Vermont. Here the pioneer, as a farmer and miller, lived and had a family of eight sons who accompanied his wife and himself on their journey up the Hudson river and thence through Lake Champlain, and one daughter, Anna, who was born after the migration.

(II) Jacob, seventh son of John Saxe, settled at Plattsburg, New York, where he was at one time engaged as an iron founder at the mouth of the Salmon river, and after years of great activity and financial reverses, he returned to Vermont, spending his declining years on a farm at Sheldon, Vermont. He married Rowena Keith, whose father was born August 2, 1783, at Rhinebeck, New York, died November 12, 1866, at Sheldon, Vermont; he married, December 23, 1812, Rowena, eldest daughter of Alfred Keith, born March 31,

1794, at Pittsford, Vermont, and died March 25, 1873, at Sheldon, Vermont.

(III) Hannah, eleventh child and fourth daughter of Jacob Saxe, was born March 19, 1834, at Sheldon, Vermont. She married, April 28, 1858, Rev. Homer Eaton, born November 16, 1834, at Enosburg, Vermont (see Eaton VIII). Mrs. Hannah (Saxe) Eaton was a first cousin of John Godfrey Saxe, who for many years was so popular as a poet and lecturer in Lyceum courses, and who died at Albany in March, 1887. She had eight brothers: Alfred, George, and Godfrey, who were in the Methodist ministry; Edward, a pioneer, settled at Saxeville, Wisconsin, was killed in the civil war; Robert J., was a merchant at Sheldon and Omaha, Nebraska, and at one time was consul of the United States at St. Johns, Province of Quebec, Canada; Arthur W., a prominent physician and state senator at Santa Clara, California; Jacob W., a merchant at Boston; Herman A., for many years a teacher at San Jose, California. Her sister, Rowena K., is now widow of Emerson W. Keyes, formerly superintendent of schools in Brooklyn. Her brother, Herman A., and Mrs. Eaton are the only survivors of a family of thirteen children.

CHAUNCEY   The surname Chauncy is of Norman origin, derived from Canchy, a place in Normandy. The ancestry of President Chauncy, of Harvard, is traced to the time of the Norman Conquest in several lines and to Charlemagne in one pedigree. The paternal ancestry is given by Sir Henry Chauncy in the History of Hertfordshire. The Chauncys occupied estates in Yorkshire as hereditary barons of Skirpenbeck from 1066 to 1399, removing then to Gedleston or Newplace in Hertfordshire.

(I) Chauncy de Chauncy came to England from Normandy in 1066 with the Conqueror.

(II) William de Chauncy, his son, was Baron of Skirpenbeck.

(III) Walter de Chauncy, his son, was also Baron.

(IV) Anfride de Chauncy, had sons Walter and Roger.

(V) Roger de Chauncy, his son, had sons Robert and Hugh.

(VI) Robert de Chauncy, his son, was Baron in the twenty-third year of Henry III.

(VII) Thomas de Chauncy, his son, married Isabel de Chauncy, of another branch of the family, daughter of Sir Philip.

(VIII) William de Chauncy, his son, was Baron of Skirpenbeck, in the second year of Edward II.

(IX) Thomas de Chauncy, his son, was Baron in the seventeenth year of Edward III.

(X) William de Chauncy, his son, married Joan, daughter of Sir Roger Bigod, son of Roger, son of Sir John. Through intermarriages with the royalty, the ancestry is traced to Charlemagne and Alfred the Great.

(XI) John de Chauncy, son of Sir William, married Margaret Gifford, whose ancestry is traced to the Earls of Northumberland and the early Saxon kings.

(XII) John Chauncy, his son, married Ann Leventhorp, died May 7, 1479, and was buried in the church at Sawbridgeworth.

(XIII) John Chauncy, his son, married a daughter of Thomas Boyce.

(XIV) John Chauncy, his son, married Elizabeth Mansfield, widow, and died June 4, 1546.

(XV) Henry Chauncy, his son, possessed great wealth in land; built a house called New Place on his manor of Gifford's of Gelston; he died April 24, 1587.

(XVI) George Chauncy, his son, was father of President Chauncy. He married (first) Jane, daughter of John Cornwall, of Yardley. He married (second) Agnes, daughter of Edward Welsh, of Great Wymondley, and widow of Edward Humberston, by whom he had George, Edward and President Charles. He had children also by his first wife. He had estates at Yardley, New Place, Giffords, Netherhall and others. His home was at Yardley Bury, Hertfordshire, where he died in 1625.

(XVII) Charles Chauncy, the second president of Harvard College, was the immigrant ancestor of the Chauncey (Chauncy) family in the United States. He was the fifth son of George Chauncy, of New Place and Yardley Bury in Hertfordshire, England. Charles Chauncy was baptized November 5, 1592, thirty-fourth year of Elizabeth, in Yardley Bury Church, Hertfordshire. He received his preparation for entrance into the University in the famous Westminster School, where on November 5, 1605, he with the other members of the school came near falling victims to the famous "Gunpowder Plot" of Guy Fawkes, because of the nearness of the school to the parliament house. He entered the University as a student of Trinity College, Cambridge, where he received the degree of B. A. in 1613, and that of M. A. in 1617. He became a fellow of the College and was honored in 1624 with the degree of Bachelor of Divinity. Because of his deep knowledge of Oriental literature, he was chosen by the heads of the houses as Professor of Hebrew, but since Dr. William, the vice-chancellor, preferred a relative of his own, Mr. Chauncy withdrew his pretensions, and was appointed Professor of Greek. While he was living at Cambridge he composed several Latin and Greek poems which are still in existence, and he had a high reputation at Cambridge for his learning. In 1627 he became vicar of Ware, Hertfordshire, probably obtaining the place through the master and fellows of Trinity College, who were patrons of the vicarage. He soon became involved in the church difficulties of the times, and in January, 1629, was questioned in the high commission court for having preached against the church; the case was referred to Bishop Laud, on condition that Mr. Chauncy submit to what the bishop decided. In 1635 he was again prosecuted in the high commission for opposing the railing in of the communion table at Ware, and he was suspended, cast into prison, condemned to costs and obliged to make a humiliating recantation; he never was able during the remainder of his life to forgive himself for conforming to their orders. He seems to have preached for a short time at Marston-Lawrence before he went to Ware.

He sailed from England late in 1637, arriving at Plymouth, Massachusetts, a few days before the great earthquake, which occurred June 1, 1638. Here he preached with the Rev. Mr. Reynor for about three years, and but for his views on the baptism of infants would have been called to settle as a minister in Plymouth. In 1641 he was elected pastor of the church at Scituate, Massachusetts, succeeding Rev. John Lathrop, who had moved to Barnstable. In addition to his duties as minister, he practiced as a physician, and Mather says that he was well fitted for that work. He also prepared young men for college, among them the celebrated Mr. Thomas Thacher. In Scituate he also had a controversy on the subject of baptism with William Vassal, who headed the church formed from those who had separated from Chauncy's church. His many trials there made him desire to change his residence, for although he had many friends there, he sometimes had not even the necessaries of life. He had received an invitation from his people in Ware, England, to return to them as their minister, for his party were in power and his old persecutor had been beheaded. While he was in Boston making preparations to remove his family to England, to accept the call to Ware, the overseers of Harvard College, unwilling to lose so valuable a man, "on November 2, 1654, deputed Mr. Richard Mather and Mr. Norton to tender to him the place of President, with the stipend of one hundred pounds, to be paid out of the county treasury, and also to signify to him, that it is expected and desired that he forbare to disseminate or publish any tenets concerning immersion baptism, and the

celebration of the Lord's Supper in the evening, or to expose the received doctrine thereon." "He made no difficulty in complying with this desire, and was ever punctual in the regard he paid to it." He was inaugurated November 29, 1654. Mather gives a description of his character which could hardly be equalled by other Puritans of the time, and shows what a highly educated and prominent man he was; he says of his preaching: "He was, indeed, an exceeding plain preacher, frequently saying *Artis est celare artem;* and yet a more learned and lively preacher has rarely been heard." In August, 1655, he petitioned the general court for a larger salary, as the one allowed him was insufficient to provide a living for his large family. On May 23, 1655, the court granted him five hundred acres of land, and this may have been the land said to have been given him on the Charles river, or the land in Marlborough, formerly called "Chauncy." On May 23, 1655, the court directed the treasurer to pay him thirty pounds. On May 27, 1663, he again petitioned the court, and the committee decided that the court had paid him all that was right, while the deputies decided to pay him five pounds a quarter out of the county treasury to supply his wants; the magistrates did not consent to this provision. Although as he grew old he became very feeble in body, his mind remained strong to the last, and even when he had almost to be carried he preached sermons occasionally. His friends begged him to cease his labors, saying he would surely die in the pulpit if he continued to work so hard, and he only replied: "How glad should I be, if what you say might prove true." He made his farewell oration at the beginning of the year 1671, and took a solemn farewell of his friends, dying February 19, 1671, aged seventy-nine years. He is remembered as one of the first ministers of New England. The principal works published by President Charles Chauncy were: "The Oration before the Spanish and Austrian Ambassadors"; "The Latin and Greek Poems"; "The Catechism"; "The Retraction of Charles Chauncy," published by him in 1641, for the satisfaction of those who might be offended with his submission before the High Commission Court, February 11, 1635; "A Sermon," 1655; "A Sermon," delivered the day after Commencement, 1655; "Twenty-six Sermons," 1659; "Antisynodalia Scripta Americana," his last published work, so far as is known.

He married, March 17, 1630, Catharine, daughter of Robert Eyre, of Sarum, Wilts, England, and Agnes or Ann his wife, daughter of the celebrated John Still, bishop of Bath and Wells. She died January 24, 1667. Children: Sarah, born at Ware, England, June 12, 1631; Isaac, born at Ware, August 23, 1632; Ichabod, born at Ware, 1635; Barnabas, in England, 1637; Nathaniel, mentioned below; Elnathan, twin of Nathaniel, born about 1639, in Plymouth, Massachusetts; Israel, born at Scituate, 1644; Hannah.

(XVIII) Rev. Nathaniel Chauncy, son of President Charles Chauncy, was born about 1639, at Plymouth, Massachusetts, twin of Elnathan, and was baptized at Scituate, Massachusetts, in 1641. He attended Harvard College, taking his first degree there in 1661, with his brother Elnathan and his youngest brother Israel. In 1664 he took the degree of Master of Arts, and afterwards was a fellow of the College. He preached in Windsor as a candidate, October 14, 1687, and was called by the members of the church, being the successor of Rev. Warham and Rev. Huit, the first pastors of the church. He was constantly engaged in controversy in Windsor, Connecticut, as the church was divided. He remained in Windsor for twelve years, and on November 10, 1679, was invited to preach as a candidate at Hatfield, Massachusetts; on January 21, 1680, the town invited him to settle as their minister, and he accepted, residing there the remainder of his life, preaching about five years. He died November 4, 1685, and on December 7, 1685, the town voted to pay the expenses of his funeral. He married Abigail, daughter of Elder John Strong, mentioned elsewhere in this work, at Northampton, November 12, 1673. She married (second) Deacon Medad Pomeroy, September 8, 1686, who died December 30, 1716, aged seventy-eight; Abigail died April 15, 1704. She had a son Samuel by her second husband, who was born in 1687, attended Yale College, and was minister at Newtown, Long Island. Rev. Nathaniel Chauncy left a very valuable library for the times, much of which he inherited from his father, and many of the books are still owned by his descendants. Children: Isaac, born September 6, 1674; Katherine, January 12, 1676; Abigail, October 14, 1677; Charles, September 3, 1679; Nathaniel, mentioned below; Sarah, 1683.

(XIX) Rev. Nathaniel (2) Chauncy, son of Rev. Nathaniel (1) Chauncy, was born in Hatfield, September 21, 1681. His father died when he was four years of age, and he was brought up by his uncle, Rev. Israel Chauncy, who agreed to educate him for the use of his father's library. He attended Yale College, as his uncle was one of the founders of that college, and his name stands on the Triennial Catalogue as the first who received a degree there. He was admitted to the church in Stratford. He taught school for a time after grad-

uation in Springfield, Massachusetts, keeping up his studies for the ministry meanwhile. He commenced preaching at Durham, Connecticut, May 23, 1706, and after serving on probation nearly five years was ordained February 17, 1711. He was one of the ablest preachers of his day. His sermons were delivered without notes, in a distinct and earnest tone. He was loved and respected by his people, and was a very strong man, with a magnetic personality. The works published by him were: A sermon entitled "Honouring God the True Way to Honour"; "Regular Singing Defended"; "The Faithful Servant Rewarded." He married, October 12, 1708, Sarah Judson, of Stratford, daughter of Captain James Judson, who was son of Joseph Judson, who came from England with his father, William Judson, when he was fifteen years of age, and lived in Concord four years and later in Stratford; Joseph Judson married Sarah, daughter of John Porter, of Windsor; Captain Judson married Rebecca, daughter of Thomas Wells, of Hartford. Mrs. Chauncy was born February 16, 1682, died May 31, 1745. Children: Elihu, mentioned below; Sarah, born February 24, 1711; Israel, died a bachelor in Durham; Charles, served in revolution; William, lived in northwestern part of Connecticut; Catharine, born September 22, 1714; Abigail, October 2, 1717; Nathaniel, January 21, 1720; Elnathan, September 10, 1724.

(XX) Elihu Chauncey, son of Rev. Nathaniel (2) Chauncy, was born in Durham, Connecticut, March 24, 1710, died April 10, 1791. He was representative from Durham in the state legislature for seventy-six semi-annual sessions. In the first part of the years in which he served, he was chosen second, Colonel James Wadsworth, an older man, being first, but in the latter part he was invariably chosen first, General James Wadsworth, a younger man, being second. He served in the French and Indian war as colonel of a regiment stationed on the northern frontier, and he was always invited to sit with the officers of the regular army in the councils of war. He was chief justice of the county court, and at the beginning of the revolution was on the committee who sat for the trial of persons suspected of being Tories. As he refused to take the oath of fidelity, he was suspected of being a Tory and resigned his place on the committee, and during the war held no public office. In addition to carrying on a farm, he engaged in mercantile business, which proved unprofitable. He was a man of great influence in the town. He inherited his father's home and left it to his son, Charles. It was situated at the east end of the street leading from the "Green."

He married, March 28, 1739, Mary, daughter of Samuel Griswold, Esq., of Killingworth. She died March 1, 1801, aged eighty-three. Children: Charles, born December 28, 1739, died January 13, 1740; Catharine, April 11, 1741; Sarah, December 22, 1742, died August 15, 1744; Sarah, May 8, 1745; Charles, mentioned below.

(XXI) Judge Charles (2) Chauncey, LL. D., son of Elihu Chauncey, was born in Durham, May 30, 1747, died April 28, 1823, in New Haven, Connecticut. He was king's attorney for the state and judge of the superior court. He studied law with James Abraham Hillhouse, Esq., and was admitted to the bar in November, 1768. In 1776 he was appointed attorney for the state, and in 1789 was on the bench of the superior court, resigning in 1793 to retire from the courts. For a time he devoted himself to study and lecturing to a class of students at law. In 1779 Yale College conferred on him the honorary degree of Master of Arts, and in 1811 he received the degree of Doctor of Laws from Middlebury College. Throughout his life he never ceased to study, and his knowledge of all kinds of literature was extensive. He married Abigail, born November 9, 1746, died December 24, 1818, daughter of Thomas and Abigail Darling, of New Haven. Children: 1. Charles, LL. D., born at New Haven, August 17, 1777, died August 30, 1849, in Philadelphia; graduated from Yale College in 1792, aged fifteen, probably the youngest person to graduate from the College; he established himself in Philadelphia, and in the first half of the eighteenth century, with Horace Binney and John Sergeant, was among the leaders of its bar. 2. Elihu, born at New Haven, January 15, 1779, died April 8, 1847; graduated from Yale College, 1796; admitted to the bar in Philadelphia; giving up law he engaged in financial enterprises and banking; he was one of the promoters of the Reading railroad and its first president; was cashier of the Bank of the United States, and after it was abolished of the Bank of Pennsylvania. 3. Sarah, born December 2, 1780; married William Walton Woolsey, December, 1814; died February 8, 1856. 4. Abigail, born June 27, 1785, died June 11, 1814. 5. Nathaniel, mentioned below.

(XXII) Nathaniel (3), son of Judge Charles (2) Chauncey, of New Haven, was born February 27, 1789, died February 7, 1865, in Philadelphia. In 1806 he was graduated from Yale College, and was admitted to the Philadelphia bar. He married, June 8, 1836, Elizabeth Sewall, daughter of Samuel and Nancy (Gardner) Salisbury, of Boston. Nancy Gardner was daughter of Rev. Francis Gardner, of

Leominster, Massachusetts, where he was pastor for over fifty years. She died May 22, 1850. For six years she was secretary and for thirteen years a directress of the Philadelphia Female Orphan Society of Philadelphia. Children: Charles; Elihu.

There were three immigrants by the name of Allyn, named Thomas, Samuel, and Matthew, brothers. They came first to Cambridge, Massachusetts, from Brampton, county Devon, England, and they are thought to have been the sons of Samuel Allyn, of Chelmsford, county Essex, England.

(I) Matthew Allyn or Allyne, the immigrant ancestor of this branch of the family, came from Brampton, county Devon, England, with his brothers, Deacon Thomas and Samuel. If he was son of Samuel, of Chelmsford, England, he was baptized in April, 1604. He came with the original Braintree company in 1632, to Charlestown, Massachusetts, where in 1633 he received forty-five acres in the division of lands at "the Common Pales," much the largest share of any settler, and he had an acre for his cow and three acres for planting ground "on the Neck." In 1635 he received a grant, or purchased five acres at Wigwam Neck, six acres of meadow land near Watertown, and five acres at Charlestown lane. In 1635 he owned five houses on the town plot at Cambridge, where he was the largest landholder. He lived near the meeting house. He was made a freeman of Massachusetts, March 4, 1635, and was a representative at the general court, March session, in 1636. He moved to Hartford probably in 1637, and was an original proprietor there, having his house lot on the road to the Neck, now on Windsor street. He owned one hundred and ten acres of land there and built the first mill at Hartford, at the foot of what is now West Pearl street. In May, 1638, he was lodging with Roger Williams, and in 1640 was a proprietor of Windsor. He owned large amounts of land in Killingworth and Simsbury, Connecticut. He was a member of Rev. Mr. Hooker's church at Hartford, but was excommunicated, doubtless for a doctrinal difference. On June 3, 1644, he appealed to the general court for redress, but the records do not show how the affair was settled, and the trouble may have been the cause of his removal to Windsor, where in 1638 he had purchased all the lands, "houses, servants, goods, and chattels" of the New Plymouth Company. This purchase took away the last right Plymouth had on the Connecticut river. His homestead at Windsor was near the company's old trading house. Soon after his removal to Windsor he set up a claim, that, since he had purchased his land from Plymouth, Connecticut had no right to tax his property in Windsor, and a committee decided that he should pay taxes only to Connecticut.

He was representative to the general court every year except 1653, from 1648 to 1658 inclusive, and from 1657 to 1667 inclusive he was a magistrate of the colony. In 1660-64 he was commissioner for the United Colonies of New England. In 1649, when the general court decided to begin hostilities against the Indians, Mr. Allyn was first of three deputies chosen to raise troops. In 1657 he and Joseph Gilbert were appointed to announce to the Indians at Pacomtuck the decision of the commissioners. In 1659 he and his son John were on the committee for dividing Indian lands at Podunk. In 1660, when the governor and deputy governor were chosen commissioners for 1661, he was chosen as a reserve, and also to act as moderator in their absence. In 1661 he was moderator and on the committee to petition for the charter, in which he was named as one of the grantees, when it was granted to Connecticut by Charles II. In 1662 he was moderator and chairman to treat with New Haven concerning a union in 1662-63. In October, 1663, he was chairman of a committee to treat with the Dutch envoys from New Amsterdam, and with Mr. Willis was chosen to settle the government of the English towns on the west end of Long Island. In 1664 the committee on the government of the towns was renewed with more members with authority to establish courts, etc. Also, in 1664, he was on the committee to settle bounds between "the Bay" and Rhode Island, and the south bounds; also, with three others he was "desired to accompany the Gov. to N. Y. to congratulate His Majesty's commissioners." In 1665, when the Connecticut and New Haven colonies were united, he and his son, Lieutenant John, were chosen assistants, and again in 1666, when he was moderator, and in 1667. In 1666 they were both on the committee having authority to levy troops, etc., in case of war. The Killingworth land records name him as a large landowner and first settler, though he probably never lived there. Hon. Matthew Allyn was one of the most prominent men in the colony, as can be seen from his many offices of trust. Hinman says, "Few men had more influence, or received more honors from the people, than Mr. Allyn." There are many evidences that he was always respected highly in Hartford, despite the fact that he was excommunicated from the church, and Mr. Hinman seems to hint that the Hartford church encouraged him to move because of his "influence with the settlers." In 1658

when there was again trouble in the Hartford church, he was chairman of the committee of the general court to conduct a correspondence on the subject.

He died February 1, 1670-71, and his will, dated January 30, 1670-71, makes his wife executrix, giving her the use of the estate; to his son John he left his Killingworth lands, confirming to him those lands in Hartford which he had already given him. He had already deeded his house in Windsor to his son Thomas, subject to life use by himself and his wife, and he gave him also a large estate. "Old Mrs. Allyn," probably his mother, was admitted to the Windsor church August 5, 1649, and "Old Mr. Allyn" died September 12, 1675. Children, born probably in England: Hon. John; Captain Thomas, mentioned below; Mary, married, June 11, 1646, Captain Benjamin Newberry.

(II) Captain Thomas Allyn, son of Hon. Matthew Allyn, lived in Windsor, on Branker place. He lived on the homestead after his father's death in 1670-71. He was a listed trooper, and was made freeman in 1658. He was the accidental cause of Henry Stile's death in 1651. He married Abigail, daughter of Rev. John Warham, October 21, 1658, and he died February 14, 1695-96. She was a member of the Windsor church. Children: John, born August 17, 1659, died October 4, 1659; Hon. and Col. Matthew, mentioned below; Thomas, March 11, 1662-63; John, June 24, 1665; Samuel, November 3, 1667; Jane, July 22, 1670; Abigail, October 17, 1672; Sarah, July 13, 1674; Hester, October 29, 1679.

(III) Hon. and Col. Matthew Allyn, son of Captain Thomas Allyn, was born June 5, 1660. He married, January 5, 1686, Elizabeth, daughter of Henry Wolcott Jr., and granddaughter of Henry Wolcott Sr. She inherited from her grandfather an estate in the parishes of Tolland and Ledyard St. Lawrence, county Somerset, England, and at Wellington, called Long Forth, England. The rents of these lands, held by her husband in her right, were disposed of by him in his will, 1740, to their three living sons, and the four sons of his deceased son Thomas. His estate amounted to £1,806, and he left four pounds to the First Society of Windsor. "The Hon. Col. Matthew Allyn Esq., who was many years one of the Council and Judge of the Superior Court, for the Colony of Conn., died Feb. 17, A. D. 1758, in ye 98th year of his age. Mrs. Elizabeth Allyn, his consort, died June ye 4th, A. D. 1734, in the 69th year of her age."

And here their Bodies sleep in Dust,
Till the Resurrection of the Just.

Children: Captain Thomas; Sergeant Matthew, August 9, 1687; Peletiah, mentioned below; Josiah, March 9, 1692-93; Henry, December 16, 1699; Theophilus, August 26, 1702.

(IV) Captain Peletiah Allyn, son of the Hon. and Col. Matthew Allyn, was born May 3, 1689, and married, August 26, 1711, Mary, daughter of Thomas and Dorothy (Talcott) Stoughton. He died November 3, 1766, aged seventy-eight. Children: Elizabeth, born November 22, 1712; Peletiah, October 4, 1714; Mary, October 11, 1716; Theophilus, August 28, died December 4, 1718; Dorothy, November 5, 1719; Jerusha, March 4, 1723-24; Samuel Wolcott, mentioned below; Captain Solomon, October 8, 1732; Chloe, baptized November 14, 1736.

(V) Samuel Wolcott, son of Captain Peletiah Allyn, was born December 6, 1727, and married, February 20, 1755, Joanna Mills. He died February 27, 1801, aged seventy-four, and she died July 9, 1794, aged sixty-three. Children: Clarissa, born December 21, 1756; Mary, baptized December 4, 1757; Samuel, mentioned below; Wolcott, born and baptized September 11, 1763; Clarissa, January 13, 1766; Mary, October 30, 1767.

(VI) Samuel, son of Samuel Wolcott Allyn, was born November 15, and baptized November 18, 1759. He married Jerusha, daughter of Captain Ebenezer F. Bissell. Children: Harriet, baptized February, 178—, married Odiah Loomis; Eli B. (?), baptized July 5, 1788, married Jerusha Mather; Henry, mentioned below; Richard, baptized April 15, 1792, married Julia Phelps. He probably had also: Amelia, baptized January 4, 1795; Samuel Wolcott, baptized September 20, 1801, died January 7, 1805; Samuel Wolcott, baptized March 4, 1805, died June 6, 1805, aged four years.

Ebenezer Fletcher Bissell, mentioned above, was first lieutenant of the Fourth Company, Captain Elihu Humphrey from Connecticut in 1775; captain in Colonel Huntington's regiment in 1776; on guard duty against Burgoyne's army as they went southward in 1777.

(VII) Henry, son of Samuel Allyn, was born at Windsor, Connecticut, in March, 1790, and baptized May 30, 1790. He died in Alabama, October 12, 1826. He removed to Bennington, Vermont, and married there, Ruth, daughter of Isaac and Anna (Robinson) Webster. (See Robinson IV). Children, born at Bennington: Emily, July 16, 1814; Henry Webster, March 27, 1816; Ann Jerusha, August 21, 1818; Isaac Webster, mentioned below; Ruth Eliza, August 23, 1823, died October 25, 1825; John Newton, September 4, 1825, died October 28, 1826.

(VIII) Isaac Webster, son of Henry Allyn,

was born at Bennington, Vermont, October 18, 1821, and died February 19, 1897. He was educated in the public schools. He located at White Eyes Plains, Coshocton county, Ohio, and during most of his active life was a commission merchant. He was a member of the Presbyterian church. In politics he was a Republican. He married, at Chillicothe, Ohio, December 31, 1846, Elizabeth Long, who was born in Chillicothe, Ohio, September 21, 1847; May 18, 1882. Her parents were natives of Canada, and she was left an orphan at the age of twelve years. Children: 1. Henry Webster, born Chillicothe, Ohio, September 21, 1847; died at New Philadelphia, Ohio, August 27, 1850. 2. Frank Bissell, born at New Philadelphia, Ohio, October 14, 1849; died in Chillicothe, Ohio, May 8, 1852. 3. Henry Harvey, born at New Philadelphia, Ohio, November 8, 1852; died at Philadelphia, Pennsylvania, June 17, 1867. 4. Ruth Elizabeth, born at Cleveland, Ohio, June 20, 1857; died at Philadelphia, Pennsylvania, December 17, 1876. 5. Herman Bryden, mentioned below. 6. Fannie Webster, born in Philadelphia, Pennsylvania, July 4, 1866.

(IX) Dr. Herman Bryden Allyn, son of Isaac Webster Allyn, was born at White Eyes Plains, Coshocton county, Ohio, May 2, 1860. He came to Philadelphia when one year old, and later attended the public schools and high school of Philadelphia, and completed his preparation for college under a private tutor. He entered the University of Pennsylvania in 1879, and was graduated with the degree of Bachelor of Arts in the class of 1882. Immediately afterward he began the study of his profession in the Medical School of the University of Pennsylvania and received the degree of Doctor of Medicine in 1885. For one year he was resident physician at the Philadelphia General Hospital, and for one year resident physician at Girard College, and was afterward visiting physician at St. Joseph's Hospital and instructor in physical diagnosis in the University of Pennsylvania, clinical professor of medicine in the Woman's Medical College of Pennsylvania, and visiting physician to the Philadelphia General Hospital. He is associate in medicine in the University of Pennsylvania, and a director of the Philadelphia County Medical Society; member of the Pennsylvania State Medical Society, and of the American Medical Association; fellow of the College of Physicians of Philadelphia; member of the Pathological Society of Philadelphia; of the Medical Club of Philadelphia; of the New England Society of Philadelphia; of the Physicians' Motor Club of that city; of Harmony Lodge, No. 52, Free and Accepted Masons, of

156					NEW ENGLAND.

Philadelphia. He is an elder of the Presbyterian church. In politics he is Republican, but is non-partisan in municipal affairs. For two years he was associate editor of the *Medical and Surgical Reporter* of Philadelphia, and has contributed numerous papers on clinical medicine from time to time to various medical journals and societies. Dr. Allyn occupies one of the foremost places in the medical profession in Pennsylvania. His office is at 501 South Forty-second street, Philadelphia.

He married, June 27, 1889, Rachael Patterson, born in Philadelphia, July 6, 1856, daughter of Henry Duval and Mary (Jones) Gregory. Her mother was born in Manchester, England. Children: 1. Herman Webster, born in Philadelphia, March 20, 1891. 2. Henry Gregory, November 28, 1892. 3. Emily, February 1, 1895.

(The Robinson Line).

(I) William Robinson, the immigrant ancestor of this branch of the family, was born about 1640. The first record found of him shows that he was living in Watertown, Massachusetts, as early as 1670, when he had a farm of two hundred acres on the narrow neck of land claimed by both Concord and Watertown. He was a signer of the original petition for the separation of Newtowne and Cambridge in 1678. He married in Cambridge, as early as 1667, Elizabeth Cutter, who was born in Cambridge, July 15, 1645, daughter of Richard and Elizabeth (Williams) Cutter. Elizabeth Williams is said to have come with her father, Robert Williams, in the ship "John and Dorothy," to Massachusetts, April 8, 1637; Robert Williams was born in 1608, in Norwick, county Norfolk, England, and was a cordwainer; his wife Elizabeth was born in England, and was admitted to the church at Roxbury in 1644; she died in Cambridge, March 5, 1662. Children: Elizabeth, born at Cambridge, 1669; Hannah (Ann), born at Concord, July 13, 1671, died at Cambridge, October 5, 1672; William, born July 10, 1673; Mercy, born August 7, 1676; David, born May 23, 1678; Samuel, mentioned below; Jonathan, twin of Samuel, born April 20, 1680.

(II) Samuel, son of William Robinson, was born April 20, 1680, twin of Jonathan. Jonathan moved from Cambridge, where he was born, to Cambridge Farms, in 1706, and doubtless about 1735, when the town of Grafton was organized, Samuel, with his father and other members of the family, moved to the new town, the place they settled being set off as Hardwick in 1739. He married Sarah Manning, and he was a soldier in the French and Indian wars. He was a founder of Bennington, Vermont, with his sons, and he died there in 1767.

(III) Samuel (2), son of Samuel (1) Robinson, was born in Cambridge, Middlesex county, Massachusetts, April 1, 1707. In 1735 he moved to Hardwick, and from there to the territory known as New Hampshire Grants (Vermont), in 1761, settling at Bennington. He had been a captain in the Massachusetts troops through several campaigns in the vicinity of Lakes George and Champlain, in the French and Indian wars. He was made the first justice of the peace in Bennington, being commissioned by Governor Wentworth of New Hampshire. This appointment made him prominent in the struggles between the New Hampshire and New York authorities, and as an appointee of Wentworth he took sides in the case of two claimants in Pownal, and was supported by Samuel Ashley, a New Hampshire deputy sheriff, and both men were arrested by the authorities of the state of New York and carried to Albany, where they were placed in jail, and were indicted for resisting the New York officers, but never brought to trial, as, after an acrimonious correspondence between the governors of New York and of New Hampshire, the affair ended in a compromise. On his return to the grants, Captain Robinson was chosen by the settlers in 1765 to go to Albany and try to save the land on which they had settled from the speculators who were obtaining grants of the very same land from Lieutenant-Governor Colden, but his efforts were useless. In 1766 he was sent as agent for the settlers to England to present their claims to the British ministry and he was making favorable headway, when he caught the fatal disease, smallpox, and died in London, England, October 27, 1767. His eldest son, Colonel Samuel Robinson, was chosen one of the town committee of Bennington to succeed his father. Colonel Robinson married in Hardwick, Massachusetts, Mercy Leonard, who was born in 1713, and died June 9, 1795, at Bennington. She was daughter of Moses Leonard. Children, born in Hardwick: Leonard, born July 27, 1733; Samuel, August 15, 1738; Moses, March 26, 1741; Paul, October, 1743; Silas, April, 1746; Macy, October, 1748; Sarah, November, 1751; David, mentioned below; Jonathan, August 11, 1756; Anna, mentioned below.

(IV) General David Robinson, son of Samuel Robinson, was born at Hardwick, Massachusetts, November 22, 1754, and came to Bennington with his father in 1761, being then seven years of age. He served in the Revolution as a private at the battle of Bennington, August 16, 1771, and rose rapidly by regular promotion to the rank of major-general, resigning that office in 1817. From 1789 till 1811, a period of twenty-two years, he served as sheriff of Bennington county. He was then appointed United States marshal, holding that office for eight years, until 1819. He married Sarah Fay, daughter of Stephen Fay, and by her had three sons. Stephen Fay was a member of the state assembly for several years, and also was judge of the county court and member of the council of censors in 1834; he died in 1852, aged seventy-one years. General David Robinson died in Bennington, Vermont, December 12, 1842 (December 11, 1843, according to his gravestone), aged eighty-nine years.

General Robinson was a man of powerful constitution and great courage. Once when a desperate criminal had taken refuge in a barn loft, he insisted upon going into the barn and capturing the man in spite of the danger, and succeeded in his purpose without harm, although the criminal was noted for being a reckless man.

(IV) Anna, daughter of Samuel Robinson, was born at Hardwick, Massachusetts, October 2, 1759; married Isaac Webster, son of Joseph Webster. Joseph Webster died in 1795, aged sixty-two years. He came of an old New Hampshire family. Isaac Webster was born in 1755. Children, born at Bennington: Anna, March 2, 1781; Sarah, November 28, 1782; Joseph, July 20, 1784; Persis, November 11, 1785; Mary, March 4, 1788; Ruth, March 20, 1790, married Henry Allyn (see Allyn VII); Mary, April 18, 1792; Isaac Robinson, March 8, 1795; Harriet, January 18, 1797; Isaac, June 26, 1781, died 1817.

Isaac Webster, mentioned above was sergeant in the Bennington company from 1776 to 1783 in Colonel Seth Warner's regiment; took part in the battle of Bennington and received a grant of land at Eden, Vermont, in part payment for service. (See Vermont Revolutionary Rolls, pp. 27-107-110-623-671-672; also p. 158, Vermont Historical Gazette, vol. i).

RILEY John Riley, the immigrant ancestor, came in 1621, the year after the landing of the Pilgrims, from Stepney, England, to Wethersfield, Connecticut, where in 1643 he was a landholder. His name was spelled Riley, Rilloy and Ryly in the old records. He married Grace ———, who died November 28, 1703, aged about seventy-nine, "if she had lived till Xmas." He died in May or June, 1674, and the inventory of his estate, taken June 11, 1674, by John Kilbourn, Enoch Buck and Eleazer Kimberly, was valued at 668 pounds, 4 shillings. His will was dated May 13, 1674. He made his wife executrix

and bequeathed to her and to his children. The will was proved September 3, 1674. His widow was a member of the church in 1674. Children: John, born about August 15, 1646; Joseph, October 20, 1649; Jonathan, about March 4, 1652-53; Mary, married Benjamin Gilbert; Grace, married, November 22, 1680, William Goodrich, 2nd; Sarah, married David Sayres (or Sears); Jacob, born about 1660; Isaac, mentioned below.

(II) Lieutenant Isaac Riley, son of John Riley, was born about 1670-71, died January 29, 1737-38. The inventory of his estate was taken February 14, 1737-38, and amounted to 2,856 pounds, 13 shillings, 3 pence. His will was dated January 20, 1737-38, and his wife Ann and son Samuel were appointed executors. He married Ann, daughter of Nathaniel Butler, December 17, 1696. Children: Ann, born and baptized May 21, 1699; Josiah, born May 9, baptized May 11, 1701; Isaac, mentioned below; Mary, born February 18, 1705-06; Sarah, baptized June 13, died September 18, 1708; Lucy, born September 20, 1709; Ephraim, baptized February 18, 1711; Samuel, born April 29, baptized May 3, 1713; Nathaniel, born January 13, 1715-16, baptized January 23, 1715-16.

(III) Isaac (2), son of Lieutenant Isaac (1) Riley, was born May 18, 1704, baptized May 21, 1704, died February 26, 1768. He married (first), June 12, 1729, Jemima Sage, who died May 14, 1765, aged sixty-one years. He married (second), May 28, 1766, Hannah Young, who was probably "wid. H.," who died April 8, 1825, aged eighty-two years. Children: Lucy, born March 27, 1732; Ashbel, born January 9, baptized January 13, 1733-34; Roger, mentioned below; Justus, born June 24, 1739; Lois, born February 9, 1742-43; Melicent, born December 24, baptized December 30, 1744; Ebenezer, born December 10, 1748.

(IV) Roger, son of Isaac (2) Riley, was born February 6, 1737, died May 12, 1832. He was a farmer and magistrate of Berlin, Connecticut. He married, February 12, 1761, Comfort Loveland, who died November 17, 1773. Their children: Lucy, Roger, Comfort, Isaac, mentioned below, Cynthia.

(V) Isaac (3), son of Roger Riley, was born at Berlin, Connecticut, November 29, 1770, died at Portland, Maine, March 14, 1824. He was a shipping merchant in the city of New York, the owner of sixteen vessels; also a bookseller and publisher there and in Philadelphia. He was the owner of two townships in Maine, "Ketcham" and "Riley," to which he took a colony of settlers from Philadelphia in 1823. He married, September 30, 1794, Hannah Alsop, of Middletown, Connecticut, daughter of Richard Alsop, a merchant of New York and Middletown, with a large business in the West Indies. Richard Alsop was a brother of John Alsop, delegate from the city of New York to the First Continental Congress held in Carpenter's Hall, Philadelphia, in 1774, but who resigned on the Declaration of Independence, and who was also for many years a vestryman and was buried in the graveyard of Trinity Church, New York. Children: Emmeline Matilda, married Joseph Greenleaf; Mary Wright, married Lewis Adams; Richard Alsop; Henry Augustus, mentioned below; Julia, married William S. Rodgers; Adelaide; Theodore W.; Caroline, married Isaac Abbott; Louisa; Clara.

(VI) Rev. Henry Augustus Riley, son of Isaac (3) Riley, was born November 21, 1801, in New York City, died at Montrose, Pennsylvania, March 17, 1878. He graduated in the collegiate department of the University of Pennsylvania in 1820, studied law for a short time in the office of Horace Binney, Philadelphia, graduated in the medical department of the University of Pennsylvania in 1825, and practiced medicine in New York until 1829, when he entered the Theological Seminary of Princeton, New Jersey, and graduated in 1832. In 1835 he was installed as pastor of the Eighth Avenue Presbyterian Church of New York, and in 1839 pastor of the Presbyterian church of Montrose, Pennsylvania, which he held for twenty-five years. He married (first) September 28, 1832, Emma Vaughan Smith, born in Philadelphia, December 3, 1802, died in Montrose, Pennsylvania, February 17, 1843. Children: 1. James P. W., born August 3, 1833, died October 11, 1888; married Kate Crawford. 2. Isaac, born February 2, 1835, died October 23, 1878; married Katharine A. Parker. 3. Julia Rodgers, born January 25, 1837; married Rev. B. J. Douglas. 4. Elizabeth Smith, born June 27, 1838, died December 25, 1902; married Daniel D. Lord. Henry Augustus Riley married (second), October 29, 1845, Blendena Miller, born September 16, 1811, died August 17, 1903, daughter of Dr. John Miller, of Truxton, New York, member of legislature of New York, 1820; member of congress, 1825; constitutional convention, 1846. Children: 5. Lewis Adams, mentioned below. 6. Henry Augustus, born December 20, 1848, died June 9, 1892. 7. Samuel Miller, born November 20, 1852, died January 17, 1902.

(VII) Lewis Adams, son of Rev. Henry Augustus Riley, was born in Montrose, Pennsylvania, June 7, 1847. He attended the public schools there and the academy at Homer, New York. In 1864 he entered the engineering office of Harris Brothers at Pottsville, Pennsylvania, to learn the profession of mining and civil engineering. In 1870 he was appointed engineer and agent of the Ashland estate, and when that property passed into the hands of the Philadelphia & Reading Coal and Iron Company, he became division engineer of the company. In 1872 he was made engineer and agent of the Locust Mountain Coal and Iron Company and Coal Ridge Coal and Improvement Company, properties controlled by the Lehigh Valley Railroad Company. When the Lehigh Valley Coal Company was formed in 1875, he was appointed engineer and superintendent of the company's property in the Mahanoy region. In 1880 Mr. Riley leased the lands of the Locust Mountain Coal and Iron Company, where he subsequently opened the "Logan," "Centralia," and "Big Mine Run" collieries, and operated them under the firm name of Lewis A. Riley & Company. These properties were sold to the Lehigh Valley Coal Company in 1896. Logan mine was the first anthracite colliery to adopt the rope system of haulage. The Centralia drainage tunnel, a mile and a half long, draining several mines, was completed by Mr. Riley in 1889, and extended in 1890, and was the first of the kind in the anthracite region. It was a costly and difficult undertaking, and proved of great practical value in operating the mines. In 1885 and again in 1891, Mr. Riley was appointed one of the commissioners to revise the mining laws of the state of Pennsylvania.

He has continued in the mining business as a partner of the firm of Lentz, Lilly & Company, which was formed in 1883, and is operating collieries in the Mahanoy region. In 1896 he was elected president of the Lehigh Coal and Navigation Company, the oldest and one of the largest mining and railroad companies in America, which position he held for eleven years. He is also president of the Lehigh & Hudson River Railway Company, a director of the Westmoreland Coal Company, Penn Gas Coal Company, Huntington & Broad Top Mountain Railroad and Coal Company, Eastern Pennsylvania Railways Company, and the American Gas Company. He is a member of the Philadelphia Country Club, Merion Cricket Club, Racquet Club of Philadelphia, and president of the Devon Golf Club; also a member of the Rittenhouse Club of Philadelphia, the American Institute of Mining Engineers, and a life member of the New England Society of Philadelphia. In politics he is a Republican. He is a communicant of the Protestant Episcopal church, and a vestryman of St. Mark's Church, of Philadelphia. He resides at No. 1509 Spruce street, Philadelphia.

Louis A. Riley

He married, September 8, 1870, Margaret Morton, born April 24, 1848, daughter of Henry and Frances (Morton) Drinker, of Montrose, Pennsylvania. Her parents were members of the Society of Friends. Children: 1. Henry Drinker, born at Montrose, Pennsylvania, January 28, 1872; married, February 9, 1898, Alice, daughter of Horace Brooke Burt, of Philadelphia; children: Jean Burt, Lewis Alsop and Horace Burt. 2. Margaret Morton, born in Ashland, Pennsylvania, August 23, 1873.

WILLCOX The Willcox family is of Saxon origin, and was seated at Bury St. Edmunds, England, before the Roman Conquest. Sir John Dugals, in the Visitation of the County of Suffolk, mentions fifteen generations of the family previous to the year 1600. This traces the lineage back to the year 1200, when the surname came into use as an inherited family name. On the old records the forms of Wilcox, Wilcocks, Wilcoxon and Willcox are used interchangeably.

(I) William Willcox (or Wilcoxson, as commonly spelled), was born in 1601, at St. Albans, Hertfordshire, England. He came to America when thirty-four years old, in the ship "Planter," having a certificate from the minister at St. Albans. Another William Willcox settled at Cambridge, Massachusetts Bay, and became a proprietor of that town and a town officer; he was admitted a freeman May 25, 1636, died November 28, 1653, leaving a will mentioning various relatives and friends. William Willcox, first named, was admitted as a freeman December 11, 1636. He was a linen weaver by trade. He removed to Stratford, Connecticut, in 1639; was a representative to Hartford in 1647, and died in 1652. He married Margaret ———, born 1611. Children: 1. John, born 1633. 2. Joseph, of whom further. 3. Samuel, died March 12, 1713; was sergeant; lived at Windsor and Meadow Plain, Simsbury. 4. Obadiah, born 1641, died 1713; settled in Guilford, Connecticut. 5. Timothy, died June 13, 1713; deacon; married Johanna Birdsay, December 28, 1664. 6. Elizabeth, married, April 16, 1663, Henry Stiles, of Windsor, Connecticut. 7. Hannah, married, March 7, 1664, Lieutenant Daniel Hayden. 8. Sarah, died 1691; married, March 7, 1665, John Meigs, of Madison, Connecticut. 9. Phebe, married, December 11, 1669, John Birdsey, of Stratford.

(II) Joseph, son of William Willcox, was born about 1635, died February 9, 1703. He settled in Killingworth, Connecticut, and his descendants have been numerous in that town,

always spelling the name Wilcox or Willcox. He was one of the proprietors of Killingworth under the act of 1663, and a Widow Willcox was one of the Saybrook purchasers from Killingworth in 1687. Children, born at Killingworth: 1. Joseph, of whom further. 2. Thomas, born November 13, 1661. 3. Samuel, born 1663. 4. Hannah, born January 19, 1665. 5. Nathaniel, born August 9, 1668. 6. William, born January 8, 1671. 7. Margaret, born 1673. 8. John, born 1675.

(III) Joseph (2), son of Joseph (1) Willcox, was born at Killingworth, October 29, 1659. He married, February 14, 1683, Hannah Kelsey, of Killingworth. He died there February 2, 1726. They had seven children.

(IV) Stephen, son of Joseph (2) Willcox, was born July 12, 1706, in Killingworth, and died there December 22, 1781. He was one of the grantees of Newport, New Hampshire, in 1761, and was appointed on a committee of four at Killingworth, December 25, 1764, to allot the lands to grantees, and this duty was performed July 6, 1766, at Charlestown, New Hampshire. He was one of a committee chosen on the second Tuesday of March, 1765, to open a cart road to Newport, at the west end of the lots as laid out, and at the same time was appointed to go to Portsmouth to get an extension of the conditions of the town charter. His sons, Jesse, Uriah and Phineas, and his daughter Lydia, wife of Samuel Hurd, came to Newport after the lots were laid out, and settled on the father's grant, each being given 300 acres of land. The first meeting of the proprietors of the town was held October 13, 1767, at the house of Jesse Willcox, and Stephen Willcox was moderator, and appointed on a committee to assign lots. He seems to have returned to his home in Connecticut. He married, May 10, 1733, Mary Pierson, born May 10, 1713, died December 13, 1795. Children, born at Killingworth: 1. Mary, September 7, 1734; married ——— Hurd; died June 18, 1805. 2. Lydia, twin with Mary; married Samuel Hurd; died December 13, 1798. 3. Hepsibeth, born July 3, 1736, died June 7, 1816. 4. Sarah, born January 6, 1738, died April 17, 1819. 5. Stephen, born January 8, 1740, died January 20, 1823. 6. Asa, born December 17, 1741, died at Habana, in the French war, September 10, 1761, aged twenty years. 7. Jesse, of whom further. 8. Phineas, born January 13, 1747, died at Newport, 1819. 9. Uriah, born March 13, 1749. 10. Eunice, born June 14, 1751. 11. Mabel, born December 5, 1752. 12. Joseph, born January 22, 1755, died January 17, 1817. 13. Nathan, born November 5, 1758, died March 23, 1813.

(V) Jesse, son of Stephen Willcox, was

born at Killingworth, Connecticut, October 5, 1744, died March 12, 1823, at Newport, New Hampshire. He was one of the original settlers of Newport, coming in and breaking ground before the American revolution and just after the conquest of Canada by the English had made the Connecticut Valley fairly safe for settlement, it having been previously much traveled by Indians in their raids upon the colonists. He married, June 11, 1767, Thankful Stevens, and among their children was Oliver, of whom further.

(VI) Oliver, son of Jesse Willcox, was born in Newport, New Hampshire, about 1780-85, and died in New York City in 1837. His early life was spent in Newport, and he was brought up on a farm, but on account of delicate health he did not continue the arduous life of a farmer, but joined an older brother in business in New York City, where he spent his subsequent life. For the greater part of his residence there he was an influential officer in the Presbyterian church. He was of a peculiarly gentle and loving nature, full of genial sympathy, of playful humor, and of such youthful feeling as made him strongly attractive to children. He married, September 1, 1807, Sally Stanton, born October 19, 1786, at Killingworth, died February 2, 1843, at Norwich, Connecticut (see Stanton V). Children: 1. Albert O., born May 10, 1810; married Ann E. Hamilton. 2. Elizabeth S., born 1812; married Anthony Lane. 3. Henrietta, born 1814; married Oliver W. Norton. 5. Edwin, born August 1, 1816; married Amelia A. Whittlesey. 6. Mary Augusta, married (first) Dr. David D. Marvin, (second) Thomas C. Fanning. 7. William Henry, of whom further. 8. Giles Buckingham, born August 7, 1826; married Mary J. Cooley. 9. Hamilton.

(VII) Rev. William Henry Willcox, son of Oliver Willcox, was born January 28, 1821, in Cedar street, New York City, a region which at that date was just ceasing to be a residence quarter. He attended the public schools and at the age of twelve completed the high school course. With the exception of one year he was then in business with his father until he was sixteen years old, when his father died. His father had purposed to become a minister, but had been compelled by ill health to relinquish his studies, therefore it was his earnest wish that his son should enter the calling thus closed to him, so at the age of thirteen he returned to school for a year. Shortly after his father's death a friend of the father offered him a scholarship for four years in the University of the City of New York, now the New York University, from which he graduated with the degree of Bachelor of Arts in

1843, at the head of a class of unusual ability. Immediately after graduation he entered upon his theological studies, entering Union Theological Seminary, from which he was graduated in 1846. He afterward received the honorary degree of Doctor of Laws from Drury College. In 1846 he presented himself for license to the then Fourth Presbytery of New York. Ready for work, the opportunity soon opened to him for undertaking a mission of an unusual character in Norwich, Connecticut. On "the Plain," near the monument of Uncas, stood an unused church edifice of average size. Four gentlemen residing in the neighborhood conceived the idea of gathering a congregation for it, composed of their own families and others of like inclination, together with the people working in a factory nearby. They invited the young minister to this work. He remained at Norwich until 1848, and he spent the following two years in private reading and study, broken by preaching for a short time as a temporary supply at South Royalston, Worcester county, Massachusetts. In the spring of 1850 he accepted an invitation to Elmwood, a growing settlement near the Providence boundary line, in the town of Cranston, Rhode Island, where he remained for two years. At the time he was invited to Elmwood, he was considering a visit to the west, with a view to possible settlement, but his younger brother, Giles B., was then a student at Andover Seminary, and after graduation would be ready to join him. So the elder brother waiting, in June, 1852, after ending his connection with the Elmwood church, the two set out together for Chicago, making brief stays at several smaller places, and one of several weeks in Detroit. The climate proving unfavorable for them, the thought of permanent residence was abandoned, and they shortly turned back, the elder brother going to Kennebunk, Maine, he having been tendered the pastorate of the Union Church of that town, which he accepted, and was installed pastor October 28, 1852.

In the summer of 1856 Mr. Willcox preached for a part of his vacation in the Bethesda Church of Reading, Massachusetts, which was then without a head, but declined an invitation to become its pastor. A year later the invitation, coupled with more favorable terms, was renewed and was accepted. He was dismissed at Kennebunk, June 8, 1857, and installed at Reading, July 2, 1857. Thus began a pastorate which continued until the end of his active work as a clergyman nearly twenty-two years later. The church to which he went had about double the membership of the Kennebunk church, and throughout his pastorate continued to have a steady normal growth. In his sermons he displayed unusual ability in presenting with clearness and power the fundamental truths of Christianity, and in impressing them upon the intellects and consciences of his congregation. His preaching laid stress upon the performance of the common duties of life, not as forming the essence of religion, but as the expression of this controlling affection, as the means both of developing and manifesting the filial spirit.

He was dismissed from the Reading church March 5, 1879, in order to take up other duties which demanded his time and attention. Valeria Goodenow, an aunt of Mrs. Willcox, and in early life a member of Judge Goodenow's household in Alfred, had married Daniel P. Stone who afterwards as a drygoods merchant and private banker in Boston, accumulated a large fortune. Mr. Stone died in 1878, leaving property amounting to more than two millions of dollars, and Mr. Willcox was one of the three executors of the will. Mrs. Stone requested Mr. Willcox to resign his pastorate and become her private secretary and confidential adviser, at the same salary he had been receiving. He did so, and a few months after his dismissal from his church, removed to Malden, Massachusetts. During the following few years, after the bequests made by Mr. Stone to his relatives, and the gifts in lieu of bequests made by Mrs. Stone to her relatives and friends, had consumed nearly one-half of the estate, more than a million dollars were given to educational and religious objects. The leading beneficiaries were the American Missionary Association and Phillips Academy, Andover, each receiving $175,000. Other colleges remembered were Wellesley, Amherst, Bowdoin, Drury, Oberlin, Dartmouth, Hamilton, American, Iowa, Ripon, Olivet, Robert, Illinois, Beloit, Chicago Theological Seminary, Howard University, and the Boston Young Men's Christian Association. This distribution was made almost entirely on the recommendations of Mr. Willcox. He felt strongly this responsibility, and spared no pains to meet it wisely. This work of personal investigation and voluminous correspondence made the five years following 1878 perhaps the busiest of his life, as in the service which they rendered to the community they were the most significant. The death of Mrs. Stone occurred in 1884, and during the time between that and his own death in 1904, Mr. Willcox was much occupied in the care of various religious and educational institutions.

From October, 1877, Mr. Willcox was a corporate member of the American Board of Commissioners for Foreign Missions, and from 1887 he was president of the board of trustees of Jaffna College, Ceylon. Between 1876 and 1886 he was a trustee of Drury College, at Springfield, Missouri, and from 1879 to 1882 a trustee of Abbot Academy, Andover. In 1878 he was made a trustee of Phillips Academy, Andover, and in 1879 a trustee of Straight University. From 1891 he was a trustee of the Malden Hospital. Wellesley College made him one of its trustees in 1879, member of the executive committtee of that board in 1883, and chairman thereof in 1884. In 1894 he was made president of the Congregational Education Society. Two of his sermons, "Hope for the Country" (1863), and "A Christian—What, How, Why" (1874), were published in pamphlet form, and he was an occasional contributor to the Congregationalist, the Advance, and the American Agriculturalist.

Mr. Willcox married, May 30, 1853, Annie, daughter of Hon. Daniel Goodenow (q. v.). Children: Ella G.; Mary A., professor of zoology and biology at Wellesley College for twenty-five years; William Goodenow, of whom further; Walter F., professor of social science and statistics at Cornell University; Valeria; Frederic A.; and Henry Howard.

Hon. Daniel Goodenow, deceased, father of Mrs. William Henry Willcox, was born in Henniker, New Hampshire, October 30, 1793. His father was a farmer of too limited means to allow his five boys to hope for much assistance from him in acquiring anything more than the simplest common school education. But those boys were all possessed of that self-reliant energy and those quenchless aspirations which always proclaim mental superiority. They were determined to secure for themselves the coveted education which the poverty of their father forbade him to give them. They all became lawyers, and with the exception of John the eldest (who died soon after his admission to the Oxford bar in 1812) they were for many years prominent and honored citizens. Daniel, the third son, entered Phillips Academy at Andover, Massachusetts, to prepare himself for college. On completing his preparatory studies, his limited means forbade his immediate entrance upon a collegiate course and he left his home at Brownfield to enter the law office of Hon. John Holmes, at Alfred. This was in 1813, when he was twenty years of age. During the four years spent in Mr. Holmes' office he worked his way onward to his profession and supported himself by occasionally teaching school. He also studied the sciences and classics so successfully that in 1817 he was admitted to the senior class of Dartmouth University, and graduated a few months later.

Soon after this Mr. Goodenow, having chosen Alfred as his home, was admitted to the York county bar and rapidly gained an extensive practice. In 1825-27-30, he was chosen to the House of Representatives, and was speaker the last year. In 1831-32-33, he was the candidate of the Whig party for governor; and in 1838 and again in 1841, he held the important office of attorney-general. In December, 1841, he was appointed judge of the district court for the western district of Maine, succeeding Judge Whitman. This office he held to the very general acceptance of the bar and the community for the constitutional term of seven years.

In 1848 Judge Goodenow resumed his professional practice and for a period of seven years was the acknowledged head of the York county bar. In 1855 he was appointed one of the judges of the supreme court, and filled this most important post with such dignified ability as added materially to his reputation throughout the state. The honorary degree of LL.D. was in 1860 conferred upon him by Bowdoin College, of which institution he was a faithful and devoted trustee for the last twenty-five years of his life. In company with Chief Justice Tenney, he retired from the bench of the supreme court in 1862, at the age of sixty-nine years. He was a practical Christian, and a man of the loftiest personal character.

His first wife was a daughter of Hon. John Holmes, widely known for her beauty and accomplishments. She had four children, the youngest of whom died in infancy. The eldest was the wife of Rev. William H. Willcox. The other two were lawyers in Maine,—Hon. John Holmes Goodenow, at Alfred, and Henry Clay Goodenow, of Lewiston. The mother of these children died in 1840. The second wife of Judge Goodenow (whom he married in 1848) was a daughter of the late Judge Dana, of Fryeburg, and was the widow of Henry B. Osgood, Esq., of Portland. They had one daughter, who is still living.

(VIII) William Goodenow Willcox, son of Rev. Dr. William Henry Willcox, was born at Reading, Massachusetts, February 8, 1859. He attended the public schools of his native town and the State Normal School at Bridgewater, Massachusetts. His business career began January 1, 1884, when he entered the employ of A. O. Willcox & Son, fire and marine insurance brokers. He was admitted to partnership in 1887, and shortly after the firm name was changed to Albert Willcox & Company. Since the death of Albert Willcox, the senior partner, in 1906, the firm has consisted of William G. Willcox and William Y. Wemple, managers of the American business of the

Salamandra Insurance Company of St. Petersburg, Russia. The firm's brokerage business and the business of Charles E. and W. F. Peck, and also that of Walker & Hughes, was taken over by a corporation under the name of Willcox, Peck & Hughes, of which Mr. William G. Willcox is vice-president. He is also a director of the Assurance Company of America, and of the Battery Park National Bank of New York; member of the advisory committee of the Staten Island branch of the Corn Exchange Bank of New York; president of the board of trustees of the S. R. Smith Infirmary and of the Staten Island Academy; trustee and treasurer of the investment committee of the Tuskegee Normal and Industrial Institute, Alabama, of which Booker T. Washington is principal. He is treasurer of the Richmond County (New York) Society for the Prevention of Cruelty to Children. He is a member of the Down Town Club of New York, and of the Staten Island and Richmond County Country clubs. In religion he is a Unitarian and an independent in politics.

Mr. Willcox married, at West New Brighton, Staten Island, May 28, 1889, Mary Otis, born December 20, 1861, daughter of Sydney Howard Gay. Her father was managing editor of the New York Tribune for many years under Horace Greeley, and subsequently editor of the Chicago Tribune. He wrote "Bryant's History of the United States," for which William Cullen Bryant, the poet, wrote an introduction. Mrs. Willcox is a member of the Staten Island Chapter, Daughters of the American Revolution, and is active in the woman suffrage movement. Children, born on Staten Island: 1. Henry, born May 3, 1890. 2. Sydney Gay, born July 28, 1892. 3. Daniel Goodenow, born April 25, 1896, died March 23, 1907. 4. Elizabeth Neall, born July 11, 1899. 5. Anna Goodenow, born April 26, 1903.

(The Stanton Line).

The surname Stanton is derived from a place name, and is identical with Stonington in origin. The family is of ancient English origin. Robert Stanton, an early settler of Newport, Rhode Island, was the progenitor of Hon. Edwin M. Stanton, of Lincoln's cabinet; died in Newport in 1672, aged seventy-three. There was a John Stanton in Virginia in 1635, and Thomas Stanton, aged twenty, sailed for Virginia in 1635 in the merchantman "Bonaventura". The family historian thinks he went to Virginia, but many ships whose records state that Virginia was the destination came to New England. The "Bonaventura" may have landed some passengers in Virginia, others in Connecticut or Boston.

NEW ENGLAND. 163

(I) Thomas Stanton, immigrant ancestor, was in Boston in 1636, and is on record as a magistrate there. If he was the one who came in 1635, his age must have been understated, as men under twenty-one were not magistrates in the colony, and in 1636 he was acting as Indian interpreter for Governor Winthrop. It is reasonable to suppose that he was a trader and had been both to New England and Virginia before 1635, in order to have sufficient knowledge of the language of the Indians to become an interpreter. The services of Mr. Stanton as interpreter during the Pequot war were invaluable, says the history of New London, Connecticut: "He was, moreover, a man of trust and intelligence and his knowledge of the country and of the natives made him a useful pioneer and counsellor in all land questions, as well as difficulties with the Indians." DeForest's History of Connecticut says: "Some time in April (1637) a small vessel arrived at the fort (Saybrook), having on board Thos. Stanton, a man well acquainted with the Indian language, and long useful to the colonial authorities as interpreter." Thomas Stanton served through the Pequot war and special mention is made of his bravery in the battle of Fairfield Swamp, where he nearly lost his life. He must have returned to Boston at the close of the war, for he was one of the magistrates in the trial of John Wainwright, October 3, 1637. In February, 1639, he and his father-in-law, Thomas Lord, were settled in Hartford, Connecticut, coming there soon after the colony of Rev. Thomas Hooker established the town. He was appointed official interpreter for the general court at Hartford, April 5, 1638, and at the same session was sent with others on a mission to the Warranocke Indians and as a delegate to an Indian-English council meeting at Hartford. He was interpreter for the Yorkshire, England, colonists at New Haven, November 24, 1638, when the land on which the city of New Haven is located, was bought of the Indians. He was an Indian trader as early as 1642, when with his brother-in-law, Richard Lord, he made a voyage to Long Island to trade and collect old debts, and there is a document showing that he traded as far away as Virginia. He had the grant of a monopoly of the trading with the Indians at Pawkatuck and along the river of that name. He built a trading house there, about 1651 moved to Pequot, and in 1658 occupied his permanent residence at Stonington. In 1650 the general court appointed him interpreter to the elders who were required to preach the gospel to the Indians at least twice a year. Caulkins said of him: "From the year 1636, when he was

Winthrop's interpreter with the Nahantic sachem, to 1670 when the Uncas visited him with a train of warriors and captains to get him to write his will, his name is connected with almost every Indian transaction on record." He received several grants of land. In 1651 he was deputy magistrate. In 1658 he moved to Wequetequock Cove, east of Stonington, where he was the third settler; it was then called Southington, Massachusetts, part of Suffolk county, and in 1658 he was appointed one of the managers. In 1664 he was commissioner to try small causes, and in 1665 had authority to hold a semi-annual court at New London. In 1666 he was again commissioner of county judges, overseer-general of the Coassatuck Indians, commissioner in Indian affairs, and commissioner until his death in 1677. In 1666 he was in the general assembly and remained until 1674. He and his sons were active in King Philip's war. He was one of the founders of the church at Stonington, June 3, 1674, and his name was the first on the roll. He died December 2, 1677, and was buried in the family burial ground between Stonington and Westerly.

He married Ann Lord, born in England, daughter of Dr. Thomas and Dorothy Lord. Her father was the first physician licensed to practice in Connecticut by the general court, June 30, 1652, and the rates he could charge in Hartford, Wethersfield, Windsor, and other towns in this section were fixed in the license, a salary of fifteen pounds to be paid by the county. The Lord coat-of-arms: Argent on a fesse gules between three cinque foils azure a hind passant between two pheons or. Ann Stanton spent her last days with her daughter, Mrs. Dorothy Noyes, of Stonington, and died there in 1688. The original home site of Thomas Stanton at Hartford is now occupied by the Jewell Leather Belting Company factory. Children: Thomas, born 1638; John, 1641; Mary, 1643; Hannah, 1644; Joseph, mentioned below; Daniel, 1648; Dorothy, 1651; Robert, 1653; Sarah, 1655; Samuel, 1657.

(II) Joseph, son of Thomas Stanton, was born in 1646, baptized March 21, 1646. He went with his parents to Stonington, and settled on a large tract of land which his father had bought of a Narragansett Indian chief for a half bushel of wampum. The sachem's child was a captive and was redeemed by the aid of Thomas Stanton, so the Indian sold the land as part payment of the price. In 1669 he was appointed assistant magistrate to hold court in New London. In 1685 he leased land in Charlestown, Rhode Island, formerly part of Westerly, "where I do now live," showing that he had moved there. He married (first) June 19, 1673, Hannah Mead, of Roxbury, who died in 1676, daughter of William Mead. He married a second, and perhaps a third and fourth time. Children: Joseph, born 1674; Hannah, 1676, buried May 6, 1681; Thomas, December 16, 1678, died young; Rebecca, April, 1681; Thomas, baptized April 5, 1691; Daniel, mentioned below; Samuel, baptized July 16, 1698, died young.

(III) Captain Daniel Stanton, son of Joseph Stanton, was baptized April 1, 1694, died December 28, 1773. He married (first) Mercy, daughter of Job Babcock, of Westerly; (second) ——— ; (third) December 10, 1762, probably Prudence, daughter of Rev. Salmon and Dorothy (Noyes) Treat. Children: Daniel, married twice; Samuel, married Sarah Browning; John, mentioned below; Joseph, married Abigail Sheffield; George, died unmarried; Mary; Elizabeth.

(IV) John, son of Captain Daniel Stanton, was born in February, 1722, in Charlestown, Rhode Island, died at Paris, Oneida county, New York, September 1, 1814. He married Dorothy Richardson, born 1724, died 1790, daughter of Jonathan and Anne (Treat) Richardson, and granddaughter of Dorothy (Noyes) Treat. Children, born at Westerly: Adam, mentioned below; Daniel; Amos, born December 22, 1756; George; Prudence; Anna; Dorothy; Mary, 1769; Rachel; Rebecca, 1773.

(V) Adam, son of John Stanton, was born in Westerly in 1749, died at Clinton, Connecticut, October 15, 1834. He moved from Westerly, in 1774-75, and settled in Killingworth, Connecticut, in the southern part, now Clinton. He built his house on the lot where stood the house of Abraham Pierson, the first president of Yale College, and the timbers of the Pierson house are now in the Stanton house. His first business was making salt from the water of Long Island sound, sending it by ox trains to Boston, and selling it for two dollars a bushel. He married, December 4, 1777, Elizabeth, born May 28, 1754, at Preston, Connecticut, died May 23, 1805, daughter of Rev. Samuel Treat. Children: Mary, born October 23, 1778; Elizabeth, May 29, 1780; John, April 5, 1783; Sally, October 19, 1786, died February 2, 1843, married, September 1, 1807, Oliver Willcox (see Willcox VI); Nancy, February 18, 1790, accidentally burned to death, February 28, 1879.

COWDIN James Cowdin or Cowden, son of Thomas Cowden, was born in the north of Ireland in 1695. Thomas Cowden came thither from

Scotland. The coat-of-arms of James Cowden answers to the description of the most ancient Cowden coat-of-arms in Scotland: "Azure on a fesse argent between three annulets or, a lion passant sable. Crest: A demilion sable charged with an annulet or label. In Ireland the common spelling has been Cowdin, but Cowden is also used. Family tradition states that James Cowdin was a barrister and resided for some time in Dublin. He married young, and had one child, David. Early in 1720 he married (second) Janet Craige. It is said that his first wife was "Lady Polly Connor." Janet Craige or Craig was also of Scotch parentage, both Craigs and Cowdens coming from Scotland and locating near each other between Manor Cunningham and Newton Cunningham. In 1728 James Cowden, his wife and four or five children, also Matthew Cowden, son of William Cowden, twelve years the junior of James and probably his cousin, came from Londonderry, Ireland. Matthew located in Paxtang township in Pennsylvania, where many Scotch-Irish settled and where he doubtless had relatives and friends. In his family records we find "He had relatives in New England." Mrs. Cowden probably had relatives among the New England Scotch-Irish, for John, David and Robert Craige came with the pioneers in 1718. The Cowdens settled in Worcester, Massachusetts, whither some of the first Scotch-Irish had come, and in 1731 he purchased land at North Worcester and cleared a farm in what is now Holden. In 1740 James Cowden and his son David were petitioners for the incorporation of the town of Holden. He died October 1, 1748, "having gone to Worcester to execute his will, just written, he was taken suddenly ill, and died in a few hours." He left a considerable estate. His widow administered the estate. She married (second) Captain James Craig, a prominent citizen of Rutland, Massachusetts, April 16, 1755, and she died February 19, 1776. Children of James Cowden: David, captain in revolution; Thomas, mentioned below; Margaret; William, captain in the revolution; Samuel; Elizabeth; Robert; John; James. David, James and John invested in New York lands; John settled in Canada; David and James at Cambridge, Washington county, New York. Robert lived at Princeton, Massachusetts; William in Worcester and Rutland; Samuel in Rutland. Each of the sons learned a trade.

(II) Captain Thomas Cowdin, son of James Cowdin, was born in Ireland, December 25, 1720. His education was received chiefly in the home in North Worcester under the instruction of his father, and he became well versed in jurisprudence and in Roman, English, Scottish and Irish history. In youth he served an apprenticeship in Marlboro as a blacksmith, and afterward opened a shop on his own account on Main street, Worcester. He belonged to a company of cavalry there and was sergeant in the old French and Indian war, sailing from Boston for Louisburg, March 24, 1745, and he distinguished himself during the fight. Afterwards he was stationed at the town of Charlestown No. 4, New Hampshire, and on one occasion was detailed with two soldiers to carry despatches to Fort Dummer. Meeting hostile Indians, the little party scattered and ran for their lives. Cowdin reached what is now Keene, New Hampshire, and a company of soldiers was sent to escort him to Fort Dummer. When returning to Charlestown No. 4, they met searching parties looking for Cowdin, whom his companions supposed to have been captured or killed. Sergeant Cowdin sailed from Boston, May 20, 1755, in the expedition against Nova Scotia, and he continued in the service most of the time until the close of the French and Indian war. He was commissioned ensign, September 24, 1756, and lieutenant, February 21, 1760. He was detailed to search for deserters, April 17, 1761. He was commissioned captain by Governor Francis Bernard, April 18, 1761, and the commission is now in the possession of the Wallace library of Fitchburg, as is also his captain's commission, dated April 6, 1780, and his commission as justice of the peace.

In 1764 Captain Cowdin bought of Samuel Hunt his property in Fitchburg and removed thither in July. The house had been used as a tavern and for ten years Captain Cowdin continued to conduct an inn there. The location on Pearl street has long been known as the General Wood place. He was on the building committee and gave an acre and forty rods of land from his wheat field for a site for the new meeting house. During the winter of 1764-65 services were held in Cowdin's house. He was town clerk from 1766 to 1775, selectman for many years, and member of the school committee. He owned much real estate: some four hundred acres of land in Fitchburg, and his homestead of some two hundred acres extended from Mount Vernon street to Baker's brook. In 1770 he was the largest taxpayer. In 1775 he built a house on the site of the present American House and resided there the remainder of his days. In 1779 he was made a Free Mason in Trinity Lodge of Lancaster.

He was opposed to the war of the revolution and was at first called a Tory, but he sent his son Thomas with a load of provisions for the minute-men when on the march to Lexington. For the first time after he became a freeman of Fitchburg he was dropped from the list of town officers. But he soon joined the Whigs, and in 1777 responded to the Bennington Alarm in the Fitchburg company. In 1778 he enlisted for eight months, and in 1779 he served three months as captain in Captain James Denny's regiment which was sent to reinforce the American army in New York. He was elected representative to the first general court under the new state constitution in 1780 and several years afterward. His influence became greater than ever. During Shays' Rebellion he loyally supported the government. Until emancipation came with the constitution in 1780, Captain Cowdin owned negro slaves and afterward they remained in his employ. Two of these, Nancy, the maid servant of Mrs. Cowdin, and Mevus, the body-servant of the captain, were important figures in the family history. Mevus was something of a fiddler and his services were in demand for dances far and near.

An excellent account of the life of Captain Cowdin was written by Miss Ada L. Howard, ex-president of Wellesley College, and is published in the proceedings of the Fitchburg Historical Society in 1898. It is illustrated with engravings of the oil paintings of Captain Cowdin and his wife. "Till past threescore and ten," says Miss Howard, "Esquire Cowdin was strong in heart and intellect. He was keenly alive to the interests of the town of Fitchburg—the schools, the militia and the church. He was honored as 'one of the richest men of his time', and the great secret of his success and power was his unswerving integrity." He died at Fitchburg, April 22, 1792, and was buried in the old South Street burying ground. A monument of Quincy granite was erected to his memory by his grandson, John Cowdin, of Boston, and occupies a conspicuous place on the summit of Laurel Hill.

He married (first) November 19, 1748, Experience Gray, of Worcester. She died April 3, 1760. He married (second) October 2, 1761, Hannah Craig, of Rutland. "She was a woman of sterling character and worthy of her honored husband. * * * All traditions represent Mrs. Cowdin as endowed with strong mental power and the physical health to make that power effective in many directions." She administered her husband's estate and brought up five minor children. She spent her last years with her daughter, Mrs. Jacob Upton, and died at Fitchburg, July 30, 1822. The births of the children are recorded in Fitchburg in the father's own hand, viz:

Thomas, born March 7, 1754, at Worcester; Experience, January 10, 1757, at Worcester; Hannah, June 23, 1763, at Worcester. Born at Fitchburg: Joseph, July 5, 1765; Angier, mentioned below; Daniel, October 30, 1769; James, March 30, 1772.

(III) Angier, son of Captain Thomas Cowdin, was born at Fitchburg, July 13, 1767. A story of his youth is related by Miss Howard. He saw a bear in the woods and ran home for a gun, but his father refused to let him have it. The servant Nancy got the gun for the boy, however, and he hurried back and shot the bear, which was brought to the Cowdin home by some woodsmen. The only comment of the Squire when he was convinced that the lad had shot the bear was to say to Nancy, "You are a curious girl." He settled in Jamaica, Vermont. He married (first), Sally Farwell, who died in 1794 with her infant daughter. Married (second) Abbie ———, born in Fitchburg in 1767, died in 1830. Children of second wife: Angier, died 1795; Abel, died March 3, 1866; Jephthan R., born November 14, 1799, died December 20, 1864; Mary F., born July 29, 1801, died April 30, 1862; Martha F., twin of Mary F., born July 29, 1801, died October 10, 1856; Hannah D., born July 25, 1803, died August 15, 1875; General Robert, born September 18, 1805, died July 9, 1874, colonel of one of the first regiments to start for Washington after Fort Sumter was fired upon; John, born December 11, 1807, died March 10, 1885; Samantha, born April 9, 1809, died February 28, 1844; Caroline, born September 17, 1812, died January 3, 1832; Sarah E., born April 24, 1815, died September 15, 1833; Sylvia C., born May 13, 1817, died December 28, 1862; Elliot Christopher, mentioned below.

(IV) Elliot Christopher, son of Angier Cowdin, was born at Jamaica, Vermont, August 9, 1819. His father died when he was a child and during his boyhood he was under the care of his brother John, a Boston merchant and importer, at whose house he lived for more than twenty years. He attended the common schools, and at the age of sixteen years became a clerk in the store of Allen & Mann, dealers in ribbons and millinery, Boston. After he had been with this house for nine years, the senior partner died and he was admitted to the firm, the name of which became W. H. Mann & Company in 1844. One of the factors that contributed materially to his success in life was the education he received as a member of the Mercantile Library Association, a club of merchants' clerks then located in School street. The members declaimed, wrote compositions and had lecture courses. In October, 1842, he was elected treasurer.

In 1846 he made his first trip abroad to purchase goods for the firm and from that time as long as he lived he made frequent voyages to Europe, from New York to Paris, Lyons, St. Etienne and Basle. He crossed the Atlantic eighty-six times. He was in Paris during the French revolution of 1848. In the spring of 1853 he withdrew from the firm of W. H. Mann & Company, and established a new firm in New York under the name of Elliot C. Cowdin & Company with a branch in Paris, and he made his home in Paris and attended to the buying. Business grew and prospered. He entertained many American friends at his home in Paris, and there Charles Sumner was a guest when he sought rest and recuperation after the assault by Senator Brooks.

When the financial panic of 1857 came, he made haste to return to New York. But few merchants and manufacturers escaped failure and he expected to see his fortune wiped out, when he found that three-quarters of the customers of the firm had suspended or were unable to meet their obligations, but he weathered the storm and maintained his credit. He demonstrated the possession of that union of probity, firmness, integrity and sagacity which inspired confidence. In the autumn of 1858 he made his home in New York City and afterward made two trips abroad each year.

When the civil war came he gave his hearty support to the government. He was a Republican and made his first political speech as president of the Republican festival in New York, February 22, 1860, and was active in organizing the Union League Club of New York, the purpose of which was to make patriotism fashionable and bring into activity in the cause of freedom and union the forces of wealth and culture. "The tremendous pressure which the Union League Club of New York, strong in wealth, high in social position, dominant in intelligence, vehement in patriotism, merciless in hunting traitors to their last hiding places, brought to bear on the latent treason peeping forth in some of the highest circles of New York society has never been adequately recognized." Early in 1861 Mr. Cowdin was in Paris and his office was a center for the Union Americans, and he presided at the great American Union breakfast, May 29, 1861, at the Grand Hotel du Louvre, making the opening speech. He kept a sharp eye on the American representatives and in at least one instance detected a disloyal official. In the fall he returned to New York, visited the army in the field and

Elliott C. Cowdin

made a stirring patriotic address. In 1862 he was nominated as the Union candidate for congress in the eighth New York district, but was defeated. He was appointed one of the commissioners of the United States to the great Paris Exposition of 1867, and he prepared a report on silk and silk manufactures that proved to be of great value to American merchants and manufacturers. In 1869 he removed his family to Paris, and in May of that year he presided at a farewell banquet given by Americans to General John A. Dix. Hon. E. B. Washburne, who succeeded General Dix as ambassador, became a valued friend, and when Mr. Cowdin died, he wrote: "I never had a more sincere, unselfish and devoted friend, personal and political. As a husband, father, friend and citizen, Mr. Cowdin was almost without a peer." Mr. Cowdin came to know the Americans in Paris and the Americans visiting that city better than anyone else, for he kept open house and his dinners and receptions were the most graceful and genial acts of hospitality which the great city afforded to Americans who were only for a few weeks resident in it. When Paris was besieged Mr. Cowdin's family was on the last train that left Paris, and afterward he was in Paris during the desperate days of the Commune. He observed affairs closely and afterward gave a very valuable and instructive lecture on "The War, the Commune and the International," at Cooper Union, New York. In 1876 he was prevailed upon to accept a nomination to the state assembly, and he was elected. He introduced a bill to reduce the excessive taxation of bank stock in New York, and it was defeated by a narrow margin. This legislature, it is said, was one of the worst in temper and disposition of any in the history of the state. Mr. Cowdin supported otherwise progressive legislation, but appears to have been a generation ahead of the majority of his colleagues, and his measures met with gross personal abuse and malignant vituperation. He sought to introduce better business methods, and effect sensible economy in the administration of New York City, and he tried to organize an effective street cleaning department. Disappointed at the result of his year's work, he declined re-election.

In 1877 he retired from commercial business and went to live at Mount Kisco on a pretty farm he had bought there, and he set to work with vigor and enthusiasm to transform it into a country place of elegance and beauty as well as a highly productive farm. He was one of the active members of the Bedford Farmers' Club and one of the reunions of the club was held at his house shortly before he died. After he became a resident of Westchester county, he was urged to take the nomination for congress on the death of Hon. Alexander Smith, of Yonkers, but he declined the honor, though he took an active part in the campaign and presided at Cooper Institute at the merchants' meeting when Senator Blaine spoke.

Mr. Cowdin died at his New York home, 14 West Twenty-first street, New York, April 12, 1880, after a short illness of Bright's disease. The firm which Mr. Cowdin established was engaged chiefly in importing silks; after his withdrawal it became Hanson, Wood & Company. Mr. Cowdin was a leading member for many years of the New York chamber of commerce and was chairman of the executive committee at the time of his death. He was vice-president of the Union League Club; had been president of the New England Society; was a member of the Century Club; director of the Metropolitan Bank, the Hanover Fire Insurance Company and of the Woman's Hospital; member of the Westchester Agricultural Society.

He was the intimate and trusted friend of such statesmen as Sumner, Greeley and Henry Wilson. In a letter to Mrs. Cowdin, General Sherman wrote: "Will you permit me to intrude for a moment on your sacred threshold to mingle my grief with yours on learning the death of your good husband. You will remember that he was always kind to us who fought for our country in its day of peril, that I have been more than once your guest, notably in Paris, and that I am indebted to Mr. Cowdin for many acts of great kindness in public. Among all my acquaintances I can recall no more ardent, enthusiastic and generous patriot than Mr. Cowdin, and I lament his death as a national loss."

The *Evening Mail* paid this tribute to his citizenship: "For the public, the one great lesson of Mr. Cowdin's life was the fact that he realized and performed the duties of a citizen. If New York had twenty such men, the fight against municipal misrule and bad State legislation would be far more hopeful. He gave his money freely for all good causes. But he did far more than that. He gave himself. And he found a noble satisfaction in doing his duty as a citizen. He found in political and public activities an unfailing stimulus, a keen delight and a self-rewarding toil."

A memoir by E. P. Whipple published shortly after Mr. Cowdin died contains in addition to a biography, the funeral sermon by Rev. Dr. Bellows, newspaper obituaries and memorial editorials and resolutions and messages of condolence. He and his family attended All Souls' Church.

He married, September 13, 1853, Sarah Katharine Waldron, of Boston, born February 4, 1827, died December 6, 1903, daughter of Samuel Wallis and Martha (Melcher) Waldron. Children: 1. Katherine Waldron, born June 5, 1856; married (first) Dr. Gaspar Griswold; (second) Henry Marquand. 2. John Elliot, mentioned below. 3. Martha Waldron, born November 15, 1859; married Robert Bacon, formerly secretary of state of the United States, now United States Ambassador to France; children: Robert Low, born July 23, 1884; Gaspar Griswold, born March 7, 1886, Elliot Cowdin, born July 4, 1888; Martha, July 4, 1890. 4. Winthrop, born September 28, 1861; married (first) Lena, daughter of Bishop Henry C. Potter, (second) Lelia, daughter of Dr. Harrison, of Virginia. 5. Alice, born September 5, 1866; married Hamilton L. Hoppin; children: Hamilton Howland; Geoffrey, died November, 1903. 6. Elliot Channing, born March 28, 1872.

(V) John Elliot, son of Elliot Christopher Cowdin, was born in Boston, March 22, 1858. He received his early education in private schools in New York City. In 1869 he went abroad and studied in France and Germany, returning in 1875 to enter Harvard College from which he was graduated in the class of 1879 with the degree of Bachelor of Arts. He engaged in the manufacture of silk in New York City, as a partner in the firm of Johnson, Cowdin & Company. The business has been very successful and continues under the same name, though the senior partner died in 1887. In politics Mr. Cowdin is a Republican, in religion a Unitarian. He is a member of the University Club, the Harvard Club, the Union League Club and other clubs of New York City, and of the New England Society of New York. He resides at 13 Gramercy Park, New York.

He married, May 20, 1885, Gertrude Cheever, born May 16, 1863, in New York City, daughter of John H. and Anna (Dow) Cheever. Children: 1. Elliot Christopher, born in New York City, March 3, 1886. 2. Ethel, April 16, 1887; married, June 4, 1910, Charles Morgan, son of Charles Morgan, of New York; child: Charles Morgan, born March 18, 1911. 3. John Cheever, March 17, 1889.

SNOWDEN

Although the Snowdens of Philadelphia, Pennsylvania, claim no New England ancestry in their paternal line they trace, through intermarriage, to the oldest and most historic families in New England—the Hookers, Fitz Randolphs, Leetes, Smiths and many others of note. The Snowdens herein recorded spring from an English ancestor, whose family, although perhaps originally founded in Scotland, was long seated in Yorkshire, West Riding. Sir Walter Scott, in the "Lady of the Lake," names King James as the "Knight of Snowden" and Snowdens paid the "hearth tax" in Yorkshire as far back as Queen Elizabeth who began to reign in 1558. The name of Snowden is yet found in Yorkshire and is not an uncommon one. The American ancestor, John Snowden, was the son of William, but no record of him is found, save in papers of his son John, who speaks of land inherited from his father, William, lying in Delaware county, Pennsylvania. He probably lived and died in England, and may have invested through his son in Pennsylvania lands. He had three children: William, settled at Burlington, New Jersey, married Hannah ———, who survived him and married (second) Moses Lippincott; John, of whom further; Ann, who married John Pancoast.

(II) John, son of William Snowden, was born in Knaresboro, Yorkshire, England, in 1632, died in Philadelphia, Pennsylvania, in May, 1736. He came to America where the first definite knowledge of him is found when in 1677 he signed in a list of the proprietors of West Jersey, but he was in Pennsylvania prior to that date as there are land records in Delaware county showing his ownership of land there at an earlier date. Later he settled on lands at Burlington, New Jersey, probably to be near old friends from Yorkshire who had settled there. He also owned land across the river in Falls township, Pennsylvania, and in Philadelphia. He was associate judge of Bucks county, Pennsylvania, 1704-1712; member of the house of assembly from Bucks county, 1715-1717-1718; justice of the peace; moved from Bucks county to Philadelphia about 1720, where he remained until death. He had been brought up in the Established Church but later had joined the Quakers in Yorkshire and in New Jersey and was a member of the Burlington Meeting. When the trouble arose in that meeting with Keith he seems to have sided with the "Keithians". Later he became a Baptist and was immersed in 1704. He married in Burlington Meeting, 2mo., 13 day, 1682, Ann Barrett, probably a widow, and daughter of Benjamin and Margaret Scott. She died 1688 and was buried at what is now Fourth and Arch streets, Philadelphia. He married (second), 1718, Elizabeth Swift, evidently a daughter of Joseph

Swift, a prominent man and a leader in the Keith division. She is mentioned in his will. She married (second) William Fletcher. Children of John Snowden, all by first wife: Ann, born 1683, was unmarried and living at the time of her father's death; Margaret, born 1684, married ———— Priestley; John, of whom further; William, married Abigail Woolley; Mary, married, 6mo., 8 day, 1726, Benjamin Wright.

(III) John (2), son of John (1) Snowden, "the founder", was born in Burlington, New Jersey, 1685, died in Philadelphia, March 24, 1751. He owned large tanning interests, farm property and Philadelphia property at Second and Dock streets that remained in the family for four generations. He was one of the founders of the First Presbyterian Church of Philadelphia, and the first regularly ordained elder of the Presbyterian church in this country. He represented the first church in the Synods of 1717-1718-1719-1721-1725 and 1727. He married (first), November 10, 1709, Mary, daughter of Christopher Taylor, a leading citizen of Chester county. He married (second), October 4, 1720, in Princeton, New Jersey, Mrs. Ruth (Fitz Randolph) Harrison, widow of Edward Harrison and daughter of Benjamin Fitz Randolph. She was born at Piscataway, New Jersey, April 8, 1695, died September 25, 1780, at Maidenhead (now Lawrenceville, New Jersey). Benjamin, her father, was born in Plymouth colony at Barnstable, Massachusetts, 1663, died in Princeton, New Jersey, October 5, 1746, son of Edward Fitz Randolph, born 1615, in Nottinghamshire, England, died at Piscataway, New Jersey, 1676. He was one of the early Pilgrims and married Elizabeth, daughter of Thomas Blossom, an Englishman who joined the Puritans at Leyden, sailed in the "Speedwell" for America, but went back when the "Speedwell" was found unseaworthy. He later came to America in the "Mayflower" on her last voyage. Elizabeth, his daughter was born in Leyden, Holland, and came to America with her father, who became one of the founders of Plymouth. Benjamin Fitz Randolph married Sarah Dennis, born at Piscataway July 18, 1673, died at Princeton, New Jersey, November 22, 1732, a descendant of the early New England families of Dennis, Howland and Bloomfield.

Children of John (2) Snowden and his first wife, Mary Taylor: James, born March 8, 1711, married Catherine, daughter of Caleb North; Rebecca, born February, 1713, married, 1730, Charles Edgar; Mary, born 1715, married (first), 1735, David Murray, (second) Matthias Keen, a captain of the revolution and burgess of Bristol, Pennsylvania; Anna, died

in infancy; John, born 1718, died 1772, married, 1740, Rachel Hendrick. Children of John (2) Snowden and his second wife, Ruth (Fitz Randolph-Harrison) Benjamin, born 1721, died 1748; Jedidiah, born September 21, 1724, died 1797, married Mary Bell. He is the ancestor of Dr. Weir Mitchell, the famous physician of Philadelphia, and well known author of historical novels; Isaac, of whom further; Rachel, died in childhood.

(IV) Isaac, son of John (2) Snowden and his second wife, Ruth (Fitz Randolph-Harrison) was born in Philadelphia, April 14, 1732, died in Middletown township, Chester county, Pennsylvania, December 26, 1809. His tombstone yet standing is remarkable for its elaborate and well chosen words of eulogy. He owned a great deal of land in and around Princeton, New Jersey, and was an early friend and patron of both the town and college. He owned tanneries in Philadelphia and a parcel of land extending from the north side of Spruce street to the south side of Chestnut street, and from the west side of Ninth street to the east side of Eleventh street. He made Philadelphia his home until the British occupied Philadelphia when he took up his residence in Princeton. He was a distinguished patriot and civil officer of Philadelphia, and in Princeton is remembered for his early connection with Princeton and as a trustee for sixteen years of Princeton College. He was quartermaster of the Fourth Battalion of Philadelphia Associators in 1775, and in 1777 under Colonel Kane; although himself under arms he enlisted and paid the cost of keeping two men in the field that he might always be represented. From 1777 to 1779 he was commissioner to sign continental money and his name may be seen on many bills yet in existence. From 1780 to 1782 he was treasurer of Philadelphia county and city. He was equally prominent in the Presbyterian church, and was the first treasurer of the United Synod of Pennsylvania and New Jersey; first treasurer of the first General Assembly of the Presbyterian Church in the United States; charter member of the Second Presbyterian Church of Philadelphia, and member of the committee that prepared the form of government for the Presbyterian Church in the United States.

As stated he served sixteen years as trustee of Princeton College and with Mr. Bayard furnished the funds to send its president, Rev. John Witherspoon, to Europe in the interest of the college. He was a member of the social organization, "The State in Schuylkill," and his name appears on its first list of members, after the granting of its charter. The club was formed by wealthy gentlemen to acquire lands for fishing and shooting purposes and as a purely social body. It is still maintained as a social club, membership being derived by inheritance, no new members being admitted in any other way. Isaac Snowden was a leader in his city, maintained an elegant, hospitable mansion and in social life was very prominent.

He married (first), March 8, 1759, Mary Parker, born September 8, 1726, died May 29, 1761, a native-born Philadelphian, daughter of Benjamin Parker. He married (second), March 17, 1763, in Old Christ Episcopal Church, Philadelphia (where his first marriage was also solemnized), Mary (Cox) McCall, born 1735, died June 30, 1806, widow of Samuel McCall and daughter of William Cox (also Coxe) and Mary Francis. William Cox, was one of the early counsellors of Philadelphia, was born in England and educated in Holland. Children of Isaac Snowden and his first wife: 1. Benjamin Parker, born 1760, was lost at sea ; he was a graduate of Princeton and left a will which was not probated until three years after his loss was reported. 2. Mary, died in infancy. Children of Isaac Snowden and his second wife: 3. Isaac (2), born 1764, a graduate of Princeton College, and an elder of the Second Presbyterian Church of Philadelphia ; married Cornelia Clarkson. 4. Rev. Gilbert Tennent, born 1766, died 1797 ; graduate of Princeton, and an eloquent, forceful minister of the Presbyterian church. 5. Rev. Samuel Finley, born 1767, died 1845 ; graduate of Princeton and a prominent minister of the Presbyterian church ; married Susan Breese ; descendants are yet found in New Jersey, but are mostly in the south, particularly . Tennessee. 6. Rev. Nathaniel Randolph, of whom further. 7. Rev. Charles Tennent, born 1772, died at an advanced age ; was a graduate of Princeton and a minister of the Presbyterian church ; married Sarah Malcolm, daughter of General Malcolm, of New Jersey. 8. Mary, born 1774, died 1774. 9. William, born 1776, died unmarried.

(V) Rev. Nathaniel Randolph Snowden, son of Isaac Snowden by his second wife Mary (Cox-McCall) Snowden, was born in Philadelphia, January 17, 1770, died in Freeport, Armstrong county, Pennsylvania, November 2, 1851. He was a graduate of Princeton College, class of 1787, studied divinity and was ordained a minister of the Presbyterian church in 1792. His first pastorate was over the church at Harrisburg, Pennsylvania, where he also had charge of the churches at Derry and Paxtang, preaching in all every Sunday. His was the first English church in Harrisburg. He was a tutor for a time at Dickinson College, Carlisle, which in its early days was a Presbyterian college. He remained at Harrisburg from 1792 to 1803, then was for several years at Middletown and Williamsport, Pennsylvania. He lived for a number of years in Philadelphia, retired from the ministry, then settled in Armstrong county, at Freeport, where he died. He was of a kindly, sympathetic nature and accomplished a great deal of good for his Master's cause. He married, May 24, 1792, at Carlisle, Pennsylvania, Sarah Gustine, born June 21, 1775, in New York City, died April 2, 1856, at Freeport, Armstrong county, daughter of Lemuel (2) Gustine, born 1749, at Saybrook, Connecticut, died 1807, at Carlisle (see Gustine V). Children of Rev. Nathaniel R. Snowden: 1. Dr. Isaac Wayne, of whom further. 2. Dr. Charles Gustine, born 1796, died 1868 ; studied medicine and spent his life engaged in the practice of his profession at Freeport, Armstrong county, Pennsylvania. He married (first) Sarah Scott, (second) Margaret Given. 3. Dr. Lemuel Gustine, born 1798, died 1842. He was a regularly qualified physician. 4. Samuel, died young. 5. Mary Parker, born 1801, died 1889 ; married James Thompson, chief justice of the supreme court of Pennsylvania. 6. Nathaniel Duffield, born 1803, died 1864. He was also a regularly accredited physician, in practice all his active life. He married Jane McClelland, and their only living son is Major General George Randolph Snowden, of Philadelphia. 7. James Ross, of whom further.

(VI) James Ross, son of Nathaniel R. and Sarah (Gustine) Snowden, was born December 9, 1809, near Chester, Pennsylvania, died in Bucks county, March 21, 1878. He studied under the direction of his father at Dickinson College, Carlisle, Pennsylvania, later embraced the profession of law and at the age nineteen years was admitted to the bar. He located at Franklin, Pennsylvania, where he practiced until his entrance into public and political life. He was a Democrat in politics and was chosen a member of the assembly from Venango county. In 1842 and 1844 he was speaker of the House. In 1847 treasurer of the United States, and during 1847 and 1848 also treasurer of the United States mint at Philadelphia. In 1852 he became solicitor for the Pennsylvania railroad and removed his residence to Pittsburgh. In 1853 he was appointed director of the United States mint at Philadelphia, continuing until 1861. At that time the director of the Philadelphia mint was director of all United States mints. From 1861 to 1873 he was prothonotary of the supreme court of Pennsylvania. In the latter year he returned to the practice of his profession, locating in Philadelphia. He was a high authority on mint management, and when the government began an investigation into the condition of the several mints he was appointed to assist in the investigation. He was the author of "Mint Manual of Coins of all Nations", "Washington Memorials", "Coins of the Bible", "Life of Gyantwahia" (Cornplanter), and of innumerable pamphlets, etc., on his favorite subjects, coins and coinage and George Washington. He was colonel of a volunteer militia regiment of Pennsylvania troops, and in 1845 president of the State Military Convention and wrote the memorial that brought about much needed reforms in the military establishment of the state. He received from Jefferson College the degree of Master of Arts and from Washington and Jefferson that of Doctor of Laws. He was an elder of the Presbyterian church belonging to the old Tabernacle Church of Philadelphia. He was a member of the State in Schuylkill; the Masonic order; was corresponding secretary of the Pennsylvania Historical Society; member Numismatic Society, Philadelphia Academy of Natural Science, Presbyterian Historical Society, and others of professional and scientific nature.

He married, September 13, 1848, Susan Engle Patterson, born in Philadelphia, October 19, 1823, died there February 11, 1897, daughter of General Robert Patterson, of Philadelphia, the hero of many battles of the war of 1812, the war with Mexico and the civil war. General Patterson was born January 12, 1792, in county Tyrone, Ireland, died in Philadelphia, August 8, 1881. He was the son of Francis Patterson, an Irish patriot who escaped from Ireland to America, a price being offered for him "dead or alive" by the British government. He fled to America with his only son Robert (General) in 1798. He married Mary Graham. Both the Pattersons and Grahams trace their ancestry to the famous Scotch families bearing their names. General Robert Patterson became an eminent business man of Philadelphia and from a youth was filled with patriotism and military enthusiasm. He was captain and colonel of militia and served in the United States Regular Army during three wars. He was commissioned first lieutenant, Twenty-second Regiment Infantry, April 5, 1813; captain Thirty-second Regiment, June, 1813; serving at Lundy's Lane and in other battles of the war until 1814. He was commissioned Major General of Volunteers July 7, 1846, and was second in command during the Mexican war, gaining a high reputation as a military commander. At the outbreak of the civil war he

again offered his sword to his country and was assigned a command. At that early period, with all the commanders hampered and often harassed by the authorities at Washington, few successes came to the Union army. He was in command of Union forces at the first battle of Bull Run, and although he fought that battle bravely and well, his orders were of such a nature that success was impossible. Much has been written derogatory to the old hero's part in that battle, but he had the commendation of President Lincoln and the great generals of the war. He was a gallant, courtly gentleman, and at his mansion on Locust street, Philadelphia, (where now stands the Pennsylvania Historical Society Building) maintained a generous hospitality, celebrating every year the taking of the city of Mexico with his old companions-in-arms who gathered from all sections to join with him and live again that glorious day. General Patterson married December 12, 1817, Sarah Ann Engle, born in Philadelphia, April 2, 1792, died there in June, 1875, daughter of James Engle, a patriot of the revolution, who enlisted at the age of nineteen years; was sergeant, ensign and second lieutenant, Third Regiment Pennsylvania Line; in 1809 was speaker of the Pennsylvania house of assembly; married Margaret Adam, a descendant of the Grahams of Montrose, Scotland, and of the "Quaker Jones" family. James was a son of John and Ann (Witmer) Engle; John the son of Paul (2) and Willimker (Tyson) Engle; Paul (2), son of Paul (1) Engle, was elected burgess of Germantown in 1703, but declined on account of Mennonite principles. Children of General Robert Patterson: 1. Mary Ann Engle, born 1818, died 1874; married General John Joseph Abercrombie. 2. James Engle, died young. 3. Francis Engle, born 1821, died 1861; a veteran of the Mexican war and brigadier-general in command of Pennsylvania troops during the civil war. His was the first command to follow the Sixth Massachusetts through Baltimore, going through unmolested. 4. Susan Engle, mentioned above.

Children of James Ross Snowden: 1. Sarah Patterson, married John Stephenson Mitchell, a descendant of Governor Jennings, of New Jersey; the Stephensons of New Jersey and the Kinzey and Mitchell families of Bucks county, Pennsylvania. Mrs. Mitchell survives her husband, a highly cultured, patriotic lady, residing in Philadelphia. She is historian of Pennsylvania Chapter, Daughter of Founders and Patriots of America; member of Colonial Dames of America; Philadelphia Chapter, Daughters of the Revolution; member of the Pennsylvania State Society of Daughters of 1812; regent of General Robert Patterson Chapter, Daughters of 1812; member of the Guadaloupe Club (a society formed of descendants of the Mexican war); dame of the Military Order of the Loyal Legion; member of the Pennsylvania Society of New England Women; president of the Plastic Club (art); member of the board of managers of the Fellowship of Pennsylvania Academy of Fine Arts. 2. Robert Patterson, assistant engineer Camden & Amboy railroad; married Mary Dilbert. 3. James Ross, died young. 4. Frank Patterson, deceased. 5. Gertrude, died young. 6. Mary Thompson, married William Stansfield. 7. Llewellyn, twin of Mary Thompson, deceased. 8. Charles A., died in infancy. 9. Louisa Hortense, graduate of University of Pennsylvania, Bachelor of Science, with post-graduate courses at the Sorbonne, Paris; Leipsic, Germany, and the University of Pennsylvania; received the Woman's Table at Naples, and is still pursuing courses of study both at home and abroad; a resident of Philadelphia.

(VI) Dr. Isaac Wayne Snowden, eldest son of Rev. Nathaniel R. Snowden, was born in Harrisburg, Pennsylvania, in 1794, died at Hogestown, Cumberland county, Pennsylvania, in 1850. He was given a good education and chose the profession of medicine which he successfully practiced all his life in Cumberland county. He was the first of his brothers to adopt that profession, which was later followed by them all with the exception of James Ross Snowden. He was a Democrat in politics and a member of the Presbyterian church. He married Margery Bines Loudon, daughter of Archibald Loudon of Cumberland county. Children: 1. Nathaniel Randolph, died unmarried. 2. Sarah Gustine, married Thomas Stewart; resides in Ohio. 3. Maude, unmarried. 4. Archibald Loudon, of further mention.

(VII) Archibald Loudon, son of Dr. Isaac Wayne Snowden, was born in Cumberland county, Pennsylvania, August 11, 1837. Following a preliminary academic education he entered Jefferson, later known as Washington and Jefferson College, in western Pennsylvania, from whence he was graduated Bachelor of Arts, class of 1856. In 1880 his alma mater bestowed the honorary degree of Master of Arts and in 1902 Doctor of Laws. After completing his collegiate course he determined upon the profession of law and entered the University of Pennsylvania Law School, but was destined for a far different career. At the solicitation of his uncle, James Ross Snowden, then director of the United

States mint at Philadelphia, he accepted the appointment of register of the mint. In 1866 he was promoted chief coiner, a position he continuously filled until 1877. In the latter year he received unsought the appointment of postmaster of Philadelphia, by President Grant, holding until 1879. His administration of the Philadelphia postoffice was strictly a business one and gave great satisfaction. He returned to the mint in 1879 as superintendent, receiving the appointment from President Hayes, who twice offered him the directorship of all United States mints and was twice refused. He was unanimously confirmed by the senate as superintendent of the Philadelphia mint and entered upon his long career as chief of that institution, so noted a historic landmark of Philadelphia. As chief coiner and superintendent, his services covered a period of twenty-eight years. These were years of great advancement for the mint. Colonel Snowden installed better machinery and appliances for more rapid, accurate and artistic coinage, some of which he invented while others he suggested. He became a recognized authority on coinage and is the author of many published papers relating to these subjects.

He continued superintendent of the mint until 1885, when President Cleveland appointed a successor agreeing with himself in political faith. In 1889 Colonel Snowden was appointed by President Harrison, minister resident and consul general to Greece, Roumania and Servia. Shortly after his appointment this mission was raised to that of envoy extraordinary and minister plenipotentiary. He served under this appointment 1889-1891, with headquarters at Athens, Greece. In the latter year he was appointed United States minister to Spain and spent the years 1891-1893 at the Spanish capital, Madrid. Some grave diplomatic questions arose during his term of office, which with others of long standing he successfully settled. On his retirement from Madrid the Queen Regent in recognition of his valuable services to the two governments conferred upon him the Grand Cordon of Isabella the Catholic, one of the highest orders of Spain. Later, when a private citizen and free to accept honors without the consent of congress, he received from the King of Greece, the Grand Cordon of the Saviour, the highest order in Greece, as a mark of the personal friendship of King George. From the King of Roumania he received the Grand Cordon of the Crown of Roumania. On retiring from the diplomatic service Colonel Snowden returned to Philadelphia, which has ever since been his home. He has also rendered his country military service. At the outbreak of the civil war he organized a regiment of volunteers and was commissioned lieutenant-colonel, and Pennsylvania's quota being full the regiment was assigned to service in regiments from other states. He was urged to return to the mint in Philadelphia, by the director, and did so, but subsequently participated in the skirmishes preliminary to the battle of Gettysburg, as a member of the First City Troop of Philadelphia, an organization with which he was connected actively for fifteen years, passing through all subordinate ranks to that of colonel in command, commissioned 1877. He is an orator and writer of national repute and as stated, is a recognized authority on matters relating to coins and coinage. His services to the city of Philadelphia have been varied and continuous. He has been president of the Fairmount Park board of commissioners, and was in entire management of the great parade on December 16, 1879, that welcomed General Grant on his return from his trip around the world. For his efficient service in organizing that great parade and for the splendid work accomplished he received the cordial thanks of the city authorities. Another great public event with which Colonel Snowden was prominently connected was that to which he was appointed by the Constitutional Centennial Commission. He organized the industrial and civic departments of the great processional celebration which took place in Philadelphia, September 15-17, 1887. Both these parades were unparalleled successes and most creditable to Colonel Snowden and his city. He is a member of the American Philosophical Society and other organizations of a literary character. His clubs are the State in Schuylkill, St. Andrews, Philadelphia and the Union League. He is an ex-president of the Fire Association of Philadelphia and of the United Fire Underwriters of America. He is yet actively interested in business, occupying offices in the Land Title Building. His residence is 1812 Spruce street, Philadelphia. He is a Republican in politics.

Colonel Snowden married, February 16, 1864, Elizabeth Robinson, daughter of Isaac Robinson Smith, of Philadelphia.

(Gustine and Allied Families).

Sarah Gustine, wife of Rev. Nathaniel Randolph Snowden, was a lineal descendant of Augustin Jean, born on the Isle of Jersey at the village of Saint Ouen, 1647, died 1720, at Falmouth (Portland), Maine, son of Edward Jean, born in October, 1597, died November 12, 1674. Edward Jean, married, April 25, 1638, Esther Lerossignol, born at L'Etacq,

Isle of Jersey, January 25, 1612. Children: Katherine, born October 2, 1640; Augustin, of further mention; Marguerite, born November 24, 1656; Edmund, April 16, ――.

(II) Augustin, son of Edward Jean, was born at Saint Ouen, on the Isle of Jersey, January 9, 1647. He came to the American colonies settling at Watertown, Massachusetts. He anglicized his name to John Augustin, which through many changes finally became John Gustin or Gustine. He fought in King Philip's war in Captain Turner's company at Brookfield, and under Captain Beeres at Marlboro, ranking as sergeant or acting sergeant. He married, January 10, 1678, at Watertown, Massachusetts, Elizabeth Browne, born May 26, 1657, at Cambridge, daughter of John Browne, "the Scotchman", born presumably in Scotland in 1631, died in Watertown in 1697; married, April 24, 1655, by Captain Atherton, Esther Makepeace; children of John Browne: John (2), born 1656, died young; Elizabeth, of previous mention; Sarah, July 18, 1661; Mary, December 19, 1662; John (3), November 27, 1664; Hester, 1667, died 1677; Thomas, 1669; Daniel, 1671; Deborah, 1673; Abigail, 1675; Joseph, 1677. Esther Makepeace was a daughter of Thomas Makepeace, born in England, in 1592, died in Boston, Massachusetts, 1667; his children were: Thomas; William; Hannah; Mary; Esther, married John Browne; Wait-a-While, married Josiah Cooper; Opportunity. Children of John Gustine, born at Lynn, Massachusetts, and Falmouth, Maine: Samuel, of whom further: Sarah; John, born in 1691; Abigail, December, 1693, married Zachariah Brazier; Ebenezer, born 1696; Thomas, March 5, 1699; David, February 6, 1703.

(III) Samuel, son of John Gustine, was born about 1680 at Falmouth (Portland), Maine. He married at Stonington, Connecticut, June 12, 1712, Abigail Shaw, born in 1695. Children: Abigail, born 1713; Samuel (2), 1718; Stephen, 1720; Elizabeth, 1722; Lemuel, of whom further.

(IV) Lemuel, son of Samuel Gustine, was born in Stonington, Connecticut, 1724. He served as land commissioner and in other public capacities. He married and had four children: 1. Lemuel (2), of whom further. 2. Dr. Joel, served in the revolution and fought at Bunker Hill. 3. Hannah, married Archibald Snowden, of Carlisle, Pennsylvania, (another Snowden branch.) 4. A daughter, married William Thompson.

(V) Lemuel (2), son of Lemuel (1) Gustine, was born in Saybrook, Connecticut, 1749, died at Carlisle, Pennsylvania, 1807. He was a regular physician and a surgeon in the revolutionary war. He later settled in the Wyoming valley of Pennsylvania with his wife, and daughter Sarah. He was aide to Colonel Zebulon Butler and under Colonel Nathan Denison, who commanded the left wing of the patriot forces at the battle and massacre of Wyoming, July 3, 1778. He signed the articles of capitulation as a witness and promised with all the surrendered troops not to again take up arms in the conflict between Great Britain and the colonies. He had made some good friends among the Indians, probably through his healing art, who advised him to get away quickly, warning him of what later followed. His wife had died a month previous, leaving him with a three year old daughter, Sarah, and an infant of one month. These he placed in a boat with him, escaping down the river to Harrisburg—the infant dying before or just after reaching that city. Sarah lived to a good old age and was the last survivor of the Wyoming massacre. Dr. Lemuel Gustine is incorrectly called Samuel in the records and on the Wyoming battle monument. He spent his latter years in western Pennsylvania, near his only daughter, Sarah, wife of Rev. Nathaniel Snowden. Dr. Gustine married Susanna Smith, born at White Plains, New York, November 17, 1750, died at Forty Fort, Wyoming Valley, Pennsylvania, June 12, 1778, daughter of Dr. William Hooker Smith, a well known character in the Wyoming Valley. Children: Sarah, married Rev. Nathaniel R. Snowden (see Snowden V), and Susan, the babe before mentioned.

(The Smith Line).

(I) William Smith was born in England; married, September 4, 1661, Elizabeth Hartley, of Newport Pegnel, Buckinghamshire, England, of a distinguished English family of lawyers.

(II) Thomas, son of William Smith, was born at Newport Pegnel, Buckinghamshire, England, September 19, 1675, died at New York City, November 14, 1745. He came to New York in 1715 and was the founder of the First Presbyterian Church in that city. By the advice of the trustees of Yale College, he secured the services of Jonathan Edwards, then a youth of nineteen years, who became the first pastor of the First Presbyterian Church of New York City, which proved to be the first steppingstone to his wonderful career as a minister. Thomas Smith married, May 13, 1696, in England, Susanna Odell, who died before her husband came to New York.

Children: William, born October 5, 1697, father of William Smith, the historian of

New York; Thomas; Rev. John, of whom further; Odell, died in infancy.

(III) Rev. John Smith, son of Thomas Smith, was born May 5, 1702, at Newport Pegnel, Buckinghamshire, England, died at White Plains, New York, February 26, 1771. He was a graduate of Yale and a noted physician and minister of the Gospel (see Dexter's "Yale Graduates"). He married, May 6, 1724, Mehitable Hooker, born May 1, 1704, at Guilford, Connecticut, died at White Plains, New York, September 15, 1775, daughter of Judge James Hooker (see Hooker).

(IV) Dr. William Hooker Smith, son of Rev. John Smith, was born at Rye, New York, May 23, 1725, died July 17, 1815, in Luzerne county, Pennsylvania. He was a surgeon and physician at Rye, and in 1772 transferred his business and practice to the Wyoming Valley of Pennsylvania. He was an ardent patriot and on May 15, 1775, enlisted in the Third Company, First Regiment Connecticut Troops. He served with his regiment in the Northern New York, Lake Champlain and Canadian expeditions; re-enlisted in December, 1775, in the Tenth Connecticut Regiment, Colonel Parsons, joined Washington at New York, fought at Long Island, commissioned captain, Twenty-fourth Regiment Connecticut Line; was commissioned surgeon May 27, 1778, and at the time of the Wyoming Massacre, in July, 1778, was away with the Wyoming Battalion. He marched with General Sullivan in 1779 into the Indian country and by his cheerfulness and example greatly encouraged the soldiers on that fatiguing and dangerous mission. After the war he was chosen the first judge of the fifth district, Luzerne county, Pennsylvania, court of common pleas, taking office May 11, 1787. He erected the first iron works on the Susquehanna, having unbounded faith in the future development of the mineral wealth of Pennsylvania. After his death his heirs received from the government twenty-four hundred dollars in payment of his services as surgeon during the revolution.

He married, in 1743, at Rye, New York, Sarah Browne, born there March 13, 1725, died at Forty Fort, June 12, 1778. Children: Mary, unmarried; Sarah, born 1747, married, June 22, 1765, James Sutton; Susanna, born 1750, married Lemuel Gustine (see Gustine V); John, died young; Martha, born 1754; James, 1757; Elizabeth, 1759; Deborah, 1761; William, 1762; Jonathan, 1764; Doctor Smith had two other wives, but no more children.

(V) Susanna, daughter of Dr. William Hooker Smith, married Dr. Lemuel Gustine.

(VI) Sarah, daughter of Dr. Lemuel Gustine, married Rev. Nathaniel R. Snowden (see Snowden V).

(The Hooker Line).

Mehitable Hooker, mother of Dr. William Hooker Smith, was a descendant of Thomas Hooker, the Puritan minister and early settler of Hartford, Connecticut. He was born at Marfield, Leicestershire, England, July 7, 1576, died July 7, 1647. He was a graduate of Cambridge University and became a minister of the Gospel. He came to America in the ship "Griffin", arriving at Boston, September 4, 1633. He was chosen pastor of the church at Newtown (Cambridge) till June, 1636, when he led a company through the forests settling on the banks of the Connecticut at Hartford, Connecticut. From that time until his death he was identified with all the important public affairs of the colony. He was one of the moderators of the first New England Synod, held in Cambridge, in the famous case of Ann Hutchinson. His wife's name was Susan ———, perhaps Pym, although there is no proof. Children: Rev. John, returned to England; Joanna, married Rev. Thomas Shephard; Mary, married Rev. Roger Newton, first pastor of Farmington, Connecticut; Sarah, married Rev. John Wilson, of Medfield; a daughter, married; Rev. Samuel, of whom further.

(II) Rev. Samuel Hooker, son of Rev. Thomas Hooker, was born in 1633, died at Farmington, Connecticut, November 6, 1697. He was a graduate of Harvard College, 1653, studied divinity and on account of his earnestness and piety was known as the "Fervent Hooker." He was the second minister of the Farmington Church and a powerful, effective preacher. He married, September 22, 1658, Mary, born at Plymouth, May 4, 1643, daughter of Captain Thomas Willett, of Swansea (see Willett IV). She survived him and married (second) Rev. Thomas Buckingham, of Saybrook. Children of Mr. and Mrs. Hooker: Doctor Thomas, married Mrs. Mary (Smith) Lord; Samuel, married Mehitable Hamlen; William, married Susanna, widow of John Blackleach; Judge James, of whom further; Roger, died unmarried; Nathaniel; Mary, married Rev. James Pierpont; Hezekiah, died young; Doctor Daniel, married Sarah Standley; Sarah, married Rev. Stephen Buckingham.

(III) Judge James Hooker, son of Rev. Samuel Hooker, was born at Farmington, October 27, 1666, died at Guilford, Connecticut, March 12, 1743. He was first judge of the probate court at Guilford; representative 1702-03-05-06-07-08-09-10-12-13-16-20; justice

of New Haven courts 1712, and from 1714 to 1720, and 1722; judge 1720-1725. He married, August 1,1691, at Guilford, Mary Leete, born January 11, 1672, died October 5, 1752, daughter of William Leete of Guilford (see Leete III). Children of Judge James Hooker: 1. Mary, born November 5, 1693, married James Hart. 2. Ann, died unmarried. 3. Sarah, born February 26, 1696, died January 26, 1760; married ——— Bartlett. 4. William, born October 16, 1702. 5. Mehitable, married Rev. John Smith (see Smith III).

(IV) Mehitable, daughter of Judge James Hooker, married Rev. John Smith.

(V) Dr. William Hooker, son of Rev. John Smith, married Sarah Browne.

(VI) Susanna, daughter of Dr. William Hooker Smith, married Dr. Lemuel Gustine.

(VII) Sarah, daughter of Dr. Lemuel Gustine, married Rev. Nathaniel R. Snowden (see Snowden V).

(The Willett Line).

Mary Willett, wife of Rev. Samuel Hooker, was a descendant of a distinguished clerical family of Leicestershire, England. Rev. Thomas Willett was born in 1510, died 1598. He was rector, vicar and canon of the established church at Barley, Leicestershire, England; sub-almoner to King Edward VI; deprived of his ministerial dignities by Queen Mary and forced by his conscience to forsake church promotion; was hidden in the house of a noble friend, who on the accession of Queen Elizabeth was appointed bishop of Ely, Thomas Willett being appointed prebend. He was a most scholarly divine, holding many degrees and positions of honor.

(II) Rev. Andrew Willett, son of Rev. Thomas Willett, was born in 1562, at Ely, England, died at Hadsden, England, September 4, 1621. He was a high dignitary of the church and died full of honors. He married, in 1589, Jacobeda Goad, baptized in 1592, died July 11, 1632, daughter of Thomas Goad, Doctor of Divinity and provost of Kings College.

(III) Captain Thomas Willett, son of Rev. Andrew Willett, was born August 29, 1605, at Barley, Leicestershire, England, died at Swansea, Massachusetts, August 3, 1674. He came to Plymouth at an early day and on March 7, 1648, succeeded Miles Standish as captain of Plymouth. In 1650 he was on the committee of arbitration to settle the boundary lines between the Dutch and English; was assistant from Plymouth 1651-1664; member of council of war 1653; served on the expedition that captured New York from the Dutch, and on June 2, 1665, was appointed the first English Mayor of New York City; member of the general council 1672. He married, July 6,

1636, Mary Browne, born in England, died at Swansea, Massachusetts, January 8, 1669. Children: Mary; Martha; John; Rebecca; Esther; James; Hezekiah, first and second; David; Andrew; Samuel.

(IV) Mary, daughter of Captain Thomas Willett, married Rev. Samuel Hooker (see Hooker II).

(The Browne Line).

Mary Browne descended from Sir Anthony Browne to whom Henry VIII. presented Battle Abbey.

(II) Thomas, son of Sir Anthony Browne.

(III) Thomas (2) was a son of Thomas (1) Browne, and brother of Peter Browne who came in the "Mayflower".

(IV) John, son of Thomas (2) Browne, was born in England in 1584, died at Swansea, Massachusetts, April 10, 1662. He was one of the founders of Plymouth colony, coming in 1633 with wife Dorothy and three children. He was made freeman 1635, and in 1636 began his eighteen years' service on the board of assistants. In 1637 he became one of the proprietors of Taunton. In 1643 was serving in the train band with his sons, John and James. In 1645 he moved to Rehoboth, settling at what is now Swansea on land scrupulously purchased from the Indian sachem Massasoit. For twelve years from 1645, and from the second year of its existence, he was a member of the board of colonial commissioners.

(V) Mary, daughter of Captain Thomas Browne, married Captain Thomas Willett (see Willett III).

(Another Browne Line).

Sarah Browne, wife of Dr. William Hooker Smith, descended from Sir Anthony Browne, through Peter Browne of Plymouth, who came to New England with the Pilgrims on the "Mayflower" in 1620 (see "Mayflower Descendants"). The line of descent is through Hackaliah, son of Peter, who founded the branch known as the Brownes of Rye, New York. Peter (1), the Pilgrim, descended through a younger son of Sir Anthony Browne.

(II) Hackaliah, son of Peter Browne, "the Pilgrim", was born in Plymouth, died 1720, at Rye, New York. He married Ruth Mead.

(III) Deliverance, son of Hackaliah Browne, was born at Rye, in 1672, died in 1727 at White Plains, New York. He was a justice from 1698 to 1716; commissioner of arbitration 1697; representative 1698; married and had issue.

(IV) Jonathan, son of Deliverance Browne, was born at Rye, New York, in 1706, died at Hartford, Connecticut, June 15, 1768. He

was a justice in 1735 and prominent in Westchester county, New York; married Phoebe Kniffen.

(V) Sarah, only child of Jonathan Browne, married Dr. William Hooker Smith (see Smith IV).

(The Leete Line).

Mary Leete, wife of Judge James Hooker, was a descendant of Governor William Leete, born in Doddington, Huntingtonshire, England, in 1613, died April 16, 1683, at Hartford, Connecticut; was "bred to the law", and served for a time in Bishops Court, Cambridge, where he, observing the oppression of the Puritans and their uncomplaining submission to persecution, became himself a Puritan and resigned his office. He came to New Haven Colony in July, 1639, and became one of the most prominent figures in the colony. After holding many high offices, he was chosen governor in 1676, holding and wisely administering that high office until his death in 1683. He had three wives, his children, however, being all by his first wife, Anne, daughter of Rev. John Payne, whom he married in England. She died in Connecticut, September 1, 1668. Children: John, married Mary Chittenden; Andrew, born 1643; William, of whom further; Abigail; Caleb; Peregrine; Joshua; Anna.

(II) William (2), son of Governor William Leete, was born in 1645, died at Guilford, Connecticut, June 1, 1687. He was a member of the general court of Connecticut eight terms and a man of prominence. He married Mary Fenn, born in 1647 at Milford, died at Guilford, Connecticut, June 20, 1701.

(III) Mary, only child of William Leete, married Judge James Hooker (see Hooker III).

From these intermarriages the Snowdens of Philadelphia trace a New England ancestry even to the "Mayflower" and can prove alliance with the best blood of the colonies, and in their own paternal right are of the best blood of Pennsylvania.

APPLETON   In the two contiguous parishes of Great and Little Waldingfield (given in the local records as Waldingfield Magna and Waldingfield Parva) in the county of Suffolk, England, the family of Appleton can trace a clearly defined line back for five hundred years. Prior to that time many scattering notices of members of the family are to be found. In these there are various spellings of the name, the form Apulton being the one used in the genealogical tree from which the following account is taken. As a local appellation the name is found in old records prior to the Norman Conquest, the word being of Saxon origin and meaning orchard, or apple enclosure. This etymology is borne out by the arms of the family which contain three apples. Since the names borne by the family are Norman, it is probable that the family was a Norman one to which had been granted a Saxon estate before surnames became prevalent. The arms of the Suffolk Appletons are given as follows: Argent, a fesse sable, between three apples gules, stalked and leaved vert; Crest, an elephant's head couped sable ear'd or, in his mouth a snake vert, writhed about his trunk.

(I) John Appleton, or Apulton, was living in Great Waldingfield in 1396 and died there in 1414.

(II) John (2), son of John (1) Appleton, lived at Little Waldingfield. He confirmed lands to his son John, and Margaret, his son's wife, in 1459.

(III) John (3), son of John (2) Appleton, died in 1481 and was buried at Waldingfield. He married Margaret, daughter of Richard Wellinge and she died in 1468.

(IV) John (4), son of John (3) Appleton, was of Great Waldingfield in 1483; married Alice, daughter and co-heir of Thomas Malchier and wife, Amy. Children: John, and two sons named Thomas, a custom not uncommon.

(V) Thomas, son of John (4) Appleton, was of Little Waldingfield, died in 1507; he married Margaret, daughter of Robert Crane of Little Stonham, and she died November 4, 1504. Both are buried at Waldingfield. Children: Robert, mentioned below; Thomas, rector of Lavenham; William and Alice.

(VI) Robert, son of Thomas Appleton, was of Little Waldingfield and died in 1526. He married Mary, second daughter of Thomas Mountney. She married (second) ——— Martyn; her portrait in brass is in the Little Waldingfield church. Children: William, mentioned below; and Edward, of Edwardstone.

(VII) William, son of Robert Appleton, was of Little Waldingfield, and married Rose, daughter and heiress of Robert Sexton of Lavenham. Children: Thomas (2), mentioned below; and Frances.

(VIII) Thomas (2), son of William Appleton, died in London in 1603; he married Mary, second daughter and co-heir of Edward Isaack, of Patricksbourne, county Kent. Children: Sir Isaac, died 1608; John, buried at Chilton; Thomas (3), of London; Samuel, mentioned below; Mary, married Robert Ryece, Esq.; Judith, died 1587; Judith, mar-

ried Dr. Lewis Bayley; Sarah, married Edward Bird of Walden; and Henry Smythe.

(IX) Samuel Appleton, the immigrant ancestor of the American line, was a son of Thomas (2) Appleton, mentioned above. He was born at Little Waldingfield, England, in 1586; married at Preston, England, January 24, 1616. Judith Everard (some accounts give his wife's name as Mary). He came to Massachusetts and took the freeman's oath, May 25, 1636, and as early as July, 1636, was a resident of Ipswich. In the same year Sarah Dillingham bequeathed to Appleton and his wife, and committed the education of her child to Mr. Saltonstall and Mr. Appleton. The title Mr. indicated social position above the ordinary, and but three others in Ipswich at that time were given this prefix in the records. He was chosen deputy to the general court in May, 1637, and received several grants of land besides his great farm of four hundred and sixty acres; the ancient grant is now entirely in the possession of direct descendants. He died at Rowley, Massachusetts, in June, 1670. He married (first) Judith Everard; (second) Martha ———. Children of first wife: Mary, born at Little Waldingfield, 1616; Judith (she and all but the two youngest were also born at Little Waldingfield), 1618; Martha, 1620; John, 1622; Samuel (2), mentioned below; Sarah, born at Reydon, 1629. Child of second wife: Judith, born at Reydon, 1634, married Samuel Rogers of Ipswich.

(X) Major Samuel (2) Appleton, son of Samuel (1) Appleton, was born at Little Waldingfield, England, 1624, and came with his father to New England. He was lieutenant and deputy to the general court in 1668; and deputy with his brother John, in 1669-71, and again in 1673 and 1675. In King Philip's war he was commissioned captain, by order dated September 24, 1675, was sent to assist the Connecticut river towns, and when Major Pynchon resigned, Appleton succeeded to the command of the colonial forces in that section. He repulsed an attack on Hatfield by about eight hundred Indians. Much of his official correspondence in his own handwriting is to be found in the archives. In December, 1675, at Dedham he took command of six companies of foot and one of horse and joined General Winslow's forces for the attack on Narragansett. In October, 1676, he was appointed to command an expedition to Piscataqua, but declined it. In 1681 he took his seat in the council as an assistant and continued until the evil days of Governor Andros, when he was proscribed among those "persons factiously and seditiously inclined, and disaffected to his majesty's government," and a warrant issued for his arrest. He escaped for a time by taking refuge in the home of his son at Lynn, but in October, 1687, he was brought before the governor and council and ordered "to stand committed until he give bond in the sum of 1,000 pounds to appear at the next superior court at Salem to answer what shall be objected against him, and in the meantime to be of good behavior". He refused to give the bond and was committed to the jail in Boston and kept a prisoner from November to March. He was never tried on the complaint and it is said that he had the satisfaction, after the fall of Andros, of handing the haughty governor into the boat which conveyed him to prison in the Castle. He died May 15, 1696, and his gravestone is still preserved at Ipswich.

He married (first) April 2, 1651, Hannah, daughter of William Paine, of Ipswich. He married (second) December 8, 1656, Mary Oliver, who was then but sixteen years old, daughter of John Oliver of Newbury. She died February 15, 1698. Children by first wife: Hannah, born January 9, 1652; Judith, August 19, 1653; Samuel, November 3, 1654. Children by second wife: John, born 1660; Isaac, mentioned below; Joanna; Joseph, June 5, 1674; Oliver, June, 1676; Mary, June, 1676; Oliver, 1677; Mary, about October 20, 1679. The records also give another wife, Elizabeth, daughter of William and Mary (Lawrence) Whittingham.

(XI) Major Isaac Appleton, son of Major Samuel Appleton, was born at Ipswich, in 1664, and died May 22, 1747. He made his home at Ipswich on the farm he inherited there. He married Priscilla, daughter of Thomas Baker, of Topsfield. She died May 26, 1731. She was a granddaughter of Governor Symonds. The following account of the lineage of Priscilla Baker is taken from a book entitled, "The Ancestry of Priscilla Baker, who lived 1674-1731, and was the wife of Isaac Appleton of Ipswich, Massachusetts," by William Appleton, 1870. Condensed, the account states that John Baker emigrated from Norwich, England, in 1637, and settled at Ipswich, Massachusetts, and his son, Thomas, married Priscilla, daughter of the Lieutenant-Governor Samuel Symonds, and their eldest child was Priscilla Baker, the wife of Isaac Appleton. Samuel Symonds was the son of Richard Symonds of Great Yeldham, county Essex, England, a gentleman of good family and position. He came to New England in 1637 and held many important offices. His second wife was Martha Read, sister of the second wife of Governor John Winthrop, of

Connecticut. One child of theirs was Priscilla, who married Thomas Baker.

The children of Major Isaac and Priscilla (Baker) Appleton were: Priscilla, born March 16, 1697; Isaac, March 21, 1699; Mary, October 1, 1701; Isaac (2), mentioned below; Rebecca, 1706; Elizabeth, 1706; Martha, born July 30, 1708; Joanna, baptized November 17, 1717.

(XII) Isaac (2), son of Major Isaac (1) Appleton, was born at Ipswich, May 30, 1704, and died December 18, 1794, at the age of ninety-one. He married (first) Elizabeth Sawyer (intention dated April 25, 1730), daughter of Francis Sawyer of Wells, Maine. She was born in 1710, and died April 29, 1785. He married (second) at the age of eighty-two, December 11, 1785, Mrs. Hepzibah Appleton. Children: Isaac, baptized May 30, 1731; Francis, baptized March 25, 1733; Elizabeth, baptized October 24, 1736; Samuel, mentioned below; Thomas, baptized October 5, 1740; John, baptized December 26, 1742; Daniel, baptized April 7, 1745; William, baptized April 12, 1747; Mary, baptized July 2, 1749; Joseph, baptized June 9, 1751. Jesse Appleton, a grandson of Isaac Appleton, was president of Bowdoin College.

(XIII) Samuel (3), son of Isaac (2) Appleton, was born in 1739. He inherited his father's farm at Ipswich, and in 1794 built on the site of an older one the house which is now the summer home of Mrs. D. F. Appleton. He married (intention dated November 26, 1768) Mary, daughter of Rev. Timothy White, of Haverhill. He died May 15, 1819; she, November 10, 1834. Children, born at Ipswich: Elizabeth, December 6, 1769; Sampel Gilman, February 26, 1771; Mary, December 3, 1772; Susanna, December 21, 1774; Isaac, December 15, 1776; Timothy, November 13, 1778; John White, November 29, 1780; Rebecca, March 19, 1783; James, mentioned below; Gardiner, March 2, 1787; Joanna, July 19, 1789; Nathan Davis, May 20, 1794.

(XIV) General James Appleton, son of Samuel (3) Appleton, was born at Ipswich, February 14, 1785. He was an active and conspicuous citizen. His military career began during the war of 1812. He rose through all the grades and became brigadier-general of the Massachusetts militia. He resided in Ipswich and Gloucester in early life and removed to Portland, Maine, where he became prominent in public life, an influential member of the legislature. Although Neal Dow is given credit for being father of the Maine prohibitory law, General Appleton first introduced the measure in a report he made to the legislature in 1837, and was an earnest worker

James Appleton

Daniel Fuller Appleton

Francis Randall Appleton.

Francis Randall Appleton, Jr.

in the temperance movement. After the death of Samuel Gilman Appleton, his brother, he inherited the homestead known as "Appleton farms" at Ipswich and afterwards made his home there. He retained his interest in politics and made a memorable address to the Ipswich soldiers at the railroad station as they started for the front in the civil war. He died August 25, 1862. He married, November 15, 1807, Sarah, daughter of Rev. Daniel Fuller, of Gloucester. She died January 7, 1872.

Children: 1. Samuel Gilman, born at Gloucester, November 5, 1808, died at Morrisania, New York, November 29, 1873; he married, September 30, 1839, Sarah, daughter of Rev. Sylvester Gardner of Manlius, New York. 2. Sarah Fuller, born at Gloucester, January 20, 1811; died June 7, 1884; married at Marblehead, May 6, 1833, Rev. Stephen C. Millett, of Beloit, Wisconsin. 3. James, born at Gloucester, March 11, 1813; died March, 1884; married, June 21, 1842, Sarah Bristol, daughter of Samuel L. Edwards, of Manlius, New York. 4. Mary White, born at Gloucester, November 15, 1815; died January 14, 1905. 5. Elizabeth Putnam, born at Gloucester, December 3, 1818; died March 29, 1897, at Racine, Wisconsin; married, September 2, 1845, Shelton L. Hall, of Racine. 6. Joanna Dodge, born at Marblehead, February 23, 1821; died at Racine, April 25, 1870; married, November 9, 1843, Peyton R. Morgan. 7. Hannah Fuller, born at Marblehead, April 21, 1823; died at Orange, New Jersey, November 10, 1903; married, April 27, 1854, Robert H. Thayer. 8. Daniel Fuller, mentioned below. 9. Harriette Hooper, born at Marblehead, March 24, 1828; died August 26, 1905; married, December 9, 1849, Rev. John Cotton Smith, rector of St. John's Church, Portland, and later of the Church of the Ascension, New York City. 10. Anna Whittemore, born at Marblehead, January 31, 1831; married, June 21, 1852, Dr. Charles H. Osgood.

(XV) Daniel Fuller, son of General James Appleton, was born at Marblehead, January 31, 1826. He was educated in the public schools in Portland. In 1846 he came to New York City, and entered the employ of Royal Robbins, who afterward admitted him to partnership under the firm name of Robbins & Appleton. In 1857 this firm became the owners of the new and small watch factory at Waltham, and this was the beginning of the American Waltham Watch Company. Mr. Appleton retained his interest in the business until his death, and his sons have succeeded him in the company. He was a delegate to the first national convention of the Republican party when General John C. Fremont was

nominated for president, and he was one of those invited to sit on the platform at the convention when President McKinley was nominated for the second time. While his business interests were in New York City, he spent his vacations in Ipswich at the old homestead to the ownership of which he succeeded after his father's death. He died February 4, 1904.

He married (first) June 9, 1853, Julia, daughter of Nicholas P. Randall, of Manlius, New York. She died August 20, 1886, aged sixty years (see Randall V). He married (second) December 17, 1889, Susan Cowles, daughter of Professor John P. Cowles, of Ipswich. Children of first wife: 1. Francis Randall, mentioned below. 2. Ruth, born May 30, 1857; married, April 15, 1880, Charles Sanders Tuckerman, A.B., Harvard, 1874, who died August 27, 1904; children: Muriel, born in Brookline, March 6, 1881; John Appleton, in Boston, November 26, 1884; Julia Appleton, in Ipswich, May 17, 1888; Leverett Saltonstall, in Salem, December 3, 1892. 3. Mary Eliza, born April 21, 1860; married, November 22, 1881, Gerald Livingston Hoyt, of Staatsburg, New York, A.B., Yale, 1872; children: Julia Marion, born in New York, March 3, 1883; Lydig, in New York, December 21, 1883. 4. Randolph Morgan, January 4, 1862, A.B., Harvard, 1884; married, June 2, 1888, Helen Kortwright Mixter; children: Madeline, born in Ipswich, July 8, 1891; Julia, in Ipswich, June 5, 1894; Sybil, in Boston, December 28, 1899. 5. James Waldingfield, June 4, 1867, graduate of Harvard, 1888.

(XVI) Francis Randall, son of Daniel Fuller Appleton, was born in New York, August 5, 1854. He attended private schools, and was fitted for college in Phillips Academy, Andover, Massachusetts. He was graduated from Harvard College, in the class of 1875, and from the Columbia Law School, in 1877, and was admitted to the bar in New York in 1877. He practiced his profession in New York City for several years. From 1884 to 1910, when he retired, he was a member of the firm of Robbins & Appleton, agents for the Waltham Watch Company. His winter home is in New York. His summer home is on the old homestead at Ipswich, of which he is the present owner. He is a member of the Society of Colonial Wars, and was an overseer of Harvard College during 1903-1909. In politics he is a Republican; in religion, an Episcopalian.

He married at Lenox, Massachusetts, October 7, 1884, Fanny Lanier, born at Lenox, August 17, 1864, daughter of Charles Lanier, of New York, and of his wife Sarah Egleston, a great-granddaughter of Major-General Paterson of General Washington's staff in the revolutionary war. Children: Francis Randall Jr., born in Lenox, July 9, 1885, graduate of Harvard College in 1907; Charles Lanier, born in New York, September 25, 1886; graduate of Harvard College, 1908; Ruth, born in New York, January 10, 1891; Alice, born in New York, December 8, 1894; James, born in New York, March 6, 1899.

(The Randall Line).

(I) John Randall, the immigrant ancestor, settled at Westerly, Rhode Island, and died there 1684-85. He married Elizabeth ——. Children, born at Westerly: John, mentioned below; Stephen, Matthew, and Peter.

(II) John (2), son of John (1) Randall, was born in 1666 at Westerly, and died at Stonington, Connecticut. He married (first) at Stonington, in 1695, Abigail ——, who died at Stonington, in 1705. He married (second) at Stonington, November 25, 1706, Mary, daughter of John and Rebecca (Palmer) Baldwin. She was born February 24, 1675. Children, born at Stonington: Elizabeth, July 4, 1696; Jonathan, December 16, 1698; Mary, 1700; John, December 2, 1701; Dorothy, December 7, 1703; Abigail, December 4, 1705; Sarah, November 10, 1707; Nathan, mentioned below; Ichabod, October 21, 1711; Sarah, March 12, 1714; Joseph, June 2, 1715; Benjamin, twin of Joseph; Rebecca, July 31, 1717, Joseph, July 17, 1720.

(III) Nathan, son of John (2) Randall, was born at Westerly, July 7, 1709, and died at Voluntown, Connecticut. He was admitted a freeman at Westerly, May 4, 1736, and was a farmer there until about 1750, when he settled at Voluntown, Connecticut, and bought lands of Amos Kinney and others. He married (first) December 16, 1730, Mary Cottrell, and (second) her sister, Eleanor Cottrell, July 22, 1736. Children: Nathan, born September 18, 1731; Joseph, September 8, 1733; Nathan, October 10, 1735; Reuben, April 24, 1737; Amos, October 11, 1739; Dorothy, June 5, 1741; Eleanor, February 24, 1743; Amy, December 26, 1745; Peleg, October 19, 1748; Lydia, June 3, 1751; Nicholas, mentioned below; Jonas, September 8, 1756.

(IV) Nicholas, son of Nathan Randall, was born May 21, 1753, at Voluntown, Connecticut, and died at Bridgewater, New York, September 23, 1814. He married at Voluntown, Content Phillips, born at Voluntown, died at Bridgewater, January 14, 1815. He was a farmer. He took the freeman's oath, September 9, 1777; was selectman of Voluntown, 1795-97 and 1798-1804; member of the school

committee, 1796-97 and 1801-02, and an assessor. He was appointed, in 1803, on a committee to fix a place for holding the county and superior courts. In 1805 he removed to Bridgewater. Children: Nicholas Phillips, mentioned below; Rebecca, November 2, 1780; Mary, June 17, 1782; Rodley, May 24, 1783; Jenevereth, 1785; Jason, March 24, 1787; Jonathan, August 21, 1789; John, October 20, 1792; Betsey, 1795; Charles, August 20, 1806.

(V) Nicholas Phillips, son of Nicholas Randall, was born in Voluntown, July 25, 1779, and died in Manlius, New York, March 7, 1836. He prepared for college and graduated with honor at Yale College, in the class of 1803. He then entered the law office of Hotchkiss & Simons, at Clinton, New York, and in due course was admitted to the bar. In 1807 he opened an office in New Hartford, New York, and in 1811 removed to Manlius, New York, forming a partnership with James O. Wattles. He continued to practice law the rest of his life with marked ability and success. He was a member of the Baptist church in his younger days, but afterward became a communicant of the Protestant Episcopal church and for a number of years was vestryman and warden of the church at Manlius.

He married (first) at Clinton, 1809, Sarah Bristol, born at Clinton, 1787, died there February, 1815; (second) at Sandy Hill, New York, 1815, Belvidera Hitchcock, born at Sandy Hill, 1789, died at Manlius, November, 1818; (third) at Caldwell, New York, 1819, Eliza Norman, born in England, 1791, died at Manlius, June, 1822; (fourth) at Manlius, 1823, Sybil Dyer, born at Rutland, Vermont, May 29, 1800. Children of first wife: Francis, born at New Hartford, New York, June 15, 1810; Sarah Bristol, born at Manlius, October 1, 1812. Child of second wife: Belvidera Hitchcock, November 3, 1816. Child of third wife: Nicholas Norman, July 14, 1820. Children by his fourth wife: Eliza, November 16, 1823; Julia, April 9, 1827, married at Manlius, June 9, 1853, Daniel Fuller Appleton (see Appleton XV); Charles, September 30, 1833; Nicholas Dyer, May 30, 1835.

COX   Jacob Dolson Cox, son of Michael and Mary (Dolson) Cox, was born in Dutchess county, New York, June 2, 1792. He became a carpenter and builder in New York City and was noted for his skill in building churches and warehouses and in roofing large areas without using internal columns of support. He was called to Montreal, Canada, at the age of thirty-three to superintend the carpenter work on the great church of Notre Dame and planned the remarkable concealed trusses which support both the roof and ceiling of that imposing building. He was engaged on this work four years, returned to New York City, carried on his business as architect and builder there for twenty years, then went to California with the "Argonauts" and died at Yuba, November 5, 1852. He married Thedia Redelia Kenyon, whose acquaintance he made at Albany, New York, a direct descendant of Elder William Brewster, of the "Mayflower" colony (see Brewster X). They had eleven children, four of whom died in infancy, and five of whom achieved distinction in business and in public life.

(II) Major General and Governor Jacob Dolson (2) Cox, son of Jacob Dolson (1) Cox, was born in Montreal, October 27, 1828, died at Magnolia, Massachusetts, August 4, 1900. When he was a year old the family returned to New York City and he received his early education there. He graduated from Oberlin College, Ohio, with the class of 1851. In the fall of that year he was appointed superintendent of the public schools in Warren, Ohio. While superintendent he completed the study of law, which he had commenced before going to college, and was admitted to practice in 1853. In 1859 he was elected to the Ohio state senate to represent the Trumbull-Mahoning district. He foresaw the coming civil war and prepared for it by extensive reading of military works. When Sumter was fired upon, Mr. Cox devoted his whole time to organizing and equipping the state militia. He was commissioned brigadier-general of Ohio State Volunteers, April 23, 1861, and brigadier-general of United States Volunteers, May 17, 1861. He remained at Camp Dennison, drilling and instructing volunteers, until July 6, 1861, when he was ordered to take command of an expedition up the Kanawha Valley, West Virginia. With three thousand men he encountered General Wise with four thousand men and drove him up the valley, capturing Gauley Bridge with one thousand five hundred stands of arms and quantities of ammunition. In August, 1862, he was ordered east with his Kanawha division and placed in charge of the Virginia defenses of Washington. After the defeat of General Pope and the resumption of command by General McClellan, the Kanawha division was attached to the Ninth Army Corps, to the command of which he succeeded on the death of General Reno at South Mountain. He directed all its operations at the battle of Antietam, and on October 6, 1862, was commissioned major-general "for gallant conduct at

South Mountain and Antietam". At the same time he was sent back to West Virginia, which had been overrun by the Confederate forces during his absence, and after driving them out again he remained in charge of the district until April, 1863, when he was placed in charge of the District of Ohio. During the summer of 1863 he defeated a plot for releasing the confederate prisoners on Johnson's Island, Sandusky Bay, and in the fall of 1863 he directed the operations which resulted in the capture of General Morgan and his raiders. In December, 1863, he was sent to East Tennessee and commanded the field operations of the Twenty-third Army Corps during the ensuing winter and spring. In May, 1864, the Twenty-third Corps joined General Sherman's army at Dallas and took a prominent part in the Atlanta campaign, being largely employed in turning operations on the enemy's flank and rear, which required a high degree of courage, discipline and military skill. After Sherman started on his "March to the Sea", General Cox commanded the Twenty-third Army Corps and distinguished himself anew at the battles of Franklin and Nashville, in recognition of which he was again commissioned major-general, his first commission having expired for want of confirmation by the senate. His corps was then transferred to North Carolina and took a prominent part in the capture of Wilmington and won two battles at Kinston.

General Cox was nominated for governor of Ohio, while acting as district commander of North Carolina, and was elected by a handsome majority in the fall of 1865. In March, 1869, he was appointed secretary of the interior by President Grant. He applied the rules of civil service reform to his department, and introduced various reforms in the Indian service. The patent laws of the United States were revised and amended during his term of office. He resigned and left the cabinet in October, 1870, owing to lack of support in enforcing his civil service rules as against campaign committees and clerks who had exhausted their vacations and still desired to go home and participate in the political campaigns in their respective states. He resumed the practice of law in Cincinnati, but was called to the presidency of the Toledo & Wabash Railroad Company by the unanimous voice of two factions contending for its control, in September, 1873, and decided that it was his duty to accept. He removed, with his family, to Toledo, and in 1876 was elected to congress from that district. Returning to Cincinnati at the close of his congressional term, he was appointed dean of the Cincinnati Law School, and in 1885 president of the University of Cincinnati. Both institutions prospered greatly under his management.

General Cox was the author of two volumes in the *Scribner* Campaign series: "Atlanta" and "March to the Sea; Franklin and Nashville", also of various articles in the *Century* publication: "Battles and Leaders of the Civil War". He also wrote the last half of General Force's biography of General Sherman; the "Second Battle of Bull Run", in which he sustains the findings of the first court martial against General Fitz John Porter; "The Battle of Franklin", a critical review of the entire campaign culminating in that bloody contest, and "Military Reminiscences of the Civil War", a serious review of operations with which he was connected, well fortified by authorities. He wrote many historical and military reviews and biographical notices for *The Nation, The Atlantic, The North American,* and other magazines.

His scholarship was profound, his fairness and ability as a military critic unquestioned, and his whole influence on public affairs salutary, though after 1878 he persistently refused to accept any political office. He helped organize the Republican party in Ohio and maintained his party relations to the end, though he differed with the majority as to the reconstruction measures, especially the policy of committing the welfare of the Southern States to the ignorant and incapable blacks just released from slavery. In August, 1865, he predicted, in his so-called "Oberlin Letter", extensively published, all the evil consequences which actually ensued from enfranchising the blacks in the Southern States before they were fitted by education and training for the responsibilities of civil government. He was also opposed to a high protective tariff; believing that a moderate tariff, designed chiefly to produce revenue, would furnish all the protection American manufacturers really needed. General Cox had deep religious feeling and faith in an all-wise overruling Providence. In later life he was a constant attendant of the Episcopal church, finding in its liturgy the best expression of his spiritual needs and aspirations.

General Cox married Helen Finney Cochran, the widowed daughter of Rev. Charles G. Finney, the distinguished revivalist, afterwards president of Oberlin College. They had seven children, two of whom died in infancy. Four still survive: Helen Finney, wife of Professor John G. Black, of Wooster University; Jacob Dolson (3), a prominent manufacturer of Cleveland, Ohio; Kenyon, the distinguished artist; and Charlotte Hope,

who married John H. Pope, son of Major General John Pope, United States army.

(The Brewster Line).

(I) William Brewster Sr. lived in Scrooby, Nottinghamshire, England, as early as 1570-71, in which year he was assessed in that town on goods valued at three pounds. In 1575-76 he was appointed by Archbishop Sandys receiver of Scrooby and bailiff of the manor house in that place belonging to the bishop, to have life tenure of both offices. Some time in the year 1588, or possibly before, he was appointed to the additional office of postmaster under the Crown. He was known as the "Post" of Scrooby, and was master of the court mails, which were accessible only to those connected with the court. He died in the summer of 1590. His wife was Prudence ———. Child, William, mentioned below.

(II) Elder William (2) Brewster, immigrant ancestor, who came in the "Mayflower", was born during the last half of the year 1566 or the first half of 1567, the date being fixed by the affidavit made by him at Leyden, June 25, 1609, when he declared his age to be forty-two years. The place of his birth is not known, but is supposed to have been Scrooby. The parish registers of Scrooby do not begin until 1695, and no record of his birth, baptism or marriage has ever been discovered. He matriculated at Peterhouse, which was then the "oldest of the fourteen colleges grouped into the University of Cambridge." December 3, 1580, but does not appear to have stayed long enough to take his degree. He is next found as a "discreete and faithfull" assistant of William Davison, secretary of state to Queen Elizabeth, and accompanied that gentleman on his embassy to the Netherlands in August, 1585, and served him at court after his return until his downfall in 1587. He then returned to Scrooby, where he was held in high esteem by the people, and did much good "in Promoting and furthering religion." In 1590 he was appointed administrator of the estate of his father, who died in the summer of that year, and succeeded him as postmaster, which position he held until September 30, 1607. While in Scrooby he lived in the old manor-house where the members of the Pilgrim Church were accustomed to meet on Sunday. When the Pilgrims attempted to move to Holland in the latter part of 1607, they were imprisoned at Boston. Brewster was among those imprisoned and suffered the greatest loss. After he reached Holland he endured many unaccustomed hardships, not being as well fitted as the other Pilgrims for the hard labor which was their common lot, and he spent most of his means in providing for his children. During the latter part of the twelve years spent in Holland, he increased his income by teaching and by the profits from a printing press which he set up in Leyden. When after twelve years it was decided that the church at Leyden should emigrate to Virginia, Brewster, who had already been chosen elder, was desired to go with the first company. He was, therefore, with his wife Mary, and two young sons, among the passengers of the "Mayflower" which landed at Plymouth harbor, December 16, 1620. Here he bore an important part in establishing the Pilgrim republic, was one of the signers of the famous compact, and is believed to have drafted the same. He was the moral, religious and spiritual leader of the colony during its first years, and its chief civil adviser and trusted guide until his death. His wife was Mary ———. She died April 17, 1627, somewhat less than sixty years old. Elder Brewster died April 10, 1644, in Plymouth, and a final division of his estate was made by Bradford, Winslow, Prence and Standish, between Jonathan and Love, his only remaining children. Children: Jonathan, mentioned below; Patience; Fear; Child, died at Leyden, buried June 20, 1609; Love; Wrestling, came in "Mayflower" with his parents, and brother Love, was living at time of division of cattle, May 22, 1627.

(III) Jonathan, son of Elder William (2) Brewster, was born August 12, 1593, in Scrooby, Nottinghamshire, England, and came over in the ship "Fortune" in 1621. He moved from Plymouth to Duxbury about 1630, and was deputy from there to the general court, Plymouth colony, in 1639-41-43-44. From there he moved to New London, about 1649, and settled in that part later established as Norwich, the farm lying in both towns. He was admitted an inhabitant there, February 25, 1649-50, and was deputy to the general court in 1650-55-56-57-58. He engaged in the coasting trade, and was master of a small vessel plying from Plymouth along the coast of Virginia. In this way he became acquainted with Pequot harbor, and entered the river to trade with the Indians. He was clerk of the town of Pequot, September, 1649, and received his first grant of land in that town in the same month from Uncas, Sachem of the Mohegans, with whom he had established a trading house. At this latter place, which is still called by his name, Brewster's Neck, he laid out for himself a large farm. The deed for this land was confirmed by the town, November 30, 1652, and its bounds determined. In 1637 he was a military commissioner in the Pequot war, in 1642 a member of the Duxbury

committee to raise forces in the Narragansett alarm of that year, and a member of Captain Myles Standish's Duxbury company in the military enrollment of 1643. He was prominent in the formation of the settlement of Duxbury and in the establishment of its church. He sometimes practiced as an attorney and was also styled gentleman. He died August 7, 1659, and was buried in the Brewster cemetery at Brewster's Neck, Preston. A plain granite shaft, about eight feet high, was erected to his memory and that of his wife. The original footstone is still in existence and leans against the modern monument.

No probate papers relating to his estate have been found, but bills of sale are recorded, dated in 1658, which conveyed all his property in the town plot and his house and land at Poquetannuck with his movable property to his son Benjamin, and son-in-law, John Picket. His widow was evidently a woman of note and respectability in the community. She had always the prefix of Mrs. or Mistress, and was usually recorded in some useful capacity as nurse or doctor, as a witness to wills, etc. He married, April 10, 1624, Lucretia Oldham, of Darby, doubtless a sister of John Oldham, who came to Plymouth about 1623. She died March 4, 1678-79. There is some reason to believe that he had married before at an early age, and buried his wife and child by this marriage in Leyden. Children, the first three born in Plymouth, the fourth in Jones River, the others in Duxbury: William, born March 9, 1625; Mary, mentioned below; Jonathan, July 17, 1629; Ruth, October 3, 1631; Benjamin, November 17, 1633; Elizabeth, May 1, 1637; Grace, November 1, 1639; Hannah, November 3, 1641.

(IV) Mary, daughter of Jonathan Brewster, was born April 16, 1627. She married, November 10, 1645, (November 12 by Plymouth Colony record) John Turner, of Scituate, son of Humphrey and Lydia (Gamer) Turner. Children: Jonathan, born September 20, 1646; Joseph, probably died in infancy; Joseph, January 12, 1648-49; Ezekiel, mentioned below; Lydia, January 24, 1652; John, 1654; Elisha, 1656-57; Mary, died at Hull, Massachusetts, December 10, 1738, aged eighty; Benjamin, March 5, 1660; Ruth, 1663; Isaac, not mentioned in father's will; Grace, 1667; Amos, 1671.

(V) Ezekiel, son of John and Mary (Brewster) Turner, was born January 7, 1650-51. He married Susanna Keeny and among their children was Abigail, mentioned below.

(VI) Abigail, daughter of Ezekiel and Susanna (Keeny) Turner, married Clement Minor and among their children was Lucy, mentioned below.

(VII) Lucy, daughter of Clement and Abigail (Turner) Minor, married Rev. Nathan Howard and among their children was Thedia, mentioned below.

(VIII) Thedia, daughter of Rev. Nathan and Lucy (Minor) Howard, married Payne Kenyon and among their children was Joseph, mentioned below.

(IX) Joseph, son of Payne and Thedia (Howard) Kenyon, married Sarah Allyn and among their children was Thedia Redelia, mentioned below.

(X) Thedia Redelia, daughter of Joseph and Sarah (Allyn) Kenyon, married Jacob Dolson Cox (see Cox 1).

HOWLAND The original Howlands in America were Arthur, Henry, and John. The last named was one of the "Mayflower" number, and the others appeared in the early days of the settlement of Plymouth, but how and from what place in England they came has never been definitely ascertained.

(I) Henry Howland, youngest of the three brothers mentioned above, is first heard of in Plymouth, in 1624, when his name appears in the allotment of cattle to the different families. In the court records of Plymouth the name of Henry Howland is found in a list of freemen under date of 1633. He appears in Duxbury among its earliest settlers, where he is referred to as "living by the bay side, near Love Brewster's", and the records say he was "one of the substantial landholders and freemen". He was chosen constable for Duxbury in 1635, and was for several years surveyor of highways in the town. In 1643 he was on a list of freemen and of men able to bear arms. He served on the grand jury nine years between 1636 and 1656. In 1657 he apparently joined the Friends, which was just beginning to spread in America, and as a result endured for the rest of his life the various persecutions to which this sect was subjected by the civil authorities. Towards the end of his life he became a large possessor of real estate. In 1652 he was associated with others in the ownership of a large tract of land in Dartmouth, and in 1659 he bought with twenty-six others what was then called Assonet, now Freetown. It appears by his will that he owned a house in Duxbury where he doubtless died. He married Mary Newland, who died June 6, 1674. He died January 17, 1671. Children: Joseph; Zoeth, mentioned below; John; Samuel; Sarah; Elizabeth; Mary; Abigail.

(II) Zoeth, son of Henry Howland, was born in Duxbury, and married Abigail ———, October, 1656. He was killed by Indians, January 21, 1676, at Pocaset. Abigail married (second), February 12, 1678, John Kirby Jr. He took the oath of "fidelitie" at Duxbury in 1657, and became a convert to the Friends' sect about the same time, and meetings were held at his house, for which he was fined in December, 1657. In March, 1657-58, he was sentenced to "sitt in the stockes for the space of an hour" for "speaking opprobiously of the minnesters of Gods Word." In March, 1659, his wife was fined ten shillings for not attending the meetings of the Puritans. He moved to Dartmouth, probably as early as 1662, for more congenial society. The Newport Friends' records and the inventory of his estate, dated June, 1677, refer to him as Zoeth of Dartmouth, and his mother owned a house there. Just where he was killed and how he came to be there is unknown. His sons, with the exception of Samuel, were active members of the old Apponegansett meeting. The first eight children are recorded in the Newport Friends' records. Children: Nathaniel, born October 5, 1657; Benjamin, May 8, 1659; Daniel, July, 1661; Lydia, November 23, 1663; Mary, February 23, 1665-66; Sarah, April, 1668; Henry, August 30, 1672; Abigail, August 30, 1672; Nicholas, mentioned below.

(III) Nicholas, son of Zoeth Howland, married, December 26, 1697, Hannah, daughter of Lieutenant John Woodman, of Little Crompton, Rhode Island. He died before July 7, 1722, at which date his will was admitted to probate in the Bristol county office. He was a large real estate owner and seems to have carried on a tannery as well as farming. His homestead was situated west of Apponegansett meeting house, on the opposite side of the road, and his real estate there seems to have extended from that of his brother Henry westward to what is now called the Chase road. This neighborhood was called Pascamansett, from the river that flowed through it. He owned Gooseberry Neck, at the mouth of Buzzards Bay. He was a successful business man, highly respected and trusted by the community, and held a number of town offices from 1702 to 1712. Children: Abigail, born November 3, 1698; Mary, September 21, 1700; Rebeckah, April 9, 1702; Samuel, mentioned below; Nicholas, July 13, 1706; Hannah, September 10, 1708; Joseph, October 24, 1710; Daniel, September 28, 1712; Benjamin, November 30, 1716; Job, September 26, 1719; Edith.

(IV) Samuel, son of Nicholas and Hannah

(Woodman) Howland, was born in Dartmouth, July 13, 1706. He married (first) January 9, 1723, Sarah, daughter of William Soule, of Dartmouth; (second) April 8, 1747, Ruth Davol, of Dartmouth, where he died. Children of first wife: Nicholas, mentioned below; Samuel, born May 12, 1727; Hannah, April 27, 1728; Sarah, October 31, 1731; Alice, February 6, 1733; Mary, February 14, 1736; William, December 24. 1738; Elizabeth, June 2, 1741. Children by second wife: Silas, born October 8, 1749; Eunice, September 4, 1751; Reuben, January 18, 1754; Daniel, April 3, 1757; Weston, May 23, 1759.

(V) Nicholas (2), eldest son of Samuel and Sarah (Soule) Howland, was born March 1, 1725, in Dartmouth, and married, January 4. 1750, Mary, daughter of Jonathan and Mary Sisson, of Westport. They lived in Westport, where he owned a farm on the east side of Westport river, about two and one-half miles below Westport village. Children: Mary; Alice; Anne; Jonathan; Joseph; William, mentioned below; Reuben, January 11, 1774; Benjamin.

(VI) William, third son of Nicholas (2) and Mary (Sisson) Howland, was born February 2. 1772, in Dartmouth, and married, June, 1795, Diana Smith, of that town. They moved to Saratoga, New York, where he was a hatter, living there until his death in 1832. He learned his trade in Westport, and carried on the business for a time at Smith Mills, Dartmouth. Children: Thomas, born March 20, 1797; Dorcas, June 28, 1800; Benjamin, August 12, 1803; Jonathan, February 22, 1806; William, mentioned below; Smith, October 12, 1809; Almina, August 26, 1912; Ellenor A., March 7, 1815; Reuben, March 12, 1818.

(VII) William (2), fourth son of William and Diana (Smith) Howland, was born February 11. 1808, in Saratoga, New York. He married (first) Louisa Packard, born September 28, 1817, died July 4, 1845. He married (second) November 2, 1852, Mary Ann Potter, born August 18, 1815, died April 6, 1882. His early days were spent on his father's farm, and from twelve to eighteen years of age he attended the district schools, working in his father's hat factory winters. He attended an academy at White Creek, New York, and was for a time clerk for John Cummings. Afterwards he was in a store in South Dartmouth. In 1836 he went on a voyage as supercargo for I. H. Bartlett, of New Bedford, to the Kennebec river, Maine, and afterwards commanded a coaster until he returned to Mr. Cummings and went into business with him in 1842 in the general merchandise business. Mr.

Cummings also ran a saw-mill and grist-mill, and Mr. Howland assumed a very large share of the care and oversight of the above. He remained there twenty-five years, and then moved to the William Potter homestead, the former home of his wife, a mile northwest of Smith Mills. He had one of the best farms in that locality, which greatly improved under his management, as he was a successful and progressive agriculturist. He was held in high esteem by the community. Children: Maria Packard, born June 4, 1842; Thomas Smith, mentioned below.

(VIII) Thomas Smith, only son of William (2) and Louisa (Packard) Howland, was born in Dartmouth, Massachusetts, February 13, 1844. He attended the public schools of his native town and various private schools in New Bedford, then entered the Massachusetts State Normal School at Bridgewater, from which he was graduated in 1862. He enlisted from New Bedford, Massachusetts, in Company I, Thirty-third Regiment Massachusetts Volunteer Infantry for three years, and took part in many of the important battles of the civil war, including Gettysburg and Chattanooga. He was in General Sherman's army in the famous March to the Sea, and took part in the grand review at Washington at the close of the war. He entered the service as a private, and was promoted to the grade of corporal, then sergeant, and when mustered out held a commission as second lieutenant, signed by the famous war governor of Massachusetts, John A. Andrew. He was mustered out of service June 11, 1865, and became a student in the Lawrence Scientific School of Harvard University, from which he was graduated with the degree of civil engineer in 1868. He was employed in the engineering department of the Burlington & Missouri River Railroad, with headquarters at Burlington, Iowa. In 1884 he was elected secretary of the Burlington & Missouri Railroad Company, and in 1885 moved to Boston, where he made his headquarters until 1901. In that year he was elected vice-president and treasurer of the Chicago, Burlington & Quincy Railroad Company, offices he has held to the present time, and has made his home in Chicago. He is a member of the University Club of Chicago; the Union League Club; the Exmoor Country Club; and the New England Society of Chicago. In politics he is a Republican, and in religion non-sectarian.

He married, October 3, 1871, at Burlington, Iowa, Eliza Semple Harbach, born at Pittsburgh, Pennsylvania, December 7, 1848, daughter of Abraham and Ball (Graham) Harbach. Children: 1. Abram Harbach, born

September 25, 1872; attended Hopkinson School in Boston, and entered Harvard University, from which he was graduated with the degree of bachelor of arts in 1896; married Angelica Bustamente, who is of Spanish ancestry, of the City of Mexico, where they are now living, and where he is engaged in business; children: Thomas Bustamente and Angelica.   2. Mary Potter, born at Burlington, Iowa, February 23, 1877; educated in public schools and at Miss Shaw's private school, Boston; graduated from Radcliffe College, 1898; married I. W. Linn, a nephew of Miss Jane Addams, of Hull House, Chicago; he is a professor in Chicago University; children: Jane Addams Linn and Elizabeth Howland Linn.   3. Elizabeth Harbach, born at Burlington, October 2, 1878; educated in private schools; an art student, now living in Chicago. 4. Ruth Almy, born at Burlington, October 16, 1881; fitted for college in private schools, and graduated from Radcliffe, class of 1901; married John DeWitt, and resides in Keokuk, Iowa.

LANE   William Lane, the immigrant ancestor, may have been related to Job, James and Edward Lane, who came from Yorkshire, England, and settled in Billerica, Malden and Gloucester, Massachusetts, and in Falmouth, now Portland, Maine. There was a tradition that William Lane, of Boston, and two brothers, cordwainers, came to Beverly or Gloucester, Massachusetts, and to Maine, and were nephews of William Lane, of Dorchester, who in 1635 came from county Norfolk, England. William Lane appears to have gone to Connecticut early, as a son Samuel was born in Hartford, August 8, 1648, but, if so, he returned. He was admitted a freeman in Massachusetts, May 6, 1657. He was a cordwainer by trade. His first wife, Mary, was a member of the First Church of Boston, and died in Boston, May 22, 1656. He married (second) August 21, 1656, Mary, daughter of Thomas Brewer. They were married by Deputy-governor Bellingham. Her father lived in Ipswich in 1642, afterward in Roxbury, and died in Hampton, New Hampshire, March 3, 1689-90. Children: Samuel, born in Hartford, August 8, 1648, died young; Samuel, born in Boston, January 23, 1651-2; John, born in Boston February 5, 1653-4; Mary, May 15, 1656; Sarah, June 15, 1657; William (2), of whom further; Elizabeth, February 3, 1661; Ebenezer, March 21, 1666-7.

(II) William (2), son of William (1) Lane, was born in Boston, October 1, 1659. He was a tailor by trade. He joined the North Church

in Boston in 1681, and removed in 1686 to Hampton, New Hampshire, where he settled on a grant of ten acres of land. He built a one-story house near the meeting-house on the site afterward occupied by the academy. He is said to have been a devout and godly man, living a quiet and humble life, respected by all his neighbors. He married, June 21, 1680, Sarah, daughter of Thomas Webster. She died January 6, 1745, aged eighty-five years. He died at the home of his son Joshua, February 14, 1749, aged eighty-five. Children, born in Boston: John, born in Boston, February 17, 1685; Sarah, November 6, 1688; Elizabeth, July 12, 1691; Abigail, December 9, 1693; Deacon Joshua, of whom further; Samuel, June 4, 1698; Thomas, June 8, 1701.

(III) Deacon Joshua Lane, son of William (2) Lane, was born in Hampton, June 6, 1696. He resided on a farm on the road to North Hampton, half a mile north of the present railroad station, and followed the trade of tanner and shoemaker. While standing on his doorstep after a thunder shower he was struck by lightning and killed, June 14, 1766. He had sixty grandchildren at the time of his death. He married, December 24, 1717, Bathsheba Robie, who was born August 2, 1696, daughter of Samuel and Mary Robie. He and his wife joined the Hampton Church March 10, 1718.

Deacon E. J. Lane, of Dover, wrote of him: "Deacon Joshua Lane was a good man, governed in all his conduct by the love and fear of God and good-will to men. He was just in his dealings, generous to the poor, kind and compassionate to the sick and the afflicted, rejoicing with those who rejoiced and weeping with those who wept. So he gained the love and respect of all. He had clear views of the great plan of salvation, of the depravity of man, of his own unworthiness and of the need of being born again. He trusted in the Son Jesus Christ and the power of the Holy Spirit to renew and sanctify his soul. He was eminently devout, a man of prayer, not only in the social meetings, but in the family and in the closet. He was a constant attendant at public worship, and made diligent use of the means of grace, daily studying the Bible and meditating upon its instructions. As a father he was affectionate, yet faithful, thus securing the love and the respect of his children, and a numerous posterity seemed to inherit his faith and his piety, and rose up to call him blessed." Joshua Lane died at a time when there was no minister in the parish, and at his burial his son, Deacon Jeremiah Lane, wrote and read a funeral discourse called "A Memorial and Tear of Lamentation." It was printed for the benefit of his descendants, eighty-two of whom were living at the date of his death. This has been reprinted, and on August 15, 1889, a handsome granite monument was placed on his grave, and dedicated to the memory of the early generation of the Lane family.

Bathsheba (Robie), wife of Deacon Joshua Lane, was an active, intelligent, Christian woman, an excellent mother, efficiently aiding her husband in training their children to habits of industry, sobriety and morality. Her grandfather, Samuel Robie, was born at Castle Dunington, the family seat in Yorkshire, England, February 12, 1619, and came to America as early as 1639. At the ordination of Rev. James Miltimore in Stratham, in January, 1786, the eight sons of Deacon Joshua Lane met at the house of their elder brother, Deacon Samuel Lane, who was then sixty-eight years old, and Josiah, the youngest was forty-eight. Children, born at Hampton: Deacon Samuel, of whom further; Mary, February 7, 1720; Joshua, March 16, 1721; William, June 11, 1723; Joshua, July 8, 1724; Josiah, twin of Joshua; Major John, February 14, 1726; Sarah, December 3, 1727; Bathsheba, June 6, 1729; Isaiah, December 21, 1730; Deacon Jeremiah, March 10, 1732; Ebenezer, September 28, 1733; Abigail, November 13, 1734; Elizabeth, May 25, 1736; Josiah, May 19, 1738; Anna, March 24, 1741.

(IV) Deacon Samuel Lane, son of Deacon Joshua Lane, was born at Hampton, October 6, 1718. He removed in June, 1741, from Hampton to Stratham, New Hampshire. Here he continued the business of tanner and shoemaker, and purchased first a piece of wet land on the east side of the stream, and then three acres of dry land on the opposite side, where he built his house. He afterward bought eighty acres, and followed farming as well as the trade of tanner. He was often called upon to survey land. He surveyed the township of Bow and several others. He was elected selectman in 1751, and was justice of the peace for several years. He was a member of the provincial assembly in 1766, and from 1774 until he died was town clerk. When he was seventeen years old he joined the church and drew up certain articles to govern his conduct as a christian, and throughout his life followed those rules. He was elected deacon of the Stratham Congregational Church, July 4, 1765, and held the office until May 28, 1800, when he was chosen elder, an office he held the rest of his life, "displaying an exemplary christian character and enjoying that respect which his consistent life obtained from his fellow-citizens." He was deputy from Stratham to the Fourth Provincial Congress held at Exeter, New Hampshire, May 17, 1775. * * * Deacon Lane was a great lover of good books and collected a large library, which was especially rich in the department of theology. His systematic plan of devoting two hours a day to study, enabled him to became familiar with the best writers of the age and qualified him to be useful in the affairs of the government and the church."

He married (first) December 24, 1741, Mary James, of Hampton, born March 3, 1722, died January 30, 1769, daughter of Benjamin and Susanna James. He married (second) June 22, 1774, Mrs. Rachel (Parsons) Colcord, widow of Gideon Colcord, of Newmarket. She was born at Cape Ann, Massachusetts, June 29, 1726, died January 18, 1813, daughter of Josiah and Eunice (Sargent) Parsons, and granddaughter of John Parsons, whose father Jeffry Parsons was born in Exeter, England, in 1631, died in Gloucester, August, 1689. His first wife, with whom he lived twenty-seven years, is described as a kind companion and good mother. His second wife "was an excellent Christian woman, and though she had the care of seven fatherless children by her first husband, she took a deep interest in training the children of her second husband, so that his children and grandchildren long cherished the memory of her discreet and faithful care of them and her affectionate interest in their welfare." Children by first wife: Mary, July 14, 1744; Samuel, May 8, 1746; Joshua, February 9, 1748; Susanna, July 24, 1750; Sarah, September 30, 1752; Martha, February 22, 1755; Bathsheba, May 27, 1757; Jabez, of whom further.

(V) Jabez, son of Deacon Samuel Lane, was born at Stratham, May 16, 1760, died April 3, 1810. He resided on the homestead and continued the tanning business of his father. He had planned to learn a profession and was fitting for college when the revolution broke out, and he gave up study to devote himself to his father's trade. He joined the Congregational church in Stratham, and throughout his life was a devout and zealous christian. In an obituary notice written by Hon. Paine Wingate, his neighbor, his virtues as a man and christian were highly extolled. He said: "In his domestic relations he was an example worthy of our esteem and imitation. He excelled in filial piety, conjugal affection and parental care. His household was watched over, instructed and managed with unusual assiduity and regularity, even to the minutest concerns. As a neighbor he was ever ready to friendly offices, and when occasion required he shunned not to perform the most difficult part of the duty of a friend, a neighbor and a christian, to admonish, to counsel, and with meekness endeavor to reclaim those who were deviating from the path of rectitude. In his charities to the needy and distressed, except on public occasions, when he was sufficiently liberal, he studiously avoided ostentation, but they will be gratefully remembered by many who have experienced his seasonable and bountiful relief. * * * If we consider the character of the deceased in its various relations from his youth to the grave, we shall seldom find one in the private walks of life more deserving of our esteem and imitation."

He married, October 2, 1783, his step-sister, Eunice Colcord, born March 25, 1763, died April 6, 1836, daughter of Gideon and Rachel (Parsons) Colcord. Children: Anna, born December 27, 1784; Martha, January 28, 1787; Mary, April 10, 1788; George, July 14, 1791; Elizabeth, March 7, 1794; Charles, of whom further; Andrew Colcord, July 1, 1799; Deacon Edmund, June 6, 1802; Lucy, May 12, 1805.

(VI) Charles, son of Jabez Lane, was born November 27, 1796, at Stratham, died there October 27, 1884. He went to Newmarket (Newfields) in 1817, and was one of the first class at the Methodist Seminary, afterward transferred to Wilbraham, Massachusetts, and was the last survivor of his class. He began business in Newfields as a tanner, and from selling leather and shoes proceeded to deal in groceries and dry goods. He prospered and built houses to rent and sell and became one of the most substantial and wealthy citizens of the town. He held various offices of trust and honor. He was an earnest member of the Congregational church, and when his youngest son died just after finishing his course in the Andover Theological Seminary, Mr. Lane gave $500 to found a memorial scholarship there. He retired from business in November, 1867.

He married (first) September 24, 1821, Hannah French, born in Pittsfield, February 5, 1802, died January 18, 1841, daughter of Abraham and Hannah (Lane) French. He married (second) October 9, 1842, Elizabeth Berry, of Greenland, born July 8, 1804, daughter of Isaiah Berry. Children by first wife: Olivia Emeline, born November 14, 1825; Rev. John William, of whom further; Mary Elizabeth, April 29, 1830, married Rev. Jacob Chapman; Annie Lucy, September 1, 1834; Charles Edward, December 27, 1837.

(VII) Rev. John William Lane, son of Charles Lane, was born at Newfields, New Hampshire, September 7, 1827. He was a student for a time in Princeton College, and

afterward at Amherst, from which he was graduated with the degree of Bachelor of Arts in 1856. He then entered Andover Theological Seminary, from which he was graduated in 1859. He won the prize for oratory in the speaking contest while at Amherst. He served on the Christian Commission work during the civil war. He was ordained pastor of the Congregational church at Whately, Massachusetts, October 17, 1860, and continued in that pastorate for a period of eighteen years. In May, 1878, he was installed pastor of the Second Congregational Church, at North Hadley, Massachusetts, where he continued until 1911. For some years he was connected with the Massachusetts State Agricultural College at Amherst, and the Springfield Training School, Springfield, Massachusetts, as one of the faculty.

He married, August 26, 1868, Mary Haynes, born at Townsend, Massachusetts, July 11, 1841, graduated at South Hadley, Massachusetts, now Mount Holyoke College, in 1864, and was afterward a teacher in the seminary. She was a daughter of Samuel and Eliza (Spaulding) Haynes. Her brother John Haynes was in the service in the civil war, and died at Port Hudson, Louisiana, during the service. Children: 1. Charles William, born November 16, 1869, died October 21, 1870. 2. Samuel, born and died March 6, 1871. 3. John Edward, born at Whateley, February 12, 1872; educated at Hopkins Academy; graduated from Yale University with the degree of Bachelor of Arts in 1894, and Master of Arts in 1895, and from Yale Medical School with the degree of Doctor of Medicine in 1902, now practicing at North Yakima, Washington; married Alice Treat Rogers, of Ansonia, Connecticut. 4. Aleck Forbes, born July 20, 1873, died March 18, 1875. 5. Amy Sanders, born at Whateley, October 31, 1874; educated in the public schools and at Hopkins Academy; graduated at Wellesley College in the class of 1896; received the degree of Master of Arts from the University of Michigan; now a teacher in the high school at Saginaw, Michigan. 6. Wallace Rutherford, of whom further. 7. Wilfred Clary, of whom further. 8. Susan Klein, born July 13, 1881, at North Hadley; graduate of Hopkins Academy in 1899, and from the Northampton High School, Massachusetts, in 1900; student at Wellesley College 1900-1901; graduate of the Mary Hitchcock Memorial Hospital of Hanover, New Hampshire, as a trained nurse; since then engaged in settlement work in New York City.

(VIII) Professor Wallace Rutherford Lane, son of Rev. John William Lane, was born at Whateley, Massachusetts, near Northampton, August 12, 1876. He attended the public schools of Hadley, Massachusetts, and graduated from Hopkins Academy. He completed his preparation for college at Williston Seminary, Easthampton, Massachusetts, and entered Brown University, Providence, Rhode Island. While in college he won the Carpenter prize in a speaking contest. He entered the Yale Law School, and was graduated with the degree of Bachelor of Laws in 1900. He began to practice in Des Moines, Iowa, making something of a specialty of patent, manufacturing and corporation cases. For nearly ten years he was in partnership with Joseph R. Orwig. He came from Iowa to Chicago, January 1, 1910, and entered into partnership with Robert Parkinson in the practice of law. The firm has made a specialty of corporation, patent, trade mark and unfair competition cases. The office of the firm is in the Marquette building. Mr. Lane has been a contributor to the *Yale Law Journal*, to *Law and Commerce* and to the *Illinois Law Review*. Among the articles he has published in various journals may be mentioned: "The Development of Secondary Rights in Trade Mark Cases" (*Yale Law Journal*, June, 1909), "Assignability of Trade Marks," "Legitimate Competition," "Dilatory Patent Proceedings" (*The Green Bag*). Mr. Lane was professor in the Highland Park College of Law from 1900 to 1904. At present he is a lecturer at the law schools of the University of Nebraska, and of Drake University, at Des Moines.

He is a member of the American Bar Association, and in 1908 delivered an address before that organization; and also belongs to the Iowa State Bar Association. He has been admitted to practice at the bar of the supreme court of the United States, and of the States where he has engaged in practice. He is also a member of the Patent Law Association of Chicago, and the Washington Patent Bar Association; the Pi Beta Pi fraternity; the Book and Gavel Society of the Yale Law School; the Union League and University Clubs, of Chicago; the University Club, of Evanston, Illinois; the Des Moines and the Grant Club, of Des Moines, Iowa; and other clubs. In politics he is a Republican; in religion, a Congregationalist.

He married, July 1, 1901, Gertrude Gardner, born at New Bedford, Massachusetts, December 12, 1874, daughter of William F. and Esther Marion (Cook) Gardner. Children, born at Des Moines, Iowa: 1. Esther Haynes, May 27, 1902. 2. Josephine Gardner, April 3, 1904. 3. John Wallace, October 9, 1908.

(VIII) Wilfred Clary Lane, son of Rev.

John William Lane, was born at North Hadley, Massachusetts, June 23, 1878. He attended the public schools of his native town, and was graduated from Hopkins Academy in 1896, subsequently taking courses preparatory for college at Phillips Andover Academy and Williston Seminary. He entered Brown University, but was compelled to abandon his course there before its completion on account of ill health, and went south to seek a change of climate. While there he matriculated in the Mercer University Law School, at Macon, Georgia, and was graduated with honors, receiving the degree of Bachelor of Laws with the class of 1900. He then entered Yale Law School, receiving the degree of Bachelor of Laws from that institution in 1901. He began the practice of law at Macon, Georgia, continuing his residence there from 1901 to 1905, and in connection with his professional work in Macon lectured at the Mercer University Law School for four years. In January, 1905, • he was appointed clerk of the United States circuit and district courts, and United States commissioner at Augusta, Georgia, which position he held until March 30, 1907. His resignation was then tendered for the purpose of accepting a promotion to the office of referee in bankruptcy for the southern district of Georgia, with headquarters at Valdosta. This station he continued successfully to fill, in addition to engaging in general practice, and specializing in United States court practice and patent litigation, until June, 1912, when he resigned to engage in legal practice at Des Moines, Iowa.

In politics he is a Republican, and was a delegate to the Republican National Convention at Chicago in 1908, from the Eleventh Congressional District of Georgia. He is a member of the American Bar Association; the State Bar Associations of Georgia and Florida; a member of the Bar of the Supreme Court of the United States, the supreme courts of Georgia, Florida, and Iowa, and various courts of the United States for the circuits where he has engaged in practice. He belongs to the Phi Delta Theta national college fraternity; the Capitol City Club, of Atlanta; the Country Club, of Augusta; the Alcyone-Suwannee Club, of Florida; and the Grant Club, of Des Moines, Iowa. In fraternal organizations he is a member of the Benevolent and Protective Order of Elks; a past chancellor and member of the Grand Lodge of Georgia, Knights of Pythias; is a Thirty-second Degree Mason, and a Shriner. In religion he is a Congregationalist.

He married, October 2, 1907, Lile Darling Woodbury, born in Burlington, Vermont,

March 3, 1883, daughter of ex-Governor Urban Woodbury, of Vermont. They have one child: John Woodbury, born at Valdosta, Georgia, May 30, 1909.

The name is a very ancient one FIELD and can be traced back to the conquest of England by William the Norman. Probably not a dozen families can prove so great an antiquity. The name is one of those derived from locality. Burke states that this family was originally in Alsace (then part of French, now German territory), seated at the Chateau de la Feld, or "of the field", near Colmar, in German Kolmar, from the darkest of the middle ages. Sir Hubertus de la Feld was the first of the line that immigrated to England, and in 1069 was enrolled as owner of lands by gift of the conqueror, as compensation for military services, in the county of Lancashire. He was one of the Counts de la Feld, of Colmar. In the fourteenth century, because of wars with France, the French prefixes were dropped, and the name thereafter written Field.

(I) Roger del Feld, born in Sowerby, England, about 1240, was a descendant of Sir Hubertus de la Feld. He was head of the family which settled in Lancashire and Kent counties.

(II) Thomas, son of Roger del Feld, was born about 1278, in Sowerby. He was a jeweler there in 1307.

(III) John Feld, son of Thomas del Feld, was born in 1300, in Sowerby, and had land in that place in 1336.

(IV) Thomas, son of John Feld, was born in 1330, in Sowerby. He was constable there in 1365, and greave in 1370, and also filled other public offices. His wife's name was Annabelle.

(V) Thomas (2), son of Thomas (1) and Annabelle Feld, was born in 1360, and willed lands to his wife Isabelle, in the territory of Bradford. He died in 1429 at his residence in Bradford.

(VI) William, son of Thomas (2) and Isabel Feld, was probably born in Bradford, died there April, 1480. His wife Katherine was administratrix of his estate.

(VII) William (2), son of William (1) and Katherine Feld, was born in Bradford, and lived in East Ardsley.

(VIII) Richard Felde, son of William (2) Feld, was born, probably, in East Ardsley, where he was a husbandman, and died December, 1542. His wife Elizabeth was one of his executors.

(IX) John Field, son of Richard and Elizabeth Felde, was born about 1535, at East

Ardsley. He married, in 1650, Jane, daughter of John Amyas. She died August 30, 1609, and he died May, 1587. He was an eminent astronomer, and introduced into England, in 1557, the Copernican system, against the opposition of scientists of his day, and in recognition of this service to astronomy a sphere was later added to and surmounted the family coat-of-arms.

(X) John, son of John and Jane (Amyas) Field, was born about 1568 in Ardsley. He moved away before attaining his majority. Record of his death has not been found.

(XI) Zachariah, grandson of John (1) Field, the astronomer, American ancestor of the Field family, was born in 1596, at East Ardsley, Yorkshire, England. The Field family has usually taken the liberal side of religious and political questions. In 1629 Zachariah Field left England on account of the persecutions of dissenters, and landed in Boston, settling in Dorchester. In 1636 he was one of Rev. Thomas Hooker's congregation, which settled in Hartford, Connecticut. With the more liberal members of that church he removed to Northampton, Massachusetts, in 1659. He was engaged in mercantile business and had a large trade with the Indians. He was one of the original twenty-five proprietors of Hatfield, same colony, and was a member of the committee which laid out the lands. He received a grant of land there in 1661, and resided there until his death, June 30, 1666. He married about 1640. Their children were: Mary; Zachariah; John; Samuel, of whom further; Joseph.

(XII) Sergeant Samuel Field, son of Zachariah Field, was born about 1651, at Hartford, Connecticut. He married, August 9, 1676, Sarah, daughter of Thomas and Catherine (Chapin) Gilbert, of Springfield. She married (second) October 17, 1702, Ebenezer Chapin, of Springfield. He came with his father to Northampton, Massachusetts, in 1663. He removed to Hatfield, Massachusetts, where he became a prominent and influential man, holding many town offices. He was sergeant in the Turner's Falls fight, May 19, 1676. He was slain by Indians, while hoeing corn June 24, 1697. The settlement of his estate was dated September 20, 1701. Children: Samuel (2), of whom further; Thomas, June 30, 1680; Sarah, June 30, 1683; Zachariah, August 29, 1685; Ebenezer, March 17, 1688; Mary, July 23, 1690; Josiah, November 5, 1692; Joshua, April 9, 1695.

(XIII) Deacon Samuel (2) Field, son of Sergeant Samuel (1) Field, was born September 27, 1678, at Hatfield, Massachusetts. He married, January 10, 1706, Mrs. Hannah

NEW ENGLAND.

(Edwards) Hoyt, born September 10, 1675, died July 23, 1747. She was a daughter of Joseph Edwards, and her first husband, David Hoyt, was killed by the Indians in the Meadow Fight. Deacon Field died August 25, 1762, at Deerfield, Massachusetts. He was wounded in a fight with the Indians, August 25, 1725, near where the present depot of Greenfield now stands. He was a deacon and a very prominent man in the town. He was granted by the general court, in 1736, two hundred acres of land on the east side of Northfield, probably for military services.

The following is a manuscript account of the fight with the Indians, by Reverend Stephen Williams, about 1730: "August 25, 1725, Deacon Samu Field, Deacon Samu Child, Sergt. Joseph Severance, John Wells, Joshua Wells and Thomas Bardwell, went over to Derfd river to the Green river farms, and they took a cow with them, designing to put her in the pasture, the Indians ambushed them, but Deacon Child, driving the cow, discovered them and cried out, 'Indians!' John Wells discharged his gun at an Indian, who fell upon his friend. Deacon Field, being at some distance from the company, rode towards them, but the company being before separated one from the other, retreated toward the mill and at a considerable distance from the hill, they halted, jt John Wells might load his gun, and then the Indians fird upon them, and wound Dea Samu Field, the ball passing through the right Hypocondria, cutting off three plails of the mysenteice ; a gut hung out of the wound in length almost two inches, which was cut off even with the body ; the bullet passing between the lowest and the next rib, cutting at its going forth part of the lower rib, His hand being close to his body when ye ball came forth, it entered at the root of the heel of ye thumb, cutting the bone of the forefinger, resting between the fore and second finger ; was cut out and all the wounds through the blessing of God upon men were healed in less than five weeks by Dr. Thomas Hastings," etc.

Children, born at Hatfield and Deerfield: Elizabeth, April 16, 1707; Samuel, February 20, 1709; David, of whom further ; Eunice, May 29, 1714; Thankful, 1716; Ebenezer, October 2, 1723.

(XIV) Colonel David Field, son of Deacon Samuel (2) Field, was born at Hatfield, January 4, 1712. He married, in 1740, Mrs. Thankful (Taylor) Doolittle, born July 18, 1716, daughter of Thomas Taylor, and widow of Oliver Doolittle. She died March 26, 1803. He was a merchant in Deerfield and traded with the Indians on the Mohawk river. From

his generosity and losses due to the revolution he failed, and his accounts receivable, amounting to 20,000 pounds, realized not six per cent. He was a deputy to the provincial congress at Concord in 1774, and at Cambridge in 1775. He was member of the Massachusetts council of safety. He was commissary general under Stark at the battle of Bennington, August 16, 1777. He was in the confidence of John Hancock and other leaders. He was colonel of the Fifth Hampshire County Regiment, commissioned February 8, 1776, and his regiment turned out at the battle of Ticonderoga as volunteers. His resignation on account of age was dated at Deerfield, February 4, 1778, and accepted by the general court, February 20, 1778. He was active and influential in the town and held many important offices. Children, born at Deerfield: Mary, October 31, 1741; Samuel (3), of whom further; Rufus, July 20, 1745, died young; David, May 4, 1747; Tirza, April 16, 1749; Oliver, September 13, 1751; Elihu, October 16, 1753; Thankful, March 25, 1758; Filena, September 5, 1761.

(XV) Rev. Samuel (3) Field, son of Colonel David Field, was born in Deerfield, September 14, 1743. He married April 26, 1769, Sarah Childs, born 1742, died December 31, 1831, daughter of Samuel Childs. He was graduated from Yale College in 1762, and studied divinity under Rev. Jonathan Ashley, but afterward read law in the office of Daniel Jones, at Hinsdale, New Hampshire. After being admitted to the bar he returned to Deerfield, where he was for a time a merchant. In 1771 he opened a law office in Greenfield, where he also engaged in trade. In 1774 he removed to Conway and followed farming for two years, returning thence to Deerfield, where he resided until May, 1794, and then returned to Conway to practice his profession.

"In his person, he exceeded the ordinary height of man, thickset, without inclining to corpulency. His face exhibited a relaxed appearance and his natural countenance an unusual gravity and sternness, but when enlivened by conversation a complacency and thorough good nature that was highly pleasing and could scarcely fail of persuading a stranger of the excellence of his heart. He was careless in pecuniary matters as well as in dress, but in domestic life was much beloved by all. * * * His naturally pacific disposition led him to regret the late war with its multiplied evils resulting to all parts of the social and political society. He did not take an active part in the revolution. No man rejoiced more sincerely in the establishment of the independence of his country, nor had the republican institutions which were the result of that glorious struggle any more heartfelt friends. * * * He represented the town of Deerfield in the general court for several years and was a member of the convention that adopted the Constitution of the United States, besides holding various other offices. In religious matters, he was a firm believer in the doctrines of Swedenborg and Sandemann, and was known as a Sandemanian, upon which he lectured and wrote quite a treatise upon them. He was also quite a political, prose and poetical writer. Part of his works were collected and published. * * * He possessed a mind always content with his present condition, and he could tread with equal tenor the adverse or prosperous path. He was just and upright in all his dealings; quiet and peaceful, full of compassion; and ready to do good to all men according to his abilities and opportunities."

Children: Robert Rufus, of whom further: Samuel Edwards, October 2, 1773; Samuel Edwards, July 31, 1775; Sarah, April 11, 1777, died young; Sarah, June 12, 1779; George Plumb, July 22, 1781; Tirza, February 13, 1784.

(XVI) Robert Rufus, son of Rev. Samuel (3) Field, was born August 22, 1771, at Deerfield. He married, January 15, 1795, Patty Hoyt, born 1775, died July 23, 1859, daughter of Jonathan and Abigail (Nash) Hoyt. He removed to Conway, Massachusetts, in 1791, and in 1796 to Phelps, Ontario county, New York. In 1800 he went to Geneva, New York, and in 1808 returned to Deerfield, where he died. He was for many years toll-gatherer of the Deerfield river bridge at Cheapside, and during most of his life followed farming. Children: Richard Edward, of whom further; Abigail Field, September 19, 1799; Robert Rufus, June 29, 1806; Tirza Ann, baptized April 21, 1809.

(XVII) Richard Edward, son of Robert Rufus Field, was born at Conway, Mass., September 5, 1796.

He married (first) June 21, 1820, Elizabeth Wait, born March 10, 1797, died April 4, 1864, daughter of William and Hepsibeth Wait. He married (second) Mrs. Sarah T. (Snow) Thompson, daughter of David and Sarah R. (Wait) Snow, of Heath, and widow of John Thompson. Mr. Field lived most of his life in Greenfield, where he was a manufacturer of carriages and sleighs. He removed for about two years to Guilford, Vermont, where he engaged in the manufacture of woodenware, returning to Greenfield and his former business. He was a Whig in politics and held the office of justice of the

peace for many years. For a time he accepted an appointment in the customs service under President Fillmore. For upwards of forty years he was connected with St. James Episcopal Church, as vestryman, warden, superintendent of Sunday-school, and lay reader, his license for the latter dating about 1827. His private journal records many sermons and addresses delivered in churches at his home and neighboring towns. It also mentioned that, in 1831-2, as lay reader at Guilford, Vermont. he walked every other Sunday to the West Village, a distance of four miles, for over a year, to hold service for which he "received one quarter of veal" as compensation. He was a frequent contributor to the press, writing under the nom de plume of "Saturday Night". He died November 14, 1884.

Children born at Deerfield: Richard, October 5, 1821; David Griswold, August 9, 1823; James Edward, December 25, 1825; Charles Reed, of whom further; Martha Elizabeth, March 23, 1836.

(XVIII) Charles Reed, son of Richard Edward Field, was born September 24, 1828, in that part of Deerfield that has since become a part of Greenfield. He attended the public schools and the then famous Fallenberg Academy, at Greenfield. Engaging in the grocery and forwarding business, that took him to Boston frequently, he there saw some children's cabs made in England. Purchasing one as a pattern he brought it home to his father, who was then manufacturing carriages and sleighs. Several were made and sold so readily in Boston, that he, in copartnership with his father, as R. E. Field & Son, engaged in their manufacture, one of the first of their kind in this country. Later disposing of all other business interests he founded the Charles R. Field Manufacturing Company, in which he remained as its head for the balance of his life. He was many times selectman of Greenfield, vestryman of St. James Church, executor of several estates, director of First National Bank, trustee of Franklin Savings Institution, and at one time candidate for auditor on the Democratic state ticket of Massachusetts.

He married, July 5, 1854, Martha Hinkley, daughter of Phineas Wait and Mary (Pierce) Barr. She was born June 7, 1835, at Petersham, Massachusetts. Her brother George served in the Fifty-second Massachusetts Regiment in the civil war. Children: 1. Harry Ledyard, born at Greenfield, October 31, 1861, associated with his brother Charles E., in Chicago; married Elizabeth Wait, of Greenfield. 2. Frank Russell, residing in Denver, Colorado; married Jessie McElheney, of LaSalle, Illinois. 3. Charles E., of whom further.

(XIX) Charles Edward, son of Charles Reed Field, was born at Greenfield, Massachusetts, June 3, 1857. He attended the public schools there. In 1870 he entered Norwich University, and was graduated in 1874 with the degree of Bachelor of Science. He was employed in the construction of the Hoosac Tunnel line of Fitchburg railroad, 1874-5. Then he became associated with his father in manufacturing children's carriages at Greenfield until 1877, when he entered the employ of the D. B. Shipman White Lead Works, at Chicago, Illinois, was elected secretary and treasurer of the company. When this company was merged with the National Lead Company he was made comptroller of its Chicago branch and later assistant manager. In November, 1910, he was elected manager and a director of the company. He is a member of the Protestant Episcopal church, was vice-president of the Chicago Church Club, a member of the board of missions, diocese of Chicago, and for many years a trustee of the Church Home for the Aged. He has held the office of president in the Massachusetts Society of Chicago, the National Paint, Oil & Varnish Association, and the Chicago Paint, Oil & Varnish Club. In addition to this he is a member of the New England Society of Chicago, the Chicago Athletic Association, and the Evanston Golf Club. He married, January 3, 1883, Helen Ledyard Powers, born at Coldwater, Michigan, May 11, 1858, daughter of David Cooper and Margaret (Ledyard) Powers. Children: 1. Margaret Ledyard, born at Coldwater, Michigan, August 18, 1884. 2. Charles Barr, born at Chicago, February 4, 1888; married, April 10, 1912, Ann Lamont, daughter of Reuben and Elizabeth (Wood) Dugan.

KEYES Robert Keyes, the immigrant ancestor, settled in Watertown, Massachusetts, before or in the year 1633. The records there say that he moved to Sudbury, Massachusetts, June 16, 1645, and died there in 1647, while another record gives his death as July 16, 1647. His death was recorded in Watertown, Newbury, Plymouth and Sudbury. He seems to have been in Watertown in 1633 or earlier, to have moved to Newbury between 1643 and 1645, and to Sudbury in 1645. His widow married, in 1658, John Gage (in November, 1664, according to Plymouth record.) Children, recorded at Watertown, except Peter and the second Mary, born in Newbury: Sarah, born May 26, 1633; Peter, probably son of Robert;

Rebecca, March 17, 1637; Phebe, June 17, 1639; Mary, 1641, died 1642; Elias, mentioned below; Mary, June 16, 1645.

(II) Elias, son of Robert Keyes, was born in Watertown, Massachusetts, May 20, 1643. He married, September 11, 1665, Sarah, daughter of John Blanford, or Blanchard. Children, born in Sudbury: Elias, November 15, 1666; John, probably, 1668, supposed son of Elias; James, mentioned below; Sarah, April 9, 1673; Thomas, February 8, 1674.

(III) James, son of Elias Keyes, was born in Sudbury, Massachusetts, September 13, 1670, and died in Bolton, Massachusetts, September 25, 1746. He was one of the proprietors of the Indian Plantation in Marlboro in 1693. He was third in the list of twenty-two town clerks of Bolton. He married Hannah ———, of Marlboro, and she died March 19, 1742. Children, born at Sudbury: Elias, mentioned below; James, born 1696; Mathias and Jonathan, twins, 1698; Elizabeth, 1701; Hannah, 1704.

(IV) Elias (2), son of James Keyes, was born in 1694, at Sudbury, and died February 27, 1756. He was one of the sixteen founders of the church in Shrewsbury, Massachusetts. About 1742 or 1743 he moved to New Marlboro, and was dismissed from the Shrewsbury church to that place. He married, at Marlboro, December 13, 1718, Keziah Brigham. Children: Elias, born July 22, 1719; Mary, April 13, 1721, died 1724; David, born September 20, 1722; Robert, mentioned below; Mary, December 12, 1726; Charles, April 29, 1728; Keziah, February 13, 1730; Paul, September 16, 1731; Zenas, March 9, 1733, died 1740; Martha, June 27, 1736; Thaddeus, June 17, 1738; Deliverance, 1740.

(V) Robert (2), son of Elias Keyes, was born April 18, 1725, at Marlborough, and went with the family into Berkshire county, Massachusetts. He settled in Sheffield. He married Azubah ———. Children: David, mentioned below; Elizabeth, born October 20, 1754; Hannah, September 26, 1756; Phebe, August, 1759; Mary, born March 5, 1767, died May 10, 1769; Jane, June 22, 1769.

(VI) David, son of Robert (2) Keyes, was born at Sheffield, August 28, 1753. He removed to Middletown, Vermont, when a young man. He married ——— Stevens. He was a soldier in the revolution, from Vermont, and took part in the battle of Ticonderoga. Children: Robert, born September 6, 1783; Tolman, went west and has many descendants there; Stephen, mentioned below; Hiram, went west, where he has descendants; Lyman, born 1796, lived at Middletown, where he died January 23, 1833, leaving one son; Jonas C., left home young; Sally, married —— Beals; Azubah; Polly, died in Middletown; Emmeline, went west; Azubah and Polly, never married.

(VII) Stephen, son of David Keyes, was born in 1790-1, at Middletown, and settled in his native town. His brother Robert lived in Poultney, and afterward in Knox county, Ohio. Stephen Keyes was a farmer. He married Polly Waldo, born 1789, died 1864, daughter of Gamaliel Waldo. The Waldo family was prominent in Windham county, Connecticut. He died at Middletown, December 28, 1865. Children, born at Middletown: 1. Harley C., 1813; lived in East Rutland, Vermont, died March, 1878; married Emily Mallory; children: Merrett, and Laura C., reside in West Rutland. 2. Mary Ann, 1814, died October 31, 1848. 3. Sally Maria, married Lucius B. Adams, and resided at Castleton, Vermont; children: John Quincy, Charles, Mary Ann, and Jennie, wife of Almer Gardner, and resides in Rutland, Vermont. 4. Isaac B., 1822, died June 15, 1862; his widow lives at Spencerport, New York; had a daughter who died in infancy. 5. Annis J., born 1827, died January 13, 1842. 6. Lovisa, married Alanson Adams, and had Alphonso, Adelaide, and Emma Adams, all deceased, and she died in Poultney about 1866. 7. David H., mentioned below.

(VIII) David Harrison Keyes, son of Stephen Keyes, was born at Middletown, Vermont, August 11, 1833, in the village of Middletown Springs. He attended the public and select schools of his native town, and worked during his youth on his father's farm there. His first business venture was as salesman traveling for a patent medicine concern. Subsequently he became sales agent of Johnson & Browning, of New York, map publishers. He then entered partnership with Nelson Ransom, of Poultney, Vermont, where they established a general store, and continued in business as Ransom & Keyes until the store was burned in February, 1862. In the autumn following he went to Chicago and opened an agency of the Universal clothes wringer. Afterward he represented the Amsterdam wringer, and was a jobber in other similar goods. He established a business as contractor in gravel-roofing, and carried it on for a period of twenty-five years. Among other important contracts he had that for the roofing of the buildings on the entire system of the Chicago & Northwestern railroad for a period of twenty-six years. He was also for many years a part owner of the Artesian Stone and Lime Works of Chicago, Keyes & Thatcher, proprietors. In 1902 the firm leased its

plant for twenty years, and since then Mr. Keyes has been virtually retired from active business, devoting himself to his private affairs and to the enjoyment of well-earned leisure. He was formerly a member of the Douglas Club and the Oakland Club of Chicago. He attends the Evangelical church. In politics he is a Progressive Republican. He is a member of the New England Society of Chicago.

He married, in January, 1873, Ella Jewell, born 1847, daughter of Jefferson and Susan (Fuller) Jewell, of Rockford, Illinois. Her mother was a cousin of Margaret Fuller, the transcendental thinker, scholar and author. Mr. and Mrs. Keyes have no children. They reside at 4420 Oakenwald avenue, Chicago, and Mr. Keyes has an office at 145 Roanoke Building.

DUTTON The family of Dutton or Dunton takes its name from the ancient town of Dutton, England, mentioned three times in the Domesday Book. One part of this town was held by Odard or Udard, also spelled Hodard and Hudard. The family has borne a coat-of-arms from the earliest days, and from 1060 to the present time has ranked among the leading noble families. Hodard, the progenitor of the family in England, came from Normandy in 1066 with William the Conqueror. In the distribution of the conquered lands he received a good part of the town of Dutton in Cheshire, and settled there. This grant came from Hugh Lupus, formerly Earl of Avranches, later Earl of Chester. The sister of Hugh Lupus married William of Normandy. One authority makes Hodard a nephew of Hugh Lupus, and therefore a nephew by marriage to the King. Hodard had five brothers—Edward, Wolmere, Horswyne, Wolfarth, and Nigell. Hodard held Aston under William FitzNigell, Baron of Halton. Hodard was Lord of Dutton; according to the family record in 1665 the land was then in the custody of his lineal descendant, Lady Elinor Vicomptess Kilmorey, daughter of Thomas Dutton. His descendants added the name of the town to their Christian names, after he received the land.

(I) John Dutton, the American ancestor, came to America in 1630. He was before the general court of Massachusetts, October 29, 1640. The names of Dunton and Dutton have the same origin, and in the same families the two spellings were used as late as the revolution. It is presumed therefore that the Dutton and Dunton pioneers at Reading, Massachusetts, may have been sons of John Dutton; Thomas, born 1621, mentioned below; Josiah, lived in Reading; Robert of Reading; Samuel of Reading, born about 1620.

(II) Thomas, son of John Dutton, was born in England in 1621. Most of the New England families of the name are traced to him as their ancestor. Thomas Dutton lived in Reading seven years, and in 1668 had lived ten years in Woburn. He removed to Billerica in 1669, and was accepted as an inhabitant November 22, 1669. He settled on the south side of Fox brook by the old and abandoned road to the Great plain, northwest of the Davis place. He was living in Billerica in 1675, and died there January 22, 1687. His wife Susannah died August 27, 1684, aged fifty-eight years. He married second, November 10, 1684, Ruth Hooper, probably widow of William Hooper of Reading. Children by first wife, born at Reading: Thomas, mentioned below; Mary, born September 14, 1651; Susanna, February 27, 1653-4; John, March 28, 1656-7. Born at Woburn: Elizabeth, born January 28, 1658-9; Joseph, January 25, 1660-1; Sarah, March 5, 1661-2; James, August 22, 1665; Benjamin, February 19, 1667.

(III) Thomas (2), son of Thomas (1) Dutton, was born in Reading, Massachusetts, September 14, 1648. He married (first) in Billerica, January 10, 1678-9, Rebecca Draper, a widow, of Concord. She died March 16, 1720-1. He married (second), November, 1721, Sarah Converse. He bought or had land of his father in Billerica in 1670; also purchased land of John Stearns. He was in Sergeant Hill's garrison in 1675, and in the center squadron in 1707. In 1677 he served in the ill-starred expedition to the Eastward, as the Kennebec country was called. His petition to the general court (Mass. Archives, vol. lxix, page 209) contains the best account of this expedition. Two hundred Christian Indians from Natick and forty English soldiers took part under Captain Benjamin Sweat of Hampton. Of these, fifty men were killed by the Indians and a score more wounded. Dutton was shot through the side of his belt and through the left knee, "and fell down not able to help himself". His escape from death was marvelous. Children, born at Billerica: Rebecca, born November 13, 1679; Thomas, mentioned below; John, February 24, 1683-4, died December 14, 1687; Susannah, born April 30, 1686, died September 3, 1688; Susan, born November 4, 1687.

(IV) Thomas (3), son of Thomas (2) Dutton, was born at Billerica, Massachusetts, August 2, 1681, and died at Westford in

1759. He moved to Westford after 1738, and he and his sons lived in the vicinity of the Jonathan T. Colburn place. He married at Billerica, January 31, 1710-1?, Hannah Burge of Chelmsford, Massachusetts. Children, born in Billerica: Joseph, born December 1712; Thomas, mentioned below; John, born February 13, 1715; Josiah, February 21, 1716-17; Hannah, August 10, 1718, died October following; Rebecca, twin of Hannah, died young; Benjamin, born May 2, 1720; James, May 5, 1721; Hannah, June 13, 1723; Rebecca, May 18, 1726; Ephraim, January 1, 1728; David, 1731; Susanna, March 10, 1732-3.

(V) Thomas (4), son of Thomas (3) Dutton, was born at Billerica, August 28, 1713, and moved to Westford, Massachusetts, about 1746. He married (first) Mary Hill, who died about 1754. He married (second), September 9, 1756, Sarah Fitch, a daughter of Joseph and Mary (Clark) Fitch. She was born in Boston, May 8, 1731. Thomas Dutton remained in Westford, but a change of town lines placed him among the residents of Lunenburg near the present line of Fitchburg. Children, by first wife: Mary, born at Billerica, December 14, 1737; Silas, born at Westford, November 23, 1739; Sarah, March 18, 1741. Born in Lunenburg: Hannah, January 28, 1744-5; Sybil, December 9, 1749; Elizabeth, December 18, 1752. Children by second wife: Joseph Fitch, born July 3, 1757; Susanna, March 7, 1759; John, mentioned below; James, baptized November 20, 1773, at Rockingham, Vermont. The family removed to Rockingham, Vermont, before the revolution, and Sarah, wife of Thomas, was admitted to the Rockingham church by letter from the Lunenburg church; at this time Thomas was refused admission because of irregular attendance, but was afterward admitted. As early as December 31, 1746, Thomas Dutton appears to have been interested in Charlestown, New Hampshire (township No. 4), as his name appears among the petitioners for the protection of the town during the French and Indian war. Another signer was John Dutton of Townsend, Massachusetts.

(VI) John, son of Thomas (4) Dutton, was born in Lunenburg, July 9, 1761, and died March 10, 1826. He married (first), in Fitchburg, August 31, 1786 (intention published August 13, 1786, at Putney, Vermont), Betsey Hodgkin of Fitchburg. She was born in 1761 and died May 11, 1818, at Vergennes, Vermont. He married (second), at Lowville, New York, February 15, 1820, Lucy Hamilton of Nova Scotia. She was born October

20, 1770, and died at Auburn, Ohio, November 9, 1864. John Dutton was a soldier in the war of 1812, assistant to the surgeon, in 1814, and took part in the battle of Bennington. Children by first wife: Betsey, born September 24, 1787, died May 18, 1805; Sally, born May 22, 1789, died September 18, 1811; James M., born in Claremont, New Hampshire, September 11, 1790, died April 13, 1859; Lucy, January 19, 1793, died February 8, 1825; Charles Olcott, February 25, 1795, died September 11, 1818; Rufus, mentioned below; Sybil, July 22, 1801, died April 12, 1820; Thomas R., October 13, 1803, died January 24, 1829.

(VII) Rufus, son of John Dutton, was born in Rutland, Vermont, October 13, 1797. When a young man he was a manufacturer of hats and in later life a farmer. He died November 26, 1880. He married, February 28, 1828, Mary Campbell Ball, who was born June 20, 1798, in Pittsfield, Massachusetts, a daughter of Jonas Ball; she died May 27, 1872. Children: 1. Catherine Elizabeth Browning, born in Norfolk, St. Lawrence county, New York, December 31, 1828, died January 28, 1906. 2. Charles Frederick Ball, mentioned below. 3. James Rufus, born at Canton, St. Lawrence county, February 22, 1833, died January 12, 1904; he was auditor and afterward purchasing agent of the Michigan Central Railroad Company; he married Deborah Adams and had three children: Alfred, who lives in Detroit, Michigan; Robert, who lives in Toledo, Ohio; and Edith May, who married Frank Wilcox. 4. John Byron, born at Bainbridge, Geauga county, Ohio, July 1, 1835; married Emily Russell and had four children: Russell, Rufus, Mabel and Elsie Dutton. John B. Dutton, the father of these children, enlisted as private and rose through all the grades to the rank of captain of the Second Ohio Regiment of Volunteer Cavalry, serving the full term of three years and three months in the civil war. He also served as private in the First Ohio Infantry, first call for three months' volunteers. 5. George Whipple, born at Bainbridge, Cleveland, Ohio, October 28, 1837, and died November 4, 1869, unmarried. 6. Betsey Ann, born at Newburg, Cleveland, Ohio, August 13, 1840.

(VIII) Charles Frederick Ball, M. D., son of Rufus Dutton, was born in Norfolk, St. Lawrence county, New York, January 5, 1831. He attended the public schools and Shaw Academy in Euclid, Ohio, and entered Hudson Preparatory School, now Western Reserve College, where he fitted for college. He entered Oberlin College and was a student there in 1854-5, leaving his class to take up the study of medicine at the Cleveland Medical College and afterward at the Bellevue Hospital Medical College in New York City, from which he was graduated with the degree of Doctor of Medicine in 1864. He began to practice medicine in Cleveland, but after a short time enlisted in the One Hundred and Fiftieth Regiment, Ohio Volunteer Infantry, from Cleveland, as a private. Subsequently he took the United States medical examination at Columbus, Ohio, and was appointed first assistant surgeon in his own regiment and served in that rank to the end of the war. He was detailed to take charge of one of the military hospitals in the suburbs of Washington. After he was mustered out, he took a post-graduate course at the College of Physicians and Surgeons in New York City, 1866-1867. Since that time he has been in general practice in Cleveland, Ohio. In 1884 he was appointed lecturer on diseases of the chest at the College of Physicians and Surgeons in Cleveland and afterward he was appointed professor of Obstetrics and Diseases of children. He also occupied the chair of Medical and Clinical Medicine. He resigned June 15, 1901, and retired after seventeen years of faithful and brilliant service. Upon his retirement from the faculty, his associates passed a resolution of appreciation of his fidelity and ability and of regret at his retirement.

Dr. Dutton is a member of the American Medical Association, of the Cuyahoga County Medical Society, of which he was at one time president, and the Cleveland Medical Society. From time to time he has contributed to various medical journals and publications articles and papers of a technical nature. He has been a member of the Congregational church since the age of fourteen and he is a member of the Congregational Club of Cleveland. In politics he is an independent Republican. He is a member of the New England Society of Cleveland and the Western Reserve.

He married, August 12, 1857, at Cleveland, Mary Sophia Newton, born in Jefferson county, New York, died May 9, 1904, a daughter of William H. and Alvira (Coughlin) Newton. They had one child, Charles Frederic, mentioned below.

(IX) Charles Frederic, son of Charles Frederick Ball Dutton, was born in Cleveland, April 5, 1870. He was educated in the public schools of his native city and at Oberlin College, from which he was graduated in the class of 1893 with the degree of Bachelor of Arts. Since then he has been a teacher in the public schools of Cleveland and is now on the faculty of the Cleveland High School of Commerce. In religion he is a Congregationalist. He married, June 25, 1902, Elma Edwina Booth, born at Litchfield, Medina county, Ohio, July 12, 1882, a daughter of Sherman William Booth. They have one child, Frederic Booth Dutton, born in Cleveland, December 24, 1906.

WEBB   Samuel Webb, the immigrant ancestor, was born in Redriff, near London, England, December 25, 1696, son of Captain Samuel Webb, who served in the reign of Queen Anne, and who was lost at sea in 1708. Samuel Webb was left an orphan, his mother having died in 1706, and he was "bound out" to learn his trade. As his master or guardian did not allow him as much liberty as he desired, in 1713 he ran away, taking passage on a ship for America, but where he went first after reaching this country has not been ascertained. It is likely that he followed the sea for a time.

In an account of him, written by his grandson, Seth Webb, it states that he landed in Rhode Island and was taken into the family of Mr. McIntyre, a blacksmith, of Tiverton, Rhode Island, and there learned his trade, and though his name is not found on Tiverton records, he could have been there at that time, for he was a minor. The first public record of him is in Braintree and Weymouth, giving his first marriage, September 15, 1721, to Susanna, born in Weymouth, January 14, 1702-03, died there December 22, 1724, daughter of John and Susanna (Porter) Randall. He married (second), August 11, 1726, Bethiah (Farrow) Spear, born at Hingham, Massachusetts, November 29, 1704, died at Little Isle of Holt, November 30, 1770, daughter of John and Persis (Holbrook) Farrow, of Hingham, and widow of David Spear, of Braintree, Massachusetts. Rev. Nehemiah Hobart officiated at these marriages, and they were recorded in the Weymouth town records. Samuel Webb may have been distantly related to the other Webbs of Braintree and Weymouth. It is a curious coincidence that he should have chosen for his residence on leaving Rhode Island the same town in which Richard Webb settled as early as 1640, but a mile or so from the home of Christopher Webb, of Braintree. But a thorough search shows that he was not a direct descendant of any of the pioneers of this name. There is no reason to doubt the family record of his birth in England. About 1730 Samuel Webb moved away from Weymouth, leaving his

sons Samuel and Thomas with their grandfather, John Randall, who was chosen guardian for the son Samuel, March 14, 1736, according to the Suffolk probate records. The history of Deer Isle states that he once lived in the vicinity of Salem, Massachusetts. He was in that part of Falmouth, now Westbrook, in 1740. The history of Gorham states that he was in Boston in 1744. He moved to what is now Windham in 1745 and settled on home lot No. 23. He was a blacksmith there and the first schoolmaster. He served as a soldier in the Indian wars of 1747-48 and in 1757. He probably moved from Windham to North Yarmouth about 1760, and about 1764 to Little Isle of Holt. After the death of one of his sons in 1784, he moved to Deer Isle, where he died February 15, 1785. In the burying ground of North Weymouth, Massachusetts, is a large granite monument erected by his descendants over the spot where his first wife lies buried, and upon this is the following inscription: "Samuel Webb, son of Samuel Webb, born in London, England, 1696, died in Deer Isle, Maine, Feb. 15, 1785." Other family names are inscribed thereon, including that of his first wife. He and his second wife are buried in the old graveyard at Deer Isle.

Children of first wife: Samuel, born July 31, 1722; Thomas, December 21, 1723, died January 31, 1724; Thomas, December 1, 1724. Children of second wife: David, born March 29, 1727; Susannah, March 29, 1729; Ezekiel; Seth, mentioned below; John, born about 1735; Eli, November 17, 1737; James; Elizabeth, June 14, 1743; Josiah, January 21, 1745; Elizabeth, March 4, 1746-47.

(II) Seth, son of Samuel Webb, was born in 1732. He settled in Windham, Maine. He was surprised and captured by Indians, August 22, 1750, and carried to Canada, but returned home before the next Indian war. In 1756 he took part in the Indian fight at Windham. He was on military duty again with Elisha Webb in 1758. He bought lot No. 16 at Windham, May 29, 1760, for forty pounds, and sold it in 1761. He bought land at Gorham, Maine, May 28, 1763. In 1764 he was of New Gloucester, Maine, according to a deed in which he conveyed part of his Gorham land to Ebenezer Hall, of Falmouth, and in the same year he removed to the Isle of Holt, now Kimball's Island, on which he was the first settler. He was at what is now Hampden, Maine, in 1776-77, for a short time. He was a famous hunter and was on excellent terms with the Penobscot Indians. He was killed by the accidental discharge of his gun in the autumn of 1784 while hunting sea fowl on the Little Isle of Holt. Solomon Kimball was appointed administrator in 1791 and sold the island to Moses Brackett, of Haverhill, receiving a deed of it himself on the same day from Brackett. Mr. Webb's family removed to Deer Isle and in 1790 the widow Hannah and four females comprised the family, according to the first federal census. He married Hannah Winship, of Windham (published at Falmouth, November 12, 1759). She was born in 1742, died at Deer Isle, April 18, 1815. Children: Josiah, mentioned below; Susannah, married, in 1784, James Saunders; Mehitable, married Francis Kimball; Bethiah, married Daniel Moore; Hannah, married Joshua Emerson; Samuel, born May 31, 1770; Mary, 1774; William, 1776, lived at Deer Isle; Sarah.

(III) Josiah, son of Seth Webb, was born at Isle of Little Holt in 1765, died in 1849, aged eighty-three. (Bangor Hist. Reg., vol. iii, p. 33). He settled at Windham. His name is reported as of Windham in the census of 1790, and also Eli, Ezekiel, Seth, John, Josiah and James, mentioned above, or sons of those mentioned.

(IV) John, son of Josiah Webb, was born about 1785-90. He was doubtless born in Windham, and settled early in what is now Skowhegan, Cumberland county, Maine. He married ———. Children: Josiah, mentioned below; Sumner, Seth, John, Cornelia, and two others who died young.

(V) Josiah (2), son of John Webb, was born at Skowhegan, Maine, September 19, 1811. He was the eldest of the family and during his youth attended school and worked on his father's farm in his native town until he was nearly of age. His father for many years was in ill health and the care and management of the farm devolved upon the eldest son, giving him at an early age the burden of much work and responsibility but affording him an invaluable training in business, in self-reliance and practical administration of affairs. The old farmhouse did not fit his notion of a proper home for the family, so he set to work with the aid of his younger brothers to erect a better house, getting the funds for material largely by working out on neighboring farms and themselves performing the carpentering and other labor. Six months before he was twenty-one, following the example of many ambitious young men of his day, he purchased his "freedom" of his father for the sum of fifty dollars. He contracted to work for a year at $12 a month for Mr. Hill. In November, 1832, he came to Boston, and for several months was employed in a box factory in Roxbury. Early

in the spring of 1833, when he was just recovering from a severe illness, he was accosted by a stranger on the street, a man from Milton looking for help. Mr. Webb was engaged on the spot to come to work as soon as he was strong enough. His employer was Benjamin Dickerman, proprietor of what was then known as the Red Mill, occupying the present site of the chocolate mill of the Baker Company. After working here a few months he worked for some time in the paper mills of Deacon Lyon. He was next employed by H. G. Durell as clerk in his grocery store. Here his native enterprise and sagacity asserted itself. With the co-operation of Mr. Durell he made a trip to Maine, chartered a vessel, which he loaded with produce from the farms and brought to the markets of Milton. The experiment was so successful that it was repeated. So highly did Mr. Durell value his young clerk that he offered him a partnership, but Mr. Webb declined, having larger things in view. Late in 1838 or early the following year, Mr. Webb engaged in partnership with Josiah F. Twombly to manufacture chocolate and he continued in this business with remarkable success and profit until he retired from business in 1881, a period of nearly forty years. He laid the foundations and built up one of the great industries of New England.

Rev. C. S. Rogers, D. D., pastor of the Dorchester Methodist Episcopal Church, in a memorial sermon, spoke thus of his religious life:

"He was a Christian man. He accepted the scriptures as the word of God. He rested his faith on Christ as the world's Redeemer and his personal savior. His life was built upon this foundation. In religion, as in other matters, his convictions were positive and he was not ashamed of them. His piety was fashioned after the model of St. James rather than the more deeply spiritual model of St. John. It was eminently practical and common sense. It expressed itself in deeds rather than in words, but it rested on a firm belief. His religious life began before he left the parental roof. When about eighteen years of age he was converted and united with the Baptist Church, of which his parents were members. When he came to Dorchester, he did not forget his habit of attending church. The first Sabbath morning he attended the Congregational Church and heard a sermon by Rev. Mr. Sanford. In the afternoon he was invited by Mr. Dickerman, who was a Methodist, to attend the Methodist Church. It was the first time that he had ever heard of the Methodist Church, but he consented to go. The preacher was Rev. John T. Burrill. The subject of the discourse was 'the doctrine of free grace.' He had been accustomed to hear only the hard and stern doctrine of predestination and unconditional election and reprobation. The doctrine of Methodism as preached by Mr. Burrill was a new revelation. He accepted it joyfully, and passed in his lot with the despised and persecuted people.

Josiah Webb

It was a characteristic act and he never regretted it. His musical taste and talent soon drew him into the choir. For several years he led the singing, and in order to make the choir more efficient taught a singing school. From that early day his life and the life of this church has been closely identified. Besides serving as chorister, he was for a time superintendent of the Sunday school, and for many years until his death, a trustee. He has been a blessing to the church, and the church has been an unspeakable blessing to him.

"He has given generously of his time and money, but what he has given returned in showers of blessing on himself and his family. Especially is this true of the part he took in the erection of this beautiful edifice. I may be allowed in this connection a word that is personal.

"In the year 1872 he came as one of a committee of two to invite the speaker to return to this church for a second pastorate, with a view to erection of a new church edifice, then greatly needed. On being told that before I could give an affirmative answer I must know how much he would pledge in the enterprise, without hesitation and with the decision so characteristic of himself, he named a sum so generous that the project seemed possible, and an affirmative answer was given.

"Soon after entering upon this pastorate, unforeseen obstacles presented themselves. The great Boston fire, followed by a fearful financial panic and other difficulties, delayed the work. We came nearly to the end of the second year of the pastorate without breaking ground. The pastor had nearly decided to leave at the end of the year, but Mr. Webb understood the crisis, and, in the face of great discouragement, threw the weight of his influence and counsel in favor of an immediate advance. The way had been prepared by the purchase of property on either side of the lot then occupied, in which purchase the trustees received valuable assistance from that old and tried friend of the society, Mr. Edmund J. Baker. Another serious problem was what disposal could be made of the old church. Mr. Webb and Mr. Joseph E. Hall settled this problem by purchasing the property at considerable financial risk.

"The church was erected after years of preparatory work and many discouragements, but Mr. Webb never faltered. With tireless vigilance he watched the progress of the work until it was complete. Even then he did not rest. In accomplishing so great a work, there has been incurred a considerable debt. He could not be content until this was canceled. Largely by his generous liberality, but generously aided by others within and outside of the society, the result was at last achieved. It was one of the brightest days of his life when the last dollar of the debt was paid. * * * The fact remains that without the large contributions which Mr. Webb had the ability to make and which his generous heart prompted him to bestow, no such edifice as this would have been reared. This church, I trust, will stand and fulfil its beneficent mission for generations to come. As long as it stands it will be a monument to the Christian character and generous liberality of Josiah Webb. By it, he being dead will yet speak.

"Our brother, our neighbor, our friend is gone. We shall miss him in the place of business, in the sweet associations of the home and in the sacred precincts of the church. We shall miss his wise counsels and his welcoming smile, but he has not passed out of the circle of earthly affection and influence. To us, who have known and loved him in the various relations and associations of life, 'he being dead shall yet speak.'

"His words were always wholesome, true and pure, such shall his influence continue to be. He has wrought well his part, and he has entered upon his reward. The faith that made him strong for duty did not fail him in the time of his weakness. His last days were days of wonderful peace. As earth faded away, Heaven became real. He delighted in the word of God, and lingered with ever deepening interest over its sacred page. He was ready to go."

At an informal meeting of the Dorchester Methodist church trustees, October 14, 1888, the following resolutions were adopted:

"Whereas, Divine Providence has removed from our midst Bro. Josiah Webb, who has for sixteen years been president of this board,

First. That in his death we mourn the loss of one, who by his untiring zeal and interest has built himself into this church, and as long as this church shall stand will be a memorial of his devotion to the cause which this society represents.

Second. That as trustees wish to leave on record that without his long and continued efforts we should have been unable to rear this beautiful and commodious church building, and to express our gratitude to God, who so kindly spared his life until the completion of this work.

Third. That we kindly tender to the bereaved family and especially to the widow, our deepest sympathy in their hour of grief.

Fourth. That these resolutions be spread upon our records and a copy of them sent to the family of our deceased brother."

In dealing with the business career and character of Mr. Webb, the preacher said:

"It was no accident that Josiah Webb became prosperous in business. He did not believe in what is commonly called luck. He believed in making his own luck by the blessing of God upon honest endeavor. When he came to Milton his entire possessions were five dollars in cash and a scanty wardrobe, carried in the not very modern style of gripsack then in common use by poor boys going out from a humble country home to seek their fortune in the world. * * * The foundations of his prosperity were laid on a solid basis. He had inherited from his mother a rare endowment of energy and business tact. This natural endowment he used with the greatest faithfulness. He was faithful in that which was least. He had no idea of beginning at the top of the ladder. He was content to begin at the lowest round, but he had no idea of remaining there. * * *

"If the relation that existed between Josiah Webb and his employers, and at a later date between Josiah Webb and his employees, might generally characterize the relation of employer and employee, there would be no labor troubles, and strikes would become a thing of the past. The child is father of the man; the young man a prophecy of the man of middle and later years. A shrewd observer of human life might with tolerable accuracy have prophesied Mr. Webb's future from the characteristics of his young manhood. What he was then he substantially continued to be in all the essential qualities of life. He only grew. To his natural endowments he added qualities which were of his own choosing. He was a tireless worker. He expected no success that did not come as the reward of faithful toil. He was thoroughly honest. It is safe to say that no man who knew him ever suspected him of giving short measure or of any of the tricks of trade. He was faithful to all trusts. In business circles his name was a synonym for veracity and fidelity. It was a fit expression of the confidence reposed in him when he was called to fill the responsible position of a director in the Blue Hill National Bank, which position he held for a quarter of a century. His counsel was highly valued and widely sought, especially by young men entering upon business life. And not a few who have been favored with a good degree of success are largely indebted to his advice and in some cases financial aid. From first to last his business record was clean and honorable. He made money not for its own sake. It gave him more pleasure to use it for wise and benevolent purposes than it did to amass it.

"As a friend Mr. Webb was no less reliable than as a man of business. He was appreciative of real merit wherever it was found, and such was his keen insight into human nature that he was rarely deceived.

"He hated all sham and pretense, but delighted in genuine worth. The friends that he had and had proved were friends for life. No one who knew him intimately can forget with what deep and tender regard he always spoke of Deacon Lyons and his family, of Mr. H. G. Durell, Mr. Sampson and of others, some living and some departed, whom he held in lasting esteem. His friendships were an essential part of his life. As a friend he was able to give as well as receive. He had positive convictions on most subjects.

"He was not widely or profoundly read. He might not always express himself in faultless grammar, but he always had something to say that was worth hearing, and he never failed to make his thoughts clear. You always knew what he meant.

"At his pleasant home he dispensed a generous hospitality. He was always glad to see his friends and it was his delight to share with them the best he had. As we stand here to-day and turn our thoughts backward, how many beautiful memories of sunny hours spent beneath his roof-tree come thronging about us! With what animation and cheerful smile he always welcomed us! How deeply interested was he in all that interested us! He was a true friend."

He married, April 24, 1835, Betsey Crowell, of Chatham, Massachusetts, daughter of James Crowell. She survived him, after fifty-three years of married life together. Children: 1. Louisa, died young. 2. Charles Henry, born January 11, 1841, died June 22, 1872. Mr. Rogers said: "Charles Henry Webb was a young man of rare promise. To much of his father's business tact and energy, he added the advantages of a superior education. He had a fine musical ear and culture. With what significant and exquisite taste did he conduct the singing in the old church that stood on this thrice consecrated spot! Dear young man! It is fitting that we remember him now under these impressive circumstances and drop this simple chaplet of undying affection on his early grave." 3. John, died

young. 4. Josiah Sumner, born January 23, 1847, died February 11, 1898; he was in business with his father; he was interested in church work; he was a member of Macedonian Lodge, Free and Accepted Masons, thirty-second degree. 5. Eliza Jane, mentioned below.

(VI) Eliza Jane, daughter of Josiah Webb, was born April 16, 1849. She married, July 27, 1882, Alliston Belding Clum, born May 20, 1845, in Troy, New York, son of John and Mary E. (Belding) Clum. Mr. Clum was in the stationery business in Boston. He was a member of Macedonian Lodge, Free and Accepted Masons, and of the Methodist Episcopal church. Children: 1. Bessie Webb, born October 31, 1866; married, April 16, 1906, Charles Edward Marden, and has two children: Webb Randolph, born March 12, 1909, and Dorothy Foster, born November 5, 1910.

BRONSDON
Robert Bronsdon, immigrant ancestor, was born in 1638-39 in England, died in Boston, November 22, 1701. His death is recorded by Samuel Sewall in his diary as follows: "November 23, 1701, Mr. Bronsdon died the night before." The first mention of Robert Bronsdon in the colonial records, as far as yet discovered, was in 1667, when he was twenty-nine years of age. He is mentioned in the records as a merchant, and there is no doubt that he was a man of wealth and influence, and added much to the commercial importance of Boston. He was an active and important factor in the upbuilding of the North End of Boston, and erected several handsome brick houses and also buildings for commercial purposes. He held public office only once, March, 1675-76, when he was elected constable. He took the oath of allegiance, November 11, 1678, and was made freeman in 1690. He was a member of the Second Church of Boston, the church of the Mathers. He was an educated man, and is mentioned by Rev. Cotton Mather in his Magnalia, together with others, as having been of assistance to him in getting the book together. According to the deeds of the property which have been preserved, he did a large and lucrative business in real estate. In 1673 he was one of a company of public-spirited men of Boston who commenced the construction of the "out wharves", which were situated about where Atlantic avenue now stands, and were of great financial importance to the builders. His will was dated November 6, 1701, and the inventory of his estate was five thousand pounds. The inven-

tory shows that his possessions were varied and unusual and his brick mansion luxuriously appointed. He was buried in the old burying ground on Copp's Hill.

Robert Bronsdon married (first), April 15, 1667, Bathsheba, daughter of Edward Richards, of Lynn, Massachusetts. The latter was born in 1616, admitted a freeman, 1641, died January 26, 1689-90. His wife was Ann ———. He was a joiner or builder by trade. Robert Bronsdon married (second), January, 1677, Mrs. Rebeckah Cooley, widow of Henry Cooley. She was living in 1689. He married (third), April 12, 1694, Hannah Breeme, born July 26, 1668, died in 1730. She was daughter of Benjamin and Anne Breeme, of Hingham. They were married by Rev. Cotton Mather. Children of first wife, born in the North End of Boston: Mary, September 22, 1668, died young; Elizabeth, twin, August 27, 1670; Mary, twin of Elizabeth; Joseph, born August 7, 1672, died 1697. Children of second wife: Rebeckah, October 7, 1679, died young; Sarah, 1682; Robert, July 28, 1684, died October 13, 1695; Benjamin, mentioned below.

(II) Benjamin, son of Robert Bronsdon, was born August 30, 1686, in Boston. After his father's death, he chose as his guardian William Clark, who had married his sister. Benjamin Bronsdon was well educated for the times, and upon coming of age became a merchant. He owned warehouses and a brew house, and a large section of the "out wharves." In 1707 he also owned "three neagroes." In 1708 he served a term as constable, but does not appear to have held any other public office. He died intestate, April 12, 1757, and was buried in Copp's Hill burying ground. The tomb which he built about 1717 is still standing. He married (first), March 25, 1707, Mary, born March 22, 1681-82, in Boston, died there, October 6, 1751, daughter of Captain Bilbert and Mercy (Whitwell) Bant. He married (second) Elizabeth ———, before 1756. She survived him.

Children: Mercy, born September 15, 1708; Mary, August 12, 1710, died October 15, 1721; Rebecca, April 12, 1712, died July 4, 1712; Robert, July 12, 1713, died December 11, 1713; Gilbert, February 2, 1714-15; Benjamin, February 28, 1715-16; Robert, August 9, 1717, died October 16, 1721; William, April 6, 1719, died August 25, 1719; William, May 2, 1720, died October 1, 1721; Bant, mentioned below; Robert, March 10, 1723; William, July, 1724, died before 1728; Mary, baptized December 19, 1726; Sarah, baptized February 26, 1728; William, baptized June 16,

1729; Elizabeth, February 28, 1731; Rebecca, November, 1732.

(III) Bant, son of Benjamin Bronsdon, was born October 23, 1721, in Boston, family tradition says that Bant Bronsdon died away from home about 1765, and his wife before 1790, but there is no authentic record of their deaths. He was a mariner by occupation and therefore took small part in the affairs of his home town. There is no record of real estate in Boston belonging to Bant Bronsdon except his interest in the Bant estate, which he deeded to Ezekiel Goldthwait in 1756. He married, in 1750, Elizabeth, daughter of John and Lydia (Story) Box, of Boston (see Box). Children, recorded in books of King's Chapel: John Box, mentioned below; Sarah Box, born 1753; Rebecca, baptized August 31, 1755; Benjamin, baptized October 23, 1757; Bant, baptized January 30, 1760; William, baptized 1761; Elizabeth, baptized September 5, 1764.

(IV) John Box, son of Bant Bronsdon, was born May 21, 1751, on Hancock street, Boston, near Mount Vernon street. He attended the Mayhew School on Hawkins street, but was early apprenticed to a bootmaker in Boston.

Before his marriage he had accumulated sufficient means to enable him to purchase a house and land in Milton, and turned his attention to farming. He acquired considerable land and appears to have possessed industry and perseverance as well as business ability. He also engaged in boot and shoe making and met with a good degree of success. During two years of the revolution he served as a soldier, his service being as follows: Milton, December 21, 1775. Captain John Bradley's company, Colonel Lemuel Robinson's regiment, for seventeen days. Captain John Bradley's company, Colonel Gill's regiment, that marched from Milton to Dorchester Neck, March 4, 1776, to the assistance of the army when the forts were erected at Dorchester, service, five days. Captain Josiah Vose's company of militia from Milton that guarded the sea shore from April 13 to 26, 1776. He took an active part in the doings of that eventful time, and spared neither himself nor his possessions. On the night of March 4, 1776, when the fortification on Dorchester Heights was erected, he drove his own team, loaded with material for the construction of breastworks. He died February 22, 1823, and his wife June 18, 1827, and both are buried in Milton cemetery. He was of medium height and weight, dark hair and eyes, and of dignified presence. His wife was fair with blue eyes, and possessed much natural ability and refinement. In temperament she was quiet and serene, a marked contrast to her outspoken and impulsive husband.

John Box Bronsdon married, August 9, 1774, Abigail, daughter of Elijah and Hannah (Puffer) Baker, of Stoughton. Children, born in Milton, Massachusetts: Phinehas, born May 7, 1775, died June 22, 1776; Benjamin, mentioned below; Abigail, born December 31, 1779; Samuel, mentioned below; Sarah Curtis, born February 24, 1783; Elizabeth Box, November 7, 1784; Rebecca, June 10, 1786; John, April 9, 1788; Phinehas, April 6, 1790; Hannah, August 27, 1792; Elijah, December 16, 1796; William Bant, September 21, 1798.

(V) Benjamin, son of John Box Bronsdon, was born in Milton, Massachusetts, July 1, 1778. He was named for his Uncle Benjamin. From boyhood he was very fond of hunting and fishing, and often as a young boy he accompanied his father about the Blue Hills, where game was abundant. When he became of age he after a time purchased Brush Island at Cohasset, and had a camp there, where he went on hunting expeditions. After his marriage he lived in a house about two miles from his father's house, in Scott's Woods. He died suddenly of heart disease, July 18, 1832, and his wife survived him many years. She was buried beside him in the Milton cemetery. On his tombstone is the following inscription: "Behold my wife and children dear, This was your friend who slumbers here. Though death to me no warning gave But suddenly laid me in the grave Yet mourn not for your God is near He will to you a friend appear." Benjamin Bronsdon married, July, 1805, Nancy Wade Damon, born in Scituate, Massachusetts, May 4, 1780, died February 6, 1862, in Milton, aged eighty-two. She was daughter of Zadock and Thankful (Wade) Damon. Children, born in Milton: Jane, born August 13, 1806, married Aaron Bullock Drake; George Curtis, born May 17, 1810, died unmarried; Lewis Vose, mentioned below; Enos Fobes, born December 5, 1819, married Annah N. Coffin.

(V) Samuel, son of John Box Bronsdon, was born in Milton, Massachusetts, August 9, 1780, died June 10, 1840. He lived in Milton all his life. He and his wife were members of the Unitarian church there. They were noted for their generosity and hospitality. He married, February 4, 1812, Mary (Polly), born August 10, 1785, died August 25, 1867, daughter of William and Experience (Pittee) Brewer, of Hingham, Massachusetts. Children, born in Milton: Charles, born April 20, 1813, married Lydia Maria Jenness; Mary Elizabeth, December 28, 1814, married William Henry Swan; Francis Henry, born September 3, 1817, married Sarah Ann Kennison; Samuel, born November 29, 1819, married Deborah K. Whiton; William Brewer, mentioned below; Amos Holbrook, born September 24, 1824; Joseph Warren, born April 2, 1829, was in civil war, Thirteenth Massachusetts Regiment, died in the service.

(VI) Lewis Vose, son of Benjamin Bronsdon, was born at Milton, August 5, 1814, died April 4, 1907, at Milton. He was a farmer and lived on his father's homestead in Scott's Woods. He married, February 6, 1844, Louisa McDuffee, born in Bradford, Vermont, April 11, 1817, died June 13, 1900, daughter of John and Martha (Doak) McDuffee, of Bradford, Vermont. Both the Doak and McDuffee families were of Scotch-Irish descent. The name McDuffee traces back to the time of Shakespeare's Macbeth, where the name is spelled McDuff; for his services to the King, McDuff received a large tract of land in county Fife, with other gifts, and the "fee" was added to his name. The family appears in the north of Ireland about 1612: in 1689 "Matchless Martha" McDuffee was made famous by saving a quantity of meal during the siege of the city of Londonderry and distributing it among the starving people; she and her husband, John McDuffee, and several children came to America in 1720. Among the children was Daniel McDuffee and his wife and daughters, who in the spring of 1721 settled with other Scotch-Irish friends, in Londonderry, New Hampshire. John McDuffee, grandson of Daniel, was born in Londonderry, and when a young man moved to Bradford, Vermont, where he owned a large tract of land and a ferry across the Connecticut river; he was a civil engineer and surveyed many of the first railroads in America; he was the father of Mrs. Bronsdon. Children of Lewis Vose and Louisa (McDuffee) Bronsdon: 1. Louise, born January 24, 1849; lives in Milton where she formerly taught school. 2. Lewis, born May 6, 1852; married, September 6, 1894, Delia Riley, of Braintree, Massachusetts. 3. Peleg, born August 13, 1854; unmarried; farmer at Milton.

(VI) William Brewer, son of Samuel Bronsdon, was born at Milton, Massachusetts, May 4, 1822. He was educated in the public schools and Milton Academy, and learned the trade of carpenter. During his active life he was a carpenter and builder and has always lived on the homestead, Brook road, Milton. He served nine months in the civil war, enlisting in September, 1862, in Company B, Forty-fifth Regiment Massachusetts Volunteer Militia, and was mustered out July 7,

Lewis Vose Bronsdon

Louisa McDuffee Bronsdon

1863, with an honorable record in the service. In politics a Republican, in religion a Congregationalist. He married, in Milton, July 19, 1853, Margaret Thompson Willey, who died January 9, 1898, daughter of Simeon and Deborah (Hopkins) Willey, of Mattapan. Children: 1. Arthur Edgar, born April 17, 1854, died September 4, 1854. 2. William Franklin, April 23, 1857, died April 26, 1857. 3. Walter Lincoln, April 7, 1865; married, June 17, 1896, Madeline Robina Findlater, born December 4, 1873, daughter of James Alexander and Margaret (Burns) Findlater; children, born in Milton: Howard Allen, born February 5, 1897; Winslow Brewer, January 6, 1898.

(The Box Line).

(I) John Box, immigrant ancestor, was descended from the English gentry, and was born in London in 1697. The first mention found of him in America is in 1730, at Charlestown, Massachusetts, where he asked for a settlement. Through his marriage he acquired a part of the Story homestead, and his wife's mother lived with them, dying in 1741. John Box was a rope-maker. In 1743 he borrowed money of Joseph Smith to extend his business, and in 1755 he purchased of Ebenezer Storer a piece of land on Beacon Hill. On June 10, 1741, his storehouse was destroyed by fire, the loss being estimated at about two thousand pounds. When the land was purchased in 1755 it was taken in the name of Box & Austin, showing that the partnership was formed about that time. In 1758 and 1760 they bought still more land. Their business was for the most part in the merchant's line, and they supplied many vessels with cordage. They had a sail loft at the North End where sails were cut and fitted. Their warehouse and office at King street just escaped the great fire of 1760. Mr. Box was sometimes called major, though no military service has been found credited to him. His brother was a naval commander in Egypt under Nelson. He was vestryman in 1741-42-45-64-65-74, and warden, either senior or junior, from 1746 to 1754, inclusive. With Mrs. Box and others he acted as sponsor to various infants at baptism. He gave two hundred pounds towards rebuilding the present chapel and later gave a hundred pounds more, as well as contributing for the organ. He was a prominent member of St. John's Grand Lodge, Free and Accepted Masons, Boston, having joined July 23, 1740, and he held various offices of importance. He died October 31, 1774, "of a consumptive disorder." "He was a man of a fair unblemished character, strictly just in his dealings, a Constant at-

tender of Divine worship." He was buried in the family tomb under King's Chapel. Owing to the litigation concerning his estate, the whole was lost to the heirs. His will was dated September 28, 1774. Mrs. Box returned to the Story homestead after the Beacon Hill home was sold. According to tradition Mrs. Box was a Tory in her sympathies, but was not harmed because of the esteem in which her husband had been held. She died March 9, 1788, aged seventy years, and was buried from Trinity Church.

John Box married Lydia, daughter of Elisha Story, who is said to have come from England about 1700, accompanied by a sister Sarah, who later married Thomas Dawes. Elisha Story lived in Boston where the "Revere House" is now situated, and he was a cordwainer (shoemaker). In 1705 he became a member of the Old South Church. He married (first) October 17, 1706, Lydia, daughter of Benjamin and Mary Emmons, and had two sons named Elisha, by her, who both died young; she died July 27, 1713, and he married (second) Sarah, widow of Charles Renouf, or Renough, October 1, 1713. Elisha Story died September 20, 1725, aged forty-two, and she died June 28, 1741; his will was dated January 6, 1723, and proved September 30, 1725. When he was living on King street as a crown officer, a mob attacked and plundered his house and destroyed his papers. Mr. Story resigned his office as deputy register of the court of the admiralty. His children were: Sarah, born September 8, 1714, died young; Elizabeth and Elisha, born March 3, 1717-18, died young; Lydia, baptized March 26, 1718-19, married John Box; William Story, born April 25, 1720. Children of John and Lydia (Story) Box: Elizabeth, married Captain Bant Bronsdon (see Bronsdon III) ; John, baptized October 5, 1737; Lydia, baptized March 4, 1738-39, buried September 11, 1743; Elisha, baptized April 11, 1740, buried September 11, 1743; Lydia, baptized April 24, 1745; Sarah, baptized October 28, 1747; Ann, baptized November 22, buried November 27, 1749; Mary, baptized 1757.

(The Baker Line).

(I) Richard Baker, immigrant ancestor, came to Boston, November 28, 1635, from London, England, in the "Bachelor", as master's mate. He was a man of superior mould and capacity. He settled in Dorchester, and became influential in town and church affairs; freeman, 1642; member of the Ancient and Honorable Artillery Company in 1658; town officer nearly every year from 1642 to 1685; selectman in 1653. He married Faith, daughter of Henry Withington, immigrant in 1636, and a prominent citizen of Dorchester; he signed the church covenant with Rev. Richard Mather, in 1636, and was soon after chosen ruling elder, which office he held twenty-nine years; his first wife was Elizabeth ———, and his second wife Mrs. Marjorie (Turner) Paul; he died February 2, 1666-67, aged seventy-nine years. Richard Baker died October 25, 1689, and his wife February 3, 1688-89.

(II) John, son of Richard and Faith (Withington) Baker, was born in Dorchester, April 30, 1643, died August 26, 1690. He married, July 11, 1667, Preserved, born 1646, died November 25, 1711, daughter of Thomas and Sarah (Proctor) Trott, of Dorchester. Thomas Trott came from Bristol, England, in the "James", May 23, 1635; he was made freeman in 1641, joined the church the same year, was selectman in 1646, died July 28, 1696, aged eighty-two years. Sarah (Proctor) Trott died May 27, 1712; she was daughter of George and Edith Proctor, who came from England and settled in Dorchester. Mr. Proctor was granted land in 1634-37-56, and was town bailiff in 1642.

(III) John (2), son of John (1) and Preserved (Trott) Baker, was born November 25, 1671. He married, May 16, 1708, Hannah, born December 19, 1686, daughter of Captain John Withington, who commanded the Dorchester company on the disastrous expedition to Canada in 1690, and his wife, Elizabeth (Preston) Withington. Captain Withington was the son of Deacon Richard Withington, who was the only son of Elder Henry Withington by his wife, Elizabeth (Eliot) Withington, the latter the daughter of Philip Eliot, brother of the famous apostle to the Indians, John Eliot. Philip Eliot was the son of Bennet and Lettice (Agar) Eliot.

(IV) Elijah, son of John (2) and Hannah (Withington) Baker, was born May 14, 1720, died November 2, 1802. He married Hannah Puffer, who was descended from Rachel Farnsworth, of Braintree, first wife of Matthias Puffer, the immigrant, who was in Dorchester as early as 1663.

(V) Abigail, daughter of Elijah and Hannah (Puffer) Baker, married, August 9, 1774, John Box Bronsdon (see Bronsdon IV).

BLANCHARD   Thomas Blanchard, the immigrant ancestor, was a yeoman, born in England. He came to this country from Penton, Hants, England, sailing from London in the ship "Jonathan", and landing at Charlestown, Massachusetts, June 23, 1639. He settled at Braintree and lived there until 1650, when he

returned to Charlestown and bought land there in 1651 and also land in Boston. He married (second) in London, Agnes (Bent) Barnes, a widow, who died during the voyage to America, as did also her child and her mother. He died at Charlestown, May 21, 1654. He bequeathed by will to his wife Mary, three sons, a grandson, Joseph Blanchard, and to the church in Malden. His third wife, Mary, died in 1676. His son George settled in Malden, and Samuel in Andover, Massachusetts. Children: George, born 1618, died March 18, 1700; Thomas, 1625, died 1651; Samuel, 1629, died April 22, 1707; Nathaniel, mentioned below; child, born 1639, died in infancy; John (?).

(II) Nathaniel, son of Thomas Blanchard, was born in England, in 1630. He settled in Weymouth, and died in 1676. He married Susannah ———. Children, born at Weymouth: John, March 27, 1660; Mary, December 1, 1662; Nathaniel, September 25, 1665; Edward, mentioned below; Mercy, April 14, 1674.

(III) Edward, son of Nathaniel Blanchard, was born at Weymouth, June 7, 1668. According to the history of Northfield, New Hampshire, Edward Blanchard was one of the men furnished by the province of New Hampshire for scouting purposes under Captain Jeremiah Clough, who kept the old fort at Canterbury. This protection was given from 1721 to 1746. According to the Northfield history he was killed by the Indians in 1738. According to the history of Canterbury, of which Northfield was originally a part, there is doubt about his name, Benjamin and Richard both being given in records. There appears to be no doubt that Edward had sons Benjamin and Richard, however, or rather that Benjamin and Richard were brothers and early settlers. The Canterbury history states that Benjamin's father (Benjamin of Northfield, mentioned below) was scalped by the Indians in their raid on Canterbury in 1746, near his home not far from the fort. The Northfield history tells us that his wife was Bridget, of Scotch-Irish descent, and that once she was taken captive by the Indians when she was out after the cows, but eluded her captors and showed such fleetness in running that the Indians stopped their pursuit and "shook their sides with laughter while she safely arrived at the fort." Children: Sergeant Richard, who married (second) ——— Hancock, in 1768, and had Jacob, Hannah, Benjamin, and Edward, besides other children by his first wife; lived on the east slope of Zion's Hill; Benjamin, mentioned below.

(IV) Benjamin Blanchard, one of the founders of Northfield, was born about 1720. He was probably a scout in Canterbury in 1746 after the date of his father's death, and he signed with others a petition to the provincial government in 1748, asking protection for the grist mill of Henry Lovejoy in West Concord. He came from the Canterbury fort in 1760 through the unbroken forest to the foot of Bay Hill and settled on the farm later owned by Judge Peter Wadleigh. After making a clearing and erecting a cabin he brought thither his wife and nine children. He paid for his farm in part by services as surveyor and the rest in furs valued at $750. For several years Benjamin Blanchard and family were the only settlers in Northfield. "Blanchard's residence was a log house—then and for many years after the fashionable style of architecture among the pioneers of Bay Hill, and of the town generally. It was a convenient style—not showy, but having a severe Doric simplicity, while in keeping with the character of the early inhabitants. They were not capacious—containing but one or at most two rooms, and with the big families of those days, they must at times have furnished rather close quarters. But they were warm and cosy —easily constructed, for the timber was close at hand and a few days' labor only was required to transform it into the settler's modest mansion. Here then, Blanchard lived for several years, cut off from mankind by many miles of intervening forest. * * * He must have suffered privations, we know—all settlers did in those times."

His wife was buried in the orchard, close by a tree that was known to later generations as the "Granny Tree." He died at the home of his son Edward, on the Byron Shaw place, but was buried on the old homestead. When the present Wadleigh house was built, his gravestone was unearthed in digging the cellar. His son Edward sold the homestead to Lieutenant Charles Glidden in 1805 for $2,000.

Mr. Blanchard was a man of great industry and mechanical skill. In his old age he spent much of his time in whittling: "He wore pantaloons patched with woodchuck skins to protect them from wear, and he seemed a patriarch, with his thick white hair hanging long over his shoulders. He had a brother or uncle Joseph, an officer in the French and Indian war, who in 1754 marched six hundred men to the Salisbury Fort, now the site of the Orphans' Home, and thence through the wilderness to Crown Point and Canada. He had another brother who kept a hotel in Concord in 1785, who directed the Hills to Bay Hill when they came up from Haverhill seeking new homes." Before the town was divided, we

find on the tax list in 1767, Benjamin Blanchard, Benjamin Blanchard (2d), Edward Blanchard and Richard Blanchard. Benjamin (2d) was a distant relative (Benjamin (5), Benjamin, Jonathan, Samuel, Thomas (1).) Richard was the brother and Edward a son. Benjamin Blanchard recorded his cattle mark November 28, 1760; Edward Blanchard in 1771.

Children: 1. Elizabeth, married William Glines, who lived in Northfield, near Canterbury; Mayor Glines, of Somerville, Massachusetts, is a descendant. 2. Benjamin, mentioned below. 3. Richard, married Polly Webster and lived on the River road. 4. Edward, succeeded to the homestead, selectman of Northfield for many years; married Azubah Keazer, and his widow married Lieutenant Thomas Clough.

(V) Benjamin (2), son of Benjamin (1) Blanchard, was born about 1744, died 1826, aged eighty-two years. Among the signers of the Association Test in 1776, an act that entitles descendants to membership in the various revolutionary societies, we find the names of Benjamin Blanchard, Richard Blanchard and Edward Blanchard. It is difficult to discriminate between the records of the various Benjamin Blanchards of Canterbury and Northfield in the revolutionary war. In Canterbury, Benjamin Jr. and Benjamin (3d) were very active. He married Mary Wells, of New Hampshire.

(VI) Joshua, son of Benjamin (2) Blanchard, was born in Sandwich, New Hampshire, on a farm owned by Dr. Moses Hoyt. July 16, 1777, he settled in Eaton, New Hampshire, and conducted a farm there. He married Elizabeth Calfe, who was born at Belfast, Maine, June 15, 1787, daughter of John Calfe and Tamsen (Evans) Calfe. Her father, Rev. Thomas Evans, a clergyman, was a graduate of Edinburgh University, Scotland. Children, all born at Sandwich, New Hampshire, excepting John Calfe: 1. George Sullivan, born March 5, 1813; married (first) Mary Linscott, (second) Lucy Russell. 2. Joshua Wells, born August, 1816; married Lucy Ellis. 3. Thomas Calfe, born November 21, 1818; married Sarah Vittum. 4. Stephen Danforth, born November 21, 1822; married Jane Sommersville. 5. Sarah West, born November 21, 1824; married Cyrus Jones. 6. John Calfe, mentioned below.

(VII) John Calfe, son of Joshua Blanchard, was born December 2, 1831, at Eaton, New Hampshire. He received his early education in the public schools of his native town. In 1866 he came to Hyde Park, Massachusetts, before it was incorporated, and engaged in business at his trade as a carpenter. He became a builder of prominence, beginning to take contracts in 1867 and continuing with uniform success for a number of years. He had charge as millwright of the mill machinery of the mills of Glover & Willcomb, manufacturers of curled hair in Boston, for a period of twenty-five years. He devised machinery for removing dirt from curled hair. Since 1906 he has been retired from active labor, making his home in Hyde Park. In the civil war he enlisted in the Eighth Regiment New Hampshire Volunteer Infantry, November 13, 1861, and served his term of enlistment under Captain Alphonso G. Colby. He is a member of Timothy Ingraham Post, No. 121, Grand Army of the Republic. In politics he is a Progressive. His residence is at 5 Childs street, Hyde Park, Massachusetts.

He married, June 23, 1856, Mary E. Cranston Atchison, who was born in England, March 4, 1832. Children: 1. Mary Elizabeth, born July 27, 1859; married Edgar H. Wright of Hyde Park; children: Edgar H. Jr., born May 4, 1881, and Lilly Blanchard Wright, May 9, 1885. 2. John Calfe Jr., born January 13, 1861, manager of the clothing department of the Walpole Rubber Company, of which company he is a director.

HOUSE Walter House, the first of this surname in Connecticut, died in 1670 at New London, leaving a widow and son John, of whom we know nothing further.

(I) William House, perhaps a relative of Walter House, settled in Glastonbury, Connecticut, and died in 1703-4. His will was dated February, 1703-4, at Glastonbury. The inventory amounted to £119 13s., taken by Joseph Smith and Thomas Hale Sr. In the settlement of the estate the ages of his children are given. (Page 83, Vol. II, Hartford county probate records.) Children: John, born 1674; Sarah, 1676; Mary, 1678; Anne, 1684; William, 1685; Joseph, mentioned below; Eunice, not mentioned in estate, married Thomas Loveland.

(II) Joseph, son of William House, was born at Glastonbury, in 1687. He was administrator of his brother's estate. He married Rachel Pitkin, born December 14, 1692. See will of Roger Pitkin, her father, January 1, 1733. (Page 620, Hartford probate records, III.) The home of the House family has been at Glastonbury, Connecticut.

Charles Andrew House, a descendant of the Glastonbury branch, and lineal descendant of William House, the immigrant, was born at East Glastonbury, Connecticut, June 12, 1845.

He attended the public schools there and the Bryant & Stratton Business College. He came to Hyde Park, Massachusetts, in 1873, and after conducting a grocery store for a few years he purchased the plant of the Fairmount Manufacturing Company, a business that he conducted successfully during the remainder of his life. He was an active and prominent member of the Methodist Episcopal church, serving on the official board and teaching in the Sunday school, and for many years superintendent of the Sunday school. He was a member of Neponset Council, Royal Arcanum, of which he was at one time the regent and for many years secretary. He was a member of Riverside Lodge, Ancient Order of United Workmen, the Business Men's Association and of the Anti-Saloon League. He died at Hyde Park, January 20, 1908.

He married, January 13, 1869, Annetta Faunce, born October 29, 1841, at Sandwich, Massachusetts, daughter of Elisha Benjamin and Thankful (Toby) Bradford. Children: 1. Nettie Burnham, born June 26, 1870; married Henry A. Norris, of Hyde Park, June 7, 1893, and had children: Bradford Faunce Norris, born February 3, 1896; Myra Norris, January 29, 1900; Marian, died aged three years; Jeanette Norris, born March 29, 1905. Mr. Norris is in the insurance business in Boston. 2. Charles Bradford, born January 5, 1873; in partnership with his brother-in-law, William Garfield Nunn, in the Fairmount Manufacturing Company at Hyde Park. 3. Ethel Faunce, born October 30, 1880; married, June 7, 1905, William Garfield Nunn, and they have one child, Edward Andrew Nunn, born December 9, 1908.

(The Bradford Line).

The surname Bradford is derived from the name of a place, Broadford or Bradenford. There are two very ancient towns of this name, one in Wiltshire, England, near Bath, and one in Yorkshire, near Leeds. Near the latter was the home of the ancestors of the American family. The family dates back in England, doubtless, to the beginning of surnames in the eleventh or twelfth centuries. One of the first martyrs burned at the stake during the reign of Bloody Mary was John Bradford, Prebend of St. Paul, and a celebrated preacher. He was born in Manchester, Lancashire, 1510, and was executed July 1, 1555. He was a friend of Rogers, Hooper, Saunders, Latimer, Cranmer, and Ridley, who also died at the stake about the same time.

The Bradford coat-of-arms is: Argent on a fesse sable three stags' heads erased or. The Right Rev. Father in God, Samuel Bradford, Lord Bishop of Rochester and Dean of Westminster, bore these arms as well as those of his Episcopal See.

The ancestry of Governor William Bradford has-not been traced beyond his grandfather, mentioned below, though it is known that the family is ancient.

(I) William Bradford, grandfather of Governor William Bradford, lived at Austerfield, (Osterfeldt), county Nottingham, England, and in 1576 he and John Hanson were the only subsidiaries located there. Bradford was taxed twenty shillings on land; Hanson the same amount on goods. His grandson William lived with him after the death of William, his son. The date of his burial at Austerfield was January 10, 1595-6. Children: William, mentioned below; Thomas, had a daughter Margaret; Robert, baptized at Austerfield, June 25, 1561, (Governor Bradford lived with him after death of grandfather); Elizabeth, baptized July 15, 1570.

(II) William (2), son of William (1) Bradford, was born at Austerfield, probably about 1560, and died when yet a young man, July 15, 1591. He married Alice Hanson. Children, born at Austerfield: Margaret, baptized March 8, 1585, died young; Alice, baptized October 30, 1587; William, mentioned below.

(III) Governor William (3) Bradford, son of William (2) Bradford, was born in England, and baptized at Austerfield, March 19, 1590. After his father's death he lived at first with his grandfather, and at his death in 1596 went to live with his uncle, Robert Bradford, who lived in Scrooby, five miles from Austerfield, near the estate of the Brewsters, in county Nottingham. He joined the church where Rev. Richard Clifton and Rev. John Robinson preached, and soon became one of the leading "separatists". His early educational advantages were limited, but by diligent study he became very proficient in Dutch, Latin, French and Greek, and also devoted himself to the study of Hebrew, that he might read the Bible in its original form. He went with the company which migrated to Holland, and was a most influential power among them. On coming of age he received considerable property from his father's estate, but did not succeed him in his commercial undertakings. He learned the art of "fustian or frieze weaving". On November 15, 1613, he was affianced to Dorothea May, from Wisbeach, Cambridge, England. The banns were published in Leyden, and they were married in Amsterdam, Holland, December 9, 1613. His age is given as twenty-three, hers as sixteen. They embarked for England, July 22,

1620, and after many trials sailed from Plymouth, England, September 6, 1620, on the ship "Mayflower", reaching Cape Cod harbor the November following. While they were at anchor and he was absent from the vessel, Dorothea fell overboard and was drowned, December 9, 1620. Soon after the death of Governor Carver, William Bradford was elected governor of the colony, an office which he held by annual election until his death, with the exception of the years 1633-34-36-38-44. He took a prominent part in all the councils, which were held at his house, and in all civic, political, and military affairs. From his house at the foot of Burial Hill each Sunday morning, the company of people who assembled there marched up to the fort at its top, where religious services were held. The history of the times which he left gives a correct and valuable picture of the events of that day. He married (second) Alice, widow of Edward Southworth, and daughter of Alexander Carpenter, of Wrentham, England. She died March 26, 1670, and he died May 9, 1657. Children: John of Duxbury, 1645. By second wife: William, mentioned below; Mercy, married Benjamin or Joseph Vermages; Joseph, born 1630.

(IV) Major William (4) Bradford, son of Governor William (3) Bradford, was born in Plymouth, Massachusetts, June 16, 1624, and died there February 20, 1700. He removed to Kingston, Massachusetts, for a time. He was assistant deputy governor, and was one of Governor Andros' council in 1687. He was the chief military officer of Plymouth colony. His will was dated January 29, 1703. He married (first) Alice Richard, who died at Plymouth December 12, 1671, daughter of Thomas and Wealthyan Richards, of Weymouth, Massachusetts. He married (second) the widow Wiswell; (third) Mrs. Mary Holmes, who died June 6, 1714-5, widow of Rev. John Holmes, of Duxbury, and daughter of John Atwood, of Plymouth. Children: John, born February 20, 1653; William, born March 11, 1655, died 1687; Thomas, of Norwich; Samuel, born 1668; Alice, married Major James Fitch; Hannah, married Joshua Ripley; Mercy, married ——— Steel; Melatiah, married John Steel; Mary; Sarah, married Kenelm Baker. By second wife: Joseph, of Norwich, mentioned below; Israel, married Sarah Bartlett; David, married Elizabeth Pinney; Ephraim; Hezekiah.

(V) Joseph, son of William (4) Bradford, was born in 1674, and died January 18, 1747. He lived in Norwich and removed to Lebanon, and thence to the North Parish of New London in 1717. He was a very active and energetic citizen. His farm was lately owned by J. Randolph Rogers, and was formerly called the Perez Bradford place. He was elder of the New London church in 1724. He married (first) October 5, 1698, Anna Fitch, who died October 17, 1715, daughter of Rev.. James and Priscilla Fitch. He married (second) Mary (Sherwood) Fitch, widow of Captain Daniel Fitch. She died September 10, 1752.

Children: Anne, born July 6, 1699; Joseph, born April 9, 1702; Priscilla, twin of Joseph; Althea, born April 6, 1704; Irena, twin of Althea; Sarah, born September 21, 1706; Hannah, May 24, 1709; Elizabeth, October 21, 1712; Althea, September 19, 1715; Irena, twin of Althea. By second wife: John, mentioned below.

(VI) John, son of Joseph Bradford, was born May 20, 1717, and died March 10, 1787. He was a farmer, and lived in the North Parish, now Montville, New London. He married, December 15, 1736, Esther Sherwood. Children: Samuel, born January 4, 1738; John, December 7, 1739; Joseph, June 17, 1742; Sarah, July 27, 1744; Perez, October 11, 1746; Benjamin, mentioned below; Eleanor, died young; Rebecca, born January, 1754; Mary, January 17, 1756.

(VII) Benjamin, son of John Bradford, was born in New London, October 8, 1748. He lived in the north part of the North Parish, in Salem Society, where he owned a farm. He married Parthenia, daughter of Thomas and Sarah (Fitch) Rogers. Child: Thomas, mentioned below.

(VIII) Thomas, son of Benjamin Bradford, was born November 16, 1776. He was a farmer, and lived in New Salem Society, in North Parish, now Salem, Connecticut. He married, April 23, 1806, Mercy, daughter of Elisha and Anna '(Fitch) Fox. Children: Parthenia, born January 13, 1807; Rachel, April 3, 1808; Anna F., November 22, 1809; Elisha B., mentioned below; Mary E., June 18, 1815.

(IX) Elisha B., son of Thomas Bradford, was born September 22, 1811, at Salem, Connecticut, and died October 8, 1895. He was a Methodist minister, and lived for a time in Uncasville, moving later to Massachusetts. He was living at Hyde Park in 1884. He married, in West Duxbury, May 30, 1838, Thankful Toby Faunce. Children: 1. William Fish, born March 27, 1839, died October 4, 1839. 2. Anetta Faunce, born October 29, 1841; married, January 13, 1869, Charles A. House (see House). 3. Ella Albertine, born March 29, 1846; married, December 4, 1883, Waterman R. Burnham, of Norwich.

HERRESHOFF Karl Friedrich Herreshoff (original form of family name), progenitor of the American family of Herreshoff, was a native of Germany. He married Agnes Muller, and they had one child, Charles Frederick (further mentioned below). His wife died when the child was three years old, and he entrusted the latter to the care of a friend near Berlin, and went to Italy, where he died soon afterward.

(II) Charles Frederick Herreshoff, son of Karl Friedrich and Agnes (Muller) Herreshoff, was born in Germany, December 27, 1763, and when three years old was left to the care of a friend of his father, a professor and author, by whom he was brought up. April 1, 1779, he entered the Philanthropin, an educational institution which had been recently founded at Dessau. After remaining there eight years he emigrated in 1787 to the United States and located in New York City. For a number of years he was engaged in business with a Mr. Goch, and after 1801 was associated with his father-in-law, John Brown, particularly in the development of a tract of land in Herkimer county, known as the "John Brown Tract." He was a man of unusual education, an accomplished linguist, versed in seven languages, a good musician, and of polished address. He married, in 1801, Sarah, daughter of John and Sarah (Smith) Brown (see Brown). Children: 1. Anna Frances, born April 2, 1802, died in Bristol, Rhode Island, unmarried, September 4, 1887. 2. Sarah, born April 27, 1803, died in Bristol, unmarried, June 2, 1882. 3. John Brown, born March 27, 1805, died in Bristol, unmarried, June 11, 1861; graduated from Brown University, 1825. 4. Agnes, born July 6, 1807, died in Providence, Rhode Island, unmarried, March 5, 1849. 5. Charles Frederick, of whom further. 6. James Brown, born December 20, 1811, died January 4, 1812. All these children were born in Providence, Rhode Island.

(III) Charles Frederick Herreshoff, son of Charles Frederick and Sarah (Brown) Herreshoff, was born in Providence, Rhode Island, July 26, 1809. He graduated from Brown University in 1829, and lived many years on Point Pleasant farm, Bristol, Rhode Island, where all his children were born. In 1856 he removed to the town of Bristol. He married, May 15, 1833, Julia Ann, daughter of Joseph Warren and Ann (Lane) Lewis, born March 20, 1811. Her father, son of Captain Winslow Lewis, was born September 20, 1784, died May 11, 1844, married, May 1, 1808, Ann, daughter of Levi and Elizabeth

(Giles) Lane, of Boston, born June 21, 1786, died in Bristol, July 13, 1856. Captain Winslow Lewis, born in Wellfleet, July 3, 1741, died at sea, July, 1801; he was son of Rev. Isaiah Lewis, and married, September 12, 1765, Mary, daughter of Willard and Bethia (Atwood) Knowles, of Eastham, born October 20, 1746, died in Boston, January 31, 1807. Rev. Isaiah Lewis, born in Hingham, was son of John Lewis, and married, June 25, 1730, Abigail, daughter of Kenelm and Abigail (Waterman) Winslow, born June 25, 1707, died April 13, 1776. John Lewis, son of James Lewis, was born October 29, 1656, died November 8, 1715, settled in Hingham, and married there, November 17, 1682, Hannah, daughter of Daniel and Susannah Lincoln, of Hingham, born September 10, 1659, died October 30, 1715. James Lewis, born in East Greenwich, England, died at Hingham, Massachusetts, 1726, was son of George, and married Sarah, daughter of George and Sarah Lane, of Hingham, born 1638. George Lewis was born in East Greenwich, county Kent, England, died at Barnstable, Massachusetts, and married, in England, Sarah Jenkins, and settled in Scituate, Plymouth county, Massachusetts, between 1633 and 1636. Children of Charles Frederick and Julia Ann (Lewis) Herreshoff, born in Bristol, Rhode Island: James Brown, Caroline Louise, Charles Frederick, and John Brown, all of whom are further mentioned below; Lewis, born February 3, 1844, and Sally Brown, born December 1, 1845, both unmarried, and reside at the family homestead, Bristol; also Nathaniel Greene, John Brown Francis and Julian Lewis, all further mentioned below.

(IV) James Brown Herreshoff, chemist and mechanical engineer, son of Charles Frederick and Julia Ann (Lewis) Herreshoff, was born March 18, 1834. He was educated in the schools of Bristol and Providence and Brown University, which he entered in 1852, there pursuing a special three-year course, mainly in chemistry. After leaving the university he became superintendent of the Rumford Chemical Works, Providence, and remained as such eight years. From 1863 to 1870 he was variously concerned in commercial enterprises and with inventions, obtaining several patents for various improvements. In 1870 he traveled abroad. For two years he resided in Brooklyn, New York, later resided several years in England and France, returning home in 1883, and lived at Bristol ten years, in Coronado, California, eleven years, afterwards taking up his residence in New York City, where he is engaged in study and mechanical research. His residence is at 1415 Sedgwick avenue. He married, May 14, 1875, Jane, daughter of William and Jane (Morrow) Brown, of Ireland, born August 22, 1855. Children:

1. Jane Brown, born in Brooklyn, New York, July 13, 1876.

2. James Brown, born in London, England, March 18, 1878; educated in Bristol schools and Coronado, California, later at University of California, where he took a full course and a post-graduate course in chemistry and metallurgy. About 1900 he entered the employ of the Nichols Copper Company, near Brooklyn, New York, where he is now superintendent, and has inaugurated many improved processes. He married, January 11, 1906, Constance Mills, of San Diego, California, born July 15, 1879. Children: Constance Walden, born February 11, 1907; James Brown, January 5, 1909; Margaret, March 21, 1910.

3. Charles Frederick, born in Nice, France, May 28, 1880; educated in schools of Bristol, and Coronado, California; took special course in naval architecture and marine engineering at University of Glasgow, Scotland. In 1902 he returned home and established himself in New York City as a naval architect and mechanical engineer, and built many yachts and power launches. He later resided in Bridgeport, Connecticut, and was concerned in the construction of gasoline engines and other appurtenances of motor boats and automobiles. In 1908 he removed to Detroit, Michigan, and is engaged in manufacturing automobiles. He married, in Glasgow, Scotland, April 9, 1902, Elizabeth McCormick, born in New York, February 11, 1884. Children: Allan Stuart, born February 8, 1903; Elizabeth, June 22, 1904.

4. William Stuart, born in Hampton Wick, England, April 21, 1883; educated in schools of Bristol, and Coronado, California; and graduated from University of California as mechanical and civil engineer. In 1904 he entered the employ of the Nichols Copper Company, but later established himself as designer and builder of special gasoline engines for motor launches and flying machines. He resides at 1415 Sedgwick avenue, New York City.

5. Anna Frances, born in Bristol, Rhode Island, July 5, 1886; is a graduate of Barnard College.

(IV) Caroline Louise, daughter of Charles F. and Julia Ann (Lewis) Herreshoff, was born February 27, 1837. She married, August 16, 1866, Lieutenant E. Stanton Chesebrough, born in New York City, August 17,

1841, died in Bristol, October 22, 1875. Their only child, Albert Stanton Chesebrough, born in Bristol, January 11, 1868, is a naval architect and mechanical engineer, and since 1891 has been a designer of steam and sailing yachts and supervisor of their construction. He married, May 6, 1897, Emma, daughter of Hon. J. Russell and Emma (Westcott) Bullock, of Bristol, born September 25, 1869, in Bristol, died there December 6, 1908. Children: Edith Russell, born July 7, 1903; Westcott Herreshoff, March 16, 1908.

(IV) Charles Frederick Herreshoff, son of Charles F. and Julia Ann (Lewis) Herreshoff, was born February 26, 1839. He resides on the Point Pleasant farm, Poppasquash, Bristol, and has always been a farmer. This beautiful property was bought by John Brown, in November, 1781, the State of Rhode Island being the grantor. He married (first), December 3, 1868, Mary Potter, born March 3, 1843, died March 24, 1866; (second) Alice Almey. Child by first marriage: Julia Ann, born August 20, 1864, resides at home.

(IV) John Brown Herreshoff, naval architect and mechanical engineer, son of Charles F. and Julia Ann (Lewis) Herreshoff, was born April 24, 1841. He is president and treasurer of the Herreshoff Manufacturing Company, established in Bristol, Rhode Island, in 1863. The company began with the construction of sailing craft of all sizes, mainly for pleasure, and the reputation of their yachts for excellence of design and construction and also for high speed, soon placed them as foremost in the world. In 1876 Nathanael Greene Herreshoff became a member of the company as designer and superintendent. The character of work was now changed, and steam vessels (yachts, motor boats and torpedo boats) largely took the place of sailing vessels. During the '90's the international races gave an impetus to the construction of the well-known defenders of the America's cup—the "Vigilant," "Defender," "Columbia" and "Reliance," and the cup race off New York attracted the attention of the entire marine world, the Herreshoff vessels showing the result of the highest skill in design, as well as sailing qualities. Since that period the Herreshoff Company has continued the construction of pleasure craft to be sent to all parts of the world, as well as serviceable vessels for the United States and foreign governments.

Mr. Herreshoff resides in High street, Bristol, Rhode Island. He married, April 22, 1892, Eugenia Tams Tucker, of Providence, Rhode Island. He has a daughter by a former marriage—Katherine Kilton, born July 31, 1871, married, April 29, 1896, Lewis Henry, born October 4, 1855, died September 6, 1900, son of Algernon Sidney and Clara (Diman) De Wolf. She married (second) Walter J. Tubbs, of Bristol, and (third) Charles K. Amidon, of Brookline, Massachusetts. Child by first marriage: Louise Henry, born August 9, 1898.

(IV) Nathaniel Greene Herreshoff, naval architect, steam and mechanical engineer, son of Charles F. and Julia Ann (Lewis) Herreshoff, was born in Bristol, Rhode Island, in 1848. He was educated in the Bristol schools and the Massachusetts Institute of Technology. From early childhood he displayed taste and ability in nautical affairs, and at the early age of ten years was a skillful manager of sailboats. In the autumn of 1869, having just attained his majority, he entered the employ of the Corliss Steam Engine Company, of Providence, Rhode Island, doing expert and experimental work on the steam engine. In 1876 he became associated with his brother, John Brown Herreshoff, in the Herreshoff Manufacturing Company, for whom he had previously done designing. He gave to his profession the highest skill and all that scientific experimentation could suggest, with the result that the vessels of all descriptions turned out by the Herreshoff Company proved to be examples of perfection from every point of view. Added to his skill in designing and construction, he was conceded to be the most skillful sailor of yachts in the United States, and without a superior in the world. He reached his zenith of skill in the production of the Defenders of the America's Cup, which, in design, construction and mechanical appliance surpassed any vessel for its purpose ever produced in this or any other country. His attainments in the designing of steam engines for special work in steam yachts, torpedo boats and other high speed vessels, have placed him in the front rank of steam engineers. In 1896 Brown University conferred upon him the degree of Master of Science, in recognition of his many inventions and improvements in naval architecture and steam engineering. He is an honorary member of the New York Yacht Club, the Boston Yacht Club, the Rhode Island Yacht Club and the Bristol Yacht Club; and a member of the Institute of Naval Architects, London; of the Royal Society of Arts, London; the Society of Naval Architects and Marine Engineers of New York; and the Franklin Institute of the State of Pennsylvania.

Mr. Herreshoff married, December 26,

1883, Clara Anna De Wolf, born September 5, 1853, died November 28, 1905, daughter of Algernon Sidney and Clara Anna (Diman) De Wolf, of Bristol, Rhode Island. Children: 1. Agnes Muller, born October 19, 1884. 2. Algernon Sidney, born November 22, 1886; educated in Bristol schools and Institute of Technology, Boston; now assistant superintendent of Herreshoff Manufacturing Company. 3. Nathaniel Greene Jr., born February 5, 1888; educated at Bristol schools, and Institute of Technology, Boston; mechanician and electrician; now in employ of General Electric Company, Lynn, Massachusetts. 4. Alexander Griswold, born in Bristol, April 16, 1889; educated in Bristol schools and Institute of Technology, Boston; now draftsman for Herreshoff Manufacturing Company. 5. Lewis Francis, born November 11, 1890; educated in Bristol schools and at College of Agriculture and Mechanic Arts, Kingston, Rhode Island; has charge of farm of family in Bristol, at Ferry Hill. 6. Clarence De Wolf, born February 22, 1895, in Bristol.

(IV) John Brown Francis Herreshoff, a distinguished chemist and metallurgist, son of Charles F. and Julia Ann (Lewis) Herreshoff, was born in Bristol, Rhode Island, February 7, 1850. He was educated in the Bristol (Rhode Island) schools, and Brown University, from which he received the honorary degree of Master of Arts in 1890. He has long been recognized as one of the foremost chemists and metallurgists in the world. From 1875 to 1890 he was associated with the firm of G. H. Nichols & Company, and as superintendent of the Laurel Hill (Long Island) Chemical Works. From 1890 to 1900 he was with the Nichols Chemical Company, and from the latter year to the present time he has been identified with the Nichols Copper Company as vice-president, and with the General Chemical Company as consulting engineer. During these thirty years of active industrial development he has applied his mind to a great variety of chemical and metallurgical industries, and has perfected many radical improvements, replacing old methods with scientific processes founded upon his practical experience and experimentation. In 1883 he patented the copper smelting furnace which bears his name, and is of world-wide fame. Later he developed the most advanced process for the manufacture of sulphuric acid. In 1896 he patented a furnace for roasting fine iron pyrites, and made a marked improvement upon it in 1899. His next great work was the development of the electrolytic refining of copper, which attracted the admiring attention of the scientific world, and in 1908, at a notable meeting of the Chemists' Club, on behalf of the American Chemical and Electro-Chemical Society, Mr. Herreshoff was presented with the "Perkins Gold Medal," provided for award to that chemist residing in the United States who had accomplished the most valued work in applied chemistry during his career. The presentation (the first in America) and a review of Mr. Herreshoff's scientific attainments, were given in full in the *Journal of the Society of Chemical Industry,* and reprinted in pamphlet form in England as well as in the United States.

A further honor came to him in 1909, when Brown University conferred upon him the honorary degree of Doctor of Science—a degree most sparingly bestowed, and only in recognition of the most scientific attainments.

Mr. Herreshoff is a member of the American Society of Mechanical Engineers, the American Chemical Society, the Society of Chemical Industry, the Scientific Alliance, the Brown University Alumni Association, the University and Chemistry Clubs of New York City, the New York Yacht Club and the Hamilton Club of Brooklyn. His offices are at 25 Broad street, and his residence at 620 West End Avenue, New York City.

Mr. Herreshoff married (first), February 9, 1876, Grace Eugenia Dyer; born March 20, 1851, died December 2, 1880, daughter of John Dyer, of Providence, Rhode Island. He married (second) Emily Duval Lee, daughter of Richard Henry Lee, of Philadelphia, Pennsylvania. Child of first marriage: 1. Louise Chamberlain, born November 29, 1876; married Charles C. Eaton, of Providence, now of Schenectady, New York, a descendant of Chad Brown. Children of second marriage: 2. Francis Lee, born in Brooklyn, October 2, 1883; married Mildred Master, of Brooklyn, New York, and has one child, Norman F. Herreshoff. 3. Frederick, born in Brooklyn, March 7, 1888; he is a leading American golf player; he was runner up with H. H. Hilton, of England, in the International Amateur Golf Championship finals in 1911. He is a partner in the firm of Frenaye & Herreshoff, bankers and brokers, 60 Broadway, New York; he married Mary Faulkner. 4. Sarah Lothrop, born in Brooklyn, October 17, 1889; married Luigi Masnada, of Bergamo, Italy, and they reside in his native place; they have one child, a daughter, born July, 1911.

(IV) Julian Lewis Herreshoff, an accomplished musician, son of Charles Frederick and Julia Ann (Lewis) Herreshoff, was born at Point Pleasant Farm, Bristol, Rhode

Island, July 29, 1854. His musical education was under the supervision of the best teachers the country afforded, and in 1886 he went with his family to Europe for further and advanced study in music, giving special attention to the piano, studying with Professor Kullak. He also perfected himself in the German language, and entered the University of Berlin. On his return to America in 1888 he established in Providence, Rhode Island, the Westminster School of Languages and Music, where all the modern languages and vocal and instrumental music are taught, and which is to-day in a flourishing condition. The School is in the Butler Exchange Building, and his home is at 146 Lloyd Avenue, Providence, Rhode Island. He married, September 11, 1879, Ellen Frances, daughter of James Madison and Frances E. (Mowry) Taft, of Pawtucket, Rhode Island, born January 3, 1852. They have one child, Grace, born in Bristol, March 31, 1881.

(The Brown Line).

(I) Chad Brown, immigrant ancestor, came from England in the ship "Martin," which arrived in Boston, Massachusetts, July, 1638. He brought with him his wife Elizabeth, son John, then eight years old, and perhaps younger ones. A fellow passenger died on the voyage, and Chad Brown witnessed the will soon after his arrival. He did not long remain in Massachusetts, probably because of his religious views, but soon removed to Providence, where he became at once a leader and one of the most valued citizens of that colony. That same year (1638) he and twelve others signed a compact relative to the government of the town. In the capacity of surveyor he was soon after appointed on a committee to compile a list of the home lots of the first settlers of the "Towne Streete," and the meadows allotted to them. His own home lot fronted on the "towne streete," now South Main and Market Square, with the southern boundary to the southward of College and South Main streets. The college grounds of Brown University now comprise a large portion of this lot. In 1640, he served on a committee with three others in regard to the disputed boundary between Providence and Pawtuxet. That same year, he, with Robert Cole, William Harris and John Warner, was the committee of Providence Colony to report their first written form of government, which was adopted and continued in force until 1644, in which year Roger Williams returned from England with the first charter. Chad Brown was the first of the thirty-nine signers of this agreement. In 1642 he was

ordained as the first settled pastor of the Baptist church. In 1643 he was on a committee to make peace between the Warwick settlers and Massachusetts Bay, but their efforts were unavailing. He died September 2, 1650, on which date the name of his widow occurs in a tax list. Children: John, mentioned below; James and Jeremiah, both of whom removed to Newport, Rhode Island; Judah, or Chad, died May 10, 1663, unmarried; Daniel.

(II) John Brown, son of Chad Brown, was born 1630, and died about 1706. He married Mary, daughter of Rev. Obadiah and Catharine Holmes, of Newport, Rhode Island. He lived in Providence, at the north end, in a house afterwards occupied by his son James. He served the town in various official capacities—juryman, commissioner on union of towns in 1654, surveyor of highways, 1659; was freeman in 1655; moderator, member of the town council, deputy in legislature, assistant. He took the oath of allegiance, May 31, 1666. In 1672 he sold the home lot of his father to his brother James, of Newport, who resold the same day to Daniel Abbott. Nearly one hundred years later a part of it was repurchased by his great-grandsons John and Moses Brown, and by them presented to the College of Rhode Island at the time of its removal from Warren to Providence. The corner-stone of University Hall, for many years the only building, was laid by John Brown, May 31, 1770. Children: Sarah, married, November 14, 1678, John Pray; John, born March 18, 1662; James, mentioned below; Obadiah; Martha; Mary and Deborah.

(III) James Brown, son of John Brown, was born in 1666, and died October 28, 1732. He married, December 17, 1691, Mary, daughter of Andrew and Mary (Tew) Harris, granddaughter of William and Susannah Harris, and also of Richard and Mary (Clarke) Tew, born December 17, 1671, and died August 18, 1736. He served as a member of the town council almost continuously from 1705 to 1725, and from 1714 to 1718 as town treasurer. He was pastor or elder of the First Baptist Church, and in 1726 succeeded Rev. Ebenezer Jenkes in the ministry, a position which he held until his death. One historian says, "He was an example of piety and meekness worthy of admiration." In his will, made March 3, 1728, he provides well for his children. His father had deeded to him, July 6, 1690, three home lots, dwelling house and other land. Children: John, born October 8, 1695; James, mentioned below; Joseph, May 5, 1701; Martha, October 12, 1703; Andrew, September 20, 1706; Mary, April 29, 1708, died February 20, 1729; Anna, born 1710; Obadiah, October 2, 1712; Jeremiah, November 25, 1715; Elisha, May 25, 1717.

(IV) James Brown, son of James Brown, was born March 22, 1698, and died April 27, 1739. He married Hope, daughter of Nicholas and Mercy (Tillinghast) Power, and granddaughter of Elder Pardon and Lydia (Tabor) Tillinghast, born January 4, 1702, died June 8, 1792. Shortly after his marriage he entered into business and later with his younger brother Obadiah became partners. They were the founders of the commercial house of the Browns. Children: James, born February 12, 1724, died unmarried, 1750; Nicholas, born July 28, 1729; Mary, 1731; Joseph, December 3, 1733; John, mentioned below; Moses, September 12, 1738. The names of these four sons are those of the "four brothers," whose history is intimately connected with that of the times in which they lived.

(V) John Brown, son of James Brown, was born January 27, 1736, and died September 20, 1803. He was the third of the "Four Brothers," and was associated with them in business until 1782, when he withdrew and established himself at India Point, where he began direct trade with the East Indies and China. He became a wealthy merchant, and at the time of the breaking out of the Revolution had large interests at stake. This did not, however, prevent him from supporting the patriot cause and contributing largely to it. The Hope Furnace at Cranston, built mostly by him and his brothers, manufactured cannon for use in the Continental army. He furnished the ships and was leader of the party which destroyed the British armed schooner "Gaspee," in Narragansett Bay, June, 1772. On suspicion of being concerned in this affair he was sent in irons to Boston, but was released through the efforts of his brother Moses. It is said that at this time, to avoid arrest, he did not sleep two nights in succession under the same roof, but made the rounds of his country seats, of which he possessed several about Providence. In 1767, he and his brother Moses served on the committee appointed by the town of Providence to prepare for the introduction of free schools. With his brothers he was influential in the removal of the College of Rhode Island from Warren to Providence, and was its constant benefactor. He laid the cornerstone of its first building, May 14, 1770. He also gave liberally to the support of the Baptist Church. He secured the building of the Washington bridge across the Seekonk, at the lower ferry, and his brother Moses that

of the Red or Central Bridge, at the upper ferry. He was a member of the Assembly in 1789, in which year that body increased the import duty on many foreign goods for the purpose of encouraging home manufacture. In January of that year he appeared at the Assembly dressed in a suit, the cloth of which was made from the wool of his own sheep. His town residence was on South Main Street, and here he gave a famous dinner party in honor of General Nathaniel Greene, the largest, it is said, that had ever been given in Rhode Island. In 1787 he built his Power street mansion, then the finest in the city. In 1790 he was a member of the society for promoting abolition in the United States and for improving the condition of the African race. In 1799 he was elected a member of Congress and served two years.

He married, November 27, 1760, Sarah, daughter of Daniel and Dorcas (Harris) Smith, born May 13, 1738, died February 25, 1825, granddaughter of Benjamin and Mercy (Angell) Smith, great-granddaughter of John and great-great-granddaughter of John Smith, the miller. She was also granddaughter of William and Abigail Harris. Children: James, born September 22, 1761, died unmarried, December 12, 1834; Benjamin, February 13, 1763, died July 7, 1773; Abigail, November 26, 1764, died October 16, 1766; Abby, born November 20, 1766, died March 5, 1821, married, 1788, John Francis, of Philadelphia; Sarah, September 5, 1773, married, July 2, 1801, Charles Frederick Herreshoff (see Herreshoff); Alice, January 1, 1777, died October 23, 1823; married James Brown Mason.

COFFIN In Fallaise, a town in Normandy, stands the old chateau of Courtitout, once the home of the Norman Coffins; the name is now extinct in that vicinage. The chateau is now owned by Monsieur Le Clere, who is the grandson of the last Mademoiselle Coffin, who married a Le Clere in 1796. Until her marriage the chateau had always been owned by a Coffin. (The above information came through Admiral Henry E. Coffin, of the English navy, who is the nephew of Admiral Sir Isaac Coffin, who was born in Boston, Massachusetts, May 16, 1759, made a baronet, and granted a coat-of-arms in 1804).

The family traces its ancestry to Sir Richard Coffin, Knight, who accompanied William the Conqueror from Normandy to England, in the year 1066, to whom the manor of Alwington in the county of Devonshire was assigned. There are various branches of the family in county Devon. The English records show the name Covin, whence it was changed to Cophin, and is also found as Kophin, Coffyn and Coffyne.

Before 1254 the family was flourishing at Portledge near the sea, in the parish of Alwington, five miles from Biddeford, England. For a period of two hundred years the heir always received the name of Richard and so the family was perpetuated for many generations through that name. The name was early brought to the Massachusetts Bay Colony and has been borne by many leading men. The Coffin family were not as conspicuous during the revolution as they undoubtedly would have been if their location had been different. The island was visited by the British warships on several occasions, and the inhabitants were intimidated, and for their own safety were obliged to preserve a neutrality. The Portledge family bore these arms: Vert, five cross-crosslets argent, between four plates. These arms are also used by the American families.

(I) Tristram Coffin, a descendant of Sir Richard Coffin, married and lived in Brixton, county of Devonshire, England. In his will he left legacies to Anne and John, children of his son Nicholas Coffin; Richard and Joan, children of Lionel Coffin; Philip Coffin and his son Tristram; and appointed Nicholas Coffin, of whom further, as his executor.

(II) Nicholas, son of Tristram Coffin, lived in Butler's parish, Devonshire, England, where he died in 1603. In his will, which was proved at Totnes, in Devonshire, November 3, 1603, mention is made of his wife and five children, namely: Peter, of whom further; Nicholas, Tristram, John and Anne.

(III) Peter, eldest son of Nicholas and Joan Coffin, was born on the Coffin estate at Brixton, Devonshire, England, about 1580, and died there in 1627-28. He married Joan or Joanna Thember, and their six children were born and baptized in the parish of Brixton, Devonshire, England, in the order following: 1. Tristram, of whom further. 2. John, born about 1607; he was a soldier and died in the service from a mortal wound received in battle during the four years' siege of the fortified town during the civil war, and he died within the town about 1642. 3. Joan, born in England, about 1609, and probably died there. 4. Deborah, died probably in England. 5. Eunice, born in England, came to Massachusetts Bay Colony with her parents; married William Butler, and died in 1648. 6. Mary, married Alexander Adams, and had children: Mary, Susannah, John and Samuel; she died in 1677 or thereabouts. Widow Joan with

her children, Tristram, Eunice and Mary, her two sons-in-law, husbands of her daughters who were married in England, her daughter-in-law, Dionis, and five grandchildren, came to Salisbury in 1642. She died in Boston in May, 1661, aged seventy-seven years, and in the notice of her family it is quaintly stated that the Rev. Mr. Wilson "embalmed her memory".

(IV) Tristram (2), eldest son of Peter and Joan (Thember) Coffin, was born in the parish of Brixton, Devonshire, England, probably in 1605. He was of the landed gentry of England, being heir to his father's estate in Brixton, and he was probably a churchman after the order of the time of Elizabeth. He died at his home on Nantucket Island, October 2, 1681. It is a strange fact that the christian name of the immigrant forefather of all the Coffins in America, Tristram, is repeated and multiplied in every family in every generation, while the name of the foremother, Dionis, is repeated but once in all the generations, and that was when it was given to the eldest daughter of Stephen, but when she married Jacob Norton her name appears as Dinah. It is not known on which of the early ships conveying emigrants from England to New England the Coffin family took passage, but it is generally believed that it was the same ship that brought Robert Clement, the emigrant, who owned the ships "Hector", "Griffin", "Job Clement," and "Mary Clement," and if Robert Clement, the immigrant, took passage on one of his own ships, Tristram Coffin, the immigrant, was a passenger in the same ship, and both men settled in Haverhill in 1642.

The early settlers of Salisbury, which town was established October 7, 1640, commenced a settlement at Pentucket the same year, and the Indian deed for this land was witnessed by Tristram Coffin in 1642, and in 1643 he removed to the place which was established as the town of Haverhill, Norfolk county, Massachusetts Bay Colony. He settled near Robert Clement. Tradition has it that Tristram Coffin was the first man to plow land in the town of Haverhill, he constructing his own plow. He changed his residence to the "Rocks" in the following year, and in 1648-49 removed to Newbury where he kept an ordinary and sold wine and liquors and kept the Newbury side of Carr's Ferry. In September, 1643, his wife Dionis was prosecuted for selling beer for threepence per quart, while the regular price was but twopence, but she proved that she had put six bushels of malt into the hogshead while the law only required the use of four bushels, and she was discharged. He returned to Salisbury and was commissioner of the town, and while living there purchased or planned the purchase of the island of Nantucket, where he with his associates removed on account of religious persecution. At least Thomas Macy, who was the pioneer settler on Nantucket Island, "fled from the officers of the law and sold his property and home rather than submit to tyranny, which punished a man for being hospitable to strangers in the rainstorm even though the strangers be Quakers." Mr. Macy returned to Salisbury and resided there in 1664, and when he left he sold his house and lands and so the story of his fleeing from persecution would seem to be spoiled and history perhaps gives the true reason for his migration, the search for a milder climate and better opportunities for cultivating the soil. Early in 1654 Tristram Coffin took Peter Folger, the grandfather of Benjamin Franklin, at the time living in Martha's Vineyard, as an interpreter of the Indian language, and proceeded to Nantucket to ascertain the "temper and disposition of the Indians and the capabilities of the island, that he might report to the citizens of Salisbury what inducements were offered emigrants." A grant of the Island had been given to Thomas Mayhew by William Earl, of Sterling, and recorded in the secretary's office of the state of New York, July 2, 1659. Thomas Mayhew deeded the Island to Tristram Coffin, Richard Swain, Peter Coffin, Stephen Greenleaf, William Pike, Thomas Macy, Thomas Barnard, Christopher Hussey, John Swain, retaining an interest of one-twentieth for himself, the consideration being "£30 and two Beaver Hats, one for myself and one for my wife." Later the same parties purchased from one Wanackmamak, head Sachem of Nantucket, a large part of their lands, consideration £40. James Coffin accompanied Thomas Macy and family, Edward Starbuck and Isaac Coleman to the island later the same year, and they all took up their residence there. The Coffin family that settled at Nantucket included Tristram Sr., James, Mary, John, and Stephen, each the head of a family. Tristram Coffin was thirty-seven years old when he arrived in America, and fifty-five years old at the time of his removal to Nantucket, and during the first year of his residence he was the richest proprietor. The property of his son Peter is said soon after to have exceeded in value that of the original proprietor, the family together owning about one-fourth of the island and the whole of Tuckernock. On the 29th of June, 1671, Francis Lovelace, governor of New York, granted a commission to Tristram Coffin to be chief magistrate on and over the island of Nantucket and Tuckanuckett (Deeds

III, secretary's office, Albany, New York). At the same time Thomas Mayhew was appointed the chief magistrate of Martha's Vineyard through commissions signed by Governor Lovelace, of New York, bearing date June 29, 1671, and the two chief magistrates, together with two assistants for each island, constituted a general court, with appellative jurisdiction over both islands. The appointment was made by Governor Francis Lovelace, of New York, and his second commission, September 16, 1677, was signed by Edward Andros, governor-general of the province of New York. Tristram, when he died, left his widow Dionis, seven children, sixty grandchildren, and a number of great-grandchildren, and in 1728 there had been born to him one thousand five hundred and eighty-two descendants, of whom one thousand one hundred and twenty-eight were living.

He married Dionis (the diminutive for Dionysia and afterwards written Dionys), daughter of Robert Stevens, of Brixton, England. The children were nine in number, the first five having been born in England, as follows: Peter, Tristram Jr., Elizabeth, James, of whom further; John, Deborah, Mary, John, Stephen.

(V) James, son of Tristram (2) and Dionis (Stevens) Coffin, was born in 1640 in England, died at Nantucket, July 28, 1720, aged eighty years. He came to Nantucket with the first settlers, but subsequently removed to Dover, New Hampshire, where he resided in 1668, being a member of the church there in 1671 and the same year, May 31, he was there made a freeman. Soon after this date, however, he returned to Nantucket and resided there until his death. He filled several important public positions at Nantucket, among them judge of the probate court. The first records of the probate office are under his administration. He was the father of fourteen children all of whom except two grew to maturity and married. From him have descended perhaps the most remarkable representatives of the Coffin family, as doubtless the most numerous and generally scattered. This branch furnished the family that remained on the side of Great Britain in the revolution and General John Coffin, as well, rendered service against the colonies. Sir Isaac Coffin, brother of General John Coffin, did not take an active part in the war of the revolution against the colonies. He was in the British navy at the breaking out of the war, and at his own request was assigned to service in the Mediterranean, that he might not have to fight against his own kindred. Although the highest honors had been conferred on him in the Spanish navy, and he had been chosen a member of parliament, he cherished a regard for the land of his nativity. In 1826 he visited Boston and Nantucket, and was honorably and hospitably received. Harvard University conferred on him the honorary degree of M.A. At Nantucket he founded a school, chiefly in the interest of the Coffin family. The land on which the school stands was given by Gorham Coffin, who was one of the trustees, and had been the site of the residence of his father, Abner Coffin. The school is still in existence, and at the present time is a Mechanical Training School for the inhabitants of the Island. One of the most distinguished women that America has produced, Lucretia Mott, was also descended from this line, her father, Thomas Coffin, being the seventeenth child of Benjamin, and not the youngest either.

James Coffin married, December 3, 1663, Mary, daughter of John and Abigail Severance, of Salisbury, Massachusetts. Children: Mary, James, Nathaniel, of whom further; John, Dinah, Deborah, Ebenezer, Joseph, Elizabeth, Benjamin, Ruth, Abigail, Experience, Jonathan.

(VI) Nathaniel, son of James and Mary (Severance) Coffin, was born at Dover, New Hampshire, in 1671, died August 29, 1721. He married, October 17, 1692, Damaris, born October 24, 1673, died September 6, 1764, daughter of William and Dorcas Gayer, of Nantucket. Children: Dorcas, Christian, Lydia, William, Charles, Benjamin, of whom further; Gayer, Nathaniel, Catharine.

(VII) Benjamin, son of Nathaniel and Damaris (Gayer) Coffin, was born in Nantucket, April 3, 1705, died in Nantucket, November 3, 1780. He married (first) Jedidah, daughter of Batchelor Hussey, (second) Deborah, daughter of Thomas Macy. Children: Reuben, Nathaniel, William, Benjamin, Abigail, Joseph, Anna, Seth, Paul, Elihu, Isaiah, Abraham, Abner, of whom further; an infant died young, Isaac, Thomas, Deborah.

(VIII) Abner, son of Benjamin and Deborah (Macy) Coffin, was born at Nantucket, March 20, 1753, died there February 15, 1802. He was for many years judge of the probate court at Nantucket. He married Elizabeth, born February 27, 1751, died June 19, 1826, daughter of Peleg Gardner. Children: Kezia, Elizabeth, Alfred, Roland, Gorham, of whom further. Elizabeth (Gardner) Coffin is a descendant of "Mayflower" ancestry, tracing her line from John Howland, who married Elizabeth Tilley; their daughter Desire married Captain John Gorham; their son John married Mary Otis; their son Stephen married Elizabeth Gardner; their daughter Eunice

married Peleg Gardner, and they were the parents of Elizabeth (Gardner) Coffin.

(IX) Gorham, youngest son of Abner and Elizabeth (Gardner) Coffin, was born at Nantucket, January 25, 1785, died December 17, 1849. He was a ship master by the time he was twenty-one and was also engaged in the mercantile marine as commander of a ship. During the Napoleonic wars he was captured by French forces when coming out of the Thames river, having landed a cargo in London, the vessel and crew being taken into Boulogne, France, and held for some time before he could get the ship released, when her American ownership was shown. Afterwards he became a member of the firm of Christopher Mitchell & Sons, shipowners, engaged in the whaling business, and who also had a refinery making sperm candles. The "Globe", one of their ships, was taken by mutineers, the captain and other officers killed, and then went to Mulgrave Islands where it was intended to form a colony. One night, while the vessel was being dismantled, some of the crew slipped the cables and succeeded in navigating the ship to Valparaiso, where she was taken charge of by the United States consul. Later a United States cruiser went in search of the mutineers, and they found all had been killed by the natives except two boys. These two were rescued by the United States ship. Gorham Coffin married Rebecca, born February 25, 1788, died February, 1842, daughter of Christopher Mitchell. Children: Eliza, Stephen, Harriet, Andrew Gardner, of whom further; Lydia, Phebe, Alfred, Arthur, Mary Ann.

(X) Andrew Gardner, son of Gorham and Rebecca (Mitchell) Coffin, was born at Nantucket, September 4, 1816, died July 31, 1897. As a boy he went round the world in one of his father's ships and was away four years. At the age of twenty or twenty-one he came to New York and engaged as a clerk in an insurance office and an importing concern, and finally engaged in the wholesale drug business. In 1852 he put a stock of drugs on a vessel and sailed for San Francisco and engaged in the drug business. Later he joined the firm of Redington & Company, and came to New York as the purchasing and shipping agent of the firm, which business exists today, having been incorporated in New York in 1907, under the name of Coffin, Redington Company. He continued with this firm until he retired from active work. He married (first) Elizabeth M., born March 14, 1817, died January 10, 1856, daughter of Isaac and Elizabeth Sherwood, (second) Sarah, died August, 1880, daughter of Chandler Pierson,

of Avon, New York. Children: Isaac Sherwood, of whom further; Elizabeth Rebecca, born September 9, 1850; Grace, child by second marriage, born June 6, 1859.

(XI) Isaac Sherwood, son of Andrew Gardner and Elizabeth M. (Sherwood) Coffin, was born at Nantucket, February 28, 1842. He was educated in a private school, and came to New York with his parents. He went with his father to California at the age of fifteen. He remained there two years and then returned to New York and has continued in the business ever since, succeeding his father. He has been president of the Electro-Silicon Company, manufacturers of polishing preparations, and vice-president of the Coffin, Redington Company. He is an independent Republican, and attends the Unitarian church in Brooklyn, where he lives. He belongs to the Downtown, Hamilton, Rembrandt (Brooklyn) and Lorentian Fishing clubs.

He married (first) Emma, daughter of Abraham Leggett, and had daughter Adele, born May 8, 1870, died April 10, 1911, and a son, Frederick Leggett, born 1873, with father in business. He married (second) Ida E., daughter of Joseph Willetts. Children by second marriage: Sherwood, born in Brooklyn, February 15, 1883; Willets, born January 29, 1885, with father in business; Mitchell, born September, 1889, graduated from Massachusetts Institute of Technology in 1912; Helen, born December 20, 1898.

John Alden, immigrant ancestor, ALDEN was born in England in 1599.
He joined the Pilgrims on the "Mayflower" at Southampton as the ship was on its way to America. When the ship stopped there for supplies, he was hired as cooper. He had not been with them at Leyden and was probably not a member of the independent church, but soon joined. He cast his fortunes with the Pilgrims, after enduring the hardships of that first terrible winter at Plymouth when so many died. He was doubtless influenced in this decision by his love for Priscilla Mullens, the story of which, with some embellishments, is told in the "Courtship of Miles Standish". She was the daughter of William Mullens who came on the "Mayflower" with his family. John and Priscilla were married in the spring of 1621. When the common property of the colony was divided in 1627, Alden went with Captain Standish, Elder Brewster, John Howland, Francis Eaton and Peter Brown to Mattakeeset, the Indian name of that territory now included in Duxbury, Marshfield, Pembroke, Hanson and Bridgewater, Massachusetts. For several

years they were obliged to return to Plymouth during the winter season to combine all their forces against the possible Indian attacks. The residence at Plymouth in the winter also gave them an opportunity to attend worship, and the records show a written agreement of Alden and others in 1632 to remove their families to Plymouth in the winter. In 1633 Alden was appointed assistant to the governor, an office which he held for nearly all of the remainder of his life, serving with Edward Winslow, Josiah Winslow, Bradford, Prince and Thomas Hinckley. From 1666 until his death he held the office of first assistant, was often called the deputy governor, and was many times acting governor in the absence of the governor. From 1640 to 1650 he was also deputy to the colonial council from Duxbury. Winslow's "History of Duxbury" says of him, "Holding offices of the highest trust, no important measure was proposed, or any responsible agency ordered in which he had not a part. He was one of the council of war, many times an arbitrator, a surveyor of lands for the government as well as for individuals, and on several important occasions was authorized to act as agent or attorney for the colony. He was possessed of a sound judgment and of talents which, though not brilliant, were by no means ordinary. Writers who mention him bear ample testimony to his industry, integrity and exemplary piety, and he has been represented as a worthy and useful man of great humility, and eminent sanctity of life, decided, ardent, resolute and persevering, indifferent to danger, stern, austere and unyielding, and of incorruptible integrity. He was always a firm supporter of the Church and everything of an innovating nature received determined opposition." From the Puritan point of view Alden was a model if this description of his virtues is truthful. He took his part in making the lives of the Quakers at Plymouth colony intolerable. On the Alden farm stands the house built by his son Jonathan, having been occupied by eight generations in direct line. It is the oldest house in New England, with three exceptions; the old fort at Medford, built in 1634, the Fairbanks house at Dedham, built in 1636, and the old stone house at Milford, Connecticut, built in 1640. Here Alden spent his declining years. He died in Duxbury, September 1, 1686, aged eighty-seven years, the last of the famous band of Pilgrim Fathers, and the last of the "Mayflower" company.

John Alden had eleven children, only eight of whom are known, namely: John, born about 1622 at Plymouth; Joseph, of whom further; Elizabeth, 1625; Jonathan, about 1627; Sarah, married Alexander Standish, son of Captain Miles Standish; Ruth, married John Bass, of Braintree, from whom the presidents Adams descended; Mary; David, prominent man of Duxbury.

(II) Joseph, son of John Alden, was born in Plymouth in 1624, died February 2, 1697. He inherited land at Bridgewater where he settled, and also at Middleborough, Massachusetts. He was admitted a freeman in 1659. He married Mary, daughter of Moses Simmons Jr., who came in the "Fortune" in 1621 and settled at Duxbury. Joseph Alden's will was dated December 14, 1696, proved March 10, 1697. Children: Isaac, married, December 2, 1695, Mehitable Allen; Joseph, mentioned below; John, born about 1675; Elizabeth, married, 1691, Benjamin Snow; Mary, married, 1700, Samuel Allen.

(III) Joseph (2), son of Joseph (1) Alden, was born in 1667 at Plymouth or Duxbury, died at Bridgewater, December 22, 1747. He settled in South Bridgewater, Massachusetts. He was deacon of the church and a prominent citizen. His will was dated November 12, 1743. He married, in 1690, Hannah Dunham, of Plymouth, daughter of Daniel Dunham. She died January 13, 1748, aged seventy-eight years. Children, born at Bridgewater: Daniel, January 29, 1691; Joseph, August 26, 1693, died December 9, 1695; Eleazer, September 27, 1694; Hannah, February, 1696; Mary, April 10, 1699; Joseph, September 5, 1700, died October 5, 1700; Jonathan, December 3, 1703, died November 10, 1704; Samuel, mentioned below; Mehitabel, October 18, 1707; Seth, July 6, 1710.

(IV) Samuel, son of Joseph (2) Alden, was born at Bridgewater, August 20, 1705, died in 1785. He resided at Titicut, Bridgewater. He married (first) 1728, Abiah, daughter of Captain Joseph Edson. He married (second) in 1752, a daughter of Josiah Washburn. Children, born at Bridgewater: Abiah, 1729; Mehitable, 1732; Sarah, 1734; Samuel, mentioned below; Josiah, 1738; Simeon, 1740; Silas, died aged twenty-one; Mary; Hosea, killed by kick of a horse.

(V) Samuel (2), son of Samuel (1) Alden, was born in Bridgewater in 1736, died in 1816. He was a carpenter and lived in Abington, Massachusetts. He was a very worthy man and was a member of the Baptist church in Randolph, now East Stoughton, Massachusetts. He married Hannah Williams, of Raynham, Massachusetts. Children: Daniel; Silas, born 1765; Joseph; Samuel; William, 1772; Hosea, died young; Hannah; Seth, mentioned below; Hosea.

(VI) Deacon Seth Alden, son of Samuel

(2) Alden, was born November 3, 1777, died June 3, 1838. He was a deacon of the Baptist church. He was a carpenter of East Stoughton, Massachusetts. He married (first) January 11, 1802, Harmony, born in 1781, died May 24, 1823, daughter of Perez Southworth. He married (second) Betsey, born October 3, 1790, died January 28, 1842, daughter of Nathaniel Littlefield. Children by first wife: Lysander, born August 12, 1804, died November 28, 1808; Eunice, November 27, 1806; Azel, March 1, 1809; twins, February 22, 1811, died same day; Lysander, January 21, 1812; Samuel, September 12, 1814; Adoniram Judson, May 30, 1817, burned to death, November 22, 1819; Adoniram Judson, November 25, 1819; Southworth and Seth, twins, May 13, 1823. Children by second wife: Ann Amelia, born August 3, 1826; Nathaniel Littlefield, June 13, 1828; Isaac, mentioned below; James, September 7, 1835.

(VII) Isaac, son of Deacon Seth Alden, was born at Randolph, Massachusetts, December 10, 1830. He was educated in the public schools, and learned the trade of shoemaking. For about ten years of his life he was a manufacturer of boots and shoes. In 1865, at the close of the civil war, he went west and followed farming for five years at Malcom, Iowa. In 1873 he returned to Boston, but a few years later returned to the west, locating at Minneapolis, Minnesota, where he spent his last years. He married, in 1855, Hannah S., daughter of Alphonso and Mary (Cardell) Rice, of Randolph, Vermont. Children: 1. Carrie Florence, born June 12, 1856; married Frank H. Nutter; children: William, Frank H. and Hannah Nutter, all living in Minneapolis. 2. Charles L., mentioned below. 3. John Willard, mentioned below.

(VIII) Charles L., son of Isaac Alden, was born November 29, 1858, at East Stoughton, now Avon, Massachusetts. He was educated in the public schools. He engaged in business as a grocer in Roxbury in 1876, and from time to time added other grocery stores to his business until he had a very large and flourishing trade. He also engaged in the milk business and in the course of time devoted all his attention to his dairy and sold his grocery stores one by one. Under the name of "the Oak Grove Farm" he built up a very extensive and widely known business. Perhaps no similar concern in Boston has a higher reputation for the excellence of its products. The business was incorporated in 1910 under the name of the Alden Brothers Company, with main offices at 1171 Tremont street. The company has a large wholesale business and a large number of retail stores in Greater Boston for the disposal of its dairy products. His home for many years has been at Hyde Park, now a part of the city of Boston. He has been a director of the Hyde Park National Bank since its organization in 1906. He was president of the Hyde Park Young Men's Christian Association its first two years. He is a prominent member of the First Congregational Church of Hyde Park, and in 1911 he was chairman of the building committee of the church and aided materially in securing the funds for the erection of a new edifice costing $80,000. Mr. Alden is keenly interested in family history and local affairs. He is treasurer of the Alden Kindred of America, an association of the descendants of John and Priscilla Alden.

He married, September 13, 1883, Bessie L., daughter of Abijah and Mary (Bryant) Wheeler, of Bethel, Maine. Children: 1. John, born July 25, 1884. 2. Priscilla, born June 30, 1886; married, January 1, 1910, Webster Brewer Evans, a graduate of Dartmouth College, class of 1908, now engaged in the life insurance business in Boston, a son of L. S. and Emily (Tripp) Evans. 3. Arthur W., born September 28, 1888. 4. Charles L. Jr., born June 6, 1890. 5. Rachel, born December 23, 1892. 6. Esther, born June 7, 1894. 7. Myles Standish, born December 13, 1897. 8. Bradford, born and died May 4, 1903.

(VIII) John Willard, son of Isaac Alden, was born in Unity Springs, New Hampshire, April 18, 1863. He was educated in the public schools. He has been associated in business with his brother, is also engaged in the cake baking business at No. 2220 Washington street, Boston, and is a manufacturer of the celebrated "Berwick Cake Specialties" and has built up a large wholesale and retail trade in loaf cake throughout New England. He married, October 10, 1892, Rachel, daughter of Rev. Austin and Adelaide (Churchill) Craig. Her father was pastor of the Congregational church at Rochester, New York. Children: Craig, Josephine, Rachel, Priscilla.

PURINTON George Purinton, immigrant ancestor, was born in England, and settled as early as 1640 in York, Maine. He was deputy to the general court in 1640 for the town of York. He died about 1647. His widow was licensed to sell wine in that jurisdiction in 1649. His will was dated June 25, 1647. It mentions his wife Mary and five children; also "my brother Robert Purrinton." Robert Purinton, brother of George, married Amy Davis, and had children: John and Robert; was land-

holder of Portsmouth in 1640 and 1657. Mary Purinton, widow of George, married (second) before 1661, Captain John Davis, of York; she was living in 1690. Children: John, mentioned below; Elias, was living in 1698; Mary, Frances, Rebecca. One of the daughters married John Penwell.

(II) Lieutenant John Purinton, son of George Purinton, was born about 1640. He was a fisherman. He married Mary Scammon and removed from York to Cape Porpoise, where he lived until 1678. He took the oath of allegiance in 1680, had a grant of land in 1681, was town clerk and selectman until the town was abandoned in 1690, when he left. He died a few years later. Children: John, house carpenter, removed to Salisbury; James, mentioned below; Joshua, married ——— Derrell, a shoemaker, of Hampton; George; Elizabeth, married John Conner, of Salisbury; Mary, married Sanders Carr, of Salisbury.

(III) James, son of John Purinton, was born about 1663. He was lost at sea. His estate was administered October 2, 1718. He was a member of the Society of Friends. He married (first) Elizabeth ———; (second) Lydia Mussey. Children: James, born July 8, 1693; Elizabeth, born December 8, 1695, married Phillip Rowell; John, mentioned below; Elisha, born 1698-1705; Daniel; Mary, living in 1719; Hannah, born April 14, 1708, married Josiah Dow, son of Joseph and Mary Dow; Ruth.

(IV) John (2), son of James Purinton, was born 1700. He married Theodate ———. Among their children was James, born January 22, 1722-23.

(V) Jonathan, son or nephew of John (2) Purinton, was born about 1725. The family remained comparatively small until 1800 or later and in the census of 1790 but few adults are reported. The largest settlement was at Dover, New Hampshire; at Weare we find Chase, Elisha, Elisha Jr. and Hezekiah Purrinton or Purrington; at Dover, Zachariah, Elijah, Elisha, John, Zaccheus and Winthrop at Weare and Henniker; James at Pittsfield, New Hampshire. Jonathan settled at Kensington. He was doubtless a brother of Elijah, who came to Weare, New Hampshire. The records do not give us the families at this period.

(VI) Chase, nephew of Elijah and doubtless son of Jonathan Purinton, came from Kensington, New Hampshire, and settled on lot 46, range 6, in Weare, New Hampshire, afterward removing to Lincoln, Vermont. He married ———. Children: Jonathan, mentioned below; Elijah, born July 18, 1781; James, November 12, 1783; Judith, April 19, 1786; Elizabeth, August 3, 1788; Chase, July

19, 1792; Lydia, October 3, 1795; Mary, September 7, 1799.

(VII) Jonathan (2), son of Chase Purinton, was born at Weare, New Hampshire, December 3, 1779. He married Hannah Huntington and settled at Lincoln, Vermont. They had five sons: Benjamin, Eleazer, John, Thomas, mentioned below, and Jacob, and a daughter Huldah. Some of the descendants are living on the old homestead at Lincoln.

(VIII) Thomas, son of Jonathan (2) Purinton, was born in February, 1812, died in April, 1894 or 1896. He married Martha Chandler, born in May, 1818, died in January, 1888. Children, born at Lincoln, Vermont: Luther, born in June, 1841, died in June, 1883; Edgar Jerome, mentioned below; Edna Salome, twin of Edgar Jerome, born July 21, 1846, married Royal Smith, of Bristol, Vermont.

(IX) Edgar Jerome, son of Thomas Purinton, was born July 21, 1846, in Lincoln, Vermont, died at Starksboro, Vermont, March 4, 1897. He was educated in the public schools. During the greater part of his life he followed farming in Starksboro. He represented the town and in 1886 was selectman, serving for a number of years. In early life he was a member of the Free Will Baptist church, but in later life joined the Society of Friends and was active in the affairs of the Friends church. He married Henrietta Wood, born at Starksboro, Vermont, January 15, 1848, daughter of Artemas and Harriet Wood. Children: 1. Riley Harris, mentioned below. 2. Luther Artemas, born in September, 1873; a merchant at Burlington, Vermont; married Carrie, daughter of Edwin Meader; children: Vira, Charles and Kenneth. 3. Child, died in infancy. 4. Harriet, born January 12, 1891; married Frank Darrow and has one child, Burchard Darrow.

(X) Riley Thomas, son of Edgar Jerome Purinton, was born in Bristol, Vermont, December 17, 1871. When he was but six months old his parents removed to Starksboro, where he attended the public schools. He followed farming in Starksboro until he was twenty-four years old and then went to New York state, where he had charge of Dr. Brush's farm for a year. Returning to Vermont he bought a farm in Lincoln, and followed farming there from 1897 to 1902. In 1905 he came to Rutland, where he has resided since. In 1907 he engaged in business at Rutland as a dealer in groceries, meats, provisions, wood and hay. He also conducts a farm there. While residing in Lincoln he was road commissioner of the town for two years. In politics he is a Republican. He married,

April 30, 1892, Lena Lafayette, born August 9, 1874, in Starksboro, daughter of Israel and Celia (Wicklaw) Lafayette. Children: 1. Celia Alice, born April 1, 1893; married Lewis M. Buffum. 2. Henrietta Jessie, born August 2, 1894, died in 1905. 3. Edgar Israel, born August 30, 1896. 4. Edna Vida, born May 9, 1898. 5. Emma Gladys, born July, 1899. 6. Child, died in infancy. 7. Raymond Datus, born May 14, 1904. 8. Child, died in infancy.

SEAVER According to tradition, the earliest member of the Seaver family came in Cromwell's army into Ireland. He settled in the Town of Trea, county Armagh, and his name was Charles Seaver. The coat-of-arms borne by the branch of the family in Ireland is the only one known, and is as follows: Argent, a chevron gules between three doves pecking sheaves of wheat, proper. Crest: A hand and arm, holding a sword erect, encircled by a laurel wreath, all proper. Motto: "The highest praise to merit."

(I) Robert Seaver, immigrant ancestor, was born about 1608, in England. On March 24, 1633-34, at the age of about twenty-five, he took the oaths of supremacy and allegiance to pass for New England in the ship "Mary and John" of London, Robert Saymes, master. In the same ship came William Ballard, and in 1633 also came Elizabeth Ballard. She soon "joyned the church, and was afterwards married to Robert Sever of this church, where she led a godly conversation". (Church records.) He settled in Roxbury and was admitted a freeman April 18, 1638. His name was spelled variously in the records. Sever, Seaver, Civer, Seaver. He was married twice, his second wife being Elizabeth Ballard, who was buried December 18, 1689. His will was dated January 16, 1681, and proved July 5, 1683. He died May 13, 1683, aged about seventy-five years. Children: Shubael, mentioned below; Caleb, born August 30, 1641; Joshua, twin, August 30, 1641; Elizabeth, November 19, 1643; Nathaniel, January 8, 1645; Hannah, February 14, 1647, died June 3, 1647; Hannah, born October 13, 1650, buried March 3, 1653.

(II) Shubael, son of Robert Seaver, was born January 31, 1639, and died January 18, 1729-30. He married, February 7, 1668, Hannah, daughter of Nathaniel Wilson, and she died February 13, 1721-2, aged seventy-five years. Children: Robert, born June 7, 1670; Joseph, mentioned below; Hannah, September 1, 1674; Abigail, July 23, 1677; Shubael, October 10, 1679; Thankful, April 6, 1684.

(III) Joseph, son of Shubael Seaver, was

born June 1, 1672, in Roxbury, Massachusetts, died before August 26, 1754, on which date his will was proved. He married in Sudbury, Massachusetts, December 10, 1701, Mary Read. Children: Robert, mentioned below; Mary, born October 5, 1706; Nathaniel, born April 1, 1709; Hannah, born 1712; Elizabeth, born January 31, 1714; Abigail, married Azariah Walker.

(IV) Robert, son of Joseph Seaver, was born in 1703, died probably early in 1752. He and his two oldest sons enlisted in the first Louisburg expedition and were at the surrender of the fortress, June 28, 1745. In October, 1748, his house in Sudbury was burned, and he appealed for help from the colonial legislature. Soon after this he moved to Narragansett No. 2, settling upon right lot No. 70 in the southeast part of the town. This land he bought of Josiah Brown of Sudbury on November 20, 1750. In the spring of 1751 he had "a frame of a house, 3 acres of land fenced, 2 cleared and 1 broken up ready for planting." In 1755 his widow sold his land to Luke Brown, but she continued to live in Westminster until her death in 1773 or 1774. He married, September 2, 1726, Eunice Norman, of Boston, daughter of Captain Norman, whose ship was wrecked outside of Boston Harbor, on the rocky ledge since known as Norman's Woe. Children: Joseph, born in Sudbury, June 10, 1727; Benjamin, born in Framingham, October 8, 1728; Thankful, Framingham, October 6, 1731; Norman, mentioned below; Hannah; Samuel, born in Sudbury, April 8, 1747.

(V) Lieutenant Norman Seaver, son of Robert Seaver, was born in 1734 or 1735, according to his tombstone, whether at Framingham or Sudbury. He seems to have come to Narragansett No. 2 with his father and money was paid to him for work for the proprietors in 1751. He returned to Sudbury after his father's death and lived there a few years, then moving to Shrewsbury, now Boylston. Early in 1773 probably, he returned to Westminster (Narragansett No. 2), where he bought lots No. 76 and 122. This land was occupied for years by his grandson Isaac, and was situated between Prospect and Beech Hills. He served in the revolution as lieutenant in Captain Ebenezer Belknap's company, Colonel Nathaniel Wade's regiment, July 25, 1778, to January 1, 1779, Rhode Island. He served from Westminster as sergeant in Captain Noah Miles' company, Colonel John Whitcomb's regiment, April 19, 1775; ensign in Captain Francis Wilson's company, Colonel Danforth Keyes' regiment, 1777; finally as first lieutenant in Captain Belknap's company.

He was a carpenter by trade, and had the contract for part of the work on the second meeting house of Westminster. During the "raising", July 31, 1787, he fell from the frame and received injuries which resulted in his death almost immediately. He married, at Sudbury, March 14, 1754, Sarah, daughter of Jacob and Experience Reed, and she died in 1808. Children: Eunice, born May 3, 1755; Benjamin, April 21, 1757; Sarah, January, 1759; Joseph, March 13, 1761; Isaac, February 18, 1763; Ethan, September 24, 1765; Daniel, June 28, 1767; Heman, mentioned below; Luther, April 13, 1771; Relief, September 25, 1774; Asahel R., October 2, 1775; Faithful, August 2, 1777; Lucinda, March 23, 1780.

(VI) Heman, son of Lieutenant Norman Seaver, was born May 6, 1769, died at Marlboro, Massachusetts, December 19, 1835. For years he was a very successful teacher in Marlboro. He moved to Montreal, Canada, where he became a wealthy man. He married (first) Elizabeth Weeks, (second) Sarah Rice. Child by first marriage: Norman, mentioned below. Children by second marriage: Sarah R., married Professor Horace Day, of New Haven, Connecticut; Hannah; Elizabeth; William Rufus, a clergyman in Pontiac, Michigan.

(VII) Norman (2), son of Heman Seaver, was born in Groton, Massachusetts, in 1806, and died at St. Louis, Missouri, in 1839. He was a lawyer by profession. He received his education at the Jesuits College in Montreal and then attended Middlebury College for two years, and Harvard College for four years. He married Anna Maria, born in 1806, died in 1893, daughter of Luther and Lucy (Bigelow) Lawrence. Children: Edwin Lowell, deceased; Norman, mentioned below; Emily, deceased.

(VIII) Rev. Norman (3) Seaver, son of Norman (2) Seaver, was born in Boston, April 23, 1834. He attended the public schools there and the Boston Latin School and was admitted to Williams College from which he was graduated with the degree of Bachelor of Arts in 1854. He studied law and was admitted to the bar of Suffolk county at the age of twenty-one years, but he preferred the ministry as a profession and entered the Andover Theological Seminary from which he was graduated. He was ordained and for more than fifty years has been in the ministry continuously. He preached for eight years at Rutland, Vermont; for eight years was pastor of the First Presbyterian Church of New York City, and had a pastorate for eight years in Syracuse, New York. He also had pastorates in Philadelphia; Chicago; St. Paul, Minnesota, where he preached for five years, and at Montpelier, Vermont, where he was a pastor for eight years, since then he has been minister at large, preaching every Sunday.

He married (first) in Rutland, Vermont, in 1865, Caroline Keith Daniels, he married (second) Ellen (Stocker) Pond, widow of Erasmus Abbott Pond of Rutland. He has no children.

BROOKS Thomas H. Brooks is a member of one of the old colonial families of America that has been represented in the Western Reserve, Ohio, from pioneer times. His father, the late Dr. Martin L. Brooks, was one of Cleveland's beloved physicians for nearly half a century. Hezekiah Brooks, the pioneer of the family in the Western Reserve, came from Berlin, Hartford county, Connecticut, in 1818, bringing with him his wife and children, three in number, and several relatives. They made a seven weeks' journey through the almost unbroken wilderness with teams, and settled near LaPorte, in Carlisle township, Lorain county, Ohio, where Hezekiah Brooks followed farming through the remainder of his life.

Dr. Martin L. Brooks was born December 7, 1812, in Berlin, Connecticut, and was six years of age when the family came to Ohio. He was the eldest of thirteen children. Soon after the arrival of the Brooks family in the new country, other pioneer residents came, and the parents, ambitious to educate their children, soon opened a school which Martin L. Brooks attended to the age of sixteen years, when an accident occurred which probably had much to do with the shaping of his future life. While hauling logs he in some manner sustained a fracture of the leg. When he had partially recovered but was not yet fitted for manual labor, his father, not wishing his son to remain idle, placed him as a student in the academy of the Rev. Henry Lyon, at Brownhelm—the first classical school in the entire section. His ambitions once aroused, there was no return to the farm for him, and, after spending two years at the academy, he continued his education at Elyria, Ohio, and afterward went to Oberlin, remaining a student there for two years, during which time Charles G. Finney also entered that institution. While attending school at Oberlin it was Mr. Brooks' good fortune to hear William Lloyd Garrison, and as the result of the interest in the slavery question which the latter awakened, Dr. Brooks early became imbued with the anti-slavery spirit of that great champion of human liberty, and on July 4th, 1833, he made

the first speech on abolition ever delivered at Oberlin, coming out firm and square against slavery. This caused much excitement and talk in the little town which was destined afterward to become one of the greatest abolition centers of the north. It is popularly supposed that Oberlin College was founded on anti-slavery principles from the first, but this is erroneous, as the trustees did not adopt the principles of anti-slavery until some time after Dr. Brooks made his maiden speech in defense of it.

After leaving Oberlin Dr. Brooks went to Cincinnati, where he engaged in teaching school, and subsequently taught a large school for negroes at Gallipolis, Ohio, numbering among his pupils many freed slaves. This school, of which he had charge, was under the patronage of the presbytery of Chillicothe. While there he aroused the antipathy of the townsfolk by his outspoken defense of the colored race. At one time a number of his friends had to guard his house from ruffians who threatened his life, and on another occasion he was attacked on a lonely road, but, being mounted on a good horse, made his escape. Contrary to the advice of his friends, he boldly came forth and had his assailant arrested and placed in jail. During his sojourn there he was also a member of the famous underground railway system, and many fugitive slaves had occasion to thank him for his aid in assisting them to freedom in Canada. In this connection, Dr. Brooks related how one night, just as he was starting from a friendly farm house with a load of hay, under which there was a small colony of little darkies, the good hostess came out to him and, raising both hands to heaven, brought them down on his strong young shoulders with a fervent "God bless you, my boy!"

On the conclusion of his labors in Gallipolis, Dr. Brooks attended a course of lectures at the Medical College of Ohio, Cincinnati, but as his funds became exhausted he went to Kaskaskia, Illinois, where he remained in business for three years. During that period he was at one time brought into close contact with Abraham Lincoln, who even at that early day impressed Dr. Brooks as a remarkable man. In 1842 he returned to Cincinnati and completed his medical studies, being graduated in 1844. After spending some time in a hospital in that city, he located at Patriot, Indiana, a small town on the Ohio river, where he remained until the spring of 1848, when, feeling that his labors were circumscribed by the narrow borders of the place, he removed to Cleveland, which city remained his home throughout the rest of his days. His practice steadily grew, as did his medical reputation, and as steadily he advanced in the respect and affection of the community. His practice in Cleveland covered a period of more than forty-five years, during which time he enjoyed well-earned distinction as a successful and capable family physician.

During the civil war Dr. Brooks had charge of the United States Marine Hospital as surgeon, and he was for years a censor in the medical department of the University of Wooster, while later he was censor of the medical department of the Western Reserve University. He was also honored with the first presidency of the Cuyahoga County Medical Society. For a number of years after the close of the civil war Dr. Brooks was associated in practice with Dr. H. J. Herrick, his son-in-law, but during the last quarter of a century his active connection with the profession was alone. He practiced in all departments, never confining his attention to a specialty, but engaged in family practice, office consultation being of secondary consideration. His life was ever an extremely busy one. Aside from his profession, he took great interest in politics and public questions, though he never sought political preferment. Originally he was connected with the Whig party, but on the formation of the Republican party to prevent the further extension of slavery, he identified himself with that organization. He was also deeply interested in religious matters, and was an elder in the Second Presbyterian Church of Cleveland, for forty years.

At Kaskaskia, Illinois, December 8th, 1839, Dr. Brooks was married to Miss Rebecca F. Hope, a daughter of Captain Thomas Hope, of Hampton, Virginia, the Hope family being one of the oldest and most pronounced pro-slavery families of that state. Mrs. Brooks passed away about twelve years prior to the death of her husband, who about seven years before his demise retired from active practice because of advancing age. He died after a few weeks' illness, on June 10, 1899, sincerely mourned and beloved by all who knew him. Under the caption of "A Beloved Physician", a Cleveland paper said editorially of Dr. Brooks:

"Full of years and rich in the garnered friendships of a half-century's busy life, Dr. Martin L. Brooks has passed from an earth that he did much to make pleasant for poor humanity. He was an honor and an ornament to the noblest of professions, and in that branch of the service which he made peculiarly his own, that of family physician, he endeared himself to grateful thousands. His smile was a light in the sickroom and his cheering words have brought hope to countless despairing souls. He had schooled himself to conceal his natural fears and anxieties—perhaps it was a heaven-sent faculty—and to the ailing ones he seemed more the tender sympathetic friend than the watchful and heavy burdened phytor Brooks,' but it was ever a term of affectionate sician. For many years he was known as 'Old Doctor Brooks,' but it was ever a term of affectionate regard. He early aged in appearance, and many of our older citizens well remember that he bore a venerable air for a quarter of a century or more. But though time left its impress freely on the outer crust of the man it never touched his heart. There was sadness in many homes when the news of his death was read, for no man beyond the border of the hearthstone is quite so dear as he who has lightened the pain, or mayhap, shared the sorrow of the family circle, and it is as such a friend and comforter that the dear old doctor's memory will be best revered and long cherished."

To Dr. and Mrs. Brooks were born a daughter and two sons: Mary, who became the wife of Dr. H. J. Herrick, of Cleveland; Martin, who was a physician engaged in practice in Newburg, where he died, and Thomas H.

The last-named son was born in Patriot, Indiana, October 10, 1846, and was but one year of age when his parents established their home in Cleveland. His early education was acquired in the public schools, and afterward he entered Williams College, from which he was graduated in 1870. In 1875 he established the T. H. Brooks Foundry and structural iron business. In 1890 the firm name was changed to T. H. Brooks & Company, which stands to-day as one of the foremost representatives of this line of business in the middle west, being exclusively engaged in the manufacture of structural iron and ornamental steel work. The plant is one of the most important productive industries of the city, and the modern business methods which are employed and the high commercial principles which are followed in its conduct, constitute this one of the leading business concerns of Cleveland. Mr. Brooks has also figured prominently in connection with financial interests, being one of the organizers of the East End Banking & Trust Company in 1890, while for several years he served as president of the organization until the same was merged with the Cleveland Trust Company. He is interested in a number of banks and manufacturing concerns in Cleveland.

Mr. Brooks married Miss Anna M. Curtiss. He is a member of the Second Presbyterian church, and for a number of years has served on its board of trustees. In politics he is a Republican, and is a well-known club man, belonging to the University Club of New York, and the Union, Country and Euclid Clubs of Cleveland. In that city, where his residence has been maintained from early childhood days, he has a wide acquaintance, and such has been his course in life that young and old, rich and poor, speak of him in terms of highest respect.

This surname was TOLMAN-TURNER originally "le Tollere," or "le Toller," the term applied to those employed in gathering the king's levy. Tradition asserts that the Tolmans are of remote German origin, and that their Teutonic ancestors settled in England at a very early date. In the year 825 A. D., during the reign of Egbert, first king of the United Saxons, Sir Thomas Tolman was grand almoner of that sovereign. The recognized head of the family in England during the first half of the seventeenth century was Sir Thomas Tolman, of North Lincolnshire, and a nephew of the latter was a favorite of the ill-fated Charles I. A Sir Thomas Tolman of the same period commanded a Puritan regiment under Cromwell at the battle of Marston Moor, in 1644. The family coat-of-arms is thus described: "Sa. a martlet ar. between three ducal crowns or; crest: two arms armour embowed, wielding a battle axe, all ppr."

(I) The American descendants of the English Tolmans now being considered are undoubtedly the posterity of Thomas Tolman, of Salcomb Regis, Devonshire, who according to the Parish register, was buried there August 24, 1622.

(II) Thomas (2), son of Thomas (1) Tolman, of Devonshire, England, was born in England, December 9, 1608, died June 8, 1690; his will was dated October 29, 1688. The family tradition says that he came to New England in the ship "Mary and John" in 1630. He settled in Dorchester, and owned land extending from the sea to the Dedham line. He owned also land in what is now Canton, Stoughton and Sharon. The first mention of him on the Dorchester records is: "It is ordered that Goodman Tolman's house be appointed for the receiving any goods that shall be brought in whereof the owner is not known." He signed the church covenant in 1636, and was admitted a freeman, May 13, 1640. He located near Pine Neck, now Port Norfolk, and his house stood within a hundred feet of Pine Neck creek, on the west side, and on the north side within about two hundred feet, the creek forming an elbow there. In 1852 the Old Colony railroad removed the most of the cellar of the house. The land is still or was lately in possession

of the family, and some of his descendants still reside there. He probably built also the house in which his son Thomas lived, between what is now Ashmont and Washington streets. He married (first) Sarah ———; (second) Katherine ———, who died November 7, 1677. Children: 1. Thomas, born 1633, died September 12, 1718, aged eighty-five years; married, November 4, 1654, Elizabeth, daughter of Richard Johnson, of Lynn, Massachusetts; she died December 15, 1726; Thomas was admitted with his wife into the Dorchester church, May 17, 1674; he was made a freeman in 1678; his house stood about one hundred feet from "Ashmont street" in "Tolman's Lane"; children: Thomas, Mary, Samuel, Daniel. 2. John, mentioned below. 3. Sarah, married, March 18, 1659, Henry Leadbetter; died April 20, 1722. 4. Rebecca, married James Tucker. 5. Ruth, married Isaac Royal; died May 1, 1681. 6. Hannah, born July 27, 1642, died August 4, 1729; married (first) George Lyon, (second) William Blake. 7. Mary, married ——— Collins, of Lynn.

(III) John, son of Thomas (2) Tolman, died January 1, 1724-25. He was made a freeman in 1678. He was one of the selectmen of Dorchester for 1693-94-95. He married (first) Elizabeth, daughter of John Collins; she died October 7, 1690. He married (second) June 15, 1692, Mary Paul, widow, who died August 25, 1720. Children of first wife: 1. Elizabeth, born October 14, 1667; married, October 28, 1692, Moses Hewse, or Hewes. 2. John, mentioned below. 3. Joseph, born June 7, 1674. 4. Benjamin, born December 6, 1676; went to Scituate, Massachusetts. 5. Henry, born March 13, 1678-79; married Hannah ———, by whom he had nine children, all born in Dorchester; he afterwards removed to Attleboro, Massachusetts, where he died at an advanced age; his wife Hannah died November 11, 1735. 6. Ann, born February 1, 1681. 7. Ebenezer, born March 27, 1683. 8. Ruth, born January 1, 1685; married Joseph Burt, January 18, 1711. 9. William, born September 2, 1687.

(IV) John (2), son of John (1) and Elizabeth (Collins) Tolman, was born January 2, 1671, died October 23, 1759. He married (first) February, 1696-97, Susanna, daughter of John Breck; she died January 20, 1712. He married (second) April 1, 1714, Elizabeth White, who died June 25, 1768, aged eighty-nine years. Among his children was John, mentioned below.

(V) John (3), son of John (2) and Susanna (Breck) Tolman, was born April 6, 1700, died from the sting of bees, May 29,

Jacob A. Turner

Jacob Lee Turner

Roger Felix Turner

1779. He was a wheelwright by trade. He married, January 2, 1735, Hannah Clap, who died March 16, 1799. Children: 1. Hannah, born May 11, 1736; married Deacon Edward Pierce, November 1, 1763. 2. John, born April 13, 1738; married (first) Elizabeth Baker, April 16, 1761, who died November 23, 1762, aged twenty-five; married (second) Hannah Hall, May 31, 1764, and she died April 22, 1828, aged eighty-two. 3. Ezekiel, mentioned below. 4. Jemima, born May 28, 1743, died May 24, 1774. 5. Ruth, born November 5, 1745, died January 9, 1750. 6. Susannah, born August 16, 1749, died January 12, 1750. 7. Nathaniel, born March 16, 1752.

(VI) Ezekiel, son of John (3) and Hannah (Clap) Tolman, was born October 24, 1740, died December 31, 1827. He served as selectman for four years, and representative to general court for six years. He married Sarah Harrington, who died October 16, 1821, aged eighty years. Children: 1. Sarah, born July 13, 1767; married ———— Clap Jr., 1800. 2. Ezekiel, born January 22, 1769; removed to Maine, married and had children. 3. Lemuel, born October 8, 1770; married (first) Mary Tolman, May 11, 1797; (second) June 4, 1840, Lydia Brewer; he died at Roxbury, Massachusetts. 4. Nathaniel, born August 9, 1772, drowned in Portland Harbor, October 10, 1804; married Lydia Pratt, January 28, 1796. 5. Moses, born April, 1774; went to Industry, Maine, to live, was a justice of the peace, married and had children. 6. Phineas, born November 9, 1775; married Lydia (Pratt) Tolman, widow of his brother, Nathaniel, on December 8, 1809. 7. Ruth, born June 17, 1777; married John Dickerman, of Stoughton, Massachusetts, June 10, 1795. 8. John, born May 29, 1779; went to Portland, Maine, married, but had no children. 9. Enos, mentioned below.

(VII) Enos, son of Ezekiel and Sarah (Harrington) Tolman, was born January 19, 1784, died in 1868. He married Esther Treat, who died in Medway, Massachusetts, in 1859, and was buried in the Codman cemetery, Norfolk street, Dorchester, Massachusetts. Children: 1. Sarah Ann, born January 18, 1807; married, November 29, 1832, Benjamin F. Turner, and had a son, Jacob Arthur, mentioned below. 2. Hannah Merrill, born May 18, 1809; married, March 26, 1834, Thomas Cook. 3. Enos, born March 21, 1811; married Irene ————, and had children: Charles Edwin, George Enos, Elbridge, Harriet Newell and Irene. 4. Ezekiel, born September 29, 1812, died young. 5. Ezekiel, born April 3, 1814. 6. Esther, born February 9, 1816. 7. Harriet Newell, born

January 17, 1818; married William B. Pierce. 8. Ezekiel James, born May 16, 1819. 9. John, born December 12, 1820. 10. Amos David, born January 4, 1823. 11. Elizabeth, born December 5, 1824. 12. Charles, born October 28, 1827.

Jacob Arthur Turner, son of Benjamin F. and Sarah Ann (Tolman) Turner, was born April 15, 1849. He married, May 20, 1891, in Milton, Massachusetts, Mary Delia, daughter of Daniel G. Corliss, of Milton, and Maria Lydia (Whittier) Corliss, and a relative of John Greenleaf Whittier, the poet. Her grandfather was Elijah Corliss. Jacob A. Turner came to Milton in 1865 and in 1872 he formed a partnership with John Tolman to conduct the ice business, which continued until the autumn of 1876, when the firm was dissolved. Then Mr. Turner went into the ice business on his own account. In 1883 he formed a partnership with J. Frank Pope and the firm was Pope & Turner, which has been in existence ever since. They are well known ice dealers and conduct an extensive business. Mr. Turner is a member of the Sons of Veterans, the Ancient and Honorable Artillery Company of Boston, the Fusileers Veteran Association of Boston, the Thomas G. Stevenson Post, No. 26, Grand Army of the Republic, Macedonian Lodge, Free and Accepted Masons, of Milton, Washington Lodge, Free and Accepted Masons, of Roxbury, Massachusetts, Mount Vernon Chapter, Roxbury Council, Joseph Warren Commandery, and is a Scottish Rite thirty-second degree Mason. Mrs. Turner is a member of the Milton Historical Society, Women's Relief Corps, Eastern Star, Milton Educational Society, the Milton Women's Club and the Social League of Milton. Their children are: Jacob Lee, born January 5, 1899, and Roger Felix, born March 3, 1901. They reside on Central avenue, Milton, Massachusetts.

BACHELDER   The English surname Batchelder is identical with Batcheller, and is, of course, variously spelled in the early records. The English registers of the thirteenth and fourteenth centuries, where the name is first found, use the French prefix, "le". At a later date the "le" was dropped, as in the case of similar surnames. Before 1600 the name is common in Kent, Surrey, Sussex, Wilts, Hampshire, Bucks, Middlesex, Norfolk and Suffolk, all in southeastern England. There were seven immigrants of this surname to New England: Alexander, of Portsmouth, New Hampshire; Rev. Stephen, of

Lynn, Massachusetts, and Hampton, New Hampshire; Henry, of Ipswich; Joseph and John, of Salem; William, of Charlestown, and John, of Watertown, Denham and Reading.

(1) Rev. Stephen Batchelder, the immigrant ancestor of this line, was born in England, in 1561. He matriculated at St. John's College, Oxford, in 1581, and in 1586, at the age of twenty-six years, was presented by Lord de la Warr with the living of Wherwell (Horrell), a pretty village in Hampshire, on the river Test. The Oxford registers do not give Mr. Batchelder's name, but there were at Kingselere, Burgolere and Highclere, a few miles from Wherwell, a large family of Bachilers; and at Upper Clatford, in 1571, there died a Richard Bachiler, whose will mentioned several family names early found in Hampton, New Hampshire. While Stephen Bachiler was at Wherwell, there was living at Andover and Weyhill, a few miles away, Rev. James Samborne, whose son, Rev. James Samborne Jr., was rector of Grately, nearby, in 1604, and of Upper Clatford, 1610-28. Mr. Bachiler was deprived of his living in 1605, presumably for holding Calvinistic or Puritan beliefs, and he took refuge in Holland, it is said, but no record of his life there has been found. His son-in-law, Rev. John Wing, was the first pastor of the English church at Middleburgh, in Holland, from 1620, and it is worth noting that Mr. Samuel Bachilor, minister to Sir Charles Morgan's fighting regiment in Holland, was the same year called to a pastorate in Flushing, Holland, and declined. Samuel is thought by some genealogists to have been son of Stephen; he was author of a book called "Miles Christianus," perhaps the same volume that Rev. Stephen sent to the wife of Governor Winthrop in October, 1639, from Hampton. He said in this letter:

"I present my great respect and thankfulness unto you in a little token. And though it be little in itself, yet doth it contain greater worth of true worth than can easily be comprehended but of a spiritual man. * * * Looking among some special reserved books, and lighting on this little treatise of one of mine own poor, I conceived nothing might suit more to my love, nor your acceptance. As God gives you leisure to read anything that may further your piety, and hope of a better life than this, if you shall please to vouchsafe a little part of that time to read this by degrees, I shall judge it more than sufficient to my love and desire of furthering you in the way of grace."

When in London in 1631, making preparation to come to New England, permission was granted him, his wife Helen, and daughter, Ann Sandborn (Samborne) widow, who lived in the Strand, London, to go to Flushing for two months to visit his sons and daughters there. Soon after leaving Wherwell, Mr. Batchelder settled at Newton Stacy, the nearest hamlet to the eastward and bought land there in 1622, selling it in 1631. He sailed for Boston, March 9, 1632, on the ship "William and Francis", being pastor of the colony sent over by the Plow Company to settle the Plow Patent in Maine. His son-in-law, Christopher Hussey, of Dorking, settled in Lynn, where he was joined by Mr. Batchelder, who formed a small church there, baptizing first his grandson, Stephen Hussey, born 1630. The Plow colony was a failure. At Lynn, Mr. Batchelder came into collision with the authorities and for a time was restricted to preaching to those that came with him. He was admitted a freeman May 6, 1635. In February, 1636, he moved to Ipswich, where he was granted fifty acres of land. He was one of the founders of Sandwich, Massachusetts, and, though seventy-six years old at that time, walked from Ipswich to Sandwich. But he soon moved again, this time to Newbury, Massachusetts, where he had a grant of land July 6, 1638. Finally he and his company who petitioned therefor were granted liberty to begin a plantation at Winnicunnet, later called Hampton, New Hampshire. The settlement was begun October 16, 1638, the town incorporated June 7, 1639, and soon afterward named Hampton. In 1639 Ipswich voted to give Mr. Bachiler sixty acres of upland and twenty of meadow if he would reside in that town as preacher three years, but he preferred Hampton, where he had three hundred acres for a farm, besides his house lot. He gave the town a church bell which was used until it cracked in 1703, and was sent to England to help pay for a new bell. Soon trouble arose in the church, and even the personal character of the aged preacher was assailed. He was called to Exeter, New Hampshire, and Casco, Maine, but finally accepted neither. He left Hampton and resided in Portsmouth in 1647. He gave all his property to his grandchildren in that year and returned to England between 1650 and 1658, settling in Hackney, part of London, where he died in 1660. He married (first) in England ———, and (second) in England, Helen ———, born 1583, died 1642. He married (third), about 1648, Mary ———, and this marriage was unfortunate. Grave charges were made against her and he sued for divorce. When he went to England he left her behind. He may have erred, but in the main his life was clean and honorable. He was learned and had a very long and eventful, if not entirely successful life.

A description of his coat-of-arms is given in Morgan's "Sphere of the Gentry," printed 1661: Vert a plough in fesse and in base the sun rising or. Motto: *Sol justiter exoritur.* Children: Nathaniel, mentioned below; Deborah, born 1592; Stephen, 1594; Theodate, 1596 daughter; Ann, 1601.

(II) Nathaniel, son of Stephen Batchelder, was born in England and resided there. He married Hester Mercer, of Southampton, a niece of Rev. John Priaulx, archdeacon of Sarum. Children: Stephen, merchant of London; Anna, married Daniel DuCornet; Francis, resided in England; Nathaniel, mentioned below; Benjamin, resided in England.

(III) Nathaniel (2), son of Nathaniel (1) Batchelder, was born in 1630, in England, and was the immigrant ancestor. He lived in Hampton, New Hampshire, where he held many offices of trust. He was some time constable, and selectman nine years. It is said that after the death of his first wife, when he determined to marry again, he resolved to be governed in his choice by the direction in which his staff, held perpendicularly over the floor, should fall, when dropped from his hand. The experiment being tried, the staff fell to the southwest, and in that direction he bent his steps, travelling to Woburn, where he offered the widow Wyman his hand. His will was dated February 14, 1706-7; he died suddenly January 2, 1710. He married (first) December 10, 1656, Deborah, daughter of John Smith, of Martha's Vineyard, sister of John and niece of Ruth Dalton. She died March 8, 1675, and he married (second) October 31, 1677, Mrs. Mary (Carter) Wyman, daughter of Rev. Thomas Carter, and widow of John Wyman, of Woburn. She was born July 24, 1648, and died 1688, probably cousin of his first wife. He married (third) October 3, 1689, Elizabeth B. Knill, widow of John Knill. She survived her husband, and was admitted to the Charlestown church September 2, 1677. Children: Deborah, born October 12, 1657; Nathaniel, mentioned below; Ruth, May 9, 1662; Esther, December 22, 1664; Abigail, December 28, 1667; Jane, January 8, 1669; Stephen, July 31, 1672, died December 7, 1762; Benjamin, born September 19, 1673; Stephen, March 8, 1675; Mercy, December 11, 1677; Mary, September 18, 1679, died young; Samuel, January 10, 1681; Jonathan, 1683; Thomas, 1685; Joseph, August 9, 1687; Mary, October 17, 1688, died young; Theodate.

(IV) Deacon Nathaniel (3) Batchelder, son of Nathaniel (2) Batchelder, was born in Hampton, December 24, 1659, and died in 1745, in Hampton Falls. In 1719-20 he was an assessor, and in 1722 selectman; he and his

sons Nathaniel, Joseph and Josiah were original proprietors of Chester, New Hampshire. He married, probably in 1683, Elizabeth Foss, of Portsmouth, born 1666, died 1746. Children, born in Hampton: John, July 28, 1684; Deborah, April 9, 1686; Nathaniel, February 19, 1690; Elizabeth, 1694; Josiah, July 1, 1695; Jethro, January 2, 1698; Nathan, July 2, 1700; Phinehas, November 1, 1701; Ebenezer, mentioned below.

(V) Deacon Ebenezer Batchelder, son of Nathaniel (3) Batchelder, was born December 10, 1710, and died in 1784. He lived in East Kingston, New Hampshire, where he was prominent; deacon of the church; in 1774, representative to general court. He married Dorothy ———. Children: Nathan, mentioned below; Richard, October 5, 1736; William, November 2, 1738; Nathaniel, February 21, 1740; Betty, August 2, 1741; Dorothy, May 23, 1743; Ebenezer, February 6, 1746; Josiah, December 25, 1749; Joanna, October 7, 1750; Ann, January 13, 1758.

(VI) Major Nathan Bachelder, son of Ebenezer Batchelder, was born in East Kingston, October 25, 1734. He was an early settler of Loudon, New Hampshire, and served in the revolution as major. He married, April 8, 1756, Margaret Bean, daughter of Joseph, son of James, son of John Bean. She was born in Kingston, August 12, 1738. He married (second) September 16, 1781, Dorothy Page, of Deerfield. Children: Richard, born December 8, 1756; Phineas, November 16, 1760; William, March 19, 1762; Joseph, January 2, 1764; Ebenezer, October 2, 1769; Dolly, February 13, 1772; Josiah, mentioned below; Ebenezer, died in infancy.

(VII) Josiah, son of Nathan Bachelder, was born in Loudon, January 24, 1775. He married Mary Blake. Children, born in Loudon: Moses, mentioned below; Mathais; Joseph.

(VIII) Moses, son of Josiah Bachelder, was born in Loudon, August 3, 1802, and died April 1, 1830. He lived in Gilmanton, New Hampshire. He was a lumber dealer. He married, in Gilmanton, 1824, Sally Parsons Gilman, born February 28, 1803, died February 8, 1871. Child: John Badger, mentioned below.

(IX) Colonel John Badger Bachelder, son of Moses Bachelder, was born at Gilmanton, New Hampshire, November 29, 1835, and died at Hyde Park, now Boston, Massachusetts, December 23, 1894. He was educated in the public schools. His life was devoted to literary work. He became a writer of national reputation, as the government historian of the battle of Gettysburg. Shortly after the battle he went to the field of action, by order of the United States government, and began what proved to be the work of a lifetime, for throughout his life he was engaged in collecting the facts and writing the history of the battle. He prepared for publication and preservation thousands of pages of manuscript: He had traversed the field day after day, and from personal interviews with the men engaged on both sides in the battle, he could tell any combatant just where his place was in that great struggle. He could point out the location and trace the movements of every regiment, Federal and Confederate. He was author of various other works: "The Tourist's Guide;" "Gettysburg, What to See and How to See It;" "Geometrical Drawing of the Gettysburg Battlefield;" "Historical Paintings of the Battle of Gettysburg;" "Last Hours of Lincoln;" and "Popular Resorts and How to Reach Them." In politics he was a Republican, in religion a Congregationalist. For many years he made his home in Hyde Park.

He married, at Nottingham, New Hampshire, November 2, 1854, Elizabeth Barber Stevens, who was born August 5, 1828, daughter of Daniel B. Stevens (see Stevens). They had one child, Charlotte Butler, born May 16, 1861, died June 2, 1874.

(The Stevens Line).

(I) William Stevens, the immigrant, was born in England, in 1617, and came from Gonsham, county Oxford, England, at the age of twenty-one years, with his mother Alice Stevens, and his wife Elizabeth, and servants, in the ship "Confidence", sailing April 24, 1638. He settled in Newbury, Massachusetts, and was admitted a freeman of the colony May 18, 1642. He was a yeoman and a proprietor of the town. He died May 19, 1653. His will, proved June 30, 1653, bequeathed to his wife Elizabeth and sons John and Samuel. His widow married, March 3, 1653-4, William Titcomb. Children of William and Elizabeth Stevens: Bitfield, born March 16, 1649, died July 23, 1649; John, born November 19, 1650; Samuel, November 18, 1652, killed at Bloody Brook, September 18, 1675, by the Indians.

(II) John, son of William Stevens, was born at Newbury, November 19, 1650. He married, March 9, 1669-70, Mary Chase. He took the oath of allegiance at Newbury in 1669 and again in 1678, aged thirty. His will was dated January 15, 1724-5, and proved April 6, following. Children, born at Newbury and Haverhill: Mary, February 10, 1670; John, mentioned below; Thomas, July 3, 1676; Moses; daughter, September 7, 1680; Aaron, April 7, 1685; Joseph, November 19,

1689, died young; Benjamin, January 15, 1692-3; Sarah; Hannah.

(III) John (2), son of John (1) Stevens, was born at Newbury, March 22, 1673-4. He settled at Haverhill, Massachusetts. He married (first) May 18, 1697, Hannah Currier; (second) May 30, 1700, Mary Bartlett; (third) Miriam Jackson. Children, born at Haverhill, by first wife: Child, February 8, 1697-8, died young; child, January 1699-1700, died young. Children by second wife: Abigail, born July 4, 1701; Moses, mentioned below; Hannah, March 16, 1704-5; Jonathan, March 25, 1707; Joseph, July 12, 1709; Mary, April 14, 1710; John, July 26, 1712, died 1717; Susanna, May 17, 1716; Samuel, March 29, 1718; Timothy, June 20, 1721; Ruth, February 20, 1724-5. Child by third wife: Ann, May 13, 1729.

(IV) Moses, son of John (2) Stevens, was born at Haverhill, November 13, 1702. He married, at Haverhill, April 23, 1724, Mary Roberts. Children, born in Haverhill: Moses, September 29, 1726; Mary, baptized May 7, 1727; David, October 10, 1728; Mary, October 29, 1730; Hannah, October 3, 1732; Reuben, December 1, 1734; Joshua, mentioned below; Susanna, baptized August 27, 1738; Amos, baptized December 21, 1740; Mary, baptized October 24, 1742; Daniel, May 3, 1747.

(V) Joshua, son of Moses Stevens, was born at Haverhill, and baptized there June 9, 1737. He lived in Stratham, Newmarket and Nottingham, New Hampshire. He was in Newmarket in 1787. In 1790 the first federal census shows Joshua at Nottingham with four males over sixteen, and three females in his family. He died at Nottingham, September 16, 1816, aged seventy-nine years. He came to Nottingham from Stratham, according to the town history, and settled on the farm afterward owned by his grandson Daniel Stevens. He married Anna Harvey, born August 12, 1741, daughter of Robert Harvey; (second) Anna Watson. Children by first wife: Molly, married Elijah Mathes; Thomas, mentioned below; John, married Mary Avery, of Deerfield; Robert, married Mary Gile; Nancy, married Robert Harvey. Children by second wife: Hannah and Harvey.

(VI) Thomas, son of Joshua Stevens, was born at Nottingham, New Hampshire, February 2, 1764, and died September 24, 1847. He married Betsey, daughter of Daniel Barber, of Epping, New Hampshire, and succeeded to the homestead.

(VII) Daniel Barber, only son of Thomas Stevens, was born at Nottingham, March 14, 1803. He married, March 2, 1827, Betsey M., daughter of Captain John Butler. Children: 1. Elizabeth Barber, born August 5, 1828; married, November 2, 1854, Colonel John Badger Bachelder (see Bachelder). 2. Thomas, born February 16, 1830; married Sarah Jane Sanborn, of Deerfield, and they lived near the homestead; children: Alice Butler, married Dr. C. G. Carleton of Lawrence, Massachusetts, and have one child, Frances Coggswell Carleton; Edward Sanborn, married Caroline Pike, and they have one child, Charlotte Butler; Blanche; and Andrew Butler, married Grace Pike, and they have one child, Thomas Benjamin Stevens. 3. Amanda, born April 16, 1833, unmarried. 4. John Butler, born October 19, 1837; married Jennie Lucy, and lived in San Jose, California. 5. Charlotte Butler, born March 9, 1840, lived at Washington, D. C. 6. Joanna Mary, born February 17, 1842, died in Pennsylvania, April 11, 1860. 7. Walter Daniel, born November 10, 1849; married Martha Gault Shute, of Derry, New Hampshire, November 16, 1871; children: Mabel B., born July 29, 1874, deceased; Bessie Butler, February 15, 1876, married Fred Bachelder, and had one child, Helen Louise Bachelder; Harold Edward; Mildred, married Harry C. Kimball.

BUCK Among the earliest names in New England this has borne an honorable part in the development of that section, as well as of other states in the Union. While not so universally represented as some others, it has carried its full share in the spread of civilization. The name is supposed to be of German origin, and is found with many forms of spelling in the early records of England and the United States.

(I) William Buck was born in 1585, in England, and died in Cambridge, Massachusetts, December 24, 1658. He came to New England in the bark "Increase" in 1635, being then fifty years old, accompanied by his son Roger, a young man of eighteen years. He was a manufacturer of plows and set up his shop in the "West Field," Cambridge, on the former highway to the great swamp, now called Raymond street. No mention appears in the records of his wife or other children, and he may have been a widower or may have preceded his family to the new world, anticipating their subsequent arrival.

(II) Roger, son of William Buck, was also born in England, and came with his father at the age of eighteen and settled in Cambridge in 1643. His wife Susanna died in 1685, and he afterward moved to the adjacent town of Woburn, Massachusetts, where he died November 10, 1693. Children born

at Cambridge: Samuel, February 6, 1643, died September 21, 1690; John, September 3, 1644, died young; Ephraim, July 26, 1646; Mary, January 23, 1648, died August 31, 1669; Lydia, married Henry Smith; Ruth, November 6, 1653, married T. Bathrick; Elizabeth, July 5, 1657, married Joshua Wood.

(III) Ephraim, son of Roger Buck, was born at Cambridge, July 26, 1646. He settled in Woburn, Massachusetts, and had a farm in what is now the town of Wilmington, later called the "old Buck farm," one mile south of the meeting house. Children, born in Woburn: Sarah, January 11, 1673; Ephraim, July 13, 1676; John, died young; John, February 7, 1679-80; Samuel, November 13, 1682; Eunice, July 7, 1685; Ebenezer, mentioned below; Mary, October 28, 1691.

(IV) Ebenezer, son of Ephraim Buck, was born at Woburn, Massachusetts, May 20, 1689. In 1723 he settled at Haverhill, Massachusetts. He married, January, 1713, Lydia Eames (or Ames). Children born at Woburn: Lydia, May 28, 1715; Ebenezer, February 22, 1717-18; Colonel Jonathan, mentioned below.

(V) Colonel Jonathan Buck, son of Ebenezer Buck, was born at Woburn, February 20, 1719, and died at Bucksfield, Maine, March 18, 1795. He was the founder of Bucksfield, which was named for him. He resided for a time in Haverhill, Massachusetts, and went to Penobscot country in 1762 and located in what was later the town of Bucksfield. He is described as a thin, spare figure, five feet ten inches in height, of expressive face, with a Roman nose, arching eyebrows and dark penetrating eyes. He was of an ardent temperament and iron will. In politics he was a staunch Whig, and aided the revolution with all his power. His houses and saw mills were burned by the British in 1779, and he himself barely escaped capture when Castine was taken. He traded with the Indians and had a reputation for absolute honesty in his transactions with them. It is said that he never deceived any man. During the war he was colonel of the Fifth Regiment. He married, October 19, 1742, in Haverhill, Lydia Morse, of Newbury, born August 17, 1718, in Newbury, daughter of Philip and Mary (Brown) Morse. She died December 15, 1789, aged seventy-one. Children: 1. Jonathan, mentioned below. 2. Mary, born September 29, 1749, married Colonel Dustin, and lived at Camden, Maine. 3. Ebenezer, April 25, 1752; a bold pioneer, captain in the revolution, carpenter by trade; married, in 1780, Mary Brown, of Belfast; children: Ebenezer, Mary, William, Jane, George, Alice, Jonathan, Charles, Henry and Caroline; he died April

20, 1824. 4. Amos, July 24, 1754; settled in Bucksfield, near Orland; a blacksmith; married, September, 1778, Lydia Chamberlain, of Plaistow. 5. Daniel, September 2, 1756, at Haverhill; followed the sea and became a captain; settled in Bucksfield, and was a trader from 1798 to 1812, built a store and wharf there in 1805; married, in 1783, Mary, daughter of Colonel Dummer Sewall, of Bath; children: Samuel, Eliza, Harriet, Maria, Jonathan, Sewall, Lucy, Rufus, Daniel and Richard Pike. 6. Lydia, October 22, 1761; married Joshua Treat, of Frankfort, and had eleven children. Three other children died in youth.

(VI) Jonathan, son of Colonel Jonathan Buck, was born at Haverhill, April 3, 1748, and died at Bucksfield, March 27, 1824. In character he was much like his father, an earnest Christian, and deacon of the First Congregational Church of Bucksfield. He held various offices of trust and represented the town in the general court, 1804, and again from 1811 to 1813. He served in the revolution. He married, November, 1768-9, Hannah Gale. Children, born at Bucksfield: Rev. Benjamin, 1768, settled at Orland; John, mentioned below; Ruth, August 9, 1775; Lydia, October 25, 1777; Hannah, June, 1780; Amos, October, 1782; Joseph, May, 1785, had ten children; James, April 29, 1787; Nancy, December, 1789; David, May, 1792; Moses, July, 1794.

(VII) John, son of Jonathan Buck, was born in Bucksfield, October 27, 1771, and died there November 25, 1835. He married at Bucksfield, Elizabeth Bartlett, of Newburyport, Massachusetts, December 28, 1794. His wife died May 12, 1850, aged seventy-nine years. Children, born at Bucksfield: Eliza, in 1796; John, mentioned below; Edmund, 1805; Hannah G., 1809, died February 26, 1880; Joseph W., 1811; Charles, 1813; Nancy O'-Brien, 1815, married J. Gorham Lovell.

(VIII) John (2), son of John (1) Buck, was born June 9, 1816. He may have been the second child of the same name, for the printed genealogy in the *Bangor Historical Magazine* gives the date of birth of a son John as 1803. He was educated in the public schools, followed farming for a living, and died in Bucksfield in 1899. He married Abby Matilda Morse, born in Newfane, Vermont, February 5, 1827, daughter of Jacob and Ada Morse. She survives her husband (1912).

(IX) Orlando Jacob, son of John (2) Buck, was born in Bucksfield, Maine, December 30, 1852. He attended the public schools of his native town and the State Normal School at South Paris, Maine. He was for a number of years a dealer and manufacturer of oils and

paints. In 1881 he went to Chicago, and is general superintendent and second largest stockholder of the William Wrigley Jr. Company, manufacturers of Wrigley's spearmint pepsin gum, which has a world-wide reputation. The company has extensive factories in Chicago, New York, and at Toronto, Ontario, in Canada. The headquarters in Chicago is at No. 727 W. Van Buren street. Mr. Buck is also vice-president of The Otis Lithograph Company of Cleveland, Ohio. He resides at No. 9900 Longwood Drive, Chicago. He is a member of the New England Society of Chicago, and a life member of the Art Institute of Chicago; the Hamilton Club; the Illinois Athletic Club; Beverley Country Club; regular member of South Shore Country Club and Swan Lake Shooting Club. In politics he is a Republican; in religion a Universalist.

He married, January 21, 1880, Lillian Louise Brewer, of Cleveland, Ohio, born December 26, 1856, daughter of Nelson C. and Caroline C. Brewer. Children: 1. Hazle, born in Cleveland, December 25, 1880; married Davis Ewing, of Bloomington, Illinois. 2. Nelson LeRoy, December 2, 1882, at Chicago; assistant factory manager of the William Wrigley Jr. Company; married, March 13, 1909, Rena Alice Hooper, of Chicago. 3. Ellsworth Brewer, at Chicago, July 3, 1892.

CLARK Clark, also written Clarke, Clerk, Clerke and Clearke, is a name of great antiquity in England. Originally any person who could read and write was given the name and it came to be the surname of learned persons generally, but particularly of officers and ecclesiastical courts and parish churches who were entrusted with recording and preserving the records. In medieval days, the name was one to be respected, hence it is of frequent use in Domesday Book, either written in one of the various spellings given above or Clericus—"clerk or clergyman", "one of the clerical order". In the early settlement of New England by the English Puritans, 1625 to 1640, we find men of the name who became founders of large and distinguished families, not only in the New England colonies, but in Virginia, Maryland and New York, the family in the southern section of the United States generally adopting the spelling with the final "e". The most numerous of the Christian names appears to have been William, with John, Thomas and Samuel, in abundant evidence. Irish emigrants to America have added to the name either from Scotch-Irish or from the families of O'Clery or O'Clersach, not only common but distinguished names in the

Emerald Isle, and literally indicating "the son of the cler". Four brothers from Bedfordshire, England, came to New England in the first quarter of the seventeenth century; they were: Thomas, John, Carew and Joseph Clark. Thomas Clark (1593-1697), a carpenter in Plymouth colony, 1623, and Susannah Ring, wife, have among their illustrious descendants: Alvan Clark (1804-1887) of telescope fame, and his son Alvan Graham Clark (1832-1897) the lens maker of Cambridge, Massachusetts; Alonzo Howard Clark, born 1850, the scientist; George Bassett Clark (1827-1891) the mechanician; James Freeman Clarke (1810-1888) the clergyman, author and anti-slavery advocate; Samuel F. Clarke (1851) the naturalist. John, with Roger Williams, was a founder of Rhode Island, and also founder of the Baptist church in Newport, 1638; he has numerous descendants. Nathaniel Clarke, of Newbury (1642) and Elizabeth (Somerby) Clarke, his wife, have among their descendants: Thomas March Clark (1812-1903), second bishop of Rhode Island; Rufus Wheelwright Clark (1813-1886), Yale 1838, clergyman and author; Samuel Adams Clark (1822-1875), clergyman; and others equally notable. William Clark (1609-1690); in Nantucket, Massachusetts Bay colony, 1630, Dorchester, 1636, and Northampton, 1659, is the progenitor of the Clarks of western Massachusetts and Connecticut, and has numerous descendants in the far west. Among his more distinguished descendants we may name: General Emmons Clark (1827-1905) commander of the Seventh Regiment, National Guards, New York State Militia, 1864-89; Edson Lyman Clark, born 1827, clergyman and author, Yale, 1853; Ezra Clark (1883-1896), representative in the thirty-fourth and thirty-fifth congresses and president of the Hartford Water Board; Governor Myron H. Clark (1806-1892), governor of New York, 1854-55, and others.

(I) Joseph Clark was born in county Suffolk, England, and married, in the first half of the seventeenth century, Alice Pepper. He settled in Dedham, Massachusetts, signed the Dedham covenant and was one of the thirteen original grantees and founders of the adjoining town of Medfield, where he was admitted a freeman, May 15, 1653. His homestead in Medfield was on the west side of South street; an old cellar hole near the corner of Oak street has for many years marked the site of his former dwelling. He was a man of property and influence and was selectman in 1660. He died January 6, 1664, and his wife died March 17, 1710. Children: 1. Joseph (2),

mentioned below. 2. Benjamin, February 9, 1643, married Dorcas Morse. 3. Ephraim, February 4, 1646, married, March 6, 1669, Maria Butler. 4. Daniel, September 29, 1647, mortally wounded by Indians in King Philip's war, dying April 7, 1676. 5. Mary, June 12, 1649. 6. Sarah, February 21, 1651, married, January 7, 1673, John Bavers. 7. John, October 28, 1652. 8. Nathaniel, October 6, 1658, married Experience Hinsdell. 9. Rebecca, born August 16, 1660, died February 17, 1738-39; married (first), May 1, 1679, John Richardson; married (second) John Hall.

(II) Joseph (2), son of Joseph (1) and Alice (Pepper) Clark, was born in Dedham, February 27, 1642, and died in 1702. His father received a grant of land for a house lot for Joseph, junior, in 1663. In 1674 his house was situated near Pine Swamp, near the junction of Curve and Spring streets, Medfield, and he built a malt house near it. He married, April 8, 1663, Mary Allen, born 1641, died September 4, 1702, daughter of James Allen, of Medfield, cousin of Rev. John Allen, of Dedham. Allen bequeathed a house to his son-in-law, Joseph Clark, on the site of the house of C. W. Kingsbury. At the time of his death he owned besides his homestead, land at the planting field and at Wrentham. He was selectman of the town for some years, deputy to the general court, and held other offices of importance. Children: 1. Joseph, born 1664. 2. John, 1666, died 1691. 3. Jonathan, 1668, died 1690. 4. Esther, 1670, married Thomas Thurston. 5. Thomas, 1672, died 1690. 6. Mary, 1674-75. 7. Daniel, 1676, died 1694. 8. Leah, 1677. 9. Solomon, mentioned below. 10. David, 1680, died 1714; married, 1703, Mary Wheelock. 11. Moses, born and died, 1685. 12. Aaron, 1686, died 1751; he settled in Wrentham.

(III) Solomon, son of Joseph (2) and Mary (Allen) Clark, was born in Medfield, in 1678, and died in 1748. He settled at the planting field now owned and occupied by Thomas S. Clark. He was for three years selectman; was trustee of Province Loan, 1721, and deputy to general court, 1725. He married (first), 1698, Mary White, who died April 16, 1740; (second) October 7, 1740, Elizabeth Adams, born 1694, died 1766. Children by first wife: 1. Mary, born April 7, 1699; died 1718. 2. Jonathan, June 14, 1700. 3. Solomon (2), mentioned below. 4. Daniel, August 7, 1703. 5. David, January 19, 1705. 6. Ann, March 4, 1706, died 1764; married, 1726, Ephraim Carey. 7. Hannah, December 8, 1708; died 1710. 8. Daniel, April 25, 1710. 9. Hannah, September 30, 1711, married, 1730, Aquila Robbins. 10. Sarah, born and died

May 5, 1713. 11. John, May 14, 1715. 12. Sarah, July 3, 1718; married, 1736, Daniel Clark.

(IV) Solomon (2), second son of Solomon (1) and Mary (White) Clark, was born August 11, 1701, in Medfield, and died there March 24, 1747. He lived in the southern part of the town, near the head of Noon Hill street, where lilacs, garden pinks and a grapevine still mark the site. All traces of the cellar and well have been obliterated. He married, December 25, 1723, Mary Lovell, born January 26, 1704, in Medfield, daughter of Alexander and Elizabeth (Dyer) Lovell. She married (second) October 11, 1753, Eleazer Morse of Sherborn. Children of Solomon (2) Clark: Solomon, born July 29, 1726; Marah and Silence (twins), May 8, 1729; Mary, October 4, 1730; Thankful, February 13, 1733; Elizabeth, October 4, 1734; Sybil, July 10, 1737; Dyer, July 30, 1740, lived in Franklin, Massachusetts; Stephen, January 29, 1742; Cephas, mentioned below.

(V) Cephas, youngest child of Solomon (2) and Mary (Lovell) Clark, was born January 7, 1745, in Medfield, and settled in Keene, New Hampshire, where he was a member of the "company of foot" 1773, and signed the association test. He was a soldier of the revolution and was also a Baptist clergyman. He married in Dedham, Massachusetts, December 4, 1766, Jemima Griggs, born there November 17, 1747, daughter of John and Mehitable (Ellis) Griggs. Children: 1. Cephas, died in his third year. 2. Rufus, born April 22, 1770, married, April 13, 1793, Hannah Kingsbury. 3. Paul, died one year old. 4. Silas, twin of Paul, died eleven days later. 5. Paul, April 25, 1774, married, June 25, 1799, Hannah Hodgman. 6. Mehitable, April 4, 1776, married, April 28, 1795, Wilkes Richardson, and removed to Champion, New York. 7. Silas, November 30, 1777, married, February 20, 1805, Betsy Wyman. 8. Samuel, May 22, 1780. 9. Abigail, May 23, 1782. 10. Cephas (2), mentioned below. 11. Gideon, May 15, 1786, resided in Keene, where he died, September 6, 1859; he married, October 15, 1813, Delana Ware, who died October 22, 1867. 12. Caleb Ellis, May 29, 1788. Caphas Clark died August 8, 1858.

(VI) Cephas (2), eighth son of Cephas (1) and Jemima (Griggs) Clark, was born July 17, 1784, in Keene; he settled finally in Glover, Vermont, having previously resided in Rutland, Vermont, and Westmoreland, New Hampshire. He served as a soldier in the war of 1812 in Colonel Steele's regiment, which was stationed at Portsmouth, New Hampshire. After the war he settled upon a farm in Glover, and there continued until his death, in July, 1858. When he removed from Westmoreland to Glover, in October, 1818, his household goods were transported on a sled drawn by two oxen, and his first dwelling was a log house built after his arrival there. An heirloom still preserved in the family is a flax wheel used in Cephas Clark's family. He married, September 26, 1805, in Westmoreland, Deborah Wilbur, born April 18, 1790, in Westmoreland, and died in Glover, July 23, 1850, daughter of Rev. Nathaniel and Deborah (Aldrich) Wilbur, of Westmoreland (see Wilbur VI). Children: Caleb Aldrich, born December 14, 1807, in Westmoreland, died in Glover, July 10, 1883; Cephas Cheney, September 30, 1809, in Rutland, Vermont, died in Glover, October 23, 1869; Amasa Ford, June 22, 1811, in Rutland, died September 5, 1879, in Wilmington, Massachusetts; Alvah Ward, July 9, 1813, in Keene, died in Glover in June, 1884; Deborah Wilbur, May 31, 1815, in Westmoreland, died March 13, 1882, in Greensboro, Vermont, wife of Moses Haines; Nathaniel Evelyn, June, 1817, in Keene, died in Glover, October 11, 1820; Frederick P. A., mentioned below; Betsy Alfreda, August 27, 1821, in Glover, died there in July, 1889; Abigail Richardson, May 14, 1824, died in November, 1891; Nathaniel Evelyn, March 10, 1826; Fannie Candace, June 18, 1828, died September 8, 1860; Ezra Leonard, August 29, 1830, died in April, 1896, in Wakefield, Massachusetts.

(VII) Frederick Plummer Abbott, sixth son of Cephas (2) and Deborah (Wilbur) Clark, was born May 21, 1819, in Glover, Vermont, where he died February 6, 1889. Throughout the active years of his life he was engaged in agriculture. He married, December 9, 1845, Eliza Jennette King, born November 6, 1823, in Glover, died January 19, 1907. The history of her family reads much like a tale of romance. Her great-grandfather, George King, was the son of a southern slave holder and was disinherited because of his marriage to a northern woman. He settled in Portsmouth, New Hampshire, and was a soldier of the revolution, losing his life in battle. George King, his son, was born in Portsmouth, and was for many years a sailor in the merchant marine and on privateers. At one time he was captured by a British vessel and held a prisoner seven months in the West Indies. He was a selectman of Portsmouth in 1776 and 1777. In 1776 he was a seaman on the Continental frigate "Raleigh," enlisting July 15, at a wage of eight dollars per month, and is described as an American "of dark complexion, five feet and six inches in height".

W. F. Clark

George William, son of George King Jr., was born in Gilmanton, New Hampshire, and married Hannah Pierce, of Tuftonboro, same state. They were the parents of Eliza Jennette King, wife of Frederick P. A. Clark. (VIII) William Frederick, son of Frederick P. A. and Eliza J. (King) Clark, was born January 7, 1849, in Glover, Orleans county, Vermont, and was a student at the Montpelier Seminary, and the Orleans Liberal Institute in his native town, after which he took up the study of law. His youth was passed upon the paternal homestead and his early occupation was that of a farmer. Before completing his legal studies he became interested in the real estate and insurance business with which he has been prominently connected down to the present time. He wrote "History of Methodism in Glover," and several poems of merit—"Glover Boys at Gettysburg", "God on the Deep", and others. His political affiliations are with the Republican party, of which he has always been a strong and highly valued supporter. His interest in the public affairs of the town has been a beneficial one for that section and he has served in the following offices: Town superintendent, town grand juror, member of the Vermont state legislature in 1896, and justice of the peace. In 1898 he had charge of the leading bill making provision for the expenses and conduct of the Spanish-American war, and was assistant judge of Orleans county, Vermont, 1902-6. He is a member of the Methodist Episcopal church, and holds a high rank in the Masonic fraternity, being a member of Orleans Lodge, No. 55, Free and Accepted Masons, of Barton, Vermont; Keystone Chapter, No. 16, Royal Arch Masons; Malta Commandery, No. 10, Knights Templar, of Newport, Vermont; Mount Sinai Temple, Nobles of the Mystic Shrine, of Montpelier, Vermont.

Mr. Clark married, September 27, 1871, Elizabeth Marston, born in Craftsbury, Vermont, June 6, 1848, daughter of Deacon Charles Marston and Emeline B. (Emery) Marston, the former a member of the Vermont state legislature. Mr. and Mrs. Marston had two other children: Jeremiah and Ellen. Mr. and Mrs. Clark have had children: 1. Charles F., born in 1873; was graduated from the University of Vermont, took a post-graduate course at Cornell University, and is now an instructor in the agricultural department of that institution. 2. Arthur W., 1879, was graduated from the University of Vermont, and is now first assistant chemist in the New York State Agricultural Experimental Station at Geneva, New York; he

married, October 6, 1909, Muriel Blood, and has one child: Ruth Elizabeth. 3. Eliza E., 1889, now attending the William Smith College, Geneva, New York. 4. James G., 1891, is now attending Cornell College.

(The Wilbur Line).

One of the many notable characters in early New England history was the founder of the family bearing the surname of Wilbur, but which in the time of the ancestor himself was spelled Wildbore. This rendition is said to have been continued through one or two generations of some branches of the family after that of Samuel, and in various early records in towns where some of his descendants became settled the name appears in different forms, and Savage gives account of Wildboar, Wildboare, Wilbur, Wilbore and Wildbore. The name Wilbur now represents a majority of the descendants of Samuel Wildbore, of Boston and Portsmouth, Rhode Island, and Taunton, Massachusetts, where the scene of his life was chiefly laid. It may be said, however, that so good an authority as Austin in his genealogical dictionary gives the family name of Samuel as Wilbur. In the present work the name will be mentioned as known to the several generations holding it.

(I) Samuel Wildbore was born in England, and is believed to have come to this country before 1633, with his wife and several children. The Christian name of his first wife was Ann and reliable accounts mention her as a daughter of Thomas Bradford, of Doncaster, Yorkshire, England, from which part of the dominion Samuel himself is said to have come. His second wife was Elizabeth, widow of Thomas Lechford. The year of Samuel's birth is not known, but he died September 29, 1656. He was made freeman in Boston in 1633, and with his wife Ann was admitted to the church in December of the same year. In 1634 he was assessor of taxes, and on November 20, 1637, was one of the several persons disarmed "in consequence of having been seduced and led into dangerous error by the opinion and revelations of Mr. Wheelwright and Mrs. Hutchinson," and therefore being given license to depart from the colony he took up his place of abode in the colony of Rhode Island. He is next recorded in Portsmouth, Rhode Island, where on March 7, 1638, he was one of eighteen who entered into the following compact: "We whose names are underwritten do here solemnly in the presence of Jehovah incorporate ourselves into a Bodie Politick, and as He shall help, will submit our persons, lives and estates, unto our Lord Jesus Christ, the King of Kings and Lord of Lords, and to all those perfect and absolute laws of His given us in His holy word of truth, to be guided and judged thereby." It is evident that Samuel Wildbore was a person of some consequence in the plantation at Portsmouth, for, in 1638 he was present at a public meeting, upon notice, and in the same year was chosen clerk of the train band. In 1639 he was made constable and given an allotment of a neck of land lying in the great cove, containing about two acres. In 1640 he and Ralphe Earle, who seems to have been in some way associated with him, were ordered to furnish the town of Newport with new sawed boards at eight shillings per hundred feet, and half-inch boards at seven shillings, to be delivered at the "pit," by the waterside. On March 16, 1641, he was made freeman in Portsmouth, became sergeant of militia in 1644 and in 1645 returned with his wife to Boston. On November 29, 1645, Samuel Wildbore and his wife were received into the church in Boston, and in a deposition made May 2, 1648, he made oath that when he married the widow of Thomas Lechford he received no part of her former husband's estate. In 1655 he was again in Portsmouth, but at the time of the making of his will he lived in Taunton and at the same time had a house in Boston. His will was recorded in both Massachusetts and the Plymouth colony. That instrument bore date April 30, 1656, and was admitted to probate November 1, following, which fact determines the year in which he died. His will made provision for his sons Samuel, Joseph and Shadrach, but does not mention a son William, who is ascribed to him in family records. It is probable that if he had a son of that name he died before his father, and so far as the records disclose he had no female issue. The estate and property inventoried two hundred and eighty-two pounds, nineteen shillings, six pence. The children just mentioned were sons of Samuel by his first marriage; none were born of the second marriage.

(II) Shadrach Wilbur, of Taunton, Massachusetts, son of Samuel Wildbore, died in 1698, and in some respects enjoyed a prominence equal to that of his father. He succeeded to all the lands in Taunton that had been his father's and for thirty-five years was clerk of the town. In 1674 he was grand juror and in 1685 was licensed to sell strong liquor by the gallon if "careful not to sell to such as will abuse the same". In 1687 he was taken into custody on a warrant which charged that he "hath lately in the name and

with the consent of the said town written and published a certain scandalous, factious and seditious writing, therein very much reflecting upon and contemning the laws, authority and government of his Majesty's territory and dominion of New England." This was during the time of Sir Edmund Andros and under the charge mentioned Shadrach was kept in prison for some time. His will, dated September 12, 1696, was admitted to probate, March 1, 1698, and named as executors his sons Joseph and Shadrach. His property was inventoried at seven hundred and twenty pounds, nine shillings, hence he must have been a man of considerable means. He married twice, but the name of his first wife, by whom all his children were born, is unknown. The Christian name of his second wife was Hannah, who died in 1696. The ten children of Shadrach Wilbur were: Sarah, Mary, Samuel, Rebecca, Hannah, Joseph, Shadrach, John, Eleazer, Benjamin.

(III) Shadrach (2), third son of Shadrach (1) Wilbur, was born December 5, 1672, in Taunton. He settled on a farm in that part of the town which was afterwards set off as the town of Raynham. No record of his marriage appears. He had six sons: Shadrach, Meshach, Joseph, Jacob, Abyah and Philip. The first two settled in Raynham.

(IV) Joseph, third son of Shadrach (2) Wilbur, was born about 1712, in Raynham, and settled in Westmoreland, New Hampshire. He was the first representative of that town in the state legislature, and was elected highway surveyor, March 5, 1775. He married and among his children was Nathaniel.

(V) Rev. Nathaniel Wilbur, son of Joseph Wilbur, was born October 23, 1755. He was a Baptist preacher, serving forty years as pastor of a church in Westmoreland. He married, October 19, 1782, in Westmoreland, Deborah, born March 17, 1750. in Abington, Massachusetts, daughter of Caleb and Deborah (Niles) Aldrich (see Aldrich III). Children: Nathaniel Azel, Joseph, Deborah, Caleb Alvah, Warren.

(VI) Deborah, only daughter of Rev. Nathaniel and Deborah (Aldrich) Wilbur, was born April 18, 1790, in Westmoreland, and became the wife of Cephas (2) Clark of that town (see Clark VI).

(The Aldrich Line).

The family of Aldrich in this country was founded by George Aldrich, of Braintree and Mendon, Massachusetts, and Henry Aldrich, of Dedham, same colony, who was presumably a brother of George. The latter came from Devonshire, England, in 1631, arriving on the Massachusetts coast, November 6th, and settled first at Dorchester, whence he removed to Braintree. He was among the pioneer settlers of Mendon, Massachusetts, in 1663, and passed the remainder of his life there. Henry Aldrich died in Dedham, Massachusetts, in 1645, leaving a son Samuel and probably other sons. As most of the members of this family were Quakers they were ignored in the Puritan records and very little can be found concerning them. There are but four entries under this name in the vital records of Braintree and very few in Dedham and other towns, which were originally a part of Dedham. There is mention of a Benjamin Aldrich in Braintree in 1651, and he may have been the grandfather of the Benjamin with whose name the line herein traced must begin, but all circumstances go to indicate that he was more probably descended from Henry, of Dedham. A Thomas Aldrich lived in Dedham, where he was married (first) in 1675 and (second) in 1678.

(I) Benjamin Aldrich, born about 1694, settled in Walpole, Massachusetts, formerly a part of Dedham, and was one of the grantees of Westmoreland, New Hampshire, to which town he removed after 1749, and there died in 1763. He married, in Bridgewater, Massachusetts, August 24, 1721, Mary Shaw. The births of ten children were recorded in Walpole: Mary, June 8, 1725; Susannah, October 27, 1727; Caleb, mentioned below; Elizabeth, April 3, 1732; Benjamin, March 17, 1734; Luke, March 23, 1736; George, March 13, 1738; Ebenezer, March 5, 1740; Joel, July 18, 1743; Sarah, March 24, 1749. The last three sons resided in Westmoreland.

(II) Caleb, eldest son of Benjamin and Mary (Shaw) Aldrich, was born March 4, 1730, in Walpole. He resided in Weymouth, Massachusetts, from 1755 to 1758. The next ten years were spent in Abington, Massachusetts, and in 1768 he settled in Westmoreland, where he resided until his death. His farm was in the eastern part of the town and was successively owned by his son Niles, grandson Niles and great-grandson Allen Aldrich. He married, in Weymouth, January 30, 1755, Deborah Niles, born October 11, 1734, in Braintree, daughter of Joseph and Anne (Cornish) Niles, of that town. She was descended from John Niles, who settled in Dorchester, Massachusetts, in 1634, was in Braintree as early as 1639 and was admitted freeman, May 26, 1647. His wife Jane died there May 16, 1654. He died February 8, 1694. They had sons: John, Joseph, Nathaniel, Samuel, Increase,

Benjamin and Isaac. Joseph, son of John and Jane Niles, was born August 15, 1640, in Braintree, and married, November 2, 1662, Mary Mical. Their children were Hannah, Joseph, Mary, John and Benjamin. John (2), son of Joseph and Mary (Mical) Niles, was born about 1671 in Braintree, and had a wife named Catherine. He was a member of the Second Church of Braintree. His children were: Hannah, Susannah, Joseph, Sarah, Deborah, John, Jane, Catherine, Abigail. Joseph (2), senior son of John (2) and Catherine Niles, was born May 1, 1700, in Braintree, and lived in that town where he married, July 15, 1731, Anne Cornish. Children: Anne, Deborah, Mary, Hannah and probably others. Deborah, second daughter of Joseph (2) and Anne (Cornish) Niles, was born October 11, 1734, and became the wife of Caleb Aldrich, as above noted. They had children born in Abington; two are recorded in Weymouth in 1755 and 1757.

(III) Deborah, daughter of Caleb and Deborah (Niles) Aldrich, was born March 17, 1750, in Abington, and became the wife of Rev. Nathaniel Wilbur, of Westmoreland (see Wilbur V.).

UPSON   Thomas Upson, the immigrant ancestor, was born in England, and was in Hartford, Connecticut, as early as 1638, though his name does not appear among the original settlers of the town. He with others "had the privilege of getting wood and keeping cows on the common". In 1640 he owned four acres of land in the division east of the Connecticut river. His name appears among the first settlers and proprietors of Farmington. He married, in 1646, Elizabeth Fuller, who married, after his death, Edmund Scott. He died July 19, 1655, leaving a small estate which was distributed in 1671 to his children and to Edmund Scott, whom his widow had married, in her right. Children: Elizabeth, born at Hartford probably, died July 20, 1655, unmarried; Thomas; Stephen, mentioned below; Mary; Hannah.

(II) Sergeant Stephen Upson, son of Thomas Upson, was born in Farmington, about 1650; married, December 29, 1682, Mary, daughter of John and Mary (Hart) Lee, of Farmington (see Lee). Upson settled at Waterbury, Connecticut, before his marriage, and became a substantial citizen, holding the offices of surveyor, school committee, grand juror, and was three times elected deputy to the General court. He was a sergeant of the militia company in 1715. He died in 1735, and his wife February 15, 1715-

16. Children, born at Farmington: Mary, born November 5, 1683, married Richard Walton; Stephen, September 30, 1686, married Sarah Bronson; Elizabeth, February 14, 1689-90, married Thomas Bronson; Thomas, March 1, 1692, married Rachel Judd; Hannah, March 16, 1695, married Thomas Richards and (second) John Bronson; Tabitha, March 11, 1698, married John Scoville; John, mentioned below; Thankful, March 14, 1706, married James Blakeslee.

(III) John Upson, son of Stephen Upson, was born in Farmington, December 13, 1702; married, July 1, 1725, Elizabeth, daughter of Deacon Thomas Judd, and great-granddaughter of Thomas Judd, of Farmington. From this marriage was descended Daniel Upson, born at Southington, Connecticut, March 13, 1786, father of Hon. William H. Upson, of Akron, Ohio, judge of the circuit court. The Upsons lived in Waterbury and afterward in the southwest part of Southington, Connecticut. In seating the congregation in 1786, Mr. John Upson was assigned to a front pew with the dignitaries of the town. His will was dated in 1763. He died November 2, 1789, aged eighty-seven years. His wife died January 28, 1798, aged ninety-six years. Children, born at Waterbury: Daniel, March 19, 1726; Elijah, February 11, 1727, died young; Elijah, February 5, 1730, died young; Hannah, November 17, 1733, married Silas Merriman; Martha, May 1, 1736, married William Barnes; John, mentioned below; James, November 4, 1742; Elijah, May 6, 1745; Jessie, December 4, 1748, died young.

(IV) John (2), son of John (1) Upson, was born at Farmington, March 31, 1739, buried in Tallmadge, Ohio. He was executor of his mother's will and sold land in Southington, formerly part of Farmington, in 1796-97. His last deed is dated January 31, 1798, when he was living in Blandford, Massachusetts. He and his wife were dismissed from the Southington church in 1796. He married Lois Atwater. Children, born in Southington: Freeman; Reuben; Sylvia; Stephen; Horatio, of whom further; Huldah; Lucinda; John; Daniel, baptized May 21, 1786; Lois, baptized June 15, 1788; Alfred, baptized July 4, 1790.

(V) Horatio, son of John (2) Upson, was born in Southington or Waterbury, died December 12, 1849, buried at Tallmadge, Ohio. He was a soldier from Connecticut in the war of 1812 in Captain John Buckingham's company from Watertown, formerly part of Waterbury, and served at New Haven in October, 1814. He married, and his children were: 1. Elias C., born December 16, 1797,

died March 15, 1879; married Orra Blakeslee, in 1824, who died July 21, 1860. 2. Charles, born January 26, 1800, died May 16, 1840; married, January 15, 1823, Emma Clark, who died September 1, 1824. 3. Lois, born March 22, 1802, now deceased; married, in 1822, William Church, died February 23, 1884. 4. Edwin, of whom further. 5. Jenette, December 18, 1806, died January 21, 1884; married Heman Parsons, October, 1833. 6. Frederick, October 7, 1809, died at Norwalk, Ohio; married, October 3, 1835, Mary Powers. 7. Lucy, July 24, 1812; married, February 1, 1835, Harvey Strong. 8. William, August 8, 1815, died March 16, 1816. 9. George, July 21, 1819, died July 24, 1847.

(VI) Edwin, son of Horatio Upson, was born in Waterbury, Connecticut, May 21, 1804, died at Cleveland, May 1, 1885, buried at Tallmadge, Ohio. He attended the public schools in his native town and when a young man left home and walked with a knapsack on his back all the way from Waterbury to New Connecticut, now Tallmadge, Summit county, Ohio. He married, September 15, 1833, Betsey Augusta, born in Litchfield, Connecticut, daughter of Jacob N. Blakeslee, a prominent citizen of Watertown, and Electa (Weed) Blakeslee. Edwin Upson became one of the prominent and influential men in Summit county. Children: 1. Mary M., born May 20, 1836; married Rufus P. Upson; lives in Tallmadge, Ohio. 2. Jacob E., September 11, 1838, died June 8, 1844. 3. Joseph Edwin, of whom further.

(VII) Joseph Edwin, son of Edwin Upson, was born at Tallmadge, Summit county, Ohio, August 14, 1842. He attended the public schools of his native town and the Eastman Business College of Poughkeepsie, New York. His business career began in the town where his grandfather was born, Waterbury, and for the first year he was clerk and bookkeeper in the Waterbury Savings and Loan Association. Afterward he went to New York City in a similar position with the firm of Abbott Brothers, manufacturers of and dealers in photographic supplies. Soon after the beginning of the civil war he returned to his old home in Ohio and assisted his father on the farm. At the age of twenty he enlisted in the famous "Squirrel Hunters", a company organized under a call for volunteers by Governor David Tod. The company was sent to the vicinity of Covington, Kentucky, to check the raids of General Kirby in northern Kentucky and southern Ohio. He re-enlisted in 1864 as a private in the 164th Regiment Ohio Volunteer

Infantry, under Colonel John C. Lee, and went to Arlington Heights, Virginia, where he served for a hundred days in defending Washington. At the time this regiment was mustered out it was reviewed by President Lincoln at the White House.

After he left the service, he entered the employ of William Bingham & Company, hardware merchants, Water street, Cleveland, and continued with this firm until 1866, when he became a clerk for L. L. Lyon, of the same city, in the ship chandlery business. In 1871 he started in business as a ship chandler in partnership with John W. Walton, under the firm name of Upson & Walton. The business flourished and the name of the firm is widely and favorably known. The business was incorporated some years ago as The Upson-Walton Company, of which Mr. Upson is president. In other enterprises he has also taken an important part. He is president of the Wilson Transit Company, the Cleveland Block Company, and vice-president of the Mahoning & Lake Erie Coal Company. He is also a director of the Central Grain Elevator Company; the Cleveland Grain Company; the Keller Transit Company; Lake Carriers' Association, and Volunteer Transit Company. He has large financial interests in lake commerce, and has been prominent in promoting the business growth and prosperity of the city of Cleveland. His home was 11447 Euclid avenue, but in October, 1912, he moved to Los Angeles, California. He is a member of the Cleveland Chamber of Commerce, and both he and his wife are members of the Euclid Avenue Presbyterian Church. In politics he is a Republican.

He married, September 22, 1868, Cornelia Maria Lyman, born at Newton Falls, Trumbull county, Ohio, August 31, 1846, daughter of Luther F. and Harriet (Stevens) Lyman (see Lyman). Children: 1. Frances Emma, born in Cleveland, January 8, 1870; married Robert Young; living at Los Angeles, California; children: Mary Frances and Clarence Young. 2. Mira Augusta, born December 23, 1872, died December 7, 1874. 3. Oliver Welton, born in Cleveland, January 25, 1875; married Helen Burkert, of Detroit, Michigan; he is now associated in business with his father in the Upson-Walton Company. 3. Walter Lyman, born in Cleveland, July 3, 1877; graduate of Princeton University with degrees of electrical engineer and master of science; formerly professor of electrical engineering at Ohio State University, now residing at Schenectady, New York, as professor of electrical engineering in Union College; married Anna Leigh Richardson, of

Cleveland; has one child, Joseph Edwin (2d). 4. Clara Cornelia, born in Cleveland, January 3, 1879; now living with her parents in California.

(The Lee Line).

(I) John Lee, the immigrant ancestor, was born in county Essex, England, probably in Colchester, in 1620, between April 10 and August 8. He was thirteen years of age when he sailed for America, according to the official shipping list of passengers sailing from Ipswich. His great-grandson, Seth Lee, A. M., wrote that he was sent over when under age by his father from Colchester, England, among some of the first settlers; his father intended to come later with the family, but never came after all. John lived at Hartford, Connecticut, and when Farmington was settled he became one of the eighty-four proprietors to whom the land was granted. William Westwood was his guardian on his arrival, and he remained a year with him at Cambridge before he went to Hartford in 1635. He was just twenty-one years of age when he joined the Farmington settlers. On March 4, 1657, he was made constable at a particular court at Hartford. His home lot was on the west side of the main street of Farmington, on ground now occupied by the ladies' school of the Misses Porter. Part of the land which he owned in the original grant of Farmington is still in possession of descendants in Southington, Bristol and New Britain. He died August 8, 1690, and was buried in the old cemetery at Farmington. The old headstone on his grave was replaced in 1876 by a monument erected by William H. Lee, of New York. His son John inherited the homestead. The inventory of his estate was presented November 5, 1690, at Hartford. John Lee married, in 1658, Mary, daughter of Deacon Stephen Hart. She is said to have been born about 1635, but as her brother Stephen, who was younger than she, was born in 1634, the first date must be wrong, and she was probably born in 1630-1. She and her husband joined the Farmington church July 15, 1660. She married (second), January 5, 1692, Jedediah, son of Elder John Strong, of Northampton, Massachusetts, as his third wife. He was born May 7, 1637, and after her death lived with his children at Coventry, Connecticut, where he died May 22, 1733. Jedediah Strong and his wife "set out early in the morning to visit their children at Coventry (Ct.), but when they came against the Falls at South Hadley among the broad, smooth stones, the horse's feet slipped up, and he fell flat on the off side, and by the fall killed the woman, tho' she was not quite dead then, but had life in her till the next day, yet never spoke a word"; she died October 10, 1710. Children of John and Mary (Hart) Lee, born at Farmington: John, June 11, 1659; Mary, mentioned below; Stephen, April 2, 1669; Thomas, August, 1671; David, 1674; Tabitha, 1677.

(II) Mary, daughter of John Lee, was born at Farmington, Connecticut, August 14, 1664. She married, December 29, 1682, Sergeant Stephen Upson, of Mattatuck, or Waterbury (see Upson).

(The Lyman Line).

(IV) Richard Lyman, son of Richard Lyman (q. v.), was born in April, 1678, at Northampton, Massachusetts, and died June 6, 1748. He removed to Lebanon in 1696. He married, April 7, 1700, Mary Woodward. Children: Israel, born February 22, 1701; Ebenezer, August 4, 1702; Thomas, July 6, 1704; Mary, October 27, 1706; Hannah, September 13, 1708; John, January 10, 1711; David, mentioned below; Elizabeth; Richard, March 23, 1721.

(V) David, son of Richard Lyman, was born in 1711, and died December 27, 1787. He married, May 27, 1732, Anna Lee, who died December 5, 1736. He married (second), March 1, 1740, Mary Benton, of Tolland. She died May 29, 1741, and he married (third), April 8, 1742, Mary Gittau, of Woodbury. He removed in 1745 to Bethlehem, Litchfield county, Connecticut. Mary was a daughter of Francis Gittau, M. D., a French Huguenot whose family was banished from France and came to America from England. She died in 1803, aged eighty-five years. Children by second wife: David, born May 20, 1741, died young; John, born at Lebanon, February 14, 1744; David, born at Bethlehem, May 20, 1747; Francis, 1755, died in Ohio, in 1840; Josiah, settled in Ohio; Elizabeth; Anna; a daughter, married ———— Steele.

(VI) David (2), son of David (1) Lyman, was born May 20, 1747, and died July 29, 1813. He married, October 20, 1773, Mary Brown, of Torrington, a relative of John Brown, the Abolitionist, and a descendant of Peter Brown, who came in the "Mayflower" to Plymouth. Her descendants are eligible to the Society of Mayflower Descendants. She died July 22, 1820. David was a soldier in the revolution, and was discharged in order to have him operate a grist mill in New Haven for the American troops. He was called "General". Children: Elijah, born August 16, 1774; David, June 14, 1776; John, October 5, 1778; Rev. Orange, July 26, 1780;

Daniel, April 15, 1784; Norman, September 6, 1787; Mary, August 18, 1789; Samuel, February 8, 1793.

(VII) David (3), son of David (2) Lyman, was born June 14, 1776, at New Haven. He married, April 9, 1801, Rhode P. Belden. Children, born at New Haven: David B., July 28, 1803, a missionary; George, April 18, 1806, of Cleveland; Elijah, February 6, 1808, of Ohio; Edward, August 5, 1810, of Ohio; Luther F., mentioned below; Rhoda P., November 22, 1816, of Ohio; James, February 14, 1818, died young; Benjamin, July 18, 1819, of Iowa; Gaylord P., September 6, 1821, of Ohio; Julia A., May 22, 1822.

(VIII) Luther F., son of David (3) Lyman, was born at New Haven, October 1, 1814. He married Harriet Stevens and settled in Cleveland, Ohio. Their daughter, Cornelia Maria, born at Newton Falls, Trumbull county, Ohio, August 31, 1846, married Joseph Edwin Upson (see Upson).

———————————

CUTTING   This is one of the English families which came to America in the period following the Puritan emigration, but must nevertheless be credited with enterprise and energy. The conditions prevailing at the time of the Pilgrims must seem appalling even to the stoutest hearts, and one can readily see that it requires much enterprise at any time for one to cross three thousand miles of ocean, leaving behind friends and ties of every association, to make a beginning in a new world.

(I) Richard Cutting, immigrant ancestor of this line, was admitted freeman April 18, 1690, in Watertown, Massachusetts, where he settled about 1640. He was a wheelwright by occupation. He died March 21, 1696, "an aged man". His wife Sarah died November 4, 1685, aged sixty years. In his will, dated June 24, 1694, are named sons Zachariah and James, and daughter Susan Newcomb and Lydia Spring. His son John and his daughter Sarah, wife of John Barnard, died before the date of the will.

(II) Zachariah, son of Richard Cutting, was born about 1645, in Watertown, and lived there many years. He sold land there in 1709, which indicates that he moved from the town, and no record of his death is found. The name of his wife was Sarah ————.

(III) Zachariah (2), son of Zachariah (1) Cutting, was born about 1670, in Watertown, and probably passed his life there. The name of his first wife is not on record. He married (second), May 5, 1701, Elizabeth Wellington, born April 27, 1685, daughter of Joseph and Elizabeth (Strait) Wellington, of

Hon. Charles S. Cutting

Watertown. His first wife was the mother of Jonas, Sarah (died young), and Lydia; the second wife, of Elizabeth, Susannah and Sarah.

(IV) Jonas, son of Zachariah (2) Cutting, was born about 1695, and lived in Watertown until about 1734, when he removed to Shrewsbury, Massachusetts. He married, March 6, 1720, Dinah Smith, born January 24, 1695, daughter of Jonathan and Jane (Peabody) Smith, of Watertown. Children: Jonas; Zachariah; James; Lydia; Francis, mentioned below; Dinah; Salmon; Eliphalet.

(V) Francis, son of Jonas Cutting, was born September 24, 1728, in Watertown, and lived in Shrewsbury for a time. He was a soldier in the revolution, and served in the siege of Boston in 1775, and at Rutland, Massachusetts, in 1779, guarding prisoners. After living in Shrewsbury he lived in Worcester and vicinity. He married, May 11, 1750, Thankful Warren, born May 29, 1730, in Weston, Massachusetts, daughter of Jonathan and Sarah (Whitney) Warren. Children, born in Worcester: James, October 20, 1754; James, May 1, 1756; Francis, November 20, 1758; Benjamin, baptized August 26, 1760; Susannah, born October 5, 1762; John, March 12, 1765; Benjamin, August 19, 1766; David and Jonathan, August 19, 1768; Reuben, September 16, 1771.

(VII) Francis Cutting, doubtless a grandson of Francis, and son probably of Francis Jr., was born in the vicinity of Croydon or Claremont, New Hampshire, about 1790 (not shown in New Hampshire records). He married, May 4, 1817, in Croydon, Keziah Hudson. Benjamin Cutting, a son of Francis (V), settled in Croydon and served in the revolution. His son Francis, born at Croydon, lived there all his life and left children: Irena, Alfred, Freeman, Elon, Francis M., Shepherd H., Philinda, Diantha S. and Addison. Francis was register of deeds of Sullivan county, New Hampshire.

(VIII) Charles Albert, son of Francis Cutting, was born in Claremont, New Hampshire, in 1818, and died in 1897. He was educated at Highgate Springs, Vermont, and later kept a hotel at St. Albans, same state. Thence he removed to Minnesota and kept a hotel at Hastings. Following this he was in the same business at Salem, Oregon. Going to Tama City and Cedar Rapids, Iowa, he was there a hotel keeper, and later moved to Palatine, Illinois, where he died. He married Laura Elizabeth Averill, daughter of John Averill, a Quaker and member of Vermont legislature. She was born in 1818 at Highgate Springs, and died in Chicago in

1901. Child, Charles Sidney, mentioned below.

(IX) Hon. Charles Sidney, son of Charles Albert Cutting, was born at Highgate, Franklin county, Vermont, March 1, 1854. He attended the public schools and Willamette University at Salem, Oregon. In 1907 the University of Michigan conferred on him the degree of LL.D. He began his career as a newspaper man, as assistant editor of the *Cedar Rapids Times* in Cedar Rapids, Iowa. Afterward he was for a time in educational work and for six years was principal of the high school at Palatine, Cook county, Illinois. In 1874 he went to Chicago, and in 1877 began to study law in the office and under the instruction of Judge Joshua C. Knickerbocker. He was admitted to the bar of Illinois, January 8, 1879, and began to practice law in Chicago. From 1887 to 1890 he was master in chancery of the circuit court of Cook county, Illinois. For one year he was attorney for the town of Cicero, Illinois. For many years he was a partner in the firm of Cutting, Castle & Williams. Since 1900 has been judge of the probate court of Cook county, having been four times re-elected to this office. In politics he is a Republican. For nine years he was a member of the board of education of Cook county and for three years its president. He was also for three years a member and president of the board of education of Palatine, Illinois, while living in that town. He is a member of the American Bar Association, the Illinois Bar Association, the Chicago Bar Association, the Union League Club, of which he was formerly president, the Hamilton Club, the City Club, the Law Club, the Chicago Literary Club, the Oaks Club of Austin, Illinois, the Twentieth Century Club, Westward Ho! Club, and the New England Society of Chicago. In religion he is nonsectarian and liberal. He married, June 27, 1876, Annie Elizabeth, born in Cook county, Illinois, July 17, 1854, daughter of Myron H. and Ann L. (Bradwell) Lytle. They have one child, Robert Myron, mentioned below.

(X) Robert Myron, son of Hon. Charles Sidney Cutting, was born at Palatine, Cook county, Illinois, February 18, 1882. He attended the public schools of his native county and entered the University of Michigan, from which he was graduated in the class of 1903 with the degree of Bachelor of Arts. He studied law at the Northwestern University and was graduated in 1906 with the degree of Bachelor of Laws. In the same year he was admitted to the Illinois bar. After practicing law for a time, he engaged in the manufacture of automobiles in Chicago, a business in which he has continued to the present time. He married, November 10, 1909, Mary, daughter of Ferdinand E. Bartelme, of Chicago.

Edward Bangs, the immigrant BANGS ancestor, was born in England, about 1592, and came to Plymouth, Massachusetts, in the "Anne", which landed there in July, 1623, one of the first three vessels which arrived at Plymouth, the two which preceded her being the "Mayflower" and the "Fortune". There is a tradition that Edward Bangs came from Chichester, county Sussex, England. The year of his arrival he received four acres of land for a garden plot on the other side of Eel river, and in 1627, at a division of cows and goats and also at a division of land, he received a share. He was at this time one of the surveyors appointed to lay out the lots of land, together with Edward Winslow, John Howland, Francis Cook and Joshua Pratt. In 1633 he was a freeman, and in 1634-35 one of the assessors. October, 1636, he was on a jury "to try actions and abuses" and 1636-37 and 1638, 1640, and 1641, one of the great inquest, or grand jury. In the latter year he was appointed, with the governor and assistants, as a committee to divide the meadow lands. In 1642 he contributed one-sixteenth part of the money to build a barque of forty or fifty tons to cost £200. As compensation the court at Plymouth granted him eighty acres of land. It is said that he superintended the building of this vessel. In 1645 he had removed to Eastham, the oldest town on Cape Cod, and was that year a freeman there. He was town treasurer of Eastham, 1646-1665, and selectman for about two years. In 1650-52 he was a deputy to the old Colony Court, and in the latter year one of the jurors to lay out a convenient way from Sandwich to Plymouth. In 1657 he was licensed as a merchant, and it is said that for many years he engaged extensively in trade. He had formerly been a shipwright. He married (first), Lydia, daughter of Robert and Margaret Hicks. Robert Hicks came from Southwark, England, where he was a dealer in hides and leather, in 1621, in the "Fortune," and settled at Plymouth. At an early date he had one acre of land assigned to him, and is called "merchant". He settled at Duxbury before 1634, and subsequently removed to Scituate. He died at Plymouth, and left a will dated May 28, 1645. His first wife was Elizabeth, and his second Margaret, who survived him. Edward Bangs married (second) Rebecca ———. He died at Eastham, in

1678. Child of first wife: John, married, January 23, 1660, Hannah Smalley, daughter of John, of Eastham; children of the second wife: Lieutenant Joshua, born at Plymouth, 1637; Rebecca, married, October 16, 1654, Captain Jonathan Sparrow, died before 1677; Sarah, married at Eastham, 1656, Captain Thomas Howes, of Yarmouth, Massachusetts; Captain Jonathan, mentioned below; Lydia, married (first), December 24, 1661, Benjamin Higgins; Hannah, married, April 30, 1662, John Doane; Bethia, May 28, 1650; Apphia October 15, 1651; Mercy, twin with Apphia.

(II) Captain Jonathan Bangs, son of Edward Bangs, was born at Plymouth, 1640, and died at Brewster, November 9, 1728. He lived in early life at Eastham, where he was selectman for three years, and deputy to the Old Colony Court, 1674-76-82-83-87. In 1692 he was representative to the general court. He was also for some time treasurer of Eastham. He was captain of the military company. In 1680, on a document relating to the boundaries of certain lands lying at Sautuckett (later Harwich) and adjacent places, and signed by him and others concerned, he used a crest which belonged to the Bankes or Bangs family of England. He married (first), July 16, 1664, Mary, daughter of Captain Samuel and Thomasine (Lumpkin) Mayo, baptized at Barnstable, February 3, 1649-50, died at Brewster, January 26, 1711. Her father, Captain Samuel, mariner, was born about 1625, settled at Boston, 1658, and died 1663 or 1664. He was the son of Rev. John, of Boston and Barnstable, and lastly of Yarmouth. Jonathan Bangs married (second) Sarah ———, who died June, 1719, aged seventy-eight. He married (third), 1720, Ruth Young, of Eastham, daughter of Daniel Cole, of Eastham. Children: Captain Edward, born September 30, 1665, at Eastham; Rebecca, February 1, 1667, at Eastham; Mary, April 14, 1671; Jonathan, May 4, 1673; Hannah, March 14, 1676; Tamson, or Thomasine, May 5, 1678; Captain Samuel, mentioned below; Mercie, January 7, 1682; Elizabeth, May 16, 1685; Sarah, August, 1687; Lydia, October 2, 1689.

(III) Captain Samuel Bangs, son of Captain Jonathan Bangs, was born July 12, 1680, at Harwich, and died June 11, 1750, at the same place. He married (first), January 13, 1703, Mary, daughter of Samuel and Sarah (Pope) Hinckley, born July 22, 1678, died January 7, 1741, at Harwich. Her father was the son of Governor Thomas Hinckley and his first wife. Her mother was the daughter of John Pope, of Sandwich. He married (second), April 1, 1742, widow Mary

Rider, who married (third) Thomas Huckins. Children, Seth, born June 29, 1705; Samuel, July 11, 1707; David, March 29, 1709; Mary, May 2, 1711, at Harwich; Joseph, mentioned below; Melatiah, March 4, 1714-15; Sarah, October 23, 1716; Lemuel, June 2, 1719; Abijah, July 29, 1743.

(IV) Joseph, son of Captain Samuel Bangs, was born at Harwich, January 30, 1713, and married, September 18, 1735, Thankful Hamblen, of Barnstable. He died at Phillips' Patent (Oblong), New York, in 1757. Children: Tabitha, born September 20, 1736; Ellice, or Alice, about 1737; Hannah, June 21, 1738; Lemuel, mentioned below; Lydia, October 5, 1741; Joseph; Jonathan, baptized December 9, 1744; Heman, baptized April 3, 1748; Thankful, baptized May 12, 1750.

(V) Lemuel, son of Joseph Bangs, was born December 31, 1739, at Harwich, and died May 9, 1824, near the present town of Genesee Falls, New York. He married (first) —— Hall; (second) Rebecca, daughter of Elijah and Sarah Keeler, born at Ridgefield, Connecticut, April 23 or April 29, 1751, died February 24, 1812, at Grand River, Upper Canada. He was by trade a blacksmith. He was a commissary in the French war, and an adjutant in the revolution. In religion he was an Episcopalian. He lived at Stratford, Connecticut, till 1782; in Fairfield till 1791; in Stamford, New York, till 1809; then removed to Grand River, Upper Canada. Children of first wife: Richard, born August 1, 1764; Phebe, September 5, 1765; Lemuel Hamblin, February 14, 1767; Sarah, April 25, 1766, probably died young; Eliakim, July 25, 1768; Sarah, born at Ridgefield, March 7, 1774; children of second wife: Rev. Joseph, born at Stratford, Connecticut, April 25, 1776; Rev. Nathan, mentioned below; Captain Elijah Keeler, Stratford, June 4, 1780; Rev. John, Stratford, August 8, 1782; Hannah, Stratford, about 1786, died at Fairfield, about September 6, 1786; Priscilla, Fairfield, July 20, 1787.

(VI) Rev. Nathan Bangs, son of Lemuel Bangs, was born at Stratford, Connecticut, May 2, 1778, and died in New York, May 3, 1862. In May, 1799, he removed to Upper Canada, where he taught school and practiced surveying for two years. In 1800 he joined the Methodists, and in August, 1801, was licensed to preach. Until December 1st of that year he travelled on the Niagara circuit, and until June, 1802, on Long Point circuit. He then joined the New York Annual Conference on trial and was assigned the Bay Quinte and Home District until June, 1804. He then at-

tended the New York Annual Conference, was received into full communion, ordained a deacon and two days later an elder, and assigned the river Thames district, including part of Michigan and Ohio. In 1805 he was assigned the Oswegatchie circuit with Sylvanus Keeler; in 1806, Quebec; in 1807, Niagara. On his way to the latter place he was turned back by the presiding elder to Montreal for the year. In 1808 he returned to New York and was assigned to the Delaware circuit, the following year to Albany, and in 1810 to New York City. In 1812 he was prevented by the war from returning to Montreal, where he had been assigned as pastor and presiding elder, and lived part of the year in Troy and part in Bedford, New York. In 1813 he was presiding elder of Rhinebeck district, and in 1817 returned to New York City. Here he served as pastor of the Duane Street Church from 1817 till 1819; presiding elder of New York district till 1820; book agent till 1828; editor of the *Christian Advocate and Journal* till 1832; editor of books till 1836; resident corresponding secretary of the Missionary Society till 1841; president of Wesleyan University till September, 1842; pastor of Second Street Church till 1844; of Green Street Church till 1846; of Sands Street Church, Brooklyn, till 1848; presiding elder of New York East district till 1852. At that time, after having taken fifty consecutive annual appointments, he was reported superannuated. He was a great man in the Methodist church, and its recognized historian. He was a Doctor of Divinity, the founder of their periodical literature, and their educational institutions, the first editor of their *Quarterly Review*, chief editor of their monthly magazine and their book publications. He was their greatest missionary advocate, and during twenty years wrote all the reports of their missionary society.

He married, April 23, 1806, at Edwardsburg, Upper Canada, Mary, daughter of Henry and Margaret (Lateur) Bolton, born at Terrebonne, L. C., December 23, 1787, died in New York City, May 16, 1864. Children: Nancy, born in Upper Canada, April 25, 1807, died there, June 10, 1807; Lemuel, born in Stamford, New York, March 26, 1809; William McKendree, born in New York City, December 15, 1810; Nathan, born at Sharon, Connecticut, October 21, 1813; Mary Eliza, born at Rhinebeck, New York, October 30, 1815; Elijah Keeler, born at New York, July 12, 1817; Grace Shatwell, born at New York City, June 30, 1819; Susan Cornelia, at New York, April 17, 1821, died December 12, 1822; Joseph Henry, New York, January 17,

1823; Rebecca, June 17, 1825; Francis Nehemiah, February 23, 1828.

(VII) Lemuel, son of Rev. Nathan Bangs, was born at Stamford, New York, March 26, 1809. For many years he was a publisher and book auctioneer and dealer in New York City. He married (first) Sarah Almira Disbrow, born July 17, 1814. He married (second) Julia Anderson Merwin, born December 2, 1814, daughter of Samuel Merwin, of Connecticut.

(VIII) Dr. Lemuel Bolton Bangs, son of Lemuel Bangs, was born in New York City, August 9, 1842. He attended the public schools of New York, and the College of City of New York. He did not graduate in arts and received the degree of M. D. from the College of Physicians and Surgeons of Columbia University in 1872. Since then he has practiced in New York City, and won distinction as a surgeon and teacher. He is consulting surgeon of St. Luke's Hospital, of Bellevue Hospital, City Hospital, St. Vincent's Hospital and the Methodist Episcopal Hospital. He was professor of genito-urinary diseases in the New York Post-Graduate Medical School and Hospital; professor of genito-urinary surgery in the University and Bellevue Hospitals Medical School, 1898-1901. In 1885 he was president of the American Association of Genito-Urinary Surgeons. He edited a text-book on genito-urinary diseases. He is a member of the New York County Medical Society, the New York State Medical Society, the American Medical Association, of the Society of Colonial Wars, St. Nicholas Society, and of the University, Century and Quill clubs of New York City. His home is in New York City. In politics he is a Republican, in religion Protestant Episcopalian.

He married (first), October 26, 1876, Frances Augusta Edwards, born May 25, 1845, daughter of William Edwards, of New York. She died December 27, 1885, and he married (second), December 5, 1894, Isabel Hoyt, born September 6, 1861, daughter of Reuben and Rhoda E. Hoyt, of New York. Children by his first wife: 1. Merwin Bolton, born August 29, 1877. 2. Mary Edwards, born January 31, 1880. 3. Helen Augusta, born June 14, 1882. Child of second wife: 4. Nesbitt Hoyt, born September 28, 1896.

THURBER John Thurber, immigrant ancestor of the American family, came from England with his wife Priscilla and six of his eight children, leaving James and Mary in his old home at Stanton, Lincolnshire. In 1672, the following year, the other two joined the family. They settled at Rehoboth, Massachusetts, on a place at New Meadow Neck, now in Barrington, Rhode Island. Children: Abigail, John, Thomas, Edward, Charity, Elizabeth, James, Mary.

(I) Captain George Winchester Thurber, a descendant of John Thurber, was born in 1830 and lived at Lubec, Maine. He followed the sea from early youth and became a master mariner. He was lost at sea in 1871. He was an able and experienced mariner and taught navigation to many seafaring men on shore and at sea. He married Abigail Matilda, daughter of Jonathan (4) and Abigail (Reed) Dawes (see Dawes VII). Her mother was born at Mount Desert, Maine. Children: 1. Mary Frances, born in Ellsworth, in 1853, now deceased; married Orient Richardson, of Mount Desert. 2. Susan Elizabeth, born in Ellsworth, now deceased. 3. George W., born in Ellsworth. 4. Alexander B., born in Ellsworth. 5. Frank Leslie, mentioned below.

(II) Frank Leslie, son of Captain George Winchester Thurber, was born in Ellsworth, Hancock county, Maine, March 22, 1861. He attended the public schools of his native town. When a young man he entered the hotel business as clerk and manager and was employed in these capacities at Ellsworth, at Moosehead Lake and at Bangor and Portland, Maine, for a period of twelve years. In 1893 he entered the employ of the Union Mutual Life Insurance Company of Maine as representative and general manager of the company in the maritime provinces and continued in this position for five years. In November, 1898, he came to Cleveland, Ohio, for the Union Mutual Life Insurance Company, and since July, 1910, he has been superintendent of agencies for the Prudential Insurance Company. He is a member of Lakewood Lodge, Free and Accepted Masons, of Lakewood, Ohio, and of Webb Chapter, Royal Arch Masons, of Cleveland, Ohio. He is a member of the New England Society of Cleveland and the Western Reserve. His home is at Lakewood, Ohio, and he is a member of the city council there. In politics he is a Republican, in religion a Christian Scientist.

He married (first), November 29, 1882, Helen McFarland, born in Ellsworth, Maine, August 9, 1860, died in Cleveland, Ohio, 1900, daughter of Robert P. and Ann (Anderson) McFarland. He married (second), 1901, May Lavina (Brown) Bishop, a widow, daughter of George and Anne Jeanette Brown. She was born in Fremont, Ohio, November 18, 1874. Children by second wife:

Frances May, born in Cleveland, Ohio, 1902; Thornton, born in Lakewood, Ohio, 1909.

(The Dawes Line).

(I) William Dawes, immigrant ancestor of the American family, came to America from England with the first body of Massachusetts Bay Colony in 1628-29, the founders of Boston and Salem, but soon returned. Family tradition says that he was accompanied by his wife and that she gave birth to a child during the voyage, and that the child was named Ambrose for the vessel on which he was born, but nothing further is known of either father or son. The coat-of-arms of the English family of Dawes is described: Argent on a band azure, cottised gules, three swans or, between six pole-axes.

(II) William (2), son of William (1) Dawes, was born in Sudbury, county Suffolk, England, in 1620. He came to America in the ship "Planter" in April, 1635, at the age of fifteen years. He married, at Braintree, Massachusetts, Susanna, daughter of John and Susanna Mills, of that town, about 1641, and his eldest son was born there. He was a mason by trade. About 1652 he moved to Boston, where he lived the remainder of his life, buying an estate on the east side of Sudbury street. Part of this estate was deeded to his son Ambrose and the mansion house remained in the possession of his descendants fully five generations; was at one time known as "The Parrot", and was finally destroyed by the British during the siege of Boston in 1776. Mr. Dawes was admitted a freeman, May 6, 1646, and both he and his wife were among the founders of the Third or Old South Church in 1669 and former members of the First Church. He died March 24, 1703. Children: Ambrose, born July 24, 1642; William, March 8, 1655, died young; Hannah, January 7, 1659, died January 14 following; Jonathan, mentioned below; Daughter, married John Nicholls, whom Ambrose calls "my brother".

(III) Jonathan, son of William (2) Dawes, was born in Boston, November 3, 1661. He was a mason and bricklayer. He married Hannah, daughter of John and Elizabeth Morse. His wife joined the Old South Church, January 29, 1688. Jonathan Dawes died October 5, 1690, leaving some debts, including ninety pounds due his father, and property amounting to £226. His widow was appointed administratrix. Children: Hannah, baptized January 13, 1683, probably died young; Hannah, baptized August 9, 1685, died young; Jonathan or Joanna, born April 21, 1687, baptized April 24 following; Han-

nah, baptized May 19, 1689; Jonathan, mentioned below; Samuel, probably twin of Jonathan.

(IV) Jonathan (2), son of Jonathan (1) Dawes, was born January 11, 1691. He settled at East Bridgewater, Massachusetts. He married Lois Stetson, at Pembroke, February 10, 1714. They had a daughter Margaret, born July 27, 1715. They probably moved to Maine and had other children.

(V) John, believed to be son of Jonathan (2) Dawes, settled in Boothbay, Maine. He was a prominent citizen and active during the revolution. He served on the committee on correspondence in 1778 and 1781 and on the committee on ammunition from Boothbay, Maine, in 1782. A John Dawes, of Boothbay, was a seaman on the brigantine "Warren" in 1777 and was captured by the British, March 12, 1777. According to the first federal census, taken in 1790, Jonathan and John Dawes were heads of families in Boothbay, Lincoln county, Maine. Jonathan had in his family two males over sixteen, one under age and eight females.

(VI) Jonathan (3), son of John Dawes, was of Boothbay, Maine.

(VII) Jonathan (4), son of Jonathan (3) Dawes, married Abigail Reed, of Mount Desert, Maine. Their daughter, Abigail Matilda, married Captain George Winchester Thurber (see Thurber I).

ALLISON The family of Allison is of very old date in the parish of Avondale, county of Lanark, Scotland, where the name is still prevalent. Mac Alister, the original form of the surname Alison, was the name or title of the clan that inhabited the south of Knapdale and the north of Kintyre in Argyleshire. They are traced to Alister or Alexander, son of Angus Nor, or Angus the Great, of the clan Donald. Their name is spelled in conformity with the universal practice of higher families among the ancient Gaels, who took their surnames from the names of the greater chieftains among their ancestors, calling themselves their sons or descendants, and confining the use of occupational names like MacGowan (smith), MacBaird (minstrel) now Ward, to families of no social position. Exposed to the encroachments of the Campbells the principal possessions of the MacAllisters or Allisons became ere long absorbed by different branches of that powerful clan. Their clan badge was the five-leafed heather. The Highland name of the MacAllisters was changed into the anglicized form of Allison, when the family or a branch of it was driven from Loupe, near Oban, in Argyleshire, by the followers of King Robert Bruce. From their descent from Alexander (Alister), eldest son of Angus Nor, Lord of the Isles and of Kintyre in 1284, grandson of Somerled, thane of Argyle, the MacAllisters claim to be representative, after the MacDonells of Glengarry, of the ancient Lords of the Isles, as heirs male of the grandson of Somerled. Alexander of Loupe, last mentioned, took the side of Baliol, competitor for the Scottish throne, and was attacked by King Robert Bruce in his chief castle, Sweyn of Knapdale. This was not a great distance from Oban. He was overcome, compelled to flee, taken prisoner on his way to Ayrshire, and confined in the Dundonald Castle, where he died in 1309. This castle is in the parish of Dundonald, Ayrshire, four miles from Prestwick, four from Kilmarnock and seven from Ayr. His two sons and a few of their followers escaped, and to preserve them from the wrath of the followers of Bruce they settled in the parish of Avondale and changed their name to Allison. This was in 1310. There they have continued for six hundred years, and at the present day a great many of the farms and small estates in that neighborhood are owned by Allisons, and the wilderness has now to some extent become a fruitful field.

(I) Lawrence Allison, immigrant ancestor and progenitor of the branch of American Allisons here dealt with, died in 1664. He was a Puritan. He is first heard of in Watertown, Massachusetts, whence he went to Wethersfield, Connecticut, removing again from there to Stamford, and thence to Hempstead, Long Island, with several other newly landed immigrants, who had accompanied Rev. Richard Denton in 1644. Most of the early families of Hempstead were under his leadership and came from Hemel, Hempstead, England, about twenty miles from London. Some, however, went to Halifax. These immigrants are supposed to have been part of a colony which came across the sea with Robert Winthrop and Sir Richard Saltonstall in 1630. In June, 1645, Lawrence Allison obtained a verdict of four pounds' damages against Thomas Mansfield in particular, in the court of Connecticut. In 1657 he was taxed in Hempstead, Long Island, for twenty-nine acres. In 1658 Lawrence and John Allison became sureties for the good behavior of Lawrence's son-in-law and John's brother-in-law, John Ellington. On November 29, 1658, he had ten acres of land allotted him in Hempstead, Long Island, and in 1659 was chosen townsman. Not long did he continue with his youthful settlement, for at the court

of sessions held at Hempstead, January 2, 1665, letters of administration on his estate were granted to his three sons, their father having died in the previous year. This is the oldest record but one in legal archives of the surrogate office in New York City. In legal documents Lawrence signed his name by his "mark". Children: Richard, born about 1620; Thomas, 1622; John, of whom further.

(II) John, son of Lawrence Allison, was born about 1624, died after 1678. When a young man, in company with his father, Rev. Richard Denton and several other immigrants, composing a colony which was aggrieved at the limited franchises granted the town of Stamford by the New Haven colony, he left the jurisdiction of England and took up land under the Dutch government on the south side of Long Island. This was in 1644, and three years later land was apportioned to them in Hempstead. On November 29, 1658, ten acres of land were allotted to John, who like his father signed legal documents with his "mark". In 1662 he was elected townsman, and a year later land was granted him and others at Nad Nan's Neck. He was taxed this same year for thirty acres in one place and for ten acres in another, as well as for two oxen and four cows. In 1676 he was chosen overseer and was granted four acres of land, for which he was required to furnish the town two gallons of rum to drink at a public meeting on Hempstead Plains. In 1678 he was chosen constable and real estate valuer. He made no will and his estate went to relatives. Children: John, of whom further; Thomas.

(III) John (2), son of John (1) Allison, was born in Hempstead, Long Island, died in 1754 between June 6 and October 21. He was the immediate founder of the family of Allisons who for a number of generations have lived and been buried at Haverstraw, Rockland county, New York. John Allison was one of a company which purchased land in the north part of the Kakiat patent of land in Orange county. He became owner of the greater part of De Hart's patent, which included the present townships of Haverstraw and Grassy Point in Orange county, now Rockland county. In the heyday of his life he removed with his family to New Hempstead, later to Haverstraw, and founded his home, which remained such until his death. From the knowledge we have of his enterprises he appears to have been a man of push and executive ability. He was probably buried in the old cemetery called "Neck", near Miniscongo creek, or in the old Allison burying-ground, near the former house of Benjamin Allison. Children, all born in Haverstraw: Benjamin, about 1717; John; Joseph, of whom further; William; Elizabeth; Deborah; Mary; Hannah; Richard.

(IV) Captain Joseph Allison, son of John (2) Allison, was born at Haverstraw, Orange county, New York, about 1721, died January 2, 1796. He resided in Haverstraw, New York, where he owned a large farm and much landed estate. The headstone of Mr. Allison appears in the old Allison burial ground, though his remains now rest in the Mount Repose cemetery. He married (first) Elizabeth, daughter of Matthew Benson, died December 12, 1767; (second) May 4, 1769, Elsie Parcells, who died April 16, 1815. Children by first marriage: Matthew, born July 13, 1745; Elizabeth, 1746; Mary, 1747; Hannah, 1750; Joseph, 1752; John, 1754; William, 1756; Thomas, 1760; Deborah, 1762; Benjamin, 1764. Children by second marriage: Peter, 1770; Amos, 1771; Michael, 1773; Parcells, 1777; Richard, of whom further; Elsie, 1783; Abraham, 1783.

(V) Richard, son of Captain Joseph and Elsie (Parcells) Allison, was born in Haverstraw, Rockland county, New York, October 23, 1780, died December 26, 1825, in New York City. He resided in both Haverstraw and New York City. He was married, at St. John, New Brunswick, to Miss Eliza Ruckel, died May, 1870, in New York City. Children, all born in New York City: Mary Caroline, February 5, 1808, died in 1878 at Newark, New Jersey; Michael, of whom further; Susan Elizabeth, March 29, 1811, died in 1883 at Glendale, Ohio; Richard, August 7, 1813; Jasper H., July 12, 1815, died in 1883 at Newark; Edgar, November 22, 1817, died in 1818 in New York City; Amelia Southard, May 13, 1820, died in 1877 at Glendale, Ohio; Abram Stagg, February 17, 1823, died in 1872; Sarah Jane, February 17, 1823, died in 1873 in New York.

(VI) Michael, son of Richard and Eliza (Ruckel) Allison, was born in New York City, June 22, 1809, died at Tappan, New York, April 5, 1876. He was educated in the public schools, and left school to engage in the furniture business in New York, where he made his home till 1868. He then moved to Tappan, at which place he lived until the year of his death. He married (first) in New York City, Susan Gentil, born in New York about 1812, died there April 5, 1846; (second) Harriet M., daughter of Andrew Calhoun, born in 1764 in the parish of Ray, near the towns of Rahpoe and Lubadisk, county Donegal, Ireland, son of William Calhoun. The

church he attended was at Manor Cunningham. Andrew Calhoun came to America in 1790, lived in Boston, Massachusetts, and is buried in Concord, New Hampshire. Mrs. Harriet M. (Calhoun) Allison was born in Canajoharie, New York, May 5, 1827, and in 1880 removed to Nebraska, where she now resides. Children by first marriage: Jane Amelia, born in New York City, June 20, 1833; William Gentil, of whom further; Richard, July 7, 1838; Thomas, of whom further. Children by second marriage: Howard Calhoun, born in New York City, April 7, 1852; Harriet, born May 29, 1853; Michael, April 1, 1856; Lilia, July 19, 1857; Irving, December 18, 1859; Winthrop, August 26, 1861; Eliot, July 1, 1866; Mabel Hitchcock, born in New York City, September 12, 1867.

(VII) William Gentil, eldest son of Michael and Susan (Gentil) Allison, was born in New York City, August, 1835, died there April 5, 1869. He was in the twine and cordage business practically all his life, the title of the firm being G. H. & W. G. Allison, of New York. The firm broke up when W. G. Allison died, and the business was surrendered to Lewis C. Glover. William Gentil Allison was a member of the Seventh Regiment, and one of the first volunteers to enlist in the civil war. He was affected by a sunstroke when in active service, and died shortly after he had been honorably discharged. He married, March 30, 1863, Hester Julia Manwaring, born in New York City, June 16, 1843 (see Manwaring VII). Children: Ida, born January 14, 1867, married Rt. Rev. C. T. A. Pise, D. D., dean of St. Philip's Cathedral, Atlanta, Georgia; William Manwaring, of whom further.

(VII) Judge Thomas Allison, third son of Michael and Susan (Gentil) Allison, was born in New York City, September 19, 1840. He received his preliminary education in the public schools of the city, and from ward school No. 35 in West Thirteenth street entered the Free Academy, now the College of the City of New York, being graduated in 1860. He was admitted to the bar in 1861, having studied in the office of the Hon. John W. Edmonds, and has since been in active practice of his profession, ranking high as a lawyer. He was offered by Mayor Edson in 1884 the appointment as corporation counsel of New York City, but declined to accept. He was nominated for judge of the court of common pleas for the city and county of New York in 1889, endorsed by the Republicans, and polled some ninety-two thousand votes, but was defeated by the Tammany Hall Democratic candidate. In 1895 he was appointed by Governor Morton to fill a vacancy as judge of the court of general sessions until 1896, when he again took up his practice. In 1902 he was appointed by the appellate division to the position of commissioner of jurists, which he has held ever since. The degrees of Bachelor and Master of Arts have been conferred upon him. He married, August 30, 1871, Mary E., daughter of William E. Millet. Children: Mary A., born April 27, 1873; Florence A., October 15, 1874; Albert, January 17, 1876, died 1876; Olive, October 16, 1877; Thomas, September 23, 1879, died 1882.

(VIII) William Manwaring, only son of William Gentil and Hester Julia (Manwaring) Allison, was born in King street, New York City, March 12, 1869, only three weeks before the death of his father. He was educated in the public schools and the College of the City of New York, attending the latter only one term, preferring to enter commercial life. On January 4, 1885, he entered the employ of the firm of Combs, Crosby & Eddy, one of the largest exporting firms of American manufactures, where he rose from office boy to be head of one of their important departments. He continued in the employ of this concern until 1894, in which year he entered into partnership with Charles William Jacob, in the business of importing crude drugs and other foreign raw products. The firm of Charles W. Jacob & Allison has been steadily successful, being recognized authorities in the lines they specialize.

William Manwaring Allison married, June 15, 1901, Alice, daughter of George L. and Fannie (Edwards) Crosby, of Brooklyn, New York, who was born in Paris, France, August 13, 1876. Children: Crosby, born March 28, 1903; William Manwaring, January 9, 1905; Frances Doris, February 21, 1908; Alice Eileen, June 28, 1911. After his marriage Mr. Allison, who had always resided in New York City, took up his residence in Brooklyn, and has also a summer residence at Bay Shore, Long Island. He and his family are members of St. Peter's Protestant Episcopal Church, of Brooklyn, where he is a member of the vestry. He is a member of the Crescent Athletic Club of Brooklyn.

(The Manwaring Line).

The line of descent of Mrs. William G. Allison is from Oliver Manwaring. One of his descendants, Miss Frances Caulkins, has written a "History of New London" in which she refers to the old homestead which has been in the possession of the Manwaring family for nearly two hundred and forty-one years. She says: "The first record relating to the

Manwarings in this country of which we have any knowledge bears date November 3, 1664, when Joshua Raymond purchased house, home lot and other land in New London belonging to Mr. William Thompson, missionary to the Indians near New London, for Oliver Manwaring, his brother-in-law." In front of this house was the common that figured in the defense of New London against the traitor, Benedict Arnold, on September 6, 1781. The invaders drove the Americans out of Fort Nonsense and entered the town where only a small body of men armed with one field-piece opposed them. The English soldiers ransacked the Manwaring house, destroyed the furniture and set fire to the structure. The fire was soon discovered and extinguished by a man after the English left, and a barrel of soap was used to put out the flames. The house is still of distinct colonial architecture, and surrounded by wide grounds. It descended in course of time to Dr. R. A. Manwaring, son of Christopher (2) Manwaring.

(I) Oliver Manwaring, the progenitor, married Hannah, daughter of Richard Raymond, and sister of Joshua Raymond, referred to above. Their children were: Hannah, Elizabeth, Prudence, Love, Richard, of whom further; Judith, Oliver, Bathsheba, Anne, Mercy.

(II) Richard, son of Oliver Manwaring, married Elinor, daughter of Richard Jennings. Their children were: Richard, Asa, Henry, Hannah, an unnamed infant; Christopher, of whom further; Love.

(III) Christopher, son of Richard Manwaring, married Deborah, daughter of Robert Denison, January 31, 1745 (see Denison V). Their children were: Robert, of whom further; Deborah, Hannah, Eleanor, Anna, Elizabeth, Asa, Roger, Sybil, Sarah, John, Lois.

(IV) Robert, son of Christopher Manwaring, married (first), October 8, 1772, Elizabeth, daughter of Captain James Rogers; (second) Elizabeth Raymond; (third) Susan Bushnell. Children by first marriage: Deborah, Christopher, of whom further; Fanny, Elizabeth, Eleanor, Lucretia, Phebe. Child by second marriage: Caleb Baker. Child by third marriage, William Hubbard.

(V) Christopher (2), son of Robert Manwaring, married (first) Sarah Bradley; (second) January 21, 1807, Mary, daughter of Dr. Simon Wolcott (see Wolcott VII). Children of first marriage: Sally, Christopher C., Lucretia, and an infant. Children of second marriage: Mary, Simon Wolcott, of whom further; Dr. Robert Alexander, who inherited the Manwaring homestead, referred to above, and left it to his son Wolcott B. Manwaring, who willed it on his death to the city of New London, Connecticut, for a children's hospital, with the remainder of the family estate for its support.

(VI) Simon Wolcott, son of Christopher (2) Manwaring, was born in September, 1810, died March 2, 1871. He married Sarah Banta, in New York City, November 2, 1837. Children: Mary Ellen, Sarah Frances, Hester Julia, of whom further; Caroline, Martha Pitkin.

(VII) Hester Julia, daughter of Simon Wolcott Manwaring, was born in New York City, June 16, 1843. She married William Gentil Allison (see Allison VII).

(The Denison Line).

(I) The record of the Denison family begins with William Denison, who was born about 1586 in England. He came to America in 1631, and settled in Roxbury, Massachusetts. He married Margaret ———, and had children: Daniel, Edward, George, of whom further.

(II) George, son of William Denison, married (first) Bridget Thompson; (second) Ann Borodell. Children by first marriage: Sarah, Hannah. Children by second marriage: Captain John, of whom further; Ann Borodell, George, William, Margaret, Mercy.

(III) Captain John Denison, son of George and Ann (Borodell) Denison, married Phebe, daughter of Robert and Sarah Say, of Saybrook, Connecticut. Children: John, George, Robert, of whom further; William, Daniel, Samuel, Ann, Phebe, Sarah.

(IV) Robert, son of Captain John Denison, married Joanna, daughter of Robert and Joanna (Gardner) Stanton. Their children were: Deborah, of whom further; Robert, Elizabeth, died young; Elizabeth, Daniel, Andrew, Mary, Robert, David, Sherman, Mercy, Robert, Gurdon, Samuel, Sarah, Eunice.

(V) Deborah, daughter of Robert Denison, married Christopher Manwaring (see Manwaring III).

(The Wolcott Line).

(II) Henry Wolcott, American progenitor of this family, was born in England, son of John Wolcott. His marriage to Elizabeth, daughter of Thomas Saunders, and also born in England, occurred on January 19, 1606. Their children were: John, Anna, Henry, George, Christopher, Mary, Simon, of whom further.

(III) Simon, son of Henry Wolcott, married (first) Joanna Cook, by whom he had no children. He married (second) October 17,

1661, Martha Pitkin, by whom he had nine children: Elizabeth, Martha, Simon, Joanna, Henry, Christopher, Mary, William, Roger, of whom further.

(IV) Roger, son of Simon Wolcott, married, December 3, 1702, Sarah Drake. Children: Roger, Elizabeth, Alexander, died young; Samuel; Alexander, of whom further; Sarah, died young; Sarah, Hepzibah, Josiah, Erastus, Ursula, Oliver, Marianne.

(V) Alexander, son of Roger Wolcott, married (first) Lydia Atwater; (second) Mrs. Mary Allen; (third) in 1745, Mary Richards, of New London, Connecticut. Children by first marriage: Jeremiah, Alexander, Lydia. Children by third marriage: Esther, Simon, of whom further; Esther, George, died young; George, Christopher, Mary, Alexander, Guy, Elizabeth.

(VI) Simon (2), son of Alexander Wolcott, is referred to as Dr. Simon Wolcott. He married (first) in 1774, Lucy Rogers; (second) Mrs. ——— Mumford. Children by first marriage: Lucretia, Alexander, Lucy, Mary, of whom further; Lucy, Charlotte, Catherine, Elizabeth. Child by second marriage: Frances Caroline.

(VII) Mary, daughter of Dr. Simon (2) Wolcott, married, January 21, 1807, Christopher (2) Manwaring, as his second wife (see Manwaring V).

———

BUFFUM The Buffum family, now represented in Rutland, Vermont, by Charles Paris Buffum, long identified with the agricultural interests of the county, is one of the oldest in New England, whither it was transplanted, early in the seventeenth century, from the Mother country across the sea.

(I) Robert Buffum, progenitor of the family in America, came in 1630 from England to Massachusetts, and died in 1679.

(II) Caleb, son of Robert Buffum, was born in 1650.

(III) Benjamin, son of Caleb Buffum, was born in Salem, Massachusetts, in 1686, and subsequently removed to Smithfield, Rhode Island.

(IV) Benjamin (2), son of Benjamin (1) Buffum, was one of the first settlers of Richmond, New Hampshire. He belonged to the Society of Friends, and was in his day regarded as one of the foremost men in the county, being an advanced thinker and of sterling integrity of character.

(V) Caleb (2), son of Benjamin (2) Buffum, was born in 1759, in Smithfield, Rhode Island.

(VI) Caleb (3), son of Caleb (2) Buffum,

was born February 1, 1781, in Providence, Rhode Island, and in 1797 settled in Danby, Vermont. He was a blacksmith by trade, and in 1806 purchased the triphammer and shop of Samuel Dow. For ten or twelve years thereafter he followed his trade in Danby, and in 1818 removed to a farm at Mount Tabor, where he lived for many years. He was a man of note in the town and for twenty-nine years held the office of justice of the peace, also serving as town clerk and selectman for several years. In 1841 he returned to Danby, where for a number of years he cultivated a farm. Later he came to Rutland, where his last years were spent in the home of his son Caleb. He married, December 15, 1803, Huldah Paris, born December 15, 1779, and the following were their children: 1. Lucy, born November 16, 1804, died in 1895; married (first) Larned Bowen, (second) Josiah M. Dayton. 2. Sophia, born January 26, 1806, died August 6, 1866; married Andrus Bowen. 3. Almira, born October 10, 1807, died December 16, 1872; married Hartwell Kendall. 4. Paris E., born December 2, 1809, died April 16, 1891. 5. Daniel, born March 18, 1812, died April 13, 1853. 6. Hemon M., born April 6, 1814. 7. Huldah Melissa, born February 29, 1816, died July 12, 1908; married Dr. Myron Knowlton. 8. Amanda Maria, born June 7, 1818, died February 23, 1844; married William W. Pierce. 9. Caleb, mentioned below. 10. Hannah, born April 15, 1823, died March 4, 1830. 11. Larned, born February 26, 1827, died March 31, 1831. Caleb Buffum, the father, died October 8, 1857, in Rutland, and his widow passed away May 27, 1866.

(VII) Caleb (4), son of Caleb (3) and Huldah (Paris) Buffum, was born June 4, 1820, in Danby, Vermont. He received a common school education. He came as a young man to Rutland and there carried on an extensive business as a butcher, having also large farming interests. He married (first), March 6, 1842, Nancy, daughter of Hiram Griffith, (second) April 23, 1848, Sally Ann, daughter of ——— Slocum, of Manchester, Vermont. By his second marriage Mr. Buffum became the father of the following children: 1. Charles Paris, mentioned below. 2. Albert R., died in infancy. 3. John S., died in infancy. 4. Fannie S. 5. Sarah Ann. 6. Huldah, married William Dolan. The three daughters are deceased. Mr. Buffum died in Rutland, April 15, 1896, and the death of Mrs. Buffum occurred in 1897, she being then seventy-five years old.

(VIII) Charles Paris, son of Caleb (4) and Sally Ann (Slocum) Buffum, was born May

31, 1854, in Rutland, Vermont. He received his education in the schools of the town. He has always made farming his occupation and has also engaged in business as a butcher. He lives on a large farm situated within the city limits and comprising one hundred and fourteen acres. On this estate he conducts an extensive dairy business and keeps a large amount of young stock. Mr. Buffum married, May 31, 1887, Julia, daughter of Lewis and Hannah (Arnold) Walker, of Clarendon, Vermont, and they are the parents of four children: 1. Thomas Caleb, born June 22, 1888; carries on the home farm; married Jessie Jasamond, and has two children: Clarence Caleb, born November 25, 1908, and Charlotte Lois, born May 23, 1911. 2. Lewis Merritt, born November 12, 1890; married Celia Purinton and has had one child, Harold, deceased. 3. Ada Walker, born October 12, 1892. 4. Florence Natalie, born September 5, 1896.

HANRAHAN Dr. John David Hanrahan, of Rutland, Vermont, who has been for more than a quarter of a century one of the leading physicians in his section of the state, is descended from Irish ancestors and is himself a native of the Green Isle.

(I) James Hanrahan, grandfather of Dr. Hanrahan, of Rutland, was born in Ireland and passed his entire life in his native country. He married Mary Brown, and their children were: John, died in Ireland; Michael, came to America; James, mentioned below; David, came to America; Honora, married John Mahoney and died in Ireland; Bridget, married John Daley; Mary, married Richard Brady; Margaret, married (first) Thomas Mangan, (second) Michael Collins. The three last-named daughters came to America.

(II) James (2), son of James (1) and Mary (Brown) Hanrahan, was born in county Limerick, Ireland, and in 1856 emigrated to the United States. He married Ellen, daughter of Michael and Mary (Dalton) O'Connor, of County Kerry, Ireland, and the following children were born to them: Honora; John David, mentioned below; Margaret; David; James. James Hanrahan, the father, died in Rutland, Vermont.

(III) John David, son of James (2) and Ellen (O'Connor) Hanrahan, was born June 18, 1844, in Rathkeale, county Limerick, Ireland. At the age of eleven years he came with his parents to the United States, making the voyage to Quebec, and then going by way of Montreal and Troy to New York City by boat. His earliest education was received

in the national schools of Ireland, and after coming to this country he attended the public schools and Free Academy of New York City. In 1860 he began the study of medicine with Dr. John K. Wright, of Yorkville, New York. He attended four courses of lectures in the medical department of the University of the City of New York, graduating in March, 1867. In June, 1861, Dr. Hanrahan was, on examination, not having yet graduated, appointed surgeon in the United States navy, and served throughout the civil war, being stationed on vessels which did duty mostly on the rivers of Virginia and North Carolina, where his time and services were divided between the army and navy. He thus received the benefit and experience of both branches of the service, especially in the surgical line. In August, 1863, the vessel on which he was serving was captured at the mouth of the Rappahannock river, and all on board were made prisoners. They were taken overland to Richmond, Virginia, and confined in Libby prison. The Confederates at that time were much in need of surgeons and medical supplies, and Dr. Hanrahan was asked if he would go over to Belle Isle and attend the Union prisoners. After consulting with his fellow captives he consented, and for six weeks faithfully attended the sick and wounded prisoners, laboring under great disadvantages, the supply of medicine and surgical appliances being very limited. He was subsequently paroled, having been treated during his imprisonment with the greatest courtesy by the medical staff and officers of the Confederacy.

After the close of the war Dr. Hanrahan practiced for about one year in New York City, and then for the same length of time in Montreal, coming, April 12, 1869, to Rutland, where he has ever since remained, building up a most enviable reputation both as a physician and a citizen. He was the first Catholic professional man in the state, and his practice, especially in the surgical and obstetrical line, has been remarkably extensive. He was for many years town and city physician of Rutland, and has served as physician and medical examiner for the following organizations: St. Peter's Hibernian Society, American Order of Foresters, Catholic Order of Foresters, Rutland Council, Knights of Columbus; and Queen of Vermont Circle companies, Foresters of America. He has also served at different times as examiner for several life and accident insurance companies. He was surgeon of the Third Regiment Vermont National Guard until it was mustered out of service. Dr. Hanrahan is the author

of several medical papers, has performed many surgical operations and has served conspicuously through several epidemics of small-pox and diphtheria.

Dr. Hanrahan has always been active in state and national politics, and for a number of years was chairman of the county committee, also serving for twelve or fifteen years on the state committee. For eight years he was village trustee, and for one year served as president of the board. For the same length of time he was president of the village, and for one year held the office of county commissioner, the only Democrat ever elected to that position in Rutland county. He has acted as delegate to four national conventions, and in 1888 was chairman of the Vermont delegation. He was president of the United States pension examining board under the Cleveland administration, and for four years served as its treasurer under Harrison. He was appointed by President Cleveland postmaster of Rutland and held the office throughout the four years of the second Cleveland administration.

Since its organization Dr. Hanrahan has been an active member of the Grand Army of the Republic, and is one of the charter members of Roberts Post, for which he has been surgeon, having also served as medical director of the Department of Vermont. He has served on the staffs of three commanders-in-chief, Veazey, Palmer, and Weissert, and in 1911 was elected at Rochester, New York, surgeon-general of the Grand Army of the Republic. Dr. Hanrahan is a member of the American Medical Association, the Vermont State Medical Society and the Rutland County Medical and Surgical Society, of which he was the first president. He is a director and consulting surgeon of the Rutland Hospital, the Fanny Allen Hospital at Winooski, Vermont, and a member of the Vermont Sanitary Association. Among the Irish Nationalists Dr. Hanrahan has always been conspicuous and he was at one time president of the Land League. He belongs to the American Catholic Historical Society, and the Irish-American Historical Society, of which he was at one time vice-president for the state of Vermont. He was appointed by Bishop De Goesbriand a delegate from the diocese of Vermont to the first American Catholic Congress and Catholic Centennial Celebration, held in Baltimore, November 10, 1889. Dr. Hanrahan has always taken a public-spirited interest in the welfare and advancement of his home city, and was at one time a member of the Rutland board of trade. He was also a director of the original electric light company of Rutland,

and for several years held the same office in the New England Fire Insurance Company. He is a life member of the Rutland County Agricultural Society, and is identified with the Rutland Lodge of Elks, St. Peter's Hibernian Benevolent Union, the American Order of Foresters, the Catholic Order of Foresters, Rutland Council, Knights of Columbus, the Young Men's Catholic Union and the Ancient Order of Hibernians.

Dr. Hanrahan married (first), February 12, 1870, Mary A., daughter of Bernard and Elizabeth (Halpin) Riley, of Tinmouth, Vermont. Dr. Hanrahan married (second), 1883, Frances M., daughter of John C. and Mary (Hughes) Keenan, becoming by this marriage the father of the following children: 1. Mary F., born October 31, 1883; married Walter K. Barber, of Rutland, and has one child, John F. 2. James, born December 28, 1885, died in infancy. 3. Anna, born September 14, 1886; married Nelson Dwire, of Bristol, Vermont, now of Springfield, Massachusetts. 4. Hugh, born November 4, 1887; graduate of St. Lawrence College, Montreal, and of the University of Vermont. 5. Frances, born April 14, 1889. 6. John P., born September 8, 1891. Dr. Hanrahan married (third) Mary E. (Lynch) Griffin.

GRISWOLD   Griswold is an ancient English surname derived from the name of a place, like many other English patronymics. The ancient seat of the family was at Solihull, Warwickshire, prior to the year 1400. The ancient coat-of-arms is: Argent a fesse gules between two greyhounds current Sable. About the middle of the fourteenth century John Griswold came from Kenilworth and married a daughter and heiress of Henry Hughford, of Huddersly Hall at Solihull, and the family has since been known as the Griswolds of Kenilworth and Solihull. Solihull is on the northwest border of Warwickshire and Yardly in Worcestershire on the south and west. It is but eight miles from Kenilworth to the westward and twelve miles northwest of Stratford-on-Avon, and was a place of importance before the Norman conquest. The two American immigrants, Edward and Mathew Griswold, came to Connecticut from Kenilworth. Mathew came over in 1639 and settled at Windsor, Connecticut; died at Lyme, Connecticut, September 21, 1698, and was buried at Saybrook; assisted in the settlement of Lyme and was a large land-owner; was deputy to the general assembly in 1664 and afterwards.

(I) Edward Griswold, immigrant ancestor,

son of George Griswold, and brother of Mathew Griswold, was born in Warwickshire, England, about 1607. He came to Connecticut at the time of the second visit of George Fenwick, when many other settlers came. He was attorney for Mr. St. Nicholas, of Warwickshire, who had a house built for him at Windsor, and a tract of land impaled, as had also Sir Richard Saltonstall. Mr. Griswold later had a grant of land at Poquonock to which he removed in 1649, when his house was the outpost of the colony. It was on the site of the Eliphalet S. Ladd house, having the Tunxis river on the south and east. He was active in public affairs. In 1650 he helped build the fort at Springfield for Pyncheon. He was a deputy to the general court from Windsor in 1656, and every season but one afterward until the new charter was granted. He was a prominent settler of Homonosett or West Saybrook, whither about 1663 he removed with his younger children, deeding to his sons George and Joseph his Windsor property, reserving a small annuity. The settlement was organized as a town in 1667 and received the name of his English home, Kenilworth, which became strangely perverted in the spelling to Killingworth, now Clinton, Connecticut. He was the first deputy from the town, magistrate and deputy for more than twenty years, 1662 to 1678-89, and was succeeded in office by his son John. The colonial records show him to have been an active and influential member of the legislature, accomplishing much good. He had the pleasure of meeting his own son Francis and brother Mathew in office, and there has been scarcely a time since when the family has not been represented in the legislature of the province and state. He served frequently as commissioner. In 1678 he was on the committee to establish a Latin school at New London. He was deacon of the Killingworth church, and died in Killingworth in 1691, aged eighty-four years.

He married (first) in England in 1630, Margaret ———; she died August 23, 1670; her gravestone is the oldest in the burial ground at Clinton, formerly Killingworth. He married (second), 1672-73, Sarah, widow of James Bemis, of New London. Children, all by first wife, recorded in Kenilworth, England: Sarah, born 1631; George, 1633; Francis, mentioned below; Lydia, 1637; Sarah, 1638; Ann, born in Windsor, baptized June 19, 1642; Mary, born in Windsor, baptized October 13, 1644; Deborah, baptized at Windsor, June 28, 1646; Joseph, baptized March 12, 1647; Samuel, baptized November 18, 1649; John, baptized August 1, 1652.

(II) Francis, son of Edward Griswold, was born in England in 1635, died in October, 1671. He was made freeman in 1657. He moved to Saybrook, Connecticut, before his father went to Killingworth, and later he settled in Norwich, Connecticut, where he was a first proprietor and an active citizen. He was deputy to the general court from 1661 inclusive to 1671. Children: Sarah, born March 28, 1653; Joseph, June 4, 1655, died July, 1655; Mary, August 26, 1656; Hannah, December 11, 1660; Deborah, May, 1662; Lydia, June, 1663, died 1664; Samuel, mentioned below; Margaret, born October, 1668; Lydia, October, 1671.

(III) Captain Samuel Griswold, son of Francis Griswold, was born September 16, 1665, died December 9, 1740, at Norwich, Connecticut. He was captain of the Second Company of the Train Band of Norwich. He married (first), on her seventeenth birthday, December 10, 1685, Susanna, daughter of Christopher Huntington. She died March 6, 1727, and he married (second) Hannah ———, who died February 25, 1752. Children: Francis, born September 9, 1691; Samuel, mentioned below; Lydia, May 28, 1696; Hannah, April 30, 1699; Sarah, January 19, 1700-01; John, December 16, 1703; Joseph, born October, 1706; Daniel, April 25, 1709, died December 22, 1724.

(IV) Samuel (2), son of Captain Samuel (1) Griswold, was born February 8, 1693. He married, April 2, 1719, Elizabeth Abell. Children: Samuel, born April 21, 1720, died June, 1726; Elisha, May 6, 1722; Ebenezer, mentioned below; Samuel, April 7, 1728; Simon, August 14, 1731; Elizabeth, May 19, 1734.

(V) Ebenezer, son of Samuel (2) Griswold, was born July 29, 1725, died in 1810. He married, November 7, 1748, Hannah Merrill. Children: Ebenezer, born July 16, 1749; Eunice, April 20, 1752; Hannah, August 23, 1754; Rhodilla, October 31, 1756; Samuel, March 29, 1759; Ruth, July 16, 1761; Jedediah, March 11, 1764; Joshua, April 19, 1766; Alvin, October 24, 1768; Rufus, mentioned below.

(VI) Dr. Rufus Griswold, son of Ebenezer Griswold, was born in Norwich, March 8, 1773, died in Wallingford, Vermont, May 10, 1849, aged seventy-five years. He was a physician, and practiced in various towns in the state of Vermont. He was very successful in his practice. He married Catharine Obert, who died March 26, 1865, aged eighty-four years. Children: Margaret, married Elnathan Mattox; Mary, married Darius Bucklin; Eliza, married Dennis Cavanaugh;

Harriet; Caroline, married Joseph Hawkins; Samuel H., mentioned below.

(VII) Dr. Samuel Henry Griswold, son of Dr. Rufus Griswold, was born in Chester, Massachusetts, September 14, 1818, died in Rutland, Vermont, July 13, 1896. He came to Wallingford, Vermont, with his parents when a mere infant and was educated there in the public schools and one term in Ludlow Academy. Later he studied medicine in Rutland and taught school there in the winter terms. He attended lectures at the Medical School at Castleton, Vermont, and received his diploma of Doctor of Medicine. He practiced first at Clarendon Springs, Vermont, for five years and then came to West Rutland, Vermont, where he continued in general practice for a period of twenty-five years. From 1875 until he died he made his home in Rutland. In politics he was a Republican, in religion a member of the Congregational church. He was a member of the Vermont State Medical Society.

He married, April 28, 1845, Laura Ann Tenney, born in Sudbury, Vermont, November 29, 1822, died October 28, 1893, daughter of Alvin and Mary (Barnes) Tenney. They had one child, Carrie E., born in West Rutland, Vermont, July 11, 1858, now living on the homestead at Rutland.

DUTTON This old New England family, through marriage, is intimately connected with the Day, Dalliba, Dwight, Brewster, Perkins and Huntington lines, a brief genealogical record of each of which is given in the following context. Savage, in his "Genealogical Dictionary of New England," states that John Dutton arrived in 1630 but that it is not known where he seated himself. Thomas Dutton, of Woburn, perhaps a son of John, was born in England about 1621 and lived for some time at Reading, Pennsylvania, where by his wife Susan it is thought he had the following children:

Thomas, born in 1648; Mary, November 14, 1651; Susannah, February 27, 1654; John, March 2, 1656. The following were probably born at Woburn, Massachusetts: Elizabeth, January 28, 1659; Joseph, January 25, 1661; Sarah, March 5, 1662; James, August 22, 1665; Benjamin, February 19, 1669. Thomas Dutton removed from Woburn to Billerica and was there with his sons Thomas and John in 1675. His son Thomas was wounded and had a remarkable escape in 1677, when Captain Swett and many of his men were killed in the Indian war at the east. His wife died May 27, 1684, aged fifty-eight years, and he married (second), November 9, 1684, Ruth Hooper.

From the genealogy furnished by Chester Dutton, of Lake Sibley, Kansas, the following facts are gleaned. The Dutton ancestry is traced with certainty to Thomas Dutton, of Wallingford, Connecticut, who in the early part of the eighteenth century was living there with three brothers, Samuel, Benjamin and David. These four brothers are understood to have been sons of David Dutton, who at a still earlier date was living with his brother Jonathan at Barnstable, Massachusetts. It is thought that David and Jonathan may have been grandsons of Thomas Dutton, of Woburn and Billerica.

(I) Samuel Dutton, supposedly son of David and brother of Thomas, Benjamin and David (2) Dutton, is the earliest ancestor of this particular branch of the family of whom anything definite is known. He was born February 13, 1704-05, at East Haddam or Farmington, Connecticut, died December 30, 1790. He served in the French and Indian war from 1755 to 1757 and was a member of Captain Ephraim Preston's Company, the Thirteenth, Colonel Tyman's regiment, in November of the latter year. This company consisted of men from New Haven and Wallingford, Connecticut. It would seem from a document concerning the last will and testament of Samuel Dutton, entered in "Public Records State of Connecticut," and bearing upon expenses incident to the settlement of his estate, that he was the owner of property in the vicinity of Farmington. He married, March 17, 1726, Rachel, daughter of Jarad and Elizabeth Cone. Jarad Cone was born in March, 1668, at East Haddam; married, in 1693, Elizabeth ———, died April 11, 1718. He was a son of Daniel and Mehitable (Spencer) Cone, the latter of whom was born at Lynn, in 1642, died at Haddam in 1691, and the former of whom died October 24, 1706. Mehitable Spencer was a daughter of Jarad Spencer, who married Alice ———, and died in 1685. He was commissioned ensign of the Haddam, Connecticut, Train Band, in 1675, and was ensign of the Train Band of Lynn in 1656; he served in King Philip's war and was deputy for Haddam in 1674-75-78-79-80-83. Samuel and Rachel Dutton had a son, Ebenezer, mentioned below.

(II) Ebenezer, son of Samuel and Rachel (Cone) Dutton, was born January 22, 1732-33. He was ensign of the Sixteenth Company of Train Band, Twelfth Regiment, in 1768; was lieutenant of the Sixteenth Company in 1772; and was captain of the company in 1774. He married, April 26, 1753,

Phoebe Beebe, of Haddam. Among their children was Amasa, mentioned below.

(III) Amasa, son of Ebenezer and Phoebe (Beebe) Dutton, was born in East Haddam, January 27, 1754, died October 24, 1842. He served in the war of the revolution, having enlisted as an orderly in August, 1776. In October, 1780, he was commissioned ensign, and in 1783 captain at Fort Trumbull. He married Mary Rogers, born June 17, 1752, died May 4, 1796. Among their children was George, mentioned below.

(IV) George, son of Amasa and Mary (Rogers) Dutton, was born August 20, 1789, died December 20, 1854, aged sixty-five years. He resided for two years after his marriage (January 1, 1817) in Philadelphia, Pennsylvania, but afterwards he removed to Utica, New York, and lived there until his death. He married Sarah Dwight Day, born March 20, 1796, died September 2, 1877 (see Day VI). Children: George, born December 13, 1818, died July 10, 1864; William Henry, mentioned below; Mary Day, October 12, 1823, married Dr. Theodore Pomeroy; Sarah Dwight, August 18, 1825, married Rev. Dr. J. McIlvaine; Elizabeth Bushnell, April 28, 1829, died July 20, 1847.

(V) William Henry, son of George and Sarah Dwight (Day) Dutton, was born December 25, 1820, in Philadelphia, Pennsylvania, died at Long Branch, New Jersey, July 21, 1904. Most of his life was spent in Utica, New York. In 1865 he engaged in business at Philadelphia, Pennsylvania. He married, December 30, 1846, Mary Huntington Dalliba, born June 20, 1826, died January 30, 1877 (see Dalliba II). Children: William Dalliba, mentioned below; Edward Tracy, born January 6, 1850, died August 31, 1857.

(VI) William Dalliba, son of William Henry and Mary Huntington (Dalliba) Dutton, was born at Utica, New York, December 1, 1847. He received his early educational training in the public schools and in the Academy of Utica, New York. When he was seventeen years of age his father removed to Philadelphia, Pennsylvania, where the family home was maintained for a number of years. While in that city Mr. Dutton was a member of many prominent clubs, including the Penn Club, the Art Club, and the Union League Club. He was also a member of the Historical Society, and took an active interest in municipal reform. He was one of the founders and one of the committee of five on organization of the Art Club, now one of the largest and most successful clubs in Philadelphia. Notwithstanding his immersion in business, he gave much time to matters relating to art and also to municipal reform, having been at one time a member of the executive committee of the committee of fifty.

In 1892 Mr. Dutton was called to New York by Mr. Leopold Peck, head of the house of Hardman, Peck & Company, manufacturers of the Hardman Piano, and he has been actively engaged in connection with the work of that corporation during the intervening years to the present time (1912) being now treasurer of the company and a member of its board of directors. He is a member of the Metropolitan Club, the Fencers' Club, Society of Mayflower Descendants, the Sons of the Revolution, and the Huguenot Society, having been a member of the executive committee of the latter organization for a number of years. He has a large social connection. In politics, in which he takes a deep though not active interest, he is an Independent Republican. He was baptized in the Episcopal church, but is now more of a Unitarian than an Episcopalian.

Mr. Dutton married (first), January 30, 1873, Evelyn Dunbar Bradley, born at Philadelphia, Pennsylvania, June 21, 1851, died April 24, 1904, daughter of Joseph W. and Amelia M. Bradley. Mr. Dutton married (second), June 1, 1911, Mrs. Augusta Temple Merritt, of New York; her maiden name was Schack. One child by first wife: Louis, born at Portland, Maine, September 1, 1873; he married, April 25, 1907, Olive Eugenia Ayer and they have two children: Olive Evelyn, born March 7, 1908; Jean, born August 1, 1911.

(The Day Line).

(I) The lineage of this family is traced back to Thomas Day, who resided at West Springfield, Massachusetts. He died December 27, 1711. He married Sarah, daughter of Thomas Cooper, born in 1619, died October 27, 1675. Thomas Cooper was a lieutenant and commanded Brookfield, Massachusetts, forces. He was killed at the burning of Springfield, Massachusetts. Mrs. Day died November 21, 1726.

(II) John, son of Thomas and Sarah (Cooper) Day, was born February 20, 1669, died August 6, 1730. He served under Captain Mosely in King Philip's war. He married, March 10, 1697, Mary Smith, born in 1677, died in 1742.

(III) Benjamin, son of John and Mary (Smith) Day, was born October 27, 1710, died in 1808. He served as captain of a company of militia at Crown Point in 1755 and in the following year was captain under Major-General Winslow. In 1757 he was captain at relief of Fort William Henry and in 1771

he held the rank of lieutenant-colonel of South Regiment. He married, October 9, 1742, Eunice Morgan, whose demise occurred in 1765.

(IV) Benjamin (2), son of Benjamin (1) and Eunice (Morgan) Day, was born April 23, 1747, died March 24, 1794. He married, July 16, 1772, Sarah Dwight, born October 30, 1751 (see Dwight IV).

(V) Henry, son of Benjamin (2) and Sarah (Dwight) Day, was born March 23, 1773, died October 10, 1811. He married, May 31, 1794, Mary Ely, born November 15, 1774, died June 15, 1859, daughter of William and Druscilla (Brewster) Ely (see Brewster VII). Cable Ely, father of William Ely, married, May 21, 1740, Mary Edwards. He was a son of John and Mary (Bliss) Ely, and Mary Bliss was a daughter of Samuel Bliss, a volunteer in the Narragansett war. Samuel Bliss was born in 1624; married, November 10, 1665, Mary Learnard, who died March 21, 1724. He died March 23, 1720.

(VI) Sarah Dwight, daughter of Henry and Mary (Ely) Day, was born March 20, 1796, died September 2, 1877. She married, January 1, 1817, George Dutton (see Dutton IV).

(The Dwight Line).

(I) Timothy Dwight, immigrant ancestor of this old Massachusetts family, was born in England in the year 1629. He immigrated to America as a young man and died in the Old Bay State, January 31, 1717-18. In 1691-93-94 he was deputy from Dedham to the general court of Massachusetts Bay. In 1676 he was commander of the Suffolk County Troop; in 1683 he was lieutenant of a Boston troop; in 1693 he was commissioned captain of a Massachusetts company. He married, January 9, 1664-65, Ann Flint, widow of John Bassett. She was born September 11, 1643, died January 29, 1685-86.

(II) Henry, son of Timothy and Ann (Flint-Bassett) Dwight, was born October 16, 1676, died March 26, 1732. He served as a scout for Hatfield, Massachusetts, and subsequently was captain of a company in Lieutenant Joseph Hawley's Regiment. He married, August 27, 1702, Lydia Hawley, born July 7, 1686, died in 1748. On her tombstone at Hartford, Connecticut, is engraved: "Dust is cast down and leveled with dust; but not the souls who trust in the Lord Jehovah; for He is the health of their countenance and their God."

(III) Edmund, son of Henry and Lydia (Hawley) Dwight, was born January 19, 1717, died October 28, 1755. He was an ensign in the colonial army and was likewise captain at Lewisburg. He married, August 23, 1742, Elizabeth Scott, born in 1724, died in 1764.

(IV) Sarah, daughter of Edmund and Elizabeth (Scott) Dwight, born October 30, 1751, married, July 16, 1772, Benjamin (2) Day (see Day IV).

(The Brewster Line).

(I) The original progenitor of the name of Brewster in America was the famous Elder William Brewster, who came over in the "Mayflower", in 1621. He was born in 1593, died April 16, 1644. He married Mary Love, who died April 17, 1627.

(II) Love, son of Elder William and Mary (Love) Brewster, was born in Holland a short time prior to his parents' immigration to America, and he died in Massachusetts, October 1, 1650. He was a member of the Duxbury Company, Massachusetts, in 1643. He married, May 15, 1634, Sarah Collier, who died April 26, 1691. She was a daughter of William Collier, who came to America from England in 1633; he was assistant at Plymouth Colony, commissioner of United Colonies, and a member of the council of wars; his demise occurred in 1670.

(III) William (2), son of Love and Sarah (Collier) Brewster, died November 3, 1693. He married, January 2, 1673, Lydia Partridge, who died February 2, 1742-43. She was a daughter of George and Sarah (Tracy) Partridge, the former of whom was a member of the Duxbury Military Company, under Miles Standish. Sarah Tracy was a daughter of Stephen and Tryphosa Tracy. Stephen Tracy was married at Leyden, January 2, 1621, and came to America in the good ship "Ann", in 1623; he was prominent in the public life in his home community and was the incumbent of many important and responsible offices.

(IV) Benjamin, son of William (2) and Lydia (Partridge) Brewster, was born July 7, 1688. He married, October 10, 1713, at Preston, Connecticut, Elizabeth Witten, born March 3, 1694, died February 21, 1741.

(V) William (3), son of Benjamin and Elizabeth (Witten) Brewster, was born September 16, 1714, died in 1742. He married, March 24, 1737, at Preston, Damaris Gates, born December 18, 1718, died September 7, 1751. She was a daughter of Joseph Gates, born March 16, 1680, at Sudbury, Massachusetts, died at Preston, 1742. Joseph Gates married, in 1711, Damaris Rose, of Preston, daughter of Thomas Rose. Thomas Rose was a grantee of Preston, and married, in 1686, Hannah, daughter of Robert Allyn, the latter

of whom was born in 1608, died in 1683, and who was in 1657 secretary of the general court of Connecticut. Thomas Gates, father of Joseph Gates, was born in 1642, married Elizabeth, daughter of Edmond Freeman, a native of England, where he was born in 1590, died in 1682. In 1642 Edmond Freeman was a member of the council of war and in 1647 he was deputy to the general court of Plymouth.

(VI) Druscilla, daughter of William (3) and Damaris (Gates) Brewster, was born November 3, 1745, died October 13, 1828. She married, October 12, 1766, William Ely, born June 15, 1743, died March 2, 1825.

(VII) Mary, daughter of William and Druscilla (Brewster) Ely, was born November 15, 1774, died June 15, 1859. She married, May 31, 1794, Henry Day (see Day V).

(The Dalliba Line).

(I) Nothing is known concerning the immigrant ancestor of this family. George Dalliba was a resident of Connecticut prior to his removal to Whitestown, New York, in 1785. He was a pioneer in that vicinity and resided there during the remainder of his life. He married and had children: James, mentioned below; Penelope, born in Whitestown, New York, in November, 1786, married, in July, 1805, at Oriskany, Asa Merrill, son of Jarad Merrill, of Whitestown; she died at Byron, New York, April 22, 1823; Major Hamilton Wilcox Merrill, United States army, a graduate of West Point, was her son; he served with the utmost gallantry in the battle of Molino del Rey; his son, Hon. Frederick J. H. Merrill, Ph.D., is the state geologist of New York.

(II) James, son of George Dalliba, was born at Granby, Connecticut, December 5, 1785, died at Port Henry, New York, October 9, 1832. After receiving a good preliminary educational training he was appointed, January 2, 1808, as a representative from Connecticut to the United States Military Academy at West Point, in which institution he was graduated (No. 9) March 1, 1811, and was commissioned second lieutenant of artillery, March 8, 1813. He was commissioned captain and deputy commissary of ordnance, August 5, 1813, and major and assistant commissary general, February 9, 1815. On the reorganization of the army, June 1, 1821, the ordnance department was abolished and he was commissioned a captain in the First Artillery with rank from August 5, 1813, and was brevet major with rank from February 9, 1815. Being dissatisfied with the reduction in his rank by the reorganization, and unable to obtain redress, he resigned from the army, May 1, 1824. During his career as officer he did garrison service in Atlantic posts in 1811 and 1812; in the campaign on the Northwestern frontier in Michigan territory he participated in the battle of Brownstown, August 9, 1812; he was surrendered as prisoner of war by General Hull at Detroit, August 16, 1812, and his name appears in various lists of United States prisoners of war in Canada, published in the newspapers of that day as James Dalliba, second lieutenant of artillery (of Utica), a prisoner of war at Chariabe, about six miles from Quebec. He was exchanged September 17, 1813, and was on ordnance duty from that time until his resignation. He was for some time in command of the United States Arsenal at Watervliet. His views on the subject of reorganization are stated in a pamphlet of thirty-six pages, Volume 102, No. 2, State Library, Albany. It is entitled: "Improvements in the Military Establishment of the United States, Suggested by James Dalliba, Brevet Major of the First Artillery on Ordnance Service, and late Major of the Corps of Ordnance, Troy. Printed by William S. Parker, 1822." It is dated "U. S. Arsenal, Watervliet, N. Y., December 29, 1821." The only other printed work of Major Dalliba in the State Library is "A Narrative of the Battle of Brownstown, Fought on the 9th of August, 1812, During the Campaign of the Northwestern Army, under the Command of Brigadier General Hull."

In company with Hon. John D. Dickerson, of Troy, Major Dalliba erected the first furnace at Port Henry, about 1822, the same yielding from fifteen to eighteen tons of iron a week. Until 1827 the iron was taken to Troy, New York, and after that the works were used for the manufacture of stoves and hollow ware. At his death the property passed into the hands of Stephen S. Keyes. Major Dalliba first lived at Port Henry in 1824 and he erected his residence there in 1825. He married, October 22, 1815, Susannah, daughter of Gurden Huntington, of Rome, New York (see Huntington V). She died at Rome, New York, March 19, 1837. One child, Mary Huntington Dalliba, born June 20, 1826, died January 30, 1877; married, December 30, 1846, William Henry Dutton (see Dutton V).

(The Huntington Line).

(I) Simon Huntington, founder of the American branch of the Huntington family, was born in England, where he was reared to maturity and where he married Margaret Baret, sister of the mayor of Norwich, England, who was a Huguenot of record in England. The name Baret or Barré appears as Huguenot in the books at the Huguenot Library, 105 East Twenty-second street, New York City. Simon Huntington died at sea in 1633.

(II) Simon (2), son of Simon (1) and Margaret (Baret) Huntington, was born in England in 1629 and was brought to America in 1633, at the age of four years. He died June 28, 1706. He served as representative in the general court of Connecticut in 1674-77-85. He married, in October, 1653, Sarah Clark, born in 1633, died in 1721, daughter of John Clark, of Saybrook and Windsor, who died in 1678 at Saybrook. John Clark was deputy to the general court of Connecticut for twenty-one sessions, beginning in 1649; he was churchman and freeman of New Haven and a sergeant; was magistrate and commissioner and was entrusted with many important commissions as a result of the confidence placed in him by his fellow citizens.

(III) Daniel, son of Simon (2) and Sarah (Clark) Huntington, was born March 13, 1675-76, died September 13, 1741. He married, July 8, 1735, Rachel Wolcott, of Windham, daughter of Jonathan and Priscilla (Bailey) Wolcott; Jonathan was a son of Jonathan and Mary (Sibley) Wolcott, the latter of whom was a daughter of John Sibley, who served in King Philip's war, was a lieutenant of Salem militia, and captain of Troop of Horse. Priscilla Bailey was a daughter of Joseph and Priscilla (Putnam) Bailey, and the latter was a daughter of John Putnam, who in 1678 was lieutenant of Troop of Horse, and was called captain.

(IV) Benjamin, son of Daniel and Rachel (Wolcott) Huntington, was born April 19, 1736, died October 16, 1800, at Rome, New York, where he was buried. He was graduated at Yale College in 1761; from 1771 to 1780 was deputy to the general assembly from Norwich; from 1775 to 1777 was a member of the committee of safety for Connecticut; in 1776-77 was clerk of the house; in 1779 was delegate to the Hartford convention; in 1780 was delegate from Connecticut to congress; from 1780 to 1784 and 1787-88 he was a member of the Continental congress; in 1778-79 was speaker of the house; member of the upper house of Connecticut legislature, 1781 to 1793, and first mayor of Norwich, Connecticut, 1784 to 1796, when he resigned. He was representative from Connecticut to the first congress of the United States of America, 1789, and judge of the superior court of Connecticut, 1793 to 1796.

He married, May 5, 1765, his cousin, Anne

Huntington, born January 10, 1740, died October 6, 1790. She was a daughter of Jabez Huntington by his second wife, Sarah Booth, who was born in 1701, died March 21, 1783. She was a widow of —— Wetmore. Jabez Huntington was born January 26, 1691, died September 26, 1752; he was a man of prominence in the public affairs of his community and was colonel of the Fifth Regiment of Connecticut. He was a son of Christopher and Sarah (Adgate) Huntington; Sarah Adgate was a daughter of Thomas and Mary (Marvin) Adgate; Mary Marvin was a daughter of Matthew and Elizabeth Marvin, who immigrated to America, April 15, 1635.

(V) Gurden, son of Benjamin and Anne (Huntington) Huntington, was born March 16, 1768, died in 1840. He was twice married. He married (second), July 6, 1794, Anne Perkins, born February 1, 1768, died April 21, 1802 (see Perkins V). Their daughter, Susannah Huntington, married James Dalliba (see Dalliba II).

(The Perkins Line).

(I) This old American family was founded in this country by John Perkins, whose birth occurred in 1590 at Newent, Gloucestershire, England. He immigrated to this country on the ship "Lyon", December 1, 1630, and landed at Nantucket, February 5, 1631. Soon after his arrival in this country he was made "Sargant of the Allied English and Friendly Indians under Mascowoma, at Agawam (Ipswich, Massachusetts), in the war with the Tarratines". He married Judith ——.

(II) Jacob, son of John and Judith Perkins, was born in England in 1624, died January 29, 1700. He came from England to America with his parents in 1631, and married, in 1647 or 1648, Elizabeth Love, born in 1629, died February 12, 1665.

(III) Joseph, son of Jacob and Elizabeth (Love) Perkins, was born at Ipswich, Massachusetts, June 21, 1647, died September 6, 1726. He married, May 22, 1700, Martha Morgan, born in 1680, died in October, 1754, daughter of Joseph and Dorothy (Parke) Morgan; Joseph was a son of James and Margery (Hill) Morgan, of Roxbury. Dorothy Parke was a daughter of Thomas and Dorothy (Thompson) Parke; Thomas was a son of Robert Parke.

(IV) Joseph (2), son of Joseph (1) and Martha (Morgan) Perkins, was born October 25, 1704, at Norwich, Connecticut, died July 7, 1794. He married, July 23, 1730, Mary Bushnall, born in 1707, died in 1795, daughter of Cable and Ann (Leffingwell) Bushnall; Cable was a son of Richard and Elizabeth

(Adgate) Bushnall; Richard was a son of Richard and Mary (Marvin) Bushnall. Ann Leffingwell was a daughter of Thomas and Mary (Bushnall) Leffingwell; Thomas was a son of Thomas and Mary (White) Leffingwell; Thomas Leffingwell served in the Connecticut general assembly for twenty-six sessions and also served in King Philip's war.

(V) Andrew, son of Joseph (2) and Mary (Bushnall) Perkins, was born at Norwich, Connecticut, July 17, 1743. He married, October 21, 1766, Anne Turner, born in 1747, died June 12, 1785, daughter of Philip and Anne (Huntington) Turner; Philip was a son of Philip and Elizabeth (Nash) Turner; Philip was a son of "Young" John and Anne (James) Turner. Humphrey Turner, father of "Young" John Turner, married Lydia Camer, at Plymouth, and was incumbent of the offices of deputy and constable. Philip Turner, who married Anne Huntington, served as cornetist and captain in the army and was at one time deputy for Norwich. His wife was Widow Adgate and daughter of Daniel Huntington, who married Abigail Bingham, daughter of Thomas Bingham. Thomas Bingham married Mary Rudd, daughter of Jonathan Rudd, who fought in the Indian wars. Anne Perkins, daughter of Andrew and Anne (Turner) Perkins, married Gurden Huntington (see Huntington V).

The family of Bissell (spelled **BISSELL** also Bisselle and Byssell) is an ancient one and is of French origin. One, at least, of its members embraced the doctrines of the Reformation, and after the Massacre of St. Bartholomew's Day, August 24, 1572, fled to England to escape the persecution which then broke out against the Huguenots.

(I) John Bissell, first settler of the name in America, arrived at Plymouth, Massachusetts, from Somersetshire, England, in 1628. He removed in 1640 to East Windsor, Connecticut, and was one of the founders of that township. He was deputy to the general court, 1648 to 1665; member of the Windsor Troop of Horse, 1657-1658; captain of the Windsor Dragoons in King Philip's War, 1675; quartermaster of the Hartford Troop of Horse, May 10, 1679. A careful investigation shows that the following coat-of-arms, used up to the present time by his descendants, was taken from France to England, by his grandfather, and is the same mentioned in Burke's "General Armory of Great Britain." Bissell arms: Gules, on a bend, argent, three escallops, sable; crest: a demi-eagle with wings displayed, charged on neck with an escallop shell,

IN RECTO DECUS

BISSELL

Edward Bissell

or. Motto: *In recto, decus* (In rectitude, honor).

John Bissell, the first settler, married in England, and died October 3, 1677, his wife having passed away May 21, 1641. The following were their children, of whom the three first were born in England: 1. John. 2. Thomas. 3. Mary. 4. Samuel. 5. Nathaniel, born in Windsor, Connecticut, September 24, 1640. 6. Joyce, married Samuel Pinney, November 7, 1665.

John, son of John Bissell, married, June 17, 1658, Isabel Mason, of Saybrook, Connecticut, daughter of Major John Mason; she died March 29, 1665. He married (second), in 1669 (name unknown). Children: 1. Mary, born February 22, 1658. 2. John, 1661. 3. Daniel, born September 29, 1663. 4. Dorothy, born August 10, 1665. 5. Josiah, born October 10, 1670. 6. Hezekiah, born April 30, 1673. 7. Ann, born April 28, 1675. 8. Jeremiah, born February 22, 1677.

Thomas, second son of John Bissell, the first settler, married, October 11, 1655, Abigail Moore, of Windsor, Connecticut, and died July 31, 1689.

Thomas, second son of Thomas (1) and Abigal (Moore) Bissell, was born October 2, 1656, and married, October 15, 1768, Esther Strong, of Northampton, Massachusetts.

Ebenezer, son of Thomas (2) and Esther (Strong) Bissell, was born August 1, 1685, in East Windsor, Connecticut; married ———— ————, who died August 1, 1726. Married (second) Mary ————, who died March 9, 1753. (Tombstone in Old East Windsor graveyard.) Ebenezer Bissell died September 5, 1750.

Captain Aaron Bissell, son of Ebenezer Bissell, married, December 5, 1757, Dorothy Stoughton; he died May 11, 1787.

Epaphras, son of Captain Aaron and Dorothy (Stoughton) Bissell, was born July 24, 1765, in East Windsor, Connecticut; married, November 30, 1794, Jerusha Wolcott, of the same place, and died November 20, 1826. His widow survived him until September 7, 1849. Children:

1. Frances, born in September, baptized October 11, 1795; married, September 22, 1819, Owen P. Olmsted, of Hartford, Connecticut; had one daughter, Frances, who was born in that city March 23, 1829, and married, November 21, 1849, Henry R. Coit, and died in Litchfield, Connecticut, March 27, 1909. 2. Edward, born January 20, 1797. 3. Frederick, born August 26, 1799, died June 5, 1870; unmarried. 4. Sidney, born January 3, 1802; died April 1, 1873. 5. Theodore, born March, 1804; married Cynthia M. Spoffard, May 16,

1827, and died December, 1876. 6. Levorett, born September, 1807; married, November 26, 1840, Julia Reed Watson, of East Windsor, Connecticut, and died September 25, 1872, leaving no children.

Edward, eldest son of Epaphras and Jerusha (Wolcott) Bissell, resided first in Geneseo, New York, moved from there to Lockport, New York, thence to Toledo, Ohio (then a part of the Connecticut Reserve), being one of the founders of that city. He married, October 15, 1823, Jane Ann Maria, daughter of Abner and Elizabeth (Loring) Reed, the former of East Windsor, Connecticut, the latter of Lansingburg, New York. The death of Edward Bissell occurred November 9, 1861, and that of his widow September 30, 1864. Hosmer's "History of Toledo" states as follows: "Whatever Toledo may become in the future, she will always owe her first start in life to Edward Bissell, a gentleman of fine education and refinement, of great foresight, sagacity and energy, who knew no such word as fail." Children: 1. Edward, born September 24, 1824. 2. Arthur Frederick, born June 14, 1826. 3. Elizabeth Reed, born February 13, 1828. 4. Charlotte, born February 21, 1830; died unmarried. 5. Mary, born December 5, 1831. 6. Henry Tudor, born August 12, 1834. 7. Julia W., born October 12, 1836.

Edward, eldest son of Edward (1), born at Geneseo, New York, entered Yale College in 1840, and was graduated in 1844; entered the Law Department of Harvard University, graduating in 1846. Moved to Galveston, Texas, for the purpose of practicing his profession. In May of the same year enlisted in the First Regiment of Texas Riflemen, then being organized for the war with Mexico. In July, 1847, after the regiment was disbanded at Camargo, he returned to Toledo, Ohio, and in 1848 was admitted to the bar. He married, December 24, 1862, Sarah A. Secor, of Toledo, Ohio, and died November 22, 1894. Children: 1. Edward A., born April 7, 1864, died May 5, 1872. 2. Frederick, born October 28, 1865. 3. Herbert Spencer, born June 2, 1868. 4. Maurice Reed, born February 11, 1870. 5. Walter Secor, born May 20, 1877. 6. Charlotte Secor, born October 22, 1880.

Frederick, second son of Edward (2), married, October 25, 1892, Katharine Latham Scott, of Toledo, Ohio. Children: Cornelia Corwin, born July 30, 1893; Edward, born July 8, 1897; Sarah Secor, born January 11, 1904; Katharine, born February 5, 1905.

Herbert Spencer married, June 10, 1902, Cora Alice Law. Children: Mary Law, born June 5, 1903; Robert Secor, born October 9,

1907, died September 9, 1909; Herbert Edward, born November 5, 1909.

(4) Maurice Reed, born February 11, 1870; married, October 26, 1899, Harriet M. Russell at Massillon, Ohio. Child: Thomas Russell, born September 25, 1905.

(5) Walter Secor, born May 20, 1877; married, October 10, 1905, at Toledo, Ohio, Harriet Maria Thorp. Children: 1. Frederick Thorp, born May 10, 1907. 2. Charlotte H., born July 24, 1911.

Arthur Frederick, second son of Edward and Jane Ann Maria (Reed) Bissell, was born at Geneseo, New York, June 14, 1826, and graduated June, 1848, from the College of Physicians and Surgeons, New York City. In the autumn of 1849 settled at Toledo, Ohio, and practiced there his profession until May 12, 1863, when he retired from the practice of medicine and moved to New York City. He married, October 29, 1851, at Rye, New York, Anna Evelyn, daughter of Judge Nehemiah and Pamela Rhoda (Sanford) Browne, of that place. Mrs. Bissell died December 22, 1900, leaving one child, Florence Sanford, born July 29, 1854.

(3) Elizabeth Reed Bissell, born February 13, 1828; married, at Toledo, Ohio, Judge William Collins, of that city, who died April 3, 1891. Elizabeth Reed (Bissell) Collins died May 7, 1907, leaving no children.

(4) Charlotte (Bissell), born February 21, 1830; died unmarried, May 21, 1855.

(5) Mary (Bissell), born December 5, 1831; married, January, 1857, at Toledo, Ohio, Alfred W. Gleason, and died December 16, 1900. Children: Mortimer Chester, born December 13, 1866, died April 30, 1879; Maud, born May 27, 1869, married, May 9, 1905, Frederick W. Pride, of New York City.

(6) Henry Tudor, third son of Edward and Jane Ann Maria (Reed) Bissell, was born August 12, 1834, in Lockport, New York; studied law at Cincinnati, Ohio; was admitted to the bar at Toledo, Ohio, in 1858; enlisted August 22, 1862, in the One Hundred and Eleventh Regiment of Ohio Volunteer Infantry; appointed sergeant-major, September 1; promoted to second lieutenant of H, November 17, 1862, and first lieutenant and adjutant of the regiment February 1, 1863. He participated in General Buell's campaign in pursuit of General Bragg's army, and in 1863 in the campaign raid after Morgan, until that general was captured. When the regiment commenced its East Tennessee campaign he was too ill from fatigue and exposure to accompany it, and died in the hospital at Louisville, Kentucky, September 9, 1863.

(7) Julia W. (Bissell), born October 12,

1836; married, December 6, 1860, Asa W. Backus, of Norwich, Connecticut, and died December 5, 1891. Children: 1. Carrie T. 2. Asa W. 3. Lizzie H. 4. Julia R. 5. Edward T. 6. Frederick T.

FLAGG   Thomas Flagg, immigrant ancestor of the American family, was born in Whenburgh, county Norfolk, England, in 1615. At the age of twenty-one years he came to America, embarking at Soratby, Norfolk, in 1637. He was then in the employ or service of Richard Carver. He settled as early as 1641 at Watertown, Massachusetts, and became a proprietor and yeoman. He had a homestall of six acres, also twenty acres originally granted to John Rose, July 25, 1636. He is ancestor of all the American families of this name as far as the genealogists know. The name in England was spelled Fleg and Flegg, a spelling that still prevails. The lineage of the family has been traced in England to William Flegg, who died in 1426, and various Fleggs and de Fleggs are mentioned in English records in the twelfth and thirteenth centuries. The head of the English family was the Lord of the Manor of Flegg Hall, Winterton, in the Hundred of East Flegg, county Norfolk. Thomas Flagg was a prominent citizen. He was selectman from 1671 to 1676, also 1678, 1681 and from 1685 to 1687. He was lieutenant of the Watertown company. He lost his left eye by a gunshot wound received previous to 1659.

He married Mary ———, who was born 1619. He died February 6, 1697-98. His will was dated March 5, 1697, and proved February 16, 1697-98. He bequeathed to wife Mary; to sons Michael, Thomas, Eleazer, Allen and Benjamin; to daughters Mary, Elizabeth Bigelow and Rebecca Cooke; to grandchild, John Flagg, and to the heirs of deceased son, Gershom. The widow's will, proved April 21, 1703, named children Mary, Elizabeth Bigelow, Rebecca Cooke and Benjamin Flagg. Children: Gershom, mentioned below; John, born June 14, 1643; Bartholomew, at Watertown, February 23, 1645; Thomas, April 28, 1646; William, 1648; Michael, March 23, 1650-51; Eleazer, May 14, 1653; Elizabeth, March 22, 1654-55; Mary, January 14, 1656-57; Rebecca, September 5, 1660; Benjamin, June 25, 1662; Allen, at Watertown, May 16, 1665.

(II) Lieutenant Gershom Flagg, son of Thomas Flagg, was born at Watertown, Massachusetts, April 16, 1641, died July 6, 1690. He settled in Woburn about 1668; he was a tanner by trade and had his tanyard and residence with an acre of land on what is now High street near the site of the first meeting-house, having Rev. Mr. Carter's house on the west, the old burying ground on the east and the training field on the south. Lieutenant Flagg was killed with Captain Wiswall and others by the Indians at Wheelwright's Pond at Lee, New Hampshire. His widow married Israel Walker. Many of the descendants of Gershom Flagg have been famous. Children: Gershom, mentioned below; Eliezer, August 1, 1670; John, May 25, 1673; Hannah, March 12, 1675; Thomas, June 22, 1677, died June 23, 1677; Ebenezer, December 21, 1678; Mary, February 28, 1682-83; Thomas, April 19, 1685; Benoni, August 19, 1687, died same day; Abigail, January 8, 1689.

(III) Gershom (2), son of Lieutenant Gershom (1) Flagg, was born at Woburn, March 10, 1669, and died there August 24, 1755. He became a leading citizen of that town. His wife Hannah died January 4, 1741. He was a constituent member of the Third Society in 1746. Children, born at Woburn: Elizabeth, born May 22, 1696; Gershom, November 22, 1698, died July 11, 1700; Zachariah, June 20, 1700; Gershom, January 25, 1702; Benjamin, died by gunshot wound, April 7, 1725; Samuel, mentioned below.

(IV) Dr. Samuel Flagg, son of Gershom (2) Flagg, was born March 21, 1735-36. He became a prominent physician of Hartford, Connecticut. He died there in 1782. He was one of the first physicians to inoculate for smallpox. Among his children was Samuel, mentioned below.

(V) Dr. Samuel (2) Flagg, son of Dr. Samuel (1) Flagg, was born April 21, 1766, at Hartford, Connecticut. He removed to Pennsylvania. He was one of the foremost physicians of his day. He married and among his children was Samuel G., mentioned below.

(VI) Samuel G., son of Dr. Samuel (2) Flagg, married Harriet Maxwell. He settled in New York, removing later to Boston.

(VII) Stanley G., son of Samuel G. Flagg, was born in Waterford, New York, April 19, 1830. He spent his childhood in Boston, where he attended the public schools. At the age of fourteen years he became clerk in a retail dry goods store and continued for ten years. In 1855 he established a malleable iron business in a small way, developing the new idea of making malleable iron fittings for gas, steam and water pipe, formerly made of brass, and his idea proved so successful that his trade grew to very large proportions in a short time. In 1863 the capacity of his plant was enlarged. In 1865 he bought the property at 19th street and Pennsylvania avenue, Philadelphia, and in 1881 greatly increased it by purchasing adjoining property. Subsequently he admitted his sons to partnership under the firm name of Stanley G. Flagg & Company. In 1896 a subsidiary factory was erected at Pittstown, Pennsylvania. The firm engaged in the manufacture of stove lining and fire brick in 1872, and in 1896 purchased a pottery on Ridge avenue. The manufacture of steel castings was added to the business and became an important part of the output of the factories. He married Adelaide Shoemaker Gordon, born in Philadelphia, Pennsylvania, 1828, daughter of Mordecai Lewis and Hannah (Marshall) Shoemaker. Hannah Marshall was also a native of Philadelphia. Child, Stanley G., mentioned below.

(VIII) Stanley G. (2), son of Stanley G. (1) Flagg, was born in Philadelphia, Pennsylvania, January 21, 1860. He was educated in private schools in his native city, and at Classical High School of Philadelphia. He is a member of the firm of S. G. Flagg & Company, Morris Building, Philadelphia. His residence is at 1723 Spruce street in that city. He is a member of the Art Club of Philadelphia; the Pennsylvania Society, Sons of the American Revolution; of the Rittenhouse Club of Philadelphia; of the Union League Club of Philadelphia. He is a vestryman of St. James' Protestant Episcopal Church.

EDSON The surname Edson is very likely a contraction of Edwardson, Edmonson, Edwinson, or some other name of the same kind. There is a theory that it is a corruption of Addison. The first mention of the name Edson is when the immigrant came, and it may be that he adopted that spelling.

(I) Deacon Samuel Edson, the immigrant ancestor, was an early settler in this country, being found in Salem, Massachusetts, in 1639, when he was acknowledged as an inhabitant and was granted a half an acre of land near Catt Cove and four acres of planting ground. In 1642 he was granted twenty-five acres of land in Mackerel Cove and two acres of meadow. About 1650 he moved to Bridgewater, Massachusetts, and was called an inhabitant there in a deed dated December 10, 1652, and died there in 1692, aged eighty years. He and his wife were buried in the old burying-ground, and the oldest monument in the graveyard is erected over their graves. Deacon Samuel Edson, and Rev. James Keith, of

Scotland, the first minister of Bridgewater, were given grants of land after the fifty-four proprietors had taken their shares, making fifty-six shares. He erected the first corn-mill in the town in 1662, on Town river, and later he deeded this mill to his five daughters; the deed was recorded April 19, 1636. His will was dated January 15, 1688-89, proved September 20, 1692. He was made freeman before 1657. His home was on the south side of the river, near his mill. It is not known that he was a millwright by trade, but it is known that he was a good farmer and had mechanical ability. In 1660 he owned three shares in the town, and he very likely conveyed two of these to his sons Samuel and Joseph, as in the great division of 1683 he had only one share. He acquired a large estate by his industry and thrift, and was well-to-do. He held several town offices; in 1666 appointed a member of the council of war; in 1676 representative to the general court at Plymouth, and in the same year was on a committee to distribute the town share of the Irish contributions for the distress of the Indian wars; in November, 1672, was on a committee which received the deed of conveyance from Chief Pomonoho of the Titicut purchase, "in and for the use of the townsmen of Bridgewater joint purchasers with them." In December, 1686, he with Ensign John Hayward and Deacon John Willis, agents for the town, received a confirmatory deed of the Indian Chief Wampatuck for the purchasers and the town of all the lands previously conveyed to them by Massasoit, on March 3, 1649. In 1667 was foreman of the jury to lay out roads, as well as in 1672; in 1680 was on a committee to settle the Bridgewater and Middleborough boundary line, and the same year to settle the Bridgewater and Taunton line. He was one of the first deacons of the town and served from about 1664 to the end of his life. Was associated with very prominent men and influential in town affairs. He is said to have been of a large, athletic frame, of medium weight and with a fine constitution which could endure almost every hardship; dignified and grave in manner, active and keen in argument and very firm in his ideas, but he was not an obstinate man and would cheerfully admit the accuracy of a different judgment. It is said that he was more inclined to listen than to debate, but when he did speak at town meetings he generally succeeded in convincing his audience that he had carefully considered his subjects. The strength and vigor of his intellect, the quickness of his perceptions, the extent and accuracy of his memory and the struggle of mental enterprise,

supplied in no inconsiderable degree the deficiencies of education. While he was respected for these attributes of his mind and character, it was to his constant practice of the christian virtues and the influence of his example that his pre-eminence was greatly due.

He married, about 1637, in England, Susanna Orcutt, probably an elder sister of William Orcutt, who came from Scituate and settled in Bridgewater before 1682. "Her education and natural abilities were said to be full equal to his, and this coupled with an expressive modesty of deportment and unaffected piety, gave to her person an elevated position and to her character a high rank among the matrons of the town. She exhibited a majestic figure, rather above the medium height, an elegant and majestic mein, with a countenance happily combining graceful dignity with cheerful benignity." Children: Susanna, born probably in England in 1638; Sarah, born in Salem about 1640; Elizabeth, born in Salem about 1643; Samuel, mentioned below; Mary, born in Bridgewater about 1647; Joseph, born about 1649; Josiah, born in Bridgewater, 1651; Bethiah, born about 1653.

(II) Samuel (2), son of Deacon Samuel (1) Edson, was born in Salem, 1645, died in 1719, aged seventy-four years. His home was on the south side of Town river in West Bridgewater, where he had forty acres given him by his father. The house and barn were burned in 1676 by the Indians in King Philip's war. He was prominent in town affairs. In the spring of 1676 he was one of a party of twenty-one men who went to join Captain Church's company during the war. They failed to meet the company, but came suddenly on a party of Indians whom they fought, taking seventeen prisoners and returning home without losing a member. The prisoners were sold and the men who captured them received the money. In 1709-12-19 he was a selectman, and in 1697 and 1713 was representative to the general court. He was highly respected by those who knew him. He married, 1678, Susannah, daughter of Nicholas Byram, and she died in 1741, aged ninety-three years. Nicholas Byram, born in England, married a daughter of Abraham Shaw, of Dedham, and settled in Bridgewater about 1660. Children: Susannah, born 1677; Elizabeth, 1684; Samuel, mentioned below.

(III) Samuel (3), son of Samuel (2) Edson, was born in 1690 in Bridgewater, died in 1771, aged eighty-one years. On January 23, 1747, he gave fourteen acres of land to the society in England for the propagation of the gospel in foreign parts, the income to be used for the support of public worship in the Protestant Episcopal church in Bridgewater. He married, in 1707, Mary, daughter of Benjamin Dean, of Taunton, Massachusetts; he was son of Walter Dean, an original proprietor and first settler of Taunton. She was born in 1687, died in 1770, aged eighty-three. Children: Susannah, born 1708; Bethiah, 1710; Mary, 1712; Samuel, 1714; Nathan, 1716; Abel, 1718; Obed, 1720; Elizabeth, 1722; Sarah, 1724; Silence, 1726; Ebenezer, 1727; John, 1729; Ezra, mentioned below.

(IV) Ezra, son of Samuel (3) Edson, was born in 1730, and lived in Bridgewater. He married, in 1756, Rebecca Johnson. Children, born in Bridgewater: Robert, 1757; Ezra, 1759; Molly, 1760; Rebecca, 1762; Vina, 1765; Libeus, 1769; Ebenezer, 1772; Hannah, 1774; Cyrus, mentioned below; Sarah, 1780.

(V) Cyrus, son of Ezra Edson, was born April 2, 1776, in Bridgewater, died September 23, 1862, in Mendon, Vermont, where he settled in 1817. He was a cabinetmaker by trade. He married (first) March 3, 1797, Hannah Hudson, born April 2, 1779, died May 2, 1850, daughter of John Hudson. He married (second) September 19, 1852, Laura Smith, born June 30, 1786. Children by first wife: Rebecca, born June 19, 1798; Annie, August 11, 1799; Hannah, December 19, 1802; Cyrus, mentioned below; Melzar and Melvin, October 11, 1807; Susan, May 18, 1810; Ezra, January 12, 1813; Galen H., June 13, 1815; Otis H., August 3, 1818.

(VI) Cyrus (2), son of Cyrus (1) Edson, was born May 26, 1805, in Minot, Maine, died in Bennington, Vermont, 1892. He came to Vermont in 1817 with his parents, and was a cabinetmaker by trade. He married (first) Sybil Wilcox, (second) Abigail French. Children by first wife: Melvin C.; Sarah A., married ―― Norton; Amos W.; Albert W., mentioned below. Child by second wife: Ara Otis.

(VII) Albert W., son of Cyrus (2) Edson, was born in South Mendon, Vermont, died in Rutland, Vermont, in 1898. For many years he lived in Norfolk, Virginia, where he was in the internal revenue service. He later moved to Rutland, where he was engaged in the lumber business until his death. He married Carro Vaughan, now deceased, daughter of James and Lucy Graves Vaughan. Children: Grace, deceased, married Thomas McGowan; Russell, mentioned below.

(VIII) Russell, son of Albert W. Edson, was born at Norfolk, Virginia, September 9, 1879. When a child he went to Plainfield, New Jersey, and there made his home with relatives, receiving his education and remaining there until 1911, when he came to his present home in Rutland, Vermont.

This name has been spelled MERRICK in at least eight different ways, such as Merrick, Meyrick, Myrick, Mirick, and so on. Four brothers bearing the name landed at Charlestown, Massachusetts, in 1636. In the early days many of the family were sailors and many others became tillers of the soil. In Burke's Peerage may be found the following paragraph:

"The Meyricks are of the purest and noblest Cambrian blood, and have possessed the same ancestral estate and residence at Bodorgan, Anglesey, Wales, without interruption, above a thousand years. They have the rare distinction of being lineally descended both from the sovereign Prince of Wales of the Welsh royal family, and from King Edward I., whose oldest son was the first Prince of Wales of the English royal family."

The family here described is supposed to have descended from Meyrick ap Llewellyn, who was captain of the guard at the coronation of Henry VIII., in 1509. He was the first high sheriff of Anglesey, and held this office until his death. From him and his position the name of Meyrick, meaning a guardian, was derived. There had been no surnames in Wales before the time of King Henry VIII. Six of the name were knighted by different English sovereigns. The family lived on the island of Anglesey for many generations, but many of them left there to follow the sea, principally the younger sons. After the advent of the family to America, fully a score of them were lost at sea from the port of Nantucket alone. Of the four brothers mentioned above, William, the eldest, born in Wales, in 1603, reached Charlestown with his three brothers in 1636, in the ship "James," and later became a member of the militia under Captain Myles Standish; the second brother was John Merrick; the third, James, spelled the name Mirick, and the fourth was Thomas, mentioned at length below.

(I) Thomas Myrick, born in Wales, in 1620, came with his three brothers and probably a sister Sarah (who married John Atkinson) in 1636, and located in Charlestown. The brothers separated, one going to Newbury, one to Plymouth, one remaining in Charlestown, and Thomas is recorded in Roxbury in 1636. He was at Hartford, Connecticut, in 1638, when he was preparing to visit Springfield, then known by the Indian name of Agawam. The first settlers at this place had grown discouraged and had returned to the older settlements in and around Boston, their places later being taken by others, and in January, 1638, Thomas Merrick was one of thirteen men who were to set out the bounds of the plantation on both sides of the river and mark the trees. He became a man of influence and prominence in the affairs of Springfield, and his name appears over eighty times in the town records. Between 1640 and 1669 he secured ninety-six acres of land in the vicinity. He helped make allotments of land, dealt with the Indians, helped build a church, surveyed lands, viewed fences, and many other public movements found him actively interested. He was a sergeant in the militia of which William Pynchon was captain, and his seat in the meeting house was the second from the front. He died September 7, 1704, and his second wife is buried by his side in the cemetery at Springfield. He married his first wife, according to the records, July 14, 1639, and she died after having had five children. He married (second) Elizabeth Tilley, August 21, 1653, who died August 21, 1684. The first wife, Sarah, was a daughter of Rowland and Sarah Stebbins, and the second wife is thought to have descended from a family that was numerous and influential in the colony at Springfield. Eight children were born of the second marriage, and from them there descended thousands of Merricks who located in many parts of the United States and Canada. The following children were born to Thomas Merrick: Thomas, April 12, 1641, died young; Sarah, born May 9, 1643; Mary, September 28, 1645, died 1646; Mary (2), born August 27, 1647; Hannah, February 10, 1649; Elizabeth, August 26, 1654, died 1659; Miriam, born May 1, 1655; John, November 9, 1658; Elizabeth, July 4, 1661; Thomas, January 2, 1664; Tilley, October 20, 1667; James; Abigail, September 1, 1673.

(II) Lieutenant James Merrick, third son of Thomas and Elizabeth (Tilley) Merrick, was born at Springfield, March 2, 1670, and died September 8, 1765, aged ninety-five years, and was buried in the old cemetery at West Springfield, where his tombstone may still be seen. He served as selectman in 1715-19, and also acted as constable, tithingman, fence viewer, and in like public offices. His name was often on the town records. He married (first) July 30, 1696, Sarah, daughter of Luke Hitchcock, of Springfield, who was born April 1, 1678, and died February 5, 1733-34. Mr. Merrick married (second) Widow Abigail Mosely, of Westfield, Massachusetts, who after his death moved to Glastonbury, Connecticut, where she died. Lieutenant James

Merrick had children: Sarah, born February 12, 1696-97; James, January 1, 1698; Thankful, October 8, 1701; Joseph; Mercy, October 21, 1706; Aaron, September 6, 1708; Noah, August 6, 1711; a son who died at birth, January 23, 1715.

(III) Deacon Joseph Merrick, second son of Lieutenant James and Sarah (Hitchcock) Merrick, was born March 27, 1704, at Springfield, and died in March, 1792, in his eighty-eighth year, having served nearly forty-two years as deacon in the church. He married (first) Mary Leonard, of Northampton, Massachusetts, November 13, 1730; she died in January, 1779, aged seventy-three years. He married (second) Widow Mary Root, in December, 1780, and she died in September, 1784, aged seventy-four years. Joseph Merrick had children: Sarah, born September 19, 1731; Mary, October 6, 1733; Rebekah, February 2, 1736; Joseph; Thankful, September 11, 1741; Mercy, September 11, 1741; Tilley, September, 1743; Margaret, December 4, 1745; Eunice, September 18, 1748, died in 1751; Daniel, January 6, 1750.

(IV) Joseph (2), first son of Deacon Joseph (1) and Mary (Leonard) Merrick, was born at West Springfield, Massachusetts, in 1739. In the records he is spoken of as Captain Joseph, but no particulars are given of the service which entitled him to this title. He married Deborah Leonard, of West Springfield. His four sons, all born at West Springfield, were: Gad, June 28, 1763; Perez; Joseph, May 12, 1769; Quartus, March, 1771.

(V) Perez, second son of Joseph (2) and Deborah (Leonard) Merrick, was born at West Springfield, January 28, 1766, and in 1789 married Hannah Williston, of the same place. Children, all born at Franklin, New York: Sylvester W.; Gordon, 1791; Perez, June 12, 1792; Roderick, August 5, 1794; Deborah, 1796; Flora, 1799; Priscilla Leonard, 1800; William Cabot, 1802; Austin Leonard, January 2, 1807; Irene, 1809; Louisa Jones, 1811.

(VI) Sylvester W., eldest son of Perez and Hannah (Williston) Merrick, was born in 1790, at Franklin, and died in March, 1850, at the age of sixty years, in Sandusky county, Ohio. In 1811 he married Mercy Loveland, who died in 1878, at Manteno, Illinois. Children, all born in Franklin, Delaware county, New York: 1. James Fordyce, 1812; married Matilda Brakefield; had five children, and died in October, 1896, at Lancaster, Missouri; he was a pioneer, a farmer, and a country merchant. 2. Williston Sylvester, born 1814; married Rowena Hathaway; lives at Fostoria, Ohio; six children. 3. Sarah Amelia, born 1816; married (first) Jesse Cook, by whom she had two children, and (second) Joseph Younglove, and died in 1888, at Manteno. 4. Frederick L., born 1821; married Nancy Chapman; became a merchant at Kankakee, Illinois, and died in 1891, at Fresno, California, having had nine children. 5. Dr. George Clinton. 6. Lyman B., born September 10, 1829; October 14, 1855, at Manteno, Illinois, married Sarah J., daughter of Henry and Susannah Harsh, who was born at Freeport, Ohio. He was a nurseryman at Topeka, Kansas, and he and his wife had eight children.

(VII) Dr. George Clinton Merrick, fourth son of Sylvester W. and Mercy (Loveland) Merrick, was born December 11, 1824, at Franklin, New York, and died July 2, 1895, at Manteno, Illinois. He was always devoted to his profession, and won the respect and esteem of all by his upright and earnest life. He graduated from Rush Medical College, Chicago, Illinois, with the class of 1851, and later practiced at Manteno from 1852 for the remainder of his life. He was not in any sense a politician, but took a keen interest in public affairs, and President Lincoln appointed him postmaster at Manteno, in which office he served in 1861-62. He married Mary Elizabeth Pęck, of Palmyra, Wisconsin. Children: 1. Charles, born September 17, 1852, at Manteno; married Laura Shidler; children: Mary, Lawrence, Ross and Sylvester; Mr. Merrick is now a broker at Seattle, Washington. 2. Frederick Williston, born October 15, 1855, at Manteno; now a merchant at Seattle; he married Grace Frisbie; one child, Oscar Briggs. 3. Mary Helen Merrick, deceased, born at Manteno, May 15, 1860; married John F. Barnard, also deceased; children as follows: Mary, George, Ruth and Merrick. 4. George Peck. 5. Oscar Peck, born at Lancaster, Missouri, April 6, 1867; now a cashier and accountant in employ of International Harvester Company; married Abigail Castile; children: Gladys and Oscar Peck Jr. The mother of these children, daughter of Joel M. and Amanda (Purdy) Peck, was born November 3, 1828, at Troy, New York, and her mother, Amanda Purdy, was the daughter of Judge Purdy, of Chenango county, New York.

(VIII) George Peck, third son of Dr. George Clinton and Mary Elizabeth (Peck) Merrick, was born October 4, 1862, at Manteno, Illinois, and is a well-known attorney-at-law of Chicago, where he represents many important interests in a legal way. He received a liberal education, and is well fitted by natural ability and training to take a leading place among the members of the Chicago bar. He was prepared for college at Evanston Academy, and in 1880 entered Northwestern University, graduating four years later with the degree of B. L. Subsequently, when he had proved his right to it, his *alma mater* conferred on him the honorary degree of LL. M. He was admitted to the Chicago bar in 1886 and at once entered upon practice, soon becoming a member of the law firm of Hanecy & Merrick, which arrangement continued four or five years. At the end of that time, by various changes, the firm became Merrick, Evans & Whitney, and Merrick & Ramsey. His first associate, Judge Hanecy, was elected to the circuit bench in 1893, and the others with whom Mr. Merrick had been associated have been men of superior ability.

Mr. Merrick won considerable prominence for his connection with the litigation concerning the Lake Front in Chicago, and took an active part in securing the decisions which established the lake front as a park, to be kept free from buildings. He resides in Evanston, where he is much interested in educational matters and other movements affecting the general welfare. He has served as alderman, has been president of the board of education of Evanston, and a trustee of Northwestern University. For some time he lectured before the Law School of the University, and has always been much interested in this branch of its work. He is now alone in the practice of law, and has won a high reputation and standing in his profession. Fraternally he belongs to Evanston Lodge, A. F. and A. M., to the Royal Arch Chapter, and to Evanston Commandery, Knights Templar. He is a member of the American, Illinois and Chicago Bar Associations; Chicago Law Institute, Chicago Law Club, Chicago Club, University Club, Mid-day Club, Glenview Club, Evanston Club, the Phi Beta Kappa society, the New England Society of Chicago, the American Historical Association, the American Geographical Society, Western Economic Society, and American Peace Society. He is an interested student of history, and feels reasonably proud of the record of his ancestors in America. He has in his possession a commission signed by John Hancock, of Massachusetts, and given to one of his ancestors who was then living there.

On January 21, 1885, Mr. Merrick was united in marriage with Grace, daughter of Judge James S. Thompson, the latter being from Richmond, Virginia. She was born at New Boston, Illinois. Children: 1. Clinton, born in Chicago, January 18, 1886; attended the public schools, graduated at Yale College with degree of A. B., class of 1909; became a student in law school of Northwestern University, of Evanston, and in 1912 graduated with degree of LL. B., and has been admitted to the bar of Illinois. 2. Grace Willetts, born in Evanston, October 1, 1896; is attending Evanston high school. 3. Thompson, born March 29, 1900, at Evanston; is being educated in public schools of that place. This family suffered bereavement in the death of the wife and mother, April 25, 1912. She is deeply mourned by many outside the family circle.

SUMNER Roger Sumner was a husband-man of Bicester, Oxfordshire, England. He married there, November 2, 1601, Joane Franklin. He died there December 3, 1608, and his widow married (second) January 10, 1611, Marcus Brian. Roger Sumner had a brother William who died at Bicester in 1597.

(II) William, only child of Roger Sumner, was born at Bicester, England, in 1605, and married there, October 22, 1625, Mary West. He came to New England in 1636 and settled at Dorchester, Massachusetts. He was admitted a freeman May 17, 1637, and became a prominent man in the province. He was selectman there in 1637 and for more than twenty years. From 1663 to 1680 he was one of the feoffes of the school land, and from 1663 to 1671 he was a commissioner to end small causes. In 1663 he was chosen clerk of the train band. He was deputy to the general court in 1658, 1666-70, 1672, 1678-81, and 1683-86, from Dorchester. His wife Mary died at Dorchester, June 7, 1676, and he died December 9, 1688. Children, first four born at Bicester, England, others at Dorchester, Massachusetts: William; Joane, married Aaron Way, of Dorchester, Boston and Rumney Marsh; Roger, mentioned below; George, 1634; Samuel, May 18, 1638; Increase, February 23, 1643.

(III) Roger, son of William Sumner, was born at Bicester, England, and was baptized there August 8, 1632. When he was less than five years of age he came to America with his father and settled in Dorchester, where he lived over twenty years. He was admitted to the church there in 1656, when twenty-four years of age. In 1659 or 1660 he moved to Lancaster, Massachusetts, with his wife and one son. He was dismissed from the church in Dorchester, August 26, 1660, "that with other Christians at Lancaster a church might be formed at that place." He was the first and only deacon of this church for sixteen years, and seems to have been very prominent in the new settlement. Lancaster was attacked and destroyed in King Philip's war, February 10, 1676, and after this dreadful affair he moved with his family to Milton, Massachusetts, where in 1682 he was chosen deacon of the church, being admitted November 20, 1681, and ordained deacon August 20, 1682. On May 6, 1657, he had been made freeman of the colony of Massachusetts. His house in Milton was situated on the east side of Brush Hill, a short distance from the house owned by Manasseh Tucker, who married his daughter Waitstill. He built the house and it is still owned and occupied by the Sumner family. On December 14, 1700, an inventory of his estate was taken by Thomas Vose, Ralph Houghton and Samuel Trescott, and Mary, his widow, was given as her share the old end of the dwelling-house in Milton, while Waitstill was given "one-third part of the chamber, and one-third part of the garret in the new end of the dwelling-house, and other estate." He married, in Lancaster, 1656, Mary Joslin (Josselyn), daughter of Thomas Joslin, of Lancaster. He died at Milton, May 26, 1698, and his widow survived him thirteen years, dying August 21, 1711. Children: Abigail, born at Dorchester, November 16, 1657, died February 19, 1658; Samuel, at Dorchester, February 6, 1659, lived in · Canada; Waitstill, at Lancaster, December 20, 1661, married, December 29, 1679, Manasseh Tucker, of Milton (see Tucker); Mary, at Lancaster, August 5, 1665; Jazaniah, at Lancaster, April 11, 1668, served in Canada expedition, 1690, and undoubtedly lost; Rebecca, at Lancaster, October 9, 1671; William, mentioned below; Ebenezer, at Dorchester, May 28, 1678.

(IV) William, son of Roger Sumner, was born at Lancaster, January 26, 1674, and died December 22, 1738. The following is quoted from the Boston News-Letter, Thursday, December 28, 1738: "Last Thursday one Mr. Sumner of Milton, being at Roxbury, on his way to Boston, was very much benumb'd by the extream Cold, whereupon he stop'd at a House to warm and refresh himself but was suddenly seiz'd with a Fit, and died in a few Minutes." He married, at Milton, June 2, 1697, Esther, daughter of Matthias Puffer, of Dorchester; she died June 27, 1748. Children, born at Milton: Mary, May 2, 1698; Abigail, January 31, 1700; Roger, March 25, 1702; William, February 7, 1705; Gershom, July 1, 1707, died July 26, 1707; Esther, August 12, 1709, died June 7, 1710; Seth, mentioned below.

(V) Seth, son of William Sumner, was born December 15, 1710, at Milton, Massa-

NEW ENGLAND.

265

chusetts, and died at that place November 11, 1771.

He married (first) October 17, 1734, Hannah, daughter of John Badcock, of Milton; she died August 13, 1739. He married (second) 1742, Lydia, daughter of William Badcock, of Milton; she died September 2, 1800. Children of first wife, born at Milton: Seth, July 8, 1735; Roger, November 1, 1737. Children of second wife, born at Milton: Lydia, December 6, 1743; Ebenezer, May 11, 1745, died same day; Enos, born September 25, 1746; William, mentioned below; Esther, September 12, 1750; Clement, February 2, 1752; Job, April 23, 1754, served in revolution; Rufus, February 19, 1756, served in revolution; Hannah, April 15, 1757; Abigail, August 18, 1760; Jesse, November 15, 1763.

(VI) William, son of Seth Sumner, was born August 6, 1748. He served in the revolution from May 20, 1775, to October, 1775, as ensign in Captain Elijah Vose's company from Dorchester. He is said to have been a lieutenant in the Massachusetts line, but the records give his rank as that of ensign, equivalent to third lieutenant. He was a paper maker and had a mill on River street, now Hyde Park, which is now owned by the Tileston & Hollingsworth Company. His brother, Job Sumner, born April 23, 1754, was graduated from Harvard College, 1778; served in the revolution as major in the Massachusetts line, and died September 16, 1789, on board a packet-ship on passage from Charlestown, North Carolina, to York; he was buried at New York by the Freemasons, with much ceremony, in the Trinity churchyard, Broadway, where there is a marble monument to his memory. Job had a son Job, born at Milton, January 20, 1776, who later changed his name to Charles Pinckney Sumner; he was graduated from Harvard College, 1796, and for many years was high sheriff of Suffolk; he married Relief Jacobs, and died in 1839. Charles Pinckney Sumner was father of Hon. Charles Sumner, who was born at Boston, January 6, 1811, graduated from Harvard College, 1830, and was the distinguished United States senator from Massachusetts.

William Sumner married (first) April 30, 1775, Elizabeth, daughter of John Minot, of Dorchester; she died in June, 1792. He married (second) at Dedham, June 12, 1794, Mary, daughter of Eliphalet Pond, of Dedham; she died October 2, 1805. He married (third) at Dorchester, October 26, 1809, Sarah, widow of Zachariah Marquand Thayer, of Braintree, Massachusetts, daughter of —— Gardiner of Hingham, Massachusetts;

she died at Braintree, March 3, 1835. They lived at Dorchester, where he died January 30, 1836. Children of first wife: William, born at Dorchester, July 10, 1775, died January 25, 1776; Elizabeth, at Dorchester, March 17, 1777; Martha, at Milton, May 24, 1779; Lucy, at Milton, November 20, 1781; Charlotte, at Milton, October 10, 1784; Clarissa, at Dorchester, October 26, 1786; William, at Dorchester, December 27, 1788; Abigail Minot, at Dorchester, May 18, 1792. Children of second wife, born at Dorchester: Mary, July 5, 1795; Charles, January 5, 1797; Rufus Pond, mentioned below; Edward, September 20, 1800; Sally Richards, August 6, 1802; Elvira, June 16, 1804.

(VII) Rufus Pond, son of William Sumner, was born at Dorchester, Massachusetts, January 17, 1799. He married, at Boston, May 17, 1819, Susan, daughter of Noah Kingsbury, of Dorchester; she died at Milton, July 23, 1875.

Children, born at Milton: 1. Frederick Augustus, March 4, 1820; married Lucy Lavinia, daughter of Thomas Gaffield, of Boston; children: Frederick Augustus, born November 7, 1844, died March 27, 1847; Lucy Gaffield, March 6, 1846, died February 9, 1849; Franklin Herbert, April 20, 1847, lives in Dorchester; Charles Pinckney, August 3, 1849, manager of Cunard Steamship Company, New York City; James Gaffield, August 16, 1851, married a daughter of Mayor Fox, of Cambridge, Massachusetts; Mary Elvira, September 18, 1852, lives at Jamaica Plain, Boston; Sarah Gaffield, November 16, 1854, lives in Boston, had two children who died young. 2. Charles Henry, born at Milton, October 16, 1822; was a merchant and died November 2, 1891; married, April 23, 1846, Sally, born August 28, 1826, daughter of Charles Tileston, of Dorchester, she died March 5, 1909; children: i. Isabel, born at Boston, May 31, 1847, married, January 31, 1877, David Albert Dunbar, who died December 14, 1895, and was a merchant in Boston, had two children—Laura Spaulding Dunbar, born May 2, 1878, married, April 7, 1902, John Edward McNammara, having Louise Otis, Betina Dunbar McNammara; and Sally Sumner Dunbar, born October 31, 1888, married, January 7, 1911, Edward Everett Richards, of Boston; ii. Josephine Maria, in Boston, August 23, 1849, married, January 7, 1874, James D'Wolf Lovett, died September 8, 1877; iii. Clara, in Boston, February 14, 1853, unmarried; iv. Lillian, in Boston, May 25, 1856, died January 30, 1857; v. Marion, in Boston, April 14, 1861, died November 3, 1869. 3. Rufus Willard, born at

Milton, November 7, 1823; married, February
17, 1858, Eliza Sumner Girard Whittier, of
Dorchester; she died March 31, 1860; child:
Rufus Willard, at Milton, February 18, 1860,
died same day. 4. Susan Jane, March 4,
1825, at Milton; married, April 11, 1844,
Ellis Anderson Hollingsworth, of Milton, a
prominent paper manufacturer and citizen;
children: Sumner, married Mary Clapp Stevens, of Gardiner, Maine; Ellis Hollingsworth, of Hollingsworth & Whitney Company,
of Boston, paper manufacturers, married Elsie Littlefield. 5. Franklin, mentioned below.
6. Gilbert, at Milton, November 26, 1827;
married, June 24, 1849, Catherine Rider, of
Dorchester; children: Albert, July 16, 1850,
died November 4, 1850; Helen Eugenia, October 11, 1854, married George W. Gould,
one child, Catherine Sumner Gould; Gilbert
was a farmer. 7. James, at Wilton, May 28,
1831; married March 3, 1864, Elizabeth Francis, daughter of William S. Spring of Cambridge; children: Georgia Beatrice, at Cambridge, March 8, 1865; Susan Hollingsworth,
at Hyde Park, April 24, 1868. 8. Edmund,
March 29, 1833; lives in Franklin, connected
with Norfolk City Mills; married, January
8, 1857, Jane, daughter of Nathaniel Thomas
Davenport, of Milton, lives at Norfolk; children: Roger Edmund, Charlotte Jane, Arthur
Malcolm, Lilly Maud and Daisy Louise, twins.
9. William, September 25, 1835, died December 11, 1855. 10. Edward, February 17,
1837; married, February 17, 1863, Harriet
A. Rogers, of Bath, Maine; lived in Brooklyn, New York; children, born there: Ralph
Edward, Grace Harriet, Howard Wilder, Agnes Humphrey, and Ruth. 11. George, June
25, 1843; married, November, 1865, Helen,
daughter of Horatio Gates, of Milton; child,
George, born there August 20, died August
30, 1866.

(VIII) Franklin, son of Rufus Pond Sumner, was born in Milton, August 4, 1826, and
died there July 4, 1898. He was educated in
the public schools of his native town, and
during the greater part of his active life he
followed farming in Milton. At one time
he had a general store and was also engaged
in farming. In 1849 he went to California,
where he resided for eighteen years. In politics he was a Republican, in religion a Unitarian. He married, at Milton, November 3,
1858, Mary Antoinette Kingsbury, born April
15, 1833, daughter of Nathaniel and Mary
(Shaw) Kingsbury. Children, born at Milton: Frank, died young; Antoinette, died
young; Florence M., who resides with her
mother on the homestead, Brush Hill road,
Milton.

STRONG John Strong, the immigrant
ancestor, was the son of John
Strong, and was born in Eng-
land in 1626, died at Windsor, Connecticut, February 20, 1697-8. He was a tanner
by trade, and an important citizen of Windsor. He married (first) November 2, 1656,
Mary Clark, baptized September 30, 1638,
died April 28, 1663, aged twenty-five years,
daughter of Joseph and Frances Clark. Frances Clark married (second) March 22, 1639,
Thomas Dewey, of Westfield. John (2)
Strong married (second) in 1664, Elizabeth
Warriner, died June 7, 1684. Children of
first wife, born at Windsor: Mary, born
April 22, 1658; Hannah, August 11, 1660.
Children of second wife: John, of whom further; Jacob, born April 8, 1673; Josiah, January 11, 1678; Elizabeth, about 1684.

(II) John (2), son of John (1) Strong,
was born at Windsor, Connecticut, December
25, 1665, died there May 29, 1749. He married, at Windsor, November 26, 1686, Hannah,
daughter of Deacon John Trumbull, of Suffield, Connecticut. Children, born at Windsor:
Mary, born May 24, 1688; Elizabeth, September 21, 1689; Deacon Jonathan, April 22,
1694; Esther, April 12, 1699; Abigail, May
11, 1701; Deacon David, of whom further;
John Warham, September 30, 1706; John, July
14, 1707; Elizabeth, August 13, 1708.

(III) Deacon David Strong, son of John
(2) Strong, was born at Windsor, Connecticut, December 15, 1704, died January 25, 1801.
He was a farmer at Bolton, Connecticut, and
for sixty-five years was deacon of the Congregational church. In 1730 he went from Windsor to Bolton, and settled three miles from
the center of the town on the road to Buckingham, then Eastbury. He married (first)
May 3, 1732, Thankful, born March 5, 1709,
died May 21, 1771, daughter of Moses Loomis,
born May 15, 1671, son of Nathaniel and
Elizabeth (Moore) Loomis. Moses Loomis
married, April 27, 1694, Joanna Gibbs, born
March 26, 1671, daughter of Samuel and
Hepzibah (Dibble) Gibbs, of Windsor. Deacon David Strong married (second) Abigail
Phelps, of Simsbury, died October 16, 1787.
He married (third) in 1793, Zilpah Davis, of
Hebron, born 1775. She was eighteen years
old and he was eighty-eight years old at the
time of their marriage. Children by first wife:
David, born May 13, 1733; Levi, December
19, 1734; Nathan, January 15, 1736-7; Judah,
November 28, 1739; Thankful, October 12,
1740; Aaron, September 21, 1743; Bathsheba,
January 20, 1747; Hepzibah, married Captain
William Hibbard; Ebenezer, of whom further.

(IV) Ebenezer, son of Deacon David

E. E. Strong

Strong, was born in 1754, died in 1824. He was a soldier in the revolution, a private in the company of Captain Thomas Pitkin, from Bolton, on the Lexington Alarm, April 19, 1775; also in 1776 under Captain J. Wells. He lived at Bolton, Connecticut. He married (first) August 24, 1779, Lucy (Kilbourne) Lawrence, died April 28, 1793, daughter of Benjamin and Lucy (Goodrich) Kilbourne, and widow of Daniel Lawrence, who was killed in the Wyoming massacre. He married (second) in August, 1793, Abigail, daughter of Ebenezer Smith, of Ashford; she died October 29, 1825. Children by first wife: Ebenezer Jr., born May 20, 1780; Solomon, July 8, 1782, settled at Rome, New York; Daniel, November 18, 1784; Eli, of whom further; Genubath, October 22, 1791. Child by second wife: Samuel, April 22, 1795, was adopted by John and Cleopatra Skinner, of Barkhamsted, and his name changed to Samuel Skinner.

(V) Eli, son of Ebenezer Strong, was born October 8, 1789, at Bolton, Connecticut, died there September 19, 1867. He was a farmer in his native town. He married (first) December 10, 1812, Betsey Cowles, of Belchertown, born July 24, 1794, died October 27, 1825, daughter of John Cowles (see Cowles VI). He married (second) Sybil Cowles, born July 19, 1802, sister of his first wife. Children, born at Bolton, by first wife: Lucy Kilburn, born August 25, 1814; Captain Ethan Eli, October 12, 1816; William Coles, of whom further; Semantha Lodemia, November 28, 1820, died March 28, 1821; John Remember Cowles, February 7, 1822; Cornelia Jane, November 1, 1824. Children by second wife: Betsey Lodinia, February 10, 1827; Semantha Azubah, January 16, 1829; Samuel Alanson, March 29, 1831, died March 26, 1842; Mary Emmeline, July 6, 1833; Horatio Bardwell, June 10, 1836; Harrison Alanson, October 16, 1840.

(VI) William Coles (as he preferred the spelling), son of Eli Strong, was born in Bolton, Connecticut, July 27, 1818. He was a paper maker at Talcottville, Vernon, Connecticut. He married, in 1839, Lucy Maria Nichols, born December 9, 1820, daughter of John and Harriet (Moulton) Nichols. Her father was of Manchester, Connecticut. Children: 1. Edgar Eugene, of whom further. 2. Jane Maria, born January 2, 1843, died September 13, 1845. 3. Charles Wesley, born October 25, 1844. 4. Ella Semantha, born March 23, 1847, died February 11, 1848. 5. Jeanie Maria, born October 4, 1849, died February 20, 1859. 6. Eva Cecil, June 9, 1853. 7. Will Nichols, August 1, 1856. 8. Clinton

Frederic, June 5, 1859, died June 21, 1862. 9. Minnie Alice, September 11, 1864.

(VII) Edgar Eugene, son of William Coles Strong, was born at Manchester, Connecticut, April 14, 1841. He attended the public schools of his native town and also the academy there, completing his preparation for college at a boarding school at East Greenwich, Rhode Island, known as the Providence Conference Seminary. He left school to enlist in the Union army, becoming a private in Company H of Manchester, Sixteenth Regiment Connecticut Volunteer Infantry. Subsequently he was transferred to Company F of the same regiment. He enlisted in August, 1862, and served through the remainder of the civil war. He was slightly wounded at the great battle of Antietam, September 17, 1862, and twice afterward during skirmishes. He was promoted from the ranks for faithful and efficient service and commissioned second lieutenant of Company H, and afterward first lieutenant of Company F of the Sixteenth Regiment. He was in command of the company during most of the time after he received his commission. His regiment was in the army of the Potomac under McClellan, Burnside and Hooker. He was honorably discharged in 1865. After the war Mr. Strong became clerk in a hardware store in Cleveland, Ohio, and he continued in this business with the same firm for a period of twenty years. Afterward he was a partner in the firm of Brown, Strong & Company in the lumber business. The lumber yard of the firm was partially destroyed by fire, and he withdrew. In 1887 the firm of Strong, Carlisle & Turney was formed to deal in mill supplies and machinery, wholesale and retail. Mr. Strong was senior partner. The business flourished and was incorporated in 1893, the name being changed five years later to the Strong-Carlisle-Hammond Company. Their offices are at No. 336 Frankfort avenue, Cleveland. Mr. Strong has been president of the company from the outset. He is also president of the Clarke Manufacturing Company, of Cleveland, and is a director in both corporations. Although his life has been devoted to business in which he has won high distinction Mr. Strong had intended before the war to study medicine and surgery. His enlistment prevented him from following his chosen career.

He is a member of Memorial Post, Grand Army of the Republic, of Cleveland; the Ohio Commandery, Military Order of the Loyal Legion; the Cleveland Yacht Club; the New England Society, of Cleveland, Ohio; and the Western Reserve. In religion he is a Presbyterian; in politics, Republican. He is a veteran member of Tyrian Lodge of Free Masons and of Cleveland Chapter, Royal Arch Masons.

Mr. Strong married, January 19, 1869, Mary Ella Clarke, who was born at Cleveland September 1, 1846, a daughter of Aaron and Caroline (Bingham) Clarke. Children, born at Cleveland: 1. Clinton Eugene, born December 14, 1869, drowned while a student at Cornell University. 2. Herbert William, June 24, 1871; married Gladys, daughter of George C. Mosher, of Kansas City; children: Ruth, born July 3, 1910, and Elizabeth, February 4, 1912. 3. Edith, born July 27, 1876, died March 2, 1879. 4. Elizabeth, born June 20, 1880; graduate of Smith College, Northampton, Massachusetts; married Warren S. Hayden; child: Sherman Strong Hayden, born February 9, 1908.

(The Cowles Line).

(I) John Cowles, the immigrant ancestor, was born in England about 1598, died in Hatfield, Connecticut, September, 1675. He was among the early settlers of Hartford, Connecticut. Not long after the year 1640 he located at Farmington, Connecticut, and in 1652 was one of the founders of the church there. He bought land at the north end of Farmington village, afterward known as the Dr. Thompson and Bodwell places, and after selling this land he bought three lots just south of the present meeting house and built a house there. He spelled his name Cowles, in order to distinguish himself from a man named Coles of the same town, and his descendants have spelled the name Cowles, Cowls and Coles to the present time. Originally Cole and Coles were of the same English family. He was a farmer, and deputy to the general assembly from Farmington in 1653-54. In 1659 he was one of the signers who started the settlement at Hadley, Massachusetts, but was probably not among the first to settle, although living there in 1662. He was one of the twenty-five "engagers" in Hadley to establish themselves in Hatfield, across the Connecticut river, before March, 1661. He was on the committee that laid out a burying ground February 14, 1669, and there was no other cemetery there until 1848. His widow Hannah after his death went to live with her son-in-law Caleb Stanley, of Hartford, where she died March 16, 1683, and is buried. Her will was dated October 27, 1680, and in it she states that her husband's will was dated December 11, 1674. The homestead in Hatfield was in possession of descendants until April, 1898. Children: Samuel, born 1639; John, of whom further; Hannah, 1644, married Caleb Stanley; Sarah, 1646, married Nathaniel Goodwin; Esther, 1649, married Thomas Bull; Elizabeth, 1651, married Edward Lyman; Mary, June 24, 1654, married Nehemiah Dickinson.

(II) John (2), son of John (1) Cowles, was born in 1641, died May 12, 1711. He was admitted a freeman in 1690. He married, November 22, 1668, Deborah, daughter of Robert Bartlett, of Hartford. Children, born at Hatfield or Hadley: Hannah, November 14, 1669; Jonathan, of whom further; Samuel, May 27, 1673; John, June 15, 1676; Abigail, February 1, 1679; Sarah, June 5, 1681; Mary, November 3, 1683; Esther, April 14, 1686.

(III) Jonathan, son of John (2) Cowles, was born January 26, 1671, at Hatfield, died there November 13, 1756. He married, January 21, 1697, Prudence Frary, died July 1, 1756. Children: Abigail, born May 24, 1698; John (3), of whom further; Jonathan, June 30, 1703; Timothy, April 9, 1706; Keziah, September 6, 1708; Nathaniel, March 31, 1711; Eleazer, September 18, 1713; Elisha, April 19, 1716; Eunice, August 18, 1719; Abia, October 27, 1722.

(IV) John (3), son of Jonathan Cowles, was born in Hatfield, December 27, 1700, died between June and November, 1735. He married Mary ——, died at Belchertown, 1795, in her eighty-ninth year. Children: Israel, born September 28, 1726, settled in Belchertown, where he died in 1797, married Lydia Bardwell; Abia, December 22, 1729, married, March 3, 1752, Gideon Hannum, of Belchertown; John (4), of whom further; Martha, November 14, 1734, married, December 12, 1754, Stephen Crawford, of Belchertown; Mary, baptized October 3, 1742.

(V) Captain John (4) Cowles, son of John (3) Cowles, was born at Hatfield July 28, 1731, died in 1811, aged eighty years, in Belchertown, where he made his home when a young man. He was a soldier in the revolution in Colonel Woodbridge's regiment on the Lexington Alarm and until fall of 1775 at Cambridge. He married, at Hatfield, September 24, 1757, Hannah Bardwell, died in 1813 at Belchertown, daughter of Joseph and Lydia Bardwell, of Hatfield and Belchertown. Her father died in 1791, aged seventy-eight; her mother in 1800, aged eighty-six. Children: John (5), of whom further; Joshua, died in 1842 aged sixty-six: Enos, removed to South Hadley; probably others.

(VI) John (5), son of Captain John (4) Cowles, was born in Belchertown about 1758, died there in 1830. He was a soldier in the revolution, a private in Captain Elijah Dwight's company, Colonel Elisha Porter's

Regiment, at Bennington in 1777, ranking as corporal. In 1782 he was sergeant in Captain Gideon Stebbin's company, Fourth Hampshire County Regiment. He married Elizabeth Smith, died in 1827, aged sixty-six. Children, born at Belchertown: Remember J.; Samantha; Betsey, born July 24, 1794, died October 27, 1825, married, December 10, 1812, Eli Strong (see Strong V); Sybil, born July 19, 1802, second wife of Eli Strong; and other children.

SKINNER   The surname Skinner is like a large class of English trade and business names adopted about the twelfth century as family names, as butcher, baker, chandler, merchant, brewer, etc. Skinner means simply a dealer in furs and hides. The Skinners Company of London received a charter of incorporation as early as the reign of Edward III., and has a coat-of-arms of ancient date. The families of Skinner are found in all parts of England. The Skinners of Le Burtons and Ledbury, county Hereford, descended from Stephen Skinner (1557), elder son of Stephen Skinner, of county Hereford. Arms: Sable a chevron or between three griffins' heads erased argent a mullet for difference. Crest: A griffin's head erased argent holding in the beak a hand couped gules on the breast a mullet for difference. The families at Cowley, Devonshire, in London, county Essex, in the Isle of Wight, in Dewlich, and various other localities, also bear arms. Thomas Skinner was lord mayor of London in 1596. A common device in various Skinner arms is: Sable three griffins' heads erased argent.

(I) Sergeant Thomas Skinner, ancestor of the Essex county (Massachusetts) families, was born in 1617, in England, and died March 2, 1703-4, in Malden, Massachusetts. He came from Chichester, county Sussex, England, bringing with him his wife and two sons. He lived at one time at Subdeaneries Parish, Chichester. He was a victualler, and May 31, 1652, was licensed to keep an inn at Malden. His house there was situated at the southeast corner of Cross and Walnut streets. It was given to Skinner's son Abraham, April 23, 1684. He was admitted freeman May 18, 1663.

He married (first) in England, Mary ———, who died April 9, 1671; (second) Lydia (Shepardson) Call, widow of Thomas Call; she died December 17, 1723, aged eighty-seven years. Children, born at Chichester, England: Thomas, July 23, 1645; Abraham, mentioned below.

(II) Abraham, son of Thomas Skinner, was born in Subdeaneries Parish, Chichester, and baptized in Pallant Parish Church, September 29, 1649. He had the homestead in Malden, Massachusetts, paying certain sums to his brother and mother Lydia. He died before his father, Sergeant Thomas Skinner, who deeded to Abraham's widow, Hannah, lot 75 in the second division, in consideration of her maintaining the grantor and his wife, May 27, 1698. He served in King Philip's war in 1676 under Captain Prentice, and his son Abraham was a grantee on account of this service in Narragansett township No. 2. A large rock at the corner of Cross and Walnut streets, on the old homestead, was known as Skinner's Rock, and was not removed until 1887. Children, born at Malden: Abraham, mentioned below; Thomas, December 7, 1688 (given 1691 in printed Malden records, but 1688 by various other good authorities); Mary, September, 1690.

(III) Abraham (2), son of Abraham (1) Skinner, was born April 8, 1681, at Malden. He removed to Woodstock late in life with his son William Skinner. He married Tabitha ———. Children, born at Malden: Abraham, May 10, 1718; William, July 16, 1720; Isaac, April 5, 1723; Tabitha, twin, August 18, 1725; Abigail, twin, August 18, 1725; Benjamin, mentioned below; Hannah, June 15, 1730; Ebenezer, March 29, 1733; Jonathan, December 12, 1735.

(IV) Benjamin, son of Abraham (2) Skinner, was born at Malden, February 26, 1727. He removed to Woodstock, Connecticut. He lived in Windham county. He was a soldier in the revolution, a fifer in Captain Experience Storrs' company (second), Colonel Israel Putnam's regiment, and was at Cambridge from May to December, 1775, and probably at the battle of Bunker Hill. He was in 1776 in Colonel Benedict Arnold's regiment. Among his children were Harvey, who settled in Royalton, Vermont, and Baxter, mentioned below. He died before 1787, as shown by appointment of a guardian to his son Harvey.

(V) Baxter, son of Benjamin Skinner, lived in Royalton, Vermont, where his brother Harvey Skinner lived. He is first mentioned there on the list of 1796, and last in 1811; in some of the intervening years his name does not appear on the list. He bought an interest in the carding and fulling mill on the First Branch, in 1811. He married, September 28, 1797, Miriam Prouty, of Langdon, New Hampshire. Children: Betsey, born 1798, in Langdon; George, May 9, 1800, in Langdon, probably; Oren, March 24, 1802; Martha, August 16, 1804; Otis Ainsworth, mentioned below; Samuel Prouty, November 16, 1809, at

Royalton; Frances Louisa, 1815; Benjamin Harvey, hotel keeper in Chicago.

(VI) Rev. Otis Ainsworth Skinner, son of Baxter Skinner, was born in Royalton, Vermont, July 3, 1807, and died at Naperville, Illinois, September 18, 1861. He received his education in the public schools, and for some years was a school teacher. In 1826 he was ordained as a Universalist minister, and in 1831 was settled in a pastorate at Baltimore, Maryland. Three years later he accepted a call to Haverhill, Massachusetts, and in 1837 went to Boston to preach. He had a pastorate in New York City from 1846 to 1849, when he returned to his former charge in Boston, where he remained until April, 1857. In that month he located in a pastorate at Elgin, Illinois, but in August of the same year he was elected president of Lombard University, Galesburg, Illinois. In October, 1858, he became pastor of a Universalist church at Joliet, Illinois. He was prominent as an editor as well as a preacher. He edited the *Southeastern Pioneer*, a religious publication at Baltimore; the *Gospel Sun*, of Haverhill; and the *Universalist Miscellany*, a monthly magazine of Boston, 1844-49. He was an efficient worker for liberal religion, for education, for temperance, and other reforms. He was the author of "Universalism Illustrated and Defended" (Boston, 1839); "Miller's Theory Exploded" (1840); "Letters in Revivals" (1842); "Prayer Book for Family Worship" (1843); "Letters on Moral Duties of Parents" (1844); "Lessons from the Death of the Young" (1844); "Reply to Hatfield" (1847); "Death of Daniel Webster" (1852). A biography of Mr. Skinner was written by Thomas B. Thayer and published in Boston in 1861. He was largely instrumental in securing the funds for the founding of Tufts College. His portrait was presented to Lombard University, of which he was at one time president, through the generosity of his grandson, Edward M. Skinner. He married, July 30, 1831, Angela Malvina, born August, 1808, at Weare, New Hampshire, daughter of Rev. Sebastian Streeter. Children: Angela Adelaide, born January 15, 1832, at Baltimore; Otis Streeter, mentioned below.

(VII) Otis Streeter, son of Rev. Dr. Otis Ainsworth Skinner, was born December 26, 1838, at Boston, and died in 1908. He married Martha L. McGinnis, born in 1842, at Brunswick, New Jersey, daughter of Isaac B. McGinnis. Children. 1. Edward McGinnis, mentioned below. 2. Otis Ainsworth, born at Madison, Wisconsin, 1869; married May McAllister; children: Edward Ainsworth, born in Chicago, 1894, student in the University of

Illinois; and Marion Streeter, born in Chicago, 1898.

(VIII) Edward McGinnis, son of Otis Streeter Skinner, was born in Boston, September 4, 1864. He attended the public schools of his native city and at Gardner, Illinois, where he went to live with his mother and brother in 1873. He removed with the family afterward to Wilmington, Illinois, and in 1879 came to Chicago, where he began his business career as a messenger boy in the wholesale store of Field, Leiter & Company. He remained with this concern in various positions for ten years. In 1891 he entered the employ of Cluett, Coon & Company, now Cluett, Peabody & Company, in charge of the credit department, and continued with that firm until 1894. Since 1894 he has been connected with the firm of Wilson Brothers as manager of the credit department, and since 1901 as a director and general manager.

He was one of the organizers and one of the first presidents of the Chicago Association of Credit Men. He was actively identified with the formation of the Chicago Commercial Association, afterwards the Chicago Association of Commerce, and served as its president in 1909, after having served at different times as chairman of almost every important committee. He was one of the founders of the Chicago Branch of the Peace Society, was a director for several years, and vice-president one year. He was for a number of years secretary of the Newsboys and Boot-blacks Association, and a member of the board of trustees of the Chicago Home for Boys, likewise a member of the board of the Anti-Cruelty Association, and director of the Chicago Immigrants' Protective League. His interest in civic matters was shown by his having been a director of the Illinois Legislative Voters' League, and a member of the finance committee of the Municipal Voters' League. Mr. Skinner was a member of the Chicago Vice Commission, a municipal body appointed by Mayor Busse, the only municipal commission ever appointed to investigate the social question. He was one of the few business men appointed to this commission, which consists of thirty members from various walks of life. The report of this commission was thorough and exhaustive, and the demand for copies came from all over the world. The report, contrary to public opinion, reaches the conclusion that the social evil is a man problem, and not a woman question.

Mr. Skinner has been a lecturer on credit and business topics at the University of Wisconsin, the University of Illinois, the Northwestern University at Evanston, and has given much time in an effort to have the retail merchant establish his business upon a more systematic, efficient and profitable basis, appearing in one year before the Retail Clothiers' Association in the states of Minnesota, Iowa and Michigan. His interest in the welfare of humanity has been repeatedly demonstrated, and he has given his voice and financial aid to every movement of importance toward social progress and betterment, although burdened by the cares and responsibilities of a great mercantile business.

In his annual address as president of the Chicago Association of Commerce, Mr. Skinner said: "It has been truthfully said that commerce can make a large city, but not a great city." That idea furnishes an index of Mr. Skinner's purposes and character. He brought about new and progressive policies in this Association which has accomplished so much good in Chicago.

He is an active member of St. Paul's Universalist Church of Chicago, of the Union League Club, the Glenview Golf Club, and the New England Society of Chicago. He was the founder of the Men's Club of St. Paul's Church. In politics he is a Progressive.

He married, July 5, 1893, Carolyn Hope Caldwald, born at Hamilton, Ohio, June 4, 1871, daughter of Robert Webster and Florence Hope (Flagg) Caldwald. They have no children.

PARKINSON William Parkinson, the first ancestor found for this family, went from Scotland with his young wife, Esther Woods, and settled in Londonderry, Ireland, about 1739. There his oldest son was born, and in 1744 the three came to America and settled in Londonderry, New Hampshire, where their kindred had settled. Children: Henry, mentioned below: born in Londonderry, New Hampshire: Aaron, Jonathan, Reuben, Esther, Elizabeth, Sylvanus, William, Katherine, Mary, Susan.

(II) Henry, son of William and Esther (Woods) Parkinson, was born in 1741, in Londonderry, Ireland, and came to Londonderry, New Hampshire, with his parents in 1744. He attended Princeton College, from which he was graduated in 1765, and then for several years taught in some department in the college, being called "Tutor Parkinson." He returned to his father's home after this and was there when the revolution broke out. He enlisted in the beginning as a private in Captain Reid's company, marched with it to the vicinity of Boston, and participated in the battle of Bunker Hill. On July 6, 1775, he

received a commission as quartermaster in the First New Hampshire Regiment under General Stark, and served with him at the battle of Bennington. In the spring of 1777, General Stark threw up his commission in anger, and in the following June his friend Parkinson received his discharge. He had anticipated this change and had arranged to have some land which he owned at Francestown, New Hampshire, cleared for him, and there built his home. It is said that his constitution was broken while in the service. In April, 1778, he was appointed town clerk, and served in this office 1778-79-80. His handwriting was very clear, and his books well kept, being distinct and legible after more than a hundred years. He was chosen justice of the peace March 23, 1780, by the legislature, on recommendation of the town, and in 1779 was chairman of the committee of safety. Early in 1781 he removed to Pembroke, New Hampshire, where he remained three years, and seems to have taught school during his stay there. He then went to Concord, and for the ten years from 1784 to 1794 "maintained a superior school," then moved to Canterbury, where he founded a classical school at which young men were fitted for college, and for many years was known as the "Canterbury school-master." There he bought a farm, built a house and mill, and spent the remainder of his life, continuing to teach until compelled to stop because of the infirmities of age, and died there May 8, 1820. He married, September 17, 1777, Jennett McCurdy, of Londonderry, New Hampshire, and by her had three sons and five daughters.

(III) Robert, eldest son of Henry and Jennett (McCurdy) Parkinson, was born in Francestown, May 18, 1781. His father gave him a good education and he was a great reader, a scholarly and capable man, and taught school for a few years in early life. In 1808 Colonel Timothy Dix employed him to superintend the building of a road through Dixville Notch, which lay in an unbroken wilderness, Colonel Dix having bought large tracts of land in Coos county, New Hampshire. Mr. Parkinson purchased a farm at East Columbia, Coos county, erected a log house thereon, and lived there alone until 1809. He then married and brought his wife to live in the wilderness. His barn, of sawed timber, was the first building in the neighborhood, and in it the first public school was conducted. Settlers soon began to pour in and all received a welcome at his home. He made heavy investments in timber, and through the war embargo and his having become security for others he became financially embarrassed. Because of this, in

1821 he removed to New Boston, and later to Nashua, New Hampshire, and died at the latter place, May 12, 1849. He married, in February, 1810, Elizabeth, daughter of Daniel Kelso, of New Boston. Children, born in Columbia: 1. Mary Jane, December 28, 1810; was a teacher, and employed some time in the School of Design, Cooper Institute, New York City. 2. Hon. Henry, October 11, 1812; married (first) Mary Alley, in 1841, (second) November 2, 1843, Lydia R. Wilson; he was a merchant and builder in Nashua. 3. Eliza Ann, March 11, 1814; married (first), 1856, Luke Nichols, (second) Leonard McKean. 4. Royal, mentioned below. 5. Frances S., March 9, 1819; was a teacher for fourteen years, beginning at the age of fifteen years; she married Rev. Melancthon G. Wheeler, May 4, 1848; children: Elizabeth P., married John R. Carter; Prof. John H., graduate of Harvard and of University of Bonn, a brilliant scholar, became professor of Greek in University of Virginia; Carrie A., graduated from Wellesley, and married Prof. Charles H. Cooper, of Carlton College, Minnesota; Cornelia F., studied at Wellesley, and married W. W. Hill, of Woburn, Massachusetts; and Edward F., graduate of Bowdoin College, taught in Hartford Theological Seminary. 6. Caroline, October 13, 1820; was for forty years a teacher in Nashua, New Hampshire, and Worcester, Massachusetts. 7. John K., in New Boston, January 31, 1822; machinist at Diamond Springs, California. 8. Clara H., September 7, 1824; was a teacher in Nashua Academy, now Smith College; married, 1849, Henry W. Herrick, of Manchester; children: Allen E., a wood engraver and artist; Rev. Robert P., graduate of Dartmouth College and Hartford Seminary, became president of Western Minnesota Seminary; and Henry A., mill engineer for the Amoskeag Corporation, Manchester.

(IV) Rev. Royal Parkinson, son of Robert and Elizabeth (Kelso) Parkinson, was born at Columbia, New Hampshire, November 8, 1815. He graduated from Dartmouth College in 1843, and from Andover Theological Seminary in 1847, and on October 18, 1848, settled over the Congregational church at Cape Elizabeth, Maine. Later he preached at West Falmouth, Maine; Sandwich and Temple, New Hampshire; and Windham, Queechy, Randolph and Milton, Vermont. In 1864-65 he served as chaplain in the Union army, and afterwards became connected with the Treasury Department at Washington, where he died December 21, 1882. He married, November 21, 1848, Joanna Z., daughter of Joseph Griffin, a publisher and bookseller of Brunswick, Maine. Children: 1. Joseph

Griffin, born at Cape Elizabeth, Maine, August 10, 1849; made deaf by scarlet fever while a child; was educated at National Institution for the Deaf and Dumb at Washington, D. C.; passed civil service examinations and was appointed to a clerkship in the Patent Office in that city, despite his handicap proving exceptionally efficient and competent. He was promoted to the position of principal examiner and after filling that position several years and having graduated from the Washington Law School, resigned to become a partner of his brother and to practice law in Cincinnati. The firm had an extensive practice, extending to the principal cities of the country. He has received the honorary degree of Master of Arts from Dartmouth College. 2. Robert Henry, twin of preceding, mentioned below. 3. George Bowen, attorney-at-law, graduate of Dartmouth College, is practicing in Cincinnati. 4. William Dwight, born August 10, 1857; graduate of Dartmouth College; now superintendent of public schools, Waltham, Massachusetts.

(V) Hon. Robert Henry Parkinson, son of Rev. Royal and Joanna Z. (Griffin) Parkinson, was born at Cape Elizabeth, Maine, August 10, 1849. He attended the public schools of Bangor, Maine, prepared for college at Randolph, Vermont, and in 1866 entered Dartmouth College, from which he graduated with the class of 1870 with the degree of bachelor of arts, taking a Phi Beta rank. He studied law in the offices of Judge Barrett, and the firm of Converse & French, of Woodstock, Vermont, and later with Cross & Burnham, of Manchester, New Hampshire, the junior partner of which firm is now United States senator from New Hampshire. In 1872 Mr. Parkinson went to St. Louis, Missouri, and was for a short time a law student in the office of E. B. Adams, now United States circuit judge of the Eighth Circuit. He took the examination in open court and was duly admitted to the bar at St. Louis in 1872. He immediately began the practice of law in that city, and was soon afterwards assistant attorney of the Atlantic & Pacific Railroad Company there. In 1874 he became junior partner of the law firm of Hatch & Parkinson, in Cincinnati, but this firm was dissolved in 1878, and he and his brother Joseph Griffin formed a partnership, pursuing the practice of law at Cincinnati and making a specialty of patent and trade-mark law. Since 1893 Mr. Parkinson has resided in Chicago, where he has been in extensive practice, arguing many important cases in the federal courts there and in New York, Boston, Cincinnati and other cities, as well as in the supreme court of the United

States. Since 1910 the firm has been Parkinson & Lane. His office is in the Marquette Building, and his residence at 110 Bellevue Place, Chicago.

Mr. Parkinson is the author of various articles on legal subjects, and is counted among the ablest patent lawyers of the country. He was appointed by the United States Court of Appeals as the Chicago representative on the committee to assist the United States Supreme Court in revising its rules for equity practice, and served by appointment of the president and secretary of state as one of the American representatives to the International Conference of 1911, to formulate a treaty relating to laws governing industrial property—a conference at which forty nations were represented. Mr. Parkinson is a member of the American Bar Association, and chairman of the patent section; of the Illinois Bar Association, the Chicago Bar Association, the Lawyers' Club of New York, and of the bar of the Supreme Court of the United States, of many other federal courts, and of the Supreme Court of Illinois. He also belongs to the Union League Club, the University Club, the Chicago Club, and the New England Society of Chicago, and of the Queen City Club of Cincinnati. In religion he is a Congregationalist and in politics a Republican.

He married, April 22, 1878, Helen B. McGuffey, born in December, 1857, in Cincinnati, daughter of Alexander H. and Elizabeth (Drake) McGuffey. Her mother was sister of Chief Justice Drake, of the Court of Claims of Missouri, and once United States Senator from Missouri, and a daughter of Dr. Daniel Drake. Her father's brother was president of the University of Virginia. Children, born in Cincinnati: 1. Elizabeth Drake, June 23, 1879. 2. June Griffin, April 6, 1881; married Alfred E. Manierre, of Chicago. 3. Stirling Bruce, January 1, 1883; married Sylvia Davidson, of Chicago; he was educated in the University of Chicago, and lives in that city. 4. Kelso Steele, August 19, 1884; perished in a storm on Lake Michigan, in August, 1893.

BARTON   Samuel Barton, immigrant ancestor of all the families of the name whch have been long in Worcester county, settled in Salem, Massachusetts, where he was a witness in one of the famous witchcraft cases. In 1638 Marmaduke Barton was in Salem, and Samuel, who was probably not born before 1650, may have been born in Salem. He was in Watertown, Massachusetts, for a short time, and received the usual "warning" that came to newcomers when moving into a Puritan colony, dated June 16,

1693. In 1699 and perhaps earlier, he was in Framingham, where his children are all recorded. He bought what is known as the Elliott grist mill at Oxford. He bought a fourth part of the corn mill, one home lot of forty acres and ten acres adjoining, also fifty acres in the second division on Long Hill, and various other lots of land in Oxford, together with the right of common October 19, 1716, for £85, of Jonathan Provender. He was then of Framingham, but his daughter was called of Oxford when she married, December 17, 1716, so he must have moved in the fall of 1716. He was formally dismissed by the Framingham church to the Oxford church, January 15, 1721, and he was one of the original members of the church there. Before his death he gave his homestead to his son Joshua. He died September 12, 1732, and his will, dated June 13, 1732, proved September 23, 1732, bequeathed to all his children, leaving lands not previously disposed of to Caleb, his third son. He married Hannah, daughter of Edmund Bridges, of Salem, probably, and Edmund Bridges Jr. also settled in Framingham. Children: 1. Samuel, born October 8, 1691. 2. Mercy, May 22, 1694. 3. Joshua, December 24, 1697. 4. Elisha, April 22, 1701. 5. Caleb, mentioned below. 6. Jedediah, September 18, 1707. 7. Mehitable, August 22, 1710. 8. Edmund, August 5, 1714; his son was Stephen, born June 10, 1740, father of Stephen, born August 18, 1774; this Stephen was father of Clarissa H. Barton, born December 25, 1821, who became so famous in the civil war for her nursing, and was founder of the Red Cross Relief; she died in May, 1912.

(II) Caleb, son of Samuel Barton, was born February 9, 1705, at Framingham. He was constable, and lived on Prospect Hill, in Oxford, until about 1763, when he moved to Charlton. He was executor of his father's will. He died at Charlton. He married (first) December 6, 1725, Mary, daughter of Peter Shumway, born at Topsfield, died August 29, 1747. He married (second) January 3, 1748, Susanna March, of Sutton, who died at Plainfield, when very aged. Children: John, mentioned below; Hannah, born 1728; Reuben, 1731, died 1733; Azubah, born 1733, died 1747; Caleb, born August 11, 1736; Abraham, October 16, 1750; Jacob, November 2, 1752; Bathsheba, October 15, 1754; Hannah, July 18, 1757; Sibley, August 18, 1760; Olive, October 14, 1763.

(III) John, son of Caleb Barton, was born October 12, 1726. He lived in the east part of Oxford, lot H., 21. In his later years he lived in Andover, Vermont, where his son

Rufus lived, and he died there. He married, July 23, 1746, Abigail, daughter of Phineas Dana, and she died at Ludlow, Vermont, before her husband died, while her son Rufus was living there.

Children of John Barton, born at Oxford: Asa, May 21, 1747; Azubah, August 15, 1749; Phinehas, mentioned below; John, January 23, 1755; Caleb, December 17, 1756; David, March 30, 1759; Abigail, May 25, 1761; Jeremiah, June 24, 1763; Edward, August 28, 1765; Hannah, July 21, 1767; Perley, March 6, 1770; Amos, June 1, 1772; Rufus, August 11, 1774; Phebe, twin, August 11, 1774.

(IV) Phinehas, son of· John Barton, was born at Oxford, May 9, 1752. He was a soldier in the revolution, from Oxford, joining the Continental army in 1777. He was in Captain Thomas Newhall's company on the Lexington alarm, and in Captain John Howard's company, Colonel Samuel Brewer's regiment, in 1777. He settled in Leicester, Worcester county, Massachusetts. He married, February 26, 1772, Elizabeth Hersey, of Leicester. He died there July 26, 1827, and she died there January 7, 1836. Children, born at Leicester: Betsey, September 3, 1776; Elijah, October· 25, 1778; Polly, March 25, 1781; Samuel H., mentioned below; Phinehas, May 12, 1785, died young; child, died February 18, 1790; child, died July 3, 1792; Phinehas, born October 27, 1795; Horace, December 17, 1799.

(V) Samuel Hersey, son of Phinehas Barton, was born in Leicester, December 21, 1782. He married Margaret Burdett, of Dutch descent, a native of New York state. He resided in Albany, New York. Children: Henry, Ann Eliza, Ira, Stephen, Thomas (all now deceased), Margaret, born in Canada, 1830, now living in Canada; Samuel Emery, mentioned below.

(VI) Samuel Emery, son of Samuel Hersey Barton, was born in Albany, New York, March, 1816, and died May, 1879. He went to Canada with his father when he was a boy, and settled at Demorestville, Ontario, where he followed farming. He married Philena Adelaide Billings, born at Pomfret, Vermont, 1821, daughter of John and Philana (Carpenter) Billings. Children: 1. James Irving, born in Canada, April 6, 1843; married Georgianna Dunning; child: Georgia, born 1879, died 1892. 2. Harriet, born in Canada, February, 1845, died in 1851. 3.· Amanda, born in Canada, 1847, died in 1849. 4. Jesse Billings, mentioned below. 5. Emily, born in Canada, July 8, 1852; unmarried, now living in Hinsdale, Illinois. 6. Margaret Adelaide,

born in Canada, August 27, 1860, now living at Hinsdale, unmarried.

(VII) Jesse Billings, son of Samuel Emery Barton, was born in Demorestville, Ontario, Canada, May 28, 1850. He attended the public schools of his native town, and was graduated in the class of 1873 with the degree of bachelor of arts from Albert College, now part of the University of Toronto. He began to study law in Chicago, and was a student in various law offices. In January, 1876, he was examined in open court and admitted to the bar. He was for two years and a half assistant corporation counsel of Chicago. He engaged in general practice afterward, and November 1, 1899, he was appointed attorney and general counsel of the Chicago Terminal Transfer Railroad Company, a position he has filled with signal ability and success to the present time. In politics he is a Democrat. He is a member of the Illinois Bar Association and of the Chicago Bar Association, of the Hinsdale Club of Hinsdale, Illinois, where he makes his home, and of Hinsdale Lodge of Free Masons. He was made a Mason in 1876, in Oriental Lodge, No. 33. He is also a member of the New England Society of Chicago. His office is in the Baltimore & Ohio Railroad station, Chicago.

He married (first) February, 1879, Ella R. Wilcox, born February 5, 1855, died December 27, 1879, daughter of Albert Wilcox, of Point Peninsula, New York. He married (second) February 25, 1885, Lucy Eudora (Thomas) Bonfield, widow, daughter of Jesse Burgess Thomas, judge of the supreme court of Illinois; she was born in Chicago, in 1845. Child by first wife: 1. Ella Wilcox, born December 20, 1879, died in infancy. Children by second wife: 2. Alice Marie (adopted), born in Paris, France, March 28, 1880; married Aldis Brainard Hatch; one child, Aldis Brainard Jr. 3. Jesse Billings, born in Chicago, September 26, 1885; educated in public schools of Hinsdale, Illinois, prepared for college at the Lewis Institute, Chicago, and entered Stanford University, California, where he was a student for two years; matriculated at University of Wisconsin, where he spent his junior and senior years; now a civil engineer with the Chicago Telephone Company. 4. Walter Irving, born in Chicago, June 8, 1888, died 1905. 5. Lucy Adelaide, born in Ogden City, Utah, September 26, 1891; educated in Lewis Institute, Chicago, the National Cathedral School (Protestant Episcopal) for Girls, Washington, D. C., of which she is a graduate, and the Ann Morgan Studio for Expression of Chicago, from which she was graduated in 1912.

HAWLEY The surname Hawley seems to have had a Norman origin. At any rate it was used by a Norman at the time of the Conquest, and appears in the Battle Abbey. The family has been prominent in Derbyshire since about A. D. 1200. We have six generations of an old pedigree in that county. Doubtless many of the families branched off from this line. John Hawley (5), of Banbridge, had an only daughter and heir, Anne, who married Thomas Blount. He was the son of Thomas Hawley, of Ersby, and grandson of Sir William, of Ersby. Sir William's father was also Sir William, and his grandfather was Robert de-Hawley. Coat-of-arms of the Derby family: Vert a satire engrailed argent. Crest: A dexter arm in armor proper garnished or holding in the hand a spear or bend spinster point downwards proper. Motto: *Suivezmoi*.

(I) The father of the three immigrants of this family who came to America and their two sisters is not known, and though it is known that they were of the Derbyshire family, the English lineage has not been traced. Children: Joseph, mentioned below; Hannah, of Milford, Connecticut, married (first) John Ufford, and (second) Captain John Beard; Elizabeth, of Stratford, Connecticut, married John Booth; Thomas, settled in Roxbury, Massachusetts, married Emma ——; Robert, of Rhode Island, married Dorothy (Harbottle) Lamb, widow of T. Lamb.

(II) Joseph Hawley, the American immigrant ancestor, was born in Derbyshire, England, in 1603, and died May 20, 1690. He was a yeoman, and evidently of good education and abilities, for he was the town recorder, 1650-66, at Stratford, Connecticut, where he settled soon after coming to this country. He married Katherine Birdsey, who died at Stratford, June 25, 1692. He bought lands at Stratford in 1650 of Richard Mills, and from time to time he received grants of land when the common lands were divided. He was representative to the general assembly thirty times in thirty-three years, and evidently one of the most prominent men of the town of that time. In his will he bequeathed land at Parwidge, in Derbyshire, to his son Samuel. This is the town of Parwich, nine miles from old Derby. Children, born at Stratford: Samuel, 1647; Joseph Jr., born January 9, 1649; Elizabeth, January 26, 1651; Ebenezer, September 16, 1654; Hannah, May 26, 1657; Ephraim, mentioned below; John Esq., June 14, 1661; Mary, July 16, 1663, married Captain John Coe.

(III) Ephraim, son of Joseph Hawley, was born at Stratford, August 7, 1659, and died there April 18, 1690. He married, December 4, 1683, Sarah, daughter of Captain Samuel and Elizabeth (Hollister) Welles, she was born September 29, 1664, and died June 29, 1694. Captain Samuel Welles was born in 1630, married Elizabeth, daughter of John and Joanna (Treat) Hollister. His mother was a sister of Governor Robert Treat. Captain Samuel was a son of Governor Thomas Welles, mentioned elsewhere in this work. Ephraim Hawley was a farmer. His inventory was dated May 14, 1690. His widow married (second) Lieutenant Agur Tomlinson. Children: Daniel, born September 20, 1684; Gideon, mentioned below; Abiah, September 19, 1690.

(IV) Gideon Hawley, son of Ephraim Hawley, was born at Stratford, January 30, 1687, and died February 16, 1730-1. He married, February 4, 1711, Anna Bennett, born in 1691, died November 14, 1727. Gideon lived at what was called Pequonnet, now Bridgeport. His estate was distributed April 23, 1734.

Children, born at Stratford: James, mentioned below; Zechariah, September 2, 1717; Gideon, 1719; Sarah, October 11, 1721; Abiah, 1723; Ann, 1724; Gideon, November 11, 1727, a missionary.

(V) Sergeant James Hawley, son of Gideon Hawley, was born at Stratford, now Bridgeport, January 29, 1713, and died October 7, 1746. He married, July 18, 1733, Eunice Jackson, born 1714, died September 6, 1796, daughter of Henry Jackson. His widow married Lieutenant Isaac Bennett. James was sergeant of militia. He followed farming in his native town. Children, born at Stratford: Benajah, 1734; Anna, November 6, 1735; Wolcott, April 15, 1737; Aaron, mentioned below; Captain David, 1741; Huldah, 1744; Deacon Elijah, December 30, 1744.

(VI) Major Aaron Hawley, son of James Hawley, was born in 1739, at Stratford, and died July 21, 1803. He was a farmer at Bridgeport. He lived in the old red house on the Hawley place from 1787 to 1803, and bequeathed it to his son Captain Samuel. He married, November 24, 1759, Elizabeth, daughter of Captain Ezra and Abigail (Hall) Hawley; she was born in 1732, and died July 8, 1776. He married (second) July 10, 1777, Sarah Comstock, born November 12, 1747, died May 3, 1786, daughter of John and Deborah (Welch) Comstock. He married (third) Rachel Pickett. Children, born at Bridgeport: Samuel, April 15, 1761; Gideon, July 20, 1763; Isaac, April 30, 1765; Hannah, August 6, 1768; Aaron, mentioned below; Anson, August 4, 1778; John, May 15, 1780; Charles and Sarah, twins, September 28, 1782; William, March 30, 1785.

(VII) Aaron (2), son of Aaron (1) Hawley, was born at Bridgeport, June 15, 1774, and died there June 28, 1810. He married Grissell, daughter of Captain Stephen and Mary (Halberton) Summers, of Stratford; she was born May 15, 1773, and died September 5, 1853. Children, born at Bridgeport: Deacon Stephen, mentioned below; Caroline, March 22, 1798; Daniel, August 12, 1800; Susan, December 28, 1802; Jane Elizabeth, September 27, 1805; Matilda, July 7, 1807.

(VIII) Deacon Stephen Hawley, son of Aaron (2) Hawley, was born at Bridgeport, September 6, 1795, and died there November 4, 1861. He was a merchant in Bridgeport, and later engaged in the insurance and banking business. He was prominent in church work, was connected with the Congregational church, and leader of a movement for the organization of the First Presbyterian Church of Bridgeport, in which he was a ruling elder to the time of his death. He married (first) in Bridgeport, Temperance Wheeler, born October 1, 1794, died 1857, daughter of Samuel and Julia (Odell) Wheeler. He married (second) in 1858, Eliza A. Rose. Children, born at Bridgeport: Captain Aaron, 1816; Daniel W., mentioned below; Frederick S., July 19, 1822; Henry, February 9, 1829.

(IX) Daniel Wheeler, son of Deacon Stephen Hawley, was born at Bridgeport, December 25, 1818, and died August 19, 1866. He was educated in the public schools of his native town, and learned the trade of saddler and harness maker. He was in business in Bridgeport for many years, making and dealing in harness and saddles. He served in the civil war as artificer of the Second Connecticut Light Battery, and so well was his work done that the harness and other equipment that was made under his charge for the battery, and the care and maintenance of same, earned him especial commendation from his superior officers, and prominent mention in the history of the battery. At the opening of the war he laid aside a prosperous business, volunteered at the enlistment of the battery, refused official honors, and gave his services for the pay of a private until the close of hostilities. He was a giant in stature. He contracted a fever in the service, and never recovered his health and died soon after returning to his home. He married, May 7, 1846, Henrietta Sarah Hopkins, born May 24, 1824, died September 3, 1887, daughter of Royal and Sally (Minton) Hopkins. Her father was in the navy in the war of 1812,

served under Commodore Perry at the battle of Lake Erie, and was at one time on the staff of General Winfield Scott. He was the original inventor of a carding machine which he manufactured in Vermont and introduced in the southern states, where it was extensively used. Later he located in Canada, and was driven out at the beginning of the war of 1812, when he enlisted in the navy. Children of Daniel W. Hawley: Roswell Mason, born September 7, 1847, died in childhood; Henry S., mentioned below.

(X) Henry S., son of Daniel Wheeler Hawley, was born at Bridgeport, August 12, 1851, and attended the public schools of his native town. From 1874 to 1883 he was engaged in bridge construction and in promoting and constructing railroads. He was a contractor on the Grand Trunk railroad, constructing the section from Valparaiso, Indiana, to Thornton, Illinois. He purchased at master's sale the Chicago & Southern railroad, now owned by the Chicago & Grand Trunk Railway Company, and was one of the promoters of the Chicago & Wisconsin railroad. In 1883 he was elected president of the Chicago, Wisconsin & Minnesota railroad during its construction from Chicago to Schleisingerville, Wisconsin. He was general agent and purchased the right of way of portions of the Chicago Great Western railroad, and upon its completion he became its general agent of traffic and leases in Chicago from 1883 to 1890. He was general agent for traffic in Chicago of the Chicago & Northern Pacific railroad from 1890 to 1893, and became general agent and treasurer for the receivers of the same railroad, 1893 to 1897. He was general agent and treasurer of the reorganized company, the Chicago Terminal Transfer railroad, 1897 to 1899, and traffic manager, treasurer and assistant secretary from 1899 to 1902. He is now president and director of the Railroad Supply Company of Chicago, manufacturers and dealers in railroad supplies. In politics he is a Republican, and was very active in the presidential campaigns of 1880, 1884 and 1888, in Illinois. He was secretary of the Union League of America in 1872-4. He is a communicant of the Protestant Episcopal Church, and senior warden of the Church of the Redeemer in Chicago. He is a member of the board of trustees of the endowment fund of the Diocese of Chicago. He is also a member of Hyde Park Council, No. 582, Royal Arcanum; the Royal League of Chicago; the South Shore Country Club; the Chicago Automobile Club; the Chicago Yacht Club; the Church Club; the Engineers' Club of New York; and the New England Society of Chi-

cago. He was lay delegate to the General Convention of the Episcopal church held at Cincinnati in 1910. His summer house is at Wicklow, Rhode Island.

He married, November 3, 1880, Lillie Leah Ferguson, born July 24, 1857, at St. Charles, Iowa, daughter of William G. and Leah (Hill) Ferguson. She removed from her native town to Rockford, Illinois, and thence to Chicago. Her father was a native of Scotland, son of Duncan Ferguson, a civil engineer, who came to America and settled in Rockford, Illinois. Children of Mr. and Mrs. Hawley: 1. Royal Duncan, born in Chicago, October 15, 1881; educated in public schools of Hyde Park; and was for three years a student in the University of Wisconsin; married, October 15, 1907, Marguerite Lewis; resides in San Francisco, California, and is a dealer in railroad supplies. 2. Philip Ferguson, born in Chicago, September 14. 1883; educated in public schools; graduated from Sheffield Scientific School of Yale University, class of 1906; now assistant purchasing agent of Railroad Supply Company of Chicago. He married, October 22, 1912, Evelyn DeWitt, of Chicago, daughter of Rev. William C. DeWitt, Dean of the Western Theological Seminary of Chicago. 3. Henry Stephen Jr., born September 20, 1897, died March 8, 1898.

BRIGHAM-SMITH The surname Brigham is from the Saxon word *brigg* (bridge) and *ham* (house). There is a manor of the name in county Cumberland, adjoining Scotland, of which in ancient days it was a part. The barony from which the family name is derived is now generally called by another name, Cockermouth. The old Brigham castle was one of the strongest in its day, built largely of material taken from an old Roman castle in the vicinity. As late as 1648 it was garrisoned, and stood siege for a month. After it was taken it was nearly destroyed, but at last accounts a small part was still habitable. From this manor the English and American Brighams get their names, and all probably are descended from the Brigham family there.

(I) Thomas Brigham, immigrant ancestor, was born in 1603, in England. He embarked at London for New England, April 18, 1635, in the ship "Susan and Ellen", Edward Payne, master. He settled at Watertown, Massachusetts. In 1637 he had a fourteen-acre lot there, bought of John Doggett, situated in a part later annexed to Cambridge. He built his house in Cambridge on a lot containing three acres and a half. His neighbors were Joseph, Simon and Isaac Crosby. His home

was about two-thirds of a mile from Harvard College, and at one point abutted on Charles river. He resided there until 1648. He was admitted a freeman April 18, 1637, and became a leading citizen. He was selectman in 1640-42-47, and constable in 1639-42. He made a specialty of raising hogs, and in 1647 owned a third of all the swine in the town. He owned a windmill for grinding corn. He died December 8, 1653. His will was dated December 7, 1653, and proved October 3, 1654. He married Mercy Hurd, who is said to have come with her sister alone from England, owing to religious differences from which they suffered annoyance and persecution at home. After the death of Mr. Brigham she married (second) March 1, 1655, Edmund Rice, of Sudbury and Marlborough, by whom she had two daughters. She married (third) William Hunt, of Marlborough, who died in 1667. She died December 23, 1693, after being in her third widowhood twenty-six years. Children: Mary; Thomas, mentioned below; John, March 9, 1644; Hannah, March 9, 1649; Samuel, January 12, 1652-3.

(II) Thomas (2), son of Thomas (1) Brigham, was born about 1640, probably in Cambridge, and died in Marlborough, November 25, 1716. When his mother married Edmund Rice, Thomas went with her to Sudbury and Marlborough, and when he came of age he settled in Marlborough near Williams Pond, in the southwest part of the town. He was one of the purchasers of the old plantation Ockoocangansett, reserved originally for the Indians in Marlborough. On the old Brigham homestead on the south side of the present Forest street, about a score of rods from the highway at the foot of Crane Hill, is a slightly raised rectangular spot where rest the remains of the last of the Marlborough Indians. The first house in the homestead was destroyed by fire. In 1706 a frame house was built and became the ell of a house built by Gershom in 1724. The old house was used for a garrison during Queen Anne's war. The old ell was taken down in 1791, and the rest of the house occupied until 1859, and soon afterward it was torn down also. Thomas Brigham was a leading citizen and held various offices. His will was dated April 21, 1716, and he died November 25 following. He married (first) December 27, 1665, Mary, daughter of Henry and Elizabeth (Moore) Rice, granddaughter of Edmund Rice, the immigrant. He married (second) July 3, 1695, Susanna Shattuck, daughter of William, of Watertown, and widow first of Joseph Morse and (second) of John Fay, whose first wife was Mary, sister of Thomas Brigham. Children, born at Marlborough: Thomas, February 24, 1667; Nathan, June 17, 1671; David, August 11, 1673; Jonathan, February 22, 1675; David, April 12, 1678; Gershom, February 23, 1680; Elnathan, mentioned below; Mary, October 26, 1687; married Captain Jonas Houghton.

(III) Elnathan, son of Thomas Brigham, was born at Marlborough, March 7, 1683, and died at Mansfield or Coventry, Connecticut, April 10, 1758. He removed from Marlborough to Mansfield in 1717. He married, in 1705, Bethiah, who died in Coventry, April 15, 1765, aged eighty-two, daughter of William and Hannah (Brigham) Ward. Children, the six elder born at Marlborough, the other two at Mansfield: Uriah, April 30, 1706, died young; Jerusha; Priscilla, born April 3, 1709; Levinah, August 31, 1711; Prudence, January 28, 1715; Elnathan, April 7, 1716; Paul; Uriah, mentioned below.

(IV) Uriah, son of Elnathan Brigham, was born about 1723, and died in Coventry, January 25, 1777. He settled in Coventry. He was a patriot, and his anxiety for his country is believed to have hastened his death. He was very plain in all his tastes. He married (first) Lydia Ward, who died December 14, 1750; (second) Ann, daughter of Amos Richardson, of Coventry, May 28, 1754. Children by first wife, born at Coventry: Hannah, April 9, 1746; Captain Gershom, 1750. Children by second wife: Roger, October 28, 1755; Bethiah, July 14, 1757; Anna, October 14, 1759; Norman, December 2, 1761; Don Carlos, February 21, 1764; Cephas, mentioned below; Martha or Marcia, January 28, 1770; Lucy or Lucia, November 6, 1771.

(V) Cephas, son of Uriah Brigham, was born December 7, 1765, in Coventry, Connecticut, and died May 17, 1841. He resided at South Coventry, where he held various offices of trust and honor, and was representative to the general assembly. Children, born in South Coventry: Anna, married Roderick Dimock; Lucia, married Horace Russ; Sally, married, November 29, 1810, Artemas Russ; Uriah, married Emily Wright and Harriet Nye; Daniel R., mentioned below; Eveline L., married Gurdon Fuller; Maria, married, July 4, 1821, Levi Allen; Emily, married Roderick Dimock; Julia, married Abner Mason; Edwin G.

(VI) Daniel R., son of Cephas Brigham, was born in South Coventry, August 6, 1795, and died December 3, 1854. He lived at South Coventry. He married Eliza, daughter of George Needham; she was born January 6, 1796.

Children, born at South Coventry: Dan-

iel Watson, April 6, 1821; Henry Gray, April 13, 1823; Emily Wright, November 1, 1826; Frederick Benton, mentioned below; George N.; Edwin G., May 2, 1831, twin of George.

(VII) Frederick Benton, son of Daniel R. Brigham, was born at South Coventry, April 13, 1829, and died in New York City. He married Jane Smith, daughter of Roswell Smith (see Smith). Children: Frederick Everett, mentioned below; Charles.

(VIII) Frederick Everett (Brigham) Smith, son of Frederick Benton and Jane (Smith) Brigham, was born in Norwalk, Connecticut, March 15, 1857. He took his mother's name, and has been known from childhood as Frederick Everett Smith. He attended the public and high schools of New Britain, Connecticut. He began his business career as a clerk in the New Britain National Bank, was promoted from time to time, and remained with the bank for eight years and a half. He was bookkeeper for several houses and clerk in a hotel for a time. In April, 1882, he became a clerk in the offices of the New York & New England Railroad Company at New Britain, remaining in that position until July 1, 1883, when he accepted a position in the city office of the Union Pacific Railroad Company. Boston. Subsequently he was appointed auditor of the Connolton Valley Railroad, with offices at Canton, Ohio. Afterward he was with the Cleveland, Akron & Columbus Railroad Company in the passenger department, and became chief clerk and afterward traveling auditor of the Cleveland, Akron & Columbus Railroad. In 1889 he was elected auditor of the Zanesville & Ohio River Railroad Company, and held the office until 1894. In that year he removed to Lynn, Massachusetts, to accept the position of auditor of the Lynn & Boston Railroad, and continued until the road was consolidated with the Boston & Northern Railroad. In 1899 Mr. Smith came to Chicago and was made auditor of the Chicago Union Traction Company, which was reorganized in 1908 under the name of the Chicago Railway Company, in which he holds the responsible office of comptroller. He is a prominent Free Mason, having taken all the degrees in Scottish Rite Masonry to and including the thirty-second. He was made a Mason in Golden Fleece Lodge, of Lynn, of which he is a life member. He is a member of Sutton Chapter, Royal Arch Masons; Zebulon Council, Royal and Select Masters; Olivet Commandery, Knights Templar. He is a member of the Hamilton Club of Chicago, and the New England Society of Chicago. He is a Republican in politics, and non-sectarian in religion. His office is at 1165 North Clark street, Chicago.

He married, May 3, 1883, Helen Josephine McCoy, born in Brooklyn, New York, December 19, 1862. Child: Helen King, born at Akron, Ohio, August 12, 1885; educated in public and private schools at Zanesville, Ohio, public schools in Swampscott, Massachusetts, and college in Kalamazoo, Michigan; married, June 26, 1909, Franklin Balch, now living in Topsfield, Massachusetts, and has one daughter, Helen Balch, born November 28, 1910.

(The Smith Line).

Sergeant Francis Smith was born at Middletown, of one of the pioneer families of Connecticut, about 1685. He married, February 8, 1711, Hannah Hubbard of Glastonbury, Connecticut, and settled at Bolton, in that colony. Children, born at Bolton: Deborah, November 24, 1711; Hannah, March 6, 1714; Frances, February 29, 1716; Prudence, March 2, 1718; Jonathan, October 11, 1722; David, mentioned below; Martha, November 28, 1727; Noah, April 14, 1730; Ebenezer, February 18, 1731-2.

(II) David, son of Francis Smith, was born at Bolton, October 3, 1725. He married Eunice Jones. Children, born at Bolton: David, and Roswell, mentioned below.

(III) Roswell, son of David Smith, was born January 19, 1758. He married, November 11, 1790, Hannah Kingsbury, born January 8, 1769, at Vernon, and lived at Vernon, Connecticut. Children: Obediah K., born July 6, 1791; Fanny, January 2, 1793; Electa, December 28, 1794; Harriet, May 25, 1797; Mabel, July 30, 1799; Anna, April 11, 1802, died 1812; Roswell, mentioned below; Emily, April 28, 1809.

(IV) Roswell (2), son of Roswell (1) Smith, was born at Vernon, October 5, 1804. He married Mariva King, at Vernon, in March, 1832. Among their children was Jane, born April 17, 1833, died November 30, 1869, married Frederick Benton Brigham (see Brigham).

FOOTE Nathaniel Foote, immigrant ancestor, was born about 1593. He came probably from Shalford, Colchester, England, and settled in Watertown, Massachusetts. He took the freeman's oath in 1633. He removed to Wethersfield, Connecticut, where he was one of the first settlers. In 1640 he had a home lot of ten acres on the east side of Broad street. He was a farmer. He was a deputy to the general court in 1644. He married, in England, about 1615, Elizabeth Deming, born about 1595, died

July 8, 1683, sister of John Deming, a first settler of Wethersfield. She married (second) Thomas Welles. Nathaniel Foote died in 1644. Children: Elizabeth, born about 1616; Nathaniel, about 1620; Mary; Robert, mentioned below; Frances; Sarah; Rebecca.

(II) Robert, son of Nathaniel Foote, was born in 1629, died in 1681. He was a lieutenant. He lived in Wethersfield and Wallingford, and in 1669 in Brandon, Connecticut. He married, in 1659, Sarah, daughter of William and Frances Potter; she married (second) in 1686, Aaron Blanchley, of Branford. Children: Nathaniel, mentioned below; Sarah, born February 12, 1662; Joseph, March 6, 1664; Elizabeth, March 6, 1666; Samuel, May 14, 1668; John, July 24, 1670; Stephen and Isaac, twins, December 14, 1672.

(III) Nathaniel (2), son of Robert Foote, was born April 13, 1660. He married Tabitha Bishop, of Guilford, Connecticut, who died 1715. He resided at Brandon, Connecticut, and died in 1714. Children: Elizabeth, baptized March, 1696; Dorcas, March, 1696; Nathaniel, June, 1696; Daniel, February, 1697; Moses, mentioned below; Abraham, 1706; Abigail, 1708.

(IV) Moses, son of Nathaniel (2) Foote, was born January 13, 1702. He married, June 22, 1726, Mary, daughter of John Byington; she died January, 1740. He married (second) November 5, 1740, Ruth, daughter of John Butler. He died February, 1770, she died August 7, 1792, at Gill, Massachusetts. He lived in that part of Waterbury, Connecticut, now Plymouth. Four of his sons were in the revolutionary war. Children: Rebecca, born April 10, 1727; Lydia, March 23, 1728; Dorothy, March 26, 1729; David, November 11, 1730; Ruth, August 1, 1732; Moses, August 4, 1734; Mary, October 9, 1739; Aaron, July 6, 1738; Ebenezer, May 21, 1740; Obed, mentioned below; Lydia, November 30, 1743; Dorothy, November 10, 1749.

(V) Obed, son of Moses Foote, was born November 25, 1741. He married, December 3, 1761, Mary, daughter of Rev. Samuel Todd; she was born September 11, 1742, and married (second) March 26, 1798, Rev. Jonathan Leavitt, of Heath, Massachusetts; she died May 16, 1816. Mr. Foote died September 21, 1797. In May, 1780, he moved to Rowe, Massachusetts, where he purchased about 1,000 acres of land. In 1784 he moved to Gill, Massachusetts, where he purchased the farm on which he lived until his death. Children: Asenath, born September 19, 1762; Mary Dorothea, June 11, 1764; Bernice, June 5, 1766; Sedate, March 5, 1768; Samuel, April 7, 1770; Chloe, March 21, 1772; Lydia, May .

15, 1774; Erastus, mentioned below; Philena, September 22, 1779; Rhoda Ann, January 1, 1781; Obed, April 27, 1787.

(VI) Erastus, son of Obed Foote, was born September 19, 1777. He married, 1812, Susan, daughter of Colonel Moses Carlton, of Wiscasset, Maine; she was born January 28, 1796, and died June 28, 1817. He married (second) July 9, 1820, Eliza, daughter of Colonel Moses Carlton, of Wiscasset, Maine; she was born July 1, 1798, and died June 27, 1880. He was admitted to the bar in Northampton, Massachusetts, and began his professional career at Camden, Maine. He was successively county attorney, senator of Massachusetts legislature, senator of Maine legislature immediately after the organization of Maine into a state and attorney-general of Maine. This last office he held for twelve successive years, and gave tone and character to the criminal jurisprudence of the state, alike honorable to himself and highly appreciated by the public. He died July 14, 1856, at Wiscasset, Maine. Children: Mary Wood, born December 20, 1813; Erastus Miles, August 31, 1815; Susan Eliza, January 1, 1817; Erastus, mentioned below; Mary Todd, December 25, 1823; Abigail, August 31, 1825; Ann Butler, October 8, 1827.

(VII) Erastus (2), son of Erastus (1) Foote, was born September 6, 1821, in Wiscasset, Maine. He married, June 1, 1847, Sarah Page Wood, daughter of Wilmot Wood, of Wiscasset, Maine. He prepared for college at Augusta, Maine, and graduated from Bowdoin in 1843, afterwards practiced law in Wiscasset. In 1868 he moved to Chicago, Illinois, where he engaged in the real estate business until the time of his death, February 20, 1893. He was a man of singularly genial character, and was highly respected and loved by the community in which he lived. Children: Wilmot Wood, born May 21, 1848; Erastus, mentioned below; Emma Louise, October 27, 1851; Eliza Carlton, November 10, 1854; Harriete Cobb, November 15, 1859.

(VIII) Erastus (3), son of Erastus (2) Foote, was born in Wiscasset, Maine, March 4, 1850, and received his early education in the public schools of his native town. When a young man he went to Boston and worked for two years as clerk in a wholesale grocery house. In 1868 he followed his father to Chicago, Illinois, and became a clerk in the iron foundry and manufacturing establishment of N. S. Bouton & Company. This concern was finally merged in the Union Foundry Company, of which Mr. Foote became an officer. In 1883 the Dearborn Foundry Company was established and Mr. Foote has been president since. His office is at the plant, 1525 Dear-

born street, Chicago. He owns a summer home in his native town and spends as much time as possible at Wiscasset. He is a member of the Union League Club of Chicago, the Western Society of Engineers, and the New England Society of Chicago. In politics he is a Republican, in religion a Presbyterian. He is unmarried.

(The Wood Line).

(I) Henry Wood, immigrant ancestor, was in Plymouth as early as September 16, 1641, when he bought of John Dunham, the younger, his house and land at Plymouth, for £7. He was among the Plymouth men reported as able to bear arms. He removed to Yarmouth, where his children Samuel and Sarah were born. In 1649 he returned to Plymouth. In 1665 he settled at Middleborough. He was not among the twenty-six original purchasers, but received the share set out to John Shaw, and part of his original homestead is still in the possession of his descendants. He was the original proprietor of the Little Lotmen's Purchase. His home was near the General Abiel Washburn place. He was admitted a freeman of the colony in 1648; was grand juror 1648-56-59-68 and often on other juries. He was one of the complainants against the rates at Plymouth. In 1665 he had one share of thirty acres on the west side of the Nenasket river. His name is sometimes spelled Wood, alias Atwood, in the records. His son Samuel and son-in-law John Nelson were appointed administrators of his estate, October 29, 1670. He married, April 25, 1644, Abigail Jenney, daughter of John, who owned land in Lakenham, now Carver, April 18, 1644. Their sons Abiel and Samuel were among the original members of the church at Middleborough. Their son John made a nuncupative will dated April 13, 1673, bequeathing to his two youngest brothers, sister Mary and mother Abigail, and later the court ordered the eldest brother Samuel to give over his land to the youngest brothers, Abiel and James. Children: Samuel, May 25, 1647; Jonathan, January 1, 1649; David, October 17, 1651; John; Joseph; Benjamin; Abiel, mentioned below; James; Sarah; Abigail; Susanna.

(II) Abiel, son of Henry Wood, was born in 1657, and died October 10, 1719. He married Abiah Bowen. Children: Elnathan, 1686; Abiah, 1688; Abiel, 1691; Timothy, 1693; Jerusha, 1695; Ebenezer, mentioned below; Judah, 1700; Thomas, 1703.

(III) Ebenezer, son of Abiel Wood, was born in 1697, died in 1768. He married Lydia Lovell. Children: Silas, born 1729; Timothy, 1732; Sarah, 1734; Ebenezer, 1736;

Lydia, 1738; Simeon, 1740; Levi, 1740; Abiel, mentioned below; Mary, 1746.

(IV) General Abiel Wood, son of Ebenezer Wood, was born July 22, 1744, and died August 11, 1811. He married, December 19, 1765, Betsey Tinkham, born July 14, 1750, died November 7, 1802. He married (second) October, 1804, Mrs. Sally Sayward, of Old York. He was a general of militia, and an officer in the revolution. Children: Ebenezer, born August 11, 1770; Abiel, mentioned below; Joseph, February 26, 1774; Ebenezer, May 4, 1776; Betsey, June 14, 1778; Joseph Tinkham, April 4, 1780; Lydia, April 13, 1782; Hartley, November 13, 1784; Ebenezer, November 29, 1786; Henry, October 9, 1788; Susan, September 2, 1790.

(V) Major Abiel Wood, son of General Abiel Wood, was born July 22, 1772, and died October 26, 1831. He was a prominent citizen, and major in the militia. He married, in 1793, Hannah Hodge, who died May 14, 1814. He married (second) Jane Anderson, November 26, 1818, who died March 15, 1827. He married (third) Lydia Theobald, in 1830. Children: Betsey, born October, 1794; Willmot, mentioned below; Helen, July 13, 1799; Isabella, 1803; Abiel, February 22, 1807; Hannah; Margaret.

(VI) Willmot Wood, son of Major Abiel Wood, was born February 2, 1796. He married, October 21, 1822, Emeline Page, who died in 1867. Among their children was Sarah Page Wood, born 1826, died 1898, married Erastus Foote (see Foote).

WALKER The surname Walker is of obvious origin, one of the oldest of English surnames. A branch of the family went to the north of Ireland early in the seventeenth century and became in later generations connected with the Scotch settlers there and known as Scotch-Irish. According to the records of 1890 the family is still numerous in the Scotch province of Ulster. Of 144 births recorded in Ireland to Walker families in that year, eighty were in the Protestant counties of Antrim, Down and Londonderry. At the time of the siege of Derry, Rev. George Walker was assistant governor and a distinguished figure. He was suspected by his men and violently opposed by his enemies. He was one of the leaders named in the act of attainder passed by King James's parliament at Dublin, May 7, 1689. He fought during the siege, and afterward was sent to King William with an address signed by the chief defenders of the town, setting out August 9, 1689, by way of Scotland. He published an account of the siege which became popular. His account was attacked in public print and defended by himself and friends. Among the signers of the memorial to King William we find the names of two George Walkers and one Robert Walker. From this Londonderry family of Walkers are descended the Walkers of this sketch.

(I) Soon after 1719, when Nutfield, New Hampshire, afterward Londonderry, was settled by the Scotch-Irish, we find among the settlers Alexander Walker. In the petition brought from Londonderry, Ireland, dated March 26, 1718, to Governor Shute, of Massachusetts, asking for a grant of land, we find the names of two Robert Walkers, James Walker and William Walker. It is reasonable to believe that the first settler at Londonderry was son or nephew of one of these Robert Walkers of Londonderry, Ireland, and that Robert, born 1708, was his son. Alexander Walker had a grant of land at Nutfield in 1720, recorded March 2, 1720-21. He probably died soon, as little is known of him.

(II) Robert Walker, believed to be son of Alexander Walker, lived at Bradford, Massachusetts, where he was elder in the church, according to his gravestone in Forest Hill Cemetery, Derry, formerly the old village of Londonderry. He died October 10, 1777, at Londonderry, aged sixty-nine. He had a pew in the Londonderry church in 1755.

(II) Andrew Walker, brother of Robert and son of Alexander, as indicated by all the evidence found, was born about 1710, in Ireland, and probably came in 1718 or 1720 with his father's family, but he may have been born after that date. He went from Londonderry soon after the town of New Boston, New Hampshire, was settled, and built a grain and saw mill to accommodate the settlers, under a contract with the town, on the site of the Dodge and Bentley mills of a later date, and he agreed to keep the mill in order and make reasonable charges. In 1753 complaints were made of his not keeping to his agreement and there was friction with the town for a time. Children: Andrew, married Ruth Woodbury, and settled at Unity, New Hampshire; Alexander, died 1776, a soldier in the revolutionary war; James, also a soldier in the revolution; Robert, mentioned below; Peggy, married Jonathan Major, a baker in the American army.

(III) Robert, son of Andrew Walker, was born at New Boston, about 1760, and died at Acworth, New Hampshire, in 1801. He married Deborah Woodbury, whose ancestors were among the early settlers of Beverly, Massachusetts, and vicinity. He settled in Acworth. Children: Asa, married Betsey

Mathewson; Jesse Woodbury, mentioned below; Sally E., married Alexander Walker; Betsey, married Kinsman Marshall; Roswell, married Florinda Clark, and (second) Lydia S. McMillan.

(IV) Jesse Woodbury, son of Robert Walker, was born September 18, 1796, at New Boston, New Hampshire, and settled early in life in Whitefield, same state, where he was a farmer. He married Polly Griffin White, born June 10, 1796, in Weare, New Hampshire, daughter of Henry and Elizabeth (Dustin) White. The latter was born in Weare, about 1771, a great-granddaughter of Hannah Dustin, whose heroic exploits in Indian warfare are commemorated by two granite monuments in New England. Children: Mary A., married Simeon Sanborn; R. Henry; Betsey J.; Calvin W.; Alice; Deborah W.; Plummer S.; Franklin P., mentioned below; Roswell M., lives at Groveton, New Hampshire; Lucetta, died unmarried in 1871.

(V) Franklin Pierce, son of Jesse Woodbury Walker, was born at Whitefield, New Hampshire, June 26, 1836. He was a farmer and hotel proprietor at Whitefield and one of the best known and most popular citizens of that town. He died there August 31, 1911. In politics he was a Democrat, in religion a Liberal. He married Betsey Wales, born February 28, 1835, in London, New Hampshire, died April 30, 1908, in Chicago, Illinois. She was a daughter of Samuel T. and Dolly E. (Staniels) Wales of Chichester, New Hampshire. Samuel T. Wales was a son of Samuel Wales, born August 29, 1771, in Canton, Massachusetts. Children: Sarah Jane, Mary Elizabeth, Ellen Maria, and Emery Staniels, mentioned below. The eldest died in Salt Lake City, wife of James Madden. The second is Mrs. William W. Sanborn, residing in Concord, New Hampshire. The third wife of Edgar Atwood died in Pembroke, New Hampshire.

(VI) Emery Staniels, only son of Franklin Pierce Walker, was born at Whitefield, New Hampshire, September 29, 1856. He attended the public schools of his native town. He commenced his business career as clerk in the department store of Jordan, Marsh & Company, of Boston, where he was employed for two years. He left this position on account of ill health, and after a prolonged sickness he began to study law. In 1875, however, at the age of nineteen, he was made a partner in the firm of Glidden & Walker, which established the business now controlled by the American Wringer Company. In 1876 he became a student in the high school of the Chicago Atheneum, entered the Union College

of Law in Chicago in 1879, and was graduated in due course in the class of 1881. He was admitted to the Illinois bar in 1881, and has been practicing law in Chicago since that time. He has been very successful and prominent in his profession, and has the reputation of being a persistent and courageous fighter in any cause which he espouses. He is, perhaps, best known to the public as the leader in the fight against the smoke nuisance in Chicago, and as the first lawyer to win a case in a prosecution under the ordinances. He secured a verdict against the New York Life Building of $1,500 for not complying with the law, and this verdict became a precedent in prosecuting other offenders. His vigorous crusade against the violators of the smoke laws ultimately made the air cleaner and the city more healthful. He has also been active in the prosecution of violations of the liquor law, especially that prohibiting selling on Sunday. Mr. Walker was a leader in the movement resulting in the contribution of a large fund for the relief of the earthquake sufferers in Italy. He is a member of the Chicago Bar Association; the Union League Club of Chicago; the Press Club of Chicago; the New England Society of Chicago. In politics he is a Republican. He is non-sectarian in religion.

He married, January 1, 1882, Placentia J. Paranteau, born in Troy, New York, November 12, 1855, daughter of Michael and Clementine Paranteau. Children: 1. Edna, born in Chicago, November 14, 1882; educated in public schools and at the Lewis Institute, Chicago. 2. Placentia (called Bessie), born April 23, 1884, a student in the University of Chicago. 3. Emery Sumner, born in Loudon, New Hampshire, June 4, 1885; educated in public and private schools and at Illinois University. 4. Stanley Franklin, born November 19, 1887; educated in public schools and at Faribault Military School, Minnesota. 5. Emerson, born April 11, 1890.

UPHAM This name occurred as a surname very early in the period of the first use of surnames. The name of Hugo de Upham occurred in the Charter Rolls in England in 1208, when he received royal grants of lands and honors. His name signified Hugo of Upham, and Upham as the name of a place was known long before the use of surnames. John Upham and Phineas, his son, of New England, added the final "e" to their names, but their descendants pretty generally dropped this final letter and the name again assumed its original form.

It is of Saxon or Norman origin, and

early became known in Ireland, as well as most other parts of the British Isles.

(I) John Upham, the first of the name known to have come to America, was born in England, it is believed in Somersetshire, but nothing is definitely known of his origin. He came with the Hull colony to Weymouth, when his family comprised the following: John Upham, aged thirty-five years; Elizabeth, aged twenty-six; John Jr., aged seven; Nathaniel, five, and Elizabeth, three. Rev. Joseph Hull was a native of Somersetshire, and from the fact that John Upham came with his colony it is probable that he also was born there. Rev. Hull had been rector at Northleigh, in Devon, and set sail with his followers, March 20, 1635, from Weymouth, England, for lands in the Massachusetts Bay colony. Forty-six days later the company arrived, and on July 2 of the same year, having gained permission of the general court, they located at Wessaguscus, their future home, which they named Weymouth, in memory of their sailing port in England. John Upham gave his age as thirty-five years, which would have made the date of his birth 1600, and although the date of his birth, according to his gravestone, would have been three years earlier, the former statement is generally believed to be correct. Sarah Upham is believed to have been his sister, and his wife, Elizabeth Upham, was the mother of his children. Her name is thought to have been Webb before her marriage, from her name appearing in the will of Richard Webb, which was made in his old age, in 1671. John Upham was admitted freeman on September 2, 1635, and in 1643 he became a selectman. The following year the general court empowered him, with two others, to "end small causes," at Weymouth, which shows him to have been a man of judgment and good sense in considering the rights of others. He also served as selectman, 1645-47. He remained in Weymouth until 1648 and from then until 1650 no record is found of his name, although between those two dates he removed to Malden, having made his home at Weymouth for at least thirteen years. Several persons from Charlestown organized themselves into a church and settled at Malden, and I mo. 22d. 1651, John Upham signed a petition as selectman in Malden. About 1654 the church members at Malden were at odds with the general court because they had elected their minister without reference to other churches, but they again found favor by making acknowledgment of their offense to the court and to the other churches. In 1657, with two others, John Upham was appointed by the general court to "end general

small causes" at Malden, for one year, and his name appears frequently in the town records in various connections. In 1671 he declared his intention of marriage with Katherine, widow of Angell Hollard, at which time he declared he had no intention of receiving any estate or appurtenance belonging to her, and especially any money or estate from her former husband. She is believed to have been Kathryn, wife of Angell Hollard, who appears on the list of passengers from England in the Hull company. In 1678 John Upham is mentioned as one of the settlers of Worcester, but his will has not been found. His first wife, Elizabeth, died between December 2, 1670, and August 14, 1671, when he was about to contract a marriage with Katherine Hollard. Each passenger and half passenger (under twelve years of age) of the Hull company was allotted a certain number of acres of land, and from the number allotted John Upham he must have one more child than mentioned in the list of passengers, so that it is supposed his son Phineas (spelled in the records also Phinehas and Phynehas), who was born in 1635, may have been born while on the voyage from England or very soon after the family arrived in their new home. Two daughters were born in America, Mary and Priscilla, and there was an adopted son, John Upham. John Upham died February 25, 1681, and was buried in the old burying ground at Malden. His gravestone and that of several of his descendants are in a very fair state of preservation. He was pious, upright in demeanor, honored and respected by his fellows, and held several important offices. He was a pioneer settler in Weymouth, Malden and Worcester, and was often called upon to settle estates or manage affairs for widows and orphans. He was a deacon in the church twenty-four years at least, and educated his sons to become useful citizens, one becoming a minister and another an officer in the army. His children were: John, Nathaniel, Elizabeth, Phineas, Mary and Priscilla, and he had an adopted son, John.

(II) Lieutenant Phineas Upham, son of John and Elizabeth Upham, was the only son in the family who left posterity. As before mentioned, he was born in 1635, but whether between the making of the passenger list of the Hull Company and the time of sailing on the voyage to the New World, or whether he was born very soon after the landing of the company, is not known. He performed valuable service in King Philip's war. According to the Malden records he became owner of land in Malden in 1663-64. In 1671-73, with others, he surveyed the road from Cambridge

284 NEW ENGLAND.

to Malden. On July 8, 1673, he was allotted land at Worcester. He received the commission of lieutenant about 1675, and his name is found frequently in the history of events during King Philip's war. He was lieutenant of the fourth company of the Massachusetts regiment of which Gen. Josiah Winslow, governor of Plymouth colony, was commander-in-chief, and Samuel Appleton, of Ipswich, was major. Captain Isaac Johnson commanded the fourth company, and when he was killed at the beginning of the storming of Fort Canonicus and battle at Great Swamp fort, Lieutenant Upham, next in rank, commanded the company until he was himself wounded. He died in Malden in 1676, and in the records of the general court at their fall term in that year it is noted that the court ordered his bills of charge from surgeons and doctors be paid, and that Ruth Upham, his widow, be paid £10 from the treasury of the county, "in consideration of the long service her husband did for his country, the great loss of the widow by his death, being left with seven small children, not able to carry on their affairs, for the support of herself and family." Ruth Upham died January 18, 1696-97, aged sixty years, and was buried at Malden. In the record of Malden marriages the following entry is to be found: "Phineas Upham and Ruth Wood, 14d. 2 m. '58, by me, Richard Russell." The children of this couple were all born at Malden, and were as follows: Phineas, May 22, 1659; Nathaniel, 1661; Ruth, 1664, died 1676; John; Elizabeth; Thomas, 1668; Richard, 1675.

(III) John (2), third son of Lieut. Phineas and Ruth (Wood) Upham, was born December 9, 1666, and died at Malden, June 9, 1733. He married Abigail Hayward (in one account written Howard), 1688, daughter of Samuel Hayward, and died August 23, 1717. John Upham married (second) Tamzen Ong, 1717-18. Children: John, born 1690; Samuel; Abigail, 1698; Ezekiel, 1700; David, 1702; Jacob, died in infancy.

(IV) Samuel, second son of John (2) and Abigail (Hayward) Upham, was born in 1691, in Malden, and his will was dated February 1, 1761, at Leicester, to which place he removed some time before. He married Mary, daughter of Lazarus Grover. Children: Mary, born 1715-16; Abigail, 1718; Mercy, 1720; Samuel, 1722; Jonathan; Ebenezer, 1726; Jacob, 1729; Phebe, 1731, died in 1738; John, 1733, died in 1736; William, 1735, died in 1738.

(V) Jonathan, second son of Samuel and Mary (Grover) Upham, was born in 1724, probably in Malden, and died March 30, 1802,

aged seventy-seven years, having lived most of the time at Charlton and Brimfield. In 1759 the town of Charlton voted him £26 13s 4d, "for setting up the frame of the church building." He married, 1750, in Leicester, Martha Tucker, and (second), probably 1752-53, at Charlton, ——— Corbin, died in April, 1816. Children: Bathsheba, born February 5, 1752; Jonathan, November 30, 1753, died young; Jonathan, December 8, 1754, died young; Martha, May 9, 1756; Jonathan; Esther, December 4, 1762; Mercy, January 14, 1765; Nancy, February 25, 1767; Hannah, July 8, 1768; Phebe, September 11, 1772, died in infancy; Phebe, April 9, 1773; Anne, February 4, 1774.

(VI) Jonathan (2), eldest son of Jonathan (1) Upham and his second wife, who reached maturity, was born February 27, 1759, and died April 2, 1840, at Westminster, Massachusetts. He lived at Brimfield and Holland, and served in the revolution. He afterwards received a pension and in his old age went to live with his son Alvin, who had settled at Westminster, where his death occurred. He lived a number of years at Holland, where four of his children were born, and the others were probably born at Brimfield. He married Sarah Upham, his second cousin, daughter of Ezekiel and Rebecca Upham, her line of descent being as follows: John, the emigrant; Phineas, John (2) and Ezekiel. Jonathan and Sarah Upham had children: Rebecca, born 1782; Patty, December 5, 1784; Walter, April 25, 1787; Calvin, June 28, 1789; Bathsheba, June 27, 1791; Sally, June 18, 1794; Erastus, September 1, 1796; Alvin; Diantha, May 4, 1802; Horace, April 14, 1806.

(VII) Alvin, fourth son of Jonathan (2) and Sarah (Upham) Upham, was born August 2, 1799, at Holland, Massachusetts, and died in 1852, at Niles, Michigan. For many years he was engaged in the manufacture of cane-seated chairs at Westminster, and his output was sold in many parts of the state, as he had wagons on the road to take orders and deliver the same. A business firm got into debt to him for a large sum of money and he employed Franklin Pierce, who afterwards became president, to recover the money owing. Owing to delay of the suit, during which time the defending firm placed a valuable piece of their property in hands where it could not be claimed in judgment, the claimant was unable to get any satisfaction, and this resulted finally in his having to give up his business at Westminster. With his wife and eight children he removed to Niles, Michigan, dying there a few months after his arrival. The remainder of the family later removed to Racine, Wisconsin, where the older ones found employment and the younger ones continued their education. Mr. Upham was a man of superior intellect and ability and was characterized as a fond, indulgent father, a courteous and hospitable host and friend, and popular with all who knew him. He said grace before meals, held family prayer, and read daily from the Scriptures to the members of his household. His mother lived with him many years and passed away at his home when over ninety years old. He was not only a good husband and father, but a loving and dutiful son, and his fifty-two years of life were filled with deeds of kindness and thought for the happiness of others. All his children became prominent and useful members of society and filled their places in the world with dignity and honor. He married Sarah Derby, born at Westminster, February 26, 1800, died at Racine, in September, 1878, daughter of Ezra and Ruth (Puffer) Derby, of Westminster. Children: 1. Calvin Hoadley. 2. Sarah Maria, born October 20, 1829; married Porter P. Heywood, at Racine, in 1856, and some years later moved to Chicago; two children. 3. Nathan Derby, born May 18, 1832; married Sarah C. Miller. 4. Angeanette, born April 5, 1834; married, at Niles, July 25, 1861, Joseph Lyford Peavy, an officer of the First Michigan Infantry in the war of the rebellion, who died, and she was in business in Racine at one time. She published a newspaper at Shawano in 1879, and was elected superintendent of public instruction in Colorado, being the first woman elected to a state office in the United States. Mr. and Mrs. Peavy had one child. 5. Ellen Pauline, born February 5, 1836; married Hiram C. Russell, of Weyauwega, Wisconsin, November 16, 1857, and died at Clinton, Illinois, April 16, 1864; two children. 6. Charles Mandell, born September 21, 1837; married Julia Parsons, and located at Shawano. 7. Erastus Roberts, died 1847, aged about eight years. 8. William Henry, born May 3, 1841; entered the Second Wisconsin Infantry in 1861, was shot through the lungs at Bull Run, in July, 1861, and reported dead, but was held a prisoner of war six months. He was appointed to the United States Military Academy by President Lincoln, and served in the regular army, but resigned and engaged in lumber business at Marshfield, Wisconsin. He was governor of Wisconsin, 1895-97. He married Mary C. Kelly. 9. Mary Eliza, born April 29, 1843; married Hiram C. Russell, of Shawano, December 19, 1867; fourteen children.

(VIII) Calvin Hoadley, eldest child of Alvin and Sarah (Derby) Upham, was born February 18, 1827, Westminster, Massachusetts, and died February 27, 1892, at Ripon, Wisconsin. He was for many years prominent in the affairs of that town and was held in high esteem by its citizens. He was an officer in the civil war, and served as captain and commissary of subsistence in the Department of the Gulf. His commission was signed by both President Lincoln and Secretary Stanton, a circumstance that gave him great satisfaction. He was educated in the public schools and Westminster Academy, and accompanied his mother to Racine in 1853. From this district he was sent to the state legislature in 1861. In 1862 he joined the army, remaining in the service of his country until the close of hostilities and winning a most honorable record. In 1866 he removed to Shawano, where he engaged in general merchandise business. In 1877 he moved to Ripon, and there the remainder of his life was spent. He became postmaster there during President Arthur's administration. He was an active, shrewd and upright business man, and very successful. He was a selfmade man in every sense, and became one of the best known men in his state.

Calvin H. Upham married, at Westminster, October 28, 1851, Amanda E. Gibbs. Children: Frederic William; Catherine Jeannette, born February 8, 1864, at Racine, married, May 2, 1890, Dr. F. A. Everhard, of Ripon, and they have one child, Frederic Upham Everhard, born at Ripon, September 20, 1891; Mary Ellen, born at Shawano, October 8, 1870, died November 19, 1870.

(IX) Frederic William, eldest child and only son of Calvin Hoadley and Amanda E. (Gibbs) Upham, was born January 29, 1861, at Racine, Wisconsin. He attended Ripon College, then went to Marshfield, where he became associated with his uncle, William H. Upham (afterwards governor of Wisconsin) in lumber business. In 1894 he removed to Chicago to engage in the same business on his own account. He soon become prominent in political affairs and was elected alderman, when he gave his support to measures for a clean administration and contributed his salary to two assistants who kept in close touch with the needs of his constituents. In 1898 he was elected a member of the Cook county board of tax review and served as its first president, he was re-elected in 1900 and again in 1906, his term expiring December 31, 1912, after fourteen years of continuous service. He has also been prominent in national politics, and in 1892 was a delegate to the Republican national convention, and in 1904 was vice-chairman of the committee on arrangements of the Republican national convention. In 1908 he was chairman of the same committee of the convention which nominated Taft, and again chairman in 1912. He was assistant treasurer of the Republican national committee during the Taft campaign, and served on the advisory staff of the Republican national committee during the campaign of 1912. Mr. Upham has varied business interests, being the principal owner of the Upham & Agler Lumber Company, president of the City Fuel Company; a director of the Peabody Coal Company, Illinois Midland Railway, Knickerbocker Ice Company, Calumet Insurance Company, Security Life Insurance Company, American Surety Company, Single Service Package Corporation of America, and a trustee of Ripon College. He is a member of the following clubs: Chicago, Union League, Commercial, Chicago Athletic, Hamilton, Mid-day, Marquette, City, Press, South Shore Country, Glen View Golf, Chicago Golf and Exmoor Golf, of Chicago; of the Lambs, Union League and Automobile Club of America, of New York; and of the Metropolitan Club, of the city of Washington. Besides, he is a director and past president of the Illinois Manufacturing Association, and chairman of the executive committee of the National Business League of America. He belongs to the Society of Colonial Wars, Sons of American Revolution, the New England Society, and the Military Order of the Loyal Legion.

Mr. Upham is much interested in the early history of the country and is reasonably proud of the part his ancestors have taken in affairs of their times. They have been pioneers in many fields and have been imbued with the spirit of progress, which led them to seek the best they could find for their own development and the future of their children. Mr. Upham is well known in many circles and has won his position by ability and hard work. His business interests are international, and he has also been one of the most active workers in the interests of the Republican party in the country. He is a typical successful American, who has built up extensive business relations, and at the same time has kept alive to political matters and has felt the incentive for the highest citizenship, for he has performed a large share of work in every campaign in which he has accepted responsibility by his appointment to important national committees. His work has been most acceptable to the Republican party and has won him wide recognition.

Mr. Upham married Miss Helen Hall, of Cedar Rapids, Iowa, in 1905; they have no children.

PORTER — Dr. Daniel Porter, the immigrant ancestor of this family, was one of the first physicians of the colony of Connecticut. He was doubtless born in England and came early to this country. He was fined March 16, 1644-45, for some trivial offense by the particular court. He was licensed to practice physic and chirurgery by the general court of Connecticut, and in 1681 a yearly salary of six pounds was ordered paid to him out of the public treasury and his "fee-table" was established by law. He was a celebrated bonesetter, as the surgeons were commonly called in his day. He settled in Farmington, Connecticut, but was required to attend the sick in Hartford, Windsor, Wethersfield and occasionally in Middletown. In 1668 he was "freed from watching, warding, tryneing (training)" and in the following year a special grant of land was made to him by the general court for his services, a hundred acres, laid out afterward in the northeast part of Wallingford. This tract proved not in the colony land, and in 1723 on petition of his grandsons, Daniel Porter, son of Daniel, and Hezekiah Porter, of Woodbury, son of Dr. Richard of New Haven, one hundred acres were granted instead, west of the Housatonic river. In 1671 his salary was raised to twelve pounds as "incouragement for setting bones," and the court "advised him to instruct some person in his art." Evidently he instructed his son Daniel, and his sons Richard and Samuel also became bonesetters. Porter was not on the list of freemen in 1669, but was in 1672. He died in 1690. He married Mary ———. Children: Dr. Daniel, mentioned below; Mary, born February 5, 1654-55; Nehemiah, October 24, 1656; Dr. Richard, March 24, 1658; Anna, 1660-61; John, November 14, 1662; Dr. Samuel, October 24, 1665, succeeded his father as surgeon at Farmington.

(II) Dr. Daniel (2) Porter, son of Dr. Daniel (1) Porter, was born February 2, 1652-53, died January 15, 1725. He married Deborah Holcomb, and settled at Waterbury, Connecticut, where she died May 4, 1765. He was for a considerable time, the only professional man in the town, there being no business for a lawyer and no means of support for a minister. Besides medicine and surgery, which he learned under the instruction of his father, he did land surveying and filled various offices the duties of which called for more than the usual amount of education. He left an estate valued at about two thou-

sand dollars and besides this he had given much to his children in life. His medical library, it may be said, consisted at the time of his death of a "bone-set" book valued at two shillings. Children, born at Waterbury: Daniel, mentioned below; James, born April 20, 1700; Thomas, April 1, 1702, died aged ninety-five; Deborah, March 6, 1703-04; Ebenezer, December 24, 1708; Ann, April 29, 1712.

(III) Daniel (3), son of Dr. Daniel (2) Porter, was born at Waterbury, March 5, 1699, died there November 14, 1772. He married (first), June 13, 1728, Hannah, daughter of John Hopkins. She died December 31, 1739, and he married (second) Joanna ————. Children by first wife, born at Waterbury: Preserved, born November 23, 1729; Dr. Daniel, March 8, 1731, died of smallpox at Crown Point, in 1759, unmarried; Hannah, June 16, 1733; Dr. Timothy, mentioned below; Susanna, July 7, 1737; Anna, December 6, 1738. Children by second wife: Elizabeth, married Ard Warner; Jemima, married Timothy Scovill.

(IV) Dr. Timothy Porter, son of Daniel (3) Porter, was born at Waterbury, June 19, 1735, died January 24, 1792. He was also a physician and surgeon. He married Margaret Skinner, born 1739, died in 1813, daughter of Gideon Skinner of Bolton, Connecticut. Children (dates from Waterbury history): Daniel, mentioned below; Sylvia C., born February 24, 1771; Dr. Joseph, September 3, 1772; Olive, July 26, 1775; Anna, April 5, 1777; Chauncey, April 24, 1779; Timothy Hopkins, November 28, 1785.

(V) Daniel (4), son of Dr. Timothy Porter, was born September 23, 1768. He lived at Waterbury. He married (first), June 9, 1789, Anna Ingham, granddaughter of Israel Clark of Southington, (second) February 1, 1834, Mrs. Leve J. Johnson. Children (from Waterbury history): Horace, born September 30, 1790; Timothy, mentioned below; Elias, May 14, 1795; Alma Anna, April 12, 1800; Dr. Daniel, May 20, 1805; Joseph, July 11, 1807.

(VI) Timothy, son of Daniel (4) Porter, was born at Waterbury, Connecticut, January 30, 1792. He was a farmer in Waterbury, on the old Porter homestead. He married (first), May 17, 1811, Clarissa, daughter of Ebenezer Frisbie. She was born at Waterbury, August 21, 1794, and died November 18, 1821. Her father was born at Waterbury, November 30, 1773; married, November 23, 1791, Deborah Twitchell, daughter of Isaac Twitchell, and died in New Haven, Ohio, May 14, 1835. Reuben Frisbie, father of Ebenezer, son of Elijah, married (first),

May 25, 1769, Hannah Waklee, daughter of Ebenezer Waklee. She died November 22, 1778, and Reuben married (second), June 3, 1779, Ruth Seward, daughter of Amos Seward. Reuben Frisbie died September 10, 1824, aged seventy-eight years.

Timothy Porter married (second), December 30, 1824, Polly Ann, born May 12, 1800, daughter of Hezekiah Todd, of Cheshire, Connecticut. Children of Timothy and Clarissa Porter: Joseph, mentioned below; Mary Ann, born August 21, 1815, married S. E. Palmer; Jane E., born February 3, 1818, married J. C. Welton. Children of Timothy and Polly Ann Porter: Timothy Hopkins, February 16, 1826; Nathan T., December 10, 1828; Thomas, February 9, 1831; David G., March 8, 1833; Samuel M., May 17, 1835.

(VII) Joseph, son of Timothy Porter, was born at Waterbury, June 5, 1812, and died in 1893. He was educated in the public schools of his native town and for many years was connected with the Seville Manufacturing Company.

He married, January 26, 1840, at Waterbury, Charlotte Ann Tompkins, of Florence, New York, daughter of Eber Tompkins of Plymouth, Connecticut. Children: Celinda Jane, born June 25, 1842, married Henry C. Robinson and had Henry P., Edith and Irene Robinson; Eleanor Medora, born May 24, 1845, married William C. Hart of New Britain, Connecticut; Joseph L., mentioned below.

(VIII) Joseph L., son of Joseph Porter, was born in Waterbury, December 19, 1846. He attended the public schools of his native town, the Waterbury High School and Bassetts' Private School at Waterbury. In 1863 he went to New York City on July 23, entered the employ of A. W. Welton & Porter, dealers in fancy goods and notions. His uncles, N. T., Thomas and S. M. Porter were partners in this firm, which subsequently became Porter Brothers & Company, and continued thus until 1897. In 1897 Mr. Porter withdrew from Porter Brothers & Company, and reorganized the old firm of Noyes, Smith & Company, dealers in fancy goods and notions, and commission merchants, under the name of Watson, Porter, Gibbs & Company. The house continues at the present time under this name, though Mr. Porter is the only survivor of the original partnership. Their place of business is at 61 Leonard street, New York City. Mr. Porter is a member of the New England Society of New York, of the Wood Club, the Greenwich Country Club, the Ardsley Club at Ardsley-on-Hudson, and with his firm, a member of the Merchants' Association of

New York. In politics he is a Republican; in religion a Baptist.

He married, October 31, 1894, Carita Highet, daughter of William Wilson Highet, and sister of Frank Brewster Highet (see Highet).

ABBOTT George Abbott, the immigrant ancestor, was probably born in England, and died in Rowley, Essex county, Massachusetts, in 1647. He was one of the first settlers there, coming about 1642 from England, with his family. The records of Rowley during the time he lived there are missing, so that not much has been found concerning him. His name was at the head of a list of fifty-nine whose house-lots were surveyed January 10, 1643. About twenty acres of land are recorded as belonging to him at that time, but he evidently owned much more than that. It is thought that the Thomas Jr. in his family was an adopted son. George Abbott died in 1647, and after his death the court at Ipswich decided to put Thomas Jr. out as an apprentice to John Boynton for seven years, and guardians were appointed for the children. Abbott left a will, according to the Massachusetts colonial records, which was referred by the general court to the Salem court, November 11, 1647, but the will has not been found. The inventory of his estate was dated August 30, 1647. About three years after his death, Thomas Sr., his son, was eighth on the list of land-owners, and was one of the leading proprietors and overseers, showing that his father must have owned a large amount of land. Children, born in England: Thomas Sr.; George, mentioned below; Nehemiah; Thomas Jr.

(II) George (2), son of George (1) Abbott, was born in England, about 1631. After coming to New England he lived at Rowley about fourteen years, and in 1655 moved to the part of Andover, later called North Andover, and now Andover Center. He was a farmer and tailor, and was well-to-do for the times, being very industrious and thrifty. There were but four men in the town who had higher taxes than he. In 1658-59 he was a member of Sergeant James Osgood's militia company, and had been before that a member of Sergeant Stevens' company, according to the Essex county court records. On May 19, 1669, he was made freeman, and was chosen constable June 5, 1680. He very likely held many other offices, but the records are too confused to tell correctly. For about thirty years he was in charge of the North meeting house at Andover, and received thirty shill-

ings a year for ringing the church bell. The first grant of land which he received from the town consisted of two parcels of about four and six acres each, the first including a house and orchard. The first record of his land at Salem is June 10, 1662, for land which his son John inherited. The Andover committee assigned many other lots of land to him at various times, and there are many deeds on records made by him. He became a large land-owner and very well-to-do. He died at Andover, intestate, March 22, 1688-89, aged about fifty-eight years, according to a deposition that he made in 1657, when he said he was twenty-six, and one in 1676 when he said he was about forty-four years old. His property was divided between the widow and the children, the agreement being signed January 20, 1689-90. George Abbott married in Ipswich, Massachusetts, April 26, 1658, Sarah Farnum, who was probably born in Massachusetts, about 1638; she was daughter of Ralph and Alice Farnum, of Andover, who sailed from Southampton, England, April 6, 1635, in the brig "James", arriving at Boston, June 3, 1635, he aged thirty-two and his wife twenty-eight years. It is thought that they were of Welsh ancestry; they went to Dracut, Massachusetts, after leaving Andover, and were the ancestors of a prominent family. Sarah Abbott married (second), August 1, 1689, Sergeant Henry Ingalls, who was born in England about 1627, son of Edward and Anna Ingalls, probably of Lincolnshire, England, who settled in Lynn, Massachuetts, in 1629. They both died at Andover, he February 8, 1718-19, aged ninety-two years, and she in 1728, aged ninety years. Ingalls' son James, who married Hannah, daughter of George and Sarah (Farnum) Abbott, was given his homestead by will of July 5, 1714, being charged with the care of the widow. Children, born in Andover: George, mentioned below; Sarah, born September 6, 1660; John, August 26, 1662; Mary, March 20, 1664-65; Nehemiah, July 20, 1667; Hannah, September 22, 1668; Mehitable, February 17, 1671, died young; Lydia, March 31, 1675; Samuel, May 30, 1678; Mehitable, April 4, 1680.

(III) George (3), son of George (2) Abbott, was born in Andover, January 28, 1658-59, and died there January 24, 1724, aged sixty-five. He was a farmer and shoemaker in Andover. He received from his father sixteen acres of upland on which he built his house. This land is now a part of the Kittredge estate. On November 9, 1723, he sold to his brother Obed land in Andover. On October 25, 1723, he sold to his son Uriah the house in which he was living, the barn, half the orchard, some plow land, and two other pieces of land. His will was dated October 1, 1724, and proved December 7, 1724. He married (first), at Andover, September 13, 1689, Elizabeth, daughter of Joseph and Elizabeth (Phelps) Ballard, and granddaughter of William Ballard, an early settler in Andover. Joseph and John Ballard started a fulling-mill in Andover, the first one there. Elizabeth (Ballard) Abbott died at Andover May 6, 1706. He married (second), July 21, 1707, Hannah Estey, of Topsfield, Essex county, Massachusetts; she was born there in 1667, daughter of Isaac and Mary (Town) Estey, and granddaughter of Jeffrey Estey. Mary Estey, a woman of "sound judgment and exalted Christian character", was executed at Salem for witchcraft, September 22, 1692. Hannah (Estey) Abbott died in Topsfield, November 5, 1741, where she had been living with John Perkins and his wife since her husband's death. Children, born in Andover: George, July 28, 1691; Uriah, November 20, 1692; Jacob, March 19, 1694; Elizabeth, November 5, 1695; Obed, March 16, 1696-97; Moses, February 14, 1698; Peter, mentioned below; Sarah, March 17, 1702-3; Hannah, April 16, 1706.

(IV) Peter, son of George (3) Abbott, was born in Andover, July 27, 1701. He was a farmer, and lived in Brookfield, Massachusetts, where, November 13, 1725, he bought eighty acres of land on the south side of Quaboag river. He served in the colonial wars, with the following record: Private, July 17, 1722, Colonel Shadrach Walton's command; private, November 22, 1724, in Colonel Thomas Westbrook's command. He served in the revolution, from the third precinct in Brookfield, June 30, 1778. He probably died in 1785. His will was dated April 27, 1744, and proved April 26, 1785, his eldest son Joel being executor. He married, in Brookfield, in 1730, Lydia, daughter of Samuel and Lydia Gilbert; Lydia was daughter of Thomas Barns. Lydia (Gilbert) Abbott was probably born at Brookfield, January 3, 1712, granddaughter of Henry and Mary (Wheat, widow) Gilbert; great-granddaughter of Thomas and Catherine (Chapin-Bliss) Gilbert of Windsor, Connecticut, and Springfield, Massachusetts. The Brookfield records show that a Peter Abbott married, in 1759, Rachel Stevens, and, as there was no other Peter there at the time, this was probably his second marriage. Children, born at Brookfield: Nathan, March 8, 1731, died January 16, 1742; Joel, born January 1 (12?), 1732-33; Damaris, March 7, 1734-35, died July 11, 1736; Gideon,

born April 20, 1738; Elizabeth, July 30, 1739; Nathan, mentioned below; Jesse, twin of Nathan; Moses, December 20, 1743, died September 2, 1748; Joshua, born April 12, 1746; Lydia, November 25, 1748; Prudence, September 13, 1752; Sarah, May 21, 1755; John, probably died young.

(V) Nathan, son of Peter Abbott, was born March 20, 1742, in Brookfield. He removed to Tyringham, Massachusetts, and later to Stockbridge, Windsor county, Vermont, where he was living in 1790, when the first federal census shows that he had two males over sixteen, two under that age, and five females in his family. Among his children were: Peter; Mathias, born August 11, 1770; Anne, October 6, 1772; Elizabeth, June 27, 1777; Danford; child born March 29, 1781; child, February, 1782.

(VI) Danford, grandson of Nathan Abbott, was born about 1800, in Stockbridge, Vermont. He married —— Burnett. His sister married the grandfather of C. W. Fairbanks, vice-president of the United States.

(VII) Luther Burnett, son of Danford Abbott, was born at Stockbridge, Vermont, in January in 1829, and died in Minnesota, 1908. He was a machinist, farmer and railroad man, able and successful. He married Marian Elizabeth Soper, born at Leicester, Rutland county, Vermont, 1827, died 1910, daughter of Jesse Soper, born 1788, a soldier in the war of 1812. Jesse Abbott, a relative, was also a soldier in this war.

(VIII) Frank D., son of Luther Burnett Abbott, was born at Bethel, Vermont, January 29, 1853. He attended the public schools of his native town, several schools in Minnesota, and the normal school at Owatonna. In 1874 he came to Chicago and found employment. Here he began his literary career as correspondent and contributor to a musical publication entitled *The Vox Humana*. In 1884 he established *The Presto*, a weekly journal of the music trades and industries, published every Thursday, at 440 South Dearborn street, Chicago. The business was incorporated in 1904 as the Presto Publishing Company, of which Mr. Abbott is president. This corporation also publishes *The Presto Buyers' Guide, the Blue Book of American Musical Instruments*. C. A. Daniell is the associate editor of *The Presto*.

Mr. Abbott is a member of the Press Club of Chicago; the Glen Oak Club of Glen Ellyn, Illinois; the Wheaton Golf Club of Wheaton, Illinois; the Automobile Club of Chicago; the New England Society of Chicago; Saint Cecilia Lodge, Free Masons; Austin Chapter, No. 14, Royal Arch Masons, Austin, Minnesota; Apollo Commandery, No. 1, Knights Templar, Medina Temple, Order of the Mystic Shrine, etc., etc. He is independent in politics, and non-sectarian in religion. He married, in 1878, Eva Shugart, who was born at Elizabeth, Pennsylvania, March 9, 1859, daughter of Fletcher Shugart, of German ancestry. They have one child, Bertha Berenice, born at Brighton, Iowa, January, 1879, who married Otto Miller, of Glen Ellyn, Illinois, and has one child, Jenny Miller, born June 1, 1910.

BROWN Many families of this name are found very early in New England, and several different families often appear in one neighborhood, making it difficult to distinguish. The family herein traced was located in the Plymouth Colony, but the continued tracing is rendered extremely difficult by the meagreness of vital records in some of the towns of that region.

(I) Among the signers of the Mayflower Compact, November 11, 1620, on board the historic "Mayflower," in Cape Cod Bay, Peter Brown was thirty-third. He is said to have been a son of Thomas and great-grandson of Anthony Brown, who was created Knight of the Bath at the coronation of Richard II., and was recipient of the famous Battle Abbey at the hands of Henry VIII. John Brown, an elder brother of Peter, became acquainted with the Pilgrims at Leyden, Holland, prior to 1620, and the year of his immigration has been fixed at about 1630. He was a resident of Duxbury, Massachusetts, in 1636, and was a man of large intelligence, great energy of character and deep and earnest piety. In 1634 he was made a freeman, and in 1636 was an assistant to the governor, an office which he held by annual election for seventeen years. He was a grand pioneer in the settlement of the towns on the west of old Plymouth. His name is found among the purchasers of Taunton in 1637, and he, with Miles Standish, erected bounds around the purchase in 1640. Thither he had probably removed with his family before 1643, for among the fifty-four males subject to military duty in that year his name stands first, followed by his two sons, James and John. During the same year he was one of the company to purchase Rehoboth, and his interest in that township was the largest of any, amounting to £600 sterling. Prior to June 9, 1645, he removed to Rehoboth. His son James removed from Taunton with him, and his son John followed in 1647. In December, 1645, John Brown, Sr. became sole proprietor of the section known by the Indians as

Wannamoisett and Wannamoisett Neck (now Bullock's Point and Riverside, Rhode Island), which originally included a portion of the present towns of Rehoboth and Swansea, with a large portion of Barrington and the south part of Sekonk and East Providence. His name appears on all of the important committees of the town of Rehoboth. In 1643 the colonies of Plymouth, Massachusetts, Connecticut and New Haven, united in a confederacy styled the United Colonies of New England, for their common defense and welfare. Each colony sent two commissioners to the meetings of this body, and John Brown represented Plymouth Colony twelve years. He was associated in deliberations with such men as John Winthrop and others, serving the colonies wisely and faithfully. He died at Wannamoisett, April 10, 1662. His widow, Dorothy Brown, died in Swansea, January 27, 1673, aged ninety years. Children: Mary, married Captain Thomas Willett; John, mentioned below; James Brown.

(II) John (2), eldest son of John (1) and Dorothy Brown, was born probably in England, and resided in Rehoboth, where he died March 31, 1662. His will was probated the same day and his father was made executor. He married Lydia, daughter of William Buckland. Children: John, born "last Friday of September, 1650"; Annah, January 29, 1657; Lydia, August 5, 1655; Joseph, mentioned below; Nathaniel, June 9, 1661.

(III) Joseph, second son of John (2) and Lydia (Buckland) Brown, was born April 9, 1658, in Rehoboth, and resided in that town until after 1702, when he removed to Attleboro, Massachusetts, and was representative from that town in 1712 and 1726-27-28. He died there May 5, 1731. He married, November 10, 1680, Hannah Fitch, born 1669-70, died October 14, 1739. Children, born in Rehoboth: Hannah and Joseph (twins), November 21, 1681 (latter died young); Joseph, died young; Jabosh (Jabez), mentioned below; John, March 13, 1685; Joseph, August 28, 1688; Lydia, December 5, 1691; Benjamin, April 13, 1694; Mary, June 28, 1696; Christopher, June 17, 1699; Jeremiah, October 7, 1702. There is reason to believe that there was another, Noah.

(IV) Jabez, third son of Joseph and Hannah (Fitch) Brown, was born December 30, 1683, in Rehoboth, and died in Providence, Rhode Island, September 9, 1724. He married at Providence, November 18, 1718, Mary, daughter of Israel and Mary (Wilmarth) Whipple, born November 3, 1699, in Attleboro, and granddaughter of John and Sarah Whipple, who came from England to Dorchester, Massachusetts, in 1632, and removed to Providence in 1658. They had sons: Ichabod, Nicholas and Jabez.

(V) Nicholas, son of Jabez and Mary (Whipple) Brown, was born February 24, 1720, in Attleboro, and resided in Cumberland and Smithfield, Rhode Island. At the time of his marriage, April 22, 1744, to Hope, daughter of William and Elizabeth (Sprague) Whipple, he was called "of Cumberland," as was also his wife. She was born April 28, 1723, in Smithfield. Children: Ichabod, mentioned below; Jeremiah, born about 1747; Nicholas, October, 1749; Elizabeth, probably 1751; Mary, about 1753; Levi, 1755.

(VI) Ichabod, eldest child of Nicholas and Hope (Whipple) Brown, was born probably 1745, in Smithfield, although not recorded in that town or elsewhere in Rhode Island. He was an officer in the revolutionary army, his commission issued by Governor Greene, of Rhode Island, in 1779. After the revolution he resided for a time in Adams, Massachusetts, and was among the early settlers of Farmington, Ontario county, New York, in 1791. He took up land there at this time, but did not remove his family until later. He seems to have lived for a time in Mansfield, New York, as his wife died there April 17, 1807. He spent his last days with his daughter, Mrs. Rhoba Wells, in Farmington, where he died September 16, 1828. He married, November 9, 1777, Hannah, eldest child of Stephen and Mehitable (Cook) Ballou, born March 15, 1752, in Cumberland, Rhode Island.

(VII) Benjamin Ballou, son of Ichabod and Hannah (Ballou) Brown, was probably born in Adams, and resided for a time in Penn Yan, New York, where he kept a store, whence he removed to Manchester, New York, where several of his children were born. After residing for a time in Auburn, New York, he removed in 1837 to McHenry, Illinois, where he was a pioneer settler. He built a log cabin which was known as Brown's "Log Cabin Tavern" on the site of the present Riverside Hotel at McHenry. His last days were spent at King City, Missouri, with his daughter, Reliance Griswold, and he died July 30, 1864. He married Anne Mary, daughter of Joshua and Reliance (Lawrence) Way, in Milo, Yates county, New York, about 1815. She was a native of Milo, New York. Children: Reliance, Henry Townsend, Susan, Homer, Mary and William W.

(VIII) Henry Townsend, eldest son of Benjamin B. and Anne Mary (Way) Brown, was born November 1, 1823, in Manchester, New York, and was a small boy when his parents removed to Illinois. At the age of sixteen years he operated the ferry conducted by his father over the Fox river at McHenry. His duties consisted of paddling a flat-bottom scow from one bank to the other. He attended the Slater Academy at Ringwood, McHenry county, Illinois, for several seasons, and subsequently took up the study of medicine with Dr. James McAllister, of that town. After three years he went to Chicago, where he entered Rush Medical College, from which he received the degree of M. D., February 7, 1850. At this time the California fever was at its height and the adventurous spirit which he had inherited from his pioneer ancestors led the young physician to cross the plains with a party of four who followed the old Mormon trail until they reached Placerville, California, then known as "Hangtown". Dr. Brown here combined the practice of medicine and surgery with gold mining, but two years of the wild western life sufficed him and he returned to Illinois. Proceeding by steamer to the Isthmus of Panama, he crossed with mule train and proceeded from Aspinwall to New Orleans by steamer, thence up the Mississippi by steamer and from there by stage to McHenry. He devoted five years to the practice of his profession in and about that town, and in 1857 again crossed the plains, going as far as Pike's Peak, Colorado, where he once more combined the occupation of physician and gold-seeker. Within a year he tired of this and returned to Illinois. On this journey the party encountered a herd of buffalo which spread as far as the eye could reach, and three days were consumed in driving through them. Great caution was necessary to prevent a stampede which might have proved fatal to the party. Settling at McHenry, Dr. Brown there continued to practice until a few years before his death, June 26, 1907. He was a man of broad and liberal mind; a Universalist in religion, and an active supporter of Republican principles in governmental affairs. He married, at McHenry, June 1, 1852, Mary Almira, daughter of Abijah and Thankful (Griswold) Smith, born April 29, 1831, in Springfield, Vermont. Their first child, born May 28, 1854, died young. The others were: Adele, born June 8, 1855, married Clarence A. Knight, at McHenry, October 31, 1877; Paul, mentioned below.

(IX) Paul, youngest son of Dr. Henry T. and Mary A. (Smith) Brown, was born December 1, 1864, at McHenry, and was educated in the public schools of his native town. He began the study of law in the office of Hoyne, Horton & Hoyne, in Chicago, which was one of the most prominent law firms in the west, and was admitted to the bar in March, 1886. Within a few months he was appointed Master in Chancery of the Circuit Court of Cook county, which position he held eight years, resigning at the end of that time in order to devote his entire time to his private practice. From 1889 to 1903 he was a member of the law firm of Knight & Brown, when the firm was dissolved and he became a member of the firm of Horton & Brown, which firm continued until 1906, when the firm became Horton, Brown, Richardson & Miller. This was dissolved in 1908, and since that time Mr. Brown has continued in practice independently. Mr. Brown has taken part in large important litigations. Among the earliest of these cases was that of Gregsten vs. City of Chicago, Mr. Brown representing the complainant. He was defeated in the Circuit and Appellate courts, but the Supreme court reversed both lower courts and sustained every contention of the complainant. This decision settled the law with reference to the rights of parties using space under sidewalks, streets and alleys in the city of Chicago under ordinance or contract. Other important cases were those of: Swigart vs. The People, 154 Illinois, 284; People vs. Lake Street, Elevated Railroad Company, 54 Illinois, Appellate 348; Llewellyn vs. Dinger, 165 Illinois, 26. The last-named case involved a large tract of valuable property at Wilmette, a suburb of Chicago, which was begun in 1871 and continued twenty-five years, a cloud upon the title to the land involved, and in the meantime the parties to the litigation and their counsel had all died. In 1896 Mr. Brown was employed by the heirs of the original defendant, Dinger, and in January of the following year obtained a decision of the Supreme court terminating the litigation in favor of his clients. He was counsel in several cases involving the Lake Street Elevated Railroad, and in that of the Inter-Ocean Publishing Company vs. the Associated Press, 184 Illinois, 348. This is the celebrated case which resulted in the dissolution of the Associated Press as an Illinois corporation and its reorganization under the laws of New York. The Circuit court dismissed the bill filed by Mr. Brown for want of equity, and this action was approved by the Appellate court, but upon appeal the Supreme court sustained every contention of the complainant, reversing the decree of the lower courts, with directions to enter a decree as prayed for in the bill. Mr. Brown was counsel in the case of Sargent Glass Company vs. The Matthews Land Company of Indiana, and other impor-

tant cases in that state, wherein large corporations were involved. He takes an active interest in political progress, being a staunch Republican, but has steadfastly declined any nomination for an elective office. His pleasing personality and professional characteristics are well described in an article from a Chicago legal paper, as follows: "Mr. Brown is a man of plain manners, fixed convictions, sterling integrity and a firm purpose to do the right. He possesses a well-balanced judgment, and a keen sense of honor. As a lawyer he is distinguished for his thoroughness and careful attention in the preparation of his pleadings, his logical arrangement and plain presentation of the issues, and his terse argument—he studies each case as if he never had one at all similar, but expected to have many more involving the same questions."

He married, April 25, 1889, at McHenry, Grace Alice, daughter of Oliver Williams and Harriett Elizabeth (Holmes) Owen, born at McHenry, Illinois, in 1864, died April 25, 1911, in Glencoe, a Chicago suburb. Their children are: Paul Donald, born July 11, 1890; Grace Dorothy, October 25, 1892; Clarence Raymond, February 16, 1896.

LANE The surname Lane is of the same class as Woods, Pond, Field, Hill, coming into use as a surname at a very early date. The personal name modified by the designation, "in the lane", "by the lane", "in lana", "ad lanam", may be found in medieval documents. The Lane family of Kings Bromley claims to be of Norman origin, descending from Sir Reginald de Lane, of the twelfth century. Many of the English branches of the Lane family have coats-of-arms.

(I) William Lane, the immigrant ancestor, was born in England, and came probably from the western part of England. He was a resident of Dorchester, Massachusetts, as early as 1635. He received grants of land there in 1637. His will, proved July 6, 1654, mentions his children, but no wife. Children, all probably born in England: Elizabeth; Mary; Avis, or Avith; George, mentioned below; Sarah; Andrew.

(II) George, son of William Lane, was an early settler in Hingham, and at the first division of land, September 18, 1635, was granted a house lot of five acres. He also had a grant of ten acres at "Nutty Hill," and thirteen shares in the common lands. He was a shoemaker, and resided on what is now North, near Beal street. He was selectman in 1669-78. He died June 11, 1689. His will was dated October 16, 1688, and proved

August 20, 1689. He married Sarah Harris, who died at Hingham, March 26, 1694-95, daughter of Walter and Mary (Frye) Harris. Her father came to Weymouth in 1632. Children, all born in Hingham: Sarah, March, 1637-38; Hannah, February 24, 1638-39; Josiah, May 23, 1641; Susannah, June 23, 1644; John, mentioned below; Ebenezer, August 25, 1650; Mary, April 11, 1653; Peter, July 21, 1656.

(III) John, son of George Lane, was born January, 1647-48, and died at Norton, Massachusetts, November 23, 1712. He married, June 4, 1674, Mehitable, daughter of Thomas and Jane Hobart; she was born July 4, 1651, and died February 15, 1689-90. He married (second), about 1693, Sarah ———, who was admitted to the church at Norton in 1718 and died November, 1727. He was known in Hingham as John Lane, the shoemaker, and was constable there in 1689. He removed to Norton, Massachusetts, about 1694, and settled near the boundary between Norton and Attleborough. He was taxed in Attleborough, November 12, 1696, £1 for paying the town's debt of £5 15s. 1d., and was chosen grand juryman March 22, 1696-97. He was rated in Norton, 1710, for building the first meeting house, and was on the committee, June 12, 1711, to secure incorporation of the precinct of Norton. Children by first wife: Samuel, born March 15, 1677; Priscilla, March 5, 1679-80; Mary, April 3, 1682; Asaph, July 21, 1685; child; children by second wife: Ephraim, mentioned below; John, born February 18, 1695-96; Sarah, January 11, 1697-98; Benjamin, February 15, 1698-99; Sarah, June 22, 1701; Melatiah, June 18, 1703; Elizabeth, July 29, 1705; Ebenezer, April 6, 1707.

(IV) Ephraim, son of John Lane, was born June 24, 1694, in Rehoboth, Massachusetts. He married, January 10, 1716-17, Ruth Shepperson, who united with the church in Norton, 1718: she was a daughter of John and Elizabeth Shepperson, of Attleborough, Massachusetts. He was admitted to full communion with the church in Norton, 1715, and was tithingman in 1719. Children: Ephraim, mentioned below; Elkanah, born April 1, 1719; Ruth, April 13, 1721, died young; Ruth, January 11, 1722-23; Jonathan, February 25, 1724; Abigail, September 11, 1727; Samuel, September 30, 1729.

(V) Ephraim (2), son of Ephraim (1) Lane, was born September 30, 1717, and died in 1800, aged eighty-two years. He married, September 21, 1738, Mehitable Stone, who joined the church in 1742. He was admitted to the church in 1734 and was made tithing-man in 1745. He kept a public house, 1754-67. Children: Ephraim, mentioned below; Nathaniel, born June 15, 1743; Isaac, May 9, 1745; Mehitable, June 3, 1747, died young; Anne, July 21, 1752; Mehitable, January 5, 1755; Chloe, February 4, 1757; Polly, May 27, 1762.

(VI) Lieutenant-Colonel Ephraim (3) Lane, son of Ephraim (2) Lane, was born July 9, 1739-40, and died in 1826. He married, February 19, 1764, Elizabeth Copeland, of Norton, daughter of Benjamin and Sarah (Allen) Copeland; she died January 12, 1818. He kept public house, 1768-73. He was lieutenant-colonel in Colonel Daggett's regiment, called out by the Lexington alarm, April 19, 1775; was appointed first captain of Norton artillery company, October 31, 1776; was lieutenant-colonel of Thomas Carpenters' regiment, Rhode Island service, July 21 to September 9, 1778; was town treasurer, 1787-88; selectman, 1789-94. He died in April, 1826. Children: William, born April 7, 1765; Elijah, April 16, 1767; Isaac, May 28, 1769; Daniel, mentioned below; Betsey, June 6, 1775; David, August 15, 1777; Allen, February 16, 1780; Calvin, March 11, 1782; George, July 26, 1786; Sarah, October 29, 1789.

(VII) Deacon Daniel Lane, son of Lieutenant-Colonel Ephraim Lane, was born April 22, 1771, and died November 1, 1857. He married, November 17, 1794, Eunice Danforth, who died in 1852. He served in the war of 1812; united with the church about 1814; was selectman, 1815-18-19-20; assessor, in 1812, for four years. He was elected deacon of the Unitarian church December 2, 1824, held the office twelve years, and then resigned. The church, September 30, 1836, "voted that the thanks of the church be presented to Deacon Daniel Lane for the long and useful services he has afforded the church in his office. * * * Like most of the young men of his time, Deacon Lane enjoyed but few advantages for obtaining an education, yet by observation and experience he succeeded in storing his mind with much practical wisdom and good sense, so that his counsel was often sought for and valued by his friends and townsmen. As an officer in the church his many virtues and his practical good sense, his love for peace and his unostentatious life, rendered his advice of great value, and especially was it so to his venerable pastor. In all the positions of life he occupied he was faithful and reliable. He retained his physical and mental faculties in a remarkable degree to the last, and labored until forty-eight hours before his death."

Children, born at Norton: 1. Eunice, July 18, 1796, died January 24, 1825. 2. Daniel, mentioned below. 3. Bradford, April 19, 1799, died December 7, 1834. 4. Lavinia, born March 14, 1801; married James Perry, and had Harry C., born 1827; George L. and Eliza. 5. Thomas Danforth, born March 14, 1803, died October 21, 1872; resided at Lawrence, Massachusetts; married (first) Mary Beals, of Canton, Massachusetts, who died January 9, 1855, and (second), about 1886, ———; had no children. 6. Clarissa, September 26, 1804, died February 17, 1825. 7. Albert, September 27, 1806, died October 5, 1863; married, February 28, 1835, Almira Gregory, of Norton, born August 26, 1814, and had Henry A., born November 2, 1835; Crawford, August 30, 1836; Ellen M., May 26, 1838; Marcus O., April 15, 1846; Herbert E., September 2, 1849; Julia Etta, January 11, 1852. 8. Ephraim, born April 1, 1809, died November 14, 1864; married, September 22, 1834, Lemira Ann Chace, who died August 6, 1868; children: Willard, born at Taunton, June 22, 1835; Seabury Nelson, March 24, 1837; Frank Ephraim, December 20, 1849. 9. Harrison, born March 26, 1810, a painter, at Taunton; married Augusta Babbitt; children: Richard B., born November 1, 1846, died July 28, 1864; Julia A., January 29, 1848. 10. Benjamin Copeland, born December 22, 1812; died unmarried, in 1890.

(VIII) Daniel (2), son of Deacon Daniel (1) Lane, was born in Norton, September 4, 1797. He was a manufacturer at Norton. He married Hannah, daughter of Daniel Bassett, of Norton. Children: 1. Daniel, mentioned below. 2. Clara E., born November 11, 1829; married Captain Martin Palmer, of New Bedford; he was thrown overboard and drowned while harpooning a whale; children: Clara A., born 1851, Fred M., 1854, Mary. 3. Frederick T., born April 12, 1832; married Serena R. Caswell, born December 10, 1827; children: Annie S., born July 12, 1857, a teacher; Serena C., June 7, 1858, an artist; Mary L., October 1, 1869, a teacher.

(IX) Dr. Daniel (3) Lane, son of Daniel (2) Lane, was born at Norton, June 9, 1825, and died in 1912, at Dighton, Massachusetts. He was a dentist in Boston. He married, April 8, 1849, Anna Elizabeth Pidge. Children:

1. Arthur Erastus, mentioned below.
2. Anna Winthrop, born July 29, 1857; married, 1881, William Henry Gilmore, a jeweler at Attleborough, Massachusetts; children: Arthur Harold, born April 12, 1882; Ernest Lenwood, August 21, 1883; Erastine Bright, May 27, 1888; Evans Winthrop, March 28, 1892. 3. Emma Frances, twin of Anna, died January 17, 1869.

(X) Arthur Erastus, son of Dr. Daniel (3) Lane, was born at Norton, January 16, 1853. He attended the public schools of his native town and the Lawrence (Massachusetts) high school. After leaving school he became a bookkeeper in a Boston house dealing in wallpapers and interior decorations, where he remained two years. He then entered the employ of Henry A. Gane & Son, a firm established in 1846, dealing in bookbinders' supplies and machinery, in 1871, as bookkeeper. This firm had a store also in New York City, and he subsequently was employed in that department as bookkeeper and salesman until 1883, when he was admitted to the firm and went to Chicago to manage the branch of the firm's business in that city. The firm also has a branch in St. Louis. It is now composed of three partners—George A. Gane, Arthur E. Lane and S. F. Gane, under the name of Gane Brothers & Company. The Chicago office is at 610 to 618 Federal street, Chicago.

Mr. Lane is a member of the Chicago Athletic Club, the South Shore Country Club, the Homewood Club, the Hamilton Club, all of Chicago, the New England Society of Chicago, and of Lodge of Free Masons. In politics he is a Republican; in religion non-sectarian. He married, December 21, 1882, Mary Louise, daughter of Benjamin and Louise (Lull) Walker; she was born at Woodstock, Vermont, November 9, 1861. Children: 1. Arthur Walker, born February, 1884; died June, 1884. 2. Marjorie, born November 9, 1887; educated in private schools and at Vassar College, where she was a student in 1904, and at Smith College, from which she was graduated with the degree of bachelor of arts in 1908.

ELLIS   Orange Ellis, the immigrant ancestor, came with his brother Richard to Bangor, Maine, and afterward settled at Pepperill, Middlesex county, Massachusetts, where he married Emily Shattuck, who was descended from one of the pioneers of the Massachusetts colony. Among their children was Jarvis C., mentioned below.

(II) Jarvis C., son of Orange Ellis, was born in Pepperill, Massachusetts, in 1812. He was a mechanic and contractor. He settled in Fort Village, town of Waterloo, Sheffield county, Province of Quebec, Canada, where he died at the ripe old age of ninety-two years. He married Euretta Rowena Warner, born in 1824, died in 1854, daughter of Seth Warner (see Warner). Children: 1. Caroline Isabella, born at Fort Village, 1844; married P. W. Hall, and was killed in a railway accident near Montreal; she was the mother of Henry and George Hall, now living at Montreal, Canada. 2. Orange Warner, mentioned below. 3. Sarah Rowena, born at Fort Village, 1848; married Alfred Leopold Maffre, of Montreal; now living at Rutherford, New Jersey; children: Ernestine and Alfred Maffre. Two others, Albert and Lorenzo, died in infancy.

(III) Orange Warner, son of Jarvis C. Ellis, was born at Fort Village, Waterloo, Sheffield county, Province of Quebec, Canada, September 4, 1846. He was educated in the public schools of his native town and in the Montreal Military School, from which he was graduated in the class of 1868. He became associated with his father in the management of lumber mills, woolen mills and a grist mill at Waterloo until 1876, when he became agent of the Goodyear Rubber Company at Montreal, Canada. After some six years in this position he entered the employ of the Montrose Wall Paper Company and continued until 1890. He then went to Chicago as manufacturers' agent representing various hardware and dry goods concerns, and has been in this business to the present time. Mr. Ellis is a member of Shepard Lodge, No. 53, Free Masons, of Waterloo, of which he was secretary; of Dorchester Chapter, Royal Arch Masons, No. 17, of which he was scribe; of the Good Roads Association of Illinois; the New England Society of Chicago; the Illinois Society, Sons of the Revolution. In politics he was a Democrat until 1896, when he became a Republican. In religion he is an Episcopalian. He married, November 15, 1876, Nancy Augusta Pierce, born in 1858, died in 1895, daughter of Henry and Mary (Benton) Pierce of Stanstead. Children: 1. Henry, born December 15, 1877; educated in public schools of Canada; now living at Derby Line, Vermont. 2. Isabella Rose, born in Montreal, 1879, died, 1897. 3. Mary Nennie, born in Montreal, 1888, now living in Chicago. 4. Margaret, born in Montreal, 1886, living at Stanstead, Canada. Mr. Ellis resides at 4300 Ellis avenue, Chicago, and his office is at 22 East Washington street, that city.

(The Warner Line).

The name Warner is an old English surname which occurs in Domesday Book and is also found in the account of the Manor of Warners, which derived its name from Edmund Warner, who held the estate in 1630. The coat-of-arms is described: A bend engrailed between six roses with three and three

gules; motto, *Non nobis tantum nati.* The coat-of-arms is found carved in several parts of the ceiling of the south aisle of the church of Great Waltham, England. The earlier Warners, the progenitors of the family, are generally supposed to have been of a fighting Christian stock. An authority has stated that several were killed in religious riots or massacres. The manor of Pakelsham, containing 418 acres, was granted to John Warner, of Warner's Hall, Great Waltham; his son John held it until 1473; his son Henry seized of it March 21, 1504; his son John, gentleman, held it until his death in 1552; he also held the Manor of Brusches; Henry, his brother, an heir, held it until his death in 1556, when it passed to the heirs of his sister. Queen Elizabeth granted in 1508 lands to Sir Edward Warner, Knight, in the manor of Gettingham, county Kent; also manor of Baxley in the same county; he married Elizabeth, daughter of Sir Thomas Brooke. William Warner, Esq., in the latter part of the reign of King Edward became possessed of Northwood Manor, county Kent, and held it until his death in 1504; then his son Humphrey seized of it, and he held it until 1513, when he willed it to his son William. John Warner, of Foot Cray, was sheriff of county Kent in 1442. He received the position from his father John, who had received it from the government in 1395.

(I) John Warner, the immigrant ancestor, at the age of twenty-one years came from England with the party which sailed on the ship "Increase" in 1635. In 1637 he performed service in the Pequot war. He became one of the original proprietors of Hartford in 1639. He became an original proprietor and settler of Farmington, Connecticut, and joined the church there in 1657. He was made freeman in 1664. In 1673 he went to Mattatuck, now Waterbury, to find if it was a desirable place to settle, and was a patentee of that place in 1674. It was his intention to move thither, but he died in 1679, leaving a widow Margaret. He married (second) Ann, daughter of Thomas Norton of Guilford, so Margaret must have been a third wife. Among his children was John, mentioned below.

(II) John (2), son of John (1) Warner, was born in Hartford or Farmington, probably the latter place, about 1645. He was brought up in Farmington and was on the list of freemen in 1669 and the list of proprietors in 1672, together with his father. He also subscribed to the articles of 1674 and made an effort to secure his right in the "Waterbury estate", of which he was a pioneer. His name occurs in all the fence divisions, and he is called "Senior" in the Waterbury records. He had recorded there February 19, 1703, one and a half acres of land on which his dwelling then stood. He called himself of Farmington in April, 1703, and again in 1706. In his will, however, dated Farmington, December 27, 1706, he speaks of himself as of Waterbury. He died soon after the latter date, in his sixty-third year, and the inventory of his estate was made in March, 1707. His real estate and homestead in Waterbury were given to his son John, and the latter, with Samuel Bronson, a son-in-law, was executor of his will. Children: John, born March 1, 1670; Ephraim, 1670; Robert; Ebenezer, mentioned below; Lydia, baptized March 13, 1680; Thomas, baptized May 6, 1683.

(III) Dr. Ebenezer Warner, son of John (2) Warner, married, December 19, 1704, Martha Galpin, who died April 17, 1745. He died April 23, 1755. Children: Ebenezer, born March 18, 1706; Martha, July 23, 1707; Benjamin, mentioned below; Margaret, December, 1712; Rebecca, December 12, 1715; Tamar, February 26, 1718; Lydia, February, 1720; Thomas, November, 1722; Frances, February, 1726; Rachael, baptized March 23, 1729.

(IV) Dr. Benjamin Warner, son of Dr. Ebenezer Warner, was born May 6, 1709. In 1763 he moved to Bennington, New Hampshire, the second year of the settlement of the town. He married, December 16, 1736, Silence Hurd, who died November 15, 1785. Children: Hannah, born August 4, 1737; Dr. Benjamin, May, 1739; Daniel, April 12, 1741; Seth, mentioned below; John, May 29, 1745; Dr. Reuben, baptized March 4, 1750; Elijah, baptized June 30, 1754; Asahel; David; Tamar.

(V) Colonel Seth Warner, son of Dr. Benjamin Warner, was born in Roxbury, May 6, 1743, and died December 26, 1784. He received a common school education in a school nearly six miles from his home, and as a young boy was remarkable for his energy and wise judgment. When his father moved to Bennington he at once became interested in hunting, and in a short time was noted for his ability in that line. He was not only experienced in hunting, but knew the other possibilities in the woods and was a skillful botanist, often relieving sickness through his knowledge of herbs. About this time the contest arose between New York and New Hampshire as to the jurisdiction of the Connecticut river to within twenty miles of the Hudson river. New York was given the

right by the crown and all would have been settled if New York had not claimed that the patents of the settlers' grants in the New Hampshire grants were invalidated by the decision. The old settlers refused to give up their land to the new patentees and the sheriff was resisted by force after the settlers found that trials at Albany brought no justice. At this time, while Ethan Allen was directing the trials, Warner was leader of the conventions of the settlers, who trusted thoroughly in his wise guidance. In 1771 a proclamation was issued by the governor of New York offering a reward of £20 for the arrest of Ethan Allen, Seth Warner, Remember Baker, and some others, and the next year Baker was taken in the night. Before his captors reached Albany, however, Warner and his party rescued him, and after a time the governor of New York offered £50 each for the arrest of Allen, Warner, and Baker, who were the most prominent leaders of the Green Mountain Boys. Warner also was prominent in the revolution, and enlisted at its beginning. He commanded the party which took Crown Point, and Allen commanded at Ticonderoga. After Colonel Hinman's regiment reached Ticonderoga, Allen and Warner went to the Continental Congress to ask for money to pay soldiers and raise a regiment from the New Hampshire grants. They were successful in their efforts, and the regiment was raised, Warner being appointed lieutenant-colonel by a practically unanimous vote. During the siege of St. John's by Montgomery, he was at the head of the regiment, September, 1775. In January, 1776, he received a letter from General Wooster, asking him to raise men in the middle of winter to go to Canada, and the request was carried out in a remarkably short time. On July 5, 1776, he was appointed lieutenant-colonel of a regiment consisting of those who had served with him in Canada, and he went at that time to Ticonderoga, where he remained till the close of that campaign. He also served in 1777 at the battles of Hubbardston and Bennington, being made colonel after the last battle. The hardships of his winter in Canada and other services had undermined his strong constitution, and when his regiment returned, November 10, 1777, he was returned "sick at Hoosick". He never was strong after this sickness, though he continued in command of his regiment until the end of the year 1781, living at Bennington with his family. In 1782 he returned to Roxbury, but his ill-health remained with him and he died December 26, 1784, after long suffering. In appearance he was six feet tall and well proportioned, showing great strength both in body and in character. His reputation for firmness and bravery protected him from being attacked single-handed except on one occasion when an officer from New York attempted to take him. Warner wounded and disarmed the officer but sent him back to New York instead of killing him. He was so much interested in the public welfare that he neglected his own affairs and his family was left destitute. Most of his grants of land were sold for taxes, but in November, 1787, his heirs received from the legislature of Vermont 2,000 acres of land in county Essex. He was highly respected and loved by everyone.

During the last few days of his life he was deprived of his reason, and imagined he was fighting his battles over again; a guard of several persons was kept at his house for two or three days before his death. He was noted for his coolness in danger, seeming to be unconscious of fear; also he was a man of great generosity and kindness to his fellowmen. He married Esther Burd. Children: Israel, Abigail, Seth, mentioned below.

(V) Seth (2), son of Colonel Seth (1) Warner, was born in 1776, in Bennington, and settled in 1813 at Henryville, Canada, then a wilderness, making his way from St. Albans by marked trees. He took up 150 acres of land lying on both sides of South river, on which he built a saw mill. At first his family lived in a log house, and he cleared land and developed a fine farm. The upper floor of his second house (still standing) was used as a Masonic hall. He died there October 27, 1854, and the place is still owned by his descendants. He was a thirty-second-degree Mason. He married (first) Lydia Barnes, and had two daughters. He married (second) Polly Hogle, and had three sons and seven daughters: Hethbert, Fanny, Aaron, Polly Ann, Henry E., Martha Louise, Euretta R., Hester M., Caroline E., and Abigail A. The second son died in infancy; all the others lived to have families. Of these children, Euretta Rowena, born 1824, married Jarvis C. Ellis, of Waterloo, Canada (see Ellis).

PEIRSON Samuel Peirson, the immigrant ancestor, was born in England, and came from Yorkshire about 1699 to Philadelphia, Pennsylvania. He belonged to the Society of Friends. He and his family removed to the back settlements of North Carolina, and in the war which ended in 1763 he is said to have been murdered with all his family except two children. By his first wife he had children: Samuel, mentioned below; Thomas; George; Mary and Elizabeth.

(II) Captain Samuel Peirson, son of Samuel Peirson, was born in Philadelphia, about 1731, and died at New Gloucester, Maine, July, 1791. He is said to have commanded the first vessel that made the passage by way of the Cape of Good Hope to China. He was afterwards a merchant in Boston. His cottage "with paling in front and garden in' the rear was on Devonshire street, the Quaker lane, between the old Exchange Coffee House and State street. The Boston Massacre took place very near his dwelling, and one of the wounded soldiers fell upon his doorstep". He married Elizabeth Cox, who was born in Boston, March, 1726, and died at Biddeford, Maine, April, 1809. Children: Samuel and George.

(III) Samuel, son of Captain Samuel Peirson, was born in Boston, February 22, 1759, and died in Biddeford, Maine, in May, 1852. He served nearly six months in the army of the revolution, and was one of General Washington's private clerks. He afterwards entered business as a merchant in Salem, Massachusetts, and in Portland, Maine. About 1792 he made his home in Biddeford, Maine, and remained there until his death. He married, in Salem, Massachusetts, Sarah Page, born at Medford, Massachusetts, October 7, 1755; (second) Sarah Hill. Children by first wife: Samuel Page, born March 5, 1784, murdered by Malays in the Bay of Bington; Elizabeth Cox, born at Falmouth, May 14, 1786, died March, 1813; George, born at Falmouth, July 17, 1789, drowned at Saco, Maine, May 6, 1797; John, born at Danvers, Massachusetts, February 3, 1791 lost at sea in 1826, master of the ship "Armadillo", which capsized; Abel Lawrence, born at Biddeford, January, 1793, died young; Abel Lawrence, mentioned below; Elizabeth, born at Biddeford, December, 1796, died 1798; Sarah Page, born at Biddeford, June, 1801, married Captain Samuel White, of Biddeford. Children by second wife: Jeremiah Hill, born June, 1806; Abigail Margaret, February, 1808; George Washington, December, 1809; Daniel Josiah, February, 1811, died June 29, 1826; Elizabeth Mary, May, 1813, married Samuel Chase; Thomas McCobb, May, 1816, married Sarah Dunn, and had Isabella, Harriet and Thomas; Harriet Lawrence, January, 1818, died February, 1837.

(IV) Abel Lawrence, son of Samuel Peirson, was born at Biddeford, Maine, November 25, 1794; married, in 1819, Harriet Lawrence, of Salem, Massachusetts. He resided in Salem, where he practiced medicine for many years. He was drowned in a railroad disaster at Norwalk, Connecticut, May 6, 1853, and was buried in Salem. Children: Dr. Edward Brooks, born at Salem, January 22, 1820, died November, 1874, married (first) Catherine Saltonstall, (second) Ellen E. Perry, by whom he had four children; Abby Lawrence, born in Salem, 1821; John L. and Sarah S., died young; Abel Lawrence, mentioned below; Harriet L., born 1831, married Rev. William Ropes, now of Andover, Massachusetts; Charles Lanman, born 1833, married Emily Russell, of Boston; James J., born 1833, died 1847.

(V) Abel Lawrence (2), son of Abel Lawrence (1) Peirson, was born July 24, 1824, and died in March, 1870. He was educated in the public schools of his native town, Salem, and engaged in the leather business in the adjacent town of Peabody, Massachusetts. At one time he was supercargo on a vessel. He married Elizabeth Teadwell Sutton, daughter of General William and Nancy (Osborn) Sutton. She was born in 1822, and died in 1892. Children: 1. Annie Osborne, born 1850, married Price W. Hasbrouck, of New York City. Children: Elizabeth H., married Oakley R. Delameter, of New York; Lawrence Hasbrouck, who married (first) Frances Reed, of New York City, and (second) Florence Reed, sister of his first wife; Harold Hasbrouck, married Mary Scott. 2. Harriet, born 1853, died 1873, married Caleb Caller, of Hamilton, Ontario, Canada. 3. Mary H., born in 1861; unmarried. 4. Elizabeth, died in infancy. 5. Abel Lawrence, mentioned below.

(VI) Abel Lawrence (3), son of Abel Lawrence (2) Peirson, was born in Peabody, Massachusetts, April 24, 1869. His father died when he was about a year old. He attended the public schools of Peabody, and graduated from the high school of that town in the class of 1886. His first business experience was as a clerk in the dry goods house of Hovey & Company, of Boston. Subsequently he was a clerk in the stock exchange concern of Putnam, Messervy & Company, of Boston. From this firm he went to the banking and brokerage house of Parkinson & Burr, New York, in 1892, and seven years later, after winning promotions from time to time to positions of greater responsibility, he was admitted to partnership, and since 1899 he has continued with this concern. He is a member of the Montclair Golf Club; the Essex Fells Club of New Jersey; the New England Society of New York, and other organizations. In politics he is a Republican. He is a communicant of the Protestant Episcopal church. At the present time he resides at Essex Fells, New Jersey, and he is a member of the common council of the municipality.

He married, October 12, 1896, Mary Perkins, born at Salem, Massachusetts, February 22, 1873, daughter of Frank A. and Caroline L. (Ives) Langmaid, of Salem. Children: Abel Lawrence, born at South Orange, New Jersey, August 3, 1897; Rebecca, born August 5, 1901, at East Orange; Charles Lawrence, January 3, 1903, at East Orange; Elizabeth, August 12, 1908, at Essex Fells.

PUTNEY   (II) Samuel Putney, son of John Putney (q. v.), was born July 13, 1689, at Salem, Massachusetts. About 1728 he was one of the pioneers of Rumford, now Concord, New Hampshire. He was elected fence viewer of the town in 1732-33. Elizabeth his wife was one of the early members of the Congregational church, joining about 1730, her number being 95. During the French and Indian war in 1746 Samuel and Henry, Joseph and William Putney were in the garrison at Joseph Hall's house; Joseph was in Rev. Timothy Walker's house, and John Putney Jr. at the house of Timothy Walker Jr. His sons were: John; Joseph, mentioned below; William; Henry, born 1721, died April 13, 1807, married Mary Wells; Dolly Jewett; Deborah Austin.

(III) Joseph, son of Samuel Putney, was born about 1710. About 1740 he and James Rogers became the first settlers of the town of Dunbarton, New Hampshire. During their hunting trips together, they discovered the Great meadows and there they erected their log houses and lived until 1746. Rumford was the nearest settlement and nothing but a blazed trail connected the two places. During the French and Indian war in 1746 word was sent to them from Rumford of a threatened Indian attack and they sought refuge with their families at Concord where they were assigned to garrison as described above. The Indians burned their houses at Dunbarton, killed their cattle and destroyed their orchards. During the war Putney was wounded. Afterward he returned to Dunbarton and rebuilt his house and barns in 1749. He lived to an advanced age. Among his children was a son Henry, mentioned below.

(IV) Henry, son of Joseph Putney, was born about 1740. He settled in Dunbarton and the town meetings of Dunbarton and Bow were held at his house. He married Dolly Jewett. Among his children was David, mentioned below.

(V) David, son of Henry Putney, was born

A. L. Peirson

about 1770 at Dunbarton. He succeeded to the homestead and followed farming in his native town. He married Rebecca Sawyer. Children, born at Dunbarton: Molly, March 23, 1791; Rebecca Sawyer, July 10, 1793; Adna, July 10, 1796; Fanny, February 27, 1799; David, mentioned below; Fanny, September 22, 1805; Henry, June 11, 1807; Louisa, December 5, 1810.

(VI) David (2), son of David (1) Putney, was born at Dunbarton, September 6, 1801. His brother Henry and he were both prominent citizens. He held various town offices and was representative to the state legislature. He married Mary Brown, a descendant of Peter Brown, who came in the "Mayflower." Peter Brown was also a progenitor of John Brown, the Abolitionist. David Putney was buried in the old graveyard on the border between Dunbarton and Bow, New Hampshire, where many of the early generations of the family lie. Children: John, soldier in the civil war; George; Charles, principal of the St. Johnsbury public school, Vermont; Albert Baker, mentioned below; Walter, now living on the homestead at Bow, New Hampshire, a prominent citizen of the town, has been representative to the state legislature and state senator; Freeman, teacher in the public schools of Gloucester, Massachusetts, for more than thirty years and superintendent of schools for twenty years; Newton; Milton; Eliza; Lucretia, married Charles Brown, of Concord.

(VII) Albert Baker, son of David (2) Putney, was born at Bow, New Hampshire, August 25, 1841. He was educated in the public schools of his native town and became a prominent merchant of Boston, Massachusetts, where he is now living, retired from business. He married Sarah Bliss Abbott, born at Manchester, New Hampshire, June 15, 1847, a descendant of one of the first settlers of Concord, New Hampshire. Her mother, Maria (Wood) Abbott, of Bow, comes of one of the pioneer families of New Hampshire. Children: 1. Carrie Maria, born in Concord, New Hampshire, October 7, 1870; married, May 5, 1892, George H. Bryant; she is a graduate of Smith College; member of the Daughters of the American Revolution. 2. Albert Hutchinson, mentioned below. 3. Sadie Josephine, died in infancy. 4. Alice Josephine, born in 1876, died unmarried in 1897. 5. Arthur Stuart, born in Boston, September 2, 1879; educated in the public schools of Newton, Massachusetts, and at the St. Johnsbury Academy, Vermont; now a mining superintendent at Manhattan, Nevada; unmarried. 6. Florence Abbott, born at Boston, January 24, 1882; married, October, 1908, Harry F. Vail, of

Chicago, and has one child, Harry F. Vail Jr., born January 24, 1910. 7. Chester Washburn, born at Newton, August 25, 1884, died young. 8. Clarence Newell, twin of Chester Washburn, died in infancy. 9. Theodora Newell, born at Newton, March 18, 1887; married, December 30, 1911, Albert Christiana.

(VIII) Albert Hutchinson, son of Albert Baker Putney, was born in Boston, September 28, 1872. He attended private schools in Boston and prepared for college in the Newton high school. In 1889 he entered Yale College and was graduated with the degree of Bachelor of Arts in the class of 1893. He then entered Boston University Law School and was graduated with the degree of Bachelor of Laws in 1895 and for three years practiced law in Boston. In 1900 he was appointed professor in the Illinois College of Law and in 1904 he became dean of the faculty. He has been a prolific writer on legal topics. In 1904 he published "Government in the United States" and in 1908 "Law Library" (twelve volumes) and "United States Constitutional History and Law." His later works have been: "Currency, Banking and Exchange" (1909); "Corporations" (1909); "Principles of Political Economy" (1909); "Bar Examination Reviews" (1910); "Foreign Commercial Law" (1910), and in collaboration with Hon. James Hamilton Lewis a "Handbook on Election Laws" (1912). He is an able and interesting public speaker and has taken an active part on the stump in various political campaigns. In politics he is a Democrat. In religion he is a Unitarian. He is a member of the Press Club of Chicago, the South Shore Country Club, the Cook County Democracy.

He married, April 6, 1911, Pearl Lyda Avery, born at Waterloo, Iowa, July 9, 1886, daughter of Jesse and Ida (Meek) Avery. She comes of New England descent on her father's side and of an old southern family on her mother's side.

HATCH Elder William Hatch, immigrant ancestor of the family, was born in Sandwich, county Kent, England. He was a merchant there, and came from there to Scituate, Massachusetts, before 1633. In the course of a year or two he returned to England to get his family and in March, 1635, sailed with his wife Jane, five children and six servants in the ship "Hercules" of Sandwich. He was a merchant of ability and was the first ruling elder of the Second Church of Scituate, founded in 1644. He was lieutenant of the militia company. His brother, Thomas Hatch, was in Dorchester, Massachusetts, in 1634, and afterward in Scituate, where he died in 1646, leaving five children: Jonathan, William, Thomas, Alice, Hannah. The home of Elder William Hatch was on Kent street, the first lot south of Greenfield lane. His widow Jane married Elder Thomas King in 1653. Children of William and Jane Hatch: Jane, married John Lovell; Anne, married Lieutenant James Torre; Walter, mentioned below; Hannah, married Samuel Utley; William, died in Virginia; Jeremiah, died in 1713.

(II) Walter, son of Elder William Hatch, was born in England about 1625, died in Scituate in March, 1701. He was a shipwright by trade, and with his brother Jeremiah bought land in what is now Hanover, Massachusetts, on Center street, a portion of which was called Hanmer's Neck. Most of the Hatch families of Hanover are descended from Walter Hatch. He married (first) May 6, 1650, Elizabeth, daughter of Thomas Holbrook, of Weymouth; (second) at Marshfield, August 5, 1674, Mary ———.

Children by first wife, all born at Scituate: Hannah, March 13, 1651; Samuel, mentioned below; Jane, March 7, 1656; Antipas, October 26, 1658, died unmarried December 7, 1705; Bethia, July 8, 1664, died in 1737; Israel, March 25, 1667, died in 1740; Joseph, December 9, 1669.

(III) Samuel, son of Walter Hatch, was born in Scituate, December 22, 1653, died in Scituate, June, 1735. He was also a shipwright. The name of his wife is unknown. Children, all born in Scituate: Samuel, born November 10, 1678; Josiah, May 30, 1680; Hannah, February 17, 1682; Ebenezer, April 6, 1684; Isaac, mentioned below; Elizabeth, June 16, 1690; Elisha, November 7, 1692; Ezekiel, May 14, 1695; Desire, September 25, 1698.

(IV) Isaac, son of Samuel Hatch, was born December 20, 1687, died in November, 1759, in Pembroke, Massachusetts. He married (first) Lydia ———, and (second) Penelope ———. Children, born at Scituate or Pembroke: Isaac, mentioned below; Josiah, baptized September 30, 1722; Lydia, baptized January 4, 1729-30; Penelope, baptized February 20, 1725; Seth, baptized December 24, 1727; Sarah, baptized September 16, 1734; Samuel, baptized August 1, 1736.

(V) Isaac (2), son of Isaac (1) Hatch, was born in 1717, baptized September 30, 1722, died 1799. He married Ann ———. Children, born at Pembroke: Josiah, mentioned below; Lydia, born January 11, 1740; Isaac, October 4, 1742; Judith, February 16, 1744; Fisher, June 28, 1751; John, June, 1756;

Jabez, December 20, 1759; Harris, September 13, 1760.

(VI) Josiah, son of Isaac (2) Hatch, was born at Pembroke, 1739, baptized June 3, 1739. He settled in Weathersfield, Vermont, about 1780. Among his children was Ebenezer, mentioned below.

(VII) Ebenezer, son of Josiah Hatch, was born in 1770, died in 1836. In 1790 Ebenezer had one male over sixteen and one female in his family, according to the first federal census. He married ——— Dennis. Among his children was Abijah B., mentioned below.

(VIII) Abijah B., eldest son of Ebenezer Hatch, was born October 29, 1799 died in 1861. He lived at Grand Isle, Vermont, and owned a farm south of the center of the town on road No. 29. In politics he was a Republican and in religion a Congregationalist. He married Abigail Lyon, born March 16, 1801, daughter of Rev. Asa Lyon, of Goshen, Connecticut, and Esther Newell, of Charlotte, Vermont. Esther Newell was daughter of Rev. Abel Newell, a graduate of Yale College in 1751, and Abigail Smith, daughter of John Smith. Children of Rev. Abel Newell: Esther, married Rev. Asa Lyon; John, Abel, Abigail, Job, Elisha. Children of Abijah B. Hatch: Asa Lyon, born September 29, 1822; Oscar, March 8, 1824; Mariet, April 9, 1826, died March, 1842; Juliet, August 5, 1827, died April, 1859; Henry Reynolds, mentioned below; Daniel M., February 18, 1832; Esther L., August 16, 1834, died September, 1856; Evelyn D., December 4, 1836; Elam A., February 25, 1839, died June, 1856; William Newell, February 21, 1842, died 1848; Arthur E., September 11, 1846.

(IX) Henry Reynolds, son of Abijah B. Hatch, was born at Grand Isle, Vermont, October 8, 1830. He worked during his early youth on his father's farm, and attended the public schools of his native town. For six months he was a student in the Vermont Episcopal Institute at Burlington, Vermont. At the age of fifteen he began his mercantile career as clerk in the general store of John Brown at North Hero, Vermont, but he returned to farm life on the homestead, continuing for two years. He then became a clerk in the employ of C. F. Staniford, merchant, at Burlington, promising his father, however, to return to assist in the summer work. He left home, finally, March 22, 1853, to go to St. Paul, Minnesota, stopping on the way at Cleveland, where he decided to remain. He entered the employ of E. I. Baldwin & Company, merchants, in Cleveland, as clerk and was soon filling a position of large responsibility there. In 1857 he was admitted as a partner and later, owing to the ill health of Mr. Baldwin, the management of the business fell upon Mr. Hatch. In the seventies W. S. Tyler and G. C. F. Haynes were admitted to the firm and the name became E. I. Baldwin, Hatch & Company. Afterward, however, the junior partners both withdrew from the firm, leaving Mr. Hatch the sole owner, after the death of Mr. Baldwin, whose interests he purchased from the estate. From a small beginning this dry goods business developed to mammoth proportions. The yearly sales came to aggregate almost a million dollars before the death of Mr. Baldwin and continued to grow afterward when the firm name was H. R. Hatch & Company. This firm has ranked for years among the foremost in its line in Ohio. He retired from business in 1906. Mr. Hatch has various other financial and business connections. He was one of the original stockholders and directors of the Cleveland National Bank, and one of the founders of the Savings and Trust Company, which was later merged with the Citizens Savings and Trust Company. He is a director of the Society for Savings and of the First National Bank, and president and trustee of the Lake View Cemetery Association. He has been an active and prominent member of the Chamber of Commerce and co-operated with all the movements to benefit the city and advance the welfare of its people. In later years he has had time to gratify a fondness for travel, both in this country and abroad. He has made extensive tours in the British Isles, in the Mediterranean countries, Russia, Norway, Sweden, Egypt, Palestine and Greece, accompanied by his family.

Mr. Hatch is well-known as a philanthropist. He has given freely to various organizations, the purposes of which he approves. He is vice-president of the Humane Society in which he has rendered valuable service to the needy and to the community itself. In 1890 he erected a Home for Waifs as a memorial to his wife, called the "Lida Baldwin Infants' Rest". He gave the library building, known as the Hatch Library, to Western Reserve University. He was one of the original members of the Bethel Associated Charities. He is a trustee of the Young Women's Christian Association, and of the Western Reserve University, and a member of the Union Club, Hunt Club, Country Club, and Colonial Club of Cleveland. He is a communicant of the Calvary Presbyterian Church, and president of the Society. Mr. Hatch has won to a remarkable degree the respect and confidence of the people of the community in which he lives. His ability, integrity, kindliness, exemplary

personal character, public spirit and wise use of his wealth and influence have placed him among the most honored and valued citizens of Cleveland. In politics he is a Republican, but he has never accepted public office.

He married (first) September 16, 1857, in New Haven, Connecticut, Eliza Newton, daughter of Silas Irving Baldwin (see Baldwin VI). She died in 1886. He married (second) in November, 1887, Mary Cummings Browne, born July 21, 1861, at Newark, New Jersey, daughter of Leonard Perkins Browne, of Newark, New Jersey. Leonard P. Browne married Matilda, daughter of Samuel and Hannah (Miner) Culver; he was son of Gurdon P. and Esther (Dean) Browne. Children by first wife: 1. Alice Gertrude, born January 29, 1859; married Charles Lathrop Pack, April 28, 1886; children: George Lathrop, deceased; Randolph G., born June 8, 1890; Arthur Newton, February 20, 1893; Beulah F., June 5, 1895. 2. Eddie Irving, born June 1, 1861, died young. 3. Freddie Baldwin, born June 1, 1861, died young. 4. Willie, died in infancy. 5. Anna Louisa, born August 30, 1865; married Edward C. Meyer. 6. Nellie Baldwin, died aged six months. Children by second wife: 7. Esther Marguerita, born October 29, 1889. 8. Henry Reynolds Jr., born December 20, 1896.

(The Baldwin Line).

(I) Richard Baldwin, immigrant ancestor, was son of Silvester Baldwin, who died on the ship "Martin" on the voyage from England to America, June 21, 1638. Richard Baldwin was baptized at Parish Ashton, Clinton, Buckinghamshire, England, August 25, 1622. He settled at Milford, Connecticut. He was well educated and versed in the law, having studied under his uncle, Henry Baldwin, it is thought. His handwriting is like engraved script. He joined the church, May 9, 1641. His homestead in 1646 was of three acres on the west side of the Wepawaug river. He was on a committee to equalize lots in 1647. He and Thomas Tibbals were granted Beaver Pond Meadow on condition that they drain it within six months. He was sergeant in the militia. He was an active, intelligent citizen. He was prominent in the settlement of the town of Derby, kept a tavern, and was licensed to sell liquor. His predecessor, it is interesting to note, had broken a court order by selling strong drink "at higher prices than allowed". The high cost of living was then a subject for court interference. Not only were prices regulated, but citizens were forbidden to buy certain luxuries unless the court considered them within their means. Men had to pay taxes on a certain minimum before they could indulge their vanity in top-boots or their wives could appear in silken bonnets. Richard Baldwin was a member of the general assembly in May, 1662, and May, 1664. He died July 23, 1665. His widow married, in 1670, William Fowler Jr. He mentioned his children in his will. He married Sarah Bryan. Children: Elizabeth, baptized at Milford, September, 1644; Sylvanus, baptized November 20, 1646; Sarah, baptized April 1, 1649; Temperance, baptized June 29, 1651; Mary, baptized November 6, 1653; Theophilus, April 26, 1659; Zachariah, September 22, 1660; Martha, April 1, 1663; Barnabas, mentioned below.

(II) Barnabas, son of Richard Baldwin, was born in 1665 at Milford. He was a grantee of the town of Derby, was selectman of Milford and collector. His will was dated May 5, 1740, proved October 19, 1741. He married (first) Sarah Buckingham, born January 8, 1664-65, daughter of Samuel and Sarah (Baldwin) Buckingham, granddaughter of Thomas Buckingham. She died before December 3, 1692. He married (second) January 1, 1696, ———. Children: Thomas, baptized January 1, 1688-89; Barnabas, mentioned below; Timothy, baptized January 1, 1698-99; Mary, baptized January 1, 1698-99; Theophilus, baptized October 22, 1699; Henry, baptized June 14, 1702; Sylvanus, born September 17, 1706.

(III) Barnabas (2), son of Barnabas (1) Baldwin, was born in Milford in 1691, baptized January 1, 1698-99. He married, January 13, 1725-26, Mehitable Beecher, of New Haven, widow of John Beecher and daughter of Thomas Tuttle Jr. She was born June 14, 1699, married (first) John Beecher, December 7, 1721, and had a son, John Beecher. Barnabas Baldwin settled at New Haven, but returned to Milford in 1738 and was in the parish of Amity. He was one of the original members of the Woodbridge church. He was an ensign in 1739 in the Sixth Company of New Haven, lieutenant in 1740 and captain in 1749. Children: Barnabas, mentioned below; Mehitable, born December 13, 1728; Esther, March 26, 1731; Elsie, March 26, 1733; Temperance, May 20, 1736; Sarah, March 16, 1737-38; Thomas, July 10, 1742; Burwell, July 11, 1745, died in 1823.

(IV) Barnabas (3), son of Barnabas (2) Baldwin, was born in New Haven, August 31, 1726, died December 24, 1804. He married Mary Turrell, of New Milford, who died January 15, 1803, aged seventy-four. They lived in what is now the town of Woodbridge and he was a man of property and a slave owner.

Children, born in Milford: Silas, born October 19, 1748, died young; Mary, baptized February 10, 1751, died young; Sarah, baptized June 3, 1753, died young; Jared; Barnabas, born 1760; Mary, March 18, 1765; Ephraim, 1766; Silas, mentioned below.

(V) Silas, son of Barnabas (3) Baldwin, was born in Amity parish, Milford, in 1770, died April 18, 1808. He married Mary ———, born June 12, 1774, died July 19, 1850. Children, born in Woodbridge: David R., August 4, 1791; Huldah, July 2, 1793; Betsey, June 18, 1795; Mary, August 26, 1797; Charlotte, July 16, 1799; Silas Irving, mentioned below; Sarah Harriet, June 20, 1803; Lucy C., August 2, 1805; Minerva, 1808.

(VI) Silas Irving, son of Silas Baldwin, was born at Woodbridge, July 5, 1801. He lived in New Haven and was a dealer in boots, shoes and dry goods. He married, March 27, 1828, Eliza E., daughter of Josiah Newton and granddaughter of Enoch Newton, of Milford. Children: Elbert I.; Eliza Newton, married Henry R. Hatch (see Hatch IX); Alice Gertrude, married John M. Richards; Adolphus Kent.

DUNCAN   Samuel Duncan, immigrant, settled in Newbury, Massachusetts. Savage says perhaps he moved to Boston. He owned land at Muddy Brook, Boston, ·now Brookline. He had a son Thomas, January 15, 1656, and others.

(I) John Duncan, the ancestor of the line herein recorded, was born in Billerica, October 28, 1678. He was a weaver by trade. He came from Billerica to Worcester, Massachusetts, among the early settlers. He bought land, one hundred and three acres on North brook, October, 1722, of Gershom Rice. He married, June 16, 1701, Sarah, daughter of John Dutton. He and his wife Sarah deeded to son, John Jr., February 10, 1731-32, part of the homestead on North brook. He died at Worcester, December 15, 1739, aged sixty-seven. John's will was dated November 30, 1739, and proved December 25, 1739, at Worcester, bequeathing to wife Sarah; children Simeon, John, Samuel, Daniel, Sarah Parmenter and Abigail. Children, born at Billerica: Sarah, June 14, 1703, married ——— Parmenter; John, April 10, 1706, married Sarah Rogers; Elizabeth, January 9, 1710-11; Daniel, mentioned below; Simeon, August 22, 1713, married, at Billerica, August 22, 1743, Bridget Richardson, and lived in Worcester; Samuel; Abigail.

(II) Daniel, son of John Duncan, was born in Billerica, February 13, 1711-12. He was a soldier in the revolution from Petersham in the guards under Colonel Loammi Baldwin in May, 1775, also in Captain Joel Fletcher's company, Colonel Ephraim Doolittle's regiment, and in Captain John Callender's company, Colonel Richard Gridley's regiment of artillery in 1775. He married Sarah Rice, of Conway, born February 9, 1703, died at Petersham, December 10, 1781, daughter of Gershom Rice, born May 9, 1667, died December 19, 1768, aged one hundred and one years, son of Thomas Rice. Gershom Rice resided in Groton, Connecticut, and removed to Marlborough, Massachusetts, before October 13, 1713; was one of those who wished to renew the settlement at Worcester, whither he went in 1715 and had a grant of eighty acres in 1718; was the second settler of the third and permanent settlement of Worcester, his brother, Jonas Rice, being the first; the first town meeting was at his house, and he planted the first orchard in Worcester; married Elizabeth Balcom, born August 16, 1672, daughter of Henry and Elizabeth (Haynes) Balcom; children: Gershom, born 1696; Elizabeth, October 20, 1698; Abraham, October 16, 1701; Sarah, February 9, 1703, mentioned above; Mathias, January 26, 1707; Ruth, April 11, 1710. Children of Daniel and Sarah Duncan, born in Worcester: Mary, December 30, 1738-39, married James Jackson; John, September 4, 1740, married Rebecca Meacham, of New Salem; Daniel, June 1, 1742, married, January 21, 1765, Zurvilla Rice, of Worcester; Elizabeth, January 26, 1743-44; Ezekiel, January 15, 1744-45; Lovinah, October 7, 1747, married, 1765, John Rice, of Petersham; Abel, mentioned below; Sally, married James Jackson, of Petersham.

(III) Abel, son of Daniel Duncan, was born in Worcester, Massachusetts, February 2, 1749-50. He married Lydia Mills, of Petersham. Children: Abel Jr., born February 22, 1772; Nathan, married Betsy Winn, of Chester; Rufus, mentioned below; Anna, married Amos Heald, of Chester; Lucy, married Jason Duncan Jr., of Dummerston; Charles, married Patty Carter, of Wethersfield; John, married Caroline Hastings, of Charlestown, New Hampshire; Arad; George; Lydia, married Daniel Church, of Chester.

(IV) Rufus, son of Abel Duncan, was born in Vermont about 1780. He married Lucy Kimball, of Chester, Vermont. They lived at Weathersfield, Vermont. Among their children was Albert Russell, mentioned below.

(V) Albert Russell, son of Rufus Duncan, was born in Weathersfield, Vermont, in 1814. He married Mary Sophia Kimball, born in Burlington, Vermont, in 1817, died in 1891. Children: 1. Frank A. 2. Henry A., enlisted

in the civil war from Vermont and served in the First Vermont Battery; died in the service, was unmarried. 3. Albert Russell, mentioned below. 4. Ellen May, born 1851; married (first) a Mr. Weston, by whom she had one child, Orville M.; married (second) Rev. J. E. Metcalf, now living near Troy, New York. 5. Kate E., born 1858; married M. A. Chase, now living in Burlington, Vermont; three children.

(VI) Albert Russell (2), Jr., son of Albert Russell (1) Duncan, was born at Winooski, Vermont, December 6, 1847. He received his early education there in the public schools. Afterward he was for six years clerk in a dry goods store at Burlington, Vermont. In 1869 he came to Cleveland, Ohio, where he was for twelve years a salesman in a dry goods house. In 1882 he established a commission business, dealing in butter, eggs and other produce in Cleveland, beginning in a modest way with small capital and being his own salesman, bookkeeper and manager. In the first year his total sales amounted to fifteen thousand dollars. From year to year, however, the business grew to large proportions and became correspondingly profitable. In 1901 it was incorporated as the A. R. Duncan Jr. Company, of which Mr. Duncan is president and general manager. The company does an aggregate business of more than a million and a half dollars a year and is the largest of its kind in Cleveland and in the state of Ohio. Mr. Duncan is a Republican in politics, but disposed to independence from party ties. He is a member of the Chamber of Commerce of Cleveland, of the Cleveland Athletic Club, the Colonial Club, the Gentlemen's Driving Club, the New England Society of Cleveland and the Western Reserve.

He married, in August, 1869, Ellen Maria Newton, born May 6, 1848, died November 24, 1911, daughter of Richard and Catherine (White) Newton. She was a member of the local chapter, Daughters of the Revolution. They had no children.

SACKETT John Sackett, the immigrant, came to New England from Bristol, England, with his brother Simon, on the ship "Lyon", in the winter of 1630-31. He brought with him his son John Sackett Jr., who was about three years old at the time. No record of any other of his immediate family has been found. Either before leaving England, or during his tedious mid-winter voyage to America, he became attached to the brilliant and popular nonconformist minister, Roger Williams, whom he followed first to Plymouth settlement, and afterwards to Rhode Island. Tiring of his life in the wilderness, he made his way to the New Haven settlement, in the records of which he is mentioned as early as 1640, and as late as 1684. On October 6, 1684, he filed an inventory of the estate of John Sackett Jr. Child, John, mentioned below.

(II) John (2), son of John (1) Sackett, was born about 1628 in England, died September 3, 1683. He was brought to New England by his father in 1631, when he was three years old. Very little is known of his boyhood days. In 1646 he was a member of the New Haven Train Band. The general court of that year first brought him to notice and gave him a place in the recorded history of Connecticut by fining him six cents "for wanting a rest at the training he attended". A rest was a stick crotched at one end which was used to steady the heavy musket then in use when taking aim. On May 20, 1652, he married Agnes Tinkham, who was probably a younger sister of the colonist, Ephraim Tinkham, of Plymouth settlement. He remained a resident of New Haven until his death in 1684. The records there show that on October 6, 1684, John Sackett made and filed an inventory of the estate of John Sackett Jr. Agnes (Tinkham) Sackett died at New Haven in the early part of the year 1707. An inventory of her estate was filed April 25, 1707, by her grandson, Lieutenant Joseph Sackett, who had previously been appointed administrator of her husband's estate. The records also show that on July 8, 1712, Lieutenant Joseph Sackett made a final accounting of said estate and was discharged from his bonds. Children: John, born April 30, 1653; Jonathan, mentioned below; Mary, September 24, 1657; Joseph, March 2, 1660; Martha, September 19, 1662.

(III) Jonathan, son of John (2) Sackett, was born June 6, 1655, and lived in New Haven, Connecticut. He married Hannah ———. Children, born at New Haven: Jonathan, married Ruth Hotchkiss; Richard, mentioned below; Hannah; John, married Hannah Smith; Joseph.

(IV) Captain Richard Sackett, son of Jonathan Sackett, was born at New Haven. In his younger days he seems to have worked in the forests in New England learning how tar was extracted from pine trees. In 1699 he lived in New York City, where he was proprietor of a malt house or brewery located on the north side of Cherry street, then known as Sackett street, named in his honor. About 1699 he was commissioned captain of the Seventh Company of the New York City Regiment under Colonel William Peartree, and he kept this command for several years. On March 11, 1703, he petitioned the Lord Cornbury government for permission to purchase some land in Dutchess county, called Wassaic, from the Indians, and the petition was granted. Richard Sackett & Company received a patent for this land, November 2, 1704, covering seven thousand five hundred acres. His name occurs often in public records of New York and Connecticut at that time, and he seems to have been very prominent. In April, 1703, he was appointed by Lord Cornbury as chief revenue officer for the southeastern section of the province of New York. In April, 1704, he filed a record of expenses incurred in seizing the sloop "Betsey" of Oyster Bay, for trading contrary to the law, and bringing her up to New York, showing that he had jurisdiction of both land and seacoast and harbor. On June 16, 1704, he was licensed to dispose by lottery of several lots of land in New York City and Dutchess county, New York. Some of his descendants say that for a time he was a sea captain. Also it is said that "having perfected his title to the Wassaic tract, he, in connection with several wealthy residents of New York City, purchased the Indian titles to several other extensive tracts in same vicinity, and the colony line between New York and Connecticut not having at the time been established, he probably availed himself of his knowledge of astronomy, acquired in the study of navigation, and made experiments and observations, based upon the treaty of partition made in 1683, but which had never been carried out by actual survey, and persuaded himself that the boundary line when surveyed would run within about two miles of the Ousatonic river. And that in this belief he purchased of Metoxan, the great chief of all the Indian tribes in that region, twenty-two thousand acres of land, more than seven thousand acres of which the survey of the boundary line showed to be in Connecticut." This probably refers to the Nine Partners tract for which, April 10, 1606, a patent was issued for him and associates. In May, 1705, he petitioned the general assembly of Connecticut for permission to transport all pine and spruce for use in his Majesty's navy, and the petition was granted. According to the census about 1708 in New York City, he lived in the east ward, and had a family which included his wife, four children and four negro slaves, one female and three males. In 1711 the family settled permanently in Dutchess county, about a mile south of Wassaic, and it is said that when he settled there was no one living within fifteen miles of him. In 1711 Governor Hunter appointed him superintendent of the manufacture of naval stores in the province of New York and later of New Jersey also, somewhat in opposition to the Lords of Trade, and he served in this office during Governor Hunter's term of office; at least twelve times the governor spoke favorably of his work in official reports to the Lords of Trade, in the first of which he said: "I have provided here by the name of Sackett, who hath lived three years in the Easterne Countries, among the manufacturers of tar, and gives me a vert rational account of the method of preparing the trees; I have also wrote to Connecticut for two more, who, as I am informed, understand ye matter very well". Mr. Sackett was one of the presiding officers of the "Court over the Palatines", which was appointed by "His Excellency, Brigadier Hunter, Captain-General and Governor-in-Chief", to manage the affairs of the Palatine villages within his jurisdiction. In 1715 he was made the first clerk of Dutchess county, being recommended by Judge Leonard Lewis, and he held that office until 1721. He petitioned the New York assembly, November 29, 1722, for a warrant of survey of land in Dutchess county. He was one of the incorporators of "The New London Society, United for Trade and Commerce", for which in 1732 the general assembly of Connecticut granted a charter. In 1734-35 the New York colonial assembly passed an act for the division of the tract of land in Dutchess county called Nine Partners. Richard Sackett died at Wassaic in 1746 and was buried in a private burying ground on the original home farm of the family. His will was proved April 28, 1746, recorded both at Albany and New York City. The last years of his life were made often disagreeable by suits against him from persons who claimed tracts of his land from deeds which they declared antedated his. Captain Sackett was employed by the British colonial government of New York state for about twenty years, and he was connected with Livingston in that service.

He married Margery L. Sleade, the marriage license being issued in New York City, May 11, 1699. Children: Richard, mentioned below; John, Catherine, Maria, Josiah Crego.

(V) Richard (2), son of Captain Richard (1) Sackett, was born in 1701. After his father's death, in 1746, he purchased a farm in New Milford, Connecticut, where he moved from Dover, Dutchess county, New York, and there spent the remainder of his life. The Dutchess county records show that he refused to qualify as an executor of his father's estate, as he wished not to be involved in several law suits pending relative to title to

large tracts of land covered by his father's will. He was a well-to-do farmer in Milford, and seems to have left a will which was not recorded. He left several pieces of land to his wife and children. The will is said to have been dated April 2, 1771, and the larger share is said to have gone to Richard. He married Mary ———. Children: Margery, married David Green; Mary, married Israel Canfield; Richard, mentioned below; Elizabeth, born October 14, 1751, died probably in infancy; Catherine, October 14, 1751, died probably in infancy.

(VI) Richard (3), son of Richard (2) Sackett, was born July 14, 1749, in Milford, died in 1789. He lived in New Milford, and in Arlington, Vermont. He seems to have been a well-to-do farmer also. On January 4, 1770, before he was of age, he bought from his father fifty acres of land near the homestead at New Milford. The deed of this land is still in possession of the family. He does not seem to have been active in public affairs, but to have preferred a quiet life. He inherited a large part of his father's estate in 1771, and in 1775 sold all the property in New Milford. He then moved to Arlington, where he was a member of the military company under Captain Ebenezer Wallace. He served in the revolution also. He married, before 1776, Martha Benedict, born 1756, died 1812; she married (second) about 1791, Jason Kellogg. Children: Richard, born April 22, 1777; Lucy, October 8, 1780; Jonathan, March 12, 1783; Anson, mentioned below; Hester, June 24, 1789. Mrs. Sackett was daughter of Jonathan Benedict, born 1723, died 1800, married Lucy Castle, who died at North Milford, Vermont; Jonathan Benedict moved after her death to Manchester, Vermont, where he married Widow Margaret Seelye (Pinnock). He was son of Joseph Benedict, who was born at Norwalk, Connecticut, and married (first) Anne ———, died 1716; they moved to Ridgefield, Connecticut; he married (second) March 21, 1720, Mary ———, mother of Jonathan. Joseph was son of John Benedict, who was born at Southold, Long Island, and married at Norwalk, Connecticut, November 11, 1670, Phebe Gregory; was made freeman in 1680, and was a deacon; selectman from 1689 to 1699. John was son of Thomas Benedict, the immigrant ancestor, who came from Nottinghamshire, England, to Massachusetts in 1638, and married Mary Bridgman; they lived several years at Southold and in 1662 lived at Jamaica, Long Island; later lived at Norwalk, where he was deacon of the church.

(VII) Anson, son of Richard (3) Sackett,

was born May 27, 1785, died in 1869. He was a farmer. In religion he was an Episcopalian, and in politics a Democrat. About 1812 he moved to Volney, Oswego county, New York, and in 1838 to Villenova, Chautauqua county, New York, where he remained until his death. Jacob Kendal, a citizen of Volney, wrote in 1899 that Anson and Jonathan Sackett came in 1812, bought a farm which they ran together, and then divided. Anson took the west part and built a house for which Jacob Kendal helped to get the timber; he also said that Anson Sackett was an officer of the Episcopal church at Fulton, four miles from his home. He married, at Poultney, Vermont, where he was born, Docia, daughter of Denison Ruggles, of Hampton, New York. They were married January 31, 1810. Children: 1. George R., born December 15, 1815, died July 15, 1848; married Clarissa (Payne) Woodbury. 2. Clarissa, September 26, 1817, died August, 1902; married Selah Seymour. 3. William D., mentioned below. 4. Ezra B., October 16, 1822, died April 16, 1896; married Simena R. Ward. 5. Martha, April 18, 1824, died April 6, 1846, unmarried. 6. Cyrus T., April 14, 1827, died May 29, 1855, unmarried. 7. Ozander A., May 12, 1829, died February 26, 1894; married Ophelia A. Gould. 8. Hester, May 2, 1832; married Medad S. Corey, M. D. 9. Phoebe D., October 8, 1834; married William J. Swits.

(VIII) William Dennison, son of Anson Sackett, was born in Oswego county, New York, August 30, 1820, died in February, 1904. When he was eighteen years of age he came with his parents to Chautauqua county, New York, in 1838; the journey was very difficult, as it was made in the winter on sleds and snowstorms and unbroken roads made traveling hard. He attended Allegheny College, Meadville, Pennsylvania, and then became principal of the Meadville Academy, which was the preparatory school for the college. His health, however, compelled him to give up this work, and he then served an apprenticeship at the carpenter and joiner trade. He became a successful contractor and builder, and in connection with his business carried on a planing mill. He had many large contracts in connection with building the Atlantic & Great Western railroad. As his business increased and he needed more capital he took a partner, and conducted business under the firm name of Sackett & Thomas. He lived for the most of his life at Meadville, but often made long stays at the home of his daughter, Mrs. Waters, at Nashville, Tennessee. Early in life he joined the Methodist Episcopal church, and was always generous towards its support. He contributed toward the building of the First Church and the State Street Church in Meadville, and for many years was a class leader. He married, December 31, 1849, Caroline, daughter of Captain Ora and Eliza (Morison) De Long. Captain De Long came from Sackett's Harbor, New York; the harbor was named from the Sackett family, and he was uncle of the well known Lieutenant De Long who headed an expedition for the North Pole. Children: 1. James De Long, mentioned below. 2. Clara Elisabeth, born January 23, 1853; resides in Meadville, Pennsylvania. 3. Ella M., born July 13, 1855, died November 9, 1891; married W. T. Waters. 4. Hattie D., November 17, 1857, died April 9, 1859. 5. Albert H., February 8, 1859; married Ida Benn. 6. Mary E., July 21, 1862; resides in Meadville. 7. Carrie M., January 13, 1866; married W. T. Waters. 8. Gertrude, E., August 4, 1868; married C. C. Laffer, M. D.

(IX) James De Long, son of William Dennison Sackett, was born at Meadville, Pennsylvania, January 26, 1851. He attended the public schools of his native town and for a time was a student in Allegheny College, Pennsylvania. After leaving school he was employed for a time as clerk in the purchasing department of the New York, Pennsylvania & Ohio Railroad Company. In 1883 he entered the Cleveland Paper Manufacturing Company, a corporation of which he is now secretary and manager. He is a prominent figure in the wholesale paper business. He is a member of the Chamber of Commerce of Cleveland and of the Cleveland Association of Credit Men and The Manufacturers and Wholesale Merchants Board. He is also a member of the Cleveland Athletic Club, the Mayfield Country Club, the Euclid Club, the Graphic Arts Club and of the New England Society of Cleveland and the Western Reserve. In religion he is an Episcopalian, in politics a Republican.

He married, December 29, 1892, at Cleveland, Clara Gertrude, born in Lancaster, Pennsylvania, March, 1866, daughter of William H. and Anna (Buckins) Hostetter. Their only child, a daughter, born July 8, 1894, died July 10, 1894.

WILEY

The surnames Wiley and Willey were originally used interchangeably in England, though the American families of Wiley, mentioned below, seem not related to the Willey families at all. Wiley or Willey is derived from the personal name William. Some others of the same derivation are Williams, Williamson, Fitz-Williams, Wilkins, Wilcox, Wilmot, Billson, Tilson (William was once nicknamed Till, as well as Bill), and Guilliam, Gillett, etc., from the French Guillaume. The surname Wiley was derived from the name of a parish in Wiltshire. The Wiley coat-of-arms is: Argent three griffins passant sable. The Willey family in various parts of the country uses a modified form of this armorial, and this seems to prove that originally the Wiley and Willey families were of the same stock. Wiley or Willey: Argent three griffins segeant in fesse sable. Also: Argent three griffins segeant in fesse sable between five trefoils slipped vert. The only crest found is: A rose bush vert bearing roses argent. The Scotch Wylie or Wiley family is especially numerous in the north of Ireland, county Antrim.

A number of the Willey family came to New England before 1650. Allen Willey was admitted to the church in Boston, November 9, 1634; Isaac Willey and wife Joanna were in Boston before 1640; she married second June 8, 1660, in Boston, Edward Burcham of Lynn. Thomas Willey settled in Dover, New Hampshire, and a large family descended from a settler of this surname at New London, Connecticut.

(I) John Wiley, the immigrant ancestor of the Wiley family, was born in England, about 1615. He settled at Reading, Massachusetts, where his descendants have been prominent to the present time. He gave bonds in the general court July 30, 1640, and was a proprietor in 1648. His wife Elizabeth was a member of the Reading church in 1648; she died August 3, 1662. He lived in "Little World", now called Woodville, Reading, and was one of the earliest settlers in that town. He died probably in 1672. Children: John Jr.; Benjamin (?), married, 1707, Mary Nichols; Elizabeth, born March 4, 1649; Timothy, mentioned below; Susanna, born July 16, 1655; Sarah, born February 4, 1658.

(II) Timothy, son of John Wiley, was born in Reading, Massachusetts, April 24, 1653. He succeeded his father on the homestead, and became a leading citizen, holding the offices of selectman and deputy to the general court. He died in 1728. He married (first) in 1678, Elizabeth Davis, who died in 1695, daughter of George Davis. He married (second) 1698, Susanna ———. Children of first wife: John, born 1679; Elizabeth, December 12, 1681, died young; Timothy, mentioned below; Elizabeth, born May 1, 1690. Child of second wife: Thomas, born June 17, 1697.

(III) Timothy (2), son of Timothy (1) Wiley, was born in 1688-92, at Reading, and

died August 19, 1749. He lived at Woodville, Reading. He married, in 1714, Mary Poole, of Lynnfield. Children, born at Reading: Sarah, 1715, baptized July 24, 1715; Susanna, 1717, baptized January 8, 1717; Mary, born September 21, 1721; Lydia, April 17, 1724; Timothy, October 5, 1725; John, 1727; Nathaniel, mentioned below; Phineas, February 8, 1730-1.

(IV) Nathaniel, son of Timothy (2) Wiley, was born at Reading, April 11, 1729, and baptized October 13, 1729. He lived in Reading, and died there in 1822, aged ninety-three years. He served in the revolution on the Lexington alarm, April 19, 1775, in Captain John Walton's company, Colonel David Green's regiment. He was a member of the train band of Reading. He married, April 5, 1751, Mary Eaton, of Andover, Massachusetts. Children, born at Wakefield, South Reading: Timothy, June 21, 1752; Mary, November 7, 1756; Nathaniel, March 29, 1759; Phineas, August 19, 1761; Benjamin, December 12, 1763; Edmund, July 12, 1766; Ephraim, August 17, 1768; Samuel, mentioned below; Eli, April 11, 1775.

(V) Samuel, son of Nathaniel Wiley, was born at Reading, Massachusetts, January 10, 1772. He married at Reading, February 19, 1795, Betsey Vinton. Children, born at Reading, except the eldest: Samuel, born in Stoneham; John, January 23, 1796; John (2d), mentioned below; Ira, March 13, 1802; Betsey, February 27, 1804; Adam, April 5, 1806; Louisa, August 2, 1808; Rebecca, October 27, 1810. Ira Wiley was captain of the famous Rifle Grays, married Eunice W. Nichols and had Horace and Eunice A. Wiley. Adam's son Herbert was a soldier in the civil war in Company K, Twenty-third Massachusetts Regiment, volunteer militia. John Wiley's farm was at Little World, Reading, now town of Wakefield. Children: Lyman, Orlando, George, Samuel, and William Henry, mentioned below.

(VII) William Henry, son of John, and grandson of Samuel Wiley, was born September 12, 1821, in or near Boston.

He was educated in the public schools and was for many years a manufacturer of shoes in Hartford, Connecticut, senior partner in the firm of William H. Wiley & Son, in his later years. He was for many years a member of the North Baptist Church of that city, and helped organize the Asylum Hill Baptist Church of which he was a member at the time of his death. An earnest Republican, never failing to vote for fifty years. He died in November, 1892, in Hartford. He married Miranda Griswold, born at Simsbury, Connecticut, in 1827, daughter of Roger and Eunice (Loomis) Griswold, a descendant of many of the early Connecticut pioneers. Children: 1. Louis Griswold, born 1849; married Carrie ————; children: Louis Griswold Jr., Robert, Herbert and Mabel. 2. Edward Norris, mentioned below. 3. Lyman A., born at Hartford, Connecticut, 1857; married Jennie Burkett, of Hartford, and had Lillian Burkett and Ralph Burkett Wiley; now living in Chicago, secretary of People's Gaslight and Coke Company of Chicago. 4. James Allen, born at Hartford, 1859; married Annie Corbin, of Hartford; children: Harry, John and Louisa Wiley. 5. Clarence Henry, born at Hartford, 1863; resides at Hartford, retired from business; married Julia Howard, and had Leland Howard Wiley. 6. Annie A., born at Hartford; married Edward C. Frisbie, of Hartford; she died March 30, 1912; children: Florence, Edward C. Jr. and Alice Frisbie. 7. Lillian, born at Hartford, died aged sixteen years.

(VIII) Edward Norris, son of William Henry Wiley, was born at Hartford, Connecticut, March 8, 1855, and was educated in the public and high schools of Hartford. He started upon his business career as clerk in a wholesale drygoods house in Hartford, and after ten years of experience went to Chicago in 1881. He entered the employ of S. M. Moore, insurance agent and broker, and was subsequently admitted to partnership. The firm afterward became Wiley, Magill & Johnson, then Webster & Wiley. Since the death of Mr. Webster, Mr. Wiley has continued in the insurance business with offices in the Insurance Exchange Building, Chicago. He is a member of the Union League Club of Chicago, the Chicago Athletic Club of Chicago, the Kenwood Club, the Midlothian Country Club, the Chicago Club of Charlevoix, Michigan, where Mr. Wiley has a summer residence; the Congregational Club, the Kenwood Evangelical Church, and the New England Society of Chicago.

He married (first) May 31, 1883, Jennie E. Moore, born in Chicago, 1860, died in July, 1903, daughter of Silas M. and Elizabeth (Davidson) Moore. He married (second) August, 1909, Mrs. Alice (Kelsey) Teall, widow of Edward M. Teall. Children by first wife: 1. Silas Moore, born in Chicago, March 15, 1884; graduate of Princeton College with the degree of bachelor of arts, and from the University of Michigan with the degree of bachelor of laws, now a member of the Illinois Bar Association, practicing law in Chicago. 2. Edward Norris Jr., born in Chicago, 1887, educated in the public schools of Chicago, the

preparatory school at Lawrenceville, New York, and now in the employ of the insurance firm of William H. Wiley & Sons, Chicago.

SCOTT George Robert White Scott, A. M., Ph. D., D. D., was of Scotch and English ancestry. He was son of John and Eliza (Boden) Scott. The family is descended from Sir Walter Scott, and his mother, Eliza (Boden) Scott, was descended from James Beattie, the poet.

Dr. Scott was born in Pittsburgh, Pennsylvania, April 17, 1842, died at Berlin, Germany, September 13, 1902, after a short illness. Although he spent his early years in Pennsylvania, he was educated in New England, and was graduated from Middlebury College, Vermont, in 1864, and from Andover Theological Seminary in 1867. After graduating he was called as pastor to the church at Newport, New Hampshire, in 1867, and was ordained September 17, 1868, remaining until 1873. He went from Newport to Boston, where he remained for two years in charge of the Chambers Street Mission which was supported by the Old South Church. In 1876 he went to Fitchburg, Massachusetts, where he was pastor of the Rollstone Church for twelve years, until 1888. He was very popular and powerful both in the parish and in the city. He was a member of several of the national councils of the Congregational churches, and spoke in those of 1898 and 1901. He was chosen moderator of the Massachusetts Association of Churches. In December, 1885, his physician insisted on his taking a trip to Europe for his health, but he retained his name as pastor of the Rollstone Church and his position as chaplain on the staff of the Sixth Massachusetts Regiment. Although he remained abroad for six years, he was not inactive, but preached in many places, at Dresden, Florence, Venice and Rome. He preached the installation sermon of Rev. Dr. Stuckenberg at the American church in Berlin, worked on the church committee, and took charge of the church during the pastor's trip to America. With Dr. Philip Schaff he traveled through Germany, becoming acquainted with many prominent people. He was a delegate to the Evangelical Alliance which met in Florence, Italy. In the year 1886 he studied at Tübingen, and was at the University of Berlin for two years, receiving the degree of Doctor of Philosophy in 1889. Already both Middlebury College and Olivet College, Michigan, had awarded him the degree of Doctor of Divinity.

On his return to America he accepted a call as pastor and preacher for six months at the

Edward N. Wiley

Congregational church of Leominster, Massachusetts, and remained there for five years and a half. A tribute to his ability as organizer and manager is shown in the fact that four colleges offered him the position of president, among them Middlebury College, and for years he was trustee of Dow Academy in Franconia, New Hampshire, and Jaffna College, Ceylon. Even after he retired from parish work to his home, Kenrick Park, Newton, he was as busy as ever with sermons, addresses and committees. In addition to all this work he found time to write. The "Italian Renaissance of To-day" is one of his writings. He also contributed much to *The Chicago Advance, The Independent, The Congregationalist, Our Day, Good Words* (English), and others. He became a member of the New England Historic Genealogical Society in 1893, and his work as chairman of the committee on papers and essays was very valuable. One of his best works was in the biographical sketch of Rev. Edwards A. Park, D. D., of Andover, who was his teacher there and a personal friend, in "Professor Park and His Friends", which he collaborated with Joseph Cook and others. He was fraternal delegate of the National Council of American Congregational Churches to the tercentenary celebration and dedication of the John Robinson Memorial Church of Gainsborough, England. He had been instrumental in raising over five thousand dollars for this church, to which Governor Crane, Bishop Lawrence, and President Eliot, of Massachusetts, contributed. He made three addresses during these services, June 8-11, 1902. Following this visit he preached several times in London, and gave addresses at Hackney College, London, and at the United Yorkshire College, Bradford, and spoke at the Congregational Union of England and Wales. On November 1 of the same year, 1902, his funeral was held in the Eliot Congregational Church, Newton, Massachusetts, at which Rev. Drs. W. D. Davis, pastor of the church, Edward L. Clark, and Samuel E. Herrick, of Boston, officiated. Among the delegations present at the funeral were those from the American Historical Association, the American Home Missionary Society, in which he was a member of the national committee, the Congregational National Council, the Massachusetts State Association of Congregational Churches, the New England Historic Genealogical Society, American Board of Foreign Missions, of which he was a corporate member, Boston Theological Library, Andover Theological Seminary, Middlesex Congregational Union, the Congregational Club of Boston, the Bostonian So-

ciety, the Monday and Tuesday Clubs of Newton, and the Board of Trustees of Jaffna College of Ceylon. He was buried in the family lot in Mt. Auburn cemetery, the Rev. Dr. James L. Barton, of the American Board, officiating. Memorial services were held at Leominster, November 9, and at the Rollstone Church, Fitchburg, November 16; at the Gainsborough church, September 28, and in the American Church at Berlin on the same day.

Wherever Dr. Scott lived he soon became powerful among the neighbors, and he made very few enemies. Everyone loved him for his manliness, his knowledge, and his genial, hearty manners. He was always a true friend and generous. He was of commanding stature, able to hold an audience through his personality. His name will always be remembered and cherished by the churches in which he preached. In his home and social life he was much beloved. He was always young in spirit, and "always a lover". On his trip to the Gainsborough church, when President Roosevelt sent him as his representative, he wrote: "Because I cannot come Dr. Scott shall be in my stead. Receive his greetings as my greetings." His ambition was to be an authority on the history of the Puritan movement that had its origin in England, its development in Holland, and its completion in America, and it was natural that he should be chosen for the important position of carrying greetings to the historic church. Rev. Alexander McKenzie, D.D., in the funeral service, said of him that he was "Called, chosen, faithful", than which no better tribute could be given.

Dr. Scott married, September 22, 1869, Mary Elizabeth, daughter of Moses Arnold Dow, of Boston, the founder of Dow Academy and a direct descendant of Molly Burr, the niece of President Aaron Burr, of Princeton. He had two sons, George Dow, mentioned below, and Arnold, and a daughter, Mary Elizabeth, who died in infancy.

(II) Dr. George Dow Scott, son of Rev. George Robert White Scott, was born at Newport, New Hampshire, January 28, 1871. He attended the public schools of his native town and Phillips Academy, Andover, Massachusetts. He then went abroad and studied at Eberhardt Ludwig's Royal Imperial Gymnasium at Stuttgart, Germany, and at the Schillmann Gymnasium in Berlin, Germany. Afterward he traveled extensively in all parts of Europe and became proficient in several European languages. In 1891 he returned to this country and entered Middlebury College, Vermont, graduating there in the class of 1895 with the degree of Bachelor of Science. In 1896 he received the degree of Bachelor of Arts at Harvard University, after which he won his degree of Doctor of Medicine at Harvard Medical School. In 1898 he served in the Boston Lying-in-Hospital; in 1900 he was assistant physician on the Boston Floating Hospital; in 1901 he was an interne in the Boston City Hospital, south department, and in the New York Infants' and Children's Hospital in 1903. For many months he served in the Vienna General Hospital and in the Poliklinik Hospital, children's department, also in Vienna, under Professor Alois Monti. Since 1904 Dr. Scott has been in practice in New York City. He is assistant visiting physician and lecturer on the diseases of infants and children as well as chief of clinic of the Post-Graduate Medical School and Hospital of New York; chief of clinic and attending physician at St. Mark's Hospital of New York, consulting specialist at the Nassau Hospital, and an eminent specialist in the diseases of children.

He is a member of the Harvard Medical Society, the Bronx Medical Society, the New York Physicians' Association, the West Side Clinical Society, the Post-Graduate Clinical Association, the Greater New York Medical Society, the New York County Medical Society, the Harlem Medical Association, the New York State Medical Society, the American Medical Association, the Society of Medical Jurisprudence, the Pediatric Section of the Academy of Medicine. His office is at 111 West Seventy-seventh street, New York. In politics he is a Republican, in religion a Congregationalist.

RUGGLES   The Ruggles family is descended from the English family of counties Suffolk and Essex, with very few exceptions. There are some who claim descent from an ancestor who came from France. In a life of George Ruggles, the famous scholar and dramatic author during the reign of King James I., written by John Sydney Hawkins, son of Sir John Hawkins, and published in London in 1787, there is a statement that the Ruggles family of Essex and Suffolk was descended from the very ancient family of Ruggeley or De Ruggeley, of Staffordshire; he states in the book that doubtless the name was derived from the town of Ruggeley or Rugeley, Staffordshire, where they first settled. The name is said to be of Anglo-Saxon origin, meaning rugged land, and it has been variously spelled De Ruggele, De Ruggeley, Ruggeley, Ruggelay, Ruggleigh, Rogyll, Rogle, Rugle, Rugles, Rug-

gles, and finally Ruggles. The first mention of the family is in Shaw's "Antiquities of Staffordshire", which states that Robert de Ruggele lived in 1220, during the reign of Henry III., and later that Humphrey de Ruggeley was owner of Hawksbeard. In the "Antiquities of Warwickshire", Sir William Dugdale speaks of the families as follows: "They were gentlemen of very good note, for so early as the twenty-sixth year of the reign of King Edward I., viz., A. D. 1298, I find William de Ruggele, de comitatu Staffordiae, recorded with an encomium for having performed faithful service to the king in his army then in Flanders; and in the tenth, thirteenth and fourteenth of Edward III., mention is made of Simon de Ruggeley, who was then sheriff of the counties of Salop and Stafford". He also states that Nicholas Ruggeley, of Hawksbeard, was appointed to the rangership of Sutton Chase, Warwickshire, in the second year of Henry IV., continuing until the tenth year of Henry VI.; about 1423 he bought the manor of Claptham, in Dunton, later called Downton Ruggeley, Warwickshire; in 1428 he was sheriff of Warwick and Leicester. A branch of this family moved to Lincolnshire, at Holton Holgate, and later some of the family moved to Essex and Suffolk, where the first known ancestor of the American family was found in 1547. The coat-of-arms of the family is as follows: "Argent, between three roses a chevron gules". Crest: "A tower or, with a beacon flaming at the top proper, and transpierced with four arrows in saltire, points downward, argent." Motto: "Struggle."

(I) Thomas Ruggles was of Sudbury, county Suffolk, England. His will was dated June 21, 1547. He had a brother William, and a sister Isabella, who married ——— Norris. Children: Nicholas, mentioned below; John, of Stanstead, Suffolk, will proved May 19, 1566; Ann; Elizabeth.

(II) Nicholas, son of Thomas Ruggles, was also of Sudbury, county Suffolk. Children: Roger, married, February 23, 1573, Margery Dandye; George, of Sudbury, will proved May 16, 1616, married, June 5, 1575, Alice Dandye; Thomas, mentioned below; Edward, married and left issue; Margery, married, January 19, 1584, John Drury; William, married October 6, 1577, Mary Brundish, (second) October 11, 1585, Lucy Grome; Robert of Lavenham, county Suffolk, died June 21, 1605, married Elizabeth ———.

(III) Thomas (2), son of Nicholas Ruggles, was of Sudbury, England. Children: Thomas, mentioned below; John, of Roxbury, Massachusetts, in 1635, born 1591.

(IV) Thomas (3), son of Thomas (2)

Ruggles, was the immigrant ancestor of the family. He was born in Sudbury, England, in 1584. He married, in Nasing, county Essex, England, November 1, 1620, Mary, sister of William Curtis, who came to Roxbury with his family in 1632. She was born about 1586, and died February 14, 1674, aged eighty-eight according to the Roxbury church records, though perhaps she was eighty-five years of age, as the Nasing records give a Mary Curtis baptized in 1589. Thomas Ruggles came to Roxbury, Massachusetts, in 1637, with his wife and children, Sarah and Samuel, his oldest son having died in England, and his second son John being brought over as a servant of Phillip Eliot. He and his wife joined the church soon after their arrival. He "had a great sicknesse the yeare after his coming", and died November 15, 1644, "of a consumption". In his will he bequeathed to his son John a lot of about sixteen acres of land, "beyond the Great Pond", Jamaica, and to Samuel he left the lot of about seven acres at Roxbury, near the lots of Phillip Eliot and Arthur Gary, and about twelve acres at Dedham, Massachusetts; his daughter Sarah received £3, and his wife had the rest of his land and his house, as well as certain provisions to be supplied by his sons, who after her death were to divide the land, John having one half and Samuel and Sarah the other half. Mary, wife of Thomas, doubtless married (second) "goodman" Roote. She survived her first husband thirty years. Children: Thomas, born about 1621-2, died in England; John, mentioned below; Sarah, baptized in Nasing, February 16, 1627-8; Samuel, born 1629.

(V) John, son of Thomas (3) Ruggles, was baptized January 8, 1624-5, in Nasing, England. When he was ten years of age, in 1635, he came to Roxbury, Massachusetts, in the ship "Hopewell", from London to Boston, with his uncle John Ruggles, being in care of Phillip Eliot. He died September 15, 1658, aged thirty-three years. His will, dated September 9, 1658, appointed his "uncle Ruggles, my father Craft, and my brother Samuel to be overseers; and if my wife mary again and my overseers do not like the usage of my children, I give them power to take them away and one half of my estate which I leave in the hands of my wife." He bequeathed the whole estate to his wife until the children should be of age, when John was to have two parts and Samuel and Thomas one part each; his wife and his father Craft were executors of the will. He married, January 24, 1650, Abigail Craft, born in Roxbury, March 28, 1634, died January 19, 1706, daughter of Grif-

fin Craft, an early settler of Roxbury, 1630, and an active man in town affairs; he married Alice ———. She married (second) November 15, 1659, Ralph Day, of Dedham, and by him had a daughter, Abigail Day, born in Dedham, April 22, 1661. She married (third) ——— Adams, and died in Medfield. Children: John, born October 16, 1651, died young; John, mentioned below; Thomas, January 28, 1655; Samuel, August 16, 1657.

(VI) John (2) Ruggles, son of John (1) Ruggles, was born January 22, 1653-4, in Roxbury, and died December 16, 1694, aged forty years. He was a yeoman in Roxbury. He married, September 2, 1674, Martha Devotion, of Muddy River, now Brookline, Massachusetts, daughter of Deacon Edward and Mary Devotion. She was baptized at Roxbury, March 13, 1653, and she married (second) April 21, 1704, John Payne, of Dedham, grandson of Thomas of Salem, Massachusetts, an emigrant in 1637; John Payne married (first) Mary, daughter of Ralph and Susan (Fairbanks) Day, of Dedham; Ralph Day married (second) Abigail (Craft) Ruggles, mother of Martha's husband. Deacon Edward Devotion, father of Martha, was a freeman and member of the church at Boston in 1645. Children: Abigail, born June 5, 1675; John, March 16, 1680; Edward, November 16, 1683; died young; Martha, December 21, 1686; Edward, mentioned below.

(VII) Edward, son of John (2) Ruggles, was born in Roxbury, October 2, 1691, and died in Cambridge, in 1765. Through Samuel Craft, father of his first wife, Edward became interested in the new settlement of Pomfret, Connecticut, and seems to have moved there about 1715, as his first child was born there in 1717, but he doubtless returned soon after to Roxbury, as his other children were born there, and he is spoken of in deeds as a yeoman of Roxbury. His later years he lived in Cambridge, where he made his will and died. The will was administered by his daughter Elizabeth Noble and stepson Joseph Williams; to his son Edward he left all his land in Pomfret; he bequeathed to his wife and children. For many years he was a deacon of the First Church at Roxbury. In 1748, "Nehemiah Walter Clerk, Edward Ruggles and Samuel Gridley, deacons of the First Church of Roxbury, sell a piece of land, being a gift to the church." He was buried by the side of his first wife, Hannah, in the Eustis street burying-ground, and their gravestones are still to be seen. He married (first) June 24, 1715-6, Hannah Craft, daughter of Samuel, and great-granddaughter of Griffin Craft, the immigrant ancestor. She was born March 15,

1697, and died in Roxbury, March 11, 1732. He married (second) January 11, 1733, Abigail, widow of Joseph Williams, and daughter of John and Mary (Torrey) Davis. Children by first wife: Samuel, born at Pomfret, March 29, 1717; Hannah, at Roxbury probably, December 22, 1718; Elizabeth, at Roxbury, October 21, 1720, died young; Elizabeth, October 20, 1722; Edward, mentioned below; Abigail, May 12, 1726; Thomas, November 15, 1729; Benjamin, February 19, 1731.

(VIII) Edward (2), son of Edward (1) Ruggles, was born in Roxbury, Massachusetts, June 22, 1724, and died in Montague, Massachusetts, December 25, 1797. He joined the church in Roxbury, March 3, 1744. He was a farmer in the west parish of Pomfret, known as Abington parish. In 1753 he, aged twenty-nine, and Samuel Craft, aged thirty-three, his cousin, were elected deacons of the Abington church soon after it was formed, and in 1782, according to church records, they asked a dismission from office, which was granted, but in 1785 they were again elected and doubtless remained in that office until Samuel Craft died in 1791, aged sixty-eight. He married, in Pomfret, Connecticut, April 2, 1747, Ann, daughter of Samuel and Elizabeth (Griffin) Sumner; Samuel was born November 13, 1695, and married Elizabeth Griffin, November 20, 1723; he was son of George Sumner, of Milton, Massachusetts, who was born February 9, 1666, and died in 1732, leaving his "eldest son Samuel all my land in Pomfret." George married Ann Tucker, and he was son of George, of Milton, who was born in England, February 14, 1634, and married Mary Baker; George Sumner was son of William Sumner, of Dorchester, Massachusetts, 1636, born in England, 1605, married Mary West; William was son of Roger Sumner, of Bicester, Oxfordshire, England, died 1608, married, November 2, 1601, Joane Franklin. Ann Sumner, wife of Edward Ruggles, was born in Pomfret, September 25, 1724, and died in Montague, July 10, 1808. Children: Benjamin, born August 18, 1747; Abigail, June 23, 1749; Samuel, mentioned below; Elizabeth, April 10, 1754; Anna, October 1, 1756; Hannah, August 15, 1758; Edward, April 3, 1763; Thomas, August 11, 1765.

(IX) Samuel, son of Edward (2) Ruggles, was born at Pomfret, February 25, 1751, and died October 23, 1778, in Killingly, Connecticut. The Connecticut revolutionary records show that Samuel Ruggles, of Willington, served on the Lexington alarm, and that Samuel Ruggles, of Fairfield county, served from May 8 to November 15, 1775, in the Eighth Company, under Captain Joseph Smith. He

married, September 17, 1772, Lucy Robison. Children: Ebenezer, mentioned below; John, born February 3, 1776, moved to Rutland, Vermont.

(X) Ebenezer, son of Samuel Ruggles, was born at Pomfret, December 17, 1773, and died June 22, 1823. He lived in Walpole, New Hampshire. He married Persis Goodell. Children: Perley, born April 21, 1796; Philarmon, mentioned below; Electa, July 16, 1800; Lucy, April 30, 1803; Louisa, April 30, 1805; Persis, March 9, 1808; Phoebe, December 5, 1811; Mary Ann, March 5, 1814; Ebenezer W., November 10, 1818.

(XI) Philarmon, son of Ebenezer Ruggles, was born in Walpole, New Hampshire, April 30, 1798, and died April 15, 1876. He lived in Milton, Massachusetts. He married (first) Eliza Burroughs, and (second) Mary Ann Burroughs. Children, all by first wife: Eliza A., born August 20, 1822, died September 29, 1863; Amanda R., November 14, 1826, died December 14, 1888; Mary A., September 4, 1830, died May 16, 1858; Thomas Edwin, mentioned below.

(XII) Thomas Edwin, son of Philarmon Ruggles, was born at Topsfield, Massachusetts, May 19, 1838, and died August 4, 1911. He was educated there in the public schools, and followed farming for an occupation. He was active in town affairs, and served six years on the school committee, and for a number of years on the board of selectmen. In politics he was a Republican, in religion a Congregationalist.

He married, September 13, 1866, Harriot W. Murray, who was born in Bristol, England, June 15, 1838, daughter of John Thomas and Harriot (Despard) Murray, granddaughter of John Murray, and great-granddaughter of Colonel John Murray, a distinguished citizen of New Brunswick, Canada. Mr. Ruggles died at Milton, August 4, 1911. He had lived there since he was about four years old. Children of Thomas Edwin and Harriot Ruggles: 1. Ellen Letitia, born November 5, 1867, died May 26, 1905. 2. Mary Frances, born March 13, 1869, died September 1, 1869. 3. Murray, born May 13, 1870; married, October 9, 1895, Caroline Barnes, daughter of Henry Barnes and Susan Shaw, and has one child, Doris, born May 3, 1897. 4. Henry Edwin, born August 13, 1871, died August 23, 1872. 5. Edwin Packenham, born January 5, 1873; married, September 2, 1896, Gertrude, daughter of Albert Bacon, of Springfield, Massachusetts, and has one child, Helen, born December 18, 1905. 6. Frank LeBaron, born September 28, 1874, died May 27, 1888. 7. Harriot Despard, born December 13, 1876;

married, September 3, 1907, Albert R. Baker, of Hartford, Connecticut; children: Edwin Ruggles, born June 21, 1908, and Harriot Baker, born November 15, 1910.

William, Count Tankerville, of Tankerville Castle, in Normandy, was the progenitor of the Chamberlain family in England. He came to England with William the Conqueror in 1066, but returned to Normandy, his descendants remaining in England on the land granted to them. (II) John De Tankerville, son of William, was lord chamberlain to King Henry I., and assumed his title as a surname. (III) Richard, son of John, was also chamberlain to King Stephen, and the surname Chamberlain has since his time been that of his family. (IV) William Chamberlain was son of Richard. (V) Robert Chamberlain was son of William. (VI) Sir Richard Chamberlain was son of Robert. (VII) Sir Robert Chamberlain was son of Sir Richard. (VIII) Sir Richard was son of Sir Robert. (IX) John Chamberlain was son of Sir Richard. (X) Thomas Chamberlain was son of John. (XI) John Chamberlain was son of Thomas. (XII) William Chamberlain was son of John. The American family of which William was the immigrant ancestor, doubtless belongs to this English family, though the line is not traced. The coat-of-arms is: Gules, an escutcheon argent between eight mullets in orle, or. Quartering: gules a chevron between three escallops or. Motto: *Virtuti nihil invium.* Seat: Dunstew, in Oxfordshire, England.

(I) William Chamberlain, the immigrant ancestor, was born in England, about 1620. His brother Thomas was one of the three original purchasers of the Dudley farm at Billerica, but settled at Chelmsford, Massachusetts. Another brother, Edmund, settled first at Woburn, then removed to Chelmsford before 1656, when he sold land at Billerica. Savage said that Edmund finally settled in Woodstock. William Chamberlain was admitted an inhabitant of Woburn, January 6, 1648, and permitted to buy land there. He removed to Billerica in 1654, about the time his brothers left that town, and spent the remainder of his life there. He died May 31, 1706, aged eighty-six years. His house in Shawshin (Billerica) was on the farm, probably near the Woburn road, in the southwest part of the village. His name first appears in the records in October, 1654, on a petition to enlarge the bounds of the town and to change the name to Billerica. A little later, when the committee on militia ordered Sergeant Hills's house to be a garrison, William Chamberlain's family was one of those assigned to it. He married Rebecca ————, who died September 26, 1692, in the prison at Cambridge, where she was held on a charge of witchcraft. Children: Timothy, born at Concord, Massachusetts, August 13, 1649-50; Isaac, at Concord, October 1, 1650; John, died March 1, 1652; Sarah, born at Billerica, May 20, 1655-56. Born at Billerica: Jacob, mentioned below; Thomas, February 20, 1659; Edmund, July 15, 1660; Rebecca, February 25, 1662; Abraham, January 6, 1664; Ann, March 3, 1665-66; Clement, May 30, 1669; Daniel, September 27, 1671; Isaac, January 20, 1681.

(II) Jacob, son of William Chamberlain, was born in Billerica, Massachusetts, January 18, 1657-58. He married Experience ————. Children: Jacob, mentioned below; John, born 1695, at Charlestown, Massachusetts; William, 1697, at Cambridge, Massachusetts; Jason, at Holliston, Massachusetts, 1701; Ebenezer, at Westborough, Massachusetts, 1704.

(III) Jacob (2), son of Jacob (1) Chamberlain, was born in 1691-92, and died July 28, 1771, in Newton, Massachusetts. He came to Newton with his father from Arlington about 1700. His name is among those on a protest dated May 20, 1720, against having but one school-house in the town. He was selectman in 1746. He married, about 1718, Susannah Stone, born at Groton, October 23, 1694, daughter of Deacon Simon and Sarah Stone, of Groton. Children, born at Newton: Jacob, mentioned below; Josiah, November 13, 1721; Susanna, September 27, 1724; Isaac, April 6, 1728; Willia, September 22, 1730; Sarah, September 19, 1733; Margaret, September 20, 1736; Simon, August 10, 1739.

(IV) Jacob (3), son of Jacob (2) Chamberlain, was born at Newton, November 28, 1719. Early in 1742 he moved to Worcester, Massachusetts, where he bought a tract of land of Richard Flagg, on Salisbury street, February 28, 1742. This land was handed down to his son John, and from him seventy-two acres were handed down to his son Thomas, since inherited by his sons Robert H. and Thomas Jr. Jacob Chamberlain was a farmer. In 1761 he held the office of selectman in Worcester. In 1774 he was a Tory protestor, numbered among "the internal enemies" by the committee of correspondence in 1775, and disarmed by that committee. Again, June 16, 1777, he was reported among others that the selectmen deemed enemies to the common cause. He was deacon of the old First

Church on the common, 1775-90. He left the church August 8, 1779, on account of the innovation of singing. He died March 17, 1790, and was buried on the common, and his headstone with the others there was taken down and placed under the sod. The stone bears the following inscription: "Sacred to the memory of Deacon Chamberlain who departed this life March 17, 1790, in the 71st year of his age. Who fulfilled the office of deacon in the Church of Christ in Worcester for about 28 years with satisfaction to the church and honor to himself. He was possessed of good natural abilities. Useful in society of which he was a member. Instructive and entertaining in conversation. Compassionate to the afflicted. Given to hospitality, sound in faith. And now, we trust, has entered into his eternal rest." After coming to Worcester, he married, at Newton, June 7, 1744, Lydia Stone, born May 4, 1724, daughter of John and Abigail (Stratton) Stone, of Newton. He married (second) Mrs. Anna Heywood, June 3, 1769, born at Brookline, Massachusetts, widow of Abel, son of Major Daniel Heywood, of Worcester, of Indian war fame. Children: John, mentioned below; Sarah, born January 26, 1746-47; Thaddeus, November 17, 1748; Susannah, June 10, 1751, died young; Jacob, September 19, 1753; Lydia, October 8, 1755; Susannah, November 22, 1757; Abigail, September 16, 1760; Mary, July 13, 1763; William, July 25, 1767. Child of second wife: Anna, born July 21, 1770.

(V) John, son of Jacob (3) Chamberlain, was born at Worcester, July 22, 1745. He received the education of the district schools in winter, and worked with his father on the farm, which later he inherited. He dealt extensively in real estate and owned considerable property. Seventy-two acres of the old homestead were handed down to his son Thomas by will dated June 5, 1806. In May, 1775, he was disarmed by the committee of safety and correspondence, he being in accord with his father's principles of loyalty to the crown. He was a selectman, 1785-95, inclusive, and in 1797-98, 1801-02. He was deacon of the First Parish church twenty-two years, succeeding his father in 1791. He died in 1813. He married, at Worcester, June 27, 1771, Mary Curtis, born October 14, 1747, daughter of Captain John and Elizabeth (Prentice) Curtis, of Worcester. Children: John Curtis, born June 5, 1772, a lawyer of note in Charlestown, New Hampshire, member of congress from his district; Elizabeth Prentice, November 8, 1774; Henry Vassall, January 11, 1777, a well-known lawyer in Mobile, Alabama, became a judge; Mary,

April 8, 1779; Thomas, mentioned below; Elizabeth, May 25, 1785, died young; Levi, May 14, 1788, lawyer in Keene, New Hampshire; Dolly, January 16, 1792.

(VI) Thomas, son of John Chamberlain, was born at Worcester, Massachusetts, March 6, 1783. He received his education in the common schools of the town. In early life and after he was married he taught school. Among the schools in his charge were those at Tatnuck and Quinsigamond. He conducted the farm formerly owned by his father and grandfather in what was known as the Chamberlain district. His purpose of advancing the science and encouraging and improving the art of horticulture was widened by the fact that he was one of the founders and first trustees of the Worcester Horticultural Society in 1840. His portrait may be seen on the wall of Horticultural Hall, Front street, Worcester. He was crier of the Worcester court for seventeen years. He was a member and first president of the common council of the city of Worcester after incorporation, and all of his public duties he discharged with ability and faithfulness. He filled most of the offices of the state militia, from corporal to brigadier-general, with highest honor to himself and satisfaction to those under his command. He was originally a Whig in politics, later a Republican. He attended the Old South Church. He married (first), May 30, 1810, Nancy Woods, of Groton, born February 19, 1781, died July 25, 1831, daughter of Colonel Sampson Woods. He married (second), October 30, 1832, Hannah Blair, born February 19, 1793, died August 23, 1873, daughter of Robert and Elizabeth (Harrington) Blair, of Worcester. He died September 5, 1855. Children of Thomas and Nancy: Charles Thomas, born May 30, 1811, died July 4, 1867, married Sarah E. Hathaway, September 21, 1841; Nancy Woods, June 16, 1813, died May 20, 1891, married June 3, 1839, A. Watson Grant; George Alexander, September 24, 1815, died July 22, 1866, married Martha W. Barnes, May 8, 1858; John Curtis, October 7, 1817, died July 23, 1884, married at Mobile, Alabama, Hannah Elizabeth Chamberlain; Mary Elizabeth, July 25, 1819, died July 25, 1886, married December 7, 1843, Andrew Kettell Hunt, (second) Herbert Curtis; Francis Henry, September 5, 1821, died August 10, 1888, married Lucy Parker; Sarah Jane, July 1, 1824, died December 4, 1891, married Massena Parker, of Mobile; Caroline Maria, October 26, 1826, died April 27, 1854, married James P. Lowe, of Washington, D. C. Children of Thomas and Hannah: Dolly Curtis, born February

10, 1834, died October 4, 1872; Thomas Jr. born June 4, 1835; Robert Horace, mentioned below.

(VII) General Robert Horace Chamberlain, son of Thomas Chamberlain, was born in Worcester, June 16, 1838, died in 1910. He was educated in the public schools of Worcester, and at the Worcester Academy. At the age of eighteen he began an apprenticeship with Ball & Ballard, machinists, School street, where he remained until the civil war, when he enlisted in Company A, 51st Regiment, Massachusetts Volunteer Militia, September 25, 1862, for nine months, and was appointed a sergeant of his company. He was in the campaign of North Carolina, taking part in the engagements of Goldsboro, Whitehall and Kingston, and was afterwards at Fortress Monroe, White House, Baltimore, Harper's Ferry, and with the Army of the Potomac after Gettysburg in pursuit of Lee. He was mustered out July 27, 1863. He enlisted again July 20, 1864, in Company F, 60th Regiment, received a lieutenant's commission, and later became a captain. The regiment was assigned to Indianapolis, Indiana, on special guard duty at the camp of five thousand Confederate prisoners. He was mustered out November 30, 1864. He then returned to Worcester and worked at his trade of machinist until 1870, when he was appointed by Mayor Blake superintendent of sewers. He held this position for eighteen years, 1870-88, during which time the system was developed and widely extended. In 1888 he was appointed master of the House of Correction, and in 1892 was elected high sheriff of Worcester county.

For twelve years after the war he was active in the state militia. In 1865 he reorganized the Worcester City Guards and was the first captain of that company, serving for two years. He also reorganized a battery of artillery in Worcester, called the Chamberlain Light Battery. He received the commission of major and afterwards of colonel of the 10th Regiment, and was made brigadier-general of the Third Brigade, December 31, 1868. He resigned and retired from the service in 1876. Before he was superintendent of sewers he had served from 1867 to 1870 in the common council of the city. He was a Republican in politics, and a member of the Union Congregational Church. He was a prominent Free Mason. On September 8, 1862, he became a member of Montacute Lodge, Free Masons; of Worcester Chapter, Royal Arch Masons, May 6, 1864; of Hiram Council, Royal and Select Masters, March 23, 1865; he received the Templar degrees in Worcester County Commandery, Knights Templar, December 1, 1865; in 1892 he was elected grand commander of the Grand Commandery of Massachusetts and Rhode Island; he was a member of Massachusetts Consistory, Thirty-second degree, of Scottish Rite Masonry; he was treasurer of the board of trustees of the Masonic fraternity for over twenty years; also treasurer of the Masonic Mutual Relief Association. He was a charter member of George H. Ward Post, No. 10, Grand Army of the Republic, and a member of the Loyal Legion, Boston. He was a member of the Hancock Club and of the Worcester Board of Trade.

He married, January 10, 1865, Esther Browning, born July 12, 1841, daughter of Joshua and Lavinia (Morse) Browning, of Hubbardston, Massachusetts. Her father was a carpenter, and captain of a company of artillery. Children: 1. Flora Browning, born August 16, 1868; married Charles B. Weatherby, June 12, 1894; children: Esther Sherman Weatherby, born July 16, 1898, Olive Benedict, August 21, 1902, and Jean Chamberlain Weatherby, December 31, 1904. 2. Mabel Susan, born at Worcester, March 15, 1872.

(VII) Thomas Chamberlain, brother of General Robert H. Chamberlain, was born in Worcester on the old Chamberlain homestead on Salisbury street, June 4, 1835. He received his early education in the public schools of his native town. He started upon his business career as a clerk in the office of the *Boston Journal*. Afterward he was for three years a clerk in the Bunker Hill Bank of Charlestown. Thence he went to Peoria, Illinois, where he was in business for five years on his own account. In 1861 he accepted a position in the State Bank of Boston, and for a period of twenty-five years was paying teller. Although he has retired from the more responsible duties of this position, on account of age, his counsel, assistance and advice are given to the bank as required. He has made his home for forty years at Hyde Park, now part of the city of Boston. In politics he is a Republican. He married, August 31, 1859, Helen Augusta Hovey, born in Charlestown, Massachusetts, December 14, 1834, daughter of Solomon and Augusta (Flint) Hovey. Children: 1. Henry Richardson, of whom further. 2. Alfred Thomas, born 1863, died November 26, 1869. 3. Helen C., born May 7, 1866. 4. Alice Louise, born January 29, 1872; married Lester W. Davis, of Winchester, Massachusetts.

(VIII) The following authentic and very complete narrative relating to Henry

Richardson Chamberlain is from *The New York Sun:*

Henry Richardson Chamberlain, who died in London, February 15, 1911, had been the London correspondent of *The Sun* for nearly twenty years, and had been a member of its staff continuously for more than thirty years.

The son of Thomas Chamberlain of Boston, he was born at Peoria, Illinois, August 25, 1859. The family, which had been spending a year in that city, went back to Boston, and there he was educated in the public schools. While he was attending the English high school he had a teacher who used as his main text books Shakespeare and *The Sun,* so that Mr. Chamberlain's acquaintance with this newspaper began early in life, and its use in the classroom he always believed gave him his taste for newspaper work. When he was graduated from the high school, at the age of sixteen, his father wished him to go to college, but a compromise was effected by the youth agreeing to try working in a chemical laboratory in Philadelphia. It took only a few months to give him enough of chemistry, and though the professor under whom he was working told Mr. Chamberlain's father that a good chemist was lost to the world by his quitting, went back to Boston.

He began his newspaper work by hunting up items of news on his own account and turning them over to the *Boston Journal,* and when he was eighteen, his appearance being that of a man of twenty-five, he got a place as a regular reporter. After a few years doing the various kinds of news gathering incident to work on a daily paper, he was appointed Boston correspondent of *The Sun.* One of his early noteworthy efforts in news getting was in a celebrated trunk mystery in which he furnished to the police the clue that enabled them to get on the track of the criminal. Then he was put on financial work and gained a good insight into the workings of banks and other financial institutions which later stood him in good stead. He covered for the *Boston Journal* and for *The Sun* many important news stories, and did a lot of writing on special subjects that attracted attention.

In 1888 he came to New York as managing editor of *The Press,* but after a year he resigned and went to Europe for a vacation. After a few months he came back and went to work again for *The Sun,* this time in New York, remaining here till 1891. That year he accepted an offer to become editor of the *Boston Journal,* and he then resumed his work for *The Sun* in New England. After he had been in that place a year he was made correspondent of *The Sun* in London, from which place he had general oversight of *The Sun's* news service in Europe. Soon after the dissolution of the United Press he took charge of the Laffan Bureau in London.

In the course of his work Mr. Chamberlain traveled about a great deal all over Europe, and his foresight was so keen that whenever a big "story" would break anywhere on the continent, he was usually to be found not far from the scene. He was in Macedonia at the time of the disturbances there, was in Rome at the time Pope Leo XIII. died, and the particulars of the Panama Canal scandal were graphically given in his despatches from Paris. At the time of the political crisis in Russia in 1909, Mr. Chamberlain went to St. Petersburg, whence his despatches and his illuminative descriptive articles reached the situation that really existed there and gave a different aspect to events there from that in which they had appeared to the American public. His investigations into conditions in Russia just prior to the Japanese war pictured such terrible conditions that he was accused of sensationalism, but subsequent events established their entire accuracy. One of Mr. Chamberlain's later achievements was his long and graphic story of the Messina earthquake. At the time he was describing conditions in Russia, flattering offers were made to him by several leading magazines to write on the subject for them, but he preferred to stick to his newspaper work. In London some of the news events he covered were the jubilee of Queen Victoria, and the coronation of King Edward VII.

Among his personal friends was the late John Hay, who got to know him well when Mr. Hay was American ambassador to the Court of St. James. Mr. Hay said that Mr. Chamberlain had a better grasp of the European situation than anybody he knew, and there were times when he was secretary of state that he asked for Mr. Chamberlain's opinion on matters of European politics, with which the correspondent kept thoroughly conversant.

Only once did Mr. Chamberlain turn his attention to other than journalistic literature. That was when he published a novel called "Six Thousand Tons of Gold." He was married, in Boston, in 1883, to Miss Abbie L. Sanger, of Boston. Mr. Chamberlain's house in Nevern Square in London was for many years a sort of headquarters for Americans abroad, many of whom are indebted to him for kindnesses shown. By his fellow correspondents in London he was greatly beloved, and those who worked under him were always enthusiastic when they spoke about him.

Mr. Chamberlain was always a hard worker, and he took a long rest last year as the result of his health giving way. He returned to work last fall seemingly in excellent condition. His one club in London was the Savage Club, an organization composed of authors, journalists, artists and persons of the best element of Bohemia, many of whom were his close friends.

(The Hovey Line).

(I) Daniel Hovey, the immigrant ancestor, was a planter in Ipswich, Massachusetts, and a proprietor of the town in 1636. He was one of Major Dennison's subscribers in 1648, and in 1664 owned a share in Plum Island. He had twenty acres of land in Topsfield in 1660, and in 1666 was given permission by the town to cut trees for a house for his son John, a shop for his son James, and for the latter's use in his trade. He married, about 1642, Abigail, daughter of Robert Andrews. In a letter to the Essex probate court, dated September 27, 1683, he names his wife, six sons and a daughter, all her children and all the sons living except James. He died May 29, 1695. His will was dated March 18, 1691-92, when he was seventy-three years old. His estate was large for the times. Children: Daniel, born 1642; John, mentioned below; Thomas, 1648; James, killed by Indians in King Philip's war, August 2, 1675; Joseph; Nathaniel, March 20, 1657; Priscilla; Abigail.

(II) John, son of Daniel Hovey, was born in Ipswich, Massachusetts, about 1645. He settled on his father's land in Topsfield. He married, August 13, 1665, Dorcas Ivory, of Topsfield. He named a son Ivory, and in almost every family of his descendants that name has been given. Children: John, born in Topsfield, December, 1666; Dorcas, January 16, 1668; child, born and died 1671; Elizabeth, January 18, 1674; Luke, mentioned below; Ivory, 1678; Abigail, April 28, 1680.

(III) Ensign Luke Hovey, son of John Hovey, was born in Topsfield, Massachusetts, May 3, 1676, recorded also in Boxford. He married, October 25, 1698, Susanna, daughter of Moses Pillsbury; she was born February 1, 1677. They came to Boxford after the birth of their first child, and built the Hovey house which was used by the family until it was torn down recently. It was situated in the Bradford road, a quarter of a mile north of the Second church, on the south slope of the hill. He died October 31, 1751, aged seventy-five years, and his widow died December 22, 1767, aged ninety years. Children, born in Boxford, except first: Susannah, July 25, 1699; Dorcas, May 20, 1701; Hannah, July 18, 1703; Elizabeth, October 3, 1706; Luke, May 18, 1708; Abigail, July 6, 1710; Joseph, July 17, 1712; Abijah, mentioned below; Daniel, December 3, 1720.

(IV) Abijah, son of Ensign Luke Hovey, was born at Boxford, December 9, 1719. He married, at Haverhill, March 21, 1744-45, Lydia Graves, of Haverhill. They removed to Lunenburg, Worcester county, Massachusetts, and she died there November 28, 1760. Children, born at Lunenburg: Dorcas, June 24, 1751; Lydia, August 17, 1753; Miriam, October 8, 1758; Abijah, October 16, 1760; Solomon, mentioned below.

(V) Solomon, son of Abijah Hovey, was born about 1750. He married Jerusha, sister of Nehemiah Wyman. Their son Solomon is mentioned below.

(VI) Solomon (2), son of Solomon (1) Hovey, was born August 14, 1781. He married, at Charlestown, Massachusetts, January 5, 1806, Sarah Johnson. Children, born at Charlestown: Solomon, mentioned below; twins, born July 3, 1808, died young; Sarah Caroline, June 19, 1809; Martha Story, September 14, 1811; James, August 16, 1815; Harriet, August 21, 1818; Joseph Faulkner.

(VII) Solomon (3), son of Solomon (2) Hovey, was born at Charlestown, November 6, 1808. He became president of the Mechanics' Fire Insurance Company. He married Augusta Flint. Their daughter, Helen Augusta, married Thomas Chamberlain (see Chamberlain).

RUNNELLS   The surname Runnells is of Scotch origin, from the word runnels, meaning a small running brook. It has been thought by some genealogists that the families of Runnells and Reynolds were identical, but they appear to be of distinctly different origin, though the spelling is often used interchangeably. Many Reynolds families spell the name Runnells, but few Runnells have changed to Reynolds. Reynolds is an English surname. The only Runnells coat-of-arms is described: Argent masoned sable upon a chief indented of the last a plate charged with a rose gules barbed and seeded between two fleur-de-lis or. Crest: A fox passant or, holding in the mouth a rose as in the arms slipped and leaved vert. Motto: *Murus aheneus esto.* One branch of the family bearing these arms came originally from Biddeford, county Devon, England. The Runnells families of New England are descended from Samuel, Job and John Runnells (Runels or Runals), settlers in New Hampshire.

Samuel Runnells was born, according to family tradition, in 1671, near Port Royal, Nova Scotia, and it is said that he and an elder brother escaped from an attack of Indians or pirates up in their father's residence near Halifax, and came in an open boat to New England. Samuel settled in Bradford, Massachusetts, and also owned a house and land in Boxford, an adjacent town. He died October 27, 1745. He married Abigail Middleton.

(I) Job Runnells, younger brother of Samuel Runnells, came doubtless of Scotch ancestry from Nova Scotia to Dover, New Hampshire. He bought land as early as November 13, 1713, in Dover, now Durham, New Hampshire. His house was near Wensday's brook a little south of the Mast road. He added to his original farm from time to time. He served on a town committee to apportion lands in 1734. He died in 1765 and his estate was inventoried April 25, 1765. He had deeded some of his property, perhaps all of it, to his son Job. He married, about 1713, Hannah ———, who joined the Durham Church, May 5, 1723. A deed of February 3, 1748-49 shows that she was a granddaughter of Robert Burnham. Children, born in Durham: Job, 1714; Abigail, 1717; Susan, 1719; Enoch, 1721; Mary, May 15, 1724; Jonathan, 1726; Hannah, June 4, 1728; Samuel, mentioned below.

(II) Samuel, son of Job Runnells, was born at Durham, New Hampshire, in 1730. He was a soldier in the French and Indian war, sentinel in Company 6 in 1755 in the

New Hampshire Regiment. He resided at
Lee, New Hampshire, whence he removed to
Woodstock, New Hampshire, among the early
settlers. He was twice married. He married (second) Love Tibbetts, but his children
were by his first wife. Children: Samuel,
mentioned below; Hannah, married ——
Drew; Lovey, died young.

(III) Samuel (2), son of Samuel (1) Runnells, was born in Lee in 1754, died December 19, 1797, at Milton, New Hampshire. He
removed from Lee to Shapleigh, now Acton,
Maine. He worked for Daniel Fox who had
married his cousin, and afterward settled
near Lovewell's pond in the north part of
Acton. He married, in 1783, Olive Farnham, of Acton, daughter of Paul Farnham,
and sister of Ralph Farnham, the last survivor of the battle of Bunker Hill (see Farnham V). She died at Lebanon, Maine. Children, born at Shapleigh: Mary, May 28,
1784; Eunice, May 6, 1786; Samuel, mentioned below; Paul, June 4, 1790; Betsey,
June 20, 1792; Olive, 1794; Asa, July, 1796.

(IV) Samuel (3), son of Samuel (2) Runnells, was born at Shapleigh, Maine, June 22,
1788. He was a farmer and deacon of the
Free Will Baptist church of Acton (Milton
Mills), and died there March 27 or 29, 1854,
of smallpox. His gravestone contains the ap-
propriate epitaph, "My record is on high."
He married, January 3, 1811, Hannah Farnham, of Acton, Maine, daughter of Ralph
Farnham (see Farnham VI). She was born
March 20, 1788, died at Acton, October 14,
1861. Her gravestone bears this inscription:
"My trust is in God." Children: Asenath,
born October 28, 1811; Eli, February 21,
1815; John, mentioned below; Asa, April 10,
1818; Hosea, July 11, 1820; Israel, July 5,
1823; Alvah, December 1, 1825; William
Buzzell, August 14, 1828; Almira, January
18, 1831.

(V) Rev. John Runnells, son of Samuel
(3) Runnells, was born March 9, 1817. He
received his academic education at the Parsonsfield Academy, Maine, 1835-37, and studied for the ministry at the Free Will Baptist
Theological School in Parsonsfield. He was
ordained in November, 1842, at Acton, Maine,
and had pastorates at North Berwick, Maine,
at Eaton, New Hampshire, until 1846, at
Milton Mills, New Hampshire, and at Newport, Rhode Island. He was settled as pastor
of the Free Baptist Church at Tamworth
Iron Works, New Hampshire, in January,
1852, and died after a long and honorable
service as minister, at Tamworth, September
2, 1877. In 1859 he was elected chaplain of
the New Hampshire house of representatives

for the June session. He was a trustee of
the New Hampton Literary and Theological
Institution and was associational officer of
his denomination in the state of New Hampshire. He married, December 15, 1842, Huldah Staples, of North Berwick, Maine, born
at North Berwick, October 3, 1819, died at
Tamworth, New Hampshire, in 1906. Children: John Sumner, mentioned below; Abby
May, born July 28, 1851, died in 1880, married Rev. Thomas M. Findley and had one
son, John Runnells Findley, now sales agent
of the American Radiator Company, Chicago.

(VI) John Sumner, son of Rev. John Runnells, was born at Effingham, New Hampshire, July 30, 1844. He attended the public
schools at Tamworth, New Hampshire, and
prepared for college at New Hampton, New
Hampshire, Academical Institute. He was
graduated from Amherst College with the
degree of Bachelor of Arts in the class of
1865. He was a teacher in the high schools
of Rochester and Dover, New Hampshire, in
1866-67. He began to study law at Dover,
New Hampshire, and was admitted to the bar
at Des Moines, Iowa, in January, 1869. He
was the private secretary of Governor Merrill, of Iowa, for one year, and in the meantime was secretary of the Iowa Republican
State Central Committee, performing the
duties of his office with "masterly and honor-
ing ability," and doing efficient service in the
campaign of 1868 with Hon. Peter Melendy,
member of congress, supporting President
Grant. He filled a consular appointment in
Tunstall, Staffordshire, near Manchester,
England, 1869-71, and from 1876 to 1881 was
official reporter of the Iowa supreme court.
He practiced law in Iowa from the time of
his admission to the bar until 1887 when
he removed to Chicago, and since then
he has been general counsel of the Pullman
Sleeping Car Company, and in May, 1905,
became vice-president of that corporation.
On the retirement of Robert T. Lincoln, son
of President Abraham Lincoln, Mr. Runnells
became president of the Pullman Company.
He is senior partner of the law firm of Runnells, Burry & Johnston, of Chicago. He was
United States district attorney for Iowa,
1881-85. He became known in Iowa as a
specialist of great prominence in railway and
telegraph law and also for his successful handling of a case which he carried through the
state courts to the supreme court of the
United States involving the constitutionality
of the prohibitory liquor law of Iowa. He was
chairman of the Iowa State Republican Committee in 1879-80 and member of the Republican National Committee from Iowa from

1880 to 1884. He was a delegate to the Republican National Convention in 1880. He is an able public speaker and has been chosen orator upon various patriotic and historical occasions. One of his best known orations is that delivered at the Grant banquet in New York City in 1893. He is a gifted writer and when a young man was for a time on the editorial staff of the *Des Moines Register*. He is a director of the Pullman Company, the Merchants Loan and Trust Company, Pullman Trust and Savings Bank and other corporations, and a member of the Chicago Club, the University Club, the Chicago Literary Club, the Onwentsia Club, the Saddle & Cycle Club, the University Club of New York and the New England Society of Chicago. He also has a summer residence at Tamworth, New Hampshire.

He married, March 31, 1869, at Des Moines, Helen Rutherfurd Baker, born at Concord, New Hampshire, May 29, 1845, daughter of Hon. Nathaniel B. Baker, who was governor of New Hampshire in 1854 and adjutant-general of Iowa during the civil war. She is a member of the Society of Colonial Dames, being a lineal descendant of John and Priscilla Alden, who came in the "Mayflower", and related to Governor Peter Stuyvesant, of New Amsterdam. Children: 1. Mabel, born in Tunstall, England, July 8, 1870; married Robert Irving Jenks, a native of New Hampshire, now living in New York City. 2. Lucy B., born at Des Moines, January 10, 1874; married Albert A. Jackson and is living at Philadelphia. 3. Clive, born at Des Moines, September 10, 1877; graduate of Harvard College in 1900, banker and broker in Chicago. 4. Alice Rutherfurd, born in Des Moines, October 4, 1884; married, January 6, 1912, William James, son of Professor William James, of Harvard University.

(The Farnham Line).

The Farnham or Farnum family is of ancient English origin. The principal family seat is at the Querndon House of Leicestershire, the lineage of which is traced back to the reign of Edward I. The Farnham arms: Quarterly or and az. in the two first quarters of a crescent countersigned. Crest: An eagle or wings, close preying on a rabbit arg.

(I) Ralph Farnham, immigrant ancestor, was born in England in 1603. He came with his wife Alice from London in the brig "James", sailing from Southampton, April 6, 1635. He gave his age as thirty-two, and his wife's as twenty-eight and they had with them three young children, Mary, Thomas and Ralph. He was a barber by trade but

followed husbandry after coming to New England. He settled first in Ipswich, of which he was proprietor in 1639. He settled finally in Andover, Massachusetts. He died January 5, 1692-93, and the inventory of his estate is dated March 29, 1693. Children: 1. Mary, born 1628, resided in Andover, where she died February 3, 1714; married Daniel Poor, of Andover, in Boston, October 20, 1650. 2. Thomas, mentioned below. 3. Ralph, born 1633, died January 8, 1691-92; married Elizabeth Holt, of Andover, October 26, 1658, she died October 14, 1710. 4. Sarah, born at Andover, married John Abbot, April 16, 1658; he was the ancestor of the most prominent Abbots in America. 5. John, born 1640.

(II) Ralph (2), son of Ralph (1) Farnham, was born 1633, in England, died January 8, 1692. He married, October 26, 1658, Elizabeth, daughter of Nicholas Holt, at Andover, Massachusetts. She died October 14, 1710. Children: Sarah, born about February, 1661; Ralph, mentioned below; John, April 1, 1664; Henry, December 7, 1666; Hannah, December 7, 1668; Thomas, July 14, 1670; Ephraim, October 1, 1675.

(III) Ralph (3), son of Ralph (2) Farnham, was born June 1, 1662. He married Sarah Sterling, October 9, 1683. Children: Sarah, born May 5, 1685; Henry, September 15, 1687; Ralph, mentioned below; Daniel, January 21, 1691; Abigail, May 3, 1692; William, August 5, 1693; Nathaniel, July 25, 1695; Barachias, March 16, 1697; Benjamin, March 14, 1699; Joseph or Josiah, February 4, 1701.

(IV) Ralph (4), son of Ralph (3) Farnham, was born May 25, 1689. He married Elizabeth, daughter of Captain Matthew Austin. Children: Joseph, born June 20, 1713; Ralph, May 21, 1715; Mary, May 14, 1717; Matthew, August 4, 1719; Elizabeth, February 27, 1721; David, died young; Jonathan, April 11, 1726; Nathaniel, May 1, 1728; Paul, mentioned below; Betty, August 14, 1732; John, May 26, 1735.

(V) Paul, son of Ralph (4) Farnham, was born April 20, 1730, died in 1820, at Acton, Maine. He married Elizabeth Dore, settled in Lebanon, Maine, afterwards moving to Acton. Children: Ralph, mentioned below; Olive, married Samuel (2) Runnells (see Runnells III); Dummer; Paul.

(VI) Ralph (5), son of Paul Farnham, was born at Lebanon, Maine, in 1756, died in Acton, Maine, in December, 1860, aged one hundred and four years and five months. He lived at Acton, Maine. He was a soldier in the revolution and was the last survivor of the battle of Bunker Hill. His great-grandson, Hon. John S. Runnells, has Ralph Farnham's portrait in the office of the president of the Pullman Car Company of Chicago. Children: Benjamin, John, Daniel, Ralph, Hannah, married Samuel (3) Runnells (see Runnells IV); Mary; Joanna.

FISHER Anthony Fisher, the first of this surname of whom there is definite record, lived in the latter part of the reign of Queen Elizabeth in the parish of Syleham, county Suffolk, England, on the south bank of the Waveney river, on a freehold estate called "Wignotte". He married Mary, daughter of William and Anne Fiske, of St. James, South Elmasham, county Suffolk, England. The Fiske family was an old Puritan family of that county which had suffered during the religious persecutions of Queen Mary's reign. Anthony Fisher was buried April 11, 1640. Children: Joshua, baptized February 24, 1585; Mary, twin sister of Joshua; Anthony, mentioned below; Amos, married Anne Morrise, widow of Daniel Locke; Rev. Cornelius, baptized August 6, 1599; Martha, married John Buckingham, of Syleham, England.

(II) Anthony (2), son of Anthony (1) Fisher, was baptized at Syleham, England, April 23, 1591. He was the immigrant ancestor, and came to New England probably in the ship "Rose", arriving in Boston, June 26, 1637. He settled at Dedham and subscribed to the covenant there, July 18, 1637. He was admitted a freeman in May, 1645, and was selectman of Dedham in 1646 and 1647; selected county commissioner, September 3, 1660, and deputy to the general court, May 2, 1649. He was woodreeve in 1653-54-55-57-58-61-62. He removed to Dorchester, and was chosen selectman there, December 5, 1664, and the two years following; was commissioner in 1666. He died in Dorchester, April 18, 1671. His wife Mary was admitted to the church at Dedham, March 27, 1642, but he was not "conformably received into ye church," "on account of his proud and haughty spirit", until March 14, 1645. He married (second), November 14, 1663, Isabel Breck, widow of Edward Breck, of Dorchester. Children, all by first wife: Anthony, mentioned below; Cornelius, married (first), at Dedham, February 23, 1653, Leah Heaton, (second) July 25, 1665, Sarah Everett; Daniel, born about 1619 in England; Nathaniel, born about 1620, at Syleham, England; Lydia, married Daniel Morse, of Sherborn; John, died in Dedham, September 5, 1638.

(III) Anthony (3), son of Anthony (2)

Fisher, came with his parents to New England, and settled in Dedham, Massachusetts, in 1637. He was a member of the Ancient and Honorable Artillery Company in 1644. He was admitted a freeman, May 6, 1646, and joined the Dedham church, July 20, 1645. He was chosen surveyor of Dedham in 1652-53-54. He removed to Dorchester and was selectman there in 1666. He married, in Dedham, September 7, 1647, Joanna, only daughter of Thomas and Jane Faxon, of Braintree, Massachusetts. Children: Mehitable, born June 27, 1648, probably died young; Experience, baptized August 11, 1650, probably died young; Josiah, born May 1, 1654; Abiah, baptized August 3, 1656; Sarah, born October 29, 1658; Deborah, baptized February 24, 1661; Judith, baptized July 5, 1663; Eleazer, mentioned below.

(IV) Eleazer, son of Anthony (3) Fisher, was born in Dedham, September 18, 1669, died there February 6, 1722. He married, at Dedham, October 13, 1698, Mary Avery, born there August 21, 1674, died in Stoughton, Massachusetts, March 25, 1749, daughter of William and Mary (Lane) Avery. Her father was baptized October 27, 1647, in the parish of Brekham, Berkshire, England, son of Lieutenant William Avery. Children: Eleazer, born September 29, 1699; William, June 28, 1701; Jemima, September 28, 1703; David, June 21, 1705; Ezra, February 8, 1707; Nathaniel, 1708; Mary, October 27, 1710; Ezekiel, October 22, 1712; Timothy, August 28, 1714; Stephen, July 11, 1715, died young; Benjamin, mentioned below.

(V) Benjamin, son of Eleazer Fisher, was born in Dedham, in May, 1721. On March 14, 1742, he joined the South Parish, now Norwood church, and his wife joined. August 23, 1741, as Sarah Everett. He died January 18, 1777, aged fifty-five years, and his widow died August 2, 1795, aged seventy-seven years. His will was dated December 23, 1776, and proved February 7, 1777. His sons Eliphalet and Jesse were executors; he left one-half the estate to his wife, and mentioned also his grandson Luther, son of Benjamin, deceased, sons Asa, Eliphalet, Jesse, Moses and Aaron, and daughter Sarah, wife of Abel Allen. The inventory was dated March 20, 1777, and the widow's third was set off September 18, 1777. He married, in South Dedham, August 11, 1742, Sarah, daughter of William and Rachel (Newcomb) Everett. She was born in Dedham, June 7, 1718. Children: Benjamin, born May 23, 1743; Asa, April 30, 1745; Eliphalet, June 2, 1747; Sarah, May 24, 1749; Jesse, July 7, 1751; Sibyl, August 21, 1753; Moses, mentioned be-

Charles Henry Fisher

Lydia M. Fisher

low; Aaron, January 16, 1758; John, March 19, 1760, died July 6, 1773.

(VI) Moses, son of Benjamin Fisher, was born at Dedham, November 27, 1755, died January 23, 1847. He settled in Francestown, New Hampshire, in 1785, on the farm which is still in possession of the family, his grandson, Moses Bradford Fisher, now occupying it. He served in the revolution in William Bullard's company, Colonel William Heath's regiment, for six days at the Lexington Alarm, and from September 25, 1777, to October 28, 1777, in Captain Abel Richard's company, Colonel Benjamin Hawe's regiment; and in Captain Abel Richard's company, Colonel McIntosh's regiment, at Boston and Roxbury, from March 23, 1778, to April 6, 1778. "One of the luxuries of his house in Francestown was a chandelier made of iron, by the blacksmith, filled with chicken oil, with a cotton wick; this lamp hung from a movable crane (hake) at the side of the room." He married (first), February 19, 1784, Louisa, daughter of Eliphalet and Hannah (Lewis) Thorp, of Dedham. She was born October 26, 1762, died at Francestown, February 9, 1811. He married (second), January 25, 1813, Mrs. Lucy (Friend) Manning, of Lyndeboro. She was born June 11, 1774, died March 14, 1841. Children, born in Francestown: John, born April 20, 1785, died November 25, 1785; Lewis, August 19, 1786; Moses, October 25, 1790; Joel, September 30, 1793, died March 10, 1796; Abijah, March 17, 1795; Aaron, August 25, 1797; Amasa, August 31, 1799, died October 25, 1800; Hannah, April 24, 1802; Thorp, mentioned below; Asa Manning, April 9, 1817.

(VII) Thorp, son of Moses Fisher, was born in Francestown, New Hampshire, April 24, 1804, died at Salem, Massachusetts, December 9, 1885. He married (first), November 6, 1832, Joanna Crombie, daughter of Benjamin and Chloe (Farrington) Jones. She was born November 27, 1806, died at Salem, October 4, 1855. He married (second), October 10, 1860, Mary Ruth, daughter of Captain Christopher and Mary (Randall) Babbidge, and widow of Henry Russell, of Salem. She was born in Salem, May 30, 1807, died there February 22, 1887. Children: Louisa, born September 5, 1833; George Augustine, June 22, 1837; Charles Henry, mentioned below; Joanna Augusta, June 3, 1843.

(VIII) Charles Henry, son of Thorp Fisher, was born in Salem, Massachusetts, September 16, 1840, died February 28, 1910. He received his education in the public schools. He learned his trade in the shops of Corliss & Nightingale, steamboat and engine builders, Providence, Rhode Island. During the civil war he was assistant engineer of the steamer "Curleu" in the government service. Reuben Avery was the chief engineer. He left the "Curleu," when the steamer "Nightingale" was built and was chief engineer of her. She was in the navy during the civil war, and at Charleston, South Carolina, during the attack on Fort Sumter. Later he went to Mexico, when the United States had trouble with that country under Maximilian, and on the same steamer as engineer. While in the South during the war and on the Suwanee river he contracted yellow fever, but was saved from death by medicine given him by an old pilot. At the end of the war he left the navy, and went to California on a prospecting trip. While there he was employed to erect quartz mills, equipped with engines manufactured by his former employers, Corliss & Nightingale, and strangely enough he worked on the very engine when it was building in the shops. He came into intimate relations with the railroad magnate of later years, Collis P. Huntington, and with Mark Hopkins, president of the Bank of California, the owners of the mine where the mill was erected. Afterward he went to China, where he was employed for a number of years by the well-known firm of Russell & Company, as engineer of one of their steamers. He returned after the death of his father and lived at Salem while settling his father's estate. He retired from active business twenty-five years before he died, devoting his time to the management of his real estate and other interests. He was a member of St. John's Commandery, Knights Templar, of Providence, and of other Masonic bodies. In politics he was a Republican, in religion a Congregationalist.

He married, March 16, 1885, Lydia Matthews (Bangs) Arey, born September 10, 1841, at South Dennis, on Cape Cod, daughter of Captain Joshua Berry and Rebecca (Matthews) Bangs (see Bangs VII). They had no children. Mrs. Fisher resides at Hyde Park, Massachusetts, where Mr. Fisher spent his later years.

(The Bangs Line).

(III) Captain Edward Bangs, son of Captain Jonathan Bangs (q. v.), was born September 30, 1665, died May 22, 1746, at Satucket, now Brewster, Massachusetts. He lived in Satucket until after his second marriage, when he moved to Eastham, Massachusetts, where he lived the remainder of his life. He was an active man, a merchant and innholder, also carrying on a tanning business. His will was dated April 14, 1746, proved June 11, 1746. He married (first) Ruth Allen, who died June 22, 1738, aged sixty-eight years. He married (second), January 16, 1739, Mrs. Ruth Mayo, of Eastham, and she died August 17, 1747. Children, born in Satucket: Captain Joshua, 1691; Mary, 1692; Edward, August 14, 1694; Ruth, 1699; Ebenezer, baptized February 8, 1702; Dr. Jonathan, mentioned below; Rebecca, baptized March 9, 1709-10.

(IV) Dr. Jonathan (2) Bangs, son of Captain Edward Bangs, was baptized May 23, 1707, died December 7, 1745. The inventory of his estate was dated March 7, 1745. His widow was administratrix of the estate. He married, January 4, 1732-33, Phebe, daughter of Stephen Hopkins and widow of Samuel Bangs Jr.; Stephen Hopkins was son of Stephen, son of Giles, son of Stephen. Only child, Allen, mentioned below.

(V) Allen, son of Dr. Jonathan (2) Bangs, was born March 23, 1733-34, at Satucket, later Harwich, now Brewster, Massachusetts, and met his death by drowning while boating hay from Brewster marshes, September 14, 1793. He was a farmer. His homestead at South Dennis, Massachusetts, is still in possession of descendants. He served in the revolution as private in Captain Jonathan Crowell's company at the Lexington Alarm; also in Captain John Nickerson's company, Colonel Nathaniel Freeman's regiment, marching on the alarm to Dartmouth and Falmouth, September, 1778; also served at other times. He married Rebecca Howes, of Yarmouth, born there April 16, 1732, died at South Dennis, September 9, 1793, daughter of Joseph and Elizabeth (Paddock) Howes; Joseph was son of Samuel, son of Jeremiah and Sarah (Prence) Howes; Sarah was daughter of Governor Thomas Prence; Jeremiah was son of the Pilgrim, Thomas Howes. Children: Jonathan, born February 13, 1755, died May 27, 1760; Joseph, July 5, 1757; Phoebe, August 17, 1758; Jonathan, July 19, 1760; Zenas, May 3, 1763; Allen, April 22, 1765, died October, 1765; Allen, mentioned below.

(VI) Allen (2), son of Allen (1) Bangs, was born at Brewster, August 15, 1770. He inherited his father's homestead at South Dennis. He married, April 1, 1792, Rebecca Berry, at Brewster. She was born at Brewster, November 22, 1773, died January 1, 1858, at South Dennis. He died there July 5, 1850. Children: Rebecca H., born November 18, 1793; Hannah, married Captain Reuben Baker; Barnabas, born December 10,

1797; Allen Jr., June 1, 1800; Phoebe, November 1, 1802; Jonathan, February 24, 1806; Joshua Berry, mentioned below; Joseph, August 21, 1810.

(VII) Captain Joshua Berry Bangs, son of Allen (2) Bangs, was born September 24, 1808, at South Dennis, Massachusetts, died at Gardiner's Island, December 29, 1853. He was a seafaring man, and while sailing from Baltimore to Providence in 1854 had his vessel wrecked at Gardiner's Island, all men being lost but Captain Bangs, who was rescued and taken to the old Gardiner house on the island, where he died from injuries and exposure; Professor Hosford died in this house. He married, May 21, 1834, Rebecca Matthews, at Yarmouth, daughter of Captain Isaac Matthews Jr. She was born September 3, 1810. Children: 1. Lydia Matthews, born at Dennis, September 10, 1842; married (first), September 9, 1869, at Cambridge, Captain John W. Arey, of Chelsea, master mariner of Bucksport, Maine, son of James and Mary Arey; married (second) Charles Henry Fisher, March 16, 1885 (see Fisher VIII). 2. Joshua, born at Providence, Rhode Island, November 11, 1844.

DRAPER The surname Draper is derived from the trade of some remote ancestor and belongs to the class of English names represented by Smith, Carpenter, Cook, Weaver, Farmer, etc. The family in England is very ancient and has produced many distinguished men. The coat-of-arms of the Heptonstall family is: Argent on a fesse engraved between three annulets gules as many covered cups or. Crest: A stag's head gules attired gold, charged on the neck with a fesse between three annulets or. Motto: *Vicit perpecit*.

(I) Thomas Draper, the progenitor of this family, lived and died in the parish of Heptonstall, vicarage of Halifax, Yorkshire, England. He belonged to an ancient and numerous family. He was a clothier by occupation. Children, born in Heptonstall: Thomas; John; William; James, of whom further; Mary; Martha.

(II) James, son of Thomas Draper, was born in Heptonstall, Yorkshire, England, in 1618. He was the immigrant ancestor, and came to New England about the time he came of age. From 1640 to 1650 he was a pioneer and proprietor of Roxbury, Massachusetts. In 1654 he became a proprietor of Lancaster, Massachusetts, but lived and died in Roxbury. He was admitted a freeman in 1690. From his exceedingly strict piety he was known in his day as James the Puritan. He was the owner of several looms and followed his trade as clothier in this country. He married, April 21, 1646, Miriam Stansfield, at Heptonstall, England. She was born there November 27, 1625, daughter of Gideon and Grace (Eastwood) Stansfield, died at Roxbury in January, 1697. Her gravestone at Roxbury is inscribed: "Here lyes ye body of Mrs. Miriam Draper, wife of Mr. James Draper, aged about seventy-seven years. Dec. Jan. 1697." The stone appears to be one of the oldest in the cemetery. He died in July, 1694, aged about seventy-six years. Children: Miriam, born in England, February 7, 1647, died there; Susannah, at Roxbury, 1650; Sarah, 1652; James (2), of whom further; John, April 24, 1656, at Dedham; Moses, September 26, 1663 at Dedham; Daniel, at Dedham, May 30, 1665, died there; Patience, at Roxbury, August 17, 1668; Jonathan, March 10, 1670.

(III) James (2), son of James (1) Draper, was born in Roxbury in 1654, died there April 30, 1698, aged forty-four years. He was a soldier in King Philip's war in 1675-76. In 1683 James Draper and Nathaniel Whiting were given permission to build a fulling mill in Dedham, below the corn mill on Mother brook. The Draper interests were gradually sold out to the Whitings in this mill property. Draper injured a sinew while wrestling and was never able to leave his house afterward. He was said to be the strongest wrestler in town. He married, February 18, 1681, Abigail Whiting, who died in Roxbury October 25, 1721, aged fifty-nine years. The gravestones of both husband and wife are to be found in the Roxbury burial ground, now partly within the city of Boston. Children, born at Roxbury: Abigail, born December 29, 1681; Nathaniel, April 2, 1684; William, May 15, 1686, died young; Eunice, June 5, 1689; James (3), of whom further; Gideon, 1694; Ebenezer, April 27, 1698.

(IV) James (3), son of James (2) Draper, was born at Roxbury, Massachusetts, in 1691. On November 14, 1734, the West Roxbury church dismissed Ebenezer Draper, James Draper and his wife, Abigail, to the Dedham church. James and Ebenezer Draper had been carrying on a house and ordinary at Baker street, Roxbury, but they did not have enough room, because of granite rocks on one side, and the wet lands of the Charles river on the other. In Green Lodge they had more room for farming, and here were with their cousin, Jeremiah Whiting, who was a carpenter, they built new houses and began farming. They were about thirteen miles from Boston, and to its market they

sent wood, charcoal, and vegetables in the summer, each of the brothers having four or five horses with which to carry in their produce. On December 19, 1733, the records of Dedham show that a road was authorized to be built from Dedham and Dorchester, by the house of Jeremiah Whiting at Green Lodge, towards the Dedham Meeting House. Green Lodge was a settlement about two miles east of Dedham, on the present Green Lodge road, on the Neponset river. It was nearer Dedham than Dorchester, and for that reason several of the inhabitants there petitioned the general court that they might attend worship there instead of at Dorchester, and James Draper signed this petition. The petition requested that they be set off from Stoughton and annexed to Dedham, and although Stoughton fought against this, the petition was granted. Captain James Draper had a negro servant named Sharper Gulder, who, July 31, 1760, married, Rev. M. Tyler officiating, Rozella Allen, a negro servant of Esther Fisher. James Draper was captain of the trainband. In 1746 he was elected to serve one year as selectman, and in 1756 was elected to serve in that office for two years. He was very prominent in Dedham and highly respected. He was very well-to-do, being the owner of large amounts of land.

He married (first), May 2, 1716, Rachel, daughter of John and Mary Aldis. She was born March 5, 1690, died May 16, 1717. He married (second), November 12, 1719, Abigail, daughter of Joshua and Elizabeth (Morris) Child, of Brookline, Massachusetts. She was a sister of Dorothy Child, who married Ebenezer Draper. Child by first wife: John, born January 26, 1716, died March 10, 1717. Children by second wife: James, at Stoughton, September 22, 1720; Abigail, at Stoughton, December 12, 1721; John, at Stoughton, June 16, 1723; Joshua, at Stoughton, December 25, 1724; Josiah, at Stoughton, April 3, 1726, died August 18, 1726; Josiah, at Stoughton, September 12, 1727; Rebecca, at Stoughton, June 30, 1729; Mary, at Stoughton, September 24, 1731; Abijah, at Dedham, July 13, 1734, died November 18, 1734; Abijah, July 11, 1735, died February 13, 1737; Abijah, of whom further; Samuel, at Dedham, December 5, 1740, died November 29, 1750.

(V) Major Abijah Draper, son of James (3) Draper, was born at Dedham, Massachusetts, May 10, 1737. He succeeded his father in his landed estate at Green Lodge, Dedham. He was an energetic, active, public-spirited citizen, always ready to help any good enterprise. He was one of the three chosen by the Dedham citizens to erect a monument to William Pitt in 1766. The base of this monument is still to be seen, and is called the "Pillar of Liberty", with the following inscription: "To the Honor of William Pitt, Esq., and other Patriots, Who saved America from impending slavery, and confirmed our most loyal Affections to King George III., by procuring the repeal of the Stamp Act, 18th March, 1766. Erected here, July 22, 1766, by Dr. Nathl. Ames, 2d, Col. Ebenr Battle, Major Abijah Draper, and other patriots friendly to the Rights of the Colonies at that day. Replaced by the Citizens, July 4, 1828." Abijah Draper held every office in the militia up to that of major, and commanded a body of minute men at Roxbury under Washington. He enlisted in the revolution from Suffolk county, as senior major of the First Regiment, and February 14, 1776, entered the army as second major, First Regiment. While at Roxbury he was exposed to smallpox, and it was supposed that he carried it to his home on one of his furloughs, as his first wife, Alice, died of that disease.

He married (first), April 8, 1762, Alice, daughter of John Eaton and Elizabeth Lovering, of Purgatory, Dedham. She was born January 31, 1741, died January 22, 1777. He married (second), March 25, 1778, Desire, widow of Nathaniel Metcalf, and daughter of Ebenezer and Desire (Cushman) Foster. She was born at Attleboro, Massachusetts, August 12, 1746, died at Dedham October 23, 1815. He and both his wives are buried in the Dedham cemetery, and the epitaph on their graves is as follows: "Ah, why so soon from me he's fled, Laments the widow, orphan, friend, You must not say, 'too soon he's dead', Who stayed to answer Life's great end." The following is on Desire's tomb: "She sleeps in Jesus, Wipe the falling tear. She lives in glory—Strive to meet her there." He died May 1, 1780, at Dedham. Children of first wife: Abijah, born June 11, 1763, died December 16, 1774; Ira, December 24, 1764; Rufus, November 27, 1766; James, April 14, 1769, died January 22. 1777; Alice, April 13, 1771; Abijah (2), of whom further. Child of second wife: Lendamine, born March 30, 1780.

(VI) Dr. Abijah (2) Draper, son of Major Abijah (1) Draper, was born September 22, 1775. He was graduated from Brown University in 1797, and taught school at Green Lodge during college vacations. He then began practice as a physician at West Roxbury, Massachusetts, and his mother, Mrs. Desire Draper, kept house for him until he married. For a period of sixty years he and his son,

Dr. Abijah Weld Draper, were practicing physicians in West Roxbury. He collected some material for a family history, but it was never published. He was a member of the Massachusetts Medical Society, and worshipful master of a Masonic lodge. He married, January 12, 1807, Lavinia Tyler of Attleboro. She was born March 25, 1778, died May 22, 1864. He died March 26, 1836. Children, born at West Roxbury: Abijah Weld, of whom further; Augusta, July 21, 1810, died September 4, 1877; Amanda, twin of Augusta, died April 26, 1879, said to have died of a broken heart.

(VII) Dr. Abijah Weld Draper, son of Dr. Abijah (2) Draper, was born at West Roxbury, January 25, 1808, died February 19, 1874. He taught school for a time before he began his profession as a physician. About 1837 he moved to Philadelphia, where he established himself as a dentist. After a few years there he returned to West Roxbury, where he began practice as a physician. He was one of the surgeons at Army Square Hospital, Washington, D. C., during the civil war. A few years before his death he was compelled to give up his practice because of failing health. He was a member of the Massachusetts Medical Society, and the New England Historic-Genealogical Society. He was especially interested in the history of the Draper family and obtained many valuable notes on the subject. He made it a duty as well as a pleasure to care for the old graves of the family in Eustis street, West Roxbury, cemetery. He was also much interested in the history of the town of Roxbury. In November, 1877, his family moved to Milton, Massachusetts.

He married (first), January 20, 1839, at Philadelphia, Pennsylvania, Lydia Frances Swain, born at Nantucket, Massachusetts, January 18, 1812, died at West Roxbury, April 29, 1846. He married (second), April 26, 1848, Sarah Hawes (Hewins) Reynolds, a widow, born at South Boston, March 19, 1819. Child by first wife: William Marshall, born June 28, 1840, at Philadelphia, died at West Roxbury, July 19, 1870; enlisted in the Twenty-second Massachusetts Regiment, was in the army hospital corps, and did work in the field and in a hospital at Baltimore, Maryland; at the close of the war he enlisted for three years more in the regular army. Children of second wife: Abijah Weld (2), of whom further; Lydia Frances, at West Roxbury, July 21, 1852; Miriam Stansfield, November 19, 1854, at West Roxbury.

(VIII) Dr. Abijah Weld (2) Draper, son

of Dr. Abijah Weld (1) Draper, was born at West Roxbury, Massachusetts, April 18, 1849. He attended the public schools of his native town and Bryant & Stratton's Business College of Boston. When a boy on his father's farm he became fond of horses and cattle and acquired practical knowledge that aided him materially in his profession. When a young man he followed farming. In 1880 he bought a farm at Foxborough, Massachusetts, and followed farming there successfully for many years. In 1891 he carried out a long-cherished ambition to study veterinary medicine, and entered the Harvard Veterinary School, in which he took a three-year-course and from which he was graduated in the class of 1894 with the degree of M. D. V. Since graduation he has practiced his profession at Milton, Massachusetts, and has held the position of agent of the Cattle Bureau of the Massachusetts State Board of Agriculture. He is also a member of the Milton board of health, of which he has been secretary since 1901. He is a member of Foxborough Lodge of Free Masons. In politics he is a Republican, in religion Unitarian.

He married, June 9, 1886, Ella Josephine Howard. Children: Alice Eaton, born February 24, 1889, died May 5, 1900; Howard, September 16, 1890.

(V) Simeon Alden, son of Samuel Alden (q. v.), was born in 1740, died at Roxbury (Canterbury) of smallpox. He lived at Titicut and Bridgewater, Massachusetts. He served in the revolution in Colonel Bailey's regiment, April 19, 1775, being in Colonel Dike's return, January-March, 1777. He was a private in Colonel Mitchell's regiment, in service in Rhode Island, and in Colonel Simeon Cary's regiment in New York, 1776; in Captain Abner Crane's company, 1779, in Boston. He served in Major Eliphalet Cary's regiment, July, 1780, from Plymouth county, and in Colonel E. Putnam's Plymouth county regiment, September-October, 1781. He married, May 23, 1763, Mary, daughter of Seth Packard, of Brockton, Massachusetts. Children: Simeon, of whom further; Alpheus, born 1765; Silas, 1766; Solomon, 1767; Mary, 1769; David, 1771; Jonathan, 1775; Isaac, 1777; Lot, 1781.

(VI) Simeon (2), son of Simeon (1) Alden, was born February 29, 1764, died April 2, 1843, aged seventy-nine years. He was a currier by trade, and lived in Randolph, Massachusetts. He served in Major Eliphalet Cary's regiment, in Rhode Island, July and August, 1780. He married, 1785, Rachel,

daughter of Joshua French, of Randolph. She was born June 30, 1765, died February 22, 1844, aged seventy-nine years. Either he or his son changed the name Simeon to Horatio Bingley, by act of the legislature in June, 1811. Children: Horatio Bingley, born March 16, 1786; John, 1787; Hosea, 1789; Rachel, 1792; Sally, 1797; John, 1799; Hiram, of whom further; Isaac, 1807.

(VII) Hiram, son of Simeon (2) Alden, was born November 14, 1804. He was a boot cutter by trade, and lived at Randolph. He married, February 29, 1824, Mary, daughter of Isaac Tower (see Tower VI). Children, born at Randolph: Julia Ann, born 1825; Hiram Carroll, of whom further; Charlotte Augusta, 1831; Margaret, 1833; Caroline Francis, 1835; Mary Celestina, 1837, died 1840; William Hart, 1839; Celestina Justina, 1841, died 1842; Mary Justina, 1846.

(VIII) Hiram Carroll Alden, son of Hiram Alden, was born in Randolph, Massachusetts, July 21, 1826, died there June 1, 1896. He was named for Charles Carroll, of Carrollton, Maryland, signer of the Declaration of Independence. He received his early education in the public schools, and when a young man began his career in a mercantile house in Boston. In 1858 he engaged in the manufacture of boots and shoes in Randolph. At the beginning of the civil war he raised a company and left his business to go to the front as captain in the Fourth Massachusetts Regiment of Volunteer Infantry, under Colonel Walker. He was commissioned September 1, 1862, and mustered out, August 28, 1863. In 1866 the railroad was opened through Randolph and he was appointed station agent there. In 1870 he was appointed treasurer of the Randolph Savings Bank, and filled the position until he died, with great fidelity and efficiency. He stood high in the opinion of his business associates as an able, upright and sagacious banker. He was well known to investors and financial men throughout the state and universally esteemed. For forty years he was town clerk and treasurer of Randolph, and at the time of his death one of the oldest in point of length of service in the state. He was a Republican in politics and active in town affairs, showing great public spirit. He was the prime mover in the project to erect a soldiers' monument in Randolph. This memorial to the soldiers of the great rebellion was appropriately dedicated in the fall of 1911. He also led the movement to organize the Women's Relief Corps, an auxiliary of the Grand Army. He was a prominent and active member of Captain Niles Post, No. 160, Grand Army of the Republic; of Norfolk Union Lodge, Free Masons, and Rising Star Lodge, Odd Fellows. In religion he was a Unitarian.

He married, June 18, 1848, Julia Caroline King, born September 28, 1828, in Randolph, daughter of John and Sarah Wales (Turner) King (see Turner VI). She died December 31, 1909. They had but one child, Sarah King, of whom further. They were members of the First Congregational Church of Randolph until 1889, when they became members of the Church of the Unity, which was organized at this time. They were among the organizers.

(IX) Sarah King, daughter of Hiram Carroll Alden, was born at Randolph, August 13, 1849. She was educated in the public schools of her native town. She married, June 18, 1872, William Porter, of Stoughton, Massachusetts, son of Ahira and Rachel (Swan) Porter. He was a farmer in Randolph, and died there November 5, 1904. Mrs. Sarah King (Alden) Porter is a member of Adams Chapter, of the Daughters of the Revolution, and has been its treasurer for fourteen years. The meetings are held in the old John Quincy Adams house in Quincy, Massachusetts. She is a member of the Ladies' Library Association, now the Women's Club, of which she has been the president four years, and was vice-president, treasurer and secretary for fourteen years. Mrs. Porter's mother was one of the charter members of the Library Association when it was organized in 1855. It is one of the oldest clubs in the United States. Mrs. Porter was a noted soprano singer in the quartette of the First Congregational Church of Randolph, for twenty years.

(The Tower Line).

(I) Robert Tower, the first ancestor to whom is traced the lineage of the American family, lived in the parish of Hingham, county Norfolk, England. While the name is found in various parts of England at an early date the ancestry has not been traced further. He married, August 31, 1607, at Hingham, Dorothy Damon, who died in November, and was buried November 10, 1629. He died in April, and was buried May 1, 1634. Child, baptized at Hingham: John, of whom further.

(II) John, son of Robert Tower, was the immigrant ancestor, baptized at Hingham, England, May 14, 1609. He came with many others from Hingham, England, to Hingham, Massachusetts, where he settled in 1637. Samuel Lincoln came with him. He became a proprietor of Hingham, and occasionally drew land with the other commoners. He bought various parcels of land and sold a few lots. He was admitted a freeman March 13, 1638-39, and was then a member of the church. During the controversies in Hingham he took an active part, and his name figures in the proceedings before the general court in 1640 and 1645. He deposed January 9, 1676, that he was aged about sixty-nine years. He was one of the incorporators of Lancaster, but never settled there. He had an Indian deed to land in Rhode Island, dated June 17, 1661, but he failed after some litigation to establish his title. He bought land of Edward Wilder in Hingham, by deed dated May 16, 1664, extending from what is now Main street, at Cole's Corner, to the brook at Tower's Bridge, and soon afterward built a house on it. Three of his sons built homes on this lot also and some of the land has remained in the possession of descendants to the present time. The old house was torn down soon after 1800. In 1657 he was a way-warden; in 1659, constable; in 1665 he was on an important town committee to lay out highways, with very full powers. He fortified his house during King Philip's war, and his sons and others formed the garrison. He was an active and enterprising man, although like many pioneers rather illiterate perhaps, as he signed his name with a mark like a capital T. He was frequently in court as plaintiff or defendant. His wife signed her own name. He died intestate February 13, 1701-02, having deeded land to his children, and thus in part settled his own estate.

He married, February 13, 1638-39, Margaret, daughter of Richard Ibrook, an early settler of Hingham. She died May 15, 1700. Children: John, of whom further; Ibrook, baptized February 7, 1643-44; Jeremiah, baptized March 9, 1645-46; Elizabeth, baptized October 9, 1648; Sarah, baptized July 15, 1650; Hannah, born July 17, 1652; Benjamin, November 5, 1654; Jemima, April 25, 1660; Samuel, January 26, 1661-62.

(III) John (2), son of John (1) Tower, was baptized December 13, 1639, died in Braintree, Massachusetts, August 30, 1693. He lived in Hingham about fourteen years after his marriage, when he removed to Braintree. He owned land in Plymouth colony, but never settled there. He married, May 14, 1669, Sarah Hardin, died October 16, 1729, daughter of John Hardin, of Braintree. Children: Benjamin, born January 25, 1673-74; Gideon, January 26, 1676-77; Sarah, October 21, 1679; John, June 18, 1682; Joseph, of whom further; Mary, April 26, 1690.

(IV) Joseph, son of John (2) Tower, was born in Braintree, February 27, 1685-86, and lived there, probably in that part of the town which became Randolph, Massachusetts. He was a farmer and his name appears in several real estate transactions, the last one when he was seventy-six years old. He died intestate, probably not long after that time. He married (first) Ruth Thayer, who died March 28, 1752. He married (second), ———, the intention being published March 27, 1756. He married (third) Hannah Jones, a widow, intention published 1759. Children, born in Braintree: Ruth, March 6, 1711; Hannah, September 18, 1713; Sarah, February 18, 1715-16; John, February 7, 1717-18; Margaret, August 21, 1721; Gideon, 1723; Joseph, of whom further; Mary.

(V) Lieutenant Joseph (2) Tower, son of Joseph (1) Tower, was born in Braintree, died in Randolph, September 7, 1801. He married Rebecca ———. He served in the revolution as sergeant in Captain Seth Turner's company, answering the Lexington Alarm April 19, 1775. In March, 1776, he served as lieutenant in Captain Eliphalet Sawin's company, and again in June of the same year; also in Captain Peter Thayer's company, which marched for the relief of Fort William Henry; and later in Captain Ward's company for five months. Tradition says that he was present at the surrender of Burgoyne. His will was dated December 18, 1800, and proved October 6, 1801. It mentions wife Rebecca and children Isaac, Joseph, Jane, Rebecca and Ruth. The others probably died young. Children, born at Braintree: Rebecca, married, 1778, Luther Spear; Jane, married, 1778, Eli Spear; Abraham; Elizabeth; Isaac, of whom further; Ruth; Rhoda; Mary; Joseph, born 1780.

(VI) Isaac Tower, son of Lieutenant Joseph (2) Tower, was born February 22, 1767, in Randolph, died there March 12, 1834. He married, July 1, 1798, Mary Thayer, who was born in 1777, died April 11, 1831, aged fifty-four years. Children, born in Randolph: Orramel, March 8, 1799; Isaac, August 22, 1801; Mary, November 23, 1803, married Hiram Alden (see Alden VII); Benjamin Franklin, April 24, 1806; Sally, December 29, 1807; Elmira, July 11, 1810; Luther, February 22, 1813; Silas D., September 23, 1815; Lorenzo, May 14, 1820.

(The Turner Line).

(I) Humphrey Turner, the immigrant ancestor, was born in England about 1593, and is said to have been from Essex, England. He came to Plymouth, Massachusetts, about 1638, and had a house lot assigned him in 1629. He built his house and lived in Plym-

outh until 1633, when he removed to Scituate, where he had a house lot granted him on Kent street. He settled, however, on a farm east of Colman's Hills. He was a tanner by trade, and is said to have possessed that "judgment, discretion, energy and perseverance of character, which eminently fitted him to be one of the pioneers in beginning and carrying forward a new settlement." Deane says in his history of Scituate: "He was a useful and enterprising man in the new settlement and often employed in public business." He was a member of the first church. He represented the town several years as deputy to the general court; was commissioner to end small causes, constable, etc. Following an infrequent and puzzling custom of his forbears he had two sons of the same name, John Turner, whom he distinguished in his will as John, and Young son John, so named, tradition says, at the instance of godfathers. Both brought up families and died at a good old age in Scituate. At last accounts a lineal descendant of the pioneer owned and occupied the Turner homestead in Scituate. His will was dated February 28, 1669, and proved June 5, 1673. Besides his children he mentioned grandchildren in the will.

He married, in England, Lydia Gamer, born in England, died in Scituate in or before 1673. Children: John, born in England, married, November 12, 1645, at Scituate; John, of whom further; Thomas, born in Plymouth, married Sarah Hiland; Mary, baptized January 25, 1634-35; Joseph, baptized January 1, 1638; Daniel, married Hannah Randall; Nathaniel, baptized March 10, 1638; Lydia, married James Doughty.

(II) John, the Younger, son of Humphrey Turner, was born about 1628, died in 1687 at Scituate. He lived northeast of Hick's Swamp, near the farm lately owned by Leonard Clapp. He married, April 25, 1649, at Scituate, Ann James. Children, born at Scituate: Japheth, February 9, 1650; Ann, February 23, 1652; Israel, February 14, 1654; Miriam, April 8, 1658; Sarah, July 25, 1665; Jacob, of whom further; David, November 5, 1670; Philip, August 18, 1673; Ichabod, April 9, 1676.

(III) Jacob, son of John Turner, was born at Scituate, March 10, 1667, died November 29, 1723, aged fifty-six years. He married, in 1692, at Weymouth, Massachusetts, Jane Vining, born at Weymouth, July 7, 1672, who married (second), in 1728, Samuel Allen, of Bridgewater, Massachusetts. Children: Jacob, born at Weymouth, April 4, 1693; Seth, of whom further; Jane, April 13, 1698; Benjamin, January 29, 1706, died March 27, 1713;

Elisha, March 5, 1708, died March 1, 1724; Micah, July 8, 1710; Mary, April 12, 1713.

(IV) Seth, son of Jacob Turner, was born at Weymouth, April 7, 1695, died there October 21, 1730, aged thirty-five years. He married, in 1720, Sarah Shaw, of Weymouth. Children, born at Weymouth: Benjamin, May 30, 1721; Sarah, January 18, 1723; Jane, March 30, 1725; Seth (2), of whom further; Merriam, May 27, 1729.

(V) Seth (2) Turner, son of Seth (1) Turner, was born at Weymouth, April 7, 1727, died at Randolph, Massachusetts, January 29, 1806, aged seventy-nine years. He married Rebecca Vinton, born at Stoughton, Massachusetts, in 1729, died at Randolph, September 22, 1801, aged seventy-two years. Children: Rebecca, born 1754; Seth (3), of whom further; Sally, 1760; Samuel Vinton, July 29, 1764; Benjamin, September 22, 1765; John, November 4, 1768; Olive, 1771.

(VI) Seth (3), son of Seth (2) Turner, was born at Randolph, November 15, 1756, died there October 2, 1842, aged eighty-six years. He married Abigail, daughter of Jonathan Wales. Children, born at Randolph: 1. Sarah Wales, October 6, 1788; married John King. Their daughter, Julia Caroline King, married Hiram C. Alden (see Alden VIII). 2. Royal, December 6, 1792.

BALDWIN   In records incident to the Conquest of England the name of Baldwin appears in the Battle Abbey, and one of the name is known as early as 672. The Earls of Flanders bearing the name date from the time of Alfred the Great. Baldwin 2nd married Elstouth, daughter of Alfred, and Baldwin 5th married the daughter of Robert of France, and their daughter Matilda married William the Conqueror. Surnames, however, were not used in England until long after the Conquest, Baldwin de Hampden of the time of the Conquest became John Hampden, the patriot of the English revolution. The name is found in Denmark, Flanders and in Normandy, and other parts of France. The Baldwins of the United States came largely from county Bucks, England, where the name "John Baldwin" is of frequent historical mention in successive generations, as is Henry and Richard. In New England we have Richard Baldwin, of Braintree, 1637; John Baldwin, of Stoughton, Connecticut, 1638; Richard Baldwin, of Milford, Connecticut, before 1639; John Baldwin, of Milford, Connecticut, 1639; Nathaniel Baldwin, of Milford, 1639; Joseph Baldwin, of Milford, Connecticut, 1639, and of Hadley, Massachusetts, 1640; John Bald-

win, of Billerica, Massachusetts, 1655; and John Baldwin, of Norwich, Connecticut. Yale University has on its alumni rolls over eighty-three Baldwins.

(I) Joseph Baldwin, son of Richard Baldwin, of Cholesbury, near Ashton Clinton, county Bucks, England, must have come to Milford, either with the original settlers from New Haven or Wethersfield, in 1639, or else almost immediately after them, as he is of record there in that year. Five years later, January 23, 1644, his wife Hannah joined the church there, and had their first four children baptized; the next year two more were baptized, and four years later a seventh. Of the last two children no record of baptism has been found. About 1663 Joseph Baldwin and his family removed to Hadley, where he and his son Joseph were admitted as freemen in 1666. Meanwhile his wife Hannah had died and Joseph Sr. married (second) Isabel Ward, sister to Deacon Lawrence Ward, of Newark, and George Ward, of Branford, the father of John Ward, the turner of Newark. As the Widow Catlin, Isabel and her son John had been among the original settlers of Newark from Branford in 1666; but while John had remained in the new settlement to become one of its foremost men and its first schoolmaster, his mother had removed to Hadley, married again, this time, James Northam, and before September, 1671, on the 2nd of which month she was granted as the wife of Joseph Baldwin and "sister", i. e., sister-in-law of Elizabeth the widow, letters of administration on the estate of her brother, Deacon Lawrence Ward, she had become widow a second time and married her third husband, Joseph Baldwin. The administration, as the East Jersey Deeds tell us, she turned over to "her son John Catline and her kinsman John Warde, turner, both of Newark". She does not appear to have borne her second and third husbands any children; she died in Hadley, December 8, 1676. Shortly after this Joseph Baldwin married (third) Elizabeth Hitchcock, widow of William Warriner, of Springfield, by whom likewise Joseph seems to have had no children, although she survived him over twelve years, dying April 25, 1696. Joseph Baldwin died November 2, 1684, but long before his death he conveyed a half interest in his homestead in Hadley to his son Joseph Jr., who died about three years before his father. The will of Joseph Sr. is recorded in Northampton, Massachusetts, and is dated December 20, 1680, and in it he gives his Milford property to his three sons, Joseph, Benjamin and Jonathan, and the remainder of his estate to his wife and other children.

Children of Joseph and Hannah Baldwin: 1. Joseph, mentioned below. 2. Benjamin, born about 1642, will proven June 19, 1729; married Hannah, daughter of Jonathan Sergeant, of Branford, who died before 1721; children: Joseph, Jonathan, Benjamin, Sarah, married Robert Young. 3. Hannah, born about 1643; married, May 6, 1659, Jeremiah, son of Richard Hull, of New Haven, and had a daughter Mary, possibly also other children. 4. Mary, born about 1644; married John Catlin, son of her stepmother, who removed from Newark, New Jersey, to Deerfield, Massachusetts, before 1684; children: Joseph, John, Jonathan, Elizabeth, married James Corse, and with brothers Joseph and Jonathan were killed by the French and Indians in the Deerfield massacre, February 29, 1704; Hannah, married Thomas Bascom; Sarah, married Michael Mitchell; Esther, married Ebenezer Smead; and Ruth. 5. Elizabeth, baptized March, 1645, died April 24, 1687; married, March 31, 1664, at Hadley, James Warriner; children: Samuel, James, Elizabeth, William, Hannah, Samuel, Ebenezer and Mary. After Elizabeth's death, James Warriner married (second) July 10, 1689, Sarah, daughter of Alexander Alvord; children: Sarah, Jonathan, John, John, Benjamin and David. Sarah (Alvord) Warriner died May 16, 1704, and James Warriner married (third) December 19, 1706, as her third husband, Mary, widow of Benjamin Stebbins. James Warriner died May 14, 1727. 6. Martha, baptized March, 1645; married, at Hadley, December 26, 1667, John, son of John Hawkes, and died January 7, 1676; children: John, John, Hannah, married Jonathan Scott, of Waterbury, Connecticut. John Hawkes married (second) November 20, 1696, Alice, widow of Samuel Allis, of Hadley, and removed to Deerfield, having by his second wife one child, Elizabeth. 7. Jonathan. 8. David, born October 19, 1651, died September, 1689; married, November 11, 1674, Mary, daughter of Ensign John Stream, of Milford, who died May 28, 1712; children: Samuel, David and Nathan. 9. Sarah, born November 6, 1653, married, as second wife, Samuel Bartlett, of Northampton, Massachusetts; both died before February 12, 1717; children: Samuel, Sarah and Mindwell.

(II) Joseph (2), eldest son of Joseph (1) and Hannah Baldwin, was born about 1640, baptized June 23, 1644, in Milford. He accompanied his father to Hadley, where he was a freeman in 1666. It is presumable that he lived with his father as the latter deeded to him a half interest in the home estate. He was named as one of the executors in his father's will, but died before the latter, November

21, 1681. His first wife, as indicated by the record of his children in Hadley, bore the name of Elizabeth. He married (second) Sarah, daughter of Benjamin Coley, of Milford, baptized 1648, died in the spring of 1689. Children: Joseph, James, Mehitable, Hannah, died young, Mary, died young, Mercy (or Mary), Hannah, died young, Samuel and Hannah.

(III) James, second son of Joseph (2) and Elizabeth Baldwin, born about 1666, in Hadley, was a weaver and resided in Milford, Connecticut, where he received a deed of property, August 5, 1692. He was admitted to the church at Milford in 1699, and his wife Elizabeth, July 18, 1703. He probably resided in Milford until after 1710, when his youngest child was baptized there. He was one of the proprietors of the town of Durham, Connecticut, when it was patented May 1, 1708, and resided in that town until after 1724, removing to Saybrook, Connecticut, where his will was made in 1748, and proved in 1756. Children: Elizabeth, died young, David, Phebe, Elizabeth, Moses and Aaron (twins), Hannah, baptized 1710, at Milford.

(IV) Moses, second son of James and Elizabeth Baldwin, was born April 15, 1705, in Milford, and settled in Saybrook, where his widow received his estate in 1756. She was Abigail, daughter of Deacon Robert Royce, of Wallingford. Children: Aaron, Moses, Hannah, James, died young, Royce, David, James, Noah and Joseph.

(V) David, fourth son of Moses and Abigail (Royce) Baldwin, was born March 8, 1740, in Saybrook (family Bible says March 28), and resided for some time in Wallingford, Connecticut, where he was in 1773. In 1804 he removed to Atwater, Portage county, Ohio, where he died September 1, 1808. He married Parnell, daughter of Joseph (2) Clark, of Chester, Connecticut. She died October 31, 1815, in Atwater. Children: Roswell, Benjamin, David, Noah, Rebecca, Lydia, Abigail, Joseph, Clark, Moses and Parnell.

(VI) Noah, fourth son of David and Parnell (Clark) Baldwin, was born April 23, 1772, in Wallingford and settled in Vermont, where he died in 1857, leaving a family. He married, May 14, 1795, Sarah Warner.

(VII) Hiram Gates, son of Noah and Sarah (Warner) Baldwin, was born June 19, 1805, died at Troy, New York, November 15, 1875. He married Roxalina Wood.

(VIII) Warner Horace, son of Hiram Gates and Roxalina (Wood) Baldwin, was born May 6, 1838, in Bristol, Vermont, and is still living in Rutland, Vermont. He married, at Brandon, Vermont, April 7, 1858, Mary Olive, born October 13, 1843, in Montpelier, Vermont, daughter of Philander Barton and Lydia (Bryant) Hatch.

(IX) LeRoy Wilbur, second son of Warner Horace and Mary Olive (Hatch) Baldwin, was born October 31, 1864, in Rutland. In January, 1883, he sought a larger field of operation in the city of New York. There he assisted in the organization of the American Automatic Weighing Machine Company, and became managing director of the business of the company in the United States. He sold the business to an English company with offices in London, England. From the time of his location in New York, he has aided in the inauguration and development of various important enterprises. One of the chief of these is the Empire Trust Company, now located at No. 42 Broadway, of which he is president. This institution includes in its directorate many prominent financiers and business men with a capital and surplus of over three million dollars. Mr. Baldwin is actively interested in various corporations, including the Ann Arbor Railroad Company, the Wisconsin Central Railroad, the Rutland Railway Light & Power Company, Union Ferry Company of Brooklyn, Biograph Company, Garden City Estates, and so forth. He is a member of the following clubs: Turf and Field, Metropolitan, Riding, Automobile of America, City Midday, Sleepy Hollow Country, Recess and Rumson Country.

He married, in New York City, October, 1889, Ettie Lucile, daughter of the late Louis W. Field, a prominent broker of that city. They have one daughter named for her mother.

SHERWIN John Sherwin, the immigrant ancestor of all the early colonial families of this surname in New England, was born in England in 1644, of ancient and honored family. He died at Ipswich, Massachusetts, October 15, 1726, aged eighty-two years. He married (first) at Ipswich, Massachusetts, where he settled, after coming to America, Frances Lomas, November 25, 1667. They both joined the church in full communion, April 12, 1674. He had granted to him by the town the right to cut trees for fencing—300 rails—January 13, 1667. He had a seat in the meeting house in 1700 and was on the list of commoners for 1707. Children: Robert, Elizabeth, Hannah, Ebenezer, mentioned below; Mary, born August, 1679; Frances, born January 27, 1682. He married (second) September 30, 1691, Mary, daughter of William Chandler. Children of second wife: John, born 1692, died 1706; Alice, born January 21, 1694; Abigail, born May 4, 1695; Eleanor, born June 28,

1696; William, born July 27, 1698; Jacob, born October 17, 1699.

(II) Ebenezer, son of John Sherwin, was born about 1675 in Ipswich, and died between 1706 and 1712 at Boxford, Massachusetts. He married, at Boxford, Massachusetts, February 1, 1700, Susanna Howlett, of Topsfield, Massachusetts. Her birth appears as Johannah Howlett, born August 27, 1679, at Topsfield, Massachusetts, daughter of Samuel and Sarah (Clark) Howlett, who were married January 3, 1670, at Topsfield. Susanna died at Boxford, October 29, 1762, aged eighty-three years. Thomas Howlett, father of Samuel and grandfather of Susanna, was born in England; settled as early as 1635 in Ipswich, which granted to him that year a house lot adjoining Thomas Hardy's in the way leading to the mill; was deputy to the general court in 1635; was a commoner in 1641; was ensign in the militia and in 1643 he was paid for active service with ten soldiers; died 1673, aged seventy-nine years; wife Alice died June 26, 1666; second wife Rebecca survived him; children: Samuel, Thomas, Sarah Cummings, Mary Perley, Nathaniel, who died April 23, 1658. Children of Ebenezer and Susanna (Howlett) Sherwin, born at Boxford and recorded also at Topsfield, Massachusetts: Susanna, born August 6, or November 9, 1701, both are town records; Jonathan, born January 8, 1704; Ebenezer, mentioned below.

(III) Ebenezer (2), son of Ebenezer (1) Sherwin, was born January 5, 1706, at Boxford, Massachusetts, died in Dunstable, Massachusetts, in 1763. He was a farmer and cooper at Boxford. He married, at Boxford, September 21, 1726, Hepsibah Cole. Children born at Boxford: Ebenezer, March 12, 1728; Daniel, mentioned below; John, May 15, 1732; Susanna, August 28, 1734; Elnathan, March 9, 1736; Sampson, August 5, 1739; Martha, December 23, 1741; Silas, November 13, 1743, died November 22, 1744; Hepsibah, April 19, 1746. Those born at Dunstable were Sarah, February 17, 1748; Jonathan, June 17, 1753.

(IV) Lieutenant Daniel Sherwin, son of Ebenezer (2) Sherwin, married Susannah Proctor and settled in Townsend, Massachusetts. They had fourteen children, among whom were Daniel Jr., born May 3, 1757; John, mentioned below; and Levi, who was sole executor of Daniel's will. He was a prominent citizen there and a soldier in the revolution, took part at the battle of Bunker Hill, was a lieutenant in command of a detachment of the Townsend militia. Colonel James Prescott's regiment, responding to the Lexington Alarm; also first lieutenant in Captain Thomas Warren's company (First Townsend) Fifth Company of the Sixth Middlesex Regiment, commissioned April 24, 1776; also first lieutenant, Captain Aaron Jewett's company, Colonel Job Cushing's regiment in 1777, marching to Bennington, Vermont, to support Stark; also Captain Aaron Jewett's company, Colonel Samuel Bullard's regiment in 1777 at the time of taking Burgoyne. His son Daniel Jr. was also in the army in 1775-76-77-78. His son Captain John was also in the revolution. Daniel Sherwin Sr. died in Townsend, June 25, 1804.

(V) John (2), son of Lieutenant Daniel Sherwin, was a soldier from Townsend in the revolution in 1780, enlisting for six months and serving from July 10 to December 8, 1780. He is described at that time as twenty-one years old, of ruddy complexion, five feet ten inches tall. He removed to Weathersfield, Vermont, where he died October 5, 1830. He was a lieutenant in the militia. He married (first) Keziah Adams, who died the same year, and (second) Lucretia Wheelock. Their children were John, mentioned below, and Polly, born October 1, 1790. The second wife died August 5, 1792, and he married (third) Eunice Farwell. They had eight children, born in Townsend, Massachusetts, and probably before the removal to Weathersfield, Vermont: Miriam, January 20, 1795; Charles, September 22, 1796; Lucy, November 2, 1798; Eunice, July 22, 1800; Fox, June 9, 1806; Harriet, May 14, 1808; Nancy, December 21, 1811; George Columbus, June 14, 1814.

(VI) John (3), son of John (2) Sherwin, was born October 12, 1788, died November 24, 1865. He resided at Weathersfield, Vermont. He married Martha Leland, of Chester, Vermont, February 17, 1814 (see Leland V), and had six children: 1. Joseph Henry, born December 9, 1814, never married, died June 3, 1866. 2. Alden Wheelock, mentioned below. 3. Martha Leland, born December 11, 1820; married George W. Alford, May 21, 1844; he died April 20, 1875; she (1912) resides in North Adams, Massachusetts. . 4. John Proctor, born July 19, 1824, never married, died July 19, 1860. 5. Lucretia Smith, born December 12, 1829; she never married; died October 9, 1853. 6. Nelson Boynton, born May 21, 1832; married Lizzie M. Kidder, July 11, 1860; he died in Cleveland, Ohio, May, 1911.

(VII) Alden Wheelock, son of John (3) Sherwin, was born at Weathersfield, Vermont, September 19, 1816, died at Cleveland, Ohio, February 17, 1889. He married, November 28, 1841, Rachel Bachelder, born November 26, 1818, daughter of Edmund Bachelder, of Baltimore, Vermont. They lived at Baltimore, Vermont, removed to Springfield, Ver-

mont, in 1846 and to Cleveland, Ohio, in 1860. They had one child, Henry Alden, mentioned below.

(VIII) Henry Alden, son of Alden Wheelock Sherwin, was born in Baltimore, Vermont, September 27, 1842. He attended the public schools in Springfield, Vermont, until he was fifteen years old, and in 1860 came to Cleveland, Ohio, with his father's family. He began his business career in Springfield as clerk in a country store. In Cleveland he found employment as clerk in a large dry goods store. His ability was promptly recognized and he was rapidly promoted, becoming head bookkeeper within a year. After his employers went out of business he held a similar position in a wholesale grocery store. Again his business sagacity and trustworthiness won the confidence of his firm and he was soon afterward admitted to partnership. He retired from this concern in 1866, however, to engage in business on his own account as a dealer in paints, oils, colors and varnishes. In 1870 he formed a partnership with E. P. Williams and A. T. Osborn, under the firm name of Sherwin, Williams & Company. The business of manufacturing paints and varnishes was developed rapidly. In 1884 the business was incorporated as The Sherwin-Williams Company, of which Mr. Sherwin was president for twenty-five years; then, when partially retiring from active management, became chairman of the board of directors. The company has the largest plant and business in its line in the world, and the paints and varnishes bearing the familiar name of the concern are in use in every civilized country. Judicious advertising, a product of superior merit, shrewd management of the manufacturing and selling departments, perfect organization and co-operation in all branches of the business have characterized Mr. Sherwin's management. Mr. Sherwin attributes his success in business to "good quality, backed by good, persistent advertising." In matters of advertising and finance, his judgment is relied upon without question in every concern with which he is connected.

Mr. Sherwin is a director of the Cleveland Trust Company, the First National Bank of Cleveland and of the Society for Savings. He is a member of the Cleveland Chamber of Commerce, trustee of the Denison University at Granville, Ohio, and of the Young Men's Christian Association of Cleveland, of which he was formerly president. He was one of the founders of the Castalia Sporting Club, near Sandusky, Ohio, famous for its trout fishing, member of the Rowfant Club and the Union Club. He is a liberal contributor to organized charity, and is a trustee of various benevolent and educational institutions. To every movement contributing to the moral and physical welfare and improvement of the community he has given freely in time, influence and money.

Mr. Sherwin is naturally of an artistic temperament and fond of good literature, and has collected a beautiful library. His collection of books on angling is said to be one of the largest in the world. He is a lover of nature and especially fond of fishing. His country home at Willoughby, Ohio, naturally a beautiful spot, has been enbellished under his own supervision until it is one of the most attractive and artistic country places in America.

He married, September 27, 1865, Frances Mary Smith, born December 16, 1843, daughter of Deacon William T. and Louise Smith, of Cleveland. Her father was a highly respected and successful merchant. Children: 1. Belle, born March 25, 1868. 2. Kate, June 11, 1870, died June 28, 1873. 3. William Alden, January 18, 1872, died August 20, 1897. 4. Prudence, born January 17, 1874. 5. Eda, born November 2, 1876; married, October 25, 1899, Orville W. Prescott, son of Charles M. and Sarah B. Prescott, of Cleveland, and had children: Henry Sherwin, born October 23, 1900; John Sherwin, born April 21, 1902; Orville W. Jr., born September 8, 1906; Sarah B., May 2, 1908.

(The Leland Line).

(I) Henry Leland, the immigrant ancestor, was born in England about 1625, died in Sherburne, Massachusetts, April 4, 1680. He seems to have been the ancestor of all in America with this surname, except for one family which adopted the surname, and one other family, whose origin is not known. He doubtless came to America in 1652, as the records of the church in Dorchester show that he joined the church there in 1653, and no earlier record has been found. After remaining a short time in Dorchester he moved to Sherburne, where he lived the remainder of his life. His will was dated May 27, 1680. He married Margaret Badcock. Their first child was either born on the way to America or very soon after their arrival, and the other children are recorded in Medfield, as Sherburne at that time was not incorporated as a town. Children: Hopestill, baptized May, 1653, died 1653 at Dorchester; Experience, born May 16, 1654; Hopestill, November 15, 1655; Ebenezer, mentioned below; and Eleazer, who was born July 16, 1660.

(II) Ebenezer, son of Henry Leland, was born January 25, 1657, died in 1742, at Sher-

burne, Massachusetts. He was a farmer. Timothy Leland, of Holliston, was administrator of his estate, appointed October 18, 1742. He spelled his name Lealand, and that spelling was used by the family for many years. He lived in Sherburne all his life. He married (first) Deborah ———, (second) Mary Hunt. Children, born in Sherburne: Deborah, in 1679; Ebenezer, 1681; Timothy, 1684; James, mentioned below; Susannah, 1690; Patience, 1695; Martha, 1699; Isaac, 1702; Sibella, 1709; Amariah, 1710.

(III) Captain James Leland, son of Ebenezer Leland, was born in Sherburne, 1687, died in 1768 at Grafton, Massachusetts. In 1723 he moved from Sherburne to Hassanamisco, later Grafton, Worcester county, Massachusetts, where he lived the remainder of his life. He had a large tract of land on the Blackstone river, which, in 1735 was in the part incorporated as Grafton, and he lived on the east bank of the river. All of his children who came of age settled near him and he gave his sons each a farm. He was a farmer and captain. He married Hannah Learned. Children, born in Sherburne: Jerusha, born 1710; Thankful, 1713, died 1714; Benjamin, 1715; Moses, 1716; James, 1720; Hannah, 1722. Born in Grafton: Thankful, 1724; Thomas, 1726; Deliverance, 1729; Phineas, mentioned below; Prudence, 1732, died 1732.

(IV) Phineas, son of Captain James Leland, was born at Grafton, 1730, died there in 1773. He was a farmer. He lived on his father's homestead on the Blackstone river in Grafton. He married (first) Lydia Fletcher, (second) Sarah Warren. His widow married (second) Ziba Abbey, of Chatham, Connecticut, and she moved to Chatham, with her daughters Sarah and Deliverance. Children, born in Grafton: Lydia, 1750; Phineas, 1753; Eleazer, 1755; Joseph, 1757; David W., 1758; Thomas, mentioned below; Sarah, 1763; Caleb, 1765; Joshua, 1765; Lydia, 1767; Deliverance, 1770.

(V) Thomas, son of Phineas Leland, was born in Grafton, 1760, died in 1830 in Chester, Vermont. He was a farmer. For a few years after his marriage he lived in Conway, Massachusetts, and he then moved to Grafton, where he lived for eight or ten years. In 1795 the family moved to Chester, Vermont, where they settled on uncultivated land, which in time became a fine farm through their hard efforts. He married Lydia Sherman. Children: Elizabeth, born 1780; Ephraim S., 1782; Thomas, 1784; Paulina, 1786; Lydia, 1788; Martha, 1790, married John Sherwin (see Sherwin VI); Jasper, 1792; Asenath, 1794;

Susannah, 1796; Phineas, 1798; Mary, 1801; Fanny, 1803.

STURGIS

The first mention of this name was in a French volume published by Abbe Mac Groghegan, which reads: "About the year 815, during the reign of Conor, who reigned fourteen years, Turgesius, a son of a king of Norway, landed a formidable fleet on the north coast of Ireland; and again, about the year 835, a fleet commanded by the same man landed on the west side of Lough Lea, where he fortified himself, and laid waste Connaught, Meath and Leinster, and the greater part of Ulster, and was declared king. He reigned about thirty years. Finally the people revolted, and under the lead of Malarlin, Prince of Meath, he was defeated by a strategem and put to death." The first authentic mention is in English history, when William de Turges had grants of land from Edward I., King of England, in the village of Turges, county of Northampton, afterwards called Northfield. The coat-of-arms: Azure, a chevron between three crosses crosslet, fitchee or, a border engrailed of the last. Crest: A talbot's head or, eared sable. Motto: *Esse quam videre.*

(I) Roger Sturges, of Clipston, Northampton, England, married Alice ———. His will was dated November 10, 1530. Children: Richard, mentioned below; Robert; Thomas; Ellen, married a Raullen; Agnes, married a Hull; Clementina, named in will.

(II) Richard, son of Roger Sturges, married in Clipston. Children: Roger, mentioned below; John, had five children, was living in 1579; Thomas, of Stannion, Northampton county, England.

(III) Roger (2), son of Richard Sturges, was of Clipston. He married Agnes ———. His will was dated September 4, 1579. Children: Robert, mentioned below; John.

(IV) Robert, son of Roger (2) Sturges, was buried at Faxon, Northampton county, England, January 2, 1611. He was church warden at Faxton in 1589, and his will was dated April 9, 1610, and proved September 19, 1611. Children: Philip, mentioned below; Alice.

(V) Philip Sturgis, son of Robert Sturges, was of Hannington, Northampton county, England. His will was dated 1615. He married twice. his second wife being Anne Lewes. Children by first wife: Edward, mentioned below; Robert; Elizabeth. By second wife: Alice, baptized January 17, 1608; Anne, born September 29, 1609; William, born October 10, 1611.

(VI) Edward, son of Philip Sturgis, was born at Hannington, England. He came to New England about 1634 and settled at Sandwich, Massachusetts. He was in Charlestown, Massachusetts, in 1634, and in Yarmouth, Cape Cod, 1639. He married (first) Elizabeth ———, though one genealogist gives her name as Alice. She died February 14, 1691. He married (second) April 20, 1692, Mary, widow of Zephaniah Rider. She was the first female child born of English parents at Yarmouth (see footnote). Edward Sturgis was constable at Yarmouth in 1640-41, member of grand inquest in 1650, and surveyor of highways in 1651. He was admitted freeman, June 5, 1651, and was committeeman on affairs of the colony in 1657. He was constable in 1662, and deputy to the general assembly in 1672. He died at Sandwich, in October, 1695, and was buried at Yarmouth. Children, born in England: Alice, December 23, 1619; Maria, October 2, 1621; Edward, April 10, 1624; Rebecca, February 17, 1636-37. Born in New England: Samuel, 1638; Thomas, mentioned below; Mary, baptized at Barnstable, January 1, 1646, married Benjamin Gorham; Elizabeth, born at Yarmouth, April 20, 1648; Sarah, married Joseph Gorham, who was born at Yarmouth in 1653; Joseph, buried March 29, 1650, aged ten days; Hannah, married (first) a Gray, (second) Jabez Gorham, moved to Bristol, Rhode Island. Otis thought there was a son John, born about 1624, who went to Connecticut.

(VII) Thomas, son of Edward Sturgis, in 1695 was appointed to the duty of "seating men, women, and others in the meeting-house." He married Abigail ———. Children: Daughter, born 1681, died in infancy; daughter, 1683, died in infancy; Edward, born December 10, 1684; Thomas, mentioned below; Hannah, September 18, 1687; John, December 2, 1690; Elizabeth, December 25, 1691; Abigail, October 28, 1694; son, died in infancy; Thankful, March 18, 1697; Sarah, January, 1699; Jacob, December 14, 1700; sons, twins, 1702, died in infancy.

(VIII) Thomas (2), son of Thomas (1) Sturgis, was born April 14, 1686, died December 18, 1763. He married, December 25, 1717, Martha, daughter of Rev. John Russell. Children: Martha, born November 19, 1718; Elizabeth, June 12, 1721, died in infancy; Thomas, mentioned below; Elizabeth, born August 26, 1725; Rebecca, October 9, 1727; Jonathan, June 17, 1730; Abigail, July 22, 1732; Hannah, August 24, 1735.

* The marriage contract with Mary, widow of Zephaniah Rider, of Yarmouth, April 20, 1692, is in Barnstable Records, Vol. 2, fol. 14; also in Pope's "Pioneers of Massachusetts," p. 440.

(IX) Thomas (3), son of Thomas (2) Sturgis, was born at Barnstable, Massachusetts, July 22, 1722. He married there, January 24, 1745, Sarah Paine, of Eastham, who died December 11, 1770. He may have had two wives, both named Sarah, for Barnstable records give the death of Sarah, wife of Thomas Sturgis Jr., September 4, 1748. Children of Thomas and Sarah Sturgis (p. 275, vol. 2, Mss. records of Barnstable, at New England Historic-Genealogical Library) : Martha, born November 6, 1745, died December 29, 1745; William, February 19, 1748; Russell, August 28, 1750; Abigail, August 3, 1752; Thomas, mentioned below; John, August 15, 1757; Elizabeth, December 13, 1759; Samuel, September 28, 1762; Josiah, September 19, 1767. These children were all baptized in the Barnstable church.

(X) Thomas (4), son of Thomas (3) Sturgis, was born at Barnstable, April 5, 1755, baptized there April 6, died there September 16, 1821 (p. 184, vol. 4, Mss. records mentioned above). He lived at Barnstable and joined the church there July 3, 1814. He married Elizabeth Jackson, who was baptized late in life and joined the church, November 7, 1813. He was a soldier in the revolution, in Captain Micah Hamlen's company, Colonel Simeon Cary's regiment, 1776, and in Captain George Lewis's company, Colonel Freeman's regiment, in 1778. He was living in Barnstable in 1790. Children, born at Barnstable : Nancy, December 27, 1786; Hezekiah Jackson, March 10, 1793; Thomas, June 24, 1795; Martha Russell, March 21, 1797; Catherine, April 20, 1801; Russell, December 6, 1804; William, mentioned below; Esther Frances, May 6, 1810.

(XI) William, son of Thomas (4) Sturgis, was born September 1, 1806, at Barnstable, Massachusetts. He obtained his education in the schools of that city. He engaged in business in Boston, in 1820, as a junior clerk with a dry goods firm, and in 1830 went to London, engaging there in the shipping of dry goods to America. He returned to America in 1837 and formed the firm of Wright, Sturgis & Shaw. Later Mr. Wright died, and the firm became Sturgis, Shaw & Company, continuing until 1862, when it dissolved. Mr. Sturgis remained out of business until 1895, when his death took place, in the city of New York. He was never in public life, but was a Republican in politics. He married (first) December 8, 1831, Elizabeth Knight Hinckley, born at Hingham, June 25, 1809, (see Hinckley VI). Children: Helen Russell, died in youth; Annie, born about 1834; Elizabeth Jackson, about 1836; Charlotte Hinckley, about 1840; William, December, 1843; Thomas, April 30, 1846; Frank Knight, of whom further. He married (second) in 1857, Catharine Gore Torrey, of Boston, who died in 1863. Children: Frances Torrey Sturgis, born April, 1859; Elliot Torrey Sturgis, September, 1863.

(XII) Frank Knight, son of William Sturgis, was born September 19, 1847. He received an excellent education and at sixteen years of age became a clerk with a mercantile firm. In January, 1868, at the age of twenty, he entered the banking house of Capron, Strong & Company, New York City. He served an apprenticeship of one year, during which he devoted himself to the theoretical and practical study of finance, and was then admitted as a partner into the firm. He has maintained his partnership with the house unbroken up to the present time. In 1871 the original firm was succeeded by Work, Strong & Company, and in 1896 the style became Strong, Sturgis & Company, which it still remains.

Mr. Sturgis has the highest standing as a banker and broker, and has been honored in many ways by those in a position to recognize his strength of character and his ability. In 1892 he was elected to the presidency of the New York Stock Exchange, of which he had been a member since 1869, and in 1893 was re-elected. He is a member of the governing committee of the Stock Exchange, and has served continuously for thirty-six years. For the last twenty years he has been chairman of the law committee. During his incumbency he acquired a brilliant reputation, second to none of his predecessors. It was largely at his suggestion and through his labors, in association with other leading financiers, that the Clearing House was established. He has also been instrumental in introducing many reforms in the administration of the business of the Stock Exchange, which have benefited both the members and the business community. He is vice-president of the Standard Trust Company.

He has been, besides, an important factor in the social, benevolent and political life of New York. Upon the organization of the Jockey Club, Mr. Sturgis became a member of the board of stewards, as well as treasurer and secretary, which position he has held continuously for nearly twenty years. He has exercised a strong and wholesome influence upon all matters connected with the turf over which the Jockey Club has had especial control.

Mr. Sturgis was one of the original party of men who organized the Madison Square Garden Company, and became its president in

1891, continuing in that office until the dissolution of the company in 1912. He always gave to this enterprise earnest care and consideration, believing that it was one of the greatest boons to the people of New York, and provided not only for their public meetings, but for the development of industrial enterprises and the support of the best class of sporting interests.

His association with club life has been extensive. He was one of the founders and an original member of the board of governors of the Metropolitan Club, of which he became president in 1911. He is the vice-president of the Knickerbocker Club, which institution he joined in 1879. He is vice-president of the Midday Club, and is a member of the Century Association, the Grolier Club, the Coaching Club, the Army and Navy Club, the Union Club, the Riding Club, the Lenox Club, the Newport Reading Room, the Coney Island Jockey Club, of which he is vice-president, the Turf and Field Club, in which organization he holds the same office, and is in addition a trustee of the Westchester Racing Association. Mr. Sturgis was one of the original founders of the Racquet Club, but retired from it after some years of administration as its secretary. He is a life member of the Metropolitan Museum of Art, of the Natural History Museum, American Geographical Society, New York Historical Society, and the New York Yacht Club. He is also a trustee and governor of the Newport Racing Association, of the Newport Casino of Rhode Island, and of the New York Zoological Garden.

Among his interests in hospital work, Mr. Sturgis is a governor of the New York Hospital, the oldest institution of its kind in the city of New York. He is also a trustee of the Bloomingdale Hospital for the Insane, at White Plains, and is president of the Burke Memorial Foundation, a charitable organization, with buildings at White Plains, and dedicated by the late John M. Burke for the use of the convalescent poor of the city of New York, who, having been discharged from the hospital, are still too infirm to pursue their daily vocations—one of the most beneficent of institutions.

Mr. Sturgis married, October 16, 1872, Florence, youngest daughter of the late Philip Mesier Lydig, of the famous old Knickerbocker family of that name. Their residence in New York City is at No. 17 East 51st street, and Mr. Sturgis also owns a summer home known as Clipston Grange, at Lenox, Massachusetts, and a villa at Newport known as Faxon Lodge, both these country residences being named for the towns in England from whence his family emigrated to America in 1634.

(The Hinckley Line).

(I) Samuel Hinckley, immigrant ancestor, was born in England. He was a Puritan, but took the oath of conformity, March 14, 1634-35. "He was honest, industrious and prudent, qualities which have been transmitted from father to son down to the present time." He was a man of good estate, but not prominent in public life. He was a juror and highway surveyor. He came from county Kent, England, in 1635, with Elder Nathaniel Tilden and others, and settled in Scituate, Massachusetts. With Hinckley came his wife Sarah and four children. He resided in Scituate until July, 1640, when he sold his property and located at Barnstable. His farm at West Barnstable was lately owned by Levi L. Goodspeed. He was admitted a freeman in 1637, and was one of the grantees of Suckinesset. He was twice indicted for his hospitality in entertaining strangers, proof that he was liberal in his religious views. He died October 31, 1662. His first wife died August 18, 1656, and he married (second) Bridget, widow of Robert Bodfish. Children: Governor Thomas, born in England, in 1618; Susannah, born in England, married John Smith; Sarah, married Henry Cobb; Mary; Elizabeth, baptized in Scituate, September 6, 1635; Samuel, baptized February 4, 1637-38, died young; daughter, born in Scituate, buried in Barnstable; twins, born in Barnstable, died young; Samuel, mentioned below; John, born in Barnstable, May 24, 1644.

(II) Samuel (2), son of Samuel (1) Hinckley, was born in Barnstable, July 24, 1642, and baptized the same day. He resided on his father's estate at West Barnstable, and followed farming. He married (first) December 14, 1664, Mary, daughter of Roger Goodspeed. She died December 20, 1666, aged twenty-two, and he married (second) January 15, 1668, Mary, daughter of Edward Fitz-Randolph. Samuel Hinckley died intestate January 2, 1786-87, aged eighty-four, and his estate was divided on the thirty-first of the same month by mutual agreement among his sons—Benjamin, Joseph, Isaac, Ebenezer and Thomas. His widow married John Bursley. Children, born at Barnstable: Benjamin, December 6, 1666; Samuel, February 6, 1669, died young; Joseph, mentioned below; Isaac, August 20, 1674; Mary, May, 1677, died young; Mercy, April 9, 1679; Ebenezer, August 2, 1685; Thomas, January 1, 1688-89.

(III) Joseph, son of Samuel (2) Hinckley, was born at Barnstable, May 15, 1672. He resided at West Barnstable, on the farm which had been his grandfather's, and at last accounts his house was still standing, lately owned by Levi L. Goodspeed. He was a man of wealth for his day, and in addition to farming was a tanner and currier. He died in 1753, aged eighty-one years. His will, dated September 11, 1751, proved August 7, 1753, bequeathed to children and grandchildren. He married, September 21, 1699, Mary Gorham. Children: Mercy, born August 19, 1700; Joseph, May 6, 1702; Mary, February 25, 1703-04; Samuel, February 24, 1705-06; Thankful, June 9, 1708; Abigail, October 30, 1710; Elizabeth, January 4, 1712-13; Hannah, June 10, 1715; John, November 16, 1717; Isaac, mentioned below.

(IV) Isaac, son of Joseph Hinckley, was born October 31, 1719. He graduated from Harvard College in 1740, a classmate of Samuel Adams and other distinguished men. He resided in West Barnstable, on his father's homestead, and during the revolution was an active patriot. He was for many years town clerk of Barnstable and one of the selectmen. He died in December, 1802, aged eighty-three. He married, December 18, 1748, Hannah Bourne. Children: Richard, mentioned below; Hannah, born March 25, 1751; Abigail, February 13, 1753; Joseph, March 6, 1755; Elizabeth, April 30, 1757; Isaac, June 18, 1760; Charles, November 1, 1762; Eunice, July 14, 1765.

(V) Richard, son of Isaac Hinckley, was born at Barnstable, October 29, 1749, died in 1790. He removed to Marblehead, Massachusetts. He married Elizabeth Knight.

(VI) Isaac (2), son of Richard Hinckley, was born at Marblehead, January 2, 1781. He married, in 1805, Hannah Sturgis, born at Barnstable, August 9, 1785, died in New York City, April 9, 1871, daughter of William and Hannah (Mills) Sturgis. She had a brother William, born at Barnstable, February 25, 1782. Isaac Hinckley was a shipmaster, and died at sea, March 13, 1818, aged thirty-seven. He came to Hingham, Massachusetts, in 1810, and lived in the George Bassett house; in April, 1811, he built a house, which was lately occupied by Joseph B. Thaxter, on Main street. Children: 1. William Sturgis, born October 4, 1806, died 1841. 2. Ann Gore, born October 13, 1807, died July 5, 1835. 3. Elizabeth Knight, born June 25, 1809, in Boston; married, at Hingham, December 8, 1831, William Sturgis, and died September 17, 1849 (see Sturgis XI). 4. Thomas Davis, born at Hingham, April 20, 1811, died at Chagres, April 20, 1835. 5. Hannah Sturgis, born at Hingham, November 10, 1813; married, September 30, 1852, Joseph M. Flye. 6. Isaac, born at Hingham, October 28, 1815; graduated at Harvard College, 1834; he became president of the Philadelphia, Wilmington & Baltimore Railway Company; he gave land for a cemetery to his native town of Hingham; he was a man of high character, broad education, and great ability. He married, October 28, 1840, Julia R. Townsend; he died at Philadelphia, Pennsylvania, March 19, 1887; had seven children.

ROBINSON Members of the Robinson family figured prominently in the annals of early American history, a number of the name having been valiant soldiers in the war of the revolution. This family has contributed many valued citizens to the state of Massachusetts, and the name has ever been one well worthy of esteem.

(I) The first representative of this particular branch of the family of whom anything definite is known was Thomas Robinson, who was in Scituate as early as 1640, when he purchased land of William Gillson and represented that town in the general court of Plymouth at its session in October, 1643. He was also deacon, probably of the Second Church in Scituate. In August and September, 1654, he purchased two estates adjoining each other, directly opposite Old South Church in Boston. Here he probably resided during the remainder of his life, though he seems to have retained his connection with the church at Scituate, as all his children by the second marriage except James were baptized there. There are reasons for believing that he was a son of Rev. John Robinson, of Leyden, pastor of the church of the Pilgrims which was established at Plymouth in 1620. Isaac Robinson, known to be a son of Rev. John Robinson, settled at Scituate at the same time or very nearly the same time that Thomas made his purchase of a homestead there, and hence it is not unreasonable to infer kinship. No authentic evidence concerning this fact, however, has been ascertained. Thomas Robinson was a stalwart citizen and wrought out a good name for himself.

Thomas Robinson was thrice married, his second wife having been Mary, widow of John Woody, and daughter of John Cogan, of Boston. They were married January 11, 1652-53, and she died October 26, 1661. Subsequently he married Elizabeth Sherman. John Cogan is said by Snow (Hist. Boston) to have "opened the first shop in Boston"; it was on the northeast corner of Washington and State streets. Children: 1. John, a merchant. 2. Samuel, a merchant, died unmarried, January

NEW ENGLAND.

337

16, 1661-62, aged twenty-four years. 3. Jo-
sian, apprentice to Joseph Rocke, died April
17, 1660. 4. Ephraim, died September 22,
1661. 5. Thomas, mentioned below. 6. James,
born at Boston, March 14, 1654-55, died September, 1676. 7. Joseph, baptized March 8,
1656-57, married Sarah ———, and died in
April, 1703. 8. Mary, baptized February 28,
1657-58, died young. 9. Mary, baptized November 6, 1659, married Jacob Green Jr., of
Charlestown.

(II) Thomas (2), son of Thomas (1) Robinson, was baptized at Scituate, Massachusetts,
March 5, 1653-54. He inherited a part of his
father's homestead, where he resided; he also
inherited from his grandfather Cogan the
house and store on the northeasterly corner
of Washington and State streets, Boston. He
was a cordwainer by trade. He died in June,
1700. He married Sarah, daughter of Edward Denison, of Roxbury; she died November 15, 1710, aged fifty-three years. Edward
Denison was the son of William Denison, one
of the earliest inhabitants of Roxbury. He
had two brothers—Daniel, major-general of
the Massachusetts colony during King Phillip's war, and George, a successful and distinguished captain of Connecticut troops during the same war; both rendered important
services as legislators and magistrates. Edward manifested no taste for military affairs,
but was useful as selectman, town clerk and
representative. Children: 1. Thomas, born
November 5, 1677; married Sarah Beswick,
and died 1729-30. 2. Sarah, baptized December 28, 1679; married (first) John Ingolds-
bury, (second) John Perry. 3. Joseph, baptized November 20, 1681, died young. 4.
Elizabeth, born September 26, 1686, died
young. 5. James, mentioned below.

(III) James, son of Thomas (2) and Sarah
(Denison) Robinson, was born March 15,
1689-90, died shortly before March 11, 1762,
when his will was approved. He was a housewright by occupation. He inherited from his
father the homestead on Washington street,
Boston, which he sold February 7, 1711-12,
and bought a house on the southerly side of
Boylston street, which he also sold April 12,
1714, and removed to Rochester, where Rev.
Timothy Ruggles, a brother of his wife, resided. He remained at Rochester until 1757,
when he exchanged his farm in Rochester for
another in Hardwick, where several of his
children had already settled. Of his eight
surviving children Dorothy alone remained in
Rochester, all the others having removed to
Hardwick and Barre. He married Patience,
daughter of Captain Samuel Ruggles, of Roxbury, July 3, 1711. She died in January,

1768, aged seventy-eight years. Captain Ruggles married Martha, daughter of Rev. John
Woodbridge, and granddaughter of Governor
Thomas Dudley, on July 8, 1680. His father
was a prominent citizen of Roxbury, where he
was selectman fourteen years, assessor during the same period, and representative for
the four critical years succeeding the revolution of 1689. He was for several years
captain of militia, and when Governor Andros
and his associates were seized and imprisoned,
Joseph Dudley (afterwards governor) was
committed to his special charge, while tempo-
rarily released from prison. His preservation
from death by lightning on May 25, 1667, was
so remarkable that an account of it was entered on the church record by Rev. Samuel
Danforth: "25 (3) 1667. There was a dreadful crack of thunder. Samuel Ruggles hap-
pened at that instant to be upon the meeting-
house hill, with oxen and horse, and cart
loaded with corn. The horse and one ox were
stricken dead with the lightning; the other ox
had a little life in it, but died presently. The
man was singed and scorched a little on his
legs, one shoe torn apieces, and the heel carried away; the man was hurled off from the
cart and flung on the off side, but through
mercy soon recovered himself and felt little
harm. There was a chest in the cart, wherein
was pewter and linen; the pewter had small
holes melted in it, and the linen some of it
singed and burnt." Captain Ruggles, father
of Patience, inherited his father's military
spirit and succeeded him in many of his offices;
he was assessor, 1694; representative, 1694;
captain of militia, 1702; and selectman continuously from 1693 to 1712, except in 1701
and 1704, nineteen years. His death occurred
after a short sickness, February 25, 1715-16,
and his funeral is mentioned in Sewall's
Diary: "Feb. 28, 1715-16. Capt. Samuel Ruggles was buried with arms. * * * He is
much lamented at Roxbury."

Children of Mr. and Mrs. Robinson, of
whom the first two were born in Boston and
the remainder in Rochester: 1. James, born
March 1, 1711-12. 2. Thomas, born September 15, 1713, died young. 3. Samuel, born
November 1, 1715. 4. Thomas, mentioned below. 5. Sarah, born July 9, 1720, married
Ebenezer Spooner, of Rochester. 6. Dorothy,
born March 10, 1722-23; married (first) David Peckham, in 1743, and (second) Major
Elnathan Haskell, in 1749, and died at Rochester, September 25, 1810. 7. Denison, born
July 16, 1725. 8. Joseph, born September 13,
1727. 9. Hannah, born November 16, 1730,
married Benjamin Green in 1764.

(IV) Thomas (3), son of James and Patience (Ruggles) Robinson, was born April 20, 1718. He settled at Hardwick as a young man, and there engaged in farming. Subsequently he removed to Furnace Village, where he kept a store and tavern and also managed a saw mill and grist mill on Moose brook. He was very prosperous in business, and was one of the wealthiest men in his neighborhood in 1776. In that year the assessment of the town of Hardwick against his property was the fourth largest upon the town's books, but he sacrificed the larger part, if not absolutely the whole, of his plentiful estate in the revolutionary war, and he also served as a distinguished soldier in that conflict from the beginning to the end. He was one of the grand jurors who refused, April 19, 1774, to be impanelled at Worcester if Peter Oliver, the chief justice, should be present. He was elected lieutenant of the Alarm List, January 9, 1775, and was afterwards styled captain. He was a selectman five years, a member of the committee of correspondence five years, and served on various other important committees during that troublous period. He sold his real estate in and near Furnace Village in five parcels to Captain Benjamin Convers, in 1780, for £20,000, in the depreciated currency of that period, and subsequently removed to Windsor, but returned again in a few years. About 1799, his mental faculties having become impaired and both his sons having left town, he and his aged wife became inmates of their daughter's home, where he died January 5, 1802, aged nearly eighty-four years, and his wife Mary died August 7, 1812, aged nearly eighty-eight years.

Thomas Robinson married Mary, daughter of Captain Eleazer Warner, November 23, 1744. Captain Warner married Prudence, daughter of Thomas Barnes, of Brookfield, December 4, 1722. He devoted several years in early life to the service of his country. A brief sketch of his military career and his single-handed deadly encounter with an Indian is given in the "History of Hardwick," by Lucius R. Paige. Acknowledgment is also made to Mr. Paige and the "History of Hardwick" for this genealogy (see below). This branch of the Robinson family was very prominent in the early history of Hardwick. Before James Robinson removed to Hardwick from Rochester after selling the family homestead on Washington street, Boston, opposite the Old South Church, several of his children had already settled in Hardwick and the family remained there until Denison removed to Windsor about 1780.

"One of the 'Principal Inhabitants' of Brookfield, whose cattle, house and household goods were de-

stroyed by the Indians, was John Warner, who fled for refuge to Hadley (where one or more of his sons then resided), and died there nearly twenty years later. His grandson, Eleazer Warner, who was born 27th January, 1686, very early entered the military service of his country and was assigned to duty on the frontiers. Whether he enlisted in that company of his own choice, or was placed in it by authority, does not appear; but the fact is certain that he was for many years captain at Brookfield (the scene of his grandfather's disasters), first as a private soldier, and afterwards by gradual promotion as sergeant, ensign and lieutenant of the company commanded by Captain Samuel Wright, of Rutland. Later in life he was captain of militia in Hardwick and New Braintree, and retained that office until 1856, when he had attained the age of three-score years and ten. About 1730, while yet in the service of the government, he removed his family from his former residence near Ditch Meadow to a farm which included a part of the old Indian fortress at Winnimisset. Soon afterwards he went to Canada to effect an exchange of prisoners. While there an Indian became offended and followed him through the wilderness to his home. According to the family tradition, as I received it from his eldest daughter, my grandmother, after the Indian had lurked about the house for a few days, Captain Warner went into the forest with his musket. He soon discovered his enemy, who stepped behind a tree, and he dropped by the side of a log. He then adopted a common strategem, placing his hat on a stick and cautiously elevating it above the log, as if to reconnoitre. Almost instantly a bullet passed through it, and he sprung upon his feet. The Indian was rushing forward with his scalping knife in hand, but his race was soon ended, and his body was consigned to a lily pond between the road and the river, about half a mile east of the Old Furnace."

Children of Mr. and Mrs. Robinson: 1. Denison, mentioned below. 2. Thomas, born February 10, 1753. 3. Mary, born December 3, 1758, married Timothy Paige, January 20, 1780, and died March 21, 1836.

(V) Denison, son of Thomas (3) and Mary (Warner) Robinson, was born September 18, 1746. He was a farmer by occupation. He was sergeant of Captain Simeon Hazeltine's company of minute-men, which marched to Cambridge on the Lexington Alarm in April, 1775, and was commissioned captain of the Second Company of militia in Hardwick, Massachusetts, June 11, 1778. He was a member also of the committee of correspondence in 1778. About 1780 he removed to Windsor and resided there for several years. Late in life he followed his sons to Adams, where he died November 17, 1827. He married (first) April 10, 1768, Millicent, daughter of Rev. Robert Cutler: she died July 5, 1798; he married (second) Elizabeth Hyde, of Lenox, about 1801; she died in 1829. Children: 1. Mary, born October 18, 1769; married Alpheus Prince, and died in September, 1829. 2. Alice, born July 1, 1771; married Daniel Felshaw, and died February 1, 1792. 3. Hannah, born

June 10, 1773, died unmarried, July 7, 1796.
4. Josiah Quincy, born July 31, 1775. 5. Sophia, born August 19, 1778, died unmarried, May 12, 1855. 6. Denison, born December 29, 1780. 7. Robert Cutler, born March 12, 1785. 8. Thomas, mentioned below.

(VI) Thomas (4), son of Denison and Millicent (Cutler) Robinson, was born December 20, 1787, at Windsor, Massachusetts. He received excellent educational advantages in his youth and was prepared for the legal profession. He held high rank at the Berkshire bar, and received from Williams College the honorary degree of Master of Arts in 1828. In the spring of 1836 he removed from the south to the north village of Adams, residing for many years and until his death, October 3, 1867, aged nearly eighty years, in the stone house on Main street, later a portion of the estate of the late Dr. N. S. Babbitt. He married (first) May 13, 1812, Nancy Wells, who died in March, 1827. He married (second) in September, 1829, Catherine Susanna McLeod, who died July 20, 1854. Children: 1. Millicent Cutler, born April 12, 1813; married F. O. Sayles, and died January 31, 1852. 2. Ann Eliza, born April 29, 1815; married Dr. Nathan Snell Babbitt. 3. Mary Sophia, born May 16, 1817; married Jackson Mason, of Richmond, Vermont. 4. James Thomas, mentioned below. 5. Nancy W., born June 20, 1826, died October 13, 1826. 6. Alexander McLeod, born September 8, 1830. 7. Margaret Maria, born March 14, 1833; married Lyndon Smith, of Terre Haute, Indiana. 8. Elizabeth Rupalee, born August 5, 1836, married Albert R. Smith. 9. John Cutler, born October 4, 1839; was captain of volunteers in the war of the rebellion. 10. Charles Henry, born September 2, 1841. 11. William Denison, born August 1, 1844.

(VII) James Thomas, son of Thomas (4) and Nancy (Wells) Robinson, was born September 7, 1822, died November 21, 1894. He attended the town schools, and was also an attendant at a Lenox institution of learning of much repute in those days, having for a fellow student Hon. Marshall Wilcox, of Pittsfield. Later he attended schools at Shelburne Falls and Worthington, and at Bennington, Vermont, and in 1840 entered Williams College, class of 1844. After remaining one year in that institution he entered the law office of his father in North Adams, remaining there two years, when he returned to take the senior year with his class in Williams College, graduating with his class in 1844, and immediately thereafter beginning the practice of law in North Adams with his father, the partnership name being Thomas Robinson &

Son, which continued until the death of the senior Robinson, after which James Thomas practiced his profession on his own account. The following is worthy of mention: During these many years of business connection there was never an accounting between father and son, and in the subsequent copartnership between James Thomas and his son Arthur there was never an accounting. Although not receiving at his graduation the degrees of Bachelor and Master of Arts, these were afterwards conferred by Williams College upon James T. Robinson.

Mr. Robinson was in sympathy with those principles which found organized expression in the Free Soil movement of 1848. His speaking for this cause was supplemented by editorial writing for the *Greylock Sentinel*. In 1852 he was elected to the state senate by a union of Free Soilers and Democrats. In 1853 he was appointed one of the secretaries of the Massachusetts constitutional convention. In 1859 he was chosen by the Republicans to the state senate for a second term, and while in this service was appointed by Governor N. P. Banks judge of probate and insolvency for Berkshire county, in which capacity he served for over thirty years; his decisions were marked for their fairness, and his court was renowned for the protection it offered the helpless; in his long period of service as a judge his decisions were hardly ever reversed. Previous to this judgeship he had been elected for a term of five years, commencing the first Wednesday of January, 1857, register of insolvency for Berkshire. He was delegate-at-large from Massachusetts to the Republican national convention that renominated President Lincoln. In the winter of 1855-56 he made a lecturing tour through the west.

In 1866 Mr. Robinson purchased, in copartnership with his brother, Major John C. Robinson, and John Dalrymple, the *Adams Transcript*, and the trenchant writings of Mr. Robinson distinguished it until his death in 1894. There was no more brilliant editorial writing done on any country paper in the United States than he gave this Berkshire weekly. This copartnership continued for a few years, after which Mr. Robinson formed another with his son Arthur, which continued until considerations for his health led to the formation of the Transcript Publishing Company and his retirement from a property interest in the concern.

Besides the opportunities for influence and distinction otherwise afforded, Judge Robinson had gifts as a public speaker that brought him appreciation and prominence. This was his strongest natural endowment. Of fine presence and unusually natural and graceful bearing before an audience, he had a voice that would swell without breaking, and his gestures were natural and effective, the expression of present feeling and never the result of premeditation. Most of his speeches were unwritten, but thought out beforehand and improved upon with repetition. Of his more important speeches, not upon party politics, were the National Anniversary Address delivered at the Baptist Church, North Adams, July 4, 1865, that delivered July 4, 1878, upon the dedication of the North Adams Soldiers' Monument, and that commemorative of the death of President Garfield, delivered at the Methodist Church, September 26, 1881.

Judge Robinson married, at Marblehead, May 6, 1846, Clara, daughter of Dr. Calvin and Rebecca (Monroe) Briggs, of that town (see Briggs). Children: Arthur, mentioned below; Calvin, died young; Thomas.

(VIII) Arthur, son of James Thomas and Clara (Briggs) Robinson, was born at North Adams, Massachusetts, March 15, 1848, died there April 13, 1900. He studied in the public schools, and fitted for college at a private school in Lanesboro, conducted by Mr. Tolman, and at Professor Griffen's preparatory school in Williamstown. He was graduated from Williams College with the class of 1870, with the degree of Bachelor of Arts, and immediately entered the office of the *North Adams Transcript*, owned and edited by his father, and mastered the mechanical part of the printing and publishing business. He was then taken into partnership, and the firm name became James T. Robinson & Son. The young man took the business management of the office and paper, Judge Robinson retaining control of the editorial department. This was in the early seventies, and the business was small in comparison with the dimensions later reached. Father and son worked together in perfect harmony, and the job department soon took and held first rank among the printing establishments of North Berkshire, while the *Transcript*, under their able direction, reached a circulation and a position of influence such as come to but few country weeklies. Although the business management took most of the time and attention of Mr. Arthur Robinson, yet he was a frequent contributor to the columns of the paper, and in this field he displayed marked ability. His style of expression was graceful and pleasing, and his writings were stamped by an individuality that made his work in that line almost as recognizable as if it had borne his name. As the director of others who worked on the *Transcript*, he

exerted a masterful influence which accrued to the benefit of the men and the paper, and gave to the latter a uniformity of style which was of much value to the publication. Mr. Robinson's connection with the paper continued until after the death of his mother in the fall of 1895, his father having died a year before. Owing to unsound health and the increase of other cares, he sold the paper and retired from business life. Mr. Robinson was held in the highest respect by all classes. He was straightforward and upright in his business dealings, and in his newspaper work the good of the community was always uppermost in his mind. No temporary gain to the paper could induce him to publish that which would result in the needless injury to others, and his career as a managing editor is gratefully remembered by all who are familiar with it.

Mr. Robinson was also gifted as a public speaker, as was demonstrated on various occasions, though he never sought for prominence in that direction, and never aspired to political honors which would have come to him readily had he so desired. In politics he was a Republican, though not fully in accord with the tendencies of the party in these later days. At the time of his death he was a trustee of Drury Academy, the North Adams Savings Bank and the Public Library. He was a pleasing conversationalist, a good neighbor, citizen and friend, and his death was universally mourned by the community.

Mr. Robinson married, December 14, 1871, Clara Ellen Sanford, born in North Adams, Massachusetts, in 1854, daughter of Michael and Caroline (Millard) Sanford; she is still living and maintains her home at North Adams. Children: 1. Sanford, mentioned below. 2. Arthur, born at North Adams, July 7, 1875; married Bertha Torrey, of Williamstown, Massachusetts; they reside at North Adams. 3. James Thomas, born at North Adams, April 1, 1879; married Myrtle Zarine Drayer; one child, Martha Lee. 4. Mary, born at North Adams, February 1, 1884; married Lawrence Smith, of Holyoke, Massachusetts; they reside at Holyoke. Mrs. Arthur Robinson is the regent of Fort Massachusetts Chapter, Daughters of the American Revolution.

(IX) Sanford, son of Arthur and Clara Ellen (Sanford) Robinson, was born at North Adams, Massachusetts, July 8, 1873. He received his early educational training in the public schools of North Adams, where he was graduated in the Drury high school. He was matriculated as a student in the old *alma mater* of his father, grandfather and great-grandfather, Williams College, in 1892, and was graduated therein with the degree of Bachelor of Arts in 1896. In the following year he entered Harvard University Law School, from which he was graduated in 1900 with the degree of Bachelor of Laws. He was admitted to the Suffolk county bar, Massachusetts, in September, 1900, and practiced for one year in the office of Lincoln & Badger, at Boston. In 1901 he removed to New York, was admitted to the New York bar, and entered the law offices of Cary & Whitridge in that city. Subsequently the law firm of Cary & Robinson was formed and that alliance continued until 1910. Mr. Robinson is now engaged in individual practice, with offices at No. 59 Wall street, New York City, where he is rapidly gaining distinction as an able attorney and well fortified counsellor. In politics Mr. Robinson is a Republican, and in a social way he is a member of the Harvard Club of New York, the Greenwich Country Club, and the Delta Kappa Epsilon fraternity. While a resident of North Adams, Massachusetts, he was a member of the Congregational church of that place.

Mr. Robinson married, April 10, 1909, Ruth, born March 17, 1886, in New York City, daughter of Dr. Cyrus and Virginia (Page) Edson. Dr. Edson was one of the foremost physicians of his time in New York City, son of Franklin Edson, Mayor of New York from 1882 to 1884. Mr. and Mrs. Robinson have one child, Priscilla, born at Greenwich, Connecticut, July 3, 1910.

(The Briggs Line).

Rev. James Briggs, son of Deacon James and Damaris Briggs, was born in Norton, January 17, 1745. He earned at the forge the means for his education as a Congregational minister; he graduated at Yale, 1775, and was settled for life, July 7, 1779, as the minister of the town of Cummington, Massachusetts, then fourteen days old. Hon. Henry L. Dawes, in his address at the Cummington Centennial, says of him: "As minister of the town he was the man of the largest influence therein, and identified with all its interests; * * * possessing great simplicity of character, he was modest and unassuming in all his ways, and godly in all his walk". He labored on his farm as long as able, writing his sermons in the winter for the year; these "were sound in the doctrine, after the straightest and strictest rules drawn from the Assembly's Catechism". A young parishioner, William Cullen Bryant, well describes this venerable man in his poem entitled, "The Old Man's Funeral". He married Anna Wiswall. Children: James Wiswall, Calvin (see forward); Sophia, Clarissa.

Dr. Calvin Briggs, second child of Rev. James Briggs, was born May 10, 1785. He graduated from Williams College as salutatorian at the age of seventeen, and from Harvard Medical School in 1805. After two years of practice with Dr. Atherton, of Lancaster, whose niece and adopted daughter, Rebecca Monroe, he married, he spent forty-five useful years in Marblehead, until his lamented death, April 21, 1852. He was indeed a "beloved physician", a leading spirit in town, church and society; eminent in his profession, as evidenced by several invitations to larger fields, and by the universal love and confidence of the community. His gentleness with the poor, his courtly bearing, kindly humor, wise judgment and self-sacrificing devotion are long remembered. He was a rare man in his own home, idolized by his children. The ruling ideal was "God first, education next". His large family formed a somewhat remarkable community of themselves, having a strong mutual interest; yet eminently hospitable, a centre of literary and religious activities, of music, and brilliant conversation.

Two sons—James C. and William M.—were graduated at Yale and Amherst respectively, the first of whom joined and followed his father as physician in Marblehead. The seven daughters, "The Pleiades", were educated at Bradford Academy, two of whom, Mary S. and Harriet, were teachers there. The last became an exceptionally able missionary of the A. B. C. F. M. in Persia, as the wife of Rev. David T. Stoddard. Her well balanced mind, culture, refinement and kindly heart, with her sweet, bright face and winning ways, gave her a wonderful influence. The sobriquet of "Sister Meekness", applied by her Bradford mates, worthily clung to her. After five years of service abroad her sudden death by cholera, while returning to this country with a sick husband and two tiny daughters, closed a fragrant life.

Several members of this family had the gift of graceful, vigorous expression in prose and in verse. The second son, William M., wrote for publication frequent sketches of his travels in many countries, besides poems of nature or deep religious feeling.

The youngest daughter, Caroline Atherton, wife of Charles Mason, Esquire, of Fitchburg, early began to write over the signature of "Caro", and a book of her poems, "Utterance", was the result. She was the "local Sibyl and seer" of her adopted city, and her poems through the anxious days of war breathed patriotism and sympathy for the oppressed, and always a broad and sensitive "interest in nature, humanity, and the divine or-

der of the world. Her lively artistic sense
was exalted by rare spirituality; her apt literary faculty was ever the servant of insight
and experience; her minstrelsy was but the
voicing of her aspiration and her love for the
true, the beautiful, and the good". Rev.
Charles G. Ames, in his introduction to "The
Lost Ring and Other Poems", a collection of
her poems gathered by her husband and published after her death.

Dr. Calvin Briggs married Rebecca Monroe, December 26, 1809. Children: Child,
died in infancy; Anna W., married Dr. Thomas S. Blood; James C., married (first) Harriet E. Glover, (second) Catharine T. Whid-
den; Rebecca M., married James C. Barrus;
Clara, married Hon. James Thomas Robinson
(see Robinson VII); Mary S., married Rev.
Daniel Wight; Elizabeth, married John Wool-
dredge; Harriet, married Rev. D. T. Stoddard; Caroline A., married Charles Mason,
Esq.; William M. and Henry A.

(The Sanford Line).

Thomas Sanford, from the environment of
a Puritan ancestry in Old England, son of
Ezekiel and grandson of Thomas Sanford, a
tradesman of Essex, was born in 1607, and
is first mentioned in New England as a landholder in Dorchester, Massachusetts, in 1634.
His brothers Robert and Andrew and cousin
Zachary also came to this country, even as
John Sanford came to Rhode Island in the
time of Roger Williams and William Sanford
to New Jersey a little later, all of whose descendants comprise the field of service for
the Sanford Association of America. Thomas
Sanford and Sarah his wife removed to Milford, Connecticut, soon after the founding of
the colony in 1639, for he is mentioned in the
town records as one of the original planters
of Milford. Children: Sarah, married, August 14, 1656, Richard Shute; Andrew, see
forward; Ephraim; Samuel; Thomas; Ezekiel.

(IV) Andrew, son of Thomas Sanford,
came to Milford, Connecticut, from Hartford;
Connecticut, in 1667. He married, and among
his children was Andrew (see forward).

(V) Andrew (2), son of Andrew (1) Sanford, came to Milford, Connecticut, with his
father in 1667. He married, January 8, 1668,
Mary Botsford, and among their children was
Andrew (see forward).

(VI) Andrew (3), son of Andrew (2) Sanford, was baptized at Milford, Connecticut,
July 16, 1673. In the church records he is
called Captain Andrew. He married, and
among his children was Samuel, (see forward).

(VII) Samuel, son of Andrew (3) San-

ford, was born at Milford, Connecticut, 1704.
He married, January 4, 1731, Ann, daughter
of Joseph and Susannah Plumb. Children:
Samuel (see forward); Henry, Hannah, Ann.

(VIII) Samuel (2), son of Samuel (1)
Sanford, was a captain in the war of the revolution, from Connecticut, serving about eight
years. The following is his service as shown
by the records of the adjutant general's office
at Hartford:

"Enlisted as a sergeant, July 10, 1775, in Captain
Peter Perritt's company, Colonel Charles Webb,
Seventh Continental Regiment; discharged December 10, 1775, for expiration of term of service. The
regiment was raised by order of the Assembly at
July session, 1775; was recruited in Fairfield, Litchfield and New Haven counties. The companies were
stationed at various points along the Sound until
September 14, 1775, when upon requisition from
General Washington the regiment was ordered to
the Boston camps, and was assigned to General Sullivan's brigade on Winter Hill, at the left of the
besieging line, and remained until the expiration of
term of service, December, 1775. The Seventh Continental Regiment, Colonel Charles Webb commanding, was reorganized for service in the army for
the second year, 1776, and was known as the Nineteenth Continental Regiment. Samuel Sanford re-
entered the service in this regiment as a lieutenant.
The regiment marched from Boston to New York
(by way of New London and vessels through the
Sound) and served in that vicinity from April to
the close of the year; assisted in fortifying the city.
Ordered to the Brooklyn front, August 27, 1776, was
closely engaged at the battle of White Plains, October 28, 1776; engaged at the battle of Trenton,
December 25, 1776, and at Princeton, January 3,
1777. A portion of this regiment continued in service with other troops at the urgent request of General Washington about six weeks after the expiration of their terms. Re-entered the service from
Milford in the Eighth Regiment, Connecticut Line,
Colonel John Chandler, commanding; was commissioned first lieutenant, January 1, 1777; captain, December 15, 1777, and continued. This regiment was
raised from January 1, 1777, to serve through the
war; went into field at Camp Peekskill, New York,
in the spring of 1777; ordered into Pennsylvania in
September, 1777, under General McDougall; fought
at Germantown, October 4, 1777, and suffered loss.
A detachment from the regiment took part in the
stubborn defense at Fort Mifflin, Mud Island, Pennsylvania, November 12-16, 1777; battle of Monmouth, June 28, 1778; storming of Stony Point,
July 15, 1779. Wintered in 1780 and 1781 at Camp
Connecticut Village, and there consolidated for the
formation of 1781-83. Captain Samuel Sanford
continued in commission with his command in the
Fifth Regiment, Connecticut Line, Colonel Isaac
Sherman, commanding, and retired by consolidation,
January 1, 1783. The regiment was composed by
the consolidation of the First and Eighth Regiments, Connecticut Line."

Soon after he returned from the war, Captain Sanford removed to Plymouth, but he
must have returned to Milford, for the town
records say that Captain Samuel Sanford was
crushed to death by a log rolling on him,
March 17, 1804, while he was getting out

ship timber. He married (first) at Milford, July 26, 1765, Parthenia Baldwin, who died in Plymouth, Connecticut, 1790, aged forty-three years. A year or two later he married again, but his second wife lived only a year. Children of first marriage: 1. Samuel, born 1766; at about ten years of age he served in the war as a body servant to his father, who was an officer. 2. Sarah or Sally, born December 29, 1767, died December, 1826; married, October 29, 1789, Oliver Stoughton. 3. Anthony. 4. Raymond, was master of a vessel, was shipwrecked off Block Island in a storm, before he was thirty years of age. 5. Elijah, resided at New Haven. 6. William (see forward). 7. Harriet, born April 15, 1786, died August 22, 1864; married, February 21, 1807, Samuel Buckingham; eleven children.

(IX) William, son of Samuel (2) Sanford, was born December 16, 1782, died at Stamford, Vermont, November 3, 1856. After his marriage he removed to South Readsboro, Vermont, among the early settlers from Connecticut. They traveled by marked trees on horseback, bringing oxen with them. He was always called Captain, as after the revolutionary war the state militia was formed, in which he served with that rank. He cleared land on a farm given to his wife by her father, and erected a log house which was later replaced by a frame one, and here all their children were born. Later he purchased an extensive farm in Stamford, where both he and his wife died, and the farm was left to Justin, his youngest son, who died there, and his widow and her children reside there at the present time. There is in this house a sword that was presented to Captain Samuel Sanford, aforementioned, by General Washington, and preserved by his descendants. William Sanford held high town office, and often went over the mountains to Bennington on horseback to transact business, returning before the other men started to work. He married, January 18, 1806, Lucy Rice, daughter of Jacob Rice, a comrade of Captain Sanford during the revolutionary war. The Rice family is of very ancient origin, having a distinguished pedigree, tracing their lineage to Robert Rice, "Puritan", born in Ipswich, England, came to this country in the "Francis", in 1694, landing at Plymouth. Children of Mr. and Mrs. Sanford: 1. Daughter, still-born, March 1, 1807. 2. Annie Parthenia, born September 11, 1808, died November 15, 1821. 3. William Henry, born August 18, 1810, died November 10, 1883. 4. Merrit, born October 11, 1812, died April 26, 1849. 5. Lucy, born February 2, 1815, died April 15,

1843. 6. Hiram, born May 25, 1817. 7. Michael (see forward). 8. Louisa, born October 20, 1821. 9. Albert, born March 17, 1824, died January 12, 1858. 10. Harriet, born February 14, 1826. 11. Alford, born June 13, 1828, died November 6, 1853. 12. Charles, born May 23, 1830, died May 23, 1905. 13. Justin, born May 21, 1834, died February 23, 1905.

(X) Michael, son of William Sanford, was born June 17, 1819, died December 5, 1900. He married, February 22, 1844, Caroline Millard, born February 13, 1824, died April 13, 1902. Children: 1. Adaline, born May 14, 1851; living at the present time (1912). 2. Clara Ellen, born January 16, 1854, widow of Arthur Robinson (see Robinson VIII). 3. William, born October 24, 1858. 4. Murrey, born October 25, 1865.

EMERSON The relationship between Thomas Emerson, the immigrant ancestor of the Ipswich family to which Ralph Waldo Emerson belongs, and Michael Emerson, mentioned below, has not been established, but there is no reasonable doubt that some relationship existed. Thomas was born in Bishop's Stortford, county Essex, England, July 26, 1584, son of Robert Emerson, of Dunmow, county Essex, and grandson of Thomas Emerson, of Great Dunmow, born before 1540.

The first to use the name Emerson in England was Johannes Emeryson, of Brancepeth parish, county Durham, and he was born before 1300. It is thought that the English Emersons are all descended from him, though the lines cannot be traced for want of complete records. The will of Alexander Emerson, of Sereby, Lincolnshire, England, yeoman, dated April 10, 1604, and proved February 10, 1605, was that of a relative of both Michael and Thomas Emerson in all probability, and it is likely that Michael given below was his grandson. He bequeathed to a son Michael Emerson his homestead and other lands; to son Robert; to son Thomas lands in Howsam and Cadvey; to his wife house at Glamford Brigges; to daughters of his son George; to son John. These names have survived in both lines of the American family. The will was witnessed by Michael and Thomas Emerson, doubtless near relatives of the testator. (See N. E. Reg., 1896, p. 527. See the English Emersons; also the Emersons' Genealogy).

It should be said that the Haverhill Emersons are not all descended from Michael. Robert Emerson, presumably his brother, married, at Haverhill, in 1660, Ann Grant; died 1694; will dated May 3, 1694, bequeathing to children: Thomas, Ephraim, Stephen, Benjamin, Joseph, Elizabeth, Lydia; his son Thomas, his wife and two children were killed by the Indians in 1697 at Haverhill; his son Benjamin died in 1733, leaving wife Sarah and children: Robert, Benjamin, Charles, Sarah and Susanna; Robert's wife Ann died in 1719, when Benjamin was the only son surviving, and Lydia and Elizabeth, her daughters, were living. Robert had many descendants in Haverhill.

(1) Michael Emerson, the immigrant ancestor, was born in England about 1630, probably in Lincolnshire as indicated in the will of Michael Emerson cited above. He came to Haverhill, Massachusetts, in 1656, and in 1661 he had a meadow lot granted to him. He was called a cordwainer in various deeds and doubtless followed this trade some of the time. In 1665 he was chosen to "view and seal all leather" in town. That was the first election of a sealer of leather in Haverhill, and for many years thereafter he was re-elected at each annual meeting. His farm was on the present site of the railroad station on the east side of Little river. Michael Emerson, of Haverhill, cordwainer, deeded to his sons, Jonathan and Joshua, of Haverhill, his homestead, including land bought of Thomas Davis and Peter Green "bounded upon ye highway that goeth over ye west Bridge and rangeth from ye little river upon ye highway on ye north side of ye old wat yt went downe to ye Bridge and soe rangeth from thence as ye fence standeth to a small black oake tree next to ye highway that goeth between this said land formerly Robert Swan's (?)." In the same deed, which is dated May 21, 1699, and executed October 18, 1714, he conveyed to the same sons other parcels therein described. Michael Emerson shortly before his death by deed of gift dated June 3, 1715, and acknowledged November 14, 1715, gave forty-four acres and the residue of his estate to his grandson, Michael (or Micah), and in case of death before Michael, whom he says was then but six years old, reached his majority, the property was to be divided among the surviving children of Joshua, brothers and sister of this youthful grantee. This deed was more like a will than the usual deed and was perhaps an attempt to adopt the English custom of entailing the estate. His sons, Jonathan and Joshua, divided the property that he deeded to them jointly. The will of Michael Emerson was dated July 18, 1709, and is on file at the Salem registry, but no record shows that it was allowed. The deed mentioned seems to have disposed of his property. The will mentions his eldest son John, his young-

est sons, Jonathan and Joshua, son Samuel; daughters, Hannah Dustin and Abigail Smith; son-in-law, ———— Mathews Jr., and his children, John, Johanna and Mary Mathews.

He married, April 1, 1656, Hannah, daughter of John Webster, of Ipswich and Newbury. Children: Hannah, born December 23, 1657, married Thomas Dustin, was the famous Hannah Dustin who killed the Indians who had captured her; John, July 30, 1659; Mary, October 5, 1660; John, March 18, 1662; Samuel, February 2, 1663; Elizabeth, January 26, 1665; Abigail, December 17, 1667; Jonathan, March 9, 1669-70; Abigail, November 20, 1671; Judith, July 2, 1673; Judith, September 29, 1674; Joshua, March 2, 1675-76, died young; Ruth, May 8, 1677; Joshua, mentioned below; Susanna, April 30, 1680.

(II) Joshua, son of Michael Emerson, was born in Haverhill, November 17, 1678. He and his brother Jonathan received by deed of gift the homestead and other real estate from their father. They appointed John Marsh, Andrew Mitchell and John Whittier a committee to divide their property owned in common and the division was effected by deed dated March 31, 1716. Joshua bought land at Methuen, June 17, 1730, of Samuel Clark, and settled in that town about that time. His will was dated May 29, 1742, and proved July 19 following. He bequeathed to wife Mary and children: Hananial, Joshua, William Reuben, Sarah Stevens, Mary, Josiah and Micah or Michael. He married, July 2, 1705, at Haverhill, Mary Clark. Children, born at Haverhill: Isaac, born January 29, 1707; Joshua, mentioned below; Josiah, December 1, 1710; Hananial, May 29, 1712; Mary, April 11, 1714; Sarah, April 22, 1716; Reuben, baptized April 24, 1720; William, baptized April 1, 1722.

(III) Joshua (2), son of Joshua (1) Emerson, was born March 24, 1708-09, at Haverhill, died June 11, 1796. He was one of the thirteen founders of the Congregational church at Salem, New Hampshire, January 16, 1740. He married (first) Sarah ————, and lived in Methuen, Massachusetts. He married (second) November 17, 1757, Mary Chase. Children, born in Salem: Mary, October 12, 1735; John, December 6, 1737; Susanna, March 2, 1739-40; Sarah, October 18, 1742; Joshua, mentioned below; Avery Sanders, born August 14, 1758.

(IV) Joshua (3), son of Joshua (2) Emerson, was born in Haverhill, July 19, 1745. He was a soldier in the revolution from Methuen, a corporal in Captain John Davis's company of minute-men, Colonel Fry's regiment, on the Lexington Alarm, April 19, 1775, and took part in the battle of Bunker Hill. He was also in Captain John Davis's company, Colonel James Fry's regiment, at the siege of Boston in 1775, and also in Captain David Whittier's company, Major Benjamin Gage's regiment in the Northern Army in 1777. He died in Salem, New Hampshire, December 16, 1824. He married, December 25, 1766, Harriet (or Hannah) Saunders, of Haverhill. He probably married (second) Mrs. Hannah Emerson (intention dated April 27, 1795). Children by first wife: 1. Sarah, born at Methuen, August 21, 1767, died at Salem, New Hampshire, February 26, 1824, married Nathaniel Webster. 2. Simeon, mentioned below. 3. Hannah, born at Methuen, July 31, 1775 or 1772 (town records).

(V) Simeon, son of Joshua (3) Emerson, was born in Methuen, March 7, 1770, died at Salem, New Hampshire, January 21, 1830. He was a taxpayer in Salem in 1800 and served on the school committee in 1824. He married (first) March 7, 1793, Sarah Chase. He married (second) April 14, 1798, Patty Mitchell, at Haverhill. She was born October 17, 1776, died May 6, 1823, daughter of John and Abigail (Hibbard) Mitchell, of Haverhill. Children, born at Salem, New Hampshire: 1. John, mentioned below. 2. Harriet, born January 17, 1802, died November 24, 1841, at Salem, unmarried. 3. Joshua, born May 26, 1804, died at Milton, September 7, 1858; married, August 29, 1830, Ann Gulliver Babcock; their children: i. Nancy, born 1831, died young; ii. Harriet A., September 9, 1832, married Rev. Edwin Leonard and had one child, Harriet A., who resides at Bangor, Maine; iii. Mary F., July 2, 1836, unmarried, died in Milton, Massachusetts; iv. Ellen M., married Edwin D. Wadsworth, of Milton; v. Alice Gulliver, married, October 17, 1867, Samuel Gannett, of Milton; vi. Jane Elizabeth, January 31, 1844, married E. P. Hatch, of the Lincoln Trust Company of Boston, no children, she died in 1911; vii. Margaret, died in infancy; viii. Joshua, died in infancy. 4. Fanny, born August 5, 1806, died at Milton, June 29, 1889, unmarried. 5. Simeon Jr., born September 9, 1812, died at Milton, February 14, 1888; he was tax collector of Milton, Massachusetts, for more than forty years, representative to the general court, deacon in the Congregational church of Milton and superintendent of the Sunday school; married, January 17, 1841, Sarah Elizabeth Babcock, who died July 12, 1889, daughter of Josiah and Nancy (Gulliver) Babcock, a sister of Joshua Emerson's wife (see Babcock VI.); children: i. Emma Cornelia, born at Milton, May 17, 1843, unmarried; ii. Fanny

Elizabeth, born May 22, 1850, married, December 25, 1877, Frederick Milton Hamlin.

(VI) John, son of Simeon Emerson, was born in Salem, September 7, 1799, died at Milton, January 18, 1866. He married Ruth (Gardner) DeMerritt, a widow. Children, born at Salem: 1. Emily Frances, born August 30, 1833. 2. Sylvester, September, 1835. 3. Anna Augusta, March 10, 1837. 4. John Henry, mentioned below. 5. Harriet Maria, July 7, 1842. 6. Joshua, June 10, 1844. 7. Mary Jane, died young.

(VII) John Henry, son of John Emerson, was born in Salem, New Hampshire, January 19, 1840, died at Milton, April 19, 1910. He was in the United States navy for three years, 1857-58-59, on board the United States flagship "Cumberland", on the west coast of Africa. He was a soldier in the civil war and for many years a member of the Huntington F. Walcott Post, No. 102, Grand Army of the Republic. He was for many years superintendent of construction of buildings for the Granite Railway Company of Quincy, Massachusetts. He enlisted, October 11, 1862, in Company B, Forty-fifth Regiment Massachusetts Volunteer Infantry, for nine months and afterward was first sergeant in Company H, Fifty-sixth Massachusetts Infantry, in which he served to the end of the civil war. He was commissioned second lieutenant, May 17, 1864, and first lieutenant of Company A, July 22, 1864. He was honorably discharged July 22, 1865. He was tax collector of Milton, Massachusetts, for about eighteen years; he took the office one year after the death of his Uncle Simeon. He married, June 6, 1891, Josephine Davis, daughter of George W. and Catherine (Davis) Clapp (see Clapp IX).

(The Babcock Line).

(I) George Babcock, brother of Robert Babcock, of Milton, Massachusetts, and probably of James Babcock, of Rhode Island, was born in England. He settled in Dorchester, Massachusetts, where he was supervisor of highways in 1656. He removed to the adjoining town of Milton and died there in 1671. He married Mary ———. His will, dated September 26, 1671, and proved February 2 following, bequeathed to wife Mary; children Benjamin, Return, George, Joseph and Enoch Babcock; Mary Ellen, Dorothy Rachel and Leah Babcock; brother Robert Babcock being appointed overseer with his neighbor, Joseph Belcher. He had land in Dartmouth as well as Dorchester and Milton. Children: Benjamin, born in Dorchester or England, about 1650; Dorothy, married, March 29, 1672, John Daniel; Return, married, December 1, 1681,

Sarah Denisch; Enoch, mentioned below; Mary Ellen; George, born February 26, 1658, died young; Rachel, born March 8, 1660; Leah; George, born June 12, 1665; Samuel, born September, 1668; Joseph, born May 13, 1670.

(II) Enoch, son of George Babcock, lived at Dorchester and Milton. He married Susannah Gregory. He died at Milton, May 25, 1695. Among their children was William, mentioned below.

(III) William, son of Enoch Babcock, was born about 1685. He married Elizabeth Lancaster. Children, all born except the eldest at Milton: Elizabeth, born December 6, 1710; Hannah, September 13, 1713; Nathan, mentioned below; William, March 3, 1718; Susannah, August 14, 1720; Lydia, September 9, 1722; Ann, August 4, 1724; Enoch, June 19, 1726.

(IV) Nathan, son of William Babcock, was born at Milton, May 15, 1716, died January 30, 1777, in that town. He married Susanna Tucker, who died at Milton, August 7, 1774. Children, born at Milton: Susanna, born February 6, 1741-42; William, mentioned below; Jane, July 28, 1744; Nathan, December 10, 1745, married, January 24, 1771, Jerusha Houghton; Enoch, August 22, 1747; Elizabeth, October 20, 1748; Lydia, November 7, 1750; Josiah, November 17, 1752; Ebenezer, November 20, 1753; Ithamar, February 8, 1755; Esther, February 9, 1758; Moses, November 16, 1761.

(V) Captain William (2) Babcock, son of William (1) Babcock, was born at Milton, May 22, 1743, died December 20, 1816. He was a soldier in the revolution. He married, in 1765, Sarah Tucker, who died February 7, 1825, aged eighty-three. Children, born at Milton: Isaac, born July 14, 1766; Mary, July 11, 1768; William, September 13, 1770; Josiah, September 1, 1773, died September 14, 1778; Sarah, August 3, 1776, died young; Josiah, mentioned below.

(VI) Josiah, son of Captain William (2) Babcock, was born about 1785. He married, January 15, 1807, at Milton, Nancy Gulliver, who died August 30, 1828, aged forty-two. Children, born at Milton: Josiah, mentioned below; Samuel, born November 5, 1812; Jeremiah William, September 30, 1816; Cornelius, January 19, 1819; Sarah Elizabeth, March 8, 1822, married Simeon Emerson Jr. (see Emerson V.); Mary Augusta, May 27, 1826.

(VII) Josiah (2), son of Josiah (1) Babcock, was born January 19, 1810, at the Milton homestead, died September, 1863. He was educated in Milton schools, and was a merchant. He married, June 27, 1841, Margaret Howe Fenno, of Milton, Massachusetts. Children: 1. Charles Fenno, born December 11, 1844, died September 1, 1906; he married, September 11, 1873, Flora Aldrich, of Bernardston, Massachusetts, and they had three children: i. Margaret Edith, born August 9, 1875, married Eugene E. Petter, October 23, 1909; he is a consulting engineer, and resides in Roxbury, Boston. ii. Ernest Josiah, born December 27, 1876, unmarried; engaged in coal business and resides in Roxbury, Boston. iii. Mary Alice, born July 16, 1882, unmarried. 2. Margaret Alice, born in Milton, January 5, 1848, unmarried; resides on Adams street, East Milton. 3. Josiah, born January 3, 1851; he married October 17, 1877, Martha E. Aldrich, of Bernardston, Massachusets; he is the tax collector of Milton, Massachusetts; children: i. Paul Aldrich, born September 18, 1878, a civil engineer and resides in Milton; married Edith Constance Mead, September 10, 1902, and have three children, Rosamond May, born July 7, 1903, Paul Aldrich Jr., born September 20, 1906; Milton Mead, born April 14, 1910. ii. Josiah Jr., born May 21, 1880; he is a member of the firm of Swan, Babcock & Company of Milton, dealers in hay, grain, etc.; succeeded Samuel Gannett who established the business; married, September 7, 1904, Blanche Chase, of Sanborn, Kingston, New Hampshire. iii. Rachel Hermia, born July 5, 1883, married, June 30, 1909, Ernest Willard Grover, engaged in the shoe business in Lynn, Massachusetts, and he resides there.

(The Clapp Line).

The surname Clapp had its origin in the proper or personal name of Osgod Clapa, a Danish noble in the court of King Canute (1017-36). The site of his country place was known afterward as Clapham, county Surrey. The spelling in the early records varies from Clapa to the present form, Clapp. The ancient seat of the family in England is at Salcombe in Devonshire, where important estates were held for centuries by this family. Their coat-of-arms: First and fourth three battleaxes second sable a griffin passant argent; third sable an eagle with two heads displayed with a border engrailed argent. A common coat-of-arms in general use by the family in America as well as in England: Vaire gules and argent a quarter azure charged with the sun or. Crest: A pike naiant proper. Motto: *"fais ce que Dois advienne que pourra."*

The American branches of this family are descended from six immigrants, brothers and cousins, who settled in Dorchester, Massachusetts, whence they and their descendants have scattered to all parts of the country.

(I) Nicholas Clapp, progenitor of the family, lived at Venn Ottery, Devonshire, England. Three of his sons and one daughter, wife of his nephew, Edward Clapp, came to America. His brother, William Clapp, lived at Salcombe Regis, England, and besides his son Edward, another son, Roger Clapp, immigrated to America and settled at Dorchester. The family genealogy gives the name of Richard instead of Nicholas. Children: Thomas, mentioned below; Ambrose, lived and died in England; Richard, remained in England; Prudence, came to New England, married her cousin, Edward Clapp; Nicholas, born at Dorchester, England, 1612, married Sarah, daughter of William Clapp; John, came to Dorchester, as well as Nicholas.

(II) Thomas Clapp, the immigrant ancestor, son of Nicholas Clapp, was born in England in 1597. He arrived from Weymouth, England, July 24, 1633, and in 1634 was at Dorchester, where Nicholas and John had settled.

He was admitted a freeman at Dorchester in 1636. He moved to Weymouth, Massachusetts, as early as 1639, and lived on the farm later owned by Hon. Christopher Webb. He removed to Scituate, Massachusetts, in 1640, and was deacon of the church there in 1647. He was admitted a freeman of Plymouth Colony, June 5, 1644. He was deputy to the general court in 1649; overseer of the poor in 1667; a useful and eminent citizen. His farm was in the southwest part of the town near Stockbridge's mill pond, later owned by Calvin Jenkins. He died April 20, 1684, aged eighty-seven years. His will was dated April 19, 1684, stating that he was in his eighty-seventh year, bequeathing to wife Abigail, children: Thomas, of Dedham, Samuel, Increase and four daughters. Children: Thomas, mentioned below; Increase, born May, 1640, probably; Samuel; Eleazer, moved to Barnstable, killed March 15, 1676, by Indians; Elizabeth, married Captain Michael P. Pierce; Prudence, unmarried; John, born October 18, 1658, died 1671; Abigail, born January 29, 1660.

(III) Thomas (2), son of Thomas (1) Clapp, was born at Weymouth, Massachusetts, March 15, 1639. He settled at Dedham, Massachusetts, living in that part incorporated in 1724 as Walpole. He was a housewright. His will was dated December 14, 1688, and proved January 29, 1691. He married, November 10, 1662, Mary Fisher, of Dedham. Children, born in Dedham: Thomas, born September 26, 1663; John, February 29, 1665-66, died March 12, 1665-66; Joshua, mentioned below; Mary, December 13, 1669;

Eleazer, November 4, 1671; Abigail; Hannah; Samuel, August 21, 1682.

(IV) Joshua, son of Thomas (2) Clapp, was born in Dedham in 1667, died in 1728. He resided in Dedham in what was later the town of Walpole, incorporated 1724. He was a farmer, inheriting part of his father's estate, including half the field near the river, bounded north by land of his brother John, six acres adjoining land of James Fales, twelve acres at north of Neponset river, also two cow rights. He married (first) Mary, daughter of Jonathan Boyden. She died May 18, 1718, and he married (second) December 4, 1718, Silence Wright, widow of William Wright, and daughter of John Bird, of Dorchester. She was born February 4, 1690. Children, born at Dedham and by first wife: Joshua, mentioned below; John, born 1709; Abigail, married ―――― Morse; Esther, married ―――― Morse; Mary, married Eleazer Robins, of Stoughton; Thankful, born 1716. Children of second wife: Silence, born 1720; Seth, born 1722.

(V) Joshua (2), son of Joshua (1) Clapp, was born in Dedham in 1707, died May 6, 1802. He was a man of high character and a distinguished citizen, captain of his company, justice of the peace and magistrate, deputy to the general court, deacon of the church at Walpole, formerly Dedham. About 1745 he marched to Boston with his company to help defend it from the attack of the French fleet, then expected. He married (first) December 12, 1728, Abigail Bullard, of Walpole. She died August 12, 1782, and he married (second) Deborah Hewins, widow of Deacon Hewins. She died November 18, 1797, aged ninety years. Children, born at Walpole: Joshua, mentioned below; Ebenezer, November 27, 1733; Eliphalet, March 6, 1736; Abigail, September 5, 1738; Elkanah, October 2, 1740; Oliver, January 13, 1743; Esther, March 23, 1746.

(VI) Joshua (3), son of Joshua (2) Clapp, was born in Walpole, Massachusetts, September 7, 1729. He married Margaret Guild. Children, born at Walpole: Margaret, born June 12, 1750; Joshua, March 11, 1753; Aaron, February 5, 1755; Olive, February 22, 1757, married John Boyden; Eliphas, mentioned below; Asa, March 26, 1763; Thomas, May 19, 1766; Oliver, September 6, 1768, married Patience Copp.

(VII) Eliphas, son of Joshua (3) Clapp, was born at Walpole, September 3, 1760. He lived at Walpole. He married ―――― Boyden. Children, born at Walpole: Nancy, born March 16, 1783; Eleanor, August 16, 1784; Lydia, August 3, 1786; Eliphas, mentioned below; Prudence, May 25, 1789; Comfort, March 12, 1793; Bradford, May 9, 1796.

(VIII) Eliphas (2), son of Eliphas (1) Clapp, was born at Walpole, May 4, 1788. He married Hannah, daughter of Lewis and Prudence (Whitney) Jones, and lived in Roxbury and Milton, Massachusetts. She was a sister of General Whitney. Children: Lewis J., a cabinetmaker in Milton, married, July, 1847, Almira Jones, of Wayland; George W., mentioned below; Edwin M., a cabinetmaker in Milton, married (first) Elizabeth Fairbanks, (second) June 20, 1866, Rosalie H. Weld, and removed to Jamaica Plain.

(IX) George W., son of Eliphas (2) Clapp, was born about 1821. He was a harnessmaker in Milton, Massachusetts. He married Catherine, daughter of William and Eunice (Vose) Davis. William Davis married (first) Catherine Kimball, (second) Eunice Vose, and (third) Marion Whitelaw. Catherine Davis was born in the old house at the corner of Canton avenue and Adams street in Milton. William Davis was engaged in the woolen business in Milton; his sister was mother of Thomas B. Thayer, the Universalist minister of Boston. William Davis had eight children. Josephine Davis, daughter of George W. Clapp, married, June 6, 1891, John Henry Emerson (see Emerson VII).

RAWSON   Edward Rawson, the English ancestor, lived at Colnbrook, Langley Marsh, Buckinghamshire. He was a wealthy merchant there. His will was dated February 16, 1603-04, and proved May 4, 1604. He married Bridget ———, probably Bridget Warde.

(II) David, son of Edward Rawson, was a merchant tailor of London. His will was dated June 15, 1616, and it showed that he was well-to-do and a generous man to those not so fortunate as he. He married Margaret, daughter of the Rev. William and Isabel (Woodhal) Wilson. She married (second) William Taylor, of London, and died before 1628. Mr. and Mrs. Rawson lived at Gillingham, Dorsetshire, England, where their son Edward, mentioned below, was born. Margaret Wilson was sister of Rev. John Wilson, minister at Boston, Massachusetts.

(III) Secretary Edward (2) Rawson, the immigrant ancestor, was born April 16, 1615, at Gillingham, Dorsetshire, England, son of David Rawson. He came to New England in 1637, and settled in Newbury, Massachusetts, where he became one of the grantees and proprietors. He was the second town clerk of Newbury; notary public and register, serving from April 19, 1638, to 1647; was also selectman of the town and commissioner to hear and determine small causes; was deputy to the general court from Newbury in 1638 and nearly every year until 1650; was clerk of the house of deputies in 1645-46 and in 1649. He had a special grant of fifteen hundred acres of land in the Narragansett country on account of his services to the general court. He and Joseph Hills revised the laws of the province. He succeeded Increase Nowell, who had been secretary of the colony from the beginning in 1636, being elected May 22, 1650, and afterwards resided in Boston, being re-elected annually until Sir Edmund Andros came into power. His home in Boston was on Rawson lane, now Bromfield street, and he owned several acres bordering on the common. He and his wife were members of the church under Rev. John Wilson, after whose death Mr. Rawson became one of the twenty-eight disaffected persons who left the First Church to form the Third or Old South Church, in May, 1669. He became the agent or steward of an English Society for the Propagation of the Gospel among the Indians in New England, in 1631. He countersigned the warrant sent to Massachusetts for the arrest of the regicides, Goffe, Whalley and Dixwell, but they were never arrested. The one blot on his good record was his participation in the persecution of the Quakers, a pretty general fault of the early Puritans. His salary as secretary was at first twenty pounds a year, later sixty pounds. He was subsequently elected recorder of Suffolk county. His family Bible is now or was lately in the possession of R. R. Dodge, of Sutton, Massachusetts, having descended in direct line. He was an efficient public officer, a useful and distinguished citizen. He died August 27, 1694.

He married Rachel, daughter of Thomas Perne, granddaughter of John Hooker, who married ——— Grindal, sister of Edmund Grindal, Archbishop of Canterbury in the reign of Queen Elizabeth. Children: Daughter, married and remained in England; Edward, graduate of Harvard in 1653; Rachel, married, January 18, 1653, William Aubrey; David, born May 6, 1644; Perne, September 16, 1646; William, mentioned below; Susan, died in Roxbury in 1664; Hannah, baptized October 10, 1653, died May 27, 1656; Rebecca, born October 19, 1654, died young; Rebecca, May 23, 1656; Elizabeth, November 12, 1657; Rev. Grindal, January 23, 1659.

(IV) William, son of Secretary Edward (2) Rawson, was born May 21, 1651. He became a prominent merchant and importer of foreign goods. In 1689 he removed to Dorchester from Boston and resided on a portion of the Newbury farm, inherited by his wife. Later he purchased of the heirs of his great-uncle, Rev. John Wilson, a tract of land at Braintree near the present village of Neponset, adjoining the homestead of Hon. Josiah Quincy, and this homestead has been passed down in the family to recent if not to the present time. He married, July 11, 1673, Anne, only daughter of Nathaniel and Mary (Smith) Glover, of Dorchester. He died September 20, 1726, and she died in 1730, aged seventy-four years. Their family Bible gives the record of their twenty children: Ann, born April 11, 1674, died young; Wilson, 1675, died young; Margaret, August 1, 1676, died young; Edward, September 6, 1677, died young; Edward, August 29, 1678, died young; Rachel, October 16, 1679, died young; Dorothy, August 8, 1681, died September 20, 1689; William, December 8, 1682, married Sarah Crosby; David, mentioned below; Dorothy, June 19, 1685, died young; Ebenezer, December 1, 1686, died August 28, 1696; Thankful, August 6, 1688, died August 21, 1688; Nathaniel, December 2, 1689, married Hannah Thompson; Ebenezer, July 25, 1691, died young; Edward, January 25, 1693, married Preserved Bailey; Ann, August 28, 1694, died young; Patience, November 8, 1695, died November 14, 1695; Peletiah, July 2, 1697, married Hannah Hall; Grindal, August 24, 1698, died young; Mary, December 16, 1699, died in infancy.

(V) David (2), son of William Rawson, was born December 13, 1683, died at Braintree, April 20, 1752. He inherited the homestead at Braintree. He was a persevering business man with much force of character. He married Mary, daughter of Captain John Gulliver, of Milton, Massachusetts. Their graves are near that of President John Quincy Adams at Quincy, formerly Braintree. Children, born at Braintree: David, September 14, 1714, married Mary Dyer; Jonathan, December 26, 1715, married Susanna Stone; Elijah, February 5, 1717, married Mary Paddock; Mary, May 20, 1718, married Captain Joseph Winchester; Hannah, April 2, 1720, died July 24, 1726; Silence, June 12, 1721, died August 17, 1721; Anne, July 30, 1722, married Samuel Bass; Elizabeth, November 30, 1723, married Peter Adams; Josiah, mentioned below; Jerusha, December 21, 1729, married Israel Eaton; Lydia, January 17, 1731, married Samuel Baxter; Ebenezer, May 31, 1734, married Sarah Chase.

(VI) Josiah, son of David (2) Rawson, was born at Braintree, January 3, 1727, died February 24, 1812. He settled first in Graf-

ton, Worcester county, then in Warwick, Franklin county, Massachusetts. He married, August 28, 1750, Hannah Bass, of Braintree, a descendant of John and Priscilla (Molines or Mullins) Alden, who came in the "Mayflower" in 1620. All of her descendants are entitled to membership in the Society of Mayflower Descendants. Children: Josiah, born 1751, married Elizabeth Barrows; Simeon, 1753, married Anna Holden; Abigail, November 14, 1755, married Joshua Garfield; Mary, November 23, 1757, married David W. Leland; Anna B., October 11, 1759, married Thomas Leland; Jonathan B., 1761, married Livonia Robinson; Lydia, 1763, died aged eighteen. Elizabeth, 1765; Lemuel, mentioned below; Amelia, 1769; Hannah, 1771, died in Warwick; Secretary, September 19, 1773, married Lucy Russell.

(VII) Lemuel, son of Josiah Rawson, was born January 18, 1767. He was a tanner by trade, and carried on his business in Warwick, Massachusetts, until about 1812. He then carried on a farm, living at Orange, New Salem, and at Erving Grant, Massachusetts, until 1836. He then moved to Bath, Summit county, Ohio, where he lived until September 20, 1844, when his wife died. Then he lived with his children in northern Ohio. He married, September 8, 1790, Sarah Barrows or Barrus, of Warwick. Children: Sally, born April 20, 1792; Lemuel, December 14, 1793; Secretary and Elizabeth, twins, born October 18, 1795; Elizabeth, died aged about two years; Abel, born May 11, 1798; Bass, April 17, 1799; Hannah, March 22, 1801; La Quinio, mentioned below; Alonzo, May 3, 1806.

(VIII) Dr. La Quinio Rawson, son of Lemuel Rawson, was born September 14, 1804. In the spring of 1824 he went to Ohio and after a short time began to study medicine, attending a course of medical lectures in Cincinnati. In 1826 he commenced practice at Tymochtee, Wyandot county, Ohio. In a short time he moved from there to Lower Sandusky, now Fremont, Ohio, where he practiced for a while. He attended lectures at the University of Pennsylvania, from which he received the degree of Doctor of Medicine, and until 1855 he continued to practice at Fremont. From 1836 to 1851 he was clerk of the court of common pleas and of the supreme court in Sandusky county, Ohio. After 1853 he spent most of his time towards the development of railroads. He was president of the Lake Erie & Louisville railroad (now the Lake Erie & Western) for several years, and the town of Rawson on that railroad was named after him. He was a man with great executive and financial ability, with the force of character needed to make him successful. He married, July 8, 1829, Sophia Beaugrand, of Maumee City, Ohio, sister of Dr. Peter Beaugrand, who was an army surgeon in the civil war. She was born in August, 1814, and is still living in Fremont, Ohio, aged ninety-eight years. Children: Milton E., born January 2, 1831, was a surgeon in the Union army; Xavier J., March 28, 1833, died in infancy; Joseph L., mentioned below; Josephine S., twin of Joseph L.; Roxine H., July 13, 1838, died August 17, 1846; Eugene A., March 14, 1840, gave up going to Yale College in order to serve in the civil war, was in the Seventy-second Regiment, Ohio Volunteer Infantry, was promoted several times and killed at the battle of Tupelo, Mississippi, while serving as major of his regiment, was very young for this command, and his steady promotions were due to his marked bravery; Estelle S., March 2, 1849.

(IX) Joseph L., son of Dr. La Quinio Rawson, was born October 6, 1835. He was educated in the public schools, and followed the profession of civil engineering. He was also in business and for a number of years was a wholesale dealer in grain. During and after the civil war he was in the internal revenue service of the United States. He married, September 15, 1859, at Fremont, Ohio, Margaret Amelia, born February 23, 1839, daughter of Judge Lyman and Martha (Stevenson) Gelpin. Children: Elizabeth Sophia, born July 4, 1860, married Theodore C. Harris, of Fremont, and has one daughter, Jane Harris; Jennie Amelia, born February 7, 1863, married Dr. O. H. Thomas, of Fremont; La Quinio, mentioned below.

(X) La Quinio (2), son of Joseph L. Rawson, was born in Fremont, Ohio, October 28, 1871. He attended the public and high school of his native town. For about a year he was a clerk in the county auditor's office and for a year and a half in the office of Gusdorf Brothers, of Fremont. During these years he devoted his evenings and spare time to the study of law and afterward he was a law student in the office of James H. Fowler, of Fremont. He was admitted to the senior class of the Cincinnati Law School, from which he was graduated in the class of 1892 with the degree of Bachelor of Laws. He began to practice law with the firm of Russell & Rice and after that firm was dissolved he continued in the office of the senior member, L. A. Russell, until 1900, after which he practiced law alone for about a year. Then he became senior partner of the firm of

Rawson & Gentsch and this firm continued until October, 1909. During these years of active and general practice, Mr. Rawson made something of a specialty of insurance cases. In October, 1909, he was chosen secretary and general counsel of the Cleveland Life Insurance Company. In this office he has become prominent in insurance circles. In politics he is a Republican, and in 1903 he was elected to the general assembly of Ohio, serving as chairman of the insurance committee. During his term many important reforms were made in the insurance laws, which were virtually rewritten. He was also a member of the finance committee of the assembly and proved an able and efficient legislator. He is a member of the Cleveland Chamber of Commerce; the Cleveland Athletic Club; the Chamber of Industry, a West Side business organization; the Tippecanoe Club; the Society of Mayflower Descendants; the New England Society of Cleveland and the Western Reserve. He is a communicant of the Protestant Episcopal church.

He married, December 26, 1895, Beatrice Frances, born September 15, 1868, daughter of George W. Floyd. They have one daughter, Beatrice, born in Cleveland, November 5, 1897.

DUFFY Hugh Duffy, who has been for more than thirty years a resident of Rutland, where he is well known in business and political circles, is of Irish parentage, his ancestors having been for more generations than can be numbered natives of the Green Isle, that beautiful land whence have come so many of our ablest citizens.

(I) Hugh Duffy, grandfather of Hugh Duffy, of Rutland, was born in county Cavan, province of Ulster, Ireland, where he spent his life as a farmer, dying in 1854, aged seventy years. He was an exceptionally good judge of horses and live stock, and at fairs was habitually called upon to give his opinion and advice in regard to their merits. He was something of a veterinary surgeon, and was withal a popular man in his community. He married Bridget, daughter of Matthew Mullen, and their children were: Mary, married Thomas McCann, and came to America; Catharine, married Patrick McGuire; Edward, died young; Hugh, died young; and Thomas, of whom further. All these children are deceased with the exception of Thomas, after whose birth the mother soon passed away.

(II) Thomas, son of Hugh and Bridget (Mullen) Duffy, was born November, 1829,

TUTUM

VERUM

in county Cavan, Ireland. He attended the public and national schools there, receiving an exceptionally good education. In 1849 he emigrated to the United States, landing in New York City, where he remained for a short time, assisting in the construction of the Hudson river railroad. Later he came to Vermont, and settled in the town of Dorset, where he learned the blacksmith's trade and subsequently engaged in quarrying. For forty years he was employed in the marble quarries of D. L. Kent & Company, of East Dorset, and for the last twenty years his home has been in Rutland, where he now lives, having retired from active life. He married, in 1853, Julia O'Donnell, born about 1830, in county Tipperary, Province of Ulster, Ireland. Children: Hugh, of whom further; James, of Rutland; Catharine, deceased, married John Lalor; Thomas F., of Glens Falls, New York; John, book publisher, of New York; Patrick, deceased; and Frank, of Rutland. The mother of the family died in Rutland, September, 1909.

(III) Hugh, son of Thomas and Julia (O'Donnell) Duffy, was born September 11, 1854, in Dorset, Vermont. He received his education in the common schools of his native town. His first employment was in the mines at Port Henry, New York, and about 1880 he came to Rutland, where in 1882 he engaged in the coal and wood business on his own account. The enterprise prospered, and he has ever since continuously conducted a flourishing business. For a long time Mr. Duffy has taken an active part in local politics, and for eight consecutive years served as alderman of his ward in the city of Rutland. He takes a lively interest in all matters pertaining to public improvement, and any plan having that end in view is always sure of his hearty coöperation.

Mr. Duffy married, October 29, 1890, Anna, daughter of Dr. J. C. and Mary (Hughs) Keenan, of Dorset, Vermont. Mr. and Mrs. Duffy are the parents of the following children: Mary, born January 23, 1894; James, died in infancy; John, also died in infancy; and Hugh, who was born October 1, 1901.

LYMAN

The arms of the Lyman family are: Quarterly, 1st and 4th: Per chevron gules and argent, in base an amulet of the first (for Lyman). Those of the Lambert family are: Gules, a chevron between three sheep argent. Of the Osborne family: Quarterly, quartered ermine and gules, over all a cross or. The crest of the Lyman family: A demi-bull argent

attired and hoofed or, langued gules. Motto: *Quod verum tutum.*

(I) Richard Lyman, the immigrant ancestor, was baptized at High Ongar, county Essex, England, October 30, 1580, died in 1640. In 1629 he sold to John Gower lands and orchards and a garden in Norton Mandeville, in the parish of Ongar, England, and in August, 1631, embarked with his wife and five children in the ship "Lion", William Pierce, master, for New England. In the ship which sailed for Bristol were Martha Winthrop, third wife of Governor Winthrop, the governor's eldest son and his family, also Eliot, the celebrated apostle to the Indians. They landed at Boston, and Richard Lyman settled first in Charlestown, and with his wife united with the church of which Eliot was pastor. He was admitted a freeman, June 11, 1635, and in October of the same year, joining a party of about a hundred persons, went to Connecticut and became one of the first settlers of Hartford. His journey was beset by many dangers, and he lost many of his cattle on the way. He was one of the original proprietors of Hartford in 1636, receiving thirty parts of the purchase from the Indians. His house was on the south side of what is now Buckingham street, the fifth lot from Main street west of the South Church and bounded apparently on Wadsworth street either on the east or west. His will was dated April 22, 1640, proved January 27, 1642, together with that of his wife, who died soon after he did. His name is inscribed on a stone column in the rear of the Centre Church of Hartford, erected in memory of the first settlers of the city. He married Sarah, daughter of Roger Osborne, of Halstead, county Kent, England. Children: William, buried at High Ongar, August 28, 1615; Phillis, baptized September 12, 1611, married William Hills; Richard, baptized July 18, 1613, died young; William, baptized September 8, 1616, died November, 1616; Richard, mentioned below; Sarah, baptized February 8, 1620; Anne, baptized April 12, 1621, died young; John, baptized 1623; Robert, baptized September, 1629, married Hepzibah Bascom, November 15, 1662.

(II) Richard (2), son of Richard (1) Lyman, was baptized at High Ongar, February 24, 1617, died June 3, 1662. He and his two brothers, John and Robert, were taxed in 1655 in Hartford in a rate assessed to build a mill. They probably removed the same year to Northampton where in December, 1655, Richard was chosen one of the selectmen. He sold his father's homestead in Hartford in 1660. He married, in Hartford, Hepzibah, daughter of Thomas Ford, of Windsor. She married (second) John Marsh, of Hadley, Massachusetts. Children: Hepzibah, born in Windsor, married, November 26, 1662, Joseph Dewey; Sarah, married John Marsh Jr., 1666; Richard, mentioned below; Thomas, removed to Durham, Connecticut; Eliza, married Joshua Pomeroy, August 20, 1672; John, settled in Hockanum, Hadley; Joanna, born in Northampton, 1658; Hannah, born 1660, married, June 20, 1677, Job Pomeroy.

(III) Richard (3), son of Richard (2) Lyman, was born in Windsor, Connecticut, in 1647, died November 4, 1708, in Columbia, Connecticut. He resided in Northampton until 1696, when he removed to Lebanon, Connecticut. He received a grant of land which he subsequently divided among his children. He married, in Northampton, May 26, 1675, Elizabeth, daughter of John Coles, of Hatfield, Massachusetts. Children: Samuel, born April, 1676; Richard, mentioned below; John, July 6, 1680; Isaac, probably February 28, 1682; Lieutenant Jonathan, January 1, 1684; Elizabeth, March 26, 1685; David, November 28, 1688; Josiah, February 6, 1690; Anne, born in Lebanon.

(IV) Richard (4), son of Richard (3) Lyman, was born in Northampton, in April, 1678, died in Lebanon, June 6, 1746. He went with his family to Lebanon in 1696. He married, April 7, 1700, Mary Woodward. Children: Israel, born February 22, 1701, died March 13, 1701; Ebenezer, August 4, 1702, farmer in Columbia, Connecticut, married Lydia Wright; Thomas, born July 6, 1704, died 1783; Mary, October 27, 1706; Hannah, September 13, 1708, married ―― Swetland; John, January 10, 1711, married (first) Hannah Birchard, (second) Mary Strong; David, 1711, died 1787; Elizabeth; Richard, mentioned below.

(V) Richard (5), son of Richard (4) Lyman, was born March 23, 1721. He married Ann Bradford, of Haddam, Connecticut, great-great-granddaughter of Governor William Bradford. He lived first at Mansfield and then at Lebanon, Connecticut. Children, born in Mansfield: Ann, born April 13, 1759; Richard, mentioned below. Born at Lebanon: Joseph Bradford, born September 1, 1767; Rachel, September 19, 1769.

(VI) Richard (6), son of Richard (5) Lyman, was born at Mansfield, Connecticut, September 22, 1761, died May 4, 1830. He served in the revolution, enlisting at the age of fifteen from Lebanon, Connecticut. He served for three years, being discharged at Springfield, New Jersey. He married, April 2, 1784, Mehitable Palmer, at Lebanon, New Hampshire, moving soon after to Kingston, now Granville, Vermont, and from there to Duxbury, Vermont, where he died. Children: Jesse, born January 22, 1785; Betsey, July 22, 1787; Joseph, June 6, 1790; Mehitable, June 9, 17―; Anna, married Lowell Greenleaf; Elijah, died unmarried; Richard, mentioned below; Lavinia, married Cyrus Morse, of Montpelier.

(VII) Richard (7), son of Richard (6) Lyman, was born in Granville, Vermont, September 12, 1801, died September 1, 1849, in Duxbury, Vermont, where he had lived for many years. He married, October 26, 1826, Ann Eliza Crosset, of Duxbury, daughter of Edward and Hannah (Carter) Crosset. Edward Crosset was born in Ireland, July 25, 1749, and married, February 24, 1774, in Killingly, Connecticut, Hannah Carter, of Dutch descent, who was born July 25, 1754; they came to Duxbury, Vermont, in 1827; moved to Crosset Hill. Children: Emilyette, died unmarried; Lowell Greenleaf, born February 28, 1830, married (first) Jane Taylor, (second) Frances B. Clark, (third) Belle C. Dotten; Cyrenius, mentioned below; Arlette, married Eli Boyce; Filette, married Charles Atherton.

(VIII) Cyrenius, son of Richard (7) Lyman, was born in Duxbury, Vermont, October 15, 1831, died October 20, 1903. He married, March 28, 1855, Mary, daughter of Henry and Mary (Turner) McClure. Children: Jennie Euretta, born October 15, 1856, married Lewis Burton Graves; Richey, born September 3, 1861, married Ruth Mary Hathaway, granddaughter of Hiram Hathaway, of Moretown, four children; Jeremiah, born May 15, 1864, married Maud Ayres; Chauncey, born December 12, 1866; Walter H., mentioned below; James McClure, May 19, 1881. Robert McClure, great-grandfather of Mary (McClure) Lyman, was a son of Richard McClure, and was born in Ireland, 1718. He came to this country when nine years of age with James Lyons and one other person. They made the first settlement in Hillsboro in 1741, but abandoned the place in 1744 on account of the Indians at the time of the breaking out of the Cape Breton war. Mr. McClure was a soldier in the revolutionary war, being nearly sixty when he enlisted. In 1785 he joined his sons in Acworth, New Hampshire. He was a stalwart man and retained his physical vigor almost to the last, dying at the age of ninety-nine. He was always punctual in attendance at the meeting house. The foregoing was taken from the records of the town history of Acworth.

(IX) Walter H., son of Cyrenius Lyman,

was born March 16, 1869, at Duxbury, Vermont. He was educated in the public schools and at Montpelier Seminary, Montpelier, Vermont. He occupies a position of trust and responsibility in one of the largest savings institutions in New York City. His home is at Mount Kisco, Westchester county, New York, on West Main street. He has been prominent there in public affairs. He was a member of the board of education for several years prior to March, 1908, when he became its president, an office he held until March, 1911, when he was elected president of the incorporated village of Mount Kisco. At the time of his election a local newspaper said: "Mr. Walter H. Lyman, the successful candidate for Village President is one of the best known and most respected citizens of the village. Of a retiring disposition, he is perhaps slow in forming acquaintances, but he has the reputation of having never lost a friend during his fifteen years' residence in the village of which he was chosen father on Tuesday." In politics he is an independent Democrat. He is a member of the New York Society, Sons of the Revolution, of the Society of Colonial Wars, of the Vermont Society of New York, and of Kisco Lodge, No. 708, Free and Accepted Masons, of which he is a past master. He is interested in church work and for several years has been a member of the official board and treasurer of the Methodist Episcopal church of Mount Kisco.

He married, June 8, 1898, in Mount Kisco, Olive Jane Washburn, born in Mount Pleasant, Westchester county, New York, August 15, 1871, daughter of Oliver J. and Emily (Tyler) Washburn. Children, born at Mount Kisco: Lowell Washburn, born December 13, 1902; Emily Louise, March 13, 1907.

GARY The Gary or Gerry family came early to Westmoreland, New Hampshire, and vicinity. As other settlers came from Worcester county, Massachusetts, to this section, there is little doubt that this family was from Lancaster or Sterling, in that county, or from the older branch in Stoneham and Lynn. Most of the family in Massachusetts used the spelling Gerry, while various Vermont families spelled their name Garey. Oliver Gary served in the revolution from Westmoreland in Captain John Cole's company in 1777. It was probably his widow who had a family there, consisting of three females, names not given, according to the census of 1790. And Seth Gary, also of Westmoreland, had four males over sixteen, one male under sixteen and three females in his family. He was doubt-

less a brother or son of Oliver. In the Massachusetts Revolutionary Rolls, Oliver Gary is credited to Northfield, Massachusetts. Seth Gary was in the revolution from Rehoboth, which is near Raynham, whence came the Brittons and others to Westmoreland. There were also Gary families in Attleborough, near Raynham and Rehoboth, Massachusetts, and the Westmoreland family was undoubtedly from that section.

(I) Benjamin Gary, the first of the family, settled during or after the revolution at Westmoreland, New Hampshire, with others of the name. Thence after 1794 he went to the Mohawk Valley in New York, but afterward returned, about 1805, making the trip both ways with ox teams. Among his children was Britton, of whom further.

(II) Britton, son of Benjamin Gary, was born in Westmoreland, New Hampshire, January 26, 1793, died there, March 20, 1853. His gravestone with that of his wife and children is in the cemetery at East Westmoreland. He married, January 28, 1821, Lucy Martin, born at Lunenburg, Massachusetts, September 19, 1793, died at Grafton, Massachusetts, January 1, 1870, a daughter of Jonathan Martin. Children, born at Westmoreland: 1. Sarah E., born September 27, 1822, died at Westborough, Massachusetts; married, May 1, 1844, E. E. Jourdan. 2. Elmira, born October 16, 1824; married Frederick Hall, and died in Minnesota. 3. Stephen B., of whom further. 4. J. Martin, born in Westmoreland, September 29, 1829; married, November 7, 1853, Jane Gilbert, of Ashburnham, 5. Harris B., born January 4, 1831, died in Minnesota in 1911; married Nancy E. Woodward at Brattleboro, Vermont, May 30, 1852. 6. George W., born June 19, 1833; married, June 13, 1859, L. M. Todd, of Rutland, Vermont, and resides there. 7. L. Arminda, born March 7, 1836, died in Grafton, Massachusetts; married, October 14, 1857, Silas E. Stowe, of Grafton.

(III) Stephen Britton, son of Britton Gary, was born in Westmoreland, New Hampshire, October 21, 1826, died there April 16, 1874. He attended the public schools of his native town, but when twelve years old left home, and went to work crimping boots in a boot and shoe factory at Grafton, Massachusetts, and remained away from home for several years. After his marriage he returned to his native town to take care of his parents and conduct the homestead. He was an industrious, progressive, enterprising and successful farmer. He also bought and sold cattle for many years for Massachusetts markets. To the old homestead which was an excellent farm, he added more land from time to time, and when he died the farm comprised four hundred and sixty acres of land, and substantial buildings of all kinds. Mr. Gary was a great power in local politics, exerting his influence for good in the affairs of the town for many years, but declining to hold public office of any kind. He supported the Republican party in politics. He was also an active and generous member of the Christian church of Westmoreland, and together with his wife sang in the church choir for many years.

Mr. Gary married, January 12, 1852, Mary Ann Woodward, of Westmoreland, born January 29, 1834, daughter of Ezekiel and Mary (Wilson) Woodward. Her father was a native of Raynham, Massachusetts, born October 18, 1801, died in Westmoreland, April 16, 1874, son of Samuel Woodward, who came from Raynham or vicinity in Massachusetts to Westmoreland. Mary (Wilson) Woodward, wife of Ezekiel Woodward, was born in Jamaica, Vermont, July 3, 1803, died in Westmoreland, March 16, 1870. Polly (Gleason) Wilson, mother of Mary Wilson, was said to be from Alstead, New Hampshire, and was doubtless of the Scotch-Irish Wilsons who came early to Londonderry and Windham, Vermont. She was a daughter of Nathaniel Wilson, formerly of Alstead. Mr. and Mrs. Gary had but one child, Frank Weston, of whom further.

(IV) Frank Weston, son of Stephen Britton Gary, was born in Westmoreland, New Hampshire, December 29, 1853. He attended the public schools of his native town and also private schools in the same town. At the age of sixteen he entered upon his business career, beginning as clerk in a general store in his native town. The railroad telegraph office was located in this store and during his leisure time he learned telegraphy. Subsequently he was placed in charge of the railroad office at South Ashburnham Junction, and continued there for eighteen months. Then he was assigned to the Western Union railroad telegraph office at Rutland, Vermont, in 1871, and he held that position for nine years. In 1880 he established a retail grocery store in Rutland, in partnership with Mr. Hoag, under the firm name of Gary & Hoag, and continued in this business until 1904, when he withdrew from the firm and sold his interests. He did special work for the New England Telephone Company at various times for the next year. He was one of the founders of the corporation of Bryant & Gary Company to manufacture in Rutland lock cover mailing boxes for small hardware and novelties

and he became the secretary and treasurer. He is the principal stockholder of this business, and to it he has devoted himself exclusively in recent years with much success, building up the business from a modest beginning to large proportions. In politics Mr. Gary is a Republican, and he has been a member of the Republican City Committtee and for four years was alderman. He is an active and prominent member of the Congregational church and for some fifteen years was a member of the prudential committee. He is also a member of Rutland Lodge of Free Masons; Davenport Chapter, Royal Arch Masons; Killington Commandery, Knights Templar.

Mr. Gary married, August 22, 1876, Carrie Willis, who was born in Rutland, Vermont, August 22, 1855, daughter of George and Orril K. (Lyman) Willis. Her father was probably born at Alstead, New Hampshire, and her mother at Norwich or Thetford, Vermont. Children: 1. Willis Britton, born May 27, 1878, died May 1, 1882. 2. Edward Woodward, born February 19, 1881; died April 30, 1882. 3. Marion, born October 31, 1882. 4. George Woodward, born January 5, 1890; died February 28, 1909.

CARPENTER This is one of the most widely distributed names of the United States, as well as one of the oldest, and has been notable among the pioneers of many states. It is traced to an early period in England, and is conspicuous in the annals of the American revolution, and also in civic life through many generations and representatives. It has carried service in many commonwealths. The Carpenters trace their ancestry to John Carpenter, born in 1303, and head of the ancient house in Herefordshire, parish of Dilwyne, England, to whom the Irish Tyrconnels also trace their descent. The Hereford family of Carpenters were prominent, taking an active part in all matters of interest to the crown, and probably no family in England has performed more deeds and received more favors. Among the most noted was John Carpenter, town clerk of London, who died in 1442. The line of Lord George Carpenter is the same as that of William Carpenter, of Rehoboth. Coat-of-arms: Argent a greyhound passant and chief sable. Crest: A greyhound's head erased per fesse sable and argent. This is the same as found on the tombstone of Daniel Carpenter, of Rehoboth, who was born in 1669.

(1) John Carpenter, born about 1303, was a member of parliament in 1325. (II) Richard, born about 1335, was a goldsmith by

trade and wealthy. (III) John (2) was a cousin of John Carpenter, town clerk of London. (IV) John (3) died about 1500. (V) William, born about 1440, died in 1520, was William of Homme. (VI) James, son of William Carpenter. (VII) John (4), son of James Carpenter. (VIII) William, son of John Carpenter, was born about 1520, and died in 1550. (IX) William, son of William (2) Carpenter, was born about 1540. (X) William (4), son of William (3) Carpenter, was born in England about 1576, and was a resident of London. He sailed from Southampton for America in the ship "Bevis", landing in May, 1638, and returned to England in the same vessel, possibly having come to this country merely to help in the settlement here of his son and his family.

(I) William (5), pioneer ancestor of the American line, son of William (4) Carpenter, was born in England in 1605, died in Rehoboth, Massachusetts, February 7, 1659. He was admitted a freeman of Weymouth May 13, 1640; was representative from Weymouth, 1641-43, and from Rehoboth, 1645; constable in 1641; was chosen proprietor's clerk of Weymouth, 1643. He drew lot No. 18, in the divisions of lands in Rehoboth, June 30, 1644, was admitted an inhabitant of the town March 28, 1645, and the following June was made freeman. It was through his influence that the grant of Seekonk, otherwise known as Rehoboth, was made by the general court, then at Plymouth. This was the tract of land selected by Roger Williams for a settlement, when driven out of the Massachusetts colony. In 1647 William Carpenter was made one of the directors of the town, and again in 1655. The legal business of the town and colony was transacted principally by him. He paid eight pounds, seventeen shillings and three pence toward defraying the expenses of King Philip's war, and was one of a committee to lay out a road from Rehoboth to Dedham. About 1642 he received a commission as captain from the governor of Massachusetts, and was called upon to act for the protection and ownership of the Pawtuxet lands. The records show him to have been a yeoman, and his estate was valued at two hundred and fifty-four pounds and ten shillings. Governor Bradford, who married his cousin Alice, favored William Carpenter in all his measures in the Plymouth court, and in all their dealings they were close friends. William Carpenter's wife, Abigail, who died February 22, 1687, had been provided for in his will of April 21, 1659. Children: 1. John, born in England about 1628, died May 23, 1695. 2. William, about 1631, died January 26, 1703.

3. Joseph, 1633, died May 6, 1675. 4. Hannah, in Weymouth, April 3, 1640. 5. Abiah, April 9, 1643. 6. Abigail, twin of Abiah, died March 5, 1710. 7. Samuel, of whom further.

(II) Samuel, son of William (5) and Abigail Carpenter, was born in 1644, died in Rehoboth, Massachusetts, February 20, 1683. He was one of the purchasers in the North Purchase, and land was allotted him in the division of February 5, 1671. May 16, 1680, he with two others was chosen to lay the land of William Blanding. The will indicates that Samuel and Abiah, who were young at the time of the father's death, were the only children left at home in charge of the mother, the others having homes of their own. His education was probably limited, as he was at an early age compelled to assist his mother in the cultivation of the home farm, but he was a man of fair ability and became a wealthy and reliable citizen. He contributed eleven pounds, nineteen shillings and five pence toward the expenses of King Philip's war. He married, May 25, 1660, Sarah Readaway, who married (second) Gilbert Brooks. Children: 1. Samuel, born in Rehoboth, September 15, 1661. 2. Sarah, January 11, 1663. 3. Abiah, February 10, 1665, died April 28, 1732. 4. James, April 12, 1668, died April 27, 1732. 5. Jacob, September 5, 1670, died in 1690. 6. Jonathan, December 11, 1672, died August 23, 1716. 7. David, April 17, 1675, died July 26, 1701. 8. Solomon, December 23, 1677, died 1750. 9. Zachariah, of whom further. 10. Abraham, September 20, 1682, died April 22, 1758.

(III) Zachariah, son of Samuel and Sarah (Readaway) Carpenter, was born July 1, 1680, in Rehoboth, where he died April 8, 1718, in his thirty-eighth year. He received lands as a share of his father's estate on November 24, 1703, and his inventory made in Attleboro, April 23, 1718, valued his estate at seven hundred and two pounds, nine shillings and six pence, including land in Attleboro and Rehoboth, valued at four hundred and fifty pounds. He married Martha, daughter of Nicholas Ide, born March 18, 1683, in Rehoboth. Children: Zachariah (2), of whom further; Keziah, born July 1, 1708; Martha, June 25, 1710; Abigail, November 14, 1714; Patience, March 9, 1717.

(IV) Zachariah (2), son of Zachariah (1) and Martha (Ide) Carpenter, was born October 18, 1706, in Rehoboth, where he was a farmer, and died July 25, 1765. He married, November 27, 1728, in Rehoboth, Mary Child. Children: Patience, born June 27, 1729; Zachariah, died young; Keziah, August 29,

1733; Zachariah (3), of whom further; Phanuel, November 19, 1736; Martha, September 1, 1738; Caleb, March 10, 1740; Simeon, September 24, 1742; Esther, June 28, 1744; Richard, June 14, 1746; Grace, July 28, 1748; Benjamin, May 3, 1751.

(V) Zachariah (3), son of Zachariah (2) and Mary (Child) Carpenter, was born February 27, 1735, in Rehoboth, where he died October 1, 1775, at the age of forty years. He was a farmer. In 1767 he was a member of the first military foot company of Rehoboth. He married, May 29, 1760, Hannah Carpenter, born June 10, 1740, died April 20, 1790, daughter of Obadiah and Bethia (Lyon) Carpenter, granddaughter of William Carpenter. Children: Bethia, born May 12, 1762; Benjamin, December 25, 1763; Zachariah (4), of whom further; Hannah, November 10, 1767; Otis, December 31, 1769; Patty, died at three years old; Esther, April 18, 1775.

(VI) Zachariah (4), son of Zachariah (3) and Hannah (Carpenter) Carpenter, was born October 16, 1765, in Rehoboth, died February 22, 1837-38, in Walpole, New Hampshire. He was a carpenter by trade and lived for a time in Providence, Rhode Island, whence he removed to Walpole at the age of about forty years. He cared for his wife's parents in their old age and conducted the hotel, which was built by his father-in-law near the present railroad station in Walpole, at the mouth of Cold river. He married, November 27, 1791, in Rehoboth, Lydia, daughter of Samuel and Amy Wightman, of Rehoboth, born there August 13, 1771, died July 28, 1847, in Walpole. Samuel Wightman removed from Rehoboth to Walpole in 1801, purchased three hundred and fifty acres of land at the mouth of Cold river, and there conducted a hotel until he was succeeded by Mr. Carpenter. Children of Zachariah (4) Carpenter: 1. Amanda, born April 28, 1796; married Captain Elijah Holbrook of Surry, New Hampshire. 2. Elmira, 1798, died at the age of twenty-four years; married, October 30, 1821, Thomas Heaton of Dansville, Vermont. 3. Amy Ann, October 15, 1802; married a Gaskill, of Clarendon, Vermont. 4. Thomas K., 1804, died in childhood. 5. Fannie, January 29, 1805, died in 1841, at Walpole; married Simon Pettis of Bellows Falls. 6. Thomas K., 1806, died at the age of fourteen years. 7. Caroline, March 1, 1808, in Walpole; married Warren Daniels, of Keene, New Hampshire, and resided in Rutland, Vermont. 8. Samuel, August 31, 1809. 9. Albert Harrison, of whom further.

(VII) Albert Harrison, son of Zachariah

(4) and Lydia (Wightman) Carpenter, was born June 10, 1814, in Walpole, died in October, 1879, in that town. He received a common school education such as his native town afforded, and in early life conducted the hotel which had been managed by his father and maternal grandfather. In later life he engaged in agriculture. He was a Whig until his party was merged in the Republican party, after which he supported the latter ticket. He was a member of the Episcopal church. He married (first) November, 1843, Mary Wilder, of Keene, New Hampshire, born about 1815, died in 1861, daughter of Jonas and Cynthia Wilder. He married (second) a Widow Gage, of Westminster, Vermont. Children: Edward A., settled in South Royalston, Massachusetts; Emily A., residing in Rutland; Sarah, deceased; Mary, deceased; Henry Otis, of whom further; Thomas, living in New York City; Frederick.

(VIII) Henry Otis, son of Albert Harrison and Mary (Wilder) Carpenter, was born January 30, 1852, in Walpole. He spent his boyhood there, receiving the education afforded by the schools of that town. Before he was twelve years old he was accustomed to work on a farm, and at that age took employment in a hotel in Rutland, Vermont. After some years he constructed the Bardwell house in Rutland, the leading hostelry of that town during the thirty-seven years he conducted it. He is extensively interested in real estate in Rutland, of which village he has been trustee and president. In 1898 he represented the town in the state legislature, and in 1904 was a member of the state senate. After the incorporation of the city of Rutland he served three times as mayor, his last term closing in March, 1911. He is president of the Rutland Savings Bank, and a member of the Vermont Historical Society. In the Masonic order, he has obtained the Knights Templar degree, and is also a member of the Rutland Lodges of Knights of Pythias, Independent Order of Odd Fellows, and the Benevolent and Protective Order of Elks.

He married, May 6, 1874, Kate Mallory, born in East Poultney, Vermont, daughter of Elias and Cynthia (Seamans) Mallory. Children: Mabel, born July 3, 1875, died June 25, 1912; Katherine, born October 1, 1882, married William Philip Prophett, an undertaker and funeral director in Bridgewater, Massachusetts.

HULL   Richard Hull, the immigrant ancestor, was a native of Derbyshire, England, and came early to Boston, Massachusetts. He was admitted a freeman in the colony, April 1, 1634. He was a carpenter by trade. After living a few years at Dorchester and Boston, Massachusetts, he removed to New Haven, where he took the oath of fidelity. He was one of the founders of the New Haven colony, living on what is now Chapel street. He died at New Haven in September, 1662. He had two sons: Dr. John, of whom further; Joseph, from whom General William Hull and Commodore Isaac Hull were descended.

(II) Dr. John Hull, son of Richard Hull, was born in New Haven in 1640, and lived there during his youth. In 1661 he came to Stratford, Connecticut, where he was a planter for several years. In 1668 he went to Pawgassett, now Derby, Connecticut, where he is said to have been one of the first settlers, and to have named the town for the ancient home of his family in England. He lived at Derby until 1677, and built several dwelling houses for himself and sons. In 1687 he removed to Wallingford, where he built the first grist mill. His farm of seven hundred acres is the present town of Cheshire. He was called "Doctor", and presumably practiced medicine. He exchanged his house and land at Stratford for the house and land of Benjamin Lewis at Wallingford in 1687. The town of Wallingford laid out to Dr. Hull a tract of land supposed to contain seven hundred acres, lying between the north side of Broad swamp and the Quinnipiac river, and the grant proved afterward to be more than a mile square, and was known as "Dr. Hull's large farm". He died at Wallingford, December 6, 1711, and was buried there.

Dr. Hull married three times. The name of his first wife is unknown. He married (second) October 19, 1671, Mary Jones, and (third) Rebecca Turner. Children by first wife: John, of whom further; Joseph, 1662; Samuel, February 4, 1663; Mary, October 31, 1664. Children by second wife: Benjamin, October 7, 1672; Ebenezer, 1673; Richard, 1674; Jeremiah, 1679; Arche.

(III) John (2), son of Dr. John (1) Hull, was born in Stratford, March 14, 1661-62. He married Mary ———, and settled in Derby. Children, born in Derby: Deborah, 1691; John, 1693; Daniel; Miles, of whom further; Priscilla, 1702; Ebenezer, married Hannah Bates; Mary; Martha.

(IV) Miles, son of John (2) Hull, was born at Derby in 1700. He married Mary Tuttle, of Wallingford. Children, born at Wallingford: Martha, November 29, 1730, died young. Martha, November 23, 1732; Esther, September 15, 1733; Elizabeth, 1735;

Elijah, March 10, 1736; Eunice, March 29, 1738; Mary, July 15, 1740; Miles, of whom further; Abigail, June 11, 1745; Abijah, June 10, 1747.

(V) Captain Miles (2) Hull, son of Miles (1) Hull, was born at Wallingford, March 24, 1743. He owned the farms afterward owned by Jared Bishop and Captain Munson Cook. He married, December 4, 1761, Eunice, daughter of Ebenezer and Hannah Hull. Children: Amzi, of whom further; Luther; Miles; Polly, married Levi Douglas; a daughter, married ——— Sizer.

(VI) Amzi, son of Captain Miles (2) Hull, was born about 1765. In 1790 Amzi (spelled Amassa) was living in Woodbridge, Connecticut, and had in his family two sons under sixteen and two females. The only other person named Hull in Woodbridge at that time was Joel, who then had no family.

(VII) Rev. Aurelius Bevil Hull, son of Amzi Hull, was born at Woodbridge, Connecticut, October 12, 1788. He graduated from Yale College in 1807, with the degree of Bachelor of Arts. Later he received the degree of Master of Arts. After six years as tutor at Yale he was ordained in Worcester, May 22, 1821, and was pastor of the First Congregational Church until he died, May 17, 1826, in the prime of life. From his epitaph we quote:

This monument is erected to commemorate the faithful services and the virtuous example of the Rev. Aurelius Bevil Hull. * * * He endeared himself to the people of his charge by his affectionate and assiduous devotion to his ministerial and pastoral duties; while the suavity of his manners, the purity of his life and the sincerity and earnestness of his efforts in advancing the cause of education, and in the promotion of the general interests of the community commanded respect and gratitude. He was a scholar of refined taste, and the style of his discourses was unusually chaste and perspicuous, earnest and direct, harmonizing with the tenor of his life, and being rendered yet more impressive, during the greater part of his ministry, by his conscious and evident nearness to the grave. Accustomed to the best forms of polished life, he was dignified without display, and courteous without dissimulation, and constantly manifesting in his private intercourse and his public labors that for himself and others, he sought first the Kingdom of God. "Cautious himself, he others ne'er deceived, Lived as he taught, and as he taught believed."

He married Abigail Darling. Children: Joseph Darling, of whom further; Aurelius Bevil, of whom further; Elizabeth; Amanda, married Aaron Atwood Hardy; Thomas, died at New Haven, while a student in Yale College.

(VIII) Joseph Darling, son of Rev. Aurelius Bevil Hull, was born February 21, 1818, at New Haven, died at Roxbury, Massachusetts, now part of Boston, in 1889. He graduated from Yale College in the class of 1837. He became a Congregational minister, retiring from the pulpit in 1858, and afterward teaching school. He had a private school in Hartford, and after 1864 on Park avenue, New York City. He returned to Hartford about 1873 and taught private pupils until his health failed. He removed to Boston afterward and died there. He married (first) Charlotte Cowles, of Farmington, Connecticut. He married (second) in 1871, Kate Brown. Children by first wife: 1. Richard Cowles, born June 5, 1845, died February, 1857. 2. Mary Hawes, born January 18, 1847; married, June 22, 1870, Josiah D. Flint, who was born at Northampton, December 29, 1835, and died March 19, 1907. Mrs. Flint was a teacher of art and history from 1893 to 1903, and afterward a lecturer in the private schools on general topics. She is now a music critic, and a woman of broad culture and liberal education. 3. Edward Hooker, born October 9, 1849, died October 21, 1851. 4. Charlotte, died in infancy, January 8, 1852. 5. Albert Thomas, resides at 76 West One Hundred and Thirty-second street, New York City. 6. Josephine Darling, living in Massachusetts.

(VIII) Aurelius Bevil (2), son of Aurelius Bevil (1) Hull, and brother of Joseph Darling Hull, was born at New Haven, Connecticut, November 1, 1819, died February 15, 1907, at Morristown, New Jersey. He was educated in the public schools in Connecticut, and at the age of fifteen came to New York with his mother, after his father died. For a time he was clerk in a store, then he was in the wholesale drug business under the name of B. A. Fahnestock, Hull & Company. A branch of the business was conducted in Pittsburgh and Philadelphia, Pennsylvania, under the name of Fahnestock & Company, composed of the same partners. The business was extensive and profitable. After a prominent career he retired, January 1, 1865. The firm manufactured white lead, specific medicines and various drugs. He was a director of the Continental Insurance Company of New York and of the Fidelity and Casualty Company of New York, and one of the founders of both. He was a director and vice-president of the Morristown Trust Company, director and vice-president of the Morristown Aqueduct Company, director and vice-president of the Morris County Savings Bank, and director of the Morristown Safe Deposit Company. From 1870 to the time of his death he made his home at Morristown. In politics he was a Republican, but he was

never active in public affairs, and accepted no public offices. He was a member of the First Presbyterian Church, then of the Plymouth Church, when Rev. Henry Ward Beecher was pastor, afterward of the Church of the Pilgrims, all of Brooklyn, and finally of the First Presbyterian Church of Morristown, and at various times treasurer and president of the board of trustees.

Mr. Hull married, at Greenfield, Massachusetts, Sarah Norris Tucker, who was born at Springfield, New Jersey, December 11, 1818, died at Morristown, February, 1890, a daughter of the Rev. James Wakefield Tucker, who died at Springfield in 1819, and was a descendant of an old New England family, a graduate of Yale College in the class of 1807, educated for the ministry in the Congregational faith, and pastor of the Presbyterian church at Springfield. Mrs. Hull's mother was of the old Atwater family, of Connecticut. Children: 1. Mary Amanda, died in infancy. 2. Charles Aurelius, of whom further. 3. George Lawrence, born April 8, 1850, died at Morristown in April, 1900; married (first) Jennie, daughter of Judge Samuel Foote, of the court of appeals; his first wife died on their wedding trip. He married (second) Elizabeth, daughter of Gratz Van Rensselaer, of Geneva, New York; her father was a civil engineer and surveyor, also an insurance agent. Child by second wife: George Lawrence Jr., born July, 1880, now with the Sanborn Map Company as draughtsman; is a deaf mute; he married Viola Lombard, also a deaf mute. 4. Harrie Tucker, born at Brooklyn, October 25, 1858, educated in the public schools of Morristown, New Jersey, was secretary and treasurer of the Morristown Savings Bank for twenty-one years, now retired; married Irene Duryea. and resides at 65 Maple avenue, Morristown. Children: i. Edith Duryee, married James Graeme Lidgerwood. ii. Howard Gillispie, graduate of Yale College in 1905 (Ph. B.), living at Morristown, and secretary of the National Company. iii. Charles Aurelius, born January 28, 1886. iv. Kenneth Duryee, born June 1, 1891, now at Yale academic class of 1915.

(IX) Charles Aurelius, son of Aurelius Bevil (2) Hull, was born at Brooklyn, May 26, 1848. He attended the Brooklyn Polytechnic Institute, then entered Yale College, and was graduated in the class of 1869 with the degree of Bachelor of Arts. For about two years he was in business as manufacturer of stationary steam engines. In 1871 he entered the employ of the Continental Insurance Company in New York City, and from time to time was promoted to positions of larger responsibility. He was elected secretary of the Howard Insurance Company in February, 1876, and afterward vice-president, an office he held until the company retired from business in 1888. During the next four years he continued in the insurance business as an agent of fire insurance companies. In February, 1892, after the reorganization of the New York Fire Insurance Company, he was elected its vice-president, and in 1904 its president. In 1906 the company was financially embarrassed by the earthquake and fire at San Francisco. In 1910 Mr. Hull organized the New Amsterdam Fire Insurance Company, and was elected president. This company was amalgamated with the Empire City Fire Insurance Company, December 1, 1910. For more than twenty years he has been vice-president of the Sanborn Map Company which makes all the insurance maps of the country. He was a director of the Fifth Avenue Bank of Brooklyn until it was absorbed by the Mechanics' Bank of Brooklyn about 1904. He is a trustee of the Brooklyn Savings Bank, which has deposits of over fifty millions of dollars. He is also a director of the Proprietors of Morristown Aqueduct, the Morristown Safe Deposit Company, the North River Fire Insurance Company, and the Nassau Fire Insurance Company. In politics he is an independent Republican, and he was a member of the Brooklyn board of education in Seth Low's administration as mayor of Brooklyn. He is a member of the Church of the Pilgrims (Congregational), of Brooklyn, of which he is a trustee, and has been a deacon for many years. He is active in the American Missionary Association of the Congregational Church and a member of its executive committee. He was first elected in 1879, resigning in 1884, was again elected in 1888, and continuing in office to the present time, and he has been the chairman of the board for fourteen years, and was secretary for five years prior to his election as chairman. He has also been chairman of the board of trustees of Fisk University of Nashville, Tennessee, since his election in 1908; trustee of Mount Holyoke College since 1900; trustee of the Brooklyn Young Men's Christian Association and Brooklyn Young Women's Christian Association since 1909, and previously a director; he is trustee of the Brooklyn City Hospital, and of the Eye and Ear Hospital of Brooklyn; corporate member of the American Board of Commissioners of Foreign Missions, and member of the Long Island Historical Society of which his father was a life member before him. He holds membership in the Royal Arcanum, the Hamilton Rem-

brandt, University, and Twentieth Century clubs of Brooklyn, and the Lawyers Club of New York. He acts as the treasurer for the Rembrandt Club.

Mr. Hull married (first) November 8, 1870, Elizabeth Amelia Stanton, born March 9, 1849, died April 6, 1889, daughter of Enoch Crandall and Lucy Jane (Shepard) Stanton. Her father was a cloth merchant in New York, and is now (1912) living in Brooklyn. He married (second) June 10, 1891, in Brooklyn, Katharine Stanton, sister of his first wife. Children by first wife: 1. Elizabeth Stanton, born August 28, 1871, died July, 1872. 2. Florence Tucker, born August 31, 1876, died April 18, 1889.

CARPENTER The family herein traced is of French origin and like the English family of that name derives its cognomen from an occupation. In French it is spelled Charpentier and in early generations had the prefix de and le; in the latter form meaning "the carpenter". It is found on record as early as 1160 and descendants of Renaud le Charpentier, a son of Roger, Sire de Gouy, were held in high esteem in Cambray and vicinity about 1200. Probably on account of political differences several of the descendants removed about 1400 to France where they have held high rank down to the present day. The family had large possessions in the Netherlands, where it is now extinct, and has been traced down to 1729 and later. It gave a bishop to Chartres; an abbot to St. Vaast, in Arras; an almoner to Count de Flanders; governors, councillors and military men of various ranks, and formed alliances with many noble houses. Jean le Charpentier was treasurer for the Emperor Charles V.; whose wife, Marguerite, was a daughter of Jean. The first ancestor to whom direct descent has been traced was Pierre or Peter Charpentier, who was born about the middle of the fifteenth century and resided in Messen, West Flanders, being treasurer of that city. He was councillor of the Prince de Chimay, who granted him the coat-of-arms of the French descendants of this family.

(I) Joseph Carpenter, a native of France, emigrated to Canada in the early part of the eighteenth century and resided in the province of Quebec. His wife's maiden name was Grenier. They had children: Joseph, Charles, Laurence, Louis and Remie.

(II) Laurence, third son of Joseph Carpenter, was born about 1788 in the province of Riviere de Lieux, in Quebec, died in 1881, at the age of ninety-three years. He married Elizabeth le Coin, born about 1801, died in

1890, aged eighty-nine years. Children: Elizabeth, Sarah, Julia, lived to be eighty years of age; Lucinda, died young; Thomas, born 1825, living in La Cole, Quebec; David, Lucinda, deceased; Harriet, born 1830, lived in Winooski, Vermont, died October 16, 1912; Medore, deceased; John, deceased; Frank and George, residing in Winooski; Mary, deceased; Henry, living in Winooski.

(III) David, second son of Laurence and Elizabeth (le Coin) Carpenter, was born March 22, 1826, in La Cole, Canada, died in Rutland, Vermont, April 11, 1910. He was a stone mason and engaged in contracting with success in his native country. In 1868 he removed to Rutland and was engaged on the construction of the first business blocks in that city, such as the Baxter Bank and residence, the original portion of the high school building and the Bardwell Hotel. He married Zoe Fauchere, born in Kingsley, province of Quebec, about 1834-35, died April 12, 1907, in Rutland, aged seventy-two years. Children: Frank Joseph, born May 10, 1856, deceased; Lumira Alma, July 22, 1858, deceased; George, May, 1860; Mary H., married Pierre Lemieux, of Rutland; Lumira Alma, December 22, 1864; Celina, May 12, 1867; married Mitchell Monette; Anna, October 22, 1869; Percival L., December 22, 1871; Henry B., of whom further.

(IV) Henry Bernard, youngest child of David and Zoe (Fauchere) Carpenter, was born June 5, 1877, in Rutland, and was educated in the public schools of that town. He served an apprenticeship with a baker and has been associated with that business for a period of fourteen years. Since 1901 he has been proprietor of the People's Bakery in Rutland, and is doing a successful business. He is a member of the Modern Woodmen of America, the Order of Foresters and the Knights of Columbus. He married, September, 1907, Anna Cline, daughter of David and Jennie (Hackett) Cline, of West Rutland. They have a son, Robert Henry, born May 19, 1911.

BAKER   Edward Baker, immigrant ancestor, was born in England. He came to this country in the large fleet under Governor Winthrop which sailed in April and arrived at Boston and Salem, June and July, 1630. "Some of them were from the western part of England, but the greater number from about London". He settled on the south side of "Baker's Hill" in Saugus, then Lynn, Massachusetts, in 1630, and he was made a freeman, March 14, 1638. In 1657 he moved to Northampton, Massachusetts, where he had several grants of land,

and he lived there many years, a "respected and influential" man. He returned to Lynn, after settling his sons Joseph and Timothy in Northampton, and died at Lynn, March 16, 1687. His will was dated October 16, 1685. He married Joan ——, who died April 9, 1693. Children: Joseph; Mary, born April 1, 1642; John, born 1645; Timothy, mentioned below; Thomas, born 1653; Edward.

(II) Timothy, son of Edward Baker, was born in 1647. He settled in Northampton, on Elm street, on land given to him by his father. He was a prominent man in town affairs, and served often as selectman, and on important town and church committees. He was called "Mr.", and later was made ensign and finally lieutenant of the Train Band. He was made freeman in 1676. He died August 30, 1729, and he and his wife were probably buried in the Old Burying Ground near "Shop Row", Northampton. He married (first) January 16, 1672, Grace, daughter of John Marsh, of Hadley, Massachusetts, and granddaughter of Governor John Webster, of Connecticut. She died May 31, 1676, and he married (second) Mrs. Sarah Atherton, widow of Rev. Hope Atherton, of Hatfield, Massachusetts, and daughter of Lieutenant and Deacon John Hollister, of Westersfield. Children by first wife, born in Northampton: Grace, 1673, died February 10, 1673; Timothy, 1675, died in infancy. Children by second wife, born in Northampton: John, mentioned below; Thomas, May 14, 1682; Edward, November 12, 1685; Prudence, May 14, 1687; Deliverance, November 13, 1689, died 1710.

(III) John, son of Timothy Baker, was born at Northampton, February 3, 1680, died January 8, 1762. He lived at the homestead on Elm street in Northampton and was influential in the town. He was known as Captain John Baker. He married, June 1, 1709, Rebecca, daughter of Deacon John Clark, and granddaughter of William Clark and Elder John Strong, of Northampton. She was born November 22, 1687, and died June 9, 1774. It is said that the Bakers and Clarks for years held a regular family prayer meeting until the families became too much scattered to keep it up. John Baker, as was his father and grandfather, was very religious. Children, born in Northampton: Two Johns, died in infancy; John, mentioned below; Timothy, born 1717; Noah, 1719; Aaron, 1726; Elisha, 1727; Elijah, 1730; Stephen, 1731; Mary, married Josiah Clark; Sarah, married Gideon Henderson.

(IV) John (2), son of John (1) Baker, was born at Northampton, December 22, 1715, died February 3, 1802. He was a captain

and as active in public affairs as his father was. Hon. Osmyn Baker says: "I have heard the late Judge Lyman say that he recollected him well, as one of the most prominent and eloquent in the meetings of the people, in early Revolutionary times. Unfortunately he became a loyalist, and that shadow darkened many years of his later life." It is said that he held some honorable office in the colonial government. He and his son Hollister are the only ones of the family known to have been Loyalists. He married Abigail, daughter of Ebenezer Clark, and she died February 29, 1792. Children, born in Northampton: John, 1744; Abigail, 1746; Hollister, 1749; Sarah, 1752; Abner, mentioned below; Susan, 1758.

(V) Abner, son of John (2) Baker, was born in Northampton in 1754, died September 15, 1845. He was a soldier in the revolution and in later years a pensioner. The Massachusetts Revolutionary Rolls show that Abner Baker, of Hampshire county, served in Captain John Kirkland's company, Colonel Ruggles Woodbridge's regiment, from August 16 to November 29, 1777, reinforcing the northern army. Until 1803 he lived in Northampton, and then moved to Deerfield, Oneida county, New York, where he lived until 1805. He then moved to Loraine, Jefferson county, New York. In 1836, when he was eighty-two years old, he moved to Norwalk, Ohio, where he lived with his sons Timothy and Theodore. He married (first) August 20, 1781, Lois Waters, of Hebron, Connecticut, and she died April 8, 1830, aged sixty-eight years. He married (second) December 16, 1830, Mrs. Sophia Colyer, and she died in 1842. Children by first wife: Asenath, born July 5, 1782; Sereno, October 28, 1784; Timothy, 1787; Susan, November 27, 1789; Abner, September 17, 1791; Edward, August 29, 1794; Waters, July 27, 1796, died August 20, 1811; Artemus, 1798; Theodore, mentioned below; Nahum, February 28, 1803, died July 9, 1811; Wells, December 8, 1805; Lois, December 29, 1807.

(VI) Theodore, son of Abner Baker, was born April 26, 1801. He moved to Norwalk, Ohio, in 1819, and became a prominent man there. In October, 1862, he moved to Cleveland, Ohio, where with his son Homer he carried on a large tanning business. He married (first) March 8, 1827, Almira Morse, who died May 28, 1840. She was a daughter of Abner Morse, a soldier of the revolution. He married (second) February 2, 1841, Margaret Williams, who died August 6, 1864. Children by first wife: Asahel Morse, born May 29, 1828, married and had a son, John

Sherman Baker, of Tacoma, Washington; Henry, mentioned below; Daniel Waters, July 27, 1832; Theodore E., December 9, 1834; Abner, October 23, 1836; Homer, June 29, 1839. By second wife: Almira Amanda, born March 12, 1842; Edward Foster, August 25, 1844; Margaret Minerva, died October 3, 1847; Holland Williams, born September 6, 1851; Howard Malcolm, August 26, 1853.

(VII) Henry, son of Theodore Baker, was born at Norwalk, Ohio, July 7, 1830. He was for many years in the tannery business at Norwalk, Ohio, and later at Cleveland, and is now living at Gates Mill, Ohio, retired from active business. He married, December 4, 1851, Clarissa Maria Hall, born August 7, 1831, died July 24, 1892, daughter of Rev. Jeremiah and Clarissa (Ransom) Hall (see Hall). Among their children was Elbert Hall, mentioned below.

(VIII) Elbert Hall, son of Henry Baker, was born in Norwalk, Ohio, July 25, 1854. He attended the public schools of his native town. When he was eleven years old he moved with his parents to Cleveland, Ohio, and attended schools also in that city. From the age of sixteen to nineteen he lived in Kansas City, Missouri. His education was profitably supplemented by the study of English and American history under the instruction of his grandfather. In 1873 he returned to Cleveland and was employed for a time in a wholesale stove concern. From 1877 to 1882 he was on the business staff of the Cleveland Herald. In 1882 he became advertising manager of the Cleveland Leader and held that position for fifteen years. Since 1898 he has been general manager of the Cleveland Plain Dealer. He is now president of the American Newspaper Publishers' Association. Mr. Baker is active in charitable and religious work. He is a member of the Euclid Avenue Congregational Church and chairman of its board of trustees; a trustee of the Cleveland Young Men's Christian Association; trustee of the Schaufler Training School of Cleveland; trustee of the City Congregational Missionary Association of Cleveland. He is prominent in various business and public organizations; member of the Cleveland Chamber of Commerce in which he has served as a member of its board and as chairman of various important committees; president of the City Investment Company and the Commercial Building Company, of Cleveland, the business of these companies being the erection of commercial and office buildings in Cleveland, and a director of The Cleveland Life Insurance Company. He is also a member of the Union Club, the Cleveland Ath-

362 NEW ENGLAND.

letic Club, the Colonial Club, and the Chagrin Valley Hunt Club. He is something of a farmer as well as owns a fine herd of Guernsey cattle on his homestead at Gates Mill, Ohio. He is president of the Ohio Guernsey Association.

He married, June 1, 1876, Ida Anna Smith, born in Cleveland, July 11, 1854, daughter of Pardon Brownlow and Eliza Jane (Hovey) Smith. Eliza Jane Hovey was a daughter of Philetus Hovey, a native of New York state, descendant of the Hoveys of Essex county, Massachusetts, pioneers of the colony. Children:

1. Louise Hall, born in Cleveland, October 20, 1877; married Benjamin Hastings, of Cleveland. 2. Frank Smith, born in Cleveland, July 27, 1879; a newspaper man, formerly business manager of the *Cleveland Plain Dealer* and now publisher of the *Tribune*, Tacoma, Washington; married Gertrude Elizabeth Vilas; children: Elizabeth Vilas, born March 7, 1905; Mary Bartlett, born November 25, 1907; Elbert Hall, July 18, 1910. 3. Elbert Hall Jr., born at Cleveland, July 29, 1889, now a college student. 4. Alton Fletcher, born in Willoughby, Ohio, February 14, 1894, and now a student at Cornell University.

(The Hall Line).

Rev. Jeremiah Hall was born in Swanzey, New Hampshire. He attended the public schools there, was a student at Middlebury College and was graduated from the Newton Theological School in 1830. He was ordained in the Baptist ministry, September 28, 1830, at Townshend, Vermont. He went thence to a pastorate in Chittenden county, Vermont, continuing for two years, and then to East Bennington. In 1836 he accepted a call to Kalamazoo, Michigan, where he organized the First Baptist Church. In association with his father-in-law, Major Ransom, he organized the Michigan Huron Literary Institute and taught ancient languages there. Afterward this institute became Kalamazoo College. He was afterward pastor of the Baptist church at Akron, Ohio, and at Norwalk, Ohio, where he became also principal of the academy, which he developed into a prosperous institution. In 1852 he became pastor of the church at Granville, Ohio. He was elected president of Granville Baptist College, which was then in a failing condition, reorganized it, raised a substantial sum to put the college on a good financial basis and changed the name to Denison University. On account of ill health, after a long and honorable service as president, he resigned, lived for a time at Waverly, Iowa, with his son.

Afterward he was pastor of the Tabernacle Church at Kalamazoo.

He married (first) September 25, 1830, Clarissa Ransom (see Ransom V), born December 30, 1808, died at Kalamazoo, June 23, 1840. He married (second) ———— ————. He died at the home of his daughter, Mrs. Henry W. Chester, at Port Huron, Michigan, May 30, 1881. His first wife was a school teacher before her marriage. Children by first wife: 1. Clarissa Maria, born August 7, 1831, at Westford, died July 24, 1892; married, December 4, 1851, at Granville, Ohio, Henry Baker (see Baker VII). 2. Fletcher B., born September 26, 1834, at Kalamazoo, died young. 3. Francis M., born January 31, 1836; married, December 1, 1859, Sarah L. Higgins. 4. Sophia, October 25, 1838, died August 20, 1839. 5. J. Ransom, June 16, 1840. Child by second wife. Mrs. Chester, mentioned above.

(The Ransom Line).

(II) Joshua Ransom, son of Robert Ransom (q. v.), was born about 1663 in Sandwich, Massachusetts, and died after 1713, when he was living at Plympton, Massachusetts. He married (first) February 26, 1686, Mercy, daughter of John and Elishua Gifford. She died October 25, 1689, and he married (second) March 10, 1692, Susanna Garner, of Plymouth. She died at Halifax, Massachusetts, March 16, 1735. Children of first wife: Robert, mentioned below; Mary, born about 1688 at North Kingston. Children of second wife: John, married Martha Ripley; Sarah, married Francis Curtis; Joshua, married Mary Wrght.

(III) Robert (2), son of Joshua Ransom, was born in Wexford, Rhode Island, or vicinity, in 1687, died January 23, 1777. He settled in Colchester, Connecticut. He married Alice, daughter of James and Mary (Hubbell) Newton, granddaughter of Sergeant Richard Hubbell, of Fairfield. She moved to Colchester with her father. She was also a descendant of Richard Smith. Children, born at Colchester: John, November 13, 1709; Mary, August 30, 1711; James, March 13, 1713; Joshua, May 3, 1715; Robert, March 25, 1717; Alice, September 6, 1719; Newton, mentioned below; Peleg, September 20, 1724; Amos, February 17, 1727; Elizabeth, May 1, 1729; Amy, August 2, 1732.

(IV) Newton, son of Robert (2) Ransom, was born at Colchester, July 21, 1722, died at Halifax, Vermont, May 31, 1796. He lived at Shelburne Falls, Massachusetts, during his active life. He married, September 1, 1742, Sarah Jones, at Colchester. She died at Shelburne Falls, June 16, 1804. Six of their sons were soldiers in the revolution, and Newton was active in the patriot's cause. Children, born at Colchester: Robert, August 26, 1743; Ezekiel, mentioned below; Jabez, December 24, 1746; John, November 11, 1748; Elinor, June 22, 1750, died November 13, 1750; Roswell, December 8, 1751; Elisha, December 24, 1753; Hazel, January 3, 1756; Calvin, June 19, 1758; Luther, twin of Calvin; Ichabod, January 2, 1760; Newton, May 11, 1762; Ezekiel, October 1, 1763; Sally, April 13, 1767.

(V) Major Ezekiel Ransom, son of Newton Ransom, was born at Colchester, October 1, 1744, died November 1, 1838, at Kalamazoo, Michigan. He and his wife were buried in the lot of their son, Samuel H. Ransom, Mountain Home cemetery, at Kalamazoo. He served in the revolution, enlisting in a Vermont militia company under Captan Samuel Fletcher when he was only fourteen years of age. He was present in the expedition against Crown Point and in the battles of Bennington and Saratoga, serving until after the surrender of General Burgoyne, which he also saw. He returned to Shelburne Falls, enlisting in a short time with the Massachusetts troops, participating in the battle of Bunker Hill, continuing with other enlistments until the end of the war. He served for a time on the non-commissioned staff of General Washington, and fought in most of the battles of the Virginia campaign, also being present at the execution of Major John André. After the close of the war he again returned to Shelburne Falls where he lived for a number of years, moving then to Townshend, Windham county, Vermont, where he purchased a farm. He exchanged this farm, after some years, with his father-in-law, for a larger one near West Townshend, where he moved about 1800. In addition to running this farm, he also engaged in business as a blacksmith and shoemaker, carried on a saddle and harness shop, also tannery and tin shop. He sold his farm in 1825 to his son-in-law, John P. Marsh, and moved to East Townshend where he engaged in business as a general trader with the Boston market until 1835. He then went to Michigan where four of his children had settled, and located near or at Bronson, now Kalamazoo. His home there was situated at the southeast corner of Park and Academy streets, and he lived there the remainder of his life. Major Ransom was a member of the Baptist church, and with his son-in-law, Rev. Jeremiah Hall, and others, he was active in founding the Michigan and Huron Literary Institute, late Kalamazoo College. In ap-

pearance he was tall and muscular, with dark hair and eyes; the effects of his military experience were shown by his commanding appearance, and he was dignified in conversation, very liberal and charitable, and loved and respected by all who knew him.

He married, May 25, 1791, Lucinda Fletcher, at Townshend. She died September 30, 1850, at Kalamazoo. Children: Miranda, born at New Fane, Windham county, Vermont, September 6, 1792, married Elijah Ransom; Philinda, February 23, 1794, at Townshend, married Jonathan Allen; Fanny Jones, January 7, 1796, at Shelburne Falls, married John P. Marsh; Epaphroditus, March 24, 1798, at Shelburne Falls, married Almira C. Ransom; F. Fletcher, August 22, 1802, at Townshend, married Elizabeth Noyes; Roswell, November 21, 1803, at Townshend, married Wealthy L. Shafter; Alexis, July 21, 1805, at Townshend, married (first) Lois H. Stone, (second) Mrs. Nancy Brown; Sophia, February 15, 1807, at Townshend, married Amariah T. Prouty; Clarissa, December 30, 1808, at Townshend, married Rev. Jeremiah Hall, D. D. (see Hall); Samuel H., December 23, 1810, at Townshend, married Eleanor B. Goddard; Lucinda L., December 7, 1812, at Townshend, married Allen Goodridge; James W., August 8, 1816, at Townshend.

WARREN   Arthur Warren, the immigrant ancestor, emigrated to America before 1638 and located at Weymouth, Massachusetts. The earliest mention of his name in the Weymouth records is in 1638, and he is next mentioned in 1645 as one of the petitioners to the general court for a grant of the Narragansett lands. His name is fourth on the list of landowners, February, 1651-2, and it is evident that he owned considerable real estate. He was one of the substantial citizens of Weymouth, but he was not named among those who were admitted as freemen, and the records do not show any activity in public affairs. From this it is inferred that he was not in harmony with the religion of the Puritans. He died before 1663, in which year land was granted to "Widow Warren". He married, about 1638, Mary ————. Children, born at Weymouth: Arthur, November 17, 1639; Abigail, October 27, 1640; Jacob, mentioned below; Joseph, living in 1671; Fearnot, June, 1655.

(II) Jacob, son of Arthur Warren, was born at Weymouth, October 26, 1642, and died in Chelmsford, Massachusetts, before 1723. Prior to 1667 he removed from Weymouth to Chelmsford, and became at once active in town affairs. In 1667-8 he was fence viewer;

one of a committee for laying out land, 1673-87-88, 1709; tithingman, 1679-94-97; selectman, 1683; and surveyor of highways, 1686-87-90. March 16, 1691-2, he served as member of the "garrison in the West regiment, in Middlesex," at Chelmsford, under Lieutenant Ephraim Hildreth. December 12, 1677, he received a grant of land in Chelmsford, and this, together with other early grants made to the Warrens, was in that part of Chelmsford since known as Westford. In 1711 he was granted land on Thomas Henchman's right, and doubtless moved into the village of Chelmsford. He married there, June 21, 1667, Mary, daughter of Sergeant Richard and his first wife Sarah (———) Hildreth. Her father, Richard Hildreth, was born 1605, and was the founder of his family in Massachusetts. He was one of the petitioners for the incorporation of Woburn and Concord, afterwards removed to Cambridge, where he was made freeman, 1643. In 1653 he was one of the original grantees of Chelmsford, where he became a large landholder and died in 1688. He married Sarah ———, who died in Cambridge, June 15, 1644, and (second) Elizabeth ———, who died at Malden, August 3, 1693. Mary Hildreth Warren died at Chelmsford, December 17, 1730. Children, born at Chelmsford; Jacob, about 1668; Joseph, of whom further; Elizabeth, March 3, 1674; Ephraim, June 24, 1680.

(III) Deacon Joseph Warren, son of Jacob Warren, was born at Chelmsford, October 25, 1670, and died there April 16, 1740. In 1699 he was chosen constable, and in 1718 tithingman. In 1718 he was one of the contributors towards the building of a school-house. He was also deacon of the church at Chelmsford. Three years after his marriage he received by deed of gift from his wife's kinsman, Thomas Henchman, the property on the Boston road in Chelmsford, upon which still stands the family homestead. It has been inherited by the eldest son of each generation, and has had numerous additions and extensions, but still retains the old kitchen with its large fireplace and ovens, and the old sitting room with its wainscoat of the colonial period. Many interesting traditions attach to it. Among them is one which relates that the patriot troops who marched to Lexington and Concord in April, 1775, mustered at the "Warren Farm." Deacon Joseph Warren married, March 11, 1696, Ruth, youngest daughter of Sergeant Thomas Wheeler, son of Lieutenant Thomas Wheeler. Children, born in Chelmsford: Elizabeth, December 9, 1696; Joseph, of whom further; Jacob, December 13, 1700; Thomas, March 5, 1704; Ephraim, December 6, 1707;

Ruth, August 23, 1711; John, July 25, 1714.

(IV) Joseph (2), son of Deacon Joseph (1) Warren, was born at Chelmsford, April 5, 1699, and died there September 28, 1769. In 1723 he was surveyor of highways; in 1726, tithingman; in 1741-42-43, assessor and selectman. In 1724, during the fourth Indian war, commonly known as the "Three years' war", or "Lovewell's war", from John Lovewell, a well-known scout, he was a member of one of the companies, equipped with snowshoes, firearms, etc., and ready at a minute's notice to go on scouting parties in pursuit of the Indians. His company was under the command of Captain Robert Richardson. He married, July 18, 1721-2, Tabitha, daughter of Benjamin and Sarah (Howard) Parker, of Chelmsford, born February, 1701, buried March 1, 1750. Her father, Benjamin, was the son of Jacob Parker, the immigrant ancestor, and his wife Sarah. Her mother, Sarah Howard, was daughter of Nathaniel and Sarah (Willard) Howard. Children, born at Chelmsford: Joseph, of whom further; Tabitha, June 10, 1727; Benjamin, August 30, 1729; Sarah, July 30, 1733; Mary, April 13, 1736; Ruth, September 4, 1741.

(V) Captain Joseph (3) Warren, son of Joseph (2) Warren, was born at Chelmsford, August 24, 1724, and died there March 17, 1792. In 1754 he was tithingman, and in 1761-70-71-73 selectman. In 1765 he bought land at Westminster, Massachusetts, and in 1773 part of another lot there which afterwards became the estate of his son Jeduthan. He married, April 15, 1752, Joanna, daughter of Josiah and Joanna (Spalding) Fletcher, born March 10, 1726, died March 3, 1763. Her father, Josiah Fletcher (4), was the son of Lieutenant William (3), the son of Ensign William (2), the son of Robert Fletcher (1), the immigrant. After her death he married (second) February 23, 1769, Sarah, daughter of Joseph and Sarah Osgood, of Billerica, born January 31, 1749-50, died October 7, 1815. Children, born at Chelmsford: Joanna, April 6, 1753; Jeduthan, mentioned below; Jeremiah, February 23, 1763; Child of the second wife: Joseph, December 7, 1769.

(VI) Jeduthan, son of Captain Joseph (3) Warren, was born in Chelmsford, November 24, 1756, and died at Westminster, October 28, 1841. He was a soldier in the revolution, from September 30, 1777, until November 8th of the same year, in Captain Ford's company, Colonel Jonathan Reed's regiment. About 1779 he removed to Westminster, where he lived on the lands formerly purchased by his father, of which he eventually became the owner. Upon this land he built the house, still standing, which is well known as the "Warren Farmstead." He is described by a contemporary as a "fine old gentleman * * * with marked peculiarities." His family were all brought up in the strictest Calvinistic faith. He married, July 22, 1779, Joanna, daughter of Simeon and Joanna (Thorndike) Moors, Simeon (2) Lieutenant Joseph (1). She was born November 17, 1761, and died June 24, 1836. Children, born at Westminster: Polly, November 30, 1780; Joseph, December 17, 1781; Jesse, mentioned below; Ezra, February 28, 1786, died January 21, 1796; Jeduthan, March 5, 1788; Micaiah, born September 23, 1790; Simeon, May 27, 1794; Joanna, October 15, 1796; Ezra, October 9, 1799.

(VII) Jesse, son of Jeduthan Warren, was born at Westminster, January 23, 1784, and died at Fitchburg, Massachusetts, June 18, 1854. He lived during his early life in his native town, where he established himself as an iron-worker. In 1809 he removed to West Dedham, Massachusetts, where he carried on the same trade until 1821. He then removed to a large farm out of the village, on Fox Hill, where he built a commodious house with farm buildings and workshops. Here he carried on an extensive business in wrought iron and the manufacture of ploughs. He was one of the earliest makers of ploughs made of cast iron, if not the inventor, and obtained castings from his own patterns at Alger's furnace in South Boston. In August, 1829, he removed to Peru, Bennington county, Vermont, at the top of the pass over Mount Bromley. At the summit of this pass was a tavern which he moved down the mountain side and set up on the new road, on the banks of a small stream. Near it he built a plough-shop and foundry. In 1837 he removed to Springfield, Vermont, and in company with his son Joseph bought a foundry which was burned to the ground the year following. He then built another foundry below the town, and manufactured there agricultural implements, among them the sidehill or swivel plough of which he was the inventor. This is still used in hill regions all over the United States and in foreign lands. The original drawings are now in the possession of the present owner of the foundry, who states that there has been no improvement on the patent. He also invented and manufactured the cast-iron hub for wagon wheels. During the winter of 1839-40 he removed to Keeseville, New York, and thence in 1841 to Brandon, Vermont. In 1844 he settled at Glens Falls, New York, where he remained until 1851. He then retired from active business and removed to Fitchburg, Massachu-

setts, where he spent the last years of his life. He married, at Westminster, September 20, 1807, Betsey, daughter of Oliver and Mary (Pierce) Jackson, of that town, born there, August 5, 1790, died October 24, 1876. Oliver (6), Josiah (5), Isaac (4), Edward (3), Sebas (2), Edward (1). Children, the eldest born at Westminster, the two youngest at Peru, and the others at Dedham: Joseph, December 15, 1808, died February 13, 1809; Mary Ann, born December 18, 1809; Joseph, February 3, 1812; Betsey, February 17, 1814; Elvira, February 10, 1817; John, September 11, 1819; Samuel Mills, February 12, 1822; Cyrus Moors, mentioned below; Herbert Marshall, January 16, 1827; Harriet Newell, January 9, 1830; Ebenezer Burgess, April 18, 1833.

(VIII) Cyrus Moors, son of Jesse Warren, was born at Fox Hill, Dedham, January 15, 1824, and died at Manchester, Vermont, August 13, 1891. When he was five years old his father removed to Peru, Vermont, which was then in the midst of a wilderness. When he was thirteen his father again removed, this time to Springfield, Vermont. He received during his early years only such schooling as the locality afforded, and for a number of years taught school during the winters and worked as a farmer in the summers. In 1847 he became associated with his brother, Samuel M. Warren, in the manufacture of tarred sheathing for roofs, at Cincinnati, Ohio. This business was so successful that other brothers were called in to help carry it on, and in 1852 Cyrus was enabled to devote himself entirely to study. In 1852 he removed to Cambridge, Massachusetts, with his family, and entered the Lawrence Scientific School, in the departments of zoology and chemistry. His first meeting with Agassiz at this time was an important event in his life. In 1855 he took the degree of S. B. with high distinction, and immediately after was elected an honorary member of the Phi Beta Kappa, on the nomination of Benjamin Pierce, seconded by Louis Agassiz. He was the first graduate of the Lawrence Scientific School upon whom this honor was conferred. Soon after he took his family to Europe and studied extensively there, first at Paris, then at Heidelberg under Bunsen, at Freiberg in Saxony, at Munich under Liebig, at Berlin under Heinrich Rose, and at London. His brothers, meantime, in their manufacture of tarred sheathing, had obtained important results and immense profits by the use of the coal-tar of gas-works at a time when this material was wholly without commercial value. Long before anyone suspected that coal-tar and the various other substances obtainable from it could be put to highly important uses in the arts, the Warren brothers had control of all the tar produced in New York and several other large cities, and when aniline dyes came into use and a great demand arose for those portions of coal-tar naphtha from which those dyes were made, they were peculiarly situated for producing the naphtha. Cyrus turned his attention to the question as to how to obtain these volatile products, and in 1864 published in the "Memoirs of the American Academy of Arts and Sciences" his process of "Fractional condensation," which was widely copied into scientific journals. One important result of his researches was the unexpected discovery that the more volatile portions of Pennsylvania petroleum contained two distinct series of hydrocarbons, the complete separation of which had been impossible before the invention of his method of fractioning. From 1863 to 1866 he had a thoroughly equipped private laboratory in Boston and gave himself up wholly to research. He then removed to Brookline, where he established another laboratory. He was appointed to the professorship of organic chemistry at the Massachusetts Institute of Technology, but resigned after a year or two on account of lack of time. Later, when his brothers turned their attention to the manufacture of refined asphalt, he gave them valuable aid in this direction. In 1888 he broke down from overwork and had a paralytic shock from which he never recovered. In recognition of his many years of association with Harvard University and the American Academy of Arts and Sciences of Boston, he left them each legacies to be used for the promotion of chemical research or the advancement of chemical science.

He married, at Cincinnati, Ohio, September 12, 1849, Lydia, daughter of Ogden and Lydia (Ludlow) Ross, born at Cincinnati, January 31, 1826. Her father came from a Scotch family and went west from New Jersey. Children: Emma Ross, born at Buffalo, New York, November 1, 1851; Charles Ross, born at Cambridge, Massachusetts, April 26, 1854; William Ross, born at London, England, October 9, 1860; Annie Ross, born at Newton, February 11, 1862; Edward Ross, born at Boston, February 14, 1864; Mary Ross, born at "Walnut Place," Brookline, January 9, 1867; Gertrude Ross, born at "Walnut Place," Brookline, June 8, 1869, died March 9, 1877.

(VII) Jonathan C. Thrall, son THRALL of Chauncy Thrall (q. v.), was born in West Rutland, Vermont, died in Rutland, 1852. For many years

he had a hotel in West Rutland, until it was burned. He then moved to Rutland, where he purchased a farm situated where the Holmes Machine Company's plant is now. After a time he sold this farm and settled on the place where George C. Thrall now lives, and there he resided the remainder of his life. He married (first) in 1821, Betsey Gates, (second) Mary Townsend. Children of first wife: Emeroy, born 1822, died May 3, 1886, married John C. Batcheller; Roseman, died young; Gates, died young. Children of second wife: Samuel T., died young; Chauncey T., died January 18, 1863, in Gallatin Hospital, Tennessee, during the civil war; went to Illinois when twenty-one years of age and enlisted in the Illinois Regiment; Lydia T., died aged sixteen; Samuel C., died young; George Calvin, mentioned below; David H., died young; Frank C., died young.

(VIII) George Calvin, son of Jonathan C. Thrall, was born in Rutland, Vermont, June 30, 1841. He attended the public schools of his native town and was graduated from the Rutland high school. During his youth he assisted his father on the homestead; he has always followed farming and lived in Rutland, in 1890 building his present residence on the homestead. Besides his farm he owns other valuable real estate in Rutland. He has taken an active part in municipal affairs, and has represented his ward in the board of aldermen. In national politics he is a Prohibitionist and he has been a delegate to various national conventions of the Prohibition party. He is an active and prominent member of the Methodist Episcopal church and has held in succession the various offices of the church.

He married, February 2, 1865, Lura B. Jefferson, of Des Plaines, Illinois, born there, daughter of Luther and Betsey (Smith) Jefferson. Children, born in Rutland: Benjamin W., January 16, 1866, died September 8, 1867; Guy B., July 21, 1868, died October 6, 1869; Jay C., April 12, 1870, died August 13, 1871; Fred B., February 24, 1872, died January 12, 1875; Alice J., June 9, 1874, died July 7, 1876; Rollin C., July 24, 1876, died September 26, 1877; John C., January 1, 1878, died March 15, 1882; Mary E., August 22, 1880, died April 19, 1889.

Dr. Joshua Poore, a descendant POORE of Daniel Poor, of Andover, Massachusetts, probably of the fifth generation, was born in 1750 in Massachusetts, and died at Stratford, Connecticut, in 1792. His gravestone gives his age as forty-two years. He settled in Stratford when a young man, and was a leading medical prac- •

titioner of that city. He married, in November, 1771, Rebecca, daughter of Thomas Lewis. Children, born at Stratford: Sally, January 8, 1779; Thomas, March 25, 1781; Daniel; Nancy, December 21, 1786; David, mentioned below; Caty, July 8, 1789, died August 18, 1863; Charles, died in the East Indies.

(II) David, son of Dr. Joshua Poore, was born at Stratford, Connecticut, in 1787, died in 1852. He was a merchant in New York City. He married Anna Taylor, born in New York City in 1800, daughter of George W. Talbot, a well known New York merchant, engaged in the China trade, and granddaughter of Commodore Silas Talbot, mentioned below. Among the children of Mr. and Mrs. Poore was Charles Talbot, mentioned below.

(III) Dr. Charles Talbot Poore, son of David Poore, was born in New York City, October 14, 1839, died suddenly at his home in New York City, April 4, 1911. He was educated at Dr. Dudley's School at Northampton, Massachusetts, and in 1857 entered Williams College, graduating in the class of 1861 with a Baccalaureate degree, and in 1891 this institution conferred upon him the honorary degree of Master of Arts. He studied medicine with Dr. Henry B. Sands, of New York City. He later became a student at the College of Physicians and Surgeons, and graduated from the medical department in 1866. After his graduation entered upon the practice of his profession in the city of New York, and it soon became evident, both to the medical fraternity and to his patients, that he was a man of ability, skill and tireless energy, which, coupled with his high character, would win for him merited distinction. From August, 1865, to 1867, he served in the surgical department of the New York Hospital; in 1872 was appointed surgeon to St. Mary's Free Hospital for Children, and served in that capacity up to his death; was consulting surgeon to the Hospital for the Ruptured and Crippled; was connected with St. Luke's Home, one of the board of managers, and associate in surgery in the College of Physicians and Surgeons. He frequently contributed to the medical journals, notably on the subject of diseases of the joints. He has also published "Osteotomy and Osteoclasis for Deformities of the Lower Extremities" (Appleton, 1886), and contributed the article on "Osteology" in Reference Handbook on Medical Sciences (William Wood & Company, 1887), and the article on "Diseases of the Major Articulations" in the Encyclopedia of Diseases of Children (Lippincott, 1890). Dr. Poore was a member of the faculty of the College of Physicians and Surgeons, the New York State Medical Society, County Medical Society, Union League Club of New York, of which he was one of the officers, the Century Association, New England Society, the St. Nicholas Society.

Dr. Poore married, October 18, 1892, Helen Talbot, born in February, 1849, daughter of Charles N. Talbot, of New York.

Commodore Silas Talbot, above mentioned, was born in Dighton, Bristol county, Massachusetts, in 1751, died in New York City, June 30, 1813, buried in Trinity churchyard, New York. He was the son of Benjamin and Zipporah (Allen) Talbot, the former of whom was a prosperous farmer of Bristol county. In early life Silas Talbot went to sea on coasting vessels. He became a merchant in Providence, Rhode Island; joined the continental army as lieutenant; was commissioned captain, June 28, 1775; took part in the siege of Boston, and accompanied the troops to New York. He proposed an attack on the British fleet in the North river, by means of a fire ship, and ascending the Hudson river in a ship filled with combustibles, made a night attack, succeeding in partly destroying the British ship "Asia", after which, although severely burned he escaped to the Jersey shore. On October 10, 1777, congress tendered him a vote of thanks, and promoted him to the rank of major. He took part in the defense of Mud Island, in the Delaware river, and was badly wounded, and on his return to duty joined the army under Sullivan, participating in the battle of Rhode Island, in August, 1778. On October 29, 1778, in command of a small sloop with two guns and sixty men, he planned and executed the capture of the British ship "Pigot", of two hundred guns, anchored off Newport for which congress awarded him a vote of thanks and promoted him lieutenant-colonel. In command of the "Pigot" and "Argo" he was detailed to guard the coast from Long Island to Nantucket. He captured the British schooner "Lively"; two letters of marque brigs from the West Indies; the privateer "King George", the sloop "Adventure", and the brig "Elliot", and later captured the "Dragon", a large armed vessel, after a severe battle of four hours. He was commissioned captain and assigned to the privateer "George Washington", and, falling in with a British fleet, he was captured, and confined in the prison ship "Jersey", and in the "Old Sugar House", New York City. In November, 1780, he was taken to England on the "Yarmouth," being kept in close confinement and suffering great cruelties. He was finally exchanged in 1781, and was sent to Cherbourg, France, where he sailed for

America in a French brig. This brig was captured by the British privateer "Jupiter," but Captain Talbot was transferred to an English brig and taken to New York. He removed to Philadelphia and later to New York; and was a representative from that state in the third congress, 1793-95. Upon the reorganization of the United States navy he was commissioned captain, May 11, 1789, and commanded a squadron in the West Indies during the war with France. He planned the expedition under Lieutenant Isaac Hull, to cut out the French privateer "Sandwich" at Port Platte, Santo Domingo. He resigned his commission, September 21, 1801.

He was twice married: (first) in 1772 to Anna, daughter of Colonel Barzillai Richmond, and (second) to Rebecca, daughter of Morris Morris, and granddaughter of Governor Mifflin.

(II) Benjamin Spaulding,
SPAULDING   son of Edward Spaulding
(q. v.), was born in Braintree, Massachusetts, April 7, 1645, died before 1708. He purchased a large piece of land in what is now Brooklyn, then in the north part of Canterbury, Windham county, Connecticut. His son Edward received the family homestead, and Edward left it to his son Ebenezer. Benjamin Spaulding married, October 30, 1668, Olive, daughter of Henry and Olive Farwell, of Concord and of Chelmsford, Massachusetts. Henry Farwell was made a freeman in 1689. Children of Benjamin and Olive Spaulding: Sarah, born January 4, 1670; Edward, mentioned below; Benjamin, July 6, 1685; Elizabeth, married Ephraim Wheeler; and Mary, who married Isaac Morgan.

(III) Edward (2), son of Benjamin Spaulding, was born June 18, 1672, died November 29, 1740. The Canterbury, Connecticut, record says he died in 1739. According to Miss E. D. Learned, in "Sketches of Windham County", Edward Spaulding was the third settler within the present boundary of Brooklyn, and he bought land north of the Canterbury bounds, at the foot of Tadwick Hill, in 1707. He was on the first committee of the Religious Society, organized in 1731, the committee consisting of three members. He married Mary Adams, who died September 20, 1754, aged seventy-eight years. Children, first born in Chelmsford, others in Canterbury, where he lived : Benjamin, mentioned below; Elizabeth, born August 15, 1698; Ephraim, April 3, 1700; Jonathan, April 15, 1704; Ezekiel, September 8, 1706; Ruth, September 28, 1710; Abigail, March 10, 1713; Ebenezer,

June 24, 1717; Thomas, August 7, 1719; John, December 1, 1721.

(IV) Benjamin (2), son of Edward (2) Spaulding, was born July 20, 1696, in Chelmsford, and lived in Plainfield, Connecticut. He married (first) March 7, 1719-20, Abigail, daughter of Ebenezer Wright, of Chelmsford, and she died January 6, 1727. He married (second) October 30, 1727, Deborah Wheeler. Children, born in Plainfield. Benjamin, mentioned below ; Abigail, born February 20, 1723; Olive, January 25, 1725; Ebenezer, December 8, 1726, died March 26, 1727; Asa, March 26, 1729; Oliver, January 17, 1731, died February 24, 1731; Mary, January 17, 1732; Sarah, December 5, 1733; David, March 27, 1736; Alice, married Isaac Morgan.

(V) Benjamin (3), son of Benjamin (2) Spaulding, was born in Plainfield, Connecticut, February 29, 1720, died March 19, 1807, at Moretown, Vermont. He was a member of the Society of Friends, and his wife was a Congregationalist in religion. They lived in Plainfield, and in' Sharon, Vermont, finally settling in Moretown, Vermont. He served in the revolution. He married, January 29, 1756, Rachel Crary, sometimes spelled McCrary and also Crery. She was daughter of John and Prudence Crary. John Crary was a probate court judge in Connecticut. Rachel Crary was born in Plainfield, January 20, 1729, died at Saranac, New York, July 14, 1824. Children, first six born in Plainfield: Wright, February 5, 1757; David, May 23, 1759, died August 15, 1759; Ellen, August 25 or 28, 1760; Infant son, June, 1762, died 1762; Zilpah, November 9, 1763, or November 6. 1764; Royal, mentioned below; Abigail, February 2, 1769; Rachel, March 22, 1771; Versal, July 15, 1773, or August 15, 1773; Levi, August 15, 1777.

(VI) Royal, son of Benjamin (3) Spaulding, was born in Plainfield, Connecticut, August 23, 1766, died in Moretown, Vermont, March 6, 1813. He married, August 19, 1789, Lucy Benton, born February 20, 1771, died August 8, 1836. Children: Wealthy Parkhurst, born February 21, 1791; Olive, October 28, 1793; Benjamin Harvey, May 11, 1797; Newell Stevens, December 3, 1799; Nathan Benton, March 24, 1802; John Rogers, mentioned below; Lucy, April 15, 1806, died January 13, 1811; Sibyl, March 22, 1809, died March 31, 1809; Azel Parkhurst, June 27, 1810, died March 1, 1813; Chastina Parkhurst, August 20, 1812.

(VII) John Rogers, son of Royal Spaulding, was born in Saranac, New York, June 24, 1804, the first white child born there, and died in Rutland, Vermont, March 22, 1879.

He was a tanner by trade, and lived in Waitsfield, Vermont, and later in Castleton, Vermont, moving from there to Rutland, Vermont, in 1859. He was a charter member of Lee Lodge, Free and Accepted Masons, of Castleton, under whose auspices he was buried at Rutland. In politics he was a strong Republican and an Abolitionist. He married Aveline Waite, born in Waitsfield, Vermont, September 10, 1810, died in Rutland, May 17, 1885, daughter of Judge Lynde and Lois Waite, of Waitsfield. Children. 1. Emily Waite, born May 3, 1831, died January 31, 1908; married Dr. Charles G. Nichols, of Castleton. 2. Richard Marvin, mentioned below. 3. Courtland, July 19, 1837, died November 23, 1858. 4. Lois Waite, January 24, 1840, died September 14, 1904. 5. Celia Etta, July 14, 1841, died January 14, 1898; married (first) Francis Fenn, (second) Amos C. Bates. 6. Aveline, October 13, 1844; married, September 6, 1871, Orlando Worcester, who died February 24, 1906; son Richard, born April 20, 1873. 7. Salome Redfield, January 11, 1850; married George Verder, deceased. 8. John, August 15, 1853, lives in Rutland.

(VIII) Richard Marvin, son of John Rogers Spaulding, was born in Waitsfield, Washington county, Vermont, May 15, 1835, died at Rutland, Vermont, February 15, 1903. He received his early education in the public schools. When a young man he engaged in the lumber business and became prominent and successful as a manufacturer of lumber and as a contractor, and for many years he was one of the leaders in his line of business in this section. He employed a large force of men and many horses, owned much timber land and had saw mills in various parts of the state. In politics he was a Republican, and in religion a Methodist. He married, December 31, 1857, Mary Ann Hopkins, born in Hampton, New York, daughter of Thomas and Alice (Burns) Hopkins. Children: 1. Alice, born September 19, 1860; married Lee S. Houghton, of Rutland, and had one daughter, Mary Reese, born April 14, 1891. 2. William Hopkins, mentioned below. 3. Hattie May, May 15, 1863, died August 4, 1864. 4. Mamie Gertrude, February 19, 1865, died May 14, 1870. 5. Hattie Gertrude, April 20, 1868, died in September, 1868. 6. George W., March 19, 1872.

(IX) William Hopkins, son of Richard Marvin Spaulding, was born in Hydeville, Vermont, June 27, 1861. He came to Rutland, Vermont, with his parents when he was two years old and has made his home there since. He attended the Rutland public schools, and began his career as clerk in the hardware store of W. C. Landon. When Mr. Landon died, the business was continued by a firm composed of his son, Charles H. Landon, and Mr. Spaulding and the old name of W. C. Landon & Company retained. The firm deals extensively in all kinds of hardware and agricultural implements. In addition to the original business of the concern, the firm maintains a large and finely equipped garage and represents several of the leading automobile manufacturers. Mr. Spaulding is one of the most enterprising and prominent business men in Rutland. He takes a keen interest in public affairs and has served the city as license commissioner. He is a director of the Killington Bank of Rutland. He is a charter member of Rutland Lodge, Benevolent and Protective Order of Elks, of Rutland, also a member of Knights of Pythias.

He married, March, 1887, Bertha Brock, of Springfield, Vermont, daughter of Samuel A. and Lucy (Taylor) Brock. They have one child, Richard Brock, born March 18, 1894.

HILLIARD William Hilliard, immigrant ancestor, was born in 1642, died January 24, 1714. He was a cooper by trade and lived in Little Compton, Rhode Island. His will was dated December 15, 1713, and proved February 1, 1714, his wife Deborah being administratrix. His widow's will was dated January 23, 1717, and proved March 3, 1718, son David executor. William Hilliard married Deborah ———, born in 1652, died February 15, 1718. Children: David, mentioned below; Deborah, born in 1685; Esther; Mary, April 3, 1687; Abigail, July 12, 1690; Sarah, June 28, 1692; Jonathan, November 8, 1696.

(II) Captain David Hilliard, son of William Hilliard, was born in 1677, died January 11, 1749. He lived in Little Compton, Rhode Island, and was called captain at the time of his death. His will was dated August 1, 1748, proved February 7, 1749, his wife Susanna being executrix. He married (first) July 13, 1699, Joanna Andros, who died April 14, 1716. He married (second) Susanna Luther, born in 1686, died April 6, 1777. Children by first wife: Deborah, born April 4, 1700; Lydia, October 4, 1702; William, October 28, 1703; Priscilla, November 2, 1705; John, November 17, 1707, died July 30, 1727. Born at Stonington: Deborah, April 8, 1708; Oliver, November 28, 1709; Joseph, August 12, 1711; Dorothy, May 24, 1713; Benoni, April 12, 1716. Children by second wife, born at Stonington or Little Compton: Mary, born June 23, 1718, died August 8, 1740; Joshua,

October 27, 1719; Hannah, October 11, 1721; Samuel, March 19, 1723, died August 6, 1741; David, September 21, 1726; John, mentioned below; Susanna, June 9, 1730; Abigail, October 11, 1732. From 1708 to 1717 the family resided at Stonington, where the parents were admitted to the church, April 4, 1708, and from which they were dismissed to Little Compton, August 16, 1717.

(III) John, son of Captain David Hilliard, was born in Stonington or Little Compton, March 12, 1729, died in Danby, Vermont, in 1793. He came to Vermont when a young man, located first at Chittendon and later at Danby, where he lived until his death. He married, May 27, 1753, Elizabeth Smith, of Norwich, Connecticut, born in 1734, died in 1791, daughter of Josiah Smith. Children: Azariah, born May 22, 1754, died in 1783; Joshua, born January 1, 1757, a soldier in the revolution; Daniel, January 31, 1759; Edna and Miner, twins, born April 29, 1764.

(IV) Miner, son of John Hilliard, was born in Connecticut, April 29, 1764, died in Danby, Vermont, February 28, 1846. He was a soldier in the revolution and drew a pension in later life, $36.19 a year. He was a captain in the Vermont militia after the war. He was fond of athletics and a skillful ball player under the old style of game. He was an upright and honored citizen, holding a high place in the esteem of his townsmen. He married Abigail Hill. Children: Azariah, mentioned below; Dimmis, born 1792, married Israel Palmer; Matilda, 1795, married John Miller; Isaac, 1797; Minerva, 1800, married ———— Allen; Melinda, 1803, married Curtis Youngs; Sally, 1806, married Samuel Stannard; Edna, 1808, married ———— Wilbur; Elizabeth, 1814, married Calvin Gifford.

(V) Azariah, son of Miner Hilliard, was born at Danby, Vermont, 1790, died in 1857. He was a farmer in Danby all his life. He married Mercy Harrington. Children: Miner, born 1815; John Harrington, mentioned below; Wyman, died young; Azariah, born 1823, died 1872; Alphonso, 1825, died 1864; Amanda, married Hiram Kelly; Dimmie, 1833, married Charles Phelps and lives at Dorset, Vermont; Maria, married A. B. Herrick, of Danby.

(VI) John Harrington, son of Azariah Hilliard, was born at Danby, Vermont, August 5, 1817, died November 5, 1895. He was educated in the public schools of his native town, lived and died there. He owned more than a dozen farms, comprising several hundred acres. Like his father and grandfather he was a farmer all his active life. In politics he was a Democrat and keenly interested in

town affairs. He married Mary Ann Smith, born at Bennington, Vermont, in 1823, died in 1900, daughter of William and Ruth (Bushnell) Smith. Children: Child, died in infancy; Wyman, born May 5, 1849, died December 13, 1896; John F., mentioned below; Smith, born October 26, 1855, lives in Spokane, Washington; Merritt B., November 13, 1857, died February 4, 1890; Alphonzo, May 28, 1865, lives in North Dakota.

(VII) John Franklin, son of John Harrington Hilliard, was born at Danby, Vermont, January 31, 1852. He attended the public schools of his native town and lived there until he was twenty-five years old. For fourteen years he lived at Dorset, Vermont, and for twelve years at Manchester. In 1904 he came to Rutland and he has made his home there since that time. He was an extensive farmer, having three large farms until he retired upon removing to Rutland. He married October 17, 1877, Hattie Elizabeth, daughter of Charles T. and Lucinda C. (Bucklin) Read, of Castleton, Vermont. Children: John Read, born December 13, 1878, graduate of Burr & Burton School of Manchester, a teacher and educator, now of Hartford, Connecticut; Carrie, born January 28, 1880, died November 2, 1901; Sarah Elizabeth, August 4, 1883; Janey Mary, April 5, 1887. The family attends the Congregational church.

SMITH John Smith, descendant of an early colonial family, was born in 1760, probably in Ware, Massachusetts, died October 2, 1840, at Clarendon, Vermont. He was a soldier in the revolution in Massachusetts, and after the war settled at Clarendon, where he was one of the pioneers. He married, in 1785, Dolly Crary, born March 15, 1767, died in August, 1846. It is thought that she was born in Connecticut. Children: Isaac, born April 6, 1788, died June 19, 1853; John, March 20, 1790, died October 2, 1840; Lemuel, mentioned below; Lyman, February 1, 1794, died April 17, 1796; Nathaniel, April 13, 1796, died December 16, 1878; Orlin, January 24, 1798; Dolly, March 31, 1800, died July 28, 1825; Nathan, September 6, 1802; Julia, June 14, 1805; Sally, June 10, 1806; Oliver, November 12, 1808, died March 26, 1848; Spencer, February 6, 1811; Alvira, August 16, 1813; Aurick, April 15, 1817.

(II) Lemuel, son of John Smith, was born in East Clarendon, Vermont, April 18, 1792, died there July 8, 1859. He was educated in the public schools of his native town. He followed farming in East Clarendon all his active life, and was a well-to-do and useful

John F. Hilliard

citizen. He married Azubah Parker, who died July 3, 1861, aged seventy-two years. Children, born at Clarendon: Hiram, died May 1, 1887, aged seventy-five years; Perry; Luther; Lemuel; Austin; Daniel; Willard G., mentioned below; Elias; Harriet, married Freedom Bailey; Olive, married Josiah Crapo.

(III) Willard G., son of Lemuel Smith, was born in Clarendon, Vermont, in 1824, died in Rutland, August 2, 1893. He was educated in the district schools of his native town, and followed farming in the eastern part of the town. After his wife died his family was parted. After spending two years in Virginia, he returned to his native town and bought the farm which he had sold before leaving town. He continued on the homestead for many years. He had an excellent farm of one hundred and fifty acres. Owing to ill health he retired some years before he died and spent his last years in the family of his son at Rutland, Vermont. In politics he was a Republican. He married Lydia Wyman Crapo, of Charlestown, Massachusetts, born April 14, 1826, died at Clarendon, August 10, 1866, daughter of John Crapo. Children: 1. Luella, born August 29, 1848, died December 23, 1881; married Oscar Potter. 2. Luna, born in 1850, died June 6, 1874; married Fitch Warner. 3. Elliott W., mentioned below. 4. Fred Grant, mentioned below.

(IV) Elliott Willard, son of Willard G. Smith, was born at Shrewsbury, Vermont, May 15, 1851. When he was two years old he came with his parents to Clarendon, Vermont, and he received his early education there in the public schools. During his boyhood he assisted his father on the homestead and after leaving school worked on the farm for ten years. He then conducted a farm at Shrewsbury for ten years. In 1888 he came to Rutland, where he has resided ever since. He learned the trade of mason and has been for many years a contractor and mason in Rutland, having many large contracts and possessing a reputation for good work and upright business methods, and he is one of the leading builders of the city. He is interested in public affairs and while living in Clarendon held various offices of trust and honor. In politics he is a Republican. He married, January 25, 1871, Mary E. Aldrich, of Shrewsbury, Vermont, daughter of Truman and Rebecca D. (Kneedham) Aldrich, and granddaughter of Jonah Aldrich. Children: 1. Etta Lydia, born January 26, 1872; married George Plumly (now deceased) and had three children: Harold Ashton, Rena May and Rheta Bell, twins. 2. Lola Mary,

born May 11, 1876; married Edgar Knight, of Rutland, and has one son, Perry Leroy.

(IV) Fred Grant, son of Willard G. Smith, and brother of Elliott Willard Smith, was born in Clarendon, Vermont, September 10, 1862. He attended the public schools of his native town. When a boy he worked on his father's farm; he came to Rutland, when a young man, and learned the trade of carpenter. In 1889 he engaged in business as a contractor and builder, and continued alone in this business until 1902. From 1902 to 1906 he was superintendent for the firm of Chaffee's Sons, lumber dealers, and since 1906 one of the directors, president and general manager of the Chaffee Lumber Company, which was incorporated in the latter named year. To the interests of this business he has devoted himself assiduously. He is also a director of the Chittenden Lumber Company, and one of the prominent business men of Rutland. He is a member of Vermont Lodge, Knights of Pythias, of Rutland. He married, 1886, Mattie Crossman, of Clarendon, born in Clarendon, daughter of Washington Russ and Martha (Howard) Crossman. Children: Burton F., born September 20, 1889; Warren E., May 25, 1891; Earl B., April 19, 1899.

———————

SEAVER (III) Shubael (2) Seaver, son of Shubael (1) Seaver (q. v.), was born October 10, 1679, in Roxbury, Massachusetts. His will was proved January 14, 1757. He married, June 12, 1704, Abigail Twelves. Children: Shubael, mentioned below; Joseph, born January 29, 1706; Peter, April 15, 1709; David, October 19, 1711, died before July 25, 1755; Abigail, twin of David; Sarah, June 26, 1715; Ebenezer, August 1, 1720, died February 14, 1726-27.

(IV) Shubael (3), son of Shubael (2) Seaver, was born April 25, 1705. He married, July 4, 1734, Mary Rogers, of Boston. He lived in Framingham, Massachusetts. Children: Abigail, born May 17, 1735; Mary, August 17, 1736; Shubael, August 11, 1740, married Deliverance Hyde, of Newton; Sarah, baptized September 8, 1754; Joseph, mentioned below.

(V) Joseph, son of Shubael (3) Seaver, was born, probably in Framingham, 1752, and settled in that town. He was a blacksmith by trade. He was a soldier from Framingham in the revolution in 1775 in Captain Thomas Drury's company, Colonel John Nixon's regiment, afterward Colonel Gardner's. He had other service, not all of which is distinguishable from the service of others of the same name. He removed from Framingham to Phillipston after the revolution. He and his wife were admitted to the Framingham church in October, 1781. He lived for a short time in Rindge, and Swanzey, New Hampshire. He married (first) Esther, daughter of Samuel Lamb; (second) Abiah or Biah Rich (intention dated at Phillipston, April 19, 1794). Children by first wife: Joseph, mentioned below; Esther, born in Framingham, October 14, 1777, married Lemuel Tinkham; William, March 4, 1779, at Framingham, died at Malaga; Keziah, February 12, 1781, married Samuel Twitchell; Sally, March 10, 1783, at Rindge; Betsey, April 19, 1785, at Swanzey, married James Cheney; Abraham, at Swanzey, March 6, 1787; Nabby, July 19, 1789, at Petersham, died young; Polly, October 19, 1792, at Petersham, married —— Haskell. Children by second wife: Samuel, March 11, 1795; Nabby, January 28, 1797; Nancy, October 11, 1799; Hannah Mackreth, May 28, 1802; William Bowdoin, January 7, 1805. (Jane, Gilbert and William given in data, but not recorded at Petersham.)

(VI) Joseph (2), son of Joseph (1) Seaver, was born in Framingham, Massachusetts, July 26, 1775. When young he went with his parents to Phillipston, Massachusetts, and when a young man went to Vermont. He died at Cavendish, Vermont, in August, 1845. He married Mary Hyde, who died in 1844. Children: Harriet, married Stillman Proctor; Mary; Joseph, mentioned below; Lydia, married Eli Dean; Salome, married Samuel Adams of Cavendish; Lorinda, married Josiah Peabody.

(VII) Joseph (3), son of Joseph (2) Seaver, was born in Cavendish, Vermont, September 6, 1806, died in Pomfret, Vermont, December 15, 1875. He was educated in the public schools, and was a farmer all his active life. In 1840 he removed to Pomfret, Vermont, where he spent the last years of his life. He married A. Evelyn Parker, born September 23, 1808, in Cavendish, died May 30, 1889. Children: 1. Judge Thomas O., of Woodstock, Vermont, born December 23, 1833, died July 11, 1912; married Nancy J. Spaulding and had children: Mary, Ethel, Gertrude, Kenneth, who alone survives. 2. Francis P., of Taftsville, Vermont, born January 24, 1835; married (first) Philinda L. Seavey, who died December 20, 1873; (second) Huldah Frink, who died August 4, 1896. 3. Richard Adam, mentioned below. 4. Charles Henry, born November 18, 1839, died November 30, 1899; married Harriet Kneen. 5. William Harris, born June 7, 1842, died

November 11, 1905; married Caroline E. Cowdrey. 6. Owen L., born March 25, 1844, at Taftsville, Vermont; married Clara E. Perkins. 7. George W., born June 1, 1846, drowned at sea, October 20, 1870, at Jupiter Inlet, off the coast of Florida. 8. Eva A., born June 2, 1848, at Taftsville.

(VIII) Richard Adam, son of Joseph (3) Seaver, was born in Cavendish, Vermont, August 5, 1836. He attended the public schools of his native town. He removed to Pomfret with his parents and assisted his father on the farm during his youth; he has always followed farming for a vocation, and is now living at Hartford, Vermont. He is a member of the Congregational church. He has a notable military record. Was a member of the Vermont state militia under the command of Peter Thatcher Washburn, of Woodstock, Vermont, when the call came from President Lincoln for 75,000 troops. He was mustered in with the state militia and left for the front, May 25, 1861. The regiment took part in the battle of Big Bethel, June 12, 1861. Thence the company went to Newport News, Virginia, on guard duty. They helped to move the first rifle cannon that were pressed into service. He was honorably discharged and the company was mustered out of service, August 16, 1861. He re-enlisted, October 1, 1861, in the First Vermont Regiment of cavalry, the only cavalry regiment raised in this state during the civil war and was mustered into service at Burlington, Vermont. Was made first sergeant of Company E, November 19, 1861, and was made orderly sergeant, March 22, 1863. Was commissioned second lieutenant, July 2, 1864, and was mustered out, November 1, 1864. During his second enlistment he saw much active picket duty and skirmishing and was also in various important battles. He took part in the battle of Gettysburg, and was taken prisoner, July 6, 1863, at Hagerstown, Maryland, and confined in the rebel prison at Belle Isle for six months. At the end of that time he was exchanged and sent to Annapolis. He took part in the siege of Richmond and was in the engagement, May 30, 1864. After he left the service he made his home in Quechee, Vermont, where he has since lived. In politics he is a Republican; in religion a Congregationalist.

He married, October 13, 1861, Maria Eliza Barber, born January 15, 1841, in Woodstock, Vermont, died February 24, 1912, daughter of Warren and Sabra (Smith) Barber. Her father, Warren Barber, was born February 16, 1799, in Springfield, Massachusetts, died December 5, 1873; married (first) May 24,

1826, Abigail Goodman, who died September 27, 1838; (second) January 16, 1840, Sabra Smith, born at Woodstock, Vermont, December 19, 1805, died March 9, 1844. Children of Warren and Abigail Barber: James W., born April 16, 1827, died May 20, 1828; James W., January 1, 1829, died May, 1877; Sophia A., March 12, 1832, died April 10, 1896; Laura G., June 23, 1834, died April 5, 1870; John N., March 17, 1837, died October 24, 1837. Children of Warren and Sabra Barber: Maria Eliza, born January 15, 1841, died February 24, 1912; George E., May 7, 1843, died June 2, 1893; Augusta G., May 18, 1844, died November 5, 1899; Julia, April 20, 1847, died August 24, 1897. Children of Richard A. and Maria E. Seaver: 1. Frank R., born October 31, 1864; resides in Springfield, Massachusetts; married, April 28, 1891, Mary Elizabeth Allen, and they have one son, Blake Allen, born July 25, 1895. 2. William H., born April 22, 1866, died April 23, 1866. 3. Fred Owen, born October 13, 1867; resides in Brooklyn, New York; married Annie L. French, born May 22, 1877; children: Helen Tyler, born August 6, 1903; Philip Barber, August 10, 1905, died August 16, 1905; Elizabeth, July 29, 1910. 4. Philip Henry, mentioned below. 5. Margaret Evelyn, born April 8, 1871; married, September 27, 1906, James L. Davis, civil engineer of New York City, and they have one child, Rebecca Margaret, born August 16, 1907. 6. Robert William, born May 24, 1873; farmer in Williamstown, Massachusetts; married, April 17, 1901, Alice L. Leach, of Pomfret, Vermont; children: Edith Rachel, born February 4, 1904; Grace Dorothy, June 10, 1905; Richard Leach, July 25, 1907. 7. James Thatcher, born January 24, 1875; a civil engineer in New York City; married (first) November 7, 1900, Mary J. Babcock, who died January 17, 1906; (second) September 14, 1909, Idella M. Benjamin; had one child by first wife. 8. Mabel Jeanne, born April 12, 1878; resides with her parents. 9. John, born July 21, 1880; a civil engineer in New York.

(IX) Philip Henry, son of Richard Adam Seaver, was born September 14, 1869, in the town of Hartford, Vermont. He received his early education in the little brick school-house in the district in which he lived in his native town. Afterward he attended the public schools in Woodstock, Vermont, for two years. He came to Rutland, Vermont, in 1888, and went into the office of Lincoln Iron Works as bookkeeper and continued for about six years. He was then made manager of the jobbing department, afterward secretary of the company, then secretary and treasurer,

and eventually treasurer, an office he now holds, and he is also a director of the corporation, and treasurer of the Steam Stone Cutting Company, which is operated under the management of the Lincoln·Iron Works. He is a member of Rutland Lodge, Free and Accepted Masons; Davenport Chapter, Royal Arch Masons; Killington Commandery, Knights Templar, of which he is a past commander. He is recorder of Cairo Temple, Mystic Shrine, secretary of Cairo Temple Associates, and was one of the prime movers in building the new temple recently erected in Rutland by that body. He is deacon of the Congregational church of Rutland.

He married (first) October 7, 1891, Christine Marion Cook, born in Ludlow, Vermont, September 22, 1867, died April 9, 1898, daughter of Francis and Myra (Adams) Cook. He married (second) September 5, 1899, Sarah A. Barclay, born in Jacket River, New Brunswick, Canada, daughter of William and Agnes (MacIntosh) Barclay. Her father was born in Perth, Scotland, April 21, 1815, died in New Brunswick at the age of ninety-two years. He was a son of Robert Barclay, of Scotland, who came to New Brunswick, Canada, in 1818, when his son William was three years old, settling in Bathhurst, New Brunswick. Her mother, Agnes (MacIntosh) Barclay, was born in Scotland, November 16, 1821, died at the age of eighty years. Mr. and Mrs. Seaver have no children.

This is one of the families DEARBORN that enjoy the distinction of being among the early colonists and founders of the commonwealth of New Hampshire, whence they spread throughout New England and the United States. The Dearborns have always maintained the reputation of being an intelligent, energetic and progressive race, and some of them have been persons of distinction.

(I) Godfrey Dearborn, patriarch of the Dearborn family in the United States, was born about 1600 in England, and Exeter in the county of Devonshire is said to have been the place of his nativity. He came to the Massachusetts colony about 1638, and died in Hampton, New Hampshire, February 4, 1686. In 1639 the Rev. John Wheelwright with a company of his friends removed from the colony in Massachusetts Bay to Exeter, in the province of New Hampshire, and founded a settlement. Supposing themselves to be out of the jurisdiction of any existing colony or government they united and signed among themselves a form of social compact, which bore the signature of thirty-five persons, of whom Godfrey Dearborn was one. He seems to have been a man of considerable standing among the colonists, which is proved by his being chosen as one of the selectmen, both of Exeter and Hampton. His farm is said to have been situated within the present limits of the town of Stratham. He had in 1644 a grant of meadowland "on the second run, beyond Mr. Wheelwright's creek, toward Captain Wiggins". In 1645 in connection with two other persons he had a grant of meadow "at the head of the Great Cove Creek, about six acres, if it be there to be found". Other land is mentioned as adjoining his "on the east side of the river". In 1648 he was elected one of the "townsmen" or selectmen. Between 1648 and 1650 he removed to Hampton, where he spent the remainder of his life. On March 4, 1650, seats in the Hampton meeting-house were assigned to "Goodman and Goodwife Godfrey Dearborn". On his arrival in Hampton Godfrey Dearborn settled at the so-called "West End", on a farm ever since occupied by his descendants. One house, built between 1650 and 1686, is still standing and constitutes a part of the present dwelling. On his removal to Hampton Godfrey became a considerable land owner and of some importance in the affairs of the town. In 1670 he had a grant of eighty acres, in addition to the extensive farm in the vicinity of his dwelling, which he already possessed. His tax in 1653 was fifteen shillings and tenpence, and he was one of the selectmen in 1655-1663-1671. He made his will in 1680. He married (first) in England, but the name of his wife remains unknown. She died some time between May 4, 1650, and November 25, 1662. On the latter date he married (second) Dorothy, widow of Philanon Dalton. She died between 1680 and 1696. Children, all by the first marriage: Henry; Thomas; John; Sarah; two other daughters, names unknown.

(II) Henry, son of Godfrey Dearborn, was born about 1633 in England. The record of Hampton states: "Henry Dearborn deceased, January ye 18, 1724-25, aged 92 years." He came to this country with his father, when about six years old. He was one of the selectmen of Hampton in 1676 and 1692. He was also a signer of the petition to the king in 1683, usually called "Weare's petition". He married, January 16, 1666, Elizabeth Marrian, born about 1644, died July 6, 1716, aged seventy-two years. She was a daughter of John Marrian, one of the first settlers of Hampton. Henry Dearborn's children were: John, of whom further; Samuel; Elizabeth,

died young; Sarah; Abigail; Elizabeth; Henry.

(III) John, son of Henry (1) and Elizabeth (Marrian) Dearborn, was born at Hampton, October 10, 1666. He settled in that part of the town now called North Hampton. He married, November 4, 1689, Abigail, daughter of Nathaniel and Deborah (Smith) Batcheller, great-granddaughter of the Rev. Stephen Bachelor, a pioneer of Hampton. She was born December 28, 1667, died November 13, 1736. Children: Deborah; Jonathan, of whom further; Elizabeth; Esther; Joseph; Abigail; Lydia; Ruth; Simon; and Benjamin.

(IV) Jonathan, son of John (1) and Abigail (Batcheller) Dearborn, was born in North Hampton, New Hampshire, in 1691, died in Stratham, New Hampshire, January 29, 1779. He removed to Stratham, where he lived a great number of years, taking a fairly active share in the affairs of the town. He married, December 29, 1715, Hannah, born April 10, 1697, died June, 1780, daughter of Deacon John Tuck. Child: John (2), of whom further.

(V) John (2), son of Jonathan (1) and Hannah (Tuck) Dearborn, was born at Stratham, New Hampshire, April 2, 1718, and died there. He was engaged partly in farming and partly in mercantile pursuits of various kinds, and took part in the public life of the community, doing the work of a pioneer in cultivating the land and building up a settled commonwealth. He moved to Chester after his son was born. He married (first) Mary, the daughter of a Mr. Chapman, living in the neighborhood; (second) Mary Cawley. Child: Jonathan (2), of whom further.

(VI) Jonathan (2), son of John (2) and Mary (Chapman) or Mary (Cawley) Dearborn, was born on farm No. 17, Stratham, New Hampshire, died in Chester, New Hampshire. He lived at Chester, where his father had removed when he was young. He filled quite a number of offices during his life, and was a participant in several stirring events. He was for a long time highway surveyor of Raymund. During the revolutionary war he was a soldier in Captain Runnell's company, in the regiment commanded by Thomas Tasker. He married Abigail, daughter of a Mr. Lovitt, who lived near Chester. Children: Jonathan (3), of whom further; Nathaniel, married Mary Cram; Sarah, married (first) Nehemiah Cram, (second) Josiah Brown, and (third) John Moody.

(VII) Jonathan (3), son of Jonathan (2) and Abigail (Lovitt) Dearborn, was born in Raymund, New Hampshire, June 4, 1768, died in East Pittston, Maine, March 6, 1847. He was a farmer, and not only did the ordinary work connected with his agricultural interests, but was engaged in a small way in several transactions relating to buying and selling real estate. He had a good stock of cattle and divided his attention to their breeding and sale, as well as to matters connected with his landed property. He was too young to take much part in the revolutionary war, but it would appear that he witnessed a great many incidents connected with it, and particularly with his father's participation. When he grew old he was fond of relating his remembrances of the times through which he had passed in his youth. He seems to have been a man of considerable ability, though his occupation did not allow him much opportunity to expand. He married Sarah, born December 31, 1758, died December 23, 1829, daughter of Robert Page, born April 13, 1732, died December 31, 1816, who married Sarah Dearborn, of Raymund, born November 25, 1735, died January 12, 1821, sister of Henry Dearborn, the patriot and highminded statesman. Child: Henry (2), of whom further.

(VIII) Henry (2), son of Jonathan (3) and Sarah (Page) Dearborn, was born in Raymund, New Hampshire, February 9, 1797, died in East Pittston, Maine, August 21, 1883. For a number of years he was a farmer and had a general store in the country, but as he was a man possessed of considerable and versatile talent his time and attention were by no means confined entirely to his business in a country community. He took considerable part in public affairs of the district and state, and sat for a time in the state legislature in Maine. He was successively clerk, selectman, treasurer, and moderator of Pittston, Maine, in the legislature. He was what was at the time called a Whig and Republican. He married, March 3, 1822, Pamela, daughter of David P. Bailey, of Pittston, Maine. Her brother, Captain David Goodwin Bailey, of the Black Ball Line of packet ships, married Mary, daughter of Major Henry Smith, who was present at the storming of Quebec, Canada, and was one of the early settlers of Pittston. Children of Henry and Pamela (Bailey) Dearborn: George, living till about 1891, at Gardiner, Maine, married and had one daughter who married; Sarah, died in 1910, aged eighty-two years, married L. S. Clark; Warren, deceased; Rachael, married George F. Jackson, and lives at Fordham Heights, New York; David Bailey, of whom further; Leonora, died in infancy; Rufus, lost at sea, was married and had three children; Henry,

a sea captain, now dead, was married and had three children: Julia, died young.

(IX) David Bailey, son of Henry (2) and Pamela (Bailey) Dearborn, was born at Pittston, Maine, April 5, 1832. He was educated in the public schools of the town in which he was born. In 1849 he entered as a clerk in a shipping office in New York, and has been in the shipping business all his life. About 1853 he entered into business on his own account and has continued carrying it on to this day. He is or was a member of the Chamber of Commerce, Produce Exchange, and Maritime Exchange, and was long connected with a number of clubs from which he has now resigned. He is a Republican, but is not active. He also belongs to Clinton Avenue Congregational Church, of Brooklyn, New York.

He married, December 25, 1856, at Pittston, Maine, Ellen A., born May 4, 1835, died February 25, 1894, daughter of Captain Samuel and Rachael (Childs) Nichols, of Pittston, Maine. Children: George Samuel, of whom further; Antoinette, who married Lewis H. Lapham; Ellen A., who has remained single; and David Bailey (2), unmarried, and with his brother in business.

(X) George Samuel, son of David Bailey and Ellen A. (Nichols) Dearborn, was born at Brooklyn, New York, March 20, 1858. He received part of his education in the Brooklyn Collegiate and Polytechnical Institute, and in 1874 entered the shipping business which preceded the present company. He is now president of the American-Hawaiian Steamship Company, incorporated in 1899. He is a Republican in politics, and is affiliated with the Episcopal church of Rye, New York. He belongs to the Racket and Tennis Club, the New York Downtown Club, the Pacific Union of San Francisco, and the Apawamis Club at Rye, New York, of which he has been president, the America Yacht Club at Rye, and one or two other associations.

He married, December 15, 1887, at Brooklyn, New York, Bessie, daughter of George B. and Henrietta (Scott) Douglas. Children: Henry, born 1892, at Rye, New York, was educated at a private school, New York City, and belongs to the Williams College class of 1913; and Douglas, born February 12, 1898, at New York City, and is now at school.

WINSLOW William Winslow, or Wyncelow, first of the line as traced in England, had children: 1. John, of London, afterward of Wyncelow Hall, was living in 1387-88; married Mary Crouchman, died in 1409-10, styled of Crouchman Hall. 2. William (2), of whom further.

(II) William (2), son of William (1) Winslow, had a son Thomas, of whom further.

(III) Thomas, son of William (2) Winslow, was of Burton, county Oxford, having lands also in Essex. He was living in 1452. He married Cecelia Tansley, one of two daughters, and the heiress of an old family. She was called Lady Agnes. Had a son, William (3).

(IV) William (3), son of Thomas Winslow, was living in 1529. Children: Kenelm, of whom further; Richard, had a grant from Edward VI. of the rectory of Elksley, county Nottingham.

(V) Kenelm, son of William (3) Winslow, purchased, in 1559, of Sir Richard Newport, an estate called Newport's Place, in Kempsey, Worcestershire. He had an older and very extensive estate, in the same parish, called Clerkenleap, sold by his grandson Richard Winslow in 1650. He died in 1607 in the parish of St. Andrew. He married Catherine ———. His will, dated April 14, 1607, and proved November 9 following, is still preserved at Worcester. Only son, Edward, of whom further.

(VI) Edward, son of Kenelm (1) Winslow, was born October 17, 1560, in the parish of Saint Andrew, county Worcester, England, and died before 1631. He lived in Kempsey and Droitwich, county Worcester. He married (first) Eleanor Pelham, of Droitwich; (second) at St. Bride's Church, London, November 4, 1594, Magdalene Oliver, the records of whose family are found in the parish register of St. Peter's, Droitwich. Children: 1. Richard, born about 1585-86. 2. Edward, born October 18, 1595, at Droitwitch, governor of Plymouth colony; married (first) at Leyden, May 16, 1618, Elizabeth Barker; (second) May 12, 1621, Susan (Fuller) White, who came in the "Mayflower" with Governor Winslow, widow of William White, and mother of Peregrine White, the first-born in the colony. 3. John, born April 16, 1597, died 1674 in Boston; married, October 12, 1624, Mary, daughter of James and Susanna Chilton, who came in the "Mayflower". 4. Eleanor, born April 22, 1598, at Droitwich, and remained in England. 5. Kenelm (2), of whom further. 6. Gilbert, October 26, 1600, came in the "Mayflower" with Edward, signed the compact, returned to England after 1623, and died there. 7. Elizabeth, March 8, 1602, buried January 20, 1604, at St. Peter's Church. 8. Magdalen, born December 26, 1604, at Droit-

wich, remained in England. 9. Josiah, born February 11, 1606.

(VII) Kenelm (2), son of Edward Winslow, was born at Droitwich, county Worcester, England, April 29, 1599, baptized at St. Peter's Church May 3, 1599, died at Salem, Massachusetts, September 13, 1672. He was the immigrant ancestor. He came to Plymouth, probably in 1629, with his brother Josiah, and was admitted a freeman January 1, 1632-33. He was surveyor of the town of Plymouth in 1640, and was fined ten shillings for neglecting the highways. He removed to Marshfield about 1641, having previously received a grant of land at that place, then called Green's Harbor, March 5, 1637-38. This grant, originally made to Josiah Winslow, his brother, he shared with Love Brewster. His home was "on a gentle eminence by the sea, near the extremity of land lying between Green Harbor and South Rivers. This tract of the township was considered the Eden of the region. It was beautified with groves of majestic oaks and graceful walnuts, with the underground void of shrubbery. A few of these groves were standing within the memory of persons now living (1854), but all have fallen beneath the hand of the woodman." The homestead he left to his son Nathaniel. Other lands were granted to Kenelm as the common land was divided. He was one of the twenty-six original proprietors of Assonet, now Freetown, Massachusetts, purchased of the Indians April 2, 1659, and received the twenty-fourth lot, a portion of which was lately owned by a lineal descendant, having descended by inheritance. Kenelm was a joiner by trade as well as a planter. He filled various town offices, was deputy to the general court from 1642 to 1644 and from 1649 to 1653, eight years in all. He had considerable litigation, as the early court records show. He died at Salem, whither he had gone on business, apparently after a long illness, for his will was dated five weeks earlier, August 8, 1672, and in it he describes himself as "being very sick and drawing nigh unto death". He may have been visiting his niece, Mrs. Elizabeth Corwin, daughter of Edward Winslow.

He married, in June, 1634, Eleanor Adams, widow of John Adams, of Plymouth. She survived him and died at Marshfield, where she was buried December 5, 1681, aged eighty-three. Children: Kenelm (3), of whom further; Eleanor or Ellen, born about 1637; Nathaniel, born about 1639; Job, about 1641.

(VIII) Colonel Kenelm (3) Winslow, son of Kenelm (2) Winslow, was born about 1636 at Plymouth, died November 11, 1715, at

Harwich, in his seventy-ninth year, according to his gravestone. He removed to Cape Cod and settled at Yarmouth, afterward Harwich, and now Brewster, Massachusetts. His homestead was on the west border of the township, now called West Brewster, Satucket, of Winslow's Mills. He was mentioned in the Yarmouth records in 1668. Harwich was then a "constablerick" of Yarmouth. In records he was called "Colonel Winslow, planter or yeoman". He bought large tracts of wild land in what is now Rochester, Massachusetts, on which several of his children settled. The water privilege remains in the family to the present day. In 1699 he deeded it to his son Kenelm, and in 1873 it was owned by William T. Winslow, of West Brewster. Kenelm Winslow bought of George Denison, of Stonington, Connecticut, one thousand acres of land in Windham, later Mansfield, March 11, 1700, for thirty pounds. He gave land October 7, 1700, to his son Samuel, who sold it to his brother Kenelm, but neither Samuel nor Kenelm lived in Windham. On October 3, 1662, he was fined ten shillings for "riding a journey on the Lord's day", yet he rode sixty miles to Scituate on three occasions to have a child baptized in the Second Church there, for Kenelm in 1668, Josiah in 1670 and Thomas in 1672. He was on the committee to seat the meeting-house October 4, 1714.

He married (first) September 23, 1667, Mercy Worden, born about 1641, died September 22, 1688, in her forty-eighth year, daughter of Peter Jr. and Mercy Worden, of Yarmouth. Her gravestone is in the Winslow graveyard at Dennis. It is of hard slate from England, and is the oldest stone in the yard. The burying-ground is near the road leading from Nebscusset to Satucket, a short distance from the Brewster line. He married (second) Damaris ———, who was living as late as March 27, 1729. His will was dated January 10, 1712, and proved December 28, 1715. Children of the first wife: Kenelm; Josiah, of whom further; Thomas, baptized March 3, 1672-73; Samuel, about 1674; Mercy, about 1676; Nathaniel, 1679; Edward, January 30, 1680-81. Children of the second wife: Damaris, married, July 30, 1713, Jonathan Small; Elizabeth, married, August 9, 1711, Andrew Clark; Eleanor, married, March 25, 1719, Shubael Hamblen; John, born about 1701.

(IX) Kenelm (4), son of Colonel Kenelm (3) Winslow, was baptized August 9, 1668; he married ——— and their youngest child was John (see following sketch).

(IX) Captain Josiah Winslow, son of Colonel Kenelm (3) Winslow, was born in Marshfield November 7, 1669, died at Free-town, Massachusetts, April 3, 1761, and was buried in the south cemetery at Berkley. He received a quarter of his father's lands by gift-deed dated February 27, 1693, and bought more land of his father west of the Taunton river and in Freetown. He lived a mile from Assonet village on the road to Taunton. By trade he was a clothier, and several generations of his descendants have followed this trade in the mill near Assonet bridge, where at last accounts one of his Winslow descendants was still in the same line of business. He was one of the proprietors of the forge at Freetown in 1704. In public affairs he was very active and prominent, having been constable in 1696; highway surveyor in 1699; moderator in 1702-08-12-16; Assessor in 1702-03-05-07-10-13-22; selectman in 1702-03-04-09-10; treasurer in 1704; on the grand jury in 1721; first lieutenant of the Assonet company and commissioned captain, February 9, 1725. He served on the committee on a new meeting-house.

His marriage intention was dated June 13, 1695, and he married (first) at Freetown, Margaret Tisdale, of Taunton, born 1676, daughter of James and Mary (Avery) Tisdale, granddaughter of John Tisdale, slain by the Indians in King Philip's war June 7, 1675, who married Sarah Walker. His wife died January 12, 1737, aged sixty-one years, and buried at Berkley South Cemetery. He married (second) November 3, 1737, Mrs. Hannah Winslow; (third) March 2, 1748-49, Hannah Booth, of Middleborough, a widow; (fourth) November 30, 1749, Martha Hathaway, of Freetown; (fifth) the intention being dated September 6, 1750, Mary Jones, of Berkley. His will was dated March 5, 1753, and proved May 5, 1761. Children, born at Freetown: Josiah, June 9, 1697; Mercy, December 19, 1700; Ebenezer, November 22, 1705; Edward, August 11, 1709; James, of whom further; Margaret, March 24, 1720; Rachel, February 9, 1722.

(X) Colonel James Winslow, son of Captain Josiah Winslow, was born at Freetown, August 10, 1712, died March 1, 1777, in his sixty-fifth year, and was buried at Berkley. He succeeded his father in the cloth-dressing business and lived at Freetown, where he erected the house lately occupied by Barnaby Winslow. He was sole executor of his father's will. He was also prominent in civil and military life, and filled the offices of justice of the peace; town treasurer in 1755; selectman in 1762; lieutenant of the first foot company of militia in Freetown, commissioned June 4, 1762; captain of the Second Regiment, of Bristol county, commissioned July

25, 1771. He was run over by an ox-sled loaded with wood, on the hill a mile from Assonet village, and killed. His will was dated June 17, 1776, and proved March 22, 1777. He married, June 8, 1738, Charity Hodges, of Norton, Massachusetts, born March 30, 1716, daughter of Major Joseph and Bethia (Williams) Hodges. Children, born at Freetown: Mehitable, April 22, 1739; Ephraim, July 7, 1741; Margaret, November 23, 1743; Joseph, March 8, 1745-46; James, September 2, 1748; Shadrach, of whom further; Bethia, August 29, 1753; Thankful, October 30, 1754; Isaac, June 23, 1759.

(XI) Dr. Shadrach Winslow, son of Colonel James Winslow, was born December 17, 1750, at Freetown, Massachusetts, died February 1, 1817, at Foxborough, Massachusetts, where he was buried. He was graduated from Yale College in 1771, and became an eminent physician and surgeon. During the revolution he helped to fit out a privateer, on which he sailed as surgeon. On the first voyage the vessel was seized by the British off the coast of Spain, and he was kept prisoner for a year in the old Jersey prison ship at Wallabout bay, Brooklyn. His health was impaired by this confinement. On his return he practiced in Foxborough. "He was much respected as a physician and man". He practiced through a large circuit, extending fully twenty miles from his home, and was widely known and popular. His college diploma, dated September 11, 1771, has been preserved.

He married, March 12, 1783, Elizabeth Robbins, who was born April 29, 1764, at Foxborough, died April 1, 1846, daughter of Eleazer and Mary (Savell) Robbins. Children, born at Foxborough: Betsey Peck, September 29, 1784; Eleazer Robbins, of whom further; James, May 14, 1788; Isaac, February 21, 1791; Jesse, May 25, 1794;· Samuel, August 15, 1797; Thomas Jefferson, June 6, 1800, drowned June 18, 1803; Mary, October 3, 1802; Fanny, March 6, 1805; Joseph, August 28, 1807.

(XII) Eleazer Robbins Winslow, son of Dr. Shadrach Winslow, was born at Foxborough, Massachusetts, March 21, 1786, died August 8, 1863, at Newton Upper Falls, in that state. "He was engaged in various manufacturing enterprises and in this pursuit showed great and thorough knowledge. He was always philosophical and the testimony of those who were associated with him was that he had few superiors in general intellectual powers". On account of ill health he lived for a time in the Catskill mountains, at Hunter, Greene county, and Ramapo, Rockland county, New York, and spent his time in hunting bears and wolves, on which the state paid a bounty at that time. During his absence his wife and children in their cabin in the wilderness feared the threatened attack of wild beasts, and life proved particularly trying to a woman who had spent her early life in the city. Mr. Winslow was at one time selectman of the town of Newton.

He married, at Boston, April 21, 1811, Ann Corbett, born there October 2, 1793, and educated there, daughter of David and Deborah (Cowin) Corbett. She died September 18, 1871, at Newton Upper Falls, Massachusetts. She was a woman of fine character and great piety, a friend of the clergy in that section, and one of the first seventeen in the Methodist Episcopal class at Newton in 1826. Children: Charles, born January 30, 1814; Ann, July 13, 1815, at Hunter; Elizabeth Robbins, October 24, 1816, died young; Clarissa Williams, March 13, 1818; David Corbett, of whom further; Emeline, November 4, 1820; Seth Collins, January 11, 1822; George, August 11, 1823; John, October 21, 1825; Samuel, February 28, 1827; Deborah Ann, August 8, 1828; Mary Pratt, April 14, 1830; Elizabeth Robbins, twin, April 14, 1830; Martha Switzer, April 14, 1832; James, August 2, 1834, at Newton; Harriet F., July 25, 1836.

(XIII) David Corbett, son of Eleazer Robbins Winslow, was born at Hunter, New York, June 9, 1819, died March 27, 1879. He attended the village schools there. He removed with the family to Newton, Massachusetts, when he was seven years old, and attended the public schools there. During the six months just before he came of age he was a student in the academy of Hancock, New Hampshire. In 1840-41 he taught school at Peterborough, New Hampshire, and then removed to Long Island, where he continued to teach school and at the same time study law in the office of Judge N. B. Morse, district attorney of Kings county, afterward judge of the supreme court. He was admitted to the bar in Brooklyn, and was soon afterward appointed assistant collector of internal revenue. Afterward he was register of bankruptcy for the eastern district of New York, by appointment of Chief Justice Chase, and also United States commissioner. He was an able lawyer and magistrate.

He married, July 25, 1841, in New York City, Harriet Adaline Stearns, born at Franklin, Massachusetts, January 14, 1817, daughter of Deacon Edwin and Harriet (Paddock) Stearns, of Millbury, Massachusetts. Children: Delia Caroline, born April 28, 1842, at Hempstead, Long Island, died June 6, 1909;

David Sidney, born April 8, 1844, at New Utrecht, New York; Frances Anna, October 30, 1846, in Brooklyn; George Edwin, September 22, 1849, at New Utrecht; Louisa, January 15, 1852, at New Utrecht; Charles Howard, of whom further; Harriet Adaline, June 2, 1856, died April 27, 1859; Frederick Kenelm, of whom further.

(XIV) Charles Howard, son of David Corbett Winslow, was born February 28, 1854, at Brooklyn, New York. He attended the public schools, and was a student in Brown University in 1874-75, and afterward at Columbia University, from which he was graduated in the class of 1877 with the degree of Bachelor of Laws. He was admitted to the bar in the same year, and began to practice law in Brooklyn, where he has continued successfully to the present time. His office is at No. 16 Court street. He has made something of a specialty of real estate business, and is vice-president, general manager and director of the Rosedale Development Company. He is an active and influential Republican in the Third Assembly district, and has been president of the Sixth Ward Republican Club and frequently its delegate to nominating conventions of his party. He attends the South Congregational Church.

Charles Howard Winslow married, May 24, 1893, at Brooklyn, Ebba M. Loewenmark Jeanson, born at Gottenburg, Sweden, November 5, 1865, daughter of Claus J. Loewenmark and Clara J. (Lindquist) Jeanson. They have one child, Dorothy Adeline, born February 16, 1899, at Brooklyn, New York, student in Packer Institute.

(XIV) Frederick Kenelm, son of David Corbett Winslow, and brother of Charles Howard Winslow, was born September 5, 1861.

He attended the public schools of Brooklyn, and entered Amherst College, from which he was graduated with the degree of Bachelor of Arts in the class of 1884. He began to read law in the office of Wright & Cullen, of New York, and was admitted to the bar in 1890. For twelve years he practiced in New York City and since then has had his office in Brooklyn. In addition to general legal work he has made a specialty of real estate practice. He is a director of the Rosedale Building Company, and the Rosedale Development Company; president of the Rosedale Hook & Ladder Volunteer Company No. 1, and president of the board of trustees of Rosedale. He is a member of the Society of Founders and Patriots, and of the Franklin Literary Society of Brooklyn. He attends the South Congregational Church.

(X) Deacon John Winslow, son of Kenelm Winslow (q. v.), was born about 1701. He was a farmer in Rochester, Massachusetts, and was elected deacon of the church there, August 5, 1748. His father, in his will dated January 10, 1712, left him all the land on the "great neck * * * not disposed of and one eighth part of one whole share of my common or undivided land, all of which said land * * * within ye township of Rochester"; also an eighth of a share of cedar and spruce swamp, with twenty-five acres of land in Rochester. His will was dated January 11, 1752, and proved July 16, 1755, and it mentioned all of his children except Bethiah and Stephen. He married, March 15, 1721-22, Bethiah Andrews, born May 26, 1699, died in Sheffield, Massachusetts, at an advanced age, at the home of her son, Prince Winslow. She was a daughter of Stephen and Bethiah Andrews, of Rochester. Children, recorded at Rochester: John, born October 31, 1722; Deborah, February 8, 1724; Jedediah, mentioned below; Nathaniel, April 22, 1730, probably died young; Lemuel, November 3, 1734; Prince, April 6, 1737; Stephen, July 5, 1739, probably died young; Elizabeth; Bethiah.

(XI) Jedediah, son of Deacon John Winslow, was born at Rochester, March 26, 1727, died April 5, 1794, at Brandon, Vermont. For twenty years he followed the sea, and was noted for his remarkable strength. Until about 1773 he lived in Barre, Massachusetts, and then for a time changed his home several times, finally going to Brandon, Vermont, where he was one of the first settlers. He built the first house there, at the south end of the place, a rod and a half east of what is now Union street, near the "Point of Rocks". The *Rutland County Herald*, in speaking of the settlement of Brandon says: "Jedediah Winslow was a man of strong mind, indomitable courage, and great shrewdness. He was regarded as a leader of the little band of early settlers." He was one of the founders of the Congregational church there, organized September 23, 1785, and was the first deacon. He seems to have held the offices of deacon, moderator and scribe at the same time. He was one of the sixty-four grantees of Pittsford, in 1762. The lots were drawn June 3, 1776, and he received lots 41 and 54. He deeded this farm to his son John, May 23, 1785. None of the sixty-four grantees lived permanently in Pittsford. He married, intentions published March 24, 1750, Elizabeth Goodspeed, of Barnstable, Massachusetts; she died in Paris, New York. Children, first six recorded at Barre: Sarah, born October 5, 1751; Elizabeth, June 19, 1756; Luther, July 30, 1757; Hannah, June 14, 1758; Bethiah, June 20, 1760; Deborah, June 24, 1762; John, married Sally Bigelow; Polly, married William Chamberlain; Justin, mentioned below; Calvin, married Sally Goodenough; Charlotte, died December 10, 1777, aged two years; Thomas Goodspeed, married Phila Daniels.

(XII) Justin, son of Deacon Jedediah Winslow, was born May 22, 1770, died November 12, 1851, at Brandon, Vermont. He was seven years of age when his father moved to Barre. He volunteered for the battle of Plattsburg, but did not arrive in time for the engagement. He was a farmer at Brandon. He married there, September 27, 1791, Abigail Underwood, of Connecticut, born August 22, 1768, died November 6, 1851, daughter of William and ——— (Horton) Underwood. Children, born at Brandon: Jeremiah, August 22, 1793; Justin, August 22, 1795; Chester, mentioned below; Sally, January 24, 1799; Erastus, August 25, 1801, died June 8, 1805; Erastus Ward, October 9, 1808.

(XIII) Chester, son of Justin Winslow, was born July 17, 1797, at Brandon, Vermont, died June 29, 1871. He followed farming there all his life. He took an active part in town affairs and was trial justice many years. He married, at Brandon, April 8, 1840, Anna Green Goss, born October 17, 1818, daughter of Rufus and Anna (Green) Goss, of Brandon. Children, born at Brandon: Charles Marius, mentioned below; Anna Goss, born October 25, 1843, died April 1, 1862.

(XIV) Charles Marius, son of Chester Winslow, was born in Brandon, Vermont, February 10, 1841. He attended the public schools there, the Phillips Academy at Andover, Massachusetts, and Middlebury Academy at Middlebury, Vermont. He has since followed farming on the homestead of which he is the present owner. This farm was cleared by his great-grandfather, Jedediah Winslow, and enlarged by his grandfather and his father until it comprises some six hundred acres, much of which is in a high state of cultivation. He has made a specialty of breeding Ayrshire cattle and for thirty years in addition to farming he has been secretary of the Ayrshire Breeders Association of the United States and Canada. He has served on the Board of Cattle Commissioners of the State and has been secretary of the State Board of Agriculture, and also secretary of the State Agricultural Society. He was lister of the town of Brandon for eighteen years, and for many years was superintendent of schools of Brandon. For two years, 1894-95, he rep-

resented the town in the state legislature and while in the house of representatives served on the committee on agriculture and was its chairman. In religion he is a Congregationalist. In politics he is a Republican.

He married (first) August 17, 1870, Mary Elizabeth Blackmer, who died August 31, 1873. He married (second) August 5, 1875, Martha Elizabeth Hamilton, of Salisbury, Vermont, daughter of Colonel Eugene H. and Martha (Bump) Hamilton, granddaughter of Amos and Mary Ann (Hapgood) Hamilton. Her grandfather was born in Massachusetts. Children by first wife: Charles Gardner, mentioned below; Mary Blackmer, born August 22, 1873, died in infancy.

(XV) Charles Gardner, son of Charles Marius Winslow, was born at Brandon, Vermont, August 28, 1871. He received his early education in the public schools of his native town and prepared for college at Phillips Academy, Andover, Massachusetts. He entered Amherst College, but afterward matriculated at the University of Vermont at Burlington, from which he graduated with the degree of Bachelor of Arts. He took special courses in electrical engineering of which he has made a specialty. After being with the Rapid Transit Company of Brooklyn for two years he was engaged in construction work on the New York Central & Hudson River railroad, in charge of installing power houses. Afterward he was engaged in construction work on a North Carolina railroad and at the present time he is an electrical engineer in the employ of the Michigan Central Railroad Company in charge of the electrical system between Chicago and Buffalo. He had charge of the electrical work in the Detroit river tunnel. In politics he is a Republican, in religion a Congregationalist, and while living at Mt. Vernon was deacon of the church there. He is a member of Free and Accepted Masons.

He married, February, 1902, Ella Beebe, of Burlington, Vermont, daughter of Charles Beebe. They have one child, Frederick Beebe, born June 16, 1904.

REMINGTON Thomas Remington, immigrant ancestor, settled in Hingham, Massachusetts. He may have been related to John Remington, the first immigrant of the name, who settled in Newbury in 1637 or earlier, and was admitted a freeman, May 22, 1638. He was a lieutenant; he removed to Rowley and was appointed to train the military company there. He removed to Roxbury and built the Roxbury meeting-house, being a carpenter by trade.

(II) Thomas (2), son of Thomas (1) Remington, removed to Connecticut. He married, March 16, 1687, Remember, born in Hingham, April 22, 1662, died there November 5, 1694, daughter of Samuel and Mary (Farrow) Stowell. Children: Jael, born at Hingham, April 22, 1688; Joshua, mentioned below; Mary, May 9, 1691; Abigail, February 27, 1692-93.

(III) Joshua, son of Thomas (2) Remington, was born in Hingham, Massachusetts, in 1689-90, died at Hingham, July 1, 1733, aged forty-three years. He was a farmer. He married Elizabeth ———. Children: Joshua, born 1714, died April 2, 1730; Elizabeth, 1716; John, 1718, died September 18, 1718; Elisha, January 17, 1720; Mary, June 13, 1722; Sarah, June 23, 1724; Thomas, May 22, 1726; Olive, September 28, 1728, died February 17, 1736-37; Joshua, mentioned below.

(IV) Joshua (2), son of Joshua (1) Remington, was born at Hingham, Massachusetts, February 14, 1730-31. He married, at Hingham, Ruth Clay. Children, born at Hingham: Ruth, August 5, 1755; Uriah, 1757; Joshua, mentioned below.

(V) Joshua (3), son of Joshua (2) Remington, was born in Hingham, Massachusetts, November, 1759, baptized September 14, 1760, died at Huntington, Vermont, October 4, 1855, aged nearly ninety-six years. He was a soldier in the revolution, and was present at the battle of Bennington. He was in Captain Nathan Harwood's company, Colonel John Dickinson's regiment, in 1777, a Massachusetts regiment, the roll of which was sworn to in Chesterfield, New Hampshire. He was also in Captain Joseph Clapp's company, and Colonel Israel Chapin's regiment (Third Massachusetts) in the fall of 1779 and marched to reinforce the northern army. He settled in Wallingford, Vermont, in 1780, and saw further service there in a Vermont regiment. His brother Uriah enlisted in 1775 in a Bridgewater, Massachusetts, company, and was also a veteran at the time they went to Vermont. Joshua and Uriah were both in Captain Stafford's company, Colonel Ebenezer Allen's regiment of Vermont militia in October, 1780, June, 1781, and again in 1781 in Captain Orange Train's company, Colonel Lee's regiment; also in Captain John Sprague's company, Colonel Gideon Warren's regiment, 1780-81. He resided for a time in Hinesburg, Vermont, and bought real estate there, September 19, 1818, sold to his son, Joshua Remington Jr., August 28, 1819, and returned to Wallingford or Huntington. Among his children were: Jeremiah, born at

Wallingford, July 25, 1783; Lydia, married Reuben Smith; Joshua, mentioned below.

(VI) Joshua (4), son of Joshua (3) Remington, was born about 1790, died at Bolton, New York, 1881, at an advanced age. He lived in Wallingford and Hinesburg, Vermont, and in later years at Huntington. He married Polly Sayles or Sales. Children: Justus; Henry; Sylvester; Hosea; Mary, married Thomas Bently; Anne, married Ransom Davis; Ziba, mentioned below; Esther, married Lindsey Davis.

(VII) Ziba, son of Joshua (4) Remington, was born in Hinesburg, Vermont, May 6, 1833. He received his early education in the public schools of his native town. At the age of fifteen he removed to northern New York, where he was employed in Scroon, North Hudson, Black Brook and Horicon, Warren county, New York, and in the latter named place he has made his home for many years. He has followed farming and lumbering in this section with a large measure of success. In town affairs he has taken an active part and has held the office of constable. He is a member of the Methodist Episcopal church. In politics he is a Republican. He married, August 27, 1857, Mary Ross, born April 27, 1837, in Bolton, New York, daughter of Myron and Nora Ross. His wife died July 1, 1899. Children: Worden M., born December 13, 1859, lives in Horicon, New York; Sydney B., born August 24, 1860, a contractor and builder at Ticonderoga, New York; Eddy J., born May 15, 1866, a merchant at Bolton, New York; Fred Homer, mentioned below; Jennie Ann, born December 25, 1871, married William Thatcher, of Ticonderoga; Burdett, born January 20, 1874, of Horicon, New York.

(VIII) Fred Homer, son of Ziba Remington, was born in Horicon, Warren county, New York, March 8, 1868. He attended the public schools of his native town and of North Hudson, New York, and was graduated from the Sherman Academy at Moriah, New York. He then learned the trade of carpenter and the art of draughting. He followed these in Warrensburg, at Glens Falls, and at Ticonderoga, New York, where he engaged in business in partnership with his brother under the firm name of S. B. Remington & Company, and continued for thirteen years in the building and contracting business, erecting houses, constructing macadam road and other similar work. Mr. Remington then came to Rutland, and has here carried on a large general contracting business. He is a member of Mount Defiance Lodge, No. 364, Ancient Free and Accepted Masons, of

Ticonderoga; of Rutland Lodge, No. 1, Knights of Pythias, and also the uniformed rank of this order; member of the Benevolent and Protective Order of Elks, No. 341, of Rutland, and of the Modern Woodmen of America. He is a communicant of the Protestant Episcopal church.

He married, October 8, 1891, Annie Heightman, of Orwell, Vermont, daughter of Hammond and Mary (Leonard) Heightman. Children: Wallace E., born September, 1893; Chester H., June 15, 1898; Wendall E., June 20, 1904.

HAYWARD Thomas Hayward, born in 1719, was doubtless of the C o n c o r d, Massachusetts, branch of the family, mentioned elsewhere in this work. He settled in Templeton, Massachusetts, before the revolution, and died there September 24, 1793, at the age of seventy-five years. His family of ten children were mostly grown to maturity. He married, his intention being dated January 18, 1773, Elizabeth Young, of Hopkinton, Massachusetts, who was doubtless a second wife, and perhaps a third. She died March 24, 1774, in her forty-fifth years. Largely from the record of the settlement of a small estate left by his daughter Huldah Hayward, a spinster, who died at Templeton March 21, 1804, we have a record of his children. At that time but three of the children remained in Templeton: Anna Jackson, William Child's wife Bethia, and Samuel Hayward. They signed a petition for the appointment of an administrator. The court ordered later that the sum of five dollars and twenty-three cents be paid to each of her nine brothers and sisters, that being their respective share of the residue of her estate. In the account is mentioned her share of the estate of her father, Thomas Hayward, late of Templeton. As far as known the children were: Huldah, died as stated; Stephen, a soldier in the revolution from Templeton; Thomas Jr., married Betty Whitney, and served in the revolution; Bethia, married, April 7, 1788, William Child; Anna, married, December 3, 1772, Jonathan Jackson; Betty, married, June, 1785, John Sprague; Eleazer, of whom further; Samuel, married Patty ——, and left one child: Ziba; one other daughter.

(II) Eleazer, son of Thomas Hayward, was born in 1752, died in Shrewsbury, Vermont, in 1789. He went with the family to Templeton, Worcester county, Massachusetts, as early as 1773. He was a soldier in the revolution from Templeton, a private in Captain John Moore's company, Colonel Rufus

Putnam's regiment, the Fifth, from April 14, 1777, to December 31, 1779; also in the same company and regiment under Colonel Gardner until December 9, 1780. He enlisted for three years. He is described 'in 1780 in the rolls as twenty-eight years old, five feet and seven inches tall, of dark complexion. He re-enlisted for three years on January 15, 1781. Directly after the revolution he removed to Shrewsbury, Vermont. He married there, his intention being dated March 1, 1784, Keziah Shedd, of "Thombleston" (Templeton?). His widow Keziah married (second) —— Gibson. The Shedd family was from Pepperell and Groton, Massachusetts. Children of Eleazer: Asa; Lucy; Benjamin; Samuel, of whom further.

(III) Samuel, son of Eleazer Hayward, was born in Shrewsbury, Vermont, in 1789, died in Clarendon, Vermont, March 21, 1862. He was a farmer. He married Patty Gibson, born October 1, 1791, died September 2, 1860, a native of Clarendon (see Gibson V). Children: Sophronia, married Edson Nelson; Clarissa, born 1824, died April 26, 1850; Martha, born in 1826, died June 22, 1877; Samuel (2), of whom further; other children died young.

(IV) Samuel (2), son of Samuel (1) Hayward, was born in Shrewsbury, Vermont, August 1, 1827, died at Rutland, Vermont, February 28, 1886. He was educated in the district schools. For some years he followed farming in Clarendon, then came to Rutland and conducted a grocery store and meat market. He owned much real estate and was a successful and prominent man of business. He was selectman and overseer of the poor and alderman of the city. He was an influential member and generous supporter of the Baptist church.

He married, February 28, 1848, Delia A. Round, who was born October 31, 1833, died March 16, 1899, daughter of Hopkins and Avis (Harrington) Round. Children: 1. James Harrington, born December 28, 1850, died March 18, 1876; married Anna Terinan and had one child, Delia. 2. Edward Dyer, of whom further. 3. George Samuel, born January 5, 1856, died March 2, 1895; married Catherine Buckley, and had children: Arthur, Martha, Samuel, James and Delia. 4. William Hopkins, born July 18, 1863, lives in Rutland. 5. Wallace Round, of whom further.

(V) Edward Dyer, son of Samuel (2) Hayward, was born in Rutland, Vermont, December 1, 1852. He attended the public schools there and from his youth followed farming. For twelve years he had a farm at Mendon,

NEW ENGLAND. 383

Vermont. In 1901 he came to Rutland, where he has since lived. He has retired from active business, but is occupied by the care and management of large real estate interests. In politics he is a Republican.

He married, February 22, 1883, Minnie Kelley, of Wallingford, Vermont, daughter of William Fox and Cynthia Vervora (Rounds) Kelley. Children: 1. Bernice Louise, born July 17, 1887. 2. James Edward, born January 15, 1891.

(V) Wallace Round, son of Samuel (2) Hayward, and brother of Edward Dyer Hayward, was born in Rutland, August 7, 1867. He received his early education in the public schools of Rutland. He is a photographer and a member of the well known firm of Moore & Hayward, of Rutland. In politics he is a Republican. He is a member of Rutland Lodge, No. 79, Free and Accepted Masons; Davenport Chapter, No. 17, Royal Arch Masons; Killington Commandery, No. 6, Knights Templar; and Cairo Temple, Ancient Arabic Order, Nobles of the Mystic Shrine.

He married, in Rutland, October 6, 1886, Catherine Hennessy, born in Bennington, Vermont, daughter of Patrick and Anna (Coyle) Hennessy, who were born in Scotland. Children, born in Rutland: 1. Avis Anna, born September 29, 1887, died September 16, 1891. 2. Wallace Samuel, born November 28, 1890. 3. Avis Pauline, born April 14, 1899.

(The Gibson Line).

(I) John Gibson, the immigrant ancestor, was born in England in 1601, died in Cambridge, Massachusetts, in 1694, aged ninety-three years. He came to New England as early as 1631, and settled in Cambridge, where he was admitted a freeman May 17, 1637. His home lot was granted in the west end of the town August 4, 1634. It was situated between Harvard and Brattle squares, in what is now an important business district, and extended to the Charles river. His house stood at the end of what is now Sparks street, not far from Brattle street, on the road to Watertown, and was built before October 10, 1636. He was doubtless a member of Rev. Mr. Hooker's church, and belonged later to the succeeding society of the First Church, February 1, 1636, under the pastorate of Rev. Thomas Shepard. He held minor town offices. His wife and daughter accused Winifred Holman, widow, and her daughter, of witchcraft, and the charge not being sustained, they were sued for damages by the Holmans. For particulars of this interesting case see history of the Holman family. The

Gibsons paid a small fine. He married (first) Rebecca ———, who was buried December 1, 1661, at Roxbury. He married (second) July 24, 1662, Joan Prentice, widow of Henry Prentice, a pioneer at Cambridge. Children, all by first wife: Rebecca, born in Cambridge in 1636, was the daughter who thought she was bewitched by the Holmans; Mary, May 29, 1637; Martha, April 29, 1639; John (2), of whom further; Samuel, October 28, 1644.

(II) John (2), son of John (1) Gibson, was born in Cambridge about 1641, died October 15, 1679, of smallpox, when only thirty-eight years old. He settled in Cambridge on the homestead deeded to him by his father November 30, 1668. He also was involved in the trial of his family for calling the Holmans witches, and had to acknowledge his error in court or pay a fine. He took the cheaper course. He was a soldier in King Philip's war under Captain Thomas Prentice. He was in the Swanzey fight June 28, 1675, and the Mt. Hope expedition later. He was also in Lieutenant Edward Oake's troop, scouting near Marlborough March 24, 1675-76, and in Captain Daniel Henchman's company September 23, 1676, which marched to Hadley in early summer time. He was possibly the John Gibson in Captain Joshua Scottow's company at Black Point, near Salem, Maine, September, 1677, where the garrison was captured the following month by the Indians. He was admitted a freeman October 11, 1670, and held a number of minor offices. He married, December 9, 1668, Rebecca Harrington, who was born in Cambridge, daughter of Abraham and Rebecca (Cutler) Harrington, or Errington, as it was spelled and perhaps pronounced. Her father was a blacksmith, born at New Castleton, Massachusetts, and died in Cambridge May 9, 1677. Her mother died in Cambridge in 1697. Children, born at Cambridge: Rebecca, born October 4, 1669, died June 10, 1698, at Woburn, unmarried; Martha, married twice; Mary, married, at Concord, October 17, 1700, Nathaniel Gates of Stow; Timothy, of whom further.

(III) Deacon Timothy Gibson, son of John (2) Gibson, was born in Cambridge in 1679, died at Stow, Massachusetts, July 14, 1757. His grave is in the lower village graveyard in the eastern part of Stow. He was brought up by Abraham Holman, of Cambridge, son of William and Winifred Holman, who were involved with his parents and grandparents. In 1689 the Holmans moved to Stow and he went with them, living in the family until 1703, when they removed to the northwest part of Sudbury, and settled on the Assabet river, on a sixty-acre farm bounded on the west by the Stow line, and on the east by the road from Concord to Jewell's Mill. Holman died in 1711. Gibson was a prominent citizen of Sudbury, Massachusetts, and owned land also at Lunenburg, laid to him and his son Timothy. Neither ever lived at Lunenburg, however; but John, Arrington, Isaac and Reuben, his younger sons, settled there, and all were noted as men of great personal prowess. He removed to Stow between December 6, 1728, and February 24, 1731-32, and was selectman there in 1734-35-36-39. His homestead in Stow lay on the south slope of Pomciticut Hill, and was deeded ten years before his death to his son Stephen, and was passed down in the family until 1823. This farm is now in the town of Maynard, which was formed from Sudbury and Stow in 1871.

He married (first) at Concord, November 17, 1700, Rebecca Gates, of Stow, born at Marlborough July 23, 1682, died in Stow January 21, 1731. She was the daughter of Stephen Jr. and Sarah (Woodward) Gates. He married (second) intentions being published November 30, 1756, Mrs. Submit Taylor, of Sudbury, died at Stow January 29, 1759, in her seventy-fifth year. Both wives are buried by his side. Children, all by first wife: Abraham, born 1701; Timothy, January 20, 1702-03; Rebecca, in Sudbury March 19, 1704; John, April 28, 1708; Sarah, October 27, 1710; Samuel, August 27, 1711; Samuel, August 27, 1713; Stephen, March 14, 1715, died young; Arrington, March 22, 1717; Stephen, at Sudbury June 16, 1719; Isaac, of whom further; Mary, born June 14, 1723; Reuben, February 14, 1725.

(IV) Isaac Gibson, son of Deacon Timothy Gibson, was born at Sudbury April 27, 1721, died at Grafton, Massachusetts, June 1, 1797. His gravestone in Middleton cemetery is inscribed: "Isaac Gibson—Died June 1st 1797—in the 77th year—of his age—White is his soul—From blemish free—Red with the blood—He shed for me". He was one of "the Gibson brothers", third of the four who settled in Lunenburg, now Fitchburg, Massachusetts. He settled there before August 1, 1728, in the westerly part of the town, which was set off as Fitchburg February 3, 1764. His father deeded to him there one hundred and fifteen acres "more or less", on October 25, 1744. His house, "Fort Gibson" in the Indian raid of 1748, was situated on the eastern slope of the hill and is still to be seen. In appearance he was of great size and strength, and in character very courageous. One of the anecdotes told of him is of an encounter with a bear whose cub he was carrying off. They rolled down the hill together and he was the victor, though he bore the marks of the struggle all the rest of his life. He was always prominent in Lunenburg. In 1748 he served as scout in the Indian troubles, and was selectman in 1767-70-74-77. In 1771 he was among the thirteen largest taxpayers, and December 1, 1773, was chairman of the committee "to respond to the Boston letter". In 1774 he was on a committee "to prepare instructions for the guidance of the town's representative in the general court". He served in the revolution as minute-man in 1775, one of the five Gibsons of the forty-four Fitchburg minute-men. In 1777 he was town moderator. He served as private in Captain Ebenezer Wood's company, Colonel Asa Whitcomb's regiment of militia, which marched from Fitchburg on the Lexington Alarm of April 19, 1775. He moved to Grafton between December 26, 1786, and September 4, 1790, as shown by an agreement made on the first date by Isaac, of Fitchburg, and his son Jonathan, of Thomlinson (Grafton), and by a power of attorney on the latter date by Isaac, of Tomlinson, to his son Jacob, of Fitchburg. Doubtless he moved in the spring of 1787 as he paid his last real and poll taxes of Fitchburg in 1785, and his last personal tax in 1786. On October 16, 1791, he withdrew his membership from the First Church of Fitchburg to become a member of the Grafton church.

He married (first) at Lunenburg, February 4, 1744-45, Keziah Johnson, their intentions being published January 5, 1744-45. She was born September 7, 1725, died at Fitchburg February 7, 1766, and is buried in the Lunenburg South yard. She was daughter of Deacon Samuel and Rebecca Johnson, of Lunenburg. Deacon Samuel Johnson was son of Edward Johnson, of Woburn, Massachusetts, son of Major William Johnson, of Woburn, son of Captain Edward Johnson, the English pioneer in Charlestown, now Woburn, in 1630. Captain Edward Johnson was a very prominent man, and wrote the "Wonder Working Providences of Sion's Saviour in N. E." Isaac Gibson married (second) at Leominster, Massachusetts, November 27, 1766, Mrs. Abigail (Darby or Stearns?) Bennett, who died at Grafton, November 26, 1808, aged eighty-one years, and was buried beside her husband. Children, by first wife, born in Lunenburg (Fitchburg): Isaac (2), of whom further; John, born July 25, 1747; Abraham, June 13, 1749, died young; Jacob, March 6, 1751; Nathaniel, February 22, 1753; Jonathan, December 22, 1754, not December 22, 1757, as entered on Lunenburg records; David, January 22, 1757; Solomon, November 19, 1758; Abraham, June 13, 1760; Keziah, died September 16, 1817; Rebecca, about 1764 probably at Lunenburg. Child of second wife: Anna, December 6, 1768.

(V) Isaac (2), son of Isaac (1) Gibson, was born at Fitchburg, November 28, 1745, died at Rindge, New Hampshire, December 6, 1811, not December 6, 1815, as inscribed on the gravestone. He lived in Fitchburg for some years, and was one of the five Gibsons who were minute-men. About 1782 he moved to the southwest of Rindge where he lived the rest of his life, dying of "spotted fever", an epidemic which swept through New England in 1811 and 1812. He married (first) at Harvard, Massachusetts, March 16, 1773, published January 29, 1773, Lois Samson, of Bolton, Massachusetts, who died at Fitchburg June 17, 1782. He married (second) Ruth Eaton, born at Reading, Massachusetts, September 27, 1757, died at Rindge February 25, 1855. She was daughter of John and Mary (McIntire) Eaton, of Jaffrey, New Hampshire. Children, by first wife, born at Fitchburg: Hannah, baptized May 1, 1774; Sally, born February 25, 1776; Joel, baptized April 25, 1779, died June 22, 1782; Lois, born March 5, 1781. Children by second wife, born at Rindge: Isaac, born August 4, 1783; Ruth, May 22, 1786; Israel, September 14, 1789; Patty, October 1, 1791, died September 2, 1860, married, August 24, 1815, Samuel Hayward of Clarendon (see Hayward III); John, April 4, 1794; Catherine, August 13, 1796; Nathaniel, August 13, 1796.

VAUGHAN George Vaughan, immigrant ancestor, was born in England in 1621, died at Middleborough, Massachusetts, October 20, 1694. He settled first in Scituate, Massachusetts, as early as 1653, then removed to Middleborough in 1663 and for a time lived also at Marshfield. He appears to have had a liking for litigation as his name appears frequently in the court records both as plaintiff and defendant. He was appointed on a committee June 1, 1669, with William Crowell, John Thomson and William Nelson, to determine the boundary line between Nantasket Men's Land, called the Major's Purchase, and the towns of Marshfield, Duxbury and Bridgewater. He kept the first licensed ordinary in the town of Middleborough. In 1671 he was placed on a town committee to view the damage done by horses and hogs of the English to property of the Indians, and in 1675 was constable. He bought part of the land in the Twenty-six Men's Purchase. He was

one of the town garrison in King Philip's war. His will was dated June 30, 1694, proved November 10, 1694. His house was in that part of the town known as Wappanucket. He married, in 1652, Elizabeth, daughter of Edmund Hincksman, of Marshfield. She died June 24, 1693, aged sixty-three years. Children: Elizabeth, born April 8, 1653; Joseph, of whom further; Daniel; John, born 1658, drowned aged eighteen; Mary, married, in 1683, Jonathan Washburn.

(II) Captain Joseph Vaughan, son of George Vaughan, was born in Middleborough, August 20, 1654, died there, March 2, 1743. He was one of the selectmen of Middleborough, elected in 1689 and continued in office for a period of twenty-five years by annual re-elections. He was ensign of the Middleborough military company as early as 1706, was lieutenant in 1712 and afterward captain of the militia of the town. He lived in the house owned at one time by Captain Nathaniel Wilder and had much land in Middleborough, being an owner in the Sixteen Shilling Purchase. He married (first) May 7, 1680, Johann Thomas, who died April 11, 1718, aged sixty-one; married (second) December 2, 1720, Mercy Fuller, widow of Jabez Fuller. Children, born in Middleborough: Elisha, born February 7, 1681; Jabez, April 30, 1682; George, October 3, 1683; Ebenezer, February 22, 1685; Elizabeth, March 7, 1686; Hannah, November 18, 1688; Joseph Jr., October 2, 1690; John, September 8, 1692; Mary, October 6, 1694; Josiah, February 2, 1698-99; Joanna, January 26, 1700-01. Child, by second wife, Peter, of whom further.

(III) Peter, son of Captain Joseph Vaughan, was born in Middleborough, February 28, 1728. He lived in his native town. He married, April 28, 1751, Johanna Barrows. Among their children was Joseph, of whom further.

(IV) Joseph (2), son of Peter Vaughan, was born in Middleborough, April 15, 1755, died June 7, 1801. He was a soldier in the revolution from Middleborough in Captain Abishai Tinkham's company, Colonel Ebenezer Sprout's regiment in 1780. He married, in 1780, Sarah Thomas. Children: Jireh, of whom further; Joseph and George.

(V) Jireh, son of Joseph (2) Vaughan, was born in Middleborough, April 24, 1787, died October 21, 1871, in Rutland, Vermont. He was educated in the schools of his native town. When a young man he came to Vermont, locating first at Southerland Falls, now Proctor, afterward in Pittsford and in Plymouth, finally making his home in Rutland where he spent his last years. He was a mechanical genius and produced many useful inventions. He invented a turbine water wheel; was the first to bring into use the slate pencil; manufactured firearms and bored the barrels in his own shop. He held patents on stoves and a large number of valuable devices. He had a shop in which he worked upon his inventions and in which he carried on all kinds of mechanical work, repairing and manufacturing.

He married Ruth Whipple Campbell, born in Rhode Island or Connecticut, daughter of Joseph and Anne (Whipple) Campbell. She died in Plainfield, New Jersey, in 1889, aged ninety-one years. Children: James; Fayette, of whom further; Amelia, married Reuben Holden; Emma, married Ceylon Dake; Lorano; Ellen, married Luther Harger.

(VI) Fayette, son of Jireh Vaughan, was born in Plymouth, Vermont, September 25, 1824, died March 31, 1907. He received his early education in the common schools. When but twelve years old he began to work for the Vermont Marble Company in Proctor. He came to Rutland when a young man and engaged in business as a general merchant, having a store at the corner of Main and West streets. After he retired from mercantile business he was for a number of years a deputy under Sheriff Peabody on duty at the courthouse. In politics he was a Democrat; in religion a Congregationalist. He married, November 11, 1861, Nellie Ladd, born February 7, 1838, in Stark or Mercer, Maine, daughter of Eben and Sylvia (Lander) Ladd. Children: Frank Leonard, of whom further; Edward, born in 1868, died in 1874; Mabel L., born January 24, 1878, married C. W. Barker, of Granville, New York; William G., born June 24, 1883.

(VII) Frank Leonard, son of Fayette Vaughan, was born in Rutland, Vermont, October 13, 1863. He was educated in the public schools. He began his business career as a clerk in his father's store and afterward engaged in business as a merchant on his own account. For some years he conducted a livery stable on West street. He afterward engaged in business as a dealer in groceries, having his store on Merchants row, whence he removed in 1907 to his present location on Church street. In politics he is a Republican. He married, August 5, 1885, Lucretia May Learned, born in Rutland, Vermont, January, 1863, daughter of John K. and Electa Jane (Kelley) Learned. Children: 1. Lafayette Learned, born January 23, 1887; now in charge of a large grain elevator in Kentucky, supervising the weighing of all in-

coming and outgoing grain; married, August 3, 1910, Leon Immogene Wooten, of Glasgow, Kentucky, daughter of James Thomas and Jennie Quintilla (Fant) Wooten. 2. Alice Sabin, born January, 1889; now with the Fairbanks Scale Company, Albany, New York.

STEARNS

(II) Isaac (2) Stearns, son of Isaac (1) Stearns (q. v.), was born January 6, 1633, died August 29, 1676. He settled at Cambridge Farms, now Lexington, Massachusetts. In 1665 he was admitted a freeman. The inventory of his estate amounted to the sum of three hundred pounds. He married, June 24, 1660, Sarah, daughter of Captain Richard and Elizabeth Beers, of Watertown, Massachusetts. Captain Beers was an original proprietor of Watertown, and served as captain in King Philip's war; he was slain in battle by the Indians at Northfield, Massachusetts, September 4, 1675. Children: Sarah, born January 14, 1662; Mary, October 8, 1663; Isaac, August 26, 1665; Samuel, of whom further; Abigail, 1670; John, 1675.

(III) Samuel, son of Isaac (2) Stearns, was born January 11, 1667-68, and was accidentally killed, November 19, 1721, by the falling of a tree, it is said. He served as tithingman and assessor in Lexington for several years. He married Phoebe ——, who was administratrix of his estate, John Stearns, of Concord, being her surety. In 1730 she moved to Littleton, Massachusetts, with some of her children. There was a "Caution of Chelmsford, July 24, 1750, against settlement of Phoebe Stearns from Littleton". Children: Sarah, born January 15, 1696-97; Mary, January 27, 1698-99; Abigail, February 8, 1700; Samuel, of whom further; Ruth, May 25, 1704; Phoebe, February 23, 1706; Rebecca, April 15, 1708; Thomas, July 4, 1710; Captain John, July 23, 1712; Joseph, baptized April 15, 1715; Benjamin, born January 6, 1718.

(IV) Samuel (2), son of Samuel (1) Stearns, was born March 7, 1702, died in 1787. He lived in New Sherborn or Littleton, Massachusetts, and finally in Hollis, New Hampshire. He married, January 1, 1731, ceremony performed by Joseph Wilder, Esq., Keziah Robbins, of Littleton. Children: Samuel, born 1732; Peter, of whom further; Isaac, 1736; Joseph, 1738; Ruth, 1741; Keziah, 1743; Ebenezer, December 25, 1744; Phoebe, 1746; John, October 15, 1750.

(V) Peter, son of Samuel (2) Stearns, was born in 1734. He served in the French and Indian war in 1762, in Lieutenant Frank Miller's company. He removed from Hollis, New Hampshire, to Plymouth in that state in 1769 and became a useful citizen there. He served from Plymouth in the revolutionary war in Captain John Willoughby's company at the Ticonderoga alarm in 1777; was sergeant in Captain Eliot's company, Colonel Hobart's regiment, at Bennington, in 1777; was lieutenant in Colonel Mooney's regiment in the Rhode Island campaign, June 30, 1779, to January, 1780, and was lieutenant in the same company in the campaign on the northern frontier under the general command of Colonel Charles Johnston. In 1793 he removed to Vermont and lived at Peru and Shelburne in that state. He died at Shelburne in 1813.

He married (first) September 8, 1764, at Hollis, Abigail, daughter of Thomas and Mary (Ball) Wheet, and sister of Rev. Joseph Wheet, of Grafton, New Hampshire. She died September 22, 1786. He married (second) in 1789, Judith, born at Newbury, January 5, 1752, daughter of Jonathan and Mary (Jones) Bartlett, and sister of Evan Bartlett, of Hebron, New Hampshire. Children by first wife: Peter, mentioned below; Polly, born April 16, 1769; Polly, June 7, 1770 (given in genealogy); Keziah, September 19, 1771; Keziah, August, 1772, married Stephen Foss; Rebecca, March 27, 1774, married ——— Clark; Sally, July 30, 1776; Elizabeth, February 23, 1778; Hannah, March 21, 1781; Nathaniel Wheet, April 22, 1784; Abigail, September 10, 1786, died at Rumsey. Children by second wife: Jonathan, October 6, 1789; Judith Bartlett, October 6, 1791, married Caleb Harding; John, November 16, 1793; Phoebe, December 8, 1795, died 1855 at Albany, New York, unmarried.

(VI) Peter (2), son of Peter (1) Stearns, was born December 14, 1767, in Hollis, New Hampshire, died January 7, 1849. He came with his parents to Plymouth. He lived in Plymouth near Meredith until 1810 when he moved to Peru, New York, where as a farmer he spent his last years. He was a carpenter by trade, a town officer of Plymouth, and deacon of the Congregational church there. He was foremost in building the First Congregational church at Peru of which he was deacon until he died. He was highly respected by all who knew him, a useful and honored citizen, and a devoted Christian. It is said that he married three times. His third wife was Irene, daughter of Marcus Barnes of Chesterfield, Essex county, New York. Children: Peter, mentioned below; Charles, born 1795, married Susan Foote; Rhoda, 1797, married Arthur H. Merrill; Thomas, married Fannie Banker and settled in Peru, New York; Sarah,

died in Chesterfield, New York; Asenath, born 1806, married Joel Smith and settled in Beekmantown, New York; John, married Lucy Hewitt and settled in Red Wing, Minnesota.

(VII) Peter (3), son of Peter (2) Stearns, was born December 11, 1793 (or December 9, 1794) at Plymouth, New Hampshire, died in Westford, Vermont, February 15, 1855. He was educated in the public schools. He removed from Plymouth to Peru, New York, with others of the family, and subsequently settled in Westford, Vermont. He followed farming all his active life. Some of his descendants spell the name Sterns. He was a soldier in the war of 1812 and was in the battle at Plattsburg, New York. He married, in 1816, Sophia Wood, of Leicester, Massachusetts, born January 9, 1793, in Leicester, died September 24 1884. Children: 1. Rev. William T. born November 17, 1817, at Peru, died May 20, 1891; settled at Fletcher, Vermont; married Phebe Beeman. 2. Mary Wood, born July 21, 1819, in Westford; married John Maxfield, of Fairfax. 3. Sally, born January 20, 1821, died August 29, 1865; married Benjamin Bell. 4. Harry Kent, born November 12, or December 16, 1822. 5. Rufus Wood, born April 18, 1824. 6. Charles A., born December 1, 1826, in Westford, died September 18, 1895; married Sarah S. Rider, of Boston. 7. Nancy T., born September 14, 1828; married Lewis Story, of Fairfax. 8. Asenath, born July 24 1830 in Westford; married Anson Story, of Fairfax. 9. Hannah A., born November 1, 1833; a school teacher; married Williams Bellews. 10. John Wesley, mentioned below. 11. Artemas A., born January 30, 1838; married Cynthia Pease; settled in Rutland. 12. Ellen M., born February 18, 1840, in Westford; married a Mr. Mills, of Peabody, Massachusetts.

(VIII) John Wesley, son of Peter (3) Stearns, was born in Westford, Vermont August 24, 1835, died in Rutland, Vermont, November 22, 1909. He attended the public schools of his native town and the Hampton Seminary, Fairfax, Vermont. About 1859 he removed to Boston, Massachusetts, and learned the carpenter's trade. In 1864 he came to Rutland, Vermont, where he resided the remainder of his days. For a number of years he worked at his trade in Rutland. In 1869 he engaged in business as a dealer in furniture and undertaker and built up a large and successful business. He was active in municipal affairs and held various offices of trust and responsibility. Under the town government he served on the board of selectmen and after the city was incorporated he was elected mayor. In politics he was a Republican. In religion a Congregationalist. He married, in 1864, Isabelle, born in Canada, December 20, 1845, daughter of John and Jane (Dunwoodie) Hammond. She died at Rutland, December 23, 1910. They had but one child, John Burnham, mentioned below.

(IX) John Burnham, son of John Wesley Stearns, was born in Rutland, Vermont, September 14, 1875. He attended the public schools of Rutland, entered Harvard College and took a special course known as the law preparatory course. He became associated in business with his father while he was a student and since leaving college shared in the management of the store and undertaking business up to the time his father died when he succeeded to the business and has conducted it to the present time. He is a member of Rutland Lodge, No. 79, Free and Accepted Masons, and of Vermont Lodge, Knights of Pythias; he is a member of the State Board of Embalming Examiners. In religion he is a Congregationalist, in politics a Republican.

He married, November 29, 1898, Henrietta Winnifred Spafford, of Rutland, Vermont, daughter of Henry W. and Ella (Kingsbury) Spafford. Children: 1. Henrietta Isabelle, born June 14, 1902. 2. Mabel Eleanor, December 11, 1906. 3. John Spafford, November 23, 1909, died August, 1910. 4. John Wesley, October 10, 1910. 5. Mary Cora, June 12, 1912.

The late John Cook, for many
COOK years prominent in the business world of Rutland and always recognized as one of her leading citizens, was a descendant of English ancestors, whose posterity have for more than two centuries and a half been resident in New England.

(I) Samuel Cook, founder of the American branch of the family, was born in 1642, in Yorkshire, England, and as a mere youth emigrated to the New World. He is known to have been in New Haven, Connecticut, in 1661, when he was but nineteen years old. He was three times married and by each union became the father of two children. By the first wife he had two sons: Samuel and Aaron. By the second wife he had a son and a daughter: Ephraim and Elizabeth. By the third wife he had two more sons: Israel, mentioned below; Ashabel.

(II) Israel, son of Samuel Cook, was born in 1694, in Cheshire, Connecticut. He married Elizabeth Clark. Their children were: Ebenezer, Sarah, Delilah, Catherine, Benjamin, Ezekiel, Ashabel, mentioned below.

(III) Ashabel, son of Israel and Elizabeth

(Clark) Cook, was born May 1, 1738, in Wallingford, Connecticut, died in Rutland, December 16, 1801. He appears to have removed to Rutland, Vermont, but at what date is not recorded. He married Rachel Rice, born May 10, 1743, and the following children were born to them: John, Simeon, Israel, Ashabel, Simon, Robert, Rice, Orel, mentioned below.

(IV) Orel, son of Ashabel and Rachel (Rice) Cook, was born June 25, 1782, in Rutland, Vermont. He was a hatter by trade and for many years conducted business in his native place, where his entire life was spent. He married Lorane Dewey, born October 27, 1791, and they became the parents of the following children: Rachel Lorane, born January 22, 1809; Maria Prudence, October 11, 1811; Orel, December 7, 1813, physician and state senator; Prudence Maria, May 21, 1816; John, mentioned below; Israel, January 24, 1822; Emily, August 5, 1824; Simeon Ashabel, November 1, 1826, physician and United States consul to Peru, South America; Elizabeth E., June 30, 1830; Maria Prudence, October 11, 1823; James Porter, July 23, 1833. The father of this family died May 21, 1861, surviving his wife, whose death occurred February 21, 1850.

(V) John, son of Orel and Lorane (Dewey) Cook, was born March 13, 1819. He studied for the legal profession and was admitted to the bar. Feeling, however, a strong inclination to enter mercantile life, and conscious that his talents were of a nature to fit him in a more than ordinary degree for a commercial career, he abandoned his project of practicing law and engaged in business. For many years he was in Troy, New York, dealing in hats, caps and furs, and later he engaged in the grocery business in Rutland. Some years before his death he withdrew from the cares and responsibilities of the commercial arena, making the latter portion of his life a season of well-earned leisure after a long period of strenuous activity. The business career of Mr. Cook was exceptionally successful, a fact due to the sound and accurate judgment, penetrating insight and vigor of execution which were among his most salient characteristics, combined with strict adherence to principle and unswerving integrity. In addition to his business in Rutland he possessed large real estate interests in that city. He was a man of extensive and varied information; and his advice in matters of local importance was frequently solicited.

Mr. Cook married Sarah Jane, daughter of Jacob Bovee, and they were the parents of one daughter, Emma Sarah, mentioned below. Mrs. Cook died June 28, 1872, and her husband survived her more than a quarter of a century, passing away September 13, 1905, at the advanced age of eighty-six. The death of Mr. Cook deprived Rutland of a most estimable citizen, ever ready to lend his aid and influence to everything which would in his judgment further her improvement and advance her best interests. Mr. Cook was very musical and at sixteen was chorister of the Congregational church choir of Rutland, Vermont, and at his death was the oldest standing member of that church.

(VI) Emma Sarah, daughter of John and Sarah Jane (Bovee) Cook, was born in Troy, New York, and resides on the old homestead in Rutland, Vermont, caring for the large real estate interests inherited from her father.

GROVER Thomas Grover, American immigrant of this family, was born in England and came to this country in 1642, making his home in Charlestown, Massachusetts. He moved to the Mystic Side, later called Malden. "Old Goodwife Grover", perhaps his mother, was admitted to the Charlestown church, November 30, 1643. John Grover, presumably his brother, settled in Charlestown about 1640 and removed to Rumney Marsh, now Chelsea, Massachusetts, and finally also to Malden, where he died February 19, 1673-74. Thomas Grover died at Malden, October 28, 1661. The inventory of his estate was filed December 17, 1661, by his widow Elizabeth and son Lazarus. Lazarus also administered on the estate of his brother John who died aged seventeen and sister Elizabeth in 1674. Children: Lazarus, mentioned below; Elizabeth, born December 27, 1642, died 1674; Thomas, born April 1, 1643, married, May 23, 1668, Sarah, daughter of John Chadwick, and had Thomas, born 1669; Sarah, 1670; Thomas, 1671; John, 1673. (The printed records of Malden make Andrew son of Thomas, but the deeds prove he was son of Lazarus); John, died February 16, 1673-74; Andrew, married Hannah Hills, February 7, 1673.

(II) Lazarus, son of Thomas Grover, was born at Malden, April 5, 1642. He married Ruth, daughter of Richard Adams. Thomas, Andrew and Ephraim Grover bought land, November 14, 1702, in that part of Taunton called the West Purchase, now Norton. Thomas Grover and Andrew Grover, of Norton, deeded to William Pain, of Charlestown, in 1716 all the right of their mother, Ruth Grover, in the estate of their grandfather, Richard Adams. This deed proves the parentage of Andrew Grover. Children, born at Malden: Lazarus, December, 1665; Thomas,

June, 1671; Andrew, mentioned below; Ruth, married William Pain; Elizabeth, married Timothy Baldwin; Ebenezer.

(III) Andrew, son of Lazarus Grover, was born in Malden, October, 1673, and settled in Norton. He married Mary ———. Children, born at Malden : John, March 12, 1697-98; James, mentioned below; Mary, September 26, 1701. Born at Norton: Ruth, August 30, 1702; Mary, February 19, 1704; Stephen, July 8, 1705; Ephraim, May 27, 1706; Hannah, December 10, 1707; Sarah, November 28, 1709; Mercy, November 1, 1712; Robert, August 18, 1714; Martha, May 9, 1716; Andrew, February 14, 1718. The following were baptized at Norton, April 10, 1720: John, James, Mary, Ruth, Stephen, Sarah, Martha.

(IV) James, son of Andrew Grover, was born at Malden, September 7, 1699, and went to Norton when a baby with the family in 1702. He was baptized April 10, 1720, at Norton. He married Sarah Austin, November 17, 1726, and lived at Norton. Children, born at Norton: James, mentioned below; Sarah, born May 3, 1731; Abigail and Elizabeth, twins, March 4, 1736; John, June 20, 1739.

(V) James (2), son of James (1) Grover, was born in Norton, August 15, 1729. He lived in that part of Norton now the town of Mansfield, and removed to Packersfield, now Nelson, New Hampshire, and finally to Bethel, Maine, with others of the family. He was a man of great piety and some learning, and was the deacon of the church. He was the first person buried in the old cemetery on the Grover homestead. He married, April 18, 1754, Sarah Wellman. Children: James, born at Norton, March 31, 1755, married Polly ———; John, came to Bethel in 1780, married Jerusha Wiley; Jedediah, married Hannah Wheeler; Eli, born in 1763, married Mehitable Austin; Elijah, mentioned below; Sarah, married Daniel Gage; Olive, born 1766, married Benjamin Killgore; Naomi, born 1770, married Joseph Wheeler.

(VI) Elijah, son of James (2) Grover, was born about 1765. He lived in Bethel, Maine. He married Mrs. Hannah Mills, daughter of Moses Wason, of Dublin, New Hampshire, and widow of James Mills. Children: Elijah Jr., born April 7, 1791, married Hadasseh Bean; Mary, March 12, 1793, married Thomas S. Paine; Nathan, mentioned below; George W., June 23, 1798, married Dolly Bean; Jeremiah, 1801, married Sophronia Blake; Elvira, December 14, 1805, married Aaron Cross.

(VII) Nathan, son of Elijah Grover, was born in Bethel, June 12, 1797, died in 1878. He was educated in the public schools. He became a thrifty farmer, owning a large farm on the road from West Bethel to Albany. He was a man of marked ability in business and of the strictest integrity. He served several years on the board of education and one term in the state legislature. He was well versed and influential in public affairs and allied with all the great movements for social welfare and progress in his day. He was industrious, prudent and charitable. Besides his own family to which he was devoted, he raised to manhood and womanhood in his own home eight orphan children. For many years his house was a tavern and a favorite resort for travelers from the Upper Coos on the way to and from Portland markets. Through a long and varied life he was one of the most active and influential men of the town. He married Lucinda, daughter of Daniel Barker, of Bethel. Children, born in Bethel: Oscar Dunnath, born May 10, 1828; Daniel Barker, mentioned below; Nathan Sumners, born May 19, 1833, died October 2, 1836.

(VIII) Daniel Barker, son of Nathan Grover, was born in Bethel, March 15, 1831, died in Redlands, California, in 1897. He was educated in the public schools of his native town and at Gould Academy. For many years he lived on the homestead at Bethel, and was an intelligent, progressive and enterprising farmer. Later in life he moved to California where he spent his last years. He married (first) May 9, 1860, Martha Matilda Eames, who died in 1879, daughter of Nathan and —— (Abbott) Eames. He married (second) October 21, 1880, Theresa, daughter of Melvin Stowe, of Newry, Maine. Children, all by first wife: Mary Lucinda, born April 13, 1861; married, August 24, 1881, George A. Cheney; Nathan Eames, May 25, 1864, died in infancy; Sumner Abbott, April 24, 1865; Nathan Clifford, January 31, 1868, graduate of Maine State College; Arthur Curtis, mentioned below; Oscar Llewellyn, born August 28, 1878, graduate of Maine State College.

(IX) Arthur Curtis, son of Daniel Barker Grover, was born at Bethel, Maine, August 21, 1870. He attended the public schools and entered the Maine State College at Orono, graduating in the class of 1892. He took a special course in civil engineering. He followed his profession for two years in Newton, eleven and one-half years in Malden, Massachusetts, and in the fall of 1895 came to Rutland, Vermont, where he has followed his profession and maintained his residence; he has had charge of much important work, and since 1897 he has been city engineer of Rut-

land. Mr. Grover is a member of Center Lodge, Free and Accepted Masons; Davenport Chapter, Royal Arch Masons; Killington Commandery, Knights Templar; Cairo Temple, Mystic Shrine; Killington Lodge, Independent Order of Odd Fellows, the Encampment and Canton; Modern Woodmen of America and of the Congregational church of Rutland. In politics he is a Republican.

He married, September 9, 1895, Susie Farington Colburn, of Orono, Maine, born there, daughter of Charles Haley and Hannah (Colburn) Colburn. Children: Arthur Newell, born December 12, 1899; Doris Elizabeth, September 26, 1905.

TOWNSEND The family of Townsend in America and England traces its ancestry to Walter atte Townshende, son of Sir Lodovic de Townshende, a Norman nobleman, who came to England soon after the Conquest. Sir Lodovic married Elizabeth de Hauteville, daughter of Sir Thomas and heiress of Raymond de Hauteville; a portion of the Hauteville estate came to the Townsend family. In 1200 William Townsend was in Taverham, county Norfolk. Thomas atte-Tunneshende (Townsend) lived in the reign of Henry III. (1217-72) at West Herling. William Atte Tunesend lived in 1292; Thomas in 1314. The family was prominent in Norfolk in the fourteenth century. The coat-of-arms of this ancient family was a chevron between three escallop shells.

John, Henry and Richard Townsend came to this country from Norwich, county Norfolk, England, several years before 1645 when John was one of the patentees of the town of Flushing, Long Island. From a petition of his widow to Governor Andros we learn that he had previously taken up land near New York, and "peacably enjoyed the same years" but Indian alarms and other troubles that she does not specify induced him to leave the property and settle at Flushing, where he was joined by his brother Henry. They were members of the Society of Friends and soon at variance with the Dutch authorities over politics rather that religion, however. John was named by Governor Stuyvesant as among the principal persons of Flushing "who resist the Dutch mode of choosing sheriff, pretending against the adopted course in the fatherland, and who refuse to contribute their share to the maintenance of Christian, pious, reformed ministers." Everywhere the Friends refused to support the established church, Congregational in New England, Dutch in New York, and other forms also. Townsend was summoned

A. C. Grover

to appear January 23, 1648, before the governor and council. Then the three Townsends, desiring a more liberal environment, settled at Warwick, Rhode Island, where all three served in the general assembly. In 1656 they were patentees of the town of Jamaica, Long Island, then called Rudorp; very soon the old religious differences arose again, and Henry was ordered to pay a fine of eight pounds or leave the province in six weeks for having "called together conventicles." The people of Flushing called a meeting and addressed a remonstrance to the governor against the judgment; the sheriff presented the paper; John Townsend was held for trial on the charge of inducing the magistrates to sign the paper, in the sum of twelve pounds, and Henry Townsend was condemned by the governor and council, January 15, 1658, to pay one hundred pounds and remain arrested until the fine was paid; the records do not show how the case ended, but in that year he was in Oyster Bay. In January, 1661, John and Henry Townsend were complained of for "Countenancing Quakers", so they evidently had not yet become members of the Society. As early as September 16, 1661, John was a townsman in Oyster Bay, and had a house there soon after. He must have been quite advanced in years when he settled there, having led a most active and laborious life since emigration. His widow petitioned Governor Andros for land which he had been forced to give up because of Indian alarms and other difficulties, but her petition was not granted. The office of overseer is the only one John Townsend is known to have held in Oyster Bay. His name appears often in deeds of land. He died intestate in 1668 and was buried on his own farm, probably the first to be interred in what was afterward the graveyard of Fort Hill.

He married Elizabeth Montgomery. His widow divided his property among the six youngest children; James received three and three-quarter acres of land in Oyster Bay, in addition to what he already had, two shares of meadow near Beaver swamp, one share of meadow near the creek, land improved by his father on Mill River swamp, with part of the swamp, six acres of the plains, and some swamp land also; the daughters received thirty pounds apiece, the eldest daughter Elizabeth also sharing in this division; Rose received half a share of meadow and commoning in Oyster Bay with twenty-six acres of land; George and Daniel had the two homesteads after her decease. In her will, after she had disposed of her husband's property, she provided that after her death the remaining property should be divided among her living chil-

dren; if she died before her two youngest children became of age, the one who brought them up should have the use of their property until they became of age; her eldest son John was to have land on Hog Island. Children: John; Thomas; Elizabeth, married Gideon Wright; James, mentioned below; Rose, married John Wicks or Weeks, of Warwick; Annel Sarah; George, married, November 17, 1684, Mary Hawkhurst; Daniel, married Susannah Furman.

(II) James, son of John Townsend, was born about 1650. He married (first) ——— Wright, daughter of Peter Wright. He married (second) Jane, daughter of Henry Ruddock, October 16, 1677. He married (third) Delivered ———. His homestead was the place now or lately owned by T. W. Burtis and heirs. He removed to Cedar swamp now or lately belonging to Robert Seaman. James and his brother George owned a tract of land at Norwich. He was a surveyor and laid out lands at Unkoway and Latting's Neck. He was overseer while living at Oyster Bay. He died in 1697-98. Children: Job, mentioned below; Thomas, died young; Daniel, married Freelove, daughter of Captain Samuel Dickinson; Ruddock, married Abigail ——— and first lived at Norwich, Connecticut, then at Oak Neck, Long Island, and after 1715 at Little Egg Harbor, New Jersey; Joseph, died young; Joshua, married Meribah Cock and lived at Duck Pond, Long Island; Ruemourn, born after his father's death, married Mary Allen.

(III) Job, son of James Townsend, joined with his brothers in providing a share in the estate of their father for the posthumous son Ruemourn. He inherited land at Cedar swamp and elsewhere. The Townsend Genealogy gives no further record of him. Presumably he went with others of the family to Norwich, Connecticut. Job, Christopher and Solomon Townsend, who appeared in Newport, Rhode Island, about 1720, were probably his sons. They were without doubt brothers. The Townsend records are incomplete at this period, partly because some of the family were Quakers, partly due to changes in residence and to defective public records.

(IV) Job (2), believed to be son of Job (1) Townsend, was born about 1700-05. He settled at Newport, Rhode Island. He was justice of the peace in Newport in 1741. He married Rebecca ———. Children, born at Newport. Some of these records were from the Friends Records. Hannah, born June 20, 1727, married, August 6, 1746, John Goddard; Sarah, March 8, 1729; Susannah, November 29, 1731; married, January 17, 1750, James

Goddard; Job, married, May 31, 1753, Deborah, daughter of Peter and Thankful Taylor, and she died January 24, 1805; Mary, 1733; Peter, January 22, 1734-35; Thomas, January 30, 1742-43, married, December 8, 1765, Mary Dyer.

(IV) Christopher, son of Job (1) Townsend, was born about 1700, probably on Long Island. He married Patience Easton, December 26, 1723, at Newport. Children, recorded at Newport: Solomon, born November 6, 1724; Christopher, March 24, 1728, died May 9, 1735; Nicholas, October 27, 1730; John, February 17, 1732-33, married Philadelphia ———— and lived at Newport; Mary, 1736, died March 11, 1783, married Andrew Cozzens; Jonathan, May 23, 1745.

(IV) Captain Solomon Townsend, brother of Job (2) Townsend, was born about 1700-05. He married, at Providence, March 8, 1730-31 (by Richard Brown), Lydia Tillinghast. His residence was given as Newport. His son Solomon settled at Portsmouth, Rhode Island, and had a large family.

The Townsend family of Rhode Island before the revolution was confined to Newport and Portsmouth, if the records are at all complete. According to the census of 1774, the following were heads of families in Newport: Thomas, John, Edmund, Christopher, all having children over sixteen; four widows, Rebecca, Alice, Flora and Mary, whose sons had all left home, and Job Townsend who had one child under sixteen. Most of these are mentioned in the lists of children, doubtless incomplete, given above. Thomas, John, Christopher and Job, and others were in Newport according to the census of 1790. William Townsend was of Providence in 1774, having four daughters, himself and wife in his family. Besides those mentioned above in the fourth generation we find Nathaniel who was old enough to be married in 1745 and must have been son of one of the three brothers above mentioned.

(V) William Townsend, son or nephew of Job (2) Townsend, was born as early as 1720 in Rhode Island or Long Island, died 1775. He removed to Haverhill, Massachusetts, as early as 1743, for in that year his name appears there on a town tax list. His name was on a muster roll of men who went to Albany in the French and Indian war, April 7 to December 12, 1755. But he returned to Providence, Rhode Island, as shown by the vital records of Haverhill, showing the birth of his son Thomas there. He married Mary ————. Children: 1. William, born about 1740; married, at Haverhill, March 4, 1762, Sarah Middleton, who died October 19, 1828,

at Haverhill, aged eighty-nine years; children, born at Haverhill: Sally, February 26, 1767, married James Greenleaf, January 17, 1786; Lydia, May 1, 1769, died September 10, 1770; William Jr., was probably in Providence in 1774. 2. Sarah, baptized at Haverhill, February 19, 1743-44. 3. Elizabeth, baptized at Haverhill, August 10, 1746. 4. Thomas, mentioned below. 5. James was a soldier in the revolution from Haverhill, and lost property in the battle of Bunker Hill.

(VI) Thomas, son of William Townsend, was born, according to the records of Salem, New Hampshire, formerly part of Haverhill, Massachusetts, April 27, 1750, and was baptized, according to the church records, May 10, 1750, at Haverhill. He married Sarah Harriman and lived in Salem, New Hampshire. He was a soldier in the revolution (p. 168, Vol. 3, New Hamps. Rev. Rolls). In 1790 he was living at Salem, according to the federal census. He is said to have moved to Henniker, New Hampshire. He died in 1814. We find the record of one child, Sarah, born March 23, 1796, at Salem. He also had James, mentioned below; Daniel, William, Mary and Lydia.

(VII) James (2), son of Thomas Townsend, was born in 1789. He lived at Henniker, New Hampshire, and West Burke and Sheffield, Vermont, dying in the latter named place in 1867. He married Zerviah Leavitt, born in Northfield, New Hampshire, in 1790. Children: Oliver Hazard Perry, mentioned below; Sally Harriman, Zerviah Leavitt, Dolly Meigs, Hannah Tilton, James LaFayette, William Franklin, Ruth Mather, Solon Smith, Lydia Ann.

(VIII) Oliver Hazard Perry, son of James (2) Townsend, was born at West Burke, Vermont, December 1, 1813, died in 1891. He was for many years in the service of the newspaper, The New York Evangelist. He married (first) Phebe Ann Geer, a native of Washington, Connecticut (see Geer IV). He married (second) Mary Ryan. Children by first wife: 1. Therina, born 1843, died 1868; married Thomas J. Crombie and had two sons, George Townsend and Clarence Hugh Crombie. 2. James, died aged eighteen years. 3. Edward, mentioned below. 4. Myra, born in 1851, unmarried. 5. Phebe Ann, born 1853, unmarried. Children of second wife: 6. Mary. 7. Margaret O. 8. Perry. 9. William. 10. Herbert. 11. Hubert. And two others, now deceased.

(IX) Edward, son of Oliver Hazard Perry Townsend, was born in New York City, July 30, 1848. He attended the public schools and the Free Academy of New York City (now the College of the City of New York). After completing his education, he was employed for a time as clerk in a stationery store, and later in a dry goods store. He began his career as a banker, April 14, 1866, as clerk in the Importers & Traders National Bank of New York City, and in 1873 he was promoted to the position of assistant cashier of this bank. In 1880 he was made cashier, and in the following year he was elected a director. Since 1902 he has been president of the institution and occupies a place of influence and importance in the financial world. He is also a director of the Bankers Trust Company of New York, of the Broadway Savings Institution of New York, of the United States Life Insurance Company and other corporations. He is a member of the Union League Club and of the Harlem Republican Club, and is a Republican in politics. He is a life member of the New York Athletic Club and of the New England Society of New York. He is also a member of the Hardware Club. He and his family attend the Protestant Episcopal church.

He married, June 2, 1874, Adelaide Louise Turner, born September 26, 1850, daughter of Myron and Louise (Sherer) Turner, of Litchfield county, Connecticut, and New York City. Children, born in New York City: 1. Therina, born April 14, 1875; married Everett L. Barnard, of the state of Maine; children: Lucy, Louise Townsend and Edward Townsend Barnard. 2. Myron Turner, born May 1, 1878; married Gertrude Colby Barnard, of Rochester, New York; children: Barnard, Turner and Eugene Colby Townsend. 3. Edward Perry, born August 25, 1881; married Fanny Proddow Simpson, born in New York City, and they have had one child, Frances. 4. Harold, born July 4, 1883; married Grace Carpenter Fox, of New York. 5. Louise, born December 19, 1889.

(The Geer Line).

(I) George Geer, immigrant ancestor, was born in England in 1621, and came to this country in charge of an uncle, with a brother Thomas, born about 1623. According to family tradition the boys were sons of Jonathan Geer, of Havitree, Devonshire, and related to John Geer, whose family bore a coat-of-arms and was prominent in that county. Another tradition, however, has Shoreham in Devonshire as the old home of the family. The surname is spelled variously, Gere, Geer, Geaves, etc. George Geer was in Boston in 1635, and at New London, Connecticut, in 1651. Thomas Geer was at Enfield, Connecticut, in 1682. George Geer married, February 17, 1658, Sa-

rah, daughter of Robert Allyn, and he settled on a tract of land adjoining Allyn's. Geer had at first a grant of fifty acres of land at New London, and in 1665 a grant of a hundred acres more. His farm was in that part of New London, now the town of Ledyard. He owned land also in what is now Preston and Griswold, Connecticut. He received land by deed from Owaneco, son of Uncas, the Indian chief, December 11, 1691. His will was dated June 5, 1723, bequeathing to wife Sarah and his children. During his last years he was totally blind. He was selectman and held other offices of trust and honor, residing in Croton until about five years before he died, removing thence to Preston to live with his daughter Margaret who married Thomas Gates. He died at the age of one hundred and five. His wife and he lived together for sixty-five years. Children: Sarah, born February 27, 1659; Jonathan, May 26, 1662, died April 30, 1742; Joseph, mentioned below; Hannah, February 27, 1666; Margaret, February, 1669; Mary, March 26, 1671; Daniel, 1673; Robert, January 2, 1675; Anne, January 6, 1679; Isaac, March 26, 1681; Jeremiah, 1683.

(II) Joseph, son of George Geer, was born in New London, October 14, 1664. With his brothers Jonathan and Daniel, and brother-in-law, Thomas Gates, Joseph moved to Preston, Connecticut, a short distance from the homestead. He received from his father, by deed dated February 23, 1706-07, a tract of land at Preston and he followed farming there as long as he lived. He died in 1743. He was often chosen as referee in disputes over property boundaries and served on various town committees of a like nature. He married, January 7, 1692, Sarah Howard. Children: Joseph, born October 17, 1692, died May 19, 1718, and his estate was administered by his father; Keziah, February 23, 1710; Sarah, September 17, 1712; Benajah, May 31, 1714; Joseph, May 29, 1719; Silas, March 26, 1722; Ezra, mentioned below. The eldest son must have had a different mother from the other children, for there is a lapse of eighteen years between the eldest and second child and the youngest is thirty-two years younger than the eldest.

(III) Ezra, son of Joseph Geer, was born at Preston, May 16, 1724. He settled in Preston, removed to Kent, Connecticut, remained there for a time and then removed. Children, born in Preston and Kent: Nathaniel, died in Kent; Susan, removed to Ohio; Sarah, married Amos Barnum; Ezra, died in Vermont; John, died in Peru, Massachusetts; Elias, died in Ohio; Elijah, resided in Kent, died in Washington; David, mentioned below; Gardner, resided in Kent; Alpheus, drowned in North river, New York, while in the service in the revolution; Margaret, never married; Hannah, married James Converse and died in Plainfield, Vermont; Elizabeth, died aged twelve years; Patience, married Daniel Day.

(IV) David, son of Ezra Geer, was born in Kent, Connecticut, December 6, 1767. He lived at one time in Bridgewater, Pennsylvania. He married, April 4, 1793, Cynthia Parks, born April 4, 1770. Children: Sally Williams, born February 5, 1794, married Orin Clemens; child, June 16, 1796, died June 17, 1798; Welcome, May 4, 1798, married Sylvia Bishop; Pamelia, October 18, 1800, married Benjamin Hickok; Eliza, March 10, 1803, married A. Beardsley; Cynthia, August 30, 1805, married a Mr. Dewey; Armaluna, October 15, 1807, married Simon Parks; Azubah, July 24, 1810, married James Helm; Phebe Ann, May 3, 1813, married Oliver Hazard Perry Townsend (see Townsend VIII.).

HARRIS The Welsh custom of adding to a name the father's name in possessive form to distinguish one from another of the same Christian name, was the origin of this patronymic. In the short four centuries that surnames have prevailed in Great Britain, time has sufficed to make many changes and modifications in the form of all classes of words, and names are no exception to the rule. In the Welsh vernacular, William was "David's," Harry was "John's," and David was "William's," and thus we have Davy's (Davis), John's (Jones), Williams and Harris, among the most common of the Welsh names. The Harris family, of whom this article gives some account, was among the earliest in New England, and has contributed much to the advancement of this region and of the nation, and is now found in connection with all worthy endeavor. It has been especially active in the fields of invention and pioneer development. Almost every state has found the name among those of its pioneer settlers, and it has spread from the Atlantic to the Pacific.

(I) Thomas Harris, born in Deal, Kent county, England, died in Providence, Rhode Island, June 7, 1686. He came to America with his brother William in the ship "Lion," from Bristol, England, December 1, 1630. On August 20, 1637, or a little later, he and twelve others signed the following compact: "We, whose names are hereunder, desirous to inhabit the town of Providence, do promise to subject ourselves in active or passive obedience to all such orders or agreements as shall be made for public good of the body in an orderly way by the major asset of the present inhabitants members incorporated together into a town of fellowship, and such others whom they shall admit unto themselves, only in civil things." On July 27, 1649, he and thirty-eight others signed an agreement for a form of government. On September 2, 1650, he was taxed one pound. From 1652 to 1657 and from 1661 to 1663 he was commissioner; in 1654, lieutenant; 1655, freeman; 1656, juryman. Bishop's "New England Judged", published in London, in 1703, has the following with reference to July, 1658:

"After these came Thomas Harris from Rhode Island into our colony, who Declaring against your pride and oppression, as we would have liberty to speak in your meeting place in Boston, after the priest had ended. Warning the people of the Dreadful, terrible day of the Lord God, which was coming upon that Town and Country, him, much unlike to Nineveh, you pulled down and hall'd him by the Hair of his Head out of your meeting, and a hand was put on his mouth to keep him from speaking forth, and then had, before your Govenor and Deputy, with other Magistrates, and committed to Prison without warrant or mittimus that he saw, and shut up in the close room, none suffered to come to him, nor to have provisions for his money; and the next day whipped him with so cruel stripes, without shewing any law that he had broken. Tho' he desired it of the Jaylor, and then shut up for Eleven Days more, Five of which he was kept without bread (Your Jaylor not suffering him to have any for his Money and threatened the other Prisoners very much for bringing him a little water on the day of his sore whipping) and all this because he could not work for the Jaylor and let him have Eight Pence in Twelve pence of what he could earn; And starved he had been in all probability, had not the Lord kept him these Five Days and ordered it so after that time that food was so conveyed him by night in at a Window, by some tender People, who tho' they came not in the Profesion of Truth openly, by reason of your Cruelty, yet felt it secretly moving in them and so were made Serviceable to keep the Servant of the Lord from Perishing, who shall not go without a reward. And tho' he was in this state of Weakness from want of Bread, and by torturing his body with cruel whippings, as aforesaid, and tho' the Day after he was whipped, the Jaylor had told him that he had now suffered the Law, and that if he would hire the Marshall to carry him out of the Country he might be gone when he would; Yet the next Sixth Day in the Morning before the Sixth Hour, the Jaylor again required him to Work, which he refusing, gave his weak and fainting body Two and Twenty Blows with a pitched rope; and the nineteenth of the Fifth Month following, Fifteen cruel stripes more with a three-fold corded Whip knotted as aforesaid. Now upon his Apprehension, your Governor sought to know of him who came with him (as was their usual manner) that so ye might find out the rest of the company, on whom ye might Execute your Cruelty and Wickedness, and your governor said he would make him do it; but his cruelties could not. Nevertheless they soon were found out (who hid not themselves but were bold in the Lord) viz: William Brend and William Ledd, etc."

In 1664-66-67-70-72-73, he was deputy to the general court; in 1664-65-66-69 member of town council, and February 19, 1665, drew lot 7, in division of town lands. In May, 1667, he as surveyor laid out the lands. August 14, 1676, he was on a committee which recommended certain conditions under which Indian captives, who were to be in servitude for a term of years, should be disposed of by the town. April 27, 1683, he made the statement that about 1661, being then a surveyor, he laid out a three acre lot for his son Thomas, at Pauquchance Hill, and a twenty-five acre lot on the south side, etc. June 3, 1686, he made his will, which was proved July 22, 1686, his son Thomas being appointed executor and his sons-in-law, Thomas Field and Samuel Whipple, overseers.

Thomas Harris married Elizabeth ———, who died in Providence, Rhode Island. Children: Thomas, William, Mary and Martha.

(II) Thomas (2), son of Thomas (1) and Elizabeth Harris, always lived in Providence, Rhode Island. February 19, 1665, he had lot forty-nine in a division of lands. In 1671-79-80-81-82-85-91-94-97, 1702-06-07-08-10, he was deputy of the general court; and in 1684-85-86 member of town council. July 1, 1679, he was taxed eight pounds nine pence; September 1, 1687, fourteen shillings, nine pence. June 21, 1708, he made his will which was proved April 16, 1711, the executors being his wife Elantha and his son Henry. He died February 27, 1711. He married, November 3, 1664, Elantha Tew, born October 15, 1644, died January 11, 1718, daughter of Richmond and Mary (Clark) Tew, of Newport, Rhode Island. Children: Thomas, Richard, Nicholas, William, Henry, Amity, Elantha, Jacob and Mary.

(III) Richard, second son and child of Thomas (2) and Elantha (Tew) Harris, was born October 14, 1668, in Providence, Rhode Island, and resided in Providence and Smithfield. He deeded to his son Richard in 1725 one hundred acres of land in the latter town, and died there in 1750. He married (first) a daughter of Clement and Elizabeth King, and his second wife, Susanna, born in 1665, was widow of Samuel Gordon and daughter of William and Hannah (Wicks) Burton. She died in 1737. Children, all born of first marriage, were: Uriah, Richard, Amaziah, Jonathan, David, Preserved, Amity, Dinah and Elantha.

(IV) Jonathan, third son of Richard Harris, was born June 12, 1710, in Smithfield, where he died September 24, 1785. These dates are found in the records of the Quaker church, and lead to the assumption that his wife was a Quakeress. No record can be found of his marriage in either town or church records. He resided in Providence.

(V) Abner, son of Jonathan Harris, was born before 1740, and died between 1785 and 1789. No record can be found of his marriage, but the vital records of Smithfield show that he had sons: David, Jonathan and William.

(VI) William, son of Abner Harris, was undoubtedly born in Smithfield; was married in that town by Rev. Edward Mitchell, October 24, 1789, to Barbara, daughter of Waterman Allen, of Cumberland. He settled in Hiram, Ohio, about 1812.

(VII) Allen, eldest son of William and Barbara (Allen) Harris, was born in Smithfield, Rhode Island, May 16, 1790, died in Worcester, Massachusetts, February 3, 1864, aged seventy-four. In 1800 he moved with his parents from Smithfield to Plainfield. He was well educated and when very young taught district school two winters, and not far from 1810 was a clerk in a store at Union Village, Connecticut. After that came a great prostration in business, which left him and his family comparatively poor. In 1817, the year after his marriage, Mr. Harris removed to Providence, Rhode Island, and went into partnership with a Mr. Richmond, in the dry goods business. Not succeeding in that, he removed to Sterling, Connecticut, in 1820, and for several years was agent for the old stone mill on a salary of six hundred dollars. In 1824 he moved to Union Village, Plainfield, and afterwards to Central Village, where he built a cotton factory for making bed ticking. He also built a double house, part of which he rented. He kept a village variety store in connection with his factory to supply the factory hands. In his new business he invested all of his funds, so that for a few years he had to work hard and practice the closest economy in order to make his business successful. He was connected with Arnold Fenner in the factory at Central Village. In 1840, after manufacturing became much depressed owing to the condition of the times, he sold his interest to Mr. Fenner, to whom he gave two thousand dollars to be released from the debts of the factory and the obligations he had entered into in connection with the business.

In 1843 he moved to Worcester and commenced business as a commission merchant, and in which he continued to the time of his death in 1864. His son William H. was associated with him for many years. He was successful and accumulated considerable property. He bought a large and substantial house at the corner of Elm and Chestnut streets.

Allen Harris was a dignified, courteous gentleman, conspicuously neat in personal appearance, and exact in every business transaction. He had a great pride of family, and spent money freely for the education of his children and for all his relatives. He desired to have all of his relatives prosper, live in good houses, and rise to positions of trust and honor. He frequently helped them in business, and to buy themselves homes. He was fond of genealogical research, and the deeds of his ancestors, from Thomas Harris down, were in his possession, and he had them framed and kept as precious relics of the past. He delighted in hunting after family relics of every description. His sister Sophia, who did not share her brother's antiquarian spirit, once remarked of him. "There is Allen ; he is always bringing home some old furniture. As for me I would not give him two cents for Adam's old bureau." When the rebellion broke out he was very patriotic, and as none of the family had gone to war, he enlisted (at the age of seventy-one years) in the Worcester State Guard, which did escort duty on various occasions. Late in January, 1864, he marched about five miles into the country with his company, to do honor to the remains of a soldier brought home for burial, and taking cold died four days afterward. After his death his company made his son Daniel an honorary member. He was a member of the Old South Church in Worcester, and at his death its oldest deacon. He taught a Bible class in its Sunday school for many years, and a member of it once said : "He was the best teacher I ever had : he made everything so plain." When the Old South Church celebrated its one hundredth anniversary in 1863, he was one of the committee of arrangements and chairman of the finance committee. As the oldest deacon he was selected to "line off the hymn," as customary in the olden times, which he did with precision and zest. A gentleman who had attended the exercises said the next day : "It was announced that the oldest deacon of the church would 'line off the hymn,' and I went to hear him ; but was surprised to find that he was only the merest boy." This was related to Mr. Harris, who on hearing it, drew himself up in his usual dignified manner, and exclaimed, "Did he! Did he !" his precision and self possession were not easily lost. Allen Harris' letters show that he was high sheriff, justice of the peace, and postmaster in Connecticut. From 1832 until 1841 he was engaged with others in manufacturing. He was always a very busy man and one that was much looked up to for advice. He was full of good Christian work, and his many letters which have been preserved abound in good counsel and kind admonition. He made many loans and handsome gifts to friends, for one who had so many discouragements in business to contend against. But with all his business cares and perplexities he never neglected his sons, whom he wished to train to be useful men. He had great energy and was a very close economist. He had faith that virtue would bring its reward, and he was not disappointed. He said, "I never will fail in business as long as I have my health." He was very kind to his sisters, always providing for them when any of them were left widows with children, and he remembered them all in his will, as well as the established benevolent associations. He was a pure, upright man, so faithful to his promise that an old friend wrote of him, "I would as soon take Allen Harris' word as a note well indorsed." He was so very conscientious that he thought everyone must do what was right ; and he died greatly beloved by all his relatives and friends.

Allen Harris married (first) May 7, 1816, at Plainfield, Hart, daughter of Colonel Timothy Lester, of Shepard Hill, Plainfield. She was born at that place, December 23, 1789, died at Central Village, August 24, 1826. He married (second) in 1827, Almira, daughter of Russell Vaughn, of Plainfield. Children by first wife : Daniel Lester, born February 6, 1818 ; William Henry, in Sterling, Connecticut, March 20, 1820 ; Joel Benedict, mentioned below. By second wife : Mary Gladden, born in Plainfield, April 17, 1829, married Edward Marsh, of the firm of Lazell, Marsh & Gardner, 8 Gold street, New York, and died July 1, 1854 ; Emma Colwell, in Plainfield, August 13, 1836, died March 12, 1845, of scarlet fever ; William, lived in Rutland, Vermont.

(VIII) Joel Benedict, son of Allen and Hart (Lester) Harris, named for their pastor, Rev. Joel Benedict, was born November 5, 1822, at Sterling, Connecticut, died October 24, 1891, in Rutland, Vermont. He learned civil engineering at the Rensselaer Polytechnic Institute, Troy, New York. He was also a bridge-builder and railroad contractor, working principally on the Boston & Albany railroad. In June, 1860, he settled in Rutland, where for twenty-five years he conducted a foundry and engaged in the manufacture of car wheels. In 1885 he retired from business. Mr. Harris married (first) December 30, 1847, Susan M., born February 28, 1830, daughter of John F. Pond, of Medway, Massachusetts, and they became the parents of two daughters and a son: Emma Hart, born October 19, 1848, died July 31, 1849; Susan Payne, born June 3, 1850, married George Mather, and died in Westfield, New Jersey, May 7, 1878, leaving an infant daughter, Susan; Charles Pond, mentioned below. Mrs. Harris died October 28, 1852, and Mr. Harris married (second) November 28, 1854, Mary Jane O., daughter of William Gardner, and the following were their children: Martha Vaughn, born August 24, 1855, married William C. Newell, of Springfield, Massachusetts; William Allen, born September 15, 1857; Harriet Lester, born December 9, 1859, died June, 1906; Nellie Seaver, born April 2, 1865, married Charles A. Bowles, of Springfield, Massachusetts; Mary Gardner, born September 7, 1871, married Frederick Sweeney, of Newton Centre, Massachusetts.

(IX) Charles Pond, son of Joel Benedict and Susan M. (Pond) Harris, was born July 2, 1852, in Springfield, Massachusetts. He received his preparatory education in the Rutland high school. In 1869 he entered the Rensselaer Polytechnic Institute, graduating in June, 1873. He then spent a year in European travel, and in 1874 returned to Rutland, where he began his business career, engaging in the manufacture of doors, sashes and blinds and also dealing in finished lumber. In 1880 he added a new feature to the business by taking up the manufacture of cane-seated chairs. In 1892 the plant was destroyed by fire, and Mr. Harris after that event retired from business. He then spent four years in the study of law and was admitted to the bar but has not practiced his profession. He is the owner of large real estate interests both in Rutland and Chicago, Ill. He took an active interest in and organized the Boy Scout movement in Rutland and was elected scout master of this. To show his further interest he offered as a gift the three upper floors of a brick block known as the Banquet house block for the perpetual use of the Young Women's Christian Association, but the public failed to take advantage of this very generous offer on the part of Mr. Harris.

Mr. Harris married, June 18, 1879, Charlotte Metcalf Sessions (see Sessions VII).

(The Sessions Line).

The Sessions family had its origin in Wantage, Berkshire, England. There is at present but one family of the name to be found in England in the county of Gloucester. The head of this family, Hon. J. Sessions, was mayor of the city of Gloucester at the age of eighty years, and his three sons were asso-

ciated with him in a large manufacturing business in both Gloucester and Cardiff (Wales) under the firm name of J. Sessions & Sons. There is also a daughter who is actively engaged in benevolent and reformatory work. The mother established and built a "Home for the Fallen", which is managed by members of the family. The entire family belongs to the Society of Friends, and Frederick Sessions, besides being at the head of a large business, gives his entire attention without salary to reformatory work, lecturing and organizing Sunday schools and temperance and other beneficent societies. The crest of the English Sessions family is a griffin's head. This mythological creature was sacred to the sun, and according to tradition kept guard over hidden treasures.

(I) Alexander Sessions, said to have been a native of Wantage, Berkshire, England, born in 1645, in a deposition recorded in the office of the clerk of the courts of Essex county, Massachusetts, in the case of Simon Bradstreet against John Gage stated that he was twenty-four years of age, and that he was in Andover in 1666. Alexander and wife Elizabeth were members of the church in Andover in 1686, and from that time until their decease. He was a witness to the will of John Aslet, of Andover, Essex county, Massachusetts, May 15, 1671, and at the court when it was proved 27 4 mo 1671, as appears from the papers in the office of the clerk of the probate court. An inventory of the estate of Alexander Sutchins (the name being spelled in the original "Elexander Seshins") who died February 26, 1687, mentions eighty acres of land and other property, valued at one hundred and nineteen pounds. Elizabeth Sutchins, widow of Alexander Sutchins, presented the inventory of the estate to which he made oath in Ipswich 25 1 mo, 1690, and letters of administration were granted her after she had given bond for two hundred pounds with John Spofford, of Rowley, and Thomas Patch, of Wenham, as sureties. Later Elizabeth Sutchins, alias Low, Admx. presented an account of her administration to the court. As she was the "Alias Low," it seems she had married again. March 8, 1697, the widow makes final settlement, received her portion and the balance is divided among the children of Alexander Sutchins, to wit: Elizabeth, John, Alexander, Timothy, Samuel, Nathaniel, Josiah, Joseph and Abel. The oldest is given as about twenty-four years old, and the youngest about eight years old. The town records give the marriage of Alexander Sessions with Elizabeth, daughter of John Spofford, of Rowley, April 24, 1672. Alexander Sessions died

398 NEW ENGLAND.

February 25, 1689. Children: John, born October 4, 1674; Alexander, October 3, 1676; Timothy, April 14, 1678; Samuel, March 8, 1680; Nathaniel, mentioned below; Josiah, born May 2, 1684; and Joseph, born March 28, 1686.

(II) Nathaniel, fifth son of Alexander and Elizabeth (Spofford) Sessions, was born August 8, 1681, in Andover. He settled in Pomfret, Connecticut, as early as 1704, being one of the first white settlers there, and died there March, 1771. His wife, Hannah, died the same year. They had eight children: John, Nathaniel, Abner, Abijah, Alexander, Amasa, mentioned below; Davies and Simon.

(III) Captain Amasa Sessions, sixth son of Nathaniel and Hannah Sessions, was born in 1715, died in 1799. He lived and died in Pomfret. He was a captain of a company with Putnam in the old French war. In his prime he was a very strong man; in his advanced age he was very corpulent. His wife's name was Hannah, and she died in 1804. They had eleven children: John, Samuel, Amasa, Nathaniel, Robert, mentioned below; Hannah, Susannah, Squire, Mary, Abner, died young; Abner.

(IV) Robert, fifth son of Captain Amasa and Hannah Sessions, was born in Pomfret, March 4, 1752. He served in the revolutionary army, attaining the rank of lieutenant, was on the Lexington Alarm, and was one of the "memorable Boston Tea Party". He removed from Pomfret, Connecticut, to Wilbraham, Massachusetts, about 1779, and lived there until his death, September 27, 1836, at which time he was in his eighty-fifth year. He was a farmer and bought a farm in 1781, on which he made improvements and among other things raised and enlarged his house. This was kept in the family up to 1911. He was a prominent citizen of the town, serving as moderator, town clerk, treasurer and selectman many times, and also as a representative in the legislature three times. He was appointed justice of the peace soon after he became a citizen and held that office until his death at age of ninety-four. He married Anna Ruggles, of Pomfret, April 16, 1778, and they had children: Betsey, Charles, Robert, mentioned below; George, Nancy, Celina, Francis, Horace, Martha Phipps, Hannah Miller, Sumner, Nabby, William Vyne.

(V) Robert (2), second son of Robert (1) and Anna (Ruggles) Sessions, was born in South Wilbraham, Massachusetts. He married, May, 1811, Charlotte Bartlet Metcalf, of Lebanon, Connecticut. Children: George Metcalf, mentioned below; Elizabeth, Ann Robert, Oscar, Charlotte, Maria, Clarissa,

Jane, Nancy, Janette, Joseph Bradford and Horace Mills.

(VI) George Metcalf, eldest child of Robert (2) and Charlotte Bartlet (Metcalf) Sessions, was born in South Wilbraham, and resided in Hartford, Connecticut, where all his children were born. He married Mary Monroe Filley, of East Windsor, Connecticut, and they had children: George Filley, Charlotte Metcalf, Mary Frances.

(VII) Charlotte Metcalf, eldest daughter of George Metcalf and Mary Monroe (Filley) Sessions, was born in Hartford, Connecticut. She married, June 18, 1879, Charles Pond Harris, of Rutland, Vermont (see Harris IX). Mrs. Harris is descended through her father's mother from the "Mayflower" families of Governor William Bradford and Elder William Brewster.

SANDERSON The Sanderson family is of ancient English origin. In America most of the Sandersons are traced to the brothers, Robert and Edward, mentioned below. Robert Sanderson and wife Lydia were among the first settlers of Hamcon, New Hampshire, in 1638. Their daughter Mary was born there in 1639, and baptized October 29, 1639. Soon afterward he removed to Watertown, Massachusetts, of which he was a proprietor in 1642, and where he married (second) about 1642, Mary Cross, widow of John Cross. He remained in Watertown until about 1653, when he removed to Boston, where he was a deacon. He was a goldsmith and silversmith by trade. John Hull, a selectman and many years town treasurer of Boston, the first mint master of New England, and the coiner of the pine tree shillings, in his diary under date of 1652-53, relates how he was chosen to make coin, and adds: "I chose my friend Robert Sanderson to be my partner, to which the court consented." September 1, 1658, he says: "my boy, John Sanderson, complained of his head aching, and took his bed; a strong fever set in and after 17 days sore sickness, he departed this life." Under date of November 8, 1658, he says: "the Lord exercised with sickness my partner Robert Sanderson, and his son Joseph, but yet was pleased to recover them both Joseph kept the house about a month and my partner 13 days."

Robert Sanderson died October 7, 1693. His will was proved October 20, 1693. He bequeathed to his wife Elizabeth; son Robert Sanderson and daughter Anne West; grandchildren Robert Darby, Mary Caswell, Joseph Jones; children of Robert and Anna, and of James Penniman; great-granddaughter Abia

Reard; son-in-law Richard West; brother Edward Sanderson; Joseph, son of William Sanderson; refers to house and land at Watertown. His wife Mary died June 21, 1681, aged seventy-four. He married (third) Elizabeth ——, who died October 15, 1695, aged seventy-eight. Children: Mary, baptized October 29, 1639; Joseph, born January 1, 1642-43; Benjamin, baptized July 29, 1649; Sarah, baptized January 18, 1651; Robert, baptized October 22, 1652; John, died September 18, 1658.

(I) Edward Sanderson, brother of Robert Sanderson, and the immigrant ancestor of this family, was born in England, and came to Watertown about the same time as his brother. He married, October 15, 1645, Mary Eggleston, believed to be the eldest daughter of Bagot and Bridget Eggleston, of Dorchester, afterwards of Windsor, Connecticut. He sold his house and land in Watertown by William Shattuck Sr., and probably removed to Cambridge. The name is frequently spelled Sanders and Saunders in the early records. Children: Jonathan, mentioned below; Hester, baptized March 20, 1686-87.

(II) Jonathan, son of Edward Sanderson, was born in Watertown, September 15, 1646, died September 3, 1735, aged eighty-nine years. He moved to Watertown about 1689, and settled at Piety Corner, Waltham. He was constable of Watertown in 1695; selectman from 1703 to 1719. He married in Cambridge, October 24, 1669, Abia Bartlett, born May 28, 1651, youngest daughter of Ensign Thomas and Hannah Bartlett, of Watertown. She died September 13, 1723. Their graves are in the old or lower graveyard at Waltham, Massachusetts, formerly Watertown. His will was dated April 2, 1728, appointing his sons John and Jonathan executors. His children, all born in Cambridge: Abia, born October 28, 1673, twin; Jonathan, twin of Abia; Thomas, March 10, 1674-75; John, March 25, 1677; Benjamin, May 28, 1679; Samuel, mentioned below; Edward, March 3, 1683-84; Hannah, May 31, 1689.

(III) Samuel, son of Jonathan Sanderson, was born in Cambridge, May 28, 1681, was killed by lightning, July 8, 1722. He married, April 13, 1708, Mary Gale, born September 16, 1683, died May 8, 1776, daughter of Abraham and Sarah (Fiske) Gale, and granddaughter of the pioneer, Richard Gale. Children: Samuel, born December 29, 1709; Abraham, March 28, 1711; Jonathan, February 24, 1714; Mercy, November 26, 1718; Moses, mentioned below.

(IV) Moses, son of Samuel Sanderson, was born February 22, 1722. He married (first)

January 1, 1750-51, Mary Flagg, born February 2, 1728-29, daughter of John and Hannah Flagg, and granddaughter of John and Anna Flagg, descendant of Thomas Flagg, the pioneer of Watertown. Moses Sanderson and his wife were dismissed from Waltham to Littleton church, April 13, 1766, and had been living at Littleton for some time. He was a soldier at the Lexington call, a private in Lieutenant Aquila Jewett's company, Colonel James Prescott's regiment, and served two days. His son Moses was also a soldier in the revolution. He married (second) February 7, 1766, Elizabeth Goddard. Children of first wife: Sarah, born February 9, 1752, at Littleton; Lois, March 17, 1754; Moses, July 14, 1756, married, November 25, 1777, Mary Proctor; Sarah, July 12, 1757; Stephen, August 24, 1758; John, mentioned below; Samuel, April 30, 1762, married Lydia Whitcomb; Mary, September 16, 1763. Children of second wife: Hannah, July 12, 1767; Mercy, February 3, 1769.

(V) John, son of Moses Sanderson, was born at Littleton, Massachusetts, April 15, 1760, died at Phillipston, November 15, 1833. He married, at Littleton, April 28, 1785, Lucy Fletcher, the ceremony being performed by Jonathan Reed, justice of the peace. Children, born at Littleton: John, March 18, 1786; Peter, mentioned below; Lucy, July 5, 1790; Jonathan Fletcher, December 9, 1792.

(VI) Peter, son of John Sanderson, was born at Littleton, Massachusetts, July 26, 1788. He located at Phillipston, Worcester county, Massachusetts, where he died February 5, 1849, aged sixty years, five months, two days (gravestone). He married (intention dated at Phillipston, April 22, 1814) Chloe Robbins, of Athol, Massachusetts. Children, born at Phillipston: Courtland, mentioned below; Mary Caroline, born February 21, 1817; Lucia, January 4, 1823; Frances, died January 24, 1833, aged one year, ten months, eleven days.

(VII) Courtland, son of Peter Sanderson, was born in Phillipston, Massachusetts, April 9, 1815. He settled in his native town. He married (intention dated at Phillipston, November 11, 1837) Lydia Hunt Clapp, of Montague, Massachusetts, born in 1815, descendant of the Clapp family of Dorchester, pioneers of the colony. Children, born in Phillipston: Frederick Milton, mentioned below; Peter, September 9, 1842; Julius, September 15, 1846.

(VIII) Frederick Milton, son of Courtland Sanderson, was born in Phillipston, Massachusetts, November 5, 1838. He attended the public schools of his native town and entered Amherst College from which he was graduated in the class of 1861. He enlisted immediately afterward in the Twenty-first Regiment Massachusetts Volunteer Infantry and served faithfully for three years, taking part in the various battles in. which his regiment was engaged. He was wounded once in the hand. Since the war he has been for more than thirty-six years connected with the White Sewing Machine Company of Cleveland, Ohio, and at the present time is treasurer of the corporation. In politics he is a Republican, and for two years he was a member of the board of education of Cleveland. He is a member of Memorial Post, Grand Army of the Republic, of Cleveland, and of Cleveland Commandery, Military Order of the Loyal Legion, and of the New England Society of Cleveland, Ohio, and the Western Reserve. His office is at 2105 East Eighty-third street, Cleveland.

He married, in 1869, Harriet Pierce White, born in Templeton, Massachusetts, in 1838, daughter of Windsor White, and sister of President Thomas H. White, of the White Sewing Machine Company (see White VII). Children: 1. Eugene Windsor, born in 1870, died in 1876 in Cleveland. 2. Lydia Elizabeth, born in Cleveland in 1874; married Edward Warren Capen, son of Dr. Capen, of Boston. 3. Rev. Edward Frederick, born in Cleveland in 1876; married Ethel Eames, of Brooklyn, New York. 4. Gertrude Elmira, born in Cleveland in 1879. 5. Lucia Harriet, born in Cleveland in 1881. 6. Julius Courtland, born in Cleveland in 1882; married Mary Van Epps.

(The White Line).

(I) Thomas White, immigrant ancestor, was born in England about 1595. He settled among the first at Cambridge, Massachusetts. He was admitted a freeman, March 3, 1635-36. He was a deputy to the general court in 1637. In 1638 he had a house and a half acre of land on the west side of Garden street, Cambridge, between Mason street and Phillips place. He was also a proprietor of the adjoining town of Watertown, and in 1640 sold a house he had bought of William Swift. He removed to Sudbury where he bought land and was proprietor in 1640, town officer in 1642. He sold land in Sudbury in 1654 and in 1658 located at Charlestown where he was constable in 1659. Either he or his son Thomas, was appointed by Edward Shepard "to drive the Neck", March 23, 1662-63. His wife Margaret died at Sudbury, November 17, 1640. He married (second) Susanna Miller, who died March 6, 1686-87, aged eighty-nine. He died May 6, 1664. His will

was proved March 29, 1667. Children: Thomas, of Charlestown; John, mentioned below; Mary, married John Woodward; Sarah.

(II) John, son of Thomas White, was born in 1628 (aged forty years in 1668). He lived at Sudbury and Charlestown, and in 1664, according to his father's will, was of Cambridge. His father's widow Susanna bequeathed to his children. He died in 1676 and his administrator's account was filed October 3, 1676. His widow's account was filed again in 1700. He married Elizabeth, granddaughter of Thomas Goble, of Charlestown and Concord. She married (second) June 7, 1682, at Sudbury, Thomas Carter. Children, recorded at Charlestown and Sudbury: John, born August 8, 1653; Thomas, September 9, 1655; Elizabeth, June 10, 1658, married Lodowick or Lewis Dowse, January 9, 1676; Daniel, mentioned below; Hannah, February 13, 1669; Abigail, October 2, 1676, married Peter Thorp; Mary, married Benjamin Twitchell; Hannah; three others died young.

(III) Daniel, son of John White, was born in 1668. He lived with his mother until nineteen years old (aged eight in 1676). He settled in Cambridge Farms, now Lexington, and was a taxpayer there in 1696; constable in 1713-14. He was a man of high standing and character, as evidenced by the fact that he was assigned to the second seat below in the meeting house among the leading men in 1731. His will was dated in 1738 and he died March 14, 1739. He bequeathed to children: Hannah, Joseph, John Stephen, Samuel, Sybel Mansfield and Sarah Locke. He married (first) Mary ———, who died January 20, 1722-23; (second) Hannah ———. Children by first wife: Daniel, born May 18, 1695; Mary, October 24, 1697; John, February 16, 1699; Mary, baptized September 8, 1700; Thomas, February 2, 1701; Joseph, mentioned below; Sybel, May 1, 1706, married Theophilus Mansfield; Stephen, April 27, 1709; Sarah, August 23, 1711; Hannah. Born at Lexington: Samuel, September 2, 1714.

(IV) Joseph, son of Daniel White, was born at Cambridge, April 17, 1704, died at Lexington, August 4, 1777. He married (first) Hannah ———, who died April 7, 1731; (second) Mary ———. Children, born at Lexington by first wife: Hannah, December 10, 1728; Mary, March 25, 1731. By second wife at Lexington: Susanna, October 10, 1735; Joseph, October 11, 1737; William, April 23, 1740; Jonathan, baptized May 24, 1741; Jonathan, born April 15, 1742; Thomas, mentioned below; Benjamin, May 9, 1744; Ebenezer, July 10, 1746; John, June 1, 1748; Nathan, June 16, 1750.

(V) Thomas (2), son of Joseph White, was born at Lexington, April 15, 1742, baptized there April 18 following. His brother Joseph and wife Lucy, of Gerry, deeded to Thomas White and Thaddeus Brown, of Gerry (Phillipston), May 25. 1787. Joseph White, of Lexington, deeded to Thomas White, of Templeton, land in Templeton, forty-three acres, Lot No. 52, in the right of Daniel White (uncle or grandfather) in 1760 (Worcester Deeds, Book 48, p. 248). He lived at Templeton and was one of the first settlers of Gerry (Phillipston) where he died February 26, 1827, aged eighty-five years (gravestone). His will with codicil dated November 4, 1825, bequeathed to children of daughter Mary Smith, deceased; Hannah Fletcher; Eudoxa Nickerson; Simeon H. (confirming deed of 1806 providing for the support of self and wife as long as they lived), sons John, Abel and Thomas. He married (intention dated November 17, 1766) Prudence Hayward, of Concord. Children, born at Templeton: Susanna and Hannah, August 31, 1772; Simeon Hayward, September 14, 1776; Susanna, July 8, baptized August 29, 1779; Thomas, October 2, 1781; Eudoxa, January 10, 1783.

(VI) Simeon Hayward, son of Thomas (2) White, was born at Templeton, September 14, 1776. He received from his father deed of the homestead in Gerry, April 10, 1806, and this land was confirmed to him in his father's will. He also deeded to other sons. He married, at Phillipston, March 25, 1798, Lectty (Electa) Warner. Children, born in Phillipston: Electa, April 16, 1799; Howard, October 31, 1801; Howard, December 27, 1803; Rosamond, August 8, 1806; Windsor, mentioned below; Rebeckah, December 28, 1810; Elijah, May 13, 1813; Harriet, October 21, 1815.

(VII) Windsor, son of Simeon Hayward White, was born at Phillipston, December 2, 1808. He lived in Templeton. He married (first) at Phillipston, September 6, 1834, Betsey Pierce, of Petersham, who died September 22, 1838, aged twenty-six. He married (second) September 11, 1841, Frances H. Whitney, who died February 16, 1842. He married (third) December 7, 1842, at Templeton, Elizabeth P. Whitney. Children: Harriet Pierce, married Frederick Milton Sanderson (see Sanderson VIII); Thomas Howard, mentioned below.

(VIII) Thomas Howard, son of Windsor White, was born at Phillipston, April 26, 1836. He was educated in the public schools of Phillipston, including the high school. At the age of nineteen he began his active business career, working as chair maker at East

Templeton. At the age of twenty-two he married and moved to Orange, Massachusetts, engaging in business with William L. Grout. Later he moved to Templeton and embarked in the manufacture of hand sewing machines, remaining there three years, at the expiration of which time he returned to Orange, continuing the same line of work on his own account, remaining until 1865, when he removed to Cleveland, Ohio, and established a factory, employing thirty men, but as his business increased from year to year he added materially to his force and at the present time (1912) gives regular employment to eight hundred hands, thus being one of the leading industries of that thriving city. His executive ability and thorough business methods have brought him into prominence, and he has been chosen to fill important positions, serving now in the capacity of president of the White Sewing Machine Company, and director of the White Company, manufacturers of automobiles, and of the Park Drop Forge Company. He holds membership in the New England Society and the Western Reserve.

Mr. White married, in 1858, Elmira Greenwood, of East Templeton, Massachusetts. Children: Windsor, Clarence, Walter, Rollin, Alice, deceased; Mabel, deceased; Maude, deceased; Ella.

LANDON The name of Landon is of Welsh origin, and has not been very widely distributed in this country. It has sometimes taken the form of Langdon, and is now found in many parts of New England as well as in other sections of the United States. It was especially identified with Long Island and Connecticut in very early days.

(I) Nathan Landon, of Southold, Long Island, was born in 1664, in Herefordshire, near the Welsh border in England. According to family tradition he was fifteen years old when he sailed from Liverpool to Boston; thence he made his way to Southold, Long Island, where he died March 9, 1718. His wife Hannah (surname unknown) born 1671, died January 26, 1701, at the same time with her youngest child. Among their children were James, Elizabeth and Nathan.

(II) James, son of Nathan and Hannah Landon, was born about 1690, in Southold, Long Island. He settled in Litchfield, Connecticut, before 1737, in which year he was admitted a freeman there, and died September 19, 1738. He married (first) in May, 1717, Mary Vaile, who died August 20, 1722. He married (second) Widow Mary Wilmot, who bore him six sons and four daughters.

Among his children were sons James, Daniel, David and John. The first and last removed from Litchfield to Salisbury, Connecticut, in 1749.

(III) James (2), eldest son of James (1) and Mary (Vaile) Landon, was born about 1720, in Southold, and resided for a time in Litchfield, Connecticut, where he married Sarah Bishop. He resided on what was later known as Tory Hill, in Salisbury, owing to the allegiance of his son James to the British crown. He was one of the first magistrates, and in 1758-59-65-70-72-73-74, he represented Salisbury in the Connecticut legislature. Children: Sarah, James, Samuel, Luther, Nabby, Nancy, Asa, Ezekiel, Thomas, Rachel, Andrew, Lois and Ashbel.

(IV) Ezekiel, son of James (2) and Sarah (Bishop) Landon, was born August 31, 1738, in Litchfield, Connecticut, and resided in Salisbury, Connecticut. No record of his marriage has been found, but his wife bore the name of Azubah, and they had sons recorded in Salisbury: John, born July 7, 1763; Ezekiel, January 9, 1765; Elisha, mentioned below.

(V) Elisha, third son of Ezekiel and Azubah Landon, was born June 3, 1766, in Salisbury, Connecticut, and soon after attaining his majority removed to Sunderland, Vermont, where he died April 12, 1817. He married Alice Bingham, April 16, 1789.

(VI) Noah, eldest child of Elisha and Alice (Bingham) Landon, was born May 10, 1790, in Salisbury, died in South Dorset, Vermont, January 24, 1881. He married, April 30, 1820, Pamelia Wilcox, of Manchester, Vermont, born 1794, died December 26, 1879. Children: Warren E., born May 5, 1824, now residing in Stoughton, Massachusetts; Walter Chipman, mentioned below; Fanny P., August 20, 1838, married Samuel B. Nichols, of Brooklyn, New York.

(VII) Walter Chipman, second son of Noah and Pamelia (Wilcox) Landon, was born August 17, 1831, in Sunderland, died in Rutland, Vermont, April 10, 1910, At the early age of fourteen years he left home and worked for two years on a farm in Arlington, Vermont. Thence he went to Bennington, where he passed four years as clerk in the general store of P. L. Robinson. In the spring of 1852 he came to Rutland, and became clerk in the hardware and grocery store of Landon & Graves, which was known as "the old red store", and stood on the site of Sawyer's block. The firm soon after became J. & A. Landon, but because of his experience and abilities, and being a cousin of the proprietors, Walter C. Landon retained his position,

in all about five years. Then, with Chester Kingsley as junior partner, he opened a grocery store in the same building, which J. & A. Landon vacated for a new building. After the lapse of three years Mr. Landon sold out to Mr. Kingsley, and with J. W. Cramton bought in the Central House, which stood on the present site of Clement's bank building. Mr. Landon assumed the management of this house, and remained there until March, 1863. In the meantime, however, he enlisted for three months in the First Vermont Regiment (Infantry) and was detailed as color sergeant, and after went out as captain of Company K, Twelfth Regiment. The First Vermont regiment was among the first Union troops to invade rebel territory, and marched to Hampton, Virginia, May 23, 1861. Sergeant Landon participated in the full campaign of the regiment in the vicinity of Fortress Monroe, Hampton, Newport News, and Little Bethel, engaged in building forts, and making frequent expeditions within the enemy's lines. At the battle of Big Bethel, June 10, 1861, his company was detailed for special service, intended to cover the left flank of the attacking column, to act as skirmishers and endeavor to turn the right flank of the enemy's position. The regiment was soon after mustered out, having fulfilled its term of enlistment. When the Second Vermont Brigade was recruited under the president's call of August 4, 1862, the Twelfth was the first of the five regiments raised, ready to respond to orders. The Rutland members were in Company K, and Sergeant Landon was elected lieutenant. On September 25th, the ten companies forming the regiment were assembled at Brattleboro, and the following day the organization was completed. Captain Kingsley, of Company K, was elected major, and Lieutenant Landon became captain by succession. His commission with that rank is dated September 27, 1862. In the following month he was again in the field, and the brigade was incorporated in General Casey's division for the defense of Washington. For eight months it occupied encampments, and the Twelfth Vermont gave a good account of itself in repulsing the attempt of General J. E. B. Stewart's cavalry to capture supplies at Fairfax.

After he sold his interest in the hotel to Mr. Cramton, he entered into partnership with J. N. Baxter, in September, 1863, and opened a grocery store in the building now occupied for a like purpose by E. D. Keyes & Company. In the following May Mr. Landon obtained control of the entire business and carried on the store until November, 1865. He then removed his business to the Perkins block, on the corner of West street, and Merchants row, which he had purchased. In January, 1868, with C. F. Huntoon as junior partner, he originated his present business in the same building now occupied by W. C. Landon & Company. Mr. Huntoon's health failed in October, 1875, and he sold his interest to Mr. Landon. He again returned to the handling of hardware and became proprietor of one of the largest stores of its kind in the state.

Having shown an executive capacity, Mr. Landon was naturally called upon to serve his town in the management of public affairs. From 1864 to 1875 he served his town and village as school treasurer, and was one of the listers in 1874-81-82-83-84. For more than nine years he filled the office of water commissioner, and was also a member of the board of selectmen. For twenty years he was an active member of the Rutland fire department, and ten years preceding 1882 was its chief engineer. In the legislative session of 1882-83 he represented the town of Rutland. From its organization he was one of the directors of the Baxter National Bank, and was one of the directors of the True Blue Marble Company, and the Evergreen Cemetery Association. He was a member of the Grand Army of the Republic, one of the first members in Vermont of the order of Knights of Pythias, and was a trustee of the Elks club. At the time of his death he was commander of Roberts Post, No. 14, Grand Army of the Republic, and was a member of the Military Order of the Loyal Legion.

He married, June 16, 1862, Mary M. Manly, born August 1, 1842, in South Dorset, Vermont, died August 29, 1894, daughter of Thomas D. and Ursula (Soper) Manly, and granddaughter of William Manly, of Dorset, Vermont.

(VIII) Captain Charles Huntoon Landon, only child of Walter Chipman and Mary M. (Manly) Landon, was born April 3, 1867, in Rutland. He was educated in the public schools of his native town, graduating from the high school in 1885. Following this he spent two years in New York City, and completed a course in the Packard Business College, after which he returned to Rutland and entered the store of his father as clerk. He continued in this capacity until 1898, when he became a partner at the same time with William H. Spaulding, and the firm became W. C. Landon & Company. This title is still retained, and the firm conducts one of the largest wholesale and retail businesses in the state. Captain Landon has been active in military life and has occupied various responsible positions in both line and staff. On May

11, 1886, at the age of nineteen years, he enlisted in Company A, First Regiment Vermont National Guard, and was promoted successively to the grades of corporal, sergeant and first sergeant. He was elected first lieutenant, February 5, 1893, and captain March 19, 1894, but declined the captain's commission and continued in service as first lieutenant. At the outbreak of the Spanish-American war he volunteered for service, and on May 16, 1898, was commissioned first lieutenant of his company in the First Regiment, Vermont Infantry United States Volunteers. His regiment was not called into active service, but remained in camp at Chickamauga, Tennessee, until the restoration of peace. He served for a time as regimental quartermaster and commanded Company A on its return to Vermont, in the absence of Captain Dyer, who was home on leave. He was honorably mustered out of United States service, November 3, 1898. On September 30, 1899, he was appointed state inspector of rifle practice, with the rank of captain in the staff of Colonel J. G. Estey. He resigned from the service, September 30, 1902, after sixteen years continual service, and was retired as captain on the same date. Mr. Landon takes an active part in social organizations, being a member of Rutland Lodge, No. 79, Free and Accepted Masons; Davenport Chapter, No. 17, Royal Arch Masons; Killington Commandery, No. 6, Knights Templar. He is a member of Cairo Temple, Ancient Arabic Order Nobles of the Mystic Shrine. For five years he served as treasurer of Rutland Lodge, No. 345, Benevolent Order of Elks, and was also for a term of years treasurer of the local camp, Sons of Veterans. He is affiliated with the Military Order of Foreign Wars, in which he served two years as secretary and treasurer, one year as vice-commander, and is now commander of the Vermont department. He is past commander of Camp Harold F. Foyles, Spanish War Veterans. In March, 1911, he was elected school commissioner for a term of three years.

He married, April 26, 1892, Mattie M. Gordon, of Dalton, Georgia, daughter of Charles P. and Maggie (Manly) Gordon. Children: Gordon, born July 31, 1896; Mary Margaret, December 23, 1901.

Tristram Dodge, the founder of
DODGE this family, emigrated from county Suffolk, England, to Newfoundland in 1647, and later removed to Massachusetts. He sailed in April, 1661, from Taunton, Massachusetts, with the original fifteen settlers of Block Island and their families.

His sons followed him in 1667, and according to the best preserved family tradition they came originally from the north of England near the river Tweed. Tristram Dodge was a freeman of Block Island, May 4, 1664, and sergeant in 1676. He died intestate in 1720. The name of his wife is unknown. Children: 1. John, born in 1644, died in 1729; married, February 4, 1696, Mary ———. 2. Israel, living in 1730; married Hannah ———. 3. Tristram, born in 1647, died August 18, 1733; married, January 7, 1680, Dorcas Dickens. 4. William, of whom further. 5. Margaret, born in 1654; married John Rathbone. 6. Ann, married, November 11, 1686, John Rathbone.

(II) William, son of Tristram Dodge, was a freeman of Block Island in July, 1670. He married Sarah, daughter of Peter and Mary George, and perhaps (second) April 24, 1694, ———. Children: 1. William, born March 7, 1680. 2. Elizabeth, born May 31, 1683. 3. Mary. 4. Samuel, of whom further. 5. Sarah, born January 24, 1695.

(III) Samuel, son of William Dodge, of Block Island, was born there September 9, 1691, died at Cow Neck (now Port Washington), Long Island, in 1761. He removed to Cow Neck about 1718. He married Elizabeth ———. Children: 1. Wilkie, died before March 25, 1761; married Mary Hunt. 2. Jeremiah, born in May, 1716, died in 1800; married, October 6, 1737, Margaret Vanderbilt. 3. Samuel, of whom further. 4. Deborah, married before 1761 ——— Mott. 5. Mary, married Dr. Robert North.

(IV) Samuel (2), son of Samuel (1) and Elizabeth Dodge, of Block Island and Cow Neck, Long Island, was born at Cow Neck, March 29, 1730, died in Poughkeepsie, New York, October 4, 1807. He was a noted astronomer, a man of literary tastes and author of various poems of merit. In 1779 he was a member of the legislature from Dutchess county, New York, and at that time wrote the following which was read in the house. It should be read twice, the first time reading each line straight across; the second time reading the first half of the two lines and then the second half of the same two, and so on. The political sentiments of the author, 1779.

Hark; hark; the trumpet sounds	The din of War's alarms
O'er seas and solid grounds,	Do call us all to arms
Who for King George do stand,	Their honors soon will shine,
Their ruin is at hand,	Who with the Congress join.
The acts of Parliament,	In them I much delight,
I hate their curst intent,	Who for the Congress fight,
Who non-resistance hold,	They have my hand and heart,
May they for slaves be sold,	Who act a Whiggish part.
The Tories of the day,	They are my daily toast,
They soon shall sneak away,	Who independence boast.
The Congress of the States,	I hate with all my heart,
Blessing upon them waits,	Whoe'er take Britain's part.
To General Washington	Confusion and dishonor,
May numbers daily run,	To Britain's royal banner.
On Mansfield, North and Bute,	May daily blessings pour
Confusion and dispute,	On Congress evermore.
To North that British lord,	May honors still be done,
I wish a block or cord,	To General Washington.

Samuel Dodge was a captain in the New York line during the revolution and keeper of the Almshouse, City Hall Park, New York City, 1793 to 1802. He married, in New York City, August 4, 1753, Helena Amerman, born May 1, 1735, died in 1817. Children, first seven born in New York City, the others in Poughkeepsie: 1. Samuel, born September 1, 1754, died October 27, 1795; married, about 1769, Mary Forbes. 2. Henry, born April 12, 1756, died December 19, 1820; married Sarah Rosecrans. 3. William, of whom further. 4. Catharine, born December 7, 1760, died November 4, 1762. 5. Richard, born December 31, 1762, died December 3, 1832; married, February 4, 17—, Ann Sarah, daughter of William and Sarah Irving, and sister to Washington Irving, the author. 6. Daniel, born December 14, 1764, died April 2, 1841; married, March 17, 1796, Ann Turner. 7. Ezekiel, born February 17, 1767, died April 13, 1839; married, May 20, 1806, Jane Power. 8. Jane, born August 15, 1769, died December 4, 1772. 9. James, born December 16, 1771, died October 10, 1804; married ———. 10. Jane, born December 19, 1773, died October 14, 1794. 11. Helena, born June 20, 1776, died November 25, 1830. 12. John, born December 29, 1777, died November 25, 1830; married, April 9, 1801, Margaret E. Wood.

(V) William (2), son of Samuel (2) and Helena (Amerman) Dodge, was born in New York City, March 5, 1758, died in 1847. His wife's name is unknown. Children: 1. William, referred to below. 2. Samuel, died unmarried. 3. Helen, died unmarried. 4. Eliza,

James Mapes Dodge

died unmarried. 5. Jane A., died unmarried. 6. Mary. 7. Alexander Forbes, born about 1800, married Helen Amerman.

(VI) William (3), son of William (2) Dodge, married, May 11, 1814, Susan Johnson. Children: 1. William, of whom further. 2. John Turner, born November 3, 1816, died unmarried. 3. Samuel, born June 21, 1818, died February 23, 1827. 4. Alexander Forbes, born February 17, 1820; married Barbara Herwick. 5. Helen Mary, born December 18, 1821. 6. Jane Eliza, born October 15, 1823. 7. Robert Johnson, born May 4, 1825, died June 30, 1892; married, June 9, 1853, Antoinetta C. Arnold.

(VII) William (4), son of William (3) and Susan (Johnson) Dodge, was born in New York City, March 7, 1815, died there October 28, 1858. He graduated from Columbia University in 1834, received his M. A. degree in 1837, studied law and was assemblyman for New York in 1849. He married, September 13, 1851, Mary Elizabeth, daughter of Professor James Jay and Sophia (Furman) Mapes, of New York City (see Mapes XIV). Children: 1. James Mapes, of whom further. 2. Harrington Mapes, born November 15, 1855, died in 1881, unmarried.

(VIII) James Mapes, son of William (4) and Mary Elizabeth (Mapes) Dodge, was born in Waverley, near Newark, Essex county, New Jersey, June 30, 1852, and is now living on McKean avenue, Germantown, Pennsylvania. He received his education in the schools of Waverley, graduated from the Newark Academy, and entered the class of 1872 at Cornell University, but after remaining there for three years he went to Rutgers College, New Brunswick, New Jersey, and took a year's course in chemistry, and afterwards served an apprenticeship of about five years with John Roach, of New York. He next formed the engineering firm of Copeland & Dodge, from which he withdrew two years later to become connected with the furniture manufacturing firm of A. H. Andrews & Company of Chicago, which became the Link Belt Company with plants in Chicago, Illinois, Indianapolis, Indiana, and Philadelphia, Pennsylvania. Of this company Mr. Dodge is chairman of the board of managers. He is also president of the J. M. Dodge Company of Connecticut, a firm which stores and handles coal, and has offices in Philadelphia. He is vice-president of the Franklin Institute of Philadelphia, a former president of the American Society of Mechanical Engineers, and honorary member of the Engineers Society of Western Pennsylvania, a member of the Union League Club of Philadelphia, of the Germantown Cricket Club and of Franklin Lodge, No. 134, Free and Accepted Masons, of Philadelphia. He has taken all the rites in Free Masonry up to and including the thirty-second degree. He inherits the inventive genius of his maternal grandfather and has taken out over one hundred and fifty patents for inventions. He is a Republican in national and an independent in city politics, and a Unitarian in religion. He is a member of the Auto Club of Philadelphia.

He married, in October, 1879, Josephine, daughter of Charles Kern, of Chicago, Illinois, who was born in Terre Haute, Indiana, in 1857. Children: 1. Kern, born in Chicago, Illinois, in 1880, married Helen Peterson, daughter of Frank B. Greene, of Providence, Rhode Island, and Jane (Deacon) Greene, of Philadelphia, Pennsylvania. 2. Dorothy, died in infancy. 3. Fayelle, born in Philadelphia, Pennsylvania, in 1886; married Henry S. Paul Jr., of Philadelphia. 4. Karl, born in Philadelphia, in 1891; a student at Haverford College. 5. Josephine, born in Philadelphia, 1895.

(The Mapes Line).

John Mapes, the first member of this family of whom we have definite information, was living in Feltham, county Norfolk, England, about 1350. He bears arms: Quarterly: One and four, sable, four fusils in fesse or; two and three, Or, two bars nebulee sable. Crest: An arm in armour e, bowed or, holding in the gauntlet a spur, argent leathered sable. He married Joice, daughter and heir of John, son of Sir Hugh Blout. Children: Robert, of whom further; Thomas.

(II) Robert, son of John and Joice (Blout) Mapes, of Feltham, county Norfolk, England, lived there and married Elizabeth Gray. Children: John, of whom further; William, Anna, Elizabeth.

(III) John (2), son of Robert and Elizabeth (Gray) Mapes, of Feltham, lived there and married Jane Higham. Children: Christopher, of whom further; Eleanor.

(IV) Christopher, son of John (2) and Jane (Higham) Mapes, of Feltham, lived there and married Thomazine Heron. Child, John.

(V) John (3), son of Christopher and Thomazine (Heron) Mapes, of Feltham, lived there and married (first) Ann Moore, and (second) Alice Wolmer. Children, two by first marriage: Robert; Elizabeth; Leonard, of whom further; John, married, May 11, 1585, Anna Cater; Elizabeth.

(VI) Leonard, son of John (3) and Alice (Wolmer) Mapes, was born in Feltham about 1558. He married Catharine, daughter of

Richard Southwell, of St. Faith's, county Norfolk, England. Children: Francis, of whom further; Robert, Thomas, John, Rebecca, Elizabeth, Richard.

(VII) Francis, son of Leonard and Catharine (Southwell) Mapes, was born about 1588. In 1620 he was one of the nine hundred administrators for Virginia, named by Captain John Smith, and his occupation was that of land surveyor. He returned to England before 1625 and settled at Rowlesby, county Norfolk, where he died. He married, before 1611, Anna, daughter of Richard Loveday, of Norwich, England. Children: Catharine, born in 1611; John, born in 1613, died in 1682, emigrated to New England, and Southold, Long Island; Thomas, of whom further; Joseph, died in 1707, married Ruth ———, emigrated to Southold, Long Island.

(VIII) Thomas, son of Francis and Anna (Loveday) Mapes, was born in Rowlesby, county Norfolk, England, in 1628, died in Southold, Long Island, before October 19, 1687. He is first mentioned on the town records of Southold in 1657 as a surveyor. He also served as justice of the peace and in other town offices. He married, in 1650, Sarah, daughter of Captain William and Alice Purrier, of Southold, who was born in 1630. Children: Thomas, born in 1651, died in 1711; Rebecca, born in 1655; William, born in 1655, twin of Rebecca; Abigail, born in 1659; Sarah, born in 1660; Mary, born in 1662; Jabez, of whom further; Naomi, born in 1667; Caroline, born in 1668; Jonathan, born June 20, 1670, died January 4, 1747; married (first) in 1696, Hester Horton; (second) in 1711, Abigail ———, and (third) in 1733, Mary Terry.

(IX) Jabez, son of Thomas and Sarah (Purrier) Mapes, was born in Southold, Long Island, in 1664, died in 1732. He lived in Mapes Neck, Southold, Long Island. He married (first) Elizabeth, daughter of John Roe, who died before May 25, 1717, and (second) the Widow Hannah Case. Children, all by first marriage: Sarah, born in 1686, married John Beers; Elizabeth, born in 1690, married Elias Bailey; Hannah, born in 1693, married ——— Osman; Elce; Jabez, died in 1716; Thomas, died in 1717; Joseph, of whom further; Mary, married Joseph Goldsmith; Abiah; Bethia.

(X) Joseph, son of Jabez and Elizabeth (Roe) Mapes, was born on Mapes Neck, Southold, Long Island, in 1705, died in 1783. He married, January 12, 1727, Keziah, daughter of Captain Israel Parshall and granddaughter of James Parshall and also of Elizabeth, only daughter of David Gardiner, the

second proprietor of Gardiner's Island. Children: Keziah, born in 1729; Joseph, born in 1733; Josanna, married Peter Hallock; James, of whom further; Phineas; Anne.

(XI) James, son of Joseph and Keziah (Parshall) Mapes, of Southold, Long Island, was born there in 1744, died there in 1783. He married, May 14, 1764, Deliverance Hawkins. Children: James Hawkins, born in 1766, married ———; Jonas, of whom further; Joanna.

(XII) General Jonas Mapes, son of James and Deliverance (Hawkins) Mapes, was born in Southold, Long Island, September 6, 1768, died in New York City, July 10, 1827. He was commissioned ensign in the New York militia, October 15, 1794, and when the war of 1812 broke out had risen to the rank of lieutenant-colonel. October 10, 1816, he was commissioned major-general commanding the first division of New York state troops. He was a founder and first director of the Bank of Savings in Bleecker street, and a principal promoter of the movement which resulted in the establishment of the New York Institute for the Instruction of the Deaf and Dumb at Washington Heights, which was incorporated in 1817. He was treasurer of the committee of arrangements for the reception of General Lafayette in 1824. For many years he was senior partner of the firm of Mapes, Son & Waldron, importers and merchant tailors, of New York City. He married, October 12, 1796, Elizabeth, daughter of James Tylee, of New York City. Children: Charles, born in 1800, died in July, 1852, married Abigail Luff; Catharine A.; James Jay, of whom further; Catharine.

(XIII) Professor James Jay Mapes, son of General Jonas and Elizabeth (Tylee) Mapes, was born in New York City, May 29, 1806, died there January 10, 1866. From a child his mental activity and inventive powers were remarkable and he became one of America's most prominent scientists and inventors, also acquiring unusual prominence as chemist, civil engineer, author, editor, lecturer and artist. He was the first to manufacture Epsom salts from hydrobisilicate of magnesia, and invented many improvements in distilling, dyeing, tempering steel, and color manufacture. In 1832 he invented a new system of sugar refining. For a time he was professor of chemistry and natural philosophy to the National Academy of Design and later to the American Institute. In 1844 he was president of the Mechanics Institute of New York. He is said to have been the first person in New York to open an office as consulting engineer and he was an expert in patent cases. He published many able articles in scientific journals, which attracted attention both abroad and in this country, and he founded and edited four volumes of the *American Repertory of Arts, Sciences and Manufactures.* He was a member of the New York Lyceum of Natural History, of the National Institute at Washington, of the Scientific Institute of Brussels, of the Royal Society of St. Petersburg, of the Geographical Society of Paris, of the Artists' Fund Society, of Philadelphia, and of numerous horticultural and agricultural societies of Europe and America. He was among the first in the United States to advocate a federal department of agriculture. In 1847 he removed to New Jersey and established near Newark the farm known later as the "Mapes Model Farm", which he occupied until his death. He married Sophia, daughter of Judge Garrett Furman, of New York City, who survived her husband nearly twenty years. Children: Mary Elizabeth, of whom further; Sophia, married Cornelius W. Tolles; Catharine Furman, married James Sterling Bunnell; Charles Victor, born July 4, 1836, married, in 1863, Martha Meeker Halstead.

(XIV) Mary Elizabeth, daughter of Professor James Jay and Sophia (Furman) Mapes, was born in New York City in 1838. She was educated under private tutors in New York City. Her husband dying, left her a young widow with two sons. With Donald G. Mitchell and Harriet Beecher Stowe, she was one of the earliest editorial writers on *Hearth and Home* and for several years conducted the children's department of the paper. In 1873, with the issue of its first number, she became editress of *St. Nicholas,* the now famous children's magazine. She has contributed to English and American periodicals and has published "Irvington Stories" in 1864, "Hans Brinker or the Silver Skates" in 1865, a new edition in 1876, which has been translated into French, Dutch and other European languages; "A Few Friends and How They Amused Themselves Together" in 1869, "Rhymes and Jingles", in 1874; "Theophilus and Others", in 1876; "Along the Way", a volume of poems, in 1879; and "Donald and Dorothy", in 1883. She is the author of "Miss Malony on the Chinese Question", published in *Scribner's Monthly* in 1870. She married, September 13, 1851, William, son of William and Susan (Johnson) Dodge (see Dodge VII).

WEED Jonas Weed, the immigrant ancestor, came from near Stamford, Northampton county, England, in the fleet with Winthrop, in the ship "Ara-

bella", in company with Sir Robert Saltonstall, landing at Boston Bay in 1630. He settled in Watertown, Massachusetts, in 1631. He was admitted a freeman May 18, 1631, showing an earlier admission to the church, which was a requisite to be a freeman. As a freeman he had the right to vote and hold public office. He was given a letter of dismissal from the Watertown church to the church at Wethersfield, Connecticut, dated May 29, 1635:

"Whereas there was a dismission granted by the (church) of Watertown in the Massachusetts, dated 29 of May last (1635) to Andrewe Warde, Jo: Sherman, Jo: Strickland, Rob'te Coo, Rob'te Reynoll & Jonas Weede, w th intent to forme anewe in a ch: Covennte on this River of Connectecott, the said prties have soe accordingly done w th the publicke allowance of the rest of the members of said Churches, as by certificate nowe prodouced apprs. It is therefore in this prsent Cort ratified & confirmed, they prmissing shortlie publiquely to renewe the (said) Covennte uppon notice to the rest of the Churches. April 26, 1636." Col. Rec. of Conn., vol. I, p. 2.

From Wethersfield, Jonas Weed removed to Stamford, Connecticut, about 1641. His name appears in the list of pioneers of Stamford in 1642, and he had land granted that year. He died in Stamford, in 1676. His will, on record at Fairfield, was dated November 26, 1672, and his inventory was dated June 5, 1676. His administrators were his wife, Mary and his sons Daniel and Jonas. His legatees were his wife Mary and his children. His widow died in 1689 or 1690. Her inventory was brought in March 10, 1690. Children: 1. John Weed, mentioned below. 2. Daniel, married Ruth ———; (second) Mrs. Clapp, or Platt; mentioned in his father's will he was named in town records, 1677; awarded land by town 1677; appointed with others to attend the work of fortification in a threatened raid of Indians upon Stamford, March, 1675-76; on committee to engage Rev. John Davenport, of New Haven, as minister. He lived in Rye, New York, for twenty years. He owned land there and probably married Ruth in Rye. He died November 29, 1697, at Stamford, Connecticut. 3. Jonas Weed, named in father's will as administrator, married Bethia, daughter of John Holly, of Stamford, November 16, 1670; she died December 29, 1713. Jonas was townsman for eleven years; he died November 19, 1704. 4. Mary, wife of George Abbott, Norwalk, Connecticut. 5. Dorcas, wife of James Wright, Wethersfield, Connecticut. 6. Samuel. 7. Sarah. 8. Hannah, married Benjamin Hait, January 5, 1670. A child of Jonas Weed Sr. died July 15, 1656.

(II) John Weed, mentioned as eldest son in father's will, married, in 1665, Joanna, daughter of Richard Westcott, of Wethersfield, and Fairfield after 1657. John bought land in Stamford from Elias Bayley, April 20, 1657. John and Daniel Weed bought house and land from Joseph Mead in 1658. He died in 1688. Inventory of his estate recorded January 15, 1689. Land which had accrued to his estate since his death was divided among his heirs January 8, 1710. Children: 1. Jonas Weed, born February 5, 1667; mentioned below. 2. Daniel, born February 11, 1669. 3. John, born 1673. 4. Samuel, born 1675. 5. Joseph, born 1678. 6. Isaac, born 1682. 7. Mary, born 1684. 8. Hannah, born 1687. All of the sons of John Weed were living on the 25th day of June, 1705.

(III) Jonas Weed, son of John Weed, was born February 5, 1667. Married and had children. He was living June 25, 1705, and had died before 1710.

"Know all men by these Presents yt We underwritten appointed & Impowered by ye Court of Probates in Fairfield December 25, 1707, to make Distribution of what Land is fallen to John Weed late of Stamford Dec'd. since his Death amongst his children or their Legal Representatives do approve of an agreement made & concluded ye 25 Day of June 1705 with ye hands & seals of all ye sons of sd John Weed to say Jonas Daniel John Samuel—Joseph & Isaac—& agreeably to sd agreement have made distribution of ye first Dividend as followeth * * * & unto ye Legal Representatives of Jonas Weed Dec'd the exact half of ye Remainder of sd Dividend * * * by sd agreement belonging unto sd Jonas Weed now Dec'd & in witness * * * have sett to our hands & seals this eight day of January anno Dom 1710/11 in Stamford * * *". Town Clerk's office, Stamford, Connecticut, Town Record Book B, page 212.

Jonas Weed had a son Nathan.

(IV) Nathan Weed, son of Jonas (3) (John 2, Jonas 1), was born May 20, 1705. He married, May 28, 1730, Isabel Youngs, daughter of John Youngs and Ruth Elliott (daughter of John Elliott). Isabel Youngs Weed died November 11, 1748. Children: 1. Nathan Weed, born June 5, 1731, died July 24, 1731. 2. Abigail, born May 31, 1732. 3. Youngs Weed, born June 3, 1736; married Mary Scofield, April 4, 1758. 4. Rebecca, born June 6, 1740. 5. Ebenezer, born April 20, 1743, mentioned below. 6. Samuel, born August 31, 1745, died December 24, 1750. 7. James, born July 22, 1748, died October 19, 1748. Nathan Weed married (second) Judith Rillige, October 16, 1750. Child: Sarah, born November 10, 1751.

(V) Ebenezer Weed, born April 20, 1743; married Sarah Fairweather, of Norwalk, December 23, 1769. He was a revolutionary sol-

dier. The records of the adjutant-general's office of the War Department, Washington, D. C., show that Ebenezer Weed, rank not stated, served in 9th Company, 9th Regiment of Connecticut Militia, Revolutionary War. His name appears on a company pay-roll dated at Norwalk, April 1, 1777, which shows that he entered service October 25, 1776; was discharged December 25, 1776, and that he was in service two months. Children: 1. Mary, born May 25, 1770. 2. Hannah, born June 22, 1771. 3. Henry, born January 14, 1774, died January 30, 1775. 4. Sarah, born March 30, 1778. 5. William Henry, born July 4, 1782, mentioned below. 6. Frederick, born September 25, 1785.

(VI) William Henry Weed, son of Ebenezer Weed, was born at Norwalk, Connecticut, July 4, 1782. He settled in New York City in 1800. Merchant. Married Frances Reeder, daughter of John and Margaret Reeder, of New York, March 29, 1805. He died at 17 Ludlow street, New York City, September 9, 1845. (Frances Reeder born October 12, 1784, died in 1860.) His will was dated October 3, 1844. He owned land between Fourth and Fifth avenues, and Ninetieth and Ninety-first streets, New York City, and farm lands in Montgomery county, New York. Children: 1. Harriet Frederica, born June 20, 1806; married Alvah Finch, October 15, 1824. 2. Frances Susan, born December 29, 1808; married Alexander Thomson, July 4, 1832. 3. William Weed, born January 15, 1811, mentioned below. 4. Julianna, born April 18, 1813; married Thomas W. Faulkner, March 26, 1838. 5. Frederick L. Weed, born November 3, 1815; married Caroline Abrams, May 10, 1835. 6. Augustus C. Weed, born October 28, 1818; married Lucinda Burnstead, July 2, 1848. 7. John Reeder Weed, born August 11, 1821; married Phoebe Ann Abrams, November 20, 1842. 8. Fanny Maria, born March 3, 1824; married Eden Perrine Clark, April 26, 1846. 9. Henry F. Weed, born February 13, 1826, married ———; Edwin A. Weed, born April 5, 1828; married Arabella McPherson, April 7, 1847.

(VII) William Weed, son of William Henry Weed, was born in New York City, New York, January 15, 1811; merchant; married (first) March 26, 1832, Sarah Ann Rogers, daughter of Joseph and Eliza O'Brien Rogers; she was born December 8, 1814, and died May 1, 1841. He married (second) December 25, 1842, Anna Jemima Willson, born in London, England, July 1, 1821, died in New York City, February 2, 1887. William Weed died in New York City, May 26, 1888.

Children by first wife: 1. Harriet Finch Weed, mentioned below. 2. William Rogers, born March 2, 1835, died February 8, 1841. 3. Sarah Ann, born August 26, 1837; married January 6, 1864, Abraham Garrison; she died May 12, 1883. 4. Selim Edward, born November 5, 1839; died March 25, 1840. 5. William Edward, born April 24, 1841; married, August 5, 1871, Margaret Eugenia McCarthey; he died July 12, 1878. He was first lieutenant of Company K, Eighth Regiment, New York State Militia, in 1861. Child, Joseph Blumenthal Weed, born May 10, 1872, in New York City; married June 27, 1900, Mary Agnes Cahill; their children are: Joseph Weed, born April 11, 1901; Mary, born October 21, 1902; and Cornelius Cahill Weed, born October 9, 1906. Children of William Weed by second wife: 6. Gertrude Emily, born March 21, 1849; died May 26, 1893. 7. Lavinia Willson, born July 1, 1851. 8. Bertha Eva, born April 7, 1853, died February 19, 1888.

(VIII) Harriet Finch Weed, daughter of William Weed, was born in New York City, March 30, 1833. She married, May 20, 1856, in St. Mark's Protestant Episcopal Church, New York City, St. John Divine Van Baun, who was born in Philadelphia, Pennsylvania, September 21, 1828, and died February 25, 1889. He was a merchant in his native city. He was a son of William Donaldson and Jane (Ellis) Van Baun. William Donaldson Van Baun was born at Tortola, British West Indies, June 4, 1775, and died October, 1857, at Philadelphia. He was the son of William Thomas Van Baun and Catherine Blyden Van Baun, formerly of St. Eustatius, Dutch West Indies. Catharine Blyden was born in 1752, and married in 1773. His parents dying in 1785, he was sent to his mother's sister, Sarah Blyden, who had married at St. Eustatius, D. W. I., Joseph Donaldson Jr., of Philadelphia, December 8, 1777. He landed in Philadelphia in 1785, and lived many years with his uncle, Joseph Donaldson Jr., at the northeast corner of Sixth and High (Market) streets, Philadelphia. His mother was the daughter of Peter Zeagers Blyden, who was born July 17, 1729, at Sandy Point, at that time the English capital of St. Kitts, British West Indies, where he married, July 11, 1748, Elizabeth Warner, at St. Ann's church. He removed to St. Eustatius in 1752. Peter Zeagers Blyden was the son of John Blyden, planter, Sandy Point, St. Kitts, and his wife Mary Zeavers, married in 1722, at St. Ann's church. Children of St. John Divine and Harriet Finch Weed Van Baun: 1. Jane Ellis, born May 25, 1857, died January 23, 1876. 2. William Weed, mentioned below. 3. Sarah

Donaldson, born July 14, 1862. 4. John Blyden Van Baun, born June 25, 1869, married, November 10, 1894, Alice May Cannon, daughter of Johnson W. and Meranda Cannon, at Gloria Dei, Old Swedes church, Philadelphia. (Children: 1. Anna Elizabeth, born August 22, 1895. 2. Harriet Meranda, born August 22, 1895, died May 12, 1896. 3. Blyden, born March 21, 1900, died June 30, 1900.) 5. Harriet Rogers Van Baun, born February 8, 1879.

(IX) Dr. William Weed Van Baun, son of St. John Divine and Harriet Finch (Weed) Van Baun, was born in Philadelphia, Pennsylvania, August 20, 1858. He attended the public schools of Philadelphia and various private schools. He entered the Hahnemann Medical College of Philadelphia, and was graduated with the degree of Doctor of Medicine, March 10, 1880. He served as resident physician at the Hahnemann Medical College Hospital for a number of months. In December, 1880, he began practice at Vicksburg, Mississippi, returning after one year to Philadelphia, where he engaged in general practice. He took a post-graduate course at the University of Austria in Vienna in 1888. He was also a visitor and student in various London and Paris hospitals in 1891, making a specialty of internal medicine after his return. He is widely known and ranks among the foremost physicians of the country. He is a member of the Philadelphia County Homeopathic Medical Society, of the Homeopathic Medical Society of the State of Pennsylvania, and of the American Institute of Homeopathy. He was editor-in-chief of the *Hahnemannian Monthly* from 1888 to 1901, and under his administration this journal was recognized as one of the most valuable and important homeopathic publications. He has written on medical subjects for various other journals. He was president of the Homeopathic Medical Society of Philadelphia County from 1892 to 1893, and secretary from 1887 to 1892; president of the Homeopathic Medical Society of the State of Pennsylvania in 1896, and he has held various chairmanships in the American Institute of Homeopathy. He is a trustee and visiting physician of the Hahnemann Hospital of Philadelphia; professor of pediatrics at the Hahnemann College from 1904 to 1912; and is now associate professor of medicine; charter member and consulting physician of St. Luke's Homeopathic Hospital of Philadelphia; consulting Physician of the Women's Southern Hospital, Philadelphia, and of the West Philadelphia Homeopathic Hospital. He organized the Alumni Association of Hahnemann Medical

College, was its secretary for thirteen years and its president in 1898. He is a member of various other medical clubs and associations, of the Union League of Philadelphia, the Penn Club, the Pennsylvania Historical Society, the American Academy of Political and Social Sciences, charter member of the Church Club of Philadelphia, member of the Netherlands Society of Philadelphia, the New England Society of Philadelphia, and the Pennsylvania Society, Sons of the Revolution. He belongs to Lodge No. 51, Free and Accepted Masons, of Philadelphia, and is a member of Holy Trinity Church (Protestant Episcopal) of Philadelphia.

PERRY Though it is said by some that the Perry family were settled in the southern half of England, chiefly in Somersetshire, Cornwall, Gloucester, and Essex counties, it is thought by some that they are of Welsh origin. The Hon. Amos Perry, of the Rhode Island Historical Society, and for many years its librarian, was strongly inclined to this opinion. Among Welsh surnames appears Ap Harry (or the son of Harry) which later became Parry, and was soon corrupted to Perry. On early records in England and America the name was written Pury, Pary, Perrie and Parrie, but Perry has since been universally adopted.

(I) John Perry, a native of England, came over in 1631-32, probably in company with Rev. John Eliot, the apostle to the Indians. He is referred to by Eliot in a letter as his cousin. He was made a freeman at Boston, March 4, 1633, and settled in Roxbury, where he died and was buried September 21, 1642. His name is the fifteenth on the list of members of Rev. John Eliot's church at Roxbury. He was survived by his wife, Anna, and they had children born in Roxbury: Elizabeth, January 25, 1638; John, mentioned below; Samuel, March 1, 1641. Besides these, three children died in infancy, names not recorded.

(II) John (2), eldest surviving son of John (1) and Anna Perry, was born September 7, 1639, in Roxbury, and died in Sherborn, Massachusetts, May 4, 1713. As a young man he resided for a time in Medfield, and settled in that part of the town which subsequently became Sherborn. His residence was four miles distant from the Indian church, established by the Apostle Eliot in Natick, Massachusetts. He was rated for the Indian title in Sherborn in 1666, and seems to have taken a fair share in the public business in the colony, serving as selectman in 1692-93. He married, May 23, 1665, Bethiah Morse, born March 24, 1648, in Sherborn,

daughter of Daniel Morse, of that town, died June 3, 1717, in Sherborn. His first five children were recorded in Medfield, namely: John, born December 24, 1667; Nathaniel, May 18, 1671, died young; Samuel and Joseph (twins), August 25, 1674; Eleazer, June 1, 1680; Nathaniel; Bethiah, 1685.

(III) Joseph, son of John (2) and Bethiah (Morse) Perry, was born at Sherborn, Massachusetts, August 25, 1674. He resided and owned land near what was called the Brush Hill in Sherborn. He was a farmer, engaging, however, in all the vocations which the pioneers of that time had to undertake. He married, April 26, 1698, Martha Lovet, the sister of Joanna Lovet, whom his brother Samuel married the same day. Children: Joseph, Esq., born December 1, 1699, died May 7, 1789, married Abigail Holbrook, whose family resided north in the vicinity of the Brush Hill; James, mentioned below; David, born April 22, 1706, died September 27, 1793, aged eighty-seven, and resided north of the Brush Hill in Sherborn, Massachusetts, where the late Uriel Cutler resided for a number of years.

(IV) James, son of Joseph and Martha (Lovet) Perry, was born May 15, 1703. He resided in Sherborn, Massachusetts, near the upper depot in Holliston, as the locality stands under modern conditions. He was a busy and energetic man and applied himself vigorously to the improvement of his property, though he took a considerable interest in public affairs and attended many meetings though there is no record of his having taken office. He married Elizabeth Death, February 8, 1727-28. Children: Abner, mentioned below; Elizabeth, born October 25, 1731; James, August 12, 1734; Martha, September 18, 1736; Ruth, October 15, 1739; Barak, August 11, 1743, married Submit Sprague, February 10, 1768.

(V) Colonel Abner Perry, eldest son of James and Elizabeth (Death) Perry, was born at Holliston, Massachusetts, January 17, 1728-29. He served as commander of a regiment on an expedition to Rhode Island in 1780, during which several exciting incidents occurred. He took a great interest in military affairs and his services in that line earned for him the promotion to the rank of colonel during the revolutionary war. But military affairs did not absorb all the attention that was not devoted to business. He also took a great interest in general politics and in public affairs. He appears to have been a man of more than usual ability, and he was evidently so regarded by his fellow townsmen, and indeed also by men belonging to more distant neighborhoods. In Holliston, Massachusetts, which was his birthplace and his home, he was long regarded as foremost among the leading citizens and the distinction was conferred on him of representing the district in the general court. He married Mary Adams, January 23, 1752. Children, all born at Holliston, Massachusetts: Nathan, October 31, 1752, married Lydia Parker in 1773, and had Nathan, born February 28, 1780, Lydia, 1782, Fanny, 1784, John, February 24, 1786, Timothy, September 14, 1788; Ruth, April 15, 1754; Abner, mentioned below; Moses, May 28, 1758, married Hannah Adams in 1778; Eli, June 10, 1762; Adams, married Anna Wait, August 21, 1790, inherited the homestead, the children of the marriage being, Barah born August 21, 1793, Abner, July 24, 1795, Polly, July 15, 1797, Emery, July 25, 1799, and others.

(VI) Abner (2), son of Colonel Abner (1) and Mary (Adams) Perry, was born at Holliston, Massachusetts, July 17, 1755. Abner Perry went to what is now Dover, Wyndham county, Vermont, from Holliston, Massachusetts, some time before 1790. He had been a soldier in the revolutionary war like his father, the colonel, before him, nor was he yet done with war as far as his own family were concerned, for his son Calvin was destined also to be a soldier and even a general in the war of 1812. Abner died suddenly while attending a firemen's meeting in 1834. He married Anna Phipps, born December 9, 1762, and she attained before she died the age of nearly one hundred years. She was the daughter of Deacon Aaron Phipps, the son of John Phipps, who was a blacksmith in Holliston, Massachusetts. Aaron Phipps was born January 12, 1729-30, died of the smallpox at Holliston, Massachusetts, October 28, 1792. He was a descendant of Solomon Phipps, of Charlestown, who took the freeman oath, May 18, 1642, and died July 25, 1671, aged fifty-two years. The children of Abner Perry and Anna (Phipps) Perry were Calvin, Phipps, and others.

(VII) Phipps, son of Abner (2) and Anna (Phipps) Perry, was born at Holliston, Massachusetts, about 1778. He moved to Dover, Vermont, with his father, and between them they built a hotel which the grandson of Phipps still owns, though it is now used as a farmhouse and is calculated to have been built one hundred and twenty-five years ago. Phipps was also a farmer and owned several portions of land in the neighborhood of Dover on which were also many kinds of stock.

(VIII) Martin Phipps, son of Phipps Perry, was born at Dover, Wyndham county,

Vermont, August 12, 1812, died in the same village, June 14, 1874. He was educated in the home schools of the neighborhood, and also privately, and when he was old enough helped his father in the conduct of his hotel business as well as on the adjacent farm. He himself combined with a good knowledge of practical farming considerable business acumen, and when he grew up to man's estate branched out into the general store business, which he worked in connection with his farm. Thus he was able both to grow and to sell in the recognized commercial way a variety of products, combining in his own person the capacities of producer, middleman and retailer. His store was for many years one of the great rendezvous of the small community and subjects of the most abstruse kind used to engage the controversial abilities of the local artisans and tradespeople. Thus it came about that Martin Phipps Perry became a spiritualist in religion, though in a broad and inquiring way. He married (first) a Miss Warner, by whom he had several children; (second) in August, 1861, Lucie Clarinda Burr, born June 14, 1834, at Dover, Wyndham county, Vermont, died at Brooklyn, New York, May 11, 1898. Children by second marriage were: Wilton Hunter, mentioned below; Burton Martin, born at Dover, Wyndham county, Vermont, April 5, 1865, died February 20, 1896, at Brooklyn, New York, having been most of his life in the baking business; Enola Eliza, living at Brooklyn, New York, married twice, her second husband being Frederick Kranger; Florence, died in infancy.

(IX) Wilton Hunter, eldest son by the second marriage of Martin Phipps and Lucie Clarinda (Burr) Perry, was born at Dover, Wyndham county, Vermont, September 22, 1862, the day Abraham Lincoln issued his proclamation freeing all slaves in the territory of the United States. He was educated in the public school at Dover, and when he left school was given a course of farming on the old farm which he now owns. This old farm and the property attached to it comprises over three hundred acres and on it still stands the old hotel conducted by his grandfather, though now used as a farmhouse. Wilton Hunter Perry left the farm twenty-six years ago and came to Brooklyn, New York, to engage in the baking business with his brother. He now owns three stores, specializing in pastry, cake, and pies, probably the largest in that line in the city. Most of his time has been given to the development of his large business, but Mr. Perry has also taken considerable interest in public affairs. He is in politics a Republican, but is not active, and is an Independent. As a rule he forms his own opinion on the questions of the day. He is a strong believer in the benefits of the initiative and referendum. In religion he is broadminded and attends different churches. He is a member of the New England Society, the Vermont Society, the New York Retail Bakers' Association, and of this latter society he was elected vice-president in 1912. He is also a Mason.

He married, October 30, 1907, Barbara Joeig, born in Brooklyn, New York, December 1, 1874, died February 17, 1909. He has no children.

FAIRCHILD Thomas Fairchild, the immigrant ancestor, was born in England. He married there (first) about 1639, a daughter of Robert Seabrook; married (second) Katharine Craig, of London, England. He died December 14, 1670, and his widow married (second) Jeremiah Judson. His first wife was sister of William Preston's wife, of New Haven. Thomas Fairchild was among the first settlers of New Haven. Children of first wife: 1. Samuel, born August 31, 1640, was probably the first white child born in Stratford, Connecticut, where he lived all his life; he married there Mary, daughter of Moses Wheeler, and she married (second) Benjamin Beach Jr., in December, 1705; their children were: Robert, born 1681; Samuel, 1683; Edward, of Newtown, Connecticut; and Jonathan. 2. Sarah, born February 19, 1641-42. 3. John, born May 1, 1644. 4. Thomas, February 21, 1645. 5. Dinah, July 14, 1648. 6. Zachariah, December 14, 1651. 7. Emma, October, 1653. Children of second wife: Joseph, born April 18, 1664; John, born June 8, 1666; Priscilla, born April 20, 1669.

(I) George Edwin Fairchild, descendant of Thomas Fairchild, in the Connecticut line, was born at New Haven, Connecticut. He was educated in the public schools. He died in 1854, on one of his trips to Havana, Cuba, where he had business interests. He married Emily Dole, daughter of Dr. and Harriet (St. Clair) Pitts. Her father was a prominent physician and surgeon of New York City. Her mother, Harriet (St. Clair) Pitts, was a native of Westchester county, New York. The St. Clairs came from England and made their home in this section of New York. Children: Georgianna, Clarence, Marie C., died in 1866, married Clement S. Parsons; John Edwin, mentioned below.

(II) John Edwin, son of George Edwin Fairchild, was born in New York City, on

White street, July 12, 1844. His father died when he was a boy of nine years. He attended the Friends' School in Stuyvesant Square, New York City. During his youth he lived at Somerset, Bristol county, Massachusetts, and attended the public schools of that town. He completed his education at Pierce Academy, Middleborough, Massachusetts, during the time Elisha Jenks, a well known educator of his day, was the principal. Afterward he removed with the family to Brooklyn, New York. When he was eighteen years old he engaged in business as a broker on Wall street, New York. He is a member of the New England Society of New York City, of the Society of Colonial Wars, and of the Christian Science Church. He is a descendant through maternal lines of Major Elisha Burgess, a soldier in the revolution, of an old Massachusetts family, and is descended also from the Reed and Hartwell families of the Massachusetts Bay Colony.

He married, December 12, 1866, Harriet Lucretia Parker, who was born in Yorkville, now Eighty-third street, New York City, November 14, 1843, daughter of John Christopher and ——— (Prince) Parker. Her mother died in 1897. They had one child, Harriet St. Clair, born November 27, 1870, in the old Parker homestead, Eighty-third street. She married C. F. Ogden, of New York, and has three children: Dorothy St. Clair Ogden, St. Clair Frances Ogden, William Burnett Ogden.

CLAPP The surname Clapp or Clap had its origin in the proper or personal name of Osgod Clapa, a Danish noble of the court of King Canute (1007-1036). The site of his country place was known as Clapham, county Surrey. The ancient seat of the family in England is at Salcombe, in Devonshire, where important estates were owned for many centuries by this family. Coat-of-arms of this branch: First and fourth, three battle-axes; second, sable a griffin passant argent; third, sable an eagle with two heads displayed with a border engrailed argent. A coat-of-arms in common use by the Clapp family in England and America is: Vaire gules and argent a quarter azure charged with the sun or. Crest: A pike naiant proper. Motto: *Fais ce que dois advienne que pourra.* The American family is descended from six immigrants, Edward and Captain Roger, sons of William Clapp, and John, Nicholas, Thomas and Ambrose, sons of Nicholas Clapp, of Venn Ottery, Devonshire, England. The fathers, William and Nicholas were brothers. All came to Dorchester, Massachusetts, May 30, 1630, and formed one of the most prominent and influential families of that town.

(I) William Clapp, of the ancient Devonshire family, lived at Salcombe Regis, Devonshire. Two of his sons were prominent among the pioneers of Dorchester, Massachusetts, Captain Roger, mentioned below; and Edward, who came over with his brother about 1630, admitted freeman December 7, 1636, proprietor, town officer, deacon; married Prudence, daughter of his uncle, Nicholas Clapp, of Venn Ottery.

(II) Captain Roger Clapp, son of William Clapp, was born in Salcombe Regis, Devonshire, England, April 6, 1609. He sailed from Plymouth on the ship "Mary and John" for New England, March 20, 1630, arriving at Nantasket, May 30, 1630. He was one of the first settlers of Dorchester in 1630. He was a proprietor and was admitted a freeman, May 14, 1634. He was chosen selectman in 1637, and fourteen times afterward previous to 1665, when he took command of the fort (Fort Independence) and held that position continuously until his death. He was appointed August 10, 1665, "Captain of the Castle," with a salary of fifty pounds a year. He was several times deputy to the general court. At the first regular organization of the militia in 1644 he was lieutenant of the Dorchester company and was afterward captain. He was one of the founders of the Dorchester church and a member for sixty years. He was a kind and considerate officer, and honored and respected by all under his authority. Such was the affection in which he was held that on one occasion when he was seriously ill a day of fasting and prayer was ordered by the town of Dorchester that they might pray for his recovery. On his restoration to health a day of thanksgiving was set apart. He removed to Boston in 1686 and died there February 2, 1691. He married, November 6, 1633, Johanna, daughter of Thomas Ford, of Dorchester, England, who was a passenger in the same ship. She was born June 8, 1617, died in Boston, June 29, 1695. Children: Samuel, born October 11, 1634; William, July 5, 1636, died September 22, 1638; Elizabeth, June 22, 1638; Experience, August 23, 1640, died young; Waitstill, October 22, 1641, died August 9, 1643; Preserved, mentioned below; Experience, December, 1645, died young; Hopestill, November 6, 1647; Wait, March 17, 1649; Thanks, baptized August 25, 1650, died young; Desire, October 17, 1652; Thomas, April, 1655, died 1670; Unite, October 13, 1656, died March 20, 1664; Supply, October 30, 1660.

(III) Preserved, son of Captain Roger Clapp, was born November 23, 1643, and died September 20, 1720. He lived in Dorchester until he was about twenty years old, when he removed to Northampton and became one of the leading citizens there. He was captain of the militia, ruling elder of the church, and deputy to the general court. He married, June 4, 1668, Sarah, daughter of Major Benjamin Newberry, of Windsor, Connecticut, who died October 3, 1716, aged sixty-six. Children: Sarah, born February 24, 1669, died young; Wait, November 8, 1670; Mary, December 14, 1672, died November 2, 1691; Preserved, April 29, 1675; Samuel, 1677; Hannah, May 5, 1681; Roger, May 24, 1684, mentioned below; Thomas, June 16, 1688.

(IV) Captain Roger (2) Clapp, son of Preserved Clapp, was born May 24, 1684, and died January 9, 1762. He married Elizabeth, daughter of Samuel Bartlett, born October 27, 1687, and died August 9, 1767. He was captain in the militia and representative to the general court. He lived in Northampton. Children: Roger, born April 3, 1708; Elizabeth, May 29, 1710; Jonathan, 1713; Aaron, January 30, 1715; Asahel, about 1717; Supply, mentioned below; Charles, in 1725; Noah, died about 1751; Simeon, born 1728.

(V) Supply, son of Captain Roger (2) Clapp, was born in Northampton, 1721, died October 11, 1784. He married his second wife, Sarah Lyman, December 30, 1756, in Northampton; she was born in 1730, died March 21, 1810. He was a soldier in the French and Indian war, 1755, a sergeant in the regiment of Colonel Seth Pomeroy, and was taken prisoner at Lake George, in the capture of which fort that regiment took an important part. His name was on the sick list returned by Thomas Williams, surgeon, November 23, 1755. He was also in the expedition to Crown Point, Captain Elisha Hawley's company. Children: Supply, mentioned below; Lydia, Sarah, Abigail, Martha.

(VI) Supply (2), son of Supply (1) Clapp, was born February 22, 1767, died June 20, 1800. His first wife was Lucretia, daughter of Deacon Martin Clark, of Westhampton, a man whom everybody loved and respected. She was baptized July 24, 1770, died September 20, 1795. Their children were: Justice, mentioned below; Moseley, Sarah, Hannah, Lucretia.

(VII) Justice, son of Supply (2) Clapp, was born August 26, 1795, died in Becket, Massachusetts, October 15, 1849. He married, June 3, 1823, Lucretia Clark, born January 26, 1802, daughter of Julius Clark, fifth descendant from Lieutenant William Clark;

she died May 14, 1840. Children: Lorenzo Harlan, born May 21, 1824, died April 7, 1890; George Moseley, born August 24, 1825, died July 24, 1897; Sarah Gillett, June 29, 1827, died February 20, 1887; Julius Clark, December 2, 1829, died 1888; Oliver Martin, October 17, 1831, died July 4, 1897; Hannah Lucretia, December 9, 1833, died January 19, 1881; Edward Everett, January 5, 1838.

(VIII) Edward Everett, son of Justice Clapp, was born in Holyoke, Massachusetts, January 5, 1838. His mother died when he was two years old, and his father when he was eleven. At the age of fifteen he came to Newburg, New York, and attended the Newburg Academy under Professor Reed, living with his brother, George M. In April, 1861, he sailed for China with the purpose of seeing more of the world and securing a suitable business opening. He found his opportunity in the cotton trade in China, where, owing to the civil war in America, cotton was in demand for export to supply the cotton mills of England and other countries. In 1875, after spending most of the intervening years abroad, he established an insurance agency in Albany, New York, representing twelve fire insurance companies, one life, and the Fidelity & Casualty Company of New York, and enjoyed from the outset an excellent patronage. In 1881 the president of the Fidelity & Casualty Company persuaded him to sell his Albany business and devote his entire attention to the New York business of that company. His firm, E. E. Clapp & Company, consists of Mr. E. E. Clapp and Mr. Edward Griffith, under the firm name of E. E. Clapp & Company. They are managers of the disability department of the Fidelity & Casualty Company for New York, New Jersey, Massachusetts and Rhode Island, and for many years have been first in the amount of business written among the general agents of the entire world. In 1911 this firm paid the Fidelity & Casualty Company over $1,450,000. In the special field of disability and accident insurance, Mr. Clapp is recognized as one of the foremost authorities in this country. He has taken a leading part in the development of this form of insurance from its inception. In politics Mr. Clapp is a Republican of some prominence. In religion he is an Episcopalian. He is a thirty-second-degree Mason, a member of the New York Chamber of Commerce, the Union League Club, the Down Town Assocation, the Republican Club, the Peace Society, and the Economic Club of New York, also the Essex County Country Club, the New England Society of Orange, and the Society of Colonial Wars of New

Jersey. His home is in East Orange, New Jersey.

Mr. Clapp married, while in the United States, in April, 1864, Eliza Brooks Townsend, born June 29, 1838, daughter of William Townsend, a descendant of Henry Townsend, who in 1661 settled in Oyster Bay, New York; his brother, John Townsend, received in 1645 from Governor Keift a patent for the town of Flushing, and Henry remained there with him until 1661. After his marriage Mr. Clapp returned to China, taking his wife with him. Child: Annie Brooks, born April 28, 1866, married Robert Henry Hillis, and has one child, Edward Clapp Hillis, born November 24, 1908.

WEBBER Before 1755 the Webber family settled at Mansfield, Connecticut. Whether they were immigrants or not has not been definitely settled, as there were Webbers in Massachusetts at an earlier date. An important family of this name was located at Gloucester, Massachusetts, and many descendants have lived in northeastern Massachusetts and in Maine. Richard Webber of Mansfield was a soldier in the French and Indian war with his brother Christopher. He married, March 27, 1758, Ruth Campbell, at Mansfield. She was doubtless of Scotch-Irish stock. They had children, born at Mansfield: Christopher, February 5, 1759; Sarah, December 5, 1760, married, November 26, 1780; Asa Ropes; and Amasa, February 2, 1767. His son Christopher remained in Mansfield and had: Sarah, born September 20, 1782; Lucy, August 8, 1785; Eunice, November 16, 1787. Sarah Webber, sister of Richard Webber, married at Mansfield, October 20, 1762, Silas Hanks and her children were born there. Phebe Webber, another sister, married there also, November 15, 1764, David Royce; and Mary Webber, another sister, married November 18, 1756, David Cary.

(I) Christopher Webber, brother of Richard Webber, was born in 1740. He was a soldier from Mansfield in the French and Indian wars, a private in Major John Slope's company of Mansfield at Ticonderoga in 1759; also in Captain Robert Durkee's company, and in Colonel Phineas Lyman's First Connecticut Regiment, with rank of corporal, in 1761. He was also in Captain Jonathan Rudd's company of Windham, in Colonel Shubael Conant's regiment (Fifth Connecticut) in 1757, and marched to the relief of Fort Henry. (See French and Indian War Rolls, vol. I., p. 248, 254; vol. II., p. 106, 252.) He was one of the earliest settlers in the town

of Walpole, New Hampshire, and became a prominent and influential citizen there. He represented the town in the provincial congress at Exeter in 1776-77 during the most trying time of the revolution and held offices of trust and honor in Walpole for more than twenty years. He was a captain in General Bellow's regiment at Saratoga in the revolutionary war.

He died at Walpole, February 28, 1803, aged sixty-three years. He married (first) Hannah Sumner, who died at Walpole, February 28, 1781, aged forty-three years. He married (second) Lucy ———. Children, by first wife: 1. Persis, born April 19, 1769; married, December 31, 1793, Dr. Stephen Johnson. 2. Sarah, born February 18, 1771, married, September 10, 1789, Winslow Warren. 3. Elizabeth, twin of Sarah. 4. Christopher, mentioned below. 5. Hannah, born January 19, 1775; married, February 21, 1805, Moses Cutter of Stockbridge, Massachusetts. 6. Ebenezer Sumner, born June 22, 1778; died in 1782. By second wife: 7. Richard Mayo, born August 7, 1782. 8. Amos Sherman, baptized in 1783. 9. Melzar, baptized in 1787. 10. Althea, baptized 1789 and died 1789. 11. Samuel Ruggles, baptized in 1790. 12. Lucy, baptized in 1793. 13. Orlen, baptized in 1795.

(II) Dr. Christopher (2) Webber, son of Christopher (1) Webber, was born in Walpole, New Hampshire, May 7, 1773, and died at Cavendish, Vermont, December 5, 1850. He removed to Rutland, Vermont, from Walpole, when a young man and afterward located at Cavendish, where he practiced medicine for many years. He married (first) Electa Storer; (second) Betsey Dutton, who died January 19, 1835, aged sixty years. He married (third) Achsah Wilder, who died March 17, 1846, aged fifty-seven years, and he married (fourth) Relief Wilder, sister of his third wife. His widow died September 14, 1856. Children, all by his first wife: 1. Sumner Allen, mentioned below. 2. Electa, married Captain Kenney. 3. Augusta, married Hale Bates. 4. Christopher, who died while a cadet at West Point Military Academy.

(III) Hon. Sumner Allen Webber, son of Dr. Christopher Webber, was born at Rutland, Vermont, December 19, 1798, and died in Rochester, Vermont, May 20, 1862. His parents removed to Cavendish, where he received his early education in the public schools. He entered the Norwich Military Academy at Norwich, Vermont, in 1821, and was graduated in the class of 1824. He studied law for some time in the famous law school at Litchfield, Connecticut, conducted by Hon. James Gould. Returning to Vermont

he studied in the office of Hon. Charles K. Williams in Rutland, and was admitted to the bar there in 1825. In the following year he began to practice law at Rochester, Vermont, and continued there the rest of his life. He became prominent in his profession and was deemed a wise, able and prudent counsellor and a leader of the Windsor county bar. He had convincing powers as a pleader and his appeals for justice were eloquent in their simplicity. He had a thorough knowledge of literature and was especially well versed in the English classics. In 1830 he received the honorary degree of Master of Arts from Middlebury College. He was in early life a Whig, but in his later years a Republican. He held many offices of trust and honor in Rochester, representing the town in the state legislature in 1856 and 1857, when he was a member of the judiciary committee of the house of representatives. He was a candidate for congress in the old Third district, but failed of the nomination by a small margin. Before the civil war he was active in the anti-slavery movement. He was a prominent member of the Congregational church in Rochester and for some years was a teacher of young men in the Sunday school. He was a member of Rural Lodge of Free Masons, and for several years served in the Vermont state militia.

He married, January 5, 1831, Phoebe Jefferson Guernsey of Rochester, daughter of Joseph Guernsey. She died at Rochester, September 29, 1860. Children: 1. Sumner Jefferson, born in 1834, died in 1836. 2. Christopher Allen, mentioned below. 3. Phoebe Augusta, born in January, 1840; died in September, 1849. 4. Adeline Electa, born October 9, 1842; died September 11, 1910; married Dr. Frederick Langdon Morse. 5. Charles Sumner, born in November, 1848, died in 1849.

(IV) Christopher Allen, son of Hon. Sumner Allen Webber, was born in Rochester, Vermont, August 8, 1837, and died August 15, 1878, aged forty-one years. He was educated in the public schools of Rochester, and also in a private schol at that place and in Barre Academy, at Barre, Vermont. He also spent some time in study in Philadelphia, Pennsylvania, where his uncles, Dr. Henry Guernsey and Dr. William Guernsey were prominent physicians. He studied law with his father in Rochester and was admitted to the Bar about 1861. He became prominent in his profession, and was connected with some important litigation in Windsor and Addison counties. As one of the counsel for the town of Rochester in a suit against that town brought in Addison county, he had associated with him Hon. Edward J. Phelps, who was so much pleased with the ability displayed by Mr. Webber that he tried to persuade him to locate in a larger place; but he was so largely interested in the lumber business that he found it impracticable to give up his whole time to his profession.

He represented the town of Rochester for two terms in the general assembly for the years 1868 and 1869. The Hon. James Barrett, one of the judges of the supreme court of Vermont, said of him after his death, that he was one of the most promising of the young lawyers of the state. He was an accomplished singer, having a very fine baritone voice, with large compass, and for a great many years was the leader of the choir in Rochester, where people came from the surrounding towns to hear him sing. He was a forcible and eloquent speaker, had fine literary qualities, and contributed to the magazines both prose and verse.

On October 16, 1862, he married Julia Evelyn, daughter of Phineas Sanger and Harriet (Foster) Cooper (see Cooper VI). She was born at Rochester February 22, 1835. Children: Evelyn, born August 29, 1865, married Frank V. Johnson, Esq., a lawyer in New York City, and a native of Bradford, Vermont; Marvelle Christopher, mentioned below; Phineas Lafayette, Esq., born February 4, 1870, a lawyer in New York City.

(V) Marvelle Christopher, son of Christopher Allen Webber, was born in Rochester, Vermont, January 14, 1868. He was educated in the public schools of Rochester and prepared for college at the Montpelier Seminary, Montpelier, Vermont, being graduated from that place in 1886. In the fall of 1886 he entered Williams College, Williamstown, Massachusetts, but at the end of the first term left Williams to go to Boston University, where he was graduated from the College of Liberal Arts in 1889, with the degree of Bachelor of Philosophy. He then took a course in the Law School of Boston University, being graduated from there with the degree of Bachelor of Laws in 1891. Through the influence of his uncle, the Hon. Marvelle W. Cooper, a prominent business man of New York City, and appraiser of the Port of New York during the administration of Benjamin Harrison, Mr. Webber entered the law office of Evarts, Choate & Beaman in the fall of 1891. Hon. William M. Evarts and Hon. Joseph H. Choate were the senior members of the firm at that time.

Mr. Webber served his clerkship of one year in the office of Evarts, Choate & Bea-

man and was admitted to the New York City bar in December, 1892, and continued from that time in the employment of the firm until March, 1898, acting as managing clerk for a period of two years. In 1898 he left New York, on account of ill health, and returned to Vermont. In 1901 he located in the city of Rutland and has practiced law there ever since, having been connected with important litigation there. He was associated with Joel C. Baker, Esq., and Hon. Orion M. Barber, now a judge of the United States court of customs appeals, as counsel for the plaintiff in the well known case of Patch Manufacturing Company vs. Protection Lodge, No. 215, International Association of Machinists, which was brought to recover damages on account of a strike and which resulted in a verdict in favor of the plaintiff, and was sustained finally by the supreme court of the state. In association with Hon. O. M. Barber, before his appointment to the bench, and since then, with Maxwell Evarts, Esq., of New York, he has been and still is one of the counsel for the bank in the case of the State of Vermont against the Clement National Bank, now in the supreme court of the United States, involving the constitutionality of tax legislation affecting savings deposits in national banks. On July 14, 1909, Governor George H. Prouty appointed Judge Barber, O. S. Annis, Esq., and Mr. Webber a committee to arrange and provide for the compilation and issue of a digest of the reported decisions of the supreme court of Vermont, as the result of which the "Vermont Digest Annotated, being a Digest of the Reported Decisions of the Supreme Court of the State of Vermont," was published in 1911. In 1912 Mr. Webber was appointed by Governor John A. Mead, one of the commissioners from the state of Vermont, to attend the Annual Conference of Commissioners from the various States on Uniform Legislation. He served nearly two years as city attorney for the city of Rutland, by appointment of the then Mayor, Hon. H. O. Carpenter. In March, 1912, he was elected one of the members of the board of school commissioners of the city of Rutland.

He married, April 16, 1902, Mary Rich, of Philadelphia, daughter of Oliver P. and Anna Barclay (Stevenson) Rex of that city. Anna Stevenson was daughter of John B. Stevenson, a prominent linseed oil merchant of Philadelphia. Dr. Oliver P. Rex was one of the most prominent physicians of Philadelphia, and medical director of the Penn Mutual Life Insurance Company. Children of Marvelle C. and Mary (Rex) Webber: Payson Rex, born March 22, 1903; Christopher Allen, born May

26, 1905; Marvelle Cooper, born September 20, 1906.

(The Cooper Line).

(I) Deacon John Cooper, the immigrant ancestor, was born in England in 1618, and came to Cambridge about 1636. After the death of his father, his mother Lydia married Gregory Stone, a prominent pioneer of Massachusetts. It is interesting to note that four men of this name were among the early settlers of Massachusetts, one at Lynn, afterward of Southampton, Long Island; another at Scituate, afterward of Barnstable, and a third of Weymouth. John of Cambridge was a yeoman, a proprietor of the town, deacon of the church and a town officer. He was a selectman thirty-eight years, 1646-1690; town clerk, 1669-81; deacon from 1668 until he died. He married Anna, daughter of Nathaniel Sparhawk. She was born in England and came with her parents to Cambridge. He died August 22, 1691, aged seventy-three. His son Samuel administered the estate. Children, born at Cambridge: Anna, born November 16, 1643; Mary, September 11, 1645; John, April 2, 1651; Samuel, mentioned below; John, October 3, 1656; Nathaniel, May 2, 1659; Lydia, April 8, 1662; Anna, born December 26, 1667.

(II) Samuel, son of Deacon John Cooper, was born at Cambridge, January 3, 1653. He owned his father's homestead in Cambridge and was also deacon of the church there. He was selectman twelve years, 1704-16. He died January 8, 1717. He married, December 4, 1682, Hannah, who died October 9, 1732, daughter of Walter Hastings. Children: Hannah, December 23, 1683; Lydia, March 9, 1685; Sarah, born in 1687, married Ephraim Frost; Samuel, mentioned below; Mary, Elizabeth, Walter, John and Jonathan, six of whom were baptized at Cambridge January 17, 1717-18.

(III) Deacon Samuel (2) Cooper, son of Deacon Samuel (1) Cooper, was born in Cambridge, March 23, 1689. He was a farmer and succeeded to the homestead, which he sold in 1730 and removed to Grafton, Worcester county, Massachusetts. He married, March 29, 1719, Sarah, daughter of Samuel Kidder. Children, born in Cambridge: Nathaniel, baptized September 18, 1720; Samuel, baptized October 15, 1721; Joseph, baptized October 20, 1723; John, mentioned below; Sarah, baptized January 12, 1728-29.

(IV) Deacon John, son of Deacon Samuel (2) Cooper, was born in Cambridge, March 4, 1725, and died at Croyden, New Hampshire, August 10, 1805. He married, March 15, 1748, Mary Sherman, cousin of Hon.

Roger Sherman, one of the signers of the Declaration of Independence from Connecticut. He removed from Cambridge to Grafton with his father about 1730 and afterward removed to Hardwick, Worcester county, Massachusetts, where he bought one hundred acres of land. He was selectman of Hardwick for ten years, town clerk five years, deacon twenty years, and school teacher from 1751 to 1766. About 1769 he removed to Cornish and in 1770 to Croyden, New Hampshire. Children, recorded at Hardwick: Sarah, born February 18, 1749-50; Nathaniel, November 8, 1751; Mary, July 26, 1753; John, June 15, 1755; Joel, April 3, 1757; Huldah, May 1, 1759; Sherman, April 3, 1761; Matilda, April 16, 1762; Barnabas, mentioned below; Chloe, December 20, 1766.

(V) Barnabas, son of Deacon John Cooper, was born in Hardwick, July 28, 1764, and came to Croyden, New Hampshire, with his parents in 1769-70, removing afterward in 1807 to Rochester, Vermont, where he spent the rest of his life. He married (first) October 5, 1786, Mary Sanger, who died January 11, 1805. He married (second) December 9, 1805, Lydia Powers. Among his children was Phineas Sanger, mentioned below.

(VI) Phineas Sanger, son of Barnabas Cooper, was born in Croyden, New Hampshire, September 16, 1796, and died August 22, 1877, in Rochester, Vermont. He married, May 1, 1819, Harriet, daughter of Major Rufus Foster, a revolutionary soldier. They lived together as husband and wife for fifty-nine years. They celebrated their golden wedding in 1869; he lived nine years afterward and she lived thirteen. They had seven children: Phineas L., Hiram F., Mary M., Minnie H., Marvelle W., was appraiser of the port of New York under President Harrison and an intimate friend of President Arthur, he was also one of the founders of the Union League Club and a prominent man in New York City: Julia E., February 22, 1835, married Christopher Allen Webber (see Webber IV).

STAFFORD

Thomas Stafford, the immigrant ancestor, was born at Warwickshire, England, in 1605, died at Warwick, Rhode Island, in 1677. He is said to have come to Plymouth, Massachusetts, in 1626, and to have built there the first gristmill operated by water power in this country. His name is on the list of inhabitants admitted to Newport, Rhode Island, after May 30, 1638, and he soon received a grant there of seventeen acres of land, and was mentioned as in the employ of Nicholas Easton. He was witness to a will in Portsmouth, March 18, 1647. He was received as a townsman of Warwick, June 7, 1657, having bought a house from Christopher Unthank. He bought another house and land from Mr. Unthank, March 1, 1663. In 1665 he was a freeman of the colony. He bought a house and land in Warwick from Thomas Lawton, of Portsmouth, April 16, 1657. In 1667 he was granted a lot in the division of Potawomut, and also one in the division of Toscunk. In 1673 he was a deputy to the general assembly. His will was dated November 4, 1677, and proved April 27, 1679, bequeathing to wife Elizabeth and children. He married Elizabeth ———, who died after 1677. Children: Thomas, died January 26, 1723; Samuel, of whom further; Hannah, married Luke Bromley; Sarah, married Amos Westcott; Joseph, born March 21, 1645, at Warwick, Rhode Island; Deborah, married, June 9, 1670, Amos Westcott.

(II) Samuel, son of Thomas Stafford, was born in 1636, died March 20, 1718. He lived in Warwick, Rhode Island. He served as deputy to the general assembly in 1670-72-74-79-82-86-90 and 1705, and in 1674-86 was elected assistant but refused to serve. On February 24, 1671, he and his wife sold to Richard Carder land for twenty pounds, and on September 1, 1700, he gave six shillings toward building the Friends' meeting-house at Mashapaug. He was overseer of the poor in 1687. His will was dated March 16, 1711, and proved April 16, 1718, his son Thomas being executor. He bequeathed to his son Amos, to daughters Sarah Scranton, Patience Howland, Freelove Tillinghast and Elizabeth Devotion, to granddaughters Mary Thurber and Mary Stafford and to son Thomas. He married Mercy, daughter of Stukeley Westcott, who died March 25, 1700. Children, born in Warwick: Stukeley, born November 7, 1661, died young; Amos, of whom further; Mercy, July 8, 1668; Sarah, April 18, 1671, married ——— Scranton; Samuel, November 19, 1673, died young; Patience, married Jabez Howland; Freelove, married Joseph Tillinghast; Elizabeth, married ——— Devotion; Thomas, 1682.

(III) Amos, son of Samuel Stafford, was born in Warwick, November 8, 1665, died there in 1760. In 1702 he gave six shillings for building the Quaker meeting-house at Mashapaug. He served as deputy to the general court in 1708-21. His will was dated March 24, 1753, and proved October 20, 1760, his wife Mary and son Amos (2) being executors. He bequeathed to wife, children and grandchildren. The inventory of his estate amounted to one thousand, seven hundred and four pounds, two shillings, dated December 8, 1760. He married, December 19, 1689, Mary Burlingame, who died in 1760, daughter of Roger and Mary Burlingame. Children, born in Warwick: Mary, born September 16, 1690; Samuel, September 24, 1692; Mercy, September 21, 1694; Amos (2), of whom further; Stukeley, November 7, 1704; Patience, April 21, 1707; Freelove, October 14, 1709.

(IV) Captain Amos (2) Stafford, son of Amos (1) Stafford, was born in Warwick, Rhode Island, April 24, 1702. He lived at Coventry, Rhode Island. Children, born in Coventry: Amos (3), of whom further; Mary, April 10, 1731; Catherine, April 23, 1733; Stuteley (or Stukeley), December 21, 1735; Edith, March 30, 1738; John, February 9, 1740; Ellen, August 31, 1742; Lois, August 12, 1745.

(V) Amos (3), son of Captain Amos (2) Stafford, was born at Coventry, Rhode Island, April 3, 1726. Children, born at Coventry; Abel, born April 6, 1748; Sarah, March 25, 1750; Mary, August 22, 1752; Nathaniel, May 31, 1754; Joanna, March 10, 1756; Stutely (of Stukeley), of whom further; Amos, February 18, 1761.

(VI) Stutely (or Stukeley), son of Amos (3) Stafford, was born in Coventry, Rhode Island, May 25, 1759, died in 1826. He went to Vermont when a young man, and with the two brothers who accompanied him located at Plattsburg, New York, and settled there. He married Rebecca Irish, widow of John Irish, of Tinmouth, Vermont. She died in 1836, aged eighty years. Children: Palmer; John; Holden, of whom further; Orman; Miriam; Nancy; Mercy; and Marbury.

(VII) Holden, son of Stutely Stafford, was born about 1788, in South Wallingford, Vermont, died in 1852, aged sixty-four years. He married Jane Brayton, of Hartford, New York, who died in 1874, aged eighty-four years. Children: 1. Phebe, died in 1882, aged sixty-seven; married Alexander Northrup. 2. Thomas (2), of whom further. 3. Evelyn, died in 1899, aged eighty years; married ——— Nelson. 4. Marbury, died in 1838, aged twenty-one years. 5. John, died in 1898, aged seventy-eight. 6. Mary, died in 1896, aged seventy-three; married ——— Goodwin. 7. Amanda, twin of Mary, died in 1868, aged forty-five years; married ——— Allen. 8. Sarah, died in 1898, aged sixty-eight; married ——— Colvin. 9. Stutely, died in 1853, aged eighteen years.

(VIII) Thomas (2), son of Holden Stafford, was born about 1815, at South Wallingford, Vermont, died in Tinmouth, Vermont, November 23, 1872, aged fifty-seven years. Like his father and forefathers he followed farming for his occupation. He married Hannah Craft, born July 28, 1817, died May 3, 1867. Children: 1. Bartlett, of whom further. 2. Thomas, died in infancy. 3. Rollin C., born November 13, 1848; farmer of South Wallingford; married Ella L. Cook. Children: Nicholas, died in childhood; Hannah, died in childhood; Clarence Arthur, born August 31, 1881; Alice Elizabeth, March 17, 1886; Roy Holden, October 25, 1887; Sarah Norton, October 14, 1889; Clara Evelyn, February, 1892. 4. Jane Elizabeth, June 29, 1852. 5. John Stutely, June 1, 1854, deceased. 6. Holden, died in infancy.

(IX) Bartlett, son of Thomas Stafford, was born at South Wallingford, Vermont, October 16, 1839. He attended the public schools of his native town. When a young man he entered the American Machine Works and learned his trade as machinist. He was for many years employed as a mechanic in the United States arsenal at Springfield, Massachusetts, engaged in the manufacture of firearms. For one year he worked for the Colt Company, manufacturers of firearms at Hartford, Connecticut, manufacturing pistols. For the past thirty years Mr. Stafford has resided at Tinmouth, Vermont, where he has followed farming. He owns the farm known as the Judge Chipman place, comprising about six hundred acres. He has taken an active part in public affairs, and in 1884 represented the town in the state legislature, serving as a member of the committees on agriculture, bridges, and state prison, and on various special committees. He is a member of Chipman Lodge, Ancient Free and Accepted Masons, of Wallingford.

He married (first) in 1867, Mary Melony Valentine, born January 2, 1845, died October 27, 1895, daughter of Edmund and Flora (Sargent) Valentine. He married (second) May 2, 1902, Cassie, daughter of Isaac and Hortense (Odell) Porter. Children by his first wife: Edmund, died aged nineteen; Bert Linus, of whom further.

(X) Bert Linus, son of Bartlett Stafford, was born in Tinmouth, Vermont, December 14, 1877. He attended the common schools and the Wallingford high school, and graduated from the Rutland English and Classical Institute in 1897. He attended Middlebury College, and was graduated with the degree of Bachelor of Arts with the class of 1901. After graduating he taught school and began the study of law in the office of Lawrence & Lawrence, in Rutland. In 1906 he was admitted to the bar and began practice. Since 1908 he has been a law partner in the firm of Lawrence, Lawrence & Stafford. In politics he is a Republican.

He represented the town of Tinmouth in the Vermont state legislature in 1906, and served on committees on education, revision of bills, and military affairs, and on a special committee appointed by the governor to examine the status of state normal schools. He was elected state's attorney in 1910 for a term of two years, and was re-elected in 1912 to serve till 1914.

Mr. Stafford is a member of Chipman Lodge, Ancient Free and Accepted Masons, of Wallingford; of the Tinmouth Grange, Patrons of Husbandry; and is an attendant of the Universalist church.

He married, November, 1911, Mabel R., daughter of Rev. Thomas and Bertha (Barrickman) Stratton, formerly of Pennsylvania, now of Lyndonville, Vermont.

PHELPS   The surname Phelps is a variation of the spelling of the name Phillips, meaning son of Phillip, in the case of the original ancestor using it. The spelling of the surname has been varied and a number of well established family names are traced to the same origin. One branch of the Phelps family, however, claims to be of the Guelph family of Germany to which Queen Victoria belonged, but no proof of record has been found to establish the claim. Some branches of the American family of Phelps are descended from the ancient family of Tewksbury, Gloucestershire, England. Among them is the family mentioned below. The ancient coat-of-arms is described as follows: Sable lion chained and rampant. Various branches of the English family have their coats-of-arms.

(I) James Phelps, the English ancestor, was born about 1520, and is supposed to have been a brother of Francis Phylppe, of Nether Tyne, Staffordshire, England. He married Joan ———, who was given permission to administer his estate on May 10, 1588. Children, baptized in the Tewksbury Abbey Church, England: William, mentioned below; Thomas, August 10, 1563-64; George (Giles), September 5, 1566; Alice, December 24, 1572; Edward, May 10, 1578; Keneline, October 16, 1580; Richard, October 16, 1583; Robert, July 18, 1584; Nicholas.

(II) William, son of James Phelps, was baptized at Tewksbury Abbey Church, England, August 4, 1560, and probably died in 1611. He married Dorothy ———, who administered his estate and died in 1613. Chil-

dren, baptized in Tewksbury Abbey Church:
Mary, September 4, 1587, died young; Mary,
April 23, 1588; Thomas, June 24, 1590; Dorothy, February 29, 1595; William, mentioned
below; James, July 14, 1601; Elizabeth, May
9, 1603; George, born about 1606.

(III) William (2), son of William (1)
Phelps, was baptized at Tewksbury Abbey
Church, England, August 19, 1599, died at
Windsor, July 14, 1672. His will was dated
April 22, 1660, and proved July 26, 1672.
He was the immigrant ancestor. He resided
for a time in Tewksbury, and his first child,
Richard, was baptized in the church there.
Soon after this he probably removed to one
of the southern-counties, as there is no further record of him in Tewksbury. He and
his wife, six children, and his brother George,
came to New England in the ship "Mary and
John", sailing from Plymouth, England, March
20, 1630, and landing at Nantasket, now Hull,
May 30, 1630. He settled at Dorchester, and
was among the first settlers and founders of
that place. He was a prominent man and
often served on important committees to lay
out boundary lines. He applied for admission as a freeman, October 19, 1630, and
was admitted soon afterward. He was one
of the jury on the first jury trial in New
England, November 9, 1630. He was constable in 1631; deputy to the general court in
1634-35. He removed to Windsor, Connecticut, in the fall of 1635, and "William Phelps
was one of the six who formed the first town
meeting of Windsor". At a court held May
1, 1637, William Phelps presiding, it was ordered that there "shall be an offensive war
against the Pequots". He was a magistrate
from 1630 to 1643, 1645 to 1649, 1656 to 1662,
inclusive. He was deputy in 1651. In 1641
he was the governor of the Windsor colony.
He was a man of property, as shown by the
high pew rent that he paid. He subscribed
also toward the fund for the poor. Not being
able to prove his title and payment for the
land he purchased of Sehat, an Indian in
Windsor, he paid for it a second time, the
legal tender used being wampum. He resided
on the road running northerly, a short distance north of Mill River Valley, and he was
among those who suffered from the Great
Flood in 1639. Soon after the flood he removed farther south and settled on what is
known as Phelps Meadows, and his son William lived a short distance east of him. The
cellar of the old house may still be seen. He
married (first) —— ——, who died in
1633. He married (second) in 1638, Mary
Dover, who came to New England on the
"Mary and John". She died November 27,

1675. Children of first wife: Richard, baptized in Tewksbury, England, December 26,
1619; William, born in England; Sarah, born
in England about 1623; Samuel, born in England about 1625; Nathaniel, mentioned below;
Joseph, born in England about 1629; Timothy, born at Windsor, September 1, 1639;
Mary, born at Windsor, March 2, 1644.

(IV) Nathaniel, son of William (2)
Phelps, was born in England about 1627, and
came to New England with his father. He
settled first in Dorchester and then in Windsor, Connecticut. He resided on the Orton
place opposite his father's homestead, which
he purchased of his brother Samuel. About
1656-57 he removed to Northampton and was
one of the first settlers there. He was one
of the first deacons of the Northampton
church, and occupied his homestead forty-
three years. The farm was occupied by his
descendants until 1835. It comprised the
land which was formerly the site of Miss
Margaret Dwight's School, and later the College Institute of J. J. Dudley, and which is
now Shady Lawn. The old house stood a
few rods north of the present house. On
February 8, 1679, he and his sons, Nathaniel
Jr. and William, took the oath of allegiance
before Major Pynchon, and May 11, 1681,
he was admitted a freeman. He died in
Northampton, May 27, 1702, aged seventy-
five years. He married, in Windsor, September 17, 1650, Elizabeth Copley, of England,
an ancestress of Copley, the celebrated artist.
She died in Northampton, Massachusetts, December 6, 1712, and her will was proved there.
Children: Mary, born June 21, 1651, in
Windsor; Nathaniel, June 2, 1652, Windsor;
Abigail, April 6, 1655, Windsor, died aged one
hundred and one years, four months and
eleven days; William, mentioned below; Thomas, May 20, 1661, Northampton; Mercy,
May 16, 1662, Northampton, died July 15,
1662.

(V) William (3), son of Nathaniel Phelps,
was born at Northampton, June 22, 1657,
died January 1, 1745. He settled on the
homestead at Northampton, and was admitted
a freeman, May 30, 1690. He married, May
30, 1678, Abigail Stebbins, born September
24, 1660, died in 1748, daughter of John
Stebbins. Children: Abigail, born August 3,
1679; Elizabeth, February 4, 1682; William,
mentioned below; Mary, January 3, 1688;
Nathaniel, October 5, 1690; Deborah, May
17, 1694; Ebenezer, October, 1697; Joseph
Austin, December 5, 1699; Mary, May 4,
1703.

(VI) Captain William (4) Phelps, son of
William (3) Phelps, was born in Northamp-

ton, April 16, 1684. He remained in Northampton all of his life. He was one of the committee of safety there during the revolution. In his will he mentioned his wife and children Eliakim, Benjamin, Josiah, William, Elnathan, Thankful, Eunice, Lois and Experience. He married, 1706, Thankful Edwards. Children, born in Northampton: Thankful, December 17, 1707; Eliakim, January 17, 1709; Thankful, July 20, 1710; Benjamin, March 10, 1713; Josiah, May 20, 1716; Experience, March 15, 1717; Eunice, April, 1720; Lois, 1725; Joseph, 1728; William, September 12, 1731; Elnathan, mentioned below.

(VII) Rev. Elnathan Phelps, son of Captain William (4) Phelps, was born in Northampton, February 18, 1734, died January 2, 1813, aged seventy-nine years, at Pownal, Vermont, while on his way to Pittsfield, Massachusetts, to visit a son there. He moved to Pittsfield, Massachusetts, early in its settlement, about 1761, a short time after his brother William settled there, and he with his brother and six others were the founders of the First Church of Pittsfield, September 7, 1764, referred to in the Pittsfield records in 1781. He served on a committee of five to examine into the Shakers, who were "exceeding the bonds of Baptist toleration". After a time he began preaching in the Baptist churches, and in 1788 moved to Orwell, Vermont, where he kept up his preaching. He was the first Baptist preacher in the state of Vermont, and was the organizer of several congregations in various parts of the state, as well as of at least one in New York state. He married (first) December 15, 1757, Eleanor Bridgeman, born in Northampton, died in Pittsfield in 1774. He married (second) February 15, 1776, Sarah Elenthorp, widow of Jacob Elenthorp. She was born in Boston, April 6, 1743, died at Hopkinton, New Hampshire, March 22, 1828, aged eighty-five years. Children by first wife: Rhoda, born in Northampton, January 22, 1759, died October 6, 1759; Rhoda, born September 7, 1760, Northampton. Born at Pittsfield: Benjamin, born January 27, 1762; Paulina, May 1, 1764; Susannah, August 9, 1766; Elnathan, April 5, 1768, died October 13, 1769; Eleanor, baptized July 15, 1770, died 1770; Elnathan, mentioned below; Eleanor, born May 2, 1774. Children by second wife, born in Pittsfield: Sarah, January 21, 1778; Jacob, July 12, 1780; Anna, March 6, 1783.

(VIII) Elnathan (2), son of Rev. Elnathan (1) Phelps, was born in Pittsfield, Massachusetts, April 27, 1772, died in Orwell, Vermont, May 19, 1843. He married, at Orwell, Phebe Tuttle, born there July 6, 1777, died there

January 19, 1864. Children, born in Orwell: Elnathan, January 5, 1795; Polly, September 10, 1797; Amanda, September 25, 1799; Casandana, February 24, 1802, died 1803; Erastus, mentioned below; Orange, December 17, 1806; Alphonso, May 28, 1809; Levina, September 26, 1811; Harrison, May 2, 1814; Alonzo and Lorenzo, twins, May 18, 1819.

(IX) Erastus, son of Elnathan (2) Phelps, was born in Orwell, June 18, 1804, died in November, 1880. He lived in Lawrence, and Ticonderoga, New York. He married, March 15, 1827, Margaret, born in Orwell, November 23, 1804, died there May 6, 1896, daughter of Jonathan and Abigail (Merriman) Hibbard. Children: 1. Angie M., born April 22, 1833, in Lawrence; married Rev. Andrew N. Adams, a graduate of Harvard Divinity School, author of several genealogical works on the Adams family. 2. Erastus Hibbard, mentioned below. 3. Charles H., born in Ticonderoga, December 17, 1844; married Effie Brown; died 1911.

(X) Erastus Hibbard, son of Erastus Phelps, was born in Ticonderoga, New York, January 16, 1839. He came to Orwell, Vermont, with his parents when ten years old and attended the public schools of that town and of Ticonderoga, the Troy Conference Seminary at Poultney and Middlebury College, Vermont, from which he was graduated with the degree of Bachelor of Arts in the class of 1861. During the next three years he taught school at Chatham, New York. From 1864 to 1867 he was paymaster in the United States army. From 1867 to 1870 he was editor of the *Fair Haven Journal*. He entered the Albany Law School and prepared for his profession and in 1871 was admitted to the bar, but in 1872 was elected cashier of the First National Bank of Fair Haven and continued in this position until 1891. During the next two years he was in business in Montgomery and Fort Dodge, Minnesota. He then returned to Fair Haven where he was elected secretary and treasurer of the Vermont Clock Company. He held that office six years, since then engaged in the real estate business in Castleton.

In politics Mr. Phelps is a Republican and has held various offices of trust and honor. He was a delegate to the constitutional convention of Vermont in 1870, and represented the town in the state legislature in 1896-97, serving on the committee on corporations. He has been a trustee of Middlebury College since 1891. In religion he is a Congregationalist and is deacon of the Congregational church of Fair Haven. He married, at Millersburg, Minnesota, December 27, 1874, Mary Ella, daughter of Robbins and Mary (Barber) Miller (see Miller IV). Children: 1. Paul Harold, born October 30, 1877; a farmer at Hampton, New York; married Abigail Pitkin and has three children: William M., born June 12, 1904; Hamilton Hibbard, April 18, 1907; William Elnathan, March 11, 1911. 2. Philip Max Miller, mentioned below.

(XI) Philip Max Miller, son of Erastus Hibbard and Mary Ella (Miller) Phelps, was born at Fair Haven, Vermont, June 12, 1886. He attended the public schools of his native town; graduated in 1907 from the Cushing Academy at Ashburnham, Massachusetts; entered the Chicago Law School, but completed his course at the Albany Law School, from which he was graduated in the class of 1910 with the degree of Bachelor of Laws, and in the same year was admitted to the bar. The following two years he was in the adjusting department of the Travelers Insurance Company. In 1912 he began to practice law on his own account at Fair Haven. He attends the Congregational church. He is a member of the Chicago Chapter, Sons of the American Revolution; Rutland Lodge, Benevolent and Protective Order of Elks, and the national legal fraternity, Delta Chi.

(The Miller Line).

William Miller, immigrant ancestor, was a tanner and planter of Ipswich, Massachusetts, in 1638. In 1643 and 1646 he served as a soldier against the Indians. He resided in Ipswich in 1648, and in 1654 was one of the twenty-three original settlers of Northampton, Massachusetts. He resided on King street in that town, and died there July 15, 1690. He acquired a plantation at Northfield in 1672, and settled there, but returned to Northampton probably on account of the Indian war. He married Patience ———, who died, very aged, at Northampton, March 16, 1716. The Northampton records say that she was a skilled physician and surgeon. Children: John, married, March 24, 1670, Mary Alvord, killed by the Indians, October 5, 1675; Mary, married (first) Obadiah Williams, (second) Godfrey Nims; Rebecca, died August, 1657. Born in Northampton: Patience, September 15, 1657; William, November 30, 1659; Mercy, February 8, 1660; Ebenezer, June 7, 1664; Mehitable, July 10, 1666; Abraham, January 20, 1671.

(I) William Miller, descendant of William Miller, the immigrant ancestor, married in West Springfield, Massachusetts, Hannah Leonard.

(II) Captain William (2) Miller, son of William (1) Miller, was born December 15,

1757. He lived in Pittsfield, Massachusetts, until 1786, when he moved to Low Hampton, Washington county, New York, where he died December 23, 1812, in his fifty-fifth year. He served in the revolution. He married, March 22, 1781, Paulina, daughter of Rev. Elnathan Phelps (see Phelps VII). Children, born in Pittsfield: William, mentioned below; Joseph, born June 12, 1783, died February 6, 1784; Paulina, November 1, 1784. Born in Low Hampton: Sylvia, September 4, 1786; Daughter, born February 29, 1788, died in infancy; Cynthia, born February 13, 1789; Anna, December 31, 1790, died December 27, 1812; Mira M., September 12, 1792; Anna, February 10, 1794; George, February 6, 1796; Lois, January 25, 1798; Ira, December 3, 1799, died August 4, 1801; Rhoda, September 24, 1801, died February 27, 1812; Solomon P., November 27, 1803; Stella, June 30, 1806; Eleanor, April 1, 1809.

(III) Rev. William (3) Miller, son of Captain William (2) Miller, was born in Pittsfield, Massachusetts, February 15, 1782, died December 20, 1849, in Hampton, New York. The family moved to Hampton, New York, when he was four years old and during his youth he worked on his father's farm. He attended the district school, but was largely educated by his own efforts. After his marriage he settled at Poultney, Vermont. He received a captain's commission in the Thirtieth Regiment and entered the army in 1812 and had a brilliant military career in the war of 1812. He took part in the battle of Plattsburg. After the war he removed to Low Hampton, New York, and engaged in farming. In early life he was deistic in religious belief, but after attending the Baptist church at Low Hampton, of which his uncle, Rev. Elisha Miller, was pastor, and reading sermons when the pastor was absent, he became a convert to Christianity. He made a most careful and painstaking study of the Bible and came to the conclusion that the end of the world was fixed by the Scripture prophets. The public labors of Mr. Miller began in 1831 when he went from church to church delivering lectures on the second advent of Christ. He was later licensed to preach and as he went through the country, obtained converts by thousands and his reputation as preacher grew world-wide. His followers came to be known as Millerites. His sermons were published and widely circulated, and his labors resulted in the formation of the Second Adventist denomination. Though his prophecy that the world would come to an end in 1843-44 failed, his followers in large part recognized the earnestness and sincerity of the faith

John H. Frenier

and the church has remained strong and vigorous in many sections to the present time. Extensive biographies of William Miller were published in 1875 and 1895.

He married, June 29, 1803, Lucy Smith, of Poultney, Vermont. Children: William S., Bellona L., Satterlee E., Langdon, Robbins, George W., Infant, Electa M., John H., Lucy A.

(IV) Robbins, son of Rev. William (3) Miller, was born October 4, 1814. He married Mary Elizabeth Barber, October 4, 1842. They had two children: Mary Ella, born December 27, 1844, married Erastus Hibbard Phelps (see Phelps X); William R., born January 14, 1849.

Antoine Donay Frenier, the FRENIER immigrant ancestor, was the son of Louis Donay and Jeanne (Ganatte) Frenier, of Luçon, Poitou, now department of Vendée, France, born in 1647. With three hundred other colonists he left La Rochelle, France, and arrived at Quebec, October 27, 1662. They were brought over by Lord Peter Boucher, then governor of Three Rivers, at the order of King Louis XIV. to colonize New France. In the fall of 1667 he was sent by the governor to his Boucherville seigniory, to build the first log houses and fort, ready to receive the governor and his family in the spring of 1668. At the time of his marriage in 1669 he had four acres of land cleared and planted, a house in the fort, a barn and fifty acres of land. He married, contract dated August 24, 1669, Marie, daughter of Pierre and Anne (Masson) Richard, of St. Laurent, Champagne, France. They had nine children, the fifth child being Antoine Donay, of whom further.

(II) Antoine Donay (2) Frenier, son of Antoine Donay (1) Frenier, was born December 14, 1678, at Boucherville, Canada. He married, at Boucherville, November 6, 1702, Marie Robert. They had eight children, the fourth child being Jean, of whom further.

(III) Jean Frenier, son of Antoine Donay (2) Frenier, was born in 1715. He married, November 15, 1739, Marie J. Pepin, at Boucherville, province of Quebec, Canada. They had seventeen children, the fourteenth child being Joseph, of whom further.

(IV) Joseph, son of Jean Frenier, was born at Boucherville, August 4, 1757. He married (first) August 30, 1779, Marie Jourdain, and they had five children. He married (second) September 12, 1791, Marie Plouf, at Beloeil, province of Quebec, Canada. They had ten children, the second child being Charles, of whom further.

(V) Charles, son of Joseph Frenier, was born February 3, 1795, at Beloeil, died March 25, 1873, at Burlington, Vermont. He was a farmer and general carpenter. He married, at Beloeil, July 26, 1819, Marie T. Poulin. They had thirteen children, the fifth child being Isaac, of whom further.

(VI) Isaac, son of Charles Frenier, was born at St. Jean-Baptiste, province of Quebec, Canada, June 3, 1826, died at St. Hyacinthe, same province, November 4, 1875. He was a builder and contractor at St. Hyacinthe. He married (first) October 20, 1846, Marguerite Guernache, at St. Dominique, province of Quebec, and had three children. He married (second) October 4, 1852, at Ste. Marie, province of Quebec, Bibiane Rivard. Children by second wife: 1. John H., of whom further. 2. Marie, born August 8, 1855; married (first) P. Caron, and (second) Philias Boutin; residing at Holyoke, Massachusetts. 3. Marie A., died in infancy. 4. Marie E., residing at Providence, Rhode Island. 5. Joseph, residence unknown. 6. Frederic, born August 4, 1863; residing at St. Hyacinthe, province of Quebec. 7. Felix, November 20, 1865; residing at Worcester, Massachusetts. 8. Arthur, May 22, 1869; residing at St. Hyacinthe. 9. Napoleon, February 3, 1872; residing in Boston, Massachusetts.

(VII) John H., son of Isaac Frenier, was born August 19, 1853. At the age of fourteen he entered as apprentice, to learn the machinist's and moulder's trade, with the firm of Frechette & Brothers, of St. Hyacinthe, province of Quebec, in the fall of 1868. In 1870 he constructed the first mowing machine made in Canada, making the patterns, helping to construct same and put it into operation, and teaching the farmers its use. In 1871 he constructed the first automatic single raking machine, in a pattern very similar to those made now. At that time machines such as grist-mills, sawmills, steam engines, water wheels, etc., were all made in the same shop, as well as many kinds of tools, and Mr. Frenier had to learn the making of all these. After serving his time as apprentice he entered the firm of Chagnon & Company, of St. Hyacinthe, and for many years designed and built steam engines and machine tools of all kinds there. On February 25, 1880, he moved to Rutland, Vermont, where he is now living. For a time he worked as pattern maker for the firm of Mansfield & Stimson. On April 1, 1882, he entered the employ of David Shortsleeve & Company, as draftsman and pattern maker, building steam engines, machine tools and stone working machinery of all kinds.

While in the employ of this company he

invented the spiral sand pump, for feeding sand and water to marble sawing gangs. On November 1, 1885, he formed a partnership with one of his fellow machinists, Leon Leblanc, for the manufacture of this sand pump. The first pump was sold to Gilson & Woodfin, at West Rutland, Vermont, and in a few months the same company purchased seven more pumps. In a few years this labor-saving device was adopted by all the principal mills, and today it is used all over the world. By the old method the sand was fed to the sawing machine by hand, with a shovel, and one man could feed only two small gangs or one large one. By the new method one man can feed eight to ten gangs, thus saving the labor of twenty men for a fifty gang mill. The pumps are exceedingly durable, many of them having been used night and day for twenty-five years. In 1900 Mr. Frenier purchased his partner's share in the business, which he is now carrying on alone. In 1910 he invented a new modification of the spiral pump, which he has shipped to all parts of the world. It is used in gold and silver mines, and is the most durable sand pump yet invented for this purpose. Mr. Frenier has invented and patented a large number of marble working machines, but has never pushed their introduction, as he has devoted a large part of his time to the manufacture of the sand pump.

In politics Mr. Frenier is a Republican. Though never having sought office he has occasionally yielded to persuasion, and served for several years as alderman of the city, and delegate to Republican conventions. He also has held many offices in clubs and societies.

He married, at Burlington, Vermont, June 3, 1872, Octavie Menard. Children: 1. George Henry, born May 19, 1873, died September 8, 1873. 2. Henry H., February 25, 1875, died January 26, 1899; married, November 5, 1894, Celia Sammon, at Rutland, Vermont. 3. George H., January 1, 1877, died February 12, 1878. 4. Wilfred A., of whom further. 5. Maxime O., April 25, 1880; married, November 4, 1901, Mabel Morey; lives at Springfield, Massachusetts, where he is a draftsman for the Knox Automobile Company. 6. Marie O., August 13, 1881, died November 3, 1907; married, October 23, 1902, Ulric Dupuis; left five children. 7. Regina A., born March 20, 1883, died October 30, 1884. 8. Anna V., February 1, 1886; married, November 5, 1906, Thomas J. Byrne. 9. Leon L., May 17, 1889; married, June 20, 1911, Madeline Provost. 10. Irene Clara, May 31, 1891.

(VIII) Wilfred A., son of John H. Frenier, was born May 11, 1878. He attended college, and then at the age of seventeen years entered as apprentice with the Fitchburg Steam Engine Works, Fitchburg, Massachusetts, to learn the machinist's trade. After staying there for three years he worked with his father at the sand pump business until 1905, when he built the Frenier Automobile Garage, the oldest and largest garage in the city of Rutland, now situated on Cleveland avenue. He sells the Ford, Buick, Overland and Stoddard-Dayton automobiles, and carries on a general repair business.

Mr. Frenier married, June 14, 1905, Bertha A. Trask. They have one son: Richard H., born September 1, 1909.

YOUNG　This name is a very old one in America, arriving soon after the historical voyage of the "Mayflower", and has numerous representatives scattered all over the United States. It was conspicuously identified with the early settlement of many of the states, villages and towns having been named in its honor. There were representatives of the name of Scotch lineage who arrived in the early part of the eighteenth century and were located at various points in Massachusetts. The family tradition regarding the line herein traced speaks of three brothers, Robert, William and David Young, who were born on the river Tweed in Scotland, and went to Ireland, later to England, whence they came to America landing in New York, and two of them remained in that state.

(I) Robert Young was born about 1710-15 and first appears of record in Medway, Massachusetts, where he married, February 15, 1737, Sarah Corning. He had one child born in Holliston, Massachusetts, and others probably in that vicinity, perhaps in Old Mendon. He removed about 1748 to Athol, Massachusetts, where he resided until his death, November 20, 1796. He was among the early settlers of that town and at the first town meeting, upon its organization, March 29, 1762, he was elected one of its wardens. His wife Sarah, died in Athol, January 18, 1761, and he married (second) in Pelham, Massachusetts, December 20, 1764, Elizabeth (Lamond) Gray, widow of Daniel Gray. She was born about 1729-30, and died in Athol, February 23, 1825, aged ninety-five years. Children, of first marriage: 1. Hannah, born May 25, 1740, in Holliston, married Benjamin Sanders. 2. Mary, married Freeborn Raymond. 3. Samuel, resided in Athol; married (first) Rhoda Haven; (second) Mrs. Lois (Sanderson) Cotting. 4. William, married Keziah Haven, and lived in Athol. 5. Sarah, baptized November 4, 1750, in Athol, the year when the church was organized there. 6. Robert, May 6, 1753. 7. David, September 14, 1755. 8. Anna, March 5, 1758, died young. 9. Simeon, mentioned below. Of second marriage: 10. John, baptized August 10, 1766. 11. Anna, June 26, 1768. 12. Joel, August 5, 1770.

(II) Simeon, fifth son of Robert and Sarah (Corning) Young, was baptized August 8, 1760, in the First Church of Athol, and died October 28, 1846, in Orwell, Vermont. He was one of the pioneer settlers of Orwell, where he first went in 1786, before the organization of the town. He cleared up land; sowed winter wheat and built a log cabin, after which he returned to Athol for his wife, and in February following settled in Orwell, where he was a prominent and influential citizen, active in promoting the welfare of the town. He married in Athol (intention published February 13, 1786), Mary, daughter of Moses and Luce Hill, born October 4, 1767, in Athol, died in Orwell, May 4, 1850. Children: Samuel, mentioned below; Charles, born May 9, 1788; Polly, March 23, 1790; Simeon, June 9, 1792; Ira, June 2, 1794; Asa, August 18, 1796; Artemas, October 17, 1798, died before two years old; Levi, December 18, 1800, died in third year; Royal, November 9, 1802, died nine months old; Lucy, July 17, 1804, died in her third year; Fanny, April 15, 1807; Louise, August 1, 1810. All except the first were born in Orwell.

(III) Samuel, eldest child of Simeon and Mary (Hill) Young, was born September 1, 1786, in Athol, and died in Orwell, January 4, 1865. He was an infant in arms when his parents settled in Orwell, where he spent his life on the farm cleared by his father. He held the principal town offices and represented Orwell in the state legislature. He was also active in the state militia, serving as ensign lieutenant and captain. He married, September 29, 1812, Eudocia Hall of Orwell, born March 28, 1789, died July 22, 1872, daughter of Hiland Hall. Children: 1. Lucretia, born September 20, 1814, married Oliver Bascomb of Orwell. 2. Harriet, born October 14, 1816, married —— Southworth. 3. Lucina, born January 12, 1819, married —— Jennison. 4. Mary, born June 19, 1821, married Charles M. Stewart, and now resides in Franklin, Massachusetts. 5. William, November 19, 1823, died in his second year. 6. Hiland Hall, mentioned below. 7. Jane Eliza, born June 27, 1829, married Calvin Fairbanks of Medway, Massachusetts. 8. Darwin Samuel, born November 27, 1832, died in his twentieth year.

(IV) Hiland Hall, second son of Samuel and Eudocia (Hall) Young, was born May 30, 1826, in Orwell, where he resided and died October 8, 1909. He was a successful farmer living on the land occupied successively by his grandfather and father; held various town offices and was a highly respected citizen.

He married, September 10, 1850, Eliza Frances, born August 25, 1825, in Orwell, died July 7, 1903, daughter of Dr. Earl and Roxcena (Warner) Cushman, of that town (see Cushman VIII). Children: 1. Jennie L., born August 29, 1851, married James H. Thomas, of Orwell, and had a son, Edward Young Thomas, now deceased. 2. Robert Cushman, born April 29, 1855, resides on the homestead in Orwell. He married (first) in 1882, Abby Adams, of Franklin, Massachusetts, daughter of Peter and Clarissa (Richardson) Adams; she died June 5, 1885, and he married (second) January 11, 1888, Gertrude Stevens, of Greenwich, New York, daughter of Simon L. and Helen C. (Russell) Stevens. Children, all by second wife: Russell Stevens, born February 1, 1890; Anna, October 18, 1892; Robert Cushman, born in February, 1906. 3. Edward Earl, born October 26, 1856, married Ellen M. Rice, and is a farmer in Orwell. 4. George Hiland, mentioned below.

(V) George Hiland, youngest son of Hiland H. and Eliza F. (Cushman) Young, was born February 22, 1859, in Orwell, and now resides in Brandon, Vermont. He received a common school education in the schools of his native town, and later attended the Troy Conference Seminary, at Poultney, Vermont. Leaving this institution he began his business career by going into the First National Bank, at Brandon, Vermont, as teller in 1879, remaining in that capacity until 1882. He then went to Great Bend, Kansas, where he was cashier and manager of the Farmers' and Merchants' Bank, of that place, from 1882 to 1890. In the latter year he returned to Vermont, and for a year and a half, was teller in the Howard National Bank, of Burlington, Vermont. In 1893 he came to Brandon, Vermont, as cashier of the First National Bank, which position he held until 1908. In January of that year he was elected vice-president of the bank, and is still the incumbent of that office. He is also vice-president of the Cloud County Bank, of Concordia, Kansas. He is director of the Rutland Trust Company, at Rutland, Vermont. Interested also in fraternal matters, he is a member of St. Paul's Lodge, No. 25, Free and Accepted Masons, of Brandon; the Farmers' Chapter, No. 9, of the Royal Arch Masons; and the Killington Commandery, Knights Templar, of Rutland; Cairo Temple, Nobles of the Mystic Shrine, of Rutland; and is also connected with Brandon Lodge, No. 25, of the Independent Order of Odd Fellows.

He married, January 25, 1888, Cora A., a native of Orwell, daughter of Theron Bush Smith and Almeda Theodosia (Warren) Smith, of that town.

(The Cushman Line).

Robert Cushman was born in 1580 in England. He early became interested in the movement for greater freedom of religious opinion, and joined the little church at Scrooby, with Rev. John Robinson (afterwards its pastor), Elder Brewster, Governor Carver, Governor Bradford, Isaac Allerton and others, in 1602. Subsequently they removed to Holland, but were not satisfied with the conditions at Leyden and resolved to make application to the Virginia Company, whose authority extended over a considerable portion of the North American continent, for liberty to settle in the company's territory in America. For that purpose Robert Cushman and Deacon John Carver were selected to go to London in 1617 and open negotiations. The mission was not successful. Later they arranged with Thomas Weston and the Merchant Adventurers of London to go to America. The "Speedwell" was purchased in Holland, but, not being large enough to take all who wished to go, Robert Cushman hired the "Mayflower," a much larger vessel. The "Speedwell" proved unseaworthy and its passengers were left behind, there not being room for them on the "Mayflower." One of them was Robert Cushman, who went with them to London to look after their interests and arrange for passage later. In 1621 the "Fortune" was chartered, and carried thirty-six passengers, including Robert Cushman and his son, Thomas. He had arranged to return to London when the vessel went back; so he had only about a month to learn the sad news of the death of half his friends of the "Mayflower" during the first winter. The day before he sailed he preached a sermon to his old friends, designed to give them hope and courage. Though he was not a clergyman or teaching elder, it was a remarkable discourse, and the first one delivered in New England that was printed. He was most active and influential in securing a charter for the Plymouth colony and also for the first settlement of the Massachusetts Bay Colony at Cape Ann. He continued to perform his duties as agent of the colony in London, and did his best to promote its interests. He died somewhat suddenly in 1625, before he could return to America as he had planned. Governor Brad-

ford said of him: "He was our right hand with the Adventurers, who for divers years has managed all our busness with them to our great advantage". His son, Thomas, who came with him, is the only child known, and through him the line continued.

(II) Thomas, son of Robert Cushman, was born in England in February, 1608. He came to New England with his father in 1621. and remained in the family of Governor Bradford when his father returned to England. In a letter his father entreated the governor "to have a care for my boy as your own". He settled in that part of Plymouth now Kingston, and in 1635 was on the jury. He was appointed successor to Elder Brewster in 1649, continuing in the office until his death, December 11, 1691, more than forty-three years. The church records say: "He has bin a rich blessing to this church scores of years. He was grave, sober, holy and temperate, very studious and solicitous for the peace and prosperity of the church, and to prevent & heale all breaches." He married in 1636, Mary, daughter of Isaac Allerton, of the "Mayflower," who for several years was assistant to the governor, and went to London five times in the interests of the colony. He spent the latter part of his life in New Haven, where he died. She died at the age of ninety, surviving her husband, and was the last survivor of those who came over in the "Mayflower". Children, born in Plymouth: Thomas, mentioned below; Sarah; Lydia; Rev. Isaac, born February 8, 1647-48, a prominent minister; Deacon Elkanah, June 1, 1651; Feare, June 20, 1653; Eleazer, February 20, 1656-57; Mary.

(III) Rev. Isaac Cushman, second son of Thomas and Mary (Allerton) Cushman, was born February 8, 1638, at Plymouth, and died October 22, 1732, at Plympton, Massachusetts. He was a member of the church at Plymouth, and obtained a better education than most men of that day. In 1685 he was one of the selectmen of Plymouth, and in June, 1690, he was elected a deputy to the general court, being associated in the same office with John Broadforce. The same men were selected deputies to another session held in August, same year. In June following they were again elected and attended the last session previous to the union of the Plymouth and Massachusetts colonies, in 1692. At the death of his father in 1691 he was chosen ruling elder. He was called to the pastorate of the church in Middleboro, and of the new church established in Plympton. He accepted the latter and continued minister there from 1695 to 1732. His settlement there followed an extended controversy. He was more liberal in religious matters than his contemporaries, and secured the adoption of new articles of faith, which have remained to the present day with little change as the creed of the Congregational church. At the time of his settlement in Plymouth he was in the prime of life and was evidently a very able man. Little is known of his talent as a preacher, none of his sermons having been printed, but he was among the most useful members of his profession. During his ministry of thirty-seven years two hundred and forty-seven persons became members of his church and he solemnized one hundred and forty-four marriages. The history of the church, written by Louis Bradford, says: "He was a pious and godly man. He had not a college education. He used to preach without notes, but studied his sermons beforehand and committed to memory. Instead of a wig he used to wear a black velvet cap. His salary in 1701 was thirty-five pounds, and it was increased from time to time, till in 1728 it was eighty-five pounds a year." He married, about 1675, Mary Rickard, born in 1654, died September 27, 1727, at Plympton. Children: Isaac, Rebeckah, Mary, Sarah, Ichabod, mentioned below, and Fear.

(IV) Ichabod, junior son of Rev. Isaac and Mary (Rickard) Cushman, was born October 30, 1686, in Plympton, and resided in that town and in Middleboro. His estate was settled in 1736 by his widow, Patience. He married (first) Esther, daughter of Jonathan Barnes, and (second) November 27, 1712, Patience, daughter of John Holmes. She was mother of all his children, namely: Joanna, born December 17, 1713; William, October 13, 1715; Sarah, November 8, 1717; Experience, July 12, 1719; Patience, April 8, 1721; Mary, December 22, 1723; Ichabod, mentioned below; Rebeckah, July 11, 1727; Isaac, August 12, 1730.

(V) Ichabod (2), younger son of Ichabod (1) and Patience (Holmes) Cushman, was born May 12, 1725, in Plympton, and resided in Middleboro after 1754. He married (first) March 4, 1751, Patience Mackfern, and (second) Hope White. The latter was the mother of his youngest child, John, born June 9, 1775. Children of first wife: Experience, born March 9, 1752; Molly, April 20, 1754; Ichabod, mentioned below; Holmes, October 22, 1759; Robert, April 24, 1761; Sylvester, April 27, 1764; Earl, October 16, 1766.

(VI) Ichabod (3), eldest son of Ichabod (2) and Patience (Mackfern) Cushman, was born March 28, 1757, in Middleboro, and resided there until 1802, when he removed to Hartland, Vermont, where he died October 14, 1805. He had made a beginning in the clearing of a farm in Hartland, but his early death left his family in straitened circumstances. He married, November 28, 1782, Molly Morton, born November 5, 1758, died in Middlebury, Vermont, August 29, 1841, surviving her husband nearly thirty-six years. Children: Clark, born September 13, 1783; Ichabod Morton, November 7, 1787; Sally, June 7, 1789; Deborah, February 14, 1791; Eunice, September 27, 1795; Earl, mentioned below; Josiah Leonard, August 13, 1799.

(VII) Earl, third son of Ichabod (3) and Molly (Morton) Cushman, was born May 10, 1797, and was about five years old when his parents removed to Vermont, and was deprived of a father's care when eight years old. At the age of nine years he was bound out and in 1807 went to Middlebury, where he lived two years in the family of Colonel James Chipman. Following this he was two and one-half years with Holland Weeks of Salisbury. In his indenture it was stipulated that he should receive his clothing and three months' schooling each year. From fifteen to eighteen years of age he was employed at farm labor with the exception of six months spent in school and at the academy. He was determined to secure an education and made the most of his limited opportunities. In 1815 he lived with a brother in Boston and was thereafter engaged in teaching and studying until 1817, when he began the study of medicine. He attended medical lectures in Boston in 1820-21, and in the fall of the latter year passed a satisfactory examination and was licensed to practice medicine by the Addison County Medical Society of Vermont. He immediately settled in Orwell in that county, where he continued in practice until his death, and became prominent in the profession. Always a student he kept abreast of progress in medical science and was made an honorary member of the Association of Alumni of Castleton Medical College in 1846. In 1848 he was its delegate to the National Medical Association, and received the honorary degree of Doctor of Medicine from Castleton Medical College in 1854. In 1851 he was president of the Addison County Medical Society. He married (first) Roxcena (Warner), of Sudbury, Vermont, widow of Dr. James Q. McFarland, born in 1796. He married (second) September 11, 1834, Lucy R. Young, of Athol. Children, by first wife: Mary Asenath, born March 18, 1824, married William Moore, of Linleytown, New York; Eliza Frances, mentioned below; Harriet Nash, born June 12, 1829, died when twenty-two years old. Children by second wife: Roxcena, died in her seventeenth year; Sarah Young, born April 4, 1837; Lucy Ann, October 5, 1838; James Earl, March 31, 1840; Catharine Maria, May 19, 1842; Julia, died eight months old.

(VIII) Eliza Frances, second daughter of Dr. Earl and Roxcena (Warner) Cushman, was born August 25, 1825, in Orwell, and was married, September 10, 1850, to Hiland Hall Young, of that town (see Young IV).

NOBLE

The surname Noble is of great antiquity in England. It appears as early as 1199 in the reign of Richard I. and it has been common among English speaking people ever since. The name is found in Scotland and several distinguished merchants of the name lived in Edinburgh. Branches of the family in England, Ireland and Scotland bear coats-of-arms. The principal seats of the family were at Cornwall, Belson and Bishop's Tenter, Devonshire, and Marming, near Maidstone, county Kent.

(I) Thomas Noble, immigrant ancestor, born in England as early as 1632, died in Westfield, Massachusetts, January 20, 1704, aged at least seventy-two years. He was an early settler of Springfield, coming from Boston, where he was an inhabitant, January 6, 1653. He had an account at the store of John Pynchon in Springfield, and this account book proves that he visited England, soon after removing from Boston. In 1664 he and others were given leave to set up a saw mill on the brook below Ensign Cooper's farm over the Agawam river. He was an appraiser of the town; had lands granted him in Westfield in July, 1666, on condition that he settle there, and this grant was renewed January 9, 1668. He was located in Westfield as early as January 21, 1669, and served on a committee to decide the boundary lines. His homestead was about two miles and a half from the present center of the town. He served as constable and took the oath of allegiance, January 23, 1678. He joined the Westfield church, February 20, 1681, and was admitted a freeman, October 12, 1681. He was fined five shillings on one occasion for traveling on a fast day. His home was exposed to Indian attacks during King Philip's war and he was requested by authorities to move to a safer location. He was elected county surveyor, March 2, 1696. He was a tailor by trade. His will was dated May 11, 1697, and proved September 5, 1704.

He married, November 1, 1680, Hannah Warriner. born at Springfield, August 17, 1643, only daughter of William and Joanna (Scant) Warriner. She joined the Westfield church, November 11, 1680. She married

(second) January 24, 1705, Deacon Medad Pomeroy, of Northampton, Massachusetts. Children: John, born March 6, 1662; Hannah, February 24, 1664; Thomas, born in Springfield, January 14, 1666; Matthew, mentioned below; Mark; Elizabeth, February 9, 1673; Luke, July 15, 1675; James, October 1, 1677; Mary, June 29, 1680; Rebecca, January 4, 1683.

(II) Matthew, son of Thomas Noble, was born about 1668, died about 1744, aged about seventy-six years, in Sheffield, Massachusetts. On August 19, 1694, he put himself under the watch of the Westfield church, and he and his wife joined the church, November 3, 1728, after they had settled in Sheffield. It is known that Matthew Noble was in Sheffield, February 3, 1727, when he deeded land in Westfield to Captain John Ashley. In 1733 he issued a warrant for the first town meeting in Sheffield, and he was moderator of the meeting. He died intestate, and the inventory of his estate was dated April 10, 1745. He married, December 10, 1690, Hannah, born February 21, 1672, daughter of Thomas and Constant (Hawes) Dewey, and she was living July 9, 1745. The date of her death is not known. Children, born in Westfield: Joseph, October 8, 1691; Hezekiah, May 14, 1694; Matthew, September 19, 1698; Solomon, December 23, 1700; Elisha, February 9, 1703; Obadiah, mentioned below; Hannah, October 11, 1707; Hester, June 6, 1710; Rhoda, April 21, 1716, recorded in Springfield; Rhoda, born April 17, 1717.

(III) Obadiah, son of Matthew Noble, was born in Westfield, October 19, 1705, died in Sheffield, probably in 1786, aged eighty-one years. He settled early at Sheffield, and the first town meeting was held at his house in 1733. He lived about three-quarters of a mile north of the Congregational church. His will was dated October 14, 1785, and proved June 6, 1786, and in it he mentioned his sons Peter, Nathaniel, Zechariah, Obadiah, Ezekiel, and step-daughter, Susanna Fairchild, wife of Moses Fairchild, of Sheffield. He married Mary Bosworth,, daughter of Philip Callender, of Sheffield, and widow of ——— Bosworth. By her first husband she had a daughter Susanna who married, December 2, 1745, Moses Fairchild. Children, born in Sheffield: Peter, May 22, 1734; Nathaniel, October 23, 1736; Obadiah, mentioned below; Zachariah, April 16, 1742; Ezekiel, June 8, 1745.

(IV) Rev. Obadiah (2) Noble, son of Obadiah (1) Noble, was born in Sheffield, September 6, 1730, died in Tinmouth, Vermont, February 19, 1820. He attended the College of New Jersey from which he was graduated in 1763 in the class with Gov. William Patterson, of New Jersey, and Chief Justice Tappan Reeve, of Connecticut. On November 5, 1771, he was ordained pastor of the Congregational church in Orford, New Hampshire, but was dismissed December 31, 1777, as the people were unable to pay his salary. He served in the revolution as chaplain of New Hampshire troops, and was present at the surrender of Saratoga. He moved to Tinmouth soon after 1777, and for eight or ten years after the organization of the courts was clerk of Rutland county. From 1786 for nineteen years he was a justice of the peace. He survived every member of his class in college, living six years after all the others were dead, and until a few years before he died he retained all his faculties. He was a very generous and kind man in character. In appearance "He was of medium size, with broad shoulders, full, deep breast, muscular frame, stout neck, full face, dark eyes, and dark hair, slightly silvered with gray." He married, August 11, 1774, Mrs. Rebecca White, born about 1743, in Leominster, Massachusetts, died in Tinmouth, November 23, 1833, daughter of ―――― Rogers, and widow of Jonathan White, of Leominster. Children, born in Tinmouth: Jonathan White, born July 18, 1776; Obadiah, February 12, 1778; Rebecca, March 9, 1779; Daughter, January 24, 1781, died in infancy; Susanna, July 22, 1782; Samuel, mentioned below; Relief, August 19, 1786.

(V) Deacon Samuel Noble, son of Rev. Obadiah (2) Noble, was born in Tinmouth, Vermont, May 13, 1784, died there January, 1873. He was a farmer. He was deacon of the Congregational church. He married, February 26, 1815, Mary Ballard, born December 20, 1791, died in 1873, daughter of Tilly Ballard. Children, born in Tinmouth: Absalom, mentioned below; Mary, born August 20, 1822, died January 10, 1831.

(VI) Absalom, son of Deacon Samuel Noble, was born in Tinmouth, July 24, 1816. He was a farmer in Tinmouth. He married, October 6, 1842, Eliza Clark, born May 11, 1817, daughter of Theophilus Clark. Children: Samuel, born July 5, 1842; Theophilus Clark, mentioned below; John B., died 1908.

(VII) Theophilus Clark, son of Absalom Noble, was born in Tinmouth, March 5, 1848. He is now a farmer in Tinmouth, and lives on the home place which his grandfather settled. He has held several town offices such as lister and selectman. He married, September 7, 1870, Alice Cobb, born in 1848, daughter of Lyman and Jane (Cole) Cobb. Children, born in Tinmouth: Learned Ray, mentioned below; John Edwin, born January 8, 1874; Henry C., November 12, 1877; Lyman C., 1883.

(VIII) Learned Ray, son of Theophilus Clark Noble, was born July 9, 1871, in Tinmouth, Vermont. He attended the public schools of his native town and Middlebury College, from which he was graduated in the class of 1903. He studied law in the office of Judge Lawrence in Rutland, Vermont, and in due course was admitted to the bar. He remained in Judge Lawrence's office as clerk for a year and in 1911 opened an office for himself in West Rutland and began to practice there. In politics he is a Republican, in religion a Congregationalist. He is a member of the Delta Upsilon fraternity.

John Bennett, the first of the BENNETT family in this country, according to family traditions, was born in the north of England. He married in Brunswick, Maine, Sarah Lombard, and settled in that town. He followed the sea in his younger days and was afterward a farmer. In religion he was a Baptist; in politics a Democrat. During the war of 1812 he served in the American navy, a gunner on the warship "Enterprise" and took part in the engagement of Portland, when the British man-of-war "Boxer" was taken. He was wounded in the battle, a bullet passing through his body and he had a narrow escape from death. He survived, however, and lived to within a few months of the age of one hundred years. He received a pension for many years for his service in the war. Children: John; William; Silas Stearns, mentioned below; Sarah, Martha; and Louisa.

(II) Silas Stearns, son of John Bennett, was born in Brunswick, Maine, in 1817. He followed the sea from an early age, became a master mariner and commanded many vessels. He enlisted in the civil war in 1861 and was instantly killed during a charge on Petersburg, June 16, 1864. In religion he was a Free Will Baptist. He married at Brunswick in 1842, Hannah Robinson Doughty, who was born in Durham in 1823. She was of Scotch-Irish ancestry. Children: John Henry, mentioned below; Sarah Annie Elizabeth, born May 20, 1849.

(III) John Henry, son of Silas Stearns Bennett, was born at Brunswick, Maine, April 6, 1845. He attended the public schools of Bath, Maine, including the high school. For two years he was a student in the Gardiner Lyceum, Gardiner, Maine, and studied theology in the Maine Wesleyan Seminary and College. He taught school for several years and was a professor of commercial law, bookkeeping and penmanship. He entered the ministry in 1864 and joined the East Maine Conference in 1868 and for forty-seven years he has been in the Christian ministry. He has had charges at Lincolnville, Arrowsic, Searsport, Aroostook, Patten, Springfield, Lincoln, Bradford, Brownville, Franklin, Unity, Cushing, Waldoboro, Montville, Dresden, Georgetown, in the state of Maine; Hampden in the New England conference, and Putney, Mechanicsville, South Londonderry and Highgate, in the state of Vermont. At the present time he is pastor of the Methodist Episcopal Church at Waitsfield, Vermont, and a member of the Vermont Conference. He has served on important committees in both conferences. He is a member of Searsport Lodge, No. 68, Free Masons; of Royal Arch Masons of Belfast, Maine, since 1872; and the Independent Order of Odd Fellows, of which he has been chaplain.

He married at Belgrade, Maine, February 10, 1864, Laura Ella Bickford, born March 5, 1848, at Belgrade, Maine, daughter of Deacon Asa and Cynthia (Stevens) Bickford. Deacon Asa Bickford lived in Belgrade, and died there at his home on Bickford Hill in the northern part of the town at the great age of one hundred years and four months. All of his children married and had families except William Bickford, who died at Baton Rouge, Louisiana, in 1861, in the service, a soldier in the Union army; his son Elbridge was also in the service in the civil war. Children of Asa and Cynthia Bickford: Seth, Elbridge, William, Charles, Martha, Clara, Sylvina and Laura Ella, mentioned above. Children of John Henry and Laura Ella (Bickford) Bennett: 1. Carrie Emma, married F. J. Kenworthy, who is in the United States mail service at Hampden, Massachusetts; children: Dorothy Louise, Madeline, and Leonice Lillian. 2. William Hurlburt, mentioned below. 3. Lillian Wisteria, married Llewellyn W. Morrow of Davenport, Iowa, now superintendent of the United States armory at Rock Island, Illinois, and has one daughter, Helen Morrow. 4. Irving Kingsley, born at Patten, Maine, attended the public schools of Gardiner, Maine, Kent Hill Collegiate Institute and the Springfield Business College, Springfield, Massachusetts, and is now a general merchant at Long Grove, Iowa; he married Bessie Goodwill at Hampden, Massachusetts. Both last named daughters were teachers before they married.

(IV) Dr. William Hurlburt Bennett, son of John Henry Bennett, was born at Belgrade, Maine, May 21, 1868. He attended the public schools, the Kent Hill Collegiate Seminary, the Maine Wesleyan Seminary, the Medical School of the University of Vermont, the Baltimore University School of Medicine and the Polyclinic School of Medicine, New York City, from which he received the degree of Doctor of Medicine in 1892. He began to practice medicine in Maine, but soon afterward removed to Winchendon, Worcester county, Massachusetts, where he continued in general practice for four years. Since 1903 he has been practicing at Hyde Park, Massachusetts. He established the first hospital at Hyde Park, known as Dr. Bennett's Hospital and now the Hyde Park General Hospital. He enjoys a large practice and stands high in his profession, commanding the respect and confidence of the entire community. He is a member of Hyde Park Lodge, and Ancient Blue Lodge of Union, Maine, Free and Accepted Masons; North Star Chapter, of Winchenden, Massachusetts, Royal Arch Masons; Hyde Park Council, Royal and Select Masters. He is also a member of the Hyde Park Medical Club, of the Norfolk County Medical Society, the Massachusetts Medical Society and of the American Medical Association. His office and residence are at 1349 River street, Hyde Park, now Ward Twenty-six of the City of Boston.

He married, January 1, 1896, Lillian Wingate Batchelder, born in Union, Maine, daughter of George Washington and Helen (Barnard) Batchelder, and granddaughter of Dr. Nathan and Jane (Gordon) Batchelder. Dr. and Mrs. Bennett have one child, Helen Laura, born April 26, 1899.

BLANCHARD Richard Blanchard, immigrant ancestor, settled early in Hartford, Connecticut, and died there April 19, 1691. His will was dated April 19, 1691, leaving to his son William all his property.

(II) William, son of Richard Blanchard, was born June 10, 1688. He lived in Hartford and married there, October 15, 1718, Sarah Cowles. He had a daughter Sarah, born October 29, 1719, and a son Benjamin, mentioned below.

(III) Benjamin, only son of William Blanchard, settled in Simsbury, Connecticut, and married there, August 27, 1752, Ruth Wilcoxson. Children, born at Simsbury: Ruth, July 2, 1753; Nathaniel, October 17, 1755; Amasa, June 2, 1758; Lodamia, November 15, 1760; Sybil, September 15, 1763; Sarah, June 6, 1766; Lorinda, February 6, 1769; Benjamin, mentioned below.

(IV) Benjamin (2), son of Benjamin (1) Blanchard, was born October 9, 1772, died

September 14, 1851. He married Elizabeth Winchell, born August 14, 1772, died July, 1855. Children: Lodema, born February 17, 1796, married Horace Smith; Clarissa, March 9, 1798; Benjamin F., mentioned below; Caroline K., December 19, 1802, married Chauncy Thrall; Emery S., July 1, 1806, married ——— Capen.

(V) Benjamin F., son of Benjamin (2) Blanchard, was born December 7, 1800, in West Rutland, Vermont, died February 24, 1871. He was educated in the public schools, and followed farming for an occupation. He married, April 30, 1828, Charity R. Mead, born April 18, 1810, died September 3, 1896. They had one son Chalon, mentioned below.

(VI) Chalon, son of Benjamin F. Blanchard, was born November 30, 1836, in West Rutland, Vermont, died October 1, 1883. He was a farmer on the Blanchard homestead. He was a gifted musician and for eighteen years was the organist of the Congregational church, which at that time had the largest and finest organ in the state. He married, November 30, 1858, Ella Reynolds, born at Sutherland Falls, Vermont, May 5, 1838, daughter of Isaac C. and Ruth (Johnson) Reynolds. Her father was born June 19, 1805, and her mother December 28, 1810. Morris Reynolds, father of Isaac C., was a son of Jonathan Reynolds, of an old colonial family. Chalon and Ella Blanchard had one child, Franklin Reynolds, mentioned below.

(VII) Franklin Reynolds, son of Chalon Blanchard, was born at West Rutland, April 19, 1868. He attended the public schools of his native town, and early in life followed farming. In 1894 he entered the employ of the Rutland Scale Works, and for a number of years has been general foreman of the plant. He is also manager of the farm of Governor John A. Mead; director of the Howe Scale Company and a prominent citizen and business man in Rutland. In politics he is a Republican. For eight years he represented the ward in which he lives in the board of aldermen of the city of Rutland and he was during part of that time president of the board. At the present time he is commissioner of public works. He is a member of Hiram Lodge, Ancient Free and Accepted Masons, of West Rutland; Phyllis Chapter, Order of the Eastern Star; Rutland Valley Grange, Patrons of Husbandry. In religion he is a Congregationalist.

He married, October 11, 1888, Mary Persis, born in Clintonville, Wisconsin, daughter of David Dana and Martha (Clinton) Hewett. She is a descendant of Stephen Hewett, of Stonington, Connecticut, a pioneer there as early as 1647. She is a granddaughter of Elias Hewett, of Pomfret, Vermont, and of his wife, Persis Chase (David) Hewett, and great-granddaughter of Stephen and Rebecca (Mills) Hewett, of Connecticut. Children, born in Rutland: Edna Ruth, June 6, 1889; Paul Hewett, January 2, 1891; Harold Chalon, November 7, 1893, died June 3, 1911; Charity Ellen, May 8, 1902; Alice Dana, October 25, 1903.

DICKERMAN Thomas Dickerman, immigrant ancestor, came over with his wife Ellen, and settled in Dorchester, Massachusetts, as early as 1636. He owned land there in that year, and bought more the following year. He also owned a house and land in Boston Neck in 1652, to which he added in 1656. He was a tailor by trade, and also carried on a farm. The inventory of his estate was two hundred and thirty-five pounds, eleven shillings, four pence. He died June 11, 1657, in Dorchester, His widow married (second) John Bullard, and went to live in Medfield before July 14, 1663. Children: Thomas, born 1623, died before 1691; Abraham, mentioned below; Isaac, born December, 1637; John, baptized October 29, 1644, died young.

(II) Lieutenant Abraham Dickerman, son of Thomas Dickerman, was born about 1634. Soon after his marriage he moved to New Haven and received as his wife's dowry a considerable amount of real estate. On April 17, 1668, he bought a house and lot on the corner of Church and Elm streets, and made his home there. On April 26, 1669, he was chosen townsman, or selectman, and with the exception of four years was annually chosen to this office for thirty-one years, until 1699. In 1683 he was chosen deputy to the general court, and was re-elected until 1696. In October, 1683, he was confirmed and approved to be a lieutenant of the New Haven Train Band. When the town of Wallingford was settled, he was on a committee of thirteen, including his father-in-law, to lay out the boundaries, which were agreed upon, January 28, 1673-74. In 1669 he was on a committee of seven, vested with power to manage the affairs of the new settlement. On June 19, 1685, he was again on a committee "to procure a patent for the town bounds" of New Haven. On June 26, 1671, he "was by vote appointed to keep the ordinary", and continued to do so until 1680. He lived for fifty-three years in New Haven, and devoted most of that time to the public good. He was moderately prosperous, and added to the property given him by his father-in-law. He also shared with the other citizens in the various allotments of land, and received in this way at least fifty acres. He died November 2, 1711, aged seventy-seven years. His will was dated April 20, 1710, and mentions his sons Abraham and Isaac, daughters Mary Bassett, Sarah Sperry, Ruth Bradley, Abigail Sperry and Rebecca Foot, and four grandchildren, the children of Hannah, who married Caleb Chidsey.

He married, January 2, 1658-59, Mary Cooper, born about 1636 in England; died January 4, 1705-06, daughter of John Cooper. Her father had been with the New Haven colony from the first, and was a planter, freeman and signer of the "fundamental agreement". He was constantly engaged in public affairs and held many positions of dignity and honor; attorney, appraiser of estates, deputy to the general court, selectman, etc. Children of Abraham and Mary (Cooper) Dickerman: Mary, born about 1659; Sarah, July 25, 1663; Hannah, November 16, 1665; Ruth, April 5, 1668; Abigail, September 26, 1670; Abraham, January 14, 1673; Isaac, mentioned below; Rebecca, February 27, 1679.

(III) Captain and Deacon Isaac Dickerman, son of Abraham Dickerman, was born November 7, 1677. He seems to have had unusual aptitude for public affairs, and held many positions of trust and honor. He was appointed constable, October, 1710, and in October, 1713, he was ensign of militia, and in 1722, captain. On December 15, 1712, he was chosen selectman, and afterward continuously until 1719, then from 1722 until 1723, and from 1730 until 1732. He was deputy to the general court for fifty-nine terms between 1718 and 1757, and was appointed justice of the peace for New Haven in May, 1735, and every year afterward as long as he lived, for twenty-four years. In church affairs he was as prominent as in civil matters. He was chosen deacon of the First Church in 1727 and held the office until 1754, when he resigned. He then transferred his membership to the White Haven Church, and was at the same time chosen a deacon there, and retained the office until his death. On December 24, 1716, when Yale College was about to be removed from Saybrook to New Haven, and the latter town had made it a grant of eight acres of land, he was one of a committee to make the transfer. In 1718 he was one of a number of proprietors who made a gift of land for the support of the institution. In that same year he was first sent to the general assembly, and seems to have been regarded from the first as the special representative of Yale interests. During the religious upheaval which followed the visit of Rev.

George Whitefield to America, 1739, and the controversy which took place between the original church in New Haven and the Separatists, Isaac Dickerman, as a magistrate and an officer in the church, for many years preserved a neutral attitude. In 1754, however, he joined the White Haven church, and thus united with the Separatists. He showed throughout his life the traits of a good citizen, and many qualities of the statesman. He was energetic, of judicial temper, and tirelessly devoted to public interests. He died September 7, 1758. His will was dated May 11, 1756. Before his death he had transferred large portions of his real estate to his sons. The estate was appraised at seven hundred and eleven pounds, four shillings, nine pence.

He married (first) June 30, 1709, Mary, born December 31, 1686, daughter of Jonathan and Ruth (Peck) Atwater. Jonathan was the son of David Atwater. He married (second) Elizabeth (Alling) Morris, widow of John Morris, and daughter of Samuel and Sarah (Chidsey) Alling. Samuel was son of Roger Alling, the immigrant. His second wife was born November, 1691, and died in April, 1767. Children: Isaac, born March 3, 1711, died young; Samuel, January 12, 1712, died young; Ruth, December 13, 1712; Isaac, January 31, 1714; Samuel, mentioned below; Jonathan, July 4, 1719; Stephen, October 14, 1721; Mary, December 16, 1723; Rebekah, July 2, 1726; Abigail, August 4, 1728.

(IV) Samuel, son of Captain and Deacon Isaac Dickerman, was born March 4, 1716, died May 10, 1760. He was among the first settlers of Mt. Carmel, Connecticut, and owned a large amount of land there. He married, December 6, 1739, Mary, born December 28, 1717, died December 5, 1802, daughter of Captain Jonathan and Sarah (Sackett) Alling; Jonathan was son of John, son of Roger Alling. Captain Jonathan Alling advocated a different policy from that of Captain Isaac Dickerman, Samuel's father, and in less than a year after their marriage Captain Alling was sent to the general assembly in Captain Dickerman's place. Children : Isaac, mentioned below; Sarah, born December 29, 1741; Mary, September 2, 1743; Samuel, April 20, 1745; James, June 28, 1747; Rhoda, November 24, 1748; Chauncey, September 28, 1750; Jesse, June 16, 1752; Ruth, March 9, 1754; Susannah, February 1, 1756; Lucy, June 1, 1759.

(V) Lieutenant Isaac Dickerman, son of Samuel Dickerman, was born September 16, 1740, died April 3, 1801. About 1790 or before his son Simeon settled in Mt. Holly, Vermont, and in a short time, Isaac, Amasa and Lyman, all brothers, also settled there, and married three sisters there, Hannah, Abigail and Sarah Button. When Isaac married, his father said that he "had buttons enough but he must have another Button added." Isaac Dickerman served in the revolution as second lieutenant of the Third Company, Fifth Battalion, General Wadsworth's brigade. He lived in Mt. Carmel, Connecticut. He married, August 21, 1765, Sibyl, born June 10, 1744, died September 23, 1822, daughter of Daniel and Abigail Sperry, of Wallingford, Connecticut; Daniel was son of Daniel, son of Richard Sperry. Children: Simeon, born July 20, 1766; Isaac, September 20, 1769, died December 26, 1774; Amasa, October 17, 1771; Lyman, May 12, 1774; Isaac, mentioned below; Rhoda, June 2, 1778, died 1778; Allen, January 14, 1781; Sibyl, August 15, 1783; Manly, June 5, 1786.

(VI) Isaac (2), son of Lieutenant Isaac (1) Dickerman, was born April 22, 1776, at Mt. Carmel, died November 9, 1845, at Mount Holly, Vermont. He settled in Mount Holly, where three of his brothers also settled. The "Vermont Historical Magazine" says: "Deacon Isaac Dickerman was for many years a leading citizen of the town and it may be said of him that no man enjoyed to a greater degree the respect and confidence of the people. He was for many years a deacon and one of the main pillars of the Baptist church. He was also in responsible town offices, selectman, lister, etc. He was representative four years in the legislature and justice of the peace, some ten or twelve years. He was emphatically a man of peace and his influence was exerted to allay strife and promote harmony." He married, September 22, 1799, at Mount Holly, Sarah Button, born April 4, 1784, died August 16, 1846. Children, born in Mount Holly: Joel, June 29, 1800, died October 19, 1800; Hiram, December 22, 1801; Sibyl, August 27, 1803, died October 4, 1803; Laura Alena, December 10, 1804, died April 6, 1823; Harry B., April 2, 1807; Sally Mira, August 28, 1810, died June 21, 1839; Harvey Malden, July 12, 1812; Isaac Stanley, mentioned below.

(VII) Isaac Stanley, son of Isaac (2) Dickerman, was born in Mount Holly, August 1, 1817, died July 15, 1881. He was a farmer and remained in Mount Holly all his life. He married, April 14, 1841, Fidelia Barrett, born in Ashburnham, Massachusetts, April 13, 1817, died in Mount Holly, August 27, 1888, daughter of Joel and Sarah (Howard) Barrett. Children, born in Mount Holly: 1. Sylvanus M., mentioned below. 2. Elwin Isaac, born March 31, 1848, in Mount Holly; formerly a farmer, now in fruit culture in Florida; mar-

ried Susan E. Danforth; two children: i. Ernest, married Flora Allen, one child, Allen, resides in Greeley, Colorado; ii. Arthur Isaac, died aged twenty-eight.

(VIII) Sylvanus M., son of Isaac Stanley Dickerman, was born at Mount Holly, Vermont, September 1, 1843. He received his early education in the public schools. He has been a farmer all his active life, residing from 1873 to 1902 on the old homestead at Mount Holly. Since 1905 he has made his home in Rutland, Vermont, where he lived retired. He has been active and prominent in public life. For many years he was selectman and town treasurer of Mount Holly and in 1884 he represented the town in the state legislature, serving with distinction. He was a member of the committee on libraries of the house of representatives. In politics he is a Republican. He is a member of the Independent Order of Odd Fellows of Mount Holly,

He married (first) May 21, 1872, Maria C. Crowley, of Mount Holly, daughter of Dr. John and Sarah (Andrews) Crowley. She was a member of the Baptist church. His wife died January 2, 1909. He married (second) February 8, 1910, Nellie E., daughter of Cornelius and Anna (Toohey) Keith, of Athol, Massachusetts. Children by second wife: Ruth Elizabeth, born November 13, 1910; Marion Fidelia, February 7, 1912.

TERRY One authority defines the name Terry thus: "Not 'the tearful one,' as some etymologists have it, but a corruption of Theodoric, the personal name." Mr. Ferguson, in his "Teutonic Name System," classes together the old German names Tarro, Terra, Torro, ninth century Terri, the English names Darr, Darrow, Door, Dorey, Dorre, Tarr, Tarry, Terry, Torrey, and the French names Dary, Dorre, Dor, Dore, Tarie, Terray, Terre, and he derives these from the old Norse word doerr, meaning spear, probably from the Sanscrit root "tar". Samuel Terry, of New York City, has made investigation and thinks it originated among the early French, where under the form of Therry it was not an uncommon personal name, and through the Franks came to be regarded as French, and is now sometimes found there as a family name in this form, as Therry, and also Terry. The earliest information of the founder of the family in this country is an agreement formed by William Pyncheon and Samuel Terry, October 15, 1650, whereby he is to receive a certain amount for his services, and be taught the trade of "linnen spinner", he binding himself to be diligent in service. This was signed by Samuel Terry, Benjamin B. Cooley (his mark), and William Pyncheon, witnesses Richard Maund and John Benham. Hon. William Pyncheon was in England in the spring of 1650 and there made the contract, and doubtless it was then that he took into apprenticeship the boy Samuel Terry, who may have been of Barnet, a village eleven miles from London. He may have been an orphan whom Mr. Pyncheon had known, and it is unlikely that he would have taken such a boy for less than the entire term of his minority, accordingly he was probably born about the year 1633-34. Mr. Pyncheon returned to England and was relieved of the contract.

(I) Samuel Terry, born about 1633, in England, arrived in America about 1650; was of Springfield, Massachusetts, in 1654, and was granted land, consisting of ten acres on "Chuckappee Plain", January 7, 1654, on condition that he remain in the town five years; in 1658 he forfeited it by leaving. He was granted land at Wononoco town, 1664, and land at Fresh Water Brook (now Enfield) in 1665. He was granted thirty acres of upland, along by his meadow land beyond Chicopee Plain, in 1670. He with others was assessed two loads of firewood for the use of their pastor. In 1678 he was appointed a surveyor of highways. His name and that of his son Samuel appear in a list of persons who took the oath of allegiance December 31, 1678, and January 1, 1679. He married, January 3, 1660, Ann Lobdell, and the town settled with him for his claim to the land before mentioned by making him a grant a little farther south. In May, 1684, his wife died, also his adopted child, Johny Matthews. In 1685 he was one of a town committee to establish boundaries between Springfield and adjoining towns, and the records speak of him as Sergeant Samuel Terry. In 1690 he married Sarah, widow of John Scott, and daughter of Thomas and Margaret Bliss. In 1693 he made an agreement to teach the art of weaving to his stepson, Ebenezer Scott, whence it appears he still practiced it himself. He was also chosen constable this same year. He and his wife parted in 1694, and she died September 27, 1705. In 1730 the administration of his estate was granted to his sons Samuel and Thomas, and in the record he is called "husbandman", "formerly of Springfield". This was doubtless the year of his death. He signed his name in a free hand, as one much in the habit of writing, so probably he was better educated than most of the men of his time. His children were: Sam-

uel, mentioned below; Ephraim, died young; Thomas; Mary; Rebecca, died young; Ephraim; Rebecca Elizabeth; Ann.

(II) Samuel (2), eldest son of Samuel (1) and Ann (Lobdell) Terry, was born July 18, 1661, in Springfield, died in Enfield, Connecticut, about 1730. He settled in Enfield about 1683, and was a farmer. He held offices of constable and selectman, and was several years ensign of the local militia, of which he became captain in 1716. He was a man of exemplary piety, prominent in the church, and is styled "gentleman" in the public record of his appointment as administrator on his father's estate. He married (first) May 17, 1682, in Springfield, Hannah, born April 11, 1656, died January 17, 1696, daughter of Miles Morgan. He married (second) January 4, 1698, Martha, born about 1666, died May 29, 1743, in Enfield, widow of Benjamin Crane Jr. Children by first wife: Hannah; Samuel; Rebecca; twin sons who died young; Ebenezer. By second wife: Benjamin; Ephraim, of whom further; Jacob; Martha; Jonathan; Isaac.

(III) Ephraim, son of Samuel (2) and Martha (Crane) Terry, was born October 24, 1701, in Enfield, died October 14, 1783. He lived in Enfield, was a tanner and also major of militia. He married, September 13, 1723, Ann, born December 20, 1702, died September 10, 1778, daughter of Nathaniel and Alice (Adams) Collins. She was a great-great-granddaughter of Gov. William Bradford. Their children were: Mary, Samuel, Ephraim, Nathaniel, Anne, Lucy, Elijah, Alice, Sybil and Eliphalet, mentioned below. One of the sons, Nathaniel, was a captain of militia at Enfield, and started for Boston with fifty-nine men on the day following receipt of the news of the battle of Lexington. He afterward rose to the rank of colonel.

(IV) Eliphalet, youngest son of Ephraim and Ann (Collins) Terry, was born December 24, 1742, in Enfield, where he died November 2, 1812. He was a deacon of the Congregational church, a lawyer by profession, and served successively as town clerk, judge of probate and judge of the county court. For thirty years he was a member of the state legislature. He married, December 3, 1765, Mary, daughter of Daniel (2) and Mary (Dwight) Hall; she was born November 3, 1745, and survived him nearly twenty-one years, dying January 10, 1833. Children: 1. Esther, born January 5, 1767, married William Kibbe, and lived in Canandaigua, New York. 2. Simeon, October 18, 1768. 3. Mary, November 27, 1770. 4. Mabel, February 19, 1773, married (first) William Barton, (second) Rev. Evans John; lived at Canandaigua and died in Brooklyn, New York, 1858. 5. Eliphalet, December 25, 1776. 6. Lucy, died at the age of sixty years. 7. Seth, mentioned below. 8. Abigail, January 17, 1783. 9. Roderick, mentioned below.

(V) Seth, third son of Eliphalet and Mary (Hall) Terry, was born January 12, 1781, in Enfield, died November 18, 1865, in Hartford. He was a deacon of the South Congregational Church of Hartford, and gained great distinction as an attorney, being called "the needle of the law". He married (first) June 5, 1813, Ann, born May 6, 1786, in Birmingham. England, died October 22, 1835, in Hartford. daughter of John and Mary (Coltman) Grew. He married (second) June 7, 1837. Hannah Shepard, born June 2, 1795, died July 19, 1867, in Amherst, Massachusetts. Children: 1. Anne, born August 26, 1814; married Daniel Gardner and lived in Troy, New York. 2. Arthur, May 17, 1816, was a merchant in Stamford, Connecticut. 3. Seth Hall, mentioned below. 4. Elizabeth Grew, October 22, 1822, married Rev. Walter Clark. D. D., and resided in Hartford, and Buffalo, New York. 5. James, May 29, 1826; was a banker in Rochester, New York. 6. William Barton, died in his second year.

(VI) Seth Hall, second son of Seth and Ann (Grew) Terry, was born August 8, 1818, in Hartford, died July 29, 1884, at Charlotte, New York. He prepared for college at Mount Pleasant Academy, Amherst, Massachusetts, and graduated from Union College in 1839, receiving the second honors of his class. Two years later his *alma mater* conferred upon him the degree of Master of Arts. He prepared for the practice of law at Rochester, New York, and was admitted to the bar at Troy, where he first began practice. In 1843-44 he was municipal judge of that city, and from 1848 to 1854 was engaged in practice at Hartford. In the last-named year he removed to Rochester, New York, where he gained distinction as an attorney and was actively engaged in real estate operations, being one of the founders of Charlotte, as a summer resort. He was an active member of the First Presbyterian Church of Rochester, in which he served as an elder, was also affiliated with the Masonic fraternity, in which he attained the thirty-second degree. Politically he was a Democrat, but took no active part in the promotion of party matters.

He married, October 3, 1855, Harriet Leonard, born November 23, 1822, died April 29, 1900, in New York City, daughter of Joseph E. and Sarah (White) Sprague. Children: Walter Clark, died in his second year; Seth Sprague, mentioned below; Grace Bartlett, born December 31, 1864.

(VII) Seth Sprague, only surviving son of Seth Hall and Harriet (Sprague) Terry, was born September 23, 1862, in Rochester, and was educated in public and private schools of that city and Rochester Free Academy. Entering the University of Rochester, he was graduated in 1883, with the degree of Bachelor of Arts, and one year later received the degree of Master of Arts from the same institution. From 1884-86 he was a student of Harvard Law School and was admitted to the bar in the latter year at Rochester. Since that time he has been engaged in a general practice in New York City with success. He has always taken an intelligent interest in the progress of the community and is somewhat independent in political action, with Democratic tendency. Soon after coming to New York he was made a member of the executive committee of the Citizen's Union, and he was subsequently appointed by Mayor Strong as commissioner of accounts. At his home in Montclair, New Jersey, he is now (1912) president of the Shade Tree Commission.

He is a member of the International Committee of the Young Men's Christian Association, and has been ten years chairman of the Boys' Work Committee, a sub-committee of the International Committee; from its organization he was trustee of the People's Institute, until he resigned in 1911; he was also a member and trustee of the Parkhurst Society for the prevention of crime, until 1911. He is a member of the advisory board of the Altruist Society of Montclair, New Jersey, and one of the governors of the Working Girls' Vacation Society of New York City; a trustee of the Madison Square Church House, and a member of the Madison Square Presbyterian Church, of which he has been a deacon since 1904. Mr. Terry is very active along the line of betterment of conditions for all mankind and was for many years a trustee of the Reform Club of New York, which was located at the corner of Fifth avenue and Twenty-seventh street, but is now extinct. Through his interest in the reform of public abuses, he was prominent in political work during the presidency of Grover Cleveland. He is a member of the Delta Psi College fraternity and of the Phi Betta Kappa society of the University of Rochester, and is a member of the New York County Lawyers' Association.

He married (first) April 27, 1898, Gertrude Putnam, born in 1870, at Irvington, New York, died July 5, 1900, in New York City, daughter of Dean N. and Mary (Buckingham) Fenner. He married (second) June 30, 1903, at Meadville, Pennsylvania, Gertrude, daughter of Myron N. Sackett and his wife, Sarah V. (Barker) Sackett, now residing at Meadville. Children: Seth Sackett, born April 25, 1904, and Ward Edgar, July 26, 1906.

(V) Roderick, youngest child of Eliphalet and Mary (Hall) Terry, was born March 2, 1788, in Enfield, and was for many years a prominent merchant in Hartford, Connecticut. In association with his elder brother Eliphalet, in the early part of the last century, he conducted the principal grocery store in Hartford, which at that time was at the head of navigation on the Connecticut river. They were succeeded by Cheeney Brothers. The elder brother was president of the Ætna Fire Insurance Company and Roderick was a director of the Hartford Fire Insurance Company. These two gave the fire insurance companies an impetus which has developed immensely in Hartford. At the time of the great fire in New York, in 1837, the available funds of the insurance companies of Hartford were not large, but the Terry Brothers contributed of their private means and their individual credit by which the losses were covered. Eliphalet drove in a sleigh to New York accompanied by two guards armed with blunderbusses, carrying one hundred thousand dollars in gold. He opened an office representing the fire insurance interests of Hartford, and announced their readiness to pay all losses insured by them as soon as properly proven. After accomplishing the settlement of the claims he returned to Hartford with more money than he carried away, having taken in, in new premiums, a large amount. This established the insurance business at Hartford upon a sound basis, and it very rapidly increased. Both the brothers were highly esteemed in Hartford as men of sound business judgment and are still remembered by old residents there. Their methods differed somewhat from those of a later period, as shown by the following incident: The Connecticut river froze over much earlier than usual on one occasion, and when navigation closed, the stock of flour was very low in Hartford, the center of supplies for many surrounding towns. The firm of E. & R. Terry held about ninety per cent. of the supply in Hartford. Another merchant holding the next largest amount proposed to the Terrys to double the price, but this was sternly refused. Mr. Terry stated the current price gave a fair return upon the money invested, as well as a remuneration for labor and risk, and he was satis-

fied to sell at such price. The other merchant then offered to buy their entire stock, but this was also refused, and Mr. Terry furthermore informed him that he would not sell him a single barrel at double the price. This was long remembered by the people of Hartford, to the advantage of the Terrys. Roderick Terry was also president of the Hartford National Bank to the time of his death.

Roderick Terry married (first)January 11, 1814, Harriet Taylor, of Hartford, born May 18, 1794, died February 7, 1841. He married (second) at Norwich, December 25. 1844, Lucy Coit, daughter of Dwight and Elizabeth (Coit) Ripley, and widow of Backus W. Birge, of Enfield. She was born January 11, 1803. Children, all by first wife: 1. Roderick, born July 26, 1815, resided in Hartford, subsequently in Lyme, Connecticut. 2. Edmund, mentioned below. 3. Harriet, March 15, 1819; married James Henry Taylor, and resided in Charleston, South Carolina. 4. John Taylor, September 9, 1822, was a banker in New York City, residing at Irvington-on-Hudson. 5. Jane Elizabeth, March 3, 1825; married James Owen Sheldon, a banker of New York, and lived in Brooklyn. 6. Frank Henry, April 16, 1827, was a wholesale grocer in Milwaukee, Wisconsin, and died at Nassau, Bahama Island. 7. Lucius Hall, October 25, 1830, was a merchant in New Orleans. 8. Edward Wyllys, February 3, 1835, was a banker at Nebraska City.

(VI) Edmund, second son of Roderick and Harriet (Taylor) Terry, was born May 23, 1817, in Hartford, died in 1891, in Brooklyn, New York. He passed through the city schools of Hartford, including the high school, and was graduated from Yale College in 1837 with the degree of Bachelor of Arts; two years later he received from that institution the degree of Master of Arts. For one year he pursued the study of law at Harvard Law School, residing in Student's Row, and was admitted to the bar in 1840. Following this he established himself in practice in New York City, where he continued through life and attained a high standing at the bar. His residence was in Brooklyn and he was a member and trustee of the First Presbyterian Church of that city. For many years, up to the time of his death, he was chairman of the library committee of the Law Institute of New York City. Politically he was a Democrat, but never sought preferment for himself.

He married in Brooklyn, March 8, 1855, Anna, daughter of John H. and Sarah (Davis) Prentice. Her father, John H. Prentice, was one of the most prominent citizens of

Brooklyn, and among the first agitators for the establishment of public waterworks in that city, and also the establishment of Prospect Park. Being very fond of riding and driving he was thoroughly familiar with this territory before it was taken for park purposes. At his suggestion the parkways running from the park were laid out according to his plans, and when the scheme of building the Brooklyn Bridge was first taken up by a stock company he was the largest holder of its stock. During his active business life he was a partner of William S. Packer, in the firm of Packer & Prentice, fur dealers, at Albany, New York, and about 1842 retired with a competence and went to Brooklyn to live. The widow of his former partner was the founder of Packer Institute in Brooklyn, and Mr. Prentice was largely instrumental in founding the Polytechnic Institute in that city. He was one of the original park commissioners and was made treasurer of the bridge trustees, being an original member of that body, continuing until his death. In 1832, he married Sarah Davis, of Albany, and they were the parents of nine children.

Children of Edmund Terry: 1. Edmund Roderick, mentioned below. 2. Marion Jane, January 26, 1860, resides in Brooklyn, unmarried. 3. John Prentice, September 30, 1861; graduated at Yale in 1884, and is a mining and civil engineer, living in Brooklyn, when not professionally absent. 4. Arthur Hall, died in his seventh year. 5. Wyllys, mentioned below. 6. Eliphalet Bradford, October 1, 1866; graduated at Yale, in 1888; is a clergyman of the Presbyterian church, and for five years was chairman of the hospital committee of the Brooklyn Presbytery and devoted himself exclusively to that work. He resides in Brooklyn. 7. Henry Fowler, March 12, 1868; graduated from Dartmouth in 1892; spent most of his life in the west; died in his fortieth year. 8. George Davis, February 5, 1870; graduated at Yale in 1892; is engaged in a general contracting business; resides in Brooklyn, unmarried. 9. James Taylor, October 8, 1872; is associated with his brother Wyllys in the insurance business, in New York City,

(VII) Edmund Roderick, eldest child of Edmund and Anna (Prentice) Terry, was born June 11, 1856, in Brooklyn. He pursued his primary education in the College Grammar School in Brooklyn, conducted by Rev. Levi Wells Hart. Entering Yale College, he was graduated in 1878 with a degree of Bachelor of Arts, and after one year at Columbia Law School he was admitted to the bar in 1880. Since that time he has been engaged

in the general practice of law in New York City. He is much interested in literature and has written several poems for magazines and periodicals. In 1884 The Century magazine published his "Universal Language" and it has been translated into every European tongue. Mr. Terry has taken an active interest in the progress of the country and has been always an active Democrat, serving one year as president of the First Ward Democratic Club of Brooklyn. When the election district system was adopted by the county committee of Kings county, he became chairman of the committee on organization of the county general committee, which position he resigned when William J. Bryan became the national candidate of the party. Since that time he has taken no active part in politics, until 1907 when he was urged to take the nomination for assemblyman in a district of Kings which had always been controlled by the Republicans. Mr. Terry was triumphantly elected. In the following year he was again a candidate and although he ran ahead of his ticket he was defeated in the wave which carried Hon. William H. Taft into the presidency. While in the legislature he served as a member of the committee on railroads and public instruction. In 1909 he declined a renomination and a Republican was again elected. In 1910 Mr. Terry took the nomination and was elected by a plurality of eleven hundred votes, and during the following term was a member of the committees on judiciary and railroads, and chairman of the committee on claims. With Assemblyman John B. Trombley, John K. Evans, Senator Franklin D. Roosevelt, and others, he stood out against the election of William F. Sheehan as United States senator. Mr. Terry was among the most steadfast in this position and resisted all the blandishments and threats of the machine. To him may be largely attributed the choice of Senator O'Gorman, a man of high personal character with a clear record as a judge. Mr. Terry was also largely instrumental in the defeat of the new charter proposed for New York City during this session. He is a member of the Spencer Memorial Church, of Brooklyn, and has served for many years on the board of deacons of that church.

(VII) Wyllys, fourth son of Edmund and Anna (Prentice) Terry, was born December 6, 1864, in Brooklyn. He graduated from Yale University in 1885, with the degree of Bachelor of Arts. For six years he engaged in the warehouse business in New York and Brooklyn, and in 1891 entered the general insurance business, with offices in New York City. He is treasurer of the Van Brunt

Street & Erie Basin Railroad Company, a terminal railroad of Brooklyn, and president of the Monmouth Land Company of New Jersey. He is a director of the New Netherland Bank of New York and of the Thirty-fourth Street Safety Deposit Bank of that city. He was baptized in the Presbyterian church and is affiliated with Epiphany Episcopal Church of New York; is a member of the board of managers of the J. Hood Wright Hospital of that borough. His name Wyllys is derived from his ancestress Ruth Wyllys, daughter of Sir George Wyllys, governor of the colony of Connecticut. It was upon the Wyllys place in Hartford that the historic oak stood in which the charter was hidden by Ruth Wyllys and her brother. Politically he is independent and takes little part in practical politics. He married June 19, 1907, Marie Louise, daughter of Hon. Henry P. Baldwin, who was governor of Michigan, and served two terms in the United States senate from that state.

BRACKETT Captain Richard Brackett, immigrant ancestor, was born, according to his own deposition, in 1612. He died March 3, 1690, aged eighty, according to his gravestone. He was very prominent in town, church and military matters. He was one of the original members of the First Church in Boston, with Governor Winthrop at its head, August 27, 1630, and was dismissed to the church of Braintree, Massachusetts, December 5, 1641. His wife signed the covenant, September 8, 1635, in the Boston Church. He was ordained deacon of the Braintree church, July 21, 1642. In the year 1637 he was appointed keeper of the prison, and from his service there he received the name of "grim" Richard Brackett. He was made freeman, November 23, 1636, and became a member of the Ancient and Honorable Artillery on November 23, 1636. On March 21, 1636, he was granted a home lot in Boston, which he sold on moving to Braintree. He served as first town clerk of Braintree, as magistrate, and as selectman in 1652-70-72. He was deputy to the general court in 1643-55-65-67-71-72-73-74-80. He served as captain of his company during King Philip's war, and held that position for thirty years. It is also said that he taught school for a time in later life. He owned houses and lands in Braintree and Billerica, where several of his children settled. His will was proved December 19, 1690. He married Alice ———, who died November 3, 1690, aged seventy-six years. Children: Hannah, baptized January 4, 1635; Peter, baptized

May 7, 1637; John, mentioned below; Rachel, born November 3, 1639; Mary, born February 1, 1642; James, married Sarah ———; Josiah, born July 8, 1652; Sarah, married Joseph Crosby.

(II) John, son of Captain Richard Brackett, was born in Billerica and baptized May 7, 1637, twin of Peter. He lived in Billerica at the corner on the west side of the road between the two brooks. He died March 18, 1686-87.

He married (first) September 6, 1661, Hannah French, born about 1643, died May 9, 1674, daughter of William and Elizabeth French. He married (second) March 31, 1675, Ruth, widow of Joseph Ellise, and daughter of Samuel Morse, an early settler. Children of first wife: Hannah, born December 1, 1662; Elizabeth, June 7, 1664; Mary, February 12, 1666; Sarah, December 11, 1667; Rachel, September 30, 1669; Abigail, December 31, 1670, died January 11 following; Bathsheba, March 10, 1671-72, died April 24, 1673; Samuel, March 4, 1672-73; Sarah, May 9, 1674. Children of second wife: John, January 19, 1675-76, died June 24, 1675-76; Ebenezer, mentioned below; John, December 10, 1680; Bethia, May 25, 1682.

(III) Ebenezer, son of John Brackett, was born in Billerica, October 19, 1677. He did not receive a share in his grandfather's will, as did the children by his father's first wife. His mother received a large share of her father, Samuel Morse's estate, and doubtless her children were so well provided for that his grandfather did not think it necessary to mention him. Samuel Morse was son of Samuel Morse, who was born in Dedham, England, in 1587, and married Elizabeth, born 1587, died 1654, and died in Dedham, New England, in 1654, the same year his wife died. Ebenezer Brackett lived in Dedham, Massachusetts, from the time when he was a boy, until his death, December 7, 1750. He was a farmer. He married, January 21, 1712, Abigail Heale, who died January 23, 1772. He and his wife joined the church in February, 1728. Children, born in Dedham: Abigail, December 21, 1713; Ebenezer, March 6, 1716; Aaron, October 14, 1717; Samuel, mentioned below.

(IV) Samuel, son of Ebenezer Brackett, was born in Dedham, September 3, 1724, died there May 9, 1794. He was a farmer and owner of real estate. He married Elizabeth ———. Children, born in Dedham: Samuel, August 17, 1749, died in infancy; Samuel, mentioned below; Ebenezer, November 27, 1752; David, March 12, 1755; Mary, Febru-

J. Lewis Brackett.

ary 28, 1758; William, May 7, 1762; John, July 17, 1764; Solomon, October 12, 1766.

(V) Samuel (2), son of Samuel (1) Brackett, was born in Dedham, April 4, 1751. He was a farmer in Dedham. According to descendants he served in the revolution with the following record: Private in Captain Isaac Martin's company, Colonel Ezra Wood's regiment, to Rhode Island, April 17, 1777; private in Captain Theophilus Lyon's company, March 1, 1778; served thirteen days at Castle Island under Lieutenant Samuel Pierce. He married, October 7, 1779, Sarah Bullard, of Needham, born September 6, 1761, daughter of Moses and Sarah (Newell) Bullard; he was son of Benjamin and Elizabeth (Shephard) Bullard, son of George and Beatrice Bullard, the immigrant ancestors. Children, born in Dedham: Nathaniel, 1780; William; George, February 1, 1784; Rufus, mentioned below; Josiah, 1789; Ruby; Lucinda; Charles N., 1796; Newell; Daniel, August 9, 1801; Love, June 28, 1805.

(VI) Rufus, son of Samuel (2) Brackett, was born in Dedham, March 9, 1786, died July 31, 1848. He lived in or near Boston. He married (first) July 6, 1811, Mary Morris, daughter of John and Sally (Morris) Goldthwaite; John was son of Benjamin and Lois (Boardman) Goldthwaite; Benjamin was son of Major Benjamin and Charity (Edwards) Goldthwaite; Benjamin was son of Captain John and Sarah (Hopkins) Goldthwaite; John was son of Samuel and Elizabeth (Cheever) Goldthwaite; Samuel was son of Thomas Goldthwaite, the immigrant. Rufus Brackett married (second) June 30, 1818, Mary Ann Dadley, born July 25, 1796, died April 9, 1877. Child by first wife: Henry, born June 16, 1812. Children by second wife: Mary Ann, April 7, 1819, died October 30, 1871; Eliza Dadley, August 23, 1820, died September 22, 1821; James Dadley, November 25, 1822, died June 30, 1887; Rufus, December 15, 1824, died August 15, 1889; Isaiah Lewis, mentioned below; Harriet Ann Townsend Lewis, twin, November 25, 1828, married Alfred Stebbins, one child Alfred; Frances Eliza, April 12, 1831, died July 15, 1854; Anna Maria, February 18, 1833, died December 23, 1906.

(VII) Isaiah Lewis, son of Rufus Brackett, was born November 25, 1828. He attended the private schools in Brookline and George Fowle's Monitorial School, Boston. He began his business career as bookkeeper for Hunt & Hathaway, dry goods commission merchants, Milk street, Boston, and he was afterward employed by Charles L. Bartlett, importer of copper ingots. He was afterward bookkeeper for a Chicago firm of merchants. He returned to Boston, and on August 16, 1858, entered the employ of George William Bond & Company, wool brokers. He was admitted to partnership in this firm, January 1, 1864, and continued in this relation until April 1, 1894, when the firm was dissolved. Mr. Bond died May 29, 1892. Afterward Mr. Brackett engaged in business as a wool broker on his own account, with headquarters at 114 Federal street, Boston. He retired from active business in 1906. His residence is at 50 Pleasant street, Brookline.

He is a member of the Masonic Lodge of Eleusis of Boston and has taken the thirty-two degrees of Scottish Rite Masonry. Mr. Brackett was prominent in musical affairs for many years and a well known tenor soloist. He sang in the quartette of Grace Church, Temple street, Boston; in the Congregational church, corner of Washington and School streets, Brookline; in the First Parish Church, Walnut street, Brookline, during the pastorate of Rev. Howard M. Brown; in the Walnut Street Church, Brookline. He was also a composer of music, and Ditson published several pieces of sacred music written by him, namely: "Te Deum", "Jubilate", "The Lord is my Shepherd", "The Lord is my Light". He was a member for many years of the Cecilia Club and one of the original members of the Apollo Club, musical organizations of trained singers. In politics he is a Republican.

He married (first) June 15, 1859, Catherine Jackson Hall, daughter of Hiram K. and Louise (Whitman) Hall. She died July 6, 1874. He married (second) January 29, 1880, Lavinia Maxwell Prescott, daughter of Frederick William and Emily (Maxwell) Prescott (see Prescott X). Children by first wife: 1. Mary Ann Louise, born October 11, 1860; married (first) May 23, 1888, George A. Patterson; (second) Henry Eli Mygatt. 2. Kate Hall, born December 19, 1861; married, January 10, 1899, Joseph F., son of William Stephen and Margaret M. E. (Sullivan) MacGowan; no children. 3. Paul Bishop, born March 16, 1863; manager of the Hotel Kimball, Springfield, Massachusetts; married, March 28, 1884, Hedeia Helen Senter and has one child. Helen, born May 20, 1888, married Max Schaeffer, of Monroe, New York.

(The Prescott Line).

The surname Prescott is composed by the contraction of the Saxon words, priest and cottage, and it is ancient in England, having been used as a street name before being used as a surname. Also it was the name of a market town in Lancashire, and the early immigrants of the name who came to this country were from that town. There are various coats-of-arms for different branches of the family, and it is known that the family is one of the oldest in England.

(I) James Prescott, of Standish, Lancashire, England, was required by order of Queen Elizabeth dated August, 1564, to keep in readiness horsemen and armor. He married a daughter of Roger Standish, Esq., of Standish, and sister of Ralph Standish. Children: James, mentioned below; Roger; Ralph; Robert; William, grandfather of Sir John Prescott, Lord of the Manors of Radwington in Essex and Bromley in Kent; John.

(II) Sir James (2) Prescott, son of James (1) Prescott, married Alice Molineaux. Children: John, mentioned below; Ann. For his bravery and military prowess and achievements he was created Lord of the Manor of Dryby in Lincolnshire and had arms granted to him. He died March 1, 1583.

(III) John, son of Sir James (2) Prescott, was born at Dryby. Married and had children: William, James, mentioned below.

(IV) James (3), son of John Prescott, was born at Dryby and lived there. Married and had children: Mary; John, mentioned below; Anne; James; others, names unknown.

(V) John (2), son of James (3) Prescott, was the immigrant ancestor. He was baptized at Dryby, Lincolnshire, England, in 1632. He was the first settler in Nashaway, now Lancaster, Massachusetts, and when the inhabitants there asked for incorporation, they desired to name the town Prescott, but the general court refused, and finally chose Lancaster, the place in England from which Prescott came, incorporation dated May 18, 1653. Prescott left England to escape religious persecutions, and in a short time became one of the prominent colonists. He took the oath of fidelity in 1652 and was admitted a freeman in 1669. He was a farmer, a blacksmith and a millwright. In November, 1653, he received a grant of land on condition that he build a corn mill, which he had completed by May 23, 1654, and a short time after he also built a saw mill. The new town was much harassed by Indian raids, and on August 22, 1675, an Indian attack resulted in the death or capture of fifty persons, and the town was then abandoned for about three years. Mr. Prescott was among the first to return and he lived to see the town rebuilt, dying in 1683. Several interesting anecdotes are told of his bravery in resisting Indian attacks at various times. He married Mary Platts. Children: Mary, baptized at Sowerby, parish of Halifax in Yorkshire, England,

February 24, 1630; Martha, baptized March 11, 1632; John, baptized April 1, 1635; Sarah, baptized 1637; Hannah, 1639, may have been born at the Barbadoes, West Indies; Lydia, born at Watertown, Massachusetts, August 15, 1641; Jonathan; Joseph (?), born about 1645 or 1646; Jonas, mentioned below.

(VI) Captain Jonas Prescott, son of John (2) Prescott, was born at Lancaster, Massachusetts, June, 1648, died December 31, 1723. He had a mill in the south part of Groton, now in Harvard, still called the "old mill". He bought a large amount of land in Groton and became one of the largest landholders there. He was a blacksmith, and when the town was resettled after being destroyed by the Indians in 1676, he built mills and a forge for the manufacture of iron from the ore at Forge Village, so-called, then in Groton and now in Westford. He was an influential man, and in 1691 served as town clerk, selectman several years, representative to general assembly in 1699 and 1705, justice of the peace and captain. He married, December 14, 1672, Mary, born September 28, 1653, died October 28, 1735, daughter of John and Mary (Draper) Loker. The story of their courtship as handed down by the family is very interesting: her parents took strong measures to prevent their marriage, as they objected to her marrying a blacksmith, but the lovers succeeded in overcoming the obstacles finally. They were forced to begin housekeeping without the usual necessities, as her parents refused to give her a dowry. Children: Mary, born February 3, 1674; Elizabeth, January 23, 1676; Jonas, October 26, 1678; Nathaniel, December 21, 1680, died January 29, 1681; Dorothy, February 16, 1681; James, March 16, 1684, died young; Sarah, May 3, 1686; Abigail, May 8, 1688; Martha, February 20, 1690; Susannah, December 31, 1691; Deborah, March 5, 1694; Benjamin, mentioned below.

(VII) Hon. Benjamin Prescott, son of Captain Jonas Prescott, was born January 4, 1696, died August 3, 1738, as the result of over-exertion in saving some hay from an approaching shower. He lived in Groton. He was a man of commanding appearance, and early had a reputation for his sagacity, sound judgment and decision of character. In 1723 he was elected representative to the general court and held that office eight years, showing unusual ability for so young a man. In 1724 he became a justice of the peace, and in 1732 lieutenant-colonel of the militia; in 1735 justice of the superior court; in 1738 he was appointed representative from the province to the court at Great Britain, but declined; rep-

Frederick W. Prescott

resentative from 1734 to 1738. He married, June 11, 1718, Abigail, born in 1697, died September 13, 1765, from the malignant ulcerous sore throat, a fatal epidemic of that year, daughter of Hon. Thomas Oliver, of Cambridge. Children: Abigail, born April 23, 1719, died November 2, 1739; James, January 13, 1721; Elizabeth, October 1, 1723; William, February 20, 1726; Lucy, February 25, 1729; Oliver, mentioned below; Mary, August 7, 1735, died October 25, 1751.

(VIII) Dr. Oliver Prescott, son of Hon. Benjamin Prescott, was born April 27, 1731, died November 17, 1804. He was graduated from Harvard College in 1750, and then studied medicine with Dr. Roby, of Sudbury. He began practice in Groton, and was very successful, being very popular because of his moderate charges and his kindness and attention to the poor. He was one of the best known physicians in Massachusetts, and in 1781 was an original member of the Massachusetts Medical Society at its incorporation. He was an honorary member of various medical societies, and president of the Middlesex Medical Society during the whole period of its existence. He was prominent at the beginning of the revolution, receiving many important appointments. He was appointed a major by the King, then lieutenant-colonel and colonel. In 1776 he was brigadier-general for Middlesex county and a member of the board of war; in 1777 a member of the supreme executive council, and in 1778 third major-general of Massachusetts militia; town clerk from 1765 to 1777; in 1779 judge of probate, serving until his death. In 1781 he was appointed second major-general, but resigned soon for lack of time to perform his duties. He was incorporated a fellow of the American Academy of Arts and Sciences in 1780, and was a trustee and first president of the board of Groton Academy. He married, February, 1756, Lydia, born October 15, 1735, died September 27, 1798, daughter of David Baldwin, Esq., and Abigail Baldwin, of Sudbury. Children: Abigail, born February 21, 1760, died August 5, 1765; Oliver, April 4, 1762; Thomas, October 11, 1764, died August 10, 1765; Thomas, October 27, 1766, died October 26, 1785; Abigail, June 25, 1768, died October 26, 1783; Lucy, March 13, 1771; Samuel Jackson, mentioned below; Mary Jackson, November 8, 1774, became the wife of John Belknap, and their son, Henry Belknap, received honorable mention and was brevetted major for gallantry in battle during the war of the revolution.

(IX) Samuel Jackson, son of Dr. Oliver Prescott, was born March 15, 1773, in Groton, died in Brookline, Massachusetts, October 7, 1857. He was graduated from Harvard College in 1795, and then studied law, being admitted to the bar. Because of partial deafness he was obliged to give up his profession, and became a merchant. The embargo of 1807 and 1808 and the war of 1812 embarrassed his business so that he had to discontinue, and he then became an acting magistrate and notary public for Suffolk county, living in Boston. He married, November 13, 1804, Margaret Cleveland, born July 29, 1775, died August 4, 1841, daughter of Major Joseph and Margaret (Cleveland) Hiller. Her father was first collector of port of Salem. Children: Margaret Cleveland, born August 23, 1805; Susan Oliver, April 27, 1808, married William Augustus Wellman, and they had seven children; Ellen Sparhawk, March 21, 1810, died June 27, 1812; Frederick William, mentioned below; Thomas Oliver, May 29, 1814; he published some works of considerable literary merit, among them a translation of the Psalms from the Hebrew into English, aided by a Jewish rabbi, with whom he studied; his object, in part, was to consider the Psalms and their translation with reference to the meaning and bearing upon it of the Swedenborgian belief and ideas; he married (first) in Glasgow, Scotland, June 5, 1849, Jessie Mackie; she died in 1854; later, desiring to perpetuate the family name of his mother, Margaret Cleveland (Hiller) Prescott, who had been among those in Boston who early embraced the faith of the "Church of the New Jerusalem", or Swedenborgian, he had his last name legally changed, and being a minister, he was thereafter known as Rev. Oliver Prescott Hiller. In 1864 he married (second) Emma Ann Stokes, of London, England. Three children by his second marriage survive: Addison Prescott Hiller, born February 20, 1865; Margaret Cleveland Prescott Hiller, born November 9, 1866; Charles Frederick Prescott Hiller, born December 9, 1868. Rev. Hiller died May 11, 1870, in London; his widow died February 11, 1909, at Victoria Hotel, Folkestone, England.

(X) Frederick William, son of Samuel Jackson Prescott, was born October 6, 1812. From 1849 to 1856 he was in government employ at the Boston custom house, and then was with the Cunard Steamship Company, Boston, resigning therefrom on account of ill health. Admiral Joseph F. Greene, who was his next door neighbor, had him appointed his secretary, and Mr. Prescott spent a year, from 1870 to 1871, on board the United States warship, "Congress", in company with

Admiral Greene. This was an act of kindness on the part of Admiral Greene to give Mr. Prescott an opportunity to benefit his health. He was a resident of Brookline. He served as justice of the peace for a number of years, member of the school board and board of assessors in Brookline. For many years and until his death was treasurer and secretary of the Brookline Savings Bank. He was for many years a member of the New England Historic Genealogical Society, in which he was greatly interested. He was a man of the utmost integrity, universally beloved, respected and trusted. He was a chivalrous, old-fashioned gentleman, brave and gentle. He gave many points and items to the Mr. Prescott who wrote the book of "The Prescott Family", thus assisting him considerably. He married, October 18, 1841, Emily, daughter of James Maxwell, of Louisville, Kentucky, formerly of Philadelphia, where he was a well known publisher of fine books, among them "Audubon's Birds"; his wife was Susan Britton (Fleeson) Maxwell. Child of Frederick W. Prescott: Lavinia Maxwell, born at Louisville, Kentucky, July 19, 1844, married, January 29, 1880, Isaiah Lewis Brackett (see Brackett VII). Mr. Prescott died January 28, 1879, and his wife died March 14, 1889.

GREELEY Andrew Greeley, the immigrant ancestor of this family, was born about 1617, and died at Salisbury, Massachusetts, June 30, 1697. His name appears on the Salisbury records first in 1640, but he was probably settled there some time before that date. He was a miller and settled in the part which is now included in Seabrook, New Hampshire, and built his mill on Kane's river, to grind corn. About 1650 he added a saw mill, and soon after the completion of the mill he moved to Haverhill, Massachusetts. He was constable of Salisbury in 1653, and was a member of the planting and prudential committee. He was often on committees to lay out land and settle boundary lines, and was appointed to seal leather in 1677. In 1655 he entered into an agreement with Bartholomew Heath to maintain a corn mill for the inhabitants of Haverhill. In 1669 he was chosen to keep the ferry at Haverhill. He went bonds for his son Benjamin who died and left his debts unpaid, and the father was obliged to sell his house and property in Haverhill in order to pay them, returning to Salisbury, where he lived with his son Andrew on the old homestead until his death. He married Mary Moyse, daughter of Joseph and Han-

nah Moyse. She died December 24, 1703. Children, born at Salisbury: Philip, mentioned below; Andrew, born December 10, 1646; Mary, born July 16, 1649; Joseph, born February 5, 1652; Benjamin, born December 9, 1654; Westwood, born January 29, 1659, probably died young.

(II) Philip, son of Andrew Greeley, was born at Salisbury, Massachusetts, September 21, 1644, and died there, March 17, 1717-18. He took the oath of allegiance and fidelity before Captain Bradbury, December 5, 1677, and in 1690 was admitted a freeman. He bought and sold much land in Salisbury, and also owned portions of small vessels built there. In a division of land on May 18, 1681, he received Lot No. 37, containing twelve acres. In 1682, 1683 and 1684 he was surveyor of highways. His will was dated March 14, 1717-18. He and his wife were buried in the old cemetery at East Salisbury, near the road leading to the beach, where their gravestone may still be seen. He married at Salisbury, February 17, 1670, Sarah Isley, who was born there June 30, 1644, and died there July 19, 1710. She was the daughter of John and Sarah Isley. Children, born in Salisbury: John, born January 16, 1671; Jonathan, mentioned below; Sarah, born March 21, 1675-76; Mary, born June 5, 1679; Philip, born December 25, 1681; Ruth, born October 3, 1684.

(III) Jonathan, son of Philip Greeley, was born in Salisbury, February 15, 1672-73, and died there, October 25, 1750. His will was dated March 1, 1749-50, and the inventory of his estate was dated November 23, 1750. He married at Salisbury, March 21, 1697, Jane Walker, who died at Salisbury, May 21, 1721. They were married by Robert Pike, justice of the peace. Children, born in Salisbury: Patience, born September 7, 1698; David, mentioned below; Sarah, born April 3, 1703; Jonathan, born January 2, 1705-06; Benjamin, born September 26, 1708; Philip, born June 9, 1711; Jane, born January 1, 1713; Samuel, born October 20, 1716; Mary, born December 10, 1718; Hannah, born May 21, 1721.

(IV) David, son of Jonathan Greeley, was born in Salisbury, December 1, 1700, and died there November 2, 1773. He was a weaver by trade. His will was dated October 25, 1773, and he and his wife were buried in the old cemetery at East Salisbury, where the gravestone is still in evidence. He married at Salisbury, April 30, 1730, Mary Stevens, who was born there February, 1707-08, died there December 21, 1798. They were married by Rev. Caleb Cushing. She was the daughter of Benjamin and Mary (Greeley) Stevens. Benjamin Stevens, born at Salisbury October 7, 1677, was the son of Benjamin and Hannah (Barnard) Stevens; he died February 23, 1709-10. Mary (Greeley) Stevens was the daughter of Philip, son of Andrew Greeley. Children of David and Mary (Stevens) Greeley, born in Salisbury: Shubal, mentioned below; Mary, born June 7, 1733; Jane, born May 18, 1735; Hannah, born June 15, 1737; Esther, born May 11, 1739; David, born September 30, 1741; Richard, born September 1, 1743; Rachel, born February 18, 1745; Benjamin, born December 31, 1748; John, born October 6, 1752.

(V) Shubal, son of David Greeley, was baptized in Salisbury, January 10, 1731, and died at Salisbury, New Hampshire, October 22, 1814. On May 16, 1782, the town of Weare gave a note to his son David, in payment for three years which he was to serve in the Continental army; David died during service, August 5, 1783, and his father received in payment for his services, five heifers and calves. Shubal Greeley married at North Yarmouth, Maine, November 9, 1758, Hannah Pettengill, who was born at North Yarmouth, August 3, 1740, and died March 15, 1823, at Salisbury, New Hampshire. She was the daughter of Abraham and Hannah (French) Pettengill. Hannah French, born at Salisbury, Massachusetts, August 19, 1706, was the daughter of Edward and Mary (Winsley) French; Edward was the son of Joseph and Susanna French. Mary Winsley was the daughter of Ephraim and Mary (Greeley) Winsley; Ephraim was the son of Samuel and Elizabeth Winsley; Mary (Greeley) Winsley was the daughter of Andrew Greeley, the immigrant ancestor mentioned above. Children of Shubal and Hannah (Pettengill) Greeley, born at Salisbury, New Hampshire: Matthew, mentioned below; Mary, born December 18, 1760; David, born April 5, 1762.

(VI) Matthew, son of Shubal Greeley, was born in Salisbury, New Hampshire, September 3, 1759, and died at Enfield, New Hampshire, June 24, 1842. He lived at Salisbury, New Hampshire, until about April, 1787, when he moved to Canaan, New Hampshire, settling at the foot of Goose pond. He built the first mill there, known for many years as Greeley's mill. After living some years at Canaan, he went west, but returned soon afterward and settled in Enfield, where he lived the remainder of his life. His name is on the list of training soldiers of Salisbury, New Hampshire, May 27, 1776, and he served in the revolution, enlisting in Captain Gray's company, Colonel Scammel's regiment, in 1777, serving for three years. In 1780 he

enlisted again in Colonel Stickney's regiment. He and his wife are buried in Enfield. He married Abigail Stevens, who was born December 17, 1761, and died July 10, 1847, aged eighty-five years. Children, born in Salisbury: Shubal, born May 18, 1782; David, born April 20, 1784; Ephraim, born July 5, 1786. Children, born in Canaan: Matthew, born November 1, 1788; Sally, born May 28, 1790; Hannah, born July 20, 1792; Abigail, born in Salisbury, February 7, 1796; Achsah, born in Canaan, March 23, 1798; John Dustin, mentioned below; Lydia, born October 9, 1803; Ira, born July 27, 1805, died March, 1807.

(VII) John Dustin, son of Matthew Greeley, was born in Canaan, New Hampshire, August 23, 1800. He married Sema C. Choate, who was born in Enfield, New Hampshire, in 1794, daughter of Solomon and Abigail (Bray) Choate. Children: George; Charles; John Henry, mentioned below.

(VIII) John Henry, son of John Dustin Greeley, was born in Lebanon, New Hampshire, June 7, 1832, died November 16, 1910, at Hyde Park, Massachusetts. He received his early education in the public schools. At the age of fifteen he began his career as a railroad brakeman, afterward entering the employ of the Earle & Prew Express Company in Boston. After several years with this company he became a messenger for the Adams Express Company, continuing in this position with the same company for a period of forty years, on the route from Boston to New York. His fidelity and efficiency are attested to by his lengthy term of service. He won the confidence, and respect of both his employers and the patrons of the company and the respect and esteem of all who knew him. In politics he was a Republican, and in religious faith an Episcopalian.

He married, February 10, 1873, Mary Bockus, born January 31, 1845, at Hoboken, New Jersey, daughter of William and Mary (Cunningham) Bockus; the surname was formerly spelled Backus. The immigrant ancestor of the Backus family was William, born in England, settled, 1638, in Saybrook, Connecticut; removed to Norwich, Connecticut, in 1660, and was one of the original proprietors of that town; was admitted a freeman in 1663 and died in 1664. He married, (first) Sarah Charles; (second) before 1660, Ann ———, and had sons: Stephen and William, and daughters: Sarah and Mary. William Bockus, Mrs. Greeley's father, was born at Glen Cove, Long Island, New York, and had five children: Mary, of previous mention; Caroline, born September 6, 1847,

•

died October 15, 1908; Charles Jenkins, born September 7, 1856; Ida, born May 13, 1858; and Catherine, born June 9, 1860. Mrs. Greeley was the only one of these children who married.

Children of John Henry and Mary (Bockus) Greeley: 1. Horace Lincoln, born November 27, 1875; he is a machinist, now employed in the construction of the Panama Canal at Gorgona, Panama; married, June 15, 1906, Gertrude Louise Fisher, and had one child, Robert Henry, born June 18, 1908. 2. Maud Edna, born March 10, 1884, unmarried.

SAWYER Within a few years after the landing of the Pilgrims at Plymouth the name Sawyer appeared in the records of the settlements of Massachusetts Bay Colony, and for centuries in the United States it has been borne and honored by men who have been successful leaders in nearly all the walks of life. As governors, congressmen and senators, as lawyers and jurists, as manufacturers and merchants, argriculturists and skilled artisans and as pioneers, they have shown those qualities of character which planted civilization in a land inhabited by savages, and under conditions that would have disheartened any but the strongest and bravest. Their hardihood and christian fortitude made them fit instruments for the advancement of civilization upon the underlying foundation principles, whose object is the enjoyment of "life, liberty and the pursuit of happiness". As defenders of these principles they were ever ready to face death, as the records of the early Indian wars in New England show, and those of the revolution, and again in later years when their country required defenders. It is a matter of record that eighteen members of the Sawyer family from Lancaster, Massachusetts, alone were in military service at the same time during the revolution, and that one company recruited in that town was officered from captain down by Sawyers.

John Sawyer, or Sayer, was a farmer in Lincolnshire, England, where he is supposed to have been a landholder also. He was the father of three sons, William, Edward and Thomas, who left England on a ship commanded by Captain Parker, and settled in Massachusetts about 1636. William Sawyer, the immigrant ancestor, was born about 1613, probably in England. He was in Salem, Massachusetts, and later in Wenham, from 1640 to 1645. His name at that time was spelled Sayer. He subscribed to the oath of allegiance in 1678, and became a member of the

First Baptist Church in Boston, with his wife and several others of Newbury, in 1681. It is probable that he had then resided in Newbury for forty years. A branch of the First Baptist Church was formed in Newbury in 1682, and William and John Sawyer and others, were among its members. He was still living in 1697, and his estate was administered by his son-in-law, John Emery, in March, 1703. The name of his wife was Ruth, and his children were: John; Samuel; Ruth; Mary, died young; Sarah; Hannah, died young; William; Frances, died young; Mary; Stephen A.; Hannah; and Frances.

(I) James Sawyer, whose parentage and place of birth are unknown, appears in Ipswich, Massachusetts, in 1669, and removed thence to Gloucester, in the same colony, in 1677. He was a weaver by trade, and was granted a six-acre lot in Gloucester, on the west side of the Annisquan river, in 1688. In 1690 he purchased more land in the same vicinity, and there built his homestead where he died May 31, 1703. He married Sarah, daughter of Thomas Bray, and had children: Thomas, John and Mary, who were probably born in Ipswich before his removal to Gloucester; Nathaniel, born December 29, 1677; Abraham, 1680; Sarah, 1683; Isaac, 1685; Jacob, of whom further; James, 1691.

(II) Jacob, son of James and Sarah (Bray) Sawyer, was born in 1687, in Gloucester, Massachusetts, and resided in that town until 1726. He married, in 1716, Sarah Wallis, and had five children, born in Gloucester. He married (second) in Preston, Connecticut, in 1730, Prudence Standish, born May 9, 1711, daughter of Israel and Elizabeth (Richards) Standish, of Preston (see Standish IV). There were also children by this marriage, among whom was Ephraim.

(III) Ephraim, son of Jacob and Prudence (Standish) Sawyer, resided in Preston. He married ———— Smith, and had children, among whom was David.

(IV) David, son of Ephraim Sawyer, married Mary Woodruff. Children: Noah Woodruff; Olive Barker; David (2), of whom further.

(V) David (2), son of David (1) and Mary (Woodruff) Sawyer, was born September 25, 1807, in Tinmouth, Vermont, died in Moira, New York, December 31, 1859. He married, in 1831, in Danby, Vermont, Lucretia Stafford, born about 1813, died December 3, 1893, aged eighty years. Children: 1. Anson David, born February 13, 1832, in Tinmouth, died March 29, 1879, in Osborne City, Kansas. He married, July 31, 1866, Phebe Elizabeth, daughter of Isaac C. and

Elizabeth E. (Crawford) Goffe, born December 12, 1845. They had children: i. Miles S., born March 1, 1868; married, April 6, 1893, Julia E. Harlow, and has a daughter, Dorothy Standish, born December 26, 1893. ii. Oliver H., June 18, 1878. 2. Henry Arthur, of whom further. 3. Persis Lucretia, December 3, 1835, died October, 1911. 4. Melinda, July 31, 1837, died at the age of nine years. 5. Palmer Stafford, July 1, 1839, died May 20, 1904. 6. Noah Barker, September 20, 1848, now living in Hutchinson, Kansas.

(VI) Henry Arthur, son of David (2) and Lucretia (Stafford) Sawyer, was born March 19, 1834, in Tinmouth, Rutland county, Vermont, died in Rutland, same state, October 6, 1899.

He attended school as a child in his native town, and when nine years of age went with his parents to Moira, Franklin county, New York, where he continued in school until eighteen years of age. He then went to Boston, remaining a few years, and then engaged in the stationery business in Cornwall, province of Quebec. In 1861 he removed to Rutland, and was associated for a time with John W. Cramton in the conduct of the Central House. Later he was associated with Mr. Cramton and J. C. Dunn, in the wholesale and retail book and stationery trade. He sold out his interest in this business, and secured one in the Rutland Globe Printing & Publishing Company, of which he became treasurer. This establishment opened the store now occupied by H. A. Sawyer & Company, and Mr. Sawyer purchased the stock when the *Globe* was consolidated with the Rutland *Herald*. In 1873 he purchased the wholesale department of the stationery business operated by Dunn Brothers & Company, and founded the firm of H. A. Sawyer & Company. At one time he was a stockholder in the Howe Scale Works, and was interested in other business enterprises of the town. He was vice-president of the Clement National Bank, and director of the State Trust Company. A Republican in politics, he took an active part in local affairs, serving several times as village trustee, and was two years president of the board of aldermen after the incorporation of the city. He was a member of the board of trade and of the Congregational church, serving as a member of the prudential board of the latter. He was affiliated with Center Lodge, No. 34, Free and Accepted Masons, of Rutland; and figured prominently and honorably in the progress of the city. As a public-spirited citizen he supported every movement for its advancement and held the confidence of the business community.

He married, May 15, 1866, Julia A. Putnam, born November 15, 1841, in Ludlow, Vermont, died at Rutland, October 19, 1908, daughter of Colonel James M. and Sarah J. (Mason) Putnam. Children: James Putnam, of whom further; Mary Lucretia, born December 21, 1874, died July 12, 1911, wife of Henry W. Hudson, of Hoosic Falls, New York; David Henry, September 6, 1878, died December 19, 1910.

(VII) James Putnam, eldest son of Henry Arthur and Julia A. (Putnam) Sawyer, was born March 31, 1873, in Rutland, Vermont. He was educated in the schools of Rutland, later attending Philips-Andover preparatory school, at Andover, Massachusetts, from which he went to Yale College. He graduated in 1897, and immediately afterward went abroad, and traveled for a year in Europe. Two years later upon the death of his father he, together with his cousin, Miles Standish Sawyer, son of Anson D. Sawyer, succeeded to his father's business, manufacturers and dealers in wholesale paper and wooden ware, which had been conducted as H. A. Sawyer & Company. These two partners have continued the business under the original firm name of H. A. Sawyer & Company, even though the senior Mr. Sawyer has passed away. James P. Sawyer is a member of Centre Lodge, No. 34, Free and Accepted Masons, of Rutland.

He married, October 1, 1907, Helen Bradford Webb, of Chicago, daughter of Arthur Bradford and Frankie Adelaide (Sickles) Webb. Children: Henry Webb, born June 25, 1908; Barbara Standish, February 13, 1910.

(The Standish Line).

The surname Standish is derived from an ancient parish of Lancashire, England, still known as Standish, which was the seat of the family for many centuries. The earliest recorded ancestor was Thurston Standish, or de Standish, of the reign of Henry III. He inherited lands from his mother, Margaret de Standish, daughter and co-heiress of Robert de Hulton. The Standish family of Duxbury, county Lancaster, was descended from Hugh de Standish, through his son Ralph and grandson Hugh, the latter living in the reign of Edward I. The coat-of-arms of the Lancashire families was: Azure three standing dishes two and one argent. Crest: A cock argent combed and wattled gules. Another and perhaps even older coat-of-arms, also given in Burke's Armory, was: Argent a saltire within a bordure gules. To this

Lancashire family Myles Standish, the immigrant, doubtless belonged, though his ancestry in England has not been definitely traced.

(I) Captain Myles Standish, who came in the "Mayflower" in 1620, with his wife Rose, was born in England about 1586. He settled first in Plymouth, but soon removed among the early settlers of Duxbury across the bay from Plymouth, and the hill rising abruptly from the waters of Plymouth bay, upon which he built his home and lived the remainder of his life, is called Captain's Hill to this day. He signed the compact and became one of the leading men of the colony. In February, 1621, at a general meeting to establish military arrangements, he was chosen captain and vested with the command. He conducted all the early expeditions against the Indians and continued in the military service of the colony his whole life. He commanded the Plymouth troops which marched against the Narragansetts in 1645, and when hostilities with the Dutch were apprehended in 1653, he was one of the council of war of Plymouth, and was appointed to command troops which the council determined to raise. He was also prominent in the civil affairs of the colony; was for many years assistant, or one of the governor's council; and when, in 1626, it became necessary to send a representative to England to represent the colonies in business arrangements with the merchant adventurers, he was selected for this work. He was a commissioner of the United Colonies and a partner in the trading company.

His first wife, Rose, who came with him, died January 29, 1620-21. He married (second) Barbara ———, before 1627, when she and his children, Alexander, Charles and John, had shares of cattle with him. His will, dated March 7, 1655, was proved May, 1657. He desired to be buried near his deceased daughter Lora and daughter-in-law Mary. He bequeathed to his wife Barbara; eldest son, Alexander; sons Myles, Charles and Josiah: "to Marrye Robenson whom I tenderly love for her grandfather's sake"; to servant, John Swift Jr.; to son and heir apparent (under the English law), Alexander, lands in Ormsticke Borsconge, Wrightington, Maralsley, Woodburrow, Crawston, and the Isle of Man, which were detained from him, his great-grandfather being a younger brother from the house of Standish. He died October 3, 1656. An imposing monument to him has been erected on Captain's Hill, Duxbury. Captain Standish is one of the Pilgrims, known to every generation since and to the whole world, partly because of his military prominence, the first in New England, and partly, especially in the present generation, from the poem of Longfellow, "The Courtship of Myles Standish". Children: 1. Alexander. 2. Charles, living in 1627. 3. Joseph, living in 1627. 4. Myles, settled in Boston, died April 5, 1653; married Sarah, daughter of John Winslow. 5. Josiah, of whom further. 6. Lora. 7. Charles.

(II) Captain Josiah Standish, son of Captain Myles Standish and his second wife, Barbara, was born 1633-34 in Duxbury. He resided in early life in East Bridgewater, Massachusetts, where he was lieutenant of the militia company. Returning to Duxbury in 1663 he served there as selectman, deputy to the general court, and captain of the militia. In 1686 he removed to Norwich, Connecticut, and in the following year purchased one hundred and fifty acres of land in that part of the town which is now Preston. Here he died March 19, 1690. He married (first) December 19, 1654, Mary, daughter of John Dingley, of Marshfield, Massachusetts. He married (second) Sarah, daughter of Samuel Allen, of Braintree. Children: Myles; Josiah; Samuel; Israel, of whom further; Mary; Lois; Mehitable; Martha; and Mercy.

(III) Israel, fourth son of Josiah and Mary (Dingley) Standish, was born about 1675-80, in Duxbury. He removed with his father to Preston, Connecticut. He married, February 8, 1705, Elizabeth, daughter of William and Mary Richards, of Weymouth, Massachusetts. Children: Elizabeth, born February 7, 1707; Myles, November 18, 1708; Amy, March 14, 1710; Prudence, of whom further.

(IV) Prudence, youngest daughter of Israel and Elizabeth (Richards) Standish, was born May 9, 1711, in Preston. She became the second wife of Jacob Sawyer of that town (see Sawyer II).

PALMER   Walter Palmer, immigrant ancestor, was born, according to tradition, in county Nottingham, England, died in Stonington, Connecticut, November 19, 1661. The first authentic records of him in New England are in Charlestown, Massachusetts, when he and Abraham Palmer were admitted freemen May 14, 1634. He owned considerable real estate and received land in the first division in 1637 and again in the division of 1643. He was among those who met to prepare for the new settlement at Seacuncke, afterward Rehoboth, Massachusetts, and in 1653 removed to what is now Stonington, Connecticut. He bought land from Governor Haynes on the east bank of the Wequetequoc river. His whole tract of land contained about twelve hundred acres. His will was dated May 19, 1658, and proved May 11, 1662. He married (first) in England, Ann ———, (second) Rebecca Short, a member of Rev. John Eliot's church in Roxbury. Children of the first wife: Grace; John; William; Jonas; Elizabeth. Children of the second wife: Hannah, born June 16, 1634; Elihu, born January 24, 1636; Nehemiah, mentioned below: Moses, born April 6, 1640; Benjamin, born May 30, 1642; Gershom, baptized in Charlestown; Rebecca.

(II) Nehemiah, son of Walter Palmer, was born in Charlestown, Massachusetts, November 23, 1637, died in Stonington, February 17, 1718. He was made freeman at Hartford May 10, 1666, and also lived in Stonington. Connecticut, where he was a prominent man. On May 15, 1668, he was elected deputy to the general court of Connecticut, and held that office for fifteen sessions. In May, 1681. he was on a committee "for hearings on the Indian question and to buy land from the Indians". He purchased one hundred acres of land on December 11, 1683, from his brother, Benjamin Palmer, at Shownoak, and on April 23, 1706, he deeded a half of his land to his son Daniel, two acres of salt marsh to Nehemiah, the other half of the home lands to Joseph, on condition that the sons care for their mother, she to own the old house and one-third the income from the farm. On June 5, 1684, Nehemiah. Moses and Benjamin divided the land which had been left to their mother to divide. but which she had not divided, and they agreed to give five hundred acres to Gershom Palmer. On December 3, 1699, Nehemiah deeded two hundred acres on the Pawcatuck river to his son Nehemiah; in 1680 he sold land which his wife had received by will from her father. His grandsons, Nehemiah and David, sons of Daniel, received from him, September 4, 1716, because they cared for him in his old age, one hundred acres of land; also at that time he gave sixty-two acres to his son Jonathan. He deeded in 1717 one-half of his home lands to his grandsons Joseph, Benjamin and Gershom. to be divided according to their father's will; on June 27, 1717, he gave his son Daniel half his lands at home, "for his dutiful care of him". On April 10, 1718, his widow deeded to her son Ichabod and his wife, the property left her by her husband. Nehemiah Palmer married, in Stonington, November 20, 1662, Hannah, born in 1644, died in Stonington, October 17, 1727, daughter of Thomas and Ann (Lord) Stanton. He was buried in the old graveyard on the east side of Wequetequoc Cove. The stone on his grave is still to be seen and can be read. Children, born in Stonington: Joseph, mentioned below; Elihu, March 12, 1666, died young; Jonathan, August 7, 1668; Daniel, June 12, 1672; Elihu, baptized December 14, 1674; Jonathan, baptized December 14, 1674; Nehemiah, baptized July 8, 1677; Hannah, baptized April 11, 1680.

(III) Lieutenant Joseph Palmer, son of Nehemiah Palmer, was born at Stonington October 3, 1663, died January 31, 1710. On April 23, 1706, he received from his father half his home lands, provided he help take care of his mother. He was to own the house in which his father then lived. He made his will January 9, 1709, and in it he mentioned his wife and children. He married in Stonington, March 12, 1687, Frances Prentice, daughter of Thomas and Rebecca (Jackson) Prentice, who came to Stonington from Newton, Massachusetts. Children, born in Stonington: Son, died in 1688; Son, died in 1689; Joseph, born March 14, 1690; Daughter, died in 1692; Hannah, born May 31, 1694; Benjamin, mentioned below; Sarah, born April 3, 1698; Jonathan, born May 2, 1702.

(IV) Sergeant Benjamin Palmer, son of Lieutenant Joseph Palmer, was born in Stonington, March 18, 1696. In 1717 he and Joseph and Gershom received from their grandfather Nehemiah one-half his home lots to be divided among them according to their father's will. This was on the condition that Daniel Palmer should take care of Nehemiah's wife, "and that his son, Jonathan, should have liberty to cut the salt grass". On September 16, 1719, he gave to his brother Joseph his right in land which his father Joseph had received from his grandfather Nehemiah. On January 3, 1722-23, he and Benjamin, of Coventry, Connecticut, sold a hundred acres of land to Daniel Palmer, and on December 5, 1716, he joined with others in selling four hundred acres in Stonington to John Stanton. He moved to Coventry, Windham county, Connecticut, where he had the title of sergeant. He married (first) probably in Stonington, Rebecca Palmer, daughter of Gershom and Ann (Denison) Palmer. She was baptized in the First Church at Stonington, July 1, 1694, died in Coventry, March 22, 1726. He married (second), November 14 1726, Ruth Bidwell. Children by first wife, born in Coventry: Gershom, mentioned below; Ann, born February 5, 1720; Nathan, born November 27, 1723; John, February 14,

1725. Children of Sergeant Benjamin Palmer by second wife: Benjamin, October 10, 1729; Ruth, February 20, 1733-34; Rebecca, February 20, 1737-38.

(V) Gershom, son of Sergeant Benjamin Palmer, was born in Coventry, February 13, 1717. He married (first) in his native place, February 2, 1737-38, Mehitable Badger, who died there September 22, 1760. He married (second) Elizabeth ———. Children by first wife, born in Coventry: Gershom, mentioned below; Abigail, April 20, 1742; Elias, January 5, 1744; Rebecca, March 27, 1747; Amos, February 15, 1749; Mehitable, August 10, 1750; Benjamin, January 7, 1755; Abel, August 12, 1757. Child by second wife: Sally, April 28, 1767.

(VI) Gershom (2), son of Gershom (1) Palmer, was born at Coventry, December 5, 1738. He was a school teacher in Woodstock, Vermont. He married in Coventry, May 8, 1760, Lucy Fields. Children: Elizabeth, born April 19, 1761; Oliver, mentioned below; Bethiah; Hannah; Mehitable; Gershom; Bennet; Lucy; (Judge) Walter; Betsey; Nahum.

(VII) Oliver, son of Gershom (2) Palmer, was born June 25, 1763, and settled at Woodstock, Vermont. In 1790 Oliver had three females in his family and his father had two males over sixteen, two under that age and four females, according to the census. There were two other families of the Palmer name. John Palmer had two females in his family, and, according to the town history, left no descendants; he was a member of the Baptist church in 1794; constable 1799 to 1812; removed to New York about 1812 and died at Madison, New York, October, 1824, aged sixty-one years; married Joanna, only daughter of Eleazer Meacham. Ezekiel Palmer was probably born as early as 1740 and doubtless was closely related to Gershom; had two males over sixteen, two under that age and five females in his family in 1790.

(VIII) John, grandson of Gershom (2) Palmer and son or nephew of Oliver, was probably born in Woodstock, Vermont. He was a farmer in Woodstock, but afterward removed to Meredith, New Hampshire. He married ——— Russell, and among their children was Dudley Russell, mentioned below.

(IX) Dudley Russell, son of John Palmer, was born at Woodstock, Vermont, in 1809, died in 1887. For many years he was a grocer in Boston, and in later years was engaged in the real estate business. He married Ann E. Gibbs. Children: John, born in Boston in 1845, died unmarried; Percival

Bowditch, mentioned below; William Dudley, born in Boston in 1854, died unmarried.

(X) Percival Bowditch, son of Dudley Russell Palmer, was born in Boston, August 2, 1851. He attended the public schools of his native city, the Dwight Grammar School and the English High School of Boston, from which he graduated in 1868. For two years he was clerk in a woolen house in Boston and afterward was a salesman for Springer Brothers, wholesale dealers and manufacturers of cloaks. In 1879 he went to Chicago in the employ of J. W. Griswold & Company, wholesale dealers and manufacturers of cloaks and women's garments, established in 1851 at Hartford, Connecticut, removed to Milwaukee, Wisconsin, in 1857, and to Chicago, Illinois, in 1860. In that year J. W. Griswold, the founder, admitted to partnership his brother, Edward P. Griswold. In 1887 the senior partner retired from the firm, his interest being purchased by his brother and Mr. Palmer, the title becoming Griswold, Palmer & Company. This continued until the death of Mr. Griswold in 1899. At this time Mr. Palmer became head of the firm of Percival B. Palmer & Company, which relationship continues to the present (1912).

He married, December 27, 1877, Ellen Finch Chapin, who was born in March, 1851, at Charlestown, Massachusetts, now part of Boston, daughter of Nahum and Lucy (Farwell) Chapin, of Charlestown, Massachusetts. She had brothers Nahum and George F. Chapin. The Chapin family is of old Massachusetts colonial stock. Children of Mr. and Mrs. Palmer: 1. Dudley Chapin, born in Chicago, December 12, 1878, educated there in the public schools and in Yale College, from which he was graduated in 1900 with the degree of Bachelor of Arts, now a partner in his father's firm, Percival B. Palmer & Company; married, in October, 1911. Reta Dennis, of Chicago. 2. Percival Bowditch Jr., born in Chicago, July 1, 1881; educated in the public schools of Chicago, graduate of Amherst College with the degree of Bachelor of Arts in 1903; associated in business with his father in Chicago. 3. David Hamblen, born in Chicago, January 10, 1883, attended the public schools, and is now engaged in mining in Utah. 4. Nahum Chapin, born in Chicago, July 30, 1889, attended Chicago public schools and graduated from Phillips Academy, Andover, Massachusetts; engaged in the banking business in Chicago. 5. Lucy Farwell, born at Swampscott, Massachusetts, August 31, 1890; educated in private and preparatory schools and at Bryn Mawr College, Pennsylvania.

John Ball, immigrant ancestor, is
BALL said to have come from Wiltshire,
England, in 1650. He settled in
Watertown, Massachusetts, and was admitted
a freeman, May 22, 1650. He removed to
Concord, and died there in 1665. The inventory of his estate was filed in the Middlesex
court. Children: Nathaniel; John, mentioned below; Abigail, born April 26, 1656.

(II) John (2), son of John (1) Ball, was
born about 1620. He removed to Lancaster,
and with his wife and infant child was slain
by the Indians, in an attack of February 20,
1676, in King Philip's war. It appears in
the history of Lancaster that he was one of
the first three settlers as early as 1653, which
explains perhaps why so little is to be found
about him in the Watertown records. Lancaster was originally called Nashaway. It
was purchased of Sholan, sachem of the
Nashaways, by Thomas King and others, and
comprised a tract eight miles wide by ten
miles long, and the deed was approved by
the general court. The company in accordance with their agreement to make a settlement sent three men, Richard Linton, Lawrence Waters and John Ball, who were to
make preparations for the general coming of
the proprietors. In the year 1644 there were
but two dwellings in the place, occupied by
Ball, Linton and Waters.

He married (first) Elizabeth, daughter of
John Pierce, of Watertown. He married
(second) October 3, 1665, Elizabeth Fox,
of Concord. Children by first wife: John,
mentioned below; Mary; Sarah; Esther, born
about 1655. Children by second wife: Abigail, April 20, 1668, died young; Joseph,
March 12, 1669-70.

(III) John (3), son of John (2) Ball, was
born in Watertown, 1644. He married, October 17, 1665, Sarah, daughter of George
and Beatrice Bullard, of Watertown. Children: Sarah, born July 11, 1666; John, June
29, 1668; James, March 7, 1670; Joseph, May
4, 1674; Jonathan, mentioned below; Daniel,
August 2, 1683; Abigail, October 5, 1686.

(IV) Jonathan, son of John (3) Ball, was
born March 29, 1680, died about 1727. He
married, January 5, 1709-10, Sarah Whitney.
They settled in Watertown but may have
lived for some time at Lancaster. The birth
of their youngest child is recorded at Waltham although born at Watertown. Children:
Sarah, born 1710; Jonathan, mentioned below; Phinehas, 1716; Thankful, baptized
January 7, 1728, aged seven; Jane, baptized
January 7, 1728, aged four; Susannah, born
April 6, 1726.

(V) Jonathan (2), son of Jonathan (1)

Ball, was born in Watertown, and was baptized February 18, 1728, at Lexington. He
owned the covenant at Lexington. He lived
for a time at Lancaster. He married Martha
————. Child, Jonathan, mentioned below.

(VI) Jonathan (3), son of Jonathan (2)
Ball, was born at Lancaster, September 16,
1751, died in 1819. He was a soldier in the
revolution from Bolton, in Captain Sawyer's
company, Colonel Whitney's regiment. He
enlisted in the Continental army for three
years and the rolls show that in 1781 he was
twenty-nine years old, of dark complexion, a
farmer of Bolton. He married Mary Pratt,
of Bolton (intentions dated September 17,
1773). Children, born at Bolton: Becky,
April 25, 1778; Elizabeth, June 28, 1783;
Hannah, April 14, 1785; Asenath, October 20,
1788; Lucy, March 25, 1789; Silas, November 18, 1792; William, mentioned below.

(VII) William, son of Jonathan (3) Ball,
was born at Bolton, September 15, 1796. He
married Elizabeth Rice. Children, born at
Bolton: Elvira, May 2, 1815; Malinda, April
21, 1817, married William Carruth; Hannah,
June 22, 1820; Emerson, July 5, 1822; Addison, mentioned below; Elizabeth, September
7, 1826; Mary, January 6, 1830; Vilena, January 1, 1835, married Jacob Barnard; Elmina, October 7, 1839, married George Caniff.

(VIII) Addison, son of William Ball, was
born in Bolton, Massachusetts, May 3, 1824,
died there May 31, 1883. He was a farmer
by occupation and comb cutter by trade. He
married Mary Elizabeth Rice, born in Northborough, Massachusetts, November 20, 1828,
died July 2, 1907, daughter of Luther and
Zipporah (Kendall) Rice. Children: 1.
Mary Elizabeth, born April 4, 1847, died May
26, 1901; married Benjamin Rollins. 2. Angeline Olive, born October 27, 1849; married
George Augustus Billings. 3. Sylvester Addison, born March 23, 1852, died September
1, 1878. 4. Alonzo Eugene, mentioned below. 5. Clara Emma, born July 18, 1859. 6.
Edgar Franklin, born February 5, 1862. 7.
Ada Frances, twin of Edgar Franklin, died
May 16, 1863.

(IX) Alonzo Eugene, son of Addison Ball,
was born at Bolton, June 23, 1855. He attended the public schools of his native town
and the Bryant & Stratton Business College,
Boston. During most of his life he has been
in the newspaper business. He is now living
in Rutland, Vermont. In politics he is a
Republican. He married, December 24, 1876,
Lizzie Candace Rice, born April 24, 1856, in
Clinton, Massachusetts, daughter of Benjamin Franklin and Roxana (Boynton) Rice.

Children: Clarence Franklin, mentioned below; George A., born in South Lancaster, a painter, residing at Rome, New York, married Sophia Groff and has one child, John Clarence.

(X) Dr. Clarence Franklin Ball, son of Alonzo Eugene Ball, was born in South Lancaster, Massachusetts, February 24, 1878. He received his early education in the public schools of Rutland, Vermont, and Troy, New York, and in the Lancaster Academy at South Lancaster. He entered the American Medical Missionary College at Chicago and was graduated with the degree of Doctor of Medicine in 1902. For two years he was the assistant physician at the New England Sanitarium at Melrose, Massachusetts. In 1905 he began to practice at Rutland, Vermont, and he has continued there successfully in general practice to the present time. He was appointed health officer of the city of Rutland in 1907 and held the office until November 1, 1912, when he resigned. He is a member of the Rutland County Medical and Surgical Society, of which he has been president during the years 1911-12, the Vermont State Medical Society and the American Medical Association. He is on the staff of the Rutland Hospital. In religion he is a Seventh Day Adventist, and in politics a Republican. Dr. Ball married, September 21, 1902, Mary Olive Marsh, of Pontiac, Illinois, born June 12, 1878, daughter of John Wesley and Lucina (Rawson) Marsh. Children: Frances Lucinda, born August 3, 1903; Howard Alonzo, September 3, 1904; Olive May, October 23, 1906; Mildred Catherine, September 30, 1909; Clarence Franklin, March 19, 1912.

CURTIS The Curtis family, represented in the present generation by George Milton Curtis Jr., a prominent resident of Brooklyn, New York, is of English extraction, early members of the family removing from England to Ireland, locating in county Cork, where they spent active and useful lives and where their deaths occurred, among them being the grandfather of John Curtis, the first of the line here under consideration of whom we have the Christian name. The father of John Curtis emigrated to this country, settling in Berkshire county, Massachusetts, where he purchased a large tract of land.

(II) John Curtis, son of the emigrant ancestor, was a resident of Berkshire county, Massachusetts, an active and useful citizen, honored and respected by all with whom he was brought in contact. In early life he was a Roman Catholic, but later joined the Baptist church. He married and among his children was Beriah, of whom further.

(III) Beriah, son of John Curtis, was born in Berkshire county, Massachusetts, in July, 1800, died at Worcester, Massachusetts, December 24, 1865. After completing his studies in the common schools of the day, he entered into partnership with Colonel Billings and Colonel Clark and they established various stage lines in New England and, until the railroads were built, carried the mail, being awarded the contract for this work. In later life he was a banker, prospering in all his undertakings. He was very devout, but differed in belief from his Calvinistic neighbors, believing that Christ was not God, but a divine personality sent by God to redeem the world. In politics he was a staunch Democrat, and was a personal friend of President Andrew Jackson. He married Lydia Massena Dennys Hunter, daughter of Abraham Hunter, a descendant of John Hunter. Abraham Hunter was a soldier, participating actively in the revolution and in the war of 1812. His home was in Brookfield, Worcester county, Massachusetts, his being the first brick house built in that town, and there he followed agricultural pursuits. He married a niece of General Wilkinson, who established the first cotton mill in Rhode Island, and for whom the village of Wilkinsonville was named. Children of Mr. and Mrs. Curtis: Pascal Paoli; Maria Thurston Dennys; John Beriah; Lyman Wilkinson; Laura Matilda; George Milton, of whom further; Emma M.; William Henry Harrison; two children who died in early life.

(IV) Hon. George Milton Curtis, son of Beriah Curtis, was born in Worcester county, Massachusetts, June 20, 1840. He attended the public schools and the Baptist Academy of Worcester. He began the study of law in the office of Hon. John W. Ashmead, in New York City, and at the same time was occupied as a newspaper reporter. He was admitted to the bar in New York City in 1863 and immediately began the active practice of his profession there, gaining a reputation for professional ability of a high order, and achieving a large degree of success. He is a leader in his profession, and has served as counsel in many murder cases, but has devoted the greater part of his time to the trial of will cases and matters connected with the subject of insanity. During his career as a lawyer he has saved from the scaffold by successful defense no less than eighty-nine men indicted for murder. The following are some of the cases in which he has appeared as counsel in the last thirty years: The John

Anderson will case, the great tobacconist; the celebrated Senator Fair deed case, in California, taking part in the jury trial; the John Stetson will case, Mr. Stetson having been a notable theatrical manager; the Friedman will case, New York, 1874; the Bowdan will case, New York, 1876; the Buford case, the prisoner being indicted for the murder of Chief Justice Elliott, of Kentucky, in July, 1879, at Owenton, Kentucky; the Leslie will case, 1880; Commonwealth vs. Riddle, tried at Pittsburgh, Pennsylvania, 1885, Riddle being charged with looting the Penn Bank of Pittsburgh; the Helmbold insanity cases, Philadelphia and elsewhere; the Atlas Steamship case, New York, 1887; the Coffin lunacy case, New York, 1888; the Lane will case, New York, 1890; the Hayes forgery case, in February, 1893; with Grover Cleveland, Francis Leon Stetson, Charles Donohue, and other famous lawyers, he was engaged in the Louisana lottery contest, and was one of the counsel in the Jeannette inquiry before congress in which he pleaded the case of Jerome C. Collin; he also appeared in one of the celebrated Stewart will cases and was the only one to get a verdict against the Stewart estate; he was also counsel in the celebrated Philips will case, the Tigh will case and the will contest of Baker against the Sisters of Charity; he also procured for the matrons of the penitentiary an increase of their salaries under the law of the state of New York of 1903, arguing a constitutional question in their behalf which was decided in their favor. He is now engaged as counsel for a Nicaraugua company, which has large interests involved in matters connected with the state of Nicaraugua, its mahogany, rubber and *lignum-vitae* lands.

The political life of Mr. Curtis has been very exciting and interesting. He was elected to the New York legislature in 1863, and took his seat in January, 1864. It was in this session he made the celebrated speech in defense of Governor Seymour, which has become a political classic. It was warmly spoken of by the entire press, including the *New York Herald, The World, The Tribune, The Times* and *The Evening Post*, and was copied into all the prominent papers of the country. He was re-elected in 1865 and made the memorable speech on the Health Bill which has had a tremendous effect upon the legislation affecting the health of New York City. In 1867 he was elected justice of the marine court, his term beginning January 1, 1868, and he declined a second term. He was for one term assistant corporation attorney of New York City. He is a Democrat in

his political views. For more than forty years Mr. Curtis has been counsel of "On Leong Tong", a benevolent society which looks after the interests of the Chinese in the United States. He is a member of the New York Historical Society and of the New York County Bar Association. Mr. Curtis displayed his patriotism by enlisting in the Third Battalion of Rifles, Massachusetts, in 1861, and serving for three months on the Union side. A battle being expected he continued in the service after his term of enlistment expired. Later he raised the Ninety-fifth Regiment, New York Volunteer Militia, in which he expected to receive a commission, but his companies were consolidated and he decided not to return to the army.

Mr. Curtis married Caroline Gertrude Miner, of New York, and their only child was George Milton, of whom further.

(V) George Milton (2), son of Hon. George Milton (1) Curtis, was born in New York City, December 29, 1872. He received his early education at the Mount Pleasant Military Academy on the Hudson, graduating in 1889. He then entered Yale University, from which he was graduated in the class of 1893 with the degree of Bachelor of Arts. He then became a student in Yale Law School, graduating therefrom in 1895 with the degree of Bachelor of Laws. He was admitted to the bar of New York City in 1898, and began active practice of his profession in Brooklyn, New York, as assistant counsel for the Brooklyn Rapid Transit Company, a position he held for twelve years. In 1910 he was appointed assistant corporation counsel of the city of New York, and in 1911 was transferred to the Brooklyn branch of the corporation counsel's department, and at the present time (1912) is in charge of the trial bureau in the New York office of the corporation counsel. In his private practice he has made a specialty of corporation law. In politics Mr. Curtis is an active and influential Democrat, with independent tendencies, and has served his party as delegate to various state and other nominating conventions. During various political campaigns he made a reputation as an able and convincing stump speaker and his services are constantly in demand. He was for several years president of the Eighteenth Assembly District Democratic Club. From 1895 to 1898 he was one of the transfer tax appraisers. From 1893 to 1898 he was in the naval militia, First Battalion of Brooklyn, and attained the rank of gunner's mate. He is a director of the Flatbush Play-Ground Association, a private corporation for the purpose of furnishing play-grounds for the children of the city; one ground was opened in 1911 and two more in 1912. He is also a director in the Flatbush Merchants' Association. His recreation has always been found on the athletic field. In college he won distinction on the Yale track team; he played on the baseball club that won the college championship at the World's Fair, Chicago, in 1893; he also rowed in the crew that won the championship of the naval militia of the Eastern States in 1896.

He is a member of the New York State Bar Association; Phi Theta Theta, Theta Nu Epsilon (junior); Book and Gavel Society of Yale College; is a life member of the Benevolent and Protective Order of Elks; sachem of Hawk Eye Tribe, Improved Order of Red Men; member of the Montauk Club; the Knickerbocker Field Club; the Cortelyou Club; the University Club, and for many years was an active member of the New York Athletic Club and of the New Jersey Athletic Club. Mr. Curtis married Ethel Louise Kennan, niece of George Kennan, the famous Siberian writer and lecturer.

WILLIS Michael Willis or Wills, the immigrant ancestor, was born in England, and is said to have come to America in 1635, in the ship "James", from Bristol. He was admitted to the Dorchester church about 1636. He and George Willis of Cambridge, presumably a brother, were admitted freemen of the colony together in 1638. He became a founder of the Second Church of Boston, June 5, 1650. He was admitted an inhabitant of Boston in 1647, and sold his land at Dorchester in 1656. He was a shipbuilder. He married (first) in England, Joan ——— ; (second) Mildred ———, who survived him. His will was dated July 24, 1668. The will of his widow Mildred is dated September 20, 1680. Both died soon after the date of their wills. Children by first wife: Joseph, baptized February 3, 1639, in Boston; Experience, married Elizabeth Bolton or Botton; Temperance, baptized February 9, or 13, 1651; Joanna, baptized April 13, 1651. Children by second wife: Michael, mentioned below; Adingstill, died September 6, 1658; Abigail, died November 7, 1696; Lydia, married George Newell; Elizabeth, married Zachariah Phillips.

(II) Michael (2), son of Michael (1) Willis, was born November 11, 1652, in Boston and died 1711-12. He was a resident and taxpayer of Boston. He married Elizabeth Lowden, who survived him. She was admitted to the Second Church March 23, 1677.

She was a daughter of Richard Lowden. He was a seafaring man, and under date June 20, 1708, being in London, gave a power of attorney to his brother-in-law, John Ellis, of Boston. He died in London, about 1712. His widow Elizabeth was appointed administratrix, May 14, 1712. Administration was also granted to his widow in England, October 5, 1711, but her name is given as Mary. (It is still a legal custom to assume Mary when the given name of a woman is unknown, and Elizabeth, wife of Michael, being in America may have been unknown to the court.) Michael was described as late of the parish of St. Mary, Whitechapel (London), county of Middlesex. Children: Joseph, born January 4, 1680, died young; Abigail, born March 12, 1682 or 1689; Deliverance, November 1, 1684; Obadiah, March 5, 1686, died young; Hannah, June 14, 1688; Mildred, May 7, 1693; Michael, July 11, 1694; Ebenezer, 1697; Benjamin, 1702.

(III) Michael (3), son of Michael (2) Willis, was born in Boston, July 11, 1694, and was baptized in the First Church, July 15. He deeds land formerly owned by his grandfather, Michael, mentions his father and uncle Experience, and states that he was his father's only male heir, the others dying young. Michael married, December 6, 1716, Mary Mattox. She was admitted to the Second Church, February 12, 1715-16. Michael died in London, but the date is unknown.

(IV) Benjamin, only child of Michael (3) Willis, was born September 1, 1717, in Boston. He was a soldier in the French and Indian war, and was killed at the siege of Louisburg, in 1745. He lived in Medford and was town clerk. He married Ann Gammell, who was appointed administratrix April 29, 1746, in Boston. She died at Haverhill, March 14, 1780, having married twice after the death of Willis first, ——— Bowker, (second) ——— Knowlton.

(V) Benjamin (2), son of Benjamin (1) Willis, was born in Boston, January 10, 1743. He was a merchant and sea captain, living at Charlestown and Haverhill, Massachusetts. He followed the sea and was captain of a vessel at Surinam when the revolution broke out. He arrived home soon after the battle of Bunker Hill, and found his family had taken refuge in Lexington, whence he removed them to Haverhill. He married, in 1765, Mary Ball, of Charlestown, daughter of Captain Robert and Elizabeth (Davidson) Ball; she was born at Concord, September 16, 1742. Captain Willis was a representative to the general court from Haverhill, 1799-1800, and was admitted in 1780 to the

Fire Society of that town. His home was on Merrimac street, near Fleet, where the family lived until removing to Portland in 1803. Benjamin and his wife probably died here. He died at Haverhill, November 11, 1811, and was buried in the old Pentucket cemetery. On his gravestone is the epitaph: "Heaven gives us friends to bless the present scene. Removes them to prepare us for the next." He died intestate, and his widow Mary requests the court to appoint her son Robert administrator. She died at Haverhill, July 25, 1835, aged ninety-three, and her gravestone stands beside that of her husband. Children: Benjamin, mentioned below; Mary, born December 13, 1774; Ann, August 24, 1778; Elizabeth Ball, June 27, 1782; Robert Ball, March 13, 1784.

(VI) Benjamin (3), son of Benjamin (2) Willis, was born at Charlestown, Massachusetts, March 5, 1768, and was baptized March 6. After the family fled from Charlestown at the time of the battle of Bunker Hill, he lived at Haverhill. When a young man he sailed on a voyage to London on his father's brig, "Benjamin and Nancy", and met there John Dickinson, who assisted him in business. Mr. Willis became a leading merchant. His cargoes came usually to Newburyport in brigs and were transported to Haverhill in boats. In 1811 he built the Willis block just east of the bridge, the first brick block in the town. He was admitted to the Fire Society in 1794. In 1801 he was a petitioner for the aqueduct. He married, January 9, 1791, Mary McKinstry, at Governor Stark's home, Dunbarton, New Hampshire. She was born at Taunton, Massachusetts, August 17, 1770, daughter of Dr. William and Priscilla (Leonard) McKinstry. Her father was a loyalist, and at the time of the battle of Bunker Hill the family was living in Boston. Her mother Priscilla died at Haverhill, May 26, 1786, aged fifty-four. In June, 1803, Benjamin Willis made his home in Portland and remained there until 1815, when he moved to Fort Hill, Boston, 118 Purchase street, the northerly corner of Purchase and Oliver, then Belmont. He acquired much real estate in Boston, and left a large fortune for his day. He went to Europe in 1822, sailing from New York to Liverpool on the ship "Hercules", and visited St. Petersburg, Berlin, Dresden, and Vienna. His wife Mary died at her home in Boston, February 12, 1847. Portraits of Willis and his wife have been preserved. She is said to have been an estimable woman. "In her youth she was very handsome. She was a religious woman; for many years she communed at the Old South Church, Boston.

She was fond of reading and choice in the selection of books." She was buried in the Willis tomb in Portland. After her death, Benjamin Willis lived much of the time with his daughter, Mary Duncan, in Haverhill, and he died there October 1, 1853. In an obituary published at the time his character is described:

He was a man of great activity, energy and enterprise, and the success of his business transactions corresponded with the intelligence and vigour with which he pursued them. His death was calm and peaceful, and he experienced during his whole sickness a consciousness that he should not recover and an entire confidence in the goodness and resignation to the will of God, Who had preserved him so long through many and varied scenes; through the struggles of poverty in early life, and the temptations and vicissitudes of maturer years. From his quiet temperament he had enjoyed life to the full, and having exhausted it to the dregs, he was not unwilling to depart from it.

Children: 1. Benjamin, born November 16, 1791, died July 28, 1870. 2. William, born August 31, 1794, in Haverhill, died in Portland, February 17, 1870; graduate of Harvard College, in 1813; practiced law in Boston and Portland; author of "History of Portland" and many other historical works; state senator, 1855; mayor of Portland, in 1857; chairman of Maine presidential electors, 1860; railroad commissioner, president of Maine Central Railroad, vice-president of New England Historic Genealogical Society (LL.D. Bowdoin 1868). 3. George, mentioned below. 4. Thomas, March 16, 1800; 5. Henry, April 13, 1802. Born at Portland: 6. Mary, December 14, 1805; married James H. Duncan. 7. Elizabeth, October 25, 1807; married Henry Kinsman. 8. Thomas Leonard, April 4 or 14, 1812; married Charlotte E. Hall.

(VII) George, son of Benjamin (3) Willis, was born at Haverhill, Massachusetts, June 16, 1797, died October 24, 1844, at Munroe, Maine, and is buried in the family tomb at Portland. He went with the family to Portland when he was six years old. He became a merchant and entered partnership with his brother Benjamin, June 26, 1815, when their father moved to Boston. His home was on High street, Portland, in the house later occupied by the Cumberland Club. Afterward he lived on Park street.

He married (first) April 10, 1820, Caroline E. Hunnewell, born July 8, 1799, at Castine, Maine, daughter of Colonel Richard Hunnewell. She died September 1, 1821. He married (second) November 11, 1822, Clarissa May Hall, born June 3, 1799, died April 15 or 17, 1858, daughter of Caleb Brooks

Hall, of Bucksport, Maine. Her sister was wife of Thomas Leonard Willis, her brother-in-law. Child by first wife: Caroline Hunnewell, born February 21, 1821, died soon. Children by second wife: George Hall, mentioned below; Mary McKinstry, April 13, 1827, married George Warren Wyer; Clarissa May, November 11, 1828, died January 12, 1840; Caroline Hunnewell, July 8, 1830, died March 14, 1905, married Frederick Lyman; Charlotte Elizabeth, March 13, 1833, died February 23, 1885, married (first) Llewellyn True, (second) Gordon Z. Dimock; Anne Kinsman, August 2, 1834, married Samuel Parris; Benjamin, April 14, 1836, in Portland, died at Augusta, Maine, November 6, 1878, unmarried; Caleb Hall, September 4, 1837, died December 28, 1869, in Washington, D. C., unmarried; Emily Hall, born July 21, 1839, in Portland, died May 3, 1866, in Brooklyn.

(VIII) Captain George Hall Willis, son of George Willis, was born in Portland, June 28, 1825, died October 14, 1905, in Orange, New Jersey. He was educated in the public schools, and early in life began to follow the sea, becoming master of a vessel when he was about twenty-one. He married, at Portland, October 13, 1858, Harriet, daughter of Thomas Hammond, of Portland, and Sophia (Harris) Hammond, a native of Boston. After their marriage they made a voyage around Cape Horn in a sailing vessel. At the age of twenty-four he became a captain in the service of the Shippers Line of San Francisco, packets plying between San Francisco and New York. He commanded the first fast clipper, the "Ocean Telegraph", and later the "Ocean Express". This was the heyday of the Merchant Marine, and each captain exerted every effort to compass the distance between New York and San Francisco in the quickest time. Captain Willis was foremost among the navigators because of his knowledge of navigation, his skill and success. At the age of thirty-four years he retired from the sea and engaged in business in New York City as a ship broker. Twenty-one years before his death he retired from active business. In politics he was a Republican after that party was formed, though frequently supporting independent movements. His widow survives him, living at Orange, New Jersey. One who knew him wrote at the time of his death an obituary published in the *News*, from which we quote: "A firm believer in the early New England ideals, he was in his own life and character a consistent and thorough exponent of those ideals in sincerity and singleness of purpose, in freedom

from sham and cant, in rugged honesty and independence of view. No man, however, kept more thoroughly in touch with the trend of modern progress or has had a more intelligent appreciation of what is best in life to-day, while deploring those tendencies which exalt material progress at the sacrifice of the best standards of mental and moral development; his faith in the final triumph of American patriotism and good citizenship was firm and abiding. Always kindly, courteous and helpful, his loss will be keenly felt by a large number, who always found him a frank and intelligent counsellor, a sympathetic neighbor and friend." Children: Paul, mentioned below; Isabel, born December 24, 1866; Kate, January 31, 1869.

(IX) Paul, son of Captain George Hall Willis, was born in Orange, New Jersey, December 21, 1864. He attended private schools in his native town and the Stevens Institute of Technology at Hoboken, New Jersey, from which he was graduated in 1895. He was with George S. Morrison, civil engineer, for several years and since 1891 has been with the Kenwood Bridge Company, of which he is now president. He is a member of the Engineers' Club, the Union League Club, the University Club, the Kenwood Club, the Homewood Club of Chicago and the New England Society of that city. In politics he is a Republican. He is a member of St. Paul's Protestant Episcopal Church. His office is at 68 West Monroe street, Chicago.

He married, April 12, 1899, in Chicago, Daisy Jameson Hubbard, born in Chicago, October 10, 1873, daughter of Henry Hubbard. Children, born in Chicago: Marion Hubbard, born March 1, 1900; George Hall, May 3, 1904; Paul Jr., September 19, 1908.

PAIGE Probably the earliest record of the Page family was from 1151 to 1157, when John de Pagham was the fourth bishop of Worcester, England. Pagham, Pagenham and Pageham are the same names, the spelling being changed gradually in the records, until it became Page of Pageham, and finally Page and Paige. About 1600 Sir Gregory Page, Knight, had sons who came to America. Sir Gregory, created baronet December 3, 1714, of Greenwich, Kent, England, was his son; the baronetcy became extinct August 4, 1774. Their coat-of-arms was: Azure, a fesse indented between 3 martlets or, sometimes or and azure. Crest: A demi-horse per pole dancettée (or and az.). Many branches in England have used this coat-of-arms, and it may have been a late grant to the baronets. The arms give a distinct proof that the Page and Pagenham families are the same, for there is no other form given. Sir Hugo, Knight, must have had arms, and "William, the Crusader", 1271, at the time of the last crusade, also must have had arms, so they were evidently recorded as Pagenham. About 1310, in the time of Edward I., the coat-of-arms of Sir Edmon de Pagenham (Paganham or Pakenham), and later of John de Pagenham were: Quarterly or. and gules in the 1st quarter, an eagle displayed vert. mantling or and gules. Crest: Out of a mural crown or. a demi eagle gules. On one banner is placed the same coat-of-arms as on the family flag, and on another is placed that of the branch called Page or Paige, of Devonshire, England. These arms were: Argent a bend between 3 eagles displayed all sable. Crest: An eagle ermine. To this family belonged Nicholas Paige, of Rumney Marsh, colonel of the Second Regiment of Foot, Suffolk county, Massachusetts, 1717. He came from Plymouth, Devonshire, England, in 1665, and used a demi-eagle instead of eagle ermine for his crest. Deacon Robert Page married Lucia ———, and came from Ormsby, Yorkshire, England, or nearby, in Massachusetts. Francis Page, of Bedford, England, 1594-1678, had a son, Colonel John Page, of Williamsburg, Virginia, who was born at Bedfont, 1627, and died in 1692.

(I) Nathaniel Paige, the immigrant ancestor of this family, is thought to have come from England to Roxbury, Massachusetts, about 1685, with his wife and three children. The first record of him found in this country is on March 10, 1685-86, in a deposition recorded with Suffolk Deeds. On June 2, 1686, when the government was changed and the first charter cancelled, he was appointed one of the two marshals, and it was "ordered that the President have an honorable maintenance when 'tis known how the revenue will arise, and that Mr. Paige have five pounds a quarter for his attendance on the President." On August 2, 1686, he was licensed as an innholder of Roxbury. He was one of the eight original purchasers of the territory now in Hardwick from the Indian sachems, December 27, 1686, and on January 27, 1687, the same persons bought the territory now in Leicester and Spencer. On March 1, 1687-88, he purchased of George Grimes a farm of two hundred and fifty acres in the part now in eastern Bedford, then in Billerica, and on this farm he lived the remainder of his life. He was a well-to-do farmer, as shown by the inventory of his estate, which included a servant valued at fifteen pounds. He left the real estate in Billerica and lands near Quaboag

and Worcester to his two sons, the elder receiving a double portion, and his daughters received two hundred acres in Dedham which he bought of the Indians in 1687. He died in Boston, April 12, 1692. His will was dated April 11, 1692, and called him of "Bilrekey, in the County of Middlesex, New England, yeoman, being sick and weak of body." He married Joanna ———, who died in 1724. On July 4, 1724, her sons divided the land left by her. Children: Nathaniel, born about 1679; Elizabeth, born probably about 1681; Sarah, born probably about 1683; James, baptized in Roxbury, November 28, 1686, died July 31, 1687; Christopher, mentioned below.

(II) Deacon Christopher Paige, son of Nathaniel Paige, was born in Billerica, February 6, 1690-91, died March 10, 1774. He was a farmer and joiner. He lived on the east road to Gilbertville, at the place marked A. Warner on the map, and he settled there probably early in 1735, coming from Bedford. He was active in the management of the common property of the proprietors and in the organization of the town and church, and he was often the agent of the settlers in transacting business with the proprietors, especially in the final and successful effort to procure an incorporation as a town. In 1739 he was moderator of the first town meeting, selectman for seven years, assessor for five years. Until 1761 he was moderator of all the meetings of proprietors of Hardwick, and on May 16, 1757, compensation was granted to him "for service done the proprietors as their agent to the General Court." His name was first on the list of members when the church was organized, November 17, 1736, and on December 3, 1736, he was elected its first deacon, a position which he resigned April 13, 1749, when he became a member of the Nitchawag (now Petersham) church. This caused a breach between the two churches which was not healed for about twenty years. At the time of his death, the *Massachusetts Gazette* said. March 31, 1774: "At Hardwick, Deacon Christopher Paige, aged 83 years and 21 days, in a comfortable hope of a better life; he left a widow, and has had 12 children, 9 now living and 3 dead, 81 grandchildren, 66 living and 15 dead. A funeral sermon was preached by the Rev. Mr. Hutchinson at his funeral, on the Monday following." Only eleven children are found recorded.

He married (first) Joanna ———, who died October 27, 1719. He married (second) May 23, 1720, Elizabeth, daughter of Deacon George Reed, of Woburn, and she died in 1786, aged eighty-six years. Children: Joanna, born August 10, 1717; Christopher,

June 11, 1721; William, May 2, 1723; George, mentioned below; Timothy, May 24, 1727; Jonas, September 19, 1729; Elizabeth, October 3, 1731, died young; Lucy, February 22, 1733-34; Nathaniel, May 12, 1736; John, July 6, 1738; Elizabeth, June 7, 1743.

(III) George, son of Deacon Christopher Paige, was born in Billerica, June 17, 1725, died May 8, 1781. He was a farmer, and lived on his father's homestead. He married, June 4, 1752, Rosilla, daughter of Nathaniel Whitcomb. She married (second) March 17, 1790, Captain William Breckenridge, of Ware, Massachusetts, and after his death she returned to Hardwick, where she lived on the homestead with her son Paul. She and her sister Mary, who married Paul Dean, are said to have been noted for their industry and energy. She died October 29, 1807. Children: Nathaniel, born January 11, 1754; Asa, mentioned below; George, March 9, 1758; Rhoda, October 5, 1760; Nathan, August 5, 1762; Paul, February 12, 1765; Peirce, July 16, 1768; Anna, July 23, 1771.

(IV) Asa, son of George Paige, was born January 25, 1756. He moved to Barnard, Vermont, where he died December 20, 1819. He was a farmer. He married, at Barnard, February 19, 1789, Lydia, daughter of Elkanah Steward; she died June 25, 1847, aged nearly eighty years. Children, born in Barnard: Rosilla, born February 25, 1790; Martin, December 8, 1791; Anna, December 19, 1793, died September 8, 1794; Asa, mentioned below; Lydia, born October 22, 1797, died March 3, 1798; Cyrus, January 19, 1799; Leonard, April 7, 1801; Louisa, September 5, 1803; Hiram, December 3, 1805; Luthera, July 20, 1809.

(V) Asa (2), son of Asa (1) Paige, was born in Barnard, Vermont, August 18, 1795, died January 23, 1862. He married —— Fay. Children: Eliakim F., mentioned below; Martha.

(VI) Eliakim F., son of Asa (2) Paige, was born in Barnard, Vermont, October 13, 1819, died in Rutland, Vermont, in 1896. He married Alice M., born August 7, 1824, daughter of Daniel and Polly Hewitt Billings. Children: Frank, born January 6, 1857; Emma L., April 13, 1859, married Frank Russell; Charles E., mentioned below; Alice M., born June 1, 1866, married Orley S. Mason.

(VII) Charles E., son of Eliakim F. Paige, was born in Barnard, Vermont, August 31, 1862. He received his early education in the public schools of his native town, and learned the trade of carpenter. For many years he was in successful business as a contractor and builder in Rutland, Vermont, and he built the Mead Building, the Masonic Temple and the City Hall in Rutland, besides many other important buildings and residences. He was accounted one of the best architects and builders in this section of the state. He served the city of Rutland first as alderman, then president of board of aldermen, and then as mayor, and was prominent and influential in public affairs. At present he is living at Covina, California, engaged in fruit culture there, having a large orange grove. In religion he is a Methodist, in politics a Republican. He is prominent in Free Masonry, belonging to Blue Lodge, Chapter, Commandery, attaining the thirty-second degree.

He married Alice Elvira, born in Richford, Vermont, in 1859, died in Rutland, Vermont, July 14, 1912, daughter of Ahira and Sarah Jane (Newton) Heath, granddaughter of Elisha and Mary (Noyes) Heath, great-granddaughter of Samuel Heath, a native of Connecticut. Children: Wendell Arthur Heath, mentioned below; Lillian Alice Mildred, deceased; Edith Evangeline, deceased.

(VIII) Dr. Wendell Arthur Heath Paige, son of Charles E. Paige, was born in Rutland, Vermont, April 25, 1886. He attended the public schools there and was graduated from the Rutland high school. He received his medical education at the George Washington University at Washington, D. C., from which he was graduated in the class of 1910 with the degree of Doctor of Medicine. After extensive experience in hospitals as an interne, he located for general practice of medicin at Pittsford, Vermont.

BACKUS This name is one of those American patronymics that appear somewhat puzzling to the etymologist. There is no name of that kind to be found anywhere in England and yet it is claimed that the family is English in the origin of its first ancestor. The name might be Dutch, or German or belong to some other speech. One derivation given at haphazard is that it may be a corruption of Backhouse or Bakehouse. This gives the name an English look and may be its origin. At any rate the tradition seems to be to the effect that the stock from which the family sprang belonged to the old New England Puritan element. In Caulkins' "History of Norwich" is said of the Backus family: "It is interesting to observe how rapidly the settlement advanced in prosperity and comfort. This family and others in the course of a single generation grew strong and luxuriant, throwing out buds and branches of rich and noble growth". A modern genealogical publication says that the Backus family were of old Puritan stock and came from Connecticut, where they were originally owners of one-twentieth of the site of the town of Norwich, Connecticut.

(I) William Backus, the immigrant ancestor of the Backus family in America, was probably born in Norwich, England, died at Norwich, Connecticut. He came from England probably about 1636 and was living at Saybrook, Connecticut, in 1637. About 1659 he moved to Norwich in the same state, being one of the first settlers under the leadership of the Rev. James Fitch and John Mason. He brought with him three daughters and two sons and his stepson, Thomas Bingham. Since the young men were near mature age and since he made over his settlement to his son William Stephen his sons are regarded as first proprietors and his name does not appear on the records as such. He is said (by the consent of the others, he being the oldest man) to have given the town its name from the place in England where he had come. He died soon after his arrival in the colony, being of an advanced age. He is said to have been the first Englishman and the second person to die in the settlement. He married (first) Sarah Charles; (second) Mrs. Anne Bingham. The children were: William Stephen, mentioned below; a daughter, who married John Reynolds; another daughter who married Benjamin Crane, and another daughter who married John Barclay.

(II) William Stephen, son of William Backus, was born in 1660. He received in course of time the title of lieutenant and was one of the six Norwich legatees of Joshua Arma, one of the original proprietors of Norwich, Connecticut. In 1693 Lieutenant Backus settled in Windham, Connecticut, being one of the first twenty-two inhabitants of that town. The present Windham Green was part of the home lot of William Stephen Backus. He married Elizabeth, daughter of William Pratt, of Saybrook, Connecticut. The children were: William; Samuel, mentioned below; John; Joseph, married Elizabeth Huntington; Nathaniel, married Elizabeth, daughter of T. Tracy.

(III) Samuel, son of William Stephen and Elizabeth (Pratt) Backus, was born in 1693. He is described as a quiet, entertaining farmer, prosperous in his own business, but having little to do in public affairs. "He was an affectionate father and kind husband". The family had removed from the original home lot near the Landing to what is now known as the Yantic. Here he erected a grist mill— the second in the settlement—receiving special grants from the town, and commenced the erection of iron works. He married Sarah Gard in 1719, and had nine children, of whom Nathaniel, mentioned below, was one.

(IV) Nathaniel, son of Samuel and Sarah (Gard) Backus, was born January 13, 1728, died December 24, 1815. He married M. Elizabeth, daughter of Robert Hebard, the ceremony being performed probably about the year 1750.

(V) Elijah, son of Nathaniel and M. Elizabeth (Hebard) Backus, was born July 23, 1755. He was an active participant in the revolutionary war, being engaged in the battles of Germantown and Monmouth. He married, April 21, 1786, M. Trifina Cross.

(VI) Gurdon, son of Elijah and M. Trifina (Cross) Backus, was born in Windham county, Connecticut, in 1800, died at Brandon, Vermont, in 1871. He acquired a good literary education in the common schools of his native town, entered a theological seminary, and was ordained a clergyman of the Methodist Episcopal denomination. He officiated as pastor at Bridgewater and also acted in the capacity of presiding elder for a number of years. He married (first) Wealthy Ann Hoisington; (second) Perley Flint; (third) Sarah Chapman. Child by first marriage: Quimby S., mentioned below; by third marriage: Phoebe Hawkins, Caroline, Emeline, Justin, Harriet, Anna, Rev. Gurdon, Joseph, Clark, Martin.

(VII) Quimby S., son of Gurdon and Wealthy Ann (Hoisington) Backus, was born July 23, 1838, at Bridgewater, Vermont. His preliminary education was obtained in the public schools of his native town, and this was supplemented by attendance at the public schools of Brandon and Brandon Seminary, from which institution he was graduated at the age of sixteen years. He then removed to Woodstock, Vermont, where he learned the trade of machinist, which he followed with success for many years, being employed by the Howe Scale Company and having the distinction of making the first scales made in Brandon for the company. In 1861 he was engaged as a toolmaker in a gun shop in Windsor, the firm having a contract for supplying guns to the United States government. Later he was employed in the railroad shops at Rutland, Vermont, and subsequently was engaged in the manufacture of all kinds of machinery at Winchendon, Massachusetts. Mr. Backus patented and was for several years employed in the manufacture of vises; he later patented a bit brace, the first made that was adjustable to any size of bit. He then removed to Millers Falls, where he manufactured machine specialties, which were all his own patents and in this line of business he continued until 1876. He invented the Backus heater and established a manufactory in Philadelphia in 1888, remaining until 1892. He next located in Williamsport, Pennsylvania, where he conducted the business until 1901, removing at that time to Brandon, Vermont, where he erected a large manufactory and foundry, which gave employment to nearly a hundred people. The plant covers an area of five acres and they established offices and stores in Philadelphia, New York, Boston, San Francisco, and other large cities, besides giving the agency of the heater to private dealers throughout the country.

Mr. Backus is a Republican, a strong local man, and always took an active part in all campaigns. He was elected senator from Rutland county, in 1902, was a member of the committee on claims and the standing committee of the manufacturers and also served in the capacity of chairman of the committee on joint rules, taking an aggressive part in all discussions. He was a member and served as second lieutenant of the "Allen Grays", a company of Vermont militia, but being engaged in gun making during the progress of the civil war he was exempt from active service, but sent a substitute. He has attained a prominent position in the Masonic fraternity, having taken the thirty-second degree in the Scottish Rite, and is a noble of the Mystic Shrine.

He married, in 1858, Lavina A., daughter of Oliver E. and Emeline (Wood) Lawrence, the former named being born in Chittenden county, Vermont, and the latter at Brandon, Vermont. Mr. Lawrence is a member of the Baptist church as was also his wife, who died at the age of eighty-two years. Amos Lawrence, grandfather of Mrs. Backus, was a shoemaker by trade, served in the revolutionary war, and died at Brandon, Vermont, aged seventy-four. The children of Oliver E. Lawrence were Samuel L., who was a resident of Rutland, Vermont; James, a resident in Hubbardton, Vermont; Charles, an attorney of Philadelphia; Lavina A., who married Quimby S. Backus, above mentioned; Ellen; Porter Lawrence. The children of Quimby S. and Lavina A. (Lawrence) Backus are: Fred Elsworth, mentioned below; Nellie Everetta, born at Windsor, Vermont, married John O. Bowman, a prominent lawyer of Philadelphia, Pennsylvania, the children being Fred Quimby and Miriam Lawrence Bowman.

(VIII) Fred Elsworth, son of Quimby S. and Lavina A. (Lawrence) Backus, was born at Brandon, Vermont, August 3, 1861. He acquired his education at Brandon and later at Stebbins Institute, a business college of Springfield, Massachusetts. He later became a member of the firm of the Backus Company, founded by Quimby S. Backus, he having the management of the manufacturing department, while his father attended to the financial and sale department. He, like his father, is connected with all the Masonic bodies up to and including the thirty-second degree; has been secretary of the Chapter, senior deacon of Blue Lodge, and held offices in the Consistory. He married, in June, 1898, Maud M., born in Brandon, Vermont, daughter of Darwin Peck, having one daughter, Beatrice Carile Backus, born July 19, 1900.

William Adams, immigrant ancestor of this branch of the family, came to New England when he was fifteen years of age, in the ship "Elizabeth and Ann", in May, 1635, and settled at Cambridge. He was admitted a freeman May 22, 1638. He removed to Ipswich, Massachusetts, and was a member of the grand jury in 1642. He was selectman in 1646, and died in 1661. His widow was living in 1681. He probably lived in or near what is now Hamilton. Children: William; John, born about 1631; Samuel; Hannah, married, December 6, 1659, Francis Munsy; Mary, married, February 29, 1660, Thomas French; Nathaniel, of whom further.

(II) Nathaniel, son of William Adams, was born about 1641, died at Ipswich, April 11, 1715. He married, June 30, 1668, Mercy, daughter of Thomas Dickinson, of Rowley, Massachusetts. She died December 12, 1735. He was admitted a freeman May 27, 1674. Children, born at Ipswich: Nathaniel (2), of whom further; Thomas, born June 14, 1672; Mercy, April 1, 1674, died June 13, 1674; Sarah, July 19, 1675; William, June 20, 1678, probably died young; Mercy, March 18, 1680; Samuel, June 29, 1682.

(III) Nathaniel (2), son of Nathaniel (1) Adams, was born at Ipswich, July 11, 1670, died August 31, 1736. He married, in January, 1693, Abigail Kimball, died May 30, 1756, daughter of Caleb Kimball, of Ipswich. Children, born at Ipswich: Nathaniel, born March 1, 1695, died at Boston, October 25, 1712; William (2), of whom further; Abigail, December 6, 1699; Caleb, February 13, 1702; Mercy, February 25, 1704; Robert, October 14, 1705; Anna, March 25, 1708; Mary, 1714.

(IV) William (2), son of Nathaniel (2) Adams, was born at Ipswich, November 26, 1696. He married, in 1716, Mary, daughter of John Warner, of Ipswich. Children, born in Ipswich: Mary, born 1717; Abigail, 1719; William, 1723; Nathaniel, 1727; Sarah, 1729; John of whom further.

(V) John, son of William Adams, was born in Ipswich, in 1731. He married, July 20, 1754, Mary Lamson of Ipswich. Ipswich Hamlet, part of Ipswich, later called Hamilton, was the home of the family, which was later among the early settlers of Moultonborough, New Hampshire. When the church was organized Mary, wife of John Adams, was one of the original signers of the covenant. John Adams was selectman in 1779-80, and other years, and was active during the revolution in the cause of the patriots. Children: Abner, of whom further; Isaac, baptized at Ipswich, February 10, 1765; Aaron, baptized January 11, 1767; David, baptized May 7, 1769; perhaps others.

(VI) Abner, son of John Adams, was born at Ipswich, Massachusetts, October 31, 1761. He moved to Moultonborough with his parents just before the revolutionary war. He married Deborah Randall, born June 11, 1764. They had a son Abner (2), of whom further.

(VII) Abner (2), son of Abner (1) Adams, was born in Moultonborough, New Hampshire, December 10, 1789, died there December 23, 1870. He was a school teacher for many years in his native town. He married, January 6, 1830, Susan Meloon, born February 8, 1801, died March 10, 1878. Children: Alvin L., born December 11, 1830, died January 31, 1861; Thomas S., of whom further; George A., September 3, 1836, died August 1, 1870; Lavina, born February 15, 1838, died October 8, 1855.

(VIII) Thomas S., son of Abner (2) Adams, was born in Moultonborough, New Hampshire, June 10, 1834, died October 15, 1862. He received his early education in the public schools. At the beginning of the civil war he enlisted in Company K, Fourteenth Regiment New Hampshire Volunteer Infantry, and died of typhoid fever while in the service. He married Emily A. Hawkins, born in 1838, died in 1882, daughter of Jacob Hawkins. Children of Thomas S. and Emily A. Adams: Charles, died in infancy; Alvin Edgar, born March 28, 1859, died March 2, 1893; Arthur Lamson, of whom further.

(IX) Arthur Lamson, son of Thomas S. Adams, was born in Moultonborough, New Hampshire, September 2, 1860. He attended the public schools of his native town, and the commercial department of the New Hampshire Institute, at New Hampton, New Hampshire. In 1883 he engaged as a contractor in the business of laying concrete pavements, and has continued in business at Rutland since 1893.

He is a member of Center Lodge, Ancient Free and Accepted Masons; Davenport Chapter, Royal Arch Masons; Killington Commandery, Knights Templar; Cairo Temple, Mystic Shrine; Knights of Pythias; Killington Lodge, Independent Order of Odd Fellows; and Benevolent and Protective Order of Elks. He is an attendant of the Congregational church. In politics he is a Republican.

He married (first) in 1886, Lillian Page, of Bridgewater, New Hampshire, daughter of Nathaniel and Mary J. Page. He married (second) Jennie I., daughter of John Spicer, of St. Lawrence county, New York. She died December 4, 1895. He married (third) Nellie E., daughter of John S. and Helen Billings, of Rutland. Children by first wife: Donna E., born March, 1888; Gladys C., died aged five years. Child by second wife: Irene Lamson, born December 3, 1895.

ROBINSON   Robert Robinson, progenitor of this family, lived near Cambridge, New York. He belonged to the Robinson family of Vermont, the early ancestry of which will be found elsewhere in this work in connection with the Robinson family of Rutland county, Vermont. The first federal census, taken in 1790, shows that in that year a Robert Robinson was living at Watervliet, New York, and had in his family two males over sixteen, one male under that age and three females.

(II) Ira, son of Robert Robinson, was born near Cambridge, New York, December 31, 1789, died September 22, 1866. He married Betsey Cushing, born March 11, 1793, died December 20, 1872. Children: Charles, born November 21, 1815, died in 1868; Benjamin F., of whom further; Sayles, February, 1829, died February 21, 1891; Harriet, February 17, 1835, died August 23, 1909, married John Walker; Zenas; Charles; George; Hiram; Henry; Jane, married —— Corbett; Almon.

(III) Benjamin Franklin, son of Ira Robinson, was born June 25, 1817, in Salem, New York, died September 25, 1863. He was educated in the public schools and engaged in business afterward at Salem, New York, as a merchant and harness maker. He also held the office of village clerk for a number of years. He was a harness maker by trade, and enlisted in the civil war from Salem as a saddler and harness maker in a New York regiment. He married Catherine Dodd, born February 16, 1821, died December 23, 1862, daughter of Henry and Anna (Montgomery) Dodd, of Salem, New York. Children, born at Salem: 1. Anna M., born October 31, 1841; married Darwin C. Pierce, of Malone, New

York; lives in Rutland, Vermont. Children: Elizabeth A., January 20, 1862, died February 6, 1862; Lizzie A., November 6, 1865, died March 21, 1899; Henry Collins, born February 17, 1868, died April 14, 1896; Lyman Russell, February 16, 1870, died April 18, 1877; Darwin Wilson, September 2, 1873, lives in Los Angeles, California, married Bessie Faulkner. 2. Elizabeth C., September 12, 1846, died April 3, 1859. 3. Mary Dodd, June 30, 1849; married L. H. Tottingham, of Shoreham, Vermont. 4. Fannie, July 28, 1852, died April 28, 1878. 5. Delia Hall, June 14, 1855. 6. Mary Elizabeth, March 1, 1858, died April 5, 1859. 7. Frank Pierce, of whom further.

(IV) Frank Pierce, son of Benjamin Franklin Robinson, was born at Salem, New York, May 9, 1860. He received his early education in the public schools of Rutland, Vermont. He came there with his sister, Mrs. Anna M. Pierce, when a young boy, and made his home in Rutland afterwards. He worked in various establishments in Rutland as a bookkeeper. Since 1897 he has been in business on his own account, as a dealer in wood and coal. He is an enterprising and successful merchant. Mr. Robinson is a member of Center Lodge, Ancient Free and Accepted Masons; Davenport Chapter, Royal Arch Masons; Killington Commandery, Knights Templar; Cairo Temple, Nobles of the Mystic Shrine; and Rutland Lodge, Independent Order of Odd Fellows. He is an active member of the Congregational church, chairman of its music committee, and member of the prudential board. In politics he is a Republican.

He married, in 1889, Mary M. Smith, of Manchester, Vermont, daughter of James and —— (Howard) Smith. Children, born at Rutland: 1. Edward Dodd, born in 1890; in business with his father. 2. Sylvia C., 1892. 3. Frank Robert, 1897.

BURDICK There is good reason to believe that the surname Burdick is identical with Burditt (also spelled Burdett, Burdette, etc.). The spelling Burdick is not given in English works on surnames, and like many American names it is probably a variation in spelling from the English Burdette, etc. We find William Burdick master of the ship "Hopewell" which brought many colonists to this country in 1635. In the early records the immigrant ancestor of the Burdick family had his name spelled Berdick, Burdick and Burdett. Robert Burdett, who may be related to Robert Burdick, of this sketch, was born in 1633, came to Malden, Massachusetts, when a young man. The names of his children, Joseph, Thomas, Hannah, Mary, Sarah, and Ruth are similar to those of the Rhode Island family. The Burdett family in England is ancient and distinguished.

(I) Robert Burdick, the immigrant, was an early settler of Newport and Westerly, Rhode Island. He was baptized by Rev. Joseph Torrey, November 19, 1652, and was admitted a freeman in 1676. In 1660 a company of Newport men who bought of the Indians a tract at Misquamicut offered inducements to members who would settle. Massachusetts claimed jurisdiction over the territory, calling it Southerton. Burdick was one of the pioneers with Tobias Saunders and Joseph Clarke. These three were arrested by Walter Palmer, constable, November 1, 1661, and soon afterward Burdick and Saunders were brought before Governor John Endicott, charged with forcible entry and intrusion into the bounds of Southerton in the Pequot country. Both declined to recognize the jurisdiction of Massachusetts, and were committed to prison, refusing to give bail, and after a year of imprisonment they were exchanged for prisoners taken by the Rhode Island authorities. King Charles II. decided the dispute in favor of Rhode Island. Burdick became one of the twenty-four incorporators of the town of Westerly, Rhode Island, and held various town offices. He took the oath of allegiance, May 17, 1671, and again September 17, 1676. He was deputy to the assembly in 1680-83-85. During King Philip's war his family returned to Newport and lived with Samuel Hubbard, but Burdick remained most of the time at Westerly. He made an agreement with his son-in-law, Joseph Crandall, to care for him the remainder of his life, in consideration of the homestead. His estate was divided by agreement, October 25, 1692.

He married, November 2, 1655, Ruth Hubbard, born January 11, 1640, died in 1691, daughter of Samuel and Tacy (Cooper) Hubbard. Her father was born in Mendelsham, county Suffolk, England, in 1610, son of James and Naomi (Cocke) Hubbard. James Hubbard's father was declared by Samuel Hubbard to be the Thomas Hubbard mentioned in Fox's "Book of Martyrs". Naomi Cocke was a daughter of Thomas Cocke, of Ipswich, England. In 1675 Samuel Hubbard wrote in his diary: "I have a Testament of my grandfather Cocke's, printed in 1549, which he hid in his bed-straw, lest it should be found and burned in Queen Mary's days." This Testament was given by Samuel Hubbard to his granddaughter, Naomi Burdick, who married Jonathan Rogers, and it is said that this

Russell E. Burdick

Testament is now in the library of Alfred University, and known as the Rogers Bible. Samuel Hubbard came from England to Salem, Massachusetts, in October, 1633, and was in Watertown the next year. He was admitted a freeman, March 4, 1634, and joined the church about the same time. He removed to Windsor, where he married, January 4, 1636, Tacy Cooper. Hubbard removed to Springfield, May 10, 1639, and was one of the founders of the church and became a prominent citizen. He and his wife became Baptists and being threatened with imprisonment for their views while at Fairfield, Connecticut, they removed, October 2, 1648, to Rhode Island, arriving October 12, as recorded in Samuel's diary. He joined the Baptist church in Newport, November 3, 1648. Ruth Hubbard was "the first child on record at Springfield." Children of Robert and Ruth (Hubbard) Burdick: Robert, married Dorcas Lewis; Hubbard, married Hannah Maxson; Thomas, of whom further; Naomi, married Jonathan Rogers; Ruth, married John Phillips; Benjamin, married and had eight children; Samuel, married Mary Bliven; Tacy, married Joseph Maxson; Deborah, married Joseph Crandall.

(II) Thomas, son of Robert Burdick, was born about 1660, perhaps earlier, if Robert Burdick married twice. His name appears on a list of freemen of Westerly, May 18, 1669, and he took the oath of allegiance, September 17, 1679. He and his wife Martha were living in Westerly, May 19, 1694. He and four brothers were among the purchasers of vacant Indian lands in the Narragansett region, October 2, 1711. He removed to Stonington, about 1718, and bought land there of Edward Denison. The records show deeds of land to his children, among whom was Samuel Hubbard, of whom further.

(III) Samuel Hubbard, son of Thomas Burdick, was born at Westerly, or vicinity, about 1700. He was a prominent citizen of Stonington, land-owner, town officer, selectman from 1765 to 1772, and perhaps other years. He was commissioned ensign of the Fifth and later of the Sixth Company, Eighth Regiment, under Colonel Christopher Avery, in 1744. In 1750 he was commissioned captain of the Sixth Company. He married, at Westerly, November 5, 1731, Avis Maxson, born December 27, 1712, in Westerly, daughter of John and Judith (Clarke) Maxson, granddaughter of Rev. Joseph and Bethia (Hubbard) Clarke, and great-granddaughter of Samuel and Tacy (Cooper) Hubbard, of previous mention. Among their children was Samuel Hubbard, of whom further.

(IV) Samuel Hubbard (2), son of Samuel Hubbard (1) Burdick, was born at Stonington, August 19, 1734, died February 4, 1813, in the seventy-ninth year of his age. Elder John S. Burdick of the Sabbatarian church was a brother. Samuel H. went to the Chenango country in 1791, returning to Rhode Island with the other pioneers for the winter. He located at Five Corners. He married, October 31, 1757, at Hopkinton, Rhode Island, Amie Maccoon (by Justice Simeon Perry). Children, born at Stonington: Stephen, born August 23, 1758; Margaret, February 17, 1761; Elizabeth, September 19, 1764; Samuel Hubbard, February 25, 1767; Amy, March 22, 1769; James Coon, of whom further; Charles, June 1, 1775.

(V) James Coon, son of Samuel Hubbard (2) Burdick, was born at Stonington, Connecticut, March 29, 1771. He was a soldier from Madison, New York, in the war of 1812. He married, September 15, 1798, Hannah Alexander, also born in Stonington. Children: 1. Harriet, born May 31, 1799, died April 28, 1839; married, September, 1817, Oliver Coon. 2. Fannie, born February 17, 1801, died September 10, 1825; married William D. Burdick. 3. Alvah, born March 3, 1803, died unmarried, September 27, 1872. 4. Stiles, born May 24, 1805, died October 25, 1830, unmarried. 5. Phylura, born May 7, 1808, died April 8, 1830, unmarried. 6. Osmond Alexander, born May 25, 1810; married, May 14, 1834, Ammorillius Vincent. 7. Russell Wells, of whom further.

(VI) Russell Wells, son of James Coon Burdick, was born at Alfred, New York, October 1, 1818. He was a farmer and general merchant at Alfred. He married Malvina Amanda Middaugh, born September 11, 1822, now living with her son, Russell Emmett. She is a daughter of Abraham and Elizabeth (Weaver) Middaugh. Children: 1. Harriet, born May 24, 1844; married Frank M. Beyea. 2. Frances, born February 5, 1846, died unmarried, aged eighteen years. 3. Russell Emmett, of whom further. 4. Elizabeth, born September 2, 1850; married A. E. Bowler, of Cleveland, Ohio. 5. Mary, born July 25, 1853; married Frederick Chase, of Alfred. 6. Estella, born November 27, 1856; married Horace Edwards, of Mentor, Ohio, and had Cedric and Leita Edwards. 7. Herbert Wells, born at Alfred, May 19, 1860; married Stella Pease, and had Herbert E., Marie and Mildred. 8. Myra E., born December 8, 1862, of Cleveland, unmarried.

(VII) Captain Russell Emmett Burdick, son of Russell Wells Burdick, was born at Alfred, New York, May 28, 1848. He attended the public schools of his native town and Alfred University, graduating in the class of 1869. He settled in Cleveland, Ohio, in 1869, and then for a year and a half was clerk for the Traveler's Insurance Company of Hartford, Connecticut. In 1873, in partnership with Mr. Bowler, he established the firm of Bowler & Burdick, jewelers, and the business has been prosperous to the present time. It was incorporated in 1881 as the Bowler & Burdick Company, of which Mr. Burdick is now the president and treasurer. The company makes a specialty of the importation of diamonds and precious stones, maintaining a purchasing office at No. 6 Tulpstraat, Amsterdam, Holland, where Captain Burdick spends a portion of his time each year in the interest of his company. The place of business is 627-31 Euclid avenue, Cleveland.

Captain Burdick was for many years active in the state militia and was captain of Troop A of the Ohio National Guard Cavalry. His troop was mustered into the federal service at the beginning of the Spanish war as part of the First Ohio Cavalry. Captain Burdick served with his command through the war, rendezvousing in Chickamauga, Tennessee, Lakeland, Florida, and Huntsville, Alabama. During the seventeen years in which he served in the militia Captain Burdick took part with his troop in every presidential inaugural parade, beginning with that of Garfield. He has served on the staffs of General Horace Porter, 1897, General Francis Greene, 1901, General Granville M. Dodge, 1905, and General J. F. Bell, 1909. He has had the honor of giving his name to a camp of the United Spanish War Veterans in Cleveland, Russell E. Burdick Camp, No. 41, Department of Ohio, United Spanish War Veterans. He is a prominent Free Mason, having taken the thirty-two degrees of Scottish Rite Masonry, and is a member of Lodge, Chapter, Council, Commandery and Mystic Shrine.

He is also a member of the Chamber of Commerce of Cleveland, the Union Club, the Clifton Club, the Colonial Club, the Euclid Golf Club. In 1909-10 he was commander of the Ohio Commandery of the National Military Order of Foreign Wars of the United States. He is a member of the Naval Military Order of the Spanish American War. For several years he was on the boards of directors of several Cleveland banks. He is a president of the Clifton Park Land Improvement Company; trustee of Alfred University, of Alfred, New York; member of the New England Society of Cleveland and the Western Reserve. In politics he is a Republican. He resides at 1945 East Seventy-fifth street.

He married, in May, 1873, Mary Hoyt McCutcheon, born in March, 1852, daughter of Joseph and Mary McCutcheon. Children: 1. Arling E., born July 14, 1875, in Cleveland, died aged seven years. 2. Bessie May, born at Cleveland, September 12, 1878; married Robert C. Rathburn, of Englewood, New Jersey, and has three children: Mary and Elizabeth (twins), born in 1908, and Juliette Bleeker Rathburn. 3. Arline, born in Cleveland, March 7, 1887. 4. Joseph, born in Cleveland, March 1, 1889, died in infancy. 5. Carlton Wheeler, born in Cleveland, October 11, 1892.

RICHMOND The surname Richmond had its origin in Brittany, France, and is derived from the French words "riche" and "monte" or "monde". In English history it first appears as Rychemond, afterwards as Richemounte and Richemonte, and ultimately as Richmond. Among the various lines of ancestors in England are found those of the Ashton-Keynes and other Wiltshire Richmonds: the former for five generations bore the alias of Webb, first assumed by William Richmond about 1430, when he married Alice, daughter and heiress of Thomas Webb, of Draycott, Wiltshire, England. It is claimed by some eminent genealogists that the Richmonds of New England (though perhaps not in all of the branches in that region, or elsewhere in America) descended through one Roald, son of Roaldus "le Ennase", while others of equal celebrity state that they descend from Alan, another son of Roaldus "le Ennase", asserting that son Roald had no children.

The Richmond genealogy informs us that Roaldus de Richmond was granted lands by the crown in Yorkshire, and tradition has it that this Richmond was a relative of Alan Rufus. Alan Rufus was a kinsman of the Conqueror, and was granted lands in Yorkshire, where he built his castle and was the first duke of Richmond. Tradition also says that John Richmond was born in Ashton-Keynes, and one reputable writer states that in an examination of the old church records at Ashton-Keynes he found the date of baptism of John Richmond, in 1597.

(I) This John Richmond was the American ancestor of the particular branch of the family to be treated of in these annals, and it is believed that he came to this country with a colony of cadets of noble English families on the western coast of Ireland, who had chosen this remote region that they might be able to "engage in commercial and other pursuits without shocking their aristocratic relatives". It is believed that John Richmond came to America in a trading vessel, and it is known that he was engaged in carrying on an extensive and flourishing trade with Saco, Maine, in 1635, for the records show that in 1636 he was in court with a suit brought by him, "to collect from Thomas Lewis six pounds and ten shillings for two barrells of beife". In 1637 he was one of the purchasers and proprietors of Taunton, Massachusetts, and there his daughter Sarah was probably born in 1638, and his daughter Mary in 1639. From the fact that nothing is known of him between the years 1643 and 1655, it is thought that he returned to England and took part in the wars, for family tradition runs to that effect, and also says that he was referred to as Colonel John Richmond. He probably married before coming to New England. He was away from Taunton much of the time, and is known to have been in Newport and other places, but eventually returned to Taunton and died there March 20, 1664, aged seventy years. His children were: 1. John, of whom further. 2. Captain Edward, born about 1632, in England, died in November, 1696; married (first) Abigail Davis, daughter of James Davis; (second) Amy Bull, daughter of Governor Henry and Elizabeth Bull. 3. Sarah, born about 1638, in Taunton, Massachusetts, died in 1691; she married (first) Edward Rew, who died July 16, 1678; married (second) November 4, 1678, James Walker, the immigrant, born in 1618, died February 15, 1690-91; married (third) Nicholas Stoughton. 4. Mary, born about 1639, in Taunton, died October 3, 1715; she married William Paul, of Berkley, Massachusetts, born in 1624, died November 6, 1704.

(II) John (2), eldest son and child of John (1) Richmond, the immigrant, was born about the year 1627, before his father came to America, and died in Taunton, Massachusetts, October 7, 1715, aged eighty-eight years. He appears to have been a man of importance and was chosen to serve in various capacities. In 1672 he was appointed, with James Walker, to purchase lands of the Indians; was member of the town council in 1675-76 and 1690, and also served as constable, commissioner and surveyor in March, 1677; he was distributor of ten pounds "Irish charity", sent from Dublin, Ireland, in 1676, to be divided among the sufferers during King Philip's war. "He was a member of every important committee in Taunton for the purchase, division and settlement of land and other matters of public interest. He was interested in several extensive purchases of land from the Indians in both

Massachusetts and Rhode Island". He married Abigail Rogers, daughter of John Rogers, of Duxbury, Massachusetts. She was born about 1641 and died August 1, 1727; both she and her husband are buried in Taunton. Their children: 1. Mary, born June 2, 1654, in Bridgewater. 2. John, born June 6, 1656, in Bridgewater, was killed by the upsetting of a cart September 20, 1672. 3. Thomas, born February 2, 1659, in Newport, Rhode Island, died unmarried, in Middleboro, December 14, 1705. 4. Susanna, born November 4, 1661, in Bridgewater. 5. Joseph, born December 8, 1663, in Taunton. 6. Edward, of whom further. 7. Samuel, born September 23, 1668, in Taunton. 8. Sarah, born February 26, 1671, in Taunton. 9. John, born December 5, 1673, in Taunton. 10. Ebenezer, born May 12, 1676, in Newport, Rhode Island. 11. Abigail, born February 26, 1679, in Newport.

(III) Edward, son of John Richmond, was born in Taunton, February 8, 1665, and died in 1741. In 1687 he and Joseph Richmond bought of John Rogers of Duxbury, one hundred and fifty acres of land in Middleboro. He married (first) Marcy ——, (second) May 6, 1711, Rebecca Thurston, born November 28, 1689, daughter of Jonathan and Sarah Thurston, and (third) Mary ——. His will was dated June 3, 1738, and proved December 9, 1741. Children by first wife: Marcy, born 1693; Edward, born 1695; Richard; Josiah, of whom further; Nathaniel, born about 1700; Seth; Elizabeth; Phebe, born 1706. Children, by second wife: Sarah, born December 20, 1712; Mary, born 1714; Priscilla, born February 27, 1718; Eunice, born September 23, 1722, died young.

(IV) Josiah, son of Edward Richmond, was born in 1697 in Taunton. He died in 1763, and his will dated January 26, 1762, was proved April 5, 1763. He was a blacksmith by trade and resided in Middleboro. He married (first) Mehitable, born June 6, 1697, daughter of Benjamin and Sarah (Williams) Deane. He married (second) February 5, 1745-6, Lydia (Eddy) Crocker, widow of Theophilus Crocker and daughter of James Eddy. Children, born in Middleboro: Mary; Josiah, born 1711; Gershom; Benjamin, born 1727; George; Lemuel, of whom further; Miriam, born 1733; Ephraim, born February 12, 1736; Eleazer, born February 27, 1737; Zekiah; Mercy; Mehitable, died young.

(V) Lemuel, son of Josiah Richmond, was born in Middleboro in 1733, and died April 2, 1802. He was a man of small stature, but one of the strongest and most athletic men in the town. It was said that when he was born he was so small that he could be put into a quart tankard. He married Molly (Richmond) Lincoln, daughter of Ebenezer and Mary (Walker) Richmond and twin of Miriam Richmond, who married Elisha Walker. She was born in 1731 and died in Barnard, Vermont, April 9, 1820. Children, born in Taunton: Amaziah, born March 22, 1758; Rachel; Polly, born April 6, 1766; Job, born 1767; Major Lemuel (see below); Betsey.

(VI) Major Lemuel (2) Richmond, son of Lemuel (1) Richmond, was born in Taunton, Massachusetts, October 27, 1771. In 1793 he was apprenticed in Dighton, Massachusetts, and later moved to Barnard, Vermont, where he became a prominent man. He held every town office, some of them for several years. He also served as high bailiff of Windsor county. He entered in the war of 1812 as a volunteer with those who marched to the relief of Plattsburg, and was major in the state militia. He was a very successful man, and made "the one dollar he inherited at the age of twenty-one increase forty thousand-fold". He married, February 24, 1805, Joanna Briggs, who was born in Barnard, Vermont, March 13, 1787. Children, born in Barnard: Rollin, born July 1, 1806; Asa Whitcomb, born March 18, 1808; Alaphal, born April 9, 1810, died November 1, 1810; Joanna Raymond, born August 7, 1811; Rhoda Briggs, born November 8, 1814; Elvira J., born April 2, 1817; Lemuel Carlton, of whom further.

(VII) Lemuel Carlton, son of Major Lemuel (2) Richmond, was born in Barnard, Vermont, October 25, 1819. He was prominent in the town and held most of the town offices. He married, October 15, 1850, Jane Ann Richmond of Derby, Vermont, born September 19, 1830. She was daughter of Dr. Lemuel Richmond, who was born in Barnard, July 26, 1804, and married, September 14, 1826, Ruth Emma, daughter of Benjamin Hinman Esq., of Derby, Vermont. Dr. Lemuel Richmond was graduated from the Vermont Medical College, and began practice in Derby in 1826: he was representative from the town to the legislature several times and also held other offices; he was one of the founders of Derby Academy. His children were: Jane Ann, married Lemuel Carlton Richmond, and Mary, born May 2, 1837, married Otis Hinman. Dr. Lemuel Richmond was son of Captain Amasiah Richmond, born March 22, 1758, died September 30, 1825; he married, November 25, 1780. Hannah, daughter of Billings and Hannah Throope of Bristol, Rhode Island. She was born January 24, 1763, and died December 26, 1845, in Wood-

stock, Vermont. Captain Richmond served in the revolution, volunteering when he was sixteen years of age and serving in several campaigns. One of his uncles on one occasion offered to take his place, because of his youth, but he declined the offer; he was afterwards captain of the militia. "Physically he was the most athletic and powerful Richmond ever known in Barnard, Vermont, and a remarkably fine-looking man. He had sound judgment, strict integrity, was temperate in all things, and so regular in his attendance at church meetings that his horse would leave the pasture and go to the church at the ringing of the bell". His children were: Sarah, Mahala, Amaziah, Hannah, Clarissa, Mary, Abigail, Job, Loring, Lucy, Dr. Lemuel, who was father of Jane Ann Richmond, and Lauriston. Captain Amasiah Richmond was son of Lemuel (1) Richmond, mentioned above. Children of Lemuel Carlton and Jane Ann (Richmond) Richmond: Willis H., born August 5, 1852; Rollin Lemuel, of whom further.

(VIII) Rollin Lemuel, son of Lemuel Carlton Richmond, was born in Barnard, Vermont, November 10, 1858. He attended the public schools of his native town and the academy at Bethel, Vermont, also Kimball Union Academy and the State Normal School at Randolph, Vermont, from which he was graduated in 1878. He learned the business of druggist and followed it for a period of seventeen years, first at Ludlow, Vermont, then at Springfield, Vermont, and in St. Louis, Missouri, and lastly at Proctor, Vermont. Since 1899, he has been in the insurance business in Rutland, Vermont.

He is a director in the Rutland County National Bank of Rutland, Vermont, director of the Proctor Trust Company of Proctor, and director and vice-president of the West Rutland Trust Company of West Rutland. In politics he is a Republican and he was mayor of Rutland in 1907. In religion he is a Universalist and he is treasurer of the Universalist Society. He is a member of Rutland Lodge of Free Masons, of Rutland, and of Beaver Lodge, No. 47, Independent Order of Odd Fellows, of Proctor, Vermont.

He married, January 11, 1883, Grace E. Eaton, of Springfield, Vermont, born November 6, 1862, daughter of Calvin M. and Cynthia A. (Lockwood) Eaton. Children: Dena, born March 8, 1895; Carlton E., died aged seven years.

GOWEN   John Gowen, the immigrant ancestor, was born in Scotland about 1755-60, according to family tradition. He came to this country about the time of the revolution. Several of the name John Gowen served in the revolutionary army, but it is not known whether or not he was a soldier. He settled in Franklin, Massachusetts, where he died February 20, 1794. He married Lydia ———. Children: 1. Major Asa Henry, married Mary ———; children, all at Franklin: Mary Ann, April 9, 1807; Horatio Kingsbury, July 11, 1811; Louisa S., June 9, 1815. 2. John, born August 9, 1780. 3. Luther, of whom further.

(II) Luther, son of John Gowen, was born at Franklin, August 14, 1782, died there at an advanced age. He was educated in the district schools and followed farming in Franklin all his active life. He married there (first) December 3, 1811, Elvira, descendant of Michael Metcalf, one of the early pioneers of Dedham, whose descendants have been numerous in the vicinity of Franklin. He married (second) April 10, 1823, Polly Hartshorn. Children, born at Franklin: 1. Artemas Warren, born October 22, 1812. 2. Luther. 3. George M., of whom further. 4. Charles M., born at Franklin, December 22, 1819; married, at Franklin, June 10, 1841, Harriet Phillips. 5. Horace, born April 30, 1822.

(III) George Metcalf, son of Luther Gowen, was born in Franklin, Massachusetts, August 10, 1816, died in South Acworth, New Hampshire. He was a farmer. He went to New Hampshire when a young man and spent most of his life in Alstead and Acworth, New Hampshire. He married Hannah Permelia Chase, daughter of Benjamin Chase, of Alstead. Children: 1. George Milan, of whom further. 2. Harriet A., married ——— Ruddy, and lived in Springfield, Massachusetts. 3. Lydia A., married John Rogers, of Brattleborough, Vermont, where she now lives. 4 and 5. Frank and Frances, twins, the former living in Warwick, Massachusetts. 6. Charles R., born about 1847; married, February 2, 1869, at Franklin, Kate M. Hills, and lives in Franklin. 7. Emily A., married Charles Emerson, and lives in South Acworth.

(IV) George Milan, son of George Metcalf Gowen, was born in Alstead, New Hampshire, February 21, 1841, and is now living at Keene, New Hampshire. He attended the schools in Acworth, and followed farming until he came of age. On August 22, 1862, he enlisted for the civil war in Company B, Fourteenth New Hampshire Infantry, and was mustered in September 22, 1862. Most of the time during the war he was in Washington, D. C., as severe attacks of rheumatic fever prevented active service. He was hon-

orably discharged from service, for disability, on October 8, 1863. He was unable to do any work for about two years after he left service. He moved to Keene in 1865 and has remained there since. For several years he worked as teamster and then became a fireman on the railroad, being promoted to engineer after a time. After remaining four years on the railroad he began work for the Beaver Mills in Keene, driving a team for them for nine years. He retired from active life several years ago. In 1877 he joined Beaver Brook Lodge, No. 36, Odd Fellows, and he is also a member of John Sedgewick Post, No. 6, Grand Army of the Republic, of Keene.

He married, September 13, 1864, Mary Ellen Loomis, born in Stoddard, New Hampshire, May 26, 1845, died December 24, 1910, in Keene. She was daughter of William F. and Nancy (Green) Loomis. Children, born in Keene. 1. Will Loomis, born July 4, 1865; a farmer in Acworth; married, November 1890, Hattie Blanchard, and has one son, Harry. 2. George Burton, of whom further. 3. Fred Alonzo, August 21, 1869; lives in Waverly, Massachusetts, a railroad engineer; married, May 18, 1893, Jennie B. Eagles. Children: Burton Walter, George Niles, Daniel, Robert, Evelyn and May. 4. Ernest Milan, March 27, 1872, died August 9, 1872. 5. Loomis Clinton, elsewhere in this work. 6. Earl Henry, July 11, 1878, lives in Charlestown, Massachusetts, a railroad man. 7. Mary Imogene, July 27, 1880, died August 25, 1883.

(V) George Burton, son of George Milan Gowen, was born in Langdon, New Hampshire, Cheshire county, March 7, 1867. He received his early education in the public schools of Keene, New Hampshire. He began work at an early age as messenger boy in the telegraph office in Keene, and was afterward employed in the railroad office at South Acton, Massachusetts, for two years. At the age of nineteen he was appointed train despatcher in Boston on the Fitchburg railroad, and he filled that responsible position for a period of fifteen years. In 1901 he was appointed trainmaster and despatcher at Rutland, Vermont, and since then he has held that position. He is a member of the Beaver Brook Lodge, Odd Fellows, of Fitchburg. In politics he is a Republican; in religion a Universalist.

He married, January 13, 1886, Carrie Hayward, of South Acton, Massachusetts, daughter of Cyrus and Mary Pettingill (Edwards) Hayward (see Hayward VII). They had one son, Carroll Alvin, born at South Acton, May 24, 1888.

(The Hayward Line).

(I) John Hayward, the immigrant ancestor, was probably born in London about 1620, died January 11, 1707. He settled in Concord, Massachusetts, and was admitted a freeman in 1670. He married (first) August 17, 1656, Rebecca, daughter of Thomas Atkinson. She died in 1665, and he married (second) August 5, 1665, Sarah Simonds. He married (third) Priscilla ———, who survived him. Children of the first wife: Rebecca, born September 9, 1657, died young; Rebecca, May 13, 1660; John (2), of whom further; Persis, April 11, 1664; Benoni, July 31, 1665, died young. Children of the second wife: Sarah, August 30, 1666; Judith, January 3, 1667; Mary, November 3, 1669; Abigail, April 9, 1672; William, April 17, 1674; Huldah, September 17, 1675; James, January 27, 1678-9; Joseph, January 3, 1680-1; Benjamin, March 17, 1682-3.

(II) Deacon John (2) Hayward, son of John (1) Hayward, was born in Concord, April 5, 1662, died there January 2, 1718. He was constable of Concord in 1686, and in his later years kept an ordinary òr inn. He married Sarah ———. Children: Sarah; Thomas, born July 3, 1686; Samuel, of whom further; Edmund, July 31, 1689; Josiah, November 15, 1691; Daniel, April 15, 1694; Eleazer, August 3, 1696; Nathan, September 24, 1698; Sarah, January 18, 1700-1; John, March 14, 1703; Mary, March 23, 1704; Phinehas,. July 18, 1707; Benjamin, October 25, 1709.

(III) Deacon Samuel Hayward, son of Deacon John (2) Hayward, was born October 11, 1687, died October 28, 1750, aged sixty-three years. He resided in Concord, where he was a prominent citizen, serving as deacon of the church, town clerk, and in other town offices. He married, with Rev. Joseph Estabrook officiating, January 19, 1709-10, Elizabeth Hubbard, who died December 25, 1757, aged sixty-six years and six months, according to her gravestone. Children, born at Concord: Samuel, born October 18, 1710, died January 12, 1712-3; Amos, February 18, 1711-2, died young; Elizabeth, June 3, 1714; Samuel (2), of whom further; Jonathan, December 3, 1717; Amos, October 3, 1719; Jonas, August 21, 1721; Charles, December 24, 1723; Rebecca, December 23, 1725; Aaron, September 24, 1727, died young; Aaron, November 11, 1728; John, June 22, 1730; Sarah, June 19, 1731; Mary, April 8, 1733.

(IV) Captain Samuel (2) Hayward, son of Deacon Samuel (1) Hayward, was born March 4, 1715-16, at Concord. He appears to have moved to Chelmsford, Massachusetts, and perhaps later to Acton. He was presumably the Samuel Hayward in a Chelmsford company at the battle of Bunker Hill. He was known as captain, and probably commanded a company before or during the revolution. He was too old, however, for much active service in the war. Children: Benjamin, of whom further; Stephen; James; Samuel; Paul; Mary, married (first) Ebenezer White, and (second) Jonas Brooks.

(V) Benjamin, son of Captain Samuel (2) Hayward, was born at Chelmsford or Acton, about 1750. He was in Captain Davis's company of Acton, on the Lexington Alarm, April 19, 1775. He was also in Captain Simon Hunt's company, Colonel Eleazer Brooks's regiment, in March, 1776, and later at White Plains, New York, doubtless serving in the campaign at Long Island and Harlem (page 806, Volume VII, Massachusetts Sailors and Soldiers in the Revolution). He was credited to Chelmsford, and served at Ticonderoga under Captain John Ford in 1776-77. Among his children was Moses, of whom further.

(VI) Moses, son of Benjamin Hayward, was born probably at Acton, about 1785-90. He married and had a son Cyrus, of whom further.

(VII) Cyrus, son of Moses Hayward, lived at South Acton, Massachusetts. He married Mary Pettingill Edwards. Their daughter, Carrie, married George Burton Gowen (see Gowen V).

———

PROCTOR The origin of the surname Proctor would appear to be found in the Latin word "procurator", meaning anyone who acts for another or takes care of his interests; in other words, a proxy. Another meaning which the word began to take was "one who collected alms for lepers", or for others unable to do it themselves. From a "History of Northumberland", published by Andrew Reid and Company, of Newcastle-on-Tyne, England, it appears that "the Proctor family, originally settled in Yorkshire, was established at Shawdon, at the beginning of the sixteenth century, through the marriage of William Proctor, of Nether Bordley, to Isabel, daughter of John Lilburn, of Shawdon". Arms were granted to a family in England bearing the name of Proctor, in 1436, and the shield is described as: "Argent with two chevrons sable, between three martlets sable". There is evidence that John, Richard, George and Robert Proctor came across the water and settled in Massachusetts between the years 1636 and 1643. It is not certain that any of the four was related to any of the others. It seems reasonable, however, to suppose that some, if not all, of them were brothers, or at least that there was relationship existing among them.

(1) Robert Proctor, immigrant ancestor in America of the Proctor family here dealt with, was probably born in England, and died at Chelmsford, Massachusetts, April 28, 1697. He first appears in this country at Concord, Massachusetts, where he was made a freeman in 1643. He may have come from England with the three other Proctors already named. There is, however, another tradition concerning his ancestry. Under date of July 26, 1897, Mrs. Lucretia H. Lawrence, of Leominster, a daughter of Jacob Proctor, of Littleton, Massachusetts, writes as follows: "My father in his last days dwelt much upon the history of his family and events of his early life. He said his grandfather" (who was Nathaniel Proctor, a great-grandson of Robert, of Concord) "told him that three brothers from a wealthy family in Scotland came to this country in a ship of their own. One of the brothers settled in or near Chelmsford. The Littleton branch descended from this brother. My father remembered visits back and forth with the Chelmsford relations". The conflict between these traditions must remain unsettled, at least until additional evidence in favor of one or the other can be obtained.

In 1653 Robert Proctor, in connection with Richard Hildreth and twenty-seven others, petitioned the general court for a grant of land six miles square, "to begin at Merrimack river at a neck of land next to Concord River, and so run up by Concord River south and west into the country to make up the circumference or quantity of land as above expressed". The petition was granted. In 1654 Mr. Proctor removed to the new plantation which was organized November 22, 1654, as a town under the name of Chelmsford. The first four or five of his children were born in Concord, the others in Chelmsford. His descendants resided in many of the neighboring towns, and at an early date some of them pushed back into the wilderness and settled in New Hampshire, Vermont, and New York, and have since scattered over the west. Letters of administration on his estate were granted to Jane Proctor, executrix, July 13, 1697. Some of his children settled in what afterwards became the West Precinct, and later the town of Westford.

Robert Proctor married, December 31, 1645, Jane, eldest daughter of Richard Hildreth, of Concord and Chelmsford, ancestor of the Hildreths of America, who died at Chelmsford in 1688. Children: 1. Sarah, born October 12, 1646; married, August 10, 1666, Thomas Chamberlain. 2. Gershom, May 13, 1648. 3. Mary, April 20, 1650; married, 1685, John Bourne. 4. Peter, 1652. 5. Dorothy, 1654; married, December 18, 1679, John Barret Jr. 6. Elizabeth, December 16, 1656; became, in 1705, the third wife of Samuel Fletcher. 7. James, January 8, 1658. 8. Lydia, February 19, 1660, died August 13, 1661. 9. John, August 17, 1663. 10. Samuel, of whom further. 11. Israel, April 29, 1668. 12. Thomas, April 30, 1671, went to sea, and there is no evidence that he returned.

(II) Samuel, son of Robert and Jane (Hildreth) Proctor, was born in Chelmsford, Massachusetts, September 15, 1665, died April 12, 1740, at Townsend. He was one of the petitioners for a grant of land which became Townsend. He married one Sarah, whose maiden surname remains unknown, and who died January 17, 1757. Children, all born at Chelmsford: 1. Sarah, born April 15, 1694. 2. Samuel, January 16, 1697. 3. Thomas, of whom further. 4. David, February 1, 1701; married, December 31, 1730, Hannah Farrah, of Concord. 5. Rachel, January 5, 1702. 6. William, August 14, 1704. 7. Daniel, November 30, 1706. 8. Lucy, August 19, 1708. 9. Charles, June 30, died October 21, 1710. 10. Sarah, September 30, 1715. 11. Hannah Jones.

(III) Thomas, son of Samuel and Sarah Proctor, was born at Chelmsford, Massachusetts, December 12, 1698, died at Proctorsville, Vermont, June 3, 1750. He married, in 1722, Hannah, daughter of Isaac and Sarah Barron, born October 14, 1703, died September 3, 1774. Children: 1. Philip, born January 3, 1726. 2. Lucy, February 10, 1733. 3. Leonard, of whom further. 4. Olive, January 22, 1738; married, November 27, 1780, Thomas Scott.

(IV) Captain Leonard Proctor, second son of Thomas and Hannah (Barron) Proctor, was born at Chelmsford, January 16, 1734, died at Proctorsville, Vermont, June 3, 1827. He was one of the selectmen of Westford in 1770, 1778 and 1779. He was an officer in the revolutionary war and took part in many important battles, including those of Lexington, Trenton and Monmouth. He was second lieutenant in Captain Minot's company, which marched from Westford in consequence of the alarm of April 19, 1775. He was one of the committee of correspondence for 1780, and was chosen the same year as one of a committee of thirteen "to take under consideration the new form of government". In 1781 he was a "captain" and was "head" of one of the five "classes" into which the town was divided for the purpose of procuring soldiers to serve in the continental army. After the war Captain Proctor removed to Cavendish, Vermont, where he founded in an unbroken forest the village of Proctorsville.

He married (first) in 1760, Lydia Nutting, of Westford, who died November 16, 1767; and (second) December 25, 1769, Mary, daughter of Captain Jabez Keep, who died September 3, 1827. Children: 1. Philip, born September 2, 1761; with his brother Abel in the six months levy of soldiers from Westford in 1780. 2. Abel, December 28, 1762, died in the West Indies; married Elizabeth Clark, of New London, Connecticut. 3. Leonard, October 8, 1764, died at Cavendish in 1848. 4. Asa, November 26, 1766, died at sea, unmarried. 5. Mary, October 20, 1770. 6. Lydia, July 7, 1772. 7. Solomon, July, 1774. 8. Thomas, May 19, 1776. 9. Hannah, July 3, 1778. 10. Jabez, of whom further. 11. Experience, September 25, 1783. 12. John, September 13, 1785.

(V) Jabez, son of Captain Leonard and Mary (Keep) Proctor, was born at Westford, Massachusetts, April 22, 1780, died November 22, 1839, at Proctorsville, Vermont. He went to Vermont with his parents when he was three years old. He married, November 26, 1817, Betsey Parker, born at Cavendish, Vermont, August 5, 1792, died at Rutland, February 5, 1871, daughter of Isaac Parker, of Westford, Massachusetts. Children: 1. Harriet, born at Proctorsville, Vermont, in January, 1819; married February 10, 1840, Stoddard B. Colby, late register of the United States treasury; and died in the burning of the steamboat "Henry Clay" on the Hudson river, July 28, 1852. 2. Arabella, December 18, 1820, died August 21, 1822. 3. Lucien, October 28, 1822, died January 25, 1851, in California. 4. Araballa G., June 3, 1825, died August, 1846, unmarried. 5. Redfield, of whom further.

(VI) Colonel Redfield Proctor, youngest son of Jabez and Betsey (Parker) Proctor, was born at Proctorsville, Vermont, June 1, 1831, died in Washington, D. C., March 4, 1908. He represented the state of Vermont in the United States senate for several years. His early education was obtained in the public schools and at the Derby Academy, preparing for Dartmouth College, from which he graduated in 1851, receiving later the degree of A. M. Choosing the profession of law he entered the law school at Albany, New York, and graduated in 1859, being admitted to the bar that year at Albany and also in Woodstock, Vermont. Opportunity knocked at his

door and he was taken into the office of his cousin, Judge Isaac F. Redfield, one of the leading railroad lawyers of Boston.

At the beginning of the civil war Mr. Proctor gave up his chosen vocation, returning to Vermont and enlisting, in June, 1861, in the Third Vermont Volunteers, receiving a commission as lieutenant and quartermaster of his regiment. The Vermonters were sent to the front at once, but Lieutenant Proctor was soon withdrawn from his company to join the staff of General "Baldy" Smith, from which about a month later he was promoted to become major of the newly organized Fifth Vermont Regiment. He served with distinction in the Peninsular campaign, but suffered disabling hardships which made it necessary to resign his commission and return home. Early the next year having regained his health, he was anxious to return to the front. On the organization of the Fifteenth Vermont Regiment he was made its colonel. He went south with his new command and reached Gettysburg after dark on the first day of the battle. On the following day to his regret the regiment was sent to the rear to guard the baggage train.

Directly after the surrender of General Lee Colonel Proctor returned to the home place in Proctorsville and took up the occupation of farming. At this period it is recalled that as farmer and countryman he was often seen clad in a blue and white striped frock reaching down below his boot tops, trousers tucked in his boot legs, whip in hand, travelling beside a pair of large red and white oxen, going to his farmland in another part of the village. He was very democratic in all he did. Later he returned to law in a partnership with Colonel Wheelock G. Veazee, at Rutland. In after years Colonel Proctor had a hard fight to keep his head out of the financial maelstrom but he had faced too many bullets to be easily defeated, and he weathered the tempest and became rich. In 1880 consolidation of the principal marble interests at Southerland Falls took place, with Redfield Proctor as president of the new Vermont Marble Company. The name Southerland Falls had been changed to Proctor, and in 1886 after a bitter fight in the legislature the town was separated from Rutland, to become a community of strictly individual interests. Today it is the marble centre of the world.

The first public office which Colonel Proctor held was that of selectman of the town of Rutland. In 1867 he represented the town in the state legislature, serving as chairman of the committee on elections in the lower house. He was elected to the state senate in

1874, being chosen president *pro tempore* of that body. In 1876 he was elected lieutenant-governor of Vermont, and in 1878 was nominated by the Republican party and elected governor of Vermont. In 1888 the Vermont legislature unanimously recommended him for a cabinet position and in March, 1889, President Harrison appointed him secretary of war. Senator Proctor won national reputation by his control of the war portfolio, his administration being considered one of the ablest in the history of the department. On the retirement of Senator George F. Edmunds from the United States senate, Governor Page appointed Secretary Proctor to fill the unexpired term, and on October 18, 1892, he was elected by the Vermont legislature to fill both the unexpired term and the full term, the latter ending March 4, 1899. During this period he went to Cuba to look over the situation, returned and made out a lengthy report which was read before the senate and that resulted in war being declared. He was after that returned twice to the United States senate, where he had great influence.

He married, May 26, 1858, Emily J., daughter of the Hon. Salmon F. and Sarah (Barlow) Dutton. Children: 1. Arabella, born at Proctorsville, June 26, 1859, died March 30, 1905; married Fred G. Holden. 2. Fletcher D., of whom further. 3. Fanny G., May 2, 1863, died September 26, 1883. 4. Emily D., at Rutland, Vermont, November 21, 1869. 5. Redfield (2), of whom further.

(VII) Hon. Fletcher Dutton, eldest son of Redfield Proctor and Emily J. (Dutton) Proctor, was born at Proctorsville, Vermont, November 7, 1860, died at Proctor, Vermont, September 27, 1911. He was educated in the Rutland Military Institute, Middlebury high school and Amherst College. During his early years his father, Colonel Redfield Proctor, had been organizing and establishing on a firm basis, from the shattered remnants of several unfortunate attempts to develop their marble deposits in Rutland county, what became under his hand the Vermont Marble Company, the largest single producer of marble in the world. It was natural for the son to embrace the great opportunity before him of mastering this business in all its details and assuming the responsibility of its management. From college he went, not into the company's offices, but into its shops. He worked at the trade of a machinist, and later gained a thorough knowledge of every practical step that enters into the quarrying, manufacture and marketing of the superb marble that the company owned in abundance. In 1885 he became superintendent of the com-

pany. In 1889 his father retired from its presidency and Fletcher succeeded to that position, which he held for a period of twenty-two years up to his death. Under his control, and with the assistance of aides chosen with sagacity, the company grew and prospered to an extent that made it the largest single industry in Vermont, and the largest of its kind in the world, with branches in many cities of the United States. With it have grown and prospered the communities in which its main activities have centred.

Fletcher D. Proctor early developed a talent for serving others and the community and the public, which called for much of his time and energy. He began with town office, in the capacity of selectman in Rutland. Education early awakened his interest, and for a long period from 1883 down to his death he served on the school board of his town. These and other local duties gave him practical knowledge of community conditions that served him well in the higher positions that awaited him. He represented Proctor in the legislatures of 1890, 1900 and 1904. In the session of 1892 he was a senator from Rutland county. In the session of 1900 he was speaker of the house of representatives, his service being marked by a modest bearing and thorough efficiency that not only won him favor but despatched business without delay. In 1902 Fletcher D. Proctor was an unsuccessful candidate before the Republican state convention for the nomination as governor. He entered the canvass, but was urged to withdraw and did so in favor of Hon. John G. McCullough, who was elected. In 1906 he was his party's regular candidate for the governorship, being opposed by an independent fusion movement. It is said that it was in this campaign that the people of Vermont really discovered Fletcher D. Proctor. Though untrained as a public speaker Mr. Proctor in his many addresses made a most favorable impression and was elected to the governorship by a majority over all of 15,171, after a campaign which at the outset to many Republicans looked very discouraging.

But Mr. Proctor's interest did not end with his elevation to the governorship. He steadily pushed forward the reforms he had outlined in his inaugural address. In the midst of his other activities he had found time, during the years before he was governor, to give to duties of a most varied nature. He served three years in Company A, Vermont National Guard, rising to the rank of first lieutenant by appointment of Governor Ebenezer J. Ormsbee. He was secretary of civil and military affairs, 1886-1888. In 1883 he was chosen colonel at the head of the Vermont division, Sons of Veterans. Among his connection with enterprises of large magnitude and usefulness, aside from the Vermont Marble Company, he was president of the Vermont Forestry Association; a director of the New England Telephone and Telegraph Company, the National Life Insurance Company, and the Rutland Railroad Company; a trustee of Norwich University, and of Middlebury College, from both of which institutions he held the title of LL. D., as he did also from the University of Vermont. He was a trustee of T. N. Vail's agricultural school at Lyndon.

He married, May 26, 1886, Minnie E., daughter of the Hon. Asher C. and Erminie Robinson, of Westford, Vermont. Children: Emily, born May 24, 1887; Mortimer R., of whom further; and Minnie, January 18, 1895.

(VII) Redfield (2), youngest son of Colonel Redfield (1) and Emily J. (Dutton) Proctor, was born at Proctor, Vermont, April 13, 1879. He was educated in the town schools, and also attended schools in Pennsylvania and in Washington, D. C., as well as the Massachusetts School of Technology. He has always been identified with the Vermont Marble Company, and is a director in the company. He is vice-president of the Proctor Trust Company, a director in the Rutland County National Bank in Rutland and is a trustee in the University of Vermont and the State Tuberculosis Hospital. He has served on the board of selectmen of the town, and is president of the village, which he represented in the legislature in 1912. He is a member of the Loyal Legion.

He married, October 24, 1906, Mary. S., daughter of John A. and Margaret M. (Young) Hedrick, of Salisbury, North Carolina. There has been one child, Margaret, born March 30, 1911.

(VIII) Mortimer Robinson, son of Fletcher Dutton and Minnie E. (Robinson) Proctor, was born in Proctor, Vermont, May 30, 1889. He graduated from Yale College in 1912, and is now in the office of the Vermont Marble Company.

THRALL   William Thrall, the immigrant ancestor, was born in England in 1605. In March, 1630, a Congregational church was formed at Plymouth, England, the minister being Rev. John Warham. The minister and his people sailed for New England in the ship "Mary and John", on March 20, 1630, and landed at Nantasket Point, May 30, of the same year. They settled in Dorchester and soon afterward went to Windsor, Connecticut. Among the number

who went to Connecticut was William Thrall. He lived in what was known as Hoytes Meadow, Windsor, and some of his descendants still live on the property. He was a soldier in the Pequot war, at the time when Windsor was required to furnish thirty men. The great battle of the war was fought on May 26, 1637, and the victory was so important that "a grant of land was given to each soldier and officer; and to this day the memory of an ancestor who was in the Pequot fight, is an honorable heir-loom in every Connecticut family." William Thrall married ——— Goode, and she died July 30, 1676. He died August 3, (Sabbath), 1678, aged seventy-three years. Children: Timothy, mentioned below; David; perhaps others.

(II) Timothy, son of William Thrall, was born July 26, 1641, died in June, 1697, aged fifty-six years. He was a prominent citizen in Windsor, and his name is found often on the records. He owned much property in the town. There were four generations by the name of Timothy. He married, November 10, 1659, Deborah Gun, who died January 7, 1694. Children, born in Windsor: Deborah; Timothy; Mehitable; Elizabeth; John, mentioned below; Martha; Thomas; Samuel, Abigail, twins.

(III) John, son of Timothy Thrall, was born June 5, 1671, died April 18, 1732, aged sixty-one years and nine months. There were five generations by the name of John. He married, January 6, 1697, Mindwell Moses. Children, born in Windsor: John, mentioned below; Moses; Aaron; Amy; Joseph; David; Joel; Charles; Jerusha.

(IV) John (2), son of John (1) Thrall, was born October 13, 1699, in Windsor, died in 1762, aged sixty-three years. He, his father, and some of their descendants, were buried in the Turkey Hills parish of Windsor, where several descendants still live. John Thrall married Mary Roberts. Children, born in Windsor: John; Mary; Aaron; Lucy; Samuel, mentioned below; Mindwell; Ezekiel; Benjamin.

(V) Captain Samuel Thrall, son of John (2) Thrall, was born in Windsor, July 11, 1737, died December 3, 1821, aged eighty-four years and five months. He was the last survivor of his generation, and in 1820 there were living six of his sons and daughters, sixty-two grandchildren, twenty-eight great-grandchildren and several of the fifth generation, making over a hundred descendants. Samuel Thrall was a farmer. He was an active and industrious man, and was influential in the town, having a reputation for honesty and common sense. In height he was about five feet, nine inches, and in weight about one hundred and fifty pounds. He was for years a member of the Congregational church in West Rutland, Vermont. He served in the French and Indian war of 1762 as an officer in the English service, and in the revolution as captain. He moved from Windsor to Granville, Massachusetts, before the revoluton. In 1784 he was a sympathizer with Shays, and suffered much as a result. In 1788 he was a member of the legislature of Massachusetts, and in 1790 moved to Rutland, Vermont, where he remained the rest of his life. His children moved there about the same time with the exception of Samuel, Lucy and Worthy. He married Lucy Winchell, daughter of Martin and Lucy Winchell. Children: Theodosia; Lucy; Mary, died young; Samuel; Aaron; Jesse; Eliphas; Worthy; Chauncy, mentioned below; Mary; James, died young.

(VI) Chauncy, son of Captain Samuel Thrall, was born December 6, 1772. At the time of his death, April 4, 1844, in West Rutland, at the age of seventy-two years, the *Rutland Herald* said:

The inhabitants of this place have been called of late to mourn the departure of an unusual number of leading men; men who have occupied such stations and taken such a part in the affairs of the community, as to cause their deaths to be universally felt and lamented. The deceased was one of that number. The equanimity of his temper, and his uniform kindness as a father, can be realized only by those who sustained to him the relation of children, and are left to lament their loss. But as a citizen and a Christian, his example has been before all, and was such as to gain the respect and love of his neighbors, and inspire them with the hope that death did not find him unprepared.

He served as a representative to the legislature, and for the most of his life held some public office. He married Polly Chipman, who died a few years before him. Children, born in Rutland: Jonathan C., died in 1852, an influential citizen; Chauncy, mentioned below; Samuel R., a Presbyterian clergyman in Illinois; Lurena, married Henry Hewett, both deceased; Theodosia, married Judson Gorham; Mary, married Jacob Bailey.

(VII) Chauncy (2), son of Chauncy (1) Thrall, was born September 17, 1801, in Rutland, Vermont, in the part now West Rutland, died September 18, 1875. He was a farmer and a very industrious and active man. He lived in Rutland all his life, and was a member of the Congregational church and of its prudential committee. He married Caroline Blanchard, born December 29, 1802, died October 10, 1880. Children, born in Rutland: Rollin Chauncy, mentioned below; Lura, born 1833, died November 23, 1837; Mary Eliza-

beth, born 1834, died July 25, 1838; Lura Elizabeth, born 1837, died October 31, 1838; Benjamin Blanchard, born 1841, died January 12, 1866; Samuel Hanson, born 1843, died November 27, 1847.

(VIII) Rollin Chauncy, son of Chauncy (2) Thrall, was born in Rutland, June 25, 1828, died at West Rutland, May 12, 1895. He received his early education in the public schools of his native town and at the West Rutland Academy. During his youth he assisted his father in the work of the farm. He succeeded to the farm, and always lived on the homestead. He was gifted musically, had a well-trained voice and for many years taught singing school. He was deacon of the Congregational church and especially active and prominent in all forms of church work. He was keenly interested in public affairs and for many years was a justice of the peace. In politics he was a Republican.

He married, November 23, 1853, Aurilla L. Deland, born in West Rutland, November 8, 1830, died December 29, 1893, daughter of Joseph Appleton and Martha (Reynolds) Appleton. Children, born at West Rutland: 1. William Appleton, mentioned below. 2. Charles Rollin, born September 23, 1858; died September 15, 1862. 3. Caroline Martha, born October 9, 1860; now engaged in Young Women's Christian Association work in Providence, Rhode Island. 4. Rollin Benjamin, born June 11, 1864; died September 11, 1865. 5. Walter Chauncy, mentioned below. 6. Aurilla Deland, born December 20, 1872, general secretary of the Young Women's Christian Association at Nashua, New Hampshire. 7. Lucy Frances, born September 4, 1874; died August 27, 1875.

(IX) William Appleton, son of Rollin Chauncy Thrall, was born at West Rutland, Vermont, June 29, 1855. He attended the public schools of his native town and the Eastman Business College at Poughkeepsie, New York. He has been in business as a general merchant since 1878, formerly in partnership with others, but alone since 1897. In addition to his mercantile business, he conducts a farm of three hundred and twenty-five acres in West Rutland and is one of the best known farmers of this section. He is director of the West Rutland Trust Company, and one of the incorporators. He is a justice of the peace and has been treasurer of the town, member of the school board and in 1900 represented the town in the state legislature. While in the house he served on the committee on claims. In politics he is a Republican. He is a member and past master of Hiram Lodge, No. 101, Free Masons, of West Rutland. He is an active member of the Congregational church and chairman of the prudential committee.

He married, November 19, 1884, Carrie B. North, of West Rutland, daughter of Aaron Eugene and Jane (Baldwin) North. Children, born in West Rutland: 1. Jennie Grace, born September 3, 1885, died July 29, 1886. 2. Edith Lillian, born January 1, 1887; married June 26, 1907, Thomas Charles Ross, of West Rutland, and has one child, Mildred Thrall Ross, born October 21, 1908. 3. Rollin William, born June 11, 1889, died October 9, 1889. 4. Helen Aurilla, born May 24, 1891; died January 8, 1892. 5. William North, born August 31, 1898.

(IX) Walter Chauncy, brother of William Appleton Thrall, was born in West Rutland, March 22, 1867. He received his early education there in the public schools and at the State Normal School at Castleton, Vermont. During his boyhood and youth he worked on his father's farm, and afterward followed farming on his account. For five years he was a clerk in his brother's general store at West Rutland. Since 1910 he has been in the milk business in West Rutland and conducts a farm there. He is active in public affairs and has served on the board of school directors of West Rutland. In politics he is a Republican. He is a member of Hiram Lodge, No. 101, Free Masons, of West Rutland, and of the Congregational church of that town.

He married, February 6, 1889, Chandleretta Clark, who was born February 23, 1868, daughter of Elias and Carolina Henrietta (Morrill) Clark, granddaughter of Daniel and Maria (Salisbury) Clark, and great-granddaughter of Daniel and Sybil (Fitch) Clark. Children: 1. Mabel Henrietta, born March 3, 1890. 2. Rollin Clark, born January 7, 1892. 3. Wayne Edwin, born June 9, 1893. 4. Walter Deland, born January 5, 1899.

William Burke was born in county BURKE Tipperary, Ireland, about 1762, died there in 1842. He was a farmer, and an energetic and industrious man. Children: William; Patrick; John, in British service and died in India; Michael, of whom further; Mary.

(II) Michael, son of William Burke, was born in 1818, in Newport, county Tipperary, Ireland, died in Saratoga, New York, in 1849, aged thirty-one years. He attended school but a short time, and in 1847 came to America by way of Quebec, Canada. He settled in Litchfield, Connecticut, where he was employed in railroad construction work. After

remaining two years in America he sent for his family, and when they arrived he went to Saratoga to meet them. While there he was taken sick with cholera and died. He married, in Ireland, Honora Casey, born in 1822 in county Limerick, near the city of Limerick, died in 1905, aged eighty-three years. She was a daughter of Michael Casey. Children, born in Ireland: James, of whom further; Alice, married Michael Malar, superintendent of slate quarry at Hydeville, Vermont; John, deceased; Michael, deceased; William, deceased.

(III) James, son of Michael Burke, was born January 5, 1839, in the parish of Bird Hill, county Tipperary, Ireland. He attended school in Ireland, but most of his education has been gained through his own efforts, as he was but ten years of age when the family came to America in 1849. Owing to the sudden death of his father he was obliged to go to work when only eleven years of age. Until 1851 he lived in Philadelphia, Pennsylvania, and then moved to Whitehall, New York, remaining there about a year and a half. He then moved to West Castleton, Vermont, and was employed in the slate works for about two years. In 1854 he moved to West Rutland, Vermont, where he has lived since. He began there to work in the marble quarries, and from the lowest position attained that of foreman. He held that position for several years, and in 1906 retired from active work. He has held the offices of lister, selectman and justice of the peace.

He married, July 6, 1859, Mary Gleason, who was born in Youngtal, county Tipperary, Ireland, December 16, 1834, and came to America in 1857. She was daughter of Michael and Sarah (Hogan) Gleason. Children, born in Rutland: 1. Mary, born May 10, 1860; married P. J. Lonergan, of New York City. 2. Michael B., April 1, 1862; in the marble and granite business at Mansfield, Ohio. 3. William G., March 28, 1864, died December 11, 1901; sergeant of police in New York, and promoted to captain the day before he died. 4. James E., of whom further. 5. John, October 19, 1868, died January 6, 1898. 6. Malachi, February 22, 1871, died September, 1873. 7. Patrick Francis, September 27, 1873, died April 24, 1897. 8. Sarah A., May 29, 1876; in charge of the stenographers in the office of the Aetna Insurance Company, New York.

(IV) James Edward Burke, son of James Burke, was born May 5, 1866, in West Rutland, Vermont, then part of Rutland. He received his education in the public schools of his native town. He was clerk in a general store there for five years, and in the employ of the True Blue Marble Company, of Rutland, for fourteen years. In 1897 he became connected with the New York Life Insurance Company, of which he is now the general agent, with offices in the Mead Building, Rutland. He organized the Orvillo Marble Quarrying Company in 1902, and is its secretary and treasurer. He was one of the organizers of the Clarendon Marble Company, and is secretary of the company and one of its board of directors. He had charge of the construction of the railroad leading to the quarries of the company. Always keenly interested in politics and public affairs, he was one of the prime movers in securing an adequate public water system for the village of West Rutland. He has served on the grand jury, on the board of school directors for five years, and has been justice of the peace many years. In 1902 he represented his town in the state legislature, and served on important committees, including the committee on claims. He is serving his third year as selectman of the town. In politics he is a Democrat. Mr. Burke is exceedingly popular both in business and social life, and he possesses in the highest degree the esteem and confidence of his townsmen. In religion he is a Roman Catholic. He is a member of the Knights of Columbus, and the Ancient Order of Hibernians.

Mr. Burke married, April 1, 1888, Theresa Ollivette, of Port Henry, New York, daughter of Ignatius and Mary (McKenna) Ollivette. Children, born at West Rutland: 1. Mary C., born February 21, 1890; married Harold E. Thompson, of Rutland. Children: Yvonne Elizabeth, born October 10, 1911; Mary, October 7, 1912. 2. James Francis, October 9, 1893. 3. Frederick Leo, twin, October 9, 1893. 4. Theresa E., June 15, 1896. 5. Margaret Ollivette, May 7, 1902. 6. William J., January 31, 1912.

GANNETT   The Gannett family is of English origin. Two brothers and a sister were among the early settlers in this country. Judith Gannett, aged twenty-six, came in the ship "Francis" to Ipswich, April 30, 1634, and lived in the family of John Coggeshall, being admitted to the Boston church, September 7, 1634; she married at Scituate, September 20, 1636, Robert Shelley. She was received into the church at Barnstable, Massachusetts, in 1644, being dismissed from the Boston church, July 14, 1644. Anne Shelley, sister of Robert, also lived in the Coggeshall family. Thomas Gannett appears to have come from England about 1638. He and his brother Matthew settled

first at Hingham, Massachusetts. In 1642 Thomas became one of the first settlers and proprietors of Duxbury, Massachusetts, but in 1651, having obtained a grant of land in Bridgewater, he became one of the first five settlers of that town where he died in 1655. He married Sarah Jarmill, who married second, September 6, 1655, William Saville, and third, July 5, 1670, Thomas Faxon, both of Bridgewater. She died there in 1697. Thomas made his will, June 19, 1655, and it was proved, August 7, 1655, bequeathing to his wife and brother Mathew, as he had no children.

(I) Matthew Gannett, the immigrant ancestor, was born in 1617, and came with his brother Thomas, of previous mention, and located first at Hingham, Massachusetts, removing in 1651 to Scituate, Massachusetts, where he had purchased half a share in the Conihasset lands of Anna Vinal. He resided at Scituate the remainder of his life, in a house situated at the west end of the dam at Lincoln's Mills, near Captain Wallis' house. He died there in 1694 at the age of seventy-seven. His will is dated August 23, 1694, and was proved November 15th of the same year. He bequeathed to his grandsons, Matthew and Joseph, the lands at Bridgewater that he inherited from his brother, and he gave his homestead and land at Scituate and Hingham to his son Matthew. He married probably at Hingham, Hannah Andrews, who died at Scituate, July 10, 1700, aged seventy-eight, daughter of Joseph and Elizabeth Andrews. Children: 1. Matthew, of whom further. 2. Rehoboth, settled in Morristown, New Jersey, and died without issue. 3. Hannah, married —— Adams. 4. Abigail, married Jonathan Dodson. 5. Elizabeth, married —— Leavitt. 6. Joseph, born in Scituate about 1660, died August 14, 1693; married at Marblehead, August 15, 1682, Deborah Sharp, widow, the daughter of Henry Coombs who died in 1660 and his wife Elizabeth who died 1709. 7. Benjamin.

(II) Matthew (2), son of Matthew (1) Gannett, was born in 1652, died at Scituate, Massachusetts, February 9, 1703, aged fifty-one years. He erected a house near his father's in 1675. He had sons: Matthew (3), of whom further; Joseph and probably others.

(III) Matthew (3), son of Matthew (2) Gannett, was born about 1675. He married (first) June 30, 1702, Mary Chapin, who died April 9, 1703. He married (second) —— Children of second marriage, born in Scituate: Samuel, born February 13, 1714, died May 13, 1715; Seth, born September 18, 1716, died March 20, 1717; Elizabeth, born February 1,

1718; Samuel, of whom further; Mary, baptized April 15, 1722.

(IV) Samuel, son of Matthew (3), Gannett, was born at Scituate, April 26, 1721. Another Samuel, son of a Matthew Sr., was baptized there July 15, 1722, with Mary Gannett. Matthew Sr. was the son of Joseph, and so-called to distinguish him from Matthew (3). Samuel married at Scituate, November 2, 1752, Sarah Cole. Children of Samuel and Sarah, born at Scituate: Benjamin, baptized July 14, 1754; Joseph, baptized December 4, 1757, died young; Hannah, baptized November 4, 1759; Hannah, baptized October 9, 1763; Sarah, baptized September 28, 1766; Joseph, of whom further; Lucy, baptized September 26, 1773.

(V) Joseph, son of Samuel Gannett, was born July 1, 1768, at Scituate. His gravestone proves his parentage. He also lived at Scituate. He married, first, January 1, 1792, Ruth Gannett, who was born March 20, 1771, daughter of Matthew Jr. and Submit (Joy) Gannett, at Scituate. Her mother was of Hingham, and the intention of marriage of her parents was dated February 9, 1755. Her father, Matthew Jr., was born December 17, 1718. Ruth died November 10, 1823, aged fifty-three years, according to her gravestone. Joseph married, second, August 1, 1824, at Scituate, Betsey Battles, a widow; he married, third, March 26, 1832, at Scituate, Judith Briggs. Joseph was a farmer at Scituate. Children, all by his first wife: Cole, born April 6, 1794; Becky, March 18, 1796; Joy, of whom further; Nabby, June 25, 1800; Freeman, October 6, 1803; Seth, March 1, 1806; Howard, May 23, 1808; Joseph, September 21, 1810.

(VI) Joy, son of Joseph Gannett, was born in Scituate, June 10, 1798. He was a miller by trade. He married at Scituate, intention dated October 7, 1826, Mary King, of Littleton, Massachusetts, daughter of Roger King. Mrs. Gannett was a school teacher before her marriage. They were both members of the Baptist Church. Children: 1. Louisa Joy, born at Cohasset, November 31, 1827 (thus recorded at Scituate); married John Littlefield. 2. George King, married Rebecca H. W. Whitney. 3. Mary Rogers, born at Cohasset, December 29, 1832; married William Osgood of Boston. 4. Samuel, of whom further.

(VII) Samuel (2), son of Joy Gannett, was born at Cohasset, Massachusetts, November 27, 1834. He attended Miss Smith's private school, the public schools, Mr. Marsh's private school at Dorchester, the famous Allen School of Newton, Massachusetts, Milton Academy

at Milton, Massachusetts, and completed his academic education at Chauncy Hall School, Boston, in 1851, then kept by Thayer & Cushing, masters. He engaged in business as a dealer in flour, feed, hay and grain at Milton, Massachusetts, in 1858, and continued in business for fifty years, selling out in 1908 to the new firm of Swan, Babcock & Company. Since then he has lived in retirement from active business. He was elected a director of the Blue Hill National Bank, January 14, 1879, and became its president, January 16, 1893. He resigned as director and president, January 10, 1911, after serving as director for thirty-two years and as president for eighteen years. In politics he is independent, and he served one-year terms as assessor, surveyor of highways and selectman of Milton, declining re-election. He is a member of no secret societies, but belongs to the Milton Club. His father and mother were both members of the Neponset Baptist Church and he attended the Baptist church in his youth. Afterward he attended Methodist and Congregational churches in Milton, but in later years he has attended the Protestant Episcopal church, of which his wife is a communicant. The old Gannett house near the north Scituate depot is now owned by Mr. Samuel Gannett, of Milton.

He married, October 17, 1867, in Milton, Alice G. Emerson, who was born in East Milton, April 17, 1842, a daughter of Joshua and Ann (Babcock) Emerson. Her father was a foreman on the Granite Railway at Quincy. She had four sisters: Harriet, Mary Frances, Ellen N. and Jane E. Emerson. Children of Mr. and Mrs. Gannett: Mary King, Alice Emerson, Hattie Louise, Margaret Emerson, married Harold W. French, and they have one child, Samuel Gannett French.

ROSS (V) Abram or Abraham Ross, son of John Ross (q. v.), was born in Sudbury, Massachusetts, January 2, 1749-50, died July 14, 1841, at the great age of ninety-seven years. He removed to Bolton, Massachusetts, and thence as early as 1777 to Jaffrey, New Hampshire. In that year he was road surveyor at Jaffrey. He was a soldier in the revolution. His farm at Jaffrey was lot 4, range seven. He married Persis Welch, of Bolton. Children: Betsey, born 1775, married Jonathan Stanley; Paul, mentioned below; John, married (first) May 8, 1804, Abigail Merriam, (second) Mary Ware; Abram, born 1781, married Nancy Maynard, and lived on the homestead; Jonas, 1784; Persis, married, January 22, 1812, Thomas Browning; Pru-

Samuel Gannett

dence, married, July 11, 1809, Jedediah Stanley.

(VI) Paul, son of Abram or Abraham Ross, was born at Jaffrey, New Hampshire, 1777. He moved to Barre, Vermont. He married (first) Olive Moore, who died October 15, 1800; (second) Tryphena Chandler, September 4, 1803. The only child by the first wife was Paul Moore, mentioned below. Children by second wife: Abram, born June 27, 1804; Stephen, August 24, 1806; Ozias, December 28, 1811; John, May 2, 1813.

(VII) Paul Moore, son of Paul Ross, was born at Barre, Vermont, October 15, 1800, died at Poultney, Vermont, July 20, 1870. At the age of sixteen he was apprenticed to Judge Ellis, of Barre, and when he came of age he removed to Burlington, Vermont, thence to Vergennes in that state. In 1825, at the request of Reuben Wheeler, he came to East Poultney and entered into partnership with Olcott Sherman in the harness and saddlery business. After a few years this firm was dissolved, Ross remaining in the business at East Poultney and Sherman at West Poultney. In 1852 Mr. Ross bought what is known as the Cleveland Hill farm and conducted it until 1848 when he sold it. He manufactured Dewey's Spring Tooth Rake and Tin Spoons and in 1850 entered into partnership with Elijah West to make melodeons and he continued in this business until he died. He was a quaint, unpretending man, we are told by the old history of Poultney, and a man of wit and humor, joking without offense. He succeeded Elisha Ashley as town treasurer and he was overseer of the poor for eleven years. He married, February 14, 1827, Charlotte Moseley Dewey, born September 8, 1804, died April 5, 1897 (see Dewey VI). They had one child, Lucretius Dewey, mentioned below.

(VIII) Dr. Lucretius Dewey Ross, son of Paul Moore Ross, was born at Poultney, Vermont, July 4, 1828, died in 1902. He attended the public schools of his native town, and studied his profession at the Medical College at Castleton, Vermont, after graduating from Middlebury College. He married, July 4, 1860, Adeline A. Baldwin, born at Bristol, Vermont, in 1832, died at Poultney, Vermont, October 28, 1874, daughter of Hiram G. and Roxanna (Strong) Baldwin. Children: Carroll B., mentioned below; Willis Moore, born at Poultney, May 8, 1863; Anna Drew, April 14, 1865; Lucretius Henry, Benson, Vermont, September 29, 1867, physician at Bennington, Vermont; Paul Gilbert, October 6, 1869, postmaster at Poultney; Charles Leffingwell, November 16, 1871,

druggist at Ticonderoga, New York, married Esther E. Abbott, April 22, 1903.

(IX) Dr. Carroll Baldwin Ross, son of Dr. Lucretius Dewey Ross, was born at Poultney, Vermont, August 23, 1861. He was educated in the public schools of his native town and at Troy Conference Seminary, from which he was graduated in 1878; and at Middlebury College from which he was graduated with the degree of Bachelor of Arts in 1882. He received his medical training at the Harvard Medical School, from which he was graduated with the degree of Doctor of Medicine in 1886. Since then he has been in active practice in West Rutland, Vermont. He is a member of the Rutland County Medical Society, the Vermont State Medical Society and the American Medical Association. He has been active in public affairs and has held various offices of private and public trust. He is a director of the West Rutland Trust Company. He has been for a number of years on the school board of West Rutland. He has taken the thirty-two degrees of Scottish Rite Masonry and is a member of Hiram Lodge, No. 101, Free and Accepted Masons, of West Rutland; Davenport Chapter, Royal Arch Masons; also of the Council, Royal and Select Masters; Killington Commandery, Knights Templar, and Cairo Temple, Mystic Shrine, of Rutland, and of other Masonic bodies. In politics he is a Republican.

He married (first) 1886, Ada Dunton, of Rutland, died 1891, daughter of William H. and Sarah (Randall) Dunton. He married (second) 1897, Harriet, daughter of Rev. W. H. and Roline (Mayo) Stewart. Her father is a chaplain in the United States navy. Children by first wife: Paul Dunton, born August 8, 1888, graduate of Middlebury College in the class of 1910, now in the auditing department of the Hill systems of railroad; Adelaide, October 26, 1891, a student of Middlebury College, class of 1915. Children by second wife: Stewart, born November 7, 1898; Donald, born September 3, 1900.

(The Dewey Line).

(I) Thomas Dewey, immigrant ancestor, came from Sandwich, county Kent, England, and was one of the original grantees of Dorchester, Massachusetts, in 1636. He was here as early as 1633, however, and was a witness in that year of the nun-cupative will of John Russell, of Dorchester. He was admitted a freeman of the colony, May 14, 1634. He sold his lands at Dorchester, August 12, 1635, and removed with other Dorchester men to Windsor, Connecticut, of which he was one of the earliest settlers. He was granted land at Dorchester in 1640, and his home lot there was the first north of the Palisado, and extended from the main street eastward to the Connecticut river. He was juryman in 1642-43-44-45. He died intestate and the inventory of his estate was filed May 19, 1648, amounting to two hundred and thirteen pounds. The estate was divided by the court, June 6, 1650. He married, March 22, 1639, at Windsor, Frances, widow of Joseph Clark. She married (third) as his second wife, George Phelps, and she died September 27, 1690. Children: Thomas, mentioned below: Josiah, baptized October 10, 1641; Anna, baptized October 15, 1643; Israel, born September 25, 1645; Jedediah, born December 15, 1647.

(II) Cornet Thomas (2) Dewey, son of Thomas (1) Dewey, was born February 16, 1640, in Windsor, Connecticut, died April 27, 1690. He was living in Windsor as late as January 18, 1660. He moved to Northampton, Massachusetts, where he was granted a home lot, November 12, 1662, of four acres, on condition that he make improvement on it and possess it three years; also a lot of twelve acres. In August, 1666, he was connected with a mill. He moved to Waranoak, then a part of Springfield, under the direction of a settling committee appointed in February, 1665, and is first mentioned there as third on a list of twenty grantees of land, of which his part was three acres, upon certain conditions. This land was laid out April 24, 1667, and confirmed January 9, 1668. From then on he became an influential citizen in the new town, and was called upon to fill many important positions. On January 21, 1669, he was appointed with others to go to Springfield to a town meeting there to lay before the general court matters connected with the boundaries and settlement of their new town, and February 2, 1669, he was again appointed with others to lay out an additional grant. The town was incorporated as Westfield, May 28, 1669. In 1672, with his brothers Josiah and Jedediah and Joseph Whiting, he completed the second mill in the town, in the Little River district, and in December of the same year the town agreed to allow them the toll of one-twelfth part of the corn they ground. The Deweys afterward had extended litigation in the court respecting these mills, which terminated in their favor. On March 12, 1677, he was appointed fence-viewer for the ensuing year. He was representative to Boston in 1677-79; selectman, 1677 and 1686; licensed by the court to "keep a public house of entertainment", September 26, 1676. He took the freeman's oath,

September 28, 1680; was on a committee to locate a county road to Windsor, March 30, 1680; appointed cornet of the Hampshire Troop at the general court, July 8, 1685; joined the church, May 9, 1680. On December 17, 1680, he was granted, with his brother Josiah and Lieutenant Mosely, the right to set up a saw and grist mill on Two Mile brook. On February 1, 1681, he was chosen constable; February 2, 1686, warden for the town ways, and on March 7, 1687, with others was chosen to measure the bounds of the town; he also held other offices of trust and responsibility.

He married, June 1, 1663, at Dorchester, Constant, daughter of Richard and Ann Hawes. She was born July 17, 1642, at Dorchester, died April 26, 1703, by town records. She joined the Westfield church, March 24, 1680. Her father, Richard Hawes, came to Dorchester in the ship "Freelove", in 1635, with his wife and daughter Ann, aged two and one-half years, and son Obadiah, six months. He was twenty-nine years, and his wife twenty-six years old. He signed the church covenant in 1636, and was granted land in 1637 and 1646. He died in 1656. Children of Mr. and Mrs. Dewey, born at Northampton: Thomas, March 26, 1664; Adijah, mentioned below; Mary, January 28, 1668. Born at Westfield: Samuel, June 25, 1670; Hannah, February 21, 1672; Elizabeth, January 10, 1676; James, July 3, 1678, died February 27, 1682; Abigail, February 14, 1681; James, November 12, 1683, died May 5, 1686; Israel, July 9, 1686.

(III) Captain Adijah Dewey, son of Cornet Thomas (2) Dewey, was born at Northampton, March 5, 1666, died March 24, 1742, at Westfield. He was appointed surveyor of the bridge at Mill brook, September 22, 1691; county surveyor in 1693; constable, 1697; tithingman, 1702. On October 31, 1718, he was on a committee to treat with John Gunn Sr. concerning a place for the new meetinghouse. He was in command of the South Company, and August 20, 1723, they were ordered "to do scouting duty for 14 days"; September 18, "to relieve the Frontiers"; October 11, he was ordered to "get your troop ready and march to the relief of Deerfield and the other river towns" for eight weeks. He had thirteen acres in the general field in 1723; was selectman in 1730 and 1740; joined the church April 20, 1729. He served on many committees and was one of the most prominent men in the town. On March 23, 1733, he deeded various lots of land to his three sons. His will was dated March 23, 1733. He married, in 1688, Sarah, born September 27, 1670, at Westfield, daughter of John and Mary (Ashley) Root; Mary was daughter of Robert Ashley, of Springfield. Children, born at Westfield: Child, born November 13, died November 17, 1689; Thomas, mentioned below; Adijah, September 30, 1693; Sarah, March 17, 1696; Esther, January 20, 1699; Mary, September 18, 1701; Abigail, January 28, 1703; Bethiah, August 11, 1706; Ann, March 22, 1709; Moses, January 6, 1715.

(IV) Thomas (3), son of Adijah Dewey, was born at Westfield, January 9, 1691, died April 12, 1742, at Sheffield, Massachusetts. He was a farmer and cooper by trade. He settled in Sheffield, now Great Barrington, about 1726, and had land in the fourth division, on the east side of the Housatonic river, north of Roaring brook. He died intestate, and Adijah Dewey, his brother, was administrator of his estate. He married, August 6, 1718, at Westfield, Abigail, born March 23, 1685, in Westfield, daughter of Nathaniel and Mary Williams. Children, born at Westfield: Abigail, September 4, died September 20, 1719; Azariah, August 12, 1722. Born at Sheffield: Zebediah, January 29, 1725, died in infancy; Zebediah, mentioned below; Abigail, about 1729.

(V) Captain Zebediah Dewey, son of Thomas (3) Dewey, was born in Sheffield, October 8, 1727, died October 28, 1804, at Poultney, Vermont, where he settled about 1773. He lived on the site now occupied by Beaman's Hotel, but sold out, because, as he said "the neighbors became too near and too numerous". He then lived at the head of Hampshire Hollow, and the family still owns his farm. He was one of the men with Ethan Allen at the taking of Fort Ticonderoga, May 10, 1775. The French and Indians drove the settlers from Poultney and the neighboring towns, and Mrs. Zebediah Dewey, at the head of a company of women and children, demanded shelter in Pownal. During the night some of the enemy were reported, and she commanded the men who were present, bringing about the retreat of the Redcoats. Zebediah Dewey was lieutenant in Captain Daniel Whiting's company, Colonel Jonathan Brewer's regiment, June 17, 1775; enlisted as lieutenant from Tyringham, Massachusetts, April 24, 1775; also in a list of officers in a Massachusetts regiment, the Middlesex County Regiment, Captain Daniel Whiting. In appearance he was about five feet, ten inches tall, slim but very strong, small keen black eyes, dark hair; was of good mind and judgment, with sound common sense. He was chosen, January 15, 1777, to represent Poult-

ney at the convention which adopted the "Vermont Declaration of Independence" and declared that the district be known as the New Hampshire Grants, as a free state to be known as "New Connecticut, alias Vermont". He was on the committee of safety, March 11, 1777. He was the third richest man in town, October 4, 1781. He is said to have attained the rank of major at the battle of Hubbardtown. He married (first) widow of Solomon Jackson, who had a daughter who married Jacob Catlin. He married (second) Beulah Stearns, of Mendon, Massachusetts, born 1737, died December 31, 1820, at Poultney. Children: Thomas; Zebediah, born 1757 or 1767; Beulah; Charlotte; Anna; Artemesia; Azariah, 1765; Jonathan, about 1770; David, mentioned below; Keziah, August 28, 1782.

(VI) Dr. David Dewey, son of Captain Zebediah Dewey, was born at Poultney, March 1, 1778, died October 2, 1841, of stomach trouble, at Poultney, where he was a physician, farmer, inventor and manufacturer. He invented and patented in 1809 the first implement for shearing cloth by machinery. In order to make it he learned how to weld iron on steel in Connecticut and taught his blacksmith in Poultney how to do it. He built a dam, trip-hammer and shops for manufacturing his machines. He also engaged extensively in farming, and in 1814 patented a Vibrating Shearing Machine. He built a cotton factory near his other factories, and engaged in the manufacture of cloth. In 1818 he again received letters patent for a second improvement on the shearing machine and continued manufacturing them, although he ceased after a time to manufacture cloth. He went into the mercantile business with William Wheeler, and also about the same time, about 1818, he built and carried on one of the ten distilleries of the town. However, he stopped the last business after a time, as he became convinced that it was a crime against society. When the price of cotton goods went down, he changed the factory into a clothier's works, and put a carding machine in. At one time he owned a share of the printing office and fixtures of the *Northern Spectator*, an East Poultney paper. He kept up his farming all the time, running at least six farms at a time. In 1837 he received letters patent for the Spring Tooth Horse Rake. He was an active strong man, and never seemed to be tired. He frequently walked to Whitehall, New York, rather than tire out his horse, when he was over sixty years old. He was always generous and liberal with his wealth. He was the first secretary of the Washington Benevolent Society, brought out in interest of the Federalists in 1808. After the death of his youngest daughter he joined the Congregational church in Poultney.

He married, March 1, 1802, Anna, born about 1778, living in 1875, daughter of Joseph and Anna (Coleman) Morse. Children, born at Poultney: Charlotte Moseley, September 8, 1804, married Paul Moore Ross (see Ross VII); Esther, February 2, 1807; Jacob Catlin, January 10, 1808; David, 1810, died 1814; William, died in infancy; Zebediah, August 16, 1813; Thomas David, October 7. 1815; Laura Augusta, February 14, 1820; Harriet, 1822; James C., died in infancy; Lucretia, 1829, died March 6, 1832.

DAVIS John Davis, the immigrant ancestor, settled in Gloucester. The historian of Gloucester thinks he was formerly of Ipswich, but if so he must have been son of John Davis, of Ipswich, a shoemaker and herdsman, who was there in 1638 and sold land at Jabaque (Chebacco) in 1648. John Davis, of Gloucester, was living in 1682 and was then called John Sr. In deeds the name of his wife was given as Alice, but signed Frances. Children, born at Gloucester: John, March 10, 1660; James, born March 12, died March 23, 1662; James, mentioned below; Joseph, April 25. 1665, died May 4. 1665; Elizabeth, September 2, 1669; Abigail, April 13, 1672; Joseph, January 25, 1674; Susanna, November 20, 1676; Hannah, May 28, 1679; Ebenezer, March 26, 1681; Mark, May 20, 1683.

(II) Lieutenant James Davis, son of John Davis, was born in Gloucester, March 16, 1663. He bought house and land in Gloucester of William Somes in 1706, on the road from tide mill to the town parish. He was deacon of the church. Children: Deacon James, born December 5, 1691, died August 15. 1776, leaving sons James, John, Elias and Andrew; Elias, mentioned below; Solomon, March 3. 1696; Ebenezer.

(III) Elias, son of Lieutenant James Davis, was born at Gloucester, January 26, 1694. He was a merchant of large means and he left the largest estate of any of his townsmen, aggregating four thousand five hundred pounds. He had a warehouse, wharf and fishery room at Canso and owned ships named "John", "Molly", "Mary", "Flying Horse", "Greyhound" and "Elizabeth". Children: Mark; Job, mentioned below; Elizabeth, married David Harraden; Hannah, married Jonathan Brown Jr.

(IV) Job, son of Elias Davis, was born at Gloucester, about 1715. He married, in 1740, Thomasine Greenleaf, of Newbury. He had at Gloucester: Elias, mentioned below; Job.

(V) Captain Elias (2) Davis, son of Job Davis, was born at Gloucester, in 1746, died at Newburyport, September 15, 1783, aged thirty-seven. He was second lieutenant in Captain Moses Nowell's company on the Lexington Alarm, April 19, 1775; first lieutenant in the same company in the summer of 1775; from January to July, 1776, was stationed at Newburyport. He was captain of the Seventh Company in Colonel Jonathan Titcomb's regiment (Second Essex County) commissioned May 3, 1776. In the same year he was a captain under Colonel Timothy Pickering Jr. Another Elias Davis was in the revolution from Gloucester and was undoubtedly a cousin. It is not known whether the Gloucester or Newburyport man was captain of the privateeers "Fanny", 1780, "Peacock", 1781, "Favorite", 1782, and "Tybout", 1783. In 1790 the other Elias was living in Gloucester. He married, at Newburyport, December 26, 1669, Phebe Woodman, according to the town records. Children, born at Newburyport: Mary, April 12, 1771; Phebe, April 29, 1773; Samuel, mentioned below; Elias, September 14, 1777, died July 29, 1778; Elizabeth, April 17, 1779, baptized July 13, 1783; Nancy, March 22, 1781; Elias, June 14, 1782; Catherine, April 17, 1784.

(VI) Samuel, son of Captain Elias (2) Davis, was born at Newburyport, June 20, 1775, died in Boston, in December, 1856. He was a merchant in Boston, an importer of silverware and jewelry from Birmingham and Sheffield, England. He was in partnership with Robert Brown under the firm name of Davis & Brown at the corner of Milk and Washington streets, Boston, on the site of the building now occupied by the *Boston Transcript*. He came to Boston about 1800 and was married in the Old South Church, in October, 1807, by Rev. Dr. Eckley, to Lucy, daughter of Dr. Abraham Watson (see Watson VI). Children of Samuel Davis: William Charles, died aged nineteen years; Samuel, died aged nineteen years; Katherine, Elizabeth, Lucy, Mary, Martha, George Peabody, mentioned below.

(VII) George Peabody, son of Samuel Davis, was born in Boston, November 23, 1830. He was educated in the public schools of Boston. He married, September 7, 1864, Sarah Carlton Emerson, born October 1, 1832, in Methuen, Massachusetts, daughter of Elijah Carlton Emerson, who was for many years a manufacturer of boots and shoes, in partnership with Amasa Walker, in Boston.

He was born in Chester, New Hampshire, and lived in Brookline, Massachusetts, a descendant of Michael Emerson, one of the early settlers of Haverhill, Massachusetts. Children: 1. Katherine, born July 26, 1866; married William Cullen Snell, a son of William Snell, cousin of William Cullen Bryant, the poet, and they have three children: Sarah Emerson, Francis, George Snell. 2. Lucy Watson, born March 3, 1868; unmarried; superintendent of Children's Island Sanitarium, Marblehead, Mass. 3. Carlton Emerson, born November 14, 1869; graduate Massachusetts Institute of Technology; hydraulic engineer, in charge of water department, Philadelphia, Penn.; married Grace Bennett.

(The Watson Line).

(IV) Abraham (2) Watson, son of Abraham (1) Watson (q. v.), was born in Cambridge, in 1696, baptized in 1696-97, died at Cambridge. October 7, 1775. He was a tanner by trade; selectman of the town nine years between 1745 and 1760. He lived on the southwest side of what is now Massachusetts avenue, near Cogswell street. He married (first) Mary ———, and (second) Mary Butterworth, widow of John Butterworth, and previously of Abraham Hull. She died March 17, 1789. Children by first wife: Abraham, mentioned below; Daniel, born February 14, 1731-32; Mary, September 2, 1734; Samuel, December 22, 1745.

(V) Abraham (3), son of Abraham (2) Watson, was born at Cambridge, March 21, 1728-29. He was also a tanner. He lived on the homestead and was a prominent, energetic and intelligent citizen. He died December 11, 1781. after a long illness. Of him the *Boston Gazette* said at the time of his death: "He was a gentleman of superior abilities, which early introduced him into public life, being honored with a commission for the peace and much employed in the public affairs of the town, parish and church. In the American revolution he was an early and decided patriot, representing the town in the Provincial Congress and in the first General Court and the Convention for forming the Constitution of the Commonwealth. In domestic life, the tender passions were conspicuous in that circle as his manly virtues on the public stage. In his death, the family have to lament an affectionate husband and an indulgent parent and the public to regret the loss of a useful member of society." He married, March 28, 1751, Lucy, daughter of Rev. Nathaniel Prentice, of Dunstable, Massachusetts, now Nashua, New Hampshire. She was descended from Henry Prentice, one

of the founders of Cambridge, and from other prominent families of that town. Children: Abraham, mentioned below; Lucy, born May 26, 1754, died October 5, 1760; Samuel, November 11, 1757, died April 26, 1760; Samuel, September 19, 1759, died October 9, 1760; Lucy, February 13, 1762; Mary, February 11, 1763; Nathaniel Prentice, born October 21, 1764; Ruth, September 19, 1765; Lydia, July 20, 1768; Catherine, December 31, 1771; William Tyng, November 16, 1773, died young.

(VI) Dr. Abraham (4) Watson, son of Abraham (3) Watson, was born March 5, 1752, at Cambridge. He graduated from Harvard College in the class of 1771. He studied medicine and practiced at Littleton, Massachusetts, and Acworth, New Hampshire, whither he removed in 1787. He was a surgeon in Colonel Gardner's regiment in the revolution. He married ——— ———. Children: Lucy, married, in October, 1807, Samuel Davis (see Davis VI); she died September 12, 1867; Sophia.

———

The Champlin family in the CHAMPLIN United States is of Norman-French, rather than of English origin, it is thought. Families of this name are still found in Normandy, but few if any in England. Samuel de Champlain, the distinguished navigator and explorer, founder of Quebec and first governor of New France, was a Norman. A celebrated French painter, born at Les Andelys in 1825, bore the name Charles J. Champlin.

(I) Geoffrey Champlin, first of the Champlin name in this country, was in Rhode Island as early as 1638, within a year after the earliest white settlers made their homes there. He may have landed in Boston or some other Massachusetts port, and have left with the company of Dissentients, who followed Coddington and Arnold into the wilderness. We find him at first a resident of Portsmouth, Rhode Island, but he soon made his home at Newport. On January 24, 1638, he was admitted an inhabitant, and was made freeman, September 14, 1640. While at Newport, if not before, he acquired property, and in 1661 removed to Misquamacut, now known as Westerly, Rhode Island. His home lot and dwelling in Newport, with forty acres of land, he sold in 1669. His name appears in the list of free inhabitants of Westerly in 1669. In 1661 he took the oath of fidelity to the colony. During King Philip's war, 1675-76, he probably returned to Newport. He died in or before 1695, as in that year he is mentioned in a confirmation of a deed by his son Jeffrey as "my deceased father". Previous to 1650 Geoffrey Champlin married, probably in Newport, but the name of his wife is unknown. His children, so far as they are known, were: Jeffrey, of whom further; William; Christopher.

(II) Captain Jeffrey Champlin, son of Geoffrey Champlin, was born probably at Newport, about 1650, some say in 1652. On May 17, 1671, he was called to take the oath of allegiance to the colony, but did not appear. He took the oath, September 17, 1679. The same year he was chosen a member of the town council in Westerly. In 1680 he was moderator of the town meeting. His is the earliest record of a moderator in Westerly. He was also moderator of the meetings in 1681-84, and with the exception of 1683 he represented Westerly in the general assembly from 1681 to 1685. In 1685 he purchased of Anthony Low six hundred acres of land in Kingston, Rhode Island, and removed there in 1686. In 1690 when captain of the train band of Kingston he was appointed on a commission to raise money to pay soldiers to be used "against their Majesty's enemies". The government of Rhode Island, as organized in 1647 in accordance with the terms of the patent brought from England in 1644 by Roger Williams, consisted of a president and an assistant from each town. In case of the absence or death of the president, his place was to be taken by the assistant from the town from which the president was chosen. Jeffrey Champlin was the Kingston assistant from 1696, with the exception of 1697 to 1715, the year in which he died. He had sons Jeffrey and William, and a daughter Hannah, born about 1677, married John Watson Jr., April 8, 1703.

(III) Jeffrey (2), son of Captain Jeffrey (1) Champlin, was born probably in Westerly about 1672. About 1700, while residing in Kingston, he married (first) Susanna, daughter of Thomas and Susanna (Cole) Eldred, and granddaughter of Susanna Hutchinson, youngest child of the well-known Anne Hutchinson. Susanna (Eldred) Champlin died about 1705-06. He married (second) Hannah Hazard, died March 5, 1713, daughter of Robert and Mary (Brownell) Hazard, of Kingston, and granddaughter of the first Thomas Hazard, of Boston, Massachusetts, and Portsmouth, Rhode Island. He married (third) Susanna ———. Jeffrey Champlin died in 1718, and his will, dated February 14, 1717-18, was proved March 10, 1718. His widow married (second) May 26, 1720, Samuel Clarke, of Westerly. The inventory of Jeffrey Champlin amounted to one

thousand, four hundred and fifty-seven pounds, seven shillings, one penny. Children, by first wife: Enblin, born January 30. 1701-02; Jeffrey, February 2, 1702-03. By second wife: Thomas, September 3, 1708; Stephen, February 16, 1709-10; William, March 3, 1712-13. By third wife: Hannah, January 11, 1715; John, of whom further.

(IV) John, son of Jeffrey (2) Champlin, was born February 12, 1716-17, died September 8, 1772. He married Freelove, daughter of John Watson, of South Kingstown. She was born at South Kingstown, died in Exeter, May 10, 1773. Children: John, born July 30, 1744; Samuel, of whom further; William, August 15, 1749; Stephen, August 27, 1751; Thomas, January 23, 1754; Abigail, June 23, 1756; Elisha, November 11, 1758; Susannah, October 31, 1761; Freelove, June 15, 1767.

(V) Samuel, son of John Champlin, was born July 17, 1746, died in Exeter, Rhode Island, November 1, 1818. He married, December 10, 1782, Alice B., daughter of Benjamin and Alice (Waite) Reynolds, of Exeter. She was born July 21, 1755, died October 23, 1825. Children: John, of whom further; Benjamin, born May 9, 1786; Hannah, December 30, 1788; Waity, March 30, 1791; Russel, July 23, 1793; Samuel, August 24, 1796.

(VI) John Aldrich Champlin, of the family described above, was, it is thought son of Samuel Champlin, mentioned above, born March 26, 1784. He married (first) Lucy Green; (second) ——— ———. Children: William; John; Edwin; Esther; Maria; Katherine; Mary Jane; Martha; and Charles, of whom further.

(VII) Charles, son of John Aldrich Champlin, was born at Greenwich, or Wakefield, Rhode Island, in 1826, died in 1905. He was superintendent of various woolen mills at Potter's Hill, Rhode Island. He married (first) ——— ———; (second) Eliza Angelina Cottrell, born at Potter's Hill, Rhode Island, in 1828, died in 1893, daughter of Lebbeus and Lydia (Maxson) Cottrell (or Corthrell). She had brothers Calvert B. and Lebbeus M. Cottrell. Children of first wife: Charles B.; Arabella, married (first), Edwin Stillman, (second) Edward Clark; Giles Aldrich died at Providence. Child of second wife: Daniel H., of whom further.

(VIII) Daniel Henry, son of Charles Champlin, was born at Potter's Hill, Rhode Island, August 7, 1861. He attended the public schools of his native town and the high school at Asheway, Rhode Island. He then entered Alfred University at Alfred, New

York, and was a student there for three years. He entered the employ of Cottrell & Babcock, printing press manufacturers, of Westerly, Rhode Island, remaining with that concern for about ten years. In 1889 he came to Chicago, Illinois, as the western representative of C. B. Cottrell & Sons, manufacturers of printing presses. In 1899 he engaged in business for himself, representing various manufacturers of printing, bookbinding and lithographing machinery, and since then has been in this business in Chicago, with headquarters at 343 South Dearborn street, Chicago. His residence is in Highland Park, Illinois. Mr. Champlin is a member of the Chicago Athletic Club, the Exmoor Country Club, and the New England Society of Chicago. In politics he is a Republican. In early life he attended the Seventh Day Baptist Church, but in later years has been nonsectarian.

He married, August 25, 1886, Anna Lewis Stanton, who was born in Charlestown, Rhode Island, June 30, 1864, daughter of Hon. George A. and Bridget B. (Browning) Stanton (see Stanton VII). Her father was a cousin of Hon. Edwin M. Stanton, who was a member of Lincoln's cabinet. They have had one child, Marjorie Stanton, born in Chicago, August 25, 1896, died in infancy.

(The Stanton Line).

The surname Stanton is derived from a place name, and is identical with Stonington in origin. The family is of ancient English origin. Robert, an early settler of Newport, Rhode Island, was the progenitor of Hon. Edwin M. Stanton of Lincoln's cabinet. There was a John Stanton in Virginia in 1635, and Thomas, aged twenty, sailed for Virginia in 1635 in the merchantman "Bonaventura". The family historian thinks he went to Virginia, but many ships whose records state Virginia as their destination, came to New England. The "Bonaventura" may have landed some passengers in Virginia, others in Connecticut or Boston.

(I) Thomas Stanton, the immigrant ancestor, was in Boston in 1636, and is on record as a magistrate there. If he was the one who came in 1635, his age must have been understated, as men under twenty-one were not magistrates in the colony, and in 1636 he was acting as Indian interpreter for Governor Winthrop. It is reasonable to suppose that he was a trader and had been both to England and Virginia before 1635, in order to have sufficient knowledge of the language of the Indians to become an interpreter. The services of Mr. Stanton as interpreter during the Pequot war were invaluable, says the history of New London, Connecticut: "He was, moreover, a man of trust and intelligence and his knowledge of the country and the natives made him a useful pioneer and counsellor in all land questions, as well as difficulties with the Indians". DeForest's history of Connecticut says: "Some time in April (1637), a small vessel arrived at the fort (Saybrook) having on board Thos. Stanton, a man well acquainted with the Indian language, and long useful to the colonial authorities as interpreter." Stanton served through the Pequot war and special mention is made of his bravery in the battle of Fairfield Swamp, where he nearly lost his life. He must have returned to Boston at the close of the war, for he was one of the magistrates in the trial of John Wainwright, October 3, 1637. In February, 1639, he and his father-in-law, Thomas Lord, were settled in Hartford, Connecticut, coming there soon after the colony of Rev. Thomas Hooker established the town. He was appointed official interpreter for the General Court at Hartford, April 5, 1638, and at the same session was sent with others on a mission to the Warranocke Indians and as a delegate to an Indian-English council meeting at Hartford. He was interpreter for the Yorkshire, England, colonists at New Haven, November 24, 1638, when the land on which the city of New Haven is located, was bought of the Indians. He was an Indian trader as early as 1642, when with his brother-in-law, Richard Lord, he made a voyage to Long Island to trade and collect old debts, and there is a document showing that he traded as far away as Virginia. He had the grant of a monopoly of the trading with the Indians at Pawkatuck and along the river of that name. He built a trading house there and about 1651 moved to Pequot, and in 1658 occupied his permanent residence at Stonington. In 1650 the General Court appointed him interpreter to the elders who were required to preach the gospel to the Indians at least twice a year. Caulkins said of him: "From the year 1636, when he was Winthrop's interpreter with the Nahantic sachem, to 1670 when the Uncas visited him with a train of warriors and captains to get him to write his will, his name is connected with almost every Indian transaction on record." He received several grants of land. In 1651 he was deputy magistrate. In 1658 he moved to Wequetequock Cove, east of Stonington, where he was the third settler; it was then called Southington, part of Suffolk county, and in 1658 he was appointed one of the managers. In 1664 he was commissioner to try small causes and in 1665 had authority to hold a semi-annual court at New London. In 1666 he was again commissioner of county judges, overseer-general of the Coassatuck Indians, commissioner in Indian affairs, and commissioner until his death in 1677. In 1666 he was in the General Assembly, until 1674. He and his sons were active in King Philip's war. He was one of the founders of the Stonington church, June 3, 1674, and his name was first on the roll. He died December 2, 1677, and was buried in the family burial ground between Stonington and Westerly. He married Ann Lord, born 1621, in England, daughter of Dr. Thomas and Dorothy Lord. Her father was the first physician licensed to practice in Connecticut, by the general court, June 30, 1652, and the rates he could charge in Hartford, Wethersfield, Windsor, and other towns in that section were fixed in the license, a salary of fifteen pounds to be paid by the county. Ann Stanton spent her last days with her daughter, Mrs. Dorothy Noyes of Stonington, and died there in 1688. The original home site of Thomas Stanton at Hartford is now occupied by the Jewell Leather Bolting Company factory. Children: Thomas, born 1638; John, 1641; Mary, 1643; Hannah, 1644; Joseph, mentioned below; Daniel, 1648; Dorothy, 1651; Robert, 1653; Sarah, 1655; Samuel, 1657.

(II) Joseph, son of Thomas Stanton, was born in Hartford, Connecticut, in 1646, baptized March 21, 1646. He moved to Stonington with his parents, and settled on a large tract of land which his father had purchased from a Narragansett sachem for a half bushel of wampum. Joseph had helped to redeem the sachem's child from captivity, and the land was part payment for this. It was situated where Charlestown, Rhode Island, formerly part of Westerly, is situated, and the lease was dated November 20, 1685. In 1669 Joseph was appointed assistant magistrate, from Stonington, to hold court at New London with his father, who was magistrate. In May, 1714, Ben Uncas and fifty-four other Mohegans signed a paper declaring that Oweneco had sold the land unlawfully, in the western part, and they consigned what was left to Joseph Stanton and four others. This was probably this Joseph, though he died in 1714. He married (first) June 19, 1673, Hannah, daughter of William Mead, of Roxbury, Massachusetts, and she died in 1676. William Mead, in a will dated 1683, left half his estate to his wife and half to Joseph Stanton. He married (second) August 23, 1677, Hannah Lord, of Hartford,

and she was buried May 6, 1681. There is a record in the Stonington church of the admission of the wife of Joseph Stanton, March 16, 1683. She probably was his third wife, and she seems to have died childless. He, however, had children after 1690, so they must have been by this third wife, as Savage thinks, or by a fourth wife. Savage and Hon. John D. Baldwin think he married ———— Prentice, who may have been the third, or perhaps a fourth wife. Children, by first wife: Joseph (2), of whom further; Hannah, born 1676. By second wife: Thomas, December 16, 1678, died young; Rebecca, April, 1681. By third (or fourth) wife: Thomas, baptized April 5, 1691; Daniel, baptized April 1, 1694; Samuel, baptized July 17, 1698, died young.

(III) Joseph (2), son of Joseph (1) Stanton, was born in 1674, and lived in Westerly, Rhode Island, where he was a justice. An interesting letter written by him as justice has been preserved by the family. He married, January 3, 1705, Esther, daughter of Benadam and Hester (Prentice) Gallup. Children, born at Westerly: Esther, born 1708; Mary, 1711; Hannah, 1714; Nancy, 1716; Joseph (3), of whom further; Sarah, 1719; Lucy, September 22, 1722.

(IV) Colonel Joseph (3) Stanton, son of Joseph (2) Stanton, was born at Westerly, April 23, 1717. He served in the French and Indian war, and was present at the capture of Louisburg in 1745. He married (first) August 9, 1738, Mary, daughter of William Champlin. She was born July 13, 1722, died in 1750. She was admitted to the Stonington church, July 11, 1742. He married (second) in 1752, ———— ————, daughter of Henry Gardiner, of South Kingston, Rhode Island. Children, by first wife, born in Westerly: Joseph, born July 19, 1739; Esther, November 23, 1741; Mary, June 18, 1743; Augustus, of whom further; Hannah; February 24, 1746; Lodowick, May 27, 1749. By second wife: Gardiner, died single; Marlborough, died single; Henry; Abigail.

(V) Augustus, son of Colonel Joseph (3) Stanton, was born at Westerly, March 22, 1745, died April 10, 1822, aged seventy-seven years, at Hancock, Massachusetts, where he lived. He married, February 6, 1765, Eunice Crandal, born in Westerly, January 24, 1745, daughter of James and Damaris (Kenyon) Crandal. Children: General Joseph, born about 1766; Robert, August 14, 1768; Oliver, married Hannah Dewey; Ethan, married Nancy Stanton; Lucy, born March 29, 1777; Marlboro, of whom further; Esther, married Appleton Tracy; Cynthia, married Henry

King; Damaris, married Anderson Martin Jr.; Charlotte, married Jeremiah King, brother of Henry.

(VI) Marlboro, son of Augustus Stanton, was born in Rhode Island in 1779, died at Charlestown, Rhode Island, December 21, 1835, aged fifty-six years. He married Martha Hazzard, of Charlestown, Rhode Island, born in 1782, died April 11, 1860, in Charlestown. Her father and grandfather were both named George Wanton Hazzard, and her grandfather once served as mayor of Newport, Rhode Island. Children, born in Charlestown: Albert Wanton, born 1807; George A., of whom further.

(VII) Hon. George A. Stanton, son of Marlboro Stanton, was born at Charlestown, Rhode Island, January 24, 1809. He lived in Charlestown and Westerly, Rhode Island. He served for two years as state senator from Rhode Island, and two years in the house of representatives. For three years he was Indian commissioner. About 1888 he retired from the boot and shoe business, in which he was engaged. In religion he was an Episcopalian. He married (first) March 8, 1835, Catherine, daughter of William P. Sands, of Block Island. She was born on Block Island, November 9, 1813, died September 30, 1846, at Charlestown, Rhode Island. He married (second) June 5, 1848, Sarah M. Brown, of Stonington, born there December 16, 1822, died April 16, 1849. He married (third) February 14, 1857, Bridget Babcock Browning, born January 10, 1832, at Charlestown, Rhode Island. Children, by first wife: Dr. Nathaniel G., born July 8, 1836, at Newshoreham, Block Island; Kate Sands, April 1, 1838; Mary Elizabeth, February 29, 1841, died January 17, 1867, married Nathan B. Haile, of Providence; George A., June, 1844, married Harriet Aldrich, of Wrentham, Massachusetts, and she died 1883; Martha Babcock, 1845, died in infancy; Benjamin Franklin, September 20, 1846, married ——— Harris, of Providence. By second wife: Child, died in infancy. By third wife: Martha Babcock, October 22, 1857, died March 10, 1858; Harriet Babcock, February 12, 1859; Fanny Potter, October 16, 1861; Anna Lewis, June 30, 1864, married, August 25, 1886, Daniel Henry Champlin (see Champlin VIII).

BROWN Moses Brown was born before 1750 in Connecticut. During his boyhood he was bound out as an apprentice. He came to Ware, formerly Western, Worcester county, Massachusetts, when he was twenty-one years old, and spent the years of his manhood there. His later years were spent at the home of his son Warner at Ware, where he died in 1808. He was a prominent citizen and was on an important town committee with Captain Breckinridge to confer with General Lincoln and Captain Shays to secure peace at the time of Shays' rebellion. He served in the revolution in Captain Hooker's company, Colonel Ruggles' Regiment, in 1777 and had other service.

He married (first) ——— Bushnell, of Connecticut; married (second) a widow named Luce. Children by first wife: Eliza, married ——— Pomeroy; Roswell, died in 1850; Huldah; Hannah, married ——— Dimon; Cyrus; Ceeley, married ——— Aiken; Abigail, married ——— Witherell; Warner, mentioned below.

(II) Warner, son of Moses Brown, was born in Ware, Massachusetts, June 17, 1776. He followed farming in Ware, and took an active part in church matters, being a deacon. He later came to Hampton, New York, and was a farmer there for seven years. In 1829 he came to Vermont, and afterward lived at Wells and Poultney, dying at the latter named place. He married, December 1, 1808, Rhode Potter, born June 10, 1785, in North Brookfield, Massachusetts, died March 26, 1856, daughter of John and Rhoda (Burnett) Potter. Children: Caroline Burnett, born November 8, 1809, died January 1, 1813; Moses B., mentioned below; Catherine Burnett, April 2, 1812, died December 6, 1902; Harriet N., February 7, 1813, died May 23, 1816; Betsey Pomeroy, December 25, 1816, married ——— Platt; John Potter, August 17, 1818; Lorenzo, born April 27, 1820, died in 1885; Rhoda, October 17, 1822; Esther, February 17, 1826; Sarah Augusta, September 22, 1828, lives in East Poultney, Vermont.

(III) Moses Bushnell, son of Warner Brown, was born at Ware, Massachusetts, July 23, 1811, died at Castleton, Vermont, September 18, 1899. He received his early education in his native town, and came with his parents to New York state and afterward to Vermont. He lived in Rutland for six years. He was a farmer all his active life. He married (first) January 1, 1833, Louisa W. Hotchkiss, who died February 27, 1854. He married (second) December 19, 1854, Catherine Ross, born October 22, 1828, in Shrewsbury, Vermont, died April 5, 1894, daughter of Walter and Eliza (Webb) Ross. Children by first wife: Chalon, deceased; Herbert A., lives in Iowa. Children by second wife: Laura, born December 11, 1855, married Abram Smith Cramton; Harry Moses, mentioned below.

(IV) Harry Moses, son of Moses Bushnell Brown, was born December 3, 1866, in Rutland, Vermont. During his boyhood he lived in Clarendon and Castleton, Vermont. He attended the public schools of both towns. Since coming to Castleton he followed farming there until 1900 and still retains large farming interests, owning one farm of fourteen hundred acres, probably the largest single farm in the state. He also owns another farm of two hundred and forty acres. He made a specialty of raising cattle and dairying. In addition to his agricultural interests he has been engaged since January 1, 1900, in the manufacture of lumber at Castleton, where he operates a saw and grist mill. He is also a dealer in all kinds of feed and grain.

He married (first) October 6, 1897, Della Pond, of Castleton, who died March 5, 1898, daughter of Oscar and Evelyn Pond. He married (second) October 3, 1900, Edith Mary Wright, born at Warnersburg, New York, daughter of Martin and Sarah (Brown) Wright. Children by second wife: Harold Wright, born May 26, 1902; Mortimer Bertrand, May 24, 1905; Catherine Ross, November 12, 1912.

CLARK Elisha Clark, of one of the early pioneer families of Connecticut, was born at Suffield, Connecticut, about 1740. He came to Pawlet, Vermont, in 1784, and settled on the farm next south of the town farm. In 1795 he removed to Orwell, Vermont, where he spent his last years, living to an advanced age. His sons who remained in Pawlet were: Colonial Ozias, deacon of the church, founder of the Pawlet Manufacturing Company; Daniel, mentioned below; Joseph and Asahel.

(II) Daniel, son of Elisha Clark, was born in Suffield, Connecticut, December 15, 1770, died at Pawlet, Vermont, October 1, 1842. He was a soldier in the war of 1812. He followed farming all his active life. He married, January 31, 1788, Sybil Fitch, born February 24, 1772, died June 14, 1850, daughter of William and Alta (Wheeler) Fitch. Children: Elisha, born June 29, 1791; William Fitch, June 17, 1793; Philip Reed, June 7, 1795, died May 27, 1872; Wheeler, April 18, 1797, died October 29, 1874; John, April 5, 1799; Cyrus Austin, July 28, 1801; Darius, December 11, 1803; Cornelia, June 6, 1806; Corrilla, twin of Cornelia; Senia, August 29, 1808; Daniel, mentioned below.

(III) Daniel (2), son of Daniel (1) Clark, was born in Pawlet, Vermont, August 13, 1812, died in West Rutland, Vermont, March

3, 1889. He had a common school education, and followed farming. About 1839 he went west and located in Michigan. After eight years of pioneer life there, he returned to Vermont and lived for a time at Tinmouth. Afterward he made his home at West Rutland, where he spent his later years and died. He was a member of the Methodist Episcopal church.

He married Maria Salisbury, of Tinmouth, Vermont, born August 10, 1818, died in 1894, daughter of Elias and Fannie (Livingston) Salisbury. Children: Elias Edwin, mentioned below; Sarah F., born in 1845, married (first) M. C. Kelsey, (second) Charles H. Slason, (third) Henry G. Post.

(IV) Elias Edwin, son of Daniel (2) Clark, was born September 17, 1840, in La Pierre, Michigan. He came east with his parents when he was seven years old, and received his education in the public schools of Vermont. For twenty years he was a farmer, and then he engaged in the meat and provision business for twenty years with a market at West Rutland, Vermont. He was a soldier in the civil war, enlisting June 29, 1861, in Company I, Fifth Regiment Vermont Volunteer Militia, from the town of Poultney, and served three years. He was honorably discharged and mustered out of service in September, 1864. He took part in the battle of Savage Station and was wounded there. He was in the second battle of the Wilderness, at Spottsylvania and in the North Anna and South Anna engagements in which his regiment took an active part; also in the battle of Cedar Creek and of Petersburg and the battle of Winchester. He was taken prisoner and confined in the Rebel Prison at Belle Isle and also in Libby Prison. He was finally exchanged after enduring much hardship and suffering. He is a member of Hiram Lodge, No. 101, Free and Accepted Masons, of West Rutland. In politics he is a Republican; in religion a Congregationalist.

He married, September 7, 1865, Henrietta Caroline, born in Philadelphia, Pennsylvania, September 26, 1841, daughter of George Perry and Anna Eliza (Rose) Worrell. Children: 1. Chandleretta, born February 23, 1868; married Walter C. Thrall, of West Rutland, and has children, Mabel Henrietta, Rollin Clark, Wayne Edwin and Walter Deland. 2. Wayne Salisbury, born July 31, 1870, proprietor of an automobile garage in Rutland, married, January 1, 1901, May Angeline Morgan, of Harrisonville, Missouri, daughter of Elisha Rounds and Hannah Jane (McKisson) Morgan; children: Elsie May, born May 4, 1902; Wayne Morrell, May 20, 1903.

Charles H. Campbell

CAMPBELL The Vermont branch of the family bearing this ancient name so renowned in Scottish history is now represented in Rutland by Charles Henry Campbell, a well known business man of that city. On his mother's side Mr. Campbell is descended from ancestors the record of whose line has been for fourteen centuries interwoven with the history of England.

(I) Argyle Campbell, of Rutland, is thought to have been a native of Scotland, and is known to have emigrated at the beginning of the nineteenth century to the United States and settled in Chesterfield, New York. Soon after the birth of his youngest child he left his family and set out for the west, thinking that he might find in that then sparsely settled region more favorable opportunities. This was about 1818. His family watched in vain for his return, and year after year went by with no message from him and no tidings in regard to his fate, which ever remained a mystery. Mr. Campbell married, in Chesterfield, New York, Betsey Jaycox, born in 1790, daughter of Joseph Jaycox, who lived to the extraordinary age of one hundred and three years. The following children were born to Mr. and Mrs. Campbell: Joseph; John; Alexander, mentioned below; Charles. Mrs. Campbell, though she did not equal her father in longevity, lived to a very advanced age, dying in 1877, in her eighty-eighth year.

(II) Rev. Alexander Campbell, son of Argyle and Betsey (Jaycox) Campbell, was born September 28, 1816, in Chesterfield, New York. He belonged to the ministry of the Methodist Episcopal church, having graduated from the Troy Conference Seminary, Poultney, Vermont. For a number of years he was identified with Rutland, preaching in Centre Rutland in a church which was afterward purchased by the Vermont Marble Company and used for a store, and still later was destroyed by fire. Mr. Campbell caused to be erected on land given by General Ripley in what was then East Rutland the first Methodist Episcopal church ever built in Rutland. He married (first) October 9, 1842, Alma Tracy (see Tracy VII), and they became the parents of the following children: 1. Merritt Bates, born November 29, 1843, died December 1, 1911, in Heber, California; he was a physician and during the civil war served as a surgeon in the Union army; he was instrumental in the building of an asylum for the insane at Joliet, Illinois, and for fifteen years had charge of the institution; he married and had the following children: Alma, Bessie, Cora, a missionary to Japan; Robert, a physi-cian in Los Angeles; Mary. 2. Charles Henry, mentioned below. 3. Elizabeth P., born February 6, 1848; now living in Los Angeles. 4. William A., born July 22, 1858, died March 10, 1862. Mrs. Alma (Tracy) Campbell died August 4, 1864, in Rutland, and Mr. Campbell married (second) May 1, 1866, Laura M., widow of Caleb W. Ensign. The death of Mr. Campbell occurred May 8, 1882, at North Granville, New York, and he is buried at Shelburn, Vermont.

(III) Charles Henry, son of Rev. Alexander and Alma (Tracy) Campbell, was born December 9, 1845, in Morrisville, Vermont. He received a common school education, afterward attending the commercial college in Rutland. He was for a time engaged in the headstone and monument business, but has for forty years conducted the leading undertaking and livery establishment in West Rutland. He has extensive agricultural interests, being the owner of two farms, one in Rutland and the other in Ira. Since 1864 his home has been in West Rutland and he is prominently identified with the real estate interests of the town. Mr. Campbell married, June 30, 1868, Alta C. Ensign (see Ensign X), and they are the parents of two children: 1. Alma L., born October 5, 1869; married, March 4, 1890, Richard W. Smith Jr., of West Rutland, and has one son, Richard W., born August 21, 1898. 2. Kleber Alexander, born December 26, 1873; physician in Hopedale, Massachusetts; married, August 10, 1900, Mary Brewster Safford, of Ohio, and they have two children: Kleber Alexander, born October 18, 1902, and Katharine, born June 1, 1908.

(The Tracy Line).

(I) Cedric the Saxon, earliest known progenitor of this ancient race, sailed for England with five ships, in 495 Anno Domini, and the line of his descendants is traced below:

(II) Cuthwin, (III) Cuth, (IV) Chewald, (V) Kenred, (VI) Ingills, (VII) Eoppa, (VIII) Easa, (IX) Alkmund, (X) Egbert, (XI) Ethelwulf, (XII) Alfred the Great, came to the throne in 872, (XIII) Edward, (XIV) Edmund, (XV) Edgar, (XVI) Ethelred, (XVII) Princess Goda, married Walter, (XVIII) Rudolph, or Ralph, (XIX) Harold, Earl of Chester, married Matilda.

(XX) John, eldest son of Harold and Matilda, inherited the lands of his father and became Lord of Sudely and Toddington. He married Grace, daughter of Henry de Tracy, feudal lord of Devonshire, and they had two sons: Ralph, William, mentioned below.

(XXI) Sir William, son of John, Earl of Chester, and Grace de Tracy, inherited the lands of his mother and assumed the Tracy name. He was one of the knights who assassinated Thomas à Becket at the supposed instigation of King Henry the Second. The line of Sir William Tracy's descendants is as follows:

(XXII) Oliver, (XXIII) William, (XXIV) Henry, (XXV) Henry, (XXVI) Sir William, was in the Scotch war, (XXVII) William, (XXVIII) William, (XXIX) Sir John, was in parliament in 1357, (XXX) Sir John, was in parliament, (XXXI) William, (XXXII) William, (XXXIII) William, (XXXIV) Henry, (XXXV) Sir William, (XXXVI) Richard, of Stanway, married Barbara Lucy, (XXXVII) Nathaniel, of Tewksbury.

From the period of the emigration the line is as follows:

(I) Lieutenant Thomas Tracy, son of Nathaniel Tracy, of Tewksbury, was born in England, in 1610, and in April, 1636, came to the American colonies, settling at Salem, Massachusetts.

(II) Sergeant Thomas (2) Tracy was born in 1646.

(III) Nathaniel Tracy was born in 1675; married Sarah Minor.

(IV) Joseph Tracy was born in 1712; married Mary Fuller.

(V) Hezekiah Tracy was born in 1746; married Eunice ———.

(VI) Cyrus Tracy was born March 20, 1785; married Alma ———.

(VII) Alma, daughter of Cyrus and Alma Tracy, was born March 24, 1822, in Shelburn, Vermont, on a part of what is now the well known Webb farm; she became the wife of the Rev. Alexander Campbell (see Campbell II).

(The Ensign Line).

The line of descent of Mrs. Alta C. (Ensign) Campbell is traced as follows from William Bradford:

(I) William Bradford, born in 1590, in Austerfield, England, was a passenger on the "Mayflower," in 1620, and became the second governor of the Plymouth Colony. He married Alice Carpenter.

(II) Lieutenant-Governor William Bradford married Alice Richards.

(III) Mercy, daughter of William and Alice (Richards) Bradford, married Samuel Steele.

(IV) Thomas, son of Samuel and Mercy (Bradford) Steele, married Susannah Webster.

(V) Susannah, daughter of Thomas and Susannah (Webster) Steele, married Thomas Hosmer.

(VI) Susannah, daughter of Thomas and Susannah (Steele) Hosmer, married Joel Kellogg.

(VII) Deborah, daughter of Joel and Susannah (Hosmer) Kellogg, married Gideon Deming.

(VIII) Orpah, daughter of Gideon and Deborah (Kellogg) Deming, married Dr. Caleb W. Ensign.

(IX) Caleb W. (2), son of Caleb W. (1) and Orpah (Deming) Ensign, married Laura M. Safford.

(X) Alta C., daughter of Caleb W. (2) and Laura M. (Safford) Ensign, was born October 15, 1846, in Rootstown, Ohio, and became the wife of Charles Henry Campbell (see Campbell III).

MARSHALL Thomas Marshall, emigrant ancestor of Dr. George Morley Marshall, came in 1634 or 1635 from Boston, England, to Boston, Massachusetts. He had been mayor of the city first named. For thirteen years he was deacon of the First Church, the oldest church in Boston, Massachusetts. He was selectman eleven years and dean (or oldest member of the board) in later life.

(II) Captain Samuel Marshall, son of Deacon Thomas Marshall, settled in Windsor, Connecticut, whence the family spread to Torrington, Connecticut. He commanded the Windsor company in General Josiah Winslow's campaign against the Indian conspirator, King Philip, in December, 1675. At the head of this force, while storming Philip's fort in the Great Swamp Fight, Captain Samuel Marshall was killed. He was called "Brave Captain Samuel," and he had honorable mention in Bancroft's History, Hollister's "Connecticut", Hutchinson's "Massachusetts", Drake's "Indians", etc. He married, May 1, 1652, Mary, daughter of Lieutenant David Wilton. Children: Samuel, born May 27, 1653; Lydia, February 18, 1655; Thomas, April 23, 1659; David, July 24, 1661; Thomas (2d), of whom further; Mary, May 8, 1667; Eliakim, July 10, 1669; John, April 10, 1672; Elizabeth, September 27, 1674.

(III) Deacon Thomas (2) Marshall, son of Captain Samuel Marshall, was born February 23, 1663, died November 8, 1735. He was an original proprietor of Torrington, Connecticut, but did not settle there. He married Mary Drake, daughter of Job Drake, of the family of the famous Sir Francis Drake; her mother was daughter of the distinguished Henry Walcott. Children of Deacon Thomas and Mary (Drake) Marshall: Thomas, born January 14, 1686, died August 26, 1689; Mary, born February 21, 1689; Samuel, July

23, 1691; Thomas (3d), of whom further; Rachel, April 12, 1696; Catharine, April 11, 1699; John, April 3, 1701; Noah, April 24, 1703; Rev. Daniel, 1705; Benjamin, August 8, 1707; Eunice, May 3, 1709.

(IV) Thomas (3), son of Deacon Thomas (2) Marshall, was born in Windsor, Connecticut, February 6, 1693, died February 4, 1772. He settled in the southwestern part of Torrington some time before 1757, on a farm just south of the old Jonathan Coe place. He married, October 9, 1725, Elizabeth Tudor, born in 1700, died February 8, 1790, daughter of Owen Tudor, who migrated from Wales in 1649. Children: Thomas, born October 13, 1726, died young; Gad, February 18, 1732; Job, April 22, 1736; Thomas, of whom further.

(V) Thomas (4), youngest son of Thomas (3) Marshall, was born September 5, 1738. He settled on a farm in Newfield, adjoining the Winchester line, which his father gave him in 1761, and started the first large dairy in Newfield. He was one of the first settlers there, and a man of great influence among his neighbors. He served in the revolution in Captain Griswold's company, in 1777, and in Captain Amos Cook's company in 1775. He married (first) January 30, 1764, Desire Tuttle, born May 16, 1743, died August 14, 1808. He married (second) Sarah Butler, a widow, of Harwinton, Connecticut. Children, all by his first wife: Raphael, born May 14, 1765; Reuben, born November 29, 1766, died February 13, 1814; Harvey, born June 29, 1768; Sarah, born June 10, 1770, died April 17, 1816; Levi, born April 19, 1772, died December 25, 1818; Rosel, born December 30, 1773, died November 23, 1845; Seth, of whom further; Rachel, born June 19, 1781, died January 15, 1849; Susannah, born August 14, 1783.

(VI) Seth, son of Thomas (4) Marshall, was born in Newfield, Connecticut, December 2, 1775, died October 11, 1841. He lived for many years in Colebrook, Connecticut, and was representative in the Connecticut general assembly from Colebrook, 1809-16. He removed to Painesville, Ohio, where he died. He married, June 3, 1802, Susan Frisbie, born March 10, 1783, who survived him thirty years, dying at the age of ninety-seven. Children: Helen Maria, born April 9, 1803; Abigail Elisa, August 31, 1805; Raphael, July 21, 1807; Stephen, September 9, 1809; Sarah, July 4, 1811; Horace, December 1, 1813; Seth, of whom further; Anna, July 23, 1817; Edward, November 24, 1820.

(VII) Seth (2), son of Seth (1) Marshall, was born in Colebrook, Litchfield county, Connecticut, September 3, 1815. He went to the Western Reserve, Ohio, with his parents, in 1837, whither two married sisters had preceded him. As purser on a line of boats which traversed the Great Lakes, he spent one or two seasons, at which time he saw the hamlet of a few dwellings which later became Chicago. He then took a position in the Geauga Bank of Painesville, Ohio, which later became the First National Bank, of which he was president for many years. He early entered the hardware business, in which he remained the greater part of his business life. He was a Republican in politics and was one of the electors who elected Lincoln. He was an early Abolitionist, of strong principle and fearless. He did not hesitate to imperil large business interests that he might protect the fugitive slaves in their flight to Canada, although it was in defiance of the law and pro-slavery sentiment. His home was regarded as one of the stations on the "underground railroad," and there still stands on the Marshall homestead, the old barn with its massive frame of hewn timber, where many of the unfortunates were given food and shelter. He married, May 26, 1842, Esther Philena, born in 1815, daughter of Albert and Esther (Healy) Morley. She was descended on her maternal side from William Healy, who came with the Pilgrims and settled in Roxbury, afterwards Cambridge, Massachusetts. Children of Seth Marshall: Juliet Gillet, born April 12, 1843; Thomas Healy, November 13, 1845; Mary Woolley, April 21, 1848, died in infancy; Seth, April 25, 1850; Albert Morley, December 25, 1851; Emma Caroline, August 8, 1853; Charles Edward, born May 17, 1856, died 1864; George Morley, of whom further.

(VIII) George Morley, son of Seth (2) Marshall, was born March 13, 1858, in Painesville, Lake county, Ohio. He taught one year while preparing for college, and graduated from Adelbert College of Western Reserve University in 1883, with the degree of Bachelor of Arts. In the same year he entered the medical department of the University of Pennsylvania, from which he received the degree of Doctor of Medicine in 1886; taking at once the competitive examination at St. Joseph's Hospital, he became its first resident physician under the management of the Sisters of Charity. After remaining with that institution one year he continued his professional studies in Vienna and Berlin until the winter of 1888-89. In January, 1889, he returned to Philadelphia and began the active practice of his profession, and that year was appointed attending physician and laryngologist to St. Joseph's Hospital. Two years later he was also appointed laryngologist to the Philadelphia Hospital. Although Dr. George M. Marshall remains in Philadelphia in active practice, he has a country home and farm in Solebury, Bucks county, Pennsylvania, where his children Harriet, Celia and Thomas were born, and where the family live a portion of each year. His country property is among farmers whose ancestors received grants and were among the original followers of William Penn. It includes the historic Phillips mill, which began operation before the revolutionary war and continued with the same water power and wooden machinery to the time of its purchase in 1896, and later. Around this mill has come a colony of artists and friends.

He married, June 7, 1893, Harriet Putnam, daughter of Heman and Mary (Day) Ely, of Elyria, Ohio. Her paternal grandfather, Heman Ely, went early to the Western Reserve to develop a large tract of land inherited from his father, one of the original members of the Connecticut Land Company, and gave the name Lorain to the county, and laid out and named the town of Elyria. Her maternal grandfather, Thomas Day, of Hartford, brother of Jeremiah Day, president of Yale College, was for twenty-two years secretary of state in Connecticut. Children of George Morley and Harriet Putnam (Ely) Marshall: George Morley Jr., born March 19, 1894, died March 7, 1905; Esther Philena, born June 8, 1895; Harriet Ely, September 7, 1896; Margaret Ely, April 24, 1898; Edith Williamson, August 3, 1900, died August 16, 1901; Celia Belden, born January 29, 1902; Thomas, October 8, 1905.

Nathaniel Ely, the immigrant ancestor, was born in England, doubtless at Tenterden, county Kent, in 1606. He received a common school education, as evidenced by the records left behind him. He married, in England, Martha ———, and had a son and daughter before leaving his native land. He came to America, it is thought, in 1634, in the bark "Elizabeth", from Ipswich, England. His name is not on the passenger list, but that of his friend Robert Day appears, and as they settled on adjoining lots in Newtown, Massachusetts Bay, now the city of Cambridge, May 6, 1635, it is reasonable to believe that they came together. In June, 1636, Rev. Thomas Hooker and about a hundred others, men, women and children, probably including Nathaniel Ely, made their way through the wilderness to a fertile spot on the Connecticut river and made the first settlement at Hartford. It appears from the early records and from a map made in 1640 that

Ely owned a homestead there. In 1639 he was one of the constables, and in 1643-49 one of the selectmen. The name of Nathaniel Ely is on the monument to the memory of the first settlers of Hartford. He afterwards removed to what is now Norwalk, Connecticut, of which he was one of the founders and first settlers, where he remained until 1659 when he sold his property and removed to Springfield, Massachusetts, where he passed the rest of his life. Here, as at Hartford, he was called to serve the public soon after his arrival, and was selectman in 1661-63-66-68-71-73. His place of residence in that town from 1660 to 1665 is not certainly known, though it is most likely that he lived in what is now Chicopee. In 1665 he became keeper of the ordinary, or tavern, a business which he continued to follow to the time of his death, December 26, 1675. Martha, his wife, died in Springfield, October 23, 1688. Children: Samuel, mentioned below; Ruth, died October 12, 1662.

(II) Samuel, son of Nathaniel Ely, was born probably at Hartford, Connecticut, or Cambridge, Massachusetts, and died March 19, 1692. He removed to Springfield with his parents and married there, October 28, 1659, Mary, youngest child of Robert Day and his second wife, Editha (Stebbins) Day; she was born in Hartford in 1641. Samuel Ely was quite successful in acquiring property, and at his death left a considerable estate. He died in Springfield. Ten of their sixteen children died in infancy or in early youth. Children: child, born and died in 1660, Springfield; Samuel, born March 1, 1662, died March 22, 1662; Joseph, born August 20, 1663; Samuel, November 4, 1664, died February 18, 1665; Mary, March 29, 1667, died April 19, 1667; Samuel, born May 9, 1668; Nathaniel, January 18, 1670, died March 16, 1671; Jonathan, July 1, 1672, died July 10, 1672; Jonathan, January 24, 1676, died February following; Martha, October 28, 1677, died November 25, 1677; John, mentioned below; Mary, June 20, 1681, died December 21, 1681; Jonathan, born January 21, 1683; Mary, February 29, 1684; Ruth, 1688. All were born at Springfield.

(III) Deacon John Ely, son of Samuel Ely, was born at Springfield, January 28, 1678, died at West Springfield, January 15, 1758. He married, December 30, 1703, Mercy, daughter of Samuel and Mary (Leonard) Bliss, born July 18, 1680, died in West Springfield, May 5, 1763. Her sister Martha married Samuel Ely, a brother of John. Children, born at West Springfield: Twin sons, born November 5, 1704, died November 5-10, 1704;

Abel, November, 1706, died January 17, 1707; John, mentioned below; Reuben, January 12, 1710; Abner, September 26, 1711; Mercy, January 22, 1713; Caleb, November 25, 1714; Rachel, November 11, 1716; Noah, July 4, 1721.

(IV) Ensign John Ely, son of John Ely, was born at West Springfield, December 3, 1707, died there May 22, 1754. He married, November 15, 1733, Eunice, daughter of John and Joanna Colton, born at Longmeadow, February 22, 1705, died March 29, 1778. She married (second) June 19, 1759, Major Roger Wolcott, son of Governor Roger and Sarah (Drake) Wolcott. She married (third) April 3, 1761, Captain Joel White, of Bolton, Connecticut. Children, born at West Springfield: John, April 6, 1735; Eunice, January 19, 1737; Justin, mentioned below; Eunice, September 11, 1741; Heman, January 8, 1744, died May 9, 1754; Rhoda, May 12, 1746.

(V) Justin, son of Ensign John Ely, was born at West Springfield, August 10, 1739, and died there June 26, 1817. He married (first) November 9, 1762, Ruth, daughter of Captain Joel and Ruth (Dart) White, of Bolton, Connecticut, born February 29, 1744, died April 6, 1809. He married (second) December 11, 1809, Marion Lane, daughter of Governor Matthew and Ursula (Wolcott) Griswold, of Lyme, Connecticut, born there, April 17, 1750. She married (first) Charles Church Chandler, (second) Captain Ebenezer Lane. She died in West Springfield, June 17, 1829. Justin Ely graduated from Harvard College, 1759, and became a successful merchant in his native town, where he did a larger business than any other merchant. He was interested to a great extent in real estate in Massachusetts, Vermont, the District of Maine, and New York, and was an original proprietor of the Connecticut Western Reserve in Ohio, under the Connecticut Land Company. He represented his native town in the general court in 1777-80-85-90-97, and was otherwise prominent in public affairs. During the revolution he was active in aiding the country, especially in collecting men who were drafted into the service and in providing for them afterwards. Children, born at West Springfield: Theodore, August 10, 1764; Anna, May 12, 1767, died January 6, 1776; Justin, September 22, 1772; Heman, mentioned below.

(VI) Heman, son of Justin Ely, was born in West Springfield, April 24, 1775, and died in Elyria, Ohio, February 2, 1852. Early in the nineteenth century he became interested in the purchase of lands in central and western New York, and under his direction large

tracts there were surveyed and sold to settlers. At about the same time he entered into partnership with his brother Theodore in New York City, and was for ten years engaged with him in commerce in Europe and the East Indies. During this time he visited England, Holland, France and Spain, largely in the interests of his business. In France he lived long enough to acquire the language, and was in Paris from July, 1809, to April, 1810, where he was witness of many social and political events of historical interest. He saw in August, 1809, the grand fete of Napoleon and the Empress Josephine, and in the evening attended a ball at the Hotel de Ville, where a cotillion was danced by a set of kings and queens. The following April, the Empress Josephine having in the meantime been divorced and dethroned, he witnessed the formal entrance into Paris of Napoleon and Marie Louise of Austria, and the religious ceremony of marriage at the chapel of the Tuilleries. At that time all Europe was under arms and passage from one country to another was attended with the greatest difficulty and danger. Mr. Ely and a friend, Charles R. Codman, of Boston, in 1809 embarked for Holland from England in a Dutch fishing boat, were fired upon by gendarmes as they tried to land, and only after a long journey on foot reached Rotterdam and finally Paris. In 1810 he returned to America and the following year visited Ohio, and returned to New England by way of Niagara Falls, the St. Lawrence, and Montreal. Most of this journey was performed on horseback; part of it on the Hudson by a steamboat he mentions with special interest. In 1816 he again visited Ohio and made arrangements to open the territory owned by his father, No. 6, range 17, Connecticut Western Reserve. In February, 1817, accompanied by a large company of skilled workmen and laborers, he left the east for his future home. He and his stepbrother Ebenezer Lane rode in a covered wagon, the others walked or rode on the ox cart which carried provisions, and arrived at their destination March 17, 1817. The new settlement was named by Mr. Ely, Elyria, and owed its prosperity to his lifelong efforts. In laying out the town he arranged for broad streets and ample public grounds, with suitable lots for a church and school-house. Later he erected a high school building, also a house for boarding pupils from surrounding towns. In 1818 he built a house for himself. He encouraged all christian institutions, and contributed liberally for their maintenance, although he was not himself a member of any church until 1841. In 1831-32 he served on the state board of equalization, and from 1835 to 1845 was one of the associate judges under the old state constitution. In politics he was a Federalist, of the school of George Cabot, Harrison Gray Otis and Thomas Handyside Perkins.

He married, in West Springfield, October 9, 1818, Celia, daughter of Colonel Ezekiel Porter and Mary (Parsons) Belden, born in Wethersfield, Connecticut, October 5, 1796, died at Elyria, January 7, 1827. He married (second) in Mansfield, Connecticut, August 20, 1828, Harriet M., daughter of General John Salter, born in Mansfield, March 20, 1792, died in Elyria, August 6, 1846. He married (third) in Elyria, December 7, 1846, Cynthia, widow of John Sergeant, of Stockbridge, Massachusetts, and daughter of Dr. Jeremiah and Amelia (Ely) West, of Tolland, Connecticut, born July 21, 1791, in Tolland, died in Hartford, August 5, 1871. Children of first wife, born at Elyria: Heman, mentioned below; Albert, January 7, 1825; Mary Belden, January 7, 1827, died same day; child of second wife: Charles Arthur, May 2, 1829.

(VII) Heman (2), son of Heman (1) Ely, was born at Elyria, October 30, 1820. His mother died in 1827, and he was brought up by Rev. Emerson Davis, D. D., and his wife, of Westfield, Massachusetts. Later he attended the high school at Elyria and Mr. Simeon Hart's school in Farmington, Connecticut. He then returned to Elyria and entered his father's office, where he received a business training particularly in the care of real estate. He soon assumed the entire business. He assisted in the organization of the first bank in Elyria, was chosen a director in 1847 and from that time has been connected with it as director, vice-president and president. It became in 1883 the National Bank of Elyria. In 1852, with Judge Ebenezer Lane and others, he secured the building of that section of the present Lake Shore & Michigan Southern railway, then known as the Junction railroad, from Cleveland to Toledo. From 1870 to 1873 he was a member of the state legislature, and interested himself especially in the formation of the state insurance department. He was a member of King Solomon's Lodge, Free and Accepted Masons, and was worshipful master from 1852 to 1871; of the Grand Commandery of Knights Templar of Ohio, grand commander from 1864 to 1871; Supreme Council of the Ancient Accepted Scottish Rite of Free Masonry for the Northern Jurisdiction of the United States, and treasurer for some years. He was also a member of the Congregational church in Elyria, and for many years one of its officers.

For ten years he served as superintendent of the Sunday school. He has spent some time in compiling the records of the Ely family.

He married, in Elyria, September 1, 1841, Mary, daughter of Rev. John and Abigail (Harris) Montieth, born in Clinton, Oneida county, New York, November 12, 1824, died in Elyria, March 1, 1849. He married (second) in Hartford, May 27, 1850, Mary Frances, daughter of Hon. Thomas and Sarah (Coit) Day, born in Hartford, May 7, 1826. Children of first wife, born in Elyria: Celia Belden, November 24, 1842, died October 18, 1861; George Henry, November 15, 1844; Mary Montieth, February 20, 1849, died November 1, 1849. Children of second wife, born in Elyria: Edith Day, November 27, 1851; Charles Theodore, October 27, 1856; Albert Heman, mentioned below; Harriet Putnam, October 9, 1864.

(VIII) Dr. Albert Heman Ely, son of Heman Ely, was born in Elyria, Ohio, November 22, 1860. He prepared for college at Phillips Academy, Andover, Massachusetts, and entered Yale University, where he was graduated in the class of 1885 with the degree of bachelor of arts. He entered upon the study of his profession at the College of Physicians and Surgeons of Columbia University, and was graduated there with the degree of M. D. in 1888. He received his hospital experience as interne at St. Luke's Hospital in New York City. For about two years he traveled and studied abroad, attending lectures and acquiring hospital experience at Vienna. Since his return to this country he has been engaged in general practice in New York City. He is a member of the County and State medical societies and the American Medical Association. He is a Republican in politics. He belongs to the New England Society of New York, the University, Yale and Southampton clubs, and is a communicant of the Protestant Episcopal church.

He married, at Rochester, New York, October 7, 1891, Maude Louise Merchant, born at Rutland, Illinois, daughter of George Eugene Merchant and Frances Sherburne. Children: 1. Reginald Merchant, born August 10, 1892, died August 21, 1892. 2. Albert Heman Jr., born March 21, 1894. 3. Gerald Day, born October 7, 1896, died December 29, 1900. 4. Francis Sherburne, born November 7, 1902.

GRISWOLD

The English Griswolds were an ancient county family established at Solihull, Warwickshire, England, before 1400. They were descended from John Griswold, who came from Kenilworth about the middle of the four-

teenth century, and settled in Solihull. They were of local distinction, and held many county offices. They possessed a coat-of-arms as follows: Argent, a fesse gules between two greyhounds current, sable. The name was originally written Greswold and Gryswild.

(I) Michael Griswold, the immigrant ancestor of this branch, was born in England, and owned lands in Wethersfield, Connecticut, as early as 1640. There were two other Griswold immigrants, Matthew and Edward, whom we know were brothers; both came in 1639 and settled in Windsor, Connecticut. Another brother of Matthew and Edward remained in England, Thomas, as proved by the deposition of George Griswold, son of Edward, in 1700. The father of the beforementioned Matthew, Edward and Thomas, was Edward Griswold, of Kenilworth, Warwickshire. Michael Griswold, the immigrant ancestor of Frank D. Griswold, was not a brother of the before-mentioned Griswolds, though some early writers have assumed that he was. It is probable that he was a cousin.

Michael Griswold, the immigrant ancestor, was the only freeman of the name in Wethersfield, Connecticut, in 1659. He held the offices of constable, assessor and appraiser of land, and was a mason by trade. He owned land at Two-Stone Brook, which had been granted him by the town, together with other lots. He died September 26, 1684, and left a will, probated November 18, 1684, in which he mentioned his wife Ann, sons Thomas, Michael, Isaac and Jacob, daughters Hester, Abigail and Sarah, and grandchildren. Children, born in Wethersfield: Thomas, October 22, 1646; Hester, May 8, 1648; Mary, January 28, 1650; Michael, February 14, 1652, died young; Abigail, June 8, 1655; Isaac, September 30, 1658; Jacob, of whom further; Michael, March 7, 1666-67.

(II) Jacob, son of Michael Griswold, was born in Wethersfield, April 15, 1660, died July 22, 1737. He married, December 10, 1685, Mary, daughter of Deacon Joseph and Mary (Stoddard) Wright; she died April 25, 1735, aged seventy years. He inherited land from his father at Two-Stone Brook, now Griswoldville, and was doubtless the first settler there. This land, together with other parcels purchased by him, has remained in the family to this day. In his will, dated February 10, 1735-36, he gave his home lot to his son Ephraim, and made it appear that he had already given to sons Jacob, Michael, and Ebenezer, their portions in advance. His estate inventoried at £268, 17s. 9d. Children, born at Wethersfield: John, September 25, 1686; Mary, June 19, 1688; Jacob, March 26, 1690;

Anna, August 14, 1693; Sarah, March 18, 1695; Hester, March 13, 1696; Joseph, baptized August 21, 1697 (?); Josiah, August 20, 1698, probably died young; Josiah, January 4, 1700; Ebenezer, of whom further; Ephraim, September 23, 1704; Lydia, September 4, 1707.

(III) Lieutenant Ebenezer Griswold, son of Jacob Griswold, was born in Wethersfield, October 25, 1702, died December 7, 1772. He married, December 13, 1734, Deborah, daughter of Henry Grimes. She died June 7, 1765, aged forty-nine. Children, born in Wethersfield: Elias, February 22, 1736, died May 18, 1741; Zehiel, June 22, 1738; Elizur, August 10, 1742, died November 9, 1744; Timothy, October 24, 1744; Anne, October 10, 1746; Elias, of whom further; Elizur, October 30, 1753; Sarah, May 7, 1758.

(IV) Elias, son of Lieutenant Ebenezer Griswold, was born in Wethersfield, October 6, 1750. He came to Buckland, Massachusetts, in 1785. He married, December 8, 1773, Rhoda, daughter of Joseph Flower. Children: Elias, June 4, 1775; Horace, May 27, 1777; Joseph, of whom further; Simeon; Whiting.

(V) Joseph, son of Elias Griswold, was born about 1785. He lived with his father at Buckland, Massachusetts. In 1828 he located at Colerain, Massachusetts, and began to manufacture sash, doors and blinds. In 1830 he also began to make gimlets, augers and shaving boxes, and in 1832 he erected the cotton mill with sixteen looms, but before the end of the first year he doubled its capacity. In 1835 he added the second cotton mill, and in 1840 incorporated his business under the name of the Griswoldville Manufacturing Company. In 1851 the mill that was built first was destroyed by fire, but such was the enterprise and energy of the owners that within twelve days the structure was rebuilt. In 1856 another mill, the structure built in 1835, was burned to the ground, and its place was taken by a new mill built in 1858. The main mill is fifty by two hundred and fifty feet, two stories and a half in height, with an ell forty by sixty feet, a boiler house, cotton house and other out-buildings. In 1865 the company erected at Willis Place, a second brick mill for the manufacture of cotton, fifty by two hundred feet, three stories high, with a forty by seventy extension. Both mills are on North river and have excellent water power, with auxiliary steam power for emergencies. Several hundred hands are employed, making print cloth and sheeting. The company owns a large part of the village, and leases the tenements to the millhands.

Mr. Griswold married Louise Denison, born

in Mystic, Connecticut, and had a family of thirteen children, Joseph, Lorenzo and Wayne are the only survivors; among the others was Ethan Denison, of whom further.

(VI) Ethan Denison, son of Joseph Griswold, was born at Griswoldville, a village named for the family, in the town of Colerain, Massachusetts, March 11, 1831, died July 22, 1910. He was for many years president of the Griswoldville Manufacturing Company. At the time of his death his brother Joseph Griswold was vice-president, Lorenzo Griswold was treasurer, and F. D. Griswold was agent. He was a Republican, a Mason, and a member of the Congregational church. He married, in 1853, Sarah Wilson, born in 1833, died in 1865, daughter of Captain John Wilson, of Adamsville, Massachusetts, and Rebecca, his wife. Children, not in order of birth: Eliza; Carrie; Mary; Rebecca; Sarah; Frank D., of whom further.

(VII) Frank D., son of Ethan Denison Griswold, was born at Griswoldville, Massachusetts, September 10, 1855. He attended the public schools of his native town and of Brooklyn, New York. In 1868 he entered the Polytechnic Institute of Brooklyn, New York, and was graduated from that institution in the class of 1872. He was for a time a clerk in the dry goods commission business, and afterward entered the employ of the Griswoldville Manufacturing Company, which was founded by his grandfather. Since 1883 he has been agent of the company, and since the death of his father has been treasurer of the concern. The company makes a specialty of sterilized absorbent gauze for surgical purposes. The New York office is at 75 Worth street. His home is in Brooklyn. He attends the Central Congregational Church, of Brooklyn. In politics he is a Republican. He is a member of the Crescent Athletic Club and the Atlantic Yacht Club, of Brooklyn.

He married, October 17, 1883, Cordelia Hickok, born November 17, 1865, died February 13, 1898, daughter of William C. and Sarah Hickok. Mr. and·Mrs. Griswold had no children.

CLARK   In the same section of New England three pioneers by the name of Edward Clark settled. Edward Clark, at Wells, Maine, took the freemen's oath July 5, 1653, and served on a jury at Cape Porpoise in 1656. He died in 1661, leaving a wife Barbara, and children: Samuel, Sarah, William and Edward. The second Edward, perhaps son of Edward of Wells, had land assigned to him at Portsmouth, New Hampshire, October 19, 1659, and was

drowned at Portsmouth, June 17, 1675. By his first wife he had children: John and Sarah, and by his second wife, Mary, he had three children.

(I) Edward Clark, immigrant ancestor, settled early at Haverhill, Massachusetts, where he died February 13, 1681. He was a proprietor and drew land in the fourth division in 1659, in what is now Salem, New Hampshire. Before 1653 he married (first) Dorcas Bosworth. His second wife was Mary Davis, a widow. He had at least three children: Haniel, mentioned below; Joseph, born March 6, 1653-54; Matthew, married, April 2, 1679, Mary Wilford, widow.

(II) Haniel, son of Edward Clark, was born about 1650. He married, at Haverhill, August 2, 1678, Mary Gutterson. Children, born at Haverhill: Mary, July 15, 1680; Haniel, August 28, 1682; Sarah, December 3, 1686; William, March 25, 1689; Josiah, March 8, 1691-92; Edward, mentioned below; John, April 23, 1696; Samuel, July 10, 1699; Timothy, April 9, 1701; Elizabeth, May 29, 1705; Zabdiel, baptized July 3, 1715.

(III) Edward (2), son of Haniel Clark, was born at Haverhill, March 29, 1694. He settled in his native town and was a prominent citizen. He was sharer in division of lands in what is now Salem in 1721; was on the committee of the proprietors in 1737; selectman in 1752. In 1740 he was one of the thirteen founders of the church at Salem, signing the covenant, January 16, 1740. He married Sarah Stevens. Children, born at Haverhill: Edward, mentioned below; Priscilla, born September 6, 1718; Joseph, January 18, 1720-21; Mary, May 1, 1726; Israel, November 24, 1727, died November 30, 1727; John, August 7, 1730, died August 15, 1730; William, July 2, 1732.

(IV) Edward (3), son of Edward (2) Clark, was born in Haverhill, Massachusetts, January 15, 1715-16. He lived in that part of Haverhill set off to New Hampshire as the town of Salem. He married Ruth ———. Children, born at Salem: Joseph, July 29, 1751, a carpenter, associated with his brother Edward; Mary, April 5, 1754; Phebe, October 24, 1756; Edward, mentioned below.

(V) Edward (4), son of Edward (3) Clark, was born at Salem, New Hampshire, November 9, 1759. He was an early settler at Haverhill, New Hampshire. He was a soldier from Haverhill, Grafton county, New Hampshire, in the revolution, in Colonel Moses Hazen's regiment in 1779. He doubtless had other service, as the revolutionary records show various enlistments of Edward Clark, but in most cases fail to designate the

Mr. and Mrs. Edward R. Clark

residence of the soldier. He appears in a list of New Hampshire soldiers in Massachusetts regiments. He was a scout on the staff of the great General Lafayette. (See vol. 3, pp. 45 and 301, "Revolutionary Rolls of New Hampshire"). He learned the trade of carpenter and was a builder and contractor. He erected most of the public buildings between Brattleborough, Vermont, and Stanstead, Canada. His brother Joseph was associated with him. He was at one time sheriff of Grafton county. About 1800 he removed to Vermont and located in the town of Peacham. He died at Walden, Vermont, January 9, 1840, and was buried at Peacham.

He married, in Plymouth, New Hampshire, February 23, 1792, Elizabeth Wesson, born at Haverhill, New Hampshire, September 16, 1766, died at Peacham, Vermont, March 10, 1828, daughter of Captain Ephraim Wesson (see Wesson IV). Children, born at Haverhill: Russell, mentioned below; Edward, born December 18, 1796; Ephraim Wesson, April 25, 1799; Eliza W., September 13, 1800; Lydia P., November 12, 1802; Howard W., January 3, 1804; Joseph, October 19, 1806.

(VI) Russell, son of Edward (4) Clark, was born at Haverhill, New Hampshire, April 10, 1795, died August, 1867, at Peacham, Vermont. He was educated in the public schools, and learned the trade of carpenter, at which he worked for many years. He came to Vermont with his parents when a young child and his life was spent principally in the town of Peacham in that state. In later years he followed farming. He was a soldier in the war of 1812, and received a grant of land for his service. He married (first) Florilla Foster, born in 1799, died January 7, 1832. He married (second) Apphia W. Gilson. Children by first wife, born at Peacham: Sarah Jerusha, born April 6, 1824, died January 23, 1853; Elizabeth, February 1, 1826, died February 21, 1899, married Lafayette Strowbridge; Ephraim Wesson, mentioned below; Florilla, died in infancy.

(VII) Ephraim Wesson, son of Russell Clark, was born in Peacham, Vermont, February 9, 1828, died there, April 23, 1900. He received his education in the common schools of his native town and the Caledonia county grammar school, which he attended for two terms. He followed farming for a vocation in Peacham. At the time of the discovery of gold in California he went thither and stayed in the gold fields for about three years. He was a highly respected and useful citizen. For many years he was justice of the peace. He was active and prominent in the Congregational church, in which he held in succession

the various offices of the society. He married Clarissa, born November 7, 1833, in Peacham, Vermont, daughter of Leonard and Betsey (Merrill) Johnson, and granddaughter of Ziba and Sally (Lincoln) Johnson, and a descendant of Samuel Lincoln, weaver, who came from England and settled at Hingham, Massachusetts, about 1637. It is interesting to note that the late President Lincoln was descended from the same immigrant ancestor. Children: 1. Edward Russell, mentioned below. 2. Jessie Merrill, born May 8, 1859, died in 1906. 3. Florilla Foster, born November 9, 1860; proprietress of a private school in Plainfield, New Jersey, in which she has taught for thirty-two years (1912). 4. Martha Johnson, born September 11, 1862; married Hilton Pedley, a missionary, located at Malbashi, Japan. 5. Mary Caroline, born October 12, 1864, died in 1901; married Martin H. Gibson, of Ryegate, Vermont. 6. Charles Allen, born October 6, 1866; a merchant at Newton Highlands, Massachusetts. 7. Ephraim Wesson, born July 18, 1869; resides in Wakefield. Massachusetts; a civil engineer in the service of the West End Street Railway Company of Boston; prepared plans for the first subway of the Boston Elevated Railroad Company in Boston. 8. Elizabeth, February 27, 1872, died February, 1912.

(VIII) Dr. Edward Russell Clark, son of Ephraim Wesson Clark, was born in Peacham, Vermont, December 3, 1857. He attended the district schools of his native town and the Caledonia county grammar school. He studied his profession at Dartmouth Medical College, from which he was graduated with the degree of Doctor of Medicine in 1885. For six months he was a student and assistant in the office of Dr. Gile, of Felchville, Vermont. He then entered upon the practice of his profession at McIndoe's Falls, Vermont, where he remained three years. Thence he went to Arlington, Vermont, where he practiced for five years. In 1893 he removed to Castleton, Vermont, where he has practiced since that time. He is one of the leading physicians of the county. He is a member of the Rutland County Medical and Surgical Society and its president at the present time, member of the Vermont State Medical Society and of the American Medical Association. He has been a member of the United States pension examining board for fourteen years, and for six years the health officer of Castleton. He is a member of the Sons of the American Revolution. For thirty years he has belonged to the Independent Order of Odd Fellows and is affiliated with Hope Lodge, No. 50, of Manchester, Vermont. He is also a member of Lee Lodge, No

30, Free and Accepted Masons, of Castleton. In politics he is a Republican; in religion a Congregationalist.

He married, September 17, 1885, Susan Belknap Bliss, of Lyme, New Hampshire, born there, daughter of George and Dora (Goodell) Bliss. Children: 1. Dora Mildred, born June 30, 1886; graduate of Castleton State Normal School and the Massachusetts General Hospital Training School for Nurses, now practicing her profession. 2. Edward Bliss, born March 28, 1889; employed by the Vermont Marble Company for seven years, now residing at Tacoma, Washington, in charge of the finances of the company there; married Mildred Cornish, of Wisconsin. 3. Florilla Foster, born January 9, 1895.

(The Wesson Line).

(I) John Wesson, immigrant ancestor, was born in 1630 or 1631 in Buckinghamshire, England, died about 1723, aged over ninety years. About 1644, when he was only thirteen years old, he sailed as a stowaway in a ship bound for America, as his father was dead at that time. He settled in Salem, Massachusetts, where in 1648, at the age of eighteen, he was a member of the First Church. About 1653 he moved to that part of Reading now known as Wakefield, and accumulated one of the largest estates in the town. His lands adjoined the Meeting House square, extending southerly. He was a Puritan, very earnest in his piety, and his gravestone in the Reading graveyard shows that he was one of the founders of the church there. He served in King Philip's war. In 1653 he married Sarah, daughter of Zachariah Fitch, of Reading, and this is the first marriage there of which record exists. He had at least eight children, four sons among them, each of whom became the head of a family, and he has many descendants in all parts of the country. Children: Sarah, born July 15, 1656; Mary, May 25, 1659, probably died young; John, March 8, 1661; Elizabeth, February 7, 1662; Samuel, April 16, 1665; Stephen, mentioned below; Thomas, November 20, 1670.

(II) Stephen, son of John Wesson, was born at Reading, Massachusetts, December 6, 1667, died April 30, 1753, at Reading. His wife Sarah died at Reading, March 1, 1740, aged sixty-eight years. Children, born at Reading: Stephen, mentioned below; Isaac, September 14, 1699; John, October 19, 1707, died August 27, 1708. There may have been other children.

(III) Stephen (2), son of Stephen (1) Wesson, was born at Reading, Massachusetts, April 10, 1697. He married there, December 6, 1721, Elizabeth Parker, of Reading. Children, born at Reading: Ephraim, mentioned below; Stephen, February 28, 1724-25; Lydia, 1732. There may have been other children unrecorded.

(IV) Captain Ephraim Wesson, son of Stephen (2) Wesson, was born at Reading, Massachusetts, September 9, 1722. He moved to Pepperell, formerly a part of Groton, Massachusetts, and thence to Haverhill, New Hampshire, before the revolution. He saw much service in the old French and Indian war. In 1755 he was in the expedition against Crown Point, entering the army as lieutenant. Subsequently he was at the capture of Louisburg, and in the attack on Ticonderoga and served in all the important battles of that section. During his residence in Haverhill he was a very prominent citizen of the town, according to the town history, and took a leading part in public affairs. He held many offices of trust and honor, including those of selectman and moderator. He was a delegate to the provincial congress at Exeter and a special delegate to that body to procure arms for the Haverhill settlers. In the revolution he was intimately associated with Colonel Charles Johnson and others in the stirring events of that period, serving on the committees of safety and correspondence of the town. At the close of the revolution Captain Wesson moved to Groton, Vermont. Captain Wesson was a brave and conscientious officer and was highly esteemed and trusted by his superiors, a man of excellent character and of Puritan mould and principles, we are told by the town historian. He was at the battle of Yorktown at the surrender of Cornwallis as a scout on the staff of General Lafayette. He died March, 1814, at Peacham, Vermont.

He married, at Reading, December 5, 1746, Susanna Upham. Children: 1. Lydia, born 1747, died 1776; married Benjamin Wells. 2. Belle, born 1749; married, 1766, John Way; resided in Ryegate, Vermont. 3. Experience, born 1753; married, 1787, Judith Morse. 4. James, born 1758; married Keziah Bailey, and lived in Stanstead, Canada. 5. Peter, twin of James, died in Franconia, New Hampshire, 1792. 6. Aaron, born 1760; married Caroline Hosmer. 7. Samuel, born 1762; never married. 8. Sally, married Captain Edmund Morse; died November 12, 1843. 9. Elizabeth, born September 16, 1766; married Edward Clark (see Clark V).

SEWARD Lieutenant William Seward, the immigrant ancestor, was born in England in 1627, died March 29, 1689, in Guilford, Connecticut. He came to this country from Bristol and is said to have been in Taunton, Massachusetts, in 1643. Shortly after his arrival in America he settled in New Haven, Connecticut, but did not live there long. He moved to Guilford, where he took the oath of fidelity, May 4, 1654, and resided there the remainder of his life. For many years he was commander of the train band of the town, and he seems to have been influential in town affairs, to have possessed considerable property, and to have been a tanner. He served frequently as representative to the general assembly. His will was dated March 29, 1689, the day of his death, and it was proved June 7, 1689. His son Stephen, who seems to have been incapable of taking care of himself, was left a life estate in the home, and thirty acres, under the trusteeship of John, who was to inherit the property after Stephen's death. The other sons were also mentioned in the will, as well as his wife and daughter Hannah, and children of his daughter Mary. The tanyard and meadow land were to be equally divided among the sons.

Lieutenant Seward married, April 2, 1651, in New Haven, Grace, daughter of Thomas Norton, of Guilford. Children: Mary, born February 28, 1652, at New Haven; John, February 14, 1653-54; Joseph, 1655; Samuel, August 20, 1659, died young; Caleb, mentioned below; Stephen, August 6, 1664; Samuel, February 8, 1666-67, died April 8, 1689; Hannah, February 8, 1669-70; Ebenezer, December 13, 1672.

(II) Caleb, son of Lieutenant William Seward, was born March 14, 1662-63, died August 2, 1728. He lived for some years in Guilford, where he owned ten acres of land at East Creek. On May 4, 1699, he moved to Durham, Connecticut, where he was the first settler. He married, July 14, 1686, Lydia, daughter of William Bushnell, of Saybrook, Connecticut. She died August 24, 1753. Children, born in Guilford: Daniel, October 16, 1687, died April 28, 1688; Lydia, May 12, 1689; Caleb, January 12, 1692; Thomas, mentioned below; Noahdiah, August 22, 1697. Born in Durham: Ephraim, August 6, 1700, first white child born in the town; Ebenezer, June 7, 1703, second white child born in the town.

(III) Thomas, son of Caleb Seward, was born in Guilford, December 19, 1694. He lived in Durham and Wallingford, Connecticut, dying in the latter named city. He married, March 31, 1720, Sarah, daughter of Samuel Camp, of Durham. She married (second) Daniel Benton, and she died March 12, 1762. Children: Solomon, mentioned below;

Phebe, born February 3, 1723-24; Amos, March 25, 1726; Catharine, December 28, 1727; Nathan, baptized June 14, 1730.

(IV) Deacon Solomon Seward, son of Thomas Seward, was born January 19, 1721, and baptized January 21, 1721. He lived in Southbury, Connecticut, and in Scipio, New York. He married Alenor Baldwin, of Branford, Connecticut. Children: Samuel; Benjamin.

(V) Stephen Seward, born about 1755, is thought to have been son of Deacon Solomon Seward. In 1790 the only persons in Vermont, heads of families, according to the first federal census, were Solomon and Stephen Seward. Solomon was of Rutland and had in his family two males under sixteen and two females. Children of Stephen: Stephen, Edward; Harvey, who was killed in the Seminole war, an officer; Ira, mentioned below.

(VI) Ira, son of Stephen Seward, was born in 1785, probably in Rutland, died in Mendon, Vermont, July 28, 1860. He was a carpenter and contractor in Rutland for many years. After removing to Mendon he followed farming. He married (first) Mary Blanchard; (second) Abigail Rollins, who died May 19, 1868, aged eighty-one years. Child by first wife: Ira. Children by second wife: Edward, William Horace, mentioned below.

(VII) William Horace, son of Ira Seward, was born in Rutland, Vermont, August 27, 1827, died in Mendon, March 20, 1908. He was a farmer and his entire life was spent in his native town, and in the adjoining town of Mendon. He married, March 20, 1850, Augusta Sargent, of Hubbardton, born May 21, 1830, died May 7, 1903, daughter of Fernando Sargent. Children: William, born May 9, 1852; Henry E., mentioned below; Frances E., June 8, 1856, died February 3, 1883; Ira F., October 6, 1858; Jennie R., January 12, 1864, married Ethan Hulett; Blanche M., December 5, 1875, died July, 1911.

(VIII) Henry Eugene, son of William Horace Seward, was born at Mendon, Vermont, September 1, 1854. He was educated in the public schools of Rutland in that state. He began to learn his trade in the Baker shops in Rutland when he was sixteen years old and he worked for this concern for six years. He then located in Rutland and followed farming until 1901, when he started in his present business under the firm name of H. E. Seward & Sons, dealers in groceries and provisions. He is a prominent and successful merchant. He is a member of the Order of the Golden Cross. For thirty-three years he has been an active member of the Baptist church and he is a trustee of the society.

He married, March 21, 1877, Hattie A.

Hale, of Rutland, born October 3, 1858, daughter of Frank S. and Nancy A. (Lincoln) Hale. Children: 1. Frank Henry, born December, 1877, died in infancy. 2. Hubert Frank, born September 3, 1879; married, February 14, 1898, Ella A. Soulia, of Proctor, Vermont, and had Lillian Ella, born September 28, 1899; Frank Henry, May 20, 1901; Hazel May, October 2, 1903; Alice Harriet, November 25, 1905; Harry Rollin, May 5, 1907; Lena Belle, November 25, 1908; Child, June 24, 1912. 3. Herbert Henry, born September 3, 1879, twin of Hubert Frank, married, September, 1904, Clara Inez Bashaw, of Brandon, and had Clarence Herbert, born June 20, 1905. 4. Walter William, born May 11, 1882; married, January 21, 1907, Eva Stratton: children: Lloyd William, born September 10, 1907; Eva May, March 17, 1910; Walter Thompson, May 14, 1912. 5. Minnie, born December 16, 1885; married, January 16, 1907, Almo B. Frazoni; children: Raymond Seward, born October, 1907; Ella Lillian, October, 1908, died in 1909; Almo B., born March, 1911. 6. Pauline A., born August 26, 1887; married William L. Stickney; children: Edgar William, born August 23, 1910; Irene Pearl, born August 7, 1912. 7. Irene, born June 2, 1889; married Joseph E. Marceau; children: Theodora H., born October 20, 1909; Joseph Edward, born April 19, 1912. 8. Henry E. Jr., born November 13, 1892; married, August 6, 1912, Louise Maheux. 9. Charles Reese, born December 27, 1894. 10. Florence E., born September, 1899. 11. Clarence Erven, born April 5, 1901.

ALDEN (VII) Southworth Alden, son of Deacon Seth Alden (q. v.), was born in Randolph, Massachusetts, May 13, 1825. He was educated in the public schools. In early life he was in business as a shoe manufacturer, and afterward as a house painter at East Stoughton, Massachusetts. He married, July 10, 1850, Elizabeth Curtis, daughter of George and Betsey (Curtis) Winchester. She died August 19, 1899, aged seventy-one years, two months. He died at East Stoughton, Massachusetts, November 3, 1890, aged sixty-seven years, six months. Children: 1. Rhoda Ann, born January 19, 1852, died April 17, 1853. 2. Mary Elizabeth, born November 27, 1853; married, May 30, 1876, Henry Homer Snow; children: Mabelle Florence, born at South Braintree, July 6, 1877, died May 4, 1878; Eva May, born October 19, 1878, married, October 21, 1903. Robert T. Elliott, of Newport, Rhode Island, and they have one child, Priscilla Alden Elliott: Harry Shaw, born May 8, 1880, now of East Bridgewater, Massachusetts, married, June 16, 1908, Corinne Myrtle Dill, of Rockland, Massachusetts; Addie Williams, born March 6, 1883, died February 12, 1884. 3. Edward Southworth, mentioned below.

(VIII) Edward Southworth, son of Southworth Alden, was born October 26, 1859, at East Stoughton, Massachusetts. He was educated in the public schools of his native town. After working in a shoe factory in his native town and Brockton, Massachusetts, he came to Hyde Park, Massachusetts, in 1883, as bookkeeper for his cousin, Charles L. Alden, who was in the grocery business, and a few years later was admitted to partnership. In 1893 he withdrew from the firm to establish a grocery business on his own account at Readville, in the town of Hyde Park. In addition to this store he also conducts a store at Roslindale, purchased in October, 1910. He is an energetic and substantial merchant, and a public-spirited citizen. For the past ten years he has been deacon of the Baptist church.

He married, June 1, 1881, Francelia M. Madan, born at East Stoughton, now Avon, Massachusetts, daughter of Abram and Eliza (Ridgway) Madan. Children: 1. Merton Ridgway, born at Hyde Park, November 29, 1884. 2. Edward Southworth Jr., born January 28, 1888; married, June 1, 1910, Una, daughter of Samuel T. Elliott; she is a graduate of Wellesley College; they have one child, Barbara, born June 5, 1912. 3. Ruth Francelia, born November 9, 1891.